Excel 2003 VBA Programmer's Reference

Excel 2003 VBA Programmer's Reference

Paul Kimmel
Stephen Bullen
John Green
Rob Bovey
Robert Rosenberg

WILEY

Wiley Publishing, Inc.

Excel 2003 VBA Programmer's Reference

Published by
Wiley Publishing, Inc.
10475 Crosspoint Boulevard
Indianapolis, IN 46256
www.wiley.com

For general information on our other products and services please contact our Customer Care
Department within the United States at (800) 762-2974, outside the United States at (317) 572-3993
or fax (317) 572-4002.

Trademarks: Wiley, the Wiley Publishing logo, Wrox, the Wrox logo, Programmer to Programmer, and
related trade dress are trademarks or registered trademarks of John Wiley & Sons, Inc. and/or its
affiliates. All other trademarks are the property of their respective owners. Wiley Publishing, Inc., is
not associated with any product or vendor mentioned in this book.

*Wiley also publishes its books in a variety of electronic formats. Some content that appears in print may not be
available in electronic books.*

Library of Congress Cataloging-in-Publication Data

Excel 2003 VBA Programmer's Reference / Paul Kimmel . . . [et al.].
    p. cm.
  Includes index.
  ISBN 0-7645-5660-6 (paper/website)
  1. Microsoft Excel (Computer file). 2. Microsoft Visual BASIC. 3. Business—Computer programs.
4. Electronic spreadsheets. 5. Computer software—Development. I. Kimmel, Paul.
  HF5548.4.M523E92986 2004
  005.54—dc22
                                        2004007598

Printed in the United States of America

10 9 8 7 6 5 4 3 2

About the Authors

Paul Kimmel

Paul Kimmel founded Software Conceptions, Inc in 1990 and has been designing and building software and writing computer books ever since. Paul Kimmel is the author of several books on VBA, VB, VB.NET, C#, Delphi, and C++. Paul is also the bi-monthly columnist for www.codeguru.com's VB Today column and a frequent contributor to periodicals and online publications, including wwww.InformiT.com. You may contact him at pkimmel@softconcepts.com for help designing and building software.

Stephen Bullen

Stephen Bullen is based in Carlow, Ireland and in London, England. He has been running his own company, Business Modelling Solutions Ltd since 1997, specializing in Excel development and consulting and has worked for some of the worlds largest companies. The BMS web site, www.BMSLtd.co.uk, contains a large number of examples of his work, including tools and utilities to extend Excel's functionality and many examples of Excel development techniques.

Stephen devotes a lot of his spare time to helping other Excel users by answering questions in the CompuServe Excel forum and Microsoft's Internet Newsgroups. In recognition of his contributions and knowledge, Microsoft has awarded him the status of 'Most Valuable Professional' every year since 1996.

Stephen wrote most of the later chapters in the Excel 2000 and Excel 2002 VBA.

Programmers References, which have been carried forward to this book and updated by Paul Kimmel where appropriate. Stephen has not directly contributed to this edition.

John Green

John Green, Sydney Australia, is an independent consultant specializing in Excel and Access. With 30 years of computing experience, a Chemical Engineering degree and an MBA, he draws from a diverse background. He has led training courses for software applications and operating systems both in Australia and overseas. Microsoft has awarded him the status of 'Most Valuable Professional' every year since 1995.

John was the principal author of the Excel 2000 and Excel 2002 VBA Programmers References, which have been carried forward to this book and updated by Paul Kimmel where appropriate. John has not directly contributed to this edition.

Rob Bovey

Rob Bovey is a software developer specializing in Microsoft Office, Visual Basic, and SQL Server applications. He is founder and president of the custom application development firm Application Professionals. Rob developed several Addins shipped by Microsoft for Excel. He also co-authored the Microsoft Excel 97 Developer's Kit. Microsoft has awarded Rob the status of 'Most Valuable Professional' every year since 1995. Rob authored the chapter on Data Access with ADO for the Excel 2002 VBA Programmer's Reference. He has not directly contributed to this edition.

Robert Rosenberg

Robert Rosenberg runs his own consulting business, which specializes in providing custom solutions and advanced training in Microsoft Office. His clients include fortune five hundred companies in the entertainment, financial, and legal fields. As a Microsoft Valuable Professional in Excel, he also continually offers advanced online support in Excel on behalf of Microsoft to users of their Internet newsgroups. Robert was responsible for updating the content for the Excel and Office Indexes for the 2002 version of this book. This included updating example code and listings for existing VBA objects as well as listing new object descriptions, their methods, properties and/or arguments along with code examples.

Brian Patterson (Contributor)

Brian Patterson (Contributor) currently works for Illinois Mutual Life as a Software Development Coordinator where he is generally working with C# in WinForms or the Corporate Internet site. Brian has been writing for various publications since 1994 and has co-written several .NET related books including "Migrating to Visual Basic.nET" and ".NET Enterprise Development with VB.NET." You can generally find him posting in the MSDN Newsgroups or hanging out with his lovely wife and 3 children. You can reach him via email at bdpatterson@illinoismutual.com.

Credits

Vice President and Executive Group Publisher
Richard Swadley

Vice President and Executive Publisher
Bob Ipsen

Vice President and Publisher
Joseph B. Wikert

Executive Editorial Director
Mary Bednarek

Acquisitions Editor
Katie Mohr

Editorial Manager
Kathryn A. Malm

Senior Production Editor
Fred Bernardi

Development Editor
Adaobi Obi Tulton

Production Editor
Pamela Hanley

Media Development Specialist

Permissions Editor

Text Design & Composition
Wiley Composition Services

Acknowledgments

Paul Kimmel

I would like to acknowledge my good friend and editor Sharon Cox, Katie Mohr, and Adaobi Obi Tulton at Wiley. Without them (and David Fugate, my agent at Waterside) and the book's original authors I wouldn't have had a chance to work on this project. It has been a pleasure working with the professionals at Wiley.

While working on this project I had the good fortune of working on a C# project at Pitney Bowes with some intelligent folks. Edward Ronga is a great manager; he can work wonders with engineers that can sometimes be a bit fussy. It was my pleasure to work at Pitney with Leonard Bertelli, Jay Fusco, Enzo Maini, Peter Gomis, Kip Stroble, Carl Dalzell, Debra Alberti, Sanjay Gulati, and my cellmate Charles Haley (I played Norah Jones for four months and Charles never complained.) As always I make every effort to leave things better than I found them but always seem to be the beneficiary of these new, great relationships.

Happy New Year to new and old friends and family. Eric Cotter has a sharp mind and more enthusiasm than anyone I know, and Robert Golieb is steadfast and someone I am lucky to call friend. Greetings to my hosts at Porky's in Shelton, Connecticut for the most excellent chicken wings and adult beverages.

My greatest blessing is my family. My wife Lori is a rock and my greatest cheerleader, and I am blessed to have four healthy and beautiful children (Trevor, Douglas, Alex, and Noah). My greatest wish is that everyone can know the blessings of a loving, healthy family.

Stephen Bullen

I would like to start by thanking all those who purchased a copy of the Excel 2000 VBA Programmer's Reference and sent e-mails of congratulations and suggestions for this update. It is your support that convinced us to comprehensively update the book for Excel 2002. I'd like to thank John Green for agreeing to co-author the update, Rob Bovey for contributing the ADO chapter, and Robert Rosenberg for taking over the Reference sections. As always, the people at Wrox Press and the book's technical reviewers worked wonders, and it is their contribution that has made this the excellent book that I hope you'll agree it is.

On a personal note, I'd like to dedicate my chapters to the eye specialists, doctors, and nurses at the Temple Street Children's Hospital in Dublin for dealing with Jane's tumour so well, and to everyone in the Ford ProPrima team for their friendship and support over the past year.

Rob Bovey

I would like to thank my wife Michelle for putting up with my insatiable computer habit and my dog Harley for keeping my feet warm while I work.

Acknowledgments

Robert Rosenberg

I'd like to thank John Green, Stephen Bullen, and Rob Bovey for allowing me on the same project as three of the most brilliant minds in Excel today. It was an honor to take up the challenge. Special thanks goes to Rob Bovey, my mentor, who has always been there for me, answered all of my annoying questions, taught me countless techniques, and provided me with this opportunity.

To my best friend and brother Elliot, who has stuck by me through thick and thin.

And finally, for my Mom and Dad, their love never stops.

Contents

Contents

Contents

Contents

Contents

Contents

Contents

Introduction

Excel made its debut on the Macintosh in 1985 and has never lost its position as the most popular spreadsheet application in the Mac environment. In 1987, Excel was ported to the PC, running under Windows. It took many years for Excel to overtake Lotus 1-2-3, which was one of the most successful software systems in the history of computing at that time.

There were a number of spreadsheet applications that enjoyed success prior to the release of the IBM PC in 1981. Among these were VisiCalc, Quattro Pro, and Multiplan. VisiCalc started it all, but fell by the wayside early on. Multiplan was Microsoft's predecessor to Excel, using the R1C1 cell addressing which is still available as an option in Excel. But it was 1-2-3 that shot to stardom very soon after its release in 1982 and came to dominate the PC spreadsheet market.

Early Spreadsheet Macros

1-2-3 was the first spreadsheet application to offer spreadsheet, charting, and database capabilities in one package. However, the main reason for its runaway success was its macro capability. Legend has it that the 1-2-3 developers set up macros as a debugging and testing mechanism for the product. It is said that they only realized the potential of macros at the last minute, and included them into the final release pretty much as an afterthought.

Whatever their origins, macros gave non-programmers a simple way to become programmers and automate their spreadsheets. They grabbed the opportunity and ran. At last they had a measure of independence from the computer department.

The original 1-2-3 macros performed a task by executing the same keystrokes that a user would use to carry out the same task. It was, therefore, very simple to create a macro as there was virtually nothing new to learn to progress from normal spreadsheet manipulation to programmed manipulation. All you had to do was remember what keys to press and write them down. The only concessions to traditional programming were eight extra commands, the /x commands. The /x commands provided some primitive decision making and branching capabilities, a way to get input from a user, and a way to construct menus.

One major problem with 1-2-3 macros was their vulnerability. The multisheet workbook had not yet been invented and macros had to be written directly into the cells of the spreadsheet they supported, along with input data and calculations. Macros were at the mercy of the user. For example, they could be inadvertently disrupted when a user inserted or deleted rows or columns. Macros were also at the mercy of the programmer. A badly designed macro could destroy itself quite easily while trying to edit spreadsheet data.

Despite the problems, users reveled in their newfound programming ability and millions of lines of code were written in this cryptic language, using arcane techniques to get around its many limitations. The world came to rely on code that was often badly designed, nearly always poorly documented, and at all times highly vulnerable, often supporting enterprise-critical control systems.

The XLM Macro Language

The original Excel macro language required you to write your macros in a macro sheet that was saved in a file with an `.xlm` extension. In this way, macros were kept separate from the worksheet, which was saved in a file with an `.xls` extension. These macros are now often referred to as XLM macros, or Excel 4 macros, to distinguish them from the VBA macro language introduced in Excel Version 5.

The XLM macro language consisted of function calls, arranged in columns in the macro sheet. There were many hundreds of functions necessary to provide all the features of Excel and allow programmatic control. The XLM language was far more sophisticated and powerful than the 1-2-3 macro language, even allowing for the enhancements made in 1-2-3 Releases 2 and 3. However, the code produced was not much more intelligible.

The sophistication of Excel's macro language was a two-edged sword. It appealed to those with high programming aptitude, who could tap the language's power, but was a barrier to most users. There was no simple relationship between the way you would manually operate Excel and the way you programmed it. There was a very steep learning curve involved in mastering the XLM language.

Another barrier to Excel's acceptance on the PC was that it required Windows. The early versions of Windows were restricted by limited access to memory, and Windows required much more horsepower to operate than DOS. The Graphical User Interface was appealing, but the tradeoffs in hardware cost and operating speed were perceived as problems.

Lotus made the mistake of assuming that Windows was a flash in the pan, soon to be replaced by OS/2, and did not bother to plan a Windows version of 1-2-3. Lotus put its energy into 1-2-3/G, a very nice GUI version of 1-2-3 that only operated under OS/2. This one horse bet was to prove the undoing of 1-2-3.

By the time it became clear that Windows was here to stay, Lotus was in real trouble as it watched users flocking to Excel. The first attempt at a Windows version of 1-2-3, released in 1991, was really 1-2-3 Release 3 for DOS in a thin GUI shell. Succeeding releases have closed the gap between 1-2-3 and Excel, but have been too late to stop the almost universal adoption of Microsoft Office by the market.

Excel 5

Microsoft took a brave decision to unify the programming code behind its Office applications by introducing *VBA (Visual Basic for Applications)* as the common macro language in Office. Excel 5, released in 1993, was the first application to include VBA. It has been gradually introduced into the other Office applications in subsequent versions of Office. Excel, Word, Access, PowerPoint, FrontPage, Visio, Project, and Outlook all use VBA as their macro language in Office XP. (Microsoft is clearly expanding their commitment to VBA among their product offerings.)

Since the release of Excel 5, Excel has supported both the XLM and the VBA macro languages, and the support for XLM should continue into the foreseeable future, but will decrease in significance as users switch to VBA.

VBA is an object-oriented programming language that is identical to the Visual Basic 6.0 programming language in the way it is structured and in the way it handles objects. In future versions of VBA you will likely see VBA become increasingly similar to Visual Basic .NET. If you learn to use VBA in Excel, you know how to use it in the other Office applications.

The Office applications differ in the objects they expose to VBA. To program an application, you need to be familiar with its *object model*. The object model is a hierarchy of all the objects that you find in the application. For example, part of the Excel Object Model tells us that there is an `Application` object that contains a `Workbook` object that contains a `Worksheet` object that contains a `Range` object.

VBA is somewhat easier to learn than the XLM macro language, is more powerful, is generally more efficient, and allows us to write well-structured code. We can also write badly structured code, but by following a few principles, we should be able to produce code that is readily understood by others and is reasonably easy to maintain.

In Excel 5, VBA code was written in modules, which were sheets in a workbook. Worksheets, chart sheets, and dialog sheets were other types of sheets that could be contained in an Excel 5 workbook.

> **A module is really just a word-processing document with some special formatting characteristics that help you write and test code.**

Excel 97

In Excel 97, Microsoft introduced some dramatic changes in the VBA interface and some changes in the Excel Object Model. From Excel 97 onwards, modules are not visible in the Excel application window and modules are no longer objects contained by the `Workbook` object. Modules are contained in the VBA project associated with the workbook and can only be viewed and edited in the Visual Basic Editor (VBE) window.

In addition to the standard modules, class modules were introduced, which allow you to create your own classes. Commandbars were introduced to replace menus and toolbars, and UserForms replaced dialog sheets. Like modules, UserForms can only be edited in the VBE window. As usual, the replaced objects are still supported in Excel, but are considered to be hidden objects and are not documented in the Help screens.

In previous versions of Excel, objects such as buttons embedded in worksheets could only respond to a single event, usually the `Click` event. Excel 97 greatly increased the number of events that VBA code can respond to and formalized the way in which this is done by providing event procedures for the workbook, worksheet and chart sheet objects. For example, workbooks now have 20 events they can respond to, such as `BeforeSave`, `BeforePrint`, and `BeforeClose`. Excel 97 also introduced ActiveX controls that can be embedded in worksheets and UserForms. ActiveX controls can respond to a wide range of events such as `GotFocus`, `MouseMove`, and `DblClick`.

The VBE provides users with much more help than was previously available. For example, as we write code, popups appear with lists of appropriate methods and properties for objects, and arguments and parameter values for functions and methods. The *Object Browser* is much better than the previous versions, allowing us to search for entries, for example, and providing comprehensive information on intrinsic constants.

Microsoft has provided an Extensibility library that makes it possible to write VBA code that manipulates the VBE environment and VBA projects. This makes it possible to write codes that can directly access code modules and UserForms. It is possible to set up applications that indent module code or export code from modules to text files, for example.

Excel 97 has been ported to the Macintosh in the form of Excel 98. Unfortunately, many of the VBE Help features that make life easy for programmers have not been included. The VBE Extensibility features have not made it to the Mac either.

Excel 2000

Excel 2000 did not introduce dramatic changes from a VBA programming perspective. There were a large number of improvements in the Office 2000 and Excel 2000 user interfaces and improvements in some Excel features such as PivotTables. A new PivotChart feature was added. Web users benefited the most from Excel 2000, especially through the ability to save workbooks as Web pages. There were also improvements for users with a need to share information, through new online collaboration features.

One long awaited improvement for VBA users was the introduction of modeless UserForms. Previously, Excel only supported model dialog boxes, which take the focus when they are on screen so that no other activity can take place until they are closed. Modeless dialog boxes allow the user to continue with other work while the dialog box floats above the worksheet. Modeless dialog boxes can be used to show a "splash" screen when an application written in Excel is loaded and to display a progress indicator while a lengthy macro runs.

Excel 2002

Excel 2002 has also introduced only incremental changes. Once more, the major improvements have been in the user interface rather than in programming features. Microsoft continues to concentrate on improving Web-related features to make it easier to access and distribute data using the Internet. New features that could be useful for VBA programmers include a new `Protection` object, SmartTags, RTD (Real Time Data), and improved support for XML.

The new `Protection` object lets us selectively control the features that are accessible to users when we protect a worksheet. We can decide whether users can sort, alter cell formatting, or insert and delete rows and columns, for example. There is also a new `AllowEditRange` object that we can use to specify which users can edit specific ranges and whether they must use a password to do so. We can apply different combinations of permissions to different ranges.

SmartTags allow Excel to recognize data typed into cells as having special significance. For example, Excel 2002 can recognize stock market abbreviations, such as MSFT for Microsoft Corporation. When Excel sees an item like this, it displays a SmartTag symbol that has a popup menu. We can use the menu to obtain related information, such as the latest stock price or a summary report on the company. Microsoft provides a kit that allows developers to create new SmartTag software, so we could see a whole new class of tools appearing that use SmartTags to make data available throughout an organization or across the Internet.

RTD allows developers to create sources of information that users can draw from. Once you establish a link to a worksheet, changes in the source data are automatically passed on. An obvious use for this is to obtain stock prices that change in real time during the course of trading. Other possible applications include the ability to log data from scientific instruments or industrial process controllers. As with SmartTags, we will probably see a host of applications developed to make it easy for Excel users to gain access to dynamic information.

Improved XML support means it is getting easier to create applications that exchange data through the Internet and intranets. As we all become more dependent on these burgeoning technologies, this will become of increasing importance.

Excel 2003

The Web is a ubiquitous part of modern life. With the Web's increasing importance in the world, Microsoft has shifted focus to providing revisions that respond to this growing relevance in the computing world. For this reason, you will see that many of the changes to Excel 2003 are changes that reflect an increasingly connected world.

In addition to new Internet features, you will find extended workbook capabilities, new functionality for analyzing data, better support for XML and sharing workbooks on the Internet, and an improved user experience.

XML, or *eXtensible Markup Language*, is a self-extensible hypertext language. Ultimately, XML is text and a public, non-proprietary industry standard that is easy to extend for a wide variety of uses and moves easily over the Internet. Due to the greater support for XML Excel data it will become increasingly easier to share spreadsheet data with other Enterprise solutions that use XML too.

Greater support exists for managing ranges as list and the user interface experience is enhanced by adding features that permit modifying, filtering, and identifying these lists.

You can more easily share and update your Excel data with Windows Sharepoint Services. For example, changes made in Excel to lists shared on Sharepoint Services are automatically updated on Sharepoint Services. Support for modifying data offline and resynchronizing the data next time you connect makes it easier for busy users to work disconnected, for example, during the *Great Blackout of 2003*.

A couple dozen new and powerful statistical functions have been added to Excel, in conjunction, with side-by-side workbook comparison, greater reference information, and support for linking to wireless devices like Tablet PCs will offer you and your users with a more productive total user experience.

What This Book Covers

This book is aimed squarely at Excel users who want to harness the power of the VBA language in their Excel applications. At all times, the VBA language is presented in the context of Excel, not just as a general application programming language.

The pages that follow have been divided into three sections:

❑ Programming

❑ Advanced features for Excel

❑ New features that facilitate online information sharing

And, a comprehensive, updated object model reference has been included in Appendixes A, B, and C.

This book has been reorganized, moving almost all of the programming information upfront. In addition, new chapters have been added with a greater emphasis on object-oriented programming, error handling, and writing bulletproof code. In these chapters you will learn about everything, from encapsulation, interfaces, error handling and debugging, to writing AddIns, programming to the Windows API, and managing international issues.

The middle section of the book describes new and advanced features for Excel users. These features—like new support for ranges and lists—are essential to making the most out of Excel as a productivity and programming tool.

The third part of this book talks about increased resources for sharing Excel data on the Internet.

Because this book is primarily a programmer's reference, the greatest emphasis is on programmers. However, because so many of you like features geared more toward users we left these chapters in and updated them where it was appropriate to do so.

Version Issues

This book was first written for Excel 2000 and has now been extended to Excel 2003 as a component of Office XP. As the changes in the Excel Object Model, compared to Excel 97, have been relatively minor most of this book is applicable to all three versions. Where we discuss a feature that is not supported in previous versions, we make that clear.

What You Need to Use this Book

Nearly everything discussed in this book has examples with it. The entire code is written out and there are plenty of screenshots where they are appropriate. The version of Windows you use is not important. It is important to have a full installation of Excel and, if you want to try the more advanced chapters involving communication between Excel and other Office applications, you will need a full installation of Office. Make sure your installation includes access to the Visual Basic Editor and the VBA Help files. It is possible to exclude these items during the installation process.

Note that Chapters 13 and 14 also require you to have VB6 installed as they cover the topics of COM AddIns and SmartTags.

Conventions

To help you get the most from the text and keep track of what's happening, we've used a number of conventions throughout the book.

> **Boxes like this one hold important, not-to-be forgotten information that is directly relevant to the surrounding text.**

Tips, hints, tricks, and asides to the current discussion are offset and placed in italics like this.

As for styles in the text:

❑   We *highlight* important words when we introduce them

❑   We show keyboard strokes like this: *CtrlA*

- ❏ We show file names, URLs, and code within the text like so: `persistence.properties`
- ❏ We present code in two different ways:

> In code examples we highlight new and important code with a gray background.

The gray highlighting is not used for code that's less important in the present context, or has been shown before.

Source Code

As you work through the examples in this book, you may choose either to type in all the code manually or to use the source code files that accompany the book. All of the source code used in this book is available for download at `http://www.wrox.com`. Once at the site, simply locate the book's title (either by using the Search box or by using one of the title lists) and click the Download Code link on the book's detail page to obtain all the source code for the book.

> *Because many books have similar titles, you may find it easiest to search by ISBN; for this book the ISBN is 0-764-55660-6.*

Once you download the code, just decompress it with your favorite compression tool. Alternately, you can go to the main Wrox code download page at `http://www.wrox.com/dynamic/books/download.aspx` to see the code available for this book and all other Wrox books.

Errata

We make every effort to ensure that there are no errors in the text or in the code. However, no one is perfect, and mistakes do occur. If you find an error in one of our books, like a spelling mistake or faulty piece of code, we would be very grateful for your feedback. By sending in errata you may save another reader hours of frustration and at the same time you will be helping us provide even higher quality information.

To find the errata page for this book, go to `http://www.wrox.com` and locate the title using the Search box or one of the title lists. Then, on the book details page, click the Book Errata link. On this page you can view all errata that has been submitted for this book and posted by Wrox editors. A complete book list including links to each book's errata is also available at `www.wrox.com/misc-pages/booklist.shtml`.

If you don't spot "your" error on the Book Errata page, go to `www.wrox.com/contact/techsupport.shtml` and complete the form there to send us the error you have found. We'll check the information and, if appropriate, post a message to the book's errata page and fix the problem in subsequent editions of the book.

In Case of a Crisis . . .

There are number of places you can turn to if you encounter a problem. The best source of information on all aspects of Excel is from your peers. You can find them in a number of newsgroups across the Internet. Try pointing your newsreader to the following site where you will find people willing and able to assist:

- ❏ `msnews.microsoft.com`

Subscribe to `microsoft.public.excel.programming` or any of the groups that appeal. You can submit questions and generally receive answers within an hour or so.

Stephen Bullen and Rob Bovey maintain very useful Web sites, where you will find a great deal of information and free downloadable files, at the following addresses:

- ❑ `http://www.bmsltd.co.uk`
- ❑ `http://www.appspro.com`

Another useful site is maintained by John Walkenbach at:

- ❑ `http://www.j-walk.com`

Wrox can be contacted directly at:

- ❑ `http://www.wrox.com`—for downloadable source code and support
- ❑ `http://p2p.wrox.com/list.asp?list=vba_excel`—for open Excel VBA discussion

Direct queries can be sent to:

- ❑ pkimmel@softconcepts.com

(Keep in mind that efforts would be made to answer all queries but you may find yourself in a line behind others. It is a good idea to post your query to several sources at once to get the fastest help and a diverse set of responses to choose from.)

Other useful Microsoft information sources can be found at:

- ❑ `http://www.microsoft.com/office/`—for up-to-the-minute news and support
- ❑ `http://msdn.microsoft.com/office/`—for developer news and good articles about how to work with Microsoft products
- ❑ `http://www.microsoft.com/technet`—for Microsoft Knowledge Base articles, security information, and a bevy of other more admin-related items

p2p.wrox.com

For author and peer discussion, join the P2P forums at `p2p.wrox.com`. The forums are a Web-based system for you to post messages relating to Wrox books and related technologies and interact with other readers and technology users. The forums offer a subscription feature to e-mail you topics of interest of your choosing when new posts are made to the forums. Wrox authors, editors, other industry experts, and your fellow readers are present on these forums.

At `http://p2p.wrox.com` you will find a number of different forums that will help you not only as you read this book, but also as you develop your own applications. To join the forums, just follow these steps:

1. Go to `p2p.wrox.com` and click the Register link.
2. Read the terms of use and click Agree.

3. Complete the required information to join as well as any optional information you wish to provide and click Submit.

4. You will receive an e-mail with information describing how to verify your account and complete the joining process.

You can read messages in the forums without joining P2P but in order to post your own messages, you must join.

Once you join, you can post new messages and respond to messages other users post. You can read messages at any time on the Web. If you would like to have new messages from a particular forum e-mailed to you, click the Subscribe to this Forum icon by the forum name in the forum listing.

For more information about how to use the Wrox P2P, be sure to read the P2P FAQs for answers to questions about how the forum software works as well as many common questions specific to P2P and Wrox books. To read the FAQs, click the FAQ link on any P2P page.

Primer in Excel VBA

This chapter is intended for those who are not familiar with Excel and the Excel macro recorder, or who are inexperienced with programming using the Visual Basic for Applications (VBA) language. If you are already comfortable with navigating around the features provided by Excel, have used the macro recorder, and have a working knowledge of VBA and the Visual Basic Editor (VBE), you might want to skip straight to Chapter 3.

If this is not the case, this chapter has been designed to provide you with the information you need to be able to move on comfortably to the more advanced features presented in the following chapters. We will be covering the following topics:

❑ The Excel macro recorder

❑ User-defined functions

❑ The Excel Object Model

❑ VBA programming concepts

Excel VBA is a programming application that allows you to use Visual Basic code to run the many features of the Excel package, thereby allowing you to customize your Excel applications. Units of VBA code are often referred to as macros. We will be covering more formal terminology in this chapter, but we will continue to use the term macro as a general way to refer to any VBA code.

In your day-to-day use of Excel, if you carry out the same sequence of commands repetitively, you can save a lot of time and effort by automating those steps using macros. If you are setting up an application for other users, who don't know much about Excel, you can use macros to create buttons and dialog boxes to guide them through your application as well as automate the processes involved.

If you are able to perform an operation manually, you can use the macro recorder to capture that operation. This is a very quick and easy process and requires no prior knowledge of the VBA language. Many Excel users record and run macros and feel no need to learn about VBA.

However, the recorded results might not be very flexible, in that the macro can only be used to carry out one particular task on one particular range of cells. In addition, the recorded macro is likely to run much more slowly than the code written by someone with knowledge of VBA. To set up interactive macros that can adapt to change and also run quickly, and to take advantage of more advanced features of Excel such as customized dialog boxes, you need to learn about VBA.

> **Don't get the impression that we are dismissing the macro recorder. The macro recorder is one of the most valuable tools available to VBA programmers. It is the fastest way to generate working VBA code. But you must be prepared to apply your own knowledge of VBA to edit the recorded macro to obtain flexible and efficient code. A recurring theme in this book is to record an Excel macro and then show how to adapt the recorded code.**

In this chapter you will learn how to use the macro recorder and you will see all the ways Excel provides to run your macros. You will see how to use the Visual Basic Editor to examine and change your macros, thus going beyond the recorder and tapping into the power of the VBA language and the Excel Object Model.

You can also use VBA to create your own worksheet functions. Excel comes with hundreds of built-in functions, such as SUM and IF, which you can use in cell formulas. However, if you have a complex calculation that you use frequently and that is not included in the set of standard Excel functions—such as a tax calculation or a specialized scientific formula—you can write your own user-defined function.

Using the Macro Recorder

Excel's macro recorder operates very much like the recorder that stores the greeting on your telephone answering machine. To record a greeting, you first prepare yourself by rehearsing the greeting to ensure that it says what you want. Then, you switch on the recorder and deliver the greeting. When you have finished, you switch off the recorder. You now have a recording that automatically plays when you leave a call unanswered.

Recording an Excel macro is very similar. You first rehearse the steps involved and decide at what points you want to start and stop the recording process. You prepare your spreadsheet, switch on the Excel recorder, carry out your Excel operations, and switch off the recorder. You now have an automated procedure that you and others can reproduce at the press of a button.

Recording Macros

Say, you want a macro that types six month names as three letter abbreviations, "Jan" to "Jun", across the top of your worksheet, starting in cell B1. We know this is rather a silly macro as you could do this easily with an AutoFill operation, but this example will serve to show us some important general concepts:

❑ First, think about how you are going to carry out this operation. In this case, it is easy—you will just type the data across the worksheet. Remember, a more complex macro might need more rehearsals before you are ready to record it.

❑ Next, think about when you want to start recording. In this case, you should include the selection of cell B1 in the recording, as you want to always have "Jan" in B1. If you don't select B1 at the start, you will record typing "Jan" into the active cell, which could be anywhere when you play back the macro.

❑ Next, think about when you want to stop recording. You might first want to include some formatting such as making the cells bold and italic, so you should include that in the recording. Where do you want the active cell to be after the macro runs? Do you want it to be in the same cell as "Jun", or would you rather have the active cell in column A or column B, ready for your next input? Let's assume that you want the active cell to be A2, at the completion of the macro, so we will select A2 before turning off the recorder.

❑ Now you can set up your screen, ready to record.

In this case, start with an empty worksheet with cell A1 selected. If you like to work with toolbars, use View ⇨ Toolbars to select and display the Visual Basic toolbar as shown in Figure 1-1 in the top right of the screen. Press the Record Macro button, with the red dot, to start the recorder. If you prefer, start the recorder with Tools ⇨ Macro ⇨ Record New Macro . . . from the Worksheet menu bar.

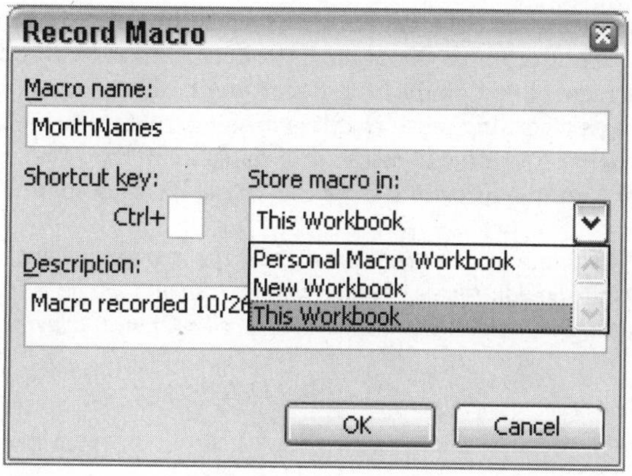

Figure 1-1

In the Macro name: box, replace the default entry, such as Macro1, with the name you want for your macro. The name should start with a letter and contain only letters, numbers and the underscore character with a maximum length of 255 characters. The macro name must not contain special characters such as !, ?, or blank spaces. It is also best to use a short but descriptive name that you will recognize later. You can use the underscore character to separate words, but it is easy to just use capitalization to distinguish words.

> Note that distinguishing words within a variable name by an initial uppercase letter is called Pascal-casing, as in ThisIsPascalCased. Making the first word's first letter lowercase and all subsequent word's first letter uppercase is called camel-casing, as in thisIsCamelCased. With case-sensitive languages like C++, Pascal or C# using variations on name-casing is a convention that many programmers follow. Because VBA is not case-sensitive you may use any standard you like, just be consistent.

Call the macro MonthNames1, because we will create another version later.

In the Shortcut key: box, you can type in a single letter. This key can be pressed later, while holding down the *Ctrl* key, to run the macro. We will use a lower case *m*. Alternatively, you can use an upper case *M*. In this case, when you later want to run the macro, you need to hold down the *Ctrl* key and the *Shift* key while you press *M*. It is not mandatory to provide a shortcut key. You can run a macro in a number of other ways, as we will see.

In the Description: box, you can accept the default comments provided by the recorder, or type in your own comments. These lines will appear at the top of your macro code. They have no significance to VBA but provide you and others with information about the macro. You can edit these comments later, so there is no need to change them now. All Excel macros are stored in workbooks.

You are given a choice regarding where the recorded macro will be stored. The Store macro in: combo box lists three possibilities. If you choose New Workbook, the recorder will open a new empty workbook for the macro. Personal Macro Workbook refers to a special hidden workbook that we will discuss next. We will choose This Workbook to store the macro in the currently active workbook.

When you have filled in the Record Macro dialog box, click the *OK* button. You will see the word Recording on the left side of the Status Bar at the bottom of the screen and the Stop Recording toolbar should appear on the screen. Note that the Stop Recording toolbar will not appear if it has been previously closed during a recording session. If it is missing, refer to the following instructions under the heading *Absolute and Relative Recording* to see how to reinstate it. However, you don't really need it for the moment because we can stop the recording from the Visual Basic toolbar or the Tools menu.

If you have the Stop Recording toolbar visible, make sure that the second button, the Relative Reference button, is not selected. It shouldn't have a border, that is, it should not be as it appears in this screenshot in Figure 1-2. By default, the macro recorder uses absolute cell references when it records.

Figure 1-2

You should now click cell B1 and type in "Jan" and fill in the rest of the cells, as shown in Figure 1-3. Then, select B1:G1 and click the Bold and Italic buttons on the Formatting toolbar. Click the A2 cell and then stop the recorder.

You can stop the recorder by pressing the Stop Recording button on the Stop Recording toolbar, by pressing the square Stop Recording button on the Visual Basic toolbar—the round Start Recording button changes to the Stop Recording button while you are recording—or you can use Tools ➪ Macro ➪ Stop Recording from the menu bar. Save the workbook as Recorder.xls.

> **It is important to remember to stop the recorder. If you leave the recorder on, and try to run the recorded macro, you can go into a loop where the macro runs itself over and over again. If this does happen to you, or any other error occurs while testing**

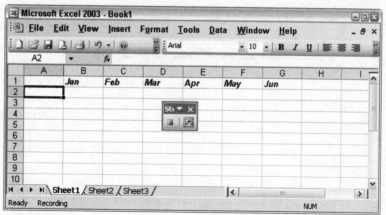

Figure 1-3

your macros, hold down the *Ctrl* key and press the *Break* key to interrupt the macro. You can then end the macro or go into debug mode to trace errors. You can also interrupt a macro with the *Esc* key, but it is not as effective as *Ctrl+Break* for a macro that is pausing for input.

The Personal Macro Workbook

If you choose to store your recorded macro in the Personal Macro Workbook, the macro is added to a special file called `Personal.xls`, which is a hidden file that is saved in your Excel Startup directory when you close Excel. This means that `Personal.xls` is automatically loaded when you launch Excel and, therefore, its macros are always available for any other workbook to use.

If `Personal.xls` does not already exist, the recorder will create it for you. You can use Window ⇨ Unhide to see this workbook in the Excel window, but it is seldom necessary or desirable to do this as you can examine and modify the `Personal.xls` macros in the Visual Basic Editor window. An exception, where you might want to make `Personal.xls` visible, is if you need to store data in its worksheets. You can hide it again, after adding the data, with Window ⇨ Hide. If you are creating a general-purpose utility macro, which you want to be able to use with any workbook, store it in `Personal.xls`. If the macro relates to just the application in the current workbook, store the macro with the application.

Running Macros

To run the macro, either insert a new worksheet in the `Recorder.xls` workbook, or open a new empty workbook, leaving `Recorder.xls` open in memory. You can only run macros that are in open workbooks, but they can be run from within any other open workbook.

You can run the macro by holding down the *Ctrl* key and pressing *m*, the shortcut that we assigned at the start of the recording process. You can also run the macro by clicking Tools ⇨ Macro ⇨ Macros... on the Worksheet menu bar and double-clicking the macro name, or by selecting the macro name and clicking Run, as shown in Figure1-4.

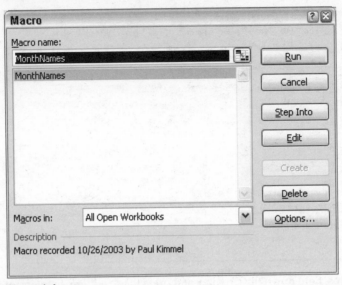

Figure 1-4

The same dialog box can be opened by pressing the Run Macro button on the Visual Basic toolbar, as shown in Figure 1-5.

Figure 1-5

Shortcut Keys

You can change the shortcut key assigned to a macro by first bringing up the Macro dialog box, by using Tools ➪ Macro ➪ Macros, or the Run Macro button on the Visual Basic toolbar. Select the macro name and press *Options*. This opens the following dialog box shown in Figure 1-6.

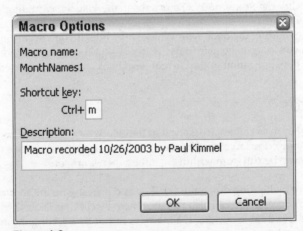

Figure 1-6

It is possible to assign the same shortcut key to more than one macro in the same workbook using this dialog box (although the dialog box that appears when you start, the macro recorder will not let you assign a shortcut that is already in use).

> It is also quite likely that two different workbooks could contain macros with the same shortcut key assigned. If this happens, which macro runs when you use the shortcut? The answer is, it is always the macro that comes first alphabetically that runs.

Shortcuts are appropriate for macros that you use very frequently, especially if you prefer to keep your hands on the keyboard. It is worth memorizing the shortcuts so you won't forget them if you use them regularly. Shortcuts are not appropriate for macros that are run infrequently or are intended to make life easier for less experienced users of your application. It is better to assign meaningful names to those macros and run them from the Macro dialog box. Alternatively, they can be run from buttons that you add to the worksheet, or place on the toolbars. You will learn how to do this shortly.

Absolute and Relative Recording

When you run MonthNames1, the macro returns to the same cells you selected while typing in the month names. It doesn't matter which cell is active when you start, if the macro contains the command to select cell B1, then that is what it selects. The macro selects B1 because you recorded in absolute record mode. The alternative, relative record mode, remembers the position of the active cell relative to its previous position. If you have cell A10 selected, and then turn on the recorder and you go on to select B10, the recorder notes that you moved one cell to the right, rather than noting that you selected cell B10.

We will record a second macro called MonthNames2. There will be three differences in this macro compared with the previous one:

- ❑ We will use the Relative Reference button on the Stop Recording toolbar as our first action after turning on the recorder.

- ❑ We will not select the "Jan" cell before typing. We want our recorded macro to type "Jan" into the active cell when we run the macro.

- ❑ We will finish by selecting the cell under "Jan", rather than A2, just before turning off the recorder.

Start with an empty worksheet and select the B1 cell. Turn on the macro recorder and specify the macro name as MonthNames2. Enter the shortcut as uppercase *M*—the recorder won't let you use lowercase m again. Click the *OK* button and select the Relative Reference button on the Stop Recording toolbar.

> If the Stop Recording toolbar does not automatically appear when you start recording, click View ⇨ Toolbars from the worksheet's menu and select Stop Recording. The Stop Recording toolbar will now appear. However, you will need to immediately click the Stop Recording button on the Stop Recording toolbar and start the recording process again. Otherwise, the recorded macro will display the Stop Recording toolbar every time it is run. The Stop Recording toolbar will now synchronize with the recorder, as long as you never close it while recording.

If you needed to resynchronize the Stop Recording toolbar using the instructions above, upper case M will already be assigned. If you have difficulties assigning the uppercase M shortcut to `MonthNames2` on the second recording, use another key such as uppercase N, and change it back to M after finishing the recording. Use Tools ⇨ Macro ⇨ Macros . . . and, in the Macro dialog box, select the macro name and press the *Options* button, as explained earlier in the *Shortcut Keys* section.

Type "Jan" and the other month names, as you did when recording `MonthNames1`. Select cells B1:G1 and press the *Bold* and *Italic* buttons on the Formatting toolbar.

> **Make sure you select B1:G1 from left to right, so that B1 is the active cell. There is a small kink in the recording process that can cause errors in the recorded macro if you select cells from right to left or from bottom to top. Always select from the top left hand corner when recording relatively. This has been a problem with all versions of Excel VBA. (Selecting cells from right to left will cause a Runtime error 1004 when the macro runs.)**

Finally, select cell B2, the cell under "Jan", and turn off the recorder.

Before running `MonthNames2`, select a starting cell, such as A10. You will find that the macro now types the month names across row 10, starting in column A and finishes by selecting the cell under the starting cell.

Before you record a macro that selects cells, you need to think about whether to use absolute or relative reference recording. If you are selecting input cells for data entry, or for a print area, you will probably want to record with absolute references. If you want to be able to run your macro in different areas of your worksheet, you will probably want to record with relative references.

If you are trying to reproduce the effect of the *Ctrl+Arrow* keys to select the last cell in a column or row of data, you should record with relative references. You can even switch between relative and absolute reference recording in the middle of a macro, if you want. You might want to select the top of a column with an absolute reference, switch to relative references and use *Ctrl+Down Arrow* to get to the bottom of the column and an extra *Down Arrow* to go to the first empty cell.

Excel 2000 was the first version of Excel to let you successfully record selecting a block of cells of variable height and width using the Ctrl key. If you start at the top left hand corner of a block of data, you can hold down the Shift+Ctrl keys and press Down Arrow and then Right Arrow to select the whole block (as long as there are no gaps in the data). If you record these operations with relative referencing, you can use the macro to select a block of different dimensions. Previous versions of Excel recorded an absolute selection of the original block size, regardless of recording mode.

The Visual Basic Editor

It is now time to see what has been going on behind the scenes. If you want to understand macros, try to modify your macros, and tap into the full power of VBA, you need to know how to use the Visual Basic Editor (VBE). The VBE runs in its own window, separate from the Excel window. You can activate it in many ways.

First, you can run VBE by pressing the Visual Basic Editor button on the Visual Basic toolbar. You can also activate it by holding down the *Alt* key and pressing the *F11* key. *Alt+F11* acts as a toggle, taking you between the Excel Window and the VBE window. If you want to edit a specific macro, you can use Tools ➪ Macro ➪ Macros . . . to open the Macro dialog box, select the macro, and press the *Edit* button. The VBE window will look something like Figure 1-7.

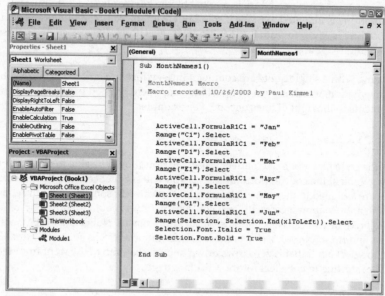

Figure 1-7

It is quite possible that you will see nothing but the menu bar when you switch to the VBE window. If you can't see the toolbar, use View ➪ Toolbars and click the Standard toolbar. Use View ➪ Project Explorer and View ➪ Properties Window to show the windows on the left. If you can't see the code module on the right, double-click the icon for Module1 in the Project Explorer window.

Code Modules

All macros reside in code modules like the one on the right of the VBE window shown in Figure 1-7. There are two types of code modules—standard modules and class modules. The one you see on the right is a standard module. You can use class modules to create your own objects. See Chapter 6 for more details on how to use class modules.

Some class modules have already been set up for you. They are associated with each worksheet in your workbook and there is one for the entire workbook. You can see them in the Project Explorer window, in the folder called "Microsoft Excel Objects". You will find out more about them later in this chapter.

You can add as many code modules to your workbook, as you like. The macro recorder has inserted the one above, named Module1. Each module can contain many macros. For a small application, you would probably keep all your macros in one module. For larger projects, you can organize your code better by filing unrelated macros in separate modules.

Procedures

In VBA, macros are referred to as procedures. There are two types of procedures—subroutines and functions. You will find out about functions in the next section. The macro recorder can only produce subroutines. You can see the MonthNames1 subroutine set up by the recorder in the above screenshot.

Subroutines start with the keyword Sub followed by the name of the procedure and opening and closing parentheses. The end of a sub procedure is marked by the keywords End Sub. By convention, the code within the subroutine is indented to make it stand out from the start and end of the subroutine, so that the whole procedure is easier to read. Further indentation is normally used to distinguish sections of code such as If tests and looping structures.

Any lines starting with a single quote are comment lines, which are ignored by VBA. They are added to provide documentation, which is a very important component of good programming practice. You can also add comments to the right of lines of code. For example:

```
Range("B1").Select 'Select the B1 cell
```

At this stage, the code may not make perfect sense, but you should be able to make out roughly what is going on. If you look at the code in MonthNames1, you will see that cells are being selected and then the month names are assigned to the active cell formula. You can edit some parts of the code, so if you had spelled a month abbreviation incorrectly, you could fix it; or you could identify and remove the line that sets the font to bold; or you can select and delete an entire macro. Notice the differences between MonthNames1 and MonthNames2. MonthNames1 selects specific cells such as B1 and C1. MonthNames2 uses Offset to select a cell that is zero rows down and one column to the right from the active cell. Already, you are starting to get a feel for the VBA language.

The Project Explorer

The Project Explorer is an essential navigation tool. In VBA, each workbook contains a project. The Project Explorer displays all the open projects and the component parts of those projects, as you can see in Figure 1-8.

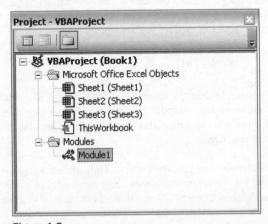

Figure 1-8

You can use the Project Explorer to locate and activate the code modules in your project. You can double click a module icon to open and activate that module. You can also insert and remove code modules in the Project Explorer. Right-click anywhere in the Project Explorer window and click Insert to add a new standard module, class module, or UserForm.

To remove Module1, right-click it and choose Remove Module1 . . . . Note that you can't do this with the modules associated with workbook or worksheet objects. You can also export the code in a module to a separate text file, or import code from a text file.

The Properties Window

The Properties window shows you the properties that can be changed at design time for the currently active object in the Project Explorer window. For example, if you click Sheet1 in the Project Explorer, the following properties are displayed in the Properties window. The ScrollArea property has been set to A1:D10, to restrict users to that area of the worksheet.

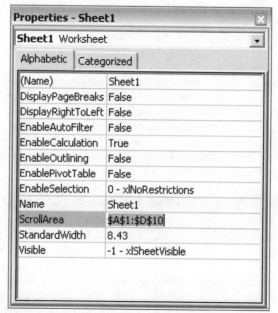

Figure 1-9

You can get to the help screen associated with any property very easily. Just select the property, such as the ScrollArea property, which is shown selected in Figure 1-9, and press *F1*.

Other Ways to Run Macros

You have seen how to run macros with shortcuts and how to run them from the Tools menu. Neither method is particularly friendly. You need to be very familiar with your macros to be comfortable with these techniques. You can make your macros much more accessible by attaching them to buttons.

If the macro is worksheet specific, and will only be used in a particular part of the worksheet, then it is suitable to use a button that has been embedded in the worksheet at the appropriate location. If you want to be able to use a macro in any worksheet or workbook and in any location in a worksheet, it is appropriate to attach the macro to a button on a toolbar.

There are many other objects that you can attach macros to, including combo boxes, list boxes, scrollbars, check boxes and option buttons. These are all referred to as controls. See Chapter 10 for more information on controls. You can also attach macros to graphic objects in the worksheet, such as shapes created with the Drawing toolbar.

Worksheet Buttons

Excel 2003 has two different sets of controls that can be embedded in worksheets. One set is on the Forms toolbar and the other is on the Control Toolbox toolbar. The Forms toolbar has been inherited from Excel 5 and 95. The Forms controls are also used with Excel 5 and 95 dialog sheets to create dialog boxes. Excel 97 introduced the newer ActiveX controls that are selected from the Control Toolbox toolbar. You can also use these on UserForms, in the VBE, to create dialog boxes.

For compatibility with the older versions of Excel, both sets of controls and techniques for creating dialog boxes are supported in Excel 97 and above. If you have no need to maintain backward compatibility with Excel 5 and 95, you can use just the ActiveX controls, except when you want to embed controls in a chart. At the moment, charts only support the Forms controls.

Forms Toolbar

Another reason for using the Forms controls is that they are simpler to use than the ActiveX controls, as they do not have all the features of ActiveX controls. For example, Forms controls can only respond to a single, predefined event, which is usually the mouse-click event. ActiveX controls can respond to many events, such as a mouse click, a double-click or pressing a key on the keyboard. If you have no need of such features, you might prefer the simplicity of Forms controls. Display the Forms toolbar by selecting View ➪ Toolbars ➪ Forms, and to create a Forms button in a worksheet, click the fourth button from the left in the Forms toolbar as shown in Figure 1-10.

Figure 1-10

You can now draw the button in your worksheet by clicking where you want a corner of the button to appear and dragging to where you want the diagonally opposite corner to appear. The dialog box shown in Figure 1-11 will appear, and you can select the macro to attach to the button.

Click *OK* to complete the assignment. You can then edit the text on the button to give a more meaningful indication of its function. After you click a worksheet cell, you can click the button to run the attached macro. If you need to edit the button, you can right-click it. This selects the control and you get a shortcut menu. If you don't want the shortcut menu, hold down *Ctrl* and left-click the button to select it. (Don't drag the mouse while you hold down *Ctrl*, or you will create a copy of the button.)

If you want to align the button with the worksheet gridlines, hold down *Alt* as you draw it with the mouse. If you have already drawn the button, select it and hold down *Alt* as you drag any of the white boxes that appear on the corners and edges of the button. The edge or corner you drag will snap to the nearest gridline.

Control Toolbox Toolbar

To create an ActiveX command button control, click the sixth button from the left side of the Control Toolbox toolbar, as shown in Figure 1-12.

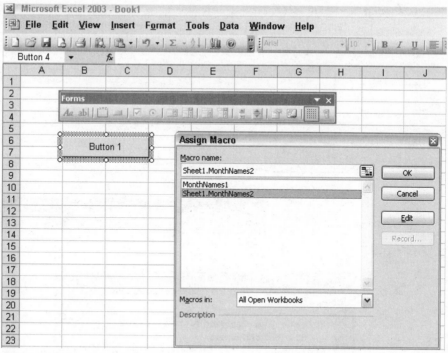

Figure 1-11

Figure 1-12

When you draw your button in the worksheet, you enter into the design mode. When you are in the design mode, you can select a control with a left-click and edit it. You must turn off the design mode if you want the new control to respond to events. This can be achieved by unchecking the design mode icon on the Control Toolbox toolbar or the Visual Basic toolbar, as shown in Figure 1-13.

You are not prompted to assign a macro to the ActiveX command button, but you do need to write a click-event procedure for the button. An event procedure is a sub procedure that is executed when, for example, you click a button. To do this, make sure you are still in the design mode and double-click the command button. This will open the VBE window and display the code module behind the worksheet. The Sub and End Sub statement lines for your code will have been inserted in the module and you can add in the code necessary to run the MonthName2 macro, as shown in Figure 1-14.

To run this code, switch back to the worksheet, turn off the design mode, and click the command button.

If you want to make changes to the command button, you need to return to the design mode by pressing the Design Mode button. You can then select the command button and change its size and position on the worksheet. You can also display its properties by right-clicking it and choosing Properties to display the window, as shown in Figure 1-15.

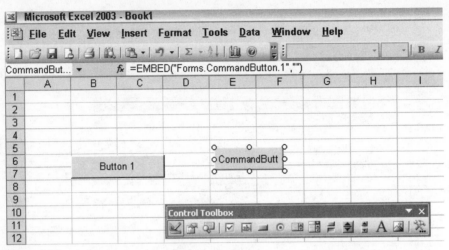

Figure 1-13

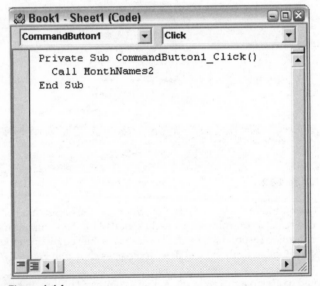

Figure 1-14

To change the text on the command button, change the Caption property. You can also set the font for the caption and the foreground and background colors. If you want the button to work satisfactorily in Excel 97, it is a good idea to change the TakeFocusOnClick property from its default value of True to False. If the button takes the focus when you click it, Excel 97 does not allow you to assign values to some properties such as the NumberFormat property of the Range object.

Toolbars

If you want to attach a macro to a toolbar button, you can modify one of the built-in toolbars or create your own. To create your own toolbar, use View ⇨ Toolbars ⇨ Customize ... to bring up the Customize dialog box, click New ... and enter a name for the new toolbar (see Figure 1-16).

Figure 1-15

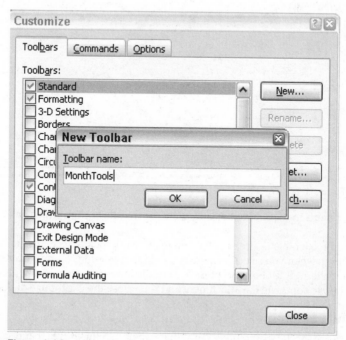

Figure 1-16

Staying in the Customize dialog box, click the Commands tab and select the Macros category. Drag the Custom Button with the smiley face icon to the new toolbar, or an existing toolbar. Next, either click the Modify-Selection button, or right-click the new toolbar button to get a shortcut menu.

Select Assign Macro... and then select the name of the macro, MonthNames2 in this case, to be assigned to the button. You can also change the button image by clicking Change Button Image and choosing from a library of preset images, or you can open the icon editor with Edit Button Image. Note that the Customize dialog box must stay open while you make these changes. It is a good idea to enter some descriptive text into the Name box, which will appear as the ScreenTip for the button. You can now close the Customize dialog box.

To run the macro, select a starting cell for your month names and click the new toolbar button. If you want to distribute the new toolbar to others, along with the workbook, you can attach the toolbar to the workbook. It will then pop up automatically on the new user's PC as soon as they open the workbook, as long as they do not already have a toolbar with the same name.

> *There is a potential problem when you attach a toolbar to a workbook. As Excel will not replace an existing toolbar, you can have a toolbar that is attached to an older version of the workbook than the one you are trying to use. A solution to this problem is provided in the next section on event procedures.*

To attach a toolbar to the active workbook, use View ⇨ Toolbars ⇨ Customize... to bring up the Customize dialog box, click the Toolbars tab, if necessary, and click *Attach...* to open the Attach Toolbars dialog box as shown in Figure 1-17.

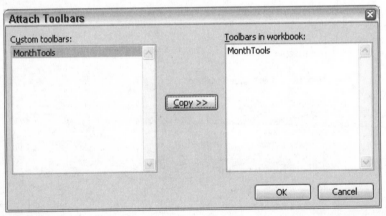

Figure 1-17

Select the toolbar name in the left list box and press the middle button, which has the caption Copy >>.

If an older copy of the toolbar is already attached to the workbook, select it in the right-hand list box and press *Delete* – shown when you select an item in the right-hand-side column – to remove it. Then select the toolbar name in the left list box and press the middle button again, which will now have the caption Copy >>. Click *OK* to complete the attachment and then close the Customize dialog box.

Event Procedures

Event procedures are special macro procedures that respond to the events that occur in Excel. Events include user actions, such as clicking the mouse on a button, and system actions, such as the recalculation of a worksheet. Versions of Excel since Excel 97 expose a wide range of events for which we can write code.

The click-event procedure for the ActiveX command button that ran the MonthNames2 macro, which we have already seen, is a good example. We entered the code for this event procedure in the code module behind the worksheet where the command button was embedded. All event procedures are contained in the class modules behind the workbook, worksheets, charts, and UserForms.

We can see the events that are available by activating a module, such as the ThisWorkbook module, choosing an object, such as Workbook, from the left drop-down list at the top of the module and then activating the right drop-down, as shown in Figure 1-18.

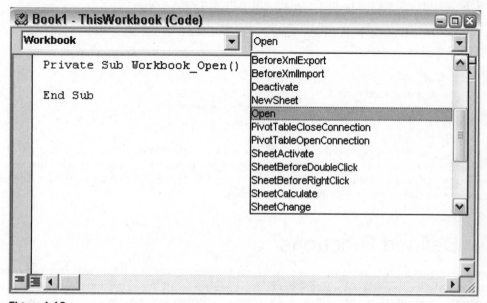

Figure 1-18

The Workbook_Open() event can be used to initialize the workbook when it is opened. The code could be as simple as activating a particular worksheet and selecting a range for data input. The code could be more sophisticated and construct a new menu bar for the workbook.

> For compatibility with Excel 5 and 95, you can still create a sub procedure called
> **Auto_Open()**, in a standard module, that runs when the workbook is opened. If you
> also have a **Workbook_Open()** event procedure, the event procedure runs first.

As you can see, there are many events to choose from. Some events, such as the BeforeSave and BeforeClose, allow cancellation of the event. The following event procedure stops the workbook from being closed until cell A1 in Sheet1 contains the value True.

```
Private Sub Workbook_BeforeClose(Cancel As Boolean)
  If ThisWorkbook.Sheets("Sheet1").Range("A1").Value <> True _
    Then Cancel = True
End Sub
```

This code even prevents the closure of the Excel window.

Removing an Attached Toolbar

As mentioned previously in this chapter, if you have attached a custom toolbar to a workbook, there can be a problem if you send a new version of the toolbar attached to a workbook, or the user saves the workbook under a different name. The old toolbar is not replaced when you open the new workbook, and the macros that the old toolbar runs are still in the old workbook.

One approach that makes it much less likely that problems will occur, is to delete the custom toolbar when the workbook is closed:

```
Private Sub Workbook_BeforeClose(Cancel As Boolean)
    On Error Resume Next
    Application.CommandBars("MonthTools").Delete
End Sub
```

The On Error statement covers the situation where the user might delete the toolbar manually before closing the workbook. Omitting the On Error statement would cause a runtime error when the event procedure attempts to delete the missing toolbar. On Error Resume Next is an instruction to ignore any runtime error and continue with the next line of code.

User Defined Functions

Excel has hundreds of built-in worksheet functions that we can use in cell formulas. You can select an empty worksheet cell and use Insert ➪ Function... to see a list of those functions. Among the most frequently used functions are SUM, IF, and VLOOKUP. If the function you need is not already in Excel, you can write your own user defined function (or UDF) using VBA.

UDFs can reduce the complexity of a worksheet. It is possible to reduce a calculation that requires many cells of intermediate results down to a single function call in one cell. UDFs can also increase productivity when many users have to repeatedly use the same calculation procedures. You can set up a library of functions tailored to your organization.

Creating a UDF

Unlike manual operations, UDFs cannot be recorded. We have to write them from scratch using a standard module in the VBE. If necessary, you can insert a standard module by right-clicking in the Project Explorer window and choosing Insert ➪ Module. A simple example of a UDF is shown here:

```
Function CentigradeToFahrenheit(Centigrade)
    CentigradeToFahrenheit = Centigrade * 9 / 5 + 32
End Function
```

Here, we have created a function called `CentigradeToFahrenheit()` that converts degrees Centigrade to degrees Fahrenheit. In the worksheet we could have column A containing degrees Centigrade, and column B using the `CentigradeToFahrenheit()` function to calculate the corresponding temperature in degrees Fahrenheit. You can see the formula in cell B2 by looking at the Formula bar in Figure 1-19.

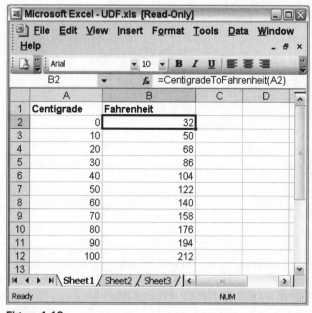

Figure 1-19

The formula has been copied into cells B3:B13.

The key difference between a sub procedure and a function procedure is that a function procedure returns a value. `CentigradeToFahrenheit()` calculates a numeric value, which is returned to the worksheet cell where `CentigradeToFahrenheit()` is used. A function procedure indicates the value to be returned by setting its own name equal to the return value.

Function procedures normally have one or more input parameters. `CentigradeToFahrenheit()` has one input parameter called `Centigrade`, which is used to calculate the return value. When you enter the formula, `= CentigradeToFahrenheit(A2)`, the value in cell A2 is passed to `CentigradeToFahrenheit()` through `Centigrade`. In the case where the value of `Centigrade` is zero, `CentigradeToFahrenheit()` sets its own name equal to the calculated result, which is 32. The result is passed back to cell B2, as shown earlier. The same process occurs in each cell that contains a reference to `CentigradeToFahrenheit()`.

A different example that shows how you can reduce the complexity of spreadsheet formulas for users is shown in Figure 1-20. The lookup table in cells A2:D5 gives the price of each product, the discount sales volume (above which a discount will be applied), and the percent discount for units above the discount volume. Using normal spreadsheet formulas, users would have to set up three lookup formulas together with some logical tests to calculate the invoice amount.

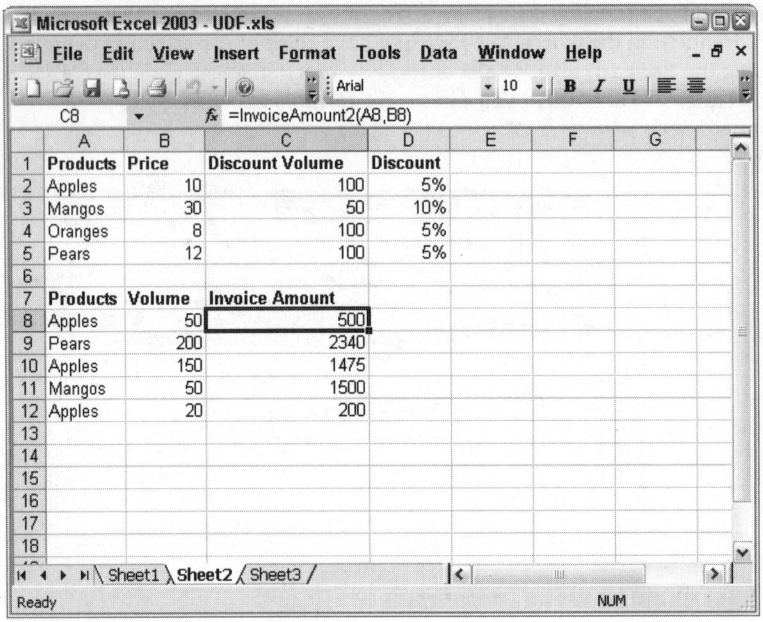

Figure 1-20

The `InvoiceAmount()` function has three input parameters: `Product` is the name of the product; `Volume` is the number of units sold, and `Table` is the lookup table. The formula in cell C8 defines the ranges to be used for each input parameter:

```
Function InvoiceAmount(ByVal Product As String, _
   ByVal Volume As Integer, ByVal Table As Range)

   ' Lookup price in table
   Price = WorksheetFunction.VLookup(Product, Table, 2)

   ' Lookup discount volume in table
   DiscountVolume = WorksheetFunction.VLookup(Product, Table, 3)

   ' Compare volume to discount volume to determine if customer
   ' gets discount price
   If Volume > DiscountVolume Then
      ' calculate discounted price
      DiscountPercent = WorksheetFunction.VLookup(Product, Table, 4)
      InvoiceAmount = Price * DiscountVolume + Price * _
         (1 - DiscountPercent) * (Volume - DiscountVolume)
   Else
      ' calculate undiscounted price
      InvoiceAmount = Price * Volume
   End If
End Function
```

The range for the table is absolute so that the copies of the formula below cell C8 refer to the same range. The first calculation in the function uses the `VLookup` function to find the product in the lookup table and return the corresponding value from the second column of the lookup table, which it assigns to the variable Price.

If you want to use an Excel worksheet function in a VBA procedure, you need to tell VBA where to find it by preceding the function name with WorksheetFunction and a period. For compatibility with Excel 5 and 95, you can use Application instead of WorksheetFunction. Not all worksheet functions are available this way. In these cases, VBA has equivalent functions, or mathematical operators, to carry out the same calculations.

In the next line of the function, the discount volume is found in the lookup table and assigned to the variable DiscountVolume. The If test on the next line compares the sales volume in Volume with DiscountVolume. If Volume is greater than DiscountVolume, the calculations following, down to the Else statement, are carried out. Otherwise, the calculation after the Else is carried out.

If Volume is greater than DiscountVolume, the percent discount rate is found in the lookup table and assigned to the variable DiscountPercent. The invoice amount is then calculated by applying the full price to the units up to DiscountVolume plus the discounted price for units above DiscountVolume. Note the use of the underscore character, preceded by a blank space, to indicate the continuation of the code on the next line.

The result is assigned to the name of the function, InvoiceAmount, so that the value will be returned to the worksheet cell. If Volume is not greater than DiscountVolume, the invoice amount is calculated by applying the price to the units sold and the result is assigned to the name of the function.

Direct Reference to Ranges

When you define a UDF, it is possible to directly refer to worksheet ranges rather than through the input parameters of the UDF. This is illustrated in the following version of the InvoiceAmount2() function:

```
Public Function InvoiceAmount2(ByVal Product As String, _
  ByVal Volume As Integer) As Double

    Dim Table As Range
    Set Table = ThisWorkbook.Worksheets("Sheet2").Range("A2:D5")
    Dim Price As Integer
    Price = WorksheetFunction.VLookup(Product, Table, 2)

    Dim DiscountVolume As Integer
    DiscountVolume = WorksheetFunction.VLookup(Product, Table, 3)

    Dim DiscountPercent As Double
    If Volume > DiscountVolume Then
      DiscountPercent = WorksheetFunction.VLookup(Product, Table, 4)
      InvoiceAmount2 = Price * DiscountVolume + Price * _
        (1 - DiscountPercent) * (Volume - DiscountVolume)
    Else
      InvoiceAmount2 = Price * Volume
    End If
End Function
```

Note that Table is no longer an input parameter. Instead, the Set statement defines Table with a direct reference to the worksheet range. While this method still works, the return value of the function will not be recalculated if you change a value in the lookup table. Excel does not realize that it needs to recalculate the function when a lookup table value changes, as it does not see that the table is used by the function.

Excel only recalculates a UDF when it sees its input parameters change. If you want to remove the lookup table from the function parameters, and still have the UDF recalculate automatically, you can declare the function to be volatile on the first line of the function as shown in the following code:

```
Public Function InvoiceAmount2(ByVal Prod As String, _
    ByVal Volume As Integer) As Double

    Application.Volatile
            Dim Table As Range
Set Table = ThisWorkbook.Worksheets("Sheet2").Range("A2:D5")
...
```

However, you should be aware that this feature comes at a price. If a UDF is declared volatile, the UDF is recalculated every time any value changes in the worksheet. This can add a significant recalculation burden to the worksheet if the UDF is used in many cells.

What UDFs Cannot Do

A common mistake made by users is to attempt to create a worksheet function that changes the structure of the worksheet by, for example, copying a range of cells. Such attempts will fail. No error messages are produced because Excel simply ignores the offending code lines, so the reason for the failure is not obvious.

> **UDFs, used in worksheet cells, are not permitted to change the structure of the worksheet. This means that a UDF cannot return a value to any other cell than the one it is used in and it cannot change a physical characteristic of a cell, such as the font color or background pattern. In addition, UDFs cannot carry out actions such as copying or moving spreadsheet cells. They cannot even carry out some actions that imply a change of cursor location, such as an Edit ⇨ Find. A UDF can call another function, or even a subroutine, but that procedure will be under the same restrictions as the UDF. It will still not be permitted to change the structure of the worksheet.**

A distinction is made (in Excel VBA) between UDFs that are used in worksheet cells, and function procedures that are not connected with worksheet cells. As long as the original calling procedure was not a UDF in a worksheet cell, a function procedure can carry out any Excel action, just like a subroutine.

It should also be noted that UDFs are not as efficient as the built-in Excel worksheet functions. If UDFs are used extensively in a workbook, recalculation time will be greater compared with a similar workbook using the same number of built-in functions.

The Excel Object Model

The Visual Basic for Applications programming language is common across all the Microsoft Office applications. In addition to Excel, you can use VBA in Word, Access, PowerPoint, Outlook, FrontPage, PowerPoint, and Project. Once you learn it, you can apply it to any of these. However, to work with an application, you need to learn about the objects it contains. In Word, you deal with documents, paragraphs, and words. In Access, you deal with databases, record sets, and fields. In Excel, you deal with workbooks, worksheets, and ranges.

Unlike many programming languages, you don't have to create your own objects in Office VBA. Each application has a clearly defined set of objects that are arranged according to the relationships between them. This structure is referred to as the application's object model. This section is an introduction to the Excel Object Model, which is fully documented in Appendix A (available online at www.wrox.com).

Objects

First, let's cover a few basics about Object-Oriented Programming (OOP). This not a complete formal treatise on the subject, but it covers what you need to know to work with the objects in Excel.

OOP's basic premise is that we can describe everything known to us as classes. Instances of classes are called objects. You and I are objects of the Person class, the world is an object and the universe is an object. In Excel, a workbook is an object, a worksheet is an object, and a range is an object. These objects are only a small sample of around 200 object types available to us in Excel. Let us look at some examples of how we can refer to Range objects in VBA code. One simple way to refer to cells B2:C4 is as follows:

```
Range("B2:C4")
```

If you give the name Data to a range of cells, you can use that name in a similar way:

```
Range("Data")
```

There are also ways to refer to the currently active cell and selection using shortcuts.

In the screenshot shown in Figure 1-21, ActiveCell refers to the B2 cell, and Selection refers to the range B2:E6.

Collections

Many objects belong to collections. A city block has a collection of buildings. A building has a collection of floor objects. A floor has a collection of room objects. Collections are objects themselves—objects that contain other objects that are closely related. Collections and objects are often related in a hierarchical or tree structure.

Excel is an object itself, referred to by the name Application. In the Excel Application object, there is a Workbooks collection that contains all the currently open Workbook objects. Each Workbook object has a Worksheets collection that contains the Worksheet objects in that workbook.

> Note that you need to make a clear distinction between the plural **Worksheets** object, which is a collection, and the singular **Worksheet** object. They are quite different objects.

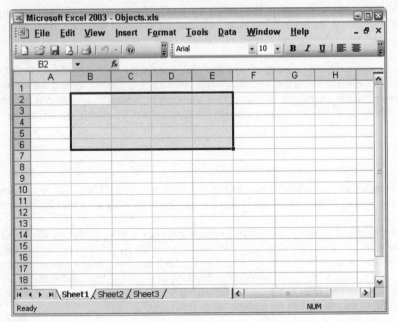

Figure 1-21

If you want to refer to a member of a collection, you can refer to it by its position in the collection, as an index number starting with 1, or by its name, as quoted text. If you have opened just one workbook called `Data.xls`, you can refer to it by either of the following:

```
Workbooks(1)
Workbooks("Data.xls")
```

If you have four worksheets in the active workbook that have the names North, South, East, and West, in that order, you can refer to the second worksheet by either of the following:

```
Worksheets(2)
Worksheets("South")
```

If you want to refer to a worksheet called `DataInput` in a workbook called `Sales.xls`, and `Sales.xls` is not the active workbook, you must qualify the worksheet reference with the workbook reference, separating them with a period, as follows:

```
Workbooks("Sales.xls").Worksheets("DataInput")
```

In object-oriented speak special characters like >, <, =, and . are called operators. The period (.) is called the member of operator. For example, we say that the Worksheets collection is a member of the Workbook class.

When you refer to the B2 cell in `DataInput`, while another workbook is active, you use:

```
Workbooks("Sales.xls").Worksheets("DataInput").Range("B2")
```

The preceding code is understood to mean that `Workbooks("Sales.xls")` returns an instance of the Workbook class. The `.Worksheets("DataInput")` part returns a single Worksheet, and the `.Range("B2")` part returns a single range. As you might have intuitively guessed, we are getting one Workbook, one Worksheet from that Workbook, and a specific Range.

Let us now look at objects more closely and see how we can manipulate them in our VBA code. There are four key characteristics of objects that you need to be aware of to do this. They are the fields, properties, methods, and events associated with an object.

Fields

Fields are variables that capture the state of an object. Fields can be anything that helps describe what instances of a class should know. For example, a `Customer` class may need to know the name of the customer. The reason we say a `Customer` class "may need to know" something is because what a class needs to know is subjective and relative to the problem domain. Extending our example further a `Customer` class may need to contain the Employer Identification Number (EIN). However, if the Customers were not business then the EIN doesn't make any sense, but perhaps a Social Security Number would be a better field.

An example of our EIN field might be:

```
Private FEmploymentIdentificationNumber As String
```

By convention, we will use an F-prefix simply to denote that a name is a field (and drop the F for properties, described in the next section.) Another convention is that fields are declared private and accessed indirectly through a Property. We will talk more about access modifiers like Private in Chapter 5. Let's look at properties next.

Properties

Properties are an evolution. Originally, classes contained fields and methods. It was soon discovered that fields needed associated methods to ensure that proper values were being assigned to the fields. The dichotomy of ease-of-use and validation converged, resulting in a property. The property is really a special method that looks like a field to the consumer (class user), but behaves and is coded like a method by the producer (class author). Properties are purely about controlling access to state information about an object.

Consequently, properties are attributes just like fields that implicitly combine the technical behavior of a method call with the notational convenience of a field. By convention, we will drop the F-prefix of a field to derive each field's property name.Other conventions exist by other contributors to this book. Rather than pretend these philosophical differences to naming styles don't exist, you will see a couple of conventions and can choose for yourself which one makes sense. (Other naming conventions used include a prefix notation that includes information about the data type of a field or property. Pick one convention and use it consistently.)

Examples of properties in Excel include worksheet `Range` object, which has a `RowHeight` property and a `ColumnWidth` property. A `Workbook` object has a `Name` property, which contains its file name. Some properties can be changed easily, such as the `Range` object's `ColumnWidth` property, by assigning the property a new value. Other properties, such as the `Workbook` object's `Name` property, are read-only. You can't change the `Name` property by simply assigning a new value to it.

You refer to the property of an object by referring to the object, then the property, separated by a period (the member-of operator). For example, to change the width of the column containing the active cell to 20 points, you would assign the value to the ColumnWidth property of the ActiveCell using

```
ActiveCell.ColumnWidth = 20
```

To enter the name Florence into cell C10, you assign the name to the Value property of the Range object:

```
Range("C10").Value = "Florence"
```

If the Range object is not in the active worksheet in the active workbook, you need to be more specific:

```
Workbooks("Sales.xls").Worksheets("DataInput").Range("C10").Value = 10
```

> **VBA can do what is impossible for us to do manually. It can enter data into worksheets that are not visible on the screen. It can copy and move data without having to make the sheets involved active. Therefore, it is very seldom necessary to activate a specific workbook, worksheet, or range to manipulate data using VBA. The more you can avoid activating objects, the faster your code will run. Unfortunately, the macro recorder can only record what we do and uses activation extensively.**

In the previous examples, we have seen how we can assign values to the properties of objects. We can also assign the property values of objects to variables or to other objects' properties. We can directly assign the column width of one cell to another cell on the active sheet using

```
Range("C1").ColumnWidth = Range("A1").ColumnWidth
```

We can assign the value in C1 in the active sheet to D10 in the sheet named Sales, in the active workbook, using

```
Worksheets("Sales").Range("D10").Value = Range("C1").Value
```

We can assign the value of a property to a variable so that it can be used in later code. This example stores the current value of cell M100, sets M100 to a new value, prints the auto recalculated results and sets M100 back to its original value:

```
OpeningStock = Range("M100").Value
Range("M100").Value = 100
ActiveSheet.PrintOut
Range("M100").Value = OpeningStock
```

Some properties are read-only, which means that you can't assign a value to them directly. Sometimes there is an indirect way. One example is the Text property of a Range object. You can assign a value to a cell using its Value property and you can give the cell a number format using its NumberFormat property. The Text property of the cell gives you the formatted appearance of the cell. The following example displays $12,345.60 in a Message box:

```
Range("B10").Value = 12345.6
Range("B10").NumberFormat = "$#,##0.00"
MsgBox Range("B10").Text
```

This is the only means by which we can set the value of the Text property.

Methods

While properties are the quantifiable characteristics of objects, methods are the actions that can be performed by objects or on objects. If you have a linguistic bent, you might like to think of classes as nouns, objects instances of those nouns, fields and properties as adjectives, and methods as verbs. Methods often change the properties of objects. A zoologist might define a Homosapien class with the verb Walk. Walk could be implemented in terms of Speed, Distance, and Direction, yielding a new Location. A credit card company may implement a Customer class with a Spend method. Charging items (spending, a method) reduces my available credit line (AvailableCredit, a property).

A simple example of an Excel method is the Select method of the Range object. To refer to a method, as with properties, we put the object name first, a period, and the method name with any relevant arguments. Backtracking to our Walk method, we might pass in the direction, speed, and time to the walk method, yielding a new Location (assuming our present location is known). The following method invocation (or call) selects cell G4:

```
Range("G4").Select
```

Another example of an Excel method is the Copy method of the Range object. The following copies the contents of range A1:B3 to the clipboard:

```
Range("A1:B3").Copy
```

Methods often have parameters (or arguments) that we can use to modify the way the method works. For example, we can use the Paste method of the Worksheet object to paste the contents of the clipboard into a worksheet, but if we do not specify where the data is to be pasted, it is inserted with its top left-hand corner in the active cell. This can be overridden with the Destination parameter (parameters are discussed later in this section):

```
ActiveSheet.Paste Destination:=Range("G4")
```

> Note that the value of a parameter is specified using :=, not just =.

Often, Excel methods provide shortcuts. The previous examples of Copy and Paste can be carried out entirely by the Copy method:

```
Range("A1:B3").Copy Destination:=Range("G4")
```

This is far more efficient than the code produced by the macro recorder:

```
Range("A1:B3").Select
Selection.Copy
Range("G4").Select
ActiveSheet.Paste
```

Events

Another important concept in VBA is that objects can respond to events. A mouse click on a command button, a double-click on a cell, a recalculation of a worksheet, and the opening and closing of a workbook are examples of events. In plain English, events are things that happen. In the context of VBA, events are things that happen to an object.

All of the ActiveX controls from the Control Toolbox toolbar can respond to events. These controls can be embedded in worksheets and in UserForms to enhance the functionality of those objects. Worksheets and workbooks can also respond to a wide range of events. If we want an object to respond to an event, then we have to write the event handler for a specific event. An event is really nothing more than an address (a number). All things in computers are just numbers. How those numbers are used is what is important to the computer. An event's number is the address—that is, the number—that can refer to the address (again just a number) of a method. When the event is raised, the address associated with the event is used to call the method referred to by its number. These special methods are called event handlers. Fortunately, the compiler manages the assignment of numbers internally. All we need to know is the grammar used to indicate that we want a particular object's event to respond using a specific event handler, a method. Fortunately, the VBE environment goes one step further: the VBE will automatically manage generating and assigning event handlers on our behalf. Of course, we also have the option of assigning event handlers manually, which is useful when we define events for classes that are not Excel or ActiveX controls.

For example, we might want to detect that a user has selected a new cell and highlight the cell's complete row and column. We can do this having the VBE generate the SelectionChange event handler and then by entering code in the event handler. By convention, the VBE precedes an event handler's name with the object's name and an underscore prefix; thus SelectionChange is coded as Worksheet_SelectionChange. Complete the following steps to create this event handler:

❑ First activate the VBE window by pressing *Alt+F11* and double-clicking a worksheet in the Project Explorer

❑ From the Object drop-down list on the left select Worksheet, and from the Procedure drop-down list on the right select SelectionChange.

❑ Enter the following code in the generated subroutine:

```
Private Sub Worksheet_SelectionChange(ByVal Target As Range)
  Rows.Interior.ColorIndex = xlColorIndexNone
  Target.EntireColumn.Interior.ColorIndex = 36
  Target.EntireRow.Interior.ColorIndex = 36
End Sub
```

This event handler runs every time the user selects a new cell, or block of cells. The parameter, Target, refers to the selected range as a Range object. The first statement sets the ColorIndex property of all the worksheets cells to no color, to remove any existing background color. The second and third statements set the entire columns and entire rows that intersect with the selected cells to a background color of pale yellow. The predefined color xlColorIndexNone can yield a color other than a creamy yellow if you have modified Excel's color palette.

The use of properties in this example is more complex than we have seen before. Let's analyze the constituent parts. If we assume that Target is a Range object referring to cell B10, then the following code uses the EntireColumn property of the B10 Range object to refer to the entire B column, which is the range B1:B65536, or B:B for short:

```
Target.EntireColumn.Interior.ColorIndex = 36
```

Similarly, the next line of code changes the color of row 10, which is the range A10:IV10, or 10:10 for short:

```
Target.EntireRow.Interior.ColorIndex = 36
```

The Interior property of a Range object refers to an Interior object, which is the background of a range. Finally, we set the ColorIndex property of the Interior object equal to the index number for the required color.

This code might appear to many to be far from intuitive. So how do we go about figuring out how to carry out a task involving an Excel object?

Getting Help

An easy way to discover the required code to perform an operation is to use the macro recorder. The recorded code is likely to be inefficient, but it will indicate the objects required and the properties and methods involved. If you turn on the recorder to find out how to color the background of a cell, you will get something like the following:

```
With Selection.Interior
    .ColorIndex = 36
    .Pattern = xlSolid
End With
```

This With...End With construction is discussed in more detail later in this chapter. It is equivalent to:

```
Selection.Interior.ColorIndex = 36
Selection.Interior.Pattern = xlSolid
```

The second line is unnecessary, as a solid pattern is the default. The macro recorder is a verbose recorder, rather than rely on implicit values and behaviors it includes everything explicitly. The first line gives us some of the clues we need to complete our code. We only need to figure out how to change the Range object, Selection, into a complete row or complete column. If this can be done, it will be accomplished by using a property or method of the Range object.

The Object Browser

The Object Browser is a valuable tool for discovering the fields, properties, methods, and events applicable to Excel objects. To display the Object Browser, you need to be in the VBE window. You can use

View ➪ Object Browser, press *F2*, or click the Object Browser button on the Standard toolbar to see the window shown in Figure 1-22.

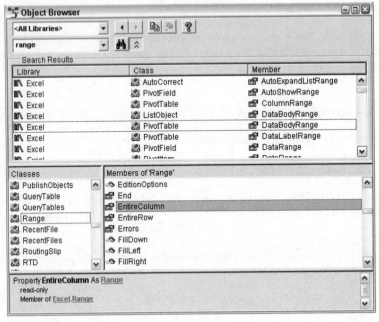

Figure 1-22

The objects are listed in the window with the title Classes. You can click in this window and type an *r* to get quickly to the Range object.

Alternatively, you can click in the search box, second from the top with the binoculars to its right, and type in range. When you press *Enter* or click the binoculars, you will see a list of items containing this text. When you click Range, under the Class heading in the Search Results window, Range will be highlighted in the Classes window below. This technique is handy when you are searching for information on a specific property, method, or event.

We now have a list of all the fields, properties, methods and events for this object, sorted alphabetically. If you right-click this list, you can choose Group Members, to separate the properties, methods, and events, which makes it easier to read. If you scan through this list, you will see the EntireColumn and EntireRow properties, which look likely candidates for our requirements. To confirm this, select EntireColumn and click the ? icon at the top of the Object Browser window to go to the window shown in Figure 1-23.

Also this can often lead to further information on related objects and methods. Now, all we have to do is connect the properties we have found and apply them to the right object.

Experimenting in the Immediate Window

If you want to experiment with code, you can use the VBE's Immediate window. Use View ➪ Immediate Window, press *Ctrl+G*, or press the Immediate Window button on the Debug toolbar to make the

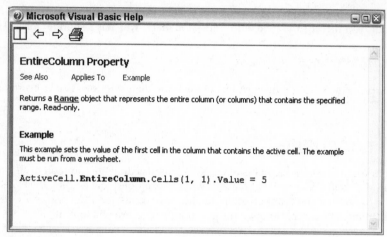

Figure 1-23

Immediate window visible. You can tile the Excel window and the VBE window so that you can type commands into the Immediate window and see the effects in the Excel window as shown in Figure 1-24.

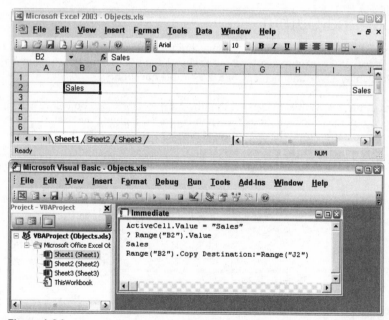

Figure 1-24

When a command is typed in the Immediate window (see lower right corner of Figure 1-24), and *Enter* is pressed, the command is immediately executed. To execute the same command again, click anywhere in the line with the command and press *Enter* again.

Here, the `Value` property of the `ActiveCell` object has been assigned the text "`Sales`". If you want to display a value, you precede the code with a question mark, which is a shortcut for `Print`:

```
?Range("B2").Value ` is equivalent to Print Range("B2").Value
```

This code has printed "Sales" on the next line of the Immediate window. The last command has copied the value in B2 to J2.

The VBA Language

In this section, you will see the elements of the VBA language that are common to all versions of Visual Basic and the Microsoft Office applications. We will use examples that employ the Excel Object Model, but our aim is to examine the common grammar. Many of these structures and concepts are common to other programming languages, although the grammar varies. We will look at:

❑ Storing information in variables and arrays

❑ Conditional statements

❑ Using loops

❑ Basic error handling

Basic Input and Output

First, let's look at some simple communication techniques that we can use to make our macros more flexible and useful. If we want to display a message, we can use the `MsgBox` function. This can be useful if we want to display a warning message or ask a simple question.

In our first example, we want to make sure that the printer is switched on before a print operation. The following code generates the dialog box shown in Figure 1-25, giving the user a chance to check the printer. The macro pauses until the *OK* button is pressed:

```
MsgBox "Please make sure that the printer is turned on"
```

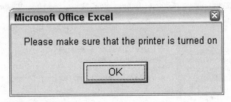

Figure 1-25

If you want to experiment, you can use the Immediate window to execute single lines of code. Alternatively, you can insert your code into a standard module in the VBE window. In this case, you need to include `Sub` and `End Sub` lines as follows:

```
Sub Test1()
   MsgBox "Please make sure that the printer is turned on"
End Sub
```

An easy way to execute a sub procedure is to click somewhere in the code to create an insertion point, then press *F5*.

`MsgBox` has many options that control the type of buttons and icons that appear in the dialog box. If you want to get help on this, or any VBA word, just click somewhere within the word and press the *F1* key. The Help screen for the word will immediately appear. Among other details, you will see the input parameters accepted by the function:

```
MsgBox(prompt[, buttons] [, title] [, helpfile, context])
```

Parameters in square brackets are optional, so only the `prompt` message is required. If you want to have a `title` at the top of the dialog box, you can specify the third parameter. There are two ways to specify parameter values, by position and by name.

Parameters Specified by Position

If we specify a parameter by position, we need to make sure that the parameters are entered in the correct order. We also need to include extra commas for missing parameters. The following code provides a title for the dialog box, specifying the title by position (see Figure 1-26):

```
MsgBox "Is the printer on?", , "Caution!"
```

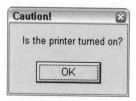

Figure 1-26

Parameters Specified by Name

There are some advantages to specifying parameters by name:

❑ We can enter them in any order and do not need to include extra commas with nothing between them to allow for undefined parameters

❑ We do need to use : = rather than just = between the parameter name and the value, as we have already pointed out

The following code generates the same dialog box as the last one:

```
MsgBox Title:="Caution!", Prompt:="Is the printer on?"
```

Another advantage of specifying parameters by name is that the code is better documented. Anyone reading the code is more likely to understand it.

If you want more information on `buttons`, you will find a table of options in the VBE help screen for the `MsgBox` function as follows:

Constant	Value	Description
VbOKOnly	0	Display OK button only
VbOKCancel	1	Display OK and Cancel buttons
VbAbortRetryIgnore	2	Display Abort, Retry, and Ignore buttons
VbYesNoCancel	3	Display Yes, No, and Cancel buttons
VbYesNo	4	Display Yes and No buttons
VbRetryCancel	5	Display Retry and Cancel buttons
VbCritical	16	Display Critical Message icon
VbQuestion	32	Display Warning Query icon
VbExclamation	48	Display Warning Message icon
VbInformation	64	Display Information Message icon
VbDefaultButton1	0	First button is default
VbDefaultButton2	256	Second button is default
VbDefaultButton3	512	Third button is default
VbDefaultButton4	768	Fourth button is default
VbApplicationModal	0	Application modal; the user must respond to the message box before continuing work in the current application
VbSystemModal	4096	System modal; all applications are suspended until the user responds to the message box
VbMsgBoxHelpButton	16384	Adds Help button to the message box
VbMsgBoxSetForeground	65536	Specifies the message box window as the foreground window
VbMsgBoxRight	524288	Text is right aligned
VbMsgBoxRtlReading	1048576	Specifies text should appear as right-to-left reading on Hebrew and Arabic systems

Values 0 to 5 control the buttons that appear (see Figure 1-27). A value of 4 gives Yes and No buttons:

```
MsgBox Prompt:="Delete this record?", Buttons:=4
```

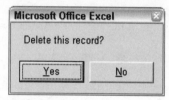

Figure 1-27

Values 16 to 64 control the icons that appear (see Figure 1-28). 32 gives a question mark icon. If we wanted both value 4 and value 32, we add them:

```
MsgBox Prompt:="Delete this record?", Buttons:=36
```

Figure 1-28

Constants

Specifying a `Buttons` value of 36 ensures that our code is indecipherable to all but the most battle-hardened programmer. This is why VBA provides the constants shown to the left of the button values in the Help screen. Rather than specifying `Buttons` by numeric value, we can use the constants, which provide a better indication of the choice behind the value. The following code generates the same dialog box as the previous example:

```
MsgBox Prompt:="Delete this record?", Buttons:=vbYesNo + vbQuestion
```

> The VBE helps you as you type by providing a popup list of the appropriate constants after you type Buttons:=. Point to the first constant and press + and you will be prompted for the second constant. Choose the second and press the Spacebar or Tab to finish the line. If there is another parameter to be specified, enter a "," rather than Space or Tab.

Constants are a special type of variable that do not change. They are used to hold key data and, as we have seen, provide a way to write more understandable code. VBA has many built-in constants that are referred to as intrinsic constants. We can also define our own constants, as we will see later in this chapter.

Return Values

There is something missing from our last examples of `MsgBox`. We are asking a question, but failing to capture the user's response to the question. That is because we have been treating `MsgBox` as a statement, rather than a function. This is perfectly legal, but we need to know some rules if we are to avoid syntax errors. We can capture the return value of the MsgBox function by assigning it to a variable.

However, if we try the following, we will get a syntax error:

```
Answer = MsgBox Prompt:="Delete this record?", Buttons:=vbYesNo + vbQuestion
```

The error message, "Expected: End of Statement", is not really very helpful. You can press the *Help* button on the error message, to get a more detailed description of the error, but even then you might not understand the explanation.

Parentheses

The problem with the above line of code is that there are no parentheses around the function arguments. It should read as follows:

```
Answer = MsgBox(Prompt:="Delete this record?", Buttons:=vbYesNo + vbQuestion)
```

The general rule is that if we want to capture the return value of a function, we need to put any arguments in parentheses. We can avoid this problem by always using the parentheses when calling a procedure. If you aren't capturing a return value you can skip the parentheses or precede the procedure call with the keyword *Call*, as in

```
Call MsgBox(Prompt:="Delete this record?", Buttons:=vbYesNo + vbQuestion)
```

The parentheses rule also applies to methods used with objects. Many methods have return values that you can ignore or capture. See the section on object variables later in this chapter for an example.

Now that we have captured the return value of MsgBox, how do we interpret it? Once again, the help screen provides the required information in the form of the following table of return values:

Constant	Value	Description
VbOK	1	OK
VbCancel	2	Cancel
VbAbort	3	Abort
VbRetry	4	Retry
VbIgnore	5	Ignore
VbYes	6	Yes
VbNo	7	No

If the Yes button is pressed, MsgBox returns a value of six. We can use the constant vbYes, instead of the numeric value, in an If test:

```
Answer = MsgBox(Prompt:="Delete selected Row?", Buttons:=vbYesNo + vbQuestion)
If Answer = vbYes Then ActiveCell.EntireRow.Delete
...
```

InputBox

Another useful VBA function is `InputBox`, which allows us to get input data from a user in the form of text. The following code generates the dialog box shown in Figure 1-29.

```
UserName = InputBox(Prompt:="Please enter your name")
```

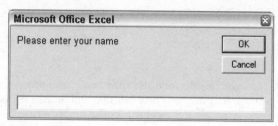

Figure 1-29

`InputBox` returns a text (string) result. Even if a numeric value is entered, the result is returned as text. If you press *Cancel* or *OK* without typing anything into the text box, `InputBox` returns a zero length string. It is a good idea to test the result before proceeding so that this situation can be handled. In the following example, the sub procedure does nothing if `Cancel` is pressed. The `Exit Sub` statement stops the procedure at that point. Otherwise, it places the entered data into cell B2:

```
Sub GetData()
    Sales = InputBox(Prompt:="Enter Target Sales")
    If Sales = "" Then Exit Sub
    Range("B2").Value = Sales
End Sub
```

In the code above, the `If` test compares `Sales` with a zero length string. There is nothing between the two double quote characters. Don't be tempted to put a blank space between the quotes.

There is a more powerful version of InputBox that is a method of the Application object. It has the ability to restrict the type of data that you can enter. It is covered in Chapter 3.

Calling Functions and Subroutines

When you develop an application, you should not attempt to place all your code in one large procedure. You should write small procedures that carry out specific tasks, and test each procedure independently. You can then write a master procedure that runs your task procedures. This approach makes the testing and debugging of the application much simpler and also makes it easier to modify the application later.

The following code illustrates this modular approach, although, in a practical application your procedures would have many more lines of code:

```
Sub Master()
  Dim SalesData As String
  SalesData = GetSalesData()
```

```
    If (SalesData <> "") Then
      Call PostInput(SalesData, "B3")
    End If
End Sub

Function GetSalesData()
    GetSalesData = InputBox("Enter Sales Data")
End Function

Sub PostInput(InputData, Target)
    Range(Target).Value = InputData
End Sub
```

Master uses the GetSalesData function and the PostInput sub procedure. GetSalesData is the one passes the prompt message for the InputBox function and returns the user's response. Master tests for a zero length string in the response. If the value is not an empty string then PostInput adds the data to the worksheet.

> Note that subroutines and functions can both accept arguments. However, you cannot subroutine with input parameters directly by pressing *F5*.

The Call Statement

The Call keyword is as old as procedures. Call is actually a carry over from an assembly language instruction with the same name. By using Call and parentheses, it is clear that your code is invoking a method and that the parameters are arguments to the procedure call.

Variable Declaration

We have seen many examples of the use of variables for storing information. Now we will discuss the rules for creating variable names, look at different types of variables, and talk about the best way to define variables.

> Variable names can be constructed from letters and numbers, and the underscore character. The name must start with a letter and can be up to 255 characters in length. It is a good idea to avoid using any special characters in variable names. To be on the safe side, you should only use the letters of the alphabet (upper and lower case) plus the numbers 0-9 plus the underscore (_). Also, variable names can't be the same as VBA key words, such as **Sub** and **End**, or VBA function names.

So far we have been creating variables simply by using them. This is referred to as implicit variable declaration. Most computer languages require us to employ explicit variable declaration. This means that we must define the names of all the variables we are going to use, before we use them in our code. VBA allows both types of declaration. If we want to declare a variable explicitly, we do so using a Dim statement or one of its variations, which we will see shortly. The following `Dim` statement declares a variable called `SalesData`:

```
Sub GetData()
   Dim SalesData As String
   SalesData = InputBox(Prompt:="Enter Target Sales")
   ...
```

Implicit variable declaration is supported but should be avoided. Your code should be as explicit as possible. Explicit code and variable declaration conveys more meaning and makes your code more precise. In addition, implicit variables are invariant data types. The problem with using invariant data types is that extra code must be added behind the scenes to determine the type of the data each time it is used. This extra decision code is added automatically, and in addition to conveying less meaning, it adds unnecessary overhead to execution time.

Option Explicit

There is a way to force explicit declaration in VBA. We place the statement `Option Explicit` at the top of our module, as demonstrated in Figure 1-30.

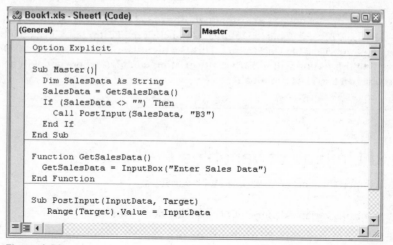

Figure 1-30

> **Option Explicit** only applies to the module it appears in. Each module requiring explicit declaration of variables must repeat the statement in its declaration section.

When you try to compile your module or run a procedure, using explicit variable declaration, VBA will check for variables that have not been declared, highlight them, and show an error message. This has an enormous benefit. It picks up spelling mistakes, which are among the most common errors in programming. Consider the following version of `GetSalesData`, where there is no `Option Explicit` at the top of the module and, therefore, implicit declaration is used:

```
Sub GetData()
    SalesData = InputBox(Prompt:="Enter Target Sales")
    If SaleData = "" Then Exit Sub
    Range("B2").Value = SalesData
End Sub
```

This code will never enter any data into cell B2. VBA happily accepts the misspelled `SaleData` in the `If` test as a new variable that is empty, and thus considered to be a zero length string for the purposes of the test. Consequently, the `Exit Sub` is always executed and the final line is never executed. This type of error, especially when embedded in a longer section of code, can be very difficult to see.

If you include `Option Explicit` in your declarations section, and `Dim SalesData` at the beginning of `GetSalesData`, you will get an error message, "Variable not defined", immediately after you attempt to run `GetSalesData`. The undefined variable will be highlighted so that you can see exactly where the error is.

> You can have **Option Explicit** automatically added to any new modules you create. In the VBE, use Tools ➪ Options… and click the Editor tab. Check the box against Require Variable Declaration. This is a highly recommended option. Note that setting this option will not affect any existing modules, where you will need to insert **Option Explicit** manually.

Scope and Lifetime of Variables

There are two important concepts associated with variables:

❑ The scope of a variable defines the accessibility of the variable

❑ The lifetime of a variable defines how long that variable retains the values assigned to it

The following procedure illustrates the lifetime of a variable:

```
Sub LifeTime()
   Dim Sales As Integer
   Sales = Sales + 1
   Call MsgBox(Sales)
End Sub
```

Every time `LifeTime` is run, it displays a value of one. This is because the variable `Sales` is only retained in memory until the end of the procedure. The memory `Sales` is released when the `End Sub` is reached. Next time `LifeTime` is run, `Sales` is recreated and treated as having a zero value. The scope of `Sales` is procedure scope and the lifetime of `Sales` is the time taken to run the procedure within which it is defined. We can increase the lifetime of `Sales` by declaring it in a `Static` statement:

```
Sub LifeTime()
  Static Sales As Integer
  Sales = Sales + 1
  MsgBox Sales
End Sub
```

The lifetime of `Sales` is now extended to the time that the workbook is open. The more times `LifeTime` is run, the higher the value of `Sales` will become.

The following two procedures illustrate the scope of a variable:

```
Sub Scope1()
  Static Sales As Integer
  Sales = Sales + 1
  MsgBox Sales
End Sub

Sub Scope2()
  Static Sales As Integer
  Sales = Sales + 10
  MsgBox Sales
End Sub
```

The variable `Sales` in `Scope1` is not the same variable as the `Sales` in `Scope2`. Each time `Scope1` is executed, the value of its `Sales` will increase by one, independently of the value of `Sales` in `Scope2`. Similarly, the `Sales` in `Scope2` will increase by 10 with each execution of `Scope2`, independently of the value of `Sales` in `Scope1`. Any variable declared within a procedure has a scope that is confined to that procedure. A variable that is declared within a procedure is referred to as a procedure-level variable.

Variables can also be declared in the declarations section at the top of a module as shown in the following version of our code:

```
Option Explicit
Dim Sales As Integer

Sub Scope1()
  Sales = Sales + 1
  MsgBox Sales
End Sub

Sub Scope2()
  Sales = Sales + 10
  MsgBox Sales
End Sub
```

`Scope1` and `Scope2` are now processing the same variable, `Sales`. A variable declared in the declarations section of a module is referred to as a module-level variable and its scope is now the whole module. Therefore, it is visible to all the procedures in the module. Its lifetime is now the time that the workbook is open.

If a procedure in the module declares a variable with the same name as a module-level variable, the module-level variable will no longer be visible to that procedure. It will process its own procedure-level variable.

Module-level variables, declared in the declarations section of the module with a `Dim` statement, are not visible to other modules. If you want to share a variable between modules, you need to declare it as `Public` in the declarations section:

```
Public Sales As Integer
```

`Public` variables can also be made visible to other workbooks, or VBA projects. To accomplish this, a reference to the workbook containing the `Public` variable is created in the other workbook, using Tools, References... in the VBE.

Variable Type

Computers store different types of data in different ways. The way a number is stored is quite different from the way text, or a character string, is stored. Different categories of numbers are also stored in different ways. An integer (a whole number with no decimals) is stored differently from a number with decimals. Most computer languages require that you declare the type of data to be stored in a variable. VBA does not require this, but your code will be more efficient if you do declare variable types. It is also more likely that you will discover any problems that arise when data is converted from one type to another, if you have declared your variable types.

The following table has been taken directly from the VBA Help files. It defines the various data types available in VBA and their memory requirements. It also shows you the range of values that each type can handle:

Data type	Storage size	Range
`Byte`	1 byte	0 to 255
`Boolean`	2 bytes	`True` or `False`
`Integer`	2 bytes	−32,768 to 32,767
`Long` (long integer)	4 bytes	−2,147,483,648 to 2,147,483,647
`Single` (single-precision floating-point)	4 bytes	−3.402823E38 to −1.401298E-45 for negative values; 1.401298E-45 to 3.402823E38 for positive values
`Double` (double-precision floating-point)	8 bytes	−1.79769313486231E308 to −4.94065645841247E-324 for negative values; 4.94065645841247E-324 to 1.79769313486232E308 for positive values
`Currency` (scaled integer)	8 bytes	−922,337,203,685,477.5808 to 922,337,203,685,477.5807

Data type	Storage size	Range
Decimal	14 bytes	+/−79,228,162,514,264,337,593,543,950,335 with no decimal point;
		+/−7.9228162514264337593543950335 with 28 places to the right of the decimal; the smallest non-zero number is +/−0.0000000000000000000000000001
Date	8 bytes	January 1, 100 to December 31, 9999
Object	4 bytes	Any Object reference
String (variable-length)	10 bytes + string length	0 to approximately 2 billion characters
String (fixed-length)	Length of string	1 to approximately 65,400 characters
Variant (with numbers)	16 bytes	Any numeric value up to the range of a Double
Variant (with characters)	22 bytes + string length	Same range as for variable-length String
User-defined (using Type)	Number required by elements	The range of each element is the same as the range of its data type

If you do not declare a variable's type, it defaults to the Variant type. Variants take up more memory than any other type because each Variant has to carry information with it that tells VBA what type of data it is currently storing, as well as store the data itself.

Variants use more computer overhead when they are processed. VBA has to figure out what types it is dealing with and whether it needs to convert between types in order to process the number. If maximum processing speed is required for your application you should declare your variable types, taking advantage of those types that use less memory when you can. For example, if you know your numbers will be whole numbers in the range of −32000 to C32000, you would use an Integer type.

Declaring Variable Type

You can declare a variable's type on a Dim statement, or related declaration statements such as Public. The following declares Sales to be a double precision floating-point number:

```
Dim Sales As Double
```

You can declare more than one variable on a single line:

```
Dim SalesData As Double, Index As Integer, StartDate As Date
```

The following can be a trap:

```
Dim Col, Row, Sheet As Integer
```

Many users assume that this declares each variable to be Integer. This is not true. Col and Row are Variants because they have not been given a type. To declare all three as Integer, the statement should be written as follows:

```
Dim Col As Integer, Row As Integer, Sheet As Integer
```

Declaring Function and Parameter Types

If you have input parameters for subroutines or functions, you can define each parameter type in the first line of the procedure as follows:

```
Function IsHoliday(WhichDay As Date)

Sub Marine(CrewSize As Integer, FuelCapacity As Double)
```

You can also declare the return value type for a function. The following example is for a function that returns a value of True or False:

```
Function IsHoliday(WhichDay As Date) As Boolean
```

Constants

We have seen that there are many intrinsic constants built into VBA, such as vbYes and vbNo discussed earlier. You can also define your own constants. Constants are handy for holding numbers or text that do not change while your code is running, but that you want to use repeatedly in calculations and messages. Constants are declared using the Const keyword, as follows:

```
Const Pi = 3.14159265358979
```

But, you should include the constant's type in the declaration:

```
Const Version As String = "Release 3.9a"
```

Constants follow the same rules regarding scope as variables. If you declare a constant within a procedure, it will be local to that procedure. If you declare it in the declarations section of a module, it will be available to all procedures in the module. If you want to make it available to all modules, you can declare it to be Public as follows:

```
Public Const Error666 As String = "It's the end of the world as we know it."
```

Variable Naming Conventions

The most important rule for naming variables in VBA (or any programming language) is to adopt one style and be consistent. Many programmers are habituated to use a prefix notation, whereby the first couple of letters are an abbreviation for the data type. This prefix notation is attributed to Charles Simonyi at Microsoft. It was invented for the very weakly typed C programming language and is called the Hungarian notation.

(A strongly typed language is a language whose compiler makes a careful distinction between the types of the arguments declared and the types actually passed to methods.) Because languages are much more strongly typed now, even Microsoft is encouraging programmers to use explicit declarations, rely on strong types, and context to clearly indicate what a variable is used for and to drop prefix notations.

You may certainly use whatever naming convention you like but computers don't care and humans aren't particularly good at reading abbreviations. If you want to include the variables type then we would encourage the use of the complete class name, for example, `ButtonUpdateStatus` rather than `btnUpdateStatus`. Alternatively, you can use `UpdateStatusButton` which is very readable. Consistency counts here.

Object Variables

The variables we have seen so far have held data such as numbers and text. You can also create object variables to refer to objects such as worksheets and ranges. The `Set` statement is used to assign an object reference to an object variable. Object variables should also be declared and assigned a type as with normal variables. If you don't know the type, you can use the generic term `Object` as the type:

```
Dim MyWorkbook As Object
Set MyWorkbook = ThisWorkbook
MsgBox MyWorkbook.Name
```

It is more efficient to use the specific object type if you can. The following code creates an object variable `aRange` referring to cell B10 in `Sheet1`, in the same workbook as the code. It then assigns values to the object and the cell above:

```
Sub ObjectVariable()
  Dim aRange As Range
  Set aRange = ThisWorkbook.Worksheets("Sheet1").Range("C10")
  aRange.Value = InputBox("Enter Sales for January")
  aRange.Offset(-1, 0).Value = "January Sales"
End Sub
```

If you are going to refer to the same object more than once, it is more efficient to create an object variable than to keep repeating a lengthy specification of the object. It is also makes code easier to read and write.

Object variables can also be very useful for capturing the return values of some methods, particularly when you are creating new instances of an object. For example, with either the `Workbooks` object or the `Worksheets` object, the `Add` method returns a reference to the new object. This reference can be assigned to an object variable so that you can easily refer to the new object in later code:

```
Sub NewWorkbook()
  Dim aWorkbook As Workbook, aWorksheet As Worksheet

  Set aWorkbook = Workbooks.Add
  Set aWorksheet = aWorkbook.Worksheets.Add( _
    After:= aWorkbook.Sheets(aWorkbook.Sheets.Count))
  aWorksheet.Name = "January"
  aWorksheet.Range("A1").Value = "Sales Data"
  aWorkbook.SaveAs Filename:="JanSales.xls"
End Sub
```

This example creates a new empty workbook and assigns a reference to it to the object variable aWorkbook. A new worksheet is added to the workbook, after any existing sheets, and a reference to the new worksheet is assigned to the object variable aWorksheet. The name on the tab at the bottom of the worksheet is then changed to "January", and the heading "Sales Data" is placed in cell A1. Finally, the new workbook is saved as JanSales.xls.

Note that the parameter after the Worksheets.Add method is in parentheses. As we are assigning the return value of the Add method to the object variable, any parameters must be in parentheses. This is a convention we prefer. If the return value of the Add method was to be ignored, you might see other developers write the statement without parentheses as follows:

```
Wkb.Worksheets.Add After:=Wkb.Sheets(Wkb.Sheets.Count)
```

Again, consistency counts here. A good policy is to adopt a coding style you are comfortable with and use it consistently. (Keep in mind few other languages support method calls without parentheses. Hence, if you begin programming in some other language then you may stumble on method calls without parentheses. Because we program in several languages it is easiest for us to use parentheses everywhere.)

With . . . End With

Object variables provide a useful way to refer to objects in short-hand, and are also more efficiently processed by VBA than fully qualified object strings. Another way to reduce the amount of code you write, and also increase processing efficiency, is to use a With...End With structure. The previous example could be rewritten as follows:

```
With aWorkbook
    .Worksheets.Add After:=.Sheets(.Sheets.Count)
End With
```

VBA knows that anything starting with a period is a property or a method of the object following the With. You can rewrite the entire NewWorkbook procedure to eliminate the aWorkbook object variable, as follows:

```
Sub NewWorkbook()
   Dim aWorksheet As Worksheet
   With Workbooks.Add
      Set aWorksheet = .Worksheets.Add(After:=.Sheets(.Sheets.Count))
      aWorksheet.Name = "January"
      aWorksheet.Range("A1").Value = "Sales Data"
      .SaveAs Filename:="JanSales.xls"
   End With
End Sub
```

You can take this a step further and eliminate the Wks object variable:

```
Sub NewWorkbook()
   With Workbooks.Add
      With .Worksheets.Add(After:=.Sheets(.Sheets.Count))
         .Name = "January"
         .Range("A1").Value = "Sales Data"
      End With
      .SaveAs Filename:="JanSales.xls"
   End With
End Sub
```

If you find this confusing, you can compromise with a combination of object variables and `With...End With`:

```
Sub NewWorkbook4()
  Dim aWorkbook As Workbook, aWorksheet As Worksheet

  Set aWorkbook = Workbooks.Add
  With aWorkbook
    Set aWorksheet = .Worksheets.Add(After:=.Sheets(.Sheets.Count))
    With aWorksheet
      .Name = "January"
      .Range("A1").Value = "Sales Data"
    End With
    .SaveAs Filename:="JanSales.xls"
  End With
End Sub
```

`With...End With` is useful when references to an object are repeated in a small section of code.

Making Decisions

VBA provides two main structures for making decisions and carrying out alternative processing, represented by the `If` and the `Select Case` statements. `If` is the more flexible, but `Select Case` is better when you are testing a single variable.

If Statements

`If` comes in three forms: the `IIf` function, the one line `If` statement, and the block `If` structure. The following `Tax` function uses the `IIf` (Immediate `If`) function:

```
Function Tax(ProfitBeforeTax As Double) As Double
  Tax = IIf(ProfitBeforeTax > 0, 0.3 * ProfitBeforeTax, 0)
End Function
```

`IIf` is similar to the C, C++, and C# programming languages' ternary operator (?:), as in, `test ?if-true: if-false` and the Excel worksheet IF function. `IIf` has three input arguments: the first is a logical test, the second is an expression that is evaluated if the test is true, and the third is an expression that is evaluated if the test is false. In this example, the `IIf` function tests that the `ProfitBeforeTax` value is greater than zero. If the test is true, `IIf` calculates 30 percent of `ProfitBeforeTax`. If the test is false, `IIf` returns zero. The calculated `IIf` value is then assigned to the return value of the `Tax` function. The `Tax` function can be rewritten using the single line `If` statement as follows:

```
Function Tax(ProfitBeforeTax As Double) As Double
  If ProfitBeforeTax > 0 Then Tax = 0.3 * ProfitBeforeTax Else Tax = 0
End Function
```

One difference between `IIf` and the single line `If` is that the `Else` section of the single line `If` is optional. The third parameter of the `IIf` function must be defined. In VBA, it is often useful to omit the `Else`:

```
If ProfitBeforeTax < 0 Then MsgBox "A Loss has occured", , "Warning"
```

Another difference is that, while `IIf` can only return a value to a single variable, the single line `If` can assign values to different variables:

```
If JohnsScore > MarysScore Then John = John + 1 Else Mary = Mary + 1
```

Block If

If you want to carry out more than one action when a test is true, you can use a block `If` structure, as follows:

```
If JohnsScore > MarysScore Then
   John = John + 1
   Mary = Mary - 1
End If
```

Using a block `If`, you must not include any code after the `Then`, on the same line. You can have as many lines after the test as required, and you must terminate the scope of the block `If` with an `End If` statement. A block `If` can also have an `Else` section, as follows:

```
If JohnsScore > MarysScore Then
   John = John + 1
   Mary = Mary - 1
Else
   John = John - 1
   Mary = Mary + 1
End If
```

A block `If` can also have as many `ElseIf` sections as required:

```
If JohnsScore > MarysScore Then
   John = John + 1
   Mary = Mary - 1
ElseIf JohnsScore < MarysScore Then
   John = John - 1
   Mary = Mary + 1
Else
   John = John + 1
   Mary = Mary + 1
End If
```

When you have a block `If` followed by one or more `ElseIf`s, VBA keeps testing until it finds a true section. It executes the code for that section and then proceeds directly to the statement following the `End If`. If no test is true, the `Else` section is executed.

A block `If` does nothing when all tests are false and the `Else` section is missing. Block `If`s can be nested, one inside the other. You should make use of indenting to show the scope of each block. This is vital—you can get into an awful muddle with the nesting of `If` blocks within other `If` blocks and `If` blocks within `Else` blocks etc. If code is unindented, it isn't easy, in a long series of nested `If` tests, to match each `End If` with each `If`:

```
If Not ThisWorkbook.Saved Then
   Answer = MsgBox("Do you want to save your changes", vbQuestion + _
                                                vbYesNo)
```

```
      If Answer = vbYes Then
        ThisWorkbook.Save
        MsgBox ThisWorkbook.Name & " has been saved"
      End If
    End If
```

This code uses the `Saved` property of the `Workbook` object containing the code to see if the workbook has been saved since changes were last made to it. If changes have not been saved, the user is asked if they want to save changes. If the answer is yes, the inner block `If` saves the workbook and informs the user.

Select Case

The following block `If` is testing the same variable value in each section:

```
Function Price(Product As String) As Variant
  If Product = "Apples" Then
    Price = 12.5
  ElseIf Product = "Oranges" Then
    Price = 15
  ElseIf Product = "Pears" Then
    Price = 18
  ElseIf Product = "Mangoes" Then
    Price = 25
  Else
    Price = CVErr(xlErrNA)
  End If
End Function
```

If `Product` is not found, the `Price` function returns an Excel error value of `#NA`. Note that `Price` is declared as a `Variant` so that it can handle the error value as well as numeric values. For a situation like this, `Select Case` is a more elegant construction. It looks like this:

```
Function Price(Product As String) As Variant
  Select Case Product
    Case "Apples"
      Price = 12.5
    Case "Oranges"
      Price = 15
    Case "Pears"
      Price = 18
    Case "Mangoes"
      Price = 25
    Case Else
      Price = CVErr(xlErrNA)
  End Select
End Function
```

If you have only one statement per case, the following format works quite well. You can place multiple statements on a single line by placing a colon between statements:

```
Function Price(Product As String) As Variant
  Select Case Product
    Case "Apples":  Price = 12.5
    Case "Oranges": Price = 15
```

```
        Case "Pears":    Price = 18
        Case "Mangoes": Price = 25
        Case Else:       Price = CVErr(xlErrNA)
    End Select
End Function
```

`Select Case` can also handle ranges of numbers or text, as well as comparisons using the keyword `Is`. The following example calculates a fare of zero for infants up to 3 years old and anyone older than 65, with two ranges between. Negative ages generate an error:

```
Function Fare(Age As Integer) As Variant
    Select Case Age
        Case 0 To 3, Is > 65
            Fare = 0
        Case 4 To 15
            Fare = 10
        Case 16 To 65
            Fare = 20
        Case Else
            Fare = CVErr(xlErrNA)
    End Select
End Function
```

Looping

All computer languages provide a mechanism for repeating the same, or similar, operations in an efficient way. VBA has four constructs that allow us to loop through the same code over and over again. They are the `While...Wend`, `Do...Loop`, `For...Next`, and `For Each`loop.

The `While...Wend` and `Do...Loop` place the test at the beginning of the loop. The `While...Wend` loop places the test at the beginning, and consequently, the test while run 0 or more times. The `Do...Loop` can place the test at the beginning or the end. If the test is at the end then the loop will run at least once. The `For...Next` loop is typically used when a specific number of iterations are known, for example, looping over an array of 50 items. The `For Each` statement is used to process objects in a collection. Check out the subsections that follow for examples of each.

While . . . Wend

The syntax of the `While...Wend` loop is `While(test)...Wend`. Place lines of code between the statement containing `While` and `Wend`. An example of a `While Wend` loop that changes the interior color of alternating rows of cells is show next.

```
Public Sub ShadeEverySecondRowWhileWend()
    Range("A2").EntireRow.Select
    While ActiveCell.Value <> ""
        Selection.Interior.ColorIndex = 10
        ActiveCell.Offset(2, 0).EntireRow.Select
    Wend
End Sub
```

Do ... Loop

To illustrate the use of a `Do...Loop`, we will construct a sub procedure to shade every second line of a worksheet, as shown in Figure 1-31, to make it more readable. We want to apply the macro to different report sheets with different numbers of products, so the macro will need to test each cell in the A column until it gets to an empty cell to determine when to stop.

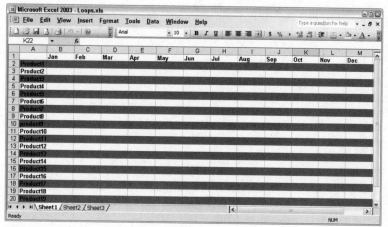

Figure 1-31

Our first macro will select every other row and apply the following formatting:

```
Public Sub ShadeEverySecondRow()
  Range("A2").EntireRow.Select
  Do While ActiveCell.Value <> ""
    Selection.Interior.ColorIndex = 15
    ActiveCell.Offset(2, 0).EntireRow.Select
  Loop
End Sub
```

ShadeEverySecondRow begins by selecting row 2 in its entirety. When you select an entire row, the left-most cell (in column A) becomes the active cell. The code between the Do and the Loop statements is then repeated While the value property of the active cell is not a zero length string, that is, the active cell is not empty. In the loop, the macro sets the interior color index of the selected cells to 15, which is gray. Then, the macro selects the entire row, two rows under the active cell. When a row is selected that has an empty cell in column A, the While condition is no longer true and the loop terminates.

You can make ShadeEverySecondRow run faster by avoiding selecting. It is seldom necessary to select cells in VBA, but you are led into this way of doing things because that's the way you do it manually and that's what you get from the macro recorder.

The following version of ShadeEverySecondRow does not select cells, and it runs about six times faster. It sets up an index i, which indicates the row of the worksheet and is initially assigned a value of two. The Cells property of the worksheet allows you to refer to cells by row number and column number, so when the loop starts, Cells(i,1) refers to cell A2. Each time around the loop, i is increased by two. We can, therefore, change any reference to the active cell to a `Cells(i,1)` reference and apply the `EntireRow` property to `Cells(i,1)` to refer to the complete row:

```
Public Sub ShadeEverySecondRow()
  Dim i As Integer
  i = 2
  Do Until IsEmpty(Cells(i, 1))
    ` use different color for contrast
    Cells(i, 1).EntireRow.Interior.ColorIndex = 23
    i = i + 2
  Loop
End Sub
```

To illustrate some alternatives, two more changes have been made on the `Do` statement line in the above code. Either `While` or `Until` can be used after the `Do`, so we have changed the test to an `Until` and we have used the VBA `IsEmpty` function to test for an empty cell. The slight variations in the two preceding examples was made to illustrate that `Do While` loops execute as long as the condition is `True`, and the `Do Until` will stop executing when the test condition is `True`.

> The `IsEmpty` function is the best way to test that a cell is empty. If you use `If Cells(i,1) = ""`, the test will be true for a formula that calculates a zero length string.

It is also possible to exit a loop using a test within the loop and the `Exit Do` statement, as shown below, which also shows another way to refer to entire rows:

```
Public Sub ShadeEverySecondRow()
  i = 0
  Do
    i = i + 2
    If IsEmpty(Cells(i, 1)) Then Exit Do
    Rows(i).Interior.ColorIndex = 15
  Loop
End Sub
```

Yet another alternative is to place the `While` or `Until` on the `Loop` statement line. This ensures that the code in the loop is executed at least once. When the test is on the `Do` line, it is possible that the test will be `false` to start with, and the loop will be skipped.

Sometimes, it makes more sense if the test is on the last line of the loop. In the following example, it seems more sensible to test `PassWord` after getting input from the user, although the code would still work if the `Until` statement were placed on the `Do` line.

```
Public Sub GetPassword()
  Dim PassWord As String, i As Integer
  i = 0
  Do
    i = i + 1
    i = i + 1
    If i > 3 Then
```

```
        MsgBox "Sorry, Only three tries"
        Exit Sub
      End If
      PassWord = InputBox("Enter Password")
      Loop Until PassWord = "XXX"
    MsgBox "Welcome"
  End Sub
```

GetPassword loops until the password XXX is supplied, or the number of times around the loop exceeds three.

For... Next Loop

The For...Next loop differs from the Do...Loop in two ways. It has a built-in counter that is automatically incremented each time the loop is executed and it is designed to execute until the counter exceeds a predefined value, rather than depending on a user-specified logical test. The following example places the full file path and name of the workbook into the center footer for each worksheet in the active workbook:

```
Public Sub FilePathInFooter()
  Dim i As Integer, FilePath As String

  FilePath = ActiveWorkbook.FullName
  For i = 1 To Worksheets.Count Step 1
    Worksheets(i).PageSetup.CenterFooter = FilePath
  Next i
End Sub
```

Versions of Excel prior to Excel 2003 do not have an option to automatically include the full file path in a custom header or footer, so this macro inserts the information as text. It begins by assigning the FullName property of the active workbook to the variable FilePath. The loop starts with the For statement and loops on the Next statement. i is used as a counter, starting at one and finishing when i exceeds Worksheets.Count, which uses the Count property of the Worksheets collection to determine how many worksheets there are in the active workbook.

The Step option determines the increment value. By default, For...Next increments the counter by 1. You can use any positive or negative integer to count by 2s, 3s, −1, 5s, etc. In the example loop, i is used as an index to the Worksheets collection to specify each individual Worksheet object. The PageSetup property of the Worksheet object refers to the PageSetup object in that worksheet so that the CenterFooter property of the PageSetup object can be assigned the FilePath text.

The following example shows how you can step backwards. It takes a complete file path and strips out the filename, excluding the file extension. The example uses the FullName property of the active workbook as input, but the same code could be used with any file type. It starts at the last character in the file path and steps backwards until it finds the period between the filename and its extension and then the backslash character before the filename. It then extracts the characters between the two:

```
Public Sub GetFileName()
  Dim BackSlash As Integer, Point As Integer
  Dim FilePath As String, FileName As String
  Dim i As Integer
```

```
      FilePath = ActiveWorkbook.FullName
      For i = Len(FilePath) To 1 Step -1
        If Mid$(FilePath, i, 1) = "." Then
          Point = i
          Exit For
        End If
      Next i
      If Point = 0 Then Point = Len(FilePath) + 1
      For i = Point - 1 To 1 Step -1
        If Mid$(FilePath, i, 1) = "\" Then
          BackSlash = i
          Exit For
        End If
      Next i
      FileName = Mid$(FilePath, BackSlash + 1, Point - BackSlash - 1)
      MsgBox FileName
    End Sub
```

The first `For...Next` loop uses the `Len` function to determine how many characters are in the `FilePath` variable and `i` is set up to step backwards, counting from the last character position, working towards the first character position. The `Mid$` function extracts the character from `FilePath` at the position defined by `i` and tests it to see if it is a period.

When a period is found, the position is recorded in `Point` and the first `For...Next` loop is exited. If the file name has no extension, no period is found and `Point` will have its default value of zero. In this case, the `If` test records an imaginary period position in `Point` that is one character beyond the end of the file name.

The same technique is used in the second `For...Next` loop as the first, starting one character before the period, to find the position of the backslash character, and storing the position in `BackSlash`. The `Mid$` function is then used to extract the characters between the backslash and the period.

For Each... Next Loop

When you want to process every member of a collection, you can use the `For Each...Next` loop. The following example is a rework of the `FilePathInFooter` procedure:

```
  Public Sub FilePathInFooter()
    Dim FilePath As String, aWorksheet As Worksheet

    FilePath = ActiveWorkbook.FullName
    For Each aWorksheet In Worksheets
      aWorksheet.PageSetup.CenterFooter = FilePath
    Next aWorksheet
  End Sub
```

The loop steps through all the members of the collection. During each pass a reference to the next member of the collection is assigned to the object variable `aWorksheet`.

The following example lists all the files in the root directory of the C drive. It uses the Microsoft Office `FileSearch` object to generate a `FoundFiles` object containing the names of the required files. The following example uses a `For Each...Next` loop to display the names of all the files:

```
Public Sub FileList()
  Dim File As Variant
  With Application.FileSearch
    .LookIn = "C:\"
    .FileType = msoFileTypeAllFiles
    .Execute
    For Each File In .FoundFiles
      MsgBox File
    Next File
  End With
End Sub
```

If you test this procedure on a directory with lots of files, and get tired of clicking *OK*, remember that you can break out of the code with *Ctrl+Break*.

Arrays

Arrays are VBA variables that can hold more than one item of data. An array is declared by including parentheses after the array name. An integer is placed within the parentheses, defining the number of elements in the array:

```
Dim Data(2) As Integer
```

You assign values to the elements of the array by indicating the element number as follows:

```
Data(0) = 1
Data(1) = 10
Data(2) = 100
```

The number of elements in the array depends on the array base. The default base is zero, which means that the first data element is item zero. `Dim Data(2) As Integer` declares a three element array of integers if the base is zero. Alternatively, you can place the following statement in the declarations section at the top of your module to declare that arrays are one based:

```
Option Base 1
```

With a base of one, `Dim Data(2) As Integer` declares a two element integer array. Item zero does not exist.

You can use the following procedure to test the effect of the `Option Base` statement:

```
Public Sub Array1()
  Dim Data(10) As Integer
  Dim Message As String, i As Integer

  For i = LBound(Data) To UBound(Data)
    Data(i) = i
  Next i
  Message = "Lower Bound = " & LBound(Data) & vbCr
```

```
      Message = Message & "Upper Bound = " & UBound(Data) & vbCr
      Message = Message & "Number of Elements = " & WorksheetFunction.
   Count(Data) _
                                                              & vbCr

      Message = Message & "Sum of Elements = " & WorksheetFunction.Sum(Data)
      MsgBox Message
   End Sub
```

`Array1` uses the `LBound` (lower bound) and `UBound` (upper bound) functions to determine the lowest and highest index values for the array. It uses the `Count` worksheet function to determine the number of elements in the array. If you run this code with `Options Base 0`, or no `Options Base` statement, in the declarations section of the module, it will show a lowest index number of zero and 11 elements in the array. With `Options Base 1`, it shows a lowest index number of one and 10 elements in the array.

> Note the use of the intrinsic constant vbCr, which contains a carriage return character . vbCr is used to break the message text to a new line.

If you want to make your array size independent of the `Option Base` statement, you can explicitly declare the lower bound and upper bounds as demonstrated:

```
   Dim Data(1 To 2) As Integer
```

Arrays are very useful for processing groups of items. If you want to create a short list, you can use the `Array` function as follows:

```
   Dim Data As Variant
   Data = Array("North", "South", "East", "West")
```

You can then use the list in a `For...Next` loop. For example, you could open and process a series of workbooks called `North.xls`, `South.xls`, `East.xls`, and `West.xls`:

```
   Sub Array2()
      Dim Data As Variant, aWorkbook As Workbook
      Dim i As Integer

      Data = Array("North", "South", "East", "West")
      For i = LBound(Data) To UBound(Data)
         Set aWorkbook = Workbooks.Open(FileName:=Data(i) & ".xls")
         'Process data here
         aWorkbook.Close SaveChanges:=True
      Next i
   End Sub
```

Multi-dimensional Arrays

So far we have only looked at arrays with a single dimension. You can actually define arrays with up to 60 dimensions. While computers can easily manage the complexities of n-dimensional arrays greater than 4 or 5, people find this very difficult to do. The following statements declare two-dimensional arrays:

```
   Dim Data(10,20) As Integer
   Dim Data(1 To 10,1 to 20) As Integer
```

You can think of a two-dimensional array as a table of data. The previous example defines a table with 10 rows and 20 columns.

Arrays are very useful in Excel for processing the data in worksheet ranges. It can be far more efficient to load the values in a range into an array, process the data, and write it back to the worksheet, than to access each cell individually.

The following procedure shows how you can assign the values in a range to a Variant. The code uses the LBound and UBound functions to find the number of dimensions in Data. Note that there is a second parameter in LBound and UBound to indicate which index you are referring to. If you leave this parameter out, the functions refer to the first index:

```vba
Public Sub Array3()
  Dim Data As Variant, X As Variant
  Dim Message As String, i As Integer

  Data = Range("A1:A20").Value
  i = 1
  Do
    Message = "Lower Bound = " & LBound(Data, i) & vbCr
    Message = Message & "Upper Bound = " & UBound(Data, i) & vbCr
    MsgBox Message, , "Index Number = " & i
    i = i + 1
    On Error Resume Next
    X = UBound(Data, i)
    If Err.Number <> 0 Then Exit Do
    On Error GoTo 0
  Loop
  Message = "Number of Non Blank Elements = " _
    & WorksheetFunction.CountA(Data) & vbCr
  MsgBox Message
End Sub
```

The first time round the Do...Loop, Array3 determines the upper and lower bounds of the first dimension of Data, as i has a value of one. It then increases the value of i to look for the next dimension. It exits the loop when an error occurs, indicating that no more dimensions exist.

By substituting different ranges into Array3, you can determine that the array created by assigning a range of values to a Variant is two-dimensional, even if there is only one row or one column in the range. You can also determine that the lower bound of each index is one, regardless of the Option Base setting in the declarations section.

Dynamic Arrays

When writing your code, it is sometimes not possible to determine the size of the array that will be required. For example, you might want to load the names of all the .xls files in the current directory into an array. You won't know in advance how many files there will be. One alternative is to declare an array that is big enough to hold the largest possible amount of data—but this would be inefficient. Instead, you can define a dynamic array and set its size when the procedure runs.

You declare a dynamic array by leaving out the dimensions:

```vba
Dim Data() As String
```

You can declare the required size at runtime with a ReDim statement, which can use variables to define the bounds of the indexes:

```
ReDim Data(iRows, iColumns) As String
ReDim Data(minRow to maxRow, minCol to maxCol) As String
```

ReDim will reinitialize the array and destroy any data in it, unless you use the Preserve keyword. Preserve is used in the following procedure that uses a Do...Loop to load the names of files into the dynamic array called FNames, increasing the upper bound of its index by one each time to accommodate the new name. The Dir function returns the first filename found that matches the wild card specification in FType. Subsequent usage of Dir, with no parameter, repeats the same specification, getting the next file that matches, until it runs out of files and returns a zero length string:

```
Public Sub FileNames()
   Dim FName As String
   Dim FNames() As String
   Dim FType As String
   Dim i As Integer

   FType = "*.xls"
   FName = Dir(FType)
   Do Until FName = ""
     i = i + 1
     ReDim Preserve FNames(1 To i)
     FNames(i) = FName
     FName = Dir
   Loop
   If i = 0 Then
     MsgBox "No files found"
   Else
     For i = 1 To UBound(FNames)
       MsgBox FNames(i)
     Next i
   End If
End Sub
```

If you intend to work on the files in a directory, and save the results, it is a good idea to get all the filenames first, as in the FileNames procedure, and use that list to process the files. It is not a good idea to rely on the Dir function to give you an accurate file list while you are in the process of reading and overwriting files.

Runtime Error Handling

When you are designing an application, you should try to anticipate any problems that could occur when the application is used in the real world. You can remove all the bugs in your code and have flawless logic that works with all permutations of conditions, but a simple operational problem could still bring your code crashing down with a less than helpful message displayed to the user.

For example, if you try to save a workbook file to the floppy disk in the A drive, and there is no disk in the A drive, your code will grind to a halt and display a message that may be difficult for the user to decipher.

If you anticipate this particular problem, you can set up your code to gracefully deal with the situation. VBA allows you to trap error conditions using the following statement:

```
On Error GoTo LineLabel
```

LineLabel is a marker that you insert at the end of your normal code, as shown below with the line label errorTrap. Note that a colon follows the line label. The line label marks the start of your error recovery code and should be preceded by an Exit statement to prevent execution of the error recovery code when no error occurs:

```
Public Sub ErrorTrap1()
    Dim Answer As Long, MyFile As String
    Dim Message As String, CurrentPath As String

    On Error GoTo errorTrap
    CurrentPath = CurDir$

    ` Try to change to the A: drive
    ChDrive "A"
    ChDrive CurrentPath
    ChDir CurrentPath
    MyFile = "A:\Data.xls"
    Application.DisplayAlerts = False
    ` Try to save the current worksheet to the A: drive
    ActiveWorkbook.SaveAs FileName:=MyFile

TidyUp:
    ChDrive CurrentPath
    ChDir CurrentPath
Exit Sub

errorTrap:
    Message = "Error No: = " & Err.Number & vbCr
    Message = Message & Err.Description & vbCr & vbCr
    Message = Message & "Please place a disk in the A: drive" & vbCr
    Message = Message & "and press OK" & vbCr & vbCr
    Message = Message & "Or press Cancel to abort File Save"
    Answer = MsgBox(Message, vbQuestion + vbOKCancel, "Error")
    If Answer = vbCancel Then Resume TidyUp
    Resume
End Sub
```

Once the On Error statement is executed, error trapping is enabled. If an error occurs, no message is displayed and the code following the line label is executed. You can use the Err object to obtain information about the error. The Number property of the Err object returns the error number and the Description property returns the error message associated with the error. You can use Err.Number to determine the error when it is possible that any of a number of errors could occur. You can incorporate Err.Description into your own error message, if appropriate.

In Excel 5 and 95, Err was not an object, but a function that returned the error number. As Number is the default property of the Err object, using Err, by itself, is equivalent to using Err.Number and the code from the older versions of Excel still works in Excel 97 and later versions.

The code in ErrorTrap1, after executing the On Error statement, saves the current directory drive and path into the variable CurrentPath. It then executes the ChDrive statement to try to activate the A drive. If there is no disk in the A drive, error 68 (Device unavailable) occurs and the error recovery code executes. For illustration purposes, the error number and description are displayed and the user is given the opportunity to either place a disk in the A drive, and continue, or abort the save.

If the user wishes to stop, we branch back to TidyUp and restore the original drive and directory settings. Otherwise, the Resume statement is executed. This means that execution returns to the statement that caused the error. If there is still no disk in the A drive, the error recovery code is executed again. Otherwise, the code continues normally.

The only reason for the ChDrive "A" statement is to test the readiness of the A drive, so the code restores the stored drive and directory path. The code sets the DisplayAlerts property of the Application object to False, before saving the active workbook. This prevents a warning if an old file called Data.xls is being replaced by the new Data.xls. (See Chapter 18 for more on DisplayAlerts.)

The Resume statement comes in three forms:

❑ Resume—causes execution of the statement that caused the error

❑ Resume Next—returns execution to the statement following the statement that caused the error, so the problem statement is skipped

❑ Resume LineLabel—jumps back to any designated line label in the code, so that you can decide to resume where you want

The following code uses Resume Next to skip the Kill statement, if necessary. The charmingly named Kill statement removes a file from disk. In the following code, we have decided to remove any file with the same name as the one we are about to save, so that there will be no need to answer the warning message about overwriting the existing file.

The problem is that Kill will cause a fatal error if the file does not exist. If Kill does cause a problem, the error recovery code executes and we use Resume Next to skip Kill and continue with SaveAs. The MsgBox is there for educational purposes only. You would not normally include it:

```
Public Sub ErrorTrap2()
    Dim MyFile As String, Message As String
    Dim Answer As String

    On Error GoTo errorTrap

    Workbooks.Add
    MyFile = "C:\Data.xls"
    Kill MyFile
    ActiveWorkbook.SaveAs FileName:=MyFile
    ActiveWorkbook.Close

    Exit Sub

errorTrap:
    Message = "Error No: = " & Err.Number & vbCr
    Message = Message & Err.Description & vbCr & vbCr
```

```
      Message = Message & "File does not exist"
      Answer = MsgBox(Message, vbInformation, "Error")
      Resume Next
   End Sub
```

On Error Resume Next

As an alternative to `On Error GoTo`, you can use:

```
   On Error Resume Next
```

This statement causes errors to be ignored, so it should be used with caution. However, it has many uses. The following code is a rework of `ErrorTrap2`:

```
   Sub ErrorTrap3()
      Dim MyFile As String, Message As String

      Workbooks.Add
      MyFile = "C:\Data.xls"
      On Error Resume Next
      Kill MyFile
      On Error GoTo 0
      ActiveWorkbook.SaveAs FileName:=MyFile
      ActiveWorkbook.Close
   End Sub
```

We use `On Error Resume Next` just before the `Kill` statement. If our `C:\Data.xls` does not exist, the error caused by `Kill` is ignored and execution continues on the next line. After all, we don't care if the file does not exist. That's the situation we are trying to achieve.

`On Error GoTo 0` looks a little confusing. All `On Error GoTo` really does is reset the `Err` object.

You can use `On Error Resume Next` to write code that would otherwise be less efficient. The following sub procedure determines whether a name exists in the active workbook:

```
   Public Sub TestForName()
      If NameExists("SalesData") Then
        MsgBox "Name Exists"
      Else
        MsgBox "Name does not exist"
      End If
   End Sub

   Public Function NameExists(myName As String) As Boolean
      Dim X As String
      On Error Resume Next
      X = Names(myName).RefersTo
      If Err.Number <> 0 Then
        NameExists = False
        Err.Clear
      Else
        NameExists = True
      End If
   End Function
```

`TestForName` calls the `NameExists` function, which uses `On Error Resume Next` to prevent a fatal error when it tries to assign the name's `RefersTo` property to a variable. There is no need for `On Error GoTo 0` here, because error handling in a procedure is disabled when a procedure exits, although `Err.Number` is not cleared.

If no error occurred, the `Number` property of the `Err` object is zero. If `Err.Number` has a non-zero value, an error occurred, which can be assumed to be because the name did not exist, so `NameExists` is assigned a value of `False` and the error is cleared. The alternative to this single pass procedure is to loop through all the names in the workbook, looking for a match. If there are lots of names, this can be a slow process.

Summary

In this chapter we have seen those elements of the VBA language that enable you to write useful and efficient procedures. We have seen how to add interaction to macros with the `MsgBox` and `InputBox` functions, how to use variables to store information and how to get help about VBA keywords.

We have seen how to declare variables and define their type, and the effect on variable scope and lifetime of different declaration techniques. We have also used the block `If` and `Select Case` structures to perform tests and carry out alternative calculations, and `Do...Loop` and `For...Next` loops that allow us to efficiently repeat similar calculations. We have seen how arrays can be used, particularly with looping procedures. We have also seen how to use `On Error` statements to trap errors.

When writing VBA code for Excel, the easiest way to get started is to use the macro recorder. We can then modify that code, using the VBE, to better suit our purposes and to operate efficiently. Using the Object Browser, Help screens, and the reference section of this book, you can discover objects, methods, properties, and events that can't be found with the macro recorder. Using the coding structures provided by VBA, we can efficiently handle large amounts of data and automate tedious processes.

For VBA programmers the primary tool is the VBE. In the next section we will spend some time getting accustomed to the capabilities of this editor. Familiarity and comfort here will aid us when we begin more advanced programming topics in Chapter 4.

Programming in the VBE

At least as far back as Borland's early Turbo Pascal editor for DOS, modern programmers have had the luxury of Integrated Development Environments (IDEs). An IDE is an editor like Notepad or MS-Word that is customized specifically for writing programming language code. The Visual Basic Editor (VBE) is an IDE that ships with every application supporting VBA, including MS-Excel. Thus, if you know how to use one VBE and VBA then you know how to use them all. All that remains is to learn the object model for each Office application you want to write code for, fortunately the Help documentation will answer many of your questions here.

This is a programming book, so it will be helpful for you to become familiar with the VBE. If you are an experienced VBA programmer and have used the VBE before, then just browse the sections of this chapter to see if there are any new techniques that you weren't previously aware of, or you can skip to Chapter 4. If you are a new VBA programmer, then reading this chapter will help you optimize your code writing and debugging experience.

Writing Code

Computers don't care about words or grammar. A computer only cares about bits and bytes. Even low-level languages that have a very simple grammar, like assembler, aren't treated any differently than the more high- level languages. Only the compiler and people care about programming languages and grammar. Since the compiler's job is to convert the programming language into bits and bytes so that the code may be executed, the grammar must be correct for the compiler to do its job. And, the easier code is for a person to read, the easier it will be to maintain. Consequently, we must master the grammar for the compiler's benefit, and we must adapt a readable style for the human reader's benefit. All of this is best accomplished in the editor.

Programming for People

The compiler is an exacting taskmaster; the code will have to be grammatically correct to run. There is little we can do about writing code for its benefit. However, we can write for the human reader by thinking about a few simple concepts and responding accordingly.

People aren't especially good at reading abbreviations, so use whole words instead. In addition, nouns and verbs make up whole sentences in the English language, so pick good nouns for class names and good verbs for method names. Furthermore, the compiler wouldn't care if we were to write one whole monolithic procedure to solve a problem as long as the grammar is correct. People, on the other hand, would likely find such code indecipherable. People are not especially good at grappling with more than a few ideas at once and are exceptionally good at focusing on one thing at a time. So make your methods and properties singular and short as opposed to plural and monolithic—that is, make sure your procedures and properties do one thing and make sure that thing is what the procedure name purports it to be.

Code will be much more difficult to comprehend if you have more than a few lines of code per procedure. If you must write many lines of code in a procedure, or the code is arguably ambiguous in its purpose, then write a comment. Comments aren't always necessary. The compiler doesn't use them, so add comments if they clarify an algorithm and not when they redundantly state what it is obvious the algorithm does. Providing many brief procedures makes each larger procedure easier to debug, and permits us to reorganize existing procedures to solve new problems. Often, monolithic procedures can only be used in one context.

People also find visual cues and organization helpful. That's why you should use indentation for subordinate ideas and remain consistent about the amount of whitespace used. The code is the programmer's work-product and should be organized.

Be explicit and precise to the greatest extent possible. Use `Option Explicit` at the top of each module and declare all variables explicitly with the most appropriate data type. If a value is immutable then use constants. Constants can't change, so if they are initialized with an appropriate value then that value will always be the correct one and as a result always reliable.

Finally, test code in small doses. Each procedure or property should be as independent as possible. We can accomplish this by limiting dependency on arguments outside the scope of the procedure itself. When you code a procedure (including property procedures), test each procedure to ensure that the inputs and outputs yield the desired result. The Immediate window is a good way to quickly test a new procedure. (Refer to Chapters 7 and 8 for techniques on writing bulletproof code, testing, and debugging.)

If you follow the preceding guidelines your code will be orderly, coherent, and as a result, easier to comprehend. Consequently, when you do run into trouble other programmers will be more inclined and able to provide assistance.

Writing Code

Reading and writing a lot of code is the best way to get good at it. You can import existing code, which we will discuss in later in this chapter (see *"Importing and Exporting Visual Basic Code"*), but most, if not all, of your programming will be done in the VBE. Let's start there.

The VBE is a separate program. It is associated with the particular Office tool you are using, and you can start up the VBE in Excel (and other MS-Office applications) by pressing *Alt+F11* or by selecting Tools ➪ Macro ➪ Visual Basic Editor. Having started the VBE, simply think of it as a special word- processing tool that is aware of the VBA grammar. The text you type will have meaning to the VBE, in that the VBE can detect special keywords, and will respond to grammatical constructs. For example, the VBE will automatically convert procedure names to Pascal-cased names.

Keep in mind that all programmers have some opinion or bias about what code should look like because coding styles is a completely subjective concept. A good rule of thumb here is that one is more likely to be successful by emulating those that are demonstrably successful or that have good reason for using one technique over another.

Where Does My Code Go?

All code is written in a module, class module, or UserForm. These are all special word-processing windows that the VBE can interact with in an effort to catch grammar errors, and through the compiler, programming errors. Think of the module as a blank sheet of paper and your keyboard as a typewriter. If you were writing a short story then you might jump right in. Most programming requires some planning though.

There are several ways to approach writing code. Experienced programmers might start with a design tool like Rational's Unified Modeling Language (UML) modeling tool. This tool promotes a methodical approach to problem solving by permitting one to figure out the solution with graphic symbols. However, it takes a considerable amount of time to master UML as it is a language in its own right. The benefit of using a modeling tool is that pictures convey more meaning and are easier to produce and change than code. A more rudimentary form of the modeling tool is a flowcharting tool, like Visio. (Visio also supports UML now.) A flowcharting tool enables users to draw pictures that describe a workflow. Again, a flowcharting tool is less desirable than a UML modeling tool and takes some time to learn. There is also the low-tech concept of simply writing your ideas on a piece of paper as plain English algorithms. If you attended computer science courses in the last 20 years, you might have been taught this technique. Ultimately, a special kind of programmer, called an architect, should know all of these tools, but they can be an unsuitable starting point for a beginner for one reason or another. Possibly the best way for a beginner to start is by writing code. However, you should write code in a directed way. Let's clarify what we mean here.

If you need to add a few basic macros then you can record them first. This approach is fast and easy. If you need to make changes, then switch to the VBE and modify the recorded macros. If you are writing an Excel-based application then you may combine recorded macros with customized procedures and UserForms. Then, mentally group each category of problem and create a separate module, class module, or UserForm for each group of problem. Finally, begin adding the fields, properties, methods, and events that solve each group of problem. This approach will work reasonably well for modest complexity problems. For very large problems however, you will likely discover that a just write it approach will ultimately be too hard to understand. If you get to this point then a technique referred to as refactoring can help unravel complex code. You can read about refactoring in Martin Fowler's *Refactoring: Improving the Design of Existing Code* (Addison-Wesley, 1999). Unfortunately, refactoring is a complex subject beyond the scope of this book.

As a final word of advice: if you know from the inception that you are writing a mission-critical enterprise application in Excel and have never done so successfully before, then get help early in the process. A mentor, and architect, or an experienced cohort will help you prevent problems that may later be intractable. Refactoring is a great aid in factoring out, reusing, and simplifying code, but even refactoring has its limitations. Mission-critical enterprise applications need to be guided by an experienced architect or a person that has successfully implemented a similarly complex application in the past. It's best to know your own limitations and address these accordingly.

Managing a Project

VBA applications are project-centric. The code you write in modules comprises a bigger project, which includes the workbook and worksheets. From within the VBE you can determine the modules that are in your project by opening the Project Explorer. You can open the Project Explorer by selecting

View ⇨ Project Explorer in the VBE or by pressing *Ctrl+R*. When you create a new workbook the Project Explorer should look like the one in Figure 2-1.

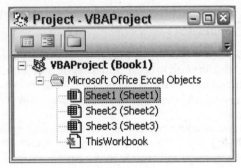

Figure 2-1

Sheet1 is a class module that represents Worksheet1. Sheet2 represents Worksheet2, and Sheet3 represents Worksheet3. ThisWorkbook is the class module that represents the currently opened workbook. These modules are VBA's view of the workbook and worksheets in that workbook. Thus, if we add a new worksheet to the default group of three worksheets then we will see a new class module Sheet4 in the Project Explorer.

While a typical user may never know or care that there are class modules representing each worksheet and the workbook, we need to know. The Project Explorer is the means by which we organize all of the modules and forms in our application. As you need to you can add additional modules, class modules, and UserForms to the project from the VBE's Insert menu of the Project Explorer's context menu. (Context menus are activated by right-clicking over the context item: in this case by right-clicking over the Project Explorer itself.)

Managing Control Layout

When you add a UserForm to a project, a new form module will be added and shown (see Figure 2-2). In addition, the Toolbox will be opened too. Adding controls to a form is a lot like using a paint

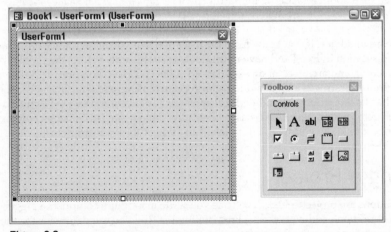

Figure 2-2

program—click the control in the Toolbox and click a location on the form where you want that control to be painted. You may also use the left-mouse button to drag an outline around the region that the control should fill, as shown in Figure 2-2.

The dots that appear on the form while you're designing it enable you to easily align the controls visually to aid in creating a uniform presentation. In addition, the VBE's Format menu contains several menu items for aligning, sizing, centering, ordering, and managing the horizontal and vertical spacing of controls. These menu items operate on a group of controls. To select multiple controls, left click and drag a dashed-line around the controls to format. (Alternatively, you can use *Shift+Left-click* to add controls to a group.) For example, to align all Label controls on the left, select the desired Label controls and choose Format ⇨ Align ⇨ Left from the menu. These menu items explain their operation for the most part and with a modest amount of practice you will find them easy and convenient to use.

Adding Classes

A class module is a special kind of module that actually describes a Component Object Model (COM) class. When we talk about object-oriented programming or object-based programming in VBA, we are referring to the code written in class modules and the code we write that interacts with existing classes, such as Workbooks, Worksheets, and Ranges.

If you define a class module, then you will need to declare variables of that class's type using the name of the module, and use the Set and New operators to create and initialize an instance of the class. A plain vanilla module does not require you to use Set or New. Members of plain modules are technically static members—that is, a procedure in a plain module is considered to be a member of a single instance of a class, which is the module containing it. Let's digress for a moment here.

In C++, static members are members that are accessible without an object instance; these members are also shared by all instances of the class. For a language like C++, the programmer has to write everything explicitly, and using static members in C++ requires more effort on the part of the programmer. Contrarily, languages like VBA are designed to be a bit easier to use but less powerful. For example, a module in VBA is really a static class—not in the VBA sense, but in the C++ sense—and all members can be accessed with the module name but without an instance of the module. To add to the confusion, VBA has its own use for the word static.

VBA uses the word static to mean that procedure variables are not created on the CPU's stack memory; instead static in VBA means that variables are created in the data memory. The reason procedure variables normally have procedure scope is that the memory for these variables is created in the CPUs stack space, which grows and shrinks each time a procedure is started and finished. The stack memory is reused each time one procedure finishes and another starts, overwriting what was there previously, including the previous procedures variables. Static in VBA also means that a procedure's variable is stored in the data memory and is consequently not overwritten by the accordion-like expanding and contracting of the stack memory. For this reason, VBA static variables maintain their value between successive calls to their containing procedure.

If you've ever had to suffer from a C++ programmer scoffing at VBA, then you know it's important to understand that in reality the amount of knowledge required to program in C++ (or Delphi, VB .NET, or C#) is significantly greater than that required to program in VBA (which occasionally may swell an immature ego). However, it is equally important to note that there are many problems that can more quickly and easily be solved by VBA, and good and bad programmers can be found writing code in all languages. If you really want to know about things like pointers, addresses, operator overloading, static members, interfaces, inheritance, multiple inheritance, multithreading, stack frames, polymorphism, abstract classes, templates, and generics, then learn C++ and assembler. If you need to learn how to crunch numbers and data, then you are already in the right place.

Modifying Properties

You will recall from Chapter 1 that classes and modules contain properties. This applies to new and existing classes. As part of the concept of a visual design tool, a special category of class called controls can be modified in the VBE. These control classes can be selected and their state changed at design time via the Properties window.

The Properties window can be opened in the VBE by pressing *F4* or clicking View ⇨ Properties window from the menu. In the Properties window you will find a drop-down list of controls with the current control selected and an alphabetized list of the public properties, which can be modified for that control. Change the property and the value will be reflected in the control at design time. For example, to change the caption of `UserForm1` from the last section to My Form, click the `UserForm`, find the `Caption` property and modify the text in the editable region to the right.

Some properties are easy to modify like the `Caption` property, and others are more complicated. Other properties like `Fonts` have several subproperties and an editor is provided. For instance, to change the Fonts for a UserForm, select the UserForm, open the Properties window, find the `Font` property and click the ellipse in the edit region (see Figure 2-3).

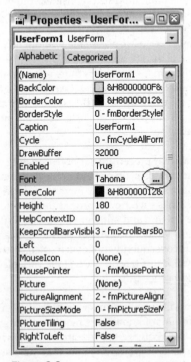

Figure 2-3

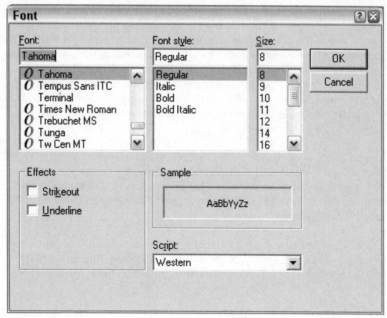

Figure 2-4

Clicking the ellipse will invoke the Property Editor for that property (see the Font Editor in Figure 2-4). Click *OK* when you are finished modifying the property and all changes will be updated in the Properties window and reflected in the control.

Importing and Exporting Visual Basic Code

VBA code and Visual Basic Code are almost identical. This means that when you are inclined to share code or are hunting for code, you can search code explicitly written for Microsoft Office and code written for VB6. This means that there are several million other VB programmers in the world with which you can pool your resources. (For example, Paul Kimmel writes a free newsletter for codeguru.com on VB called *Visual Basic Today* and much of the code in those articles can be used almost directly in your Excel VBA.)

A good rule of thumb is to share as much code as possible before writing any new code. Existing code has likely been read and debugged a couple of times, and may ultimately aid in solving a problem much more expediently. If nothing else, reuse your own code. You can import and export existing VB code from the File menu or the Project Explorer's context menu. For instance, select Sheet1 in the Project Explorer click File ➪ Export File to save Sheet1 as Sheet1.cls. (The .cls extension indicates that Sheet1 is a class module.)

Keep in mind that different tools and environments have differing defaults. For example, objects readily accessible as a Workbook project, like Workbook and Worksheets, will not automatically be referenced in a tool like Visual Basic 6. In this case, you would need to add a Reference to MS-Excel in the VB6 project. Sharing Excel VBA code among Excel users is relatively straightforward; sharing code between other versions of Visual Basic will require a bit more legwork on your part. (See Chapter 14 for more information on using VB6 code in Excel.)

Editing

The editing capabilities of the VBE contain features found in word processors and additional features pertinent to programming language editors. The Edit menu contains the features for copying, cutting, and pasting, as well as text search and replace and undo features. You will also find the Edit ⇨ Indent and Edit ⇨ Outdent menu items for block indenting and outdenting code. Consistent with other word processors, the Edit menu contains a Bookmark item for tagging locations in code. This feature will permit you to quickly move back and forth between locations of interest in code. Check out the Edit ⇨ Bookmarks menu item for available options.

Another feature unique to code editors is the Complete Word—Edit ⇨ Complete Word, or *Ctrl+Space*—feature; this menu item will display a drop-down list of choices, but does not apply to keywords. For example, if you are looking for a list of members of a Worksheet, simply type the Worksheet object's name, followed by a period, and press *Ctrl+Space*. A list of all of the members of the Worksheet class will be displayed.

Modern object models are usually way too vast to become extemporaneous knowledge. The best programmers will master the grammar, common idioms, and powerful design patterns and let the Help documentation and intelligent editors remember the nuts and bolts of parameter type, order, and count.

Managing Editor Options

We seldom monkey about with the VBE options. The most significant change we like to make is to Tab Width 2 characters instead of four (see Figure 2-5). To explore or modify editor options select Tools ⇨ Options from the VBE main menu.

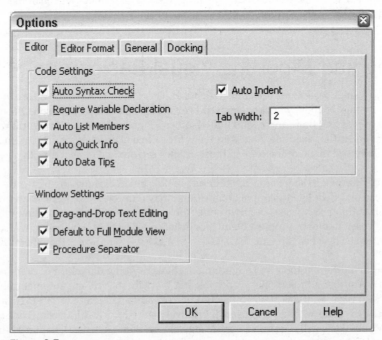

Figure 2-5

In our experience, the most common reason for changing an item is to increase the font size when making a presentation—the default font size of 10 pixels doesn't seem big enough when projected on an overhead. You won't find significant productivity gains to be had in the editor Options dialog box, but it is worth knowing about.

Running and Debugging Code

Becoming adroit with the running and debugging options in the VBE can lead to good productivity gains. The Run menu contains the Run Sub/UserForm (*F5*), Break, Reset, and Design Mode menu items, and the Debug menu contains Compile VBAProject, Step Into, Step Over, Step Out, Run To Cursor, Add Watch, Edit Watch, Quick Watch, Toggle Breakpoint, Clear All Breakpoints, Set Next Statement, and Show Next Statement menu items. All of these menu items are useful, but typically we find the Run (*F5*), Step Into (*F8*), Quick Watch (*Shift+F9*), and Toggle Breakpoint (*F9*) menu items the most useful.

VBA is an interpreted language that can also be compiled to PE-code (or portable executable code). The Run and Step Into menu options begin the debugging process. The Quick Watch (*Shift+F9*) menu item will open a dialog box displaying the value of the name under the cursor. The Breakpoint (*F9*) inserts a low-level interrupt 3 and a visible red dot—think Stop sign—and highlights the line containing the breakpoint in a dark red color. Interrupt 3 is a lower level debug interrupt added by your PCs BIOS. Using breakpoints permits you to run a long process breaking exactly before a point where you want to begin evaluating the state of your application. (Refer to Chapters 7 and 8 for more information on debugging and testing.)

Using Watches

Watches, Locals, and Quick Watch are all useful for evaluating the state of your application. Watch windows can be activated from the View and Debug menus. The View menu contains the Immediate window, Locals window, Watch window, and Call Stack, and the Debug menu contains Add Watch, Edit Watch, and Quick Watch.

The Immediate window permits a programmer to enter code directly in this simplified editor and test the code with immediate results one statement at a time. The Locals window (see Figure 2-6) displays the variables that are visible in the local or, procedural, scope. For example, inside of a class like the

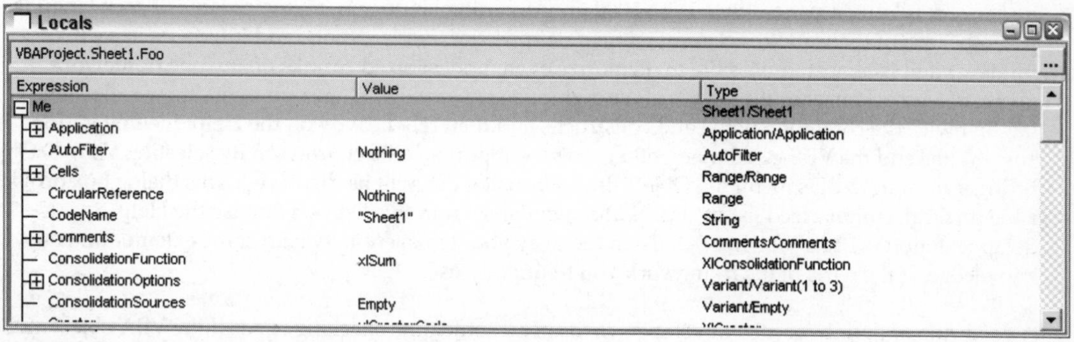

Locals		
VBAProject.Sheet1.Foo		
Expression	Value	Type
⊟ Me		Sheet1/Sheet1
⊞ Application		Application/Application
— AutoFilter	Nothing	AutoFilter
⊞ Cells		Range/Range
— CircularReference	Nothing	Range
— CodeName	"Sheet1"	String
⊞ Comments		Comments/Comments
— ConsolidationFunction	xlSum	XlConsolidationFunction
⊞ ConsolidationOptions		Variant/Variant(1 to 3)
— ConsolidationSources	Empty	Variant/Empty

Figure 2-6

Worksheet class, the Locals window will always display at least the internal reference to itself, the Me object. Me is an object's pointer to itself.

The Watch window behaves just like the Locals window except that the programmer places the objects to watch in the Watch window. The benefit of the Watch window is that an object's state will automatically update as your program runs, permitting you to evaluate the evolving state of your application. In contrast, the Quick Watch will only display one watch at a time and is displayed in a model dialog box; thus the program execution is suspended when a Quick Watch is displayed. Each of the Locals, Watch, and Quick Watch windows will permit you to drill down into an object's state.

The Call Stack window portrays the list of program execution branches in reverse order with the most recent branch listed first followed by the previous branch. One can use the Call Stack to see the exact order in which methods are called and quickly navigate in the editor between branched locations. The Call Stack Window can be invaluable tool for debugging code.

The Add and Edit Watch windows are model dialog boxes used to add and modify values in the watch window. Watch values can be simple variables, complex objects, or valid expressions. For example, A= 10 is a valid watch value that will yield a Boolean True or False depending on the value of A. (Chapters 7 and 8 contain practical examples for debugging and testing your code.)

Using the Object Browser

There are probably dozens of object models for each language and framework in existence. We program very well in C++, C, C#, Delphi, Visual Basic, VBA, and reasonably well in languages like assembly, Jscript, VBScript, Java, Clipper, Fox Pro, and can adequately survive with languages like Cobol. The key to programming in any language is to master the grammar. Fortunately, most grammars have similarities, so the trick is to become comfortable with a particular language's object model or frameworks and the language's incumbent idioms and constructs.

Delphi has its own framework, the Visual Control Library or VCL. C# and Visual Basic .NET have the .NET Framework. Microsoft's C++ has the Microsoft Foundation Classes, and Borland's C++ (prior to C++ Builder) had the Object Windows Library, and there are frameworks for other languages like Java, as well as third party frameworks for language vendors. (Any C++ programmers remember the Zinc library for early versions of C++?)

It is worth mentioning all of these languages and frameworks, so that mastery of any particular framework is kept in perspective. With 1000 programming languages, many variants of each language, potential tens of thousands of classes, methods, properties, fields, events, and interfaces in each framework, it is almost impossible to memorize even modest-sized chunks of any one framework. A good strategy is to master the keywords and grammar of each language you intend to use. Become familiar with the common idioms and constructs, and then rely heavily on the Help documentation. Toward this end the VBE—and many other tools—support an Object Browser. By selecting View ⇨ Object Browser from the VBE's menu the Object Browser dialog box will be displayed. This dialog box provides a hierarchical, summarized list of classes and members. From this list you can use the Help documentation to obtain further details. In this way you will eventually gain some extemporaneous knowledge of the parts of the framework you frequently use.

A good rule of thumb for new developers is to spend some time checking to see if the VBA object model already supports a feature before you build a solution from scratch. If a VBA object model and Help documentation search doesn't bear fruit then check the Windows API (see Chapter 16). Further still, before you build it from scratch, check the Internet and existing third party solutions, again, before building a custom solution. Finally, build a solution only if you must. Even a couple of hours searching for an existing code will be time more productively spent than building all but the most trivial algorithms from scratch.

Summary

Programming is a sport that requires practice. Like all mental and physical activities, there seems to be a certain amount of learning that occurs in the body and mind. This chapter provided you with a quick tour of some key features in the VBE that we will use throughout the book. We took the time to point these features out because we were recently surprised to work with a group of developers that had been programming for a year and didn't know about the Quick Watch window. Now you know.

The VBE is a powerful word processing tool designed to function with the Visual Basic for Applications programming language. We encourage you to spend some of your own time exploring each main menu item and the context menus and toolbars for each part of VBA. You will likely find some features that you haven't used before, and these will enable you to work more productively with this book and as a programmer.

The Application Object

In this chapter we will examine a range of Excel functionality, looking at features that are not necessarily related to each other. In general, the Excel object model contains objects designed to address quite specific tasks. The `Application` object sits at the top of the Excel object model hierarchy and contains all the other objects in Excel. It also acts as a catch-all area for properties and methods that do not fall neatly into any other object, but are necessary for programmatic control of Excel. There are `Application` properties that control screen updating and toggle alert messages, for example. There is an `Application` method that calculates the formulas in the open workbooks.

Globals

Many of the `Application` object's methods and properties are also members of `<globals>`, which can be found at the top of the list of classes in the Object Browser as shown in Figure 3-1.

If a property or method is in `<globals>`, you can refer to that property or method without a preceding reference to an object. For example, the following two references are equivalent:

```
Application.ActiveCell
ActiveCell
```

However, you do need to be careful. It is easy to assume that the frequently used `Application` object properties, such as `ScreenUpdating`, are globals when they are not. The following code is correct:

```
Application.ScreenUpdating = False
```

You will get unexpected results with the following:

```
ScreenUpdating = False
```

This code sets up a new variable and assigns the value `False` to it. You can easily avoid this error by having the line of code `Option Explicit` at the top of each module so that such references are flagged as undefined variables when your code is compiled.

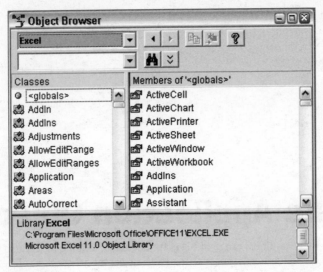

Figure 3-1

Remember that you can have Option Explicit automatically inserted in the new modules if you use Tools ➪ Options in the VBE window and, under the Editor tab, tick the Require Variable Declaration check box.

The Active Properties

The `Application` object provides many shortcuts that allow you to refer to active objects without naming them explicitly. This makes it possible to discover what is currently active when your macro runs. It also makes it easy to write generalized code that can be applied to objects of the same type with different names.

The following `Application` object properties are also global properties that allow you to refer to active objects:

- ❑ `ActiveCell`
- ❑ `ActiveChart`
- ❑ `ActivePrinter`
- ❑ `ActiveSheet`
- ❑ `ActiveWindow`
- ❑ `ActiveWorkbook`
- ❑ `Selection`

If you have just created a new workbook and want to save it with a specific filename, using the `ActiveWorkbook` property is an easy way to return a reference to the new `Workbook` object:

```
Workbooks.Add
ActiveWorkbook.SaveAs Filename:="C:\Data.xls"
```

If you want to write a macro that can apply a bold format to the currently selected cells, you can use the `Selection` property to return a reference to the `Range` object containing the selected cells:

```
Selection.Font.Bold = True
```

Be aware that `Selection` will not refer to a `Range` object if another type of object, such as a `Shape` object, is currently selected or the active sheet is not a worksheet. You might want to build a check into a macro to ensure that a worksheet is selected before attempting to enter data into it:

```
If TypeName(ActiveSheet) <> "Worksheet" Or _
   TypeName(Selection) <> "Range" Then _
      MsgBox "You can only run this macro in a range", vbCritical
   Exit Sub
End If
```

Display Alerts

It can be annoying to have to respond to system alerts while a macro runs. For example, if a macro deletes a worksheet, an alert message appears and you have to press the *OK* button to continue. However, there is also the possibility of a user clicking the *Cancel* button, which would abort the delete operation and could adversely affect subsequent code where we assumed the delete operation was to be carried out.

You can suppress most alerts by setting the `DisplayAlerts` property to `False`. When you suppress an alert dialog box, the action that is associated with the default button in that box is automatically carried out, as follows:

```
Application.DisplayAlerts = False
ActiveSheet.Delete
Application.DisplayAlerts = True
```

> It is not necessary to reset **DisplayAlerts** to **True** at the end of your macro as VBA does this automatically. However, it is usually a good idea, after suppressing a particular message, to turn the alerts back on so that any unexpected warnings do appear on screen.

`DisplayAlerts` is commonly used to suppress the warning that you are about to overwrite an existing file using File ➪ SaveAs. When you suppress this warning, the default action is taken and the file is overwritten without interrupting the macro.

Screen Updating

It can be annoying to see the screen change and flicker while a macro is running. This happens with macros that select or activate objects and is typical of the code generated by the macro recorder.

> It is better to avoid selecting objects in VBA. It is seldom necessary to do this and your code will run faster if you can avoid selecting or activating objects. Most of the code in this book avoids selecting where possible.

If you want to freeze the screen while your macro runs, you use the following line of code:

```
Application.ScreenUpdating = False
```

The screen remains frozen until you assign the property a value of `True`, or when your macro finishes executing and returns control to the user interface. There is no need to restore `ScreenUpdating` to `True`, unless you want to display screen changes while your macro is still running.

There is one situation where it is a good idea to set `ScreenUpdating` to `True` while your macro is running. If you display a UserForm or a built-in dialog box while your macro is running, you should make sure that screen updating is on before showing the object. If screen updating is off, and the user drags the UserForm around the screen, the UserForm will act as an eraser on the screen behind it. You can turn screen updating off again after showing the object.

> A beneficial side effect of turning off screen updating is that your code runs faster. It will even speed up code that avoids selecting objects, where little screen updating is required. Your code runs at maximum speed when you avoid selecting and turn off screen updating.

Evaluate

The `Evaluate` method can be used to calculate Excel worksheet formulas and generate references to `Range` objects. The normal syntax for the `Evaluate` method is as follows:

```
Evaluate("Expression")
```

There is also a shortcut format you can use where you omit the quotes and place square brackets around the expression as follows:

```
[Expression]
```

`Expression` can be any valid worksheet calculation, with or without the equal sign on the left, or it can be a reference to a range of cells. The worksheet calculations can include worksheet functions that are not made available to VBA through the `WorksheetFunction` object, or they can be worksheet array formulas. You will find more information about the `WorksheetFunction` object later in this chapter.

For instance, the `ISBLANK` function, which you can use in your worksheet formulas, is not available to VBA through the `WorksheetFunction` object, because the VBA equivalent function `IsEmpty` provides the same functionality. All the same, you can use `ISBLANK`, if you need to. The following two examples are equivalent and return `True` if A1 is empty or `False` if A1 is not empty:

```
MsgBox Evaluate("=ISBLANK(A1)")
MsgBox [ISBLANK(A1)]
```

The advantage of the first technique is that you can generate the string value using code, which makes it very flexible. The second technique is shorter, but you can only change the expression by editing your code. The following procedure displays a True or False value to indicate whether the active cell is empty or not, and illustrates the flexibility of the first technique:

```
Public Sub IsActiveCellEmpty()
   Dim FunctionName As String, CellReference As String
   FunctionName = "ISBLANK"
   CellReference = ActiveCell.Address
   MsgBox Evaluate(FunctionName & "(" & CellReference & ")")
End Sub
```

Note that you cannot evaluate an expression containing variables using the second technique.

The following two lines of code show you two ways you can use Evaluate to generate a reference to a Range object, and assign a value to that object:

```
Evaluate("A1").Value = 10
 [A1].Value = 10
```

The two expressions are equivalent. You can further shorten the expressions by omitting the Value property, as this is the default property of the Range object:

```
[A1] = 10
```

More interesting uses of Evaluate include returning the contents of a workbook's Names collection and efficiently generating arrays of values. The following code creates a hidden name to store a password. Hidden names cannot be seen in the Insert ⇨ Name ⇨ Define dialog box, so they are a convenient way to store information in a workbook without cluttering the user interface:

```
Names.Add Name:="PassWord", RefersTo:="Bazonkas", Visible:=False
```

You can then use the hidden data in expressions like the following:

```
UserInput = InputBox("Enter Password")
If UserInput = [PassWord] Then
...
```

The use of names for storing data is discussed in more detail in Chapter 21.

The Evaluate method can also be used with arrays. The following expression generates a Variant array with two dimensions, 100 rows and one column, containing the values from 101 to 200. This process is carried out more efficiently than using a For...Next loop:

```
RowArray = [ROW(101:200)]
```

Similarly, the following code assigns the values 101 to 200 to the range B1:B100, and again does it using fewer lines of code than a For...Next loop:

```
[B1:B100] = [ROW(101:200)]
```

InputBox

VBA has an `InputBox` function that provides an easy way to prompt for input data. There is also the `InputBox` method of the `Application` object that produces a very similar dialog box for obtaining data, but which is more powerful. It allows you to control the type of data that must be supplied by the user, and allows you to detect when the *Cancel* key is pressed.

If you have an unqualified reference to `InputBox` in your code, as follows, you are using the VBA `InputBox` function:

```
Answer = InputBox(prompt:="Enter range")
```

The user can only type data into the dialog box. It is not possible to point to a cell with the mouse. The return value from the `InputBox` function is always a string value and there is no check on what that string contains. If the user enters nothing, a zero length string is returned. If the user clicks the *Cancel* button, a zero length string is also returned. Your code cannot distinguish between no entry and the result of pressing *Cancel*.

The following example uses the `Application` object's `InputBox` method to prompt for a range:

```
Answer = Application.InputBox(prompt:="Enter range", Type:=8)
```

The `Type` parameter can take the following values, or any sum of the following values if you want to allow for multiple types.

Value of Type	Meaning
0	A formula
1	A number
2	Text (a string)
4	A logical value (`True` or `False`)
8	A cell reference, as a `Range` object
16	An error value, such as `#N/A`
64	An array of values

The user can point to cells with the mouse or type in data. If the input is of the wrong type, the `InputBox` method displays an error message and prompts for the data again. If the user clicks the Cancel button, the `InputBox` method returns a value of `False`.

If you assign the return value to a `Variant`, you can check to see if the value is `False`, for most return types, to detect a Cancel. If you are prompting for a range, the situation is not so simple. You need to use code like the following:

```
Public Sub SelectRange()
    Dim aRange As Range

    On Error Resume Next
```

```
    Set aRange = Application.InputBox(prompt:="Enter range", Type:=8)
    If aRange Is Nothing Then
      MsgBox "Operation Cancelled"
    Else
      aRange.Select
    End If
  End Sub
```

When you run this code, the output should look something like Figure 3-2.

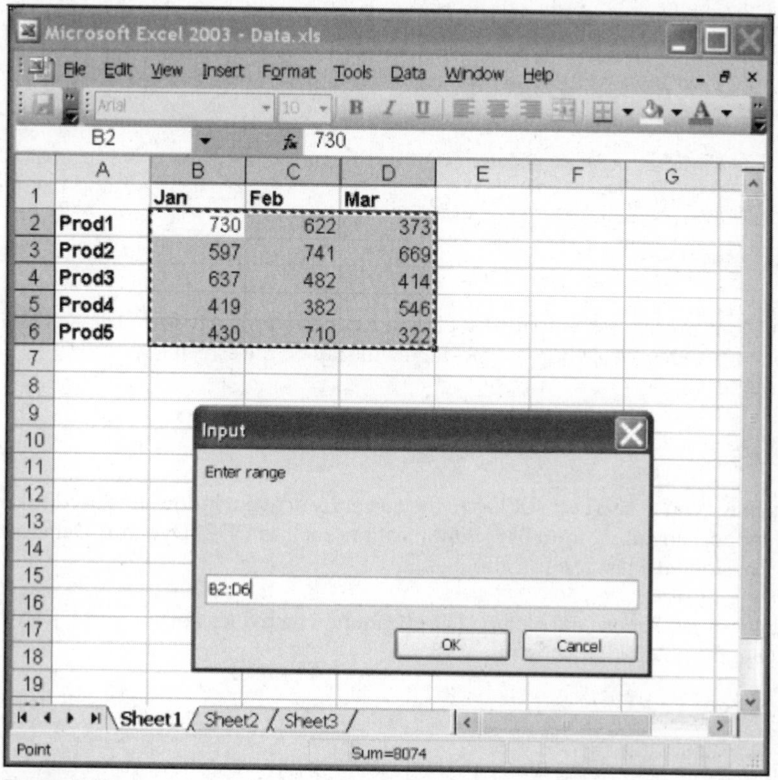

Figure 3-2

The problem is that you must use the Set statement to assign a range object to an object variable. If the user clicks *Cancel* and a False value is returned, the Set fails and you get a runtime error. Using the On Error Resume Next statement, you can avoid the runtime error and then check to see if a valid range was generated. You know that the in-built type checking of the InputBox method ensures a valid range will be returned if the user clicks *OK*, so an empty range indicates that *Cancel* was pressed.

StatusBar

The StatusBar property allows you to assign a text string to be displayed at the left-hand side of the Excel status bar at the bottom of the screen. This is an easy way to keep users informed of progress during a lengthy macro operation. It is a good idea to keep users informed, particularly if you have screen updating turned off and there is no sign of activity on the screen. Even though you have turned off screen updating, you can still display messages on the status bar.

The following code shows how you can use this technique in a looping procedure:

```
Public Sub ShowStatus()

  Application.ScreenUpdating = False

  Dim I As Long
  For I = 0 To 10000000
    If I Mod 1000000 = 0 Then
      Application.StatusBar = "Processing Record" & I
    End If
  Next I
  Application.StatusBar = False

  Application.ScreenUpdating = True

End Sub
```

At the end of your processing, you must set the `StatusBar` property to `False` so that it returns to normal operation. Otherwise, your last message will stay on the screen.

SendKeys

SendKeys allows you to send keystrokes to the currently active window. It is used to control applications that do not support any other form of communication, such as DDE (Dynamic Data Exchange) or OLE. It is generally considered a last resort technique.

The following example opens the Notepad application, which does not support DDE or OLE, and writes a line of data to the notepad document:

```
Public Sub SendKeyTest()
  Dim ReturnValue As Double
  ReturnValue = Shell("NOTEPAD.EXE", vbNormalFocus)
  Call AppActivate(ReturnValue)

  Application.SendKeys "Copy Data.xls c:\", True
  Application.SendKeys "~", True
  Application.SendKeys "%FABATCH~", True
End Sub
```

> It is important to note that **SendKeys** sends keys to the active application. If you run this macro in VBE then VBE will reobtain the focus after the first call to **SendKeys** and the text will be sent to the VBE itself. Run the macro from Excel for it to properly set and maintain focus on Notepad.

SendKeyTest uses *Alt+F+A* to perform a File ⇨ SaveAs and enters the file name as BATCH. The symbol % is used to represent *Alt* and ~ represents *Enter*. The symbol ^ is used to represent *Ctrl* and other special keys are specified by putting their names in braces, for example, the *Del* is represented by {Del} as shown in the next example. You can also send keystrokes directly to Excel. The following procedure clears the VBE's Immediate window. If you have been experimenting in the Immediate window or using Debug.Print to write to the Immediate window, it can get cluttered with old information. This procedure switches focus to the Immediate window and sends *Ctrl+a* to select all the text in the window. The text is then deleted by sending *Del*:

```
Public Sub ImmediateWindowClear()
    Application.VBE.Windows.Item("Immediate").SetFocus
    Application.SendKeys "^a"
    Application.SendKeys "{Del}"
End Sub
```

> It is necessary for you to have programmatic access to your Visual Basic project for this macro to work. This can be set from the Excel (not VBE) menu Tool ⇨ Macros ⇨ Security and selecting the Trusted Sources tab.

OnTime

You can use the OnTime method to schedule a macro to run sometime in the future. You need to specify the date and time for the macro to run, and the name of the macro. If you use the Wait method of the Application object to pause a macro, all Excel activity, including manual interaction, is suspended. The advantage of OnTime is that it allows you to return to normal Excel interaction, including running other macros, while you wait for the scheduled macro to run.

Say, you have an open workbook with links to Data.xls, which exists on your network server but is not currently open. At 3.00 P.M.. you want to update the links to Data.xls. The following example schedules the RefreshData macro to run at 3.00 P.M. which is 15:00 hours using a 24-hour clock, on the current day. Date returns the current date and the TimeSerial function is used to add the necessary time:

```
Public Sub RunOnTime()
    Application.OnTime Date + TimeSerial(15, 0, 0), "RefreshData"
End Sub
```

> It is worth noting that if you attempt to run this macro when it is currently after 3.00 P.M. you will receive an error message as you cannot schedule a task to run in the past. If necessary, change the time to one in the future.

The following RefreshData macro updates the links to Data.xls that exist in ThisWorkbook using the UpdateLink method. ThisWorkbook is a convenient way to refer to the workbook containing the macro:

```
Public Sub RefreshData()
  ThisWorkbook.UpdateLink Name:="C:\Data.xls", Type:=xlExcelLinks
End Sub
```

If you want to keep refreshing the data on a regular basis, you can make the macro run itself as follows:

```
Dim ScheduledTime As Date

Public Sub RefreshData()
  ThisWorkbook.UpdateLink Name:="C:\Data.xls", Type:=xlExcelLinks
  ScheduledTime = Now + TimeSerial(0, 1, 0)
  Application.OnTime ScheduledTime, "RefreshData"
End Sub

Public Sub StopRefresh()
  Application.OnTime ScheduledTime, "RefreshData", , False
End Sub
```

Once you run `RefreshData`, it will keep scheduling itself to run every minute. In order to stop the macro, you need to know the scheduled time, so the module level variable `ScheduledTime` is used to store the latest scheduled time. `StopRefresh` sets the fourth parameter of `OnTime` to `False` to cancel the scheduled run of `RefreshData`.

> When you schedule a macro to run at a future time using the **OnTime** method, you must make sure that Excel keeps running in memory until the scheduled time occurs. It is not necessary to leave the workbook containing the **OnTime** macro open. Excel will open it, if it needs to.

The `OnTime` method is also useful when you want to introduce a delay in macro processing to allow an event to occur that is beyond your control. For example, you might want to send data to another application through a DDE link and wait for a response from that application before continuing with further processing. To do this, you would create two macros. The first macro sends the data and schedules the second macro, which processes the response to run after sufficient time has passed. The second macro could keep running itself until it detects a change in the worksheet or the environment caused by the response from the external application.

OnKey

You can use the `OnKey` method to assign a macro procedure to a single keystroke or any combination of *Ctrl*, *Shift*, and *Alt* with another key. You can also use the method to disable key combinations.

The following example shows how to assign the `DownTen` macro to the *Down-Arrow* key. Once `AssignDown` has been run, the *Down-Arrow* key will run the `DownTen` macro and move the cell pointer down 10 rows instead of one:

```
Public Sub AssignDown()
  Application.OnKey "{Down}", "DownTen"
End Sub

Public Sub DownTen()
  ActiveCell.Offset(10, 0).Select
End Sub

Public Sub ClearDown()
  Application.OnKey "{Down}"
End Sub
```

ClearDown returns the *Down-Arrow* key to its normal function.

OnKey can be used to disable existing keyboardshortcuts. You can disable the *Ctrl+c* shortcut, normally used to copy, with the following code that assigns a null procedure to the key combination:

```
Sub StopCopyShortCut()
  Application.OnKey "^c", ""
End Sub
```

Note that a lower case c is used. If you used an upper case C, it would apply to *Ctrl+Shift+c*. Once again, you can restore the normal operation of *Ctrl+c* with the following code:

```
Sub ClearCopyShortCut()
  Application.OnKey "^c"
End Sub
```

> The key assignments made with the **OnKey** method apply to all open workbooks and only persist during the current Excel session.

Worksheet Functions

There are two sources of builtin functions that you can use directly in your Excel VBA code. One group of functions is part of the VBA language; the other group of functions is a subset of the Excel worksheet functions.

Excel and the Visual Basic language, in the form of VBA, were not merged until Excel 5. Each system independently developed its own functions, so there are inevitably some overlaps and conflicts between the two series of functions. For example, Excel has a DATE function and VBA also has a Date function. The Excel DATE function takes three input arguments (year, month, and day) to generate a specific date. The VBA Date function takes no input arguments and returns the current date from the system clock. In addition, VBA has a DateSerial function that takes the same input arguments as the Excel DATE function and returns the same result as the Excel DATE function. Finally, Excel's TODAY function takes no arguments and returns the same result as the VBA Date function.

As a general rule, if a VBA function serves the same purpose as an Excel function, the Excel function is not made directly available to VBA macros (although you can use the Evaluate method to access any

Excel function as pointed out previously in this chapter). There is also a special case regarding the Excel MOD function. MOD is not directly available in VBA, but VBA has a Mod operator that serves the same purpose. The following line of code uses the Evaluate method shortcut and displays the day of the week as a number, using the Excel MOD function and the Excel TODAY function:

```
MsgBox [MOD(TODAY(),7)]
```

The same result can be achieved more simply with the VBA Date function and the Mod operator as follows:

```
MsgBox Date Mod 7.
```

The Excel CONCATENATE function is also not available in VBA. You can use the & operator as a substitute, just as you can in an Excel worksheet formula. If you insist on using the CONCATENATE function in VBA, you can write code like the following:

```
Public Sub ConcatenateExample1()
    Dim X As String, Y As String
    X = "Jack "
    Y = "Smith"
    MsgBox Evaluate("CONCATENATE(""" & X & """,""" & Y & """)")
End Sub
```

On the other hand, you can avoid being absurd and get the same result with the following code:

```
Public Sub ConcatenateExample2()
    Dim X As String, Y As String
    X = "Jack "
    Y = "Smith"
    MsgBox X & Y
End Sub
```

The VBA functions, such as Date, DateSerial, and IsEmpty can be used without qualification, as they are members of <globals>. For example, you can use the following:

```
StartDate = DateSerial(2003, 9, 6)
```

The Excel functions, such as VLOOKUP and SUM, are methods of the WorksheetFunction object and are used with the following syntax:

```
Total = WorksheetFunction.Sum(Range("A1:A10"))
```

For compatibility with Excel 5 and Excel 95, you can use Application rather than WorksheetFunction:

```
Total = Application.Sum(Range("A1:A10"))
```

> **WorksheetFunction.VLookup** does not work properly in all versions of VBA. The errors can be avoided by using **Application.VLookup**.

For a complete list of the worksheet functions directly available in VBA, see the `WorksheetFunction` object in the reference section

Caller

The `Caller` property of the `Application` object returns a reference to the object that called or executed a macro procedure. It had a wide range of uses in Excel 5 and Excel 95, where it was used with menus and controls on dialog sheets. From Excel 97 onwards, commandbars and ActiveX controls on UserForms have replaced menus and controls on dialog sheets. The `Caller` property does not apply to these new features.

`Caller` still applies to the `Forms` toolbar controls, drawing objects that have macros attached and user-defined functions. It is particularly useful in determining the cell that called a user-defined function. The worksheet shown in Figure 3-3 uses the `WorksheetName` function to display the name of the worksheet in B2.

Figure 3-3

When used in a function, `Application.Caller` returns a reference to the cell that called the function, which is returned as a `Range` object. The following `WorksheetName` function uses the `Parent` property of the `Range` object to generate a reference to the `Worksheet` object containing the `Range` object. It assigns the `Name` property of the `Worksheet` object to the return value of the function. The `Volatile` method of the `Application` object forces Excel to recalculate the function every time the worksheet is recalculated, so that if you change the name of the sheet, the new name is displayed by the function:

```
Public Function WorksheetName() As String
    Application.Volatile
    WorksheetName = Application.Caller.Parent.Name
End Function
```

It would be a mistake to use the following code in the `WorksheetName` function:

```
WorksheetName = ActiveSheet.Name
```

If a recalculation takes place while a worksheet is active that is different from the one containing the formula, the wrong name will be returned to the cell.

Summary

In this chapter we have highlighted some of the more useful properties and methods of the `Application` object. As `Application` is used to hold general-purpose functionality that does not fall clearly under other objects, it is easy to miss some of these very useful capabilities.

The following properties and methods have been covered:

- ❑ `ActiveCell`—contains a reference to the active cell
- ❑ `ActiveChart`—contains a reference to the active chart
- ❑ `ActivePrinter`—contains a reference to the active printer
- ❑ `ActiveSheet`—contains a reference to the active worksheet
- ❑ `ActiveWindow`—contains a reference to the active window
- ❑ `ActiveWorkbook`—contains a reference to the active workbook
- ❑ `Caller`—contains reference to the object that called a macro
- ❑ `DisplayAlerts`—determines whether alert dialogs boxes are displayed or not
- ❑ `Evaluate`—used to calculate Excel functions and generate `Range` objects
- ❑ `InputBox`—used to prompt a user for input
- ❑ `OnKey`—assigns a macro to a single keystroke, or a combination (with *Ctrl*, *Alt*, etc.)
- ❑ `OnTime`—used to set the time for a macro to run
- ❑ `ScreenUpdating`—determines whether screen updating is turned on or off
- ❑ `Selection`—contains a reference to the selected range
- ❑ `SendKeys`—send keystrokes to the active window
- ❑ `StatusBar`—allows messages to be displayed on the status bar
- ❑ `WorksheetFunction`—contains the Excel functions available to VBA

This is but a small sample of the total number of properties and methods of the `Application` object—there are over 200 of them in Excel 2003. A full list is given in Appendix A.

Object-Oriented Theory and VBA

A wise sage once said: *divid et impera* (divide and conquer). The original statement was probably made about an impending battle, as in, divide the enemy and conquer them by divisions. Interestingly enough, this advice is apropos of the way we can conquer software engineering problems. We can divide the problem into many smaller, discrete problems and conquer them individually, or we can permit the problem to divide our attentions and the problem will conquer us.

A well-considered rule of thumb is to organize a solution by addressing the most complex and critical problems first. Generally, these challenging pieces act as a forcing function for significant portions of the solution, and an application without these critical pieces would be considered incomplete.

This chapter is about the mechanism that supports dividing and conquering a problem, the class. In Chapter 5 you will learn about general object-oriented theory and how this theory is supported in Visual Basic for Applications.

Comparing Classes and Interfaces

General object-oriented theory supports two common means of describing something. The first is the class. Classes are typically used to describe entities in the solution domain. A low-tech way of thinking about classes is that a class is used to nouns that are important to the problem's solution. A common analogy is that a class is a blueprint and an object is an example of the thing that the blueprint describes. The second descriptive construct is an interface. Interfaces typically describe a capability or an aspect of something. Comparatively, whereas a class might describe a thing like a television, an interface might describe a capability of a television—like the ability to increase or decrease the volume—but this capability might also exist somewhere else. For example, attenuating volume is an aspect of things that make sounds. Car radios, stereos, televisions, walkmans, bullhorns, and many other things support the ability to attenuate volume, but bullhorns and walkmans have little else in common.

How does all of this tie into VBA? The answer is that the class module is a funky sort of hybrid of a class and an interface. If one only declares but does not implement—add lines of code—in a class module then the class module is exactly an interface. If one declares and provides an implementation of members in a class module, then the class module is like a class that implements an interface that exactly matches the members of the interface. (The distinction that the class implements exactly the declared members of an interface is important because in other object-oriented languages a class can implement multiple interfaces, no interfaces, or have members that aren't declared by any interface.) For the most part you can think of a class module as a class, but it is valuable to know that subtle distinction exists.

Both classes and interfaces support polymorphism. This means that the hybrid class module supports polymorphism. Class polymorphism is supported through inheritance. Inheritance exists when we define a class and a second subclass that generalizes and extends the first class. For example, the concept of a Control class exists and a Button is a kind of control. In pure object-oriented terms a Button is a kind of Control, and we call inheritance of Control by Button generalization. Generalization is synonymous with inheritance. For example, a Control might support a Click behavior and a Button would extend this behavior by including the changing appearance of the button; this revised Click behavior is one of the forms—one of many possible forms, which is the meaning of the word polymorphism—of the Click behavior. VBA does not support class inheritance.

VBA does support interface polymorphism. Interface polymorphism is orthogonal to class polymorphism. With classes we could declare the type as a Control and initialize the Control with a Button; when we called `Control.Click` the actual Click behavior would be that of the button because a Button is a kind of Control. With interface polymorphism, we declare an interface type and any class that implements that interface satisfies the interface type, but there is no requirement that any of the types implementing the interface are related. Consider a class for a Dog and a Chess piece. Dog's and Chess pieces have nothing in common, but both could be implemented with the capability of Moving: `Dog.Move` and `Queen.Move`. We might implement an interface `Imoveable`—using an I-prefix is a convention for defining interfaces but not VBA class modules—that declares a method `Move`. Subsequently, any code designed to interface with `IMoveable` could invoke `Move`, and the form of the response would depend on the underlying object.

Technically, class polymorphism supports part of the behavior being adopted from subclasses. For example, the `Control.Click` method might raise an `OnClick` event and the `Button.Click` would cause the button to repaint and then use the parent's code to raise the event. Interface polymorphism will more than likely work completely independent of other classes implementing an interface. For instance, it is unlikely that moving the Dog will have no impact on the completely unrelated Queen Chess piece.

The subtle distinctions and uses for classes and interfaces are worth mastering if you plan on programming in other languages, such as Visual Basic .NET. For now, we will set this general discussion aside and focus on what we can specifically do with VBA.

Defining an Interface

VBA supports defining an interface in one class module and implementing that interface in a second class module. Using this approach means that we can implement one, two, or more classes that support the same behavior. This is useful because we can't overload methods in the same class module.

Overload means to have more than one method with the same name but different argument signature. We can't overload methods in the same class, but we can use interface polymorphism and define multiple classes that provide a similarly named behavior.

Suppose we want to define a class that calculates the Factorial of a number. Written mathematically as N!, factorials is the product of all of the integers between 1 and N where N is the number we want to calculate the factorial of. Factorials are useful in solving multinomial equations. (You don't need to write a factorial function; you can use the Fact(n) function built into Excel. To demonstrate interfaces, we'll pretend we have to implement this method ourselves.) We could add a class module in the VBE and declare an interface IFactorial that declares one method, Calculate. Here is the code:

```
Function Calculate(ByVal N As Long) As Long

End Function
```

Class modules with empty declarations are pure interfaces in VBA. If we use the Properties window and change the Name property to IFactorial then we have effectively defined a pure interface named IFactorial that declares one method, Calculate. Calculate accepts a Long and returns a Long. Next, we can implement multiple versions of this interface.

Implementing an Interface

To implement an interface we need a second class module that uses the Implements statement. For example, to implement IFactorial from the previous section we can add a second and third class module, include the Implements IFactorial statement and provide an implementation for the Calculate method. The next two listings show two implementations of the IFactorial interface. The first method implements Factorial as a recursive method and the second implements Calculate without recursion:

```
Implements IFactorial

Private Function IFactorial_Calculate(ByVal N As Long) As Long
  If (N > 1) Then
    IFactorial_Calculate = N * IFactorial_Calculate(N - 1)
  Else
    IFactorial_Calculate = 1
  End If
End Function


Implements IFactorial

Private Function IFactorial_Calculate(ByVal N As Long) As Long
  Dim I As Long, result As Long
  result = 1

  For I = 1 To N
    result = result * I
  Next I

  IFactorial_Calculate = result
End Function
```

Anywhere IFactorial can be used we can elect to use any of the classes that implement IFactorial. The next listing demonstrates how we could invoke the second form of Calculate. To use the first version of `IFactorial_Calculate` substitute `Factorial1` for `Factorial2` in the `Set` statement in the following example:

```
Sub TestFactorial()

    Dim Factorial As IFactorial
    Set Factorial = New Factorial2
    MsgBox Factorial.Calculate(4)

End Sub
```

Clearly implementing a `Factorial` method only makes sense if a satisfactory one doesn't exist. Like any technique, you will have to determine how a specific technique can be employed in your solution.

In our example one could define a single class module with methods named `RecursiveFactorial` and `LoopFactorial`, or some such method, but defining an interface `IFactorial` and a couple of variations of the calculation method makes it easier to substitute behaviors in a polymorphic way. By using interfaces one would only need to substitute the statement that creates the object implementing the interface but not change all of the method calls; the method calls would still be `object.method`, as demonstrated in the preceding example. If we used one class and two methods then changing methods would imply that every place we called one or the other calculation method we would have to change or code. Realistically, we change the code in one place—the point of declaration—with interfaces or in many places by using the older style of using a variety of names.

A reasonable person could argue that the potential for flexibility seems marginal in this one instance, but successful programming is the concerted application of better or best practices over weaker practices. Collectively, consistently using best practices, interfaces, in this instance, adds up to yield a better total result.

Defining Methods

Methods define the behavior of your class. Whatever your class needs to be able to do is implemented in the form of a subroutine of function in your class. Subroutines and functions in classes are referred to as methods. Good method names are generally whole word verbs and nouns. If you need to return a single datum then implement a function method. If you need to complete a task but not return data then implement a subroutine method.

A function comprises an access modifier, Friend, Public, Private (see the section *Information Hiding and Access Modifiers* later in this chapter), optionally the keyword `Static`, the keyword `Function`, a Function Name, optional parameters, and a return type. A subroutine comprises an access modifier, optionally the keyword `Static`, the keyword `Sub`, and optional parameters.

The practical needs of the method pretty much dictate whether you use a function or subroutine and the types and number of parameters and the return type (if the method is a function). Some good rules of thumb are:

❑ Use verbs and noun combinations and whole words for method names

❑ Only pass the parameters you absolutely need, if the parameter is a member field in the same class as the one containing the method, then you probably don't need to pass it

- ❑ Use whole words, preferably nouns, for parameter names
- ❑ Choose your access modifiers carefully, limiting the number of `Public` methods (see *Information Hiding and Access Modifiers* in this chapter)

You can check the Help files for the grammatical rules for methods. There are plenty of examples in this and other chapters throughout the book.

Parameters

Parameters can be passed by value, by reference, and as optional parameters. By value parameters are modified with the `ByVal` keyword. `ByVal` means that any changes to the argument are not reflected after the method returns because what you are passing is a copy of the original argument. By reference parameters are modified with the `ByRef` keyword. `ByRef` arguments are references to the outer parameter; modifications to the `ByRef` parameters are reflected when the method returns. Finally, the `Optional` modifier can be used in conjunction with `ByVal` and `ByRef`. Optional parameters must follow all non-Optional parameters.

ByVal Parameters

`ByVal` parameters can be changed inside of a method, but that change is not reflected when the method returns. For example, if we define:

```
Sub DoSomething(ByVal I As Integer)
   I = 10
End Sub
```

and call `DoSomething` using the following code:

```
Dim J As Integer
J = -7
DoSomething(J)
' J still equals -7
```

then the value of the parameter J is still −7 when `DoSomething` returns. It is important to understand how the state of your application is managed in order to control application state. In short, `ByVal` parameter changes are local to the method.

ByRef Parameters

By default if you forget to use a parameter modifier then parameters are by-reference. `ByRef` parameters are clandestinely pointers to variables. Thus, if you modified `DoSomething` so that the parameter I is now `ByRef` then the parameter J would be 10 after the call to `DoSomething` returned.

To understand how `ByVal` and `ByRef` parameters work, keep in mind that everything is a number. Variables are two sets of numbers. The first set of numbers is the location of the variable in memory. The second set of numbers is the value. When you pass a parameter by-value we are passing two numbers: the first is a new variable that has a distinct location and the second is a copy of the value of the caller's parameter. When you pass a parameter by-reference you are passing the same location as the parameter value and consequently, the same value.

Optional Parameters

The guiding principle for optional parameters is: if you define a parameter that can use a particular value most of the time, then you can save consumers some work. For example, if we defined a class that calculated sales tax and the application was used primarily in Michigan then we might define an optional parameter Tax and specify a default value of 6 precent:

```
Public Function AddSalesTax(ByVal SaleAmount As Double, _
   Optional ByVal Tax AS Double = .06) As Double
   AddSalesTax = SaleAmount * (1 + Tax)
End Sub
```

> The word consumer refers to a person that uses some code. For example, if you write a class and then use that class, you are the consumer of the class. Thus, the effort you save may be your own.

As defined, we could invoke AddSalesTax with the SaleAmount or the SaleAmount and Tax. For example, if we ran this method in Oregon then we could pass 0 for the Tax because Oregon has no sales tax.

Implementing Recursive Methods

Recursive methods are methods that call themselves as part of their implementation. Generally, within the method there is some termination condition that breaks the cycle. Recursive functions like the Factorial function, discussed earlier in the chapter are enticing because they are quick and dirty to implement. The only problem is stack winding.

When a method is called, the current location is pushed into stack memory, a limited, finite resource. Then, the parameters are pushed and the method is called. The current location is used to pick up where the code branched prior to the method call. Next, local variables are pushed on the stack. Thus, each time a method is called, more is added to the stack and the information is not removed until the method returns.

Recursive methods call themselves in their middles before the method returns, piling information on the stack without taking things off the stack. If the number of iterations is very large, then you are likely to run out of stack memory, called blowing the stack. If such a condition occurs in VBA you will get a runtime error 28, "Out of stack space." Because of this potential to blow the stack, recursive methods aren't especially robust. We can usually remove recursion with loops.

Eliminating Recursion with Loops

A recursive method calls itself as part of the solution. The call to self is implicitly the loop control, and the termination condition can most likely be used as the boundary condition for the loop. For example, the recursive Factorial method calls itself until N is 1, and then terminates. This means that the boundary conditions are 1 and N. Since 1 * M is M we can also eliminate 1 from the condition, which means our boundary conditions are 2 and N. Since all we need are a low and high boundary condition to use a loop we can—and did—reimplement the Factorial recursive algorithm using a loop.

There are a couple of reasons to replace recursion with loops: the first reason is that a for loop runs much faster than stack winding and method calls, and the second is that you can loop an infinite number of times, but eventually the stack space will be exhausted. Consequently, eliminate recursive methods, considering them as a potential for headaches for your end users.

Defining Fields

Fields represent the state of an object. Fields can be any type you need to be, and as rule it is a good idea to provide an initial value for every field in the `Class_Initialize` method and a final value in the `Class_Terminate` method. By initializing fields you know that an object is in a known state when it begins life, and adding a final state is a good habit that will aid you in ensuring that your code is never trying to use an object that has been discarded.

For example, if we have a string field name `MyField` and set `MyField` to "done" when the `Class_Terminate` runs then we could always perform a check to see if `MyField` = "done" before using the object. Granted this technique is significantly more useful in languages like C++, C, and Object Pascal, but managing state is one of the most important habits one can build.

The signature of a field is the keyword `Private`—fields are private by convention—the field name, the keyword `As` and the data type. Fields are private by convention because unfettered access to state makes it difficult to control your object's state. The problem with fields is that most fields should only have a finite range of possible values. For example, a postal code should be valid. In the United States eieieo is probably not a valid postal code. In response, this implies that we should enforce the finite set of values for our fields, ensuring we both start and remain in a valid state. The challenge is that a field by itself does not run code. Enter the property.

Defining Properties

While fields are essential for managing state, any field that we want to expose to consumers should be married to a property. A property is a special method that is consumed like a field but actually invokes a method. As a result, properties are easy to use like fields, but provide us with a convenient place to ensure that the finite range of possible values is managed.

Properties have a special signature but look like methods. The signature of a property is an access modifier—usually Public by convention—followed by the keyword `Property`, the keyword `Get`, `Let`, or `Set`, the name of the property and either a function or subroutine-like tail. To define a property that returns a value we use `Get` and we add parentheses, `As`, and the data type of the value we are returning. To define the property that sets a value, we use the keyword `Set` or `Let` and define a parameter for the type of data we want to set. If the data type we are writing to is a class then we use `Set`, and if it is a non-class type then we use `Let`. For example, if we have a field for storing a first name then we might define the marriage of fields and properties as follows:

```
Private FFirstName As String

Public Property Get FirstName() As String
   FirstName = FFirstName
End Property

Public Property Let FirstName(ByVal Value As String)
   FFirstName = Value
End Property
```

By convention, we use an F-prefix to denote a field. All that is needed is to drop the F-prefix and we have a suitable property name that is easy to match to its underlying field. (Some programmers use an abbreviated data type prefix, but the inventors of this style, Microsoft, are discouraging its continued use. You will have to decide for yourself. FirstName using a prefix might be written as sFirstName, m_FirstName, or mvar_FirstName.) The Get property returns the underlying field value by assigning it to the function-like Get property. The Let property assigns the argument Value—again a convention we use is naming all property arguments value—to the underlying field. If you need to write validation code, then you would add that code between the first and last lines of the property statement.

Generally, we only need validation code in the Let or Set property methods, but if we elected to create a derived property then we could add code to the Get property method. The first listing shows how we might validate a sales tax property to ensure the sales tax is non-negative and less than 10 percent, and the second listing shows how we could create a derived FullName property from a first name and last name field:

```
Private FSalesTax As Double

Public Property Let SalesTax(ByVal Value As Double)
  If (Value < 0 Or Value > 0.1) Then
    ' do something here to indicate an error
  End If

  FSalesTax = Value
End Property
```

The preceding example shows how we might validate a property like SalesTax. It is unlikely that we will see sales taxes exceed 10 percent for at least a few months, and if we will never see a negative sales tax:

```
Public Property Get FullName() As String
  FullName = FFirstName & " " & FLastName
End Property
```

The FullName property shows how we can create a derived property. FullName is derived from two underlying fields FFirstName and FLastName (keeping in mind our F-prefix convention). If we were really ambitious then we could also write a Let FullName property that splits one string into two strings setting the underlying FFirstName and FLastName fields.

Keep in mind that properties are really just special methods. While you can write any code in a property their main job is that of data sheriff. As data sheriffs, properties are primarily responsible for reliably setting and returning the value of fields.

Read-Only Properties

A read-only property is a property that only has a Property Get definition (no Let or Set method defined). If you have a derived property or an immutable field that you want consumers to be able to read but not write, then define a Property Get method only.

Read-only properties are properties that only define a Get method, but the syntax is the same for the Get property alone as it is for a property with a symmetric write method.

Write-Only Properties

Write properties are simply properties that have a `Property Let` or `Set` method and no `Property Get` method. (`Let` is for property writers for non-object values, and `Set` is for property writers for object values.) Write-only properties are moderately rare, but you may find an occasion to use them. For example, a person may pump fuel into a car's gas tank but unless you want a mouth full of gas there is no way to remove the fuel through the same portal in which it was added. Only driving the car will normally reduce the fuel levels. All fun aside, write-only properties are technically possible but pragmatically rare.

Defining Events

Windows, and of necessity Excel, are built upon the trinity of the state, behavior, and signal. These are implemented by the idioms state and property, method, and events. Events are the way that objects signal to respondents that some action has occurred and if desired, now is a good time to respond.

It is a bit condescending to assume that because Excel is so well designed that one can program in Excel without understanding the mechanism behind events that support this mechanism. In fact, it is more likely that if we understand the event mechanism in intimate detail then we are likely to find more creative uses for events. To this end here is a conceptual explanation of events: producers—those who create classes—don't always know in advance how consumers—those that use the classes—will respond to changing state, so they incorporate events. These events give respondents almost unlimited opportunity to respond. Underneath the grammar, an event is nothing more than an uninitialized number that refers to a method. When a programmer associates an event handler—just a method—within an event, the event is no longer an uninitialized number. The event now has the number—called an address—of the event handler.

When you add a method to a class, you are adding a preinitialized number that refers to your method's code. When you add an event to a class, you are adding an uninitialized number that permits a consumer to insert some code at the point in which your event is raised. In this way events are a placeholder in your classes where you are permitting consumers an opportunity to insert their needed responses.

From a producer's perspective one has two responsibilities: define the events that act as the signature of the placeholders and raise the events in the places that consumers are permitted to insert their code. From a consumer's perspective, an event is an opportunity to respond to the changing state of an object. For example, when the value of a `TextBox` is changed a consumer might want to make sure that the value is a digit between 1 and 9 or a string in the format of a US postal code. The reality is that the producer doesn't know in advance. Consequently, the producer is programming for the general possibilities, and the consumer is filling in the necessary blanks.

Defining Events in Classes

No implementations of object-based languages are the same. Learning a couple of languages will aid in gaining perspective and exploring possibilities. Point in case, the event idiom is restricted to class modules, forms, and documents in VBA, but an event is a function pointer so this limitation is created by VBA.

In addition to event definitions and usage being limited to class modules, forms, and documents in VBA, events must be declared as subroutines, cannot use named, Optional, or `ParamArray` arguments. When you can do is define an event in a class and consume an event in a class (forms and documents being specific kinds of classes), but you cannot define or consume an event in a plain vanilla module. (The underlying idiom—function pointer—is not as restricted in other languages, with C++ being the most flexible.)

Define an event in a class when you want a consumer to be able to insert a response to the changing state of your class. An event definition uses the access modifier—generally Public, the keyword Event, and a subroutine header where the Sub keyword is supplanted by the Event keyword. The listing shows how we might define an event for a customer calculator. This event represents an insertion point where consumers of the Calculator class might want to respond to a change in the customer Discount, by perhaps recalculating totals:

```
Public Event DiscountChanged(ByVal sender As Calculator, _
    ByVal NewDiscount As Double)
```

The event definition, as demonstrated, uses the Public and Event keywords and then looks like any subroutine definition with arguments and no return type. In the example, we include a reference to containing object. (This is a technique that has proven useful in many other object-oriented languages, and consequently, is a general practice we have adopted.) The second argument is the NewDiscount value.

Raising Events

Raising custom events is, by convention, a two-step process: call a Private method that actually raises the event. By using a wrapper method we have a convenient place to incorporate any additional behavior needed and the RaiseEvent statement is used of technical necessity. The listing demonstrates how we might raise the DiscountChanged event:

```
Private FDiscount As Double

Public Property Get Discount() As Double
  Discount = FDiscount
End Property

Public Property Let Discount(ByVal value As Double)
  If (value <> FDiscount) Then
    FDiscount = value
    Call DoDiscountChanged(FDiscount)
  End If
End Property

Private Sub DoDiscountChanged(ByVal NewDiscount As Double)
  RaiseEvent DiscountChanged(Me, NewDiscount)
End Sub
```

The preceding listing shows all of the elements that are likely to play a role in the event process. The first statement is the field containing the discount rate. The Property Get statement returns the current discount rate. The Property Let statement checks to make sure we aren't running unnecessary code by setting the discount rate without changing its value. The conditional check in the Property Let statement is a convention only. If, in fact, the Discount value is changed then we call the Private method DoDiscountChanged. Finally, DoDiscountChanged raises the event. The only statement we need to actually signal the event is the statement containing RaiseEvent, but by using the wrapper we don't need to pass the first argument, the reference to self.

Conventions are adopted in one of two ways: by hard-won trial and error or by copying those that have traveled the same path before us. The convention to wrap raising events provides one locale in which we can converge any dependent code. For example, suppose by default we elected to save the discount rate to a database, file, or the registry. Rather than have this code everywhere we might raise the event, we could insert this additional code in the DoDiscountChanged method.

Lastly, we would like to address speed and quality. By following conventions like using a wrapper every time even if it isn't exactly necessary, code takes on a consistent and symmetric appearance, which lends itself to the appearance of professionalism. Those consuming or extending your code will know what to anticipate. In addition, by doing the same kind of thing in the same kind of circumstances we spend less time thinking about how or why we do something. The end result is that we build reliable habits, much faster, and can focus more on the problem and solution and less on the methodology.

Handling Events

When you define an event you are playing the role of a producer. When you write an event handler you are playing the role of a consumer. A risk occurs when the consumer and the producer is the same person. The risk is that because the producer and the consumer is the same person they are intimately aware of the internal behavior of the class to be consumed and may take shortcuts, like wiring code directly to a field rather than adding an event and consuming the event. A good device is to write classes for a general consumer following good producer rules, and then, even if you are your own customer, write good consumer code as if you didn't know about the internal details of the classes being consumed.

To handle an event, we need to declare a variable using the WithEvents keyword and then use the code editor to generate the event handler for us. The next listing shows how a worksheet might define an instance of our Calculator class and pick the class and event from the Object and Procedure drop-down list boxes in the code editor:

```
Private WithEvents theCalculator As Calculator

Public Sub TestCalculator()

  Set theCalculator = New Calculator
  theCalculator.Discount = 0.05

End Sub

Private Sub theCalculator_DiscountChanged(ByVal sender As Calculator, _
  ByVal NewDiscount As Double)

  Call MsgBox("Discount changed to " & NewDiscount)

End Sub
```

The first statement declares a calculator variable using WithEvents. This adds the theCalculator variable to the list of objects in the code editor. Select theCalculator from the list of objects and the event DiscountChanged will appear in the procedures list, and because it is the only event, the theCalculator_DiscountChanged procedure will be added to the consuming module.

In our example, we simply show the new discount value. In a practical application we might want to recalculate totals for a customer or something similar. The general rule of thumb is to insert places in your classes where consumers can write response behavior. Remember, as a producer, it is highly unlikely that you can anticipate all present and future uses for your class. By using an event you increase the likelihood that your class can be employed in new uses, resulting in greater longevity and fewer revisions.

Information Hiding and Access Modifiers

Throughout this chapter we have talked about access modifiers. Access modifiers in VBA are the keywords `Private`, `Public`, and `Friend`. Before we talk about these keywords let us say that one can define everything as `Public` in VBA, which can be especially helpful if you are just getting started. However, we also need to say that by making everything public one is missing out on one of the most useful, albeit abstruse, facets of object-oriented programming.

Before we talk about the abstruse aspects of access modifiers, let's talk about what these words mean in practice. Both consumers and producers can invoke public members. Public members are a bit like public toilets. Anyone goes in and in some cases anything goes. Private members are for producers only. The producer of the class is the only person that can invoke private members. `Friend` can only modify procedures in Form and Class modules and cannot be late bound. The `Friend` modifier means that a procedure is public within the same project and private to external projects. In the context of Excel this means you can call `Friend` procedures from anywhere within the same workbook but not across workbooks.

Why do these distinctions exist and how do they help? The basic premise is that the fewer public members a class has, the easier it is to use. In response then, only a few, necessary members should be public and every other supporting member should be private. This is a highly subjective truism. From another perspective consider this: if a member is private then making it public won't break existing, dependent code but making a public member private may break existing dependent code. Here are some general guidelines that will help you decide how to use public and private access modifiers:

❑ Try to keep the number of public members to fewer than a half dozen

❑ If you are unsure, make a member private and see if the class can still perform its primary tasks

❑ Make all fields private

❑ Make all properties public

❑ Make all events public

❑ If you find that you need more than 6 to 12 public members then consider splitting the class

❑ Break any rule if you need to; you're the boss

Encapsulation, Aggregation, and References

Let's wrap up this chapter by talking briefly about a few abstruse concepts that are important but difficult to pin down. We are referring to encapsulation, aggregation, reference, and dependency. Encapsulation is the notion of containing things. Aggregation is the notion of things comprising parts and wholes. Reference is the notion of knowing about one thing and using something else, and dependency is the notion of relying on something else.

In the object-oriented world we talk about encapsulation and mean a class containing data. For example, a Workbook encapsulates Worksheets. Encapsulation is often exhibited by a variable name, the member of operator, and the encapsulated thing. For example, a worksheet encapsulates cells and this relationship can be expressed in the Worksheet class as a `Cells` property and the code might be `Sheet1.Cells`.

Aggregation refers to wholes and parts and the sum of those parts. A car comprises wheels and tires, engine and transmission, seats and steering wheels, and more. When put together the sum of the parts comprises a new thing. The idea behind aggregation is that by having the parts we can assemble them in different ways to create different wholes. A Hummer is not a Jeep but they may have shared parts in common. At a minimum, they have shared concepts in common. A plane is not a car, but planes and cars have shared things in common like combustion engines and tires. Aggregation reminds us that the composition of parts yields more powerful results than singular, monolithic things.

The concept Reference refers to one class knowing about another class. For example, we could add an instance of the Calculator class to a Worksheet, and the worksheet could be responsible for creating the calculator or the calculator could be created by some other class and just referred to by the Calculator. If the Worksheet creates the Calculator then the Calculator is a part and the relationship is aggregation; if the Worksheet simply refers to the Calculator then the relationship is a reference relationship. A good predefined example of a reference relationship is that represented by the `Application` object. Many classes in Excel have an `Application` property, but if an object like a Worksheet goes away, the Application isn't closed. Conversely, if the Excel application is closed then the worksheet goes away too (although it is saved, or persisted, to file). Hence, the relationship between Application and Worksheet is aggregation and Worksheet and Application is reference.

Finally, we have dependency relationships. A dependency is where one object relies on the existence of another object. A Worksheet is dependent on the existence of its cells. If a class A is dependent on another class B then the class A cannot do its job without the existence of the class B. Such a dependency relationship exists between Excel (the Application) and the Worksheet: Excel is implemented to be dependent on at least one visible Worksheet. Consequently, one can always rely on the test `ThisWorkbook.Sheets.Count >= 1`. Defining and relying on dependencies is an issue of reliable conditions: where one exists you'll find the other.

We introduced these terms here because where necessary we will refer to them throughout this book. Because they are general object-oriented concepts they apply to VBA. Knowing these terms will make our discussions more concise and will help you learn more advanced programming techniques by reading specific and generally applicable object-oriented programming books.

Summary

Excel is a practical tool. It is very good at solving mathematically intense problems and creating graphic representations of those problems. However, VBA is a very powerful general-programming language. VBA is almost part and parcel Visual Basic, and Visual Basic permits a programmer to solve problems in almost every category. By introducing these general object-oriented concepts, we are providing you with the opportunity to maximize your experience with Excel and pursue more advanced concepts. If you are using Excel to solve problems that integrate with other Office applications or VB applications, then having this knowledge will be especially useful.

If you are interested in the breadth and extent of a programming language like VBA then we encourage you to read books on topics like Patterns and Refactoring such as: *Add Refactoring: Improving the Design of Existing Code* by Martin Fowler, and *Design Patterns* by Erich Gamma *et al.* Excel is a superlative number cruncher from an object-oriented perspective, VBA is much more than a macro language.

Event Procedures

Excel makes it very easy for you to write code that runs when a range of worksheet, chart sheet, and workbook events occur. In previous chapters, we have already seen how to highlight the active row and column of a worksheet by placing code in the `Worksheet_SelectionChange` event procedure (see Chapter 2). This runs every time the user selects a new range of cells. (You can also find examples demonstrating how to synchronize worksheets in a workbook using the `Worksheet_Deactivate` and `Worksheet_Activate` events in Chapter 19.)

It is easy to create workbook, chart sheet, and worksheet events, because Excel automatically provides you with code modules for these objects. However, note that the chart events that are supplied automatically in a chart module apply only to chart sheets, not to embedded charts. If you want to write event procedures for embedded charts, you can do so, but it takes a bit more knowledge and effort.

There are also many other high-level events that can be accessed, for the `Application` object, for example. These events will be covered later on in Chapters 6 and 14. Events associated with controls and forms will also be treated in the respective chapters. In this chapter we will look, in more detail, at worksheet, chart, and workbook events and related issues.

> Event procedures are always associated with a particular object and are contained in the class module that is associated with that object, such as the **ThisWorkbook** module or the code module behind a worksheet or a UserForm. Events may only be defined in class modules.

Worksheet Events

The following worksheet event procedures are available in the code module behind each worksheet:

❑ `Private Sub Worksheet_Activate()`

- ❑ `Private Sub Worksheet_BeforeDoubleClick(ByVal Target As Range, Cancel As Boolean)`

- ❑ `Private Sub Worksheet_BeforeRightClick(ByVal Target As Range, Cancel As Boolean)`

- ❑ `Private Sub Worksheet_Calculate()`

- ❑ `Private Sub Worksheet_Change(ByVal Target As Range)`

- ❑ `Private Sub Worksheet_Deactivate()`

- ❑ `Private Sub Worksheet_FollowHyperlink(ByVal Target As Hyperlink)`

- ❑ `Private Sub Worksheet_PivotTableUpdate(ByVal Target As PivotTable)`

- ❑ `Private Sub Worksheet_SelectionChange(ByVal Target As Range)`

You can use the drop-down list at the top of the code module to create the empty event handler. For example, in a worksheet code module, you can select the `Worksheet` object from the left-hand drop-down list. This will generate the following lines of code:

```
Private Sub Worksheet_SelectionChange(ByVal Target As Range)
...
End Sub
```

The `SelectionChange` event is the default event for the `Worksheet` object. If you want a different event, select the event from the right-hand drop-down list, and delete the preceding lines.

As an alternative to using the drop-downs, you can type the first line of the procedure yourself. The procedure type and arguments must correspond, in number, order, and type (referred to as the signature) with those shown in the preceding code. You are permitted to use different parameter names, if you wish, but it is better to stick with the standard names to avoid confusion.

Most event parameters must be declared with the `ByVal` keyword, which prevents your code from passing back changes to the object or item referenced by assigning a new value to the parameter. If the parameter represents an object, you can change the object's properties and execute its methods, but you cannot pass back a change in the object definition by assigning a new object definition to the parameter.

Some event procedures are executed before the associated event occurs and have a `Cancel` parameter that is passed by reference (`ByRef`). You can assign a value of `True` to the `Cancel` parameter to cancel the associated event. For example, you could prevent a user accessing the worksheet shortcut menu by canceling the `RightClick` event in the `Worksheet_BeforeRightClick` event procedure:

```
Private Sub Worksheet_BeforeRightClick(ByVal Target As Range, _
                                       Cancel As Boolean)
    Cancel = True
End Sub
```

Enable Events

It is important to turn off event handling in some event procedures to prevent unwanted implicit recursion. For example, if a worksheet `Change` event procedure changes the worksheet, it will itself trigger the Change event and run itself again. The event procedure will change the worksheet again and trigger the Change event again, and so on.

If only one event procedure is involved, Excel 2000, 2002, and 2003 will usually detect the recursion and terminate it after some hundreds of cycles (Excel 2003 repeats the Change event after about 226 repetitions, whereas Excel 97 will stop after about 40 repetitions). If more than one event procedure is involved, the process can continue indefinitely or until you press *Esc* or *Ctrl+Break* enough times to stop each process.

For example, there could be a Calculation event procedure active as well as a Change event procedure. If both procedures change a cell that is referenced in a calculation, both events are triggered into an interactive chain reaction. That is, the first event triggers the second event, which triggers the first event again, and so on. The following Change event procedure makes sure that it does not cause a chain reaction by turning off event handling while it changes the worksheet. It is important to turn event handling back on again before the procedure ends:

```
Private Sub Worksheet_Change(ByVal Target As Range)
    Application.EnableEvents = False
    Range("A1").Value = 100
    Application.EnableEvents = True
End Sub
```

> **Application.EnableEvents = False** does not affect events outside the Excel Object Model. Events associated with ActiveX controls and UserForms, for example, will continue to occur.

Worksheet Calculate

The Worksheet_Calculate event occurs whenever the worksheet is recalculated. It is usually triggered when you enter new data into the cells that are referenced in formulas in the worksheet. You could use the Worksheet_Calculate event to warn you, as you enter new data assumptions into a forecast, when key results go outside their expected range of values. In the worksheet shown in Figure 5-1, you want to know when the profit figure in cell N9 exceeds 600 or is lower than 500.

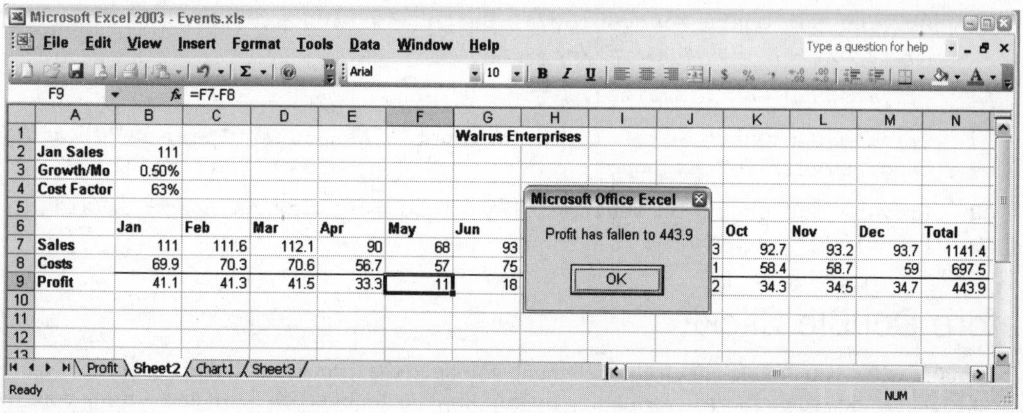

Figure 5-1

The following event procedure runs every time the worksheet recalculates, checks cell N9, which has been named `FinalProfit`, and generates messages if the figure goes outside the required band of values:

```
Private Sub Worksheet_Calculate()
   Dim Profit As Double

   Profit = Sheet2.Range("FinalProfit").Value
   If Profit > 600 Then
      MsgBox "Profit has risen to " & Format(Profit, "#,##0.0")
   ElseIf Profit < 500 Then
      MsgBox "Profit has fallen to " & Format(Profit, "#,##0.0")
   End If
End Sub
```

Chart Events

The following chart event procedures are available in the code module for each chart object:

❑   `Private Sub Chart_Activate()`

❑   `Private Sub Chart_BeforeDoubleClick(ByVal ElementID As Long, ByVal Arg1 As Long, ByVal Arg2 As Long, Cancel As Boolean)`

❑   `Private Sub Chart_BeforeRightClick(Cancel As Boolean)`

❑   `Private Sub Chart_Calculate()`

❑   `Private Sub Chart_Deactivate()`

❑   `Private Sub Chart_DragOver()`

❑   `Private Sub Chart_DragPlot()`

❑   `Private Sub Chart_MouseDown(ByVal Button As XlMouseButton, ByVal Shift As Long, ByVal x As Long, ByVal y As Long)`

❑   `Private Sub Chart_MouseMove(ByVal Button As XlMouseButton, ByVal Shift As Long, ByVal x As Long, ByVal y As Long)`

❑   `Private Sub Chart_MouseUp(ByVal Button As XlMouseButton, ByVal Shift As Long, ByVal x As Long, ByVal y As Long)`

❑   `Private Sub Chart_Resize()`

❑   `Private Sub Chart_Select(ByVal ElementID As XlChartItem, ByVal Arg1 As Long, ByVal Arg2 As Long)`

❑   `Private Sub Chart_SeriesChange(ByVal SeriesIndex As Long, ByVal PointIndex As Long)`

Before Double Click

Normally, when you double-click a chart element, you open the formatting dialog box for the element. You could provide some shortcut formatting by trapping the double-click event and writing your own code.

The following event procedure formats three chart elements when they are double-clicked. If, in the chart shown in Figure 5-2, you double-click the legend, it is removed.

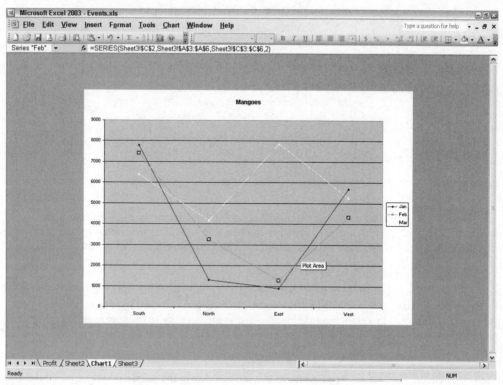

Figure 5-2

If you double-click the chart area (around the outside of the plot area), the legend is displayed. If you double-click a series line with all points selected, it changes the color of the line. If a single point in the series is selected, the data label at the point is toggled on and off:

```
Private Sub Chart_BeforeDoubleClick(ByVal ElementID As Long, _
    ByVal Arg1 As Long, ByVal Arg2 As Long, Cancel As Boolean)

    Dim theSeries As Series

    Select Case ElementID
        Case xlLegend
            Me.HasLegend = False
            Cancel = True
        Case xlChartArea
            Me.HasLegend = True
            Cancel = True
        Case xlSeries
            'Arg1 is the Series index
            'Arg2 is the Point index (-1 if the entire series is selected)
            Set theSeries = Me.SeriesCollection(Arg1)
```

```
      If Arg2 = -1 Then
         With theSeries.Border
            If .ColorIndex = xlColorIndexAutomatic Then
              .ColorIndex = 1
            Else
              .ColorIndex = (.ColorIndex Mod 56) + 1
            End If
              End With
            Else
              With theSeries.Points(Arg2)
                  .HasDataLabel = Not .HasDataLabel
              End With
         End If
         Cancel = True
   End Select
End Sub
```

The `ElementID` parameter passes an identifying number to indicate the element that was double-clicked. You can use intrinsic constants, such as `xlLegend`, to determine the element. At the end of each case, `Cancel` is assigned `True` so that the default double-click event is canceled and the Formatting dialog box does not appear.

Note the use of the keyword `Me` to refer to the object associated with the code module. Using `Me` instead of `Chart1` makes the code portable to other charts. In fact, you can omit the object reference `"Me."` and use `"HasLegend ="`. In a class module for an object, you can refer to properties of the object without qualification. However, qualifying the property makes it clear that it is a property and not a variable you have created.

If the chart element is a series, `Arg1` contains the series index in the `SeriesCollection` and if a single point in the series has been selected `Arg2` contains the point index. `Arg2` is 1 if the whole series is selected.

If the whole series is selected, the event procedure assigns 1 to the color index of the series border, if the color index is automatic. If the color index is not automatic, it increases the color index by 1. As there are only 56 colors available, the procedure uses the `Mod` operator, which divides the color index by 56 and gives the remainder, before adding 1. The only color index value that is affected by this is 56. 56 `Mod` 56 returns zero, which means that the next color index after 56 is 1.

If a single point is selected in the series, the procedure toggles the data label for the point. If the `HasDataLabel` property of the point is `True`, `Not` converts it to `False`. If the `HasDataLabel` property of the point is `False`, `Not` converts it to `True`.

Workbook Events

The following workbook event procedures are available. Again, those new to Excel 2003 are highlighted in bold:

❑   `Private Sub Workbook_Activate()`

❑   `Private Sub Workbook_AddinInstall()`

❑ Private Sub Workbook_AddinUninstall()

❑ **Private Sub Workbook_AfterXmlExport(ByVal Map As XmlMap, ByVal Url As String, ByVal Result As XlXmlExportResult)**

❑ **Private Sub Workbook_AfterXmlImport(ByVal Map As XmlMap, ByVal IsRefresh As Boolean, ByVal Result As XlXmlImportResult)**

❑ Private Sub Workbook_BeforeClose(Cancel As Boolean)

❑ Private Sub Workbook_BeforePrint(Cancel As Boolean)

❑ Private Sub Workbook_BeforeSave(ByVal SaveAsUI As Boolean, Cancel As Boolean)

❑ **Private Sub Workbook_BeforeXmlExport(ByVal Map As XmlMap, ByVal Url As String, Cancel As Boolean)**

❑ **Private Sub Workbook_BeforeXmlImport(ByVal Map As XmlMap, ByVal Url As String, ByVal IsRefresh As Boolean, Cancel As Boolean)**

❑ Private Sub Workbook_Deactivate()

❑ Private Sub Workbook_NewSheet(ByVal Sh As Object)

❑ Private Sub Workbook_Open()

❑ Private Sub Workbook_PivotTableCloseConnection(ByVal Target As PivotTable)

❑ Private Sub Workbook_PivotTableOpenConnection(ByVal Target As PivotTable)

❑ Private Sub Workbook_SheetActivate(ByVal Sh As Object)

❑ Private Sub Workbook_SheetBeforeDoubleClick(ByVal Sh As Object, ByVal Target As Range, Cancel As Boolean)

❑ Private Sub Workbook_SheetBeforeRightClick(ByVal Sh As Object, ByVal Target As Range, Cancel As Boolean)

❑ Private Sub Workbook_SheetCalculate(ByVal Sh As Object)

❑ Private Sub Workbook_SheetChange(ByVal Sh As Object, ByVal Target As Range)

❑ Private Sub Workbook_SheetDeactivate(ByVal Sh As Object)

❑ Private Sub Workbook_SheetFollowHyperlink(ByVal Sh As Object, ByVal Target As Hyperlink)

❑ Private Sub Workbook_SheetPivotTableUpdate(ByVal Sh As Object, ByVal Target As PivotTable)

❑ Private Sub Workbook_SheetSelectionChange(ByVal Sh As Object, ByVal Target As Range)

❑ **Private Sub Workbook_Sync(ByVal SyncEventType As Office .MsoSyncEventType)**

❑ Private Sub Workbook_WindowActivate(ByVal Wn As Window)

- ❑   `Private Sub Workbook_WindowDeactivate(ByVal Wn As Window)`
- ❑   `Private Sub Workbook_WindowResize(ByVal Wn As Window)`

Some of the workbook event procedures are the same as the worksheet and chart event procedures. The difference is that when you create these procedures (such as the `Change` event procedure) in a worksheet or chart, it applies to only that sheet. When you create a workbook event procedure (such as the `SheetChange` event procedure) it applies to all the sheets in the workbook.

One of the most commonly used workbook event procedures is the `Open` event procedure. This is used to initialize the workbook when it opens. You can use it to set the calculation mode, establish screen settings, alter the menu structure, decide what toolbars should appear, or enter data into combo boxes or listboxes in the worksheets.

Similarly, the `Workbook_BeforeClose` event procedure can be used to tidy up when the workbook is closed. It can restore screen and menu settings, for example. It can also be used to prevent a workbook's closure by setting `Cancel` to `True`. The following event procedure will only allow the workbook to close if the figure in the cell named `FinalProfit` is between 500 and 600:

```
Private Sub Workbook_BeforeClose(Cancel As Boolean)
  Dim Profit As Double

  Profit = ThisWorkbook.Worksheets(2).Range("FinalProfit").Value
  If Profit < 500 Or Profit > 600 Then
    MsgBox "Profit must be in the range 500 to 600"
    Cancel = True
  End If
End Sub
```

Note that if you assign `True` to `Cancel` in the workbook `BeforeClose` event procedure, you also prevent Excel from closing.

Save Changes

If you want to make sure that all changes are saved when the workbook closes, but you don't want the user to be prompted to save changes, you can save the workbook in the `BeforeClose` event procedure. You can check to see if this is really necessary using the `Saved` property of the workbook, which will be `False` if there are unsaved changes:

```
Private Sub Workbook_BeforeClose(Cancel As Boolean)
    If Not ThisWorkbook.Saved Then
        ThisWorkbook.Save
    End If
End Sub
```

If, on the other hand, you want to discard any changes to the workbook and you don't want users to be prompted to save changes in a workbook when they close it, you can set the `Saved` property of the workbook to `True` in the `BeforeClose` event procedure:

```
Private Sub Workbook_BeforeClose(Cancel As Boolean)
    ThisWorkbook.Saved = True
End Sub
```

This fools Excel into thinking that any changes have been saved.

Headers and Footers

A common need in Excel is to print information in the page header or footer that either comes from the worksheet cells, or is not available in the standard header and footer options. You might want to insert a company name that is part of the data in the worksheet and display the full path to the workbook file.

The full path and file name is available as an option in headers and footers in Excel 2003. You still need to use code like the following to insert text from worksheet cells. You can insert this information using the `BeforePrint` event procedure to ensure it is always up-to-date in reports. The following procedure puts the text in cell A2 of the worksheet named `Profit` in the left footer, clears the center footer and puts the full file name in the right footer. It applies the changes to every worksheet and chart in the Workbook:

```
Private Sub Workbook_BeforePrint(Cancel As Boolean)
   Dim aWorksheet As Worksheet
   Dim FullFileName As String
   Dim CompanyName As String

   CompanyName = Worksheets("Profit").Range("A2").Value

   FullFileName = ThisWorkbook.FullName
   For Each aWorksheet In ThisWorkbook.Worksheets
      With aWorksheet.PageSetup
         .LeftFooter = CompanyName
         .CenterFooter = ""
         .RightFooter = FullFileName
      End With
   Next aWorksheet

   Dim aChart As Chart

   For Each aChart In ThisWorkbook.Charts
      With aChart.PageSetup
         .LeftFooter = CompanyName
         .CenterFooter = ""
         .RightFooter = FullFileName
      End With
   Next aChart

End Sub
```

The footer can be seen in a Print Preview, as shown in Figure 5-3.

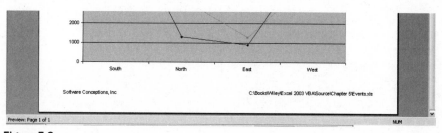

Figure 5-3

Summary

In this section you have seen some useful examples of how to utilize event procedures to respond to user actions.

You have been introduced to worksheet, chart, and workbook events. We've also delved a little deeper into the following events:

- ❑   `Worksheet_Calculate`
- ❑   `Chart_BeforeDoubleClick`
- ❑   `Workbook_BeforeClose`
- ❑   `Workbook_BeforePrint`

VBA is essentially an event-driven language, so a good knowledge of the events at your disposal can open up a whole new world of functionality you never knew existed.

To find out more, have a play with the Object Browser, and consult the object model in Appendix A.

Class Modules

6

Class modules are used in VBA to create your own customized classes. Here are some examples of problems for which you might use a custom class modules:

❑ Respond to application events; you can write code that is executed whenever any open workbook is saved or printed, for example

❑ Respond to embedded chart events

❑ Set up a single event procedure that can be used by a number of ActiveX controls such as text boxes in a UserForm

❑ Encapsulate Windows API methods to permit interaction with Windows

❑ Encapsulate standard VBA procedures in a form that is easy to transport into other workbooks

In this chapter, we will define some class to get the idea of how class modules work. Then, we will apply the principles to some more useful examples. You are already familiar with Excel's built-in objects, such as the `Worksheet` object, and you know that objects often belong to collections such as the `Worksheets` collection. You also know that objects have properties and methods, such as the `Name` property and the `Copy` method of the `Worksheet` object.

Using a class module, you can create your own "blueprint" for a new object, such as an `Employee` class. You can define properties and methods for the class, such as a `Rate` property that records the employee's current rate of pay, and a `ChangeTitle` that implicitly affects other aspects of the Employee's data. You can also create a new collection for the object, such as the `Employees` collection. The class module is a plan for the objects you want to create. From it you can create instances of your object. For example, Mary, Jack, and Anne could be instances of an `Employee` object, all belonging to the `Employees` collection.

Creating Your Own Objects

Let's proceed with creating the `Employee` object we have talked about. You want to store the employee's name, hours worked per week, and rate of pay. From this information, you want to calculate the employee's weekly pay. You can create an `Employee` object with three properties to hold the required data and a method that calculates the weekly pay.

To do this, you create a class module named `Employee` as shown in the top right of Figure 6-1.

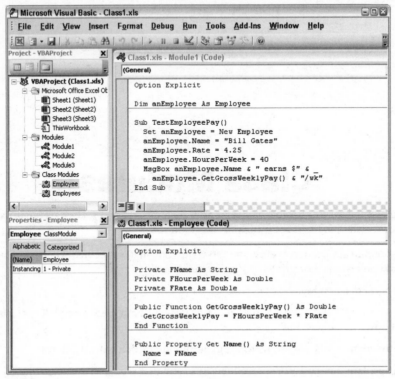

Figure 6-1

The `Employee` class module declares three public properties `Name`, `HoursPerWeek`, and `Rate` (not shown in the figure). There is also one public function, `GetGrossWeeklyPay`.

The code in the standard module (at the bottom right of the screen in Figure 6-1) creates an employee object from the `Employee` blueprint. The module declares `anEmployee` as an `Employee` type. The `TestEmployeePay` sub procedure uses the `Set` statement to assign a new instance of `Employee` to `anEmployee`.

The subroutine then assigns values to the three properties of the object, before generating the message that appears in the message box. To form the message, it accesses the `Name` property of the `Employee` object and executes the `GetGrossWeeklyPay` method of the `Employee` class.

An alternative way of setting up the standard code module, when you only need to create a single instance of the object variable, is as follows:

```
Dim anEmployee As New Employee

Sub EmployeePay()
    anEmployee.Name = "Mary"
    anEmployee.Rate = 15
```

```
   anEmployee.HoursPerWeek = 35
   MsgBox anEmployee.Name & " earns $" & anEmployee.GetGrossWeeklyPay() & "/wk"
End Sub
```

Here, the keyword New is used on the declaration line. In this case, the Employee object is automatically created when it is first referenced in the code.

Using Collections

Now that you have one Employee class, the next step might be to facilitate managing many Employee objects. VBA has a Collection class that you can use for this purpose, as demonstrated:

```
Option Explicit
Dim Employees As New Collection

Sub TestEmployeesCollection()
  Dim anEmployee As Employee

  Dim I As Long

  ' Clear any employees from collection
  For I = Employees.Count To 1 Step -1
  Call Employees.Remove(I)
Next I

Set anEmployee = New Employee
anEmployee.Name = "Paul Kimmel"
anEmployee.Rate = 15
anEmployee.HoursPerWeek = 45
Call Employees.Add(anEmployee, anEmployee.Name)

Set anEmployee = New Employee
anEmployee.Name = "Bill Gates"
anEmployee.Rate = 14
anEmployee.HoursPerWeek = 35
Call Employees.Add(anEmployee, anEmployee.Name)

MsgBox "Number of Employees = " & Employees.Count
MsgBox "Employees(2).Name = " & Employees(2).Name
MsgBox "Employees(""Paul Kimmel"").Rate = " _
  & Employees("Paul Kimmel").Rate

For Each anEmployee In Employees
  MsgBox anEmployee.Name & " earns $" _
    & anEmployee.GetGrossWeeklyPay()
Next anEmployee
End Sub
```

At the top of the standard module, we declare Employees to be a new collection. The TestEmployeesCollection procedure uses the Remove method of the collection in the For...Next loop to remove any existing objects. It removes the objects in reverse order because removing them in order would change the upper bound upon which the loop would depend. This step is normally not necessary, as the collection is initialized empty. It is only done here to demonstrate the Remove method and also allow you to run the procedure more than once without doubling-up the items in the collection.

TestEmployeesCollection creates the first employee, Paul Kimmel, and uses the Add method of the collection to place the Employee object in the collection. The first parameter of the Add method is a reference to the object itself. The second parameter, which is optional, is an identifying key that can be used to reference the object later. In this case, we have used the Employees collection's Name property. The same procedure is used with the second employee.

> If you supply a key value for each member of the collection, the keys must be unique. You will get a runtime error when you attempt to add a new member to the collection with a key value that is already in use. Using a person's name as the key is not recommended as people can have the same name. Consider a unique identifier, such as a Social Security number.

The MsgBox statements illustrate that you can reference the collection in the same way as you can reference Excel's built-in collections. For instance, the Employees collection has a Count property. You can reference a member of the collection by position or by key, if you have entered a key value.

Class Module Collection

You can also set up your collection in a class module. There are advantages and disadvantages in doing this. The advantages are that you get much more control over interaction with the collection, you can prevent direct access to the collection, and the code is encapsulated into a single module that makes it more transportable and easier to maintain. The disadvantages are that it takes more work to set up the collection, and that you lose some of the shortcut ways to reference members of the collection and the collection itself.

The following code shows the contents of a class module Employees:

```
Option Explicit

Private FEmployees As New Collection

Public Function Add(ByVal value As Employee)
  Call FEmployees.Add(value, value.Name)
End Function

Public Property Get Count() As Long
  Count = FEmployees.Count
End Property

Public Property Get Items() As Collection
  Set Items = FEmployees
End Property
```

```
Public Property Get Item(ByVal value As Variant) As Employee
   Set Item = FEmployees(value)
End Property

Public Sub Remove(ByVal value As Variant)
   Call FEmployees.Remove(value)
End Sub
```

When the collection is in its own class module, you can no longer directly use the collection's four methods (Add, Count, Item, and Remove) in your standard module. You need to set up your own methods and properties in the class module, even if you have no intention of modifying the collections methods. On the other hand, you have control over what you choose to implement and what you choose to modify, as well as what you present as a method and what you present as a property.

In Employees class, Function Add, Sub Remove, Property Get Item, and Property Get Count pass on most of the functionality of the collection's methods. There is one new feature in the Property Get Items procedure. Whereas Property Get Item passes back a reference to a single member of the collection, Property Get Items passes back a reference to the entire collection. This is to provide the capability to use the collection in a For Each...Next loop.

The standard module code is now as follows:

```
Option Explicit
Dim theEmployees As New Employees

Sub TestEmployeesCollection()
Dim anEmployee As Employee

Dim I As Long

' Clear any employees from collection
For I = theEmployees.Count To 1 Step -1
   Call theEmployees.Remove(I)
Next I

Set anEmployee = New Employee
anEmployee.Name = "Paul Kimmel"
anEmployee.Rate = 15
anEmployee.HoursPerWeek = 45
Call theEmployees.Add(anEmployee)

Set anEmployee = New Employee
anEmployee.Name = "Bill Gates"
anEmployee.Rate = 14
anEmployee.HoursPerWeek = 35
Call theEmployees.Add(anEmployee)

MsgBox "Number of Employees = " & theEmployees.Count
MsgBox "Employees.Item(2).Name = " & theEmployees.Item(2).Name
MsgBox "Employees.Item(""Paul Kimmel"").Rate = " _
   & theEmployees.Item("Paul Kimmel").Rate
```

```
For Each anEmployee In theEmployees.Items
  MsgBox anEmployee.Name & " earns $" _
    & anEmployee.GetGrossWeeklyPay()
Next anEmployee
End Sub
```

theEmployees is declared to be an instance of Employees. As before, the collection is cleared of objects and then a For...Next loop adds the two employees to the collection. As one small convenience, we no longer need to specify the key value when using the Add method of the Employees collection. The Add method code in Employees does this for us.

The second, third, and fourth MsgBox statements show the new properties needed to reference the collection and its members. You need to use the Item property to reference a member and the Items property to reference the whole collection.

Trapping Application Events

You can use a class module to trap application events. Most of these events are the same as the workbook events, but they apply to all open workbooks, not just the particular workbook that contains the event procedures. For example, in a workbook there is a BeforePrint event that is triggered when you start to print anything in that workbook. At the application level, there is a WorkbookBeforePrint event that is triggered when any open workbook starts to print.

To see what application events are available, you first insert a class module into your project. The class module can have any valid module name. The one shown in the next screenshot has been named AppEvents. You then type in the following variable declaration at the top of the module:

```
Public WithEvents App As Application
```

The object variable name, App, can be any valid variable name, as long as you use it consistently in the code that refers to the class module, as a property of the class. The WithEvents keyword causes the events associated with the application object to be exposed. You can now choose App from the left-hand side drop-down at the top of the module and then use the right-hand side drop-down to see the event list, as shown in Figure 6-2.

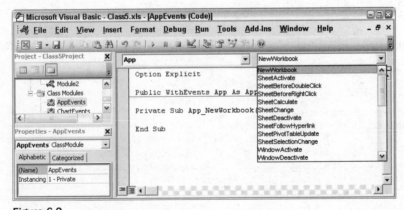

Figure 6-2

We will choose the `WorkbookBeforePrint` event and extend the event procedure that was presented in the chapter on events, using the following code in `AppEvents`:

```
Private Sub App_WorkbookBeforePrint(ByVal Wb As Workbook, _
   Cancel As Boolean)

   Dim aWorksheet As Worksheet
   Dim FullFileName As String
   Dim CompanyName As String

   With Wb
      CompanyName = "Software Conceptions, Inc"
      FullFileName = .FullName
      For Each aWorksheet In .Worksheets
        With aWorksheet.PageSetup
          .LeftFooter = CompanyName
          .CenterFooter = ""
          .RightFooter = FullFileName
        End With
      Next aWorksheet
   End With
End Sub
```

Unlike sheet and workbook class modules, the event procedures you place in your own class modules do not automatically function. You need to create an instance of your class module and assign the `Application` object to the `App` property of the new object. Code similar to the following must be set up in a standard module:

```
Public theAppEvents As New AppEvents

Sub TrapApplicationEvents()
    Set theAppEvents.App = Application
End Sub
```

All you need to do now is execute the `TrapApplicationEvents` procedure. The `WorkbookBeforePrint` event procedure will then run when you use any Print or Preview commands, until you close the workbook containing the event procedure.

It is possible to terminate application event trapping during the current session. Any action that resets module-level variables and public variables will terminate application event processing, as the class module instance will be destroyed. Actions that can cause this include editing code in the VBE and executing the `End` statement in VBA code.

> There have been (relatively rare) cases, in Excel 97, where bugs in Excel have caused variables to reset. It would be wise to expect that bugs could also exist in later versions.

If you want to enable application event processing for all Excel sessions, you can place your class module and standard module code in `Personal.xls` and execute `TrapApplicationEvents` in the

`Workbook_Open` event procedure. You could even transfer the code in `TrapApplicationEvents` to the `Workbook_Open` event procedure. However, you must keep the `Public` declaration of `theAppEvents` in a standard module.

To illustrate, you can place the following code in the (Declarations) section of a standard module:

```
Public theAppEvents As New AppEvents
```

You can place the following event procedure in the `ThisWorkbook` module:

```
Private Sub Workbook_Open()
    Set theAppEvents.App = Application
End Sub
```

Embedded Chart Events

If you want to trap events for a chart embedded in a worksheet, you use a process similar to the process for trapping application events. First, insert a new class module in your project, or you could use the same class module that you used for the application events. You place the following declaration at the top of the class module:

```
Public WithEvents aChart As Chart
```

We will set up the same `BeforeDoubleClick` event procedure that we used in Chapter 5. The class module should be as follows:

```
Public WithEvents aChart As Chart
```

```
Private Sub aChart_BeforeDoubleClick(ByVal ElementID As Long, _
  ByVal Arg1 As Long, ByVal Arg2 As Long, Cancel As Boolean)

  Dim theSeries As Series

  Select Case ElementID
    Case xlLegend
      aChart.HasLegend = False
      Cancel = True
    Case xlChartArea
      aChart.HasLegend = True
      Cancel = True
    Case xlSeries
      'Arg1 is the Series index
      'Arg2 is the Point index (-1 if the entire series is selected)
      Set theSeries = aChart.SeriesCollection(Arg1)
      If Arg2 = -1 Then
        With theSeries.Border
          If .ColorIndex = xlColorIndexAutomatic Then
            .ColorIndex = 1
          Else
            .ColorIndex = (.ColorIndex Mod 56) + 1
          End If
```

```
                  End With
            Else
                With theSeries.Points(Arg2)
                    .HasDataLabel = Not .HasDataLabel
                End With
            End If
            Cancel = True
      End Select
End Sub
```

This code allows you to double-click the chart legend to make it disappear, or double-click in the chart area to make it reappear. If you double-click a series line, it changes color. If you select a point in a series by clicking it and then double-clicking it, it will toggle the data label on and off for that point.

Say, your chart is contained in a `ChartObject` that is the only `ChartObject` in a worksheet called `Mangoes` and you have named your class module `ChartEvents`. In your standard module, you enter the following code:

```
Public theChartEvents As New ChartEvents

Sub InitializeChartEvents()
  Set theChartEvents.aChart = _
    ThisWorkbook.Worksheets("Mangoes").ChartObjects(1).Chart
End Sub
```

Figure 6-3 shows the resulting screen.

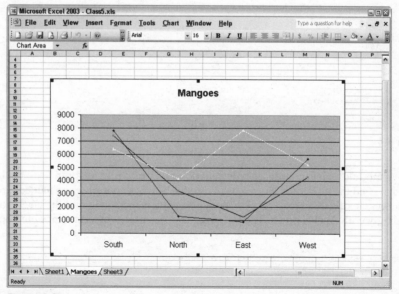

Figure 6-3

After executing `InitializeChartEvents`, you can double-click the series, points, and legend to run the `BeforeDoubleClick` event procedure.

A Collection of UserForm Controls

When you have a number of the same type of control on a form, you often write almost identical event procedures for each one. For example, say, you want to be able to double-click the label to the left of each of the TextBox in the following UserForm to clear the TextBox and set the focus to the TextBox. You would normally write four, almost identical, event procedures, one for each label control, as shown in Figure 6-4.

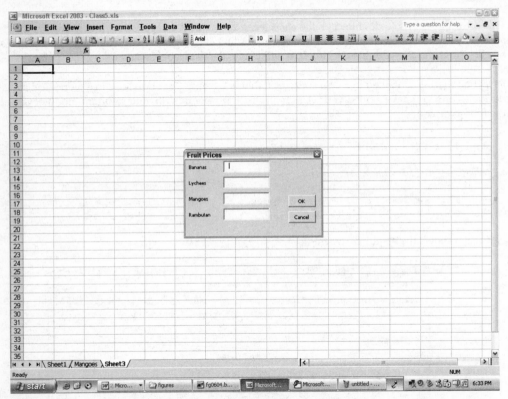

Figure 6-4

Using a class module, you can write a single generic event procedure to apply to all the label controls, or just those that need the procedure. For convenience the TextBox controls were named TextBoxBananas, TextBoxLychees, TextBoxMangoes, and TextBoxRambutan, respectively, and the labels were named correspondingly with a Label prefix. The following code is entered in a class module `ControlEvents`

```
Public WithEvents Label As MSForms.Label
Public Form As UserForm

Private Sub Label_DblClick(ByVal Cancel As MSForms.ReturnBoolean)
  Dim Product As String
  Dim TextBoxName As String
```

```
      Product = Mid(Label.Name, 6)
      TextBoxName = "TextBox" & Product
      With Form.Controls(TextBoxName)
         .Text = ""
         .SetFocus
      End With
   End Sub
```

`Label` is declared with events as a UserForm label. `Form` is declared to be the UserForm. The generic `DblClick` event procedure for `Label` uses the `Mid` function to get the product name starting with the third character of the label name, removing the "`Label`" identifier. It converts this to the TextBox name by appending "`TextBox`" in front of the product name.

The `With...End With` structure identifies the `TextBox` object by using the `TextBox` name as an index into the `Controls` collection of the UserForm. It sets the `Text` property of the `TextBox` to a zero length string and uses the `SetFocus` method to place the cursor in the `TextBox`.

The following code is entered into the class module behind the UserForm:

```
   Option Explicit

   Dim Labels As New Collection

   Private Sub UserForm_Initialize()
      Dim Control As MSForms.Control
      Dim aControlEvent As ControlEvents

      For Each Control In Me.Controls
         If TypeOf Control Is MSForms.Label Then
            Set aControlEvent = New ControlEvents
            Set aControlEvent.Label = Control
            Set aControlEvent.Form = Me
            Call Labels.Add(aControlEvent)
         End If
      Next Control
   End Sub
```

`Labels` is declared as a new collection to hold the objects that will be created from the `ControlEvents` class module. In the UserForm `Initialize` event procedure, the label controls are associated with instances of `ControlEvents class`.

The `For Each...Next` loop processes all the controls on the form. When it identifies a control that is a label, using the `TypeOf` keyword to identify the control type, it creates a new instance of `ControlEvents` and assigns it to `aControlEvent`. The `Label` property of the new object is assigned a reference to the control and the `Form` property is assigned a reference to the UserForm. The new object is then added to the `Labels` collection.

When the UserForm is loaded into memory, the `Initialize` event runs and connects the label controls to instances of the class module event procedure. Double-clicking any label clears the TextBox to the right and sets the focus to that TextBox, ready for new data to be typed in.

You need to be aware that some events associated with some controls are not made available in a class module using With Events. For example, the most useful events exposed by UserForm text boxes are BeforeUpdate, AfterUpdate, Enter, and Exit. None of these is available in a class module. You can only handle these events in the class module associated with the UserForm.

Referencing Classes Across Projects

When you want to run macros in another workbook, you can use Tools ⇨ References... in the VBE window to create a reference to the other workbook's VBA project. The reference shows as a special entry in the Project Explorer, as shown in Figure 6-5.

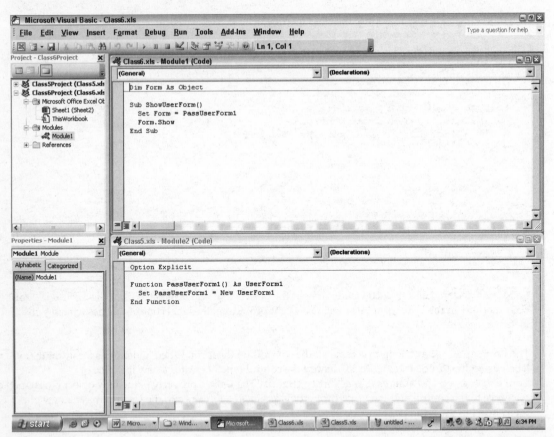

Figure 6-5

Class6.xls has a reference to Class5.xls, which contains the UserForm from our previous example. The reference allows you to run procedures in standard modules in Class5.xls from standard modules in `Class6.xls`. However, the reference does not allow you to create instances of class modules or UserForms in the referenced workbook.

> **When you create a reference to another workbook, you should make sure that the VBA Project in the referenced workbook has a unique name. By default, it will be named VBAProject. Click Tools ⇨ VBA Project Properties ... and enter a new project name.**

You can get around the limitation preventing the use of UserForms or classes if that target workbook has a function that returns a reference to the UserForm. There is an example of this type of function in the lower right-hand corner of the preceding screen. `PassUserForm1`, in `Class5.xls`, is a function that assigns a new instance of `UserForm1` to its return value. In `Class6.xls`, `Form` is declared as a generic `Object` type. `ShowUserForm` assigns the return value of `PassUserForm1` to `Form`. `Form` can then be used to show the UserForm and access its control values, as long as the UserForm is hidden, not unloaded.

Summary

Class modules are used to create blueprints for new objects, such as the `Employee` class that was presented in this chapter:

❑   `Function` and `subroutines` are used in the class module to create methods for the object

❑   `Public` variables declare the properties for the object

❑   However, if you need to take programmatic control when a property is assigned a value, you can define the property using a `Property Let` procedure

❑   In addition, `Property Get` procedures allow you to control access to property values

To use the code in your class module, you create one or more instances of your object. For example, you can create Paul and Bill as instances of an `Employee` object. You can further customize your objects by creating your own collection, where you organize objects in a single location.

Class modules are not used to create objects to the same extent in Excel VBA as they are used in a stand-alone programming language such as Visual Basic. This is because Excel already contains the objects that many Excel programmers want to use. However, Excel programmers can use class modules to:

❑   Handle application-level events, such as the `WorkbookBeforePrint` event that allows you to control the printing of all open workbooks

❑   Handle events in embedded charts

❑   Write a single event procedure that can be used by many instances of a particular object, such as a `TextBox` control on a UserForm.

❑   Encapsulate difficult code and make it easier to use

❑   Encapsulate code so that you can share the code among

❑   Different projects and users

See Chapter 16 for examples of encapsulation of API code.

7

Writing Bulletproof Code

In a sense, bulletproof code is like Superman and bulletproof vests. Superman is bulletproof unless he is in the presence of kryptonite. Bulletproof vests are bulletproof too unless someone shoots armor-piercing bullets (or interestingly, a compound bow) at it. Being bulletproof can be considered fictional and impossible and something practical, but with physical limits.

It is technically impossible with the current technology to write an algorithm that mathematically proves the efficacy of an application, and so, it is probably impossible to prove that any application is completely error free, or bulletproof. Yet Superman is believed to be the man of steel, undefeatable, and law enforcement officials prudently wear bulletproof vests. So, we too must persevere when we write code for our applications. In this chapter, we will demonstrate techniques that convey robustness and help protect your application from having a bad day—crashing, deleting files, or worse—and in the event something goes wrong you will be better prepared and able to diagnose and solve the problem. Additionally, these techniques are portable and reusable from application to application.

We will build on decades old, proven strategies for bulletproofing code using the basic tools built into VBA. Generally, you will learn (and have at your disposal) techniques for flagging assumptions that fail, tracing the actual course the CPU takes through your code, and leave "breadcrumbs" throughout your code ensuring that every path, branch, and loop your code takes has been tested. The result is that fewer things will go wrong, and when they ultimately do, you will have all of the information at your disposal necessary to quickly diagnose and solve the problem, and get back to work.

Using Debug.Print

The `Debug` object contains a couple of methods. The first stone in our foundation of testing and debugging tools is the `Debug.Print` method. The other, `Debug Assert`, will be discussed in the next section.

Simplicity itself, `Debug.Print` accepts a string message and sends this string message to the Immediate window. In addition, the `Debug.Print` method only performs its little dance when you are running the code in the debug mode (with the VBE open). This makes the `Debug.Print` statement ideally suited for tracing your code's actual progress, instead of supposed progress.

Like the inimitable Ronald Reagan said, "Trust, but verify." We are smart programmers and we trust that our code will wind its way in the order we meant it to go, but code has a relentless desire to go where we tell it to go. Debug.Print will take the guesswork out of where our code has been.

We will be building a modest toolset around Debug.Print. You can place Debug.Print statements in any property or method, and such a statement might look like this:

```
Debug.Print "You can leave your hat on"
```

However, a more practical use would be to display the name of the object and method and some useful text indicating what transpired immediately before or after the statement was executed. Here is a method that is defined in an imaginary worksheet named sheet1 and a useful Debug.Print statement:

```
Public Function CalculateFuelConsumed(ByVal Duration As Double, _
   ByVal GallonsPerHour As Double) As Double

   Debug.Print "Entered Sheet1.CalculateFuelConsumped"

   CalculateFuelConsumed = Duration * GallonsPerHour

   Debug.Print "Exiting Sheet1.CalculateFuelConsumped, result = " & _
      CalculateFuelConsumed & " gallons"

End Function
```

The preceding method calculates fuel consumed as a product of duration and fuel consumed per hour. The Debug.Print statement as used in the preceding function sends the output shown in Figure 7-1 to the Immediate window.

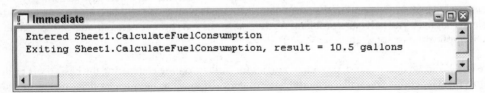

Figure 7-1

Keep in mind as we progress that the Debug object only performs its dance when debugging in the VBE. As a result we never need to remove our debug code, and users never know it is there. The benefit here is that the debug code is ready to leap into action the moment the code stumbles on some difficulty, rather than we, beleaguered programmers, having to add and remove debug code between debug cycles or periods of maintenance and growth.

We'll come back to the Debug.Print statement in the section titled *Tracing Errors*.

Using Debug.Assert

The only other method of the Debug object is the Assert method. Assert acts as the sheriff, a programmer's hired gun. Assert is designed to stop code execution in the IDE if a test passed to the Assert method fails.

When programmers are writing code we have expressed and unexpressed assumptions about the state of our application at every given statement. An example of an expressed assumption is a check to see if a file exists before we try to open it for reading. An unexpressed assumption might be that the disk drive will not be reading from a corrupt disk cluster when it tries to read the file. Either way, each programmer is most likely to know about expressed and unexpressed assumptions only when initially writing the code or when some unexpressed assumption rears its ugly head. And, when you assume these things, it is a good idea to have a sheriff on patrol. Debug.Assert is an Excel VBA programmer's best sheriff.

As you write each method of substance it is a good idea to add conditional code that makes sure certain invariant parameters are adhered to. For example, dividing by 0 is a bad thing. So, if you are employing division, then checking to ensure the denominator is non-zero is a good idea. However, because you never want to divide by 0 it is also a good idea to instruct your sheriff to assert that no denominator is 0. Keep in mind that the Debug object is a tool for programmers. Debug.Assert will suspend an application's execution if the test condition fails, but it only runs in the VBE while debugging. For this reason it never replaces reasonable and prudent conditional checks, rather it augments them from the perspective of the programmer. An If-check will not suspend the application if the check fails, but a Debug.Assert statement will. Consequently, the If-condition will prevent your code from exploding, and the Debug check will tell you while testing of an impending explosion. Used in conjunction, a Debug.Assert and conditional check will appear joined at the hip, as demonstrated in the following fragment:

```
Public Sub DivideByZero(ByVal Numerator As Double, _
    ByVal Denominator As Double)

    Dim result As Double

    Debug.Assert Denominator <> 0
    If (Denominator <> 0) Then
       result = Numerator / Denominator
    Else
       ' do something else
    End If
End Sub
```

If the assertion fails in the VBE, then execution will be suspended on the line Debug.Assert Denominator <> 0, and the programmer will immediately be notified that a consumer—a programmer using the DivideByZero subroutine—has violated an inviolate assumption, a Denominator of 0 (see Figure 7-2).

In the next section, we will employ the Debug.Print and Debug.Assert methods to build our reusable toolbox for bulletproofing code. If you are very busy you can skip over *A Brief History of PC Debugging* and go straight to *Creating Reusable Tools with the Debug Object*.

A Brief Exemplar of PC Debugging

History is important, if for nothing else then for the perspective it provides. Interestingly, the history of microcomputers has really only spanned the last 20 years or so. (Remember the first IBM PC began

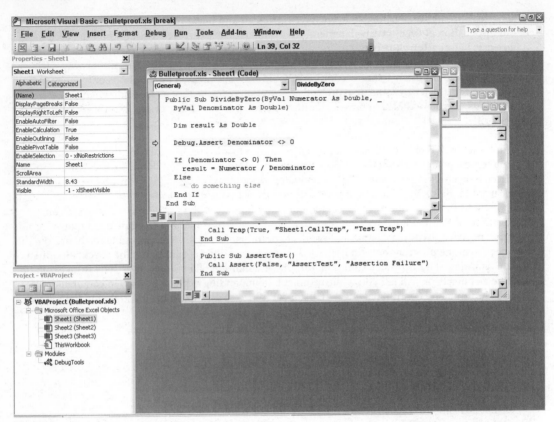

Figure 7-2

selling in August of 1981.) Hence, if you were working as a programmer in 1981 then you are a living historian of the hyperconsolidated history of microcomputers.

As the story goes, a guy named Tim Paterson sold a disk operating system he had written to Bill Gates for $25,000. That disk operating system became MS-DOS. In conjunction with the disk operating system is the PCs BIOS, or basic input output system. These two things provided the basic building blocks that permit your computer to run and programmers to write computer programs.

The BIOS comprises things called interrupts. Interrupts are essentially global functions loaded as part of the BIOS when your computer starts up, and they are still there today just buried under mountains of complex Windows code. Interrupts are numbered beginning with 0, 1, 2, 3, and so on. You might imagine that the lowest numbered interrupts came first, followed by higher numbered interrupts as features were added later. For example, the DOS interrupt is 0x21 (interrupts are generally numbered as hexadecimal numbers, 33 as a decimal number). Following the notion that lower numbers preceded higher numbers would you be surprised that interrupt 0 is the divide by 0 interrupt? Division is pretty important to programmers and division by 0 must have been a real problem if it was supported by one of the first basic system services.

It's not important to know what interrupts 1 and 2 do. Interrupt 3 is more applicable to our discussion because it is the debug interrupt. It supports breaking in the middle of program execution; it is likely the underpinnings for the Stop statement in VBA and breakpoints. (Early debugging tools called interrupt 3 the soft-ice interrupt; as in, put the program on ice.)

These basic features still exist and are employed by your computer still doing their original jobs, albeit with a lot of very nice code on top of them. You can verify that these basic capabilities exist by opening a command prompt, running the debug.exe utility and writing some basic machine code. (Be careful though. These basic capabilities are very powerful.)

Using Figure 7-3 as a guide and typing the following debug instructions and assembler code, you can try a little assembly program. (This is a great reminder of how much better VBA programmers have it now, too.)

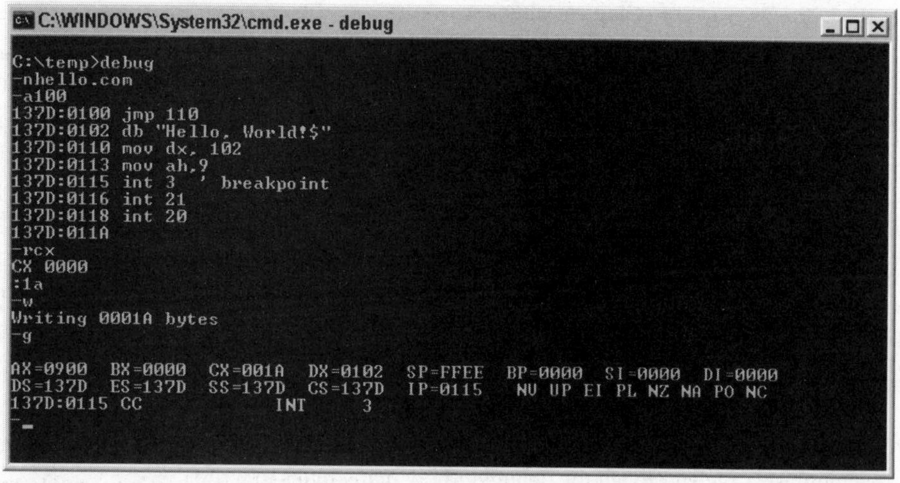

Figure 7-3

```
debug
nhello.com
a100
jmp 110
db "Hello, World!$"
mov dx,102
mov ah,9
int 3
int 21
int 20

rcx
1a
w
g
q
```

In order, the instructions and code are as follows:

❑ Debug runs the debug.exe utility when typed at the command prompt. This is actually a very basic debugger and editor, but ultimately can be very powerful.

❑ nhello.com is the name instruction. This step provides the target file name for the debug.exe utility to write the output to.

❑ a100 is the assemble instruction. We are telling the debugger we are ready to start writing code.

❑ jmp 110 is our old friend the GOTO instruction in assembly language.

❑ db "Hello, World!$" demonstrates how to declare a string variable.

❑ mov dx,102 literally places the value 102—a hexadecimal value—in your PC's CPU's DX register. Registers are analogous to the lowest level variables. They are actually switches in microprocessor, and your PC is using them millions of times a second. In this step we are pointing the DX register at our string variable

❑ mov ah,9 is actually a function in this context. Collectively, we are preparing a function call where the argument is the string "HelloWorld!" ($ is the string terminator) and the function is function 9.

❑ int 3 is a breakpoint. Our code will run to the statement containing int 3, then execution will be suspended, and the microprocessor state will be displayed. (Refer to the bottom part of Figure 7-3.)

❑ int 21 is actually the DOS interrupt. Interrupt 21, function 9 is the write string function.

❑ int 20 is the end of program interrupt. It tells the microprocessor that the program ends here and control should return to the operating system.

❑ The blank line is intentional. The blank line takes us out of the programming mode back to the instruction mode.

❑ rcx is an instruction to the debugger to dump and edit a value for the CX register. We are literally using the CX register to tell the debugger how many bytes to write.

❑ 1a is a hexadecimal number (26 in decimal). We want the debugger to write our 26 bytes of assembly language.

❑ w is the write instruction.

❑ g is like *F5* in VBA; it is the run in the debug mode instruction.

❑ q is quit. Type q and press the *Enter* key and the debug.exe utility exits.

After you exit, you will see that you have a program named hello.com in the temp folder or wherever you entered the instructions. Go ahead and type Hello at the command prompt. Notice that the text Hello, World! is written to and the command prompt returns. Also, notice that the breakpoint was ignored. Does this behavior seem familiar? It is. This is the same kind of behavior the Debug object exhibits. Debugging in the VBE and Debug object runs; outside of the VBE the Debug statements are ignored. You are now an honorary sheriff. You have some good insight right down to the hardware. (All that is left is the mechanical engineering. Fortunately, we don't have to go quite that far.) Now you know that division by zero and breakpoints and such were real concerns for early programmers, and you also know that these same capabilities are still used by your computer even though they have been made prettier by the much nicer environment of the VBE.

Creating Reusable Tools with the Debug Object

One of my favorite programming books was Dave Thielen's *No Bugs!* published by Addison-Wesley. The book was written for the C programming language after a successful release of MS DOS 5.0. Although C is a lower level language than VBA, you will be surprised that many of the core debugging aids are based on the same basic concepts presented in Dave Thielen's book, and you can employ these techniques using VBA and the Debug object. The reason you want to do this is that they work without question.

In this section, we will create three powerful, manageable tools that will systematically help you eliminate bugs, be confident that you have done so, and when something does go wrong, you will be able to diagnose and fix the problem post haste. The tools are Trace, Trap, and Assert, and just as Microsoft has built the Debug and Stop on top of fundamental BIOS capabilities (see the previous section, *A Brief History of PC Debugging*) we will layer our implementation on top of the Debug object and Stop statement.

Tracing Code Execution

Tracing is a matter of placing lines of code in your solution that output some information describing the route your code is following as it runs and the state of the code. This information can be so useful in debugging that many development tools automatically trace code execution by building a call stack—tracing method calls—showing the order of execution. VBA supports tracing with Debug.Print but does not automatically keep track of the method call order; we have to do that ourselves. With just a little effort we can build our own Trace routine and describe the kind of data we want, yielding a consistent informative result every time. From an exportable module named DebugTools.vb here is the Trace method as we implemented it:

```
Option Explicit
#Const Tracing = True
#Const UseEventLog = False

Private Sub DebugPrint(ByVal Source As String, _
  ByVal Message As String)

#If UseEventLog Then

#Else
  Debug.Print "Source: " & Source & " Message: " & Message
#End If

End Sub

Public Sub Trace(ByVal Source As String, _
  ByVal Message As String)

#If Tracing Then
  Call DebugPrint(Source, Message)
#End If

End Sub
```

In the preceding code fragment a compiler constant was defined: Tracing. The DebugPrint method is a generic method that accepts two strings, named Source and Message, respectively. Notice that we have stubbed out something controlled by the constant `UseEventLog` and the preexisting `Debug.Print` statement. (We'll come back to the `UseEventLog` branch in *Writing to the EventLog* later in this chapter.) The last method, `Trace`, accepts the same two arguments: `Source` and `Message`. `Trace` checks the value of the Debugging compiler constant. If it is `True` then `DebugPrint` is called.

A reasonable person might ask: Why are we using compiler constants and wrapping `Debug.Print` when you told me that the `Debug.Print` automatically shuts off when we are not running our code in the VBE? Glad you asked.

In our opinion, programming is a lot like building an onion from the inside out. Programming begins with a modest core, for example, your computer's basic input output system. Gradually, layers are wrapped around existing layers, slowly and judiciously adding complexity. (More subjectivity here.) These layers should be modest, easy to test, and provide useful amounts of new behavior. The new behavior does not have to be complex or large, in fact, it probably shouldn't be. The reason for this is that minor changes are easier to implement, less likely to introduce additional defects, and can be easily assessed for their utility. Put another way, if you see great globs of code—large monolithic behaviors—that try to do too much then you are probably looking at a future headache.

Singular behaviors wrapped around existing singular behaviors act like laminated wood: they combine to create something for strong and useful, yet surprisingly simple at each layer. This is what good, useful, debuggable, bulletproof code will look like. Unfortunately, last time we checked, this aspect of programming is not taught in colleges and universities. (Pardon me, if your school was the exception.) The reason for this is that our business is still quite new and not everyone has the same general opinion. (However, we would like to point out that many successful practitioners do use the same or an analogy similar to the onion layering analogy.) It takes practice to write layered, singular code, but that's what we are here for.

In keeping with the notion of layering complexity, our `Trace` method is easy to use. It takes two string parameters. In addition, it permits us to turn tracing on and off separately. From the VBE's behavior, we have expanded the definition of tracing to include a different respository. Instead of just logging to the Immediate window we have included a stub or logging to a more persistent resource, the `EventLog`. The next step is to figure out how to use the `Trace` behavior.

The programmer has to decide what to trace. You can trace everything but this gets tedious. Instead, we would subjectively elect to add `Trace` statements in places that are especially important to our solution and definitely add them wherever a bug crops up. Once you add a `Trace` statement leave it there even after the code is working well. When you change the code, new errors might rear their ugly heads, but you will already have tracing code left in place. One additional benefit is that the `Trace` statements also provide clues as to what kinds of things you or others were interested in and the problem areas in the past. That is, the `Trace` acts like breadcrumbs that you or others can follow in the future. Here is our `CalculateFuelConsumed` method from earlier in the chapter with the `Debug.Print` statements replaced by our tidier `Trace` method:

```
Public Function CalculateFuelConsumed(ByVal Duration As Double, _
   ByVal GallonsPerHour As Double) As Double

   Call Trace("Sheet1.CalculateFuelConsumped", _
      "Duration=" & Duration & " GallonsPerHour=" & GallonsPerHour)

   CalculateFuelConsumed = Duration * GallonsPerHour
```

```
    Call Trace("Sheet1.CalculateFuelConsumped", "Result=" & CalculateFuelConsumed)

End Function
```

The end result is consistent `Trace` statements and a dependable and neatly formatted output. Figure 7-4 shows the Immediate window after calling the new `CalculateFuelConsumed` method.

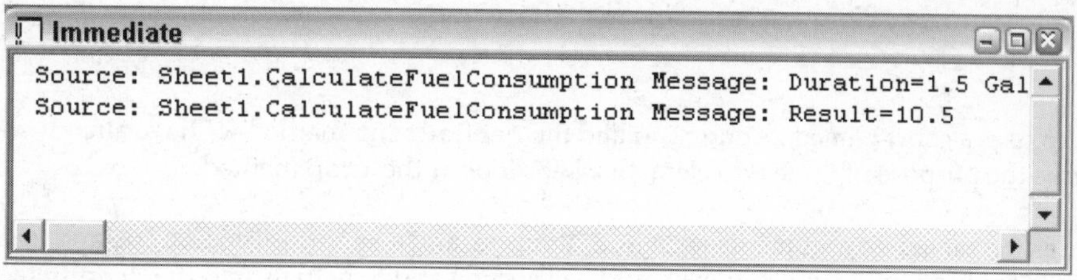

```
Immediate                                                    ⊟⬜⊠
Source: Sheet1.CalculateFuelConsumption Message: Duration=1.5 Gal ▲
Source: Sheet1.CalculateFuelConsumption Message: Result=10.5
                                                              ▼
◀ ▯                                                         ▶
```

Figure 7-4

Trapping Code Execution Paths

The next technique is called Trapping. We have to check all of the pathways our code might take, because if we don't—both `If` and `Else` conditions, all of the methods and properties, and while loops that are and aren't entered—then how can we be sure that some path we haven't checked doesn't lead us to the impending danger?

The `Trap` idiom is used to mark branches in our code to make sure that we have devised a test for every nook and cranny of our code and that we get the expected or desired results. The `Trap` idiom is layered on top of the `Stop` statement, and like the `Trace` method is wrapped to include some flexibility. Here is the code for the `Trap` idiom that we can add to our DebugTools module. We will then describe how to set the `Traps`:

```
Option Explicit

#Const Tracing = True
#Const Debugging = True
#Const UseEventLog = False

Private Sub DebugPrint(ByVal Source As String, _
  ByVal Message As String)

#If UseEventLog Then

#Else
  Debug.Print "Source: " & Source & " Message: " & Message
#End If

End Sub

Public Sub Trap(ByVal Test As Boolean, _
  ByVal Source As String, _
  ByVal Message As String)
```

135

```
#If Debugging Then

    If (Test) Then
        Call DebugPrint(Source, Message)
        Stop
    End If

#End If

End Sub
```

The `Trap` uses a const named `Debugging` and the `DebugPrint` method we have already seen. We won't redescribe the purpose of these two elements. Let's look at the `Trap` method.

`Trap` uses the same two arguments as `Trace`, `Source`, and `Message`. The `Source` and `Message` arguments are used to log which traps have been sprung and to help us find the `Trap` statement to disable it. All that happens when the `Trap` is sprung is that the source and message are logged and the program breaks (see Figure 7-5).

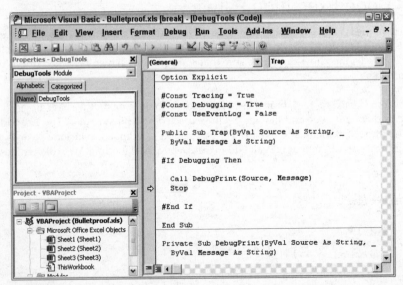

Figure 7-5

After the `Trap` is sprung we can use the value of Source to find the caller and comment out that `Trap` statement. By commenting out the `Trap` we clearly indicate that the specific path containing that `Trap` has been tested, and we can move on to other code branches to test. Again, we leave the `Trap` in place for future testing. For example, to ensure that we have devised a test for the `CalculateFuelConsumed` method, we can add a `Trap` statement. Here is how the `CalculateFuelConsumped` method looks now:

```
Public Function CalculateFuelConsumed(ByVal Duration As Double, _
    ByVal GallonsPerHour As Double) As Double

    Call Trap("Sheet1.CalculateFuelConsumed", "Tested")
```

```
    Call Trace("Sheet1.CalculateFuelConsumed", _
      "Duration=" & Duration & " GallonsPerHour=" & GallonsPerHour)

    CalculateFuelConsumed = Duration * GallonsPerHour

    Call Trace("Sheet1.CalculateFuelConsumed", "Result=" & CalculateFuelConsumed)

  End Function
```

When you devise a test for `CalculateFuelConsumed` comment out the statement containing the call to `Trap`.

Someone sensitive to neatness might not like all of the debugging and testing code intermingled with the actual labor-producing code. If you are such a person, use a consistent strategy for separating the real code from the testing code. A strategy we use is to add a private shadow method with the prefix Do. We place the real code in Do and the test code in the unprefixed method. As a result, evaluating the algorithm can be maintained separately from the bulletproof vest, the tracing, trapping, and in a moment, asserting code. Here is the revision:

```
Public Function CalculateFuelConsumed(ByVal Duration As Double, _
  ByVal GallonsPerHour As Double) As Double

  'Call Trap("Sheet1.CalculateFuelConsumed", "Tested")

  Call Trace("Sheet1.CalculateFuelConsumed", _
    "Duration=" & Duration & " GallonsPerHour=" & GallonsPerHour)

  CalculateFuelConsumed = DoCalculateFuelConsumed(Duration, FuelConsumedPerhour)

  Call Trace("Sheet1.CalculateFuelConsumed", "Result=" & CalculateFuelConsumed)

End Function

Private Function DoCalculateFuelConsumed(ByVal Duration As Double, _
  ByVal GallonsPerHour As Double) As Double

  DoCalculateFuelConsumed = Duration * GallonsPerHour

End Function
```

A casual observer might think all of this extra code is clumsy, and it is. But, as with wearing a bulletproof vest, it is nice to have the extra protection, and you'll be happy you wore it. The total effect of the code is that it shows a practiced, considered approach to a professional job, and once the basic tools are in place—DebugTools—and the habit is formed, this code is very easy to write. If you are so fortunate as to have different levels of programmers working with you, then you could write the actual behavior and junior programmer could wrap it up in the debugging and testing blanket, or it could be added later if problems are encountered.

Asserting Application Invariants

The last technique in our triad is the assertion. We happen to like policemen, but if all of these metaphors for law enforcement trouble you, keep in mind that what we are trying to convey is that programming is about what you tell the computer to do and what you are willing to enforce. Without public and private methods there is no way to safeguard data. Without debugging techniques there is no easy way to ensure things aren't going to go well. So, comparatively, like a policeman at a parade, we are trying to ensure as much as possible that things go well and the code we write behaves itself.

Assert is your highly trained, bulletproof-vest wearing, uniformed professional police officer. When you write code you will have basic assumptions about the state and behavior of your code. The Assert behavior is your way of ensuring that your assumptions are never violated. Sort of like a utopia where people don't drink and drive, litter, or commit generally annoying acts of mayhem and violence.

Use an Assert where you need to make sure things are going as expected. To be consistent, as with the other techniques, we will wrap the basic Assert up into DebugTools module to make sure we know what we expected and when our expectations are not met. Here is the code:

```
Public Sub Assert(ByVal Test As Boolean, _
   ByVal Source As String, ByVal Message As String)

#If Debugging Then
   If (Not Test) Then
       Call DebugPrint(Source, Message)
       Debug.Assert False
     End If
#End If

End Sub
```

Our Assert uses the Debugging constant defined earlier in the chapter and the DebugPrint method. Our Assert takes a Boolean test, and the Source and Message arguments. First, we check to make sure we are in the debugging mode. Then, we check to see if our assumption succeeded or failed. If the assumption failed, then we log the message and call the basic Assert, which suspends application execution. Next, we will show the assertion used in our CalculateFuelConsumed method, properly insuring that both of the GallonsPerHour and Duration are non-negative. (We have included the conditional checks in the Do method too.)

```
Public Function CalculateFuelConsumed(ByVal Duration As Double, _
   ByVal GallonsPerHour As Double) As Double

  'Call Trap("Sheet1.CalculateFuelConsumption", "Tested")

  Call Trace("Sheet1.CalculateFuelConsumed", _
    "Duration=" & Duration & " GallonsPerHour=" & GallonsPerHour)

  Call Assert(Duration > 0, "Sheet1.CalculateFuelConsumed", "Duration > 0")
  Call Assert(GallonsPerHour > 0, "Sheet1.CalculateFuelConsumed", _
    "GallonsPerHour > 0")

  CalculateFuelConsumed = DoCalculateFuelConsumed(Duration, FuelConsumedPerhour)

  Call Trace("Sheet1.CalculateFuelConsumption", "Result=" & CalculateFuelConsumed)

End Function
```

```
Private Function DoCalculateFuelConsumed(ByVal Duration As Double, _
   ByVal GallonsPerHour As Double) As Double

   If (Duration > 0 And GallonsPerHour > 0) Then
     DoCalculateFuelConsumed = Duration * GallonsPerHour
   Else
     ' Raise an error here
   End If

End Function
```

In the revised example we added two calls to Assert. The first ensures that Duration is greater than 0, as well as does the second. Note that we also added the runtime checks in the DoCalculateFuelConsumed method. As a result, this method is self-documenting, the name tells you what it does, and it is as bulletproof as we know how to make it. We have added a Trap to remind us to test the method. We can do a global search on Trap for any uncommented Traps to indicate where we still need to do testing. We have two Trace statements, so we know exactly where and in what order this method is used, and finally, we have asserted that are two parameters are within an acceptable range.

Here is one more tip before we move on. What do you do if you write a bunch of code and add Traps and Traces, but find that these Traps are never sprung and the Trace statements never show up? The answer is that you get rid of the dead weight by putting your code on a diet. That is, remove the unused code. It is just taking up precious brain cycles every time you or someone else reads it, but you know it isn't really needed.

Notice that the last revision of our method has two branch statements and an Else condition that only contains a comment. The answer is that we need to add a Trap to each branch to ensure both paths are tested, and we need to talk about raising error conditions. We will talk about raising error conditions in the next section; here is the final revision for this section that shows you how to handily incorporate the Trap statements for each branch:

```
Public Function CalculateFuelConsumed(ByVal Duration As Double, _
   ByVal GallonsPerHour As Double) As Double

   'Call Trap("Sheet1.CalculateFuelConsumption", "Tested")

   Call Trace("Sheet1.CalculateFuelConsumed", _
     "Duration=" & Duration & " GallonsPerHour=" & GallonsPerHour)

   Call Assert(Duration > 0, "Sheet1.CalculateFuelConsumed", "Duration > 0")
   Call Assert(GallonsPerHour > 0, "Sheet1.CalculateFuelConsumed", _
     "GallonsPerHour > 0")

   If (Duration > 0 And GallonsPerHour > 0) Then
     Call Trap("Sheet1.CalculateFuelConsumed", _
       "Duration > 0 And GallonsPerHour > 0")
     CalculateFuelConsumed = DoCalculateFuelConsumed(Duration, GallonsPerHour)
   Else
     Call Trap("Sheet1.CalculateFuelConsumed", "Duration > 0 And
GallonsPerHour > 0 is False")
     ' Raise Error here
   End If
```

```
     Call Trace("Sheet1.CalculateFuelConsumption", "Result=" & CalculateFuelConsumed)

End Function

Private Function DoCalculateFuelConsumed(ByVal Duration As Double, _
  ByVal GallonsPerHour As Double) As Double

DoCalculateFuelConsumed = Duration * GallonsPerHour

End Function
```

Notice that the final revision puts the If checks with the assertions and moves all of the debugging code in the outer method (the one not prefixed with Do). As a result, our algorithm is very clean and comprehensively protected.

A reasonable person might ask, do you really write all of this code for every method? The answer is no. We have written a couple of million lines of code and are pretty confident that a one-line method is so easy to test, debug, and probably write that we would not add much debugging code to something so simple. In fact, we try to keep all of our code as simple as the DoCalculateFuelConsumed method. In addition to ensuring fewer bugs, it ensures that we don't have to write a lot of comments or debugging and testing code. What we are trying to convey is that if you are just getting started you might not be so confident, or if you get yourself in a pickle, then you may have doubts about how to get out of that pickle. Ultimately, you have to decide how much debugging and testing code is enough. This subjective part is what makes good programming so hard to do.

Raising Errors

There are many good programmers that will disagree with us. Good. That's what keeps life interesting, and helps create new ideas. This is one area where thousands, perhaps millions of programmers may disagree. We hope to convince you that we are right, and they are wrong.

Years ago semantically weaker languages like C returned error codes whenever something went wrong. These error codes were simply integers, usually negative, that had some contextual but arbitrary meaning. Consequently, you will see a lot of code that returns an integer, which is some arbitrary value that means something in context. Programming like this though means everything is a function, all real return values have to be passed as ByRef arguments, and the meaning of an error code does not travel with the error; that knowledge is maintained somewhere else. Thus, if a function returns -1 to indicate an error then the consumer of that code has to go somewhere else to figure out what that -1 means. Here is our DoCalculateFuelConsumed method revised to return an error code. (Don't write code this way.)

```
Private Function CalculateFuelConsumed(ByVal Duration As Double, _
  ByVal GallonsPerHour As Double, ByRef Result As Double) As Integer

  If (Duration > 0 And GallonsPerHour > 0) Then
    Result = Duration * GallonsPerHour
    CalculateFuelConsumed = 0
  Else
    CalculateFuelConsumed = -1
  End If

End Function
```

In the revision, the return value indicates success or value and the actual result of the algorithm is a parameter. This immediately makes it difficult to use the function inline because we have to declare an extra argument for storing and retrieving the real value. Now to call `CalculateFuelConsumed` we have to write a lot of extra code:

```
Dim Result As Double
If( CalculateFuelConsumed(7, 1.5, Result) = 0) Then
  ' Yeah, it worked we can use Result
Else
  ' Sigh, it failed again Result is meaningless
End If
```

Folks, this is an especially pessimistic way to program. We are almost completely eliminating the coolness of the function return value, and we are programming as if our code is always on the verge of failing. But as you continue reading this chapter on bulletproofing, you'll know that your code is going to fail much less. So let's get back the cool factor of functions and write optimistic code where failure is an infrequent nuisance rather than a frequent guest. We accomplish this feat by getting rid of error codes and raising errors only when they occur:

```
Option Explicit

Public Function CalculateFuelConsumed(ByVal Duration As Double, _
  ByVal GallonsPerHour As Double) As Double

  If (Duration > 0 And GallonsPerHour > 0) Then
    CalculateFuelConsumed = Duration * GallonsPerHour
  Else
    Call CalculateFuelConsumedError(Duration, GallonsPerHour)
  End If

End Function

Private Sub CalculateFuelConsumedError(ByVal Duration As Double, _
  ByVal GallonsPerHour As Double)

  Const Source As String = "Sheet2.CalculateFuelConsumed"
  Dim Description As String

  Description = "Duration {" & Duration & "} and GallonsPerHour {" & _
    GallonsPerHour & "} must be greater than 0"

  Call Err.Raise(vbObjectError + 1, Source, Description)
End Sub

Public Sub Test()

  On Error GoTo Catch
    MsgBox CalculateFuelConsumed(-8, 1.5)

  Exit Sub
Catch:
  MsgBox Err.Description, vbCritical

End Sub
```

CalculateFuelConsumed performs our calculation. If either Duration or GallonsPerHour are bad then an error is raised by calling the helper subroutine CalculateFuelConsumedError. The Helper method creates a nicely formatted description and raises the error. An error is raised by calling Err.Raise and passing an optional error number, source string, description, help file name and help file context. By convention, we add a contextual error number to the constant vbObjectError (as shown) to prevent our error numbers from colliding with VBA's native error codes.

To consume the new CalculateFuelConsumed method we write an On Error Goto label statement. We always try to use some work consistently, like Catch or Handle. Next, we call the method, and add a statement to exit the method, Exit Sub for subroutines. Exit Function for functions, and Exit Property for properties. Finally, very optimistically at the end, we add the label and the error handling code. In the example we just tell the user what went wrong with the MsgBox function.

We don't have to beat a dead horse, but if someone asks you why this approach is better then you can tell them it's better because:

❑ We can use functions as they were intended, to return calculated results.

❑ We aren't adding do nothing error code that pessimistically employs conditional statements to see if things went okay. We can assume they always will run fine.

❑ We will have a safety net that catches any error not just our error codes. (For example, what if we forgot to check a zero denominator in a division statement. The code would divide by zero and not one of our error codes. The error code approach would completely miss this error; the on Error Goto statement would not.)

❑ The Error object carries the meaning of the error along with it rather than requiring that meaning be construed from just an arbitrary error code.

Clearly, if one style is better in just one way then it is better overall. Raising errors is better than returning error codes in several, non-subjective ways.

Let's look at writing error handlers next.

Writing Error Handlers

There are three forms of On Error. There is the On Error GoTo label which branches to an arbitrary line number of text label followed by a colon. There is the On Error Resume Next that branches to the line immediately following the line which caused the error, and there is the On Error GoTo 0 statement that simply clears the error.

On Error Goto Line Number

You have already seen On Error Goto used with the Catch label in the preceding section. It is important to exit the method immediately preceding the label, otherwise the label and consequently, the error code will always run. Use Exit Sub to exit subroutines. Use Exit Function to exit functions, and Exit Property to exit properties. But what if you want the error code to always run? You might.

This technique is called a resource protection block. Computers have a finite number of things collectively called resources. A resource might be a database connection, file, or a network socket. If you create instances of these resources then you must ensure they get cleaned up. You can, by using the resource protection block idiom. The way it works is simple: use an `On Error Goto` label statement after the resource is created and intentionally do not place an exit statement before the label. In this way the error handling code—in this instance resource protecting code—is always run whether or not there is an error. Here is what it looks like with the code that creates a new file and writes some text to it. (This is not the preferred way to write to files. Use the `FileSystemObject` for that purpose.)

```
Public Sub ProtectThisResource()

  Open ThisWorkbook.Path & "\dummy.txt" For Output As #1
  On Error GoTo Finally

    Print #1, "This file will always be closed"

Finally:

  Close #1

  If (Err.Number <> 0) Then MsgBox Err.Description

End Sub
```

> **Keep in mind that arbitrary line numbers can be used as labels. Simply replace the text where the label part of On Error Goto with a digit.**

The basic rhythm of a resource protection block is create the resource, insert the `On Error Goto` label statement, attempt to use the resource, and finally cleanup (both the resource and any error). In the example, we open a text file, set the `On Error Goto Finally` statement, attempt to use the resource, and then clean up every time. Notice, there is no exit statement.

On Error Resume Next

`On Error Resume Next` can be used to ignore an error and continue with the next statement. This technique is used immediately preceding a statement that can pass or fail. Kind of like a statement that isn't that important. We don't use `On Error Resume Next` that much because we'd rather not write statements that don't matter. If it doesn't matter, get rid of it.

Both `Resume` and `Resume Next` can be used by themselves. You will see `Resume` used where an error is handled and you want the code to try again. For example, if we added an extra error handling block to the `ProtectThisResource` method in the event the file couldn't be opened because its `ReadOnly` attribute was set, then we might change the attribute to the make the file readable and call `Resume` to try to open the file again. `Resume Next` is simply an instruction to skip the line of code that caused the error and proceed to the next line. You might see this in an error handler that doesn't care if an error causing line is skipped or not. The following method shows how we can use a resource protection block in

conjunction with an error handling block and specifically recover from a write-protected file and resume
trying to open the file:

```
Public Sub ProtectThisResource()

    Dim FileName As String
    FileName = ThisWorkbook.Path & "\dummy.txt"

    On Error GoTo Catch
    Open FileName For Output As #1

    On Error GoTo Finally

        Print #1, Time & " This file will always be closed"

Finally:

    Close #1
    If (Err.Number <> 0) Then MsgBox Err.Description
    Exit Sub

Catch:
    If (Err.Number = 75) Then
        Call SetAttr(FileName, vbNormal)
        Resume
    End If

End Sub
```

The first On Error Goto Catch will handler write-protected files and try a second time to open a file
after the file attributes have been cleared. The second On Error Goto ensures that the file is finally
closed.

The sample method looks kind of complicated, and it is important to note that a lot of other things might
go wrong. What if the disk is corrupted? What if we run out of memory because the file is too big? What
if the file is locked by another program? All of these things might go wrong. Quite frankly this is why
writing robust programs is so hard. It is very difficult to cover every possibility at every juncture. The
programmer has to subjectively anticipate what might reasonably go wrong and try to circumvent those
failures, but eventually we have to be done and give the code to the users. Some very smart people have
said that writing computer software is the hardest thing that people try to do. We are inclined to agree.

At this point, you have had a taste of some of the things that can go wrong with very
simple code. Now, consider trying to bulletproof the 10 or 20 million lines of code
that make up Windows and Windows NT. A lot of the onus is on Microsoft for
bulletproofing Windows, but there are a lot of very smart people that seem to delight
in trying to poke holes in Windows itself. The amazing thing is that they are
successful so few times, rather than so many.

On Error GoTo 0

On Error Goto 0 disables error handlers in the current procedure. This is another statement we don't use that often. You will likely encounter it though. Just think of On Error Goto 0 as an off switch for error handlers at the procedural level.

Using the Err Object

The Err object contains information about the most recent error. Included in this information is the error code, the origin of the error, a description about the error, and a link to a Help file document, if available.

Err is what is referred to as a Singleton object. This means that there is only one in the entire application. And, because it is an instance of a class it has methods and properties. You can invoke Err.Raise to throw an error, and Err.Clear to clear an error. The remaining properties, except for one we haven't discussed, are the values used to initialize the error. The additional property is the LastDllError property. LastDllError returns the Hresult—the error code—of an error returned from a DLL. You will need to use this property when you call into methods in external DLLs, such as those found in what is collectively referred to as the Windows API.

Scaffolding

Before we get to the section on the EventLog, let's take a minute to talk about where and when to write test code. The technique we employ is called Scaffolding. If programming is like adding stories to a building, then Scaffolding is adding test code to each story before you proceed to the next one. Scaffolding is simply the process of adding test code to ensure that new code stands alone and hasn't introduced errors on top of preexisting good code.

For example, we created the DebugTools module for general reuse. This code should and does stand alone, but we can't be sure of that until we test the debug code. To do so, we have added one test method for each public method in the DebugTools module that runs the Trace, Assert, and Trap code, making sure the code produces the desired results. (It would be sadly ironic if the debug code introduced the bugs.) Here is the complete listing for the DebugTools module with the scaffold test code shown in bold font:

```
Option Explicit

#Const Tracing = True
#Const Debugging = True
#Const UseEventLog = False

Public Sub Trap(ByVal Source As String, _
  ByVal Message As String)

#If Debugging Then

  Call DebugPrint(Source, Message)
  Stop
```

```
#End If

End Sub

Private Sub DebugPrint(ByVal Source As String, _
  ByVal Message As String)

#If UseEventLog Then

#Else
  Debug.Print "Source: " & Source & " Message: " & Message
#End If

End Sub

Public Sub Assert(ByVal Test As Boolean, _
  ByVal Source As String, ByVal Message As String)

#If Debugging Then
  If (Not Test) Then
    Call DebugPrint(Source, Message)
    Debug.Assert False
  End If
#End If

End Sub

Public Sub Trace(ByVal Source As String, _
  ByVal Message As String)

#If Tracing Then
  Call DebugPrint(Source, Message)
#End If

End Sub

Public Sub TraceParams(ByVal Source As String, _
  ParamArray Values() As Variant)

  Dim Message As String
  Dim I As Integer

  For I = LBound(Values) To UBound(Values)
    Message = Message & " " & Values(I)
  Next I

  Call Trace(Source, Message)

End Sub

  #If Debugging Then

  Public Sub TrapTest()
    Call Trap("Sheet1.CallTrap", "Test Trap")
  End Sub
```

```
Public Sub AssertTest()
  Call Assert(False, "AssertTest", "Assertion Failure")
End Sub

Public Sub TraceTest()
  Call Trace("Sheet1.TraceAssert", "Trace Test")
End Sub

Public Sub TestSuite()
  ' Comment out when each test passes
  TrapTest
  AssertTest
  TraceTest
End Sub

#End If
```

The test code is only available when Debugging is `True`. `TestSuite` calls each of our individual test methods, `TrapTest`, `AssertTest`, and `TraceTest`. Each of `TrapTest`, `AssertTest`, and `TraceTest` calls each of the debugging methods, and we can examine the perspective results in the Immediate window and step through the code to ensure we are getting the desired results before making the code generally available for other projects or to other programmers.

Scaffolding is easy. However, it is important to do it as you go. Test each layer as you add complexity rather than trying to test everything at once when you think you are all done. Layering your tests is as valuable as layering your code. Each new piece will rest firmly on a strong and sound underpinning.

Writing to the EventLog

The `EventLog` is a system resource. It is important and valuable enough that it is an integral part of Microsoft's new .NET Framework. (.NET is a framework of code for VB, C#, C++, and many other programming languages.) It is important enough as a general tool that Microsoft has incorporated in the important sounding Exception Management Application Block (EMAB) and the Enterprise Instrumentation Framework (EIF). You will have to go online for more information about the EMAB and EIF because they aren't currently available to use directly, but the `EventLog` is, so we'll talk about the `EventLog`.

The `EventLog` is a local system service that acts like a repository for information about the state of applications, security, and the running computer in general. It is useful for diagnostics because the `EventLog` persists between application runs. Consequently, even if your application crashes radically, messages to the `EventLog` will still be there, helping you diagnose and fix what went wrong. Think of it this way: the Immediate window is cool but the `EventLog` is forever.

The following code is available in `EventLog.bas`. The code uses six Windows API methods to connect to the Windows `EventLog` and simplify writing errors to the `EventLog` to a single method `WriteEntry`. Clearly, we have taken some of the flexibility out of using the `EventLog`, but we want to use it just to log errors at this point:

```
Option Explicit

Private Const GMEM_ZEROINIT = &H40 ' Initializes memory to 0
```

```vb
Private Const EVENTLOG_ERROR_TYPE = 1
Private Const EVENTLOG_WARNING_TYPE = 2
Private Const EVENTLOG_INFORMATION_TYPE = 4

Declare Function RegisterEventSource Lib "advapi32.dll" Alias
"RegisterEventSourceA" (ByVal MachineName As String, ByVal Source As String) As
Long

Declare Function ReportEvent Lib "advapi32.dll" Alias "ReportEventA" (ByVal Handle
As Long, ByVal EventType As Integer, ByVal Category As Integer, ByVal EventID As
Long, ByVal UserId As Any, ByVal StringCount As Integer, ByVal DataSize As Long,
Text As Long, RawData As Any) As Boolean

Declare Function DeregisterEventSource Lib "advapi32.dll" (ByVal Handle As Long) As
Long

Declare Sub CopyMemory Lib "kernel32" Alias "RtlMoveMemory" (ByVal Destination As
Any, ByVal Source As Any, ByVal Length As Long)

Declare Function GlobalAlloc Lib "kernel32" (ByVal Flags As Long, ByVal Length As
Long) As Long

Declare Function GlobalFree Lib "kernel32" (ByVal hMem As Long) As Long

Public Sub WriteEntry(ByVal Message As String)

  Dim Handle As Long
  Dim EventSource As Long

On Error GoTo Finally
  Handle = GlobalAlloc(GMEM_ZEROINIT, Len(Message) + 1)
  Call CopyMemory(Handle, Message, Len(Message) + 1)
  EventSource = OpenEventSource("vbruntime")

  Call ReportEvent(EventSource, EVENTLOG_ERROR_TYPE, _
    0, 1, 0&, 1, 0, Handle, 0)

Finally:
  If (Handle <> 0) Then Call GlobalFree(Handle)
  If (EventSource <> 0) Then CloseEventSource (EventSource)
End Sub

Public Function OpenEventSource(ByVal Source As String) As Long
  ' Use the local machine
  OpenEventSource = RegisterEventSource(".", Source)
End Function

Public Sub CloseEventSource(ByVal EventSource As Long)
  Call DeregisterEventSource(EventSource)
End Sub
Sub LogEventTest()
  Call WriteEntry("This is a test!")
End Sub
```

After adding the EventLog module we can change the value of UseEventLog to True and call WriteEntry to write the error information to the EventLog. Use the EventLog Viewer (Start ⇨ Run Eventvwr.msc) to view the Application log in the Event Viewer. The logged entries will be listed under the vbruntime source, as shown in Figure 7-6.

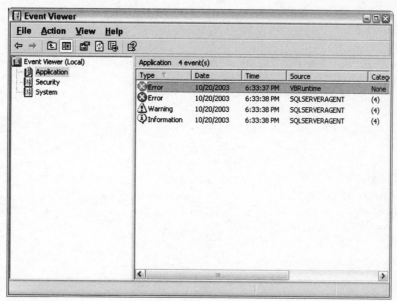

Figure 7-6

Consider the EventLog.bas module a teaser for Chapter 16. (We can't stuff everything into one chapter, so we'll reserve the discussion about using the Windows API for Chapter 16, *Programming with the Windows API*.)

Summary

Doing anything well requires a method to the madness. Doing anything well and fast is a matter of practice, habit, and a good set of tools. In this chapter, we demonstrated how we could build some useful tools for debugging and testing based on the Debug object, Stop statement, and the Windows EventLog. If you get in the habit of instrumenting your code with these debug tools, then you will write better code the first time and faster than ever.

The techniques we covered include using Assert, Trace, and Trap, and we introduced using the Windows API to write errors to the EventLog. You can easily fill in any gaps in understanding how to use the Windows API by reading Chapter 16.

8

Debugging and Testing

There are hundreds of books on programming. Interestingly, only a relatively small percentage of those books are either specifically about debugging and testing or contain chapters dedicated to it. The interesting aspect is that many reports (and our experience) suggest that more than half of a programmer's time will be spent debugging code. Given these proportions, one might think there should be a greater number of books about debugging and testing and what not to write than there would be books predominantly about code.

There are a few basic guidelines for writing bulletproof code. The first rule is if you don't write it then you won't need to test it; or, less is more. The second is that you will spend more time "fixing" what you write than "writing" what you'll fix. The third is instrument your code—add self-diagnosing code—when you initially write lines of code because you will have more ideas about the assumptions that are being made as you write than you will six months later. (By this time it's more than likely someone else will be struggling with your code, and you'll be on to something new. Sounds good, but that something new may be code someone else wrote that wasn't instrumented either.)

Being adept at finding bugs introduced by you or, more importantly, others, is an art form, like playing an instrument, or flying airplanes. Some are mechanically proficient and others demonstrate a certain grace and beauty. (If you have ever spent 30 hours debugging some C++ code and someone else only takes a minute, then they will be an object of grace and beauty.) In this chapter, we will demonstrate the tools that will help you be mechanically proficient at debugging and testing. Whether you become good at it or not is a product of practice.

Stepping Through Code

There are several kinds of testing. The terms for the kinds of testing vary, but common terms are unit testing, white box testing, gray box testing, black box testing, regression testing, integration testing, application testing, and enterprise testing. All of these terms mean something. As a programmer there are two canons that always apply: one can't be sure if the code will perform as expected unless one steps through every code path, nor can one be sure that the code will perform as expected. Perhaps the best one can offer is to write as little code as necessary; under most circumstances the code will perform as hoped, and when something goes wrong it won't go catastrophically wrong.

Your customers will find it egregious if your application barfs and dumps their hours of hard work, so to redress this catastrophic potentiality, we must meticulously walk through our code to eliminate as many possible defects as possible. Unfortunately, debugging and testing can be excruciatingly complex. It is almost impossible to convey this complexity to you if you are new to programming, and it is equally impossible to set up one of these complex scenarios in this book. However, we can demonstrate the mechanics of performing code walks and, with practice, you will become proficient.

Running Your Code

It was Robert Frost who said, "I took the road less traveled by and that has made all of the difference." This is true with software too. If you meticulously walk through code paths that may only infrequently be traveled then your code-product is likely to be more robust and offer fewer surprises to your customers. The first step in taking the road less traveled is to run your code before you ship it.

In Excel VBA the Run behavior is found on the Run menu in the VBE, or you can press *F5* in the VBE to start running your code. A good trick here is to write a co-pair test subroutine that requires no arguments that calls your method. This is called scaffolding. If you write a subroutine that exercises each (or at least most) or your methods then you are in a position to test them individually. This approach can speed up testing significantly. The next listing shows a method we might write to solve a problem and a test subroutine that calls this method, permitting a convenient test entry point:

```
Private Sub TestFahrenheitToCelsius()
  Debug.Print FahrenheitToCelsius(32)

  If (FahrenheitToCelsius(32) <> 0) Then
    Debug.Print "TestFahrenheitToCelsius: Failed"
    Debug.Assert False
  Else
    Debug.Print "TestFahrenheitToCelsius: Passed"
  End If

End Sub

Public Function FahrenheitToCelsius(ByVal TemperatureFahrenheit As Double) _
  As Double

  FahrenheitToCelsius = (5 / 9 * (TemperatureFahrenheit - 32))

End Function
```

In the example, we have a public function that converts temperatures in Fahrenheit to temperatures in Celsius. To make sure we have the equation correct, we can write a test method to verify the conversion. Knowing the sentinel boiling and freezing temperatures—212 and 100 degrees and 32 and 0 degrees, respectively—we can test the conversion algorithm, with a `private` method that compares expected results with known arguments.

In the example, `FahrenheitToCelsius` represents the desired algorithm and `TestFahrenheitToCelsius` is a `private` method that we can run and test independently of the rest of our total solution. Assuming the test method runs successfully, we can add a comment or a mark on a check list to indicate that this method runs correctly and no further examination is required. Accumulatively, if every method could be checked off as reliable then our application would perform correctly given all inputs.

In reality, we can use scaffolding to extrude many errors, but very small potential errors can accumulate and result in actual errors we never tested for. For example, what if a user entered a number that exceeded that storage capacity of the Double type? Then we would get an error we might not have anticipated and our tested code would still fail. As a result, we can eliminate a large percentage of errors with diligent testing but still cannot eliminate all errors.

As a matter of practicality it is up to you and your customers to decide what percentage of errors are permissible. If the software calculates income taxes then a minor error calculating 5 in 100 tax returns might be acceptable. If the software determines precisely when a pacemaker must fire then a 1 in 10,000,000 failure rate might be required by the product's underwriter. Because we are programming in Excel we are guessing that many of you are more likely to be calculating tax returns than writing embedded software for pacemakers. Again, though, it is important for you and your product's consumer to try to negotiate mean time between failure rates, but a zero failure rate will never be achieved given the state of current technology.

Stepping into Your Code

The `Step Into` feature is found in the VBE on the Debug menu. The shortcut for the `Step Into` feature is the *F8* key. `Step Into` single steps over each line of code. If you press *F8* on a method call then the debugger will step into that method. `Step Into` is labor-intensive process, but it permits you to check every line of code, line by line.

We can easily see where we are and the code that is coming up next. To demonstrate, open the VBE and place the cursor in the `TestFahrenheitToCelsisus` method and press *F8*. A bright yellow background will highlight the line of code that will execute next. In Figure 8-1, the subroutine header is highlighted. Press *F8* again and the line containing `Debug.Print` will be highlighted. Press *F8* a third time and the code branches to the `FahrenheitToCelsisus` method, and so on.

Step Over

The *Shift+F8* combination is the shortcut for the Debug ⇨ StepOver behavior in the VBE. For example, if we don't want to step into the `FahrenheitToCelsius` at the `Debug.Print` statement (see Figure 8-1) then we can press *Shift+F8* and the method will execute, but we won't step into `FahrenheitToCelsius` method.

Step Out

If you are in a `Long` method or a method that we have already identified as reliable, then we can use the *Ctrl+Shift+F8* shortcut to use the `Step Out` behavior. (`Step Out` is available on the Debug menu in the VBE.) `Step Out` runs the remaining code in a procedure but appears to immediately branch out of the current scope.

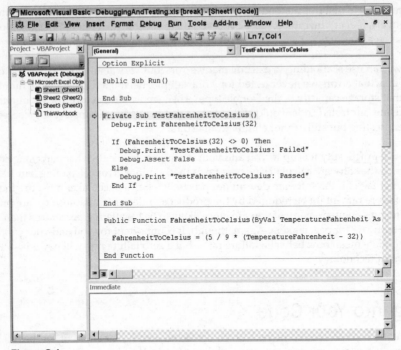

Figure 8-1

Suppose, we are stepping through a method and we figure out what's wrong. Instead of laboring through the rest of the method, we can use *Ctrl+Shift+F8* to step out of the method. We always have the option of pressing *F5* at any time, returning to the run mode.

Run to Cursor

In addition to stepping into, stepping over, and stepping out of code you can click a line of code anywhere and use the shortcut for the Debug ⇨ Run To Cursor menu—*Ctrl+F8*—to run until the debugger reaches that location and then the debugger will suspend execution. This is a good technique if you have fixed a chunk of code and don't want to belabor stepping over known good lines.

Set Next Statement

The Debug ⇨ Set Next Statement supported by the *Ctrl+F9* shortcut short circuits lines of code within the same procedure. Consider the `TestFahrenheitToCelsius` example again. Suppose, we simply want to see if the `Debug.Print` statement in the `else` condition displays the passed message correctly. We could start the `TestFahrenheitToCelsisus` method with *F8*, click on the `Debug.Print` statement in the `else` condition, and press *Ctrl+F9*. All preceding lines of code will be skipped and the debugger will jump to that line of code.

This feature is especially useful as it can help you skip lines of code that may make critical updates before you are completely sure that preparation for the modifications is perfect. After executing all of the startup and teardown code, skipping the critical, data-modifying lines of code, you can evaluate the procedure before letting the critical update execute.

Show Next Statement

Many times, while debugging you may have to pause and look up some information—for example, in a procedure you may need to look up a field in a class—and it is easy to lose track of the debugger's current position. Select Debug ⇨ Show Next Statement and the VBE editor will automatically position the cursor to the next line of code to be executed.

Collectively, Step Into, Step Over, Step Out, Run To Cursor, Set Next Statement, and Show Next statement will permit you to gracefully dance around your code like an expert, avoiding the thousands of wasted keystrokes you will use to debug code.

Using Breakpoints

In Chapter 7 we offered a brief lesson on the history of debuggers and breakpoints. In this chapter, we will use our newfound understanding of breakpoints to divide and conquer a problem. The *F9* key toggles a breakpoint—Debug ⇨ Toggle Breakpoint—on an executable line of code. A breakpoint is indicated by a red highlight on each line containing a breakpoint. During the course of a debugging session it is possible to set dozens of breakpoints. To quickly clear all breakpoints, after you have finished debugging, select Debug ⇨ Clear All Breakpoints. Clear All Breakpoints can be invoked with the *Ctrl+Shift+F9* key combination.

Now that we know the mechanics of breakpoints in the VBE, how can we employ them to the greatest effect? The answer can be found in the Latin saying Divide et impera (Divide and conquer). The fastest way to begin finding a bug whose origin is entirely unknown, especially in code that is unfamiliar to you, is to place a breakpoint anywhere and run the code. If the breakpoint is hit before the error manifests itself then the code is in the remaining half of the code that begins immediately after the breakpoint. The second step is to place a breakpoint anywhere after the first breakpoint, and repeat the process. If the second breakpoint is reached before the error then the error follows the second breakpoint. In this case, place a breakpoint after the third breakpoint. If the error manifests itself after the first breakpoint but before the second breakpoint then the error is between the first breakpoint and the second breakpoint. In this case, place a new breakpoint between the first and second breakpoint. Repeating these processes will enable you to find a defect in complete foreign terrain in a very few number of tries. (The approach is based on a logarithm of base two, also called divide and conquer.)

Many easy to find bugs will manifest themselves at their origin. These bugs tend to be pretty easy to resolve. The bugs that will require the logarithmic use of breakpoints can easily consume a large amount of time, but using breakpoints can quickly help you isolate the problem.

Using Watches

The adage "knowledge is power" is appropriate apropos for software developers. The more we know about our craft and the more we know about the state of our software the more powerful, expressive, and useful our solutions will be. We have been programming long enough to remember writing code in plain text editors, using command-line compilers, and having to implement debugging strategies in a catch as catch can manner. From that perspective we truly appreciate modern integrated development tools like the VBE, which are relatively new (within the last decade or so).

The Debug menu contains the Add Watch, Edit Watch (*Ctrl+W*), and Quick Watch (*Shift+F9*)—our favorite. To use these watch behaviors, you can select the variable, object, or expression that you want to know more about and invoke the behavior. Alternately, you can invoke the behavior and then indicate the variable, object, or expression to watch.

Add Watch

The Debug ⇨ Add Watch behavior permits you to add a variable, object, or expression to a modeless window. The Watches window is displayed while your code is running in the debug mode, and the watch expressions that are in scope are updated in the window as your program runs.

To demonstrate, here is a method that calculates the `FahrenheitToCelsius` method using the numbers 1 to 400. Instead of manually inspecting the output after each calculation, we can add a watch that will show the Fahrenheit value, represented by the loop control value, and the resultant value. The next listing shows the code we have been referring to:

```
Private Sub TestWatch()

    Dim I As Integer
    For I = 1 To 400
        Debug.Print FahrenheitToCelsius(I)
    Next I

End Sub
```

In order to add a watch for the expression `FahrenheitToCelsius(I)` we can highlight the expression in the editor and select Debug ⇨ Add Watch. The Add Watch dialog box is displayed (see the Figure 8-2). The Add Watch dialog box indicates the expression—in this context, variable, object, or expression—the context, which includes the procedure and module, and the watch type. The default watch type is just used to keep an eye on the changing value of the expression, but we also have the option of breaking when the expression evaluates to the equivalent of `True` or when the value changes. Using the watch to break on `True` or changing values is a convenient way to permit your code to run without being interrupted until some desired condition is met.

When we are done setting up a watch, click *OK*. When the Add Watch dialog box closes, the Watches window will be displayed, showing your expression. The two watches we have been discussing—the loop control I and the method call—are shown in Figure 8-3. As we step through the `TestWatch` method where these two expressions are in scope, the Watches window is constantly updated.

Another feature of the Watches window is the ability to drill down into complex objects. For example, if we place an object in the Watches window (see Figure 8-4) then we can click the [+] symbol to expand the watched object and drill down into that object's current state. Like other expressions, the watched object's state is updated as the state changes. In Figure 8-4 we can see part of the inner state of the worksheet, Sheet1.

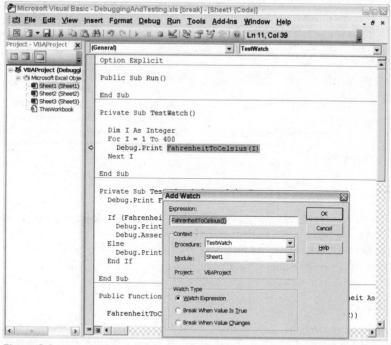

Figure 8-2

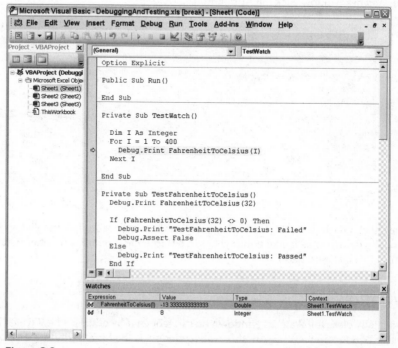

Figure 8-3

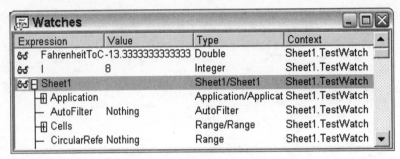

Figure 8-4

Edit Watch

The Debug ⇨ Edit Watch behavior invokes a dialog box almost identical to the add Watch dialog box. The Edit Watch dialog box permits you to change the basic watch information or delete the watch. You also have the option of editing and deleting watches directly in the Watches window. With a bit of practice you will become adept at managing watches.

Quick Watch

The Debug ⇨ Quick Watch behavior is invoked from the VBE menu or the *Shift+F9* shortcut. The Quick watch dialog box is a modal dialog box. To use it, select an expression and press *Shift+F9*. As shown in Figure 8-5, the Quick Watch dialog box shows the expression and the value. If you want to add the watch value to the Watches window click the Add button.

Figure 8-5

Because the Quick Watch dialog box is modal, execution is suspended while the dialog box is open. As with all modal windows, this modal window has to be closed to interact with other parts of the owning application, in this instance, Excel.

Locals Windows

If you accidentally close the Watches window you can reopen it by adding a new watch or selecting View ⇨ Watch Window in the VBE. Another watch window is the Locals window. The Locals window is very similar to the Add Watch window. The difference is that the values in the Locals Watch window do not reflect all of the variables, but only the variables, in the current, or local, scope. Included in the Locals window is the omnipresent reference to self-named Me (see Figure 8-6).

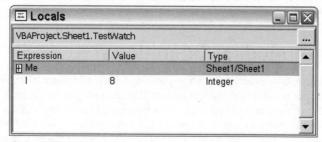

Figure 8-6

> The **Me** variable is an object's internal reference to itself. You can use **Me** as a convenient way of way of displaying the Members window. The same window can also be manually and explicitly invoked by pressing *Ctrl+Space* in the editor.

Testing an Expression in the Immediate Window

The Immediate window (View ⇨ Immediate Window or the shortcut *Ctrl+G*) is an editor-cum-interpreter. One can enter abridged commands, variables, objects, and code statements which get executed immediately. As a result, a programmer can test assumptions and alternatives immediately without running a lot of code.

A common task that we perform is to print the value of a variable in the current context. The print command is the keyword print or the symbol?. Following the print command, you can invoke just about any function, for example, ? abs(-5) will display 5 on the next line in the Immediate window. Suppose you are an old DOS (command prompt) hand, you can run the subroutine shell "cmd" to open a command prompt. For additional reference information refer to the Help topic *Immediate Window Keyboard Shortcuts* in the VBE Help documentation.

Figure 8-7 demonstrates the results of invoking the FahrenheitToCelsius function from the Immediate window. The first line shows the print command immediately followed by the function call

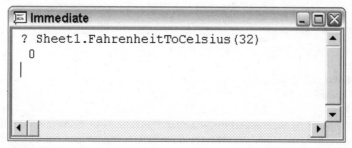

Figure 8-7

and the result. Notice in the figure we have to qualify the function call with the instance name of the class that defines the function. If the function were in a module then no object is required; because we defined the `FahrenheitToCelsius` in the Worksheet named `Sheet1` we have to use the `Sheet1` object and member-of operation (.).

Resources for Finding Definitions

At this point, you know how to meticulously explore and find out information about the state of your code. A reliable rule of thumb is to write test code that examines every code path and branch and as many negative and positive inputs as possible. As a matter of practicality this is very difficult and time consuming to do; for this reason reusing as much code as possible is one of the best ways to accelerate development and deliver timely, reliable solutions. The next piece of the puzzle is finding out what is already available and how to use it. Let's explore the VBE features that aid in achieving this end.

Edit ➡ Quick Info

The Quick Info *(Ctrl+I)* feature will manually popup a ToolTipthat will provide a hint about the item under the cursor. For instance, if we place the cursor on the word `FahrenheitToCelsius` and press *Ctrl+I* the signature of the method is displayed as a ToolTip (see Figure 8-8).

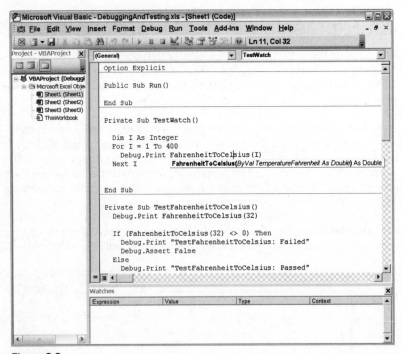

Figure 8-8

The quick information tips are enabled by default in the Tools ➡ Options menu on the Editor tab (see Figure 8-9). However, if you are relatively new to Excel or using an instance of Excel where someone else had turned the Auto Quick Info feature off then it might be a trial to know how to use any particular feature of Excel. (There are just too many classes, methods, properties, events, and fields in Excel for any one person to extemporize the information provided by the Quick Info feature.)

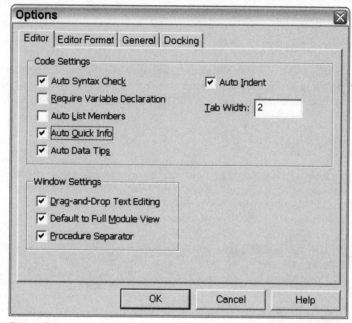

Figure 8-9

Edit ⇨ Parameter Info

The Parameter Info provides information specifically about the arguments to provide to methods. This feature is accessed through the shortcut *Ctrl+Shift+I*. When you access Quick Info, the method name is displayed in bold font. The Parameter Info feature displays the arguments in bold font. Again, modern software frameworks like Microsoft Office (the .NET Framework, Visual Control Library, or Java's J2EE) are simply too large and complex to extemporize, making programming prohibitively difficult without mastering these features of the VBE.

Edit ⇨ Complete Word

The Complete Word feature, accessed through Edit menu or *Ctrl+Space* shortcut, examines the current token and makes a stab at entering the rest of the token for you. For example, if we typed Fahre and press *Ctrl+Space* then the VBE editor will finish entering the function name for us. Generally, the VBE's guess is pretty good. Features like Complete Word can assist you in correctly entering names of things that may be difficult to spell, like Fahrenheit.

Edit ⇨ List Properties/Methods

The List Properties/Methods feature displays properties and methods that are accessible from the current context. For example, if we type the name of an object followed by the member-of operator then the properties and methods of that object are displayed in a drop-down list. By default, this feature is turned on in the Tools ⇨ Options. . . Editors tab. (The Auto List Member is checked.) If this feature becomes unchecked then *Ctrl+J* will force the drop-down list of properties and methods to be displayed.

Edit ⇨ List Constants

Ctrl+Shift+J invokes the List Constants behavior. There are hundreds of relevant constants that convey more meaning than using a literal cardinal value will. Again, it can be challenging at best to memorize even a small subset of these constants. Let the VBE do this chore on your behalf.

Edit ⇨ Bookmarks

A bookmark is precisely what it sounds like. As you bounce around in a large project it is easy to lose track of where you want to be or where you just were. Use the Edit ⇨ Bookmarks feature to toggle bookmarks and quickly scan to existing bookmarks. A bookmark is represented by a small rounded rectangle to the left of the code in the VBE, as shown in Figure 8-10.

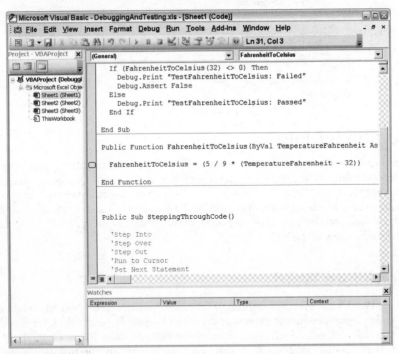

Figure 8-10

View ⇨ Definition

The Definition menu item will navigate focus in the editor to the location of the definition of the symbol. For example, in the test application, we can quickly navigate to the definition of a method by placing the cursor on the symbol and invoking the behavior from the View ⇨ Definition menu or by pressing *Shift+F2*. In our small sample project this feature might not seem so useful at first glance, but when exploring large programs or foreign code this feature can be very useful.

View ⇨ Object Browser

The Object Browser is accessed from the View ⇨ Object Browser menu or with the *F2* key. The Object Browser is a centralized location for exploring all of the classes and their constituent members. If you reference an external library then classes and members in those libraries can be explored from the Object Browser (see Figure 8-11).

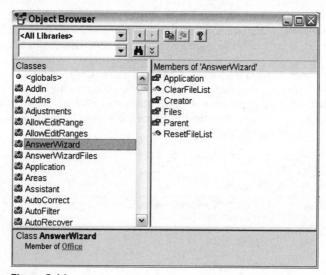

Figure 8-11

In Figure 8-11 the filter is set to all referenced libraries. The AnswerWizard class is selected in the Classes list, and the public members of the AnswerWizard class are shown in the list on the right. At the bottom, information describing what you are looking at and where this thing is defined is shown. For example, in Figure 8-11 we can tell that the AnswerWizard is a class defined in the Office library.

Default libraries for MS-Excel include Office, Excel, stdole, VBA, and VBAProject. Each of these libraries is located in a physical file on your system and introduces its own capabilities to the VBE. For example, stdole represents OLE Automation and is physically supported by the file C:\WINDOWS\System32\ stdole2.tlb. (A .tlb file is a type library file, which defines the contents of a COM object. Refer to Chapter 13 for more information on COM and Automation.)

Viewing the Call Stack

Occasionally, you may encounter a language bigot. A language bigot is someone that thinks programming in some languages is real programming and others are not. (This is sometimes a common malady suffered by C++ and Java programmers.) In reality, if you type some text and a program compiles or interprets that task and does something then you are programming; however, some tools are very general and can be used to do almost anything and others are more approachable and constrained to a specific domain. C++ can be used to do anything but will take a long time to master. VBA is very approachable and productive work can be completed very quickly. Each has its own value.

Mining this vein, many programming tools share some common capabilities. The reason is that whether the language requires rigorous study to master or is more approachable, basic operations occur and a means of exploring them must be provided. With the advent of the function—invented some time between about 1960 and 1975—programs branched to code permitting code to converge to one location rather than being copied and pasted into many locations. As a result, programmers needed a means of tracking this branching behavior. Very simply, when a function is called the current address and some state information is put in an area of memory referred to as the stack or the call stack. This area of memory is used by the computer to store the address prior to a branch and local variables after a branch. Just prior to a function exiting, the local variables are removed from the stack and the next thing remaining on the stack is the address of the previous branch location. The computer uses the branch location like breadcrumbs to return to the branch location and pick up where the execution left off prior to the branch.

The call stack can be viewed from the View ⇨ Call Stack menu (*Ctrl+L* shortcut). This feature will take the guesswork out of determining the exact path your code has taken as the CPU traipses through your code. As shown in Figure 8-12, if we step from the `TestFahrenheitToCelsius` method to the `FahrenheitToCelsisus` method then the Call Stack modal window will show branches as a reverse-order-stack—list of the methods invoked.

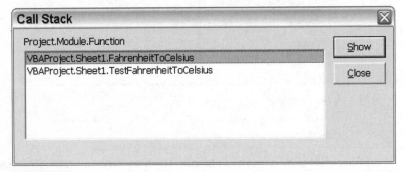

Figure 8-12

Asserting Application Invariants

Chapter 7 introduced a tool built on the Debug object's `Assert` method and adequately demonstrated how to use this feature of VBA. Before we close here, it is worth reiterating the value of assertions, in general, as a debugging aid.

When you write code you are your own best advocate. If you feel yourself writing code that feels like spaghetti then pause and think about the solution some more. If you explain your implementation to someone and the explanation sounds complex then it probably is. Finally, as you write code you will be making mental assumptions about state, inputs, and outputs. Assert these assumptions. Write a `Debug.Assert` statement or use the tool from Chapter 7 for each one of these assumptions as you write your code. A month, week, day, or even hour later these assumptions may be memories lost forever. A reasonable rule of thumb is that a method should be named using a noun and verb, should be named by what the method does, should comprise just a few lines of code, and asserted heavily. The famous Dave

Thielen says "Assert the world!" and the highly respected Juval Löwy offers a reasonable rule of thumb: Add one `aAssert` statement for every five lines of code.

Summary

A multibillion dollar study—we can't remember what the study was about but remember a promising caveat—produced the admonition that one must master the language of their field to begin to think about it creatively. This is true of programming. One must master the grammar about solutions creatively. And one must also master the framework and tools that support the language.

Writing a simple function or two is easy. Building a whole solution can be mind-bogglingly complex. The strategies in Chapter 7 and the tools discussed in this chapter will help you master the VBE.

In addition to mastering the VBE, Visual Basic, and the VBA, Office, and Excel frameworks, it will be helpful to learn about patterns and refactoring. While these subjects are beyond the scope of this book, they will help you solve complex problems. If you are implementing some very basic down and dirty worksheets then you might not need them, but elevating a few lines of VBA to a productive art form is a whole different matter altogether.

9

UserForms

Rows, columns, and cells represent a simple and utilitarian means of entering information but not a very engaging one. UserForms play the role of a blank slate, a palette, upon which you can create visual metaphors that permit you to engage your users in the process of entering data.

To create the visual metaphors, you add UserForms in the VBE using Insert ⇨ UserForm. The metaphor for adding a custom form is painting and the form is the blank canvas. This metaphor is supported by dragging controls from the Toolbox onto the UserForm. The forms and the controls you add to the forms already define methods, properties, and events that permit you to orchestrate the interaction between the user and the code. The visual appeal of any form is limited only by your imagination, as is the capability and responsiveness.

Displaying a UserForm

Historically, batch applications accepted a few input arguments and then proceeded in a linear fashion to some predetermined and constrained result. The windowing metaphor vastly improved the flexibility of computer programmers by turning mostly linear batch processing into a dynamic array of opportunistic progressions to a litany of possible outcomes. That is, the flexibility of applications has increased in a windowing environment.

Taking advantage of the window metaphor is a matter of adding UserForms to your workbook. You can add as many or as few UserForms as you need. The tempo and order in which they are displayed reflects the guided limitations and opportunities your workbook exposes as a customized Windows application. This orchestration is managed by loading, showing, hiding, and unloading UserForms based on the feedback from the user.

To load a UserForm named UserForm1 (by default) into memory, without making it visible, you use the Load statement:

```
Load UserForm1
```

You can unload UserForm1 from memory using the Unload statement:

```
UnLoad UserForm1
```

To make `UserForm1` visible, use the `Show` method of the `UserForm` object:

```
UserForm1.Show
```

If you show a UserForm that has not been loaded, it will be automatically loaded. You can use the `Hide` method to conceal a UserForm from the screen without removing it from memory call the `UserForm.Hide` method as demonstrated:

```
UserForm1.Hide
```

Figure 9-1 shows a simple UserForm in action. We will develop it over the course of this chapter. It has been designed to allow you to see the current values in cells B2:B6 and to make changes to those values. It is linked directly to the cells in the worksheet, which makes it very easy to set up with a minimum of VBA code.

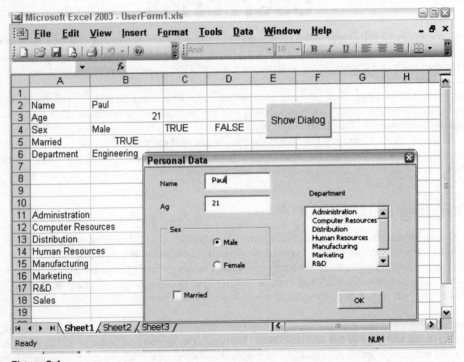

Figure 9-1

The ActiveX command button in the worksheet, with the caption Show Dialog contains the following event procedure:

```
Private Sub CommandButton1_Click()
    PersonalData.Show
End Sub
```

The default behavior of the `Show` method is to display the UserForm as a modal form. This means that the UserForm behaves like a dialog box maintaining the focus whether the form is hidden or unloaded. The user cannot interact with any other part of Excel until the UserForm is dispensed with.

We will discuss modeless UserForms, which do allow the user to perform other tasks while they are visible, later in this chapter.

Creating a UserForm

UserForms are designed in the VBE. Figure 9-2 illustrates what the design time environment of the VBE looked like while we were designing the Personal Data UserForm.

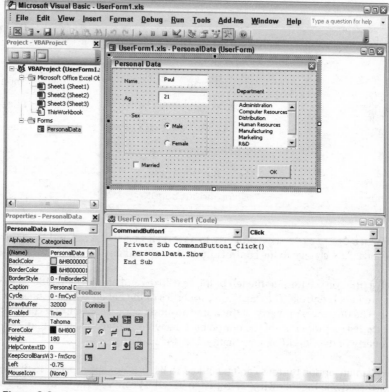

Figure 9-2

The name of the UserForm was changed from the default name `UserForm1` to `PersonalData`. You do this in the first entry, (Name), in the Properties window. The `Caption` property is changed to `Personal Data`. The controls were added from the ToolBox.

There are two TextBox controls at the top of the form for name and age data. There are two option buttons (also known as radio buttons) for Male and Female, which are inside a frame control. To create the buttons in the frame appearance, add the Frame control first and then place the `OptionButtons` in the frame. The `PersonalData UserForm` also contains a CheckBox for indicating marital status, a ListBox for Department, and an *OK* CommandButton.

It is a good idea to give a descriptive name to the controls you will be writing code to interact with. For example, you might name the TextBox for capturing the person's name, Name. If you want to know the class of the control you can introduce some additional information such as the class of the control as a prefix or suffix, resulting in the TextBox used to store the name being called NameTextBox or TextBoxName. NameTextBox reads better; TextBoxName results in all controls of the same type being sorted in the Properties window by class. The most important thing is to be consistent.

We like the controls being ordered by class in the Properties window, so we named the TextBox TextBoxName. To associate some data from the worksheet with the TextBoxName control we changed the ControlSource property to Sheet1!B2. The following table shows the revisions made to each of the controls on the PersonalData UserForm.

Control	Name	ControlSource
TextBox	TextBoxName	Sheet1!B2
TextBox	TextBoxAge	Sheet1!B3
OptionButton	OptionButtonMale	Sheet1!C4
OptionButton	OptionButtonFemale	Sheet1!D4
CheckBox	CheckBoxMarried	Sheet1!B5
ListBox	ListBoxDepartment	
CommandButton	CommandButtonOK	

When you assign a ControlSource property to a worksheet cell, the cell and the control are linked in both directions. Any change to the control affects the cell and any change to the cell affects the control.

The descriptive titles on the form to the left of the TextBoxes and above the ListBox showing the departments are Label controls. The Caption properties of the Labels were changed to Name, Age, and Department. The Caption property of the frame around the OptionButton controls was changed to Sex, and the Caption properties of the option buttons were changed to Male and Female. The Caption property of the CheckBox was changed to Married.

The Male and Female option buttons can't be linked to B4. It is not appropriate to display the values of these controls directly, so the following IF function in cell B4 converts the True or False value in cell C4 to the required Male or Female result:

```
=IF(C4=TRUE,"Male","Female")
```

Although, you only need to set cell C4 to get the required result, you need to link both option buttons to separate cells if you want the buttons to display properly when the UserForm is shown.

The RowSource property of ListBoxDepartment was entered as Sheet1!A11:A18. It is good practice to create names for the linked cells and use those names in the ControlSource, rather than the cell references used here, but this extra step has been omitted to simplify our example.

The following Click event procedure was created for the button in the code module behind the UserForm:

```
Private Sub CommandButtonOK_Click()
   Call Unload(Me)
End Sub
```

Me is a shortcut keyword that refers to the UserForm object containing the code. Me can be used in any class module to refer to the object the class module represents. If you want to access the control values later in your VBA code, you must use the Hide method, which leaves the UserForm in memory. Otherwise, the Unload statement removes the UserForm from memory and the control values are lost. You will see examples that use Hide shortly.

Clicking the [x] button in the top right corner of the UserForm will also dismiss the UserForm. This unloads the UserForm so that it is removed from memory.

Directly Accessing Controls in UserForms

Linking UserForm controls to cells is not always the best way to work. You can gain more flexibility by directly accessing the data in the UserForm. Figure 9-3 shows a revised version of our previous example. We want to display essentially the same UserForm, but we want to store the resulting data as shown. **Sex** will be stored as a single letter code, **M** or **F**. The **Department** name will be stored as a two-character code, as shown in Figure 9-3.

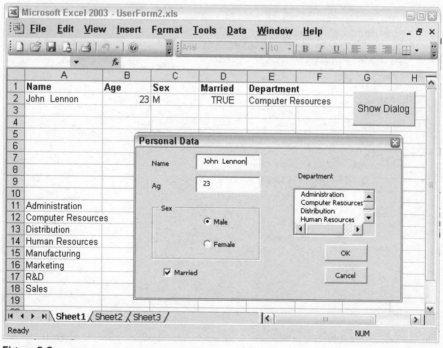

Figure 9-3

We have added a Cancel button to the UserForm so that any changes made to the controls while the UserForm is being shown can be discarded if the user wishes, rather than being automatically applied to the worksheet. The module behind `PersonalData` now contains the following code:

```
Option Explicit

Public Cancelled As Boolean

Private Sub CommandButtonCancel_Click()
  Cancelled = True
  Me.Hide
End Sub

Private Sub CommandButtonOK_Click()
  Cancelled = False
  Me.Hide
End Sub
```

The `Public` variable `Cancelled` will provide a way to detect that the Cancel button has been pressed. If the OK button is pressed, `Cancelled` is assigned the value `False`. If the Cancel button is pressed, `Cancelled` is assigned a value of `True`. Both buttons hide `PersonalData` so that it remains in memory. The following event procedure has also been added to the module behind `PersonalData`:

```
Private Sub UserForm_Initialize()

  Dim Departments As Variant
  Departments = VBA.Array("Administration", _
    "Computer Resources", _
    "Distribution", _
    "Human Resources", _
    "Manufacturing", _
    "Marketing", _
    "R&D", _
    "Sales")

  Dim DepartmentCodes As Variant
  DepartmentCodes = VBA.Array("AD", _
    "CR", _
    "DS", _
    "HR", _
    "MF", _
    "MK", _
    "RD", _
    "SL")

  Dim Data(8, 2) As String
  Dim I As Integer
  For I = 0 To 7
    Data(I, 0) = Departments(I)
  Next I
```

```
      For I = 0 To 7
        Data(I, 1) = DepartmentCodes(I)

      Next

      ListBoxDepartment.List = Data

    End Sub
```

The `UserForm_Initialize` event is triggered when the UserForm is loaded into memory. It does not occur when the form has been hidden and is shown again. It is used here to load ListBox `Department` with two columns of data. The first column contains the department names and the second column the department codes to be displayed.

`Departments` and `DepartmentCodes` are assigned arrays in the usual way using the `Array` function, except that `VBA.Array` has been used to ensure that the arrays are zero-based. `Data` is a dynamic array and the `Dim` statement is used to dimension it to the same number of elements in the `Departments` and `DepartmentCodes` arrays.

The `For...Next` loop assigns the department codes and names to the two columns of `Data`, and then `Data` is used to initialize the ListBox. If you prefer, you can maintain a table of departments and codes in a worksheet range and set the ListBox's `RowSource` property equal to the range, as we saw in the first example in this chapter.

When you have a multicolumn ListBox, you need to specify which column contains the data that will appear in a link cell and be returned in the control's `Value` property. This column is referred to as the bound column. The `BoundColumn` property of ListBox `Department` has been set to 1. This property is one-based, so the bound column is the department codes column. The `ColumnCount` property has been set to 2, as there are two columns of data in the list.

Based on the arbitrary width of the ListBox we can only see the first column in the ListBox. We can use a semicolon delimited list of widths to specify the width of each column of data in the ListBox. For example, hiding the first column and setting the second column width to 80 would be entered in the ColumnWidths field I the Properties window as 0;80. In our implementation we want to show the complete name and hide the codes, so we'll use 93;0 to use the full width of the ListBox for the long names and hide the codes.

The following code has been placed in the module behind `Sheet1`:

```
 1:  Option Explicit
 2:
 3:  Private Sub CommandButton1_Click()
 4:  Dim RangeData As Range
 5:  Dim Data As Variant
 6:
 7:  Set RangeData = Range("Database").Rows(2)
 8:  Data = RangeData.Value
 9:
10:  PersonalData.TextBoxName = Data(1, 1)
11:  PersonalData.TextBoxAge = Data(1, 2)
12:
14:    Case "F"
```

```
15:        PersonalData.OptionButtonFemale.Value = True
16:    Case "M"
17:        PersonalData.OptionButtonMale = True
18:    End Select
19:
20:    PersonalData.CheckBoxMarried.Value = Data(1, 4)
21:
22:    PersonalData.Show
23:    If (Not PersonalData.Cancelled) Then
24:        Data(1, 1) = PersonalData.TextBoxName
25:        Data(1, 2) = PersonalData.TextBoxAge
26:
27:        Select Case True
28:          Case PersonalData.OptionButtonFemale.Value
29:            Data(1, 3) = "F"
30:          Case PersonalData.OptionButtonMale.Value
31:            Data(1, 3) = "M"
32:        End Select
33:
34:        Data(1, 4) = PersonalData.CheckBoxMarried.Value
35:        Data(1, 5) = PersonalData.ListBoxDepartment.Text
36:        RangeData.Value = Data
37:    End If
38:
39:    Call Unload(PersonalData)
40: End Sub
```

Due to the length of the listing, line numbers were added for reference. Remember to remove the line numbers when you add this code to VBE.

Line 4 declares a range and line 5 declares a variant. Line 7 reads the range named Database and selects row 2 from this range, assigning the value of the range to the variant Data. Basically, we have copied the values of Sheet1 to a local array. Lines 10 and 11 copy the name and age into the appropriate controls on the form. The Select Case statement on lines 13 through 18 discerns whether the current sheet's data refers to a female or male, setting the appropriate option button. We only need to change one option button because the frame causes the buttons to be treated as a group, permitting only one button to be checked at a time. Line 20 sets the marital status Checkbox's state.

When we are ready to show the PersonalData form on line 22 we have copied all of the values from the worksheet into the UserForm, and on line 22 we show the form. If the user clicks OK on the PersonalData UserForm then the test on line 23 passes and the values are copied from the PersonalData UserForm back to the fields on the worksheet. Finally, the UserForm is unloaded. By disconnecting the worksheet and the form we have provided the user with an opportunity to cancel changes.

Stopping the Close Button

One problem with the above code is that, if the user clicks the [x] button, which is the Close button at the top right of PersonalData, the event procedure does not exit. Instead, it transfers any changes back to the worksheet. This is because the default value for Cancelled is False. Normally, clicking the [x] button would also unload the form and the code would fail when it tries to access the controls on the form.

The following example uses the UserForm's `QueryClose` event to prevent the form from closing when the user clicks the [x] close button. You can use the `QueryClose` event of the `UserForm` object to discover what is closing the UserForm and cancel the event, if necessary. Adding the following code to the `PersonalData` UserForm blocks the Close button exit:

```
Private Sub UserForm_QueryClose(Cancel As Integer, CloseMode As Integer)
    If CloseMode = vbFormControlMenu Then
            Cancel = True
    Beep
    End If
End Sub
```

The `QueryClose` event can be triggered in four ways. You can determine what caused the event by using the following intrinsic constants to test the `CloseMode` parameter:

Constant	Value	Reason for the event
VbFormControlMenu	0	The user clicked the [x] button in the Control menu on the UserForm
VbFormCode	1	The `Unload` statement was used to remove the UserForm from memory
VbAppWindows	2	Windows is shutting down
VbAppTaskManager	3	The application is being closed by the Windows Task Manager

Maintaining a Data List

The code we have developed can now be extended to maintain a datalist without too much extra effort. However, we will take a different approach to the last example. This time we will build all the code into `PersonalData`, apart from the code behind the command button in the worksheet that shows the UserForm. The code behind this button now becomes the following:

```
Private Sub CommandButton1_Click()
    PersonalData.Show
End Sub
```

It is really much easier to maintain a datalist in a proper database application, such as Microsoft Access, but it can be done in Excel without too much trouble if your requirements are fairly simple.

If we are going to manage more than one row of data, we need to be able to add new rows, delete existing rows, and navigate through the rows. `PersonalData` needs some extra controls, as shown in Figure 9-4.

We added four buttons and replaced the ListBox with a ComboBox. The button labeled `Previous Record` will be used to navigate to a previous row in the worksheet. The button labeled `Next Record` will be used to navigate to the next record in worksheet. `New Record` will be used to add a row to the worksheet, and `Delete Record` will be used to remove a row from the worksheet. The ComboBox was used to demonstrate an alternate way to permit selections.

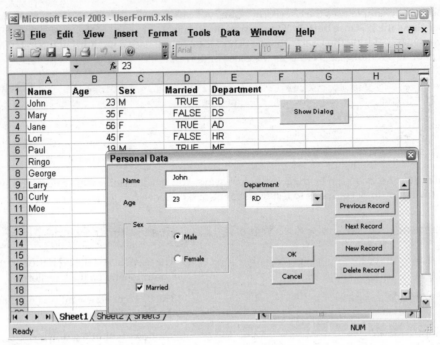

Figure 9-4

The code in `PersonalData` is discussed next. It is important to note first that the following module-level variables have been declared at the top of the PersonalData UserForm code module:

```
Dim aRangeData As Range
Dim Data As Variant
```

These variables are used in exactly the same way as they were used in the previous example, except that the row referred to can vary. The object variable `RangeData` is always set to the current row of data in the named range `Database`, which currently refers to A1:E11 in the preceding worksheet. `Data` always holds the values from `RangeData` as a VBA array.

The code from the command button event procedure in our previous example has been converted to two utility procedures that reside in `PersonalData`'s code module:

```
Private Sub LoadRecord()
   'Copy values in RangeData from worksheet to vaData array
   Data = RangeData.Value
   'Assign array values to Personal controls
   TextBoxName.Value = Data(1, 1)
   TextBoxAge.Value = Data(1, 2)

   Select Case Data(1, 3)
      Case "F"
         OptionButtonFemale.Value = True
      Case "M"
         OptionButtonMale.Value = True
   End Select
```

```
      CheckBoxMarried.Value = Data(1, 4)

      ComboBoxDepartment.Value = Data(1, 5)

  End Sub

  Private Sub SaveRecord()
      'Copy values from Personal controls to Data array
      Data(1, 1) = TextBoxName.Value
      Data(1, 2) = TextBoxAge.Value

      Select Case True
         Case OptionButtonFemale.Value
            Data(1, 3) = "F"
         Case OptionButtonMale.Value
            Data(1, 3) = "M"
      End Select

      Data(1, 4) = CheckBoxMarried.Value
      Data(1, 5) = ComboBoxDepartment.Value

      'Assign Data array values to current record in Database
      RangeData.Value = Data
  End Sub
```

As the code is in the `PersonalData` module, there is no need to refer to `PersonalData` when referring to a control, so all controls are directly addressed in the code.

`LoadRecord` and `SaveRecord` are the only procedures that are tailored to the datalist structure and the controls. As long as the datalist has the name `Database`, none of the other code in `PersonalData` needs to change if we decide to add more fields to the data list or remove fields. It also means that we can readily apply the same code to a completely different datalist. All we have to do is redesign the UserForm controls and update `LoadRecord` and `SaveRecord`.

The key navigation device in `PersonalData` is the scroll bar, which has been named `Navigator`. It is used by the other buttons when a change of record is required, as well as being available to the user directly. The `Value` property of `Navigator` corresponds to the row number in the range named `Database`.

The minimum value of `Navigator` is fixed permanently at two, as the first record is the second row in `Database`, so you need to set the `Min` property of the scroll bar in the Properties window. The maximum value is altered as needed by the other event procedures in `PersonalData` so that it always corresponds to the last row in `Database`:

```
  Private Sub Navigator_Change()
     'When Scrollbar value changes, save current record and load
     'record number corresponding to scroll bar value
     Call SaveRecord
     Set RangeData = Range("Database").Rows(Navigator.Value)
     Call LoadRecord
  End Sub
```

When the user changes the `Navigator.Value` property (or when it is changed by other event procedures) the `Change` event fires and saves the current record in `PersonalData`, redefines `RangeData` to be the row in `Database` corresponding to the new value of `Navigator.Value`, and loads the data from that row into `PersonalData`.

The `UserForm_Initialize` event procedure has been updated from the previous exercise to set the correct starting values for `sbNavigator`:

```
Private Sub UserForm_Initialize()
    'Sets up Department list values
    'and loads first record in Database
    Dim DepartmentCode As Variant
    Dim DepartmentList() As String
    Dim I As Integer

    DepartmentCode = VBA.Array("AD", _
        "CR", _
        "DS", _
        "HR", _
        "MF", _
        "MK", _
        "RD", _
        "SL", _
        "NA")

    ReDim DepartmentList(0 To UBound(DepartmentCode))

    For I = 0 To UBound(DepartmentCode)
        DepartmentList(I) = DepartmentCode(I)
    Next I

    ComboBoxDepartment.List = DepartmentList

    'Load 1st record in Database and initialize scroll bar
    With Range("Database")
        Set RangeData = .Rows(2)
        Call LoadRecord
        Navigator.Value = 2
        Navigator.Max = .Rows.Count
    End With
End Sub
```

After initializing the CheckBoxDepartment.List property, the code initializes `RangeData` to refer to the second row of `Database`, row two being the first row of data under the field names on row one, and loads the data from that row into `PersonalData`. It then initializes the `Value` property of `Navigator` to two and sets the `Max` property of `Navigator` to the number of rows in `Database`. If the user changes the scroll bar, they can navigate to any row from row two through to the last row in `Database`.

The `Click` event procedure for the button labeled Next Record is as follows:

```
Private Sub CommandButton2_Click()
    With Range("Database")
        If RangeData.Row < .Rows(.Rows.Count).Row Then
```

```
              'Load next record only if not on last record
            Navigator.Value = Navigator.Value + 1
              'Note: Setting Navigator.Value runs its Change event procedure
        End If
    End With
End Sub
```

The If test checks that the current row number in Database is less than the last row number in Database to ensure that we don't try to go beyond the data. If there is room to move, the value of Navigator is increased by one. This change triggers the Change event procedure for Navigator, which saves the current data, resets RangeData, and loads the next row's data.

The code for the button labeled Previous Record is similar to the behavior for the Next Button record (the sample shows the code without the With construct for variety):

```
Private Sub CommandButton1_Click()
  If RangeData.Row > Range("Database").Rows(2).Row Then
    'Load previous record if not on first record
    Navigator.Value = Navigator.Value - 1
    'Note: Setting Navigator.Value runs its Change event procedure
  End If
End Sub
```

The check ensures that we don't try to move to row numbers lower than the second row in Database. The if conditional checks comparing the row to the extent of the range could have been implemented using the Value, Max, and Min properties of scrollbar named Navigator, but the technique used demonstrates how to determine the row number of the last row in a named range, which is a technique that it is very useful to know. It is important to carry out these checks as trying to set the Navigator.Value property outside the Min to Max range causes a runtime error.

The code for the Delete Record button is as follows:

```
Private Sub CommandButton4_Click()
    'Deletes current record in PersonalData
    If Range("Database").Rows.Count = 2 Then
       'Don't delete if only one record left
       MsgBox "You cannot delete every record", vbCritical
       Exit Sub
    ElseIf RangeData.Row = Range("Database").Rows(2).Row Then
       'If on 1st record, move down one record and delete 1st record
       'shifting the rows below up to fill the gap
       Set RangeData = RangeData.Offset(1)
       RangeData.Offset(-1).Delete shift:=xlUp
       Call LoadRecord
    Else
       'If on other than 1st record, move to previous record before delete
       Navigator.Value = Navigator.Value - 1
       'Note: Setting sbNavigator.Value runs its Change event procedure
       RangeData.Offset(1).Delete shift:=xlUp
    End If
    Navigator.Max = Navigator.Max - 1
End Sub
```

This procedure carries out the following actions:

❑ It aborts if you try to delete the last remaining record in Database.

❑ If you delete the first record, RangeData field is assigned a reference to the second record. Navigator.Value is not reset, as row 2 becomes row 1, once the original row 1 is deleted. LoadRecord is called to load the data in RangeData into the UserForm.

❑ If you delete a record that is not the first one, Navigator.Value is reduced by one. This causes the previous record to be loaded into the UserForm.

❑ At the end, the count of the number of rows in Database held in Navigator.Max, is decreased by 1.

The code for the button labeled New Record is shown next:

```
Private Sub CommandButton3_Click()
    'Add new record at bottom of database
    Dim RowCount As Integer

    With Range("Database")
        'Add extra row to name Database
        RowCount = .Rows.Count + 1
        .Resize(RowCount).Name = "Database"
        Navigator.Max = iRowCount
        Navigator.Value = iRowCount
        'Note: Setting Navigator.Value runs its Change event procedure
    End With

    'Set default values
    OptionButtonMale.Value = True

    CheckBoxMarried = False
    CheckBoxDepartment.Value = "NA"
End Sub
```

This event procedure defines RowCount to be one higher than the current number of rows in Database. It then generates a reference to a range with one more row than Database and redefines the name Database to refer to the larger range. It then assigns RowCount to both the Max property of Navigator and the Value property of Navigator. Setting the Value property fires the Change event procedure for Navigator, which makes the new empty row the current row and loads the empty values into PersonalData. Default values are then applied to some of the PersonalData controls.

The only remaining code in PersonalData is for the code for the OK button and Cancel button click events as demonstrated:

```
Private Sub CommandButtonCancel_Click()
    Cancelled = True
    Me.Hide
End Sub

Private Sub CommandButtonOK_Click()
    Cancelled = False
```

```
    SaveRecord
    Me.Hide
End Sub
```

Both buttons unload `PersonalData`. Only the OK button saves any changes to the current record in the UserForm.

Modeless UserForms

Excel 2000, 2002, and 2003 provide the ability to show modeless UserForms. The modal UserForms that we have dealt with so far do not allow the user to change the focus away from the UserForm while it is being displayed. You cannot activate a worksheet, menu, or toolbar, for example, until the UserForm has been hidden or unloaded from memory. If you have a procedure that uses the `Show` method to display a modal UserForm, that procedure cannot execute the code that follows the `Show` method until the UserForm is hidden or unloaded.

A modeless UserForm does allow the user to activate worksheets, menus, and toolbars. It floats in the foreground until it is hidden or unloaded. The procedure that uses the `Show` method to display a modeless UserForm will immediately continue to execute the code that follows the `Show` method. `PersonalData`, from our previous example that maintains a data list, can easily be displayed modeless. All you need to do is change the code that displays it as follows:

```
Private Sub CommandButton1_Click()
    Call PersonalData(vbModeless)
End Sub
```

When the UserForm is modeless, you can carry on with other work while it is visible. You can even copy and paste data from TextBoxes on the UserForm to worksheet cells.

It is important to note that our recent example does not bind the worksheet to the form; the data is copied from worksheet top form. Thus, if we show PersonalData modeless and change data in the worksheet, the data in the form will not automatically be reflected to show the changed data. As defined, our example would necessitate us defining a scheme for manually notifying the UserForm that the worksheet had changed. Can you think of a way that we might update the PersonalData UserForm if the worksheet changed? (Here is a hint: Think about the behavior of the Worksheet `Change` event.)

Summary

In this chapter, we demonstrated how to create and use modal and modeless forms. The examples demonstrated how to refer to the data by using ranges in a worksheet or by copying data from those ranges. Several event handlers demonstrated how to add and delete data from a spreadsheet, treating the spreadsheet like a database.

In all candor, a spreadsheet is great for managing data and numbers in cells but is a weaker database. The difficulty is that database technology has evolved greatly in the last decade or so, and validation, constraints, complex relationships, indexing, search capabilities, and much more are things supported by a database. If you really need data management capabilities then we encourage you to look at Microsoft's Access. There are other database providers, but the VBA you learned in Excel works in Access.

Additionally, Excel and Access can talk to each other via the VBA language. So, consider Access for managing non-numerical data and Excel for number crunching. You know if you need to you can create forms and manage things like names and addresses in Excel, but Access will do a better job with less effort on your part. For raw number crunching, Excel is superlative.

The beauty of Microsoft Office is that the applications in Office represent some of the most powerful and complete components in each of their respective classes. In addition, they all talk to each other through a common language, VBA. If Excel is understood to be a powerful number crunching engine that is also a big component then you know that Excel can be used to build stand-alone solutions replete with forms or as a powerful math engine for enterprise solutions.

10

Adding Controls

As we have already discussed in Chapter 1, you can add two different types of controls to Excel worksheets. You can use ActiveX controls, found on the Control Toolbox toolbar, or the controls from the Forms toolbar. The Forms toolbar is an Excel 5 and Excel 95 feature, and provided controls for the dialog sheets used in those versions, as well as controls that can be embedded in a worksheet or chart. Dialog sheets have been superseded by UserForms since the release of Excel 97, and UserForms utilize the ActiveX controls.

The Toolbars

The Forms toolbar controls, shown in Figure 10-1, and dialog sheets are still supported in Excel, however. The Forms toolbar controls even have some advantages over the ActiveX controls.

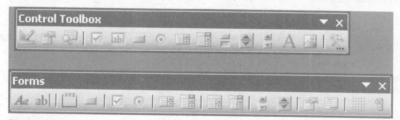

Figure 10-1

The Forms controls are less complex than the ActiveX controls and, if you want to place controls on a chart sheet, you can only use the Forms toolbar controls. However, each Forms toolbar control can only respond to a single event. In most cases, that event is the Click event—the edit box is an exception, responding to the Change event.

If you want to create controls and define their event procedures in your VBA code, as opposed to creating them manually, the Forms toolbar controls are easier to work with. A big advantage over an ActiveX control is that the event procedure for a Forms toolbar control can be placed in a standard module, can have any valid VBA procedure name, and can be created when you write the code for the application, before the control is created.

You can create the control programmatically, when it is needed, and assign the procedure name to the `OnAction` property of the control. You can even assign the same procedure to more than one control. On the other hand, ActiveX event procedures must be placed in the class module behind the worksheet or UserForm in which they are embedded, and must have a procedure name that corresponds with the name of the control and the name of the event. For example, the click event procedure for a control named `Optionbutton1` must be as follows:

```
Sub OptionButton1_Click()
```

If you try to create an event procedure for an ActiveX control before the control exists, and you try to reference that control in your code, you will get compiler errors, so you have to create the event procedure programmatically. This is not an easy task, as you will see next. In addition, see Chapter 14 for an example of adding an event procedure programmatically to a UserForm control.

On the other hand, a procedure that is executed by a Forms toolbar control does not need to have a special name and can use the `Caller` property of the `Application` object to obtain a reference to the control that executes it. The control name does not need to be included in the name of the procedure or in references to the control, as you will see later in this chapter.

ActiveX Controls

Figure 10-2 shows four types of ActiveX controls embedded in the worksheet (`Controls.xls` is available for download from `http://www.wrox.com`). We will implement the controls as follows: the scrollbar in cells C3:F3 will set the value in cell B3; the spin button in cell C4 will increment the growth percentage in cell B4; the check box in cell B5 will increase the tax rate in cell B16 from 30 % to 33%, if it is checked, and the option buttons in column I will change the cost factor in cell B15, and also change the maximum and minimum values for the scrollbar.

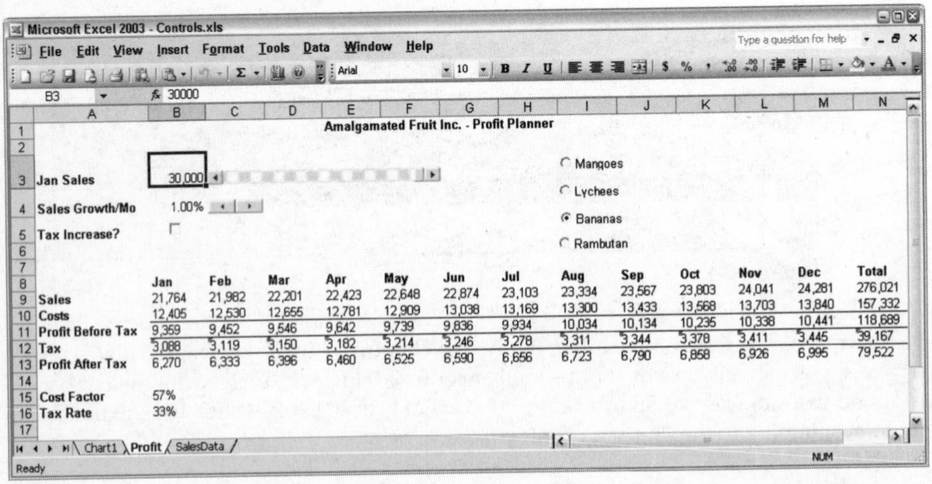

Figure 10-2

An ActiveX control can be linked to a worksheet cell, using its `LinkedCell` property, so that the cell always displays the `Value` property of the control. None of the ActiveX controls shown in Figure 10-2 use a link cell, although the scrollbar could have been linked because its value is displayed in B3. Each control uses an event procedure to make its updates. This gives you far more flexibility than a simple cell link and removes the need to dedicate a worksheet cell to the task.

Scrollbar Control

The scrollbar uses the `Change` event and the `Scroll` event to assign the `Value` property of the scrollbar to cell B3. The maximum and minimum values of the scrollbar are set by the option buttons (we'll discuss that later):

```
Private Sub ScrollBar1_Change()
   Range("B3").Value = ScrollBar1.Value
End Sub

Private Sub ScrollBar1_Scroll()
   ScrollBar1_Change
End Sub
```

The `Change` event procedure is triggered when the scrollbar value is changed by clicking the scroll arrows, by clicking above or below the scroll box (or to the left or right, if it is aligned horizontally), or by dragging the scroll box. However, there is a small glitch that occurs immediately after you change the option buttons. Dragging the scroll box does not trigger the `Change` event on the first attempt. Utilizing the `Scroll` event procedure solves this problem.

The `Scroll` event causes continuous updating as you drag the scroll bar, so that you can see what figure you are producing as you drag, rather than after you have released the scroll bar. It might not be practical to use the `Scroll` event procedure in a very large worksheet in auto-recalculation mode because of the large number of recalculations it causes.

In the above implementation, we applied the `Scroll` event in terms of the `Change` event (by calling the change event like any other method). This leads to convergent code; that is, all like behavior runs the same lines of code. An even better revision would be to implement the behavior in terms of a named method and call that named method. This makes your code more readable, adding clarity as demonstrated:

```
Private Sub ScrollBar1_Change()

  Call SetRangeValue(Range("B3"), ScrollBar1.Value)
End Sub

Private Sub ScrollBar1_Scroll()
  Call SetRangeValue(Range("B3"), ScrollBar1.Value)
End Sub

Private Sub SetRangeValue(ByVal R As Range, ByVal Value As Double)
   R.Value = Value
End Sub
```

The code adds a modest amount of overhead through the indirect call to `SetRangeValue`, but the clarity is increased and any change to `SetRangeValue` will be reflected by all code that uses it. It is important to keep in mind that the motivation for writing code this way is to directly redress the greatest cost, that of ownership, not CPU cycles.

Spin Button Control

The spin button control uses the SpinDown and SpinUp events to decrease and increase the value in cell B4. We'll use the same technique as the one at the end of the preceding section to implement the SpinButton's behavior:

```
' SetRangeValue is used from the previous section
Private Property Get SpinRange()
  Set SpinRange = Range("B4")
End Property

Private Sub SpinButton1_SpinDown()
  Call SetRangeValue(SpinRange, WorksheetFunction.Max(0, SpinRange.Value -
0.0005))
End Sub

Private Sub SpinButton1_SpinUp()
  Call SetRangeValue(SpinRange, WorksheetFunction.Min(0.01,
SpinRange.Value + 0.0005))
End Sub
```

The ReadOnly property SpinRange was created to ensure that all methods working with the SpinButton use the same range. The SpinUp and SpinDown events are implemented by reusing the SetRangeValue method from the previous section, and the WorksheetFunction.Max and WorksheetFunction.Min are used respectively to increase and decrease the range's value by 0.0005, respectively. Max ensures the value does not shrink to less than 0 and the Min function is used to ensure the value does not grow to be more than 1.

CheckBox Control

The CheckBox.Value property is equal to True when checked and False when unchecked. The following Click event procedure is implemented to toggle the value of cell B16 to 33 % checked and 30% when unchecked:

```
Private Sub CheckBox1_Click()
  If CheckBox1.Value Then
    Range("B16").Value = 0.33
  Else
    Range("B16").Value = 0.3
  End If
End Sub
```

A second clever implementation exists. You might see code like the following if it is implemented by old C programmers. It is helpful to be able to interpret code like the following but it obfuscates understanding and should be avoided for that reason in new code:

```
Private Sub CheckBox1_Click()
   ' Clever implementation
   Range("B16").Value = Array(0.3, 0.33)(Abs(CheckBox1.Value))
End Sub
```

How would you modify the first version to make the `Click` event self-documenting? (Hint: Create a named method that states what is happening; that is, the value of Range("B16") is being toggled.)

Option Button Controls

`Click` is a common event. The `OptionButton` employs the `click` event in much the same way that the CheckBox does, in response to a left mouse button press and release (and the spacebar has the same effect when the `OptionButton` has the focus). For our implementation, the `OptionButton.Click` events were each implemented to call a worker method named `SetOption`. Each of the `OptionButton Click` events are implemented as demonstrated for `OptionButton1`:

```
Private Sub OptionButton1_Click()
   Call SetOptions()
End Sub
```

The processing for all the buttons is carried out in the following procedure, which is in the class module behind the `Profit` worksheet that is holding the `Click` events for the `OptionButtons`:

```
Private Sub SetOptions()

   Select Case True
      Case OptionButton1.Value
        Call SetCostFactor(0.63)
        Call SetScrollMinMax(50000, 150000)
      Case OptionButton2.Value
        Call SetCostFactor(0.74)
        Call SetScrollMinMax(25000, 75000)
      Case OptionButton3.Value
        Call SetCostFactor(0.57)
        Call SetScrollMinMax(10000, 30000)
      Case OptionButton4.Value
        Call SetCostFactor(0.65)
        Call SetScrollMinMax(15000, 30000)
   End Select

End Sub

Private Property Get CostFactorRange()
  Set CostFactorRange = Range("B15")
End Property

Private Sub SetCostFactor(ByVal CostFactor As Double)
   Call SetRangeValue(CostFactorRange, CostFactor)
End Sub

Private Sub SetScrollMinMax(ByVal Min As Long, ByVal Max As Long)
   ScrollBar1.Min = Min
   ScrollBar1.Max = Max
   ScrollBar1.Value = Max
End Sub
```

(SetRangeValue is borrowed from earlier in the chapter.) The Select Case structure is used here in an unusual way. Normally, you use a variable reference in the first line of a Select Case and use comparison values in the Case statements. Here, we have used the value True in the Select Case and referenced the option button Value property in the Case statements. This provides a nice structure for processing a set of option buttons where you know that only one can have a True value.

Only one option button can be selected and have a value of True in the preceding worksheet because they all belong to the same group. As you add option buttons to a worksheet, the GroupName property of the button is set to the name of the worksheet – Profit, in this case. If you want two sets of unrelated option buttons, you need to assign a different GroupName to the each successive set on the same worksheet.

Forms Toolbar Controls

Figure 10-3 shows a Forms toolbar control that is being used to select a product name to be entered in column D. The control appears over any cell in column D that you double-click. When you select the product, the product name is entered in the cell "behind" the control, the price of the product is entered in column F on the same row, and the control disappears.

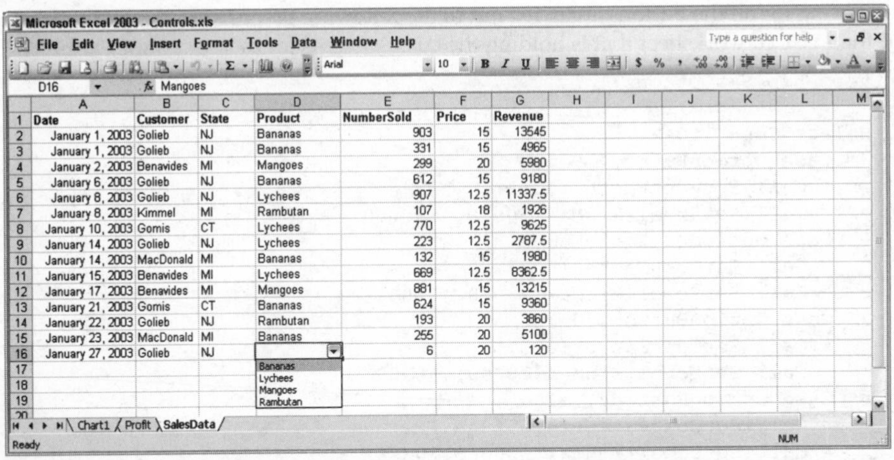

Figure 10-3

If you hover your cursor over the Forms toolbar button that creates the control in the previous figure, the ScreenTip that pops up describes this control as a Combo Box. However, in the Excel Object Model, it is called a DropDown object.

> The **DropDown** object is a hidden member of the Excel object model in Excel 97 and later versions. You will not find any Help screens for this object and it will not normally appear in the Object Browser. You can make it visible in the Object Browser if you right-click in the Object Browser window and select Show Hidden Members from the shortcut menu. You can learn a lot about the Forms toolbar controls by using the Macro Recorder and the Object Browser, but you will need to have access to Excel 5 or Excel 95 to get full documentation on them.

The drop-down control is created by a procedure called from the following `BeforeDoubleClick` event procedure in the `SalesData` sheet, which has the programmatic name `Sheet2`:

```
Option Explicit

Private Sub Worksheet_BeforeDoubleClick(ByVal Target As Range, _
  Cancel As Boolean)

  If (IsColumnSelected(Target, "D")) Then
    Call AddDropDown(Target)
    Cancel = True
  End If

End Sub

Private Function IsColumnSelected(ByVal Target As Range, _
  ByVal ColumnName As String) As Boolean

  IsColumnSelected = _
    (Intersect(Target, Columns(ColumnName)) Is Nothing = False)

End Function
```

The event procedure checks that `Target` (the cell that was double-clicked) is in column D. If so, it then runs the `AddDropDown` procedure, passing `Target` as an input argument, and cancels the double-click event.

The following two procedures are in a standard module:

```
Option Explicit

Public Sub AddDropDown(Target As Range)
  Dim Control As DropDown
  Dim Products As Variant
  Dim I As Integer

  Products = Array("Bananas", "Lychees", "Mangoes", "Rambutan")
  Set Control = SalesData.DropDowns.Add( _
    Target.Left, Target.Top, Target.Width, Target.Height)

  Control.OnAction = "EnterProductInformation"

  For I = LBound(Products) To UBound(Products)
    Call Control.AddItem(Products(I))
  Next I
End Sub

Private Sub EnterProductInformation()
  Dim Prices As Variant
  Prices = Array(15, 12.5, 20, 18)

  With SalesData.DropDowns(Application.Caller)
    .TopLeftCell.Value = .List(.ListIndex)
    .TopLeftCell.Offset(0, 2).Value = _
```

```
            Prices(.ListIndex + LBound(Prices) - 1)
        .Delete
    End With
End Sub
```

The `AddDropDown` procedure is not declared `Private`, as it would not then be possible to call it from the `SalesData` object. This would normally be a problem if you wanted to prevent users from seeing the procedure in the Tools ⇨ Macro ⇨ Macros dialog box. However, because it has an input argument, it will not be shown in the dialog box, anyway. Also, it does not matter whether `AddDropDown` is placed in the `SalesData` module or a standard module. It will operate in either location.

`AddDropDown` uses the `Add` method of the `DropDowns` collection to create a new drop-down. It aligns the new control exactly with `Target`, giving it the same `Left`, `Top`, `Width`, and `Height` properties as the cell. `AddDropDown` defines the `DropDown.OnAction` property of the drop-down to be the `EnterProductInformation` procedure. This means that `EnterProductInformation` will be run when an item is chosen from the drop-down. The `For...Next` loop uses the `AddItem` method of the drop-down to place the list of items in `Products` into the drop-down list.

`EnterProductInformation` has been declared `Private` to prevent its appearance in the Tools ⇨ Macro ⇨ Macros dialog box. Although it is private, the drop-down can access it. `EnterProductInformation` could have been placed in the `SalesData` module, but the `OnAction` property of the drop-down would have to be assigned "`SalesData.EnterProductInformation`".

`EnterProductInformation` loads `Prices` with the prices corresponding to the products. It then uses `Application.Caller` to return the name of the drop-down control that called the `OnAction` procedure. It uses this name as an index into the `DropDowns` collection on SalesData to get a reference to the `DropDown` object itself. In the `With...End With` construction, `EnterProdInfo` uses the `ListIndex` property of the drop-down to get the index number of the item chosen in the drop-down list.

You cannot directly access the name of the chosen item in a `DropDown` object, unlike a `ComboBox` object that returns the name in its `Value` property. The `Value` property of a drop-down is the same as the `ListIndex`, which returns the numeric position of the item in the list. To get the item name from a drop-down, you use the `ListIndex` property as an one-based index to the `List` property of the drop-down. The `List` property returns an array of all the items in the list.

The `TopLeftCell` property of the `DropDown` object returns a reference to the `Range` object under the top-left corner of the `DropDown` object. `EnterProductInformation` assigns the item chosen in the list to the `Value` property of this `Range` object. It then assigns the price of the product to the `Range` object that is offset two columns to the right of the `TopLeftCell` `Range` object.

`EnterProductInformation` also uses the `ListIndex` property of the drop-down as an index into the `Prices` array. The problem with this is that the drop-down list is always one-based, while the `Array` function list depends on the `Option Base` statement in the declarations section of the module. `LBound(Prices)` −1 is used to reduce the `ListIndex` value by one if `Option Base 0` is in effect or by zero if `Option Base 1` is in effect.

You can use the following code to ensure that the resulting array is zero-based under Option-Base-1 in Excel 97 and above:

```
    Prices = VBA.Array(15, 12.5, 20, 18)
```

This technique does not work in Excel 5 and Excel 95 where the above expression is influenced by the `Option Base` statement.

Dynamic ActiveX Controls

As previously stated, it is more difficult to program the ActiveX controls than the Forms toolbar controls. At the same time, the ActiveX controls are more powerful, so it is a good idea to know how to program them. We will see how to construct a combo box that behaves in a similar way to the combo box in the previous example. Just to be different, we will use the `BeforeRightClick` event to trigger the appearance of a combo box in the D column of the `SalesData` worksheet as follows:

```
Private Const ControlName As String = "Combo"

Private Sub Worksheet_BeforeRightClick( _
  ByVal Target As Range, Cancel As Boolean)

  Dim Ole As OLEObject
  Dim Control As MSForms.ComboBox
  Dim Line As Long
  Dim CodeModule As Object

  If Not IsColumnSelected(ActiveCell, "D") Then Exit Sub

  ' Disable screen updating while we add the controls
  Application.ScreenUpdating = False

  'Determine if the combo box should be built
  On Error Resume Next

  Set Ole = Me.OLEObjects(ControlName)
  If Ole Is Nothing = False Then
    GoTo Finish
  End If

  On Error GoTo 0

  'Add the combo box to the active cell
  Set Ole = Me.OLEObjects.Add( _
    ClassType:="Forms.ComboBox.1", Link:=False, _
    DisplayAsIcon:=False, Left:=ActiveCell.Left, Top:=ActiveCell.Top, _
    Width:=ActiveCell.Width, Height:=ActiveCell.Height)

  Ole.Name = ControlName
  Set Control = Ole.Object
  Control.Name = ControlName

  Call Control.AddItem("Bananas")
  Call Control.AddItem("Lychees")
  Call Control.AddItem("Mangoes")
  Call Control.AddItem("Rambutan")

  'Build the event procedure for the combo box click event
```

```
    Set CodeModule = _
        ThisWorkbook.VBProject.VBComponents(CodeName).CodeModule

    Line = CodeModule.CreateEventProc("Click", ControlName)
    Call CodeModule.ReplaceLine(Line + 1, " ProcessComboClick")

    'Make sure the Excel window is active
    Application.Visible = False
    Application.Visible = True

  Finish:
    Cancel = True
    Application.ScreenUpdating = True

  End Sub
```

We first check to see that the event took place in the D column. We also check to make sure that there is no existing combo box in the worksheet, which would mean that the user has created a combo box but has not yet selected an item from it. This did not matter in our previous example where the combo boxes were independent, even though they used the same OnAction code. Our ActiveX controls can't share the single Click event procedure we are going to create, so we need to ensure that we don't already have a control in the worksheet.

We are going to use the name Combo for our ActiveX control. The quickest way to determine if there is already a control called Combo is to create an object variable referring to it. If this attempt fails, then we know that the control does not exist. The error recovery code is used to ensure that the macro does not display an error message and stop running if the control does not exist. It would be friendlier to display an explanatory message before exiting the sub, but that is not the main point of this exercise. Setting Cancel to True suppresses the normal right-click menu from appearing.

If all is well, we add a new combo box in the active cell. You need to know that an ActiveX object is not added directly onto a worksheet. It is contained in an OLEObject object, in the same way that a chart embedded in a worksheet is contained in a ChartObject object, as you will see in Chapter 24. The return value from the Add method of the OLEObjects collection is assigned to Ole to make it easy to refer to the OLEObject object later. The Name property of the OleObject is changed to Combo to make it easy to identify later.

We then create an object variable, Control, referring to the ComboBox object contained in the OleObject, which is returned by the Object property of the OLEObject. The next line of code assigns the name Combo to the ComboBox object. This is not necessary in Excel 2000, 2002, and 2003. When you assign a name to the OLEObject, it is also automatically assigned to the embedded object in these versions. This is not the case in Excel 97, so the name needs to be explicitly assigned.

Next, we create the Click event procedure code for the combo box. You can't create the event procedure in advance. It will cause compile errors if the ActiveX control it refers to does not exist. The methodology for creating event procedures programmatically is explained in detail in Chapter 14, so check that chapter for full details.

CodeModule is assigned a reference to the class module behind the worksheet and the CreatEventProc method of the code module is used to enter the first and last lines of the

`Combo_Click` event procedure, with a blank line in between. This method returns the line number of the first line of the procedure, which is assigned to `Line`. The `ReplaceLine` method replaces the blank second line of the procedure with a call to a sub procedure named `ProcessComboClick`, which is listed in the following. The code for `ProcessComboClick` already exists in the worksheet's code module.

Unfortunately, when you add code to a code module as we have done, the code module is activated and the user could be left staring at a screen full of code. By setting the Excel application window's `Visible` property to `False` and then `True`, we make sure that the Excel window is active at the end of the procedure. There will still be some screen flicker, even though screen updating was suppressed at the start of the macro. It is possible to suppress this flicker by calls to the Windows API (discussed in Chapter 16).

The `Click` event procedure code that is created by the above code looks like the following:

```
Private Sub Combo_Click()
   ProcessComboClick
End Sub
```

When the user selects a value in the combo box, the `Click` event procedure executes and, in turn, executes `ProcessComboClick`. The code for `ProcessComboClick`, which is a permanent procedure in the worksheet's code module, contains the following:

```
Private Sub ProcessComboClick()
   Dim Line As Long
   Dim CodeModule As Object

   'Enter the chosen value
   With OLEObjects(ControlName)
      .TopLeftCell.Value = .Object.Value
      .Delete
   End With

   'Delete the combo box click event procedure
   Set CodeModule = _
      ThisWorkbook.VBProject.VBComponents(CodeName).CodeModule

   Line = CodeModule.ProcStartLine("Combo_Click", 0)
   Call CodeModule.DeleteLines(Line, 4)

End Sub
```

The combo box is the object contained in the `OLEObject` named `Combo`. The previous code enters the selected value from the combo box into the cell underneath the combo box and then deletes the `OLEObject` and its contents.

The code then deletes the event procedure. `CodeModule` is assigned a reference to the worksheet's code module. The `ProcStartLine` method returns the line number of the blank line just before the `Combo_Click` event procedure. The `Delete` method removes four lines, including the blank line.

As you can see, dynamically coding an ActiveX control requires a bit of effort. It is simpler to use a Forms toolbar control if you don't really need the extra power of an ActiveX control.

Controls on Charts

Figure 10-4 shows a chart that contains a button to remove or add the profit series from the chart, which is based on the Profit Planner figures of the Profit sheet. The control is a Forms toolbar Button object belonging to the Buttons collection (remember ActiveX controls cannot be used in charts).

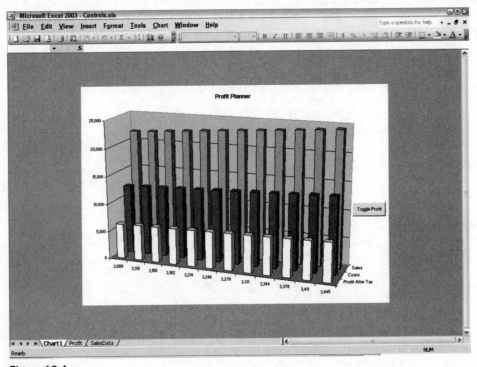

Figure 10-4

The code assigned to the OnAction property of the Button object is as follows:

```
Sub Button1_Click()
    With ActiveChart
        If .SeriesCollection.Count = 3 Then
            .SeriesCollection(1).Delete
        Else
            With .SeriesCollection.NewSeries
                .Name = Sheet1.Range("A13")
                .Values = Sheet1.Range("B13:M13")
                .XValues = Sheet1.Range("B12:M12")
                .PlotOrder = 1
            End With
        End If
    End With
End Sub
```

If the `SeriesCollection.Count` property is three, the first series is deleted. Otherwise, a new series is added and the appropriate ranges assigned to it show the profit after tax figures. The new series is added as the last series, which would plot behind the existing series, so the `PlotOrder` property of the new series is set to one to place it in front of the others.

Summary

In this chapter, we have explained some of the differences between ActiveX controls embedded in worksheets and Forms toolbar controls embedded in worksheets and chart sheets, and we've also shown how to work with them. You have seen how scroll bars, spin buttons, check boxes, and option buttons can be used to execute macros that can harness the full power of VBA and that do not need to depend on a linked cell.

You also have seen how Forms toolbar controls and ActiveX controls can be created and manipulated programmatically. ActiveX controls are more difficult to create programmatically because they are contained within `OLEObjects` and you can't create their event procedures in advance.

Data Access with ADO

ActiveX Data Objects, or *ADO* for short, is Microsoft's technology of choice for performing *client-server* data access between any data consumer (the client) and any data source (the server or provider). There are other data-access technologies of which you may have heard in relation to Excel, including DAO and ODBC. However, these will not be covered in this chapter as Microsoft intends for these older technologies to be superseded by ADO, and for the most part this has occurred.

ADO is a vast topic, easily the subject of its own book. In fact, Wrox has published several excellent books exclusively on ADO, including the *ADO 2.6 Programmer's Reference* (ISBN 1-861004-63-x) and *Professional ADO 2.5 Programming* (ISBN 1-861002-75-0). This chapter will necessarily present only a small subset of ADO, covering the topics and situations that you will frequently find useful in Excel programming. For a more detailed look at ADO, we strongly recommend one of the dedicated volumes mentioned above.

As a freestanding, universal data-access technology, ADO has evolved rapidly over the past several years, much more rapidly than the programs that use it. As of this writing, there are several versions of ADO in common use, including: 2.1, 2.5, 2.6, and 2.7. This chapter will focus on ADO 2.7. This is the version of ADO that ships natively with the newest version of Windows and Office. If you aren't running one of these applications and don't have ADO 2.7 installed, you can download it from the Microsoft Universal Data Access Web site at `http://www.microsoft.com/data`.

An Introduction to Structured Query Language (SQL)

It's impossible to get very far into a discussion of data access without running into *SQL*, the querying language used to communicate with all databases commonly in use today. SQL is a standards-based language that has as many variations as there are database vendors. This chapter will use constructs compliant with the latest SQL standard, SQL-92, wherever possible. In order to properly cover data access with Microsoft SQL Server, however, the SQL Server variant of SQL called Transact SQL, or T-SQL for short, will be touched upon.

This section will provide a brief overview of basic SQL syntax. This overview is by no means complete, but will serve to introduce you to the concepts used in this chapter. For an excellent and significantly more detailed primer on SQL, we would recommend *Beginning SQL Programming* (ISBN 1-861001-80-0) from Wrox Press.

There are four SQL commands you will use frequently, and we have added a couple that you will use less frequently but are powerful nonetheless. These are:

❑ SELECT
  Used to retrieve data from a data source

❑ INSERT
  Used to add new records to a data source

❑ UPDATE
  Used to modify existing records in a data source

❑ DELETE
  Used to remove records from a data source

❑ CREATE TABLE
  Used to create a new table

❑ DROP TABLE
  Used to remove and existing table

The terms *record* and *field* are commonly used when describing data. The data sources we'll be concerned with in this chapter can all be thought of as being stored in a two-dimensional grid. A record represents a single row in that grid, a field represents a column in the grid. The intersection of a record and a field is a specific *value*. A *resultset* is the term used to describe the set of data returned by a SQL SELECT statement.

> You will notice that SQL keywords such as **SELECT** and **UPDATE** are shown in upper case. This is a common SQL programming practice. When viewing complex SQL statements, having SQL keywords in upper case makes it significantly easier to distinguish between those keywords and their operands. The subsections of a SQL statement are called clauses. In all SQL statements, some clauses are required while others are optional. When describing the syntax of SQL statements, optional clauses and keywords will be surrounded with square brackets.

We will use the Customers table from Microsoft's Northwind demo database, as shown in Figure 11-1, to illustrate our SQL syntax examples. Northwind is installed when you install either MS-Access or MS-SQL Server (the file is usually named NWind.mdb or Northwind.mdb).

The SELECT Statement

The SELECT statement is, by far, the most commonly used statement in SQL. This is the statement that allows you to retrieve data from a data source. The basic syntax of a SELECT statement is demonstrated next:

```
SELECT  columname1, columnname2 [, columnnamen] FROM  tablename
```

Figure 11-1

The table in the preceding figure is named Customers, and contains a column named Company Name among others. To select all of the Customers by name we could write:

```
SELECT CompanyName FROM Customers
```

The SELECT clause tells the data source what columns you wish to return. The FROM clause tells the data source which table the records should be retrieved from. Extending our example, we could select the company name and contact name from the Customers table with the following query:

```
SELECT CompanyName, ContactName FROM Customers
```

This statement will notify the data source that you want to retrieve all of the values for the CompanyName and ContactName fields from the Customers table. The SELECT statement provides a shorthand method for indicating that you want to retrieve all fields from the specified table. This involves placing a single asterisk as the SELECT list:

```
SELECT *FROM Customers
```

This SQL statement will return all fields and all records from the Customers table. It's generally not considered a good practice to use * in the SELECT list as it leaves your code vulnerable to changes in field names or the order of fields in the table. It can also be very resource expensive in large tables, as all columns and rows will be returned whether or not they are actually needed by the client. However, there are times when it is a useful and time-saving shortcut.

Let's say that you wanted to see a list of countries where you have at least one customer located. Simply performing the following query would return one record for every customer in your table.

SELECT Country FROM Customers. This resultset would contain many duplicate country names. The optional DISTINCT keyword allows you to return only unique values in your query:

```
SELECT DISTINCT Country FROM Customers
```

The keyword DISTINCT may not be supported by all database vendors. You will have to check with the documentation of each provider to determine the precise grammar and keywords supported by any particular implementation of SQL. If you want to write SQL that is the most transportable, then you want to employ the GROUP BY clause. GROUP BY is ANSI SQL and performs a role similar to the DISTINCT keyword in Access; GROUP BY ensures that each column in the GROUP BY clause has a value represented just one time. You will get the same results as the preceding statement by writing the following ANSI SQL statement:

```
SELECT Country FROM Customers GROUP BY Country
```

If you only want to see the list of customers located in the UK, you can use the WHERE clause to restrict the results to only those customers:

```
SELECT CompanyName, ContactName
FROM Customers
WHERE Country = 'UK'
```

Note that the string literal UK must be surrounded in single quotes. This is also true of dates. Numeric expressions do not require any surrounding characters.

Finally, suppose that you would like to have your UK customer list sorted by CompanyName. This can be accomplished using the ORDER BY clause:

```
SELECT CompanyName, ContactName
FROM Customers
WHERE Country = 'UK'
ORDER BY CompanyName
```

The ORDER BY clause will sort columns in ascending order by default. If instead you wished to sort a field in descending order, you could use the optional DESC specifier immediately after the name of the column whose sort order you wished to modify.

The INSERT Statement

The INSERT statement allows you to add new records to a table. The basic syntax of the INSERT statement follows:

```
INSERT INTO  table_name (column1, column2 [,  columnn])
VALUES  (value1, value2 [, valuen])
```

Use of the INSERT statement is very simple. You provide the name of the table and its columns that you'll be inserting data into and then provide a list of values to be inserted. You must provide a value in the VALUES clause for each column named in the INSERT clause and the values must appear in the same order as the column names they correspond to. Here's an example showing how to insert a new record into the Customers table:

```
INSERT INTO Customers (CustomerID, CompanyName, ContactName, Country)
VALUES ('ABCD', 'New Company', 'Owner Name', 'USA')
```

Note that as with the WHERE clause of the SELECT statement, all of the string literals in the VALUES clause are surrounded by single quotes. This is the rule throughout SQL.

If you have provided values for every field in the table in your VALUES clause and the values are in the same order as they are defined in the table, the field list clause can be omitted:

```
INSERT INTO Customers
VALUES( 'ALFKJ', 'Alfreds Futterkiste', 'Maria Anders', 'Sales
Representative',
'Obere Str. 57', 'Berlin', 'Hessen', '12209', 'Germany', ' 030-0074321', '030-
0076545')
```

The UPDATE Statement

The UPDATE statement allows you to modify the values in one or more fields of an existing record or records in a table. The basic syntax of the UPDATE statement is the following:

```
UPDATE   tablename
SET   column1 = value1, column2 = value2 [, columnn = valuen]
[WHERE   filters]
```

Even though the WHERE clause of the UPDATE statement is optional, you must take care to specify it unless you are sure that you don't need it. Executing an UPDATE statement *without* a WHERE clause will modify the specified field(s) of every record in the specified table. For example, if we executed the following statement:

```
UPDATE Customers
SET Country = 'USA'
```

Every record in the Customers table would have its Country field modified to contain the value "USA." There are some cases where this mass update capability is useful, but it can also be very dangerous, because there is no way to undo the update if you execute it by mistake. Consequently, a good rule of thumb while developing queries is to make a backup copy of your database, and work on sample data. This will permit you to fix any mistakes by restoring the database from the backup.

The more common use of the UPDATE statement is to modify the value of a specific record identified by the use of the WHERE clause. Before we look at an example of this usage, we need to discuss a very important aspect of database design called the *primary key*. The primary key is a column or group of columns in a database table whose values can be used to uniquely identify each record in that table. The primary key in our sample Customers table is the CustomerID field. Each customer record in the Customers table has a unique value for CustomerID. In other words, a specific CustomerID value occurs in one, and only one, customer record in the table.

Let's say that the ContactName changed for the customer "Around the Horn", whose CustomerID is "AROUT". We could perform an UPDATE to record that change in the following manner:

```
UPDATE Customers
SET ContactName = 'New Name'
WHERE CustomerID = 'AROUT'
```

Since we have included a WHERE predicate that is based on the primary key and ensures uniqueness, then only the record belonging to the Around the Horn company will be updated.

The DELETE statement allows you to remove one or more records from a table. The basic syntax of the DELETE statement is the following:

```
DELETE FROM  tablename
[WHERE  filter]
```

As with the UPDATE statement, notice that the WHERE clause is optional. This is probably more dangerous in the case of the DELETE statement; however, because executing a DELETE statement *without* a WHERE clause *will delete every single record in the specified table*. Unless you intend to delete all rows, you should always include a WHERE clause in your DELETE statements. Again, while you are developing queries it is a good idea to work on a non-production database. For example, if you are working with an Access database, simply make a copy of the .mdb file and work on the copy. Let's assume that for some reason an entry was made into the Customers table with the CustomerID value of "BONAP" by mistake (maybe they were a supplier rather than a customer). To remove this record from the Customers table we would use the following DELETE statement:

```
DELETE FROM Customers
WHERE CustomerID = 'BONAP'
```

Once again, since we used the record's primary key in the WHERE clause, only that specific record will be affected by the DELETE statement.

The CREATE TABLE Statement

The CREATE TABLE statement is used to add new tables to an existing database programmatically. While you are likely to use this statement less frequently than the SELECT, UPDATE, INSERT, or DELETE commands, it is a good statement to know. You may want to use the CREATE TABLE statement to permit consumers to add tables after your solution is employed, to make backup tables, or to support an existing table yet replicate a new, blank table. The syntax for CREATE TABLE follows:

```
CREATE TABLE  tablename (columnname1 type1 [, columnnamen typen])
```

Keep in mind that generally tables will have a couple of useful elements. One is a primary key to aid in searchability. A second feature might be what is referred to as a foreign key. A foreign key is a unique value that is an index of another table. Suppose, for instance, we wanted to extend the Employees table in the Northwind database without changing it. We could add a new table with its own primary key, and a unique column named EmployeeID that is logically related to the Employees.EmployeeID column. Finally, we could add the new information, such as an email address. Such a query could be written as:

```
CREATE TABLE EmployeeContactInformation

(EmployeeContactInformationID Int Primary Key,
 EmployeeID Int UNIQUE,
 Email Text)
```

After running the previous query in the Northwind database we would have a new table named EmployeeContactInformation with a primary key of EmployeeContactInformationID, a unique (no duplicates permitted) `EmployeeID` that represents a logical relationship between our new table and the Employees table, and an extra column named `Email`, which could be used to store employee e-mail addresses.

Obviously, we could modify the Employees table to include such a column, but this may be undesirable, for example, if the database is provided by an outside source or such a change may break existing applications.

The DROP TABLE Statement

The first programmers were mathematicians. Mathematicians appreciate the notion of symmetry or opposites, a yin and yang, if you will. Hence, if we have a `CREATE TABLE` statement, then it only seems natural that we have a statement to uncreate tables. The statement to delete a whole table—as opposed to deleting all of the rows in a table—is:

```
DROP TABLE tablename
```

Supposing that we created the table `EmployeeContactInformation` for temporary usage then we could drop the same table with the following statement:

```
DROP TABLE EmployeeContactInformation.
```

An Overview of ADO

ADO is Microsoft's universal data-access technology. By universal they mean that ADO is designed to allow access to any kind of data source imaginable, from a SQL Server database, to the Windows 2000 Active Directory, to a text file saved on your local hard disk, and even to non-Microsoft products such as Oracle. All of these things and many more can be accessed by ADO. You can find a wealth of information on ADO in the ADO section of the Microsoft Universal Data Access Web site: `http://www.microsoft.com/data/ado/`.

ADO doesn't actually access a data source directly. Instead, ADO is a data consumer that receives its data from a lower-level technology called *OLE DB*. OLE DB cannot be accessed directly using VBA, so ADO was designed to provide an interface that allows you to do so. ADO receives data from *OLE DB providers*. Most OLE DB providers are specific to a single type of data source. Each is designed to provide a common interface to whatever data its source may contain. One of the greatest strengths of ADO is that, regardless of the data source you are accessing, you use essentially the same set of commands. There's no need to learn different technologies or methods to access different data sources.

Microsoft also provides an OLE DB provider for ODBC. This general-purpose provider allows ADO to access any data source that understands ODBC, even if a specific OLE DB data provider is not available for that data source.

ADO's object model consists of five top-level objects, all of which can be created independently. In this chapter, we'll be covering the `Connection` object, the `Command` object, and the `Recordset` object. ADO also exposes a `Record` object (not to be confused with the `Recordset` object), as well as a `Stream` object. These objects are not commonly used in Excel applications, so it's left to the interested reader to learn more about them from one of the sources mentioned at the beginning of this chapter.

In addition to the five top-level objects, ADO contains four collections, and the objects contained in those collections (for example the `Errors` collection contains `Error` objects). Master a handful of classes and you know how to use ADO. Figure 11-2 shows the ADO object model.

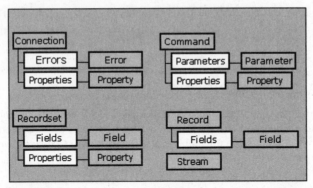

Figure 11-2

The next three sections will provide an introduction to each of the top-level ADO objects that we'll be using in this chapter. These sections will provide general information that will be applicable whenever you are using ADO. Specific examples of how to use ADO to accomplish a number of the most common data access tasks you'll encounter in Excel VBA will be covered in the sections that follow.

This is not intended to be an exhaustive reference to ADO. We will only be covering those items whose use will be demonstrated in this chapter, or which we consider particularly important to point out. ADO frequently provides you the flexibility to make the same setting in multiple ways, as both an object property and an argument to a method, for instance. In these cases, we will usually only cover the method we intend to demonstrate in the example sections.

The Connection Object

The `Connection` object is what provides the pipeline between your application and the data source you want to access. Like the other top-level ADO objects, the `Connection` object is extremely flexible. In some cases, this may be the only object you need to use. Simple commands can easily be executed directly through a `Connection` object. In other cases, you may not need to create a `Connection` object at all. The `Command` and `Recordset` objects can create a `Connection` object automatically, if they need one.

Constructing and tearing down a data source connection can be a time-consuming process. If you will be executing multiple SQL statements over the course of your application, you should create a publicly scoped `Connection` object variable and use it for each query. This allows you to take advantage of *connection pooling*.

Connection pooling is a feature provided by ADO that will preserve and reuse connections to the data source rather than creating new connections for each query, which would be a waste of resources. Connections can be reused for different queries as long as their connection strings are identical. This is typically the case in Excel applications, so we recommend taking advantage of it.

Connection Object Properties

In this section, we will examine the important `Connection` object properties.

The ConnectionString Property

The `ConnectionString` property is used to provide ADO, and the OLE DB provider that you are using with the information required to connect to the data source. The connection string consists of a semicolon-delimited series of arguments in the form of `"name=value;"` pairs.

For the purposes of this chapter, the only ADO argument that we will be using is the `Provider` argument. All other arguments in connection strings presented in this chapter will be specific to the OLE DB provider being used. ADO will pass these arguments directly through to the provider. The `Provider` argument tells ADO which OLE DB provider to use. The following sample code demonstrates a connection string to the Northwind database using the `Jet OLE DB` provider:

```
"Provider=Microsoft.Jet.OLEDB.4.0;Data Source=C:\Program Files\Microsoft
Office\OFFICE11\SAMPLES\Northwind.mdb;Persist Security Info=False"
```

The only argument specific to ADO in this string is the `Provider` argument. All other arguments are passed directly through to the SQL Server `OLE DB` provider. If a different provider were being used, the arguments would be different as well. We will see this when we begin to connect to various data sources in the example sections. The `Provider` argument to the connection string is optional. If no provider is specified, ADO uses the `OLE DB` provider for ODBC by default.

A reasonable person might be concerned about the specificity of the connection string. How on earth are you going to remember a cryptic string of text, especially if the arguments vary based on the OLE DB provider? Well, that's why you buy books like this, so we can show you.

Instead of remembering all of the possible details of any particular OLE DB provider—the proverbial fish offering, we will show you how to catch your own fish—here is a technique that will build the connection string for you. OLE DB is implemented as code in the `oledb32.dll`. This DLL has a GUI tool that is a dialog box named `Data Link` Properties (see Figure 11-3). If you create an empty text file and change the extension from `.txt` to .udl, double-clicking the file will invoke the `Data Link` Properties dialog box because files with a `.udl` extension are associated with OLE DB core services. Naturally, one of these core services is defining connections to data providers.

The `Data Link` Properties dialog box is a wizard. Start on the first tab named Provider, pick a provider and click next. The next tab is the Connection tab. This tab changes slightly based on the information each provider needs. For our example, we pick the Microsoft Jet 4.0 OLE DB Provider, the MS Access OLE DB provider. On the Connection tab we only need to browse to the location of the `Northwind.mdb` file and we are finished. After you click *OK* the dialog box is closed and the `.udl` file is updated with the connection string. Open the `.udl` file with something like Notepad and copy the connection string from the `.udl` file. Figure 11-4 shows the contents of the `.udl` file opened with Notepad. All we need is the last line of text; the first two lines of text represent comments.

Here is some code we could use to initialize an ADO connection object and assign the connection string to the connection object's `ConnectionString` property. (Remember to use Tools ➪ References in the menu item in the VBE to add a reference to the Microsoft ActiveX Data Objects 2.7 Library (ADO).)

```
Const ConnectionString As String = _
   "Provider=Microsoft.Jet.OLEDB.4.0;" + _
   "Data Source=C:\Program Files\Microsoft " + _
   "Office\OFFICE11\SAMPLES\Northwind.mdb;Persist Security Info=False"
```

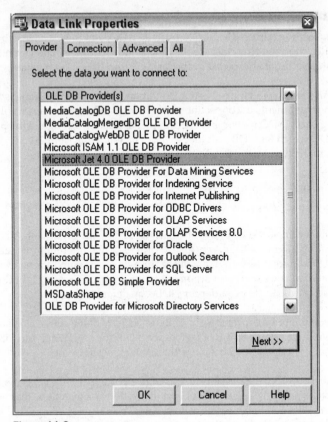

Figure 11-3

```
  connection.udl - Notepad
File   Edit   Format   View   Help
[oledb]
; Everything after this line is an OLE DB init:
Provider=Microsoft.Jet.OLEDB.4.0;Data Source=C:
|
```

Figure 11-4

```
Dim Connection As ADODB.Connection
Set Connection = New ADODB.Connection
Connection.ConnectionString = ConnectionString
```

The first statement declares a constant variable initialized with the connection string we copied from the .udl file. The second statement declares a connection object, followed by initialization of the connection object, and assignment to the connection string property.

The ConnectionTimeout Property

Almost all classes have several members. The `Connection` class has a `ConnectionTimeout` property that specifies how long ADO will wait for a connection to complete before giving up and raising an error. The default value is 15 seconds. We rarely spend any time on this value; either the connection is there or it is not. Here is how you can modify the `ConnectionTimeout` property using the connection object created from the previous section:

```
Connection.ConnectionTimeout = 30
```

The State Property

The `State` property allows you to determine whether a connection is open, closed, connecting, or executing a command. The value will be a bit mask containing one or more of the following `ObjectStateEnum` constants defined in ADO:

- ❏ `AdStateClosed`
  Means the connection is closed

- ❏ `AdStateOpen`
  Means the connection is open

- ❏ `AdStateConnecting`
  Means the object is in the process of making a connection

- ❏ `AdStateExecuting`
  Means the connection is executing a command

If you attempt to close a `connection` object that is already closed or open a connection that is already open, then your code will cause an error. You can prevent this from occurring by testing the state of the `Connection` object before closing it:

```
If Connection.State = ObjectStateEnum.adStateOpen) Then objConn.Close
```

At first, it might seem laughable that code might be written that tries to open an opened connection or close a closed connection, but attempts to open a connection might fail or if the connection is a field in the class then other code paths may have previously opened or closed an existing connection. To prevent this, it is a good idea to test the state of a connection before calling Open or Close.

Connection Methods

Methods define the behavior of objects. A connection presents a connection to a provider. As you might imagine, connections can be opened and closed, but ADO supports some additional convenience behaviors you will find useful.

The Open Method

The `Open` method establishes a connection to a provider (also called data source, though provider is the currently in vogue term). `Open` accepts several optional parameters. If we initialize the `ConnectionString` property first then we can call open with no arguments. If we don't initialize the `ConnectionString` then we can pass the `ConnectionString` and things like `UserID`, `Password`, and an additional `Options` argument that we will discuss in a minute. The following code demonstrates how we can initialize a connection object, open a connection, and test the state of that connection:

```
Const ConnectionString As String = _
    "Provider=Microsoft.Jet.OLEDB.4.0;" + _
    "Data Source=C:\ Program Files\ Microsoft " + _
    "Office\ OFFICE11\ SAMPLES\ Northwind.mdb;Persist Security Info=False"

Dim Connection As ADODB.Connection
Set Connection = New ADODB.Connection
Connection.ConnectionString = ConnectionString
Connection.Open
MsgBox Connection.State = ObjectStateEnum.adStateOpen
```

A moment ago we mentioned an additional Options argument. The Options argument allows you to make your connection *asynchronously*. That is, you can tell your Connection object to go off and open the connection in the background while your code continues to run. You do this by setting the Options argument to the ConnectOptionEnum value adAsyncConnect. The following code sample demonstrates making an asynchronous connection:

```
objConn.Open Options:=adAsyncConnect
```

This can be useful if you initialize a connection when your code begins running, but you may not need the connection for a minute and want to let the rest of your code to complete initialization in the mean time.

The Execute Method

The Execute method runs the command text provided to the Execute method's CommandText argument. The Execute method has the following syntax for an action query (one that does not return a result set, like DELETE, INSERT, or UPDATE but not SELECT):

```
connection.Execute CommandText, [RecordsAffected], [Options]
```

And for a select query, we assign the return value of the Execute method to a Recordset object:

```
Set Recordset = connection.Execute(CommandText, _
                                    [RecordsAffected], [Options])
```

The CommandText argument can contain any executable string recognized by the OLE DB provider like a SQL statement. The optional RecordsAffected argument is a return value that tells you how many records the CommandText operation affected. You can check this value against the number of records that you expected to be affected so that you can detect potential errors in your command text.

The Options argument is crucial to optimizing the execution efficiency of your command. Therefore, you should always use it even though it's nominally optional. The Options argument allows you to relay two different types of information to your OLE DB provider: what type of command is contained in the CommandText argument and how the provider should execute the contents of the CommandText argument.

In order to execute the CommandText, the OLE DB provider must know what type of command it contains. If you don't specify the type, the provider will have to determine that information for itself. This will slow down the execution of your query. You can avoid this by specifying the CommandText type using one of the following CommandTypeEnum values:

❑ AdCmdText
The CommandText is a raw SQL string.

❑ AdCmdTable
The CommandText is the name of a table. This sends an internally generated SQL statement to the provider that looks something like "SELECT * FROM *tablename*".

❑ AdCmdStoredProc
The CommandText is the name of a stored procedure (we'll cover stored procedures in the section on SQL Server).

❑ AdCmdTableDirect
The CommandText is the name of a table. However, unlike adCmdTable, this option does not generate a SQL statement and therefore returns the contents of the table more efficiently. Use this option if your provider supports it.

You can provide specific execution instructions to the provider by including one or more of the ExecuteOptionEnum constants:

❑ AdAsyncExecute
Instructs the provider to execute the command asynchronously, which returns execution to your code immediately.

❑ AdExecuteNoRecords
Instructs the provider not to construct a Recordset object. ADO will always construct a recordset in response to a command, even if your CommandText argument is not a row-returning query. In order to avoid the overhead required to create an unnecessary recordset, use this value in the Options argument whenever you execute a non-row-returning query.

The CommandTypeEnum and ExecuteOptionEnum values are bit masks that can be combined together in the Options argument using the logical Or operator. For example, to execute a plain text SQL command and return a Recordset object you would use the following syntax:

```
Const ConnectionString As String = _
  "Provider=Microsoft.Jet.OLEDB.4.0;" + _
  "Data Source=C:\Program Files\Microsoft " + _
  "Office\OFFICE11\SAMPLES\Northwind.mdb;Persist Security Info=False"

Dim Connection As ADODB.Connection
Set Connection = New ADODB.Connection
Connection.ConnectionString = ConnectionString
Connection.Open

Debug.Print Connection.State = ObjectStateEnum.adStateOpen

Const SQL As String = _
  "SELECT * FROM Customers WHERE Country = 'USA'"

Dim Recordset As Recordset
Dim RowsAffected As Long
Set Recordset = Connection.Execute(SQL, RowsAffected, CommandTypeEnum.
adCmdText)
```

The preceding code builds on our example. The `MsgBox` statement was switched to a `Debug.Print` statement because we don't want a message dialog box to interrupt the smooth flow of our code, but we might like to keep tabs on how things are going. After the `Debug.Print` statement we declared a SQL statement, a `Recordset` variable, and a long integer to store the number of rows returned. (If we didn't care whether or not there were any rows returned, we could skip the `RowsAffected` argument and use an extra comma as a placeholder in the call to Execute as follows.)

```
Set Recordset = Connection.Execute(SQL, , adCmdText)
```

The Close Method

When we are finished interacting with a provider we need to close the connection. There are only a finite number of handles for database connections, hence leaving connections open may result in an eventual inability to open future connections and make it impossible for other applications to interact with the same database. The `Close` method requires no arguments. Combining with our check for the current state being open followed by a call to the `Close` method can be written as follows:

```
If (Connection.State = ObjectStateEnum.adStateOpen) Then
  Connection.Close
End If
```

Connection Object Events and Asynchronous Programming

Synchronous means that things happen in order. Asynchronous means that things happen out of order. Asynchronous programming can be powerful because it permits your code to run background tasks while continuing to do things in the foreground. For example, if a query takes a while to execute and a user can perform other useful tasks in the meantime, then you can eliminate the need for the user to wait on a long task, doing nothing in the mean time.

The basic behavior of an asynchronous call is that the call is made and immediately returns. When an asynchronous call returns it hasn't necessarily finished. The process is actually running on a background thread (modern CPUs and Windows supports multiple threads of execution, which is why you can be listening to Coolio on your Windows Media Player while typing in Word and running a query in Access, all at the same time) and your code continues running on the foreground thread. There are many ways to support notification when an asynchronous background thread has completed; one way supported in Excel is to use an event. By associating an event with a connection the background process can call the event when it's finished permitting the foreground code to keep on running. When used correctly, asynchronous behaviors and events can enhance the performance of your solutions, resulting in a very fluid and responsive application.

To associate events with a `Connection` object we need to use a `WithEvents` statement in a class module, declaring a connection object. After we have declared the `WithEvents` statement, we can use the Object and procedure combo boxes to pick the connection object and the available events, respectively. There are several events, including `BeginTransComplete`, `CommitTransComplete`, `ConnectComplete`, `Disconnect`, `ExecuteComplete`, `InfoMessage`, `RollbackTransComplete`, `WillConnect`, and `WillExecute`. To respond to the completion of an asynchronous command execution, we will implement the `ExecuteComplete` event. The following code is a revision of the code we have been working on. The revised code shows how to execute the SQL asynchronously and populate a range from the recordset:

```
 1: Option Explicit
 2: Private WithEvents AsyncConnection As ADODB.Connection
 3:
 4: Public Sub AsyncConnectionToDatabase()
 5:
 6:   Const ConnectionString As String = _
 7:     "Provider=Microsoft.Jet.OLEDB.4.0;" + _
 8:     "Data Source=C:\Program Files\Microsoft " + _
 9:     "Office\OFFICE11\SAMPLES\Northwind.mdb;" + __
10:     "Persist Security Info=False"
11:
12:   Set AsyncConnection = New ADODB.Connection
13:
14:   AsyncConnection.ConnectionString = ConnectionString
15:   AsyncConnection.Open
16:
17:   Const SQL As String = _
18:     "SELECT * FROM Customers WHERE Country = 'USA'"
19:
20:   Call AsyncConnection.Execute(SQL, , CommandTypeEnum.adCmdText _
21:     Or ExecuteOptionEnum.adAsyncExecute)
22:
23:   Debug.Print "I ran before the query finished"
24:
25: End Sub
26:
27: Private Sub AsyncConnection_ExecuteComplete( _
28:   ByVal RecordsAffected As Long, _
29:   ByVal pError As ADODB.Error, _
30:   adStatus As ADODB.EventStatusEnum, _
31:   ByVal pCommand As ADODB.Command, _
32:   ByVal pRecordset As ADODB.Recordset, _
33:   ByVal pConnection As ADODB.Connection)
34:
35:   Debug.Print "Query finished"
36:
37:   If (adStatus = EventStatusEnum.adStatusOK) Then
38:     Call Sheet1.Range("A1").CopyFromRecordset(pRecordset)
39:   End If
40:
41:   If (pConnection.State = ObjectStateEnum.adStateOpen) Then
42:     pConnection.Close
43:   End If
44: End Sub
```

Due to the length of the listing, line numbers were added for reference. As always, don't include the line numbers in the VBE editor. The asynchronous methods comprise two statements, but the total code is very similar to what we have been using so far.

Line declares the WithEvents statement. WithEvents will permit us to generate event handlers, including the AsyncConnection_ExecuteComplete method. Calling Execute asynchronously means we don't get the Recordset back from the Execute method and the rest of the code that responds to execute is implemented in the ExecuteComplete event handler. Oring

`ExecuteoptionEnum.adAsyncExecute` on line 21 makes the `Execute` call asynchronous. The `Debug.Print` statement on line 23 was added to illustrate that line 23 runs before the query completes.

The `ExecuteComplete` event is called asynchronously when the `Execute` method actually finishes. The arguments to `ExecuteComplete` make it easy to determine which connections and commands the event is responding to and to retrieve that information. In our example, we make sure the query completed (line 37), and if so, we copy the `Recordset` into the worksheet starting at cell A1. Line 41 checks to see if the connection is opened and closes it if it is.

The `Debug.Print` statement on line 23 represents work, but we could include as much code as we'd like after the asynchronous call to `Execute`. For example, if we were deleting a table then the user would be able to delete the table in the background and continue interacting with our solution with little, if any, noticeable, deterioration in performance or wait time between the moment the delete was requested and control was returned to the user.

Exercise some care when using asynchronous behavior. For example, trying to close a connection that is processing a background request will cause an error. Asynchronous program takes a little getting used to but can yield impressive performance improvements.

Connection Object Collections

The `Connection` Object has two collections, `Errors` and `Properties`.

Errors Collection

The `Errors` collection contains a set of `Error` objects, each of which represents an OLE DB provider-specific error (ADO itself generates runtime errors). The `Errors` collection can contain errors, warnings, and messages (generated by the T-SQL `PRINT` statement, for instance). The `Errors` collection is very helpful in providing extra detail when something in your ADO code has malfunctioned. When debugging ADO problems, you can dump the contents of the `Errors` collection to the Immediate window with the following code:

```
Dim E As Error
  For Each E In pConnection.Errors
    Debug.Print E.Value
  Next
```

The Properties Collection

The Properties collection contains provider-specific, or *extended properties*, for the `Connection` object. Some providers add important settings that you will want to be aware of. Extended properties are beyond the scope of this chapter. You can find more information about them by consulting one of the ADO references mentioned earlier.

The Recordset Object

Just as the most commonly used SQL statement is the `SELECT` statement, the most commonly used ADO object is the `Recordset` object. The `Recordset` object serves as a container for the records and fields returned from a `SELECT` statement executed against a data source.

Recordset Object Properties

Learning how to use any class is a matter of learning about the Properties that describes a class's state, the methods that describe its behavior, and the events that determine what occurrences your code can respond to. We'll start our exploration of the `Recordset` by starting with the `ActiveConnection` property.

The ActiveConnection Property

Prior to opening the `Recordset` object, you can use the `ActiveConnection` property to assign an existing `Connection` object to the `Recordset` or a connection string for the recordset to use to connect to the database. If you assign a connection string, the recordset will create a `Connection` object for itself. Once the recordset has been opened, this property returns an object reference to the `Connection` object being used by the recordset.

The following code assigns a `Connection` object to the `ActiveConnection` property:

```
Set Recordset.ActiveConnection = Connection
```

The following code assigns a connection string to the `ActiveConnection` property, resulting in an implicit creation of a connection object:

```
Recordset.ActiveConnection = "Provider=Microsoft.Jet.OLEDB.4.0;" + _
    "Data Source=C:\Program Files\Microsoft " + _
    "Office\OFFICE11\SAMPLES\Northwind.mdb;" + _
                        "Persist Security Info=False"
```

The BOF and EOF Properties

These properties indicate whether the record pointer of the `Recordset` object is positioned before the first record in the `recordset` (BOF, or beginning of file) or after the last record in the recordset (EOF, or end of file). If the `recordset` is empty, both BOF and EOF will be True. The following code example demonstrates using these properties to determine if there is data in a `recordset`:

```
If (Recordset.EOF And Recordset.BOF) Then
    Debug.Print "There is no data"
End If
```

Note that there is a difference between an empty `recordset` and a closed `recordset`. If you execute a query that returns no data, ADO will present you with a perfectly valid open `recordset`, but one that contains no data. Therefore, you should consider performing a check similar to the preceding code to determine if the `recordset` is empty or not.

The `Recordset` also provides a `RecordCount` property, but some providers don't support this property. For example, `Recordset.RecordCount` always returns −1 for the Microsoft Jet 4.0 OLE DB Provider. Better checks are to use code that doesn't care if there is no data like `Worksheet.CopyFromRecordset`, use BOF or EOF, or a For Each statement (because For Each will only process records that exist in the `Recordset`).

The Filter Property

The `Filter` property allows you to filter an open recordset so that only records that meet the specified condition are visible, acting like an additional WHERE predicate on the recordset. The records that cannot be seen are not deleted, removed, or changed in any way, but are simply hidden from normal recordset operations. This property can be set to a string that specifies the condition you want to place on the records, or to one of the FilterGroupEnum constants.

You can set multiple filters, and the records exposed by the filtered recordset will be only those records that meet all of the conditions. To remove the filter from the recordset, set the Filter property to an empty string or the adFilterNone constant. The following code sample demonstrates filtering a recordset so that it displays only regions described by the abbreviation OR, as in Oregon:

```
Recordset.Filter = "Region = 'OR'"
```

You can use the logical AND, OR, and NOT operators to set additional Filter property values:

```
Recordset.Filter = "Region = 'OR' AND City = 'Portland'"
```

The State Property

The Recordset.State property has the same possible values as the Connection.State property. (Refer to the previous section entitled *"The State Property"* from earlier in the chapter.)

Recordset Methods

Classes can be large and complex, like the Recordset class. However, if you know what the most commonly used properties and methods are and you understand the general principle behind properties and methods, then you will be able to use a class effectively right away and have the tools necessary to explore further. In this section, we will cover five commonly used methods of the Recordset class.

The Open Method

The Open method retrieves the data and makes it accessible to your code, much like you open a dictionary to look up words. The Open method has the following general syntax:

```
Call Recordset.Open( Source, ActiveConnection, CursorType, LockType, Options)
```

The Source argument tells the recordset about the data source. The Source argument can be a SQL statement, a Command object, a table name, a URL, a stored procedure call, or a recordset persisted to a file. Generally, you will use something like a SQL statement.

The ActiveConnection argument can be a connection string or a Connection object that identifies the connection to be used. If you assign a connection string to the ActiveConnection argument, the recordset will create a Connection object for itself.

The CursorType argument specifies the type of cursor to use when opening the recordset. This is set using one of the CursorTypeEnum values. In this chapter, we will demonstrate two (adOpenForwardOnly and adOpenStatic) of the four (adOpenForwardOnly, adOpenStatic, adOpenkeyset, and adOpenDynamic) cursor types. It is up to the reader to devise further exploration.

adOpenForwardOnly means that the recordset can only be negotiated in a forward-only direction from beginning to end. Opening a recordset using adOpenForwardOnly is the fastest but least flexible way of traversing a recordset. Additionally, forward-only data is read-only. The adOpenStatic CursorType is used for disconnected recordsets. adOpenStatic permits random navigation and modification. If you fail to specify a CursorType then adOpenForwardOnly is used by default.

The `LockType` argument specifies what type of locks the provider should place on the underlying data source when opening the recordset. The five possible lock types are `adLockBatchOptimistic`, `adLockOptimistic`, `adLockPessimistic`, `adlockReadOnly`, and `adLockUnspecified`. Later in this chapter, we have provided examples that demonstrate `adLockReadOnly` and `adLockBatchOptimistic`. `AdlockBatchOptimistic` is required for disconnected recordsets where records are updated as a batch. `adLockOptimistic` locks records when the `Update` method is called assuming no one has changed records between the time they were retrieved and the time an update occurs. `adLockPessimistic` locks records immediately after editing begins. `adLockReadOnly` means the recordset cannot be used to modify records and is consistent with a forward-only recordset, and `adLockUnspecified` represents an unspecified locking strategy. Further exploration, apart from the examples provided later in this chapter, is left to the reader.

The `Options` argument here is the same as the `Options` argument we covered in the `Connection` object's `Execute` method earlier in the chapter. It is used to tell the provider how to interpret and execute the contents of the `Source` argument.

The Close Method

The `Close` method closes the `Recordset` object. This does not free any memory used by the recordset. To free up the memory used by the `Recordset` object, you must set the `Recordset` object variable to `Nothing`, but VBA is designed to be programmer-friendly and any object will be cleaned up when the object goes out of scope. For example, if we define a recordset in a method, then the recordset will be removed from memory when the method exits. Contrariwise, some language demand that you explicitly release objects from memory and getting in the habit of setting objects to `Nothing` (explicitly releasing them) is a good practice.

Methods for Moving the Cursor

When a recordset is first opened the *current record pointer* is positioned on the first record in the recordset. The `Move` methods are used to navigate through the records in an open recordset. They do this by repositioning the `Recordset` object's current record pointer. Listed next are the basic navigation methods that are available:

- ❑ `MoveFirst`
  Positions the cursor to the first record of the recordset.

- ❑ `MovePrevious`
  Positions the cursor to the prior record in the recordset.

- ❑ `MoveNext`
  Positions the cursor to the next record in the recordset.

- ❑ `MoveLast`
  Positions the cursor to the last record in the recordset.

The following code sample demonstrates common recordset navigation handling:

```
Public Sub RecordsetNavigation()

  Const SQL As String = _
    "SELECT * FROM Customers"
```

```
   Const ConnectionString As String = _
      "Provider=Microsoft.Jet.OLEDB.4.0;" + _
      "Data Source=C:\Program Files\Microsoft " + _
      "Office\OFFICE11\SAMPLES\Northwind.mdb;Persist Security Info=False"

   Dim Recordset As Recordset
   Set Recordset = New Recordset
   Call Recordset.Open(SQL, ConnectionString)

   Recordset.MoveFirst

   While Not Recordset.EOF
      Debug.Print Recordset.Fields("CompanyName")
      Recordset.MoveNext
   Wend

End Sub
```

Pay particular attention to the use of the MoveNext method within the While loop. Omitting this is a very common error and will lead to an endless loop condition in your code.

If we wanted to switch the order of the data in the recordset, we could add a ORDER BY clause and order the data (ORDER BY CompanyName DESC) in descending order or change the CursorType from the default of adOpenForwardOnly to adOpenDynamic and move to the last record and navigate to the first record. The revision is shown here:

```
Public Sub RecordsetNavigation()

   Const SQL As String = _
      "SELECT * FROM Customers"

   Const ConnectionString As String = _
      "Provider=Microsoft.Jet.OLEDB.4.0;" + _
      "Data Source=C:\Program Files\Microsoft " + _
      "Office\OFFICE11\SAMPLES\Northwind.mdb;Persist Security Info=False"

   Dim Recordset As Recordset
   Set Recordset = New Recordset
   Call Recordset.Open(SQL, ConnectionString, adOpenDynamic)

   Recordset.MoveLast

   While Not Recordset.BOF
      Debug.Print Recordset.Fields("CompanyName")
      Recordset.MovePrevious
   Wend

End Sub
```

The NextRecordset Method

```
Some providers allow you to execute commands that return multiple recordsets.
The NextRecordset method is used to move through these recordsets. The
NextRecordset method clears the current recordset from the Recordset object,
```

loads the next recordset into the Recordset object, and sets the current record pointer to the first record in that recordset. If the NextRecordset method is called and there are no more recordsets to retrieve, the Recordset object is set to Nothing.

Recordset Events

Recordset events must be trapped by creating a WithEvents Recordset object variable in a class module. Trapping these events is necessary whenever you are using a Recordset object asynchronously, since events are used to notify the code when an asynchronous process has completed its task. Asynchronous behavior consistently needs a mechanism to permit notification when the asynchronous behavior has completed. Blocking mechanisms and events are commonly employed in conjunction with asynchronous operations. As with the Connection object, you will be interested in the events that are raised when you invoke asynchronous recordset methods. These include FetchComplete and FetchProgress. You already know how to use the WithEvents statement, and use the VBE editor to generate event methods. We will leave it to you to explore asynchronous behavior of recordsets.

Recordset Collections

We will wrap up our look at the recordset by exploring the objects that the recordset keeps track of. These include the Fields collection, and the Properties collection. A collection is a collection is a collection. When you know how to use one collection you know how to use them all. What varies about a collection is the collected object. Thus, we will be focusing on the class stored in both of the Fields and Properties collection.

The Fields Collection

Fields describe tables, views, and recordsets. A Field is the state of the intersection of a data source's row and column. The Fields collection contains all of the fields in a recordset, referring to one row at a time. The class of the object stored in the Fields collection is the Field class. The Field class is primarily used to store the value of a single row-column intersection. Generally, what you will want to know is the value of the field, but you may need to know the name, type, size, index of the field, or constraints placed on the field. The following example demonstrates how to display the state of a field, providing a good picture of the record and field values:

```
Public Sub DescribeARow()

  Const SQL As String = _
    "SELECT * FROM Customers"

  Const ConnectionString As String = _
    "Provider=Microsoft.Jet.OLEDB.4.0;" + _
    "Data Source=C:\Program Files\Microsoft " + _
    "Office\OFFICE11\SAMPLES\Northwind.mdb;Persist Security Info=False"

  Dim Recordset As Recordset
  Set Recordset = New Recordset
  Call Recordset.Open(SQL, ConnectionString, adOpenDynamic)

  Recordset.MoveFirst

  Dim Field As Field
```

```
    For Each Field In Recordset.Fields

        Debug.Print "Name: " & Field.Name
        Debug.Print "Type: " & Field.Type
        Debug.Print "Size: " & Field.ActualSize
        Debug.Print "Value: " & Field.Value
        Debug.Print "***********************"
    Next

  End Sub
```

The first half of the method initializes the Recordset and fills it. The For Each loop walks across each column in the recordset and dumps some salient data about each field in the Immediate window.

In general, it is useful to be cognizant of every aspect of our environment if we are to master it, but it is unlikely that you will generally need to interact with specific field properties other than the name, index or value. However, these properties exist because they are useful at some level. The most common reason we have found it helpful to read the attributes of a field was to build dynamic applications. For example, in theory if one knows the name, type, size, and value of a field then it is possible to create a graphical user interface on the fly. In VBA this capability isn't opportunistically realized, but in development environments like Delphi or Visual Basic .NET, great technologies and capabilities exist to build dynamic GUIs.

The Properties Collection

The Properties collection contains provider-specific, or extended properties, for the Recordset object. Some providers add important settings that you will want to be aware of. These extended properties are even more varied than the number of database vendors. It is important to note that the properties are in a name and value pairs, like a dictionary; hence, reading one extended property is no different than reading the other. Index the Properties collection by name or number and the associated value is accessible.

The Command Class

The Command class is an object-oriented representation of an instruction to a provider. One of the first languages I programmed in (aside from RomBasic as a young boy) was Databus. Mike Groer showed me how to write Databus code. Databus is a structured language like COBOL. The language depends on state and behavior but not entities with associated behavior. Unfortunately, state and behavior don't completely mirror the physical world because in the physical world we associate state and behavior with instances of specific things. For example, all people breathe (at least those we have met so far) but only some people are pilots. From an architectural perspective, this implies that people are capable of learning but what they have chosen to learn represents the state (or knowledge) of specific people.

As an evolutionary response of greater understanding many things in programming are being wrapped in classes, this includes SQL commands. A string containing SQL text is just a string that can contain any value, but a string contained within a Command object can be required—the behavior being the validation of the string—to be valid SQL. In this section, we'll take a moment to zoom in on the Command class.

Command Properties

Everything in programming is subjective. One of my favorite analogies is Grady Booch's description of a cat. From the perspective of a veterinarian, a cat has specific genus and species and is made of certain biological attributes. From the perspective of a cat-loving grandmother, a cat is a purring, furry, loving, lap companion. (And, from my brother's perspective cats are excellent targets for blowgun practice. Just kidding.) Thus, from a programmer's perspective a cat, and every classes' state and behavior is captured relative to the domain for which we are providing a solution. For a veterinarian, the proper implementation of a cat might be biological. For pet shelters, affection, color, gender, size, and whether the animal has been spayed or neutered might be sufficient to advertise for a new home for the kitty. (And, if programming for my brother, speed, stealth, and hunting success might be sufficient attributes to describe and record cats. Still kidding.) Getting back to `Command` classes even these are likely to evolve over time. Twenty years ago all data sources may have been monolithic, flat text files. Ten years ago the notion of logical relationships may have been incorporated, and currently just about everything, including XML files, are encompassed by the concept data source. Consequently, the current notion of a `Command` includes the names of tables, SQL, and stored procedures. For our purposes, we'll look at a snapshot of the state and capabilities offered by Commands to date.

The ActiveConnection Property

The `ActiveConnection` property, as discussed earlier, represents a connection object whether explicitly initialized or implicitly created via a connection string. (Refer to earlier code examples demonstrating how to use the `ActiveConnection` property.)

The CommandText Property

The `CommandText` property is used to set the string value that will be used by the data provider to figure out what information to fill the recordset with.

The CommandType Property

The `CommandType` property represents a hint to the provider indicating the meaning of the `CommandText` property. If the `CommandText` represents a stored procedure then the `CommandType` needs to be `CommandTypeEnum.adStoredProcedure`. If the `CommandText` represents a persisted recordset file name then the `CommandType` needs to be `CommandTypeEnum.adCmdFile`. Refer to the Help documentation on Command.CommandText and Command.CommandType for more information.

Command Methods

There are only three `Command` methods. (Keep in mind that ease of use, utility, and robustness represent how we measure goodness when it comes to classes. Thus, having only three methods does not mean a class is not important or useful.) Let's take a moment to look at the utility of the `CreateParameter`, `Cancel`, and `Execute` methods.

The CreateParameter Method

This method is used to manually create `Parameter` objects that can then be added to the `Command.Parameters` collection. The `CreateParameter` object has the following syntax:

```
CreateParameter([Name As String], _
 [Type As DataTypeEnum = adEmpty], _
 [Direction As ParameterDirectionEnum = adParamInput], _
 [Size As ADO_LONGPTR], [Value]) As Parameter
```

Name is the name of the argument. You can use this name to reference the `Parameter` object through the `Command` object's `Parameters` collection. When working with SQL Server, the name of a `Parameter` should be the same as the name of the stored procedure argument that it corresponds to.

`Type` indicates the data type of the parameter. It is specified as one of the `DataTypeEnum` constants. Each of the types correlates to a type you might pass to a stored procedure. The Help documentation for `DataTypeEnum` covers these in detail.

`Direction` is a `ParameterDirectionEnum` value that indicates whether the parameter will be used to pass data to an input argument, receive data from an output argument, or accept a return value from a stored procedure. The parameter enumerations—`adParamInput`, `adParamInputOutput`, `adParamOutput`, and `adParamReturnValue`—are self-describing.

The `Size` argument is used to indicate the size of the value in bytes, and `Value` represents the value of the argument to be passed to the command.

The following code sample demonstrates how you can use the `CreateParameter` method in conjunction with the `Parameters` collection `Append` method to create a `Parameter` and append it to the `Parameters` collection with one line of code. The next exampleconnects to a SQL Server instance of the Northwind database and calls the Sales by Year stored procedure:

```
 1: Public Sub CallStoredProcedure()
 2:
 3:    Const ConnectionString As String = _
 4:      "Provider=SQLOLEDB.1;Integrated Security=SSPI;" + _
 5:      "Persist Security Info=False;Initial Catalog=NorthwindCS;" + _
 6:      "Data Source=LAP800;Workstation ID=LAP800;"
 7:
 8:
 9:    Dim Command As Command
10:    Set Command = New Command
11:
12:    Command.ActiveConnection = ConnectionString
13:    Command.CommandText = "[Sales by Year]"
14:    Command.CommandType = CommandTypeEnum.adCmdStoredProc
15:
16:    Dim BeginningDate As ADODB.Parameter
17:    Dim EndingDate As ADODB.Parameter
18:
19:    Dim StartDate As Date
20:    StartDate = #1/1/1995#
21:
22:    Dim EndDate As Date
23:    EndDate = #1/1/2004#
24:
25:    Set BeginningDate = Command.CreateParameter("@Beginning_Date", _
26:      DataTypeEnum.adDate, ParameterDirectionEnum.adParamInput, , StartDate)
27:
28:    Set EndingDate = Command.CreateParameter("@Ending_Date", _
29:      DataTypeEnum.adDate, ParameterDirectionEnum.adParamInput, , EndDate)
30:
31:    Call Command.Parameters.Append(BeginningDate)
32:    Call Command.Parameters.Append(EndingDate)
33:
34:    Dim Recordset As ADODB.Recordset
35:    Set Recordset = Command.Execute
```

```
36:
37:   Call Sheet1.Range("A1").CopyFromRecordset(Recordset)
38:
39:End Sub
```

The new connection string is defined on lines 3 through 6. Line 9 and 10 declare and initialize a `Command` object. Line 12 associates the `Command` with the connection string, which causes the `Command` object to create a `Connection` object. Alternatively, we could create a `Connection` object and assign the `Connection` object to the `ActiveConnection` property. Line 13 sets the name of the stored procedure, and line 14 sets the `CommandType` to `CommandTypeEnum.adCmdStoredProc` telling the `Command` object how to treat the `CommandText`. Lines 16 and 17 declare the two parameters we need to pass to Sales by Year. Lines 19 through 23 declare and initialize the date values that will be used to initialize the parameters. We don't need to write the code in such a verbose way, but it makes it easier to debug the code and is clearer what is going on.

Lines 25 and 26 and lines 28 and 29 use the `Command.CreateParameter` method to initialize each parameter. The parameter names can be read from the stored procedure. The parameter type can be determined in the same way. Since these two parameters will be used as input arguments, we initialize the parameters with `ParameterDirectionEnum.adParamInput` and their respective values. Finally, we finish up by adding the parameter objects to the `Command`'s Parameters collection (lines 31 and 32), execute the command (line 35), and copy the resultset into a worksheet.

The Execute Method

This method executes the command text in the `Command` object's `CommandText` property. The `Execute` method has the following syntax for an action query (one that does not return a resultset):

```
Call Command.Execute( [RecordsAffected], [Parameters], [Options])
```

And for a select query:

```
Set Recordset = Command.Execute([RecordsAffected], [Parameters], [Options])
```

The `RecordsAffected` and `Options` arguments are identical to the corresponding arguments for the `Connection` object's `Execute` method described in the *Connection Methods* section earlier. If you are executing a SQL statement that requires one or more parameters to be passed, you can supply an array of values to the `Parameters` argument, one for each parameter required. (Refer to the sample at the end of the preceding section for an example.)

Command Collections

The example in the `CreateParameter` section earlier demonstrated all of the constituent parts needed to prepare and run a command. Let's wrap up our discussion with a brief review of the Parameters and Properties collection.

The Parameters Collection

The Parameters collection contains all of the `Parameter` objects associated with the `Command` object. Parameters are used to pass arguments to SQL statements and stored procedures as well as to receive output and return values from stored procedures.

The Properties Collection

The Properties collection contains provider-specific or extended properties for the Command object. Some providers add important settings that you will want to be aware of. Find out more about provider-specific properties by exploring the Help documentation for each provider in which you are interested.

Using ADO in Microsoft Excel Applications

Here's where it all comes together. In this section, we will combine the understanding of Excel programming that you've gained from previous chapters along with the SQL and ADO techniques discussed earlier. Excel applications frequently require data from outside sources. The most common of these sources are Access and SQL Server databases. However, we've created applications that required source data from mainframe text file dumps and even Excel workbooks. As we'll see, ADO makes acquiring data from these various data sources easy.

> In the next two sections, we'll be utilizing the Northwind database. This is a sample database that is provided with both Access and SQL Server. If you don't have this database available you will need to install it to run the example code.

To run the code examples, select the Tools ➪ References menu item from within the VBE. This will bring up the References dialog box. Scroll down until you find the alphabetically located entry labeled Microsoft ActiveX Data Objects 2.7 Library. Place a checkmark beside this entry (as seen in Figure 11-5) and click OK.

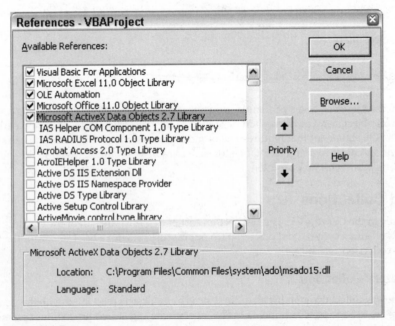

Figure 11-5

Note that it's perfectly normal to have multiple versions of the ADO object library available.

Using ADO with Microsoft Access

The rest of this chapter contains additional examples demonstrating how to use MS Access and MS SQL Server databases. We will continue our discussion with MS Access examples and wrap up with some MS SQL Server examples. (It is important to keep in mind that just about any data source can be used with ADO, but the examples in this chapter were chosen for the general availability of the sample databases.)

Connecting to Microsoft Access

ADO connects to Microsoft Access databases through the use of the OLE DB provider for Microsoft Jet (Jet refers to the database engine used by Access). We will be using version 4.0 of this provider. To connect to a Microsoft Access database, you simply specify this provider in the ADO connection string and then include any additional provider-specific arguments required. Earlier in the chapter, we used the Data Link Properties dialog box to build the connection string. Let's take a moment to dissect the connection string used to connection to an Access database:

❑ `Provider=Microsoft.Jet.OLEDB.4.0`
The Provider is a required part of the connection string that describes the OLE DB provider used for a specific connection

❑ `Data Source=[full path and filename to the Access database]`
The Data Source is a required part of the connection string used to indicate the file path to the database

❑ `Mode=mode`
The `Mode` is an optional part of the connection string that describes the kinds of operations that can be performed on the data source. Check the `ConnectModeEnum` for all of the available connection types. Three commonly used settings for this property are:

  ❑ `adModeShareDenyNone`
  Opens the database and allows complete shared access to other users. This is the default setting if the `Mode` argument is not specified.

  ❑ `adModeShareDenyWrite`
  Opens the database and allows other users read-access but prevents write-access.

  ❑ `adModeShareExclusive`
  Opens the database in exclusive mode, which prevents any other users from connecting to the database.

❑ `User ID=username`
The User ID is an optional argument used to authenticate the user. If the database requires a username and it is not supplied, then the connection will fail.

❑ `Password=password`
The password is an optional argument that can be paired with the User ID to authenticate the connection request. If the database is password protected then this argument is required.

The following example showcases a connection string demonstrating all of the elements mentioned in the preceding list:

```
Public Const ConnectionString As String = _
    "Provider=Microsoft.Jet.OLEDB.4.0;" & _
    "Data Source=C:\Files\Northwind.mdb;" & _
    "Mode=Share Exclusive;" & _
    "User ID=Admin;" & _
    "Password=password"
```

It is worth pointing out that if we initialize a Connection object with a complete connection string, then we use the representative values for elements like the Mode. For example, if we define an entire connection string then we might use the mode Share Exclusive, but if we initialized the Connection.Mode property in code then we'd use the equivalent ConnectModeEnum. adModeShareExlcusive. A reliable technique for building connection strings for any provider is to use the Data Link Properties dialog box.

Retrieving Data from Microsoft Access Using a Plain Text Query

The following procedure demonstrates how to retrieve data from a Microsoft Access database using a plain text query and place it on an Excel worksheet:

```
Public Sub PlainTextQuery()

    Const ConnectionString As String = _
        "Provider=Microsoft.Jet.OLEDB.4.0;" + _
        "Data Source=C:\Program Files\Microsoft " + _
        "Office\OFFICE11\SAMPLES\Northwind.mdb;Persist Security Info=False"

    Dim Recordset As ADODB.Recordset

    ' Define the SQL Statement
    Const SQL As String = _
        "SELECT CompanyName, ContactName " & _
        "FROM Customers " & _
        "WHERE Country = 'UK' " & _
        "ORDER BY CompanyName"

    ' Initialize the Recordset object and run the query
    Set Recordset = New ADODB.Recordset
    Call Recordset.Open(SQL, ConnectionString, CursorTypeEnum. _
adOpenForwardOnly, _
        LockTypeEnum.adLockReadOnly, CommandTypeEnum.adCmdText)

    ' Make sure we got records back
    If Not Recordset.EOF Then
        ' Dump the contents of the recordset onto the worksheet
        Call Sheet1.Range("A2").CopyFromRecordset(Recordset)

        ' Add headers to the worksheet
        With Sheet1.Range("A1:B1")
```

```
        .Value = Array("Company Name", "Contact Name")
        .Font.Bold = True
    End With


    ' Fit the column widths to the data
    Sheet1.UsedRange.EntireColumn.AutoFit
  Else
    Call MsgBox("Error: No records returned.", vbCritical)
  End If


  ' Close the recordset if it is still open
  If (Recordset.State And ObjectStateEnum.adStateOpen) Then Recordset.Close
  Set Recordset = Nothing

End Sub
```

The only ADO object used was the `Recordset` object. As mentioned at the beginning of the ADO section, all of the top-level ADO objects can be created and used independently. If we were going to perform multiple queries over the course of our application, we would have created a separate, publicly scoped `Connection` object in order to take advantage of ADO's connection-pooling feature.

The syntax of the `Recordset.Open` method has been optimized for maximum performance. We've told the provider what type of command is in the `Source` argument (`adCmdText`, a plain text query) and we've opened a forward-only, read-only cursor. The `CursorLocation` property is not specified. This type of cursor is often referred to as a *firehose cursor*, because it's the fastest way to retrieve data from a database.

We do not make any modifications to the destination worksheet until we are sure we have successfully retrieved data from the database. This avoids having to undo anything if the query fails. If we have data, then the `CopyFromRecordset` method is used to move the data from the `Recordset` into the worksheet. And, finally, we format the column headers, auto-fit the column data and close the `Recordset`.

Retrieving Data from Microsoft Access Using a Stored Query

Microsoft Access allows you to create and store SQL queries in the database. You can retrieve data from these stored queries just as easily as you can use a plain text SQL statement. The following procedure demonstrates how to invoke a query defined in the Access database:

```
Public Sub SavedQuery()

  Dim Field As ADODB.Field
  Dim Recordset As ADODB.Recordset
  Dim Offset As Long

  Const ConnectionString As String = _
    "Provider=Microsoft.Jet.OLEDB.4.0;" + _
    "Data Source=C:\Program Files\Microsoft " + _
    "Office\OFFICE11\SAMPLES\Northwind.mdb;Persist Security Info=False"

  ' Create the Recorset object and run the query.
  Set Recordset = New ADODB.Recordset
  Call Recordset.Open("[Sales By Category]", ConnectionString, _
```

```
        CursorTypeEnum.adOpenForwardOnly, LockTypeEnum.adLockReadOnly, _
        CommandTypeEnum.adCmdTable)

    ' Make sure we got records back
    If Not Recordset.EOF Then
        ' Add headers to the worksheet.
        With Sheet1.Range("A1")
            For Each Field In Recordset.Fields
                .Offset(0, Offset).Value = Field.Name
                Offset = Offset + 1
            Next Field
            .Resize(1, Recordset.Fields.Count).Font.Bold = True
        End With

        ' Dump the contents of the recordset onto the worksheet.
        Call Sheet1.Range("A2").CopyFromRecordset(Recordset)

        ' Fit the column widths to the data.
        Sheet1.UsedRange.EntireColumn.AutoFit
    Else
        MsgBox "Error: No records returned.", vbCritical
    End If

    ' Close the recordset
    Recordset.Close
    Set Recordset = Nothing

End Sub
```

Examine the differences between the `Recordset.Open` method used in this procedure and the one used in the plain text query. In this case, rather than providing a SQL string we specified the name of the stored query that we wanted to execute. We also told the provider that the type of query being executed was a table query. The Jet OLE DB provider treats stored queries and queries of entire database tables in the same manner.

Since we did not create the SQL statement ourselves, we did not know the names of the fields we were retrieving, or even how many fields there were. Therefore, in order to create the correct set of headers for each column in the destination worksheet we needed to loop the `Fields` collection of the `Recordset` object and determine this information dynamically. In order to accomplish this, the recordset had to be open, so we added the fields to the worksheet prior to closing the recordset in this case.

Inserting, Updating, and Deleting Records with Plain Text SQL in Microsoft Access

Executing plain text INSERT, UPDATE, and DELETE statements use virtually identical preparation code. Therefore, we'll examine these action queries by inserting a new record, updating that record, and then deleting it, all within the same procedure. This, of course, is not normally something you would do. You can take this generic procedure, however, and create a single purpose insert, update, or delete procedure by simply removing the sections that you don't need.

We're going to use the `Shippers` table from the Northwind database in the next procedure. The original contents of this table are shown in Figure 11-6. There are two things that you'll want to keep in mind

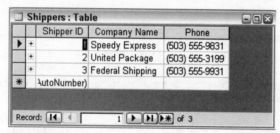

Figure 11-6

before we begin to alter this table. First, you'll notice that the column headings in the table are slightly different from the field names that we'll use in our SQL statements. This is because Access allows you to assign a `Caption` property to each field in a table, which is then displayed instead of the underlying field name. However, you must use the underlying field name in SQL statements. Second, notice that the last row in the Shipper ID column contains the value "(AutoNumber)". This isn't really a value; rather it's a prompt that alerts you to the fact that values for the Shipper ID column are automatically generated by the Jet database engine. This column is the primary key for the `Shippers` table and AutoNumber fields are a common method used to generate the unique value required for the primary key. As you'll see in the following example, you don't (and can't), set or change the value of an AutoNumber field. If you need to maintain a reference to a new record that you've inserted into the table, you'll need to retrieve the value that was assigned to that record by the AutoNumber field. We'll show how this is done in the following example:

```
1: Public Sub CheckError(ByVal RecordsAffected As Long, _
2:   ByVal Expected As Long, ByVal Description As String)
3:
4:   If RecordsAffected <> Expected Then
5:     Call RaiseError(Description)
6:   End If
7:
8: End Sub
9:
10: Public Sub RaiseError(ByVal Description As String)
11:   Call Err.Raise(vbObjectError + 1024, , Description)
12: End Sub
13:
14:
15: Public Function GetPrimaryKey(ByVal Command As ADODB.Command) As Long
16:
17:   Dim RecordsAffected As Long
18:   Dim Recordset As ADODB.Recordset
19:
20:   ' Retrieve the primary key generated for our new record.
21:   Command.CommandText = "SELECT @@IDENTITY"
22:
23:   Set Recordset = Command.Execute(Options:=CommandTypeEnum.adCmdText)
24:
25:   If Recordset.EOF Then
26:     Call RaiseError("Error retrieving primary key value.")
27:   End If
28:
```

```
29:    GetPrimaryKey = Recordset.Fields(0).Value
30:    Recordset.Close
31:
32: End Function
33:
34: Public Sub ExecuteCommand(ByVal Command As ADODB.Command, _
35:    ByVal CommandText As String, _
36:    ByVal Description As String)
37:
38:    Dim RecordsAffected As Long
39:    Command.CommandText = CommandText
40:
41:    Call Command.Execute(RecordsAffected, , _
42:       CommandTypeEnum.adCmdText Or ExecuteOptionEnum.adExecuteNoRecords)
43:
44:    Call CheckError(RecordsAffected, 1, Description)
45:
46: End Sub
47:
48:
49: Public Sub InsertRecord(ByVal Command As ADODB.Command)
50:
51:    Const CommandText As String = _
52:       "INSERT INTO Shippers(CompanyName, Phone) " & _
53:       "VALUES('Air Carriers', '(205) 555 1212')"
54:
55:    Const Description As String = _
56:       "Error executing INSERT statement."
57:
58:    Call ExecuteCommand(Command, CommandText, Description)
59:
60: End Sub
61:
62: Public Sub UpdateRecord(ByVal Command As ADODB.Command, ByVal Key As Long)
63:
64:    Dim CommandText As String
65:    CommandText = _
66:       "UPDATE Shippers SET Phone='(206) 546 0086' " & _
67:       "WHERE ShipperID=" & CStr(Key) & ";"
68:
69:    Const Description As String = _
70:       "Error executing UPDATE statement."
71:
72:    Call ExecuteCommand(Command, CommandText, Description)
73:
74: End Sub
75:
76: Public Sub DeleteRecord(ByVal Command As ADODB.Command, ByVal Key As Long)
77:
78:    Dim CommandText As String
79:    CommandText = "DELETE FROM Shippers WHERE ShipperID = " & CStr(Key) & ";"
80:
81:    Const Description As String = _
82:       "Error executing DELETE statement."
```

```
 83:
 84:    Call ExecuteCommand(Command, CommandText, Description)
 85:
 86: End Sub
 87:
 88: Private Property Get ConnectionString() As String
 89:    ConnectionString = _
 90:      "Provider=Microsoft.Jet.OLEDB.4.0;" + _
 91:      "Data Source=C:\Program Files\Microsoft " + _
 92:      "Office\OFFICE11\SAMPLES\Northwind.mdb;Persist Security Info=False"
 93:
 94: End Property
 95:
 96:
 97: Public Sub InsertUpdateDelete()
 98:
 99:    Dim Command As ADODB.Command
100:    Dim Key As Long
101:
102:    On Error GoTo ErrorHandler
103:
104:    Set Command = New ADODB.Command
105:    Command.ActiveConnection = ConnectionString
106:
107:    Call InsertRecord(Command)
108:    Key = GetPrimaryKey(Command)
109:
110:    Call UpdateRecord(Command, Key)
111:
112:    Call DeleteRecord(Command, Key)
113:
114:    ErrorExit:
115:      Set Command = Nothing
116:      Exit Sub
117:
118: ErrorHandler:
119:      Call MsgBox(Err.Description, vbCritical)
120:      Resume ErrorExit
121: End Sub
```

There are about many ways to decompose a solution. We prefer many small, self-documenting methods that can be reused, easily understood at a glance, and consequently easy to reorder and debug. The preceding listing demonstrates this style. Some programmers (and authors) will write large methods with a lot of comments, but these monolithic methods generally end up being single-purpose methods. The example program is decomposed into several parts: CheckError, RaiseError, GetPrimaryKey, ExecuteCommand, InsertRecord, UpdateRecord, DeleteRecord, and InsertUpdateDelete.

CheckError and RaiseError are used to compare the records affected and raise an error if the result doesn't match the expected result. GetPrimaryKey, InsertRecord, UpdateRecord, and DeleteRecord all rely on ExecuteCommand to send a query to the database and check the results. GetPrimaryKey is called immediately after the INSERT command (see lines 107 and 108) sending SELECT ⇨ IDENTITY to the database; this query will get the recently generated primary key from an insert statement. The UpdateRecord and DeleteRecord demonstrate how to use the primary key to find specific records. Finally, the `InsertUpdateDelete` method exercises the various queries, tying it all together by demonstrating how to factor code for reuse and employ error handling to ensure things get tidied up (see lines 114 through 121).

> Note: ⇨ **IDENTITY will only work with Access databases that are saved in Access 2000 format or above. It does not work with Access 97.**

Using ADO with Microsoft SQL Server

In the previous section on Microsoft Access, we covered the basics of performing the various types of queries in ADO. Since ADO is designed to present a common gateway to different data sources, there isn't a lot of difference in these basic operations whether your database is in Access or in SQL Server. Therefore, after a brief introduction to the few important differences that arise when using ADO with SQL Server, in this section, we'll cover more advanced topics, including stored procedures, multiple recordsets, and disconnected recordsets. We won't be going into a lot of detail on how to use SQL Server itself, as that is beyond the scope of this chapter. If you'd like to learn more about SQL Server, one of the best references available is Robert Vieira's *Professional SQL Server 2000* from Wrox press, ISBN 1-861004-48-6.

Connecting to Microsoft SQL Server

To connect to a Microsoft SQL Server database, you simply specify the OLE DB provider for SQL Server in the ADO connection string, and then include any additional provider-specific arguments required. The following is a summary of the connection string arguments you will most frequently use when connecting to a SQL Server database:

❑   `Provider=SQLOLEDB;`

❑   `Data 2Source=`*servername*`;`
In the case of SQL Server 7.0, this will almost always be the `NetBIOS` name of the computer that SQL Server is installed on. SQL Server 2000 added the ability to install multiple SQL Servers on one machine, so the server name will have the following syntax: `NetBIOS` name`\SQL Server` name. If SQL Server is installed on the same machine as your spreadsheet, you can use the name `localhost`.

❑   `Initial Catalog=`*databasename*`;`
Unlike Access, one instance of SQL Server can contain many databases. This argument will be the name of the database you want to connect to.

❑   `User ID=`*username*`;`
The username for SQL Server authentication.

❑   `Password=`*password*`;`
The password for SQL Server authentication.

❑   `Network Library=`*netlib*`;`
By default, the SQL Server OLE DB provider will attempt to use *named pipes network protocol* to connect to SQL Server. This is required for using Windows integrated security (explained next). There are many instances, however, where it is not possible to use named pipes. These include accessing SQL Server from a Windows 9x operating system and accessing SQL Server over the

Internet. In these cases, the preferred protocol for connecting to SQL Server is TCP/IP. This can be specified on each machine by using the SQL Server Client Network Utility, or you can simply use the Network Library connection string argument to specify the name of the TCP/IP network library, which is dbmssocn.

❑   `Integrated Security=SSPI;`
  This connection string argument specifies that you want to use Windows integrated security rather than SQL Server authentication. The `User ID` and `Password` arguments will be ignored if this argument is present.

A Note About SQL Server Security

There are three types of security that SQL Server can be set to use: SQL Server authentication, Windows integrated security, and mixed mode. SQL Server authentication means that separate user accounts must be added to SQL Server and each user must supply a SQL Server username and password to connect.

This type of security is most commonly used when SQL Server must be accessed from outside the network. With Windows integrated security, SQL Server recognizes the same usernames and passwords that are used to log in to the Windows NT/2000 network. Mixed mode simply means you can use either one of the first two.

The following is an example of a connection string that shows some of the elements of a basic connection. Keep in mind that you can use the Data Link Properties dialog box to build connection strings for SQL Server and many other providers too:

```
Const ConnectionString As String = _
    "Provider=SQLOLEDB.1;Integrated Security=SSPI;" + _
    "Persist Security Info=False;Initial Catalog=NorthwindCS;" + _
    "Data Source=LAP800;Workstation ID=LAP800;"
```

Microsoft SQL Server Stored Procedures

The syntax for executing plain text queries against SQL Server is identical to that which we used in the example for Access. The only difference is the contents of the connection string. Since you already know how to send text queries, we will take a closeup look at invoking stored procedures stored in a SQL Server database.

Stored procedures are simply precompiled SQL statements that can be accessed by name from the database. They are much like VBA procedures in that they can accept arguments and return values. Following is an example of a simple stored procedure that queries the Orders table and Order Subtotals view:

```
ALTER Procedure dbo.[Employee Sales by Country]
@Beginning_Date datetime,
@Ending_Date datetime AS
SELECT Employees.Country, Employees.LastName,
  Employees.FirstName, Orders.ShippedDate, Orders.OrderID,
  "Order Subtotals".Subtotal AS SaleAmount FROM Employees
INNER JOIN (Orders INNER JOIN "Order Subtotals"
 ON Orders.OrderID = "Order Subtotals".OrderID)
 ON Employees.EmployeeID = Orders.EmployeeID
WHERE Orders.ShippedDate
  Between @Beginning_Date And @Ending_Date
```

This stored procedure takes two arguments, @Beginning_Date and @Ending_Date, and returns a recordset containing the values for the fields specified in the SELECT list for Orders and Order subtotals whose ShippedDate falls between the Beginning_Date and Ending_Date parameters.

ADO provides a very quick and simple way to execute stored procedures using the Connection object. ADO treats all stored procedures in the currently connected database as dynamic methods of the Connection object. You can call a stored procedure exactly like any other Connection object method, passing any arguments to the stored procedure as method arguments and optionally passing a Recordset object as the last argument if the stored procedure returns a result set.

This method is best used for "one off" procedures rather than those you will execute multiple times, since it isn't the most efficient method. However, it is significantly easier to code. The following exampledemonstrates executing the preceding stored procedure as a method of the Connection object:

```vb
Public Sub ExecuteStoredProcAsMethod()

    Dim Connection As ADODB.Connection
    Dim Recordset As ADODB.Recordset

    Const ConnectionString As String = _
        "Provider=SQLOLEDB.1;Integrated Security=SSPI;" + _
        "Persist Security Info=False;Initial Catalog=NorthwindCS;" + _
        "Data Source=LAP800;Workstation ID=LAP800;"

On Error GoTo Cleanup
    Set Connection = New ADODB.Connection
    Set Recordset = New ADODB.Recordset

    Call Connection.Open(ConnectionString)

    Dim StartDate As Date, EndDate As Date
    StartDate = #1/1/1995#
    EndDate = #1/1/2004#
    Connection.Employee_Sales_by_Country StartDate, EndDate, Recordset

    Call Sheet1.Range("A1").CopyFromRecordset(Recordset)

    Sheet1.UsedRange.EntireColumn.AutoFit

Cleanup:
If (Err.Number <> 0) Then Debug.Print Err.Description
If (Connection.State = ObjectStateEnum.adStateOpen) Then Connection.Close
If (Recordset.State = ObjectStateEnum.adStateOpen) Then Recordset.Close

End Sub
```

In the preceding procedure, we executed our Employee_Sales_by_Country stored procedure and passed it the values #1/1/1995# for the @Beginning_Date, #1/1/2004 for the @Ending_Date. This populated the recordset with all of the employee sales between 1995 and 2004. Note that the

`Connection` object must be opened before the dynamic methods are populated and that you must instantiate the `Recordset` object prior to passing it as an argument.

The most efficient way to handle stored procedures that will be executed multiple times is to prepare a publicly scoped `Command` object to represent them. The `Connection` will be stored in the `Command` object's `ActiveConnection` property, the stored procedure name will be stored in the `Command` object's `CommandText` property, and any arguments to the stored procedure will be used to populate the `Command` object's `Parameters` collection.

Once this `Command` object has been created, it can be executed as many times as you like over the course of your application without incurring the overhead required to perform the previously described tasks with each execution.

For this example, let's create a simple stored procedure that we can use to insert new records into our `Shippers` table:

```
ALTER PROCEDURE InsertShippers
  @CompanyName nvarchar(40),
  @Phone nvarchar(24)
AS
INSERT INTO Shippers
(CompanyName, Phone)
VALUES (@CompanyName, @Phone)
RETURN @@IDENTITY

CREATE PROCEDURE InsertShippers @CompanyName nvarchar(40), @Phone
nvarchar(24) AS
INSERT INTO Shippers
```

As you can see, the stored procedure in the preceding code has two arguments, `@CompanyName` and `@Phone`, which are used to collect the values to insert into those respective fields in the `Shippers` table. However, as you may recall from our Access example, the `Shippers` table has three fields, and the stored procedure above doesn't reference the first field, `ShipperID`, anywhere.

This is because, similar to the `ShipperID` field in the Access version of the Northwind database, the `ShipperID` field in the SQL Server version of Northwind is populated automatically by the database any time a new record is inserted. We also retrieve this automatically assigned value in a similar fashion; through the use of SQL Server's `@@IDENTITY` system function. In this case, however, we won't have to make a separate query to retrieve the `Shipper ID` value since it will be returned to us by the stored procedure.

In order to present a more realistic application scenario, the following example uses publicly scoped `Connection` and `Command` objects, procedures to create and destroy the connection, a procedure to prepare the `Command` object for use, and a procedure that demonstrates how to use the `Command` object:

```
Option Explicit

Private Const ConnectionString As String = _
  "Provider=SQLOLEDB.1;Integrated Security=SSPI;" + _
```

```
      "Persist Security Info=False;Initial Catalog=NorthwindCS;" + _
      "Data Source=LAP800;Workstation ID=LAP800;"

Public Command As ADODB.Command
Public Connection As ADODB.Connection

Private Sub CreateConnection()
   Set Connection = New ADODB.Connection
   Call Connection.Open(ConnectionString)
End Sub

Private Sub DestroyConnection()
   If (Connection.State = ObjectStateEnum.adStateOpen) Then
      Connection.Close
   End If

   Set Connection = Nothing
End Sub

Private Sub PrepareCommandObject()

   Set Command = New ADODB.Command
   Set Command.ActiveConnection = Connection
   Command.CommandText = "InsertShippers"
   Command.CommandType = adCmdStoredProc

   Call Command.Parameters.Append( _
      Command.CreateParameter("@RETURN_VALUE", DataTypeEnum.adInteger, _
         ParameterDirectionEnum.adParamReturnValue, 0))

   Call Command.Parameters.Append( _
      Command.CreateParameter("@CompanyName", DataTypeEnum.adVarWChar, _
         ParameterDirectionEnum.adParamInput, 40))

   Call Command.Parameters.Append( _
      Command.CreateParameter("@Phone", DataTypeEnum.adVarWChar, _
         ParameterDirectionEnum.adParamInput, 24))

End Sub

Public Sub UseCommandObject()
   Dim Key As Long
   Dim RecordsAffected As Long

   On Error GoTo ErrorHandler

   CreateConnection
   PrepareCommandObject

   Command.Parameters("@CompanyName").Value = "Air Carriers"
   Command.Parameters("@Phone").Value = "(206) 555 1212"

   Call Command.Execute(RecordsAffected, , ExecuteOptionEnum.adExecuteNoRecords)
```

```
    If (RecordsAffected <> 1) Then
      Call Err.Raise(vbObjectError + 1024, , _
          Description:="Error executing Command object.")
    End If

    Key = Command.Parameters("@RETURN_VALUE").Value
    Debug.Print "The key value of the new record is: " & CStr(Key)

ErrorExit:

    Set Command = Nothing
    DestroyConnection
    Exit Sub

ErrorHandler:
    Call MsgBox(Err.Description, vbCritical)
    Resume ErrorExit
End Sub
```

In a normal application you would not create and destroy the Connection and Command objects in the UseCommandObject procedure. These objects are intended for reuse and therefore, would typically be created when your application first started and destroyed just before it ended.

When constructing and using the Command object's Parameters collection, keep in mind that the first parameter is always reserved for the stored procedure return value, even if the stored procedure doesn't have a return value.

Even though we didn't make any particular use of the Shipper ID value returned from the stored procedure for the new record, in a normal application this value would be very important. The CompanyName and Phone fields are for human consumption; the primary key value is how the database identifies the record. For example, in the Northwind database the Shipper ID is a required field for entering new records into the Orders table. Therefore, if you planned on adding an order that was going to use the new shipper you would have to know the Shipper ID.

Multiple Recordsets

The SQL Server OLE DB provider is an example of a provider that allows you to execute a SQL statement that returns multiple recordsets. This feature comes in very handy when you need to populate multiple controls on a form with lookup-table information from the database. You can combine all of the lookup-table SELECT queries into a single stored procedure and then loop through the individual recordsets, assigning their contents to the corresponding controls.

For example, if you needed to create a user interface for entering information into the Orders table you would need information from several related tables, including Customers and Shippers (shown in Figure 11-7).

We'll create an abbreviated example of a stored procedure that returns the lookup information from these two tables, and then use the result to populate drop-downs on a UserForm:

```
CREATE PROCEDURE GetLookupValues
AS
```

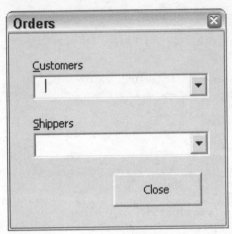

Figure 11-7

```
SELECT
  CustomerID,
  CompanyName
FROM
  Customers
SELECT
 ShipperID,
 CompanyName
FROM
  Shippers
```

Note that the stored procedure above contains two separate SELECT
statements. These will populate two independent recordsets when the stored
procedure is executed using ADO. The procedure below is an example of
a UserForm_Initialize event that populates dropdowns on the UserForm
with the results of the GetLookupValues stored procedure:Option Explicit

```
Private Const ConnectionString As String = _
   "Provider=SQLOLEDB.1;Integrated Security=SSPI;" + _
   "Persist Security Info=False;Initial Catalog=NorthwindCS;" + _
   "Data Source=LAP800;Workstation ID=LAP800;"

Private Sub UserForm_Initialize()

  Dim Connection As ADODB.Connection
  Dim Recordset As ADODB.Recordset

  Set Connection = New ADODB.Connection
  Connection.ConnectionString = ConnectionString

  Connection.Open

  Set Recordset = New ADODB.Recordset
```

```
   Call Recordset.Open("GetLookupValues", Connection, _
     CursorTypeEnum.adOpenForwardOnly, LockTypeEnum.adLockReadOnly, _
     CommandTypeEnum.adCmdStoredProc)

   Do While Not Recordset.EOF
     Call ComboBoxCustomers.AddItem(Recordset.Fields(1).Value)
     Recordset.MoveNext
   Loop

   Set Recordset = Recordset.NextRecordset

   Do While Not Recordset.EOF
     Call ComboBoxShippers.AddItem(Recordset.Fields(1).Value)
     Recordset.MoveNext
   Loop

   ' Closes the recordset implicitly
   Set Recordset = Recordset.NextRecordset

   If (Connection.State = ObjectStateEnum.adStateOpen) Then Connection.Close

End Sub
```

One thing to note about the method just demonstrated is that it requires prior knowledge of the number and order of recordsets returned by the call to the stored procedure. We have also left out any handling of the primary key values associated with the lookup table descriptions. In a real-world application, you would need to maintain these keys (we prefer using a `Collection` object for this purpose) so that you could retrieve the primary key value that corresponded to the user's selection in each drop-down.

Disconnected Recordsets

In the *Returning Data from Microsoft Access Using a Plain Text Query* section above, we mentioned that getting in and out of the database as quickly as possible was an important goal. However, the `Recordset` object is a powerful tool that you would often like to hold onto and use without locking other users out of the database. The solution to this problem is ADO's disconnected recordset feature.

A disconnected recordset is a `Recordset` object whose connection to its data source has been severed, but which can still remain open. The result is a fully functional `Recordset` object that does not hold any locks in the database from which it was queried. Disconnected recordsets can remain open as long as you need them, they can be reconnected to and resynchronized with the data source, and they can even be persisted to disk for later retrieval. We will examine a few of these capabilities in the following example.

Let's say that you wanted to implement a feature that would allow users to view any group of customers they chose. Running a query against the database each time the user specified a different criterion would be an inefficient way to accomplish this. A much better alternative would be to query the complete set of customers from the database and hold them in a disconnected recordset. You could then use the `Filter` property of the `Recordset` object to quickly extract the set of customers that your user requested. The following example shows all of the elements required to create a disconnected recordset:

```
Option Explicit

Private Const ConnectionString As String = _
  "Provider=SQLOLEDB.1;Integrated Security=SSPI;" + _
```

```
        "Persist Security Info=False;Initial Catalog=NorthwindCS;" + _
        "Data Source=LAP800;Workstation ID=LAP800;"

Public Connection As ADODB.Connection

Public Recordset As ADODB.Recordset

Public Sub CreateDisconnectedRecordset()

    Dim SQL As String

    SQL = "SELECT CustomerID, CompanyName, ContactName, Country " & _
          "FROM Customers"

    Set Connection = New ADODB.Connection
    Connection.ConnectionString = ConnectionString
    Connection.Open

    Set Recordset = New ADODB.Recordset
    Recordset.CursorLocation = CursorLocationEnum.adUseClient
    Recordset.CursorType = CursorTypeEnum.adOpenStatic

    Recordset.LockType = LockTypeEnum.adLockBatchOptimistic
    Call Recordset.Open(SQL, Connection, , , CommandTypeEnum.adCmdText)

    Set Recordset.ActiveConnection = Nothing

    Call Sheet4.Range("A1").CopyFromRecordset(Recordset)

    ' Connection intentionally left open
End Sub
```

Note that the `Recordset` object variable in the preceding example is declared with public scope. If we were to declare the `Recordset` object variable at the procedure level, VBA would automatically destroy it when the procedure ended and it would no longer be available for use.

There are six crucial steps required in order to successfully create a disconnected recordset. It's possible to combine several of them into one step during the `Recordset.Open` method, and it's more efficient to do so, but we've separated them for the sake of clarity:

❑   You must create a new, empty `Recordset` object to start with.

❑   You must set the cursor location to client-side. Since the recordset will be disconnected from the server, the cursor cannot be managed there. Note that this setting *must* be made *before* you open the recordset. It is not possible to change the cursor location once the recordset is open.

❑   The ADO client-side cursor engine supports only one type of cursor, the static cursor, so this is what the `CursorType` property must be set to.

❑   ADO has a lock type specifically designed for disconnected recordsets called Batch Optimistic. The Batch Optimistic lock type makes it possible to reconnect the disconnected recordset to the database and update the database with records that have been modified while the recordset was disconnected. This operation is beyond the scope of this chapter, so just note that the Batch Optimistic lock type is required in order to create a disconnected recordset.

❏ Opening the recordset is the next step. In this example, we've used a plain text SQL query. This is not a requirement. You can create a disconnected recordset from almost any source that can be used to create a standard recordset. There are a few capabilities that the client-side cursor engine lacks, however, multiple recordsets are one example.

❏ The final step is disconnecting the recordset from the data source. This is accomplished by setting the recordset's `Connection` object to `Nothing`. If you recall from the *Recordset Object Properties* section discussed earlier, the `Connection` object associated with a `Recordset` object is accessed through the `Recordset.ActiveConnection` property. Setting this property to `Nothing` severs the connection between the recordset and the data source.

Now that we have a disconnected recordset to work with, what kind of things can we do with it? Just about any operation that the `Recordset` object allows is the answer. Let's say the user wanted to see a list of customers located in Germany and sorted in alphabetical order. This is how you'd accomplish that task:

```
Public Sub FilterDisconnectedRecordset()
    Call Sheet4.Range("A:D").Clear
    Recordset.Filter = "Country = 'Germany'"
    Recordset.Sort = "CompanyName"
    Call Sheet4.Range("A1").CopyFromRecordset(Recordset)
End Sub
```

If you are working in a busy, multiuser environment, the data in your disconnected recordset may become out-of-date during the course of your application due to other users inserting, updating, and deleting records. You can solve this problem by requerying the recordset. As demonstrated by the following example, this is a simple matter of reconnecting to the data source, executing the `Recordset.Requery` method, then disconnecting from the data source:

```
Public Sub RequeryConnection()

    Set Recordset.ActiveConnection = Connection
    Call Recordset.Requery(Options:=CommandTypeEnum.adCmdText)
    Set Recordset.ActiveConnection = Nothing

End Sub
```

Using ADO with Non-Standard Data Sources

This section will describe how you can use ADO to access data from two common non-standard data sources (data sources that are not strictly considered databases), Excel workbooks and text files. Although the idea may seem somewhat counterintuitive, ADO is often the best choice for retrieving data from workbooks and text files because it eliminates the often lengthy process of opening them in Excel. Using ADO also allows you to take advantage of the power of SQL to do exactly what you want in the process.

Querying Microsoft Excel Workbooks

When using ADO to access Excel workbooks, you use the same OLE DB provider that you used earlier in this chapter to access data from Microsoft Access. In addition to Access, this provider also supports most

ISAM data sources (data sources that are laid out in a tabular, row, and column format). ADO will allow you to operate on workbooks that are either open or closed. However, by far the most common scenario will involve performing data access on a closed workbook.

We will be using the `Sales.xls` workbook, a picture of which is shown in Figure 11-8, for our Excel examples. You can download this workbook, along with the rest of the examples for this book, from the Wrox Web site.

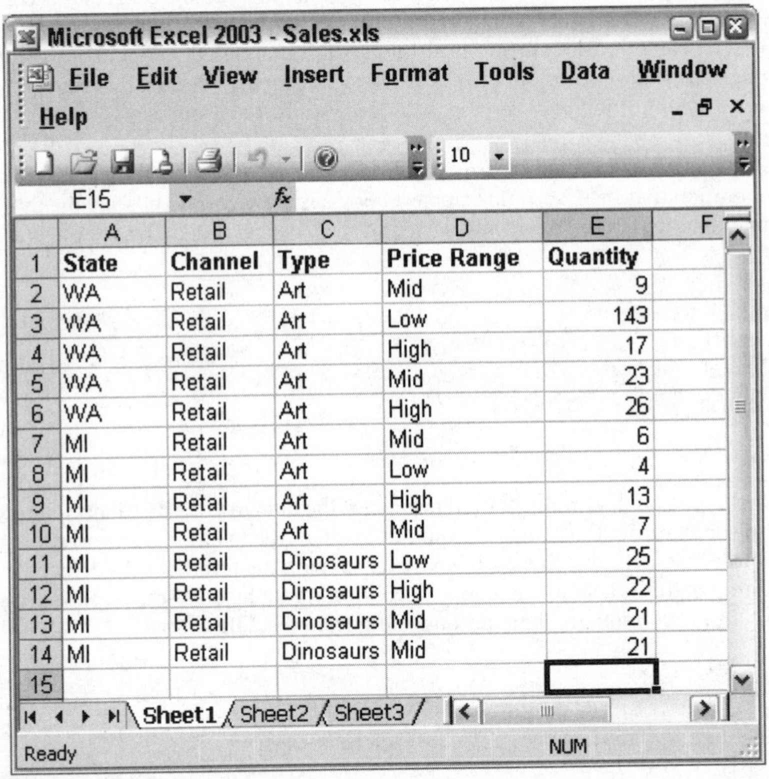

	A	B	C	D	E	F
1	State	Channel	Type	Price Range	Quantity	
2	WA	Retail	Art	Mid	9	
3	WA	Retail	Art	Low	143	
4	WA	Retail	Art	High	17	
5	WA	Retail	Art	Mid	23	
6	WA	Retail	Art	High	26	
7	MI	Retail	Art	Mid	6	
8	MI	Retail	Art	Low	4	
9	MI	Retail	Art	High	13	
10	MI	Retail	Art	Mid	7	
11	MI	Retail	Dinosaurs	Low	25	
12	MI	Retail	Dinosaurs	High	22	
13	MI	Retail	Dinosaurs	Mid	21	
14	MI	Retail	Dinosaurs	Mid	21	
15						

Figure 11-8

When using ADO to work with Excel, the workbook file takes the place of the database while worksheets within the workbook, as well as named ranges, serve as tables. Let's compare a connection string used to connect to an Access database with a connection string used to connect to an Excel workbook.

Connection string to an Access database:

```
"Provider=Microsoft.Jet.OLEDB.4.0;" & _
          "Data Source=C:\Files\Northwind.mdb;"
```

Connection string to an Excel workbook:

```
"Provider=Microsoft.Jet.OLEDB.4.0;" & _
          "Data Source=C:\Files\Sales.xls;" & _
          "Extended Properties=Excel 8.0;"
```

Note that the same provider is used and that the full path and filename of the Excel workbook takes the place of the full path and filename of the Access database. (The file paths here are artificially contrived. Replace the example file locations with the physical file path where the files are actually located on your computer.) The only difference is that when using the OLE DB provider for Microsoft Jet to connect to data sources other than Access, you must specify the name of the data source you wish to connect to in the Extended Properties argument. When connecting to Excel, you set the Extended Properties argument to Excel 8.0 for Excel 97 and higher.

You query data from an Excel worksheet using a plain text SQL statement exactly like you would query a database table. However, the format of the table name is different for Excel queries. You can specify the table that you wish to query from an Excel workbook in one of four different ways:

❑ *Worksheet Name Alone.* When using the name of a specific worksheet as the table name in your SQL statement, the worksheet name must be suffixed with a $ character and surrounded with square brackets. For example, [Sheet1$] is a valid worksheet table name. If the worksheet name contains spaces or non-alphanumeric characters, you must surround it in single quotes. An example of this is:
['My Sheet$'].

❑ *Worksheet-level Range Name.* You can use a worksheet-level range name as a table name in your SQL statement. Simply prefix the range name with the worksheet name it belongs to, using the formatting conventions described earlier. An example of this would be:
[Sheet1$SheetLevelName].

❑ *Specific Range Address.* You can specify the table in your SQL statement as a specific range address on the target worksheet. The syntax for this method is identical to that for a worksheet-level range name:
[Sheet1$A1:E20].

❑ *Workbook-level Range Name.* You can also use a workbook-level range name as the table in your SQL statement. In this case, there is no special formatting required. You simply use the name directly without brackets.

Although, our sample workbook contains only one worksheet, the target workbook can contain as many worksheets and named ranges as you wish. You simply need to know which one to use in your query. The following procedure demonstrates all four table-specifying methods discussed just now:

```vb
Option Explicit

Public Sub QueryWorksheet()

  Dim Recordset As ADODB.Recordset
  Dim ConnectionString As String

  ConnectionString = _
    "Provider=Microsoft.Jet.OLEDB.4.0;" & _
    "Data Source=" & ThisWorkbook.Path & "\Sales.xls;" & _
    "Extended Properties=Excel 8.0;"

  Dim SQL As String

  ' Query based on the worksheet name.
  SQL = "SELECT * FROM [Sales$]"
```

```
' Query based on a sheet level range name.
' SQL = "SELECT * FROM [Sales$MyRange]"
' Query based on a specific range address.
' SQL = "SELECT * FROM [Sales$A1:E14]"
' Query based on a book level range name.
' SQL = "SELECT * FROM BookLevelName"

Set Recordset = New ADODB.Recordset

On Error GoTo Cleanup

Call Recordset.Open(SQL, ConnectionString, _
    CursorTypeEnum.adOpenForwardOnly, LockTypeEnum.adLockReadOnly, _
    CommandTypeEnum.adCmdText)

Call Sheet1.Range("A1").CopyFromRecordset(Recordset)

Cleanup:
    Debug.Print Err.Description

    If (Recordset.State = ObjectStateEnum.adStateOpen) Then
        Recordset.Close
    End If

    Set Recordset = Nothing

End Sub
```

By default, the OLE DB provider for Microsoft Jet assumes that the first row in the table you specify with your SQL statement contains the field names for the data. If this is the case, you can perform more complex SQL queries, making use of the WHERE and ORDER BY clauses. If the first row of your data table does not contain field names, however, you must inform the provider of this fact or you will lose the first row of data. The way to accomplish this is by providing an additional setting, HDR=No, to the Extended Properties argument of the connection string:

```
"Provider=Microsoft.Jet.OLEDB.4.0;" & _
"Data Source=" & ThisWorkbook.Path & "\Sales.xls;" & _
"Extended Properties=""Excel 8.0;HDR=No"";"
```

Note that when you pass multiple settings to the Extended Properties argument, the entire setting string must be surrounded with double quotes and the individual settings delimited with semicolons. If your data table does not include column headers, you will be limited to plain SELECT queries.

Inserting and Updating Records in Microsoft Excel Workbooks

ADO can do more than just query data from an Excel workbook. You can also insert and update records in the workbook, just as you would with any other data source. Deleting records, however, is not supported. Updating records, although possible, is somewhat problematic when an Excel workbook is the data source, as Excel-based data tables rarely have anything that can be used as a primary key to uniquely identify a specific record. Therefore, you must specify the values of enough fields to uniquely identify the record concerned in the WHERE clause of your SQL statement when performing an update. If more than one record meets WHERE clause criteria, all such records will be updated.

Inserting is significantly less troublesome. All you do is construct a SQL statement that specifies values for each of the fields and then execute it. Note once again that your data table must have column headers in order for it to be possible to execute action queries against it. The following example demonstrates how to insert a new record into our sales worksheet data table:

```
Public Sub WorksheetInsert()

  Dim Connection As ADODB.Connection
  Dim ConnectionString As String

  ConnectionString = _
    "Provider=Microsoft.Jet.OLEDB.4.0;" & _
    "Data Source=" & ThisWorkbook.Path & "\Sales.xls;" & _
    "Extended Properties=Excel 8.0;"

  Dim SQL As String

  SQL = "INSERT INTO [Sales$] " & _
        "VALUES('VA', 'On Line', 'Computers', 'Mid', 30)"

  Set Connection = New ADODB.Connection
  Call Connection.Open(ConnectionString)

  Call Connection.Execute(SQL, , _
    CommandTypeEnum.adCmdText Or ExecuteOptionEnum.adExecuteNoRecords)

  Connection.Close
  Set Connection = Nothing
End Sub
```

Querying Text Files

The last data access technique we'll discuss in this chapter is querying text files using ADO. The need to query text files doesn't come up as often as some of the other situations that we've discussed. However, when faced with an extremely large text file, the result of a mainframe database data dump, for example, ADO can be a lifesaver.

Not only will it allow you to rapidly load large amounts of data into Excel, but using the power of SQL to limit the size of the resultset can also enable you to work with data from a text file that is simply too large to be opened directly in Excel. For our discussion on text file data access, we'll be using a comma-delimited text file, Sales.csv, whose contents are identical to the Sales.xls workbook we used in the preceding Excel examples.

The OLE DB provider for Microsoft Jet is once again used for connecting to text files with ADO. However, the connection string details are slightly different. The following example demonstrates how to construct a connection string to access a text file:

```
"Provider=Microsoft.Jet.OLEDB.4.0;" & _
          "Data Source=C:\Files\;" & _
          "Extended Properties=Text;"
```

Note that in the case of text files, the Data Source argument to the provider is set to the directory that contains the text file. Do not include the name of the file in this argument. Once again, the provider is informed of the format to be queried by using the `Extended Properties` argument. In this case, you simply set this argument to the value `"Text"`.

Querying a text file is virtually identical to querying an Excel workbook. The main difference is how the table name is specified in the SQL statement. When querying a text file, the filename itself is used as the table name in the query. This has the added benefit of allowing you to work with multiple text files in a single directory without having to modify your connection string.

As with Excel, you are limited to plain `SELECT` queries if the first row of your text file does not contain field names. You must also add the `HDR=No` setting to the `Extended Properties` argument, if this is the case, in order to avoid losing the first row of data. Our example text file has field names in the first row, and we'll assume that we need to limit the number of records we bring into Excel by adding a restriction in the form of a `WHERE` clause to our query. The following procedure demonstrates this:

```
Public Sub QueryTextFile()

    Dim Recordset As ADODB.Recordset

    Dim ConnectionString As String
    ConnectionString = _
        "Provider=Microsoft.Jet.OLEDB.4.0;" & _
        "Data Source=" & ThisWorkbook.Path & ";" & _
        "Extended Properties=Text;"

    Const SQL As String = _
        "SELECT * FROM Sales.csv WHERE Type='Art';"

    Set Recordset = New ADODB.Recordset
    Call Recordset.Open(SQL, ConnectionString, _
        CursorTypeEnum.adOpenForwardOnly, _
        LockTypeEnum.adLockReadOnly, CommandTypeEnum.adCmdText)

    Call Sheet1.Range("A1").CopyFromRecordset(Recordset)

    Recordset.Close
    Set Recordset = Nothing

End Sub
```

Summary

This concludes our discussion of data access with ADO. Due to space constraints we were only able to scratch the surface of possibilities in each section. If data access is, or might become, a significant part of your development effort, you are strongly recommended to obtain the additional resources mentioned throughout this chapter.

12

Creating and Using Add-ins

An Add-in is a chunk of code that is employed as a reusable augmentation to Excel. An Add-in might be implemented in a language like VB6 or more easily and commonly another Excel workbook containing some code that one might generally want to reuse. For example, it is practical and useful to reuse the DebugTools and EventLog modules from the `Bulletproof.xls` workbook in Chapter 7, so we might elect to add the `Bulletproof.xls` workbook to our list of Add-ins making it available to all future workbooks. In this chapter we will demonstrate how to make any workbook an Add-in, and as such, much more readily accessible to all workbooks.

Add-ins may but do not have to be compiled, external applications. However, since Office 2000 Developer Edition, support for compiling workbooks has been assisted. For more information on using compiled Add-ins refer to Chapter 13, *Automation Add-ins and COM Add-ins.*

In this chapter we will use the `Bulletproof.xls` workbook as an Add-in, and we will show you how to hide the implementation details of Add-in code to prevent it from being inadvertently changed by future consumers.

Hiding the Code

Workbooks are intellectual property. Workbooks used as Add-ins represent intellectual property that you may want to share or sell to other developers, but you may not necessarily want them to know the nuts and bolts of your solution. While you cannot prevent a consumer from knowing that your Add-in exists because it shows up in the Project Explorer window, you can prevent consumers from exploring, modifying or copying your code.

To conceal the implementation details of your intellectual property, you need to password protect your source code. To demonstrate, we have copied the `Bulletproof.xls` to the folder for Chapter 12 samples and opened the VBE. To password protect the source code (refer to Figure 12-1) in the VBE, click Tools ⇨ VBA Project Properties, switch to the protection tab, and check Lock project for viewing and providing a password. To permit you—the trusted reader—access we used the word *password* as the password.

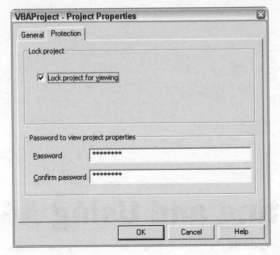

Figure 12-1

After you have entered the password and confirmed it, you will need to click OK and save the file. To see the effect, close the file and reopen it again. In Figure 12-2 you will see that the VBA Project in the Project Explorer is collapsed and cannot be expanded without providing the correct password. Password protection is only as good as the password is cryptic and the tool conceals it, but Excel VBE passwords should deter all but the most determined hackers.

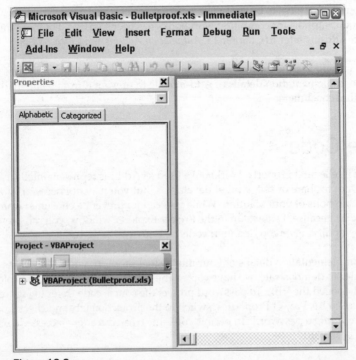

Figure 12-2

Converting the Workbook to an Add-in

To convert the workbook to an Add-in, switch to the workbook view and save the file with an `.xla` extension. Use the File ⇨ Save As menu and pick the Save As Microsoft Office Excel Add-In (`*.xla`) file type (see Figure 12-3). This will change the extension and locate the Add-In in the `C:\Document and settings\<username>\Application Data\Microsoft\Add-ins` folder.

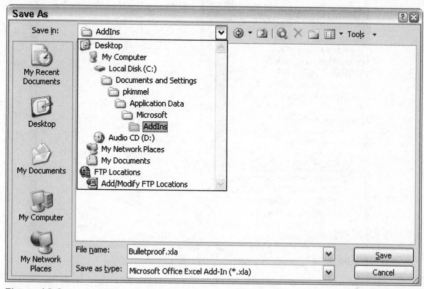

Figure 12-3

> You are not required to rename an .xls workbook extension to .xla. It is, however, a useful convention that helps Windows and consumers distinguish the file as an Add-in as opposed to a general workbook.

An alternate way to create an Add-in is to change the `IsAddin` property of the `ThisWorkbook` object in the VBE to `True` in the Properties window, as shown in Figure 12-4. (If you password-protect the workbook first then you will have to provide the password to modify the workbook's properties.)

The disadvantage to the second technique is that the workbook will be treated as an Add-in but still has the `.xls` extension. Keep in mind though that you can always use Windows Explorer to change the extension of the workbook from `.xls` to `.xla`.

Closing Add-ins

If you have just converted a workbook to an Add-in by changing its `IsAddin` property and saving it, or you have loaded the Add-in using File ⇨ Open, there is no obvious way to close the workbook from the file without exiting Excel menu because the Close menu is disabled. One way to circumvent the File

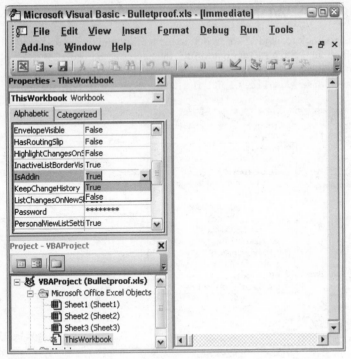

Figure 12-4

menu is to `Add-inclose` the workbook in the VBE from the Immediate window using the following command:

```
Add-inWorkbooks("Add-inBulletproof.xls").Close
```

Add-ins do not have an `Index` property value in the `Workbooks` collection and are not included in the `Count` property of the `Workbooks` collection, but they can be addressed by name as members of the `Workbooks` collection.

Another method you can use to close an Add-in is to click the file name in the recently used-file list at the bottom of the Excel File menu while holding down *Shift*. You may get a message about overwriting the copy in memory (depending on whether it has changed or not) and then you will get a message about not being able to open an Add-in for editing (a hangover from the previous versions). Click *OK* and the Add-in will be removed from memory.

Code Changes

Sometimes you need to make some changes to the VBA code that was written for a standard workbook to make it suitable for an Add-in. This is particularly true if you reference data within your Add-in workbook. Most Excel programmers write code that assumes that the workbook is the active workbook and that the worksheet is the active sheet. Nothing is active in an Add-in, so your code must explicitly reference the Add-in workbook and worksheet. Suppose our Add-in contained code like the following that assumes we are dealing with the active workbook:

```
With Range("Database")
    Set Data = .Rows(2)
    Call LoadRecord
    Navigator.Value = 2
    Navigator.Max = .Rows.Count
End With
```

This code only works if the workbook containing the name Database is active. In your Add-in code, you need to include a reference to the desired workbook and worksheet demonstrated here by a revision to the With statement: With Workbooks("workbook.xls").Sheets("Data").Range("Database"):

```
A more useful way to refer to the workbook containing the code is to use the
ThisWorkbook property of the Application object that refers to the workbook
containing the code. This makes the code much more flexible: With
ThisWorkbook.Sheets("Data").Range("Database")
```

You can also use the object name for the sheet that you see in the Project Explorer:

```
With Sheet1.Range("Database")
```

> You can edit both the workbook's programmatic name and the sheet's programmatic name in the Properties window. If you change the sheet's programmatic name, you must also change your code. If you change the workbook's programmatic name, you can use the new name if you wish, but ThisWorkbook remains a valid reference, as it is a property of the Application object and a member of <globals>.

If you want to be able to ignore the sheet name, to allow the name Database to exist on any sheet, you can use the following construction:

```
With ThisWorkbook.Names("Database").RefersToRange
```

Saving Changes

Another potential problem with an Add-in that contains data is that changes to the data will not be saved automatically at the end of an Excel session. For example, our contrived example permits changes to a range of data named Database. To ensure any modifications by the Add-in are saved we could add the following statement to the Workbook's BeforeClose or Auto_Close event handlers:

```
If Not ThisWorkbook.Saved Then ThisWorkbook.Save
```

> This technique does not work in Excel 5 or Excel 95. These versions do not allow you to save changes to an Add-in file.

Installing an Add-in

An Add-in can be opened from the worksheet File menu, as has been mentioned. However, you get better control over an Add-in if you install it using Tools ➪ Add-Ins, which displays the following dialog box shown in Figure 12-5.

Figure 12-5

Check the Bulletproof Add-in from the list of Add-Ins available. If the Add-in does not already appear in the list, you can click the Browse... button to locate it.

The friendly title and description are provided by filling in the workbook's Properties. If you have already converted the workbook to an Add-in, you can set its IsAddin property to False to make the workbook visible in the Excel window and use File ➪ Properties to display the following dialog box, as shown in Figure 12-6.

The Title and Comments boxes supply the information for the Tools ➪ Add-Ins dialog box. When you have added the required information, you can set the IsAddin property back to True and save the file.

Once the Add-in is visible in the Tools ➪ Add-Ins dialog box, you can install and uninstall the Add-in by checking and unchecking the check box beside the Add-in's description. When it is installed, it is loaded into memory and becomes visible in the VBE window and will be automatically loaded in future Excel

Bulletproof.xla Properties
General
Summary
Statistics
Contents
Custom
Title:
Bulletproof
Subject:
Author:
Paul Kimmel
Manager:
Company:
Software Conceptions, Inc
Category:
Keywords:
Comments:
Contains tools for asserting, tracing, trapping, and logging to the EventLog
Hyperlink base:
Template:
Save preview picture
OK
Cancel

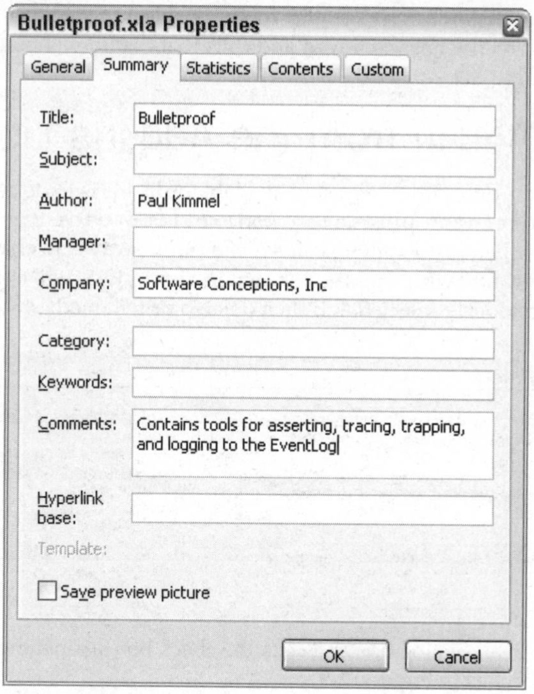

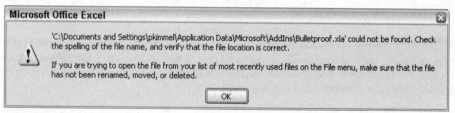

Figure 12-6

sessions. When it is uninstalled, it is removed from memory and is no longer visible in the VBE window and will no longer be loaded in future Excel sessions.

Add-in Install Event

There are two special events that are triggered when you install and uninstall an Add-in. The following code, in the `ThisWorkbook` module, shows how to display a UserForm when the Add-in is installed:

```
Private Sub Workbook_AddinInstall()
   InstallUserForm.Show
End Sub
```

The user form—named `InstallUserForm`—displays the following information for the user, as shown in Figure 12-7.

Microsoft Office Excel
'C:\Documents and Settings\pkimmel\Application Data\Microsoft\AddIns\Bulletproof.xla' could not be found. Check the spelling of the file name, and verify that the file location is correct.
If you are trying to open the file from your list of most recently used files on the File menu, make sure that the file has not been renamed, moved, or deleted.
OK

Figure 12-7

The other event is the `AddinUninstall` event. You might elect to display a UserForm that acknowledges that the Bulletproof Add-in has been removed and calls to its utilities should be removed too.

Removing an Add-in from the Add-ins List

One way to remove and Add-in from the list of available Add-ins is to delete the file from the `C:\Document and settings\<username>\Application Data\Microsoft\Add-ins` folder using Windows Explorer before opening Excel. An alternative way is to change the Add-in's file name before opening Excel. The following message, shown in Figure 12-8, will appear when you open Excel if the Add-in had been previously selected and then deleted or renamed.

Figure 12-8

Open the Tools ⇨ Add-ins ... dialog box and click the check box against the Add-in's entry. You will get the following message shown in Figure 12-9.

Figure 12-9

Click Yes and the Add-in will be deleted from the list.

Summary

Converting a workbook to an Add-in permits one to distribute code to other developers while concealing the implementation details of that code. In effect, this forces you and other consumers to use the Add-in code through its public methods and properties without focusing on the implementation details, permitting more intense focus on the details of the new problem while using the utility of an existing solution.

You will need to modify Add-in code that refers to specific workbooks and provide menu commands, controls, or toolbar buttons to provide access to macros, if they exist. Removing references to specific workbooks and worksheets was demonstrated in this chapter, and associating macros with commands and toolbar buttons is demonstrated in Chapter 26.

Automation Addins and COM Addins

Since the release of Office 2000, Microsoft introduced a new concept for creating custom Addins for all the Office applications. Instead of creating application-specific Addins (.xla files in Excel, .dot files in Word, .mde files in Access, etc.), we can create DLLs using Visual Basic, C++, or the Office Developer Edition that all the Office applications can use. Since these DLLs conform to Microsoft's Component Object Model, they are known as COM Addins. The second half of this chapter explains how to create and implement your own COM Addins.

The biggest failing of COM Addins is that the functions inside them can't be called from the worksheet. Excel 2002 and carried over to Excel 2003, Microsoft extended the concept and simplified the implementation of the COM Addin mechanism, in order for their routines to be used in the same way as worksheet functions. These new Addins are known as *Automation Addins*.

Automation Addins

Automation Addins are COM DLLs (ActiveX DLLs) that have a creatable class and a public function in the creatable class. Similarly to other objects, you need to create an instance and invoke methods. The syntax is slightly more verbose because you are invoking the method indirectly. Instead of naming the object, method, and passing parameters, you must pass this information to the CallByName method. The basic requirement is to create the COM object and invoke CallByName passing the COM object, the function name, and the parameters. The following syntax example demonstrates the ingredients needed:

```
Dim o As Object
Set o = CreateObject("objectid")
Call CallByName(o, "functionname", VbMethod, param1, param2,..., paramn)
```

We will look at several practical examples in this chapter, which will provide you with plenty of experience.

The requirements of the COM object to be an Automation object are that the object must be created with specific settings, and there must be at least one public function. You will need a copy of VB6 (or VB.NET, Delphi, C++, or some other tool that can be used to create stand-alone Automation binaries) to try some of the examples in this chapter, but you don't need these tools to use Automation objects. Even if you have little interest in learning VB6 or building custom Automation Addins, give this chapter a quick read for a better understanding of extensions to Excel.

If you can't build an Automation application then you can still use existing Automation applications like Excel, Word, PowerPoint, and SourceSafe to experiment with Automation.

Creating a Simple Addin

For the Excel VBA developer, the easiest way to create Automation Addins is to use Visual Basic 6. Unfortunately, it is not possible to create these Addins using the Office Developer Edition, as it does not allow classes to be set as `Public-Creatable`. (Public-Creatable is an instancing setting that describes how a specific object is created. Automation objects have specific rules and these instancing settings instruct compilers to add necessary information.) In this example, we'll create a simple Automation Addin using VB6. To focus on the process and not the algorithm, we will simply define a method that returns an array of sequential numbers. (You need VB6 to build the sample, but your present knowledge of VBA should help you follow along in this text.)

To build the sample project, run VB6 and create a new ActiveX DLL project. Rename the project to `MyAddin` and rename the class to `Simple` in the Properties window. Set the class's `Instancing` property to `5-MultiUse`, which is the default for ActiveX DLL projects. By setting this property, Excel will be able to create instances of the Simple class and invoke its members.

In VB6 a class is defined by the class module the code resides in. An example of a VBA class module is the Worksheet module:

```
Option Base 1
Option Explicit

Public Function Sequence(ByVal Items As Long, _
  Optional ByVal Start As Integer = 1, _
  Optional ByVal Step As Integer = 1) As Variant()

' Can't create an array of negative elements
If Items < 1 Then
  Sequence = CVErr(2015)
  Exit Function
End If

Dim result As Variant
ReDim result(Items)
Dim I As Long

For I = 1 To Items
  result(I) = Start + I - 1 * Step
Next

  Sequence = result
End Function
```

By defining the function to be `Public`, Excel will be able to see it, and we'll be able to call it from the worksheet. Save the project, then use the VB6 File ⇨ Make MyAddin.dll to create the DLL—you've just created an Automation Addin.

Registering Automation Addins with Excel

Before we can use the `Sequence` function in a worksheet, we need to tell Excel about the DLL. Microsoft has extended the Addins paradigm to include Automation Addins, making their usage extremely similar to normal Excel .xla Addins. The main difference is that instead of a filename, Automation Addins use the class's *ProgID*, which is the Visual Basic Project name, a period, then, the class name. In our example, the ProgID of the `Simple` class is `MyAddin.Simple`.

Through the Excel User Interface

To use our Addin we need to reference it in the VBE, create an instance, and invoke methods. Open the VBE and select Tools ⇨ References and search in the list of Available References. When you find MyAddin, select it by clicking in the check box, and click *OK* to add the reference. Here are the steps:

- ❑ Load Excel
- ❑ Press *Alt+F11* to switch to the VBE
- ❑ Select Tools ⇨ References to open the References dialog box
- ❑ Find the Addin MyAddin in the list of Available References
- ❑ Check it and click *OK*

After adding a reference to the Addin you can view its members through the Object Browser (available from the *F2* shortcut or the View ⇨ Object browser menu). Now we need to use the sample code from the beginning of the chapter and use our Addin.

Referencing an Addin Using VBA

If you want to reference an Addin using code, then you can reference an Automation Addin in a manner similar to that for referencing an .xla Addin. To add an Automation Addin programmatically you could write code similar to the following:

```
Sub InstallAutomationAddin()
    AddIns.Add Filename:="MyAddin.Simple"
    AddIns("MyAddin.Simple").Installed = True
End Sub
```

Incorporating an Addin by Modifying Registry

If you are distributing your code then you may want to know the registry keys and values necessary to manually install an Addin. Keep in mind though that modifying the Registry can cause headaches for others, so it is imperative that you test your settings thoroughly (and make a copy of your registry using the registries Export feature before you make any modifications).

An Addin modifies a couple of registry keys. The keys and appropriate values for adding our Addin are described next:

❑ Run the registry editor by typing `regedit` or `regedt32` in Start ⇨ Run

❑ Navigate to the registry key `HKEY_CURRENT_USER\Software\Microsoft\Office\11.0\Excel\Options`

❑ Create the string value Open—right-click New ⇨ String Value—named Open with the value `/A "MyAddin.Simple"`

Figure 13-1 illustrates an approximate view of the registry after you make the modification. The next time you open Excel, you will see the Automation Addin MyAddin in the list of (from the Excel menu) Addins available from the Tools ⇨ Addins menu item (see Figure 13-2).

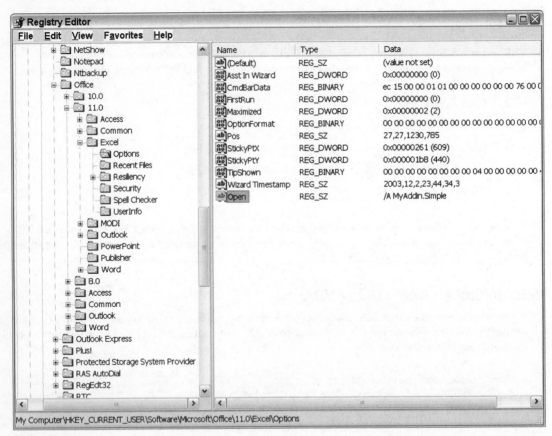

Figure 13-1

If you want the Addin listed in the Addins dialog box but not installed, then create the key `HKEY_CURRENT_USER\Software\Microsoft\Office\11.0\Excel\Addin Manager` and create the name `MyAddin.Simple`. This modification will cause the MyAddin.Simple Addin to be listed but not checked the next time you open Excel (assuming the previous entry does not also exist) and the registry after you create the new key and name will look like the image in Figure 13-3.

Figure 13-2

Using Automation Addins

Having added the Automation object think of the code in the Addin as a class. You can create instances of the class and interact with its methods and properties. You can do this by invoking the methods from Excel worksheets or in VBA code.

Invoking Sequence from a Worksheet

We installed the Addin in the last section. Next, let's invoke the Sequence method from a worksheet, displaying the sequential values—one in each cell. Suppose we want a sequence from 10 to 18, which includes 5 integers starting with 10 and incrementing by 2. We can invoke the Sequence and fill the five cells by selecting five cells, entering =Sequence(5, 10, 2), and pressing *Ctrl+Shift+Enter* to enter the formula as an array formula. The worksheet, after pressing *Ctrl+Shift+Enter*, will look very similar to Figure 13-4.

Note that if the function name in the Automation Addin conflicts with a built-in Excel function or a function defined in an .xla Addin, then Excel will defer to the function by precedence where a built-in function would be chosen first, followed by a .xla Addin function, and finally our Automation function. This tidbit can be especially useful if you get unexpected behavior.

If you want to coerce Excel to use a specific Addin then enter the fully qualified Addin name including the Automation application, class, and method name as in: =MyAddin.Simple.Sequence(5,10,2). As soon as you press *Enter*, Excel will remove the Automation Addin and class name, but it will be used to resolve the function call.

Figure 13-3

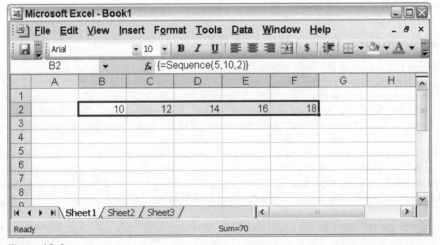

Figure 13-4

As an exercise, see if you can write an Addin that returns a sequential list of days of the week, months, or creates a simple calendar derived from a month and year value.

Invoking the Addin with VBA Code

Visual Basic for Applications is very flexible. A very easy way to reference our Addin in the VBE and with the code is to add a reference to it using the Tools ⇨ References menu. If we wanted to invoke the `Sequence` function from a `CommandButton` Click event then we could add a button to our worksheet, and in the `CommandButton`'s Click event declare and create an instance of the `MyAddin.Simple` class and call `Sequence`. The next listing demonstrates this technique:

```
Private Sub CommandButton1_Click()
  ' Assumes a reference to the MyAddin Automation Addin from the
Tools@@raReferences
  ' menu
  Dim O As MyAddin.Simple
  Set O = New MyAddin.Simple
  ActiveCell.Resize(1, 5) = O.Sequence(5, 10, 2)

End Sub@@ra
```

If we know for sure that the Addin is installed, we can use the instance that Excel has created, by implementing an alternate version of the `CommandButton1_Click` event that uses the `Application.Evaluate` method:

```
Private Sub CommandButton1_Click()
  ActiveCell.Resize(1, 5) = _
    Application.Evaluate("MyAddin.Simple.Sequence(5,10,2)")
End Sub
```

When using `Application.Evaluate`, the full ProgID is only needed if there is a risk that the function name conflicts with a builtt-in function, or one in a loaded .xla Addin. If you are reasonably sure that your function name is unique, then you can eliminate the Automation Addin and class name as demonstrated:

```
Application.Evaluate("MyAddin.Simple.Sequence(5,10,2)")
```

An Introduction to the IDTExtensibility2 Interface

The simple Addin we have been using thus far is simple in part because our Addin is independent of other classes and Automation servers. (An Automation server is just an Automation application. The term server is used to indicate that the application provides a service. Excel can be thought of as an Automation server when other applications use it.) However, as the complexity or our solutions grow, so might the complexity of implementing those solutions. This is especially true if an Automation server needs some back chatter from Excel. For example, if we want to obtain context information about the caller then our Automation Addin is aware of Excel as Excel is aware of the Addin.

In this section, we'll look at the `Application.Caller` and `Application.Volatile` properties as well as how to implement the `IDTExtensibility2` interface as a means of facilitating two-way communications between an Automation Addin and Excel.

In order to use the Excel Application object within our Automation Addin, we need to get (or be given) a reference to it, which we can store in a private variable within our Addin class. This is achieved by implementing a specific *interface* within our Addin class.

Grammatically, an interface is declarations without definitions. For example, in an interface we would supply a method header but not the method body. The interface acts as a contract, portal or facet. In the physical world, a common example everyone might understand would be a volume interface. If the volume interface defined two methods Up and Down then any class that implemented Volume would provide a definition for the Up and Down methods, although each actual implementation could vary widely. For instance, a television, MP3 player, a stereo tuner (and if we are lucky, our kids) could all implement the volume interface.

In software, when we implement an interface we are defining a programmatic contract that indicates that any class *implementing* a specific interface agrees to implement all of the things defined by that interface. Extending our volume example, then, if we implemented the volume control on any device and a universal remote control that queried devices for the volume interface, we could attenuate the volume on every device.

Prebuilt into Excel is a check for a specific interface. When Excel loads an Addin it asks the Addin, in effect, do you implement ITDExtensibility2? If the response is yes, then Excel knows it can call OnConnection because OnConnection is part of the IDTExtensibility2 interface. The OnConnection method is an opportunity for Excel to pass a reference to itself to the Addin. This handle to the Excel object permits a two-way exchange to occur. Excel can interact with the Addin by invoking its public members, and the Addin can interact with a specific instance of Excel via the reference Excel gave it.

To permit two-way communications we can store—also called cache, or assign a variable to—the reference to Excel passed to our Addin through the OnConnection method. In actuality, IDTExtensibility defines five methods, and we must implement all five methods to satisfy the contract named IDTExtensibility2. While we do not actually have to supply code for all five methods, we do have to supply an empty, or stub, method at a minimum.

The macro tasks involved here are:

❑ In VB6, create an ActiveX DLL project

❑ Add a reference to the Microsoft Excel library

❑ Implement the IDTExtensibility2 interface

❑ Declare a private variable of type Excel.Application that stores a reference to Excel passed to us in OnConnect

❑ And, implement the other four required (IDTExtensibility2) methods to do whatever you need them to do. For example, OnDisconnection it's a good idea to set the cached reference to Excel to Nothing

Let's examine each step in the macro process a bit more closely. The first step is to create an ActiveX DLL. We'll cover this step by extending the previous example, MyAddin. The next thing we will do is add a new class (.cls file) to the existing project. Name the file Complex.cls. This new class file will be the class that implements the IDTExtensibility2 interface.

Next, in VB6, we will add a reference to the Microsoft Excel library. We will also add a reference to the Microsoft Addin Designer library. The second reference contains the IDTExtensibility2 interface.

An additional precursor is that we'll set Binary Compatibility in VB6. This will ensure that our new ActiveX DLL will replace the previous DLL and registry entries rather than producing new ones each time. To set binary compatibility (see Figure 13-5), select Project ➪ MyAddin Properties, navigate to the Component tab and select Binary Compatibility.

Figure 13-5

Now that we have selected the Project ➪ References dialog box and added the Microsoft Addin Designer and Microsoft Excel 11.0 Object Library and set binary compatibility, we are ready to implement the new class. The complete listing is provided next, followed by a synopsis of the code:

```
Implements IDTExtensibility2

Private Excel As Excel.Application

Private Sub IDTExtensibility2_OnConnection(ByVal Application As Object, _
  ByVal ConnectMode As AddInDesignerObjects.ext_ConnectMode, _
  ByVal AddInInst As Object, custom() As Variant)

  Set Excel = Application
End Sub

Private Sub IDTExtensibility2_OnDisconnection( _
  ByVal RemoveMode As AddInDesignerObjects.ext_DisconnectMode, _
  custom() As Variant)

  Set Excel = Nothing
End Sub
```

```
Private Sub IDTExtensibility2_OnAddInsUpdate(custom() As Variant)
  ' Intentionally left blank
End Sub

Private Sub IDTExtensibility2_OnBeginShutdown(custom() As Variant)
  ' Intentionally left blank
End Sub

Private Sub IDTExtensibility2_OnStartupComplete(custom() As Variant)
  ' Intentionally left blank
End Sub
```

The listing provides a barebones implementation of IDTExtensibility2. The first statement of the listing indicates that we are going to implement IDTExtensibility2. VB6 is very helpful. The VB6 editor contains a list of methods defined by the interface and will generate stubs for all of the methods we have to implement to satisfy any interface we are implementing. The second statement declares a variable that represents Excel. On the first method, OnConnection, we cache the instance of Excel that created this object, and the second method, OnDisconnection, sets the instance of Excel to Nothing so we don't try to use Excel after it has shutdown.

The remaining three interface methods are intentionally left blank. Interface contracts require us to stub out every method defined by the interface, but we don't have to provide code for every method. In addition, we can add any additional members we need, including implementing more than one interface. Just keep in mind that in this case, the instance of Excel that creates the Complex object will only see the IDTExtensibility2 methods. Anything else will effectively be invisible to Excel but can be used to supplement the interface behaviors or provide new behaviors.

The important thing in the example is that we have a reliable instance of the Excel application and our Addin can poll Excel in an effort to more effectively interact with Excel. To experiment, add some code to OnConnection that requests information about the instance of Excel and injects some data. (The Excel object model is the same whether we are programming against internally, from Excel, or externally from VB6.) We will come back to a practical application of the IDTExtensibility2 interface after a brief interlude.

A Complex Addin—Generating a Unique Random Number

Now that we have a reference to the Excel Application object, we can use it in a more complex function. The Complex.GetNumbers function shown in the next code listing returns a random set of integers between two limits, without any duplicates in the set. It demonstrates calling back into Excel, using the Excel Application object in two ways:

❑ Complex.GetNumbers uses Application.Caller to identify the range of cells containing the function, and hence the size and shape of the array to create.

❑ Complex.GetNumbers uses Application.Volatile to ensure that the random number generator is recalculated each time Excel calculates the sheet.

GetNumbers works by creating an array that matches the dimensions of the selected cells, inserting a unique, random number into each element of the array. Further, the array is sorted by the value of the elements in ascending order, and then these values are used to populate the selected cells in the worksheet.

Imagine that you want to win the lottery. Many high stakes state lotteries use digits between 1 and 50 and require matching all six digits to win the jackpot. What we tried to do was figure out the least amount of money we could spend each day to cover as many numbers as possible. The result was a random number generator, which generated eight arrays of six distinct numbers between 1 and 50. This meant that with $8, 48 of the 50 numbers were covered by the matrix. Probability suggests that the numbers will arrange themselves in many random configurations and occasionally, these configurations would be linear sequences of 4, 5, and 6 (jackpot!) matching numbers. In fact, we used this technique for about six weeks and almost every week the random number generator had three winning numbers on the same ticket in at least one of the eight tickets. (We wonder what the probability is that such a technique would improve our overall chances of winning the jackpot? We wish we had paid closer attention in that Probability and Statistics class in college.)

GetNumbers has also been written to take an optional Items parameter, enabling it to be called from VBA code as well as from the worksheet. If the Items parameter is provided, the function returns a 2D array (1, n) of unique integers. If the Items parameter is not provided, the function uses Application.Caller to identify the dimensions of the array to fill. Here is the implementation (in VB6) of the random number generator:

```
Public Function GetNumbers(ByVal Min As Long, ByVal Max As Long) As Variant

  Dim aRange As Range
  Dim Values() As Double
  Dim Count As Long
  Dim I As Long
  Dim Value As Long
  Dim Rows As Long
  Dim Cols As Long

  Excel.Volatile

  Set aRange = Excel.Caller

  Rows = aRange.Rows.Count
  Cols = aRange.Columns.Count
  Count = Rows * Cols

  If (Not ValidateRange(Min, Max, Count)) Then
    GetNumbers = CVErr(xlErrValue)
    Exit Function '
  End If

  Values = GetRandomNumbers(Min, Max)
  Call Scramble(Values)

  GetNumbers = OrderValuesToCells(Rows, Cols, Values)
End Function

Private Function ValidateRange(ByVal Min As Long, _
  ByVal Max As Long, ByVal Count As Long) As Boolean
```

```vba
    ' We can't generate uniquely random numbers of the count if the
    ' number of elements is greater than the variety permitted by
    ' min and max
    Debug.Assert Min >= 0
    Debug.Assert Max > Min
    Debug.Assert Max - Min > Count

    ValidateRange = Max - Min > Count

End Function

Private Function GetRandomNumbers(ByVal Min As Long, _
    ByVal Max As Long) As Variant

    Dim Values() As Double
    Dim I As Long
    ReDim Values(1 To Max - Min, 1 To 2)

    ' We fill the first array dimension with all of the possible numbers,
    ' inclusively, between min and max.
    ' The second column is filled with random numbers. These will be used
    ' to jumble up the possible numbers later

    Randomize
    For I = 1 To Max - Min
        Values(I, 1) = I + Min - 1
        Values(I, 2) = Rnd
    Next I

    GetRandomNumbers = Values
End Function

Private Function OrderValuesToCells(ByVal Rows As Long, ByVal Cols As Long, _
    ByVal Values As Variant) As Variant

    ' Order the results so that they are in a configuration
    ' that matches the selected cell configuration
    Dim Results() As Double
    ReDim Results(1 To Rows, 1 To Cols)

    Dim R As Long
    Dim C As Long
    Dim Index As Long
    Index = LBound(Values)

    For R = 1 To Rows
        For C = 1 To Cols
            Results(R, C) = Values(Index, 1)
            Index = Index + 1
        Next C
    Next R

    OrderValuesToCells = Results
End Function
```

Scrambling the Random Numbers

The GetNumbers method fills a two-dimensional array with numbers. The first dimension contains all of the numbers from our Min to Max arguments. The second dimension contains actual random numbers between the value 0 and 1. The first dimension is in sorted order, and the second dimension is in random order. (We could just use the Rnd function to generate random numbers, but for a small set of random integers we might get duplicates. Our technique ensures we don't get duplicates.) To scramble the set of unique numbers between Min and Max, we can order the random numbers in the second dimension of the array. Thus, to scramble the first dimension we need to sort the second.

The Scramble routine we'll look at next is actually a bubble sort. Bubble sorts simple compare each element to every other element and bubble larger values toward the end. Because the bubble support compares each value against every other value it performs n * n or n² comparisons. This means for relatively small values of n—for example, n equals 1,000—we get a large number of comparisons. One thousand elements in the array would result in 1,000,000 comparisons. For this reason, bubble sorts get a bad rap. On the other hand, modern PCs are lightning fast and even the lowly bubble sort can sort 10,000 to 100,000 elements very quickly. For our purposes, this should be fast enough. (To experiment try selecting every cell on a worksheet and entering the GetNumbers (1, 10000000) method and pressing *Ctrl+Shift+Enter*. Ten million elements will take a while to scramble.)

If you really need a fast sort because you are dealing with very large sets of data, then try the Selection Sort and QuickSort. Each has attractors and detractors. For example, the QuickSort isn't much faster than the Selection sort or bubble sort for modestly sized arrays, and the QuickSort can actually be slower if the data are relatively sorted already. (If you want to learn all about sorts and advanced algorithms in general to picking up a copy of *Numerical Recipes in BASIC*.) Here is the Scramble/Sort algorithm and the Swap method:

```
Private Sub Scramble(ByRef Values As Variant)

  ' We can use an easy bubble sort here becasue it works well for
  ' arrays up to 10,000 or so elements. If you need to sort more items
  ' look at the selection sort or quick sort

  Dim I As Long
  Dim J As Long

  For I = LBound(Values) To UBound(Values) - 1
    For J = I + 1 To UBound(Values)
      If (Values(I, 2) > Values(J, 2)) Then
        Call Swap(Values, I, J)
      End If
    Next J
  Next I

End Sub

Private Sub Swap(ByRef Values As Variant, ByVal I As Long, ByVal J As Long)

  Temp1 = Values(I, 1)
  Temp2 = Values(I, 2)

  Values(I, 1) = Values(J, 1)
  Values(I, 2) = Values(J, 2)
```

```
    Values(J, 1) = Temp1
    Values(J, 2) = Temp2

End Sub
```

After making all of the changes, you will need to save and recompile the `MyAddin.dll` in VB6 using the File ➪ Make menu item. If you have both VB6 and Excel open and get a Permission Denied error then close Excel, rebuild the Addin, and then reopen Excel.

The complex Addin is used in the same way as the simple `Sequence` function shown earlier. The only difference is that we have to tell Excel to load the `MyAddin.Complex`, by clicking Tools ➪ Addins ➪ Automation Addins and selecting it from the list. When entered as an array formula, it looks something like Figure 13-6.

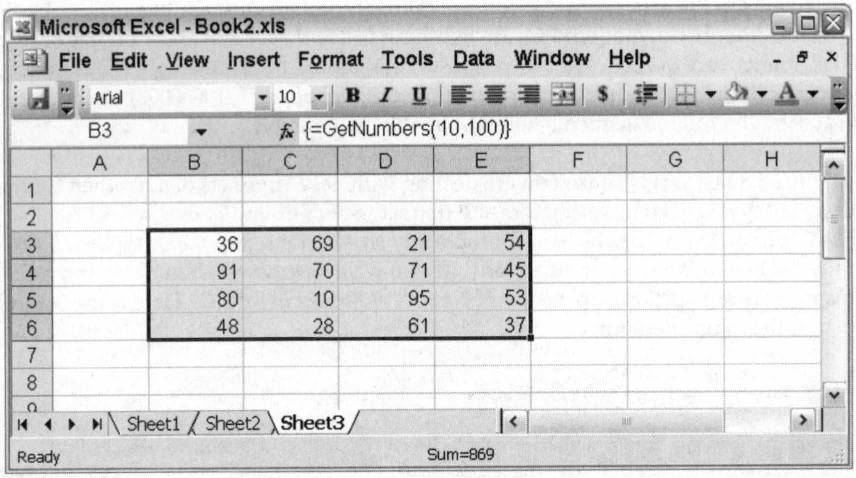

Figure 13-6

As is shown in the example, we would discourage you from selecting an entire worksheet to test the code. You would need an array of more than 16 million random numbers, and the bubble sort will fail miserably at that level. To provide you with one alternative, we have included a second implementation of scramble that uses the `QuickSort` algorithm. Here it is with the repeated `Swap` method:

```
Private Sub QuickSort(ByRef Values As Variant, _
    Optional ByVal Left As Long, Optional ByVal Right As Long)

    ' A divide an conquer algorithm that works well on large,
    ' unsorted arrays.

    Dim I As Long
    Dim J As Long
    Dim K As Long
    Dim Item1 As Variant
    Dim Item2 As Variant

    On Error GoTo Catch
```

```
   If IsMissing(Left) Or Left = 0 Then Left = LBound(Values)

   If IsMissing(Right) Or Right = 0 Then Right = UBound(Values)

   I = Left
   J = Right

   ' Get the item between left and right
   Item1 = Values((Left + Right) \ 2, 2)

   ' Explore this section of the array of values
   Do While I < J

     Do While Values(I, 2) < Item1 And I < Right
       I = I + 1
     Loop

     Do While Values(J, 2) > Item1 And J > Left
       J = J - 1
     Loop

     If I < J Then
       Call Swap(Values, I, J)
     End If

     If I <= J Then
       I = I + 1
       J = J - 1
     End If
   Loop

   'Recurse, doing the same thing to the left half
   If J > Left Then Call QuickSort(Values, Left, J)

   ' Recurse, doing the same thing to the right half
   If I < Right Then Call QuickSort(Values, I, Right)

   Exit Sub
Catch:
   MsgBox Err.Description, vbCritical

End Sub

Private Sub Swap(ByRef Values As Variant, ByVal I As Long, ByVal J As Long)

   Dim Temp1 As Double
   Dim Temp2 As Double

   Temp1 = Values(I, 1)
   Temp2 = Values(I, 2)

   Values(I, 1) = Values(J, 1)
   Values(I, 2) = Values(J, 2)
```

```
    Values(J, 1) = Temp1
    Values(J, 2) = Temp2

End Sub
```

If you are interested, it is fun to dump the array at each point with a small array. You can see how an array is split recursively, the boundary values are swapped, and the array is ultimately sorted.

COM Addins

While Automation Addins enable us to create our own worksheet functions, COM Addins provide a way to extend the user interface of Excel and all the other Office applications. They have a number of advantages over normal xla Addins:

- ❑ COM Addins load faster than .xla Excel Addins

- ❑ COM Addins don't crowd the VBE Project Explorer

- ❑ COM Addins can't be changed by users because they are compiled binaries

- ❑ COM Addins aren't specific to Excel whereas .xla Addins can only be used by Excel. A COM Addin can be used by any Office application

IDTExtensibility2 Interface Continued

The previous section introduced the IDTExtensibility2 interface, where we used the OnConnection and OnDisconnection methods to obtain a reference to the Excel Application. The remaining methods defined in the interface can be used by COM Addins to respond to specific events in Excel's lifetime. All of the methods of the IDTExtensibility2 interface are described in the following table.

Method	Occurs	Typical usage
OnConnection	When the COM Addin is loaded by Excel.	Store a reference to the Excel application, add menu items to Excel's commandbars and set up event hooks
OnStartupComplete	After Excel has finished loading all Addins and initial files.	Show a startup dialog box (such as those in Access and PowerPoint) or to change behavior depending on whether other Addins are loaded
OnAddInsUpdate	Whenever any other COM Addins are loaded or unloaded.	If the COM Addin depends on another Addin being loaded, this Addin can unload itself
OnBeginShutdown	When Excel starts its shutdown process.	Stop the shutdown in certain circumstances or perform any preshutdown tidy-up routines
OnDisconnection	When the COM Addin is unloaded, either by the user or by Excel shutting down.	Save settings. If unloaded by the user, delete any commandbar items that were created at connection

As stated previously, implementing an interface requires that we provide an implementation for every method in the interface even if that implementation is only a stub.

Registering a COM Addin with Excel

For automation Addins, we told Excel that the Addin exists by selecting it in the Tools ⇨ Addins ⇨ Automation Addins dialog box (resulting in some entries being written to the registry). We tell Excel that a COM Addin exists by writing specific keys and values to specific places in the registry. When Excel starts, it looks in those keys to see which COM Addins exist, then checks the values in those keys to see how to display them in the COM Addins list and whether to load them or not. The registry keys for COM Addins targeted for use with Excel are:

❑ Registered for the current user: HKEY_CURRENT_USER\Software\Microsoft\Office\Excel\Addins\AddinProgID

❑ Registered for all users: HKEY_USERS\.DEFAULT\Software\Microsoft\Office\Excel\Addins\AddinProgID

❑ Registered for the machine: HKEY_LOCAL_MACHINE\Software\Microsoft\Office\Excel\Addins\AddinProgID

The registry values added for each key are:

Name	Type	Use
FriendlyName	String	The name shown in the COM Addins list
Description	String	The description shown in the COM Addins dialog box
LoadBehavior	Number	Whether it is unloaded, loaded at startup, or demand-loaded
SatelliteDllName	Number	The name of a resource DLL that contains localized names and descriptions. If used, the name and description will be #Num, where Num is the numeric resource ID in the Satellite DLL. Most of the standard Office Addins use this technique for localization
CommandLineSafe	String	Whether the Addin can be called from the command prompt. This value isn't applicable to COM DLLs

Once registered correctly, the COM Addin will show up in Excel's COM Addins dialog box, where it can be loaded and unloaded like any other Addin. Unfortunately, the COM Addins menu item (to show the dialog box) is not on any of Excel's standard menus. You'll need to customize your commandbars to be able to access that dialog box, by doing the following:

❑ Right-click one of Excel's commandbars and choose Customize.

❑ Click on the Tools menu item to show its submenus.

❑ In the Customize dialog box, click the Commands tab, select the Tools item in the left-hand list and scroll down the right-hand list until you find COM Addins... (as shown in Figure 13-7).

❑ Drag the Com Addins item from the right-hand list and drop it on the Tools toolbar, below the Addins... menu item.

❑ Close the Customize dialog box.

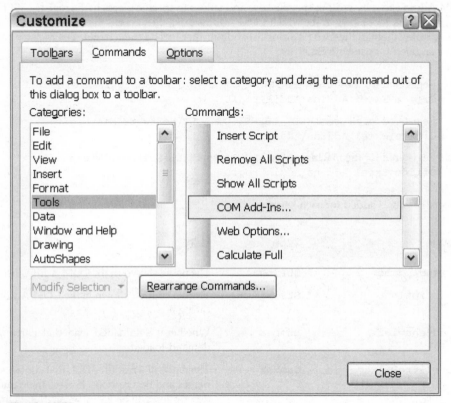

Figure 13-7

The COM Addin Designer

Microsoft has provided a COM Addin `Designer` class to assist in the creation and registration of COM Addins. The COM Addin Designer class implements the `IDTExtensibility2` interface, exposing hooks into the interface methods as events, therefore, we don't have to provide empty stubs. If we use the Designer class, we only need to implement event handlers for the behaviors that we are interested in tapping into. The Designer class providers a GUI that simplifies providing values for the registry entries. When the Designer class is compiled it automatically adds code, adding a `DllRegisterServer` entry point, which writes all of the registry keys on our behalf. (Although by default the keys are only written for the current user, `HKEY_CURRENT_USER`.) All we have to do to register the server is run `regsvr32` *application.dll*, where *application.dll* includes the path and file name of the COM binary. If you purchase a copy of the Office Developer Edition, then COM Addins can be created and compiled in the VBE instead of using Visual Basic. (If you have the Developer Edition then the Addin can be created from the VBE by selecting File ⇨ New ⇨ Project ⇨ Addin Project.)

By way of an example, we'll create a COM Addin that provides a Wizard for entering the GetNumbers Automation Addin function that we created in the previous section. We will continue to use Visual Basic, building on the MyAddin.dll from the earlier in the chapter.

Open the MyAddin project in Visual Basic. Add a new Addin class to the project by clicking Project ⇨ Add Addin Class (if that menu item doesn't exist, click Project ⇨ Components ⇨ Designers and check the Addin Class entry). This adds a new Designer class and gives it the name of AddinDesigner1. Using the Properties window, change the name to COMAddin and set the Public property to True (ignoring any warnings). Fill in the Designer form as shown in Figure 13-8.

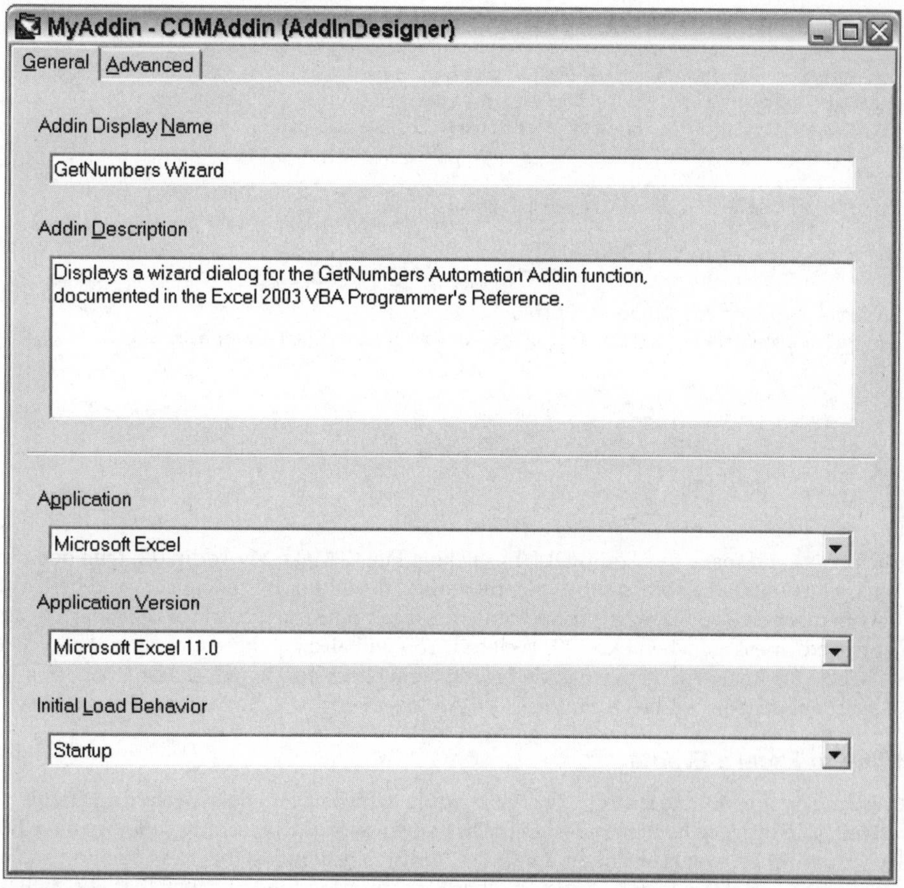

Figure 13-8

> Note that the Designer only creates registry entries for the current user. If you wish to install the Addin for all users on the machine, you will need to add your own registry entries in the Advanced tab of the Designer form, as documented in Microsoft KnowledgeBase article Q290868, at **http://support.microsoft.com/support/kb/articles/Q290/8/68.asp**.

Linking to Excel

Select the COMAddIn in the Project Explorer in VB6. Right-click the COMAddIn designer created in the preceding section, and click View ⇨ Code to get to the Designer's code module. Next, provide an implementation for the OnConnection and OnDisconnection events by selecting the AddinInstance from the Object drop-down list, and each of the OnConnection and OnDisconnection events from the Procedure drop-down list. Include a WithEvents statement that declares a variable of type Excel.Application. In short, we are simply storing an instance of the calling Excel application that is passed to us through the OnConnection event:

```
Private WithEvents Excel As Excel.Application

Private Sub AddinInstance_OnConnection(ByVal Application As Object, _
    ByVal ConnectMode As AddInDesignerObjects.ext_ConnectMode, _
    ByVal AddInInst As Object, custom() As Variant)

    Set Excel = Application
    MsgBox "Connected", vbInformation

End Sub

Private Sub AddinInstance_OnDisconnection( _
    ByVal RemoveMode As AddInDesignerObjects.ext_DisconnectMode, _
    custom() As Variant)

    Set Excel = Nothing
    MsgBox "Disconnected", vbInformation

End Sub
```

Save the project and make the Addin DLL by clicking File ⇨ Make MyAddin.dll, then open Excel 2003 (Note that you will not be able to subsequently rebuild the DLL if it is being accessed by Excel at the time). As Excel opens, you'll see a "Connected" message popup as the Addin is connected, and a "Disconnected" message when Excel XP is closed. You will also get these messages if you click the Tools ⇨ COM Addins menu item we added earlier, and check or uncheck the GetNumbers Wizard from the list of available Addins from the COM Addins dialog box, as shown in Figure 13-9.

Responding to Excel's Events

The Designer code module is a type of class module, which allows us to declare a variable WithEvents, in order to hook into designer class's events. In the preceding code, we have hooked into the Excel Application events, enabling our COM Addin to respond to the users opening and closing workbooks, changing data in cells, and any other Excel event in the same way that we can in a normal Excel Addin. See Chapter 12 for more information about these events.

Adding CommandBar Controls

Once we have a reference to the Excel Application object, we can add our commandbars and buttons in the same way as we will describe in Chapter 26. The only difference is how we respond to a button being clicked.

When adding a CommandBarButton from within Excel, we set its OnAction property to be the name of the procedure to run when the button is clicked.

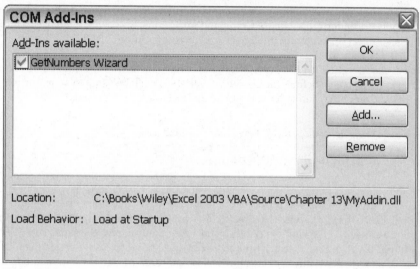

Figure 13-9

When adding a `CommandBarButton` from outside Excel (from within a COM Addin), we have to set the `OnAction` property of the button to point to the COM Addin (so Excel knows which COM Addin is responsible for that button), then hook the button's `Click` event using a variable declared with the `WithEvents` inside the Addin. The sequence of events and tasks that occur when the user clicks a button is:

- ❑ User clicks the button.
- ❑ Excel checks the button's `OnAction` property, and reads the `ProgId` of the COM Addin.
- ❑ Excel checks if that Addin is loaded. If not, it loads the Addin and runs the `OnConnection` event.
- ❑ In the Addin's `OnConnection` event, a variable is declared `WithEvents` and is set to reference the commandbar button.
- ❑ Excel fires the `Click` event for the button.
- ❑ The event handler in the Addin runs, performing the programmed action.

This sequence gives us two choices for specifying when Excel loads the Addin:

- ❑ A *demand-loaded* Addin is loaded by Excel when it is first registered and adds its menu items to Excel's menu bars, setting the `OnAction` property appropriately and leaving them in place when Excel closes. The next time Excel starts, the Addin is only loaded when the menu item is clicked. This is the preferred option if the Addin is only accessed through menu items. A demand-loaded Addin is specified by setting the Addin Designer's Load Behavior drop-down to "Load on demand."
- ❑ A *startup* Addin is loaded every time Excel starts. It will typically add its menus every time Excel opens, and remove them every time Excel closes. This is the preferred option if the Addin needs to respond to Excel's Application events. This type of Addin is specified by setting the Addin Designer's Load Behavior drop-down to "Startup."

In the following example, we'll add two menu items to show Wizard forms that will assist in the entry of our Automation Addin formulas. To use CommandBarButtons, we need a reference to the Office object library, so click Project ➪ References and check the Microsoft Office 11.0 Object Library.

Modify the declarations in the COMAddin designer code to include the additional CommandBarButton and String variables. This defines the class-level variables we'll be using to store our reference to the Excel Application object, and to hook the CommandBarButton's events:

```
Private WithEvents Excel As Excel.Application
Private WithEvents MenuButton As Office.CommandBarButton
Const AddInTag As String = "MyAddinTag"
```

When we hook a commandbarbutton's events using the WithEvents keyword, our MenuButton variable is associated with the Tag property of the button we set it to reference. All buttons that share the same Tag will cause the Click event to fire. In this way, we can handle the Click events for all of our buttons using a single WithEvents variable, by ensuring they all have the same Tag. We can distinguish between buttons by giving them each a unique Parameter property, as we create them in the OnConnection method. Modify the OnConnection and OnDisconnection methods we defined a moment ago to include the code as shown in the next listing:

```
Private Sub AddinInstance_OnConnection(ByVal Application As Object, _
   ByVal ConnectMode As AddInDesignerObjects.ext_ConnectMode, _
   ByVal AddInInst As Object, custom() As Variant)

   Set Excel = Application
   MsgBox "Connected", vbInformation

   Call InsertToolButton(AddInInst)
End Sub

Private Sub InsertToolButton( Byval AddInInst As Object)
   Dim Toolbar As CommandBar
   Dim Button As CommandBarButton

   Set Toolbar = Excel.CommandBars("Worksheet Menu Bar") _
      .FindControl(ID:=30007).CommandBar

   On Error Resume Next

   Set Button = Toolbar.Controls("Sequence Wizard")
   If (Button Is Nothing) Then
      Set Button = Toolbar.Controls.Add(msoControlButton, , "SequenceWizard")
      Button.Caption = "Sequence Wizard"
      Button.Style = msoButtonCaption
      Button.Tag = AddInTag
      Button.OnAction = "!<" & AddInInst.ProgId & ">"
   End If

   Set Button = Nothing
   If (Button Is Nothing) Then
      Set Button = ToolBar.Controls.Add(msoControlButton, , "GetNumbersWizard")
      Button.Caption = "GetNumbers Wizard"
```

```
        Button.Style = msoButtonCaption
        Button.Tag = msAddinTag
        Button.OnAction = "!<" & AddInInst.ProgId & ">"
    End If

    Set MenuButton = Button

End Sub
```

Note that the OnAction string has to be set to a specific text in order for Excel to recognize it as referring to a COM Addin. It must have the form "!<ProgID>".

The following is typical of a demand-loaded Addin, in which the menu items should only be removed if the user unloads the Addin from the COM Addins dialog box. We can determine this from the RemoveMode property. For Addins loaded at startup, the menu items would usually be removed however the Addin is closed:

```
Private Sub AddinInstance_OnDisconnection( _
    ByVal RemoveMode As AddInDesignerObjects.ext_DisconnectMode, _
    custom() As Variant)

    Dim Control As CommandBarControl

    ' If excel is being closed by the user then remove the buttons
    If RemoveMode = ext_dm_UserClosed Then
      For Each Control In Excel.CommandBars.FindControls(Tag:=AddInTag)
        Control.Delete
      Next
    End If

    Set MenuButton = Nothing
    Set Excel = Nothing
    MsgBox "Disconnected", vbInformation

End Sub
```

In the Click event for the MenuButton, we check the Parameter property of the button that was clicked and show a form we'll define based on the selected button. At this point, just add two blank forms to the project, giving them the names SequenceWizardForm and GetNumbersWizardForm:

```
Private Sub MenuButton_Click( _
    ByVal Ctrl As Office.CommandBarButton, CancelDefault As Boolean)

    If TypeOf Excel.Selection Is Range Then
      Select Case Ctrl.Parameter
        Case "SequenceWizard"
          SequenceWizardForm.Show vbModal

        Case "GetNumbersWizard"
          GetNumbersWizardForm.Show vbModal
      End Select
    Else
```

```
        MsgBox "No range of cells is selected.", vbOKOnly, _
               "Excel 2003 Wizards"
    End If
End Sub
```

Save the project and use File ⇨ Make MyAddin.dll to create the DLL, which also adds the registry entries for Excel to see it. Start Excel 2003 and click Tools ⇨ Sequence Wizard to show the blank Wizard form.

Using the COM Addin from VBA

It is possible (though, unfortunately, quite rare) for the creator of a COM Addin to provide programmatic access to the Addin from VBA. This would be done to either:

❑ Expose the Addin's functionality for use through code

❑ Provide a mechanism for controlling or customizing the Addin

Exposing an Addin to VBA achieved by setting the Addin instance's `Object` property to reference the COM Addin class (or a separate class within the Addin), then exposing the required functionality using `Public` properties and methods, just like any other class. In our example, we'll provide yet another way of getting to the `Sequence` and `GetNumbers` functions.

Add the following line to the bottom of the `AddinInstance_OnConnection` routine, to provide a reference to the Addin class using the Addin's `Object` property:

```
AddInInst.Object = Me
```

And add the following code to the bottom of the Designer's class module, to create and return new instances of our `Simple` and `Complex` classes:

```
Public Property Get SimpleObject() As Simple
  Set SimpleObject = New Simple
End Property

Public Property Get ComplexObject() As Complex
  Set ComplexObject = New Complex
End Property
```

From within Excel, we can then use the following code to access the `Sequence` function, going through the COM Addin and its `Object` property:

```
Private Sub CommandButton1_Click()

  Dim Sequence As Variant
  Sequence = Application.COMAddIns( _
    "MyAddin.COMAddIn").Object.SimpleObject.Sequence(5, 10, 2)
  ActiveCell.Resize(1, 5) = Sequence

End Sub
```

The key point about using this method is that we are accessing the same instance of the class that Excel is using for the Addin, allowing us to manipulate, query, or control that Addin from VBA. For more complex COM Addins, the same method can be used to provide access to a full object model for controlling the Addin.

Linking to Multiple Office Applications

At the start of this chapter, we mentioned that one of the fundamental advantages of COM Addins over .xla Addins is that the same DLL can target multiple Office applications. All we need to do to achieve this is to add a new Addin Designer class for each application that we want to target, in exactly the same way that we added the Designer to target Excel previously in the chapter. Of course, we still have to handle the idiosyncrasies of each application separately.

In the following simple example, we'll make the Sequence function available through the COM Addins in Access and use it to populate a list box on a form.

Start by adding a new Addin class to the project. In the Properties window, change its name to AccessAddin, set its Public property to True (ignoring any warnings) and complete the Designer's form as shown in Figure 13-10.

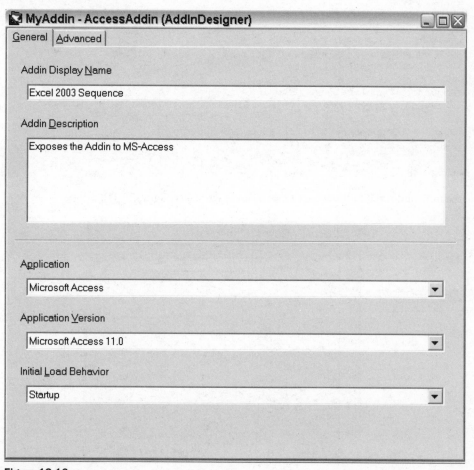

Figure 13-10

Click View ⇨ Code and copy the following into the Designer's code module:

```
Private Sub AddinInstance_OnConnection(ByVal Application As Object, _
    ByVal ConnectMode As AddInDesignerObjects.ext_ConnectMode, _
    ByVal AddInInst As Object, custom() As Variant)

    AddInInst.object = Me

End Sub

Public Property Get SimpleObject() As Simple
    Set SimpleObject = New Simple
End Property
```

Save the project and use File ⇨ Make MyAddin.dll to build the DLL. Start Access 2003 with a blank database, create a new form, add a list box and copy the following code into the form's code module:

```
Option Explicit
Option Compare Database

Private Sub Form_Load()
    Dim Sequence As Variant
    Dim I As Integer

    Sequence = Application.COMAddIns( _
        "MyAddin.AccessAddin").Object.SimpleObject.Sequence(5, 10, 2)

    For I = LBound(Sequence) To UBound(Sequence)
        List0.AddItem Sequence(I)
    Next
End Sub
```

Save the form and run it to show the COM Addin at work (see Figure 13-11).

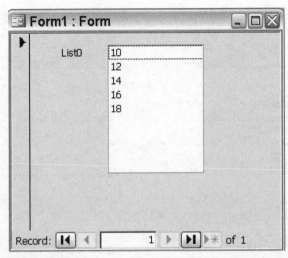

Figure 13-11

Summary

In Excel 2003, Microsoft has provided a number of ways to extend Excel using Addins written in Visual Basic, or any other language that can produce Component Object Model (COM) DLLs:

❑   With Automation Addins, we can add new functions for use in Excel worksheets and our VBA routines.

❑   With COM Addins, we can add new menu items and respond to Excel's events. We can also use these to create Addins that work across multiple Office Applications and the VBE.

❑   The COM Addin can provide programmatic access to the behavior of the Addin, such as enabling or disabling its actions, or using its functions.

❑   The performance of Automation and COM Addins is typically much faster than their VBA equivalents.

In the next chapter, we'll show a third way to extend Excel using ActiveX DLLs—SmartTags.

Customizing the VBE

There is an object library provided that is shown as Microsoft Visual Basic for Applications Extensibility 5.3 in the VBE's Tools ⇨ References list. The objects in this library and their methods, properties, and events enable us to:

❑ Programmatically create, delete, and modify the code, UserForms, and references in our own, and other workbooks

❑ Program the VBE itself, to create useful Addins to assist us in our development efforts and automate many of your development tasks

Between Office 97 and Office 2000, the Click event was added to the CommandBarButton object, which is used to respond to the user clicking the buttons that we add to the VBE's commandbars. The Addin will not, therefore work in Office 97, although all of the code that manipulates the VBE and its objects is still applicable.

The one difference introduced between Excel 2000 and Excel 2002 is related to security. Macro viruses work by using the methods shown in this chapter to modify the target file's code, thus infecting it. To prevent this, Microsoft has made it possible to disable access to all workbooks VBProjects. By default, access is disabled, so none of the code in this chapter will work. To enable access to the VBProjects, check the Trust Access to Visual Basic Project check box on Excel 2003's Tools ⇨ Macros ⇨ Security ⇨ Trusted Sources dialog box.

This chapter explains how to write code to automate the VBE by walking you through the development of a VBE Toolkit to speed up your application development. You will then add a few utilities to the toolkit that demonstrate how to programmatically manipulate code, UserForms, and references. For simplicity, most of the code examples in this chapter have not been provided with error handling.

Identifying VBE Objects in Code

All the objects that form the VBE, and their properties and methods, are contained in their own object library. You need to create a reference to this library before you can use the objects, by switching to the VBE, selecting the menu item Tools ➪ References, checking the Microsoft Visual Basic for Applications Extensibility 5.3 library, as shown in Figure 14-1, and clicking *OK*.

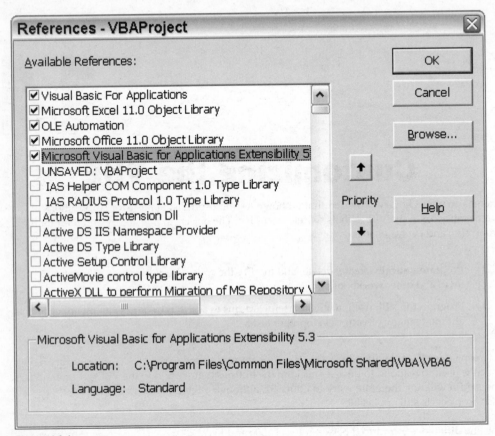

Figure 14-1

In code, this library is referred to as the VBIDE object library.

The full VBIDE Object Model is documented in Appendix B. The more important objects are summarized next.

The VBE Object

The top-level object of the Visual Basic Editor is known as the VBE object and is itself a property of the Excel Application object. Hence, to create an object variable to refer to the VBE, we need code such as:

```
Dim VBE As VBIDE.VBE
Set VBE = Application.VBE
```

The VBProject Object

This object is the container for all the "programming" aspects of a workbook, including UserForms, standard modules, class modules, and the code behind each worksheet and the workbook itself. Each VBProject corresponds to one of the top-level items in the Project Explorer. A specific VBProject object can be located either by iterating through the VBE's VBProjects collection, or through the VBProject property of a workbook.

To find the VBProject that corresponds to the workbook Book1.xls, the following code can be used:

```
Dim project As VBIDE.VBProject
Set project = Workbooks("Book1.xls").VBProject
```

When creating Addins for the VBIDE itself, we often need to know which project is currently highlighted in the Project Explorer. This is given by the ActiveVBProject property of the VBE:

```
Dim project As VBIDE.VBProject
Set project = Application.VBE.ActiveVBProject
```

Note that the ActiveVBProject is the project that the user is editing within the VBE. It is not related in any way to the ActiveWorkbook given by Excel. In fact, since the Developer Edition of Office 2000, it is possible to create self-contained VB Projects that are not part of an Excel workbook.

The VBComponent Object

The UserForms, standard modules, class modules, and code modules behind the worksheets and workbook are all represented as VBComponent objects in the extensibility model. Each VBComponent object corresponds to one of the lower-level items in the Project Explorer tree. A specific VBComponent can be located through the VBComponents collection of a VBProject. Hence, to find the VBComponent that represents the UserForm1 form in Book1.xls, code like this can be used:

```
Dim component As VBIDE.VBComponent
Set component = Workbooks("Book1.xls").VBProject.VBComponents("UserForm1")
```

The name of the VBComponent that contains the code behind the workbook, worksheets, and charts is given by the CodeName property of the related Excel object (the workbook, worksheet, or chart object). Hence, to find the VBComponent for the code behind the workbook (where code can be written to hook into workbook events), this code can be used:

```
Dim component As VBIDE.VBComponent

Set component = Workbooks("Book1.xls").VBProject.VBComponents( _
   Workbooks("Book1.xls").CodeName)
MsgBox component.Name
```

And for a specific worksheet:

```
Dim component As VBIDE.VBComponent
Dim aWorkbook As Workbook
Set aWorkbook = Workbooks("Book1.xls")
Set component = aWorkbook.VBProject.VBComponents( _
   aWorkbook.Worksheets("Sheet1").CodeName)
MsgBox component.Name
```

Note that the name of the workbook's VBComponent is usually "ThisWorkbook" in the Project Explorer. Do not be tempted to rely on this name. If your user has chosen a different language for the Office User Interface, it will be different. The name can also be easily changed by the user in the VBE. For this reason, *do not* use code such as:

```
Dim component As VBIDE.VBComponent

With Workbooks("Book1.xls")
    Set component = .VBProject.VBComponents("ThisWorkbook")
End With
```

When developing Addins for the VBE, you often need to know the VBComponent that the user is editing (the one highlighted in the Project Explorer). This is given by the SelectedVBComponent property of the VBE:

```
Dim component As VBIDE.VBComponent
Set component = Application.VBE.SelectedVBComponent
```

Each VBComponent has a Properties collection, corresponding approximately to the list shown in the Properties Window of the VBE when a VBComponent is selected in the Project Explorer. One of these is the Name property, shown in the following test routine:

```
Public Sub ShowNames()
  With Application.VBE.SelectedVBComponent
    Debug.Print .Name & ": " & .Properties("Name")
  End With
End Sub
```

For most VBComponent objects, the text returned by .Name and .Properties("Name") is the same. However, for the VBComponent objects that contain the code behind workbooks, worksheets, and charts, .Properties("Name") gives the name of the Excel object (the workbook, worksheet or chart). You can use this to find the Excel object that corresponds to the item that the user is working on in the VBE or the Excel workbook that corresponds to the ActiveVBProject. The code for doing this is shown later in this chapter.

The CodeModule Object

All of the VBA code for a VBComponent is contained within its CodeModule object. Through this object you can programmatically read, add, change, and delete lines of code. There is only one CodeModule for each VBComponent. Every type of VBComponent has a CodeModule, though this may not be the case in the future versions. For example, you may get a tool to help design, execute and debug SQL queries that only has a graphical interface, like MS query, but does not have any code behind it.

The CodePane Object

This object gives us access to the user's view of a `CodeModule`. Through this object you can identify such items as the section of a `CodeModule` that is visible on the screen, and the text that the user has selected. You can identify which `CodePane` is currently being edited by using the VBE's `ActiveCodePane` property:

```
Dim codePane As VBIDE.codePane
Set codePane = Application.VBE.ActiveCodePane
MsgBox codePane.TopLine
```

For example, the preceding code will display the top, visible line in the current code pane. If you have scrolled down the page, then the top line might actually be the 34th line in the module; this value would be displayed.

The Designer Object

Some `VBComponents` (such as UserForms) present both code and a graphical interface to the developer. While the code is accessed through the `CodeModule` and `CodePane` objects, the `Designer` object gives you access to the graphical part. In the standard versions of Office, UserForms are the only components with a graphical interface for you to control. However, the Developer Editions include a number of other items (such as the Data Connection Designer), which have graphical interfaces; these too are exposed to us through the `Designer` object.

These preceding objects are the main objects that we'll be using throughout the rest of this chapter, as we create our VBE Toolkit Addin.

Starting Up

There is very little difference in Excel 2003 between a workbook Addin and a COM Addin. The code and UserForms can be modified in the same manner, and they both offer the same level of protection (locking the Project from view). The two advantages of using a COM Addin to hold your tools are that the source is invisible within the Excel User Interface, and that it can be loaded using Excel's Tools ⇨ Addins menu (though each activated Addin will slow down Excel's startup as it is loaded). This chapter uses the term "Addin" to mean a container for tools that you're adding to Excel or the VBE. In fact, during the development of the Addin, you will actually keep the file as a standard workbook, only converting it to an Addin at the end.

This is the basic structure our Addin will have:

❑   We will add a startup module to trap the opening and closing of the Addin

❑   We will add some code to add our menu items to the commandbars on opening and remove them when closing

- ❏ We will add a class module to handle the menu items' Click events

- ❏ And, we'll add some code to perform custom menu actions.

To begin, open a new workbook and delete all of the worksheets apart from the Sheet1. Press *Alt+F11* to switch to the VBE, and find your workbook in the Project Explorer. Select the VBProject entry for it. In the Properties Window, change the project's name to VBETools. Add a new module to the project, give it the name of Common and type in the following code, which will be tasked to run when the workbook is opened and closed:

```
Option Explicit
Option Compare Text

Public Const AddinID As String = "VBETools"
Public Const Title As String = "VBE Tools"

Sub Auto_Open()
   SetUpMenus
End Sub

Sub Auto_Close()
   RemoveMenus
End Sub
```

The Auto_Open and Auto_Close procedures just call some other routines (which will be created in the following section) to add to and remove the menus and menu items from the VBE commandbars. A global constant has also been defined to uniquely identify our Addin's menus, and another to use as a standard title for the Addin's message boxes.

Adding Menu Items to the VBE

The VBE uses the same commandbar code as the rest of the Office suite, so the procedure for adding your own menus to the VBE is very little different from the examples provided in Chapter 26. There is one major difference, which is how to run your routine when the menu item is clicked. When adding menu items to Excel, we set the CommandBarButton's OnAction property to the name of the procedure to run. In the VBE, CommandBarButtons still have an OnAction property, but it is ignored.

Instead, MS has added the Click event to the CommandBarButton (and the Change event to the CommandBarComboBox). In order to use these events, we have to use a class module containing a variable of the correct type declared with WithEvents. To prepare a variable to respond to commandbar events, add a class module to the project, give it the name of CommandBarEventsClass and add the following implementation for the CommandBarEvents Click event:

```
Private WithEvents CommandBarEvents As CommandBarButton

Private Sub CommandBarEvents_Click(ByVal Ctrl As Office.CommandBarButton, _
   CancelDefault As Boolean)
```

```
      On Error Resume Next
      Application.Run Ctrl.OnAction
      CancelDefault = True
   End Sub
```

The key things to note here are:

- ❑ An object, CommandBarEvents, is declared to receive the Click event for the menu items.
- ❑ The Click event is raised by the CommandBarButtonEvents object (the only one exposed by it).
- ❑ The Click event passes the Ctrl object (the menu item or toolbar button) that was clicked.
- ❑ The code runs the routine specified in the control's OnAction property. The code is simulating the behavior that occurs when adding menu items to Excel's menus.

Here is some code that declares a reference to the CommandBarEventsClass. We create an instance of this class and associate the AboutMe event handler with the class's CommandBarEvents public variable:

```
Dim Events As CommandBarEventsClass

Public Sub AddMenu()
   Dim AddinBar As CommandBar
   Dim Button As CommandBarButton

   Set AddinBar = Application.VBE.CommandBars.FindControl(ID:=30038).CommandBar
   Set Button = AddinBar.Controls.Add(msoControlButton)

   Button.Caption = "About My Addin"
   Button.Tag = "MyAddin"
   Button.OnAction = "AboutMe"

   Set Events = New CommandBarEventsClass

   Set Events.CommandBarEvents = Button

End Sub

Sub AboutMe()
   MsgBox "About Me"
End Sub
```

In order to use this class, we have to hook it up to any CommandBarButtons we add, using the previous code, which can be typed into a new standard module. When we hook the event handler to the CommandBarButton in this way, we're actually linking the event handler (the CommandBarEvents variable in the CommandBarEventsClass class) to the *button'ss* .Tag property:

```
Option Explicit
Dim Events As CommandBarEventsClass

Public Sub AddMenu2()
```

```
    Dim AddinBar As CommandBar
    Dim Button As CommandBarButton

    Set AddinBar = Application.VBE.CommandBars.FindControl(ID:=30038).CommandBar
    Set Button = AddinBar.Controls.Add(msoControlButton)

    Button.Caption = "About My Addin"
    Button.Tag = "MyAddin"
    Button.OnAction = "AboutMe"

    Set Events = New CommandBarEventsClass
    Set Events.CommandBarEvents = Button

    Set Button = AddinBar.Controls.Add(msoControlButton)

    Button.Caption = "About My Addin Too"
    Button.Tag = "MyAddin"
    Button.OnAction = "AboutMeToo"

End Sub

Sub AboutMe()
   MsgBox "About Me"
End Sub

Sub AboutMeToo()
   MsgBox "About Me Too"
End Sub
```

All buttons that have the same `Tag` will also fire the `Click` event in the single instance of our `CommandBarEventsClass` class, as shown in the preceding example, where we're just adding a "Me Too" button. The clicks of both buttons are handled by the single `Events` object. Note that the previous code is not part of our VBE Toolkit Addin, so delete the module before continuing.

Table-Driven Menu Creation

Very few professional Excel developers write code to add their menu items one-by-one. Most use a table-driven approach, whereby a table is filled with information about the menu items we want to add, before a routine generates all the menu items based on this table. The same technique will be used here. Using a table-drive approach has the following advantages:

❏   The same menu-creation code can be reused in different projects.

❏   It is much easier and quicker to add lines to a table than to modify code.

❏   It is much easier to see the resulting menu structure by examining the table than to trace through the equivalent code.

The first thing that is needed is a table for the menu information. In Excel, rename the worksheet in our example workbook to `MenuTable` and fill out the sheet as shown in Figure 14-2.

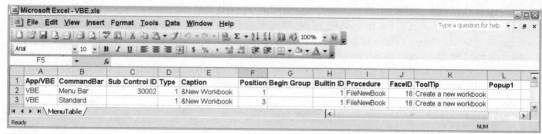

Figure 14-2

The columns of the `MenuTable` are:

Col	Title	Description
A	App / VBE	Either "App" to add items to Excel's menus or "VBE" to add them to the VBE
B	CommandBar	The name of the top-level command bar to add our menu to. See later for a list of valid names and the parts of the VBE to which they apply
C	Sub Control ID	The ID number of a built-in pop-up bar to add our menu to. For example, 30002 is the ID of the File popup menu
D	Type	The type of control to add: 1 for a normal button, 10 for a popup, etc. These correspond to the `msoControl` types listed in the Object Browser
E	Caption	The text to use for the menu item
F	Position	The position in the command bar to add the menu item. Leave this blank to add the menu to the end of the bar
G	Begin Group	`True` or `False` to specify whether to place a separator line before the item
H	BuiltIn ID	If we're adding a built-in menu item, this is the ID of that menu. Use 1 for all custom menu items
I	Procedure	The name of the procedure to run when the menu item is clicked
J	FaceID	The ID number of the built-in tool face to use for the menu. This can also be the name of a picture in the worksheet to use for the button face. 18 is the number for the standard New icon
K	ToolTip	The text of the popup ToolTip to show for the button
L	Popup1 – n	If we add our own popup menus, this is the caption of the custom popup to add further menu items to. See later for an example of its use. We can include as many levels of popup as we like, by simply adding more columns-the code will detect the extra columns

The names for each of the top-level commandbars in the VBE (i.e. the names to use in column B of the menu table) are shown in the following table. Note that Excel should always recognize these names, regardless of the user's choice of language for the Office User Interface (apart from a few rare exceptions, such as the Dutch menus, in which case we'll get a runtime error). The same is not true for the menu items placed on these toolbars. The only language-independent way to locate specific built-in menu items is to use their ID number. A routine to list the ID numbers of built-in menu items is provided in Chapter 26.

Name	Description
Menu Bar	The normal VBE menu bar
Standard	The normal VBE toolbar
Edit	The VBE edit toolbar, containing useful code-editing tools
Debug	The VBE debug toolbar, containing typical debugging tools
UserForm	The VBE UserForm toolbar, containing useful form-editing tools
MSForms	The popup menu for a UserForm (shown when you right-click the UserForm background)
MSForms Control	The popup menu for a normal control on a UserForm
MSForms Control Group	The popup menu that appears when you right-click a group of controls on a UserForm
MSForms MPC	The popup menu for the Multipage Control
MSForms Palette	The popup menu that appears when you right-click a tool in the Control Toolbox
MSForms Toolbox	The popup menu that appears when you right-click one of the tabs at the top of the Control Toolbox
MSForms DragDrop	The popup menu that appears when you use the right mouse button to drag a control between tabs in the Control Toolbox, or onto a UserForm
Code Window	The popup menu for a code window
Code Window (Break)	The popup menu for a code window, when in Break (debug) mode
Watch Window	The popup menu for the Watch window
Immediate Window	The popup menu for the Immediate window
Locals Window	The popup menu for the Locals window
Project Window	The popup menu for the Project Explorer
Project Window (Break)	The popup menu for the Project Explorer, when in Break mode
Object Browser	The popup menu for the Object Browser
Property Browser	The popup menu for the Properties window
Docked Window	The popup menu that appears when you right-click the title bar of a docked window

Name	Description
Project Window Insert	The popup menu that permits inserting a new User Form, Module, or Class to the workbook
Document	The popup menu that permits you to Save a workbook, Import a file, or invoke the document print behavior
Toggle	The popup menu that permits you to toggle a bookmark or breakpoint
Toolbox	The popup menu that permits add a tab to the toolbox, change the dockable property, and hide the toolbox
Toolbox Group	The popup menu that contains options for adding, deleting, and renaming a tab in the toolbox, and moving toolbox items up or down
Task Pane	The popup menu for the task pane
Clipboard	The popup menu for the clipboard
Envelope	The popup menu for the envelope
System	The popup system menu for minimizing, maximizing, moving, sizing, and closing a window
Online Meeting	Shows the popup for online collaboration

As this sheet will be referred to a number of times in code, it is a good idea to give it a meaningful "code name," such as MenuTable. To do this, locate and select the sheet in the Project Explorer in the VBE, probably shown as Sheet1 (MenuTable), and change its name in the Properties window. It should now be shown as MenuTable (MenuTable) in the Project Explorer. Using the code name allows you to refer directly to that sheet as an object, so the following two lines are equivalent:

```
Debug.Print ThisWorkbook.Worksheets("MenuTable").Name
Debug.Print MenuTable.Name
```

The code to create the menus from this table is shown next. The code should be copied into a new module called SetupCommandBars.

At the top of the module, a number of constants are declared, which correspond to each column of the menu table, and we will use these throughout the code. If the menu table structure changes, all you need to do is renumber these constants—you don't need to search through the code:

```
Option Explicit
Option Compare Text

Const TABLE_APP_VBE           As Integer = 1
Const TABLE_COMMANDBAR_NAME   As Integer = 2
Const TABLE_CONTROL_ID        As Integer = 3
Const TABLE_CONTROL_TYPE      As Integer = 4
Const TABLE_CONTROL_CAPTION   As Integer = 5
Const TABLE_CONTROL_POSITION  As Integer = 6
Const TABLE_CONTROL_GROUP     As Integer = 7
```

```
Const TABLE_CONTROL_BUILTIN As Integer = 8
Const TABLE_CONTROL_PROC    As Integer = 9
Const TABLE_CONTROL_FACEID  As Integer = 10
Const TABLE_CONTROL_TOOLTIP As Integer = 11
Const TABLE_POPUP_START     As Integer = 12

Dim Events As CommandBarEventsClass
```

As explained just now, the `Click` event for all our commandbars can be routed through a single instance of our event handler, by ensuring they all share the same `Tag` string.

```
Public Sub SetUpMenus()
  Dim aRange As Range
  Dim items As CommandBars
  Dim item As CommandBar
  Dim control As CommandBarControl
  Dim builtInId As Integer
  Dim column As Integer
  Dim data As Variant

  On Error Goto Catch

  RemoveMenus

  For Each aRange In MenuTable.Cells(1).CurrentRegion.Rows
    If aRange.row > 1 Then
      data = aRange.Value
      Set item = Nothing
```

The routine to actually set up the menus is called from our Addin's `Auto_Open` procedure:

```
If data(1, TABLE_APP_VBE) = "VBE" Then
  Set items = Application.VBE.CommandBars
Else
  Set items = Application.CommandBars
End If

Set item = items.item(data(1, TABLE_COMMANDBAR_NAME))

If item Is Nothing Then
  Set item = items.Add(name:=data(1, TABLE_COMMANDBAR_NAME), _
    temporary:=True)
End If
```

A single routine can be used to add menu items to both the Excel and VBE menus. The only difference is whether we are referring to Excel's `CommandBars` collection or the VBE's `CommandBars` collection:

```
If Not IsEmpty(data(1, TABLE_CONTROL_ID)) Then
  Set item = item.FindControl(ID:=data(1, TABLE_CONTROL_ID), _
    Recursive:=True).CommandBar
End If
```

```
For column = TABLE_POPUP_START To UBound(data, 2)
  If Not IsEmpty(data(1, column)) Then
    Set item = item.Controls(data(1, column)).CommandBar
  End If
Next

builtInId = data(1, TABLE_CONTROL_BUILTIN)

If builtInId = 0 Then builtInId = 1

If IsEmpty(data(1, TABLE_CONTROL_POSITION)) Or _
  data(1, TABLE_CONTROL_POSITION) > item.Controls.Count Then

  Set control = item.Controls.Add(Type:=data(1, TABLE_CONTROL_TYPE), _
    ID:=builtInId, temporary:=True)
Else
  Set control = item.Controls.Add(Type:=data(1, TABLE_CONTROL_TYPE), _
    ID:=builtInId, temporary:=True, before:=data(1, TABLE_CONTROL_POSITION))
End If

control.Caption = data(1, TABLE_CONTROL_CAPTION)
control.BeginGroup = data(1, TABLE_CONTROL_GROUP)
control.TooltipText = data(1, TABLE_CONTROL_TOOLTIP)
```

If you want to add your control to a built-in popup menu, you can recursively search for it in the CommandBars collection. For example, if you wanted to add a menu item to the Format ➪ Make same size menu, you can specify the ID of the Make same size menu (32790) in the SubControlID column of the table:

```
If Not IsEmpty(data(1, TABLE_CONTROL_FACEID)) Then
  If IsNumeric(data(1, TABLE_CONTROL_FACEID)) Then
    control.FaceId = data(1, TABLE_CONTROL_FACEID)
  Else
    MenuTable.Shapes(data(1, TABLE_CONTROL_FACEID)).CopyPicture
    control.PasteFace
  End If
End If

control.Tag = AddinID
control.OnAction = "'" & ThisWorkbook.name & "'!" & _
  data(1, TABLE_CONTROL_PROC)
```

You can either use one of the standard Office tool faces, by supplying the numeric FaceID, or provide your own picture to use. To use your own picture, just give the name of the Picture object in the FaceID column of the menu table. The picture should be 32 × 32 pixels for the small icon view, or 64 × 64 pixels when viewing large icons:

```
If builtInId = 1 And data(1, TABLE_APP_VBE) = "VBE" Then
  If Events Is Nothing Then
    Set Events = New CommandBarEventsClass
    Set Events.CommandBarEvents = control
  End If
```

```
        End If
      End If
    Next
    Exit Sub
  Catch:
    MsgBox Err.Description
  End Sub
```

(If you get an error indicating that "Programmatic access to Visual Basic Projects is not trusted" then in Excel select Tools ⇨ Options ⇨ Security and on the Security tab click Macro Security, change to the Trusted Publishers tab and check "Trust access to Visual Basic Project".) This is the code that sets up the menu event handler. It only needs to be done once, as it will respond to the `Click` events raised by *all* our buttons.

When the Addin is closed, you need to run some code to remove the menus from the VBE. Some developers just use `CommandBars.Reset`, but this removes all other customizations from the commandbars as well as their own. It is much better programming etiquette to locate all the menu items and commandbars that were created for your Addin and delete them. This takes two routines. The first removes all the menus from a specific `CommandBars` collection, by searching for its `Tag`:

```
Private Sub RemoveMenusFromBars(ByVal items As CommandBars)
  Dim control As CommandBarControl

  On Error Resume Next
  Set control = items.FindControl(Tag:=AddinID)

  Do Until control Is Nothing
    control.Delete
    Set control = items.FindControl(Tag:=AddinID)
  Loop
End Sub
```

The second removal routine calls the first to remove the menu items from the Excel commandbars and the VBE commandbars, removes any custom bars that might have been created, and clears the module-level event handler:

```
Public Sub RemoveMenus()
  Dim aCommandBar As CommandBar
  Dim aRange As Range
  Dim name As String

  On Error Resume Next

  Call RemoveMenusFromBars(Application.CommandBars)
  Call RemoveMenusFromBars(Application.VBE.CommandBars)

  For Each aRange In MenuTable.Cells(1).CurrentRegion.Rows

    If aRange.row > 1 Then
      name = aRange.Cells(1, TABLE_COMMANDBAR_NAME)
      Set aCommandBar = Nothing
```

```
        If aRange.Cells(1, TABLE_APP_VBE) = "VBE" Then
          Set aCommandBar = Application.VBE.CommandBars(name)
        Else
          Set aCommandBar = Application.CommandBars(name)
        End If

        If Not aCommandBar Is Nothing Then
          If Not aCommandBar.BuiltIn Then
            If aCommandBar.Controls.Count = 0 Then aCommandBar.Delete
          End If
        End If
      End If
    Next

    Set Events = Nothing
End Sub
```

You now have a complete template, which can be used as the basis for any Excel or VBE Addin (or just in a normal workbook where you want to modify the menu structure).

Let's add this procedure and test the Addin. Add a new module called `MenuFile` and copy in the following code. We will be adding more file-related routines to this module later:

```
Public Sub FileNewBook()
  On Error Resume Next
  Application.Workbooks.Add

  Application.VBE.MainWindow.Visible = False
  Application.VBE.MainWindow.Visible = True
End Sub
```

The `FileNewWorkbook` method just adds a new blank workbook and refreshes the VBE display. Note that the VBE Project Explorer does not always update correctly when workbooks are added and removed through code. The easiest way to refresh the VBE display is to hide and then reshow the main VBE window.

First, check that the Addin compiles, using the Debug ⇨ Compile menu. If any compile errors are highlighted, check your code against the previous listings. To run the Addin, click Tools ⇨ Macros, select the Auto_Open procedure and click the Run button. If all goes well, a new menu item will be added to the VBE File menu and a standard New icon will appear on the VBE toolbar, just to the left of the Save icon (see Figures 14-3 and 14-4).

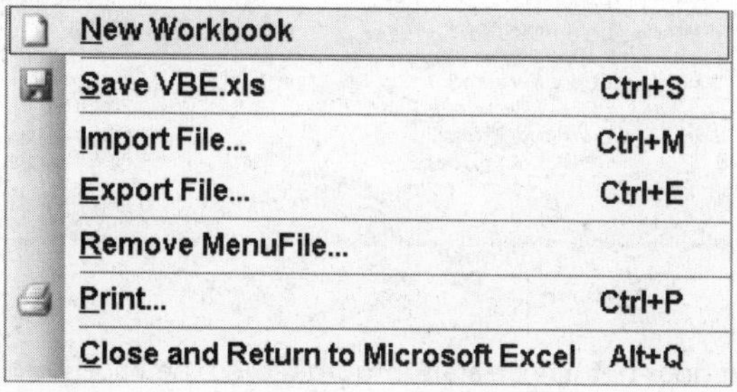

New Workbook	
Save VBE.xls	Ctrl+S
Import File...	Ctrl+M
Export File...	Ctrl+E
Remove MenuFile...	
Print...	Ctrl+P
Close and Return to Microsoft Excel	Alt+Q

Figure 14-3

Figure 14-4

When you click the button, a new workbook will be created in Excel and you will see its `VBProject`
added to the Project Explorer. Congratulations, you have successfully customized the VBE.

Displaying Built-In Dialogs, UserForms, and Messages

The ability to save a workbook from the VBE is built in to Office 2003, but you have also added the ability
to create new workbooks. For a full complement of file operations, you need to add routines to open and
close workbooks as well. Adding a "Most Recently Used" list to the VBE is left as an exercise for the
reader.

By the end of this chapter, you'll have functionality within the VBE to:

❑   Create a new workbook

❑   Open an existing workbook

❑   Save a workbook (this is built into the VBE)

❑   Close a workbook

❑   Display a workbook's `Properties` dialog box

For the `Open` routine, another menu item will be added to the File menu, and another standard button to
the toolbar. For the `Close` routine, an item will once again be added to the File menu, but it will also be
added to the Project Explorer popup menu, allowing you to close a `VBProject` by right-clicking it in the
Project Explorer. Figure 14-5 shows additions to the menu table that will achieve this.

	A	B	C	D	E	F	G	H	I	J	K	L
1	App/VBE	CommandBar	Sub Control ID	Type	Caption	Position	Begin Group	Builtin ID	Procedure	FaceID	ToolTip	Popup1 - n
2	VBE	Menu Bar	30002	1	&New Workbook	1		1	FileNewBook	18	Create a new workbook	
3	VBE	Standard		1	&New Workbook	3		1	FileNewBook	18	Create a new workbook	
4	VBE	Menu Bar	30002	1	&Open Workbook	2		1	FileOpenBook	23	Open a workbook	
5	VBE	Standard		1	&Open Workbook	4		1	FileOpenBook	23	Open a workbook	
6	VBE	Menu Bar	30002	1	Close &Workbook	3		1	FileCloseBook		Close the workbook containing the act	
7	VBE	Project Window		1	Close &Workbook			1	FileCloseBook		Close the workbook containing the act	
8	VBE	Menu Bar	30002	1	Workbook Proper&	4		1	FileBookProps		Workbook Properties	
9	VBE	Project Window		1	Workbook Proper&ties			1	FileBookProps		Workbook Properties	

Figure 14-5

Note that the Close menu does not have a standard image, so the FaceID column has been left empty, and
by not specifying a position, it is added to the bottom of the Project Explorer popup menu.

To accurately simulate Excel's functionality, a test should be made to see if the *Shift* key is held down when the menu button is clicked, and turn off any events if this is the case. Holding the *Shift* key when a workbook is opened used to kill a subroutine (see MS KnowledgeBase article Q175223 for the gory details at `http://support.microsoft.com/support/kb/articles/Q175/2/23.asp`), but this problem appears to have been fixed in Excel 2003. The best that can be done is to use the *Ctrl* key for the same effect. Back in the `Common` module, add the following declaration at the top:

```
Private Declare Function GetAsyncKeyState Lib "user32" (ByVal vKey As Long) As
Integer
```

This tells VBA about a function available in the Windows API-see Chapter 16 for more information about calling Windows API methods. At the bottom of the `Common` module, add the following function:

```
Public Function GetShiftCtrlAlt() As Integer
  Dim Keys As Integer

  Const VK_SHIFT As Long = &H10
  Const VK_CONTROL As Long = &H11
  Const VK_ALT As Long = &H12

  'Check to see if the Shift, Ctrl and Alt keys are pressed
  If GetAsyncKeyState(VK_SHIFT) <> 0 Then Keys = Keys + 1
  If GetAsyncKeyState(VK_CONTROL) <> 0 Then Keys = Keys + 2
  If GetAsyncKeyState(VK_ALT) <> 0 Then Keys = Keys + 4

  GetShiftCtrlAlt = Keys
End Function
```

For the `Open` routine, Excel's `GetOpenFilename` method will be used to retrieve the name of a file, and then open it. If the user holds down the *Ctrl* key, the application events will be turned off, so that the user can open the workbook without triggering any other code-either within the workbook being opened, or Excel's own `Workbook_Open` event. If the user is not holding down the *Ctrl* key, an attempt is made to run any `Auto_Open` routines in the workbook:

```
Public Sub FileOpenBook()
  Dim FileName As Variant
  Dim IsControlKeyPressed As Boolean
  Dim aWorkbook As Workbook

  On Error GoTo Catch

  IsControlKeyPressed = (GetShiftCtrlAlt And 2) = 2
  Application.Visible = False
  FileName = Application.GetOpenFilename
  Application.Visible = True

  If Not (FileName = False) Then
    If IsControlKeyPressed Then
      Application.EnableEvents = False

    Set aWorkbook = Workbooks.Open(FileName:=FileName, _
      UpdateLinks:=0, AddToMru:=True)
```

```
        Application.EnableEvents = True
      Else
        Set aWorkbook = Workbooks.Open(FileName:=FileName, AddToMru:=True)
        aWorkbook.RunAutoMacros xlAutoOpen
      End If
   End If

   Application.VBE.MainWindow.Visible = False
   Application.VBE.MainWindow.Visible = True
   Exit Sub

Catch:
   Application.Visible = False
   MsgBox Err.Description, vbCritical
   Application.Visible = True
End Sub
```

Whenever a dialog box is used that would normally be shown in the Excel window (including the built-in dialog boxes, any UserForms, and even `MsgBox` and `InputBox` calls), Excel automatically switches to its own window to show the dialog box. When developing applications for the VBE, however, we really want the dialog box to appear within the VBE window, not Excel's. The easiest way to achieve this effect is to hide the Excel window before showing the dialog box then unhide it afterwards:

```
Public Function ActiveProjectBook() As Workbook
   Dim project As VBIDE.VBProject
   Dim component As VBIDE.VBComponent
   Dim name As String

   On Error GoTo Finally

   Set project = Application.VBE.ActiveVBProject

   If project.Protection = vbext_pp_locked Then
     name = project.FileName

     If InStrRev(name, "\") <> 0 Then
       name = Mid(name, InStrRev(name, "\") + 1)

       If IsWorkbook(name) Then
         Set ActiveProjectBook = Workbooks(name)
         Exit Function
       End If
     End If
   Else
     For Each component In project.VBComponents
       If component.Type = vbext_ct_Document Then
         name = component.Properties("Name")
         If IsWorkbook(name) Then
           If Workbooks(name).VBProject Is project Then
             Set ActiveProjectBook = Workbooks(name)
             Exit Function
           End If
         End If
```

```
            End If
          End If
       Next
     End If

Finally:
   Application.Visible = False
   MsgBox "Workbook not found", vbExclamation
   Application.Visible = True

   Set ActiveProjectBook = Nothing
End Function
```

The Close routine presents us with a new challenge. We are adding a Close Workbook menu item to the popup menu for the Project Explorer, and hence need to determine which VBProject was clicked. The ActiveVBProject property of the VBE provides this, but a way is needed to get from the VBProject object to the workbook containing it. The method for doing this was described in the *Identifying VBE Objects in Code* section at the start of this chapter and the code is shown next. Add the following code to the Common module, along with the Auto_Open and end function:

```
Auto_Close routines, as you will be using these behaviors later:
Public Function IsWorkbook(ByVal book As String) As Boolean

   On Error GoTo Catch
   IsWorkbook = Workbooks(book).name <> ""
   Exit Function

Catch:
   IsWorkbook = False
```

Note that the Excel window is being hidden before displaying our error message, and is "unhidden" afterwards. The following routine is needed to check if the result is the name of a workbook:

```
Public Sub FileCloseBook()
   Dim aWorkbook As Workbook
   Dim isCtrlKeyPress As Boolean

   On Error GoTo Catch

   Set aWorkbook = ActiveProjectBook
   If aWorkbook Is Nothing Then Exit Sub

   isCtrlKeyPress = (GetShiftCtrlAlt And 2) = 2

   If isCtrlKeyPress Then
      Application.EnableEvents = False
      aWorkbook.Close
      Application.EnableEvents = True
   Else
      aWorkbook.RunAutoMacros xlAutoClose
      aWorkbook.Close
```

```
      End If
      Exit Sub

   Catch:
      Application.Visible = False
      MsgBox Err.Description, vbCritical
      Application.Visible = True
   End Sub
```

Now that you can get the workbook that corresponds to the active VB Project, you can use it in the `Close` routine, which should be added to the `MenuFile` module:

```
Public Sub FileBookProps()
   Dim aWorkbook As Workbook
   Dim IsAddin As Boolean
   Dim IsVisible As Boolean

   On Error Resume Next
   Set aWorkbook = ActiveProjectBook
   If aWorkbook Is Nothing Then Exit Sub

   Application.Visible = False
   IsAddin = aWorkbook.IsAddin
   aWorkbook.IsAddin = False

   IsVisible = aWorkbook.Windows(1).Visible
   aWorkbook.Windows(1).Visible = True
   Application.Dialogs(xlDialogProperties).Show
   aWorkbook.Windows(1).Visible = IsVisible
   aWorkbook.IsAddin = IsAddin

   Application.Visible = True
End Sub
```

The last workbook-related tool to be defined displays the File Properties dialog box for the active VB Project's workbook. One of the main uses for the workbook properties is to provide the information shown in the Tools ➪ Addins dialog box. The list box shows the Addin's title from its Properties dialog box, while the description shown when an Addin is selected, is obtained from its Comments box.

Excel's built-in Properties dialog box can be used for this, but we cannot tell it which workbook to show the properties for—the active workbook is used. Therefore, any Addins need to be temporarily converted to normal workbooks and "unhidden" if they are hidden. After showing the Properties dialog box, the workbooks must be converted back to Addins.

To test the Addin so far, just run the `Auto_Open` routine using Tools ➪ Macros to recreate our menu items, then check that each item works as intended.

> **Note that attempting to close the Addin itself using the menu might cause the computer to lock up.**

Working with Code

So far in this chapter, we have been working at a fairly high level in the VBIDE and Excel Object Models (limiting ourselves to the `VBProject` and `Workbook` objects), to add typical file operations to the Visual Basic environment. You now have the ability to create new workbooks (and hence their VB Projects), open existing workbooks, change a workbook's properties, and save and close workbooks from within the VBE.

In this section, we will plunge to the lowest level of the VBE Object Model and learn how to work with the user's code. We will limit ourselves to detecting the line of code the user is editing (and even identifying the selected characters within that line), and getting information about the procedure, module, and project containing that line of code. We will leave adding and changing code until the next section, where we'll be creating a UserForm, adding some buttons to it and adding code to handle the buttons' events.

To demonstrate how to identify the code that the user is working on, right-click access will be added to provide a print routine, with individual buttons to print the current selection, current procedure, module, or project. First some additional rows will be added to our menu table (see Figure 14-6).

	A	B	C	D	E	F	G	H	I	J	K	L
1	App/VBE	CommandBar	Sub Control ID	Type	Caption	Position	Begin Group	Builtin ID	Procedure	FaceID	ToolTip	Popup1 - n
2	VBE	Menu Bar	30002	1	&New Workbook	1		1	FileNewBook	18	Create a new workbook	
3	VBE	Standard		1	&New Workbook	3		1	FileNewBook	18	Create a new workbook	
4	VBE	Menu Bar	30002	1	&Open Workbook	2		1	FileOpenBook	23	Open a workbook	
5	VBE	Standard		1	&Open Workbook	4		1	FileOpenBook	23	Open a workbook	
6	VBE	Menu Bar	30002	1	Close &Workbook	3		1	FileCloseBook		Close the workbook containing the ac	
7	VBE	Project Window		1	Close &Workbook			1	FileCloseBook		Close the workbook containing the ac	
8	VBE	Menu Bar	30002	1	Workbook Proper&	4		1	FileBookProps		Workbook Properties	
9	VBE	Project Window		1	Workbook Proper&ties			1	FileBookProps		Workbook Properties	
10	VBE	Code Window		10	P&rint	4		1				
11	VBE	Code Window		1	&Selected Text	1		1	CodePrintSel	3518	Print selected text	P&rint
12	VBE	Code Window		1	&Procedure	2		1	CodePrintProc	2564	Print current procedure	P&rint
13	VBE	Code Window		1	&Module	3		1	CodePrintMod	472	Print current module	P&rint
14	VBE	Code Window		1	Pro&ject	4		1	CodePrintProj	2557	Print all modules in proje	P&rint

Figure 14-6

The first thing to note is that we're adding our own cascading menu to the Code Window popup menu (type 10 is a custom popup menu), then adding four menu items to the cascading menu, each of which has its own face ID. The result is shown in Figure 14-7.

The code for the four printing routines will be placed into their own module, so add a new module to the project called `MenuCode`.

Unfortunately, the VBIDE Object Model does not include a `Print` method for any of its objects. To provide right-click printing, there are three options:

❑ Show the VBE's `Print` dialog box and operate it using `SendKeys`

❑ Copy the code to a worksheet range and print it from there

❑ Copy the code to a private instance of Word, reformat to show the Excel reserved words, etc. in their correct colors and then print it from Word

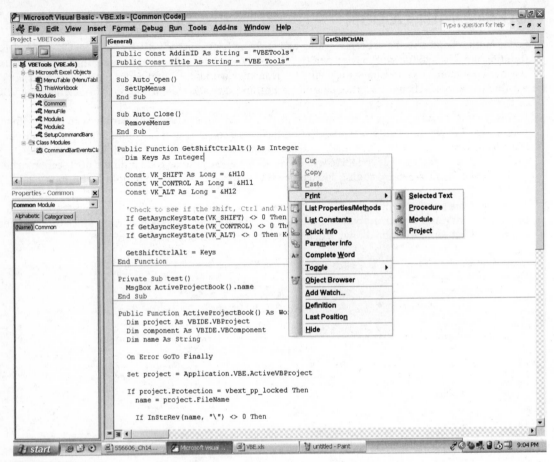

Figure 14-7

For the sake of simplicity, the first option will be implemented. The main problem that this presents is how to select the Selected Text, Module, or Project option buttons on the Print dialog box, using SendKeys, especially as the Selected Text option is only enabled when some text is actually selected.

The answer is to identify if any text is selected, then send the appropriate number of *DownArrow* keys to the dialog box to select either the Module or Project options. If we could rely on our users only ever having an English user interface language, we could send *Alt+M* or *Alt+J* keystrokes—sending *DownArrows* works with any choice of user interface language.

The code for the Selected Text menu item is the simplest and is presented next. All that is required is to identify if the user has actually selected anything and if so, to send some keystrokes to the Print dialog box to print it:

```
Option Explicit

Public Sub CodePrintSel()
  Dim StartLine As Long
```

```
      Dim StartColumn As Long
      Dim EndLine As Long
      Dim EndColumn As Long

      Application.VBE.ActiveCodePane.GetSelection StartLine, _
        StartColumn, EndLine, EndColumn

      If StartLine <> EndLine Or StartColumn <> EndColumn Then
        Application.SendKeys "{ENTER}"
        Application.VBE.CommandBars.FindControl(ID:=4).Execute
      End If
  End Sub
```

The main items to note are:

❑ The `ActiveCodePane` property of the VBE is being used to identify which module the user is editing.

❑ The variables sent to the `GetSelection` method are sent `ByRef` and actually get filled by the method. After the call to `GetSelection`, they contain the start and ending line numbers and start and ending columns of the currently selected text.

❑ A simple *Enter* keystroke is sent to the keyboard buffer. Then the VBE Print dialog box is immediately shown by running the File ➪ Print menu item (ID = 4) directly. This technique of running menu items directly is introduced in Chapter 17, in connection with the `RunMenu` routine presented there. By default (if some text is selected) when the VBE Print dialog box is shown, the Selected Text option is selected so this does not need to be changed:

```
Public Sub CodePrintMod()
  Dim StartLine As Long
  Dim StartColumn As Long
  Dim EndLine As Long
  Dim EndColumn As Long

  Application.VBE.ActiveCodePane.GetSelection StartLine, _
    StartColumn, EndLine, EndColumn

  If StartLine <> EndLine Or StartColumn <> EndColumn Then
    Application.SendKeys "{DOWN}{ENTER}"
  Else
    Application.SendKeys "{ENTER}"
  End If

  Application.VBE.CommandBars.FindControl(ID:=4).Execute
End Sub

Public Sub CodePrintProj()
  Dim StartLine As Long
  Dim StartColumn As Long
  Dim EndLine As Long
  Dim EndColumn As Long

  Application.VBE.ActiveCodePane.GetSelection StartLine, _
    StartColumn, EndLine, EndColumn
```

```
    If StartLine <> EndLine Or StartColumn <> EndColumn Then
        Application.SendKeys "{DOWN}{DOWN}{ENTER}"
    Else
        Application.SendKeys "{DOWN}{ENTER}"
    End If

    Application.VBE.CommandBars.FindControl(ID:=4).Execute
End Sub
```

To print the current module and project, very similar code can be used. The only difference is to check if any text is selected (that is, if the Selected Text option in the Print dialog box is enabled), then send a number of down keystrokes to the dialog box to select the correct option. Both of these routines can be added to the MenuCode module:

```
Public Sub CodePrintProc()
    Dim StartLine As Long
    Dim StartColumn As Long
    Dim EndLine As Long
    Dim EndColumn As Long
    Dim ProcedureType As Long
    Dim ProcedureName As String
    Dim ProcedureStart As Long
    Dim ProcedureEnd As Long

    With Application.VBE.ActiveCodePane
        .GetSelection StartLine, StartColumn, EndLine, EndColumn

        With .CodeModule
            If StartLine <= .CountOfDeclarationLines Then
                ProcedureStart = 1
                ProcedureEnd = .CountOfDeclarationLines
            Else
                ProcedureName = .ProcOfLine(StartLine, ProcedureType)
                ProcedureStart = .ProcStartLine(ProcedureName, ProcedureType)
                ProcedureEnd = ProcedureStart + _
                    .ProcCountLines(ProcedureName, ProcedureType)
            End If
        End With

        Call .SetSelection(ProcedureStart, 1, ProcedureEnd, 999)

        Application.SendKeys "{ENTER}"
        Application.VBE.CommandBars.FindControl(ID:=4).Execute
        DoEvents
        Call .SetSelection(StartLine, StartColumn, EndLine, EndColumn)
    End With
End Sub
```

The code to print the current procedure is slightly more complex, as the Print dialog box does not have a Current Procedure option. The steps we need to perform are:

❑   Identify and store away the user's current selection

❑   Identify the procedure (or declaration lines) containing the user's selection

❑   Expand the selection to encompass the full procedure (or all the declaration lines)

❑   Show the Print dialog box to print this expanded selection

❑   Restore the user's original selections

Doing this on some PCs raises an interesting issue—the final step of restoring the user's original selection sometimes gets run before the Print dialog box has been shown. This is presumably because the printing is done asynchronously. The easy fix is to include a DoEvents statement immediately after showing the Print dialog box, to let the print routine carry out its task. This will also yield control to the operating system, allowing it to process any pending or queued events.

The main item to note in this code is that the ProcOfLine method accepts the start line as input, fills the ProcedureType variable with a number to identify the procedure type (Sub, Function, Property Let, Property Get, or Property Set), and returns the name of the procedure. The procedure type and name are used to find the start of the procedure (using ProcStartLine) and the number of lines within the procedure (ProcCountLines), which are then selected and printed.

Working with UserForms

The code examples presented in this chapter so far have been extending the VBE, to provide additional tools for the developer. In this section, we move our attention to programmatically creating and manipulating UserForms, adding controls, and adding procedures to the UserForm's code module to handle the controls' events. While the example provided in this section continues to extend the VBE, the same code and techniques can be applied in end-user applications, including:

❑   Adding UserForms to workbooks created by the application

❑   Sizing the UserForm and moving and sizing its controls to make the best use of the available screen space

❑   Adding code to handle events in UserForms created by the application

❑   Changing the controls shown on an existing UserForm in response to user input

❑   Creating UserForms on-the-fly, as they are needed (for example, when the number and type of controls on the UserForm will vary significantly depending on the data to be shown)

The preceding techniques will be demonstrated by writing code to add a UserForm to the active project, complete with standard-sized OK and Cancel buttons, as well as code to handle the buttons' Click events and the UserForm's QueryClose event. The UserForm's size will be set to 2/3 of the width and height of the Excel window and the OK and Cancel buttons' position will be adjusted accordingly.

The example shown here is the difficult way to achieve the desired result, and is intended to be an educational, rather than a practical, example. The easy way to add a standardized UserForm is to create it manually and export it to disk as a .frm file, then import it using the following code (do not type this in)

```
Dim component As VBComponent
Set component = Application.VBE.ActiveVBProject. _
   VBComponents.Import ("MyForm.frm")
```

When you need to include it in another project, just import it again. The only advantage to doing it through code is that the UserForm can be given a size appropriate to the user's screen resolution and size, and its controls positioned correctly.

Start by adding another row to the menu table, which should now give you the screen shown in Figure 14-8.

	A	B	C	D	E	F	G	H	I	J	K	L
1	App/VBE	CommandBar	Sub Control ID	Type	Caption	Position	Begin Group	Builtin ID	Procedure	FaceID	ToolTip	Popup1 - n
2	VBE	Menu Bar	30002	1	&New Workbook	1		1	FileNewBook	18	Create a new workbook	
3	VBE	Standard		1	&New Workbook	3		1	FileNewBook	18	Create a new workbook	
4	VBE	Menu Bar	30002	1	&Open Workbook	2		1	FileOpenBook	23	Open a workbook	
5	VBE	Standard		1	&Open Workbook	4		1	FileOpenBook	23	Open a workbook	
6	VBE	Menu Bar	30002	1	Close &Workbook	3		1	FileCloseBook		Close the workbook containing the ac	
7	VBE	Project Window		1	Close &Workbook			1	FileCloseBook		Close the workbook containing the ac	
8	VBE	Menu Bar	30002	1	Workbook Proper&	4		1	FileBookProps		Workbook Properties	
9	VBE	Project Window		1	Workbook Proper&ties			1	FileBookProps		Workbook Properties	
10	VBE	Code Window		10	P&rint	4		1				
11	VBE	Code Window		1	&Selected Text	1		1	CodePrintSel	3518	Print selected text	P&rint
12	VBE	Code Window		1	&Procedure	2		1	CodePrintProc	2564	Print current procedure	P&rint
13	VBE	Code Window		1	&Module	3		1	CodePrintMod	472	Print current module	P&rint
14	VBE	Code Window		1	Pro&ject	4		1	CodePrintProj	2557	Print all modules in proje	P&rint
15	VBE	Standard	32806	1	&Standard Form	2		1	FormNewUserF	581	Insert standardized User	Form
16												

Figure 14-8

The result of this addition will be the Standard Form item shown in Figure 14-9.

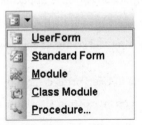

Figure 14-9

Add a new module for this routine, called `MenuForm` and copy in the following code:

```
Option Explicit
Option Compare Text

Private Declare Function LockWindowUpdate Lib "user32" _
    (ByVal hwndLock As Long) As Long
```

`Application.ScreenUpdating` does not affect the VBE, and `FormNewUserform` results in quite a lot of screen activity as the form is sized and the controls are drawn. A simple Windows API call can be used to freeze the VBE window at the start of the routine and unfreeze it at the end. See Chapter 16 for more information about using this and other API functions:

```
Public Sub FormNewUserForm()
    Dim component As VBIDE.VBComponent
    Dim DesignForm As UserForm
```

```
Dim Line As Long
Dim Button As CommandBarButton
Dim Popup As CommandBarPopup

Const Gap As Double = 6
```

Microsoft's Windows design guidelines recommend a gap of 6 points (approximately four pixels) between buttons, and between a button and the edge of a form:

```
On Error GoTo Catch
```

This is one of the more complex routines in the Addin, so some error handling code will be added to it. Every routine in this chapter should really be given similar error-handling code:

```
LockWindowUpdate Application.VBE.MainWindow.Hwnd
```

We will use the Windows API call to freeze the VBE's window. Note that HWnd is a hidden property of the MainWindow object. To display the hidden properties for an object, open the Object Browser, right-click in its window, and click the Show Hidden Members item:

```
Set component = Application.VBE.ActiveVBProject.VBComponents.Add( _
    vbext_ct_MSForm)
component.Properties("Width") = Application.UsableWidth * 2 / 3
component.Properties("Height") = Application.UsableHeight * 2 / 3
```

The VBComponent object (component in the code) provides the "canvas" (background) of the UserForm, its Properties collection, and its CodeModule. When a new UserForm is added to a project, a VBComponent object is passed back that contains the form. The VBComponent's Properties collection can be used to change the size (as shown in Figure 14-10), and change other properties like color, font, and caption of the form's background.

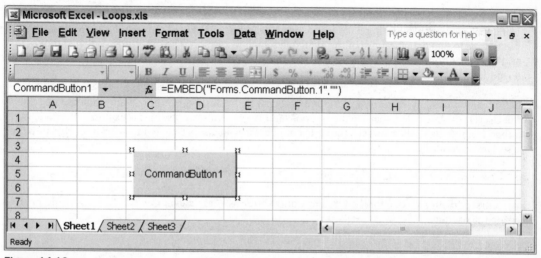

Figure 14-10

```
Set DesignForm = component.Designer

With DesignForm
  With .Controls.Add("Forms.CommandButton.1", "OKButton")
    .Caption = "OK"
    .Default = True
    .Height = 18
    .Width = 54
End With

With .Controls.Add("Forms.CommandButton.1", "CancelButton")
  .Caption = "Cancel"
  .Cancel = True
  .Height = 18
  .Width = 54
End With
```

The VBComponent's Designer object provides access to the *content* of the UserForm and is responsible for the area inside the form's borders and below its title bar. In this code, two controls are added to the normal blank UserForm, to provide standard OK and Close buttons. The name to use for the control (Forms.CommandButton.1 in this case) can be found by adding the control from Excel's Control Toolbox to a worksheet, then examining the resulting =EMBED function:

```
With .Controls("OKButton")
    .Top = DesignForm.InsideHeight - .Height - Gap
    .Left = DesignForm.InsideWidth - .Width * 2 - Gap * 2
  End With

  With .Controls("CancelButton")
    .Top = DesignForm.InsideHeight - .Height - Gap
    .Left = DesignerForm.InsideWidth - .Width - Gap
  End With
End With
```

This could be extended to add listboxes, labels, checkboxes, and other controls. From this point on, you could just as easily be working with an existing UserForm, changing its size and the position and size of its controls to make the best use of the available screen resolution. The preceding code just moves the OK and Cancel buttons to the bottom-right corner of the UserForm, without adjusting their size. The same technique can be used to move and size all of a UserForm's controls.

Now that buttons have been added to the UserForm at the desired position, some code can be added to the UserForm's module to handle the buttons' and UserForm's events. In this example, the code is being added from strings. Alternatively, the code could be kept in a separate text file and imported into the UserForm's module:

```
.AddFromString "Sub OKButton_Click()"
```

We'll first add simple code for the OK and Cancel buttons' Click events. Code like this could be used to create the routine:

```
With component.CodeModule
  Line = .CreateEventProc("Click", "OKButton")
```

```
    .InsertLines Line, "'Standard OK button handler"
    .ReplaceLine Line + 2, " mbOK = True" & vbCrLf & " Me.Hide"

    .AddFromString vbCrLf & _
    "'Standard Cancel button handler" & vbCrLf & _
    "Private Sub CancelButton_Click()" & vbCrLf & _
    " mbOK = False" & vbCrLf & _
    " Me.Hide" & vbCrLf & _
    "End Sub"
```

However, if CreateEventProc is used, all of the procedure's parameters are filled in on our behalf. There is very little difference between the two techniques. Note that the CreateEventProc adds the 'Private Sub...' line, the 'End Sub' line, and a space between them. *Do not* type this code snippet into the Addin:

```
Private Sub OKButton_Click()

End Sub
```

CreateEventProc returns the number of the line in the module where the 'Private Sub...' was added, which is then used to insert a comment line and to replace the default blank line with the code:

```
    Line = .CreateEventProc("QueryClose", "UserForm")
    .InsertLines Line, "'Standard Close handler, treat same as Cancel"
    .ReplaceLine Line + 2, " CancelButton_Click"
    .CodePane.Window.Close
  End With

  LockWindowUpdate 0&
  Exit Sub

Catch:
```

The code for the UserForm's QueryClose event is the same as that of the Cancel button, so some code will be added just to call the CancelButton_Click routine:

```
Catch:
  LockWindowUpdate 0&
  Application.Visible = False
  MsgBox Err.Description, vbExclamation
  Application.Visible = True
End Sub
```

The standard error handler unfreezes the window, displays the error message and closes. Such error handling should be added to all the routines in the Addin.

The Addin is now complete. Switch back to Excel and save the workbook as an Addin (at the bottom of the list of available file types), with an .xla extension. Then, use Tools → Addins to install it.

Working with References

One of the major enhancements in recent versions of VBA is the ability to declare a reference to an external object library (using the Tools ⇨ References dialog box), then use the objects defined in that library as if they were built into Excel. In this chapter, for example, you have been using the objects defined in the VBA Extensibility library without thinking about where they came from.

The term for this is "early binding," so named because we are binding the external object library to our application at design-time. Using early binding gives the following benefits:

❑ The code is much faster, as all the links between the libraries have been checked and compiled

❑ The New operator can be used to create instances of the external objects

❑ All of the constants defined in the object library can be utilized, thus avoiding numerous "magic numbers" throughout the code

❑ Excel displays the Auto List Members, Auto Quick Info, and Auto Data Tips information for the objects while the application is being developed

This will be explained in more detail in Chapter 16.

There is, however, one minor inconvenience to early binding. If you try to run your application on a computer that does not have the external object library installed, you will get a compiletime error that cannot be trapped using standard error-handling techniques—usually showing a perfectly valid line of code as being the culprit. Excel will display the error when it runs some code in a module, which contains:

❑ An undeclared variable in a procedure—and you didn't use Option Explicit

❑ A declaration of a type defined in the missing object library

❑ A constant defined in the missing object library

❑ A call to a routine, object, method, or property defined in the missing object library

The VBIDE References collection provides a method of checking that all the application's references are functioning correctly, and that all the required external object libraries are installed, and are the correct version. The code to check this should be put in your Auto_Open routine and the module that contains the Auto_Open must not contain any code that uses the external object libraries. If there is a broken reference, it is unlikely that any other code will run, so the routine simply stops after displaying which references are missing. Typical Auto_Open code is:

```
Public Sub Auto_Open()
   Dim o As Object
   Dim IsBroken As Boolean
   Dim Description As String

   For Each o In ThisWorkbook.VBProject.References
      If o.IsBroken Then
         On Error Resume Next
         Description = "<Not known>"
         Description = o.Description
         On Error GoTo 0
```

```
        MsgBox "Missing reference to:" & vbCrLf & _
               "    Name: " & Description & vbCrLf & _
               "    Path: " & o.FullPath & vbCrLf & _
               "Please reinstall this file."

        IsBroken = True
      End If
    Next

    If Not IsBroken Then
      ' SetupMenus
    End If
End Sub
```

Summary

The Microsoft Visual Basic for Applications Extensibility 5.3 object library provides a rich set of objects, properties, methods, and events for controlling the VBE itself. Using these objects, developers can create their own labor-saving Addins to help in their daily development tasks.

Many end-user applications can also utilize these objects to manipulate their own code modules, UserForms and references, to provide a feature-rich, flexible, and robust set of functionality.

15

Interacting with Other Office Applications

The Office application programs: Excel, Word, PowerPoint, Outlook, Access, Publisher, SourceSafe, and FrontPage all use the same VBA language. Once you understand VBA syntax in Excel, you know how to use VBA in all the other applications. Where these applications differ is in their object models.

One of the really nice things about the common VBA language is that all the Office applications are able to expose their objects to each other, and you can program interactions between all of the applications from any one of them. To work with Word objects from Excel, for example, you only need to establish a link to Word and then you have access to its objects as if you were programming with VBA in Word itself.

This chapter explains how to create the link in a number of different ways and presents some simple examples of programming the other Microsoft applications. In all cases, the code is written in Excel VBA, but it could easily be modified for any other Office application. The code is equally applicable to products outside Office that support the VBA language. These include other Microsoft products such as Visual Basic and SQL Server. There is also a growing list of non-Microsoft products that can be programmed in the same way.

We will also have cause to ponder on macro viruses at the end of this chapter.

> We will not attempt to give detailed explanations of the objects, methods, and properties of the other Office applications used in the following examples. Our aim is to show how to establish communication with them, not to study their object models. You can learn about their object models in the other Wrox publications in the Office 2000 series, namely: Word 2000 VBA Programmer's Reference by Duncan MacKenzie (ISBN: 1-861002-55-6) and Outlook 2000 VBA Programmer's Reference by Dwayne Gifford (ISBN: 1-861002-53-X). In addition, Wrox Press has published a comprehensive beginner's guide to Access VBA programming, complete with compact disk: Beginning Access 2000 VBA by Rob Smith and Dave Sussman (ISBN: 0-7645-4383-0).

Establishing the Connection

Once you have made a connection with an Office application, its objects are exposed for automation through a type library. There are two ways to establish such a connection: *late binding* and *early binding*. In either case, you establish the connection by creating an object variable that refers to the target application, or a specific object in the target application. You can then proceed to use the properties and methods of the object referred to by the object variable.

In *late binding,* you create an object that refers to the Office application before you make a link to the Office application's type library. In earlier versions of the Office applications, it was necessary to use *late binding* and you will still see it used, because it has some advantages over early binding. One advantage is that you can write code that can detect the presence or absence of the required type library on the PC running your code and link to different versions of applications based on decisions made as the code executes.

The disadvantage of late binding is that the type library for the target application is not accessed when you are writing your code. Therefore, you get no Help information regarding the application, you cannot reference the intrinsic constants in the application and, when the code is compiled, the references to the target application may not be correct, as they cannot be checked. The links are only fully resolved when you try to execute the code and this takes time. It is also possible that coding errors may be detected at this point that cause your program to fail.

Early binding is supported by all the Office applications, from Office 97 onwards. Code that uses early binding executes faster than the code using late binding, as the target application's type library is present when you write your code. Therefore, more syntax and type checking can be performed, and more linkage details can be established, before the code executes.

It is also easier to write code for early binding because you can see the objects, methods, and properties of the target application in the Object Browser and, as you write your code you will see automatic tips appear, such as a list of related properties and methods after you type an object reference. You can also use the intrinsic constants defined in the target application.

Late Binding

The following code creates an entry in the Outlook calendar. The code uses the late binding technique:

```
Public Sub MakeOutlookAppointment()
  Dim Outlook As Object
  Dim Appointment As Object
  Const Item = 1

  Set Outlook = CreateObject("Outlook.Application")
  Set Appointment = Outlook.CreateItem(Item)

  Appointment.Subject = "New Years Party"
  Appointment.Start = DateSerial(2003, 12, 31) + TimeSerial(9, 30, 0)

  Appointment.End = DateSerial(2003, 12, 31) + TimeSerial(11, 30, 0)
  Appointment.ReminderPlaySound = True
  Appointment.Save
```

```
      Outlook.Quit
      Set Outlook = Nothing
   End Sub
```

The basic technique in programming another application is to create an object variable referring to that application. The object variable in this case is conveniently named `Outlook`. You then use `Outlook` (as you would use the `Application` object in Excel) to refer to objects in the external application's object model. In this case, the `CreateItem` method of Outlook's `Application` object is used to create a reference to a new `AppointmentItem` object.

As Outlook's intrinsic constants are not available in late binding, you need to define your own constants, such as `AppointmentItem` here, or substitute the value of the constant as the parameter value. Note the times have been defined using the `DateSerial` and `TimeSerial` functions to avoid ambiguity or problems in an international context. See Chapter 17 for more details.

By declaring `Outlook` and `Appointment` as the generic `Object` type, you force VBA to use late binding. VBA cannot resolve all the links to Outlook until it executes the `CreateObject` function.

The `CreateObject` input argument defines the application name and class of the object to be created. `Outlook` is the name of the application and `Application` is the class. Many applications allow you to create objects at different levels in the object model. For example, Excel allows you to create `WorkSheet` or `Chart` objects from other applications, using `Excel.WorkSheet` or `Excel.Chart` as the input parameter of the `CreateObject` function.

It is good programming practice to close the external application when you are finished with it and set the object variable to `Nothing`. This releases the memory used by the link and the application.

If you run this macro, nothing will happen in Excel at all. However, open up Outlook and in the Calendar you will find that the appointment has been added for the morning of December 31 as shown n Figure 15-1.

Early Binding

If you want to use early binding, you need to establish a reference to the type library of the external application in your VBA project. You do this from the VBE by selecting Tools ⇨ References, which displays the dialog box shown in Figure 15-2.

You create a reference by checking the box next to the object library. Once you have a reference to an application, you can declare your object variables as the correct type. For example, you could declare `Entry` as an `AddressEntry` type as follows:

```
   Dim Entry As AddressEntry
```

VBA will search through the type libraries, in the order shown from the top down, to find references to object types. If the same object type is present in more than one library, it will use the first one found. You can select a library and click the Priority buttons to move it up or down the list to change the order in which libraries are searched. There is no need to depend on priority, however. You can always qualify an object by preceding it with the name of the main object in the library. For example, instead of using `AddressEntry`, use `Outlook.AddressEntry`.

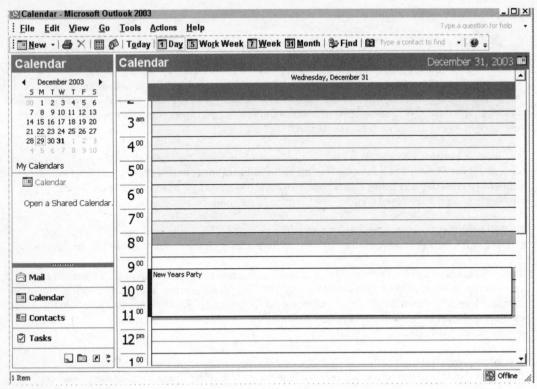

Figure 15-1

The following example uses early binding. It lists all the names of the entries in the Outlook Contacts folder, placing them in column A of the active worksheet. Make sure that you have created a reference to the Outlook object library before you try to execute it:

```
Public Sub DisplayOutlookContactNames()
    Dim Outlook As Outlook.Application
    Dim NameSpace As Outlook.NameSpace
    Dim AddressList As AddressList
    Dim Entry As AddressEntry
    Dim I As Long

On Error GoTo Finally
    Set Outlook = New Outlook.Application
    Set NameSpace = Outlook.GetNamespace("MAPI")
    Set AddressList = NameSpace.AddressLists("Contacts")
    For Each Entry In AddressList.AddressEntries
        I = I + 1
        Cells(I, 1).Value = Entry.Name
    Next

Finally:
    Outlook.Quit
    Set Outlook = Nothing
End Sub
```

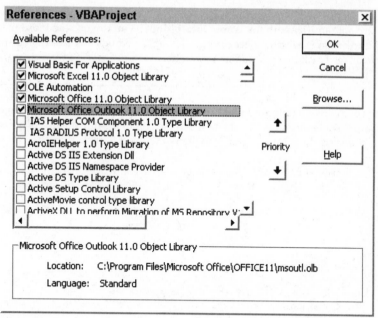

Figure 15-2

Outlook will display a warning message that a program is trying to access e-mail addresses. You can allow the operation or cancel it.

> Since Office XP protection against viruses has been improved, any attempt by programs to access e-mail addresses will invoke a warning message. Every time a program tries to send an e-mail, another warning is issued. If you need to avoid these warnings, you should consult your system administrator.

Here, we directly declare `Outlook` to be an `Outlook.Application` type. The other `Dim` statements also declare object variables of the type we need. If the same object name is used in more than one object library, you can precede the object name by the name of the application, rather than depend on the priority of the type libraries. We have done this with `Outlook.NameSpace` to illustrate the point. The `New` keyword is used when assigning a reference to `Outlook.Application` to `Outlook` to create a new instance of Outlook.

The fact that we declare the variable types specifically makes VBA employ early binding. You could use the `CreateObject` function to create the `Outlook` object variable, instead of the `New` keyword, without affecting the early binding. However, it is more efficient to use `New`.

Opening a Document in Word

If you want to open a file created in another Office application, you can use the `GetObject` function to directly open the file. However, it is just as easy to open an instance of the application and open the file from the application. We will look at another use of `GetObject` shortly.

> If you are not familiar with the Word Object Model, you can use the Word macro recorder to discover which objects, properties, and methods you need to use to perform a Word task that you can do manually.

The following code copies a range in Excel to the clipboard. It then starts a new instance of Word, opens an existing Word document, and pastes the range to the end of the document. As the code uses early binding, make sure you establish a reference to the Word object library:

```
Public Sub CopyChartToWordDocumentCopyTableToWordDocument()
  Dim Word As Word.Application

  ThisWorkbook.Sheets("Table").Range("A1:B6").Copy

  Set Word = New Word.Application

On Error GoTo Finally

  Word.Documents.Open Filename:="C:\temp\chart.doc"
  Word.Selection.EndKey Unit:=wdStory
  Word.Selection.TypeParagraph
  Call Word.Selection.PasteSpecial(Link:=False, DataType:=wdPasteOLEObject, _
    Placement:=wdInLine, DisplayAsIcon:=False)

  Call Word.ActiveDocument.Save

Finally:
  Word.Quit
  Set Word = Nothing
End Sub
```

(Make sure that you change the path—c:\temp\chart.doc—to reflect the location of Word documents located on your PC.) The New keyword creates a new instance of Word, even if Word is already open. The Open method of the Documents collection is used to open the existing file. The code then selects the end of the document, enters a new empty paragraph, and pastes the range. The document is then saved and the new instance of Word is closed.

Accessing an Active Word Document

Suppose you are working in Excel, creating a table. You also have Word open with a document active, into which you want to paste the table you are creating. You can copy the table from Excel to the document using the following code. In this example we are using early binding:

```
Public Sub CopyTableChartToOpenWordDocument()
  Dim Word As Word.Application

  ThisWorkbook.Sheets("Table").Range("A1:B6").Copy

  Set Word = GetObject(, "Word.Application")
  Word.Selection.EndKey Unit:=wdStory
```

```
      Word.Selection.TypeParagraph
      Word.Selection.Paste

      Set Word = Nothing
   End Sub
```

The `GetObject` function has two input parameters, both of which are optional. The first parameter can be used to specify a file to be opened. The second can be used to specify the application program to open. If you do not specify the first parameter, `GetObject` assumes you want to access a current instance of an object. If you specify a zero length string as the first parameter, `GetObject` assumes you want to open a new instance of Word.

You can use `GetObject`, with no first parameter, as in the preceding code, to access a current instance of Word that is in memory. However, if there is no current instance of Word running, `GetObject` with no first parameter causes a runtime error.

Creating a New Word Document

Suppose you want to use a current instance of Word if one exists, or if there is no current instance, you want to create one. In either case, you want to open a new document and paste the table into it. The following code shows how to do this. Again, we are using early binding:

```
   Public Sub CopyTableToAnyWordDocument()
      Dim Word As Word.Application

      ThisWorkbook.Sheets("Table").Range("A1:B6").Copy
      On Error Resume Next
         ' Try to open an existing instance of Word
         Set Word = GetObject(, "Word.Application")

         ' Open new instance if no running instance exists
         If Word Is Nothing Then
            Set Word = GetObject("", "Word.Application")
      End If

      On Error GoTo 0
      Word.Documents.Add
      Word.Visible = True

      Word.Selection.EndKey Unit:=wdStory
      Word.Selection.TypeParagraph
      Word.Selection.Paste

      Set Word = Nothing
   End Sub
```

If there is no current instance of Word, using `GetObject` with no first argument causes a runtime error and the code then uses `GetObject` with a zero length string as the first argument, which opens a new instance of Word, and then creates a new document. The code also makes the new instance of Word visible, unlike our previous examples where the work was done behind the scenes without showing the

Word window. The chart is then pasted at the end of the Word document. At the end of the procedure, the object variable `Word` is released, but the Word window is accessible on the screen so that you can view the result.

Access and DAO

If you want to copy data from Access to Excel, you can establish a reference to the Access object library and use the Access Object Model. You can also use ADO (ActiveX Data Objects), which is Microsoft's latest technology for programmatic access to relational databases, and many other forms of data storage. For examples of this, see Chapter 11.

Another simple and efficient way to get to Access data is provided by DAO (Data Access Objects). If you use Office 97, you will have DAO available but you might not have ADO, as ADO was released after Office 97. You can still use ADO with Excel 97, but the powerful `CopyFromRecordset` method, which is used in the following example, is not supported in Excel 97 for ADO recordsets. Here, we will show how to use DAO.

Figure 15-3 shows an Access table named `Sales` that is in an Access database file `FruitSales.mdb`.

ID	Date	Customer	State	Product	NumberSold	Price	Revenue
1	1/2/2004	Golieb	NJ	Oranges	20	12	240
2	1/2/2004	Golieb	NJ	Mangoes	30	15	450
3	1/2/2004	Golieb	NJ	Mangoes	30	15	450
4	1/2/2004	MacDonald	MI	Bananas	50	17	850
5	1/2/2004	Kimmel	MI	Apples	100	5	500
6	1/2/2004	Bourbonasi	FL	Agave	500	10	5000
7	1/2/2004	Golieb	NJ	Grapes	30	15	450
8	1/2/2004	Golieb	NJ	Olives	30	15	450
(AutoNumber)					0	0	0

Record: I◄ ◄ | 1 | ► ►I ►* of 8

Figure 15-3

The following code uses DAO to open a recordset based on the `Sales` table. It uses early binding, so a reference to the DAO object library is required:

```
Public Sub GetSalesDataViaDAO()
    Dim DAO As DAO.DBEngine
    Dim Sales As DAO.Database
    Dim SalesRecordset As DAO.Recordset
    Dim I As Integer
    Dim Worksheet As Worksheet
    Dim Count As Integer

    Set DAO = New DAO.DBEngine

    Set Sales = DAO.OpenDatabase(ThisWorkbook.Path + "\ FruitSales.mdb")
    Set SalesRecordset = Sales.OpenRecordset("Sales")
    Set Worksheet = Worksheets.Add
    Count = SalesRecordset.Fields.Count
```

```
    For I = 0 To Count - 1
        Worksheet.Cells(1, I + 1).Value = SalesRecordset.Fields(I).Name
    Next

    Worksheet.Range("A2").CopyFromRecordset SalesRecordset

    Worksheet.Columns("B").NumberFormat = "mmm dd, yyyy"
    With Worksheet.Range("A1").Resize(1, Count)
        .Font.Bold = True
        .EntireColumn.AutoFit
    End With

    Set SalesRecordset = Nothing
    Set Sales = Nothing
    Set DAO = Nothing
End Sub
```

The code opens the Access database file, creates a recordset based on the `Sales` table, and assigns a reference to the recordset to `SalesRecordset`. A new worksheet is added to the Excel workbook, and the field names in `SalesRecordset` are assigned to the first row of the new worksheet. The code uses the `CopyFromRecordSet` method of the `Range` object to copy the records in `SalesRecordset` to the worksheet, starting in cell A2. `CopyFromRecordSet` is a very fast way to copy the data compared to a looping procedure that copies record by record.

Access, Excel and, Outlook

As a final example of integrating different Office applications, we will extract some data from Access, chart it using Excel, and e-mail the chart using Outlook. The code has been set up as four procedures. The first procedure is a sub procedure named `EmailChart` that establishes the operating parameters and executes the other three procedures. Note that the code uses early binding and you need to create references to the DAO and Outlook object libraries:

```
Public Sub EmailChart()
    Dim SQL As String
    Dim Range As Excel.Range
    Dim FileName As String
    Dim Recipient As String

    SQL = "SELECT Product, Sum(Revenue)"
    SQL = SQL & " FROM Sales"
    SQL = SQL & " WHERE Date>=#1/1/2004# and Date<#1/1/2005#"
    SQL = SQL & " GROUP BY Product;"

    FileName = ThisWorkbook.Path + "\Chart.xls"
    Recipient = "pkimmel@softconcepts.com"

    Set Range = GetSalesData(SQL)
    ChartData Range, FileName

    Call SendEmail(Recipient, FileName)
End Sub
```

SQL is used to hold a string that is a SQL (Structured Query Language) command. SQL is covered in more detail in Chapter 11. In this case, the SQL specifies that we want to select the unique product names and the sum of the revenues for each product from our Access database `Sales` table for all dates in the year 2000. `FileName` defines the path and filename that will be used to hold the chart workbook. `Recipient` holds the e-mail address of the person we are sending the chart to.

The code then executes the `GetSalesData` function that is listed next. The function accepts the SQL statement as an input parameter and returns a reference to the range containing the extracted data, which is assigned to `Range`. The `ChartData` sub procedure is then executed, passing in the data range, as well as the path and filename for the chart workbook. Finally, the `SendEMail` sub procedure is executed, passing in the recipient's e-mail address and the location of the chart workbook to be attached to the e-mail:

```
Public Function GetSalesData(ByVal SQL As String) As Excel.Range
    Dim DAO As DAO.DBEngine
    Dim Sales As DAO.Database
    Dim SalesRecordset As DAO.Recordset
    Set DAO = New DAO.DBEngine

    Set Sales = DAO.OpenDatabase _
        (ThisWorkbook.Path + "\FruitSales.mdb")

    Set SalesRecordset = Sales.OpenRecordset(SQL)

    With Worksheets("Data")
        .Cells.Clear
        With .Range("A1")
            .CopyFromRecordset SalesRecordset
            Set GetSalesData = .CurrentRegion
        End With
    End With

    Set SalesRecordset = Nothing
    Set Sales = Nothing
    Set DAO = Nothing
End Function
```

The `GetSalesData` function is similar to the `GetSalesDataViaDAO` sub procedure presented earlier. Instead of getting the entire `Sales` table from the database, it uses SQL to be more selective. It clears the worksheet named `Data` and copies the selected data to a range starting in A1. It does not add the field names to the worksheet, just the product names and total revenue. It uses the `CurrentRegion` property to obtain a reference to all the extracted data and assigns the reference to the return value of the function:

```
Public Sub ChartData(ByVal Range As Range, ByVal FileName As String)
    With Workbooks.Add
        With .Charts.Add
            With .SeriesCollection.NewSeries
                .XValues = Range.Columns(1).Value
                .Values = Range.Columns(2).Value
            End With
            .HasLegend = False
            .HasTitle = True
            .ChartTitle.Text = "Year 2000 Revenue"
```

```
        End With
        Application.DisplayAlerts = False
        .SaveAs FileName
        Application.DisplayAlerts = True
        .Close
     End With
   End Sub
```

`ChartData` has input parameters to define the range containing the data to be charted and the destination for the file it creates. It creates a new workbook and adds a chart sheet to it. It creates a new series in the chart and assigns the values from the data range as arrays to the axes of the series. `DisplayAlerts` is set to `False` to prevent a warning if it overwrites an old file of the same name.

When Is a Virus not a Virus?

The following version of `SendEmail`, created in all innocence, was identified as a virus by Norton AntiVirus. In fact, this identification of the code as the `X97.OutlookWorm.Gen` virus, set us back a few hours. When Excel was closed and the work saved, Norton AntiVirus informed us that it had found a virus in the workbook and had eliminated the problem. It had deleted all the modules from the workbook. We had to turn off the AutoProtect option in Norton and start again.

Here is the code that caused the problem:

```
Public Sub SendEmail(ByVal Recipient As String, ByVal Attachment As String)
   Dim Outlook As Outlook.Application
   Dim NameSpace As Outlook.NameSpace
   Dim MailItem As Outlook.MailItem

   Set Outlook = New Outlook.Application
   Set MailItem = Outlook.CreateItem(olMailItem)
   With MailItem
     .Subject = "Year 2004 Revenue Chart"
     .Recipients.Add Recipient
     .Body = "Workbook with chart attached"

     '.Attachments.Add Attachment
     .Send
   End With

   Set MailItem = Nothing
   Set Outlook = Nothing
   End Sub
```

After some trial and error, we came up with the following code that is not identified as a virus. It escapes identification both with and without a reference to the Outlook object library. As it uses late binding, it does not require a reference to Outlook:

```
Public Sub SendEmail2(ByVal Recipient As String, ByVal Attachment As String)
   Dim Outlook As Object
   Dim NameSpace As Object
   Dim MailItem As Object
```

```
    Set Outlook = CreateObject("Outlook.Application")
    Set MailItem = Outlook.CreateItem(0)

    With MailItem
        .Subject = "Year 2004 Revenue Chart"
        .Recipients.Add Recipient
        .Body = "Workbook with chart attached"
        .Attachments.Add Attachment
        .Send
    End With
  End Sub
```

SendEMail has input parameters for the e-mail address of the recipient and the filename of the attachment for the e-mail. If your Outlook configuration requires you to logon, you will need to uncomment the lines that get a reference to the Namespace and supply the username and password. A new mail item is created using the CreateItem method. Text is added for the subject line and the body of the e-mail and the recipient and attachment are specified. The Send method sends the e-mail.

You will need to respond to three dialog boxes when executing this code in Office XP. The first two warn you that Outlook is being accessed and the second forces a five second delay and warns you that a program is sending an e-mail. The techniques you are using, while being very useful to achieve legitimate ends, are also, obviously, employed by virus writers.

While Office 2003 has strong protection against e-mail viruses, earlier versions of Office are more vulnerable. Patches are available from Microsoft to add protection to earlier versions of Outlook, but they might make it impossible to send e-mail programmatically. It can be very difficult to allow the legitimate use of programmatically generated e-mail and prevent viruses doing the same thing. The best answer is to have the latest virus protection software installed and keep it up-to-date.

Summary

To automate the objects in another application, you create an object variable referring to the target application or an object in the application. You can use early binding or late binding to establish the link between VBA and the other application's objects. Early binding requires that you establish a reference to the target application's type library and you must declare any object variables that refer to the target objects using their correct type. If you declare the object variables as the generic Object type, VBA uses late binding.

Early binding produces code that executes faster than late binding and you can get information on the target applications objects using the Object Browser and the shortcut tips that automatically appear as you type your code. Syntax and type checking is also performed as you code, so you are less likely to get errors when the code executes than with late binding where these checks cannot be done until the code is run.

You must use the CreateObject or GetObject function to create an object variable reference to the target application when using late binding. You can use the same functions when early binding, but it is more efficient to use the New keyword. However, if you want to test for an open instance of another application at runtime, GetObject can be usefully employed with early binding.

The techniques presented in this chapter allow you to create powerful programs that seamlessly tap into the unique abilities of different products. The user remains in a familiar environment such as Excel while the code ranges across any product that has a type library and exposes its objects to VBA.

You need to be aware that virus writers can use the information presented here to wreak havoc on unprotected systems. Make sure that your system is adequately covered.

Programming with the Windows API

Visual Basic for Applications is a high-level language that provides us with a rich, powerful, yet quite simple set of functionality for controlling the Office suite of products, as well as many other applications. We are insulated, some would say protected, from the "mundane minutiae" of Windows programming that a C++ programmer has to contend with.

The price we pay for this protection is an inability to investigate and control many elements of the Windows platform. We can, for example, use `Application.International` to read most of the Windows Regional Settings and read the screen dimensions from `Application.UsableWidth` and `Application.UsableHeight`, but that's about it. All the Windows-related items available to us are properties of the `Application` object and are listed in Appendix A.

The Windows platform includes a vast amount of low-level functionality that is not normally accessible from VBA, from identifying the system colors to creating a temporary file. Some of the functionality has been exposed in VBA but only to a limited extent, such as creating and using an Internet connection (for example, we can open a page from the Internet using `Workbooks.Open "<URL>"`, but we can't just download it to disk). There are also a number of other object libraries typically available on a Windows computer that provide high-level, VBA-friendly access to the underlying Windows functionality. Examples of these are the Windows Scripting Runtime and the Internet Transfer Control.

There are times, though, when we need to go beyond the limits of VBA and the other object libraries and delve into the files that contain the low-level procedures provided and used by Windows. The Windows Operating System is made up of a large number of separate files, mostly dynamic link libraries (DLLs), each containing code to perform a discrete set of interrelated functions. DLLs are files that contain functions that can be called by other Windows programs or other DLLs. They cannot be "run" like a program themselves.

These files are collectively known as the Windows Application Programming Interface, or the Windows API. Some of the most common files you'll use in the Windows API are:

File	Function Group(s)
USER32.DLL	User-interface functions (such as managing windows, the keyboard, clipboard, etc.)
KERNEL32.DLL	File and system-related functions (such as managing programs)
GDI32.DLL	Graphics and display functions
SHELL32.DLL	Windows shell functions (such as handling icons and launching programs)
COMDLG32.DLL	Standard Windows dialog functions.
ADVAPI32.DLL	Registry and NT Security functions
MPR.DLL and NETAPI32.DLL	Network functions
WININET.DLL	Internet functions
WINMM.DLL	Multimedia functions
WINSPOOL.DRV	Printing functions

This chapter explains how to use the functions contained in these files in your VBA applications and includes a number of useful examples. All of the Windows API functions are documented in the *Platform SDK* section of the MSDN Library at: http://msdn.microsoft.com/library/default.asp, which can be thought of as the online help for the Windows API.

Anatomy of an API Call

Before we can use the procedures contained in the Windows DLLs, we need to tell the VBA interpreter where they can be found, the parameters they take, and what they return. We do this using the Declare statement, which VBA Help shows as:

```
[Public | Private] Declare Sub name Lib "libname" [Alias "aliasname"]
[([arglist])]
[Public | Private] Declare Function name Lib "libname" [Alias "aliasname"]
[([arglist])] [As type]
```

The VBA Help gives a good explanation of the syntax of these statements, but does not include any example code using an API method. The following is the declaration used to find the Windows TEMP directory:

```
Private Declare Function GetTempPath Lib "kernel32" _
        Alias "GetTempPathA" ( _
        ByVal nBufferLength As Long, _
        ByVal lpBuffer As String) As Long
```

The preceding declaration tells VBA that:

- ❑ The function is going to be referred to in the code as `GetTempPath`
- ❑ The API procedure can be found in `kernel32.dll library`
- ❑ The library method we are referring to is `GetTempPathA` (case sensitive)
- ❑ `GetTempPath` takes two parameters, a `Long` and a `String` (more about these later)
- ❑ `GetTempPath` returns a `Long`

The declarations for most of the more common API functions can be found in the file `win32api.txt`. The Developer version of Office XP and any of the more recent versions of Visual Basic include this file and a small API Viewer applet to help locate the declarations. At the time of writing, the text file can be downloaded from the "Free Stuff" page of the Office Developer section of Microsoft's Web site, `http://www.microsoft.com/officedev/o-free.htm`, or directly from `http://www.microsoft.com/downloads` and searching on `win32api.exe`.

Interpreting C-Style Declarations

The MSDN library is the best source for information about the functions in the Windows API, but is primarily targeted towards C and C++ programmers and displays the function declarations using C notation. The `win32api.txt` file contains most of the declarations for the core Windows functions in VBA notation, but has not been updated to include some of the newer Windows DLLs (such as the OLE functions in `olepro32.dll` and the Internet functions in `WinInet.dll`). It is usually possible to convert the C notation to a VBA `Declare` statement, using the method shown next.

The declaration shown in MSDN for the `GetTempPath` function (at `http://msdn.microsoft.com/library/default.asp?url=/library/en-us/fileio/base/gettemppath.asp`) is:

```
DWORD GetTempPath(
    DWORD nBufferLength, // size, in characters, of the buffer
    LPTSTR lpBuffer      //  pointer to buffer for temp. path
);
```

This should be read as:

```
<Return data type> <Function name>(
    <Parameter data type> <Parameter name>,
    <Parameter data type> <Parameter name>,
);
```

Rearranging the C-style declaration to a VBA `Declare` statement gives the following (where the C-style `DWORD` and `LPSTR` are converted to VBA data types as shown):

```
Declare Function functionname Lib "libraryname" Alias "GetTempPathA" (ByVal
nBufferLength As DWORD, ByVal lpBuffer As LPSTR) As DWORD
```

On the Windows platform, there are two types of character sets. The ANSI character set has been the standard for many years and uses one byte to represent one character, which only gives 255 characters available at any time. To provide simultaneous access to a much wider range of characters (such as Far

Eastern alphabets), the Unicode character set was introduced. This allocates two bytes for each character, allowing for 65,535 characters.

To provide the same functionality for both character sets, the Windows API includes two versions of all the functions that involve strings, denoted by the "A" suffix for the ANSI version and "W" for the Unicode (or Wide) version. VBA always uses ANSI strings, so we will always be using the "A" version of the functions – in this case, `GetTempPathA`. The C-style declarations also use different names for their data types, which we need to convert. While not an exhaustive list, the following table shows the most common data types:

C Data Type	VBA Declaration
BOOL	ByVal <Name> As Long
BYTE	ByVal <Name> As Byte
BYTE *	ByRef <Name> As Byte
Char	ByVal <Name> As Byte
Char_huge *	ByVal <Name> As String
Char FAR *	ByVal <Name> As String
Char NEAR *	ByVal <Name> As String
DWORD	ByVal <Name> As Long
HANDLE	ByVal <Name> As Long
HBITMAP	ByVal <Name> As Long
HBRUSH	ByVal <Name> As Long
HCURSOR	ByVal <Name> As Long
HDC	ByVal <Name> As Long
HFONT	ByVal <Name> As Long
HICON	ByVal <Name> As Long
HINSTANCE	ByVal <Name> As Long
HLOCAL	ByVal <Name> As Long
HMENU	ByVal <Name> As Long
HMETAFILE	ByVal <Name> As Long
HMODULE	ByVal <Name> As Long
HPALETTE	ByVal <Name> As Long
HPEN	ByVal <Name> As Long
HRGN	ByVal <Name> As Long
HTASK	ByVal <Name> As Long

C Data Type	VBA Declaration
HWND	ByVal <Name> As Long
Int	ByVal <Name> As Long
int FAR *	ByRef <Name> As Long
LARGE_INTEGER	ByVal <Name> As Currency
LONG	ByVal <Name> As Long
LPARAM	ByVal <Name> As Long
LPCSTR	ByVal <Name> As String
LPCTSTR	ByVal <Name> As String
LPSTR	ByVal <Name> As String
LPTSTR	ByVal <Name> As String
LPVOID	ByRef <Name> As Any
LRESULT	ByVal <Name> As Long
UINT	ByVal <Name> As Integer
UINT FAR *	ByRef <Name> As Integer
WORD	ByVal <Name> As Integer
WPARAM	ByVal <Name> As Integer
Other	It is a probably a user-defined type, which you need to define

Some API definitions on the MSDN also include the IN and OUT identifiers. If the VBA type is shown in the table as 'ByVal <Name> As Long', it should be changed to 'ByRef...' for the OUT parameters.

> Note that strings are *always* passed **ByVal** (by value) to API functions. This is because VBA uses its own storage mechanism for strings, which the C DLLs do not understand. By passing the string **ByVal**, VBA converts its own storage structure into one that the DLLs can use.

Putting these into the declaration, conversion and removing unnecessary prefixes yields:

```
Private Declare Function GetTempPath Lib " libraryname" Alias "GetTempPathA" _
   (ByVal nBufferLength As Long, ByVal Buffer As String) As Long
```

The only thing that the declaration doesn't tell you is the DLL that contains the function. Looking at the bottom of the MSDN page, the "Requirements" section includes the line:

```
Library: Use kernel32.lib.
```

This tells you that the function is in the file kernel32.dll, giving the final declaration of:

```
Private Declare Function GetTempPath Lib "kernel32.dll" Alias "GetTempPathA" _
   (ByVal nBufferLength As Long, ByVal Buffer As String) As Long
```

The resolved function declaration is almost identical to the declaration defined in the win32api.txt file, which should be your first reference point for all API function definitions.

> **Warning: Using an incorrect function declaration is likely to crash Excel. When developing with API calls, save your work as often as possible.**

Constants, Structures, Handles, and Classes

Most of the API functions include arguments that accept a limited set of predefined constants. For example, to get information about the operating system's capabilities, you can use the GetSystemMetrics function:

```
Declare Function GetSystemMetrics Lib "user32" ( _
        ByVal Index As Long) As Long
```

Note that in the win32api.txt file, the GetSystemMetrics function is shown including an Alias clause:

```
Declare Function GetSystemMetrics Lib "user32" Alias "GetSystemMetrics" ( _
        ByVal nIndex As Long) As Long
```

The Alias clause is not required when the function name is the same as the alias, and is automatically removed when the function is copied into a code module.

The value that you pass in the Index argument tells the function which metric you want to be given, and must be one of a specific set of constants that the function knows about. The applicable constants are listed in the MSDN documentation, but their values are often not shown. Fortunately, the win32api.txt file contains most of the constants that you are likely to need. There are over 80 constants for GetSystemMetrics including SM_CXSCREEN and SM_CYSCREEN to retrieve the screen's dimensions:

```
Private Const SM_CXSCREEN As Long = 0
Private Const SM_CYSCREEN As Long = 1

Private Declare Function GetSystemMetrics Lib "user32" _
                (ByVal Index As Long) As Long

Public Sub ShowScreenDimensions()
    Dim X As Long
    Dim Y As Long

    X = GetSystemMetrics(SM_CXSCREEN)
    Y = GetSystemMetrics(SM_CYSCREEN)

    Call MsgBox("Screen resolution is " & X & "x" & Y)
End Sub
```

Many of the Windows API functions pass information using *structures*, which is the C term for a User-Defined Type (UDT). For example, the GetWindowRect function is used to return the size of a window, and is defined as:

```
Declare Function GetWindowRect Lib "user32" ( _
    ByVal hwnd As Long, _
    ByRef lpRect As Rect) As Long
```

The lpRect parameter is a RECT structure that is filled in by the GetWindowRect function with the window's dimensions. The RECT structure is defined on MSDN as:

```
typedef struct tagRECT {
    LONG left;
    LONG top;
    LONG right;
    LONG bottom;
} RECT;
```

This can be converted to a VBA user-defined type using the same datatype conversion shown in the previous section, giving:

```
Private Type Rect
    Left As Long
    Top As Long
    Right As Long
    Bottom As Long
End Type
```

The UDT definitions for most of the common structures are also included in the win32api.txt file.

The first parameter of the GetWindowRect function is shown as 'hwnd', and represents a handle to a window. A handle is simply a pointer to an area of memory that contains information about the object being pointed to (in this case, a window). Handles are allocated dynamically by Windows and are unlikely to be the same between sessions. You cannot, therefore, hardcode the handle number in your code, but must use other API functions to give you the handle you need. For example, to obtain the dimensions of the Excel window, you need to get the Excel window's hwnd. The API function FindWindow gives it to you:

```
'API call to find a window
Private Declare Function FindWindow Lib "user32" _
    Alias "FindWindowA" (ByVal ClassName As String, _
    ByVal WindowName As String) As Long
```

This function looks through all the open windows until it finds one with the class name and caption that you ask for. In Excel 2002, the hWnd property has been added to the Application object, so we no longer need to use FindWindow for that case. All of the code examples in this chapter use FindWindow, to be compatible with previous versions of Excel.

There are many different types of windows in Windows applications, ranging from Excel's application window, to the windows used for dialog sheets, UserForms, ListBoxes, or buttons. Each type of window has a unique identifier, known as its *class*. Some common class names in Excel are:

Window	Class name
Excel's main window	XLMAIN
Excel worksheet	EXCEL7
Excel UserForm	ThunderDFrame (in Excel 2003, 2002, and 2000)
	ThunderRT6DFrame (in Excel 2003, 2002, and 2000, when running as a COM Addin)
	ThunderXFrame (in Excel 97)
Excel dialog sheet	bosa_sdm_x19 (in Excel 2002 and 2000)
	bosa_sdm_x18 (in Excel 97)
	bosa_sdm_x1 (in Excel 5 and 95)
Excel status bar	EXCEL4

The FindWindow function requires the appropriate class name and the window's caption to find the window.

Note that the class names for some of Excel's standard items have changed with every release of Excel. You therefore need to include version checking in your code to determine which class name to use:

```
Select Case Val(Application.Version)
  Case Is >= 11 'Use Excel 2003 class names
  Case Is >= 9  'Use Excel 2000/2002 class names
  Case Is >= 8  'Use Excel 97 class names
  Case Else     'Use Excel 5/95 class names
End Select
```

This gives us a forward-compatibility problem. It would be nice if we could write code with a reasonable amount of confidence that it will work in the next version of Excel, but we don't know what the class names are going to be. Fortunately, the class names didn't change between Excel 2000 and Excel 2003.

Putting these items together, you can use the following code to find the location and size of the Excel main window (in pixels):

```
Private Declare Function FindWindow Lib "user32" _
   Alias "FindWindowA" (ByVal ClassName As String, _
   ByVal WindowName As String) As Long
Declare Function GetWindowRect Lib "user32" ( _
   ByVal hWnd As Long, _
   Rect As Rect) As Long

Private Type Rect
   Left As Long
   Top As Long
   Right As Long
   Bottom As Long
End Type
```

```
Public Sub ShowExcelWindowSize()
  Dim hWnd As Long, aRect As Rect
  hWnd = FindWindow("XLMAIN", Application.Caption)
  Call GetWindowRect(hWnd, aRect)
  Call PrintRect(aRect)
End Sub

Private Sub PrintRect(ByRef aRect As Rect)
  Call MsgBox("The Excel window has the following dimensions:" & _
    vbCrLf & " Left: " & aRect.Left & _
    vbCrLf & " Right: " & aRect.Right & _
    vbCrLf & " Top: " & aRect.Top & _
    vbCrLf & " Bottom: " & aRect.Bottom & _
    vbCrLf & " Width: " & (aRect.Right - aRect.Left) & _
    vbCrLf & " Height: " & (aRect.Bottom - aRect.Top))
End Sub
```

Resize the Excel window to cover a portion of the screen and run the `ShowExcelWindowSize` routine. You should be given a message box showing the window's dimensions. Now, try it with Excel maximized – you may get negative values for the top and left. This is because the `GetWindowRect` function returns the size of the Excel window, measuring around the edge of its borders. When maximized, the borders are off the screen, but still part of the window.

What if Something Goes Wrong?

One of the hardest parts of working with the Windows API functions is identifying the cause of any errors. If an API call fails for any reason, it *should* return some indication of failure (usually a zero result from the function) and register the error with Windows. You should then be able to use the VBA function `Err.LastDLLError` to retrieve the error code and use the `FormatMessage` API function to retrieve the descriptive text for the error:

```
Private Const FORMAT_MESSAGE_FROM_SYSTEM As Long = &H1000

Private Declare Function FindWindow Lib "user32" _
  Alias "FindWindowA" (ByVal ClassName As String, _
  ByVal WindowName As String) As Long
Declare Function GetWindowRect Lib "user32" ( _
  ByVal hWnd As Long, _
  Rect As Rect) As Long

Private Declare Function FormatMessage Lib "kernel32" _
  Alias "FormatMessageA" (ByVal dwFlags As Long, _
  ByVal Source As Long, ByVal MessageId As Long, _
  ByVal LanguageId As Long, ByVal Buffer As String, _
  ByVal Size As Long, ByVal Arguments As Long) As Long

Private Type Rect
  Left As Long
  Top As Long
  Right As Long
  Bottom As Long
End Type
```

```vba
Private Sub PrintRect(ByRef aRect As Rect)
  Call MsgBox("Dimensions:" & _
    vbCrLf & " Left: " & aRect.Left & _
    vbCrLf & " Right: " & aRect.Right & _
    vbCrLf & " Top: " & aRect.Top & _
    vbCrLf & " Bottom: " & aRect.Bottom & _
    vbCrLf & " Width: " & (aRect.Right - aRect.Left) & _
    vbCrLf & " Height: " & (aRect.Bottom - aRect.Top))
End Sub

Sub ShowExcelWindowSize()
  Dim hWnd As Long
  Dim aRect As Rect

  hWnd = FindWindow("XLMAIN", Application.Caption)
  If hWnd = 0 Then
    Call MsgBox(LastDLLErrText(Err.LastDllError))
  Else
    Call GetWindowRect(hWnd, aRect)
    Call PrintRect(aRect)
  End If
End Sub

Function LastDLLErrText(ByVal ErrorCode As Long) As String
  Dim Buffer As String * 255
  Dim Result As Long

  Result = FormatMessage(FORMAT_MESSAGEFROM_SYSTEM, 0&, ErrorCode, _
    0, Buffer, 255, 0)

  LastDLLErrText = Left(Buffer, Result)
End Function
```

The full code for this example can be found in the module 'Module3' in the API Examples.xls workbook, available on the Wrox Web site at http://www.wrox.com.

Unfortunately, different versions of Windows initialize Err.LastDllError with different values. For example, if you change the class name in the preceding example to XLMAINTEST in the FindWindow function call, you may expect to get an error message of "Unable to find window". This is the message you will get in Windows NT 4, but when using FindWindow under Windows 98, the error information is not populated and you get the standard message "The operation completed successfully". In most cases, you do get some error information, as will be seen in the next section.

Wrapping API Calls in Class Modules

If you need to use lots of API calls in your application, your code can get very messy very quickly. Most developers prefer to encapsulate the API calls within class modules, which provides a number of benefits:

❑　The API declarations and calls are removed from your core application code.

❑　The class module can perform a number of initialization and clean-up tasks, improving your system's robustness.

❑ Many of the API functions take a large number of parameters, some of which may be identical for each repetition of the API function call. The class module need expose only those properties that need to be changed by your calling routine.

❑ Class modules can be stored as text files or in the Code Librarian (if you're using Office Developer), providing a self-contained set of functionality that is easy to reuse in future projects.

The following code is an example of a class module for working with temporary files, allowing the calling code to:

❑ Create a temporary file in the Windows default TEMP directory

❑ Create a temporary file in a user-specified directory

❑ Retrieve the path and file name of the temporary file

❑ Retrieve the text of any errors that may have occurred while creating the temporary file

❑ Delete the temporary file after use.

Create a class module called TempFile and copy in the following code (this class can also be found in the API Examples.xls file, on the Wrox Web site at http://www.wrox.com):

```
Option Explicit

Private Declare Function GetTempPath Lib "kernel32" _
    Alias "GetTempPathA" ( _
    ByVal BufferLength As Long, _
    ByVal Buffer As String) As Long

Private Declare Function GetTempFileName Lib "kernel32" _
    Alias "GetTempFileNameA" ( _
    ByVal Path As String, _
    ByVal PrefixString As String, _
    ByVal Unique As Long, _
    ByVal TempFileName As String) As Long

Private Declare Function FormatMessage Lib "kernel32" _
    Alias "FormatMessageA" ( _
    ByVal Flags As Long, _
    ByVal Source As Long, _
    ByVal MessageId As Long, _
    ByVal LanguageId As Long, _
    ByVal Buffer As String, _
    ByVal Size As Long, _
    ByVal Arguments As Long) As Long

Const FORMAT_MESSAGE_FROM_SYSTEM As Long = &H1000

Dim TempPath As String
Dim TempFile As String
Dim ErrorMessage As String
Dim TidyUp As Boolean
```

One advantage of using a class module is that you can perform some operations when the class is initialized. In this case, you will identify the default Windows TEMP directory. The temporary file will be created in this directory, unless the calling code tells you otherwise:

```
Private Sub Class_Initialize()
  Dim Buffer As String * 255
  Dim Result As Long
  Result = GetTempPath(255, Buffer)

  If Result = 0 Then
    ErrorMessage = LastDLLErrText(Err.LastDllError)
  Else
    TempPath = Left(Buffer, Result)
  End If
End Sub
```

This is the routine to create the temporary file, returning its name (including the path). In its simplest use, the calling routine can just call this one method to create a temporary file:

```
Public Function CreateFile() As String
  Dim Buffer As String * 255
  Dim Result As Long

  Result = GetTempFileName(TempPath, "", 0, Buffer)

  If Result = 0 Then
    ErrorMessage = LastDLLErrText(Err.LastDllError)
  Else
    TempFile = Left(Buffer, InStr(1, Buffer, Chr(0)) - 1)
    ErrorMessage = "OK"
    TidyUp = True
    CreateFile = TempFile
  End If
End Function
```

In a class module, you can expose a number of properties that allow the calling routine to retrieve and modify the temporary file creation. For example, you may want to enable the calling program to set which directory to use for the temporary file. You could extend this to make the property read-only after the file has been created, raising an error in that case. The use of `Property` procedures in class modules was described in more detail in Chapter 6:

```
Public Property Get Path() As String
  Path = Left(TempPath, Len(TempPath) - 1)
End Property

Public Property Let Path(ByVal NewPath As String)
  TempPath = NewPath
  If Right(TempPath, 1) <> "\" Then
    TempPath = TempPath & "\"
  End If
End Property
```

You can also give the calling routine read-only access to the temporary file's name and full name (that is, including the path):

```
Public Property Get Name() As String
  Name = Mid(TempFile, Len(TempPath) + 1)
End Property

Public Property Get FullName() As String
  FullName = TempFile
End Property
```

Give the calling program read-only access to the error messages:

```
Public Property Get ErrorText() As String
  ErrorText = ErrorMessage
End Property
```

You'll also allow the calling program to delete the temporary file after use:

```
Public Sub Delete()
  On Error Resume Next
  Kill TempFile
  TidyUp = False
End Sub
```

By default, you will delete the temporary file that you created when the class is destroyed. The calling application may not want you to, so provide some properties to control this:

```
Public Property Get TidyUpFiles() As Boolean
  TidyUpFiles = TidyUp
End Property

Public Property Let TidyUpFiles(ByVal IsNew As Boolean)
  TidyUp = IsNew
End Property
```

In the class's Terminate code, you'll delete the temporary file, unless told not to. This code is run when the instance of the class is destroyed. If declared within a procedure, this will be when the class variable goes out of scope at the end of the procedure. If declared at a module level, it will occur when the workbook is closed:

```
Private Sub Class_Terminate()
  If TidyUp Then Delete
End Sub
```

The same function you saw in the previous section is used to retrieve the text associated with a Windows API error code:

```
Private Function LastDLLErrText(ByVal ErrorCode As Long) As String
  Dim Buffer As String * 255
  Dim Result As Long

  Result = FormatMessage(FORMAT_MESSAGE_FROM_SYSTEM, _
  0&, ErrorCode, 0, Buffer, 255, 0)

  LastDLLErrText = Left(Buffer, Result)
End Function
```

Once this class module is included in a project, the calling routine does not need to know anything about any of the API functions you're using:

```
Public Sub TestTempFile()
  Dim Object As New TempFile

  If Object.CreateFile = "" Then
    Call MsgBox("An error occured while creating the temporary file:" & _
      vbCrLf & obTempFile.ErrorText)
  Else
    Call MsgBox("Temporary file " & Object.FullName & " created")
  End If
End Sub
```

The results on Windows XP (and should be close on other versions of Windows) are similar to:

```
Temporary file C:\ WINDOWS\ TEMP\ 5024.TMP created
```

Note that the temporary file is created during the call to `CreateFile`. When the procedure ends, the variable `Object` goes out of scope and hence is destroyed by VBA. The `Terminate` event in the class module ensures the temporary file is deleted – the calling procedure does not need to know about any clean-up routines. If `CreateFile` is called twice, only the last temporary file is deleted. A new instance of the class should be created for each temporary file required.

You can force an error by amending `TestTempFile` to specify a nonexistent directory for the temp file:

```
Public Sub TestTempFile()
  Dim Object As New TempFile
  Object.Path = "C:\ NoSuchPath"

  If Object.CreateFile = "" Then
    Call MsgBox("An error occured while creating the temporary file:" & _
      Chr(10) & Object.ErrorText)
  Else
    Call MsgBox("Temporary file " & Object.FullName & " created")
  End If
End Sub
```

This time, you get a meaningful error message as shown in Figure 16-1:

Figure 16-1

Some Example Classes

This section provides a number of common API calls to include in your projects. Note that in each case the function and constant definitions must be put in the `Declarations` section at the top of a module.

A High-Resolution Timer Class

When testing your code, it can be helpful to time the various routines, in order to identify and eliminate any bottlenecks. VBA includes two functions that can be used as timers:

❑ The `Now` function returns the current time and has a resolution of about 1 second

❑ The `Timer` function returns the number of milliseconds since midnight, with a resolution of approximately 10 milliseconds

Neither of these are accurate enough to time VBA routines, unless the routine is repeated many times.

Most modern PCs include a high-resolution timer, which updates many thousands of times per second, accessible through API calls. You can wrap these calls in a class module to provide easy access to a high-resolution timer.

Class Module HighResTimer

```
Option Explicit

Private Declare Function QueryFrequency Lib "kernel32" _
    Alias "QueryPerformanceFrequency" ( _
    ByRef Frequency As Currency) As Long

Private Declare Function QueryCounter Lib "kernel32" _
    Alias "QueryPerformanceCounter" ( _
    ByRef PerformanceCount As Currency) As Long
```

Note that the `win32api.txt` file shows these definitions using the `'LARGE_INTEGER'` data type, but they are defined as `Currency` in the preceding code. The `LARGE_INTEGER` is a 64-bit data type, usually made up of two Longs. The VBA `Currency` data type also uses 64-bits to store the number, so you can use it in place of a `LARGE_INTEGER`. The only differences are that the `Currency` data type is scaled down by a factor of 10,000 and that VBA can perform standard math operations with `Currency` variables:

```
Dim Frequency As Currency
Dim Overhead As Currency
Dim Started As Currency
Dim Stopped As Currency
```

The API call itself takes a small amount of time to complete. For accurate timings, you should take this delay into account. You find this delay and the counter's frequency in the class's `Initialize` routine:

```
Private Sub Class_Initialize()
    Dim Count1 As Currency
    Dim Count2 As Currency
```

```
      Call QueryFrequency(Frequency)
      Call QueryCounter(Count1)
      Call QueryCounter(Count2)
      Overhead = Count2 - Count1
End Sub

Public Sub StartTimer()
   QueryCounter Started
End Sub

Public Sub StopTimer()
   QueryCounter Stopped
End Sub

Public Property Get Elapsed() As Double
   Dim Timer As Currency

   If Stopped = 0 Then
      QueryCounter Timer
   Else
      Timer = Stopped
End If

   If Frequency > 0 Then
      Elapsed = (Timer - Started - Overhead) / Frequency
   End If
End Property
```

When you calculate the elapsed time, both the timer and the frequency contain values that are a factor of 10,000 too small. As the numbers are divided, the factors cancel out to give a result in seconds.

The `High-Resolution Timer` class can be used in a calling routine like:

```
Sub TestHighResTimer()
   Dim I As Long
   Dim Object As New HighResTimer

   Object.StartTimer

   For I = 1 To 10000
   Next I

   Object.StopTimer

   Debug.Print "10000 iterations took " & Object.Elapsed & " seconds"
End Sub
```

Freeze a UserForm

When working with UserForms, the display may be updated whenever a change is made to the form, such as adding an item to a ListBox, or enabling/disabling controls. `Application.ScreenUpdating` has no effect on UserForms; this class provides a useful equivalent.

Class Module FreezeForm

```
Option Explicit

Private Declare Function FindWindow Lib "user32" _
  Alias "FindWindowA" ( _
  ByVal ClassName As String, _
  ByVal WindowName As String) As Long

Private Declare Function LockWindowUpdate Lib "user32" ( _
  ByVal hwndLock As Long) As Long

Public Sub Freeze(Form As UserForm)
  Dim hWnd As Long

  If Val(Application.Version) >= 9 Then
    hWnd = FindWindow("ThunderDFrame", Form.Caption)
  Else
    hWnd = FindWindow("ThunderXFrame", Form.Caption)
  End If
  If hWnd > 0 Then LockWindowUpdate hWnd
End Sub

Public Sub UnFreeze()
  LockWindowUpdate 0
End Sub

Private Sub Class_Terminate()
  UnFreeze
End Sub
```

To demonstrate this in action, create a new UserForm and add a listbox and a command button. Add the following code for the command button's Click event:

```
Private Sub CommandButton1_Click()
  Dim I As Integer
  For I = 1 To 1000
    ListBox1.AddItem "Item " & I
    DoEvents
  Next I
End Sub
```

The DoEvents line forces the UserForm to redraw, to demonstrate the problem. In more complicated routines, the UserForm may redraw itself without using DoEvents. To prevent the redrawing, you can modify the routine to use the FreezeForm class as shown:

```
Private Sub CommandButton1_Click()
  Dim Freezer As New FreezeForm
  Freezer.Freeze Me

  Dim I As Integer
```

```
   For I = 1 To 1000
     ListBox1.AddItem "Item " & I
     DoEvents
   Next I
End Sub
```

This is much easier than including several API calls in every function. The class's `Terminate` event ensures that the UserForm is unfrozen when the `Freezer` object variable goes out of scope. Freezing a UserForm in this way can result in a dramatic performance improvement. For example, the nonfrozen version takes approximately 3.5 seconds to fill the ListBox, while the frozen version of the routine takes approximately 1.2 seconds. This should be weighted against user interaction; they may think the computer has frozen if they see no activity for some time. Consider using `Application.StatusBar` to keep them informed of progress in that case.

A System Info Class

The classic use of a class module and API functions is to provide all the information about the Windows environment that you cannot get at using VBA. The following properties are typical components of such a `SysInfo` class.

> Note that the declarations for the constants and API functions used in these procedures must all be placed together at the top of the class module. For clarity, they are shown here with the corresponding routines.

Obtaining the Screen Resolution (in Pixels)

```
Option Explicit

Private Const SM_CYSCREEN As Long = 1 'Screen height
Private Const SM_CXSCREEN As Long = 0 'Screen width

Private Declare Function GetSystemMetrics Lib "user32" ( _
  ByVal Index As Long) As Long

Public Property Get ScreenHeight() As Long
  ScreenHeight = GetSystemMetrics(SM_CYSCREEN)
End Property

Public Property Get ScreenWidth() As Long
  ScreenWidth = GetSystemMetrics(SM_CXSCREEN)
End Property
```

Obtaining the Color Depth (in Bits)

```
Private Declare Function GetDC Lib "user32" ( _
  ByVal hwnd As Long) As Long
```

```
      Private Declare Function GetDeviceCaps Lib "Gdi32" ( _
        ByVal hDC As Long, _
        ByVal Index As Long) As Long

      Private Declare Function ReleaseDC Lib "user32" ( _
        ByVal hwnd As Long, _
        ByVal hDC As Long) As Long

      Private Const BITSPIXEL = 12

      Public Property Get ColourDepth() As Integer
        Dim hDC As Long
        hDC = GetDC(0)
        ColourDepth = GetDeviceCaps(hDC, BITSPIXEL)
        Call ReleaseDC(0, hDC)
      End Property
```

Obtaining the Width of a Pixel in UserForm Coordinates

```
      Private Declare Function GetDC Lib "user32" ( _
        ByVal hwnd As Long) As Long

      Private Declare Function GetDeviceCaps Lib "Gdi32" ( _
        ByVal hDC As Long, _
        ByVal Index As Long) As Long

      Private Declare Function ReleaseDC Lib "user32" ( _
        ByVal hwnd As Long, _
        ByVal hDC As Long) As Long

      Private Const LOGPIXELSX = 88

      Public Property Get PointsPerPixel() As Double
        Dim hDC As Long

        hDC = GetDC(0)

        'A point is defined as 1/72 of an inch and LOGPIXELSX returns
        'the number of pixels per logical inch, so divide them to give
        'the width of a pixel in Excel's UserForm coordinates
        PointsPerPixel = 72 / GetDeviceCaps(hDC, LOGPIXELSX)

        Call ReleaseDC(0, hDC)
      End Property
```

Reading the User's Login ID

```
      Private Declare Function GetUserName Lib "advapi32.dll" _
        Alias "GetUserNameA" ( _
        ByVal Buffer As String, _
        ByRef Size As Long) As Long

      Public Property Get UserName() As String
        Dim Buffer As String * 255
```

```
    Dim Result As Long
    Dim Length As Long

    Length = 255

    Result = GetUserName(Buffer, Length)
    If Length > 0 Then UserName = Left(Buffer, Length - 1)
End Property
```

Reading the Computer's Name

```
Private Declare Function GetComputerName Lib "kernel32" _
    Alias "GetComputerNameA" ( _
    ByVal Buffer As String, _
    Size As Long) As Long

Public Property Get ComputerName() As String
    Dim Buffer As String * 255
    Dim Result As Long
    Dim Length As Long

    Length = 255
    Result = GetComputerName(Buffer, Length)
    If Length > 0 Then ComputerName = Left(Buffer, Length)
End Property
```

These can be tested by using the following routine (in a standard module):

```
Public Sub TestSysInfo()
    Dim Object As New SysInfo
    Debug.Print "Screen Height = " & Object.ScreenHeight
    Debug.Print "Screen Width = " & Object.ScreenWidth
    Debug.Print "Colour Depth = " & Object.ColourDepth
    Debug.Print "One pixel = " & Object.PointsPerPixel & " points"
    Debug.Print "User name = " & Object.UserName
    Debug.Print "Computer name = " & Object.ComputerName
End Sub
```

Modifying UserForm Styles

UserForms in Excel do not provide any built-in mechanism for modifying their appearance. Our only choice is a simple popup dialog box with a caption and an x button to close the form, though we can choose to show it modally or non-modally.

Using API calls, we can modify the UserForm's window, to do any combination of:

❑   Switching between modal and non-modal while the form is showing

❑   Making the form resizable

❑   Showing or hiding the form's caption and title bar

❑   Showing a small title bar, like those on a floating toolbar

- ❑ Showing a custom icon on the form
- ❑ Showing an icon in the task bar for the form
- ❑ Removing the *x* button to close the form
- ❑ Adding standard maximize and/or minimize buttons

An example workbook demonstrating all these choices can be found on the Wrox Web site at http://www.wrox.com, with the key parts of the code explained next.

Windows Styles

The appearance and behavior of a window is primarily controlled by its *style* and *extended style* properties. These styles are both Long values, in which each bit of the value controls a specific aspect of the window's appearance, either on or off. We can change the window's appearance using the following process:

- ❑ Use FindWindow to get the UserForm's window handle
- ❑ Read its style using the GetWindowLong function
- ❑ Toggle one or more of the style bits
- ❑ Set the window to use this modified style using the SetWindowLong function
- ❑ For some changes, tell the window to redraw itself using the ShowWindow function

Some of the main constants for each bit of the basic window style are:

```
'Style to add a titlebar
Private Const WS_CAPTION As Long = &HC00000
'Style to add a system menu
Private Const WS_SYSMENU As Long = &H80000

'Style to add a sizable frame
Private Const WS_THICKFRAME As Long = &H40000

'Style to add a Minimize box on the title bar
Private Const WS_MINIMIZEBOX As Long = &H20000

'Style to add a Maximize box to the title bar
Private Const WS_MAXIMIZEBOX As Long = &H10000

'Cleared to show a task bar icon
Private Const WS_POPUP As Long = &H80000000

'Cleared to show a task bar icon
Private Const WS_VISIBLE As Long = &H10000000
```

While some of those for the extended window style are:

```
'Controls if the window has an icon
Private Const WS_EX_DLGMODALFRAME As Long = &H1
```

```
'Application Window: shown on taskbar
Private Const WS_EX_APPWINDOW As Long = &H40000

'Tool Window: small titlebar
Private Const WS_EX_TOOLWINDOW As Long = &H80
```

Note that this is only a subset of all the possible window style bits. See the MSDN documentation for Window Styles for the full list (http://msdn.microsoft.com/library/psdk/winui/windows_2v90.htm) and the win32api.txt file for their values.

The following example uses the above process to remove a UserForm's close button and can be found in the NoCloseButton.xls example in the code download:

```
Private Const WS_CAPTION As Long = &HC00000
Private Const WS_SYSMENU As Long = &H80000
Private Const WS_THICKFRAME As Long = &H40000
Private Const WS_MINIMIZEBOX As Long = &H20000
Private Const WS_MAXIMIZEBOX As Long = &H10000
Private Const WS_POPUP As Long = &H80000000
Private Const WS_VISIBLE As Long = &H10000000
Private Const WS_EX_DLGMODALFRAME As Long = &H1
Private Const WS_EX_APPWINDOW As Long = &H40000
Private Const WS_EX_TOOLWINDOW As Long = &H80

Private Declare Function FindWindow Lib "user32" _
  Alias "FindWindowA" ( _
  ByVal ClassName As String, _
  ByVal WindowName As String) As Long

Private Declare Function GetWindowLong Lib "user32" _
  Alias "GetWindowLongA" ( _
  ByVal hWnd As Long, _
  ByVal Index As Long) As Long

Private Declare Function SetWindowLong Lib "user32" _
  Alias "SetWindowLongA" ( _
  ByVal hWnd As Long, _
  ByVal Index As Long, _
  ByVal NewLong As Long) As Long

Const GWL_STYLE = -16

Private Sub UserForm_Initialize()
  Dim hWnd As Long
  Dim Style As Long

  If Val(Application.Version) >= 9 Then
    hWnd = FindWindow("ThunderDFrame", Me.Caption)
  Else
    hWnd = FindWindow("ThunderXFrame", Me.Caption)
  End If
```

```
      Style = GetWindowLong(hWnd, GWL_STYLE)
      Style = (Style And Not WS_SYSMENU)
      SetWindowLong hWnd, GWL_STYLE, Style
   End Sub
```

The effect of the preceding code can be seen in Figure 16-2.

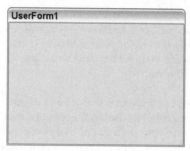

Figure 16-2

The FormChanger Class

As mentioned previously in this chapter, API calls are much easier to use when they are encapsulated within a class module. The FormChanger class included in the FormFun.xls file on the Wrox Web site (at http://www.wrox.com) repeats the preceding code snippet for all the windows style bits mentioned in the previous section, presenting them as the following properties of the class:

❑ Modal

❑ Sizeable

❑ ShowCaption

❑ SmallCaption

❑ ShowIcon

❑ IconPath (to show a custom icon)

❑ ShowCloseBtn

❑ ShowMaximizeBtn

❑ ShowMinimizeBtn

❑ ShowSysMenu

❑ ShowTaskBarIcon

To use the class on your own forms, copy the entire class module into your project and call it from your form's Activate event, as in the following example. This example can be found in the ToolbarForm.xls workbook at http://www.wrox.com:

```
   Private Sub UserForm_Activate()
      Dim Object As FormChanger
      Set Object = New FormChanger
```

```
      Object.SmallCaption = True
      Object.Sizeable = True
      Set Object.Form = Me
   End Sub
```

Resizable Userforms

In Office XP, Microsoft made the File Open and Save As dialogs resizable. They remember their position and size between sessions, greatly improving their usability. Using the same API calls shown in the previous section and a class module to do all the hard work, you can give your users the same experience when interacting with your UserForms.

One of the curiosities of the `UserForm` object is that it has a `Resize` event, but it doesn't have a property to specify whether or not it is resizable – in theory, the `Resize` event will never fire. As shown in the previous example, you can provide your own `Sizeable` property by toggling the `WS_THICKFRAME` window style bit; when you do this, the `Userform_Resize` event comes to life, triggered every time the user changes the size of the form (though not when they move it around the screen). You can respond to this event by changing the size and/or position of all the controls on the form, such that they make the best use of the UserForm's new size.

There are two approaches that can be used to change the size and/or position of all the controls on the form, absolute and relative.

Absolute Changes

Using an absolute approach, code has to be written to set the size and position of all the controls on the form, relative to the form's new dimensions and to each other. Consider a very simple form showing just a ListBox and an OK button (Figure 16-3):

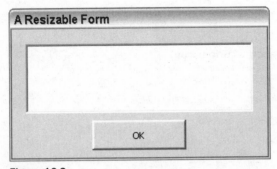

Figure 16-3

The code to resize and reposition the two controls using absolute methods is:

```
Private Sub UserForm_Resize()
   Const Gap = 6
   On Error Resume Next
   CommandButton1.Left = (Me.InsideWidth - CommandButton1.Width) / 2
   CommandButton1.Top = Me.InsideHeight - Gap - CommandButton1.Height
```

```
      ListBox1.Width = Me.InsideWidth - Gap * 4
      ListBox1.Height = CommandButton1.Top - Gap * 2
   End Sub
```

It works, but has a few major problems:

❑ Specific code has to be written for every control that changes size and/or position, which can be a daunting task for more complex forms. See the resize code in the FormFun.xls for an example of this.

❑ The size and position of controls are often dependent on the size and position of other controls (such as the height of the ListBox being dependent on the top of the OK button in the example above).

❑ If you modify the appearance of the form by adding or moving controls, you have to make corresponding changes to the resize code. For example, to add a Cancel button alongside the OK button, you have to add code to handle the Cancel button's repositioning and also change the code for the OK button.

❑ There is no opportunity for code reuse.

Relative Changes

Using a relative approach, information is added to each control to specify by how much that control's size and position should change as the UserForm's size changes. In the same dialog box, the two controls have the following relative changes:

❑ The OK button should move down by the full change in the form's height (to keep it at the bottom)

❑ The OK button should move across by half the change in the form's width (to keep it in the middle)

❑ The List's height and width should change by the full change in the form's height and width

These statements can be encoded into a single string to state the percentage change for each control's Top, Left, Height, and Width properties, and stored against the control. A convenient place to store it is the control's Tag property, which allows the resizing behavior of the control to be set at design time. Using the letters T, L, H, and W for the four properties, and a decimal for the percentage change if not 100 percent, gives the following Tag properties for the simple form:

```
   Tag=HW
   Tag=HL0.5
```

When the UserForm_Resize event fires, the code can calculate the change in the form's height and width and iterate through all the controls adjusting their Top, Left, Height, and Width as specified by their Tags. The CFormResizer class to do this is shown next.

There are a number of benefits to this approach:

❑ The resize behavior of each control is set at design time, while the form is being viewed, just like all the other properties of the control

- ❑ The change in size and position of each control is independent of any other control

- ❑ Controls can be added, moved, or deleted without having to modify the Resize code or change other controls' resize behavior.

- ❑ The resize code can treat every control in exactly the same way, hence

- ❑ Every UserForm uses exactly the same Resize code, which can be encapsulated in a separate class module

The FormResizer Class

By encapsulating all the resize code in a separate class module, any UserForm can be made resizable by adding just six lines of code, to instantiate and call into the class, and setting the resize behavior for each control in its Tag property.

The FormResizer class provides the following functionality:

- ❑ Sets the form to be resizable

- ❑ Sets the initial size and position of the form, if it has been shown before

- ❑ Resizes and repositions all the controls on the form, according to their Tag resizing string

- ❑ Stores the form's size and position in the registry, for use when the same form is shown again

- ❑ Allows the calling code to specify a key name for storing the form dimensions in the registry

- ❑ Prevents a form being resized in either direction if none of the controls are set to respond to changes in height and/or width

- ❑ Stops resizing when any control is moved to the left or top edge of the form, or when any control is reduced to zero height or width

The code for the FormResizer class is shown next, with comments in the code to explain each section. It is available for download in the FormResizer.xls workbook at http://www.wrox.com:

```
Option Explicit

Private Declare Function FindWindow Lib "user32" _
    Alias "FindWindowA" ( _
    ByVal ClassName As String, _
    ByVal WindowName As String) As Long

Private Declare Function GetWindowLong Lib "user32" _
    Alias "GetWindowLongA" ( _
    ByVal hWnd As Long, _
    ByVal Index As Long) As Long

Private Declare Function SetWindowLong Lib "user32" _
    Alias "SetWindowLongA" ( _
    ByVal hWnd As Long, _
    ByVal Index As Long, _
    ByVal NewLong As Long) As Long

Private Const GWL_STYLE As Long = (-16)
```

```vb
Private Const WS_THICKFRAME As Long = &H40000

Dim FormField As Object
Dim FormHandle As Long
Dim Width As Double
Dim Height As Double
Dim RegistryKeyField As String

Private Sub Class_Initialize()
  RegistryKey = "Excel 2003 Programmers Reference"
End Sub

Public Property Let RegistryKey(ByVal Value As String)
  RegistryKeyField = Value
End Property

Public Property Get RegistryKey() As String
  RegistryKey = RegistryKeyField
End Property

Public Property Get Form() As Object
  Set Form = FormField
End Property

Public Property Set Form(Value As Object)
  Dim StringSizes As String
  Dim Sizes As Variant
  Dim Style As Long

  Set FormField = Value
  If Val(Application.Version) < 9 Then
    'Excel 97
    FormHandle = FindWindow("ThunderXFrame", FormField.Caption)
  Else
    ' Newer versions of Excel, including Excel 2003
    FormHandle = FindWindow("ThunderDFrame", FormField.Caption)
  End If

  Style = GetWindowLong(FormHandle, GWL_STYLE)
  Style = Style Or WS_THICKFRAME
  Call SetWindowLong(FormHandle, GWL_STYLE, Style)

  StringSizes = GetSetting(RegistryKey, "Forms", FormField.Name, "")

  Width = FormField.Width
  Height = FormField.Height

  If StringSizes <> "" Then
    Sizes = Split(StringSizes, ";")
    ReDim Preserve Sizes(0 To 3)
    FormField.Top = Val(Sizes(0))
    FormField.Left = Val(Sizes(1))
    FormField.Height = Val(Sizes(2))
    FormField.Width = Val(Sizes(3))
    FormField.StartUpPosition = 0
  End If
```

```vb
End Property

Public Sub FormResize()
  Dim WidthAdjustment As Double
  Dim HeightAdjustment As Double
  Dim SomeWidthChange As Boolean
  Dim SomeHeightChange As Boolean
  Dim Tag As String
  Dim Size As String
  Dim Control As MSForms.Control

  Static Resizing As Boolean

  If Resizing Then Exit Sub
  Resizing = True
  On Error GoTo Finally

  HeightAdjustment = Form.Height - Height
  WidthAdjustment = Form.Width - Width

  For Each Control In Form.Controls
    Tag = UCase(Control.Tag)
    If InStr(1, Tag, "T", vbBinaryCompare) Then
      If Control.Top + HeightAdjustment * ResizeFactor(Tag, "T") <= 0 Then
        Form.Height = Height
      End If

      SomeHeightChange = True
    End If

    If InStr(1, Tag, "L", vbBinaryCompare) Then
      If Control.Left + WidthAdjustment * ResizeFactor(Tag, "L") <= 0 Then
        Form.Width = Width
      End If

      SomeWidthChange = True
    End If

    If InStr(1, Tag, "H", vbBinaryCompare) Then
      If Control.Height + HeightAdjustment * ResizeFactor(Tag, "H") <= 0 Then
        Form.Height = Height
      End If

      SomeHeightChange = True
    End If

    If InStr(1, Tag, "W", vbBinaryCompare) Then
      If Control.Width + WidthAdjustment * ResizeFactor(Tag, "W") <= 0 Then
        Form.Width = Width
      End If

      SomeWidthChange = True
    End If
  Next
```

```
        If Not SomeHeightChange Then Form.Height = Height
        If Not SomeWidthChange Then Form.Width = Width

        HeightAdjustment = Form.Height - Height
        WidthAdjustment = Form.Width - Width

        For Each Control In Form.Controls
          With Control
            Tag = UCase(.Tag)

            If InStr(1, Tag, "T", vbBinaryCompare) Then
              .Top = .Top + HeightAdjustment * ResizeFactor(Tag, "T")
            End If

            If InStr(1, Tag, "L", vbBinaryCompare) Then
              .Left = .Left + WidthAdjustment * ResizeFactor(Tag, "L")
            End If

            If InStr(1, Tag, "H", vbBinaryCompare) Then
              .Height = .Height + HeightAdjustment * ResizeFactor(Tag, "H")
            End If

            If InStr(1, Tag, "W", vbBinaryCompare) Then
              .Width = .Width + WidthAdjustment * ResizeFactor(Tag, "W")
            End If
          End With
        Next

        Width = Form.Width
        Height = Form.Height

        With Form
          Call SaveSetting(RegistryKey, "Forms", .Name, Str(.Top) & ";" & _
            Str(.Left) & ";" & Str(.Height) & ";" & Str(.Width))
        End With

Finally:
  Resizing = False

End Sub

Private Function ResizeFactor(ByVal Tag As String, ByVal Change As String)
  Dim I As Integer
  Dim D As Double

  I = InStr(1, Tag, Change, vbBinaryCompare)

  If I > 0 Then
    D = Val(Mid$(Tag, I + 1))
    If D = 0 Then D = 1
  End If

  ResizeFactor = D
End Function
```

Using the FormResizer Class

The code to use the `FormResizer` class in a UserForm's code module is as follows:

```
Dim Resizer As FormResizer

Private Sub UserForm_Initialize()
  Set Resizer = New FormResizer
  Resizer.RegistryKey = "Excel 2003 Programmers Reference"
  Set Resizer.Form = Me
End Sub

Private Sub UserForm_Resize()
  Resizer.FormResize
End Sub

Private Sub btnOK_Click()
  Unload Me
End Sub

Private Sub UserForm_QueryClose(Cancel As Integer, CloseMode As Integer)
  Resizer.FormResize
End Sub
```

There are a few points to remember when using this approach in your own UserForms:

❑ The resizer works by changing the control's `Top`, `Left`, `Height`, and `Width` properties in response to changes in the UserForm size, according to the control's resizing information.

❑ The control's resizing information is set in its `Tag` property, using the letters T, L, H, and/or W followed by a number specifying the resizing factor (if not 100 %).

❑ The resizing factors must be in US format, using a period as the decimal separator.

❑ If there are no controls that have T or H in their `Tag` strings, the form will not be allowed to resize vertically.

❑ If there are no controls that have L or W in their `Tag` strings, the form will not be allowed to resize horizontally.

❑ The smallest size for the form is set by the first control to be moved to the top or left edge, or to have a zero width or height.

❑ This can be used to set a minimum size for the form, by using a hidden label with a `Tag` of "HW", where the size of the label equals the amount that the form can be reduced in size. If the label is set to zero height and width to start with, the UserForm can only be enlarged from its design-time size.

Other Examples

You are not forced to put all your API calls into class modules, though it is usually a good idea. This section demonstrates a few examples where the API calls would typically be used within a standard module.

Change Excel's Icon

When developing an application that takes over the entire Excel interface, you can use the following code to give Excel your own icon:

```
Declare Function FindWindow Lib "user32" _
  Alias "FindWindowA" ( _
  ByVal ClassName As String, _
  ByVal WindowName As String) As Long

Declare Function ExtractIcon Lib "shell32.dll" _
  Alias "ExtractIconA" ( _
  ByVal Instance As Long, _
  ByVal ExeFileName As String, _
  ByVal IconIndex As Long) As Long

Declare Function SendMessage Lib "user32" _
  Alias "SendMessageA" ( _
  ByVal hWnd As Long, _
  ByVal Message As Long, _
  ByVal wParam As Integer, _
  ByVal lParam As Long) As Long

Const WM_SETICON = &H80

Public Sub SetExcelIcon(ByVal IconPath As String)
  Dim A As Long
  Dim hWnd As Long
  Dim hIcon As Long

  hWnd = FindWindow("XLMAIN", Application.Caption)
  hIcon = ExtractIcon(0, IconPath, 0)

  '1 means invalid icon source
  If hIcon > 1 Then
    'Set the big (32x32) and small (16x16) icons
    Call SendMessage(hWnd, WM_SETICON, True, hIcon)
    Call SendMessage(hWnd, WM_SETICON, False, hIcon)
  End If
End Sub

Public Sub TestExcelIcon()
  Call SetExcelIcon(ThisWorkbook.Path + "\myico.ico")
End Sub
```

Play a .wav file

Excel does not include a built-in method of playing sounds. This is a simple API call to play a `.wav` file. The `Flags` argument can be used to play the sound asynchronously or in a continuous loop, though we use a value of zero in this example to play the sound once, synchronously:

```
Declare Function sndPlaySound Lib "winmm.dll" _
  Alias "sndPlaySoundA" ( _
  ByVal SoundName As String, _
  ByVal Flags As Long) As Long
```

```
Sub PlayWav(ByVal WavFileName As String)
  Call sndPlaySound(WavFileName, 0)
End Sub

Sub TestWav()
  Call PlayWav(ThisWorkbook.Path + "\mywav.wav")
End Sub
```

Summary

The functions defined in the Windows API provide a valuable and powerful extension to the VBA developer's tool set. The `win32api.txt` file provides the VBA definitions for most of the core functions. The definitions for the remaining functions can be converted from the C-style versions shown in the online MSDN library.

Class modules enable the user to encapsulate both the API definitions and their use into simple chunks of functionality that are easy to use and reuse in VBA applications. A number of example classes and routines have been provided in this chapter to get you started using the Windows API functions within your applications. These include:

❑   Creating a TEMP file

❑   A high-resolution timer

❑   Freezing a UserForm

❑   Getting system information

❑   Modifying a UserForm's appearance

❑   Making UserForms resizable, with a minimum of code in the form

❑   Changing Excel's icon

❑   Playing a .wav file

17

International Issues

If you think that your application may be used internationally, it has to work with any supported Windows Regional Setting, on any supported language version of Windows, and with any language choice for the Excel user interface.

Any bugs in your application that arise from international issues will not occur on your development machine unless you explicitly test for them. However, they will be found immediately by your clients.

The combination of Regional Settings and Excel language is called the user's "locale" and the aim of this chapter is to show you how to write locale-independent VBA applications. In order to do this, we include an explanation of the features in Excel that deal with locale-related issues and highlight areas within Excel where locale support is absent or limited. Workarounds are provided for most of these limitations, but some are so problematic that the only solution is to not use the feature at all.

The rules provided in this chapter should be included in your coding standards and used by you and your colleagues. It is easy to write locale-independent code from scratch; it is much more difficult to make existing code compatible with the many different locales in the world today.

Changing Windows Regional Settings and the Office XP UI Language

Throughout this chapter, the potential errors will be demonstrated by using the following three locales:

Setting	US	UK	Norway
Decimal Separator	.	.	,
Thousand Separator	,	,	.
Date order	mm/dd/yyyy	dd/mm/yyyy	dd.mm.yyyy

Continues

Setting	US	UK	Norway
Date separator	/	/	.
Example number: 1234.56	1,234.56	1,234.56	1.234,56
Example date: Feb 10, 2004	02/10/2004	10/02/2004	10.02.2004
Windows and Excel Language	English	English	Norwegian
The text for the Boolean True	True	True	Sann

The regional settings are changed using the Regional Settings applet (Regional and Language Options in Windows XP) in the Windows Control Panel, while the Office XP language is changed using the "Microsoft Office Language Settings" program provided with the Office XP Language Packs. Unfortunately, the only way to change the Windows language is to install a new version from scratch.

> **Installing a virtual PC using Connectix Virtual PC or VMWare is a great way to have a non-development testing installation on your workstation and test international settings by installing an international version of Windows on your virtual PC instance.**

When testing your application, it is a very good idea to use some fictional regional settings, such as having # for the thousand separator, ! for the decimal separator, and a YMD date order. It is then very easy to determine if your application is using your settings or some internal default. For completeness, you should also have a machine in your office with a different language version of Windows from the one you normally use.

Responding to Regional Settings and the Windows Language

This section explains how to write applications that work with different regional settings and Windows language versions, which should be considered the absolute minimum requirement.

Identifying the User's Regional Settings and Windows Language

Everything you need to know about your user's Windows Regional Settings and Windows language version is found in the `Application.International` property. The online help lists all of the items that can be accessed, though you are unlikely to use more than a few of them. The most notable are:

❑   `XlCountryCode`
    The language version of Excel (or of the currently active Office language)

❑   XlCountrySetting
    The Windows regional settings location

❑   XlDateOrder
    The choice of MDY, DMY, or YMD order to display dates

Note that there is no constant that enables us to identify which language version of Windows is installed (but we can get that information from the Windows API, if required).

Note that "Windows Regional Settings" is abbreviated to WRS in the rest of this chapter and is also described as 'local' settings.

VBA Conversion Functions from an International Perspective

The online Help files explain the use of VBA's conversion functions in terms of converting between different data types. This section demonstrates how to perform explicit and implicit type conversions and how these are affected when converting data between locales.

Implicit Conversion

Implicit conversion is the most common form of type conversion used in VBA code and forces the VBA interpreter to convert the data using whichever format it thinks is most appropriate. A typical example of this code is:

```
Public Sub ImplicitConversion()
  Dim MyDate As Date
  MyDate = DateValue("Jan 1, 2004")
  Call MsgBox("This first day of this year is " & MyDate)
End Sub
```

When converting a number to a string in Office XP, VBA uses the WRS to supply either a date string in the user's "ShortDate" format, the number formatted according to the WRS, or the text for True or False in the WRS language. This is fine, if you want the output as a locally formatted string. If, however, your code assumes you've got a US-formatted string, it will fail. Of course, if you develop using US formats, you won't notice the difference (though your client will).

There is a much bigger problem with using implicit conversion if you are writing code for multiple versions of Excel. In previous versions, the number formats used in the conversion were those appropriate for the Excel language being used at runtime (buried within the Excel object library), which might be different from both US and local formats, and were not affected by changing the WRS.

Be very careful with the data types returned from, and used by, Excel and VBA functions. For example, Application.GetOpenFilename returns a Variant containing the Boolean value False if the user cancels, or a string containing the text of the selected file. If you store this result in a String variable, the Boolean False will be converted to a string in the user's WRS language, and may not equal the string "False" that you may be comparing it to.

To avoid these problems, use the Object Browser to check the function's return type and parameter types, then, make sure to match them, or explicitly convert them to your variable's data type. Applying this recommendation gives us (at least) three solutions to using Application.GetOpenFilename.

Typical code running in Norway:

```
Dim FileName As String
FileName = Application.GetOpenFilename()
If FileName = "False" Then
    ...
```

If the user cancels, `GetOpenFilename` returns a variable containing the Boolean value `False`. Excel converts it to a string to put in our variable, using the Windows language. In Norway, the string will contain "Usann". If this is compared to the string "False", it doesn't match, so the program thinks it is a valid file name and subsequently crashes.

Solution 1:

```
Dim FileName As Variant
FileName = Application.GetOpenFileName()
If FileName = False Then  'Compare using the same data types
    ...
```

Solution 2:

```
Dim FileName As Variant
FileName = Application.GetOpenFileName()
If CStr(FileName) = "False" Then       'Explicit conversion with CStr() always
                                       'gives a US Boolean string

    ...
```

Solution 3:

```
Dim FileName As Variant
FileName = Application.GetOpenFileName()
If TypeName(FileName) = "Boolean" Then      'Got a Boolean, so must have
                                            'cancelled

    ...
```

Note that in all three cases, the key point is that we are matching the data type returned by `GetOpenFilename` (a `Variant`) with our variable. If you use the `MultiSelect:=True` parameter within the `GetOpenFileName` function, the last of the preceding solutions should be used. This is because the `FileName` variable will contain an array of file names, or the Boolean `False`. Attempting to compare an array with `False`, or trying to convert it to a string will result in a runtime error.

Date Literals

When coding in VBA, you can write dates using a format of #01/01/2004#, which is obviously January 1, 2004. But what is #02/01/2004#? Is it January 2 or February 1? Well, it is actually February 1, 2004. This is because when coding in Excel, we do so in American English, regardless of any other settings we may have, and hence we must use US-formatted date literals (mm/dd/yyyy format). If other formats are typed in (such as #yyyy-mm-dd#) Excel will convert them to #mm/dd/yyyy# order.

What happens if you happen to be Norwegian or British and try typing in your local date format (which you *will* do at some time, usually near a deadline)? If you type in a Norwegian-formatted date literal,

#02.01.2004#, you get a syntax error which at least alerts you to the mistake you made. However, if you type in dates in a UK format (dd/mm/yyyy) things get a little more interesting. VBA recognizes the date and so doesn't give an error, but "sees" that you have the day and month the wrong way round; it swaps them for you. So, typing in dates from January 10, 2004, to January 15, 2004, results in:

You Typed	VBA Shows	Meaning
10/1/2004	10/1/2004	October 1, 2004
11/1/2004	11/1/2004	November 1, 2004
12/1/2004	12/1/2004	December 1, 2004
13/1/2004	1/13/2004	January 13, 2004
14/1/2004	1/14/2004	January 14, 2004
15/1/2004	1/15/2004	January 15, 2004

If these literals are sprinkled through your code, you will not notice the errors.

It is much safer to avoid using date literals and use the VBA functions DateSerial(Year, Month, Day) or DateValue(DateString), where DateString is a non-ambiguous string such as "Jan 1, 2004". Both of these functions return the corresponding Date number.

IsNumeric and IsDate Functions

These two functions test if a string can be evaluated as a number or date according to the WRS and Windows language version. You should always use these functions before trying to convert a string to another data type. We don't have an IsBoolean function, or functions to check if a string is a US-formatted number or date. Note that IsNumeric does not recognize a % character on the end of a number, and IsDate does not recognize days of the week.

CStr Function

This is the function most used by VBA in implicit data type conversions. It converts a Variant to a String, formatted according to the WRS. When converting a Date type, the "ShortDate" format is used, as defined in the WRS. Note that when converting Booleans, the resulting text is the English "True" or "False" and is not dependent on any Windows settings. Compare this with the implicit conversion of Booleans, whereby MsgBox "I am " & True results in the True being displayed in the WRS language ("I am Sann" in Norwegian Regional Settings).

CDbl, CSng, CLng, CInt, CByte, CCur, and CDec Functions

Each of the functions in the section title can convert a string representation of a number into a numeric data type (as well as converting between different numeric data types). The string must be formatted according to WRS. These functions do not recognize date strings or % characters

CDate and DateValue Functions

The CDate and DateValue methods can convert a string to a Date data type (CDate can also convert other data types to the Date type). The string must be formatted according to the WRS and use the

Windows language for month names. It does not recognize the names for the days of the week, giving a `Type Mismatch` error. If the year is not specified in the string, it uses the current year.

CBool Function

`CBool` converts a string (or a number) to a `Boolean` value. Contrary to all the other `Cxxx` conversion functions, the string must be the English "`True`" or "`False`".

Format Function

The `Format` function converts a number or date to a string, using a number format supplied in code. The number format must use US symbols (m, d, s, etc.), but results in a string formatted according to the WRS (with the correct decimal, thousand, and date separators) and the WRS language (for the weekday and month names). For example, the following code will result in "Friday 01/01/2004" in the US, but "Fredag 01.01.2004" when used with Norwegian settings:

```
MsgBox Format(DateSerial(2004, 1, 1), "dddd dd/mm/yyyy")
```

If you omit the number format string, `DateSerial` behaves in exactly the same way as the `CStr` function (even though online help says it behaves like `Str`), including the strange handling of `Boolean` values, where `Format(True)` always results in the English "`True`." Note that it does not change the date order returned to agree with the WRS, so your code has to determine the date order in use before creating the number format string.

FormatCurrency, FormatDateTime, FormatNumber, and FormatPercent Functions

The `FormatCurrency`, `FormetDateTime`, `FormatNumber`, and `FormatPercent` functions added in Excel 2000 provide the same functionality as the `Format` function, but use parameters to define the specific resulting format instead of a custom format string. They correspond to standard options in Excel's Format ⇨ Cells ⇨ Number dialog box, while the `Format` function corresponds to the Custom option. They have the same international behavior as the `Format` function in the preceding paragraph.

Str Function

`Str` converts a number, date or Boolean to a US-formatted string, regardless of the WRS, Windows language or Office language version. When converting a positive number, it adds a space on the left. When converting a decimal fraction, it does not add a leading zero. The following custom function is an extension of `Str` that removes the leading space and adds the zero.

The NumberToString Function

This function converts a number, date, or Boolean variable to a US-formatted string. There is an additional parameter that can be used to return a string using Excel's DATE function, which would typically be used when constructing `.Formula` strings:

```
Public Function NumberToString(ByVal Value As Variant, _
    Optional ByVal UseDateFunction As Boolean) As String

    Dim Temp As String
```

```
   If TypeName(Value) = "String" Then Exit Function
   If Right(TypeName(Value), 2) = "()" Then Exit Function

   If IsMissing(UseDateFunction) Then UseDateFunction = False

   If UseDateFunction Then
     Temp = "DATE(" & Year(Value) & "," & Month(Value) & "," & _
       Day(Value) & ")"
   Else
     If TypeName(Value) = "Date" Then
       Temp = Format(Value, "mm""/""dd""/""yyyy")
   Else
     Temp = Trim(Str(Value))
     If Left(Temp, 1) = "." Then Temp = "0" & Temp
       If Left(Temp, 2) = " ." Then Temp = " 0" & Mid(Temp, 2)
     End If
   End If

   NumberToString = Temp
 End Function
```

Value is a variant containing the number to convert, which can be:

❑ A number to be converted to a string with US formats

❑ A date to be converted to a string in mm/dd/yyyy format

❑ A Boolean converted to the strings "True" or "False"

UseDateFunction is an optional Boolean for handling dates. When it is set to False, NumberToString returns a date string in mm/dd/yyyy format. When it is set to True, NumberToString returns a date as DATE(yyyy,mm,dd).

Val Function

Val is the most common function that we've seen used to convert from strings to numbers. It actually only converts a *US-formatted* numerical string to a number. All the other string-to-number conversion functions try to convert the entire string to a number and raise an error if they can't. Val, however, works from left to right until it finds a character that it doesn't recognize as part of a number. Many characters typically found in numbers, such as $ and commas, are enough to stop it from recognizing the number. Val does not recognize US-formatted date strings.

Val also has the dubious distinction of being the only one of VBA's conversion functions to take a specific data type for its input. While all the others use Variants, Val accepts only a string. This means that anything you pass to Val is converted to a string (implicitly, therefore according to the WRS and Windows language), before being evaluated according to US formats.

> The use of Val can have unwanted side-effects (otherwise known as bugs), which are very difficult to detect in the code that is running fine on your own machine, but which would fail on another machine with a different WRS.

Here `myDate` is a `Date` variable containing Feb 10, 2004 and `myDouble` is a `Double` containing 1.234.

Expression	US	UK	Norway
`Val(myDate)`	2	10	10.02 (or 10.2)
`Val(myDbl)`	1.234	1.234	1
`Val(True)`	0 (=False)	0 (=False)	0 (=False)
`Val("SomeText")`	0	0	0
`Val("6 My St.")`	6	6	6

Application.Evaluate

While not normally considered to be a conversion function, `Application.Evaluate` is the only way to convert a US-formatted date string to a date number. The following two functions `IsDateUS` and `DateValueUS` are wrapper functions that use this method.

The IsDateUS Function

The built-in `IsDate` function validates a string against the Windows Regional Settings. This function provides us with a way to check if a string contains a US-formatted date:

```
Public Function IsDateUS(ByVal aDate As String) As Boolean
   IsDateUS = Not IsError( _
      Application.Evaluate("DATEVALUE(""" & Date & """)"))
End Function
```

If `aDate` is a string containing a US-formatted date then `IsDateUS` returns `True`; if the string contains an invalid US date then `IsDateUS` returns `False`.

The DateValueUS Function

The VBA `DateValue` function converts a string formatted according to the Windows Regional Settings to a `Date` type. This function converts a string containing a US-formatted date to a `Date` type. If the string can not be recognized as a US-formatted date, it returns an `Error` value, that can be tested for using the `IsError` function:

```
Public Function DateValueUS(ByVal aDate As String) As Variant
   DateValueUS = Application.Evaluate("DATEVALUE(""" & aDate & """)")
End Function
```

`aDate` is a string containing a US-formatted date. `DateValueUS` returns the date value of the given string in a `Variant`.

Interacting with Excel

VBA and Excel are two different programs that have had very different upbringings. VBA speaks American. Excel also speaks American. However, Excel can also speak in its user's language if they have the appropriate Windows settings and Office language pack installed. On the other hand, VBA knows only a little about Windows settings, and even less about Office XP language packs. Consequently, we can either do some awkward coding to teach VBA how to speak to Excel in the user's language, or we can just let them converse in American. We very much recommend the latter.

Unfortunately, most of the newer features in Excel are not multilingual. Some only speak American, while others only speak in the user's language. We can use the American-only features if we understand their limitations; the others are best avoided. All of them are documented later in the chapter.

Sending Data to Excel

By far the best way to get numbers, dates, Booleans, and strings into Excel cells is to do so in their native format. Hence, the following code works perfectly, regardless of locale:

```
Public Sub SendToExcel()
   Dim aDate As Date
   Dim Number As Double
   Dim Bool As Boolean
   Dim Str As String

   aDate = DateSerial(2004, 2, 13)
   Number = 1234.567
   Bool = True
   Str = "Hello World"

   Range("A1").Value = aDate
   Range("A2").Value = Number
   Range("A3").Value = Bool
   Range("A4").Value = Str
End Sub
```

There is a boundary layer between VBA and Excel. When VBA passes a variable through the boundary, Excel does its best to interpret it according to its own rules. If the VBA and Excel data types are mutually compatible, the variable passes straight through unhindered.

The problems start when Excel forces us to pass it numbers, dates, or Booleans within strings, or when we choose to do so ourselves. The answer to the latter situation is easy: whenever you have a string representation of some other data type, if it is possible, always explicitly convert it to the data type you want Excel to store, before passing it to Excel.

Excel requires string input in the following circumstances:

- ❑ Setting the formula for a cell, chart series, conditional format, or pivot table calculated field
- ❑ Specifying the RefersTo formula for a defined name
- ❑ Specifying AutoFilter criteria
- ❑ Passing a formula to ExecuteExcel4Macro
- ❑ Setting the number format of a cell, style, chart axis, or pivot table field
- ❑ Setting number format in the VBA Format function

In these cases, we have to ensure that the string that VBA sends to Excel is in US-formatted text – we must use English language formulas and US regional settings. If the string is built within the code, we must be very careful to explicitly convert all our variables to US-formatted strings.

Take this simple example:

```
Public Sub SetLimit(ByVal Limit As Double)
    ActiveCell.Formula = "=IF(A1<" & Limit & ",1,0)"
End Sub
```

We are setting a cell's formula based on a parameter supplied from another routine. Note that the formula is being constructed in the code and we are using US language and regional settings (that is the English IF and using a comma for the list separator). When used with different values for Limit in different locales, we get the following results:

Limit	US	UK	Norway
100	Works fine	Works fine	Works fine
100.23	Works fine	Works fine	Runtime Error 1004

It fails when run in Norway with any non-integer value for Limit. This is because we are implicitly converting the variable to a string, which you'll recall uses the Windows Regional Settings number formats. The resulting string that we're passing to Excel is:

```
=IF(A1<100,23,1,0)
```

This fails because the IF function does not have four parameters. If we change the function to read:

```
Public Sub SetLimit(ByVal Limit As Double)
    ActiveCell.Formula = "=IF(A1<" & Str(Limit) & ",1,0)"
End Sub
```

the function will work correctly, as Str forces a conversion to a US-formatted string.

If we try the same routine with a Date instead of a Double, we come across another problem. The text that is passed to Excel (for example, for February 13, 2004) is:

```
=IF(A1<02/13/2004,1,0)
```

While this is a valid formula, Excel interprets the date as a set of divisions, so the formula is equivalent to:

```
=IF(A1<0.000077,1,0)
```

This is unlikely to ever be true. To avoid this, we have to convert the Date data type to a Double, and from that to a string:

```
Public Sub SetDateLimit(ByVal Limit As Date)
    ActiveCell.Formula = "=IF(A1<" & Str(CDbl(Limit)) & ",1,0)"
End Sub
```

The function is then the correct (but less readable):

```
=IF(A1<36935,1,0)
```

To maintain readability, we should convert dates to Excel's DATE function, to give:

```
=IF(A1<DATE(2004,2,13),1,0)
```

This is also achieved by the NumberToString function presented earlier on in this chapter, when the UseDateFunction parameter is set to True:

```
Public Sub SetDateLimit(ByVal Limit As Date)
    ActiveCell.Formula = "=IF(A1<" & NumberToString(Limit, True) & ",1,0)"
End Sub
```

If you call the revised SetLimit procedure with a value of 100.23 and look at the cell that the formula was put into, you'll see that Excel has converted the US string into the local language and regional settings. In Norway, for example, the cell actually shows:

```
=HVIS(A1<100,23;1;0)
```

This translation also applies to number formats. Whenever we set a number format within VBA, we can give Excel a format string that uses US characters (such as 'd' for day, 'm' for month, and 'y' for year). When applied to the cell (or style or chart axis), or used in the Format function, Excel translates these characters to the local versions. For example, the following code results in a number format of dd/mm/åååå when we check it using Format, Cells, and Number in Norwegian Windows:

```
ActiveCell.NumberFormat = "dd/mm/yyyy"
```

This ability of Excel to translate US strings into the local language and formats make it easy for developers to create locale-independent applications. All we have to do is code in American and ensure that we explicitly convert our variables to US-formatted strings before passing them to Excel.

Reading Data from Excel

When reading a cell's value, using its Value property, the data type that Excel provides to VBA is determined by a combination of the cell's value and its formatting. For example, the number 3,000 could reach VBA as a Double, a Currency, or a Date (March 18, 1908). The only international issue that concerns us here, is if the cell's value is read directly into a string variable – the conversion will then be done implicitly and you may not get what you expect (particularly if the cell contains a Boolean value).

As is the case when sending data to Excel, the translation between US and local functions and formats occurs when reading data from Excel. This means that a cell's .Formula or .NumberFormat property is given to us in English, and with US number and date formatting, regardless of the user's choice of language or regional settings.

While for most applications, it is much simpler to read and write using US formulas and formats, we will sometimes need to read exactly what the user is seeing (in their choice of language and regional settings). This is done by using the xxxLocal versions of many properties, which return (and interpret) strings according to the user's settings. They are typically used when displaying a formula or number format on a UserForm, and are discussed in the following section.

Rules for Working with Excel

We have included some basic guidelines that help you sidestep problems related to internationalizing your worksheets and VBA code.

- ❑ Pass values to Excel in their natural format, if possible (don't convert dates/numbers/Booleans to strings if you don't have to). If you have string values representing other data types, convert them yourself before passing them to Excel.

- ❑ When you have to convert numbers and dates to strings for passing to Excel (such as in criteria for AutoFilter or .Formula strings), *always explicitly convert the data* to a US-formatted string, using Trim(Str(MyNumber)), or the NumberToString function shown earlier, for all number and date types. Excel will then use it correctly and convert it to the local number/date formats.

- ❑ Avoid using Date literals (e.g. #1/3/2004#) in your code. It is better to use the VBA DateSerial, or the Excel DATE functions, which are not ambiguous.

- ❑ If possible, use the date number instead of a string representation of a date. Numbers are much less prone to ambiguity (though not immune).

- ❑ When writing formulas in code to be put into a cell (using the .Formula property), create the string using English functions. Excel will translate them to the localized MS Office language for you.

- ❑ When setting number formats or using the Format function, use US formatting characters, for example ActiveCell.NumberFormat = "dd mmm yyyy". Excel will translate these to the localized number format for you.

- ❑ When reading information from a worksheet, using .Formula, .NumberFormat, etc., Excel will supply it using English formulas and US format codes, regardless of the local Excel language.

Interacting with Users

The golden rule when displaying data to your users, or getting data from them, is to always respect their choice of Windows Regional Settings and Office UI Language. They should not be forced to enter numbers dates, formulas, and/or number formats according to US settings, just because it's easier for you to develop.

Paper Sizes

One of the most annoying things for a user is discovering that their printer does not recognize the paper sizes used in your templates. If you use templates for your reports, you should always change the paper size to the user's default size. This can easily be determined by creating a new workbook and reading off the paper size from the PageSetup object.

Excel 2002 added the Application.MapPaperSize property, to automatically switch between the standard paper sizes of different countries (for example Letter in the US is equivalent to A4 in the UK). If Application.MapPaperSize is set to True, Excel should take care of paper sizes for you.

Displaying Data

Excel does a very good job of displaying worksheets according to the user's selection of regional settings and language. When displaying data in UserForms or dialog sheets, however, we have to do all the formatting ourselves.

As discussed earlier, Excel converts number and dates to strings according to the WRS by default. This means that we can write code like the following, and be safe in the knowledge that Excel will display it correctly:

```
TextBoxNumber.Text = 3.14159
```

There are two problems with relying on implicit type conversion (as in the preceding example, which implicitly converts floating point number to a string):

❑ Dates will get be converted using the default "ShortDate" format, which may not include four digits for the year, and will not include a time component. To force a four-digit year and include a time, use the FormatDate function shown later in this chapter. It may be better, though, to use a less ambiguous date format on UserForms, such as the "mmm dd, yyyy" format used throughout this book.

❑ Versions of Excel prior to Excel 97 did not use the Windows Regional Settings for their default formats. If you are creating applications for use in older versions of Excel, you can't rely on the correct behavior.

The solution is simple – just use the Format function. This tells VBA to convert the number to a locally-formatted string and works in all versions of Excel from 5.0 onward:

```
TextBoxNumber.Text = Format(3.14159)
```

Interpreting Data

Your users will want to type in dates and numbers according to their choice of regional settings and your code must validate those entries accordingly and maybe display meaningful error messages back to the user. This means that you have to use the Cxxx conversion functions, and the IsNumeric and IsDate validation functions.

Unfortunately, these functions all have their problems (such as not recognizing the % sign at the end of a number) that require some working around. An easy solution is to use the WinToNum and WinToDate functions shown at the end of this chapter to perform the validation, conversion, and error prompting for you. The validation code for a UserForm will typically be done in the OK button's Click event, and might be implemented like this:

```
Private Sub CommandButtonOK_Click()
   Dim result As Double

   If WinToNum(TextBoxNumber.Text, result, True) Then
      Sheet1.Range("A1").Value = result
   Else
      TextBoxNumber.SetFocus
      Exit Sub
```

```
      End If
      Me.Hide

   End Sub
```

The xxxLocal Properties

Up until now, we have said that you have to interact with Excel using English language functions and the default US formats. Now, we present an alternative situation where your code interacts with the user in his or her own language using the appropriate regional settings. How then, can your program take something typed in by the user (such as a number format or formula) and send it straight to Excel, or display an Excel formula in a message box in the user's own language?

Microsoft has anticipated this requirement and has provided us with local versions of most of the functions we need. They have the same name as their US equivalent, with the word "Local" on the end (such as FormulaLocal, NumberFormatLocal etc.). When we use these functions, Excel does not perform any language or format coercion for us. The text we read and write is exactly how it appears to the user. Nearly all of the functions that return strings, or have string arguments, have local equivalents. The following table lists them all and the objects to which they apply:

Applies To	These versions of the functions use and return strings according to US number and date formats and English text	These versions of the functions use and return locally formatted strings, and in the language used for the Office UI (or Windows version, see later)
Number/string conversion	Str	CStr
Number/string conversion	Val	CDbl, etc.
Name, Style, Command Bar	.Name	.NameLocal
Range, Chart Series	.Formula	.FormulaLocal
Range, Chart Series	.FormulaR1C1	.FormulaR1C1Local
Range, Style, Chart Data Label, Chart Axes Label	.NumberFormat	.NumberFormatLocal
Range	.Address	.AddressLocal
Range	.AddressR1C1	.AddressR1C1Local
Defined Name	.RefersTo	.RefersToLocal
Defined Name	.RefersToR1C1	.RefersToR1C1Local
Defined Name	.Category	.CategoryLocal

The Rules for Working with Your Users

❏ When converting a number or date to a text string for displaying to your users, or setting it as the `.Caption` or `.Text` properties of controls, explicitly convert numbers and dates to text according to the WRS, using `Format(arg)`, or `CStr(arg)`.

❏ When converting dates to strings, Excel does *not* rearrange the date part order, so `Format(MyDate, "dd/mm/yyyy")` will always give a DMY date order (but will show the correct date separator). Use `Application.International(xlDateOrder)` to determine the correct date order – as used in the `FormatDate` function shown at the end of this chapter, or use one of the standard date formats (for example, `ShortDate`).

❏ If possible, use locale-independent date formats, such as `Format(MyDate, "mmm dd, yyyy")`. Excel will display month names according to the user's WRS language.

❏ When evaluating date or number strings that have been entered by the user, use `CDate` or `CDbl`, to convert the string to a date/number. These will use the WRS to interpret the string. Note that `CDbl` does not handle the `%` character if the user has put one at the end of the number.

❏ Always validate numbers and dates entered by the user before trying to convert them. See the `WinToNum` and `WinToDate` functions at the end of this chapter for an example.

❏ When displaying information about Excel objects, use the `xxxLocal` properties (where they exist) to display it in your user's language and formats.

❏ Use the `xxxLocal` properties when setting the properties of Excel objects with text provided by the user (which we must assume is in their native language and format).

Excel 2003's International Options

In the Tools ➪ Options dialog box, a new "International" tab has been added in Excel 2003. This tab allows the user to specify the characters that Excel uses for the thousand and decimal separators, overriding the Windows Regional Settings. These options can be read and changed in code, using `Application.ThousandSeparator`, `Application.DecimalSeparator`, and `Application.UseSystemSeparators`.

Using these properties we can print, save (as text), or publish a workbook using local number formats, change the separators being used, print, save (as text) or publish another version for a different target country, then change them back to their original settings. It is a great pity, though, that Microsoft didn't add the ability to override the rest of the Windows Regional Settings attributes—for example, date order, date separator, or represent negatives as -10 or (10).

One problem with the International options feature is that it does not change the number format strings used in the =TEXT worksheet function, so as soon as the option is changed (either in code or through the UI), all cells that use the =TEXT function will no longer be formatted correctly. See later in this chapter for a workaround to this problem.

The addition of International options has another downside for us as developers. The problem is that while these options affect all of Excel's `xxxLocal` properties and functions (including the `Application.International` settings), *they are ignored by VBA*.

A few examples highlight the scale of the problem:

❑ The VBA Format function—used almost every time a number is displayed to the user—ignores these options, resulting in text formatted according to the Windows Regional Settings, not those used by Excel.

❑ If the user types numbers into our UserForms or InputBoxes using the override separators, they will not be recognized as numbers by conversion methods like IsNumeric and CDbl, resulting in TypeMismatch errors.

The only way to work around this problem is to perform our own switching between WRS and Override separators before displaying numbers to the users and immediately after receiving numbers from them, using the following two functions:

```
Public Function WRSToOverride(ByVal Number As String) As String

    Dim WRS As String
    Dim Thousand As String
    Dim aDecimal As String
    Dim XLThousand As String
    Dim XLDecimal As String

    If Val(Application.Version) >= 10 Then
      If Not Application.UseSystemSeparators Then
        WRS = Format(1000, "#,##0.00")
        Thousand = Mid(WRS, 2, 1)
        aDecimal = Mid(WRS, 6, 1)
        XLThousand = Application.ThousandsSeparator
        XLDecimal = Application.aDecimalSeparator
        Number = Replace(Number, Thousand, vbTab)
        Number = Replace(Number, aDecimal, XLDecimal)
        Number = Replace(Number, vbTab, XLThousand)
      End If
    End If
    WRSToOverride = Number
End Function
```

WRSToOverride converts between WRS and Excel's number formats, and returns a string using Excel's Override formatting. Number is a string containing a WRS-formatted number:

```
Public Function OverrideToWRS(ByVal Number As String) As String

    Dim WRS As String
    Dim WRSThousand As String
    Dim WRSDecimal As String
    Dim XLThousand As String
    Dim XLDecimal As String

    If Val(Application.Version) >= 10 Then
      If Not Application.UseSystemSeparators Then
        WRS = Format$(1000, "#,##0.00")
        WRSThousand = Mid$(WRS, 2, 1)
```

```
            WRSDecimal = Mid$(WRS, 6, 1)
            XLThousand = Application.ThousandsSeparator
            XLDecimal = Application.DecimalSeparator
            Number = Replace(Number, XLThousand, vbTab)
            Number = Replace(Number, XLDecimal, WRSDecimal)
            Number = Replace(Number, vbTab, WRSThousand)
        End If
    End If
    OverrideToWRS = Number

End Function
```

OverrideToWRS converts between WRS and Excel's number formats, and returns the string using WRS' formatting. Number is a string containing an Excel Override formatted number.

The final problem is that when we are interacting with the user, we should be doing so using the number formats that they are familiar with. By adding the ability to override the Windows Regional Settings, Excel is introducing a third set of separators for us, and our users, to contend with. We are, therefore, completely reliant on the user remembering that override separators have been set and that they may not be the separators that they are used to seeing (that is according to the WRS).

We strongly recommend that your application checks if Application.UseSystemSeparators is True and displays a warning message to the user, suggesting that it be turned off, and set using Control Panel instead:

```
If Application.UseSystemSeparators Then
    MsgBox "Please set the required number formatting using the Control Panel"
    Application.UseSystemSeparators = False
End If
```

Features That Don't Play by the Rules

The xxxLocal functions discussed in the previous section were all introduced during the original move from XLM functions to VBA in Excel 5.0. These functions cover most of the more common functions that a developer is likely to use. There were, however, a number of significant omissions in the original conversion and new features have been added to Excel since then with almost complete disregard for international issues.

This section guides you through the maze of inconsistency, poor design, and omission that you'll find hidden within the following of Excel 2003's features. This table shows the methods, properties, and functions in Excel which are sensitive to the user's locale, but which do not behave according to the rules we have just stated.

Applies To	US Version	Local Version
Opening a text file	OpenText	OpenText
Saving as a text file	SaveAs	SaveAs

Continues

Applies To	US Version	Local Version
Application	.ShowDataForm	.ShowDataForm
Worksheet / Range		.Paste / .PasteSpecial
Pivot Table calculated fields and items	.Formula	
Conditional formats		.Formula
QueryTables (Web Queries)		.Refresh
Worksheet functions		=TEXT
Range	.Value	
Range	.FormulaArray	
Range	.AutoFilter	.AutoFilter
Range		.AdvancedFilter
Application	.Evaluate	
Application	.ConvertFormula	
Application	.ExecuteExcel4Macro	

Fortunately, workarounds are available for most of these issues. There are a few, however, that should be completely avoided.

Using the OpenText Function

Workbooks.OpenText is the VBA equivalent of opening a text file in Excel by using File ⇨ Open. It opens the text file, parses it to identify numbers, dates, Booleans, and strings and stores the results in worksheet cells. It is discussed in more detail elsewhere in the book. Of relevance to this chapter is the method Excel uses to parse the data file (and how it has changed over the past few versions).

In Excel 5, the text file was parsed according to your Windows Regional Settings when opened from the user interface, but according to US formats when opened in code. In Excel 97, this was changed to always use these settings from both the UI and code. Unfortunately, this meant that there was no way to open a US-formatted text file with any confidence that the resulting numbers were correct. Since Excel 5, we have been able to specify the date order to be recognized, on a column-by-column basis, which works very well for numeric dates (for example, 01/02/2004).

Excel 2000 introduced the Advanced button on the Text Import Wizard, and the associated DecimalSeparator and ThousandSeparator parameters of the OpenText method. These allow us to specify the separators that Excel should use to identify numbers and are welcome additions. It is slightly disappointing to see that we can not specify the general date order in the same way:

```
Public Sub OpenTextTest()

    Dim FileName As String
    FileName = ThisWorkbook.Path & "\Data.txt"
```

```
    Call Workbooks.OpenText(FileName:=FileName, _
      DataType:=xlDelimited, Tab:=True, _
      DecimalSeparator:=",", ThousandsSeparator:=".")

End Sub
```

While Microsoft is to be congratulated for fixing the number format problems in Excel 2000, further congratulations are due for fixing the problem of month and day names in Excel 2002, and for providing a much tidier alternative for distinguishing between US-formatted and locally formatted text files.

Prior to Excel 2002, the OpenText method would only recognize month and day names according to the Windows Regional Settings, and date orders had to be specified for every date field that wasn't in MDY order. Excel 2002 introduced the Local parameter to the OpenText method with which we can specify whether the text file being imported uses US English formatting throughout, or whether it uses locally formatted dates, numbers, etc.:

❑ If Local:=True, Excel will recognize numbers, dates, and month/day names according to the Windows Regional Settings (and the Override decimal and thousand separators, if set).

❑ If Local:=False, Excel will recognize numbers, dates, and month/day name according to standard US English settings.

In either case, the extra parameters of DecimalSeparator, ThousandSeparator, and FieldInfo can be used to further refine the specification (overriding the Local parameter's defaults).

The SaveAs Function

Workbook.SaveAs is the VBA equivalent of saving a text file in Excel by using File ⇨ Save As and choosing a format of Text.

In all versions of Excel prior to Excel 2002, this resulted in a US-formatted text file, with a DMY date order, and English month and day names, etc.

In Excel, the SaveAs method has the same Local parameter described in the preceding OpenText method, resulting in a US-formatted or locally formatted text file, as appropriate. Note that if a cell has been given a locale-specific date format (that is, the number format begins with a locale-specifier, such as [$-814] for Norwegian), that formatting will be retained in the text file, regardless of whether it is saved in US or local format:

```
Public Sub SaveText()
  Dim FileName As String
  FileName = ThisWorkbook.Path & "\Data.txt"

  Call ActiveWorkbook.SaveAs(FileName, xlText, local:=True)
End Sub
```

The ShowDataForm Sub Procedure

Using ActiveSheet.ShowDataForm is exposing yourself to one of the most dangerous of Excel's international issues. ShowDataForm is the VBA equivalent of the Data ⇨ Form menu item. It displays a standard dialog box that allows the user to enter and change data in an Excel list or database. When run by clicking the Data ⇨ Form menu, the dates and numbers are displayed according to the WRS and changes made by the user are interpreted according to the WRS, which fully complies with the preceding user-interaction rules.

When used in code, `ActiveSheet.ShowDataForm` displays dates and numbers according to US formats but interprets them according to WRS. Hence, if you have a date of February 10, 2004, shown in the worksheet in the dd/mm/yyyy order of 10/02/2004, Excel will display it on the data form as 2/10/2004. If you change this to the 11th (2/11/2004), Excel will store November 2, 2004, in the sheet. Similarly, if you are using Norwegian number formats, a number of 1-decimal-234 will be displayed on the form as 1.234. Change that to read 1.235 and Excel stores 1235, one thousand times too big.

Fortunately, there is an easy workaround for this if your routine only has to work with versions of Excel since Excel 97. Instead of using `ShowDataForm`, you can select the first cell in the range, then execute the Data ➪ Form menu item itself:

```
Public Sub ShowForm()
   ActiveSheet.Range("A1").Select
   '860 is the CommandBarControl ID of the Data, Form menu item
   RunMenu 860
End Sub
```

The following `RunMenu` routine executes a given menu item, as if it had been clicked by the user. In this case, the data form behaves correctly.

The RunMenu Sub Procedure

RunMenu, defined next, will run a menu item by simulating clicking on it, given its `CommandBar.Control` ID (for example, 860 is the ID for the Data ➪ Form menu item):

```
Public Sub RunMenu(ByVal MenuId As Long)

   Dim Control As CommandBarButton

   On Error Resume Next
   With Application.CommandBars.Add
     .Controls.Add(ID:=MenuId).Execute
     .Delete
   End With
End Sub
```

The parameter `MenuId` is the control ID of the menu item we'd like to run.

Pasting Text

When pasting text from other applications into Excel, it is parsed according to the WRS. We have no way to tell Excel the number and date formats, and language to recognize. The only workaround is to use a `DataObject` to retrieve the text from the clipboard, parse it yourself in VBA, then write the result to the sheet. The following example assumes that the clipboard contains a single US-formatted number:

```
Public Sub ParsePastedNumber()
   Dim obj As DataObject
   Set obj = New DataObject
```

```
    obj.GetFromClipboard
    Dim text As String
    ActiveCell.Value = Val(obj.GetText)
End Sub
```

PivotTable Calculated Fields and Items, and Conditional Format Formulas

If you are used to using the .Formula property of a range or chart series, you'll know that it returns and accepts formula strings that use English functions and US number formats. There is an equivalent .FormulaLocal property which returns and accepts formula strings as they appear on the sheet (using the Office UI language and WRS number formats).

Pivot-table calculated fields and items, and conditional formats also have a .Formula property, but for these objects, it returns and accepts formula strings as they appear to the user, that is, it behaves in the same way as the .FormulaLocal property of a Range object. This means that to set the formula for one of these objects, we need to construct it in the Office UI language, and according to the WRS.

A workaround for this is to use the cell's own .Formula and .FormulaLocal properties to convert between the formats, as shown in the following ConvertFormulaLocale function.

The ConvertFormulaLocale Function

This function converts a formula string between US and local formats and languages:

```
Public Function ConvertFormulaLocale( _
    ByVal Formula As String, ByVal USToLocal As Boolean) As String

    On Error GoTo Catch
    With ThisWorkbook.Worksheets(1).Range("IU1")
      If USToLocal Then
        .Formula = Formula
        ConvertFormulaLocale = .FormulaLocal
      Else
        .FormulaLocal = Formula
        ConvertFormulaLocale = .Formula
      End If

      .ClearContents
    End With

Catch:

End Function
```

Formula is the text of the formula to convert from, while USToLocal should be set to True to convert US to local, and False to convert local to US.

Web Queries

While the concept behind Web queries is an excellent one, they have been implemented with complete disregard for international issues. When the text of the Web page is parsed by Excel, all the numbers and dates are interpreted according to your Windows Regional Settings. This means that if a European Web page is opened in the US, or a US page is opened in Europe, it is likely that the numbers will be wrong.

For example, if the Web page contains the text 1.1, it will appear as January 1, on a computer running Norwegian Windows.

The `WebDisableDateRecognition` option for the `QueryTable` can be used to prevent numbers being recognized as dates. Setting Excel's override number and decimal separators can ensure that numbers are recognized correctly, if the Web page is displayed in a known format

Web queries must be used with great care in a multinational application, using the following approach:

❑ Set `Application.UseSystemSeparators` to `False`.

❑ Set `Application.DecimalSeparator` and `Application.ThousandSeparator` to those used on the Web page.

❑ Perform the query, ensuring `WebDisableDateRecognition` is set to `True`.

❑ Reset `Application.DecimalSeparator`, `Application.ThousandSeparator`, and `Application.UseSystemSeparators` to their original values.

Using the TEXT Worksheet Function

The TEXT worksheet function converts a number to a string, according to a specified format. The format string has to use formatting characters defined by the Windows Regional Settings (or Excel's International Options override). Hence, if you use `=TEXT(NOW(),"dd/mm/yyyy")`, you will get "01/02/yyyy" on Norwegian Windows, since Excel will only recognize 'å' as the Norwegian number-format character used for years.

Excel does not translate the number-format characters when it opens the file on a different platform. A workaround for this is to create a defined name that reads the number format from a specific cell, then, use that definition within the TEXT function. For example, if you format cell A1 with the date format to use throughout your sheet, you can click Insert ➪ Name ➪ Define and define a name as:

```
Name:           DateFormat
Refers To:      =GET.CELL(7,$A$1)
```

Then, use `=TEXT(Now(),DateFormat)` elsewhere in the sheet. The GET.CELL function is an Excel 4 macro function—which Excel lets us use within defined names, though not on the worksheet. This is equivalent to, but much more powerful than the =CELL worksheet function. The 7 in the example tells GET.CELL to return the number-format string for the cell.

> Note that some people have experienced General Protection Faults in previous versions of Excel when copying cells that use DateFormat to other worksheets and workbooks.

The XLM functions are documented in the XLMACR8.HLP file, available from Microsoft's web site at http://support.microsoft.com/support/kb/articles/Q143/4/66.asp

Range.Value and Range.FormulaArray Properties

These two properties of a range only break the rules by not having local equivalents. The strings passed to (and returned by) them are in US format. Use the preceding `ConvertFormulaLocale` function to convert between US and local versions of formulas.

Range.AutoFilter Method

The `AutoFilter` method of a `Range` object is a very curious beast. We are forced to pass it strings for its filter criteria, and hence must be aware of its string handling behavior. The criteria string consists of an operator (=, >, <, >=, etc.) followed by a value. If no operator is specified, the "=" operator is assumed.

The key issue is that when using the "=" operator, `AutoFilter` performs a textual match, while using any other operator results in a match by value. This gives us problems when trying to locate exact matches for dates and numbers. If we use "=", Excel matches on the text that is displayed in the cell, that is, the formatted number. As the text displayed in a cell will change with different regional settings and Windows language versions, it is impossible for us to create a criteria string that will locate an exact match in all locales.

There is a workaround for this problem. When using any of the other filter criteria, Excel plays by the rules and interprets the criteria string according to US formats. Hence, a search criterion of ">=02/01/2004" will find all dates on or after February 1, 2004, in all locales. We can use this to match an exact date by using two `AutoFilter` criteria. The following code will give an exact match on February 1, 2004, and will work in any locale:

```
Range("A1:D200").AutoFilter 2, ">=02/01/2004", xlAnd, "<=02/01/2004"
```

Range.AdvancedFilter Method

The `AdvancedFilter` method does play by the rules, but, in a way, that may be undesirable. The criteria used for filtering are entered on the worksheet in the criteria range. In a similar way to `AutoFilter`, the criteria string includes an operator and a value. Note that when using the "=" operator, `AdvancedFilter` correctly matches by value and hence differs from `AutoFilter` in this respect.

As this is entirely within the Excel domain, the string must be formatted according to the Windows Regional Settings to work, which gives us a problem when matching on dates and numbers. An advanced filter search criterion of ">1.234" will find all numbers greater then 1.234 in the US, but all numbers greater than 1234 when run in Norway. A criterion of ">02/03/2004" will find all dates after February 3 in the US, but after March 2 in Europe.

The only workarounds are to populate the criteria strings from code, before running the `AdvancedFilter` method, or to use a calculated criteria string, using the =TEXT trick mentioned above. Instead of a criterion of ">=02/03/2004", to find all dates on or after February 3, 2004, we could use the formula:

```
=">="&TEXT(DATE(2004,2,3),DateFormat)
```

Here `DateFormat` is the defined name just introduced that returns a local date format. If the date is an integer (does not contain a time component), we could also just use the criteria string ">=36194", and hope that the user realizes that 36194 is actually February 3, 2004.

Using Application.Evaluate, Application.ConvertFormula, and Application.ExecuteExcel4Macro Functions

These functions all play by the rules, in that we must use US-formatted strings. They do not, however, have local equivalents. To evaluate a formula that the user may have typed into a UserForm (or convert it between using relative to absolute cell ranges), we need to convert it to US format before passing it to `Application.Evaluate` or `Application.ConvertFormula`.

The `Application.ExecuteExcel4Macro` function is used to execute XLM-style functions. One of the most common uses of it is to call the XLM `PAGE.SETUP` function, which is much faster than the VBA equivalent. This takes many parameters, including strings, numbers, and Booleans. Be very careful to explicitly convert all of these parameters to US-formatted strings and avoid the temptation to shorten the code by omitting the `Str` around each one.

Responding to Office XP Language Settings

One of the major advances starting with the release of Office 2000 is that there is a single set of executables, with a set of plug-in language packs (whereas in prior versions, each language was a different executable, with its own set of bugs). This makes it very easy for a user of Office to have their own choice of language for the user interface, Help files, etc. In fact, if a number of people share the same computer, each person can run the Office applications in a different language.

As developers of Excel applications, we must respect the user's language selection and do as much as we can to present our own user interface in their choice of language.

Where Does the Text Come From?

There are three factors that together determine the text seen by the Office user:

Regional Settings Location

The Regional Settings location is chosen on the first tab (called Regional Options) of the Control Panel's Regional and Language Options applet and defines:

- ❑ The day and month names shown in Excel cells for long date formats
- ❑ The day and month names returned by the VBA `Format` function
- ❑ The month names recognized by the VBA `CDate` function and when typing dates into Excel directly
- ❑ The month names recognized by the Text Import Wizard and the VBA `OpenText` method (when the `Local` parameter is `True`)
- ❑ The number format characters used in the `=TEXT` worksheet function
- ❑ The text resulting from the implicit conversion of Boolean values to strings, such as: `"I am " & True`.

Office UI Language Settings

The Office User Interface language can be selected by using the Start ➪ Program Files ➪ Microsoft Office Tools ➪ Microsoft Office 2003 Language Settings, installed with Office XP and defines:

❑   The text displayed on Excel's menus and dialog boxes

❑   The text for the standard buttons on Excel's message boxes

❑   The text for Excel's built-in worksheet functions

❑   The text displayed in Excel's cells for Boolean values

❑   The text for Boolean values recognized by the Text Import Wizard, the VBA OpenText method, and when typing directly into Excel

❑   The default names for worksheets in a new workbook

❑   The local names for command bars

Language Version of Windows

The language version of Windows defines:

❑   The text for the standard buttons in the VBA MsgBox function (when using the vbMsgBoxStyles constants). Hence, while the text of the buttons on Excel's built-in messages respond to the Office UI language, the text of the buttons on our own messages respond to the Windows language. Note that the only way to discover the Windows language is with a Windows API call.

There are some things in Office XP which are 100 % (US) English, and don't respond to any changes in Windows language, regional settings or Office UI language, namely:

❑   The text resulting from the explicit conversion of Boolean values to strings, that is, all of Str(True), CStr(True), and Format(True) result in "True". Hence, the only way to convert a Boolean variable to the same string that Excel displays for it, is to enter it into a cell, then read the cell's .FormulaLocal property.

❑   The text of Boolean strings recognized by CBool.

Identifying the Office UI Language Settings

The first step to creating a multilingual application is to identify the user's settings. We can identify the language chosen in Windows Regional Settings by using Application.International (xlCountrySetting), which returns a number that corresponds approximately to the country codes used by the telephone system, for example, 1 represents the USA, 44 is the United Kingdom, and 47 is Norway. We can also use Application.International(xlCountryCode) to retrieve the user interface language using the same numbering system. This method has worked well in previous versions of Excel, where there were only 30 or so languages from which to choose your copy of Office.

Beginning with Office 2000, things have changed a little. By moving each of the language configurations into separate language packs, Microsoft can support many more languages with relative ease. If you use the Object Browser to look at the `msoLanguageID` constants defined in the Office object library, you'll see that there are over 180 languages and dialects listed.

We can use the following code to find out the exact Office UI language, then decide whether we can display our application in that language, a similar language, or revert to a default language (as shown in the following code fragment):

```
LanguageID = Application.LanguageSettings.LanguageID(msoLanguageIDUI)
```

Creating a Multilingual Application

When developing a multilingual application, you have to balance a number of factors, including:

❑ The time and cost spent developing the application

❑ The time and cost spent translating the application

❑ The time and cost spent testing the translated application

❑ The increased sales from having a translated version

❑ Improved ease-of-use, and hence reduced support costs

❑ The requirement for multilingual support

❑ Should you create language-specific versions, or use add-on language packs?

You also have to decide how much of the application to translate, and which languages to support:

❑ Translate nothing

❑ Translate only the packaging and promotional documentation

❑ Enable the code to work in a multilingual environment

❑ Translate the user interface (menus, dialogs, screens, and messages)

❑ Translate the Help files, examples, and tutorials

❑ Customize the application for each location

❑ Support left-to-right languages only

❑ Support right-to-left languages

❑ Support double-byte-character-set languages, for example, Japanese

The decision on how far to go will depend to a large extent on your users, your budget, and the availability of translators.

A Suggested Approach

It is doubtful that creating a single Excel application to support all 180-plus Office languages will make economic sense, but the time spent in making your application support a few of the more common languages will often be a wise investment. This will, of course, depend on your users, and whether support for a new language is preferable to new features.

The approach that we take is to write the application to support multiple languages and provide the user with the ability to switch between the installed languages or conform to their choice of Office UI Language. We develop the application in English, and then have it translated into one or two other languages depending on the target users. We will only translate it into other languages if there is profitable demand or it is a requirement.

How to Store String Resources

When creating multilingual applications, we cannot hardcode *any* text strings that will be displayed to the user; we must look them up in a *string resource*. The easiest form of string resource is a simple worksheet table. Give all your text items a unique identifier and store them in a worksheet, one row per identifier and one column for each supported language. You can then look up the ID and return the string in the appropriate language using a simple VLOOKUP function.

You will need to do the same for all your menu items, worksheet contents, and UserForm controls. The following code is a simple example, which assumes you have a worksheet called Language that contains a lookup table that has been given a name of Translation. It also assumes you have a public variable to identify which column to read the text from. The variable would typically be set in an Options type screen.

Note that the following code is not particularly fast and is shown as an example. A faster (and more complex) routine would read the entire column of IDs and selected language texts into two static VBA arrays, then work from those, only reading in a new array when the language selection was changed:

```
Public LanguageColumn As Integer

Public Sub Test2()
  LanguageColumn = 2
  Call MsgBox(GetText(1001))
End Sub

Public Function GetText(ByVal TextId As Long) As String
  Dim Test As Variant
  Static LanguageTable As Range

  If LanguageTable Is Nothing Then
    Set LanguageTable = ThisWorkbook.Worksheets("Language") _
      .Range("Translation")
  End If

  If LanguageColumn < 2 Then LanguageColumn = 2
    Test = Application.VLookup(TextId, LanguageTable, LanguageColumn)

  If Not IsError(Test) Then GetText = Test
End Function
```

Many of your messages will be constructed at runtime. For example, you may have code to check that a number is within certain boundaries:

```
Dim Message As String
  Message = _
    "The number must be greater than " & CStr(Min) & _
    "and less than " & CStr(Max) & "."
```

```
If Value <= Min Or Value >= Max Then
  Call MsgBox(Message)
End If
```

This would mean that we have to store two text strings with different IDs in our resource sheet, which is both inefficient and much harder to translate. In the example given, we would probably not have a separate translation string for the full stop. Hence, the maximum value would always come at the end of the sentence, which may not be appropriate for many languages. A better approach is to store the combined string with placeholders for the two numbers, and substitute the numbers at runtime (using the custom `ReplaceHolders` function, shown at the end of the chapter:

```
Dim Message As String
Message = _
  "The number must be greater than %0 and less than %1."

If Value <= Min Or Value >= Max Then
  Call MsgBox(ReplaceHolders(Message, CStr(Min), CStr(Max)))
End If
```

The translator (who may not understand your program) can construct a correct sentence, inserting the values at the appropriate points.

Working in a Multilingual Environment

Here are some tips on how to work in a multilingual environment.

Allow Extra Space

In general, most other languages use longer words than the English equivalents. When designing our UserForms and worksheets, we must allow extra room for the non-English text to fit in the controls and cells. A good rule of thumb is to make your controls 1.5 times the width of the English text.

Using Excel's Objects

The names that Excel gives to its objects when they are created often depend on the user's choice of Office UI Language. For example, when creating a blank workbook using `Workbooks.Add`, it will not always be called "BookN", and the first worksheet in it will not always be called "Sheet1". With the German UI, for example, they are called "MappeN" and "Tabelle1", respectively. Instead of referring to these objects by name, you should create an object reference as they are created, then use that object elsewhere in your code:

```
Dim aWorkbook As Workbook
Dim aWorksheet As Worksheet

Set aWorkbook = Workbooks.Add
Set aWorksheet = Wkb.Worksheets(1)
```

Working with `CommandBarControls` can also be problematic. For example, you may want to add a custom menu item to the bottom of the Tools menu of the worksheet menu bar. In an English-only environment, you may write something like:

```
Public Sub AddHelloButton()
  Dim Tools As CommandBarPopup
  Dim Control As CommandBarButton

  Set Tools = Application.CommandBars("Worksheet Menu Bar") _
    .Controls("Tools")

  Set Control = Tools.CommandBar.Controls.Add(msoControlButton)
  Control.Caption = "Hello"
  Control.OnAction = "Hello"
End Sub
```

This code will fail if your user has a UI language other than English. While Excel recognizes English names for command bars themselves, it does not recognize English names for the controls placed on them. In this example, the Tools drop-down menu is not recognized. The solution is to identify `CommandBar.Controls` by their ID and use `FindControl` to locate them. 30007 is the ID of the Tools popup menu:

```
Sub AddHelloButton2()
  Dim Tools As CommandBarPopup
  Dim Control As CommandBarButton

  Set Tools = Application.CommandBars("Worksheet Menu Bar") _
    .FindControl(ID:=30007)

  Set Control = Tools.CommandBar.Controls.Add(msoControlButton)

  Control.Caption = "Hello"
  Control.OnAction = "Hello"
End Sub
```

There is an additional problem with commandbar names in some locales and object libraries (for example, the Dutch VBE commandbars), in that the commandbar name (which should always be the same US English string) has been erroneously localized. The only sure method of working with commandbars is to avoid using any names in code, using `FindControl` extensively, instead. This approach is somewhat complicated, though, as the same control can occur on many commandbars and `FindControl` may not return the control that you want. Most developers use the English commandbar names.

> **Chapter 26 of this book contains a routine to show all the commandbars and the controls on them, with their names and ID numbers. Jan Karel Pieterse has compiled a workbook containing many of the commandbar translations in a file called xlMenuFunDict, available from http://www.BMSLtd.ie/MVP.**

Using SendKeys

In the best of cases, the use of `SendKeys` should be avoided, if at all possible. It is most often used to send key combinations to Excel, in order to activate a menu item or navigate a dialog box. It works by matching the menu item or dialog control accelerator keys, in the same way that you can use *Alt+key* combinations to navigate Excel using the keyboard. When used in a non-English version of Excel, it is highly unlikely that the key combinations in the SendKeys string will match up with the menus and dialog boxes, having potentially disastrous results.

For example, SendKeys "%DB" will bring up the Subtotals dialog box in English Excel, but will quit Excel when run with the German UI. Instead of using SendKeys to trigger menu items, you should use the RunMenu routine presented earlier in this chapter to execute a menu item by its CommandBarControl ID.

The Rules for Developing a Multilingual Application

❑ Decide early in the analysis phase the level of multilingual support that you are going to provide then stick to it.

❑ Do not include any text strings within your code. Always look them up in a table.

❑ Never construct sentences by concatenating separate text strings, as the foreign language version is unlikely to use the same word order. Instead use placeholders in your text and replace the placeholder at runtime.

❑ When constructing UserForms, always make the controls bigger than you need for the English text; most other languages use longer words.

❑ Do not try to guess the name that Excel gives to objects that you create in code. For example, when creating a new workbook, the first sheet will not always be "Sheet1".

❑ Do not refer to commandbar controls by their caption. While you can refer to commandbars themselves by their English name, you must refer to the menu items by their ID (for built - in items) or tag (for custom items).

❑ Do not use SendKeys.

Some Helpful Functions

In addition to some of the custom functions already presented, such as RunMenu and IsDateUS, here are some more functions that are very useful when creating multinational applications. Note that the code has been written to be compatible with all versions of Excel from 5.0 to 2003, and hence avoids the use of newer VBA constructs (such as giving optional parameters specific data types).

Implementing WinToNum Function

My function, WinToNum, determines if a string contains a number formatted according to the Windows Regional Settings and converts it to a Double. The function returns True or False to indicate the success of the validation, and optionally displays an error message to the user. It is best used as a wrapper function when validating numbers entered by a user, as shown in the preceding *Interacting with Users* section.

Note that if the user has used Excel's International Options to override the WRS decimal and thousands separator, the OverrideToWRS function must be used to ensure we send a WRS-formatted string to this function:

```
    Private Sub Show(ByVal message As String)
      Const mask As String = _
        "This message was not recognozed as a " & message & _
        " according to your Windows Regional Settings"

      Call MsgBox(mask, vbOKOnly)
    End Sub

    Public Function WinToNum(ByVal winString As String, _
      ByRef result As Double, Optional ByVal ShowMessage As Boolean) As Boolean

      Dim Fraction As Double

      winString = Trim(winString)
      Fraction = 1

      If IsMissing(ShowMessage) Then ShowMessage = True
      If winString = " " Then winString = "0"
      If winString = "" Then winString = "0"

      If InStr(1, winString, "%") > 0 Then
        Fraction = Fraction / 100
        winString = Application.Substitute(winString, "%", "")
      End If

      If IsNumeric(winString) Then
        result = CDbl(winString) * Fraction
        WinToNum = True
      Else
        If ShowMessage Then Call Show("number")
        result = 0
        WinToNum = False
      End If

    End Function
```

WinString is the string to be converted, and Result is the converted number, set to zero if the number is not valid or empty. ShowMessage is optional, and should be set to True (or missing) to show an error message, or False to suppress the error message.

Implementing WinToDate Function

WinToDate provides similar functionality as WinToNum, but for dates instead of numbers:

```
    Public Function WinToDate(ByVal winString As String, _
      ByRef result As Double, Optional ByVal ShowMessage As Boolean) As Boolean

      If IsMissing(ShowMessage) Then ShowMessage = True

      If winString = "" Then
        result = 0
        WinToDate = True
```

```
   ElseIf IsDate(winString) Then
     result = CDbl(CDate(winString))
     WinToDate = True
   Else
     If ShowMessage Then Call Show("date")
        result = 0
        WinToDate = False
   End If
End Function
```

The `WinString` argument is the string to be converted. `Result` is the converted number, set to zero if the number is not valid, or empty. `ShowMessage` is optional, and should be set to `True` (or missing) to show an error message, or `False` to suppress the error message.

Implementing FormatDate Function

This function formats a date according to the Windows Regional Settings, using a four-digit year and optionally, including a time string in the result:

```
Public Function FormatDate(ByVal aDate As Date, _
   Optional ByVal IncludeTime As Boolean) As String

   Dim DateString As String

   If IsMissing(IncludeTime) Then IncludeTime = False

   Select Case Application.International(xlDateOrder)
     Case 0
       aDate = Format$(aDate, "mm/dd/yyyy")
     Case 1
       Date = Format$(aDate, "dd/mm/yyyy")
     Case 2
       Date = Format$(aDate, "yyyy/mm/dd")
   End Select

   If IncludeTime Then DateString = aDate & " " & Format$(aDate, "hh:mm:ss")

   FormatDate = DateString

End Function
```

The `aDate` argument is the Excel date number, and `IncludeTime` is an optional argument that can be set to `True` if you want to include the time string in the result.

Implementing ReplaceHolders Function

The `ReplaceHolders` function replaces the placeholders in a string with values provided to it:

```
Public Function ReplaceHolders(ByVal Str As String, ParamArray Args() As Variant)
As String
```

```
    Dim I As Integer

    For I = UBound(Replace) To LBound(Replace) Step 1
     Str = WorksheetFunction.Substitute(Str, "%" & I, _
        Replace(I - LBound(Args)))
    Next

    ReplaceHolders = Str

End Function
```

`Str` is the text to replace the placeholders in, and `Replace` is a list of items to replace the placeholders.

Summary

It is possible to create an Excel application that will work on every installation of Excel in the world and support all 180-plus Office languages, but it is unlikely to be economically viable.

If you have a limited set of users and you are able to dictate their language and Windows Regional Settings, you can create your application without worrying about international issues. Even if this is the case, you should get into the habit of creating locale-independent code. The requirement for locale-independence should be included in your analysis, design, and coding standards. It is much, much easier and cheaper to write locale - independent code at the onset than to rework an existing application.

At a minimum, your application should work regardless of the user's choice of Windows Regional Settings or Windows or Office UI Language or whether they have set non-standard thousand and decimal separators using Tools ⇨ Options ⇨ International. You should be able to achieve this by following the rules listed in this chapter.

The following Excel features don't play by the rules and have to be treated very carefully:

- ❑ `OpenText`
- ❑ `SaveAs` to a text file
- ❑ `ShowDataForm`
- ❑ Pasting text from other applications
- ❑ The `.Formula` property in all its guises
- ❑ `<range>.Value`
- ❑ `<range>.FormulaArray`
- ❑ `<range>.AutoFilter`
- ❑ `<range>.AdvancedFilter`
- ❑ The `=TEXT` worksheet function
- ❑ `Application.Evaluate`
- ❑ `Application.ConvertFormula`

- ❏   `Application.ExecuteExcel4Macro`
- ❏   Web queries

There are also some features in Excel that you may have to avoid completely:

- ❏   `SendKeys`
- ❏   Using `True` and `False` in imported text files

If you are building multilanguage solutions then the best way to ensure the work correctly is to test the solution in each language version you intend to support.

18

Workbooks and Worksheets

Chapter 18 is about programmatically managing workbooks and worksheets. In this chapter, you will learn about important, fundamental tasks that will aid you in effectively managing these two basic Excel objects. Specifically, we will look at workbook and worksheet collections and the code necessary to save and overwrite these core objects as their state evolves.

Using the Workbooks Collection

The Workbooks collection is a property of the `Application` object. Workbooks represent all of the open Workbooks open for each instance of Excel running. Like all collections, Workbooks is simply designed as a place to put Workbook objects. Also, like all collections you can add or remove items from the collection. Let's take a moment to look at some of the programmatic gymnastics we can perform on the Workbooks collection and Workbooks in general.

As the name suggests, a collection is just a place to collect things. All collections are pretty much the same: things are added, counted, and removed. It is the objects in the collections that provide a rich feature set. Thus, most of the cool things we'll see next are actually operations performed on individual Workbook objects.

Creating a New Workbook

A basic idea behind a good object model is to provide features that are consistent and intuitive. For example, if we have a collection of things then it is intuitive that we should be able to add things to the collection. In fact, it is intuitive that all collections support the same behavior. An easy way to add a new Workbook to an application is to invoke the `Add` method on the `Application.Workbooks` collection.

Calling

```
Workbooks.Add
```

will add a new Workbook to the instance of Excel and make that Workbook the active one. We can also declare a Workbook object and assign the result of the `Add` method to the Workbook variable, giving us a convenient reference to the new Workbook.

Saving the ActiveWorkbook

A reasonable and intuitive operation to perform on a Workbook is to save it. We can use the knowledge that a recently added Workbook is the active Workbook or assign the return value from the `Workbooks.Add` method to a variable and write the Workbook to an external file. The next couple of statements demonstrate how to add and save the active Workbook:

```
Application.Workbooks.Add
Call Application.ActiveWorkbook.SaveAs("temp.xls")
```

The preceding code creates a new Workbook, doesn't capture the returned object, but instead relies on the `Application.ActiveWorkbook` property to interact with the just-created Workbook. Other intuitive ways to perform the same task include indexing the collection to retrieve a specific Workbook or saving a reference to a recently added Workbook and using either of those references to invoke the `SaveAs` method. Both techniques are shown next:

```
` Save a copy by indexing the Workbooks collection
Application.Workbooks.Add
Call Application.ActiveWorkbook.SaveAs("temp1.xls")
Application.Workbooks("temp1.xls").SaveAs ("copy of temp1.xls")


` Store the added reference to a Workbook and save it
Dim W As Workbook
Set W = Application.Workbooks.Add
Call W.SaveAs("temp2.xls")
```

The first example demonstrates how to add a new Workbook, and use the `ActiveWorkbook` to save it, and then index the Workbooks collection by the Workbooks' name and make a backup copy. The second example demonstrates how to save the returned Workbook instance and invoke `SaveAs` on this instance. All of these operations yield roughly the same result. What is important to note is the difference between operations performed on the Workbooks collection object and a single Workbook. If you look, we consistently invoked `Add` on the Workbooks collection and consistently invoked `SaveAs` on a single instance of a Workbook object. In general, then, we think of collections as supporting an `Add` and indexing behavior and a Workbook as supporting a `SaveAs` behavior. This is true of all objects: if you know the class of the object your code is referring to then you know what behaviors can be invoked against those objects.

Activating a Workbook

However, a better technique is to use the return value of the `Add` method to create an object variable that refers to the new workbook. This provides a shortcut way to refer to your workbook and you can keep track of a temporary workbook, without the need to save it:

```
Sub NewWorkbooks()
    Dim Workbook1 As Workbook
    Dim Workbook2 As Workbook

    Set Workbook1 = Workbooks.Add
    Set Workbook2 = Workbooks.Add
    Workbook1.Activate
End Sub
```

The `Add` method allows you to specify a template for the new workbook. The template does not need to be a file saved as a template, with an `.xlt` extension – it can be a normal workbook file with an `.xls` extension. The following code creates a new, unsaved workbook called `SalesDataX`, where X is a sequence number that increments as you create more workbooks based on the same template, in the same way that Excel creates workbooks called `Book1`, `Book2`, etc. when you create new workbooks through the user interface:

```
Set Workbook1 = Workbooks.Add(Template:="C:\Data\SalesData.xls")
```

To add an existing workbook file to the `Workbooks` collection, you use the `Open` method. Once again, it is a good idea to use the return value of the `Open` method to create an object variable that you can use later in your code to refer to the workbook:

```
Set Workbook1 = Workbooks.Open(Filename:="C:\Data\SalesData1.xls")
```

Getting a FileName from a Path

When you deal with workbooks in VBA, you often need to specify directory paths and filenames. Some tasks require that you know just the path, for example, if you set a default directory. Some tasks require you to know just the filename, for example, if you want to activate an open workbook. Other tasks require both path and filename, for example, if you want to open an existing workbook file that is not in the active directory.

Once a workbook is open, there is no problem getting its path, getting its full path and file name, or just getting the filename. For example, the following code displays "`SalesData1.xls`" in the message box:

```
Set Workbook1 = Workbooks.Open(FileName:="C:\Data\SalesData1.xls")
MsgBox Workbook1.Name
```

`Workbook1.Path` returns "`C:\Data`" and `Workbook1.FullName` returns "`C:\Data\SalesData1.xls`".

However, if you are trying to discover whether a certain workbook is already open, and you have the full path information, you need to extract the filename from the full path to get the value of the `Name` property of the `Workbook` object. The following `GetFileName` function returns the name "`SalesData1.xls`" from the full path "`C:\Data\SalesData1.xls`":

```
Function GetFileName(ByVal Path As String) As String
  Dim I As Integer

  For I = Len(Path) To 1 Step -1
    If Mid(Path, I, 1) = Application.PathSeparator Or _
      Mid(Path, I, 1) = ":" Then Exit For
  Next I

  GetFileName = Right(Path, Len(Path) - I)
End Function
```

So that `GetFileName` works on the Macintosh as well as under Windows, the path separator character is obtained using the `PathSeparator` property of the `Application` object. (We also added a check for the colon explicitly to handle paths like "`c:autoexec.bat`", which is a valid Windows path.) This returns a colon (:) on the Macintosh and a backslash (\) under Windows. The `Len` function returns the number of characters in `Path` and the `For...Next` loop searches backwards from the last character in `Path`, looking for the path separator. As soon as the separator character is encountered, the `for loop` exits, and the index `I` is equal to the character position of the separator. If it does not find a separator, we will have a value of zero when the `For...Next` loop is completed.

> **When a `For...Next` loop is permitted to complete normally, the index variable will not be equal to the Stop value. It will have been incremented past the end value by 1.**

`GetFileName` uses the `Right` function to extract the characters to the right of the separator in `Path`. If there is no separator, all the characters from `Path` are returned. Once you have the file name of a workbook, you can use the following `IsWorkbookOpen` function to see if the workbook is already a member of the `Workbooks` collection:

```
Public Function IsWorkbookOpen(ByVal WorkbookName As String) As Boolean
    On Error Resume Next
    IsWorkbookOpen = Workbooks(WorkbookName) Is Nothing = False
End Function
```

In the preceding code, `IsWorkbookOpen` tries to assign a reference to the workbook to an object variable, and then sees whether that attempt was successful or not. An alternative way to achieve the same result would be to search through the `WorkBooks` collection to see if any `Workbook` object had the name indicated in the argument.

In the preceding code, the `On Error Resume Next` ensures that no runtime error occurs when the workbook is not open. If the named document is found, `IsWorkbookOpen` returns a value of `True`. If you do not define the return value of a Boolean function, it will return `False`. In other words, if no open workbook of the given name is found, `False` is returned.

The following code uses the user-defined functions `GetFileName` and `IsWorkbookOpen` functions just described. `ActivateWorkbook` is designed to activate the workbook file in the path assigned to the variable `FileName`:

```
Public Sub ActivateWorkbook()
    Dim FullName As String
    Dim FileName As String
    Dim Workbook1 As Workbook

    FullName = "C:\Temp\Books1.xls"
    FileName = GetFileName("Books1.xls")

    If IsWorkbookOpen(FileName) Then
        Set Workbook1 = Workbooks(FileName)
```

```
        Workbook1.Activate
    Else
        Set Workbook1 = Workbooks.Open(FileName:=FullName)
    End If
End Sub
```

ActivateWorkbook first uses GetFileName to extract the workbook file name, Book1.xls, from FullName and assigns it to FileName. Then, it uses IsWorkbookOpen to determine whether Book1.xls is currently open. If the file is open, it assigns a reference to the Workbook object to the Wokrbook1 object variable and activates the workbook. If the file is not open, it opens the file and assigns the return value of the Open method to Workbook1. When the workbook is opened, it will automatically become the active workbook.

Note that the preceding code assumes that the workbook file exists at the specified location. It will fail if this is not the case. You will find a function, called FileExists, in the *"Overwriting an Existing Workbook"* section that you can use to test for the files existence.

Files in the Same Directory

It is common practice to break up an application into a number of workbooks and keep the related workbook files in the same directory, including the workbook containing the code that controls the application. In this case, you could use the common directory name in your code when opening the related workbooks. However, if you "hard wire" the directory name into your code, you will have problems if the directory name changes, or you copy the files to another directory on the same PC or another PC. You will have to edit the directory path in your macros.

To avoid maintenance problems in this situation, you can make use of ThisWorkbook.Path. ThisWorkbook is a reference to the workbook that contains the code. No matter where the workbook is located, the Path property of ThisWorkbook gives you the required path to locate the related files, as demonstrated in the following code:

```
Public Sub ActivateWorkbook2()
    Dim Path As String
    Dim FileName As String
    Dim FullName As String
    Dim Workbook1 As Workbook

    FileName = "Book1.xls"

    If IsWorkbookOpen(FileName) Then
        Set Workbook1 = Workbooks(FileName)
        Workbook1.Activate
    Else
        Path = ThisWorkbook.Path
        FullName = Path & "\" & FileName
        Set Workbook1 = Workbooks.Open(FileName:=FullName)
    End If
End Sub
```

Overwriting an Existing Workbook

When you want to save a workbook using the SaveAs method and using a specific filename, there is the possibility that a file with that name will already exist on disk. If the file does already exist, the user receives an alert message and has to make a decision about overwriting the existing file. If you want, you can avoid the alert and take control programmatically.

If you want to overwrite the existing file every time, you can just suppress the alert with the following code:

```
Public Sub SaveAsTest()
   Dim Workbook1 As Workbook
   Set Workbook1 = Workbooks.Add
   Application.DisplayAlerts = False
   Workbook1.SaveAs FileName:=ThisWorkbook.Path & "\temp.xls"
   Application.DisplayAlerts = True
End Sub
```

If you want to check for the existing file and take alternative courses of action, you can use the Dir function. If this is a test that you need to perform often, you can create the following FileExists function:

```
Function FileExists(ByVal FileName As String) As Boolean
   FileExists = Len(Dir(FileName)) > 0
End Function
```

The Dir function attempts to match its input argument against existing files. Dir can be used with wild cards under Windows for matches such as "*.xls". If it finds a match, it returns the first match found and can be called again without an input argument to get subsequent matches. Here, we are trying for an exact match that will either return the same value as the input argument or a zero length string if there is no match. The following code shows how you can use the FileExists function to test for a specific filename and take alternative courses of action:

```
Public Sub TestForFile()

   Dim FileName As String
   FileName = ThisWorkbook.Path & "\temp.xls"

   If FileExists(FileName) Then
      MsgBox FileName & " exists"
   Else
      MsgBox FileName & " does not exist"
   End If

End Sub
```

What you actually do in each alternative depends very much on the situation you are dealing with. One alternative could be to prompt the user for a new filename if the name already exists. Another approach could be to compute a new file name by finding a new sequence number to be appended to the end of the text part of the filename as shown here:

```
Public Sub CreateNextFileName()
  Dim Workbook1 As Workbook
  Dim I As Integer
  Dim FileName As String

  Set Workbook1 = Workbooks.Add(Template:=ThisWorkbook.Path & "\Temp.xls")
  I = 0
  Do
    I = I + 1
    FileName = ThisWorkbook.Path & "\Temp" & I & ".xls"
  Loop While FileExists(FileName)

  Workbook1.SaveAs FileName:=FileName
End Sub
```

Here, the code in the Do...Loop is repeated, increasing the value of I by one for each loop, as long as the file name generated exists. When I reaches a value for which there is no matching file name, the loop ends and the file is saved using the new name.

Saving Changes

You can close a workbook using the Close method of the Workbook object as shown:

```
ActiveWorkbook.Close
```

If changes have been made to the workbook, the user will be prompted to save the changes when an attempt is made to close the workbook. If you want to avoid this prompt, you can use several techniques, depending on whether you want to save the changes or not.

If you want to save changes automatically, you can specify this as a parameter of the Close method:

```
Sub CloseWorkbook()
  Dim Workbook1 As Workbook

  Set Workbook1 = Workbooks.Open(FileName:=ThisWorkbook.Path & "\Temp.xls")
  Range("A1").Value = Format(Date, "ddd mmm dd, yyyy")
  Range("A1").EntireColumn.AutoFit
  Workbook1.Close SaveChanges:=True

End Sub
```

If you don't want to save changes, you can set the SaveChanges parameter of the Close method to False.

Another situation that could arise is where you want to leave a changed workbook open to view but you don't want to save those changes or be prompted to save the changes when you close the workbook or Excel. In this situation, you can set the Saved property of the workbook to True and Excel will think that there are no changes to be saved. You should make doubly sure you would want to do this before you add this line of code:

```
ActiveWorkbook.Saved = True
```

The Sheets Collection

Within a `Workbook` object there is a `Sheets` collection whose members can be either `Worksheet` objects or `Chart` objects. For compatibility with older versions of Excel, they can also be `DialogSheets`, `Excel4MacroSheets` and `Excel4InternationalMacroSheets`. Excel 5 and Excel 95 included modules as part of the `Sheets` collection, but since Excel 97, modules have moved to the VBE.

> **Modules in workbooks created under Excel 5 or Excel 95 are considered by later versions of Excel to belong to a hidden Modules collection and can still be manipulated by the code originally set up in the older versions.**

`Worksheet` objects and `Chart` objects also belong to their own collections, the `Worksheets` collection and the `Charts` collection, respectively. The `Charts` collection only includes chart sheets, that is charts that are embedded in a worksheet are *not* members of the `Charts` collection. Charts embedded in worksheets are contained in `ChartObject` objects, which are members of the `ChartObjects` collection of the worksheet. See Chapter 24 for more details.

Worksheets

You can refer to a worksheet by its name or index number in the `Sheets` collection and the `Worksheets` collection. If you know the name of the worksheet you want to work on, it is appropriate, and usually safer, to use that name to specify the required member of the `Worksheets` collection. If you want to process all the members of the `Worksheets` collection, in a `For...Next` loop for example, you would usually reference each worksheet by its index number.

The index number of a worksheet in the `Worksheets` collection can be different from the index number of the worksheet in the `Sheets` collection. In the workbook, `Sheet1` can be referenced by any of the following:

```
ActiveWorkbook.Sheets("Sheet1")
ActiveWorkbook.Worksheets("Sheet1")
ActiveWorkbook.Sheets(2)
ActiveWorkbook.Worksheets(1)
```

There is a trap, however, concerning the `Index` property of the `Worksheet` object. The `Index` property of the `Worksheet` object returns the value of the index in the `Sheets` collection, not the `Worksheets` collection. The following code iterates through all of the Worksheets in the collection to display the worksheet name and index (Figure 18-1):

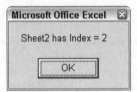

Figure 18-1

```
Public Sub WorksheetIndex()
   Dim I As Integer

   For I = 1 To ThisWorkbook.Worksheets.Count
   MsgBox ThisWorkbook.Worksheets(I).Name & _
     " has Index = " & ThisWorkbook.Worksheets(I).Index
   Next I
End Sub
```

You should avoid using the Index property of the worksheet, if possible, as it leads to confusing code. The following example shows how you must use the worksheet Index as an index in the Sheets collection, not the Worksheets collection. The macro adds a new empty chart sheet to the left of every worksheet in the active workbook:

```
Public Sub InsertChartsBeforeWorksheets()
   Dim Worksheet1 As Worksheet

   For Each Worksheet1 In Worksheets
      Charts.Add Before:=Sheets(Worksheet1.Index)
   Next Worksheet1
End Sub
```

In most cases, you can avoid using the worksheet Index property. The preceding code should have been written as follows:

```
Public Sub InsertChartsBeforeWorksheets2()
   Dim Worksheet As Worksheet

   For Each Worksheet In Worksheets
      Charts.Add Before:=Worksheet
   Next Worksheet1
End Sub
```

Strangely enough, Excel will not allow you to add a new chart after the last worksheet, although it will let you move a chart after the last worksheet. If you want to insert chart sheets after each worksheet, you can use code like the following:

```
Public Sub InsertChartsAfterWorksheets()
   Dim Worksheet1 As Worksheet
   Dim Chart1 As Chart

   For Each Worksheet1 In Worksheets
      Set Chart1 = Charts.Add
      Chart1.Move After:=Worksheet1
   Next Worksheet1
End Sub
```

Chart sheets are covered in more detail in Chapter 23.

Copy and Move

The Copy and Move methods of the Worksheet object allow you to copy or move one or more worksheets in a single operation. They both have two optional parameters that allow you to specify the destination of the operation. The destination can be either before or after a specified sheet. If you do not use one of these parameters, the worksheet will be copied or moved to a new workbook.

Copy and Move do not return any value or reference, so you have to rely on other techniques if you want to create an object variable referring to the copied or moved worksheets. This is not generally a problem as the first sheet created by a Copy operation, or the first sheet resulting from moving a group of sheets, will be active immediately after the operation.

Say, you have a workbook like the one shown in Figure 18-2 and want to add another worksheet for February—and then more worksheets for the following months. The numbers on rows 3 and 4 are the input data, but row 5 contains calculations to give the difference between rows 3 and 4. When you copy the worksheet, you will want to clear the input data from the copies but retain the headings and formulas:

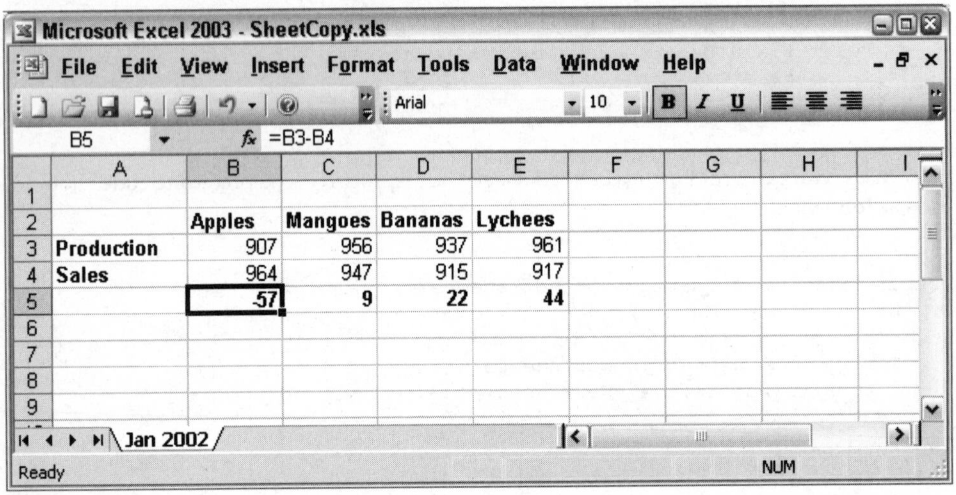

Figure 18-2

The following code creates a new monthly worksheet that is inserted into the workbook after the latest month. It copies the first worksheet, removes any numeric data from it but leaves any headings or formulas in place and then renames the worksheet to the new month and year:

```
Public Sub NewMonth()
   Dim Worksheet1 As Worksheet
   Dim FirstDate As Date
   Dim FirstMonth As Integer
   Dim FirstYear As Integer

   ' Copy the first worksheet and get a reference to
   ' the new worksheet
   Worksheets(1).Copy After:=Worksheets(Worksheets.Count)
   Set Worksheet1 = Worksheets(Worksheets.Count)
```

```
' Read the date from the worksheet
FirstDate = DateValue(Worksheets(1).Name)
FirstMonth = Month(FirstDate)
FirstYear = Year(FirstDate)

' Calculate the next sequential date and use this
' value to name the new worksheet
Worksheet1.Name = Format(DateSerial(FirstYear, _
   FirstMonth + Worksheets.Count - 1, 1), "mmm yyyy")

' Clear the old contents from the new worksheet
On Error Resume Next
Worksheet1.Cells.SpecialCells( _
   xlCellTypeConstants, 1).ClearContents
End Sub
```

The result of the copy is shown in Figure 18-3:

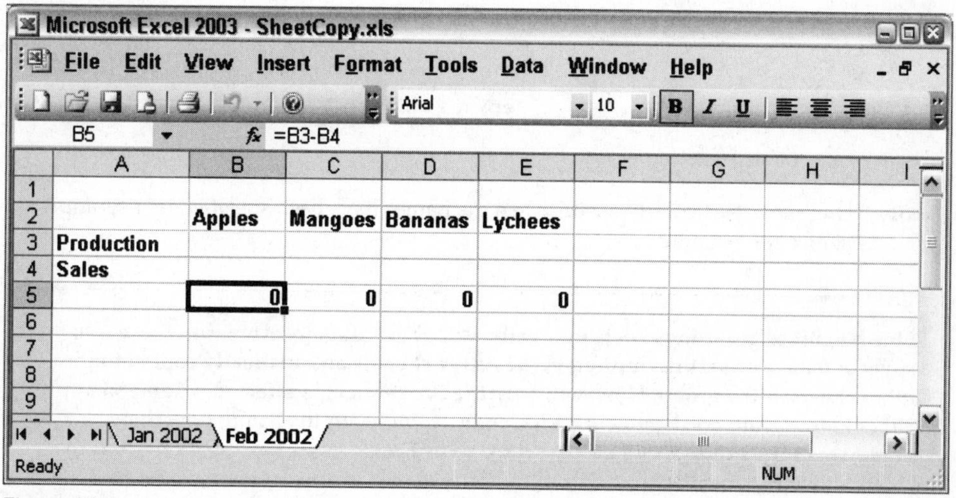

Figure 18-3

The NewMonth methods a new worksheet, and sets a reference to the new worksheet. The name of the first worksheet is read and parsed and used to increment the worksheet name to the next month and year in the sequence. Finally, all of the data is cleared form the new worksheet, leaving the headers and the equations in place.

The DateSerial method is used to calculate the next date in the sequence and the Format method uses the format string "mmmyyyy" to display the date as a three character month string and a four-digit year string. Finally, the SpecialCells method is used to clear cells containing constant numeric data. The SpecialCells method is discussed in more detail in Chapter 19.

Grouping Worksheets

You can manually group the sheets in a workbook by clicking a sheet tab then, holding down *Shift* or *Ctrl*, clicking another sheet tab. *Shift* groups all the sheets between the two tabs. *Ctrl* adds just the new sheet to the group. You can also group sheets in VBA by using the `Select` method of the `Worksheets` collection in conjunction with the `Array` function. The following code groups the first and second worksheets and makes the first worksheet active:

```
Worksheets(Array(1, 2)).Select
Worksheets(1).Activate
```

In addition to this, you can also create a group using the `Select` method of the `Worksheet` object. The first sheet is selected in the normal way. Other worksheets are added to the group by using the `Select` method while setting its `Replace` parameter to `False`:

```
Public Sub Groupsheets()
   Dim Names(1 To 3) As String
   Dim I As Integer

   Names(1) = "Jan 2002"
   Names(2) = "Feb 2002"
   Names(3) = "Mar 2002"
   Worksheets(Names(1)).Select

   For I = 2 To 3
     Worksheets(Names(I)).Select Replace:=False
   Next I
End Sub
```

The above technique is particularly useful when the names have been specified by user input, via a multiselect list box, for example.

> One benefit of grouping sheets manually, is that any data inserted into the active sheet and any formatting applied to the active sheet is automatically copied to the other sheets in the group. However, only the active sheet is affected when you apply changes to a grouped sheet using VBA code. If you want to change the other members of the group, you need to set up a For Each...Next loop and carry out the changes on each member.

The following code places the value `100` into the A1 cell of worksheets with index numbers 1, 2, and 3 bolds the numbers:

```
Public Sub FormatGroup()

   Dim AllSheets As Sheets
   Dim Worksheet1 As Worksheet
   Set AllSheets = Worksheets(Array(1, 2, 3))

   For Each Worksheet1 In AllSheets
     Worksheet1.Range("A1").Value = 100
     Worksheet1.Range("A1").Font.Bold = True
   Next Worksheet1

End Sub
```

The Window Object

In VBA, if you want to detect what sheets are currently grouped, you use the `SelectedSheets` property of the `Window` object. You might think that `SelectedSheets` should be a property of the `Workbook` object, but that is not the case. `SelectedSheets` is a property of the `Window` object because you can open many windows on the same workbook and each window, as shown in Figure 18-4:

Figure 18-4

There are many other common workbook and worksheet properties that you might presume to be properties of the `Workbook` object or the `Worksheet` object, but which are actually `Window` object properties. Some examples of these are `ActiveCell`, `DisplayFormulas`, `DisplayGridlines`, `DisplayHeadings`, and `Selection`. See the `Window` object in Appendix A for a full list.

The following code determines which cells are selected on the active sheet, makes them Red and then changes the font color to Red in corresponding ranges on the other sheets in the group:

```
Public Sub FormatSelectedGroup()
   Dim Sheet As Object
   Dim Address As String

   Address = Selection.Address
   For Each Sheet In ActiveWindow.SelectedSheets
      If TypeName(Sheet) = "Worksheet" Then
         Sheet.Range(Address).Font.Color = vbRed
      End If
   Next Sheet
End Sub
```

The address of the selected range on the active sheet is captured in `Address` as a string. It is possible to activate only the selected sheets and apply a Red format to the selected cells. Group mode ensures that the selections are the same on each worksheet. However, activating sheets is a slow process. By capturing the selection address as a string, you can generate references to the same range on other sheets using the

Range property of the other sheets. The address is stored as a string in the form "$B$2:$E$2,$A$3: $A$4", for example, and need not be a single contiguous block.

FormatSelectedGroup allows for the possibility that the user can include a chart sheet or another type of sheet in the group of sheets. It checks that the TypeName of the sheet is indeed "Worksheet" before applying the new format.

> **It is necessary to Dim Sheet as the generic Object type, if you want to allow it to refer to different sheet types. There is a Sheets collection in the Excel Object Model, but there is no Sheet object.**

Synchronizing Worksheets

When you move from one worksheet in a workbook to another, the sheet you activate will be configured as it was when it was last active. The top left-hand corner cell, the selected range of cells, and the active cell will be in exactly the same positions as they were the last time the sheet was active, unless you are in Group mode. In Group mode, the selection and active cell are synchronized across the group. However, the top left-hand corner cell is not synchronized in Group mode, and it is possible that you will not be able to see the selected cells and the active cell when you activate a worksheet.

If you want to synchronize your worksheets completely, even out of Group mode, you can add the following code to the ThisWorkbook module of your workbook:

```
Option Explicit

Dim OldSheet As Object

Private Sub Workbook_SheetDeactivate(ByVal Sht As Object)
    'If the deactivated sheet is a worksheet,
    'store a reference to it in OldSheet
    If TypeName(Sht) = "Worksheet" Then Set OldSheet = Sht
End Sub

Private Sub Workbook_SheetActivate(ByVal NewSheet As Object)
    Dim CurrentColumn As Long
    Dim CurrentRow As Long
    Dim CurrentCell As String
    Dim CurrentSelection As String

    On Error GoTo Finally
    If OldSheet Is Nothing Then Exit Sub
    If TypeName(NewSheet) <> "Worksheet" Then Exit Sub
    Application.ScreenUpdating = False
    Application.EnableEvents = False

    OldSheet.Activate 'Get the old worksheet configuration
    CurrentColumn = ActiveWindow.ScrollColumn
    CurrentRow = ActiveWindow.ScrollRow
```

```
        CurrentSelection = Selection.Address
        CurrentCell = ActiveCell.Address

        NewSheet.Activate 'Set the new worksheet configuration
        ActiveWindow.ScrollColumn = CurrentColumn
        ActiveWindow.ScrollRow = CurrentRow
        Range(CurrentSelection).Select
        Range(CurrentCell).Activate
    Finally:
        Application.EnableEvents = True
    End Sub
```

The `Dim OldSheet as Object` statement must be at the top of the module in the declarations area so that `OldSheet` is a module-level variable that will retain its value while the workbook is open and can be accessed by the two event procedures. The `Workbook_SheetDeactivate` event procedure is used to store a reference to any worksheet that is deactivated. The deactivate event occurs after another sheet is activated, so it is too late to store the active window properties. The procedure's `Sht` parameter refers to the deactivated sheet and its value is assigned to `OldSheet`.

The `Workbook_SheetActivate` event procedure executes after the `Deactivate` procedure. The `On Error GoTo Finally` statement ensures that, if an error occurs, there are no error messages displayed and that control jumps to the `Finally:` label where event processing is enabled, just in case event processing has been switched off.

The first `If` tests check that `OldSheet` has been defined, indicating that a worksheet has been deactivated during the current session. The second `If` test checks that the active sheet is a worksheet. If either `If` test fails, the procedure exits. These tests allow for other types of sheets, such as charts, being deactivated or activated.

Next, screen updating is turned off to minimize screen flicker. It is not possible to eliminate all flicker because the new worksheet has already been activated and the user will get a brief glimpse of its old configuration before it is changed. Then, event processing is switched off so that no chain reactions occur. To get the data it needs, the procedure has to reactivate the deactivated worksheet, which would trigger the two event procedures again.

After reactivating the old worksheet, the `ScrollRow` (the row at the top of the screen), the `ScrollColumn` (the column at the left of the screen), the addresses of the current selection, and the active cell are stored. The new worksheet is then reactivated and its screen configuration is set to match the old worksheet. As there is no `Exit Sub` statement before the `Finally:` label, the final statement is executed to make sure event processing is enabled again.

Summary

In this chapter, we have seen many techniques for handling workbooks and worksheets in VBA code. We have seen how to:

- ❑ Create new workbooks and open existing workbooks
- ❑ Handle saving workbook files and overwriting existing files
- ❑ Move and copy worksheets and interact with `Group` mode

You have also seen that you access some workbook and worksheet features through the Window object, and have been shown that you can synchronize your worksheets using workbook events procedures. Refer to Chapter 5 for more discussion on this topic.

In addition, a number of utility macros have been presented including routines to check that a workbook is open, to extract a file name from the full file path, and a simple macro that confirms that a file does indeed exist.

19

Using Ranges

The Range object is probably the object you will utilize the most in your VBA code. A Range object can be a single cell, a rectangular block of cells, or the union of many rectangular blocks (a non-contiguous range). A Range object is contained within a Worksheet object.

The Excel object model does not support three-dimensional Range objects that span multiple worksheets – every cell in a single Range object must be on the same worksheet. If you want to process 3D ranges, you must process a Range object in each worksheet separately.

In this chapter, we will examine the most useful properties and methods of the Range object.

Activate and Select

The Activate and Select methods cause some confusion, and it is sometimes claimed that there is no difference between them. To understand the difference between them, we need to first understand the difference between the ActiveCell and Selection properties of the Application object. The screen in Figure 19-1 illustrates this.

Selection refers to B3:E10. ActiveCell refers to C5, the cell where data will be inserted if the user types something. ActiveCell only ever refers to a single cell, while Selection can refer to a single cell or a range of cells. The active cell is usually the top left-hand cell in the selection, but can be any cell in the selection, as shown in Figure 19-1. You can manually change the position of the active cell in a selection by pressing *Tab, Enter, Shift+Tab,* or *Shift+Enter.*

You can achieve the combination of selection and active cell shown previously by using the following code:

```
Public Sub SelectAndActivate()
  Range("B3:E10").Select
  Range("C5").Activate
End Sub
```

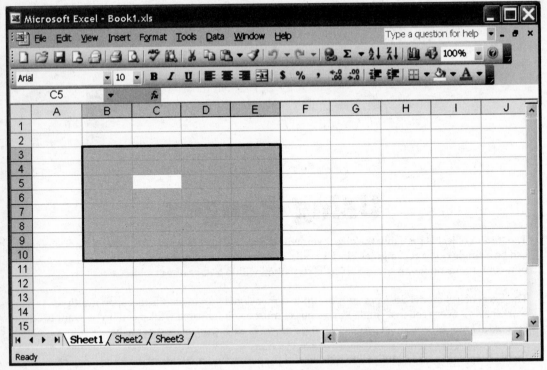

Figure 19-1

If you try to activate a cell that is outside the selection, you will change the selection, and the selection will become the activated cell.

Confusion also arises because you are permitted to specify more than one cell when you use the `Activate` method. Excel's behavior is determined by the location of the top-left cell in the range you activate. If the top-left cell is within the current selection, the selection does not change and the top-left cell becomes active. The following example will create the previous screen:

```
Public Sub SelectAndActivate2()
   Range("B3:E10").Select
   Range("C5:Z100").Activate
End Sub
```

If the top-left cell of the range you activate is not in the current selection, the range that you activate replaces the current selection as shown by the following:

```
Public Sub SelectAdActivate3()
   Range("B3:E10").Select
   Range("A2:C5").Activate
End Sub
```

In this case, the `Select` is overruled by the `Activate` and A2:C5 becomes the selection.

> To avoid errors, it is recommended that you don't use the **Activate** method to select a range of cells. If you get into the habit of using **Activate** instead of **Select**, you will get unexpected results when the top-left cell you activate is within the current selection.

Range Property

You can use the `Range` property of the `Application` object to refer to a `Range` object on the active worksheet. The following example refers to a `Range` object that is the B2 cell on the currently active worksheet:

```
Application.Range("B2")
```

Note that you can't test code examples like the previous one as they are presented. However, as long as you are referring to a range on the active worksheet, these examples can be tested by the immediate window of the VBE, as follows:

```
Application.Range("B2").Select
```

It is important to note that the previous reference to a `Range` object will cause an error if there is no worksheet currently active. For example, it will cause an error if you have a chart sheet active.

As the `Range` property of the `Application` object is a member of <globals>, you can omit the reference to the `Application` object, as follows:

```
Range("B2")
```

You can refer to more complex `Range` objects than a single cell. The following example refers to a single block of cells on the active worksheet:

```
Range("A1:D10")
```

And this code refers to a non-contiguous range of cells:

```
Range("A1:A10,C1:C10,E1:E10")
```

The `Range` property also accepts two arguments that refer to diagonally opposite corners of a range. This gives you an alternative way to refer to the A1:D10 `range`:

```
Range("A1","D10")
```

`Range` also accepts names that have been applied to ranges. If you have defined a range of cells with the name `SalesData`, you can use the name as an argument:

```
Range("SalesData")
```

The arguments can be objects as well as strings, which provides much more flexibility. For example, you might want to refer to every cell in column A from cell A1 down to a cell that has been assigned the name LastCell:

```
Range("A1",Range("LastCell"))
```

Shortcut Range References

You can also refer to a range by enclosing an A1 style range reference or a name in square brackets, which is a shortcut form of the Evaluate method of the Application object. It is equivalent to using a single string argument with the Range property, but is shorter:

```
[B2]
[A1:D10]
[A1:A10,C1:C10,E1:E10]
[SalesData]
```

This shortcut is convenient when you want to refer to an absolute range. However, it is not as flexible as the Range property as it cannot handle variable input as strings or object references.

Ranges on Inactive Worksheets

If you want to work efficiently with more than one worksheet at the same time, it is important to be able to refer to ranges on worksheets without having to activate those worksheets. Switching between worksheets is slow, and code that does this is more complex than it need be. Switching between worksheets in code is unnecessary and makes your solutions harder to read and debug.

All our examples so far apply to the active worksheet, because they have not been qualified by any specific worksheet reference. If you want to refer to a range on a worksheet that is not active, simply use the Range property of the required Worksheet object:

```
Worksheets("Sheet1").Range("C10")
```

If the workbook containing the worksheet and range is not active, you need to further qualify the reference to the Range object as follows:

```
Workbooks("Sales.xls").Worksheets("Sheet1").Range("C10")
```

However, you need to be careful if you want to use the Range property as an argument to another Range property. Say, you want to sum A1:A10 on Sheet1, while Sheet2 is the active sheet. You might be tempted to use the following code, which results in a runtime error:

```
MsgBox WorksheetFunction.Sum(Sheets("Sheet1").Range(Range("A1"), _
    Range("A10")))
```

The problem is that Range("A1") and Range("A10") refer to the active sheet, Sheet2. You need to use fully qualified properties:

```
MsgBox WorksheetFunction.Sum(Sheets("Sheet1").Range( _
                            Sheets("Sheet1").Range("A1"), _
                            Sheets("Sheet1").Range("A10")))
```

When you need to refer to multiple instances of the same value you can abbreviate your code with a `With..End With` construct as follows:

```
With Sheets("Sheet1")
    MsgBox WorksheetFunction.Sum(.Range(.Range("A1"), .Range("A10")))
End With
```

Range Property of a Range Object

The `Range` property is normally used as a property of the `Worksheet` object. You can also use the `Range` property of the `Range` object. In this case, it acts as a reference relative to the `Range` object itself. The following is a reference to the D4 cell:

```
Range("C3").Range("B2")
```

If you consider a virtual worksheet that has C3 as the top-left cell, and B2 is one column across and one row down on the virtual worksheet, you arrive at D4 on the real worksheet.

You will see this "Range in a Range" technique used in code generated by the macro recorder when relative recording is used (discussed in Chapter 1). For example, the following code was recorded when the active cell and the four cells to its right were selected while recording relatively:

```
ActiveCell.Range("A1:E1").Select
```

As the preceding code can be confusing, it is best to avoid relative cell referencing. The `Cells` property is a much better way to reference cells relatively.

Cells Property

You can use the `Cells` property of the `Application`, `Worksheet`, or `Range` objects to refer to the `Range` object containing all the cells in a `Worksheet` object or `Range` object. The following two lines of code each refer to a `Range` object that contains all the cells in the active worksheet:

```
ActiveSheet.Cells
Application.Cells
```

As the `Cells` property of the `Application` object is a member of `<globals>`, you can also refer to the `Range` object containing all the cells on the active worksheet as follows:

```
Cells
```

You can use the `Cells` property of a `Range` object as follows:

```
Range("A1:D10").Cells
```

However, the `Cells` property in the preceding statement simply refers to the original `Range` object it qualifies.

You can refer to a specific cell relative to the `Range` object by using the `Item` property of the `Range` object and specifying the relative row and column positions. The row parameter is always numeric. The column parameter can be numeric or you can use the column letters entered as a string. The following are both references to the `Range` object containing the B2 cell in the active worksheet:

```
Cells.Item(2,2)
Cells.Item(2,"B")
```

As the `Item` property is the default property of the `Range` object, you can omit it as follows:

```
Cells(2,2)
Cells(2,"B")
```

The numeric parameters are particularly useful when you want to loop through a series of rows or columns using an incrementing index number. The following example loops through rows 1 to 10 and columns A to E in the active worksheet, placing values in each cell:

```
Public Sub FillCells()
    Dim i As Integer, j As Integer

    For i = 1 To 10
      For j = 1 To 5
        Cells(i, j).Value = i * j
      Next j
    Next i
End Sub
```

Figure 19-2 shows the results of this code.

Cells used in Range

You can use the `Cells` property to specify the parameters within the `Range` property to define a `Range` object. The following code refers to A1:E10 in the active worksheet:

```
Range(Cells(1,1), Cells(10,5))
```

This type of referencing is particularly powerful because you can specify the parameters using numeric variables as shown in the previous looping example.

Ranges of Inactive Worksheets

As with the `Range` property, you can apply the `Cells` property to a worksheet that is not currently active:

```
Worksheets("Sheet1").Cells(2,3)
```

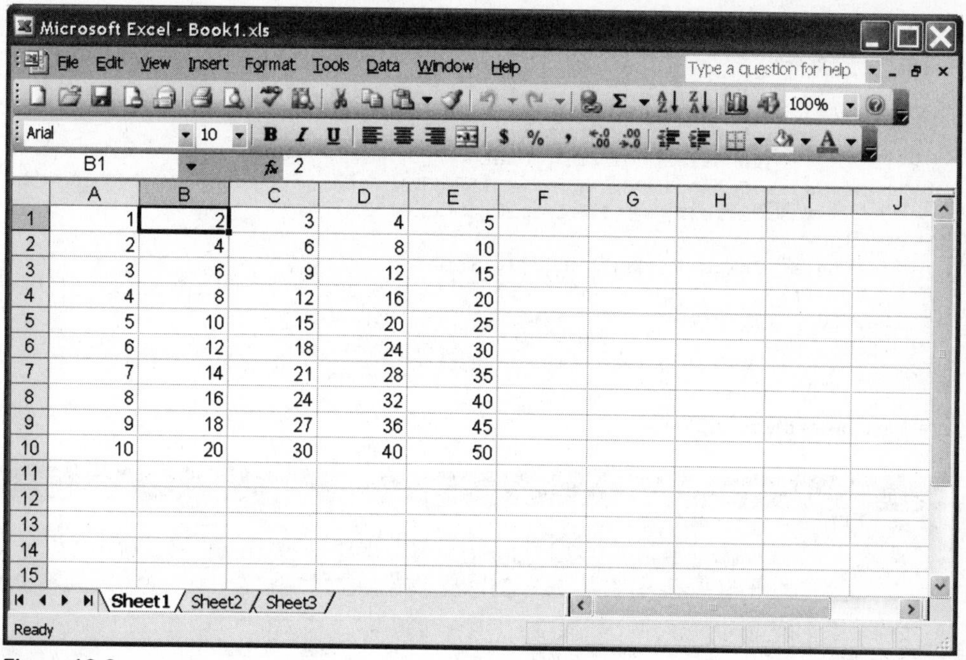

Figure 19-2

If you want to refer to a block of cells on an inactive worksheet using the `Cells` property, the same precautions apply as with the `Range` property. You must make sure you qualify the `Cells` property fully. If Sheet2 is active, and you want to refer to the range A1:E10 on Sheet1, the following code will fail because `Cells(1,1)` and `Cells(10,5)` are properties of the active worksheet:

```
Sheets("Sheet1").Range(Cells(1,1), Cells(10,5)).Font.Bold = True
```

A `With...End With` construct is an efficient way to incorporate the correct sheet reference:

```
With Sheets("Sheet1")
   .Range(.Cells(1, 1), .Cells(10, 5)).Font.Bold = True
End With
```

More on the Cells Property of the Range Object

The `Cells` property of a `Range` object provides a nice way to refer to cells relative to a starting cell, or within a block of cells. The following refers to cell F11:

```
Range("D10:G20").Cells(2,3)
```

If you want to examine a range with the name `SalesData` and color any figure under 100 red, you can use the following code:

```
Public Sub ColorCells()
   Dim Sales As Range
```

```
    Dim I As Long
    Dim J As Long

    Set Sales = Range("SalesData")
    For I = 1 To Sales.Rows.Count
      For J = 1 To Sales.Columns.Count
        If Sales.Cells(I, J).Value < 100 Then
          Sales.Cells(I, J).Font.ColorIndex = 3
        Else
          Sales.Cells(I, J).Font.ColorIndex = 1
        End If
      Next J
    Next I
  End Sub
```

Figure 19-3 shows the result:

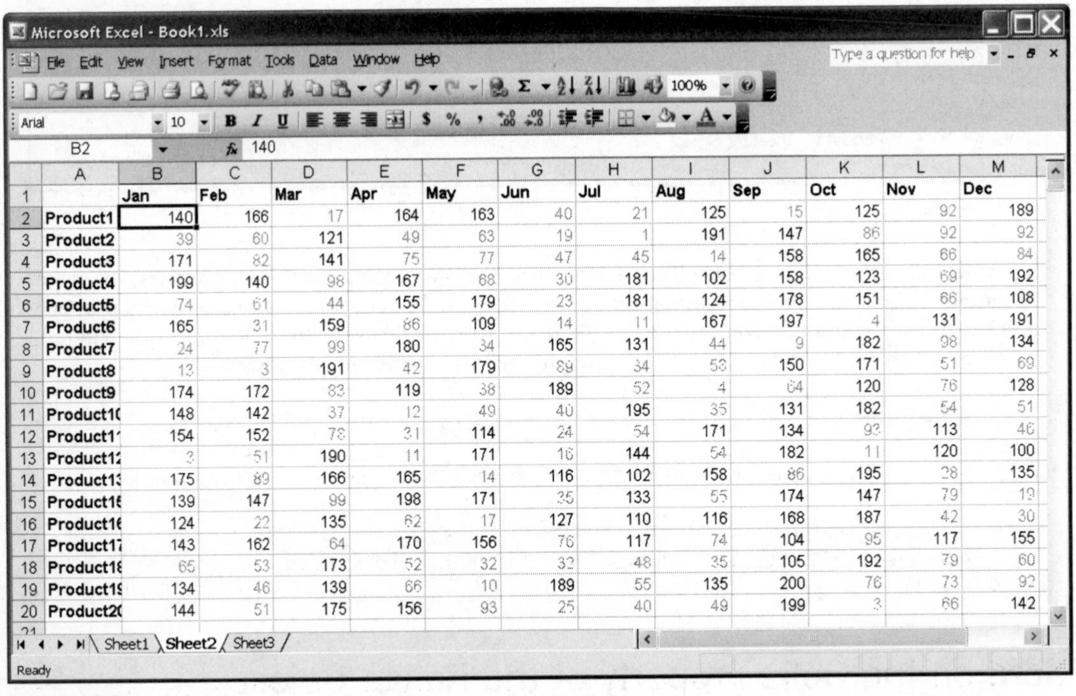

	A	B	C	D	E	F	G	H	I	J	K	L	M
1		Jan	Feb	Mar	Apr	May	Jun	Jul	Aug	Sep	Oct	Nov	Dec
2	Product1	140	166	17	164	163	40	21	125	15	125	92	189
3	Product2	39	60	121	49	63	19	1	191	147	86	92	92
4	Product3	171	82	141	75	77	47	45	14	158	165	66	84
5	Product4	199	140	98	167	68	30	181	102	158	123	69	192
6	Product5	74	61	44	155	179	23	181	124	178	151	66	108
7	Product6	165	31	159	86	109	14	11	167	197	4	131	191
8	Product7	24	77	99	180	34	165	131	44	9	182	98	134
9	Product8	13	3	191	42	179	89	34	53	150	171	51	69
10	Product9	174	172	83	119	38	189	52	4	64	120	76	128
11	Product1(	148	142	37	12	49	40	195	35	131	182	54	51
12	Product1'	154	152	78	31	114	24	54	171	134	93	113	46
13	Product1:	3	51	190	11	171	16	144	54	182	11	120	100
14	Product1:	175	89	166	165	14	116	102	158	86	195	28	135
15	Product1{	139	147	99	198	171	35	133	55	174	147	79	19
16	Product1(	124	22	135	62	17	127	110	116	168	187	42	30
17	Product1;	143	162	64	170	156	76	117	74	104	95	117	155
18	Product1{	65	53	173	52	32	32	48	35	105	192	79	60
19	Product1{	134	46	139	66	10	189	55	135	200	76	73	92
20	Product2(	144	51	175	156	93	25	40	49	199	3	66	142

Figure 19-3

It is not, in fact, necessary to confine the referenced cells to the contents of the `Range` object. You can reference cells outside the original range. This means that you really only need to use the top-left cell of the `Range` object as a starting point. This code refers to F11, as in the earlier example:

```
Range("D10").Cells(2,3)
```

You can also use a shortcut version of this form of reference. The following is also a reference to cell F11:

```
Range("D10")(2,3)
```

Technically, this works because it is an allowable shortcut for the Item property of the Range object, rather than the Cells property, as described previously:

```
Range("D10").Item(2,3)
```

It is even possible to use zero or negative subscripts, as long as you don't attempt to reference outside the worksheet boundaries. This can lead to some odd results. The following code refers to cell C9:

```
Range("D10")(0,0)
```

The following refers to B8:

```
Range("D10")(-1,-1)
```

The previous Font.ColorIndex example using Sales can be written as follows, using this technique:

```
Public Sub ColorCells()
  Dim Sales As Range
  Dim i As Long
  Dim j As Long

  Set Sales = Range("SalesData")
  For i = 1 To Sales.Rows.Count
    For j = 1 To Sales.Columns.Count
      If Sales(i, j).Value < 100 Then
        Sales(i, j).Font.ColorIndex = 4
      Else
        Sales(i, j).Font.ColorIndex = 1
      End If
    Next j
  Next i
End Sub
```

There is actually a small increase in speed, if you adopt this shortcut. Running the second example, the increase is about 5% on my PC when compared to the first example.

Single-Parameter Range Reference

The shortcut range reference accepts a single parameter as well as two. If you are using this technique with a range with more than one row, and the index exceeds the number of columns in the range, the reference wraps within the columns of the range, down to the appropriate row.

The following refers to cell E10:

```
Range("D10:E11")(2)
```

The following refers to cell D11:

```
Range("D10:E11")(3)
```

The index can exceed the number of cells in the Range object and the reference will continue to wrap within the Range object's columns. The following refers to cell D12:

```
Range("D10:E11")(5)
```

Qualifying a Range object with a single parameter is useful when you want to step through all the cells in a range without having to separately track rows and columns. The ColorCells example can be further rewritten as follows, using this technique:

```
Public Sub ColorCells()
    Dim Sales As Range
    Dim i As Long

    Set Sales = Range("SalesData")
        For i = 1 To Sales.Cells.Count
            If Sales(i).Value < 100 Then
                Sales(i).Font.ColorIndex = 5
            Else
                Sales(i).Font.ColorIndex = 1
            End If
    Next i
End Sub
```

In the fourth and final variation on the ColorCells theme, you can step through all the cells in a range using a For Each...Next loop, if you do not need the index value of the For...Next loop for other purposes:

```
Public Sub ColorCells()
    Dim aRange As Range

    For Each aRange In Range("SalesData")
        If aRange.Value < 100 Then
            aRange.Font.ColorIndex = 6
        Else
            aRange.Font.ColorIndex = 1
        End If
    Next aRange
End Sub
```

Offset Property

The Offset property of the Range object returns a similar object to the Cells property, but is different in two ways. The first difference is that the Offset parameters are zero based, rather than one based, as the term "offset" implies. These examples both refer to the A10 cell:

```
Range("A10").Cells(1,1)
Range("A10").Offset(0,0)
```

The second difference is that the Range object generated by Cells consists of one cell. The Range object referred to by the Offset property of a range has the same number of rows and columns as the original range. The following refers to B2:C3:

```
Range("A1:B2").Offset(1,1)
```

Offset is useful when you want to refer to ranges of equal sizes with a changing base point. For example, you might have sales figures for January to December in B1:B12 and want to generate a three-month moving average from March to December in C3:C12. The code to achieve this is:

```
Public Sub MoveAverage()
  Dim aRange As Range
  Dim i As Long

  Set aRange = Range("B1:B3")
  For i = 3 To 12
    Cells(i, "C").Value = WorksheetFunction.Round _
      (WorksheetFunction.Sum(aRange) / 3, 0)
    Set aRange = aRange.Offset(1, 0)
  Next i
End Sub
```

Figure 19-4 shows the result of running the code:

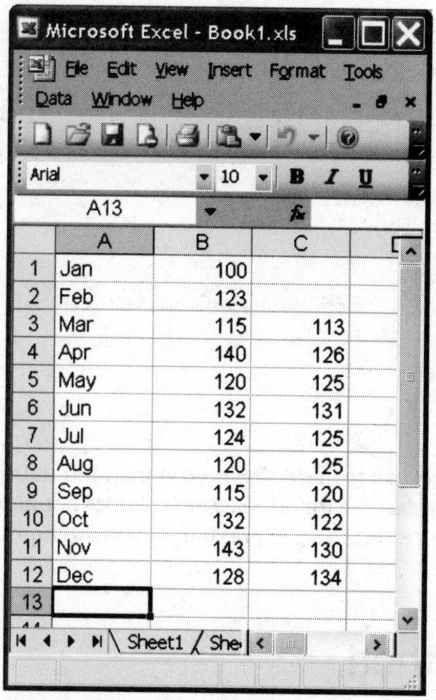

Figure 19-4

Resize Property

You can use the `Resize` property of the `Range` object to refer to a range with the same top left-hand corner as the original range, but with a different number of rows and columns. The following refers to D10:E10:

```
Range("D10:F20").Resize(1,2)
```

`Resize` is useful when you want to extend or reduce a range by a row or column. For example, if you have a data list, which has been given the name `Database`, and you have just added another row at the bottom, you need to redefine the name to include the extra row. The following code extends the name by the extra row:

```
With Range("Database")
   .Resize(.Rows.Count + 1).Name = "Database"
End With
```

When you omit the second parameter, the number of columns remains unchanged. Similarly, you can omit the first parameter to leave the number of rows unchanged. The following refers to A1:C10:

```
Range("A1:B10").Resize(, 3)
```

You can use the following code to search for a value in a list and, having found it, copy it and the two columns to the right to a new location. The code to do this is:

```
Public Sub FindIt()
  Dim aRange As Range

  Set aRange = Range("A1:A12").Find(What:="Jun", _
    LookAt:=xlWhole, LookIn:=xlValues)

  If aRange Is Nothing Then
    MsgBox "Data not found"
    Exit Sub
  Else
    aRange.Resize(1, 3).Copy Destination:=Range("G1")
  End If
End Sub
```

Figure 19-5 shows the result.

The `Find` method does not act like the Edit ⇨ Find command. It returns a reference to the found cell as a `Range` object but it does not select the found cell. If `Find` does not locate a match, it returns a `null` object that you can test for with the `Is Nothing` expression. If you attempt to copy the `null` object, a runtime error occurs.

SpecialCells Method

When you press the *F5* key in a worksheet, the Go To dialog box appears. You can then press the Special... button to show the dialog box in Figure 19-6.

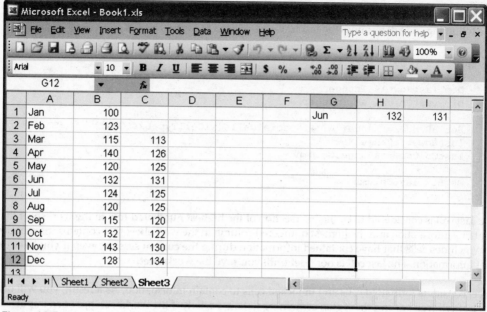

Figure 19-5

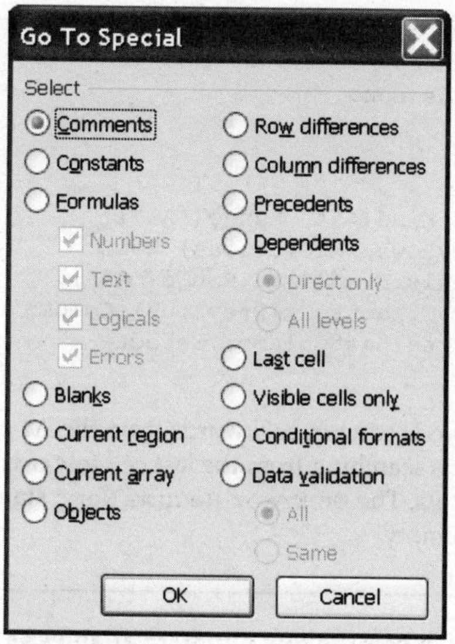

Figure 19-6

This dialog box allows you to do a number of useful things, such as find the last cell in the worksheet or all the cells with numbers rather than calculations. As you might expect, all these operations can be carried out in VBA code. Some have their own methods, but most of them can be performed using the `SpecialCells` method of the `Range` object.

Last Cell

The following code determines the last row and column in the worksheet:

```
Public Sub SelectLastCell()
   Dim aRange As Range
   Dim lastRow As Integer
   Dim lastColumn As Integer

   Set aRange = Range("A1").SpecialCells(xlCellTypeLastCell)
   lastRow = aRange.Row
   lastColumn = aRange.Column

   MsgBox lastColumn
End Sub
```

The last cell is considered to be the intersection of the highest numbered row in the worksheet that contains information and the highest numbered column in the worksheet that contains information. Excel also includes cells that have contained information during the current session, even if you have deleted that information. The last cell is not reset until you save the worksheet.

Excel considers formatted cells and unlocked cells to contain information. As a result, you will often find the last cell well beyond the region containing data, especially if the workbook has been imported from another spreadsheet application, such as Lotus 1-2-3. If you want to consider only cells that contain data in the form of numbers, text, and formulas, you can use the following code:

```
Public Sub GetRealLastCell()
   Dim realLastRow As Long
   Dim realLastColumn As Long
   Range("A1").Select

   On Error Resume Next
   realLastRow = Cells.Find("*", Range("A1"), _
      xlFormulas, , xlByRows, xlPrevious).Row
   realLastColumn = Cells.Find("*", Range("A1"), _
      xlFormulas, , xlByColumns, xlPrevious).Column
   Cells(realLastRow, realLastColumn).Select
End Sub
```

In this example, the Find method searches backwards from the A1 cell (which means that Excel wraps around the worksheet and starts searching from the last cell towards the A1 cell) to find the last row and column containing any characters. The On Error Resume Next statement is used to prevent a runtime error when the spreadsheet is empty.

> Note that it is necessary to **Dim** the row number variables as **Long**, rather than **Integer**, as integers can only be as high as 32,767 and worksheets can contain 65,536 rows.

If you want to get rid of the extra rows containing formats, you should select the entire rows, by selecting their row numbers, and then use Edit ⇨ Delete to remove them. You can also select the unnecessary columns by their column letters, and delete them. At this point, the last cell will not be reset. You can save the worksheet to reset the last cell, or execute `ActiveSheet.UsedRange` in your code to perform a reset. The following code will remove extraneous rows and columns and reset the last cell:

```
Public Sub DeleteUnusedFormats()
  Dim lastRow As Long
  Dim lastColumn As Long
  Dim realLastRow As Long
  Dim realLastColumn As Long

  With Range("A1").SpecialCells(xlCellTypeLastCell)
    lastRow = .Row
    lastColumn = .Column
  End With

  realLastRow = Cells.Find("*", Range("A1"), _
    xlFormulas, , xlByRows, xlPrevious).Row

  realLastColumn = Cells.Find("*", Range("A1"), _
    xlFormulas, , xlByColumns, xlPrevious).Column

  If realLastRow < lastRow Then
    Range(Cells(realLastRow + 1, 1), _
      Cells(lastRow, 1)).EntireRow.Delete
  End If
  If realLastColumn < lastColumn Then
    Range(Cells(1, realLastColumn + 1), _
      Cells(1, lastColumn)).EntireColumn.Delete
  End If

  ActiveSheet.UsedRange
End Sub
```

The `EntireRow` property of a `Range` object refers to a `Range` object that spans the entire spreadsheet, that is, columns 1 to 256 (or A to IV on the rows contained in the original range. The `EntireColumn` property of a `Range` object refers to a `Range` object that spans the entire spreadsheet (rows 1 to 65536) in the columns contained in the original object).

Deleting Numbers

Sometimes it is useful to delete all the input data in a worksheet or template so that it is more obvious where new values are required. The following code deletes all the numbers in a worksheet, leaving the formulas intact:

```
On Error Resume Next
Cells.SpecialCells(xlCellTypeConstants, xlNumbers).ClearContents
```

> The preceding code should be preceded by the **On Error** statement if you want to prevent a runtime error when there are no numbers to be found.

Excel considers dates as numbers and they will be cleared by the previous code. If you have used dates as headings and want to avoid this, you can use the following code:

```
Public Sub ClearNonDateCells()
  Dim aRange As Range
  For Each aRange In Cells.SpecialCells(xlCellTypeConstants, xlNumbers)
    If Not IsDate(aRange.Value) Then aRange.ClearContents
  Next aRange
End Sub
```

CurrentRegion Property

If you have tables of data that are separated from the surrounding data by at least one empty row and one empty column, you can select an individual table using the CurrentRegion property of any cell in the table. It is equivalent to the manual *Ctrl+Shift+** keyboard shortcut. In the worksheet in Figure 19-7, you could select the Bananas table by clicking the A9 cell and pressing *Ctrl+Shift+**:

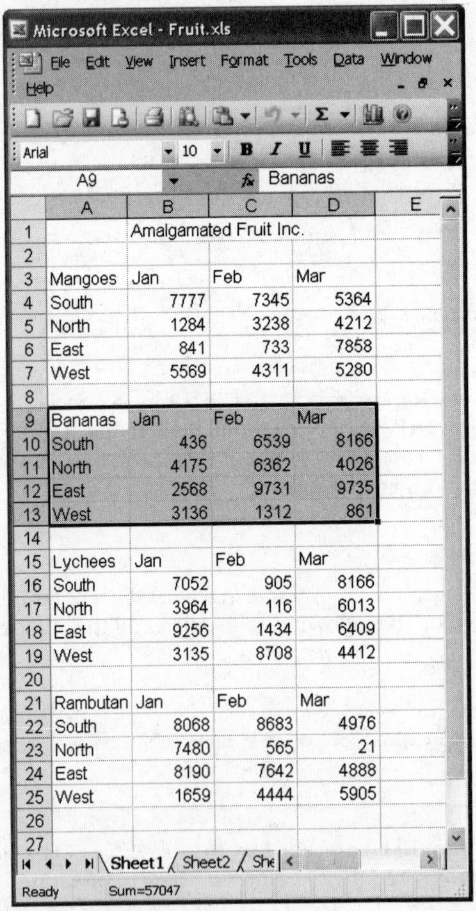

Figure 19-7

424

The same result can be achieved with the following code, given that cell A9 has been named Bananas:

```
Range("Bananas").CurrentRegion.Select
```

This property is very useful for tables that change size over time. You can select all the months up to the current month as the table grows during the year, without having to change the code each month. Naturally, in your code, there is rarely any need to select anything. If you want to perform a consolidation of the fruit figures into a single table in a sheet called Consolidation, and you have named the top-left corner of each table with the product name, you can use the following code:

```
Public Sub Consolidate()
  Dim Products As Variant
  Dim Source As Range
  Dim Destination As Range
  Dim i As Long

  Application.ScreenUpdating = False
  Products = Array("Mangoes", "Bananas", "Lychees", "Rambutan")
  Set Destination = Worksheets("Consolidation").Range("B4")
  For i = LBound(Products) To UBound(Products)
    With Range(Products(i)).CurrentRegion
      Set Source = .Offset(1, 1).Resize(.Rows.Count - 1, .Columns.Count - 1)
    End With
    Source.Copy
    If i = LBound(Products) Then
      Destination.PasteSpecial xlPasteValues, xlPasteSpecialOperationNone
    Else
      Destination.PasteSpecial xlPasteValues, xlPasteSpecialOperationAdd
    End If
  Next i
  Application.CutCopyMode = False 'Clear the clipboard
End Sub
```

Figure 19-8 shows the output:

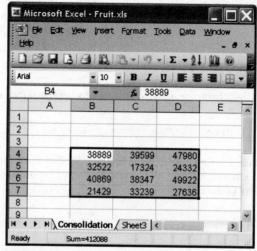

Figure 19-8

Screen updating is suppressed to cut out screen flicker and speed up the macro. The `Array` function is a convenient way to define relatively short lists of items to be processed. The `LBound` and `UBound` functions are used to avoid worrying about which `Option Base` has been set in the declarations section of the module. The code can be reused in other modules without a problem.

The first product is copied and its values are pasted over any existing values in the destination cells. The other products are copied and their values added to the destination cells. The clipboard is cleared at the end to prevent users accidentally carrying out another paste by pressing the *Enter* key.

End Property

The End property emulates the operation of *Ctrl+Arrow* key. If you have selected a cell at the top of a column of data, *Ctrl+Down Arrow* takes you to the next item of data in the column that is before an empty cell. If there are no empty cells in the column, you go to the last data item in the column. If the cell after the selected cell is empty, you jump to the next cell with data, if there is one, or the bottom of the worksheet.

The following code refers to the last data cell at the bottom of column A if there are no empty cells between it and A1:

```
Range("A1").End(xlDown)
```

To go in other directions, you use the constants `xlUp`, `xlToLeft`, and `xlToRight`.

If there are gaps in the data, and you want to refer to the last cell in column A, you can start from the bottom of the worksheet and go up, as long as data does not extend as far as A65536:

```
Range("A65536").End(xlUp)
```

In the section on rows, later in this chapter, you will see a way to avoid the A65536 reference and generalize the code above for different versions of Excel.

Referring to Ranges with End

You can refer to a range of cells from the active cell to the end of the same column with:

```
Range(ActiveCell, ActiveCell.End(xlDown)).Select
```

Say, you have a table of data, starting at cell B3, which is separated from the surrounding data by an empty row and an empty column. You can refer to the table, as long as it has continuous headings across the top and continuous data in the last column, using this line of code:

```
Range("B3", Range("B3").End(xlToRight).End(xlDown)).Select
```

The effect, in this case, is the same as using the `CurrentRegion` property, but `End` has many more uses as you will see in the following examples.

As usual, there is no need to select anything if you want to operate on a `Range` object in VBA. The following code copies the continuous headings across the top of Sheet1 to the top of Sheet2:

```
With Worksheets("Sheet1").Range("A1")
  .Range(.Cells(1), .End(xlToRight)).Copy Destination:= _
  Worksheets("Sheet2").Range("A1")
End With
```

This code can be executed, no matter what sheet is active, as long as the workbook is active.

Summing a Range

Suppose you want to place a SUM function in the active cell to add the values of the cells below it, down to the next empty cell. You can do that with the following code:

```
With ActiveCell
  Set aRange = Range(.Offset(1), .Offset(1).End(xlDown))
  .Formula = "=SUM(" & aRange.Address & ")"
End With
```

The `Address` property of the `Range` object returns an absolute address by default. If you want to be able to copy the formula to other cells and sum the data below them, you can change the address to a relative one and perform the copy as follows:

```
Public Sub SumRangeTest()
  Dim aRange As Range

  With ActiveCell
    Set aRange = Range(.Offset(1), .Offset(1).End(xlDown))
    .Formula = "=SUM(" & aRange.Address(RowAbsolute:=False, _
      ColumnAbsolute:=False) & ")"
    .Copy Destination:=Range(.Cells(1), .Offset(1).End(xlToRight).Offset(-1))
  End With

End Sub
```

The end of the destination range is determined by dropping down a row from the SUM, finding the last data column to the right, and popping back up a row.

Figure 19-9 shows the results:

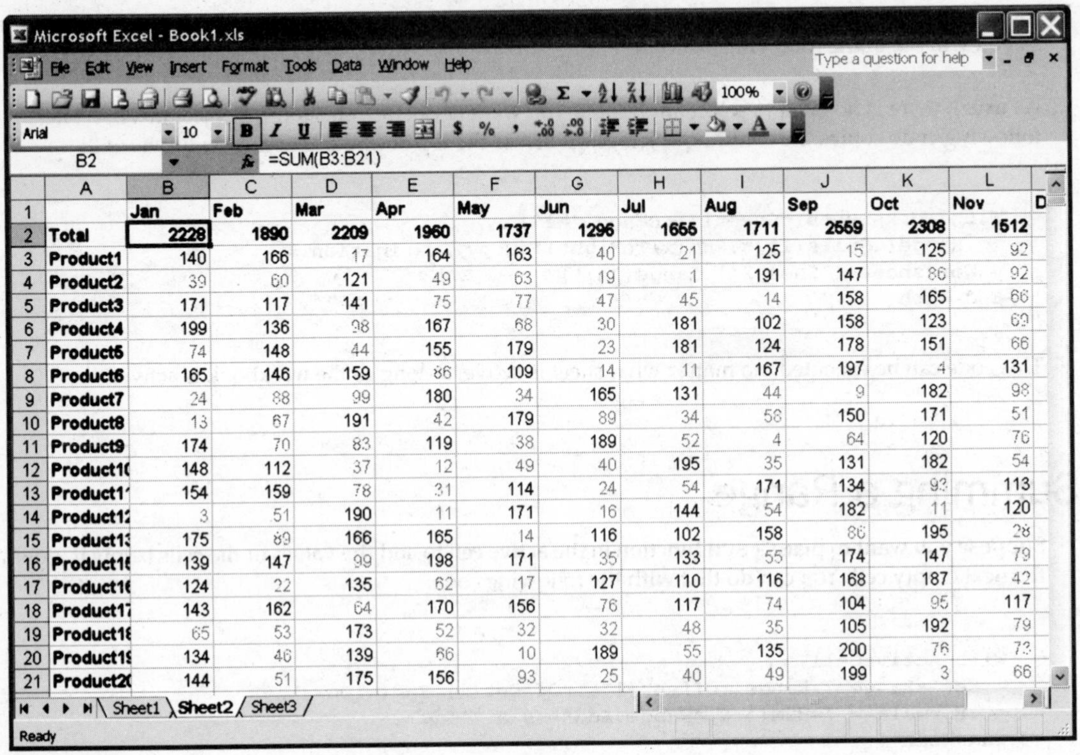

Figure 19-9

Columns and Rows Properties

Columns and Rows are properties of the Application, Worksheet, and Range objects. They return a reference to all the columns or rows in a worksheet or range. In each case, the reference returned is a Range object, but this Range object has some odd characteristics that might make you think there are such things as a "Column object" and a "Row object", which do not exist in Excel. They are useful when you want to count the number of rows or columns, or process all the rows or columns of a range.

Excel 97 increased the number of worksheet rows from the 16,384 in previous versions to 65,536. If you want to write code to detect the number of rows in the active sheet, you can use the Count property of Rows:

```
Rows.Count
```

This is useful if you need a macro that will work with all versions of Excel VBA, and detect the last row of data in a column, working from the bottom of the worksheet:

```
Cells(Rows.Count, "A").End(xlUp).Select
```

If you have a multicolumn table of data in a range named SalesData, and you want to step through each row of the table making every cell in each row bold where the first cell is greater than 1000, you can use:

```
Public Sub BoldCells()
    Dim Row As Object
```

```
    For Each Row In Range("SalesData").Rows
        If Row.Cells(1).Value > 1000 Then
            Row.Font.Bold = True
        Else
            Row.Font.Bold = False
        End If
    Next Row

End Sub
```

This gives us the results shown in Figure 19-10:

	A	B	C	D	E	F	G	H	I	J	K	L	
		Jan	Feb	Mar	Apr	May	Jun	Jul	Aug	Sep	Oct	Nov	C
1													
2	Total	2228	1890	2209	1960	1737	1296	1655	1711	2559	2308	1512	
3	Product1	140	166	17	164	163	40	21	125	15	125	92	
4	Product2	39	60	121	49	63	19	1	191	147	86	92	
5	Product3	171	117	141	75	77	47	45	14	158	165	66	
6	Product4	199	136	98	167	68	30	181	102	158	123	69	
7	Product5	74	148	44	155	179	23	181	124	178	151	66	
8	Product6	165	146	159	86	109	14	11	167	197	4	131	
9	Product7	24	88	99	180	34	165	131	44	9	182	98	
10	Product8	13	67	191	42	179	89	34	58	150	171	51	
11	Product9	174	70	83	119	38	189	52	4	64	120	76	
12	Product10	148	112	37	12	49	40	195	35	131	182	54	
13	Product11	154	159	78	31	114	24	54	171	134	93	113	
14	Product12	3	51	190	11	171	16	144	54	182	11	120	
15	Product13	175	89	166	165	14	116	102	158	86	195	28	
16	Product15	139	147	99	198	171	35	133	55	174	147	79	
17	Product16	124	22	135	62	17	127	110	116	168	187	42	
18	Product17	143	162	64	170	156	76	117	74	104	95	117	
19	Product18	65	53	173	52	32	32	48	35	105	192	79	
20	Product19	134	46	139	66	10	189	55	135	200	76	73	
21	Product20	144	51	175	156	93	25	40	49	199	3	66	

Figure 19-10

Curiously, you cannot replace `Row.Cells(1)` with `Row(1)`, as you can with a normal `Range` object as it causes a runtime error. It seems that there is something special about the `Range` object referred to by the `Rows` and `Columns` properties. You may find it helps to think of them as `Row` and `Column` objects, even though such objects do not officially exist.

Areas

You need to be careful when using the `Columns` or `Rows` properties of non-contiguous ranges, such as those returned from the `SpecialCells` method when locating the numeric cells or blank cells in a worksheet, for example. Recall that a non-contiguous range consists of a number of separate rectangular blocks. If the cells are not all in one block, and you use the `Rows.Count` properties, you only count the rows from the first block. The following code generates an answer of 5, because only the first range, A1:B5, is evaluated:

```
Range("A1:B5,C6:D10,E11:F15").Rows.Count
```

The blocks in a non-contiguous range are Range objects contained within the Areas collection and can be processed separately. The following displays the address of each of the three blocks in the Range object, one at a time:

```
For Each aRange In Range("A1:B5,C6:D10,E11:F15").Areas
   MsgBox aRange.Address
Next Rng
```

The worksheet shown next contains sales estimates that have been entered as numbers. The cost figures are calculated by formulas. The following code copies all the numeric constants in the active sheet to blocks in Sheet3, leaving an empty row between each block:

```
Public Sub CopyAreas()
   Dim aRange As Range
   Dim Destination As Range

   Set Destination = Worksheets("Sheet3").Range("A1")
   For Each aRange In Cells.SpecialCells( _
     xlCellTypeConstants, xlNumbers).Areas

     aRange.Copy Destination:=Destination
     Set Destination = Destination.Offset(aRange.Rows.Count + 1)

   Next aRange
End Sub
```

This gives us the results in Figure 19-11 and Figure 19-12:

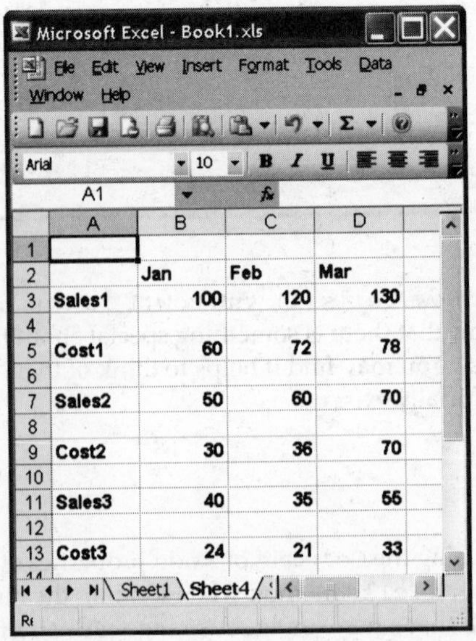

Figure 19-11

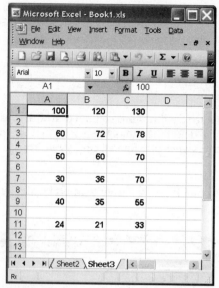

Figure 19-12

Union and Intersect Methods

Union and Intersect are methods of the Application object, but they can be used without preceding them with a reference to Application as they are members of <globals>. They can be very useful tools, as we shall see.

You use Union when you want to generate a range from two or more blocks of cells. You use Intersect when you want to find the cells that are common to two or more ranges, or in other words, where the ranges overlap. The following event procedure, entered in the module behind a worksheet, illustrates how you can apply the two methods to prevent a user selecting cells in two ranges B10:F20 and H10:L20. One use for this routine is to prevent a user from changing data in these two blocks:

```
Private Sub Worksheet_SelectionChange(ByVal Target As Range)
   Dim Forbidden As Range

   Set Forbidden = Union(Range("B10:F20"), Range("H10:L20"))
   If Intersect(Target, Forbidden) Is Nothing Then Exit Sub
   Range("A1").Select
   MsgBox "You can't select cells in " & Forbidden.Address, vbCritical
End Sub
```

If you are not familiar with event procedures, refer to the *Events* section in Chapter 2. For more information on event procedures see Chapter 10.

The Worksheet_SelectionChange event procedure is triggered every time the user selects a new range in the worksheet associated with the module containing the event procedure. The preceding code uses the Union method to define a forbidden range consisting of the two non-contiguous ranges. It then uses the Intersect method, in the If test, to see if the Target range, which is the new user selection, is within the forbidden range. `Intersect` returns `Nothing` if there is no overlap and the `Sub` exits. If there is an overlap, the code in the two lines following the `If` test are executed—cell A1 is selected and a warning message is issued to the user.

Empty Cells

You have seen that if you want to step through a column or row of cells until you get to an empty cell, you can use the `End` property to detect the end of the block. Another way is to examine each cell, one at a time, in a loop structure and stop when you find an empty cell. You can test for an empty cell with the VBA `IsEmpty` function.

In the spreadsheet shown in Figure 19-13, you want to insert blank rows between each week to produce a report that is more readable.

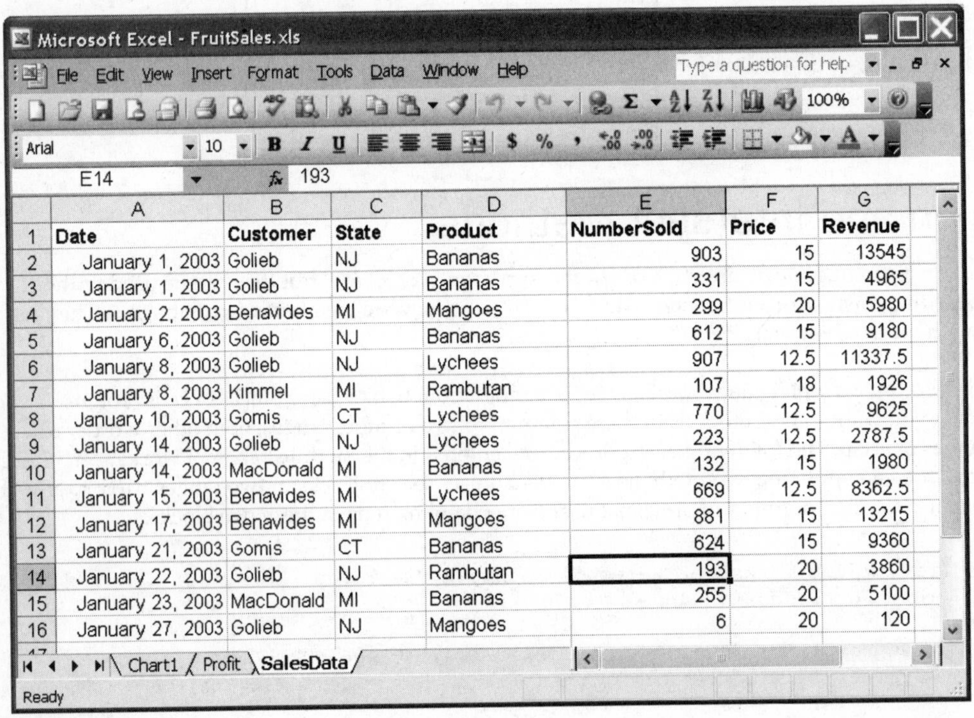

	A	B	C	D	E	F	G
1	Date	Customer	State	Product	NumberSold	Price	Revenue
2	January 1, 2003	Golieb	NJ	Bananas	903	15	13545
3	January 1, 2003	Golieb	NJ	Bananas	331	15	4965
4	January 2, 2003	Benavides	MI	Mangoes	299	20	5980
5	January 6, 2003	Golieb	NJ	Bananas	612	15	9180
6	January 8, 2003	Golieb	NJ	Lychees	907	12.5	11337.5
7	January 8, 2003	Kimmel	MI	Rambutan	107	18	1926
8	January 10, 2003	Gomis	CT	Lychees	770	12.5	9625
9	January 14, 2003	Golieb	NJ	Lychees	223	12.5	2787.5
10	January 14, 2003	MacDonald	MI	Bananas	132	15	1980
11	January 15, 2003	Benavides	MI	Lychees	669	12.5	8362.5
12	January 17, 2003	Benavides	MI	Mangoes	881	15	13215
13	January 21, 2003	Gomis	CT	Bananas	624	15	9360
14	January 22, 2003	Golieb	NJ	Rambutan	193	20	3860
15	January 23, 2003	MacDonald	MI	Bananas	255	20	5100
16	January 27, 2003	Golieb	NJ	Mangoes	6	20	120

Figure 19-13

The following macro compares dates, using the VBA `Weekday` function to get the day of the week as a number. By default, Sunday is day 1 and Saturday is day 7. If the macro finds today's day number is less than yesterday's, it assumes a new week has started and inserts a blank row:

```
Public Sub ShowWeeks()
   Dim Today As Integer
   Dim Yesterday As Integer
```

```
    Range("A2").Select
    Yesterday = Weekday(ActiveCell.Value)
    Do Until IsEmpty(ActiveCell.Value)
      ActiveCell.Offset(1, 0).Select
      Today = Weekday(ActiveCell.Value)
      If Today < Yesterday Then
        ActiveCell.EntireRow.Insert

        ActiveCell.Offset(1, 0).Select
      End If
      Yesterday = Today
    Loop
End Sub
```

The result is shown in Figure 19-14.

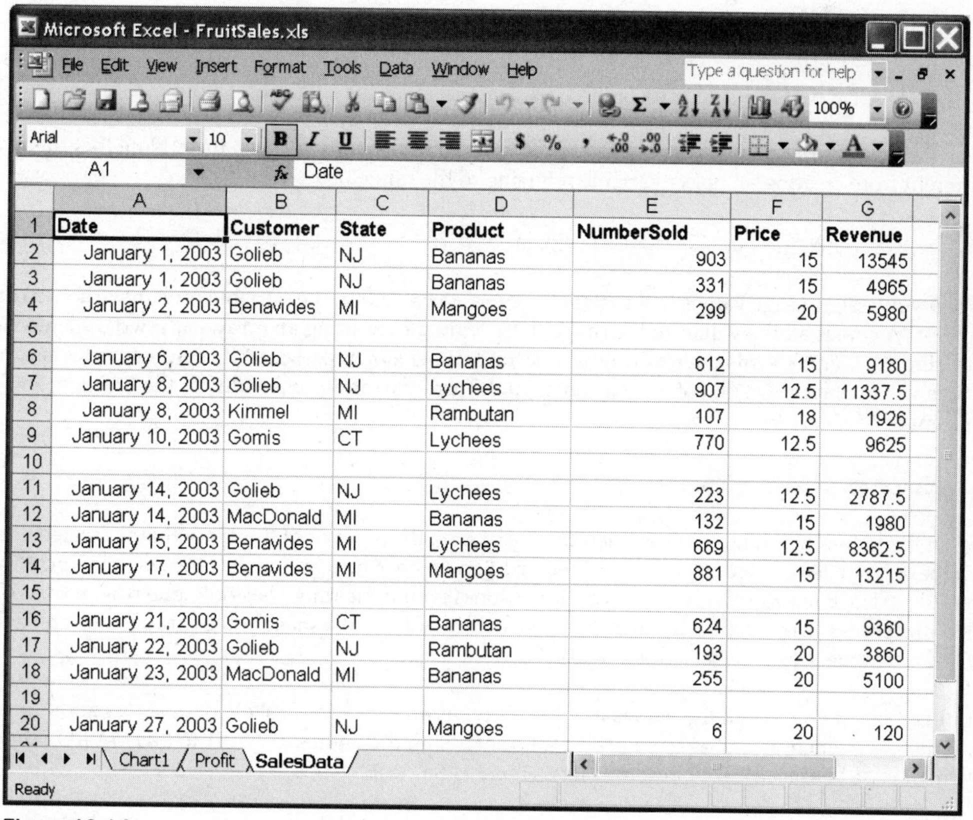

Figure 19-14

Note that many users detect an empty cell by testing for a zero length string:

```
Do Until ActiveCell.Value = ""
```

This test works in most cases, and would have worked in the previous example, had we used it. However, problems can occur if you are testing cells that contain formulas that can produce zero length strings, such as the following:

```
=IF(B2="Golieb","Trainee","")
```

The zero length string test does not distinguish between an empty cell and a zero length string resulting from a formula. It is better practice to use the VBA IsEmpty function when testing for an empty cell.

Transferring Values between Arrays and Ranges

If you want to process all the data values in a range, it is much more efficient to assign the values to a VBA array and process the array rather than process the Range object itself. You can then assign the array back to the range.

You can assign the values in a range to an array very easily, as follows:

```
SalesData = Range("A2:F10000").Value
```

The transfer is very fast compared with stepping through the cells, one at a time. Note that this is quite different from creating an object variable referring to the range using

```
Set SalesData = Range("A2:F10000")
```

When you assign range values to a variable such as SalesData, the variable must have a Variant data type. VBA copies all the values in the range to the variable, creating an array with two dimensions. The first dimension represents the rows and the second dimension represents the columns, so you can access the values by their row and column numbers in the array. To assign the value in the first row and second column of the array to Customer, use

```
Customer = SalesData(1, 2)
```

When the values in a range are assigned to a Variant, the indexes of the array that is created are always one-based, not zero-based, regardless of the Option Base setting in the declarations section of the module. Also, the array always has two dimensions, even if the range has only one row or one column. This preserves the inherent column and row structure of the worksheet in the array and is an advantage when you write the array back to the worksheet.

For example, if you assign the values in A1:A10 to SalesData, the first element is SalesData(1,1) and the last element is SalesData(10,1). If you assign the values in A1:E1 to SalesData, the first element is SalesData(1,1) and the last element is SalesData(1,5).

You might want a macro that sums all the Revenues for Golieb in our last example. The following macro uses the traditional method to directly test and sum the range of data:

```
Public Sub GoliebToAll()
    Dim Total As Double
    Dim i As Long
```

```
    With Range("A2:G20")
       For i = 1 To .Rows.Count
          If .Cells(i, 2) = "Golieb" Then Total = Total + .Cells(i, 7)
       Next i
    End With
    MsgBox "Golieb Total = " & Format(Total, "$#,##0")
End Sub
```

The following macro does the same job by first assigning the Range values to a Variant and processing the resulting array. The speed increase is very significant. It can be fifty times faster, which can be a great advantage if you are handling large ranges:

```
Public Sub GoliebTotal2()
    Dim SalesData As Variant
    Dim Total As Double
    Dim i As Long

    SalesData = Range("A2:G20").Value
    For i = 1 To UBound(SalesData, 1)
       If SalesData(i, 2) = "Golieb" Then Total = Total + SalesData(i, 7)
    Next i
    Call MsgBox("Golieb Total = " & Format(Total, "$#,##0"))
End Sub
```

You can also assign an array of values directly to a Range. Say, you want to place a list of numbers in column H of the FruitSales.xls example above, containing a 10 % discount on Revenue for customer Golieb only. The following macro, once again, assigns the range values to a Variant for processing:

```
Public Sub GoliebDiscount()
    Dim SalesData As Variant
    Dim Discount() As Variant
    Dim i As Long

    SalesData = Range("A2:G20").Value
    ReDim Discount(1 To UBound(SalesData, 1), 1 To 1)
    For i = 1 To UBound(SalesData, 1)
       If SalesData(i, 2) = "Golieb" Then
          Discount(i, 1) = SalesData(i, 7) * 0.1
       End If
    Next i
    Range("H2").Resize(UBound(SalesData, 1), 1).Value = Discount
End Sub
```

The code sets up a dynamic array called Discount, which it ReDims to the number of rows in SalesData and one column, so that it retains a two-dimensional structure like a range, even though there is only one column. After the values have been assigned to Discount, Discount is directly assigned to the range in column H. Note that it is necessary to specify the correct size of the range receiving the values, not just the first cell as in a worksheet copy operation.

The outcome of this operation is shown in Figure 19-15.

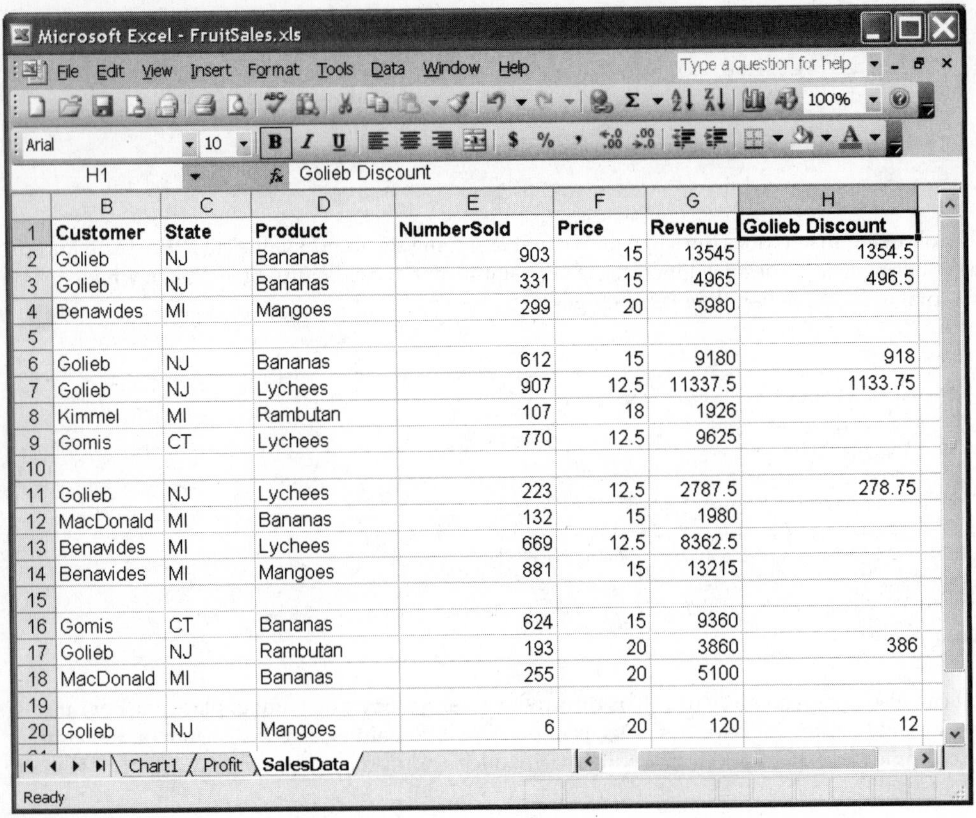

Figure 19-15

It is possible to use a one-dimensional array for `Discount`. However, if you assign the one-dimensional array to a range, it will be assumed to contain a row of data, not a column. It is possible to get around this by using the worksheet `Transpose` function when assigning the array to the range. Say, you have changed the dimensions of `Discount` as follows:

```
ReDim Discount(1 To Ubound(SalesData,1))
```

You could assign this version of `Discount` to a column with:

```
Range("H2").Resize(UBound(SalesData, 1), 1).Value = _
   WorkSheetFunction.Transpose(vaDiscount)
```

Deleting Rows

A commonly asked question is "What is the best way to delete rows that I do not need from a spreadsheet?" Generally, the requirement is to find the rows that have certain text in a given column and remove those rows. The best solution depends on how large the spreadsheet is and how many items are likely to be removed.

Say, that you want to remove all the rows that contain the text "Mangoes" in column D. One way to do this is to loop through all the rows, and test every cell in column D. If you do this, it is better to test the last row first and work up the worksheet row by row. This is more efficient because Excel does not have to move any rows up that would later be deleted, which would not be the case if you worked from the top down. Also, if you work from the top down, you can't use a simple For...Next loop counter to keep track of the row you are on because, as you delete rows, the counter and the row numbers no longer correspond:

```
Public Sub DeleteRows1()
    Dim i As Long
    Application.ScreenUpdating = False
    For i = Cells(Rows.Count, "D").End(xlUp).Row To 1 Step -1
        If Cells(i, "D").Value = "Mangoes" Then Cells(i, "D").EntireRow.Delete
    Next i
End Sub
```

A good programming principle to follow is this: if there is an Excel spreadsheet technique you can utilize, it is likely to be more efficient than a VBA emulation of the same technique, such as the For...Next loop used here.

Excel VBA programmers, especially when they do not have a strong background in the user interface features of Excel, often fall into the trap of writing VBA code to perform tasks that Excel can handle already. For example, you can write a VBA procedure to work through a sorted list of items, inserting rows with subtotals. You can also use VBA to execute the Subtotal method of the Range object. The second method is much easier to code and it executes in a fraction of the time taken by the looping procedure.

> It is much better to use VBA to harness the power built into Excel than to re-invent existing Excel functionality.

However, it isn't always obvious which Excel technique is the best one to employ. A fairly obvious Excel contender to locate the cells to be deleted, without having to examine every row using VBA code, is the Edit → Find command. The following code uses the Find method to reduce the number of cycles spent in VBA loops:

```
Public Sub DeleteRows2()
    Dim FoundCell As Range
    Application.ScreenUpdating = False
    Set FoundCell = Range("D:D").Find(what:="Mangoes")
    Do Until FoundCell Is Nothing
        FoundCell.EntireRow.Delete
        Set FoundCell = Range("D:D").FindNext
    Loop
End Sub
```

This code is faster than the first procedure when there are not many rows to be deleted. As the percentage increases, it becomes less efficient. Perhaps we need to look for a better Excel technique.

The fastest way to delete rows, that we are aware of, is provided by Excel's AutoFilter feature:

```
Public Sub DeleteRows3()
  Dim LastRow As Long
  Dim aRange As Range

  Application.ScreenUpdating = False
  Rows(1).Insert
  Range("D1").Value = "Temp"
  With ActiveSheet
    .UsedRange
    LastRow = .Cells.SpecialCells(xlCellTypeLastCell).Row
    Set aRange = Range("D1", Cells(LastRow, "D"))
    aRange.AutoFilter Field:=1, Criteria1:="Mangoes"
    aRange.SpecialCells(xlCellTypeVisible).EntireRow.Delete
    .UsedRange
  End With
End Sub
```

This is a bit more difficult to code, but it is significantly faster than the other methods, no matter how many rows are to be deleted. To use AutoFilter, you need to have field names at the top of your data. A dummy row is first inserted above the data and a dummy field name supplied for column D. The AutoFilter is only carried out on column D, which hides all the rows except those that have the text "Mangoes."

The SpecialCells method is used to select only the visible cells in column D. This is extended to the entire visible rows and they are deleted, including the dummy field name row. The AutoFilter is automatically turned off when the dummy row is deleted.

Summary

In this chapter we have seen the most important properties and methods that can be used to manage ranges of cells in a worksheet. The emphasis has been on those techniques that are difficult or impossible to discover using the macro recorder. The properties and methods discussed were:

- ❑ Activate method
- ❑ Cells property
- ❑ Columns and Rows properties
- ❑ CurrentRegion property
- ❑ End property
- ❑ Offset property
- ❑ Range property
- ❑ Resize property
- ❑ Select method
- ❑ SpecialCells method
- ❑ Union and Intersect methods

We have also seen how to assign a worksheet range of values to a VBA array for efficient processing, and how to assign a VBA array of data to a worksheet range.

This chapter has also emphasized that it is very rarely necessary to select cells or activate worksheets, which the macro recorder invariably does as it can only record what we do manually. Activating cells and worksheets is a very time-consuming process and should be avoided if we want our code to run at maximum speed.

The final examples showed that it is usually best to utilize Excel's existing capabilities, tapping into the Excel object model, rather than write a VBA-coded equivalent. And bear in mind, some Excel techniques are better than others. Experimentation might be necessary to get the best code when speed is important.

Using Names

One of the most useful features in Excel is the ability to create names. You can create a name using the Insert ➪ Name ➪ Define... dialog box. If the name refers to a range, you can create it by selecting the range, typing the name into the Name box at the left-hand side of the Formula Bar and pressing *Enter*. However, in Excel, names can refer to more than just ranges.

A name can contain a number, text, or a formula. Such a name has no visible location on the worksheet and can only be viewed in the Insert ➪ Name ➪ Define... dialog box. Therefore, you can use names to store information in a workbook without having to place the data in a worksheet cell. Names can be declared hidden so that they don't appear in the Insert ➪ Name ➪ Define... dialog box. This can be a useful way to keep the stored information unseen by users.

The normal use of names is to keep track of worksheet ranges. This is particularly useful for tables of data that vary in size. If you know that a certain name is used to define the range containing the data you want to work on, your VBA code can be much simpler than it might otherwise be. It is also relatively simple, given a few basic techniques, to change the definition of a name to allow for changes that you make to the tables in your code.

The Excel Object Model includes a Names collection and a Name object that can be used in VBA code. Names can be defined globally, at the workbook level, or they can be local, or worksheet-specific. If you create local names, you can repeat the same name on more than one worksheet in the workbook. To make a Name object worksheet-specific, you precede its Name property by the name of the worksheet and an exclamation mark. For example, you can type "Sheet1!Costs" into the top edit box of the Insert ➪ Name ➪ Define... dialog box to define a name Costs that is local to Sheet1 as shown in Figure 20-1.

When you display the Insert ➪ Name ➪ Define... dialog box you see the global names in the workbook and the local names for the active worksheet. The local names are identified by the worksheet name to the right of the name. If a local name is the same as a global name, you will only see the local name.

A great source of confusion with names is that they also have names. You need to distinguish between a Name object and the Name property of that object. The following code returns a reference

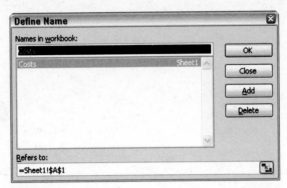

Figure 20-1

to a Name object in the Names collection:

```
Names("Costs")
```

If you want to change the Name property of a Name object, you use code like the following:

```
Names("Costs").Name = "NewData"
```

Having changed its Name property, you would now refer to this Name object as follows:

```
Names("NewData")
```

Global names and local names belong to the Names collection associated with the Workbook object. If you use a reference such as Application.Names or Names, you are referring to the Names collection for the active workbook. If you use a reference such as Workbooks("Book1.xls").Names, you are referring to the Names collection for that specific workbook.

Local names, but not global names, also belong to the Names collection associated with the WorkSheet object to which they are local. If you use a reference such as Worksheets("Sheet1").Names or ActiveSheet.Names, you are referring to the local Names collection for that worksheet.

There is also another way to refer to names that refer to ranges. You can use the Name property of the Range object. More on this later.

Naming Ranges

You can create a global name that refers to a range using the Add method of the Workbook object's Names collection:

```
Names.Add Name:="Data", RefersTo:="=Sheet1!$D$10:$D$12"
```

It is important to include the equals sign in front of the definition and to make the cell references absolute, using the $ signs. Otherwise, the name will refer to an address relative to the cell address that was active when the name was defined. You can omit the worksheet reference if you want the name to refer to the active worksheet:

```
Names.Add Name:="Data", RefersTo:="=$D$10:$D$12"
```

If the name already exists, it will be replaced by the new definition.

If you want to create a local name, you can use the following:

```
Names.Add Name:="Sheet1!Sales", RefersTo:="=Sheet1!$E$10:$E$12"
```

Alternatively, you can add the name to the `Names` collection associated with the worksheet, which only includes the names that are local to that worksheet:

```
Worksheets("Sheet1").Names.Add Name:="Costs", RefersTo:="=Sheet1!$F$10:$F$12"
```

Using the Name Property of the Range Object

There is a much simpler way to create a name that refers to a `Range`. You can directly define the `Name` property of the `Range` object:

```
Range("A1:D10").Name = "SalesData"
```

If you want the name to be local, you can include a worksheet name:

```
Range("F1:F10").Name = "Sheet1!Staff"
```

It is generally easier, in code, to work with `Range` objects in this way, than to have to generate the string address of a range, preceded by the equals sign that is required by the `RefersTo` parameter of the `Add` method of the `Names` collection. For example, if you created an object variable `aRange` and want to apply the name `Data` to it, you need to get the `Address` property of `aRange` and append it to an `=:Names.Add Name:="Data", RefersTo:="="` & `aRange.Address`

The alternative method is:

```
aRange.Name = "Data"
```

You cannot completely forget about the `Add` method, however, because it is the only way to create names that refer to numbers, formulas, and strings.

Special Names

Excel uses some names internally to track certain features. When you apply a print range to a worksheet, Excel gives that range the name `Print_Area` as a local name. If you set print titles, Excel creates the local name `Print_Titles`. If you use the Data ➪ Filter ➪ Advanced Filter... feature to extract data from a list to a new range, Excel creates the local names `Criteria` and `Extract`.

In older versions of Excel, the name Database was used to name the range containing your data list (or database). Although it is no longer mandatory to use this name, Database is still recognized by some Excel features such as Advanced Filter.

> If you create a macro that uses the Data ⇨ Form… feature to edit your data list, you
> will find that the macro does not work if the data list does not start within A1:B2. You
> can rectify this by applying the name Database to your data list.

You need to be aware that Excel uses these names and, in general, you should avoid using them unless
you want the side-effects they can produce. For example, you can remove the print area by deleting the
name `Print_Area`. The following two lines of code have the same effect if you have defined a print area:

```
ActiveSheet.PageSetup.PrintArea = ""
ActiveSheet.Names("Print_Area").Delete
```

To summarize, you need to take care when using the following names:

- ❑ `Criteria`
- ❑ `Database`
- ❑ `Extract`
- ❑ `Print_Area`
- ❑ `Print_Titles`

Storing Values in Names

The use of names to store data items has already been mentioned in Chapter 3, specifically under the
Evaluate method topic. Now it's time to look at it in a bit more detail.

When you use a name to store numeric or string data, you should *not* precede the value of the `RefersTo`
parameter with =. If you do, it will be taken as a formula. The following code stores a number and a
string into `StoreNumber` and `StoreString`, respectively:

```
Dim X As Variant
X = 3.14159
Names.Add Name:="StoreNumber", RefersTo:=X
X = "Sales"
Names.Add Name:="StoreString", RefersTo:=X
```

This provides you with a convenient way to store the data you need in your VBA code from one Excel
session to another, so that it does not disappear when you close Excel. When storing strings, you can store
up to 255 characters.

You can retrieve the value in a name using the `Evaluate` method equivalent as follows:

```
X = [StoreNumber]
```

You can also store formulas into names. The formula must start with =. The following places the COUNTA
function into a name:

```
Names.Add Name:="ItemsInA", RefersTo:="=COUNTA($A:$A)"
```

This name can be used in worksheet cell formulas to return a count of the number of items in column A, as shown in Figure 20-2.

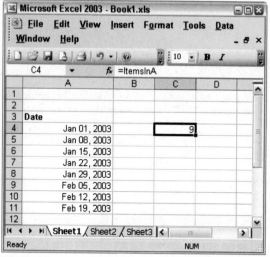

Figure 20-2

Once again, you can use the `Evaluate` method equivalent to evaluate the name in VBA:

```
MsgBox [ItemsInA]
```

Storing Arrays

You can store the values in an array variable in a name just as easily as you can store a number or a label. The following code creates an array of numbers in `MyArray` and stores the array values in `MyName`:

```
Public Sub ArrayToName()
  Dim MyArray(1 To 200, 1 To 3)
  Dim I As Integer
  Dim J As Integer

  For I = 1 To 200
    For J = 1 To 3
      MyArray(I, J) = I + J
    Next J
  Next I
  Names.Add Name:="MyName", RefersTo:=MyArray
End Sub
```

The sizes of arrays in Excel 2003 are limited only by memory and disk space available on your PC and imagination.

The `Evaluate` method can be used to assign the values in a name that holds an array to a `Variant` variable. The following code assigns the contents of `MyName`, created in `ArrayToName`, to `MyArray` and displays the last element in the array:

```
Public Sub NameToArray()
   Dim MyArray As Variant
   MyArray = [MyName]
   MsgBox MyArray(200, 3)
End Sub
```

The array created by assigning a name containing an array to a variant is always one-based, even if you have an Option Base 0 statement in the Declarations section of your module.

Hiding Names

You can hide a name by setting its `Visible` property to `False`. You can do this when you create the name:

```
Names.Add Name:="StoreNumber", RefersTo:=x, Visible:=False
```

You can also hide the name after it has been created:

```
Names("StoreNumber").Visible = False
```

The name cannot now be seen by users in the Insert ➪ Name ➪ Define... dialog box. This is not a highly secure way to conceal information, as anyone with VBA skills can detect the name. But it is an effective way to ensure that users are not confused by the presence of strange names.

You should also be aware that if, through the Excel user interface, a user creates a `Name` object with a `Name` property corresponding to your hidden name, the hidden name is destroyed. You can prevent this by protecting the worksheet.

Despite some limitations, hidden names do provide a nice way to store information in a workbook.

Working with Named Ranges

The spreadsheet in Figure 20-3 contains a data list in B4:D10 that has been given the name `Database`. There is also a data input area in B2:D2 that has been given the name `Input`.

If you want to copy the `Input` data to the bottom of the data list and increase the range referred to by the name `Database` to include the new row, you can use the following code:

```
Public Sub AddNewData()
   Dim Rows As Long

   With Range("Database")
      Rows = .Rows.Count + 1
      Range("Input").Copy Destination:=.Cells(Rows, 2)
      .Resize(Rows).Name = "Database"
   End With
End Sub
```

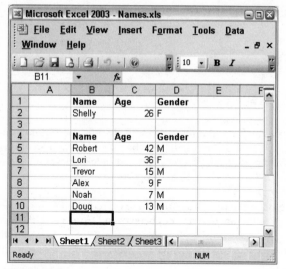

Figure 20-3

The output resulting from this code will be the same as the previous screenshot but with the data "Shelley 26 F" in cells B11:D11. The range `Database` will now refer to B4:D11.

The variable `lRows` is assigned the count of the number of rows in `Database` plus one, to allow for the new record of data. `Input` is then copied. The destination of the copy is the B11 cell, which is defined by the `Cells` property of `Database`, being `lRows` down from the top of `Database`, in column 1 of `Database`. The `Resize` property is applied to `Database` to generate a reference to a `Range` object with one more row than `Database` and the `Name` property of the new `Range` object is assigned the name `Database`.

The nice thing about this code is that it is quite independent of the size or location of `Database` in the active workbook and the location of `Input` in the active workbook. `Database` can have seven or 7000 rows. You can add more columns to `Input` and `Database` and the code still works without change. `Input` and `Database` can even be on different worksheets and the code will still work.

Searching for a Name

If you want to test to see if a name exists in a workbook, you can use the following function. It has been designed to work both as a worksheet function and as a VBA callable function, which makes it a little more complex than if it were designed for either job alone:

```
Public Function IsNameInWorkbook(ByVal Name As String) As Boolean
    Dim X As String
    Dim aRange As Range

    Application.Volatile
    On Error Resume Next
    Set aRange = Application.Caller
    Err.Clear
```

```
      If aRange Is Nothing Then
          X = ActiveWorkbook.Names(Name).Name
      Else
          X = aRange.Parent.Parent.Names(Name).Name
      End If

      If Err.Number = 0 Then IsNameInWorkbook = True
    End Function
```

IsNameInWorkbook has an input parameter Name, which is the required name as a string. The function has been declared volatile, so that it recalculates when it is used as a worksheet function and the referenced name is added or deleted. The function first determines if it has been called from a worksheet cell by assigning the Application.Caller property to aRange.

If it has been called from a cell, Application.Caller returns a Range object that refers to the cell containing the function. If the function has not been called from a cell, the Set statement causes an error, which is suppressed by the preceding On Error Resume Next statement. That error, should it have occurred, is cleared because the function anticipates further errors that should not be masked by the first error.

Next, the function uses an If test to see if aRange is undefined. If so, the call was made from another VBA routine. In this case, the function attempts to assign the Name property of the Name object in the active workbook to the dummy variable X. If the name exists, this attempt succeeds and no error is generated. Otherwise, an error does occur, but is once again suppressed by the On Error Resume Next statement.

If the function has been called from a worksheet cell, the Else clause of the If test identifies the workbook containing aRange and attempts to assign the Name property of the required Name object to X. The parent of aRange is the worksheet containing aRange and the parent of that worksheet is the workbook containing aRange. Once again, an error will be generated if the name does not exist in the workbook.

Finally, IsNameInWorkbook checks the Number property of the Err object to see if it is zero. If it is, the return value of the function is set to True as the name does exist. If there is a non-zero error number, the function is left to return its default value of False as the name does not exist.

You could use IsNameInWorkbook in a spreadsheet cell as follows:

```
=IF(IsNameInWorkbook("Lori"),"Lori is ","Lori is not ")&"an existing name"
```

You could use the following procedure to ask the user to enter a name and determine its existence:

```
Sub TestName()
    If IsNameInWorkbook(InputBox("What Name")) Then
        MsgBox "Name exists"
    Else
        MsgBox "Name does not exist"
    End If
End Sub
```

Note that, if you are searching for a local name, you must include its sheet name, in the form Sheet1!Name, in the above examples.

If you invoke `IsNameInWorkbook` as a worksheet function *and* if the name "John" is present, you will get the output shown in Figure 20-4.

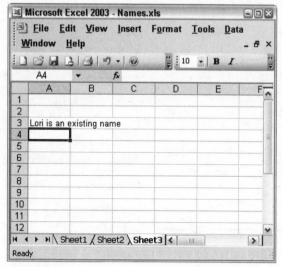

Figure 20-4

Searching for the Name of a Range

The `Name` property of the `Range` object returns the name of the range, if the range has a name and the `RefersTo` property of the `Name` object corresponds exactly to the range.

You might be tempted to display the name of a range aRange with the following code:

```
MsgBox aRange.Name
```

This code fails because the `Name` property of a `Range` object returns a `Name` object. The previous code will display the default property value of the `Name` object, which is its `RefersTo` property. What you want is the `Name` property of the `Name` object, so you must use:

```
MsgBox aRange.Name.Name
```

This code only works if aRange has a name. It will return a runtime error if aRange does not have one. You can use the following code to display the name of the selected cells in the active sheet:

```
Public Sub TestNameOfRange()
  Dim aName As Name
  On Error Resume Next
  Set aName = Selection.Name
  If aName Is Nothing Then
    MsgBox "Selection has no name"
  Else
    MsgBox "Select is named " & aName.Name
  End If
End Sub
```

If arange has more than one name, the first of the names, in alphabetical order, will be returned.

When this macro is run, the output will look something like Figure 20-5.

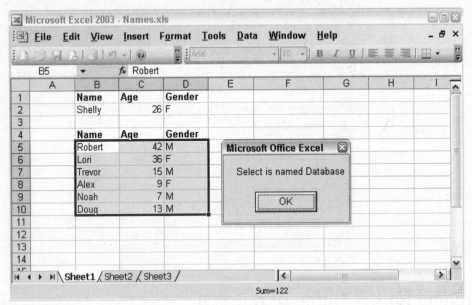

Figure 20-5

Determining which Names Overlap a Range

When you want to check the names that have been applied to ranges in a worksheet, it can be handy to get a list of all the names that are associated with the currently selected cells. You might be interested in names that completely overlap the selected cells, or names that partly overlap the selected cells. The following code lists all the names that completely overlap the selected cells of the active worksheet:

```
Public Sub SelectionEntirelyInNames()
  Dim Message As String
  Dim aName As Name
  Dim NameRange As Range
  Dim aRange As Range

  On Error Resume Next

  For Each aName In Names
    Set NameRange = Nothing
    Set NameRange = aName.RefersToRange
    If Not NameRange Is Nothing Then
      If NameRange.Parent.Name = ActiveSheet.Name Then
        Set aRange = Intersect(Selection, NameRange)
        If Not aRange Is Nothing Then
          If Selection.Address = aRange.Address Then
```

```
            Message = Message & aName.Name & vbCr
          End If
        End If
      End If
    End If
  Next aName
  If Message = "" Then
    MsgBox "The selection is not entirely in any name"
  Else
    MsgBox Message
  End If
End Sub
```

SelectionEntirelyInNames starts by suppressing errors with On Error Resume Next. It then goes into a For Each...Next loop that processes all the names in the workbook. It sets NameRange to Nothing to get rid of any range reference left in it from one iteration of the loop to the next. It then tries to use the Name property of the current Name object as the name of a Range object and assign a reference to the Range object to NameRange. This will fail if the name does not refer to a range, so the rest of the loop is only carried out if a valid Range object has been assigned to NameRange.

The next If test checks that the range that NameRange refers to is on the active worksheet. The parent of NameRange is the worksheet containing NameRange. The inner code is only executed if the name of the parent worksheet is the same as the name of the active sheet. Rng is then assigned to the intersection (the overlapping cells) of the selected cells and NameRange. If there is an overlap and aRange is not Nothing, the innermost If is executed.

This final If checks that the overlapping range in aRange is identical to the selected range. If this is the case, then the selected cells are contained entirely in NameRange and the Name property of the current Name object is added to any names already in Message. In addition, a carriage return character is appended, using the VBA intrinsic constant vbCr, so that each name is on a new line in Message.

When the For Each...Next loop terminates, the following If tests to see if there is anything in Message. If Message is a zero length string, MsgBox displays an appropriate message to say that no names were found. Otherwise, the list of found names in Message is displayed.

When this code is run in a spreadsheet with three named ranges—Data, Fred, and Mary—you get the result shown in Figure 20-6 upon running SelectionEntirelyInNames.

If you want to find out which names are overlapping the selected cells, regardless of whether they entirely contain the selected cells, you can remove the second innermost If test as in the following code:

```
Public Sub NamesOverlappingSelection()
  Dim Message As String
  Dim aName As Name
  Dim NameRange As Range
  Dim aRange As Range

  On Error Resume Next
  For Each aName In Names
    Set NameRange = Nothing
    Set NameRange = Range(aName.Name)
    If Not NameRange Is Nothing Then
```

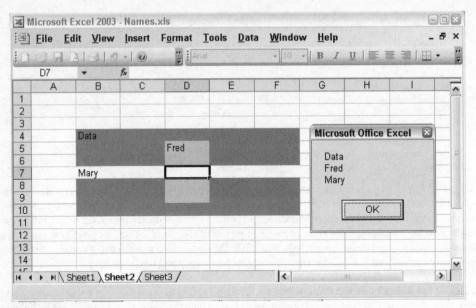

Figure 20-6

```
      If NameRange.Parent.Name = ActiveSheet.Name Then
        Set aRange = Intersect(Selection, NameRange)
        If Not aRange Is Nothing Then
          Message = Message & aName.Name & vbCr
        End If
      End If
    End If
  Next aName
  If Message = "" Then
    MsgBox "No Names are overlapping the selection"
  Else
    MsgBox Message
  End If
End Sub
```

Note that `SelectionEntirelyInNames` and `NamesOverlappingSelection` use different techniques to assign the range referred to by the name to the object variable `rgNameRange`. The following statements are equivalent:

```
Set NameRange = Name.RefersToRange
Set NameRange = Range(Name.Name)
```

Summary

This chapter has presented an indepth discussion of using names in Excel VBA. We have seen how to use names to keep track of worksheet ranges, store numeric and string data, hide names, if necessary, check for existing names in workbooks and ranges, and determine if named ranges completely or partially overlap. These skills will help you manage complex associations of overlapping and intersecting data.

21

Working with Lists

A list of items is a commonly occurring abstraction in the physical world. For example, people make lists of things to do, groceries to buy, stocks to review, places to visit, shows to watch, books to read, and on and on. In this chapter we will explore lists, the relationships lists have with ranges, and how you can publish and share your lists online.

Creating a List

A list is like a range with added features. When you create a list from a range of cells, Excel adds an auto filter list to the top of the list automatically, which permits the list to be sorted and filtered, an insert point, and a resize handle on the bottom-right side of the list which makes it easy to resize the list manually.

Creating a list couldn't be easier. Click anywhere in a contiguous range of cells and press *Ctrl+L* or select Data ➪ List ➪ Create List and the Create List dialog box (see Figure 21-1) will popup, displaying a reasonably good guess as to the cells that your list will comprise. Check "My list has headers" if the first row of your list represents header information. After you click *OK*, the list will be created with drop-down filter lists at the top of each column and an insert row at the bottom of each column.

Figure 21-1

Each of the elements described (except for the totals row) are shown in Figure 21-2. The filter drop-down list at the top of a list permits sorting in ascending or descending order, sorting by a specific item, or creating a custom sort. The dark blue border delineates the list; you can hide the borders of inactive lists by selecting Data ⇨ List ⇨ Hide Border of Inactive Lists. The resize handle works like every other resize control, snapping to the whole row and column regions. The asterisk denotes the insert point for the list, and a row total can be created by selecting the list and then selecting Data ⇨ List ⇨ Total Row.

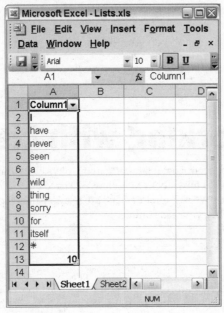

Figure 21-2

Shortcut Options for Lists

Like most features, Lists add context menus that provide shortcuts to features that are germane to Lists. The List toolbar and List context menus add features for inserting and deleting columns and rows, clearing the contents of the list, converting lists to ranges, summing, sorting, and resizing. If you right-click over a List then the context menu pops up. Of use to us, relative to a List, are the Insert and Delete menus. Each of the Insert and Delete menus contain a Row and Column submenu that will Insert or Delete a whole Column or Row.

Sorting and Filtering a List

Data generally can be twisted and contorted to convey meaning. For example, the numbers 11, 5, 3, 7, and 2 may look like random numbers, but if they are sorted in ascending order—2, 3, 5, 7, 11—then the list of numbers may represents a list of prime numbers, which may be more meaningful than a set of jumbled unordered numbers.

Placing things in context often helps give them meaning. Organizing things (or sorting and filtering) is another way that we use to understand information. The AutoFilter feature of Lists makes it easy to sort and filter data. Shown in Figure 21-3, the default options are sorting the list in ascending or descending order or filtering on one of the relevant choices in the list. For example, if we were creating an index then an alphabetic sort might make sense. (We like it better in the order D.H. Lawrence left it.)

Figure 21-3

Creating a UserForm from a List

Automatically generated forms are a mainstay of VB programming. Just a dozen years ago it took a huge amount of work to create a simple input form, and then it was done with ANSI characters. The value of an automatically created graphical user interface cannot be overstated. If we want to view our List as a UserForm all we need do is select the list and click Data ⇨ Form. As suggested by Figure 21-4, we get a zero-effort, fully function graphical user interface.

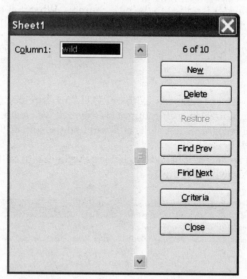

Figure 21-4

From the preceding image we can determine that the form permits adding, deleting, and filtering the data in the form. (As an interesting side note we can tell you that in the very early nineties we laminated handdrawn cutouts to simulate GUIs very similar in function to the one shown in Figure 21-4 before we spent several days to create it.)

Resizing Lists

The famous quote *change is a constant* applies to worksheets as much as anything else. Just as soon as you create a list you will likely need to resize it. A modest adjust to the size of a list can be achieved by dragging the resize icon on the lower left corner of the list, or by specifying the boundary cells. To use the latter method, click your List and click Data ⇨ List ⇨ Resize List. The Resize List dialog box will pop up (see Figure 21-5), and you can use this dialog box to express your revised list as a contiguous range of cells.

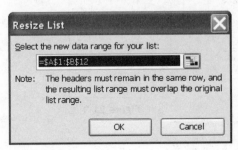

Figure 21-5

Dragging the resize handle in the bottom corner of the list

As mentioned previously, one can quickly resize a list by dragging the resize icon. For the most part, this is an easy way to reconfigure your list. When you resize a list in this manner, new columns and rows are added and an AutoFilter header is added to the new columns. What you can't do or are unlikely to need to do is span multiple worksheets or create a list from non-contiguous cells.

Totaling Rows

A common operation is to total or sum lists. With our D.H Lawrence poem, Excel makes a best guess and simply counts the number of rows in each column. However, if we created an equal number of rows of prime numbers then Excel recognizes the digits and will find the sum of the prime numbers in the list.

Summing a list can be quickly accomplished by clicking the Sigma (6) button (with the text Toggle Total Row) on the List toolbar (shown in Figure 21-6).

Figure 21-6

Converting Lists to a Range

The Data ⇨ List ⇨ Convert to Range menu option will convert a list back into a range. More importantly, you are likely to have a lot of great, well-tested code that is designed to work with ranges. Rather than throw this code out, it is better to know how to programmatically convert a list to a range so our time and effort invested in ranges isn't for naught. The next listing demonstrates how easy it is to refer to a list as a range (by displaying the cells that the list/range represents):

```
Public Sub ListToRange()

  Dim List As ListObject
  Set List = Sheet1.ListObjects(1)

  Dim R As Range
  Set R = List.DataBodyRange

  MsgBox R.Cells.Address

End Sub
```

The Worksheet's `ListObjects` property represents a collection of Lists in a specific Worksheet. We can make this aspect generic by not hardcoding a specific Worksheet; perhaps we could pass the name of the Worksheet as parameter. The `List.DataBodyRange` method returns the range of cells representing a Range. If you want a specific part of the list as a range, then you can pass a row and column index to `DataBodyRange`. From there we have a reference to a range that can be used to support any existing code you might have.

Publishing Lists

The Internet bubble burst but no one told eBay.com and Amazon.com. These companies are making money hand over fist on the Internet. While many companies may be having some trouble figuring out how to do the same, few companies deny that a Web presence is optional. Intranet sites, e-commerce, and the ubiquity of data is empowering.

A site running Microsoft's SharePoint services can host your lists. Once shared you can use Excel to refresh, synchronize, and unlink lists.

Suppose you are a hockey mom and you want to provide a list of contact information for all the other hockey moms and dads. You can quickly assembly the list of information and publish it on a SharePoint site. If someone changes his or her cell number, gets a divorce (heaven forbid), or changes jobs, then that person can browse to your list and update his or her own contact information. The old habit of writing your friends names in the back of your phonebook has been replaced with a digital method that permits them to write their own names there.

To publish your list of data, select a list and click Data ⇨ List ⇨ Publish List from the Excel menu. The Publish List to SharePoint wizard will be displayed (as shown in Figure 21-7 through Figure 21-9). Fill out any necessary information and you are finished. (At the time of this writing you could sign up for a trial SharePoint services trial offer from Microsoft.com, as demonstrated in the sample figure.)

Publishing, viewing, synchronizing, and unlinking lists is relatively easy in Excel. Simply choose the appropriate menu option and you're done. As programmers we may want to do this with code.

The following code listings demonstrate how to publish, synchronize, view, and unlink lists programmatically.

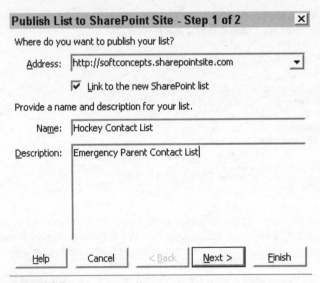

Figure 21-7

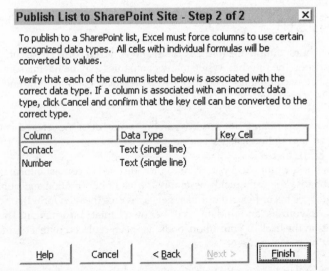

Figure 21-8

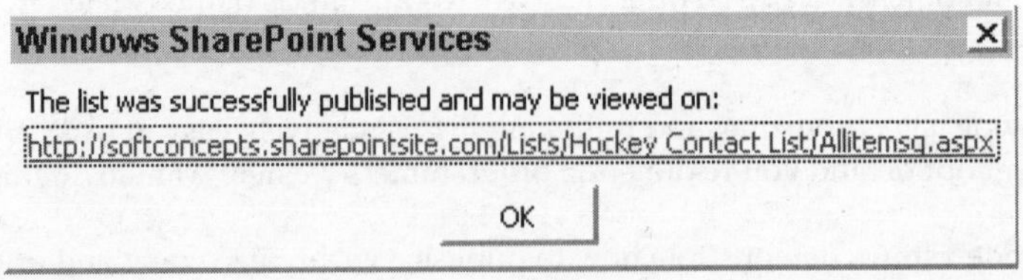

Windows SharePoint Services ☒

The list was successfully published and may be viewed on:

http://softconcepts.sharepointsite.com/Lists/Hockey Contact List/Allitemsg.aspx

OK

Figure 21-9

Publishing Your List

Suppose you are provided with a list of contact information on some predetermined interval. Instead of spending a lot of time manually publishing this list, you could write a little code that automatically publishes the list for you:

```
Public Sub PublishList()

    Dim Index As Integer
    ' hard code index for testing
    Index = 1
    Dim List As ListObject
    Set List = GetList(Index)

    Dim Url As String
    Url = List.Publish(Array("http://softconcepts.sharepointsite.com", _
        "Hockey Moms Unite", "GLAHA Contact List"), True)
End Sub
```

(Note: By the time you are reading this, my trial Sharepoint site will have been removed. You will need to replace the URL in all of the Sharepoint samples with a valid Sharepoint portal URL.) A specific list can be obtained by index or the name of the list. In the example, we request the List by index, and we'll use this very straightforward approach in the next couple of examples. (We won't relist the GetList code though.)

In the example, we obtain a specific ListObject and invoke ListObject.Publish, essentially passing the same values we'd pass in the dialog box shown in the preceding section. The Array function was used to pass an URL, Name, and Description for the list. The second argument is whether or not we should maintain a two-way link between the SharePoint server and our worksheet. If we pass True then modifications to the shared list will be reflected when we synchronize the list at a later time.

Updating Changes to Your List

Now that we have a List published on a SharePoint server we can programmatically update changes made to our worksheet. The code in the next listing demonstrates how easy this process is:

```
Public Sub SynchronizeList()
    ' Hardcoded list index for testing
    Dim Index As Integer
    Index = 1

    Dim List As ListObject
    Set List = GetList(Index)

    Call List.UpdateChanges(XLListConflict.xlListConflictDialog)
End Sub
```

Figure 21-10 shows the revised worksheet and Figure 21-11 shows the updated code on the SharePoint site after the code is run. (In the code listing we used a hard-coded index for the list and recycled the previously listed GetList method. You can make the index a parameter or in some other fashion make the index a dynamic value, which we learned how to do in earlier chapters.)

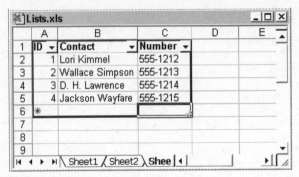

Figure 21-10

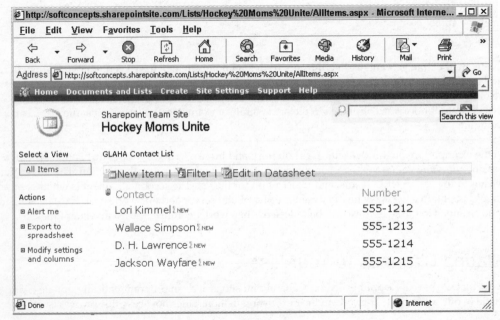

Figure 21-11

View a List on a SharePoint Server

Viewing the list on a SharePoint server is a lot like viewing any other authenticated Web page. You will need to browse the location containing your list and authenticate in the manner specified by the SharePoint host server. For our example, a trial site hosted by a Microsoft partner, we can manually browse to the URL assigned by the host server or we can select Data ⇨ List ⇨ View List on Server from Excel. The latter is a shortcut that makes it easier for developers to navigate directly to the list from within Excel.

Each host server is likely to offer a wide variety of services and may charge fees and rules of their own. You will have to explore a specific SharePoint server to figure out what the relative costs and guidelines mandated by the host are.

Unlinking the List

At some point the data will become outdated, and you will want to remove the list from the server. For our example, we probably want to remove the list at the end of the relevant hockey season. From the Excel menu we can unlink the list using Data ➪ List ➪ Unlink List and then use resources on the SharePoint site to actually delete the list. We can also delete the list after unlinking it programmatically with the following code:

```
Public Sub UnlinkList()
    ' Hardcoded list index for testing
    Dim Index As Integer
    Index = 1

    Dim List As ListObject
    Set List = GetList(Index)
    Call List.Publish
End Sub
```

Summary

Microsoft Excel and SharePoint servers permit a relatively easy way to share data online. In this chapter, you learned how to create, filter, and sort lists. We also talked about and demonstrated the intrinsic relationship between lists and ranges, demonstrating how you may use existing range-based code to work with lists. In the latter half of the chapter we talked about publishing, synchronizing, viewing, and removing lists. All of these tasks can easily be accomplished using Excel or VBA.

Yet using SharePoint services to share data is not limited to Excel or even to Microsoft Office. SharePoint offers a variety of means of publishing and sharing data. For example, SharePoint servers contain some XML Web Services that literally means anything that can speak XML—a text-based markup language like HTML—can tap into these services and manage data on a SharePoint site using other tools Microsoft Office applications and other languages besides VBA. Ultimately, technologies like SharePoint and XML Web services will promote a peaceful coexistence of tools, data, and technologies.

22

PivotTables

PivotTables are an extension of the cross tabulation tables used in presenting statistics, and can be used to summarize complex data in a table format. An example of cross tabulation is a table showing the number of employees in an organisation, broken down by age and sex. PivotTables are more powerful and can show more than two variables, so they could be used to show employees broken down by age, sex, and alcohol, to quote an old statistician's joke. PivotTables are especially useful when you need to view data in a format that is not already provided by a report. It's in your best interest to not only provide reports in your applications, but to allow the end user to extract the data so they can view and manipulate it using Excel. Following our suggestion will save you a lot of time.

The input data to a PivotTable can come from an Excel worksheet, a text file, an Access database, or a wide range of external database applications. They can handle up to 256 variables, if you can interpret the results. They can perform many types of standard calculations such as summing, counting, and averaging. They can produce subtotals and grand totals.

Data can be grouped as in Excel's outline feature and you can hide unwanted rows and columns. You can also define calculations within the body of the table. PivotTables are also very flexible if you want to change the layout of the data and add or delete variables. In Excel 2003, you can create charts that are linked to your PivotTable results in such a way that you can manipulate the data layout from within the chart.

PivotTables are designed so that you can easily generate and manipulate them manually. If you want to create many of them, or provide a higher level of automation to users, you can tap into the Excel Object Model. In this chapter, we will examine the following objects:

- ❑ `PivotTables`
- ❑ `PivotCaches`
- ❑ `PivotFields`
- ❑ `PivotItems`
- ❑ `PivotCharts`

The PivotTable feature has evolved more than most other established Excel features. With each new version of Excel, PivotTables have been made easier to use and provided with new features. As it is important for many users to maintain compatibility in their code between Excel 2002 and Excel 2003, we will discuss the differences in PivotTables between these versions.

Creating a PivotTable Report

PivotTables can accept input data from a spreadsheet, or from an external source such as an Access database. When using Excel data, the data should be structured as a data list, as explained at the beginning of Chapter 23, although it is also possible to use data from another PivotTable or from multiple consolidation ranges. The columns of the list are fields and the rows are records, apart from the top row that defines the names of the fields.

Let's take the list shown in Figure 22-1 as our input data.

	A	B	C	D	E	F	G
1	Date	Customer	State	Product	NumberSold	Price	Revenue
2	August 25, 1999	Roberts	NSW	Oranges	903	15	13545
3	August 25, 1999	Roberts	TAS	Oranges	331	15	4965
4	August 26, 1999	Smith	QLD	Mangoes	299	20	5980
5	August 30, 1999	Roberts	QLD	Oranges	612	15	9180
6	September 1, 1999	Roberts	VIC	Apples	907	12.5	11337.5
7	September 1, 1999	Pradesh	TAS	Pears	107	18	1926
8	September 3, 1999	Roberts	VIC	Apples	770	12.5	9625
9	September 7, 1999	Smith	NT	Apples	223	12.5	2787.5
10	September 7, 1999	Smith	VIC	Oranges	132	15	1980
11	September 8, 1999	Pradesh	QLD	Oranges	669	15	10035
12	September 10, 1999	Roberts	NSW	Mangoes	881	20	17620
13	September 14, 1999	Kee	SA	Pears	624	18	11232
14	September 15, 1999	Roberts	QLD	Mangoes	193	20	3860
15	September 16, 1999	Smith	SA	Mangoes	255	20	5100
16	September 20, 1999	Kee	QLD	Mangoes	6	20	120
17	September 20, 1999	Kee	VIC	Mangoes	311	20	6220
18	September 21, 1999	Roberts	NT	Oranges	9	15	135
19	September 21, 1999	Kee	TAS	Apples	706	12.5	8825
20	September 22, 1999	Kee	NT	mangoes	441	20	8820

Figure 22-1

The list contains data from August, 1999, to December, 2001. As usual in Excel, it is a good idea to identify the data by giving it a name so that it becomes easier to reference in your code. The list has been named `Database`. This name will be picked up and used automatically by Excel when creating our PivotTable. It is not necessary to use the name `Database`, but it is recognized by Excel to have special meaning, and can assist in setting up a PivotTable.

We want to summarize NumberSold within the entire time period by Customer and Product. With the cell pointer in the data list, click Data ⇨ Pivot Table and PivotChart Report... and, in the third step of the Wizard, click Layout. Drag the Customer button to the Row area, the Product button to the Column area, and the NumberSold button to the Data area, as shown in Figure 22-2.

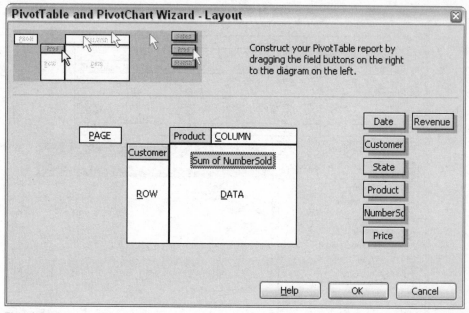

Figure 22-2

If you choose the option to place the PivotTable in a new worksheet, you will create a PivotTable report like the one in Figure 22-3.

If you use the macro recorder to create a macro to carry out this operation in Excel 2003, it will look similar to the following code that we have reformatted to be slightly more readable:

```
ActiveWorkbook.PivotCaches.Add _
    (SourceType:=xlDatabase, SourceData:="Database"). _
    CreatePivotTable TableDestination:="", _
    TableName:="PivotTable1", _
    DefaultVersion:=xlPivotTableVersion10

ActiveSheet.PivotTableWizard _
    TableDestination:=ActiveSheet.Cells(3, 1)
ActiveSheet.Cells(3, 1).Select

ActiveSheet.PivotTables("PivotTable1").AddFields _
    RowFields:="Customer", ColumnFields:="Product"

ActiveSheet.PivotTables("PivotTable1"). _
    PivotFields("NumberSold"). _
    Orientation = xlDataField
```

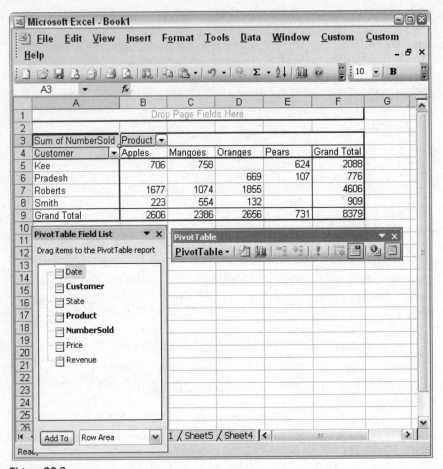

Figure 22-3

The code uses the Add method of the PivotCaches collection to create a new PivotCache. We will discuss PivotCaches next. It then uses the CreatePivotTable method of the PivotCache object to create an empty PivotTable in a new worksheet starting in the A1 cell, and names the PivotTable PivotTable1. The code also uses a parameter that is new and will only be available in Excel 2002 and Excel 2003, declaring the DefaultVersion. This parameter causes a compile error in the previous versions.

The next line of code uses the PivotTableWizard method of the worksheet to move the main body of the PivotTable to A3, leaving room for page fields above the table. Page fields are discussed later. The wizard acts on the PivotTable containing the active cell, so it is important that your code does not select a cell outside the new PivotTable range before using this method. The preceding code has no problem because, by default, the top-left cell of the range containing the PivotTable is selected after the CreatePivotTable method executes.

The AddFields method of the table declares the Customer field to be a row field and the Product field to be a column field. Finally, NumberSold is declared to be a data field, which means that it appears in the body of the table where it is summed by default.

PivotCaches

A PivotCache is a buffer, or holding area, where data is stored and accessed as required from a data source. It acts as a communication channel between the data source and the PivotTable.

Although PivotCaches are automatically created in Excel 97, you can't create them explicitly, and you don't have as much control over them as you have in the later versions.

In Excel 2003 you can create a PivotCache using the Add method of the PivotCaches collection, as seen in our recorded code. You have extensive control over what data you draw from the source when you create a PivotCache. Particularly in conjunction with *ADO* (ActiveX Data Objects), which we will demonstrate at the end of this chapter, you can achieve high levels of programmatic control over external data sources. Chapter 11 will show you the great flexibility of ADO and you can use the techniques from that chapter to construct data sources for PivotTables.

You can also use a PivotCache to generate multiple PivotTables from the same data source. This is more efficient than forcing each PivotTable to maintain its own data source.

When you have created a PivotCache, you can create any number of PivotTables from it using the CreatePivotTable method of the PivotCache object.

PivotTables Collection

Excel 2003 gives you the opportunity to use another method to create a PivotTable from a PivotCache, using the Add method of the PivotTables collection:

```
Sub AddTable()
  Dim PC As PivotCache
  Dim PT As PivotTable

  Set PC = ActiveWorkbook.PivotCaches.Add(SourceType:=xlDatabase, _
          SourceData:="Database")

  Set PT = ActiveSheet.PivotTables.Add(PivotCache:=PC, _
          TableDestination:="")

End Sub
```

There is no particular advantage in using this method compared with the CreatePivotTable method. It's just another thread in the rich tapestry of Excel.

PivotFields

The columns in the data source are referred to as fields. When the fields are used in a PivotTable, they become PivotField objects and belong to the PivotFields collection of the PivotTable object. The PivotFields collection contains all the fields in the data source and any calculated fields you have added, not just the fields that are visible in the PivotTable report. Calculated fields are discussed later in this chapter.

You can add PivotFields to a report using two different techniques. You can use the `AddFields` method of the `PivotTable` object, or you can assign a value to the `Orientation` property of the `PivotField` object, as shown below:

```
Sub AddFieldsToTable()

    With ActiveSheet.PivotTables(1)

        .AddFields RowFields:="State", AddToTable:=True
        .PivotFields("Date").Orientation = xlPageField

    End With
End Sub
```

If you run this code on our example PivotTable, you will get the result shown in Figure 22-4.

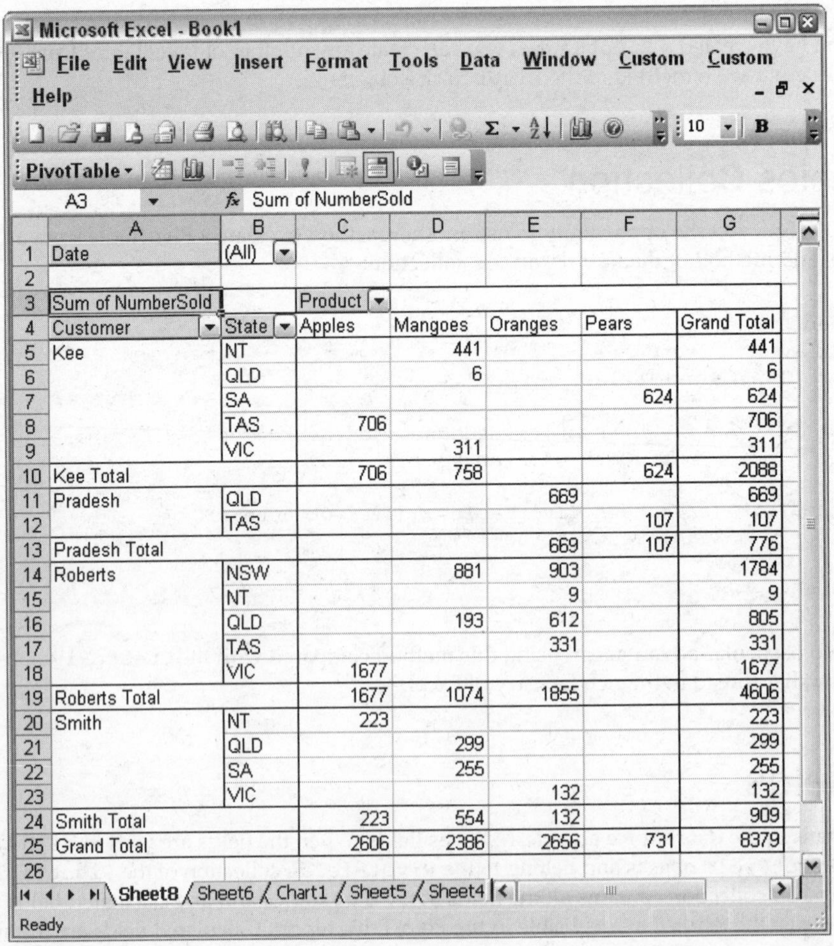

Figure 22-4

The `AddFields` method can add multiple row, column, and page fields. These fields replace any existing fields, unless you set the `AddToTable` parameter to `True`, as in the preceding example. However, `AddFields` can't be used to add or replace data fields. The following code redefines the layout of the fields in our existing table, apart from the data field:

```
Sub RedefinePivotTable()
  Dim PT As PivotTable

  Set PT = ActiveSheet.PivotTables(1)
  PT.AddFields RowFields:=Array("Product", "Customer"), _
      ColumnFields:="State", PageFields:="Date"

End Sub
```

Note that you can use the array function to include more than one field in a field location. The result is shown in Figure 22-5.

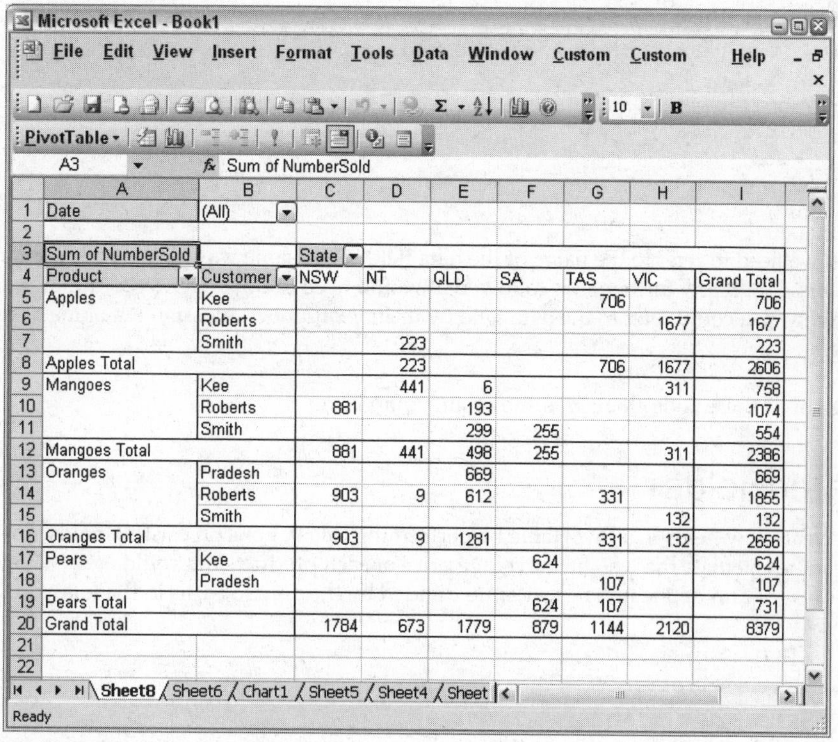

Date	(All)							
Sum of NumberSold		State						
Product	Customer	NSW	NT	QLD	SA	TAS	VIC	Grand Total
Apples	Kee					706		706
	Roberts						1677	1677
	Smith		223					223
Apples Total			223			706	1677	2606
Mangoes	Kee		441	6			311	758
	Roberts	881		193				1074
	Smith			299	255			554
Mangoes Total		881	441	498	255		311	2386
Oranges	Pradesh			669				669
	Roberts	903	9	612		331		1855
	Smith						132	132
Oranges Total		903	9	1281		331	132	2656
Pears	Kee				624			624
	Pradesh					107		107
Pears Total					624	107		731
Grand Total		1784	673	1779	879	1144	2120	8379

Figure 22-5

You can use the `Orientation` and `Position` properties of the `PivotField` object to reorganize the table. Position defines the order of fields within a particular part of the table, counting from the one on the left. The following code, added to the end of the `RedefinePivotTable` code, would move the Customer field to the left of the Product field in the previous figure, for example:

```
PT.PivotFields("Customer").Position = 1
```

You can use the `Function` property of the `PivotField` object to change the way a data field is summarised and the `NumberFormat` property to set the appearance of the numbers. The following code, added to the end of `RedefinePivotTable`, adds `Revenue` to the data area, summing it and placing it second to `NumberSold` by default. The next lines of code change the position of `NumberSold` to the second position and changes `"Sum of NumberSold"` to `"Count of NumberSold"`, which tells us how many sales transactions occurred:

```
Sub AddDataField()
  Dim PT As PivotTable

  Set PT = ActiveSheet.PivotTables(1)

  'Add and format new Data field
  With PT.PivotFields("Revenue")
    .Orientation = xlDataField
    .NumberFormat = "0"
  End With

  'Edit existing Data field
  With PT.DataFields("Sum of NumberSold")
    .Position = 2
    .Function = xlCount
    .NumberFormat = "0"
  End With

End Sub
```

Note that we need to refer to the name of the data field in the same way as it is presented in the table `Sum of NumberSold`. If any further code followed, it would need to now refer to `Count of NumberSold`. Alternatively, you could refer to the data field by its index number or assign it a name of your own choosing.

The result of all these code changes is shown in Figure 22-6.

CalculatedFields

You can create new fields in a PivotTable by performing calculations on existing fields. For example, you might want to calculate the weighted average price of each product. You could create a new field called `AveragePrice` and define it to be `Revenue` divided by `NumberSold`, as in the following code:

```
Sub CalculateAveragePrice()
  Dim PT As PivotTable

  'Add new Worksheet and PivotTable
  Worksheets.Add
  Set PT = ActiveWorkbook.PivotCaches(1).CreatePivotTable( _
           TableDestination:=ActiveCell, TableName:="AveragePrice")
  With PT

    'Remove AveragePrice if it exists
    On Error Resume Next
```

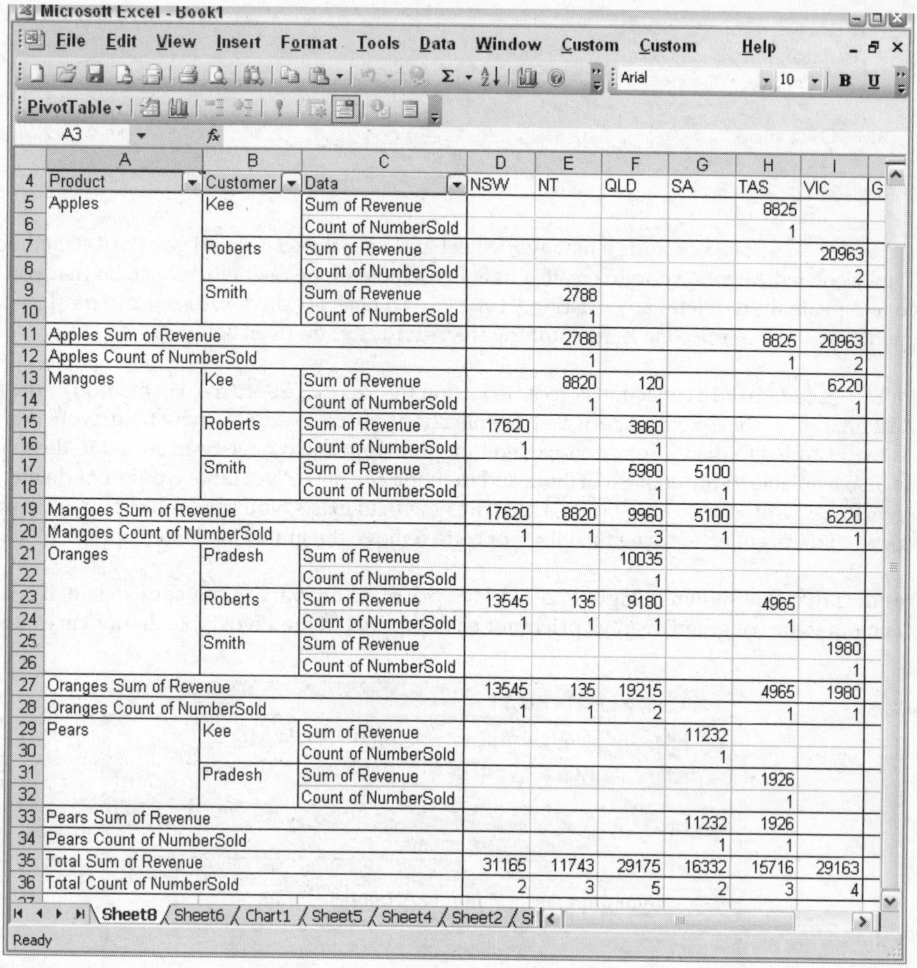

Figure 22-6

```
.PivotFields("AveragePrice").Delete
On Error GoTo 0

'Create new AveragePrice
.CalculatedFields.Add Name:="AveragePrice", _
    Formula:="=Revenue/NumberSold"

'Add Row and Column fields
.AddFields RowFields:="Customer", ColumnFields:="Product"

'Add AveragePrice as Data field
With .PivotFields("AveragePrice")
  .Orientation = xlDataField
  .NumberFormat = "0.00"
End With
```

```
      'Remove grand totals
      .ColumnGrand = False
      .RowGrand = False

   End With

End Sub
```

CalculateAveragePrice adds a new worksheet and uses the CreatePivotTable method of our previously created PivotCache to create a new PivotTable in the new worksheet. So that you can run this code repeatedly, it deletes any existing PivotField objects called AveragePrice. The On Error statements ensure that the code keeps running if AveragePrice does not exist.

The CalculatedFields collection is accessed using the CalculatedFields method of the PivotTable. The Add method of the CalculatedFields collection is used to add the new field. Note that the new field is really added to the PivotCache, even though it appears to have been added to the PivotTable. It is now also available to our first PivotTable and deleting the new PivotTable would not delete AveragePrice from the PivotCache. Once the new field exists, you treat it like any other member of the PivotFields collection. The final lines of code remove the grand totals that appear by default.

The result is the table shown in Figure 22-7. As the prices do not vary in our source data, it is not surprising that the weighted average prices for each product in the PivotTable do not vary either.

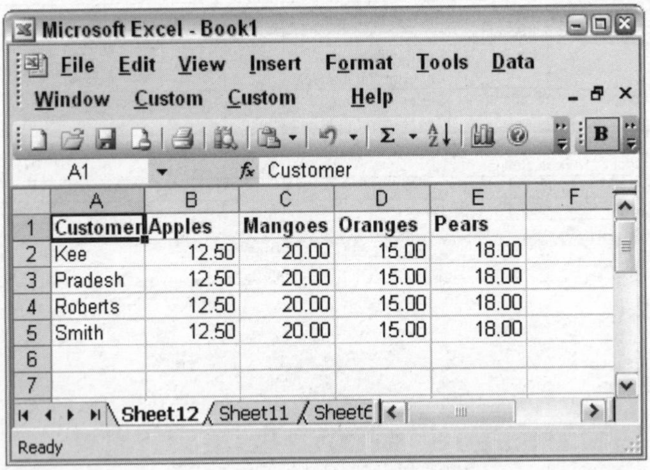

Figure 22-7

Take care when creating CalculatedFields. You need to appreciate that the calculations are performed AFTER the source data has been summed. In our example, Revenue and NumberSold were summed and one sum divided by the other sum. This works fine for calculating a weighted average price and is also suitable for simple addition or subtraction. Other calculations might not work as you expect.

For example, say, you don't have `Revenue` in the source data and you decide to calculate it by defining a `CalculatedField` equal to `Price` multiplied by `NumberSold`. This would not give the correct result. You can't get `Revenue` by multiplying the sum of `Price` by the sum of `NumberSold`, except in the special case where only one record from the source data is represented in each cell of the PivotTable.

PivotItems

Each `PivotField` object has a `PivotItems` collection associated with it. You can access the `PivotItems` using the `PivotItems` method of the `PivotField` object. It is a bit peculiar that this is a method and not a property, and is in contrast to the `HiddenItems` property and `VisibleItems` property of the `PivotField` object that return subsets of the `PivotItems` collection.

The `PivotItems` collection contains the unique values in a field. For example, the `Product` field in our source data has four unique values – "`Apples`", "`Mangoes`", "`Oranges`", and "`Pears`", which constitute the `PivotItems` collection for that field.

Grouping

We can group the items in a field in any way we like. For example, `NSW`, `QLD`, and `VIC` could be grouped as `EasternStates`. This can be very useful when we have many items in a field. We can also group dates, which have a predefined group structure including years, quarters, and months.

If we bring the `Date` field from our source data into the PivotTable as a row field, we will have nearly 400 rows in the table as there are that many unique dates (Figure 22-8).

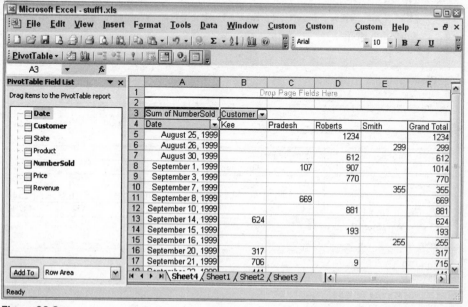

Figure 22-8

We can group the Date items to get a more meaningful summary. You can do this manually by selecting a cell in the PivotTable containing a date item, right-clicking the cell, and clicking Group and Show Detail → Group.... The dialog box in Figure 22-9 appears where you can select both Months and Years.

Figure 22-9

When you click *OK*, you will see the screen shown in Figure 22-10.

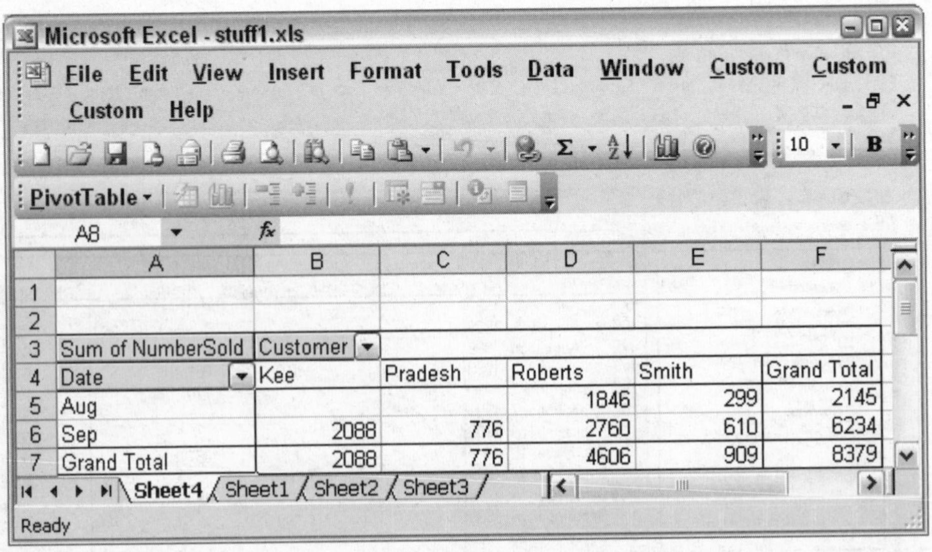

Sum of NumberSold	Customer				
Date	Kee	Pradesh	Roberts	Smith	Grand Total
Aug			1846	299	2145
Sep	2088	776	2760	610	6234
Grand Total	2088	776	4606	909	8379

Figure 22-10

The following code can be used to perform the same grouping operation:

```
Sub GroupDates()
  Dim PT As PivotTable
  Dim Rng As Range

  'Create new PivotTable in A1 of active sheet
  Set PT = ActiveSheet.PivotTableWizard(SourceType:=xlDatabase, _
      SourceData:=ThisWorkbook.Names("Database").RefersToRange, _
      TableDestination:=Range("A1"))

  With PT
    'Add data
    .AddFields RowFields:="Date", ColumnFields:="State"
    .PivotFields("NumberSold").Orientation = xlDataField

    'Find Date label
    Set Rng = .PivotFields("Date").LabelRange

    'Group all Dates by Month & Year
    Rng.Group Start:=True, End:=True, _
        Periods:=Array(False, False, False, False, True, False, True)

  End With
End Sub
```

The grouping is carried out on the Range object underneath the labels for the field or its items. It does not matter whether you choose the label containing the name of the field, or one of the labels containing an item name, as long as you choose only a single cell. If you choose a number of item names, you will group just those selected items.

GroupDates creates an object variable, Rng, referring to the cell containing the Date field label. The Group method is applied to this cell, using the parameters that apply to dates. The Start and End parameters define the start date and end date to be included. When they are set to True, all dates are included. The Periods parameter array corresponds to the choices in the Grouping dialog box, selecting Months and Years.

The following code ungroups the dates:

```
Sub UnGroupDates()
  Dim Rng As Range

  Set Rng = ActiveSheet.PivotTables(1).PivotFields("Date").LabelRange
  Rng.Ungroup
End Sub
```

You can regroup them with the following code:

```
Sub ReGroupDates()
  Dim Rng As Range

  Set Rng = ActiveSheet.PivotTables(1).PivotFields("Date").LabelRange
  Rng.Group Start:=True, End:=True, _
      Periods:=Array(False, False, False, False, True, False, True)

End Sub
```

Chapter 22

Visible Property

You can hide items by setting their Visible property to False. Say, you are working with the grouped dates from the last exercise, and you want to see only Jan 2000 and Jan 2001 (Figure 22-11).

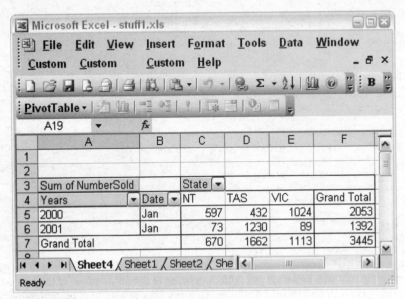

Figure 22-11

You could use the following code:

```
Sub CompareMonths()
  Dim PT As PivotTable
  Dim PI As PivotItem
  Dim sMonth As String

  sMonth = "Jan"
  Set PT = ActiveSheet.PivotTables(1)

  For Each PI In PT.PivotFields("Years").PivotItems
    If PI.Name <> "2000" And PI.Name <> "2001" Then
      PI.Visible = False
    End If
  Next PI

  PT.PivotFields("Date").PivotItems(sMonth).Visible = True
  For Each PI In PT.PivotFields("Date").PivotItems
    If PI.Name <> sMonth Then PI.Visible = False
  Next PI
End Sub
```

CompareMonths loops through all the items in the Years and Date fields setting the Visible property to False if the item is not one of the required items. The code has been designed to be reusable for comparing other months by assigning new values to sMonth. Note that the required month is made visible before processing the items in the Date field. This is necessary to ensure that the required month is visible and also so we don't try to make all the items hidden at once, which would cause a runtime error.

CalculatedItems

You can add calculated items to a field using the Add method of the CalculatedItems collection. Say, you wanted to add a new product—melons. You estimate that you would sell 50 percent more melons than mangoes. This could be added to the table created by CreatePivotTable97 using the following code:

```
Sub AddCalculatedItem()

    With ActiveSheet.PivotTables(1).PivotFields("Product")
        .CalculatedItems.Add Name:="Melons", Formula:="=Mangoes*1.5"
    End With

End Sub
```

This would give the result shown in Figure 22-12.

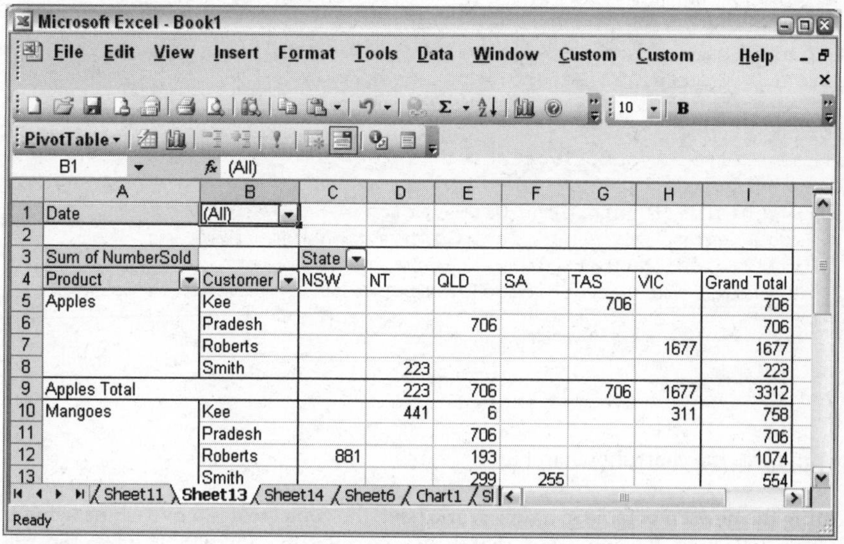

Microsoft Excel - Book1

	A	B	C	D	E	F	G	H	I
1	Date	(All)							
2									
3	Sum of NumberSold		State						
4	Product	Customer	NSW	NT	QLD	SA	TAS	VIC	Grand Total
5	Apples	Kee					706		706
6		Pradesh			706				706
7		Roberts						1677	1677
8		Smith		223					223
9	Apples Total			223	706		706	1677	3312
10	Mangoes	Kee		441	6			311	758
11		Pradesh			706				706
12		Roberts	881		193				1074
13		Smith			299	255			554

Figure 22-12

You can remove the CalculatedItem by deleting it from either the CalculatedItems collection or the PivotItems collection of the PivotField:

```
Sub DeleteCalculatedItem()
    With ActiveSheet.PivotTables(1).PivotFields("Product")
        .PivotItems("Melons").Delete
    End With
End Sub
```

PivotCharts

PivotCharts were introduced in Excel 2000. They follow all the rules associated with Chart objects, except that they are linked to a PivotTable object. If you change the layout of a PivotChart, Excel automatically changes the layout of the linked PivotTable. Conversely, if you change the layout of a PivotTable that is linked to a PivotChart, Excel automatically changes the layout of the chart.

The following code creates a new PivotTable, based on the same PivotCache used in the PivotTable in Sheet1 and then creates a PivotChart based on the table:

```
Sub CreatePivotChart()
  Dim PC As PivotCache
  Dim PT As PivotTable
  Dim Cht As Chart

  'Get reference to existing PivotCache
  Set PC = Worksheets("Sheet1").PivotTables(1).PivotCache

  'Add new Worksheet
  Worksheets.Add Before:=Worksheets(1)

  'Create new PivotTable based on existing Cache
  Set PT = PC.CreatePivotTable(TableDestination:=ActiveCell)

  'Add new Chart sheet based on active PivotTable
  Set Cht = Charts.Add(Before:=Worksheets(1))

  'Format PivotChart
  With Cht.PivotLayout.PivotTable

    .PivotFields("Customer").Orientation = xlRowField
    .PivotFields("State").Orientation = xlColumnField
    .PivotFields("NumberSold").Orientation = xlDataField
    '.AddDataField .PivotFields("NumberSold"), "Sum of NumberSold", xlSum

  End With

End Sub
```

The code produces the chart shown in Figure 22-13.

After creating the new PivotTable in a new worksheet, the code creates a new chart using the Add method of the Charts collection. It is important that the active cell is in a PivotTable when the Add method is executed. This causes Excel to automatically link the new chart to the PivotTable.

Once the PivotChart is created, you can link to the associated PivotTable using the PivotLayout object, which is now associated with the chart. It is then only a matter of setting up the fields required in the PivotTable, using the same techniques we have already used.

The last line before the End With has been commented out. It is an alternative way of adding the data field and can replace the line of code immediately before it. However, AddDataField is a new method of the PivotTable object that applies to Excel 2002 and Excel 2003 only.

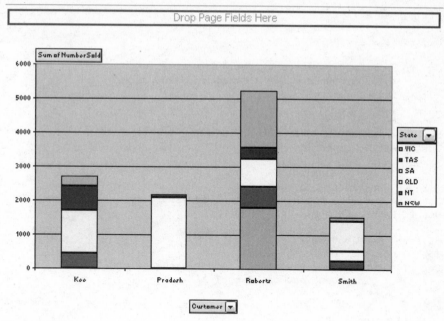

Figure 22-13

Any further programmatic manipulation of the data in the chart needs to be done through the associated PivotTable. Formatting changes to the chart can be made through the properties and methods of the Chart object.

External Data Sources

Excel is ultimately limited in the quantity of data it can store, and it is very poor at handling multiple related tables of data. Therefore, you might want to store your data in an external database application and draw out the data you need, as required. The most powerful way to do this is to use ADO (ActiveX Data Objects). We have covered ADO in greater depth in Chapter 11.

The following example shows how to connect to an Access database called SalesDB.mdb containing similar data to that we have been using, but potentially much more comprehensive and complex. In order to run the following code, you must create a reference to ADO. To do this, go to the VBE window and click Tools ➪ References. From the list, find "Microsoft ActiveX Data Objects" and click in the check box beside it. If you find multiple versions of this library, choose the one with the highest version number.

When you run the code, which will only execute in Excel 2000, 2002, and 2003 because it creates a PivotCache, it will create a new worksheet at the front of the workbook and add a PivotTable that is similar to those we have already created, but the data source will be the Access database:

```
Sub PivotTableDataViaADO()
    Dim Con As New ADODB.Connection
    Dim RS As New ADODB.Recordset
```

```
    Dim sql As String
    Dim PC As PivotCache
    Dim PT As PivotTable

    Con.Open "Provider=Microsoft.Jet.OLEDB.4.0;" & _
            "Data Source=C:\My Documents\SalesDB.mdb;"
    sql = "Select * From SalesData"

    'Open the recordset...
    Set RS = New ADODB.Recordset
    Set RS.ActiveConnection = Con
    RS.Open sql

    'Create the PivotTable cache....
    Set PC = ActiveWorkbook.PivotCaches.Add(SourceType:=xlExternal)
    Set PC.Recordset = RS

    'Create the PivotTable ....
    Worksheets.Add Before:=Sheets(1)
    Set PT = ActiveSheet.PivotTables.Add(PivotCache:=PC, _
            TableDestination:=Range("A1"))

    With PT
       .NullString = "0"
       .SmallGrid = False
       .AddFields RowFields:="State", ColumnFields:="Product"
       .PivotFields("NumberSold").Orientation = xlDataField
    End With
End Sub
```

First, we create a Connection object linking us to the Access database using the Open method of the ADO Connection object. We then define an SQL (Structured Query Language) statement that says we want to select all the data in a table called SalesData in the Access database. The table is almost identical to the one we have been using in Excel, having the same fields and data. See Chapter 20 to get more information on the SQL language and the terminology that is used in ADO.

We then assign a reference to a new ADO Recordset object to the object variable RS. The ActiveConnection property of RS is assigned a reference to the Connection object. The Open method then populates the recordset with the data in the Access SalesData table, following the instruction in the SQL language statement.

We then open a new PivotCache, declaring its data source as external by setting the SourceType parameter to xlExternal, and set its Recordset property equal to the ADO recordset RS. The rest of the code uses techniques we have already seen to create the PivotTable using the PivotCache.

Chapter 11 goes into much more detail about creating recordsets and with much greater explanation of the techniques used. Armed with the knowledge in that chapter, and knowing how to connect a recordset to a PivotCache from the preceding example, you will be in a position to utilize an enormous range of data sources.

Summary

You use PivotTables to summarize complex data. In this chapter, we have examined various techniques that you can use to create PivotTables from a data source such as an Excel data list using VBA. We have explained the restrictions that apply if your code needs to be compatible with different versions of Excel.

We have covered using the PivotTable wizard in Excel 97, and setting up PivotCaches in later versions, to create PivotTables. You can add fields to PivotTables as row, column, or data fields. You can calculate fields from other fields, and items in fields. You can group items. You might do this to summarize dates by years and months, for example. You can hide items, so that you see only the data required.

You can link a PivotChart to a PivotTable so that changes in either are synchronized. A `PivotLayout` object connects them.

Using ADO, you can link your PivotTables to external data sources.

Filtered Lists

In this chapter we will see how to set up VBA code to manage data in lists and code to filter information from lists. The features we will be looking at are the Data Form, AutoFilter, and Advanced Filter. We will demonstrate techniques for creating and managing filtered lists, generating supporting code using the macro recorder, how to use controls to display the lists, and how to side step possible problems relative to internationalization issues.

Structuring the Data

Before you can apply Excel's list management tools, your data must be set up in a very specific way. The data must be structured like a database table, with headings at the top of each column, which are the field names, and the data itself must consist of single rows of information, which are the equivalent of database records. Figure 23-1 shows a list that holds information on the sales of fruit products.

> Excel should never be considered a fully equipped database application. It is limited in the amount of data it can handle and it cannot efficiently handle multiple related database tables. However, Excel can work with other database applications to provide you with the data you need and it has some powerful tools, such as Data Form, AutoFilter, Advanced Filter, SubTotal and PivotTables, for analyzing, manipulating, and presenting that data. Examples of these elements are included in this chapter and Chapter 22.

Data Form

Excel has a builtin form that you can use to view, find, and edit data in a list. If you select a single cell in the list, or select the entire list, and click Data ⇨ Form... you will see a form like the one in Figure 23-2.

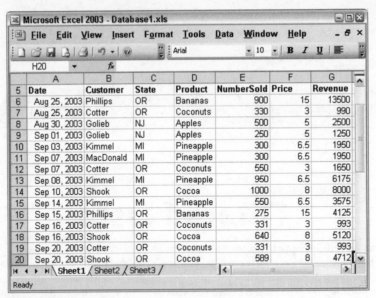

Figure 23-1

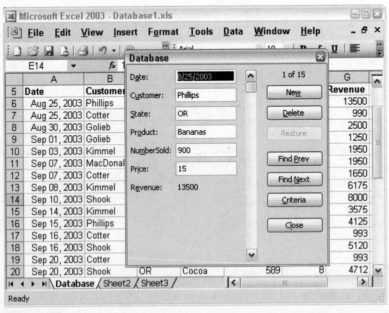

Figure 23-2

If you record this process, you will get code like the following:

```
Sub Macro1()
'
' Macro1 Macro
' Macro recorded 11/16/2003 by Paul Kimmel
'

'
    Range("B7").Select
    ActiveSheet.ShowDataForm
End Sub
```

If your list starts in the range of A5:B6, and you record selecting the first cell and showing the Data Form, then the recorded macro works. If your list starts in any cell outside the range A5:B6, and you record while selecting the top left-hand corner and showing the Data Form, the recorded macro will give an error message when you try to run it. You can overcome this problem by applying the name Database to your list.

> **If you don't work entirely with US date and number formats, the Data Form feature is quite dangerous, when displayed by VBA code using the ShowDataForm method. The Data Form, when invoked by VBA, displays dates and numbers only in US format. On the other hand, any dates or numbers typed in by a user are interpreted according to the regional settings in the Windows Control Panel. Therefore, if you set the date in the British format (dd/mm/yyyy), when you use the Data Form, the dates become corrupted. See Chapter 17 for more details.**

AutoFilter

The AutoFilter feature is a very easy way to select data from a list. You can activate AutoFilter by selecting a cell in your data list and clicking Data ➪ Filter ➪ AutoFilter. Drop-down menu buttons will appear beside each field name as shown next. If you want an exact match on a field such as Customer, all you need to do is click the drop-down beside the field and click the required match, as shown in Figure 23-3.

Custom AutoFilter

If you want a more advanced filter, such as a range of dates, you need to do a bit more work. The following screen shows how you can manually filter the data to show a particular month. Click the drop-down button beside Date and choose Custom. You can then fill in the dialog box as shown in Figure 23-4.

> **The format you use when you type in dates in the Custom AutoFilter dialog box depends on your regional settings. You can use a dd/mm/yy format if you work with UK settings, or a mm/dd/yy format if you work with US settings. Additional formats are recognized.**

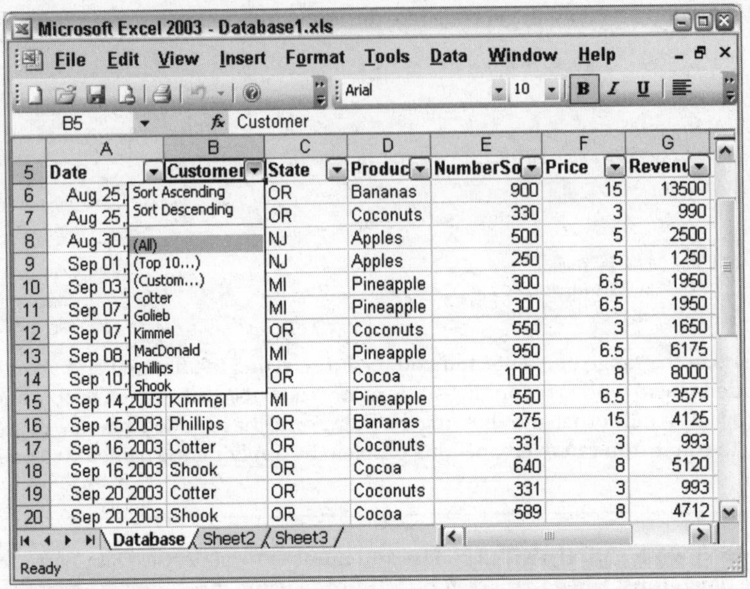

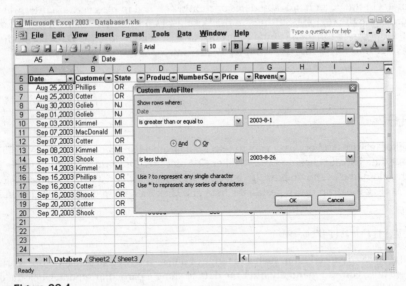

Figure 23-3

Figure 23-4

Adding Combo Boxes

You can make filtering even easier for a user by placing controls in the worksheet to run AutoFilter. This also gives you the opportunity to do far more with the data than filter it. You could copy the filtered data to another worksheet and generate a report, you could chart the data or you could delete it. Figure 23-5 shows two ActiveX combo box controls that allow the user to select the month and year required.

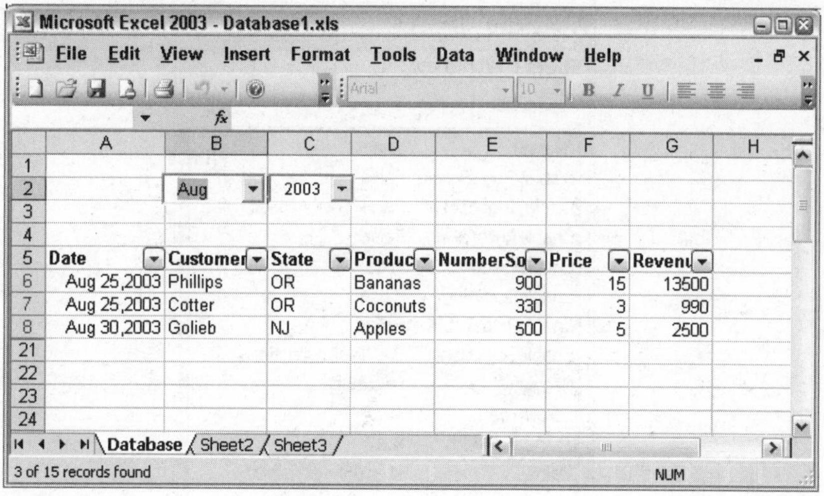

Figure 23-5

The combo boxes have the default names of ComboBox1 and ComboBox2. To place list values into the combo boxes, you can enter the list values into a worksheet column and define the ListFillRange property of the ComboBox object as something like "=Sheet2!H1:H12". Alternatively, you can use the following Workbook_Open event procedure in the ThisWorkbook module of the workbook, to populate the combo boxes when the workbook is opened:

```
Private Sub Workbook_Open()
  Dim Months() As Variant
  Dim Years() As Variant
  Dim I As Integer

  Months = Array("Jan", "Feb", "Mar", "Apr", _
    "May", "Jun", "Jul", "Aug", "Sep", _
    "Oct", "Nov", "Dec")

  Years = Array(2002, 2003, 2004)
  For I = LBound(Months) To UBound(Months)
    Sheet1.ComboBox1.AddItem Months(I)
  Next I

  Sheet1.ComboBox2.List = WorksheetFunction.Transpose(Years)

End Sub
```

The AddItem method of the ComboBox object adds the Months array values to the ComboBox1 list. To show an alternative technique, the worksheet Transpose function is used to convert the Years array from a row to a column, and the values are assigned to the List property of ComboBox2.

Note that the programmatic name of Sheet1, which you can see in the Project Explorer window or the Properties window of the VBE, has been used to define the location of the combo boxes. Even though the name of the worksheet is Database, the programmatic name is still Sheet1, unless you change it at the top of the Properties window where it is identified by (Name), rather than Name, as shown in Figure 23-6.

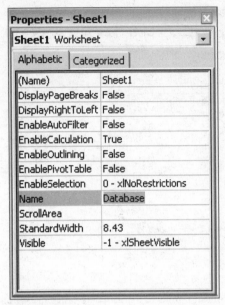

Figure 23-6

In the code module behind the worksheet, the following code is entered:

```
Private Sub ComboBox1_Change()
   Call FilterDates
End Sub

Private Sub ComboBox2_Change()
   Call FilterDates
End Sub
```

When you click an entry in their drop-down lists, each combo box executes the `FilterDates` procedure, which is described next. `FilterDates` can be in the same module, and declared `Private` if you do not want any other modules to be able to use it, or it can be in a standard code module if you want to use it as a general utility procedure.

So, how do you construct the `FilterDates` procedure? As we have shown in previous chapters, you can use the macro recorder to get something to start with, and then refine the code to make it more flexible and efficient. If you use the macro recorder to record the process of filtering the dates, you will get code like this:

```
Sub Macro4()
'
' Macro4 Macro
' Macro recorded 11/16/2003 by Paul Kimmel
'

'
   Range("A5").Select
```

```
      Selection.AutoFilter
      Selection.AutoFilter Field:=1, Criteria1:=">=8/1/2003", Operator:=xlAnd, _
        Criteria2:="<=9/15/2003"
   End Sub
```

As usual, the macro recorder selects ranges and produces precise code. What we want is slightly more generalized code that is associated with our named range rather than a specific range of cells. We can make this transformation by using our named range, Database, as shown:

```
   Public Sub FilterDates()
      Range("Database").AutoFilter Field:=1, _
        Criteria1:=">=8/1/2003", _
        Operator:=xlAnd, Criteria2:="<9/15/2003"
   End Sub
```

Working from the macro we can complete the general solution. Essentially, we need to read the month from the first combo box and the year from the second combo box. Next, we elected to add one month to the range, contriving the start and end dates as the selected month and year and the selected month + 1 and year, respectively. The final result is shown in the listing:

```
   Private Sub FilterDates()
      Dim StartMonth As Integer
      Dim StartYear As Integer
      Dim StartDate As Date
      Dim EndDate As Date
      Dim StartCriterion As String

      Dim EndCriterion As String

      StartMonth = Me.ComboBox1.ListIndex + 1
      StartYear = Me.ComboBox2.Value
      StartDate = DateSerial(StartYear, StartMonth, 1)
      EndDate = DateSerial(StartYear, StartMonth + 1, 1)

      StartCriterion = ">=" & Format(StartDate, "mm/dd/yyyy")
      EndCriterion = "<" & Format(EndDate, "mm/dd/yyyy")

      Range("Database").AutoFilter Field:=1, Criteria1:=StartCriterion, _
        Operator:=xlAnd, Criteria2:=EndCriterion
   End Sub
```

FilterDates assigns the values selected in the combo boxes to StartMonth and StartYear. The Me keyword has been used to refer to the sheet containing the code, rather than the object name Sheet1. This permits the code to be copied and pasted into another worksheet without worrying about the name of the sheet.

StartMonth uses the ListIndex property of ComboBox1 to obtain the month as a number. As the ListIndex is zero-based, 1 is added to give the correct month number. The DateSerial function translates the year and month numbers into a date and assigns the date to StartDate. The second DateSerial function calculates a date that is one month ahead of StartDate and assigns it to EndDate.

The `Format` function is used to turn `StartDate` and `EndDate` back into strings in the US date format of `mm/dd/yyyy`. The appropriate logical operators are placed in front and the resulting strings are assigned to `StartCriterion` and `EndCriterion`, respectively. `FilterDates` finally executes the `AutoFilter` method on the range `Database`, using the computed criteria.

Getting the Exact Date

There is another tricky problem with AutoFilter that occurs with dates in all language versions of Excel. The problem arises when you want to get an exact date, rather than a date within a range of dates. In this case, AutoFilter matches your date with the formatted appearance of the dates in the worksheet, not the underlying date values.

Excel holds dates as numeric values equal to the number of days since January 1, 1900. For example, January 1, 2003, is held as 37622. When you ask for dates greater than or equal to January 1, 2003, Excel looks for date serial numbers greater than or equal to 37622. However, when you ask for dates equal to January 1, 2003, Excel does not look for the numeric value of the date; Excel checks for the string value "Jan 1, 2003" as it appears formatted in the worksheet.

The following adaptation of `FilterDates` will handle an exact date match in our list, because `ExactCriterion` is assigned the date value, as a string in the format "mmm dd, yyyy" and the dates are formatted in the worksheet as mmm dd, yyyy:

```
Private Sub FilterExactDate()
  Dim ExactMonth As Integer
  Dim ExactYear As Integer
  Dim ExactDate As Date
  Dim ExactCriterion As String

  ExactMonth = Sheet1.ComboBox1.ListIndex + 1

  ExactYear = Sheet1.ComboBox2.Value
  ExactDate = DateSerial(ExactYear, ExactMonth, 1)
  ExactCriterion = Format(ExactDate, "mmm dd,yyyy")
  Range("Database").AutoFilter Field:=1, Criteria1:=ExactCriterion
End Sub
```

Note that if you change the date format used in the worksheet you also need to change the date format in the code or the code will no longer work.

The preceding code will give all the entries for the first of the month, as 1 is specified as the third parameter in the DateSerial function. To select any day of the month, a third combo box could be added to cell A2 and some code added to the ComboBox1_Click event procedure to list the correct number of days for the month specified in ComboBox1.

Copying the Visible Rows

If you want to make it easy to create a new worksheet containing a copy of the filtered data, you can place an ActiveX command button at the top of the worksheet and enter the following `Click` event procedure in the worksheet module. This procedure copies the entire `Database` range, knowing that, by default, only the visible cells will be copied:

```
Private Sub CommandButton1_Click()
  Dim NewWorksheet As Worksheet
  Dim WorksheetName As String
  Dim Month As String
  Dim Year As String
  Dim TempWorksheet As Worksheet

  Month = Sheet1.ComboBox1.Value
  Year = Sheet1.ComboBox2.Value
  On Error Resume Next
  WorksheetName = Format( _
    DateValue(Year & " " & Month & " 1"), "mmm yyyy")

  Set TempWorksheet = Worksheets(WorksheetName)

  If Err.Number = 0 Then
    MsgBox "This data has already been copied"
    Exit Sub
  End If

  On Error GoTo 0

  Set NewWorksheet = Worksheets.Add
  Range("Database").Copy Destination:=NewWorksheet.Range("A1")
  NewWorksheet.Columns("A:G").AutoFit
  NewWorksheet.Name = WorksheetName
End Sub
```

The Click event procedure first calculates a name for the new worksheet in the format mmm yyyy. It then checks to see if this worksheet already exists by setting a dummy object variable to refer to a worksheet with the new name. If this does not cause an error, the worksheet already exists and the procedure issues a message and exits.

If there is no worksheet with the new name, the event procedure adds a new worksheet at the end of the existing worksheets. It copies the Database range to the new sheet and AutoFits the column widths to accommodate the copied data. The procedure then names the new worksheet.

Finding the Visible Rows

When you use AutoFilter, Excel simply hides the rows that do not match the current filters. If you want to process just the rows that are visible in your code, you need to look at each row in the list and decide if it is hidden or not. There is a trick to this. When referring to the Hidden property of a Range object, the Range object must be an entire row, extending from column A to column IV, or an entire column, extending from row 1 to row 65536. You can't use the Hidden property with a single cell or a 7 column row from the list shown in Figure 23-7.

The following code checks each row that is visible on the screen and shades the background of any row that has an invalid Revenue calculation:

```
Private Sub CommandButton1_Click()
  Dim Database As Range
  Dim Row As Range
```

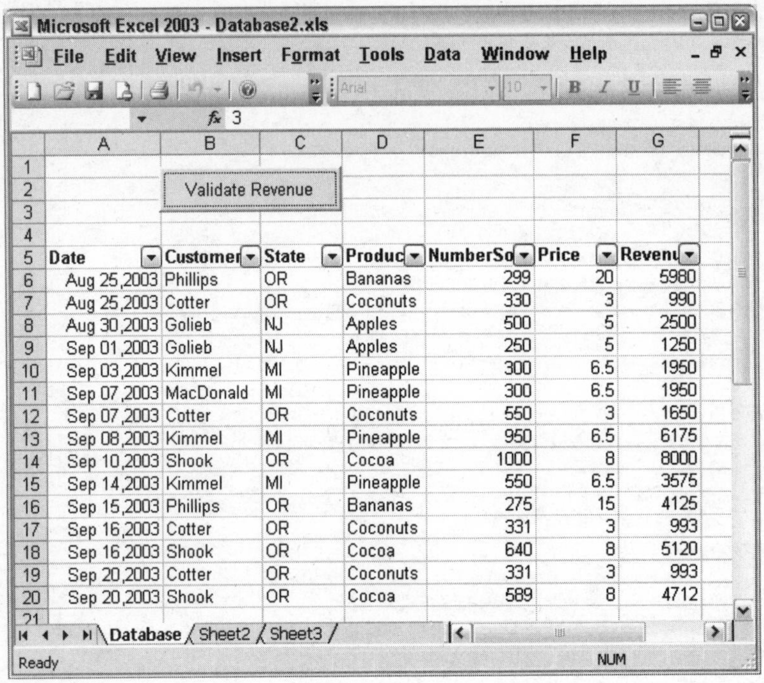

Date	Customer	State	Product	NumberSold	Price	Revenue
Aug 25,2003	Phillips	OR	Bananas	299	20	5980
Aug 25,2003	Cotter	OR	Coconuts	330	3	990
Aug 30,2003	Golieb	NJ	Apples	500	5	2500
Sep 01,2003	Golieb	NJ	Apples	250	5	1250
Sep 03,2003	Kimmel	MI	Pineapple	300	6.5	1950
Sep 07,2003	MacDonald	MI	Pineapple	300	6.5	1950
Sep 07,2003	Cotter	OR	Coconuts	550	3	1650
Sep 08,2003	Kimmel	MI	Pineapple	950	6.5	6175
Sep 10,2003	Shook	OR	Cocoa	1000	8	8000
Sep 14,2003	Kimmel	MI	Pineapple	550	6.5	3575
Sep 15,2003	Phillips	OR	Bananas	275	15	4125
Sep 16,2003	Cotter	OR	Coconuts	331	3	993
Sep 16,2003	Shook	OR	Cocoa	640	8	5120
Sep 20,2003	Cotter	OR	Coconuts	331	3	993
Sep 20,2003	Shook	OR	Cocoa	589	8	4712

Figure 23-7

```
    Dim NumberSold As Double
    Dim Price As Double
    Dim Revenue As Double

    With Range("Database")
      Set Database = .Offset(1, 0).Resize(.Rows.Count - 1)
    End With

    For Each Row In Database.Rows
      If Row.EntireRow.Hidden = False Then
        NumberSold = Row.Cells(5).Value
        Price = Row.Cells(6).Value
        Revenue = Row.Cells(7).Value
        If Abs(NumberSold * Price - Revenue) > 0.000001 Then
          Row.Select
          MsgBox "Error in selected row"
          Row.Interior.ColorIndex = 15
        End If
      End If
    Next Row
  End Sub
```

The `Click` event procedure for the command button first defines an object variable `Database` referring to the range named `Database`, excluding the Header Row. It then uses a `For Each...Next` loop to process all the rows in `Database`. The first `If` test ensures that only rows that are not hidden are processed. The `NumberSold`, `Price`, and `Revenue` values for the current row are assigned to variables and the second `If` tests that the `Revenue` figure is within a reasonable tolerance of the product of the `NumberSold` and the `Price`.

As worksheet computations are done with binary representations of numbers to an accuracy of about 15 significant figures, it is not always appropriate to check that two numbers are equal to the last decimal point, especially if the input figures have come from other worksheet calculations. It is better to see if they differ by an acceptably small amount. As the difference can be positive or negative, the Abs function is used to convert both positive and negative differences to a positive difference before comparison.

If the test shows an unacceptable difference, the row is selected and a message displayed. The row is also given a background color of light gray.

Advanced Filter

The most powerful way to filter data from a list is to use Advanced Filter. You can filter the list in place, like AutoFilter, or you can extract it to a different location. The extract location can be in the same worksheet, another worksheet in the same workbook, or in another open workbook. In the following example, we have extracted the data for OR and MI for the third quarter of 2003. The data has been copied from the workbook containing the data list to a new workbook.

When you use Advanced Filter, you specify your criteria in a worksheet range. An example of a `Criteria` range is shown in A1:C3 of Figure 23-8. This workbook is in a workbook called

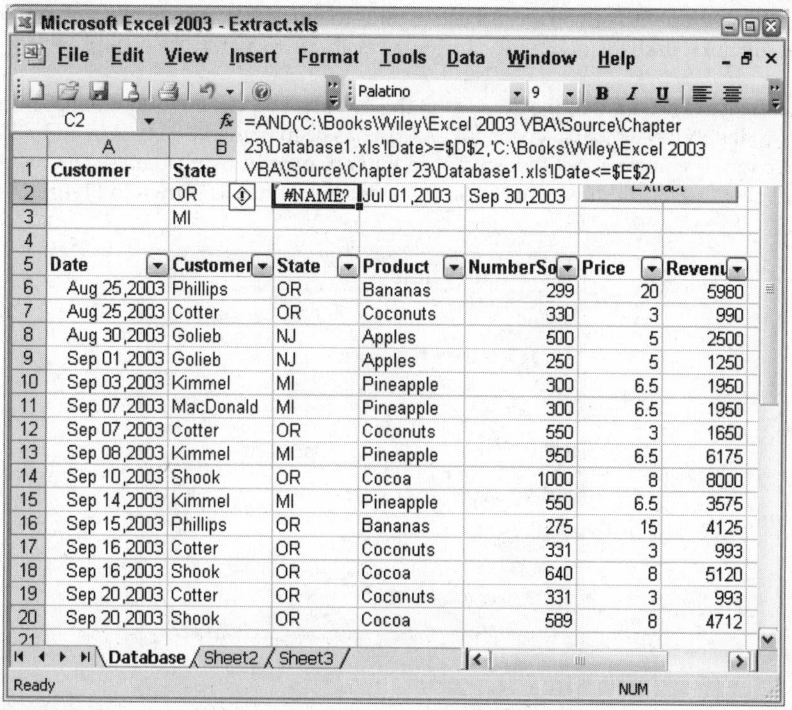

Figure 23-8

493

`Extract.xls`. The data list is in `Database1.xls` that contains data that is the same as the data we used in the AutoFilter examples.

The top row of the `Criteria` range contains the field names from the list that you want to filter on. You can have as many rows under the field names as you need. Criteria on different rows are combined using the OR operator. Criteria across a row are combined using the AND operator. You can also use computed criteria in the form of logical statements that evaluate to `True` or `False`. In the case of computed criteria, the top row of the `Criteria` range must be empty or contain a label that is not a field name in the list, such as `Calc` in this case.

When you create computed criteria, you can refer to the data list field names in your formulas, as you can see in the formula bar above the worksheet. The formula bar shows the contents of C2, which is as follows:

```
=AND(Database1.xls!Date>=$D$2,Database1.xls!Date<=$E$2)
```

The formula in C3 is identical to the formula in C2.

The criteria shown can be thought of as applying this filter:

```
(State=OR AND Date>=Jul 1,2003 AND Date<Sep 30,2003) OR _
   (State=MI AND Date>=Jul 1,2003 AND Date<Sep 30,2003)
```

As the data list is in the file `Database1.xls`, the references to the `Date` field are entered as external references, in the same format you would use to refer to workbook names in another workbook. As the field names are not workbook names, the formulas evaluate to a `#NAME?` error.

To facilitate the Advanced Filter, the data list in the `Database1.xls` workbook has been named `Database`. In the `Extract.xls` workbook, A1:C3 has been named `Criteria` and A5:G5 has been named `Extract`. If you carry out the Advanced Filter manually, using Data ➪ Filter ➪ Advanced Filter, you see the following dialog box, where you can enter the names as shown in Figure 23-9.

Figure 23-9

To automate this process, the command button with the Extract caption runs the following `Click` event procedure:

```
Private Sub CommandButton1_Click()
  Dim Database As Range
  Dim Criteria As Range
  Dim Extract As Range

  Set Database = Workbooks("Database1.xls"). _
    Worksheets("Database").Range("Database")

  Set Criteria = ThisWorkbook.Worksheets(1).Range("Criteria")
  Set Extract = ThisWorkbook.Worksheets(1).Range("Extract")
  Database.AdvancedFilter Action:=xlFilterCopy, _
    CriteriaRange:=Criteria, CopyToRange:=Extract

End Sub
```

The event procedure defines three object variables referring to the `Database`, `Criteria`, and `Extract` ranges. It then runs the `AdvancedFilter` method of the `Database Range` object.

Summary

The Data Form feature makes it very easy to set up a data maintenance macro. However, you should apply the name `Database` to your data list if the top left-hand corner of the list is not in the range A1:B2.

As you have seen, the AutoFilter and Advanced Filter features can be combined with VBA code to provide flexible ways for users to extract information from data lists. By combining these features with ActiveX controls, such as combo boxes and command buttons, you can make them readily accessible to all levels of users. You can use the macro recorder to get an indication of the required methods and adapt the recorded code to accept input from the ActiveX controls.

However, you need to take care, if you work with nonUS date formats. You need to bear in mind that VBA requires you to use US date formats when you compare ranges of dates using AutoFilter. If this interests you, you should check out Chapter 17, which deals with international programming issues.

Also, when you want to detect which rows have been hidden by AutoFilter, you need to be aware that the `Hidden` property of the `Range` object can only be applied to entire worksheet rows.

Advanced Filter provides the most powerful filtering in Excel. You can set up much more complex criteria with Advanced Filter than you can with AutoFilter and you can copy filtered data to a specified range. You can also use Advanced Filter to copy filtered data from one workbook to another.

Generating Charts

In this chapter we will see how you can use the macro recorder to discover what objects, methods, and properties are required to manipulate charts. We will then improve and extend that code to make it more flexible and efficient. This chapter is designed to show you how to gain access to `Chart` objects in VBA code so that you can start to program the vast number of objects that Excel charts contain. You can find more information on these objects in Appendix A. We will look specifically at:

❑   Creating `Chart` objects on separate sheets

❑   Creating `Chart` objects embedded in a worksheet

❑   Editing data series in charts

❑   Defining series with arrays

❑   Defining chart labels linked to worksheet cells

You can create two types of charts in Excel: charts that occupy their own chart sheets and charts that are embedded in a worksheet. They can be manipulated in code in much the same way. The only difference is that, while the chart sheet is a `Chart` object in its own right, the chart embedded in a worksheet is contained by a `ChartObject` object. Each `ChartObject` on a worksheet is a member of the worksheet's `ChartObjects` collection. Chart sheets are members of the workbook's `Charts` collection.

Each ChartObject is a member of the Shapes collection, as well as a member of the ChartObjects collection. The Shapes collection provides you with an alternative way to refer to embedded charts. The macro recorder generates code that uses the Shapes collection rather than the ChartObjects collection.

Chart Sheets

Before creating the chart as described, turn on the macro recorder. Create a new chart sheet called `Mangoes` using the Chart Wizard to create a chart from the data in cells A3:D7, as shown in Figure 24-1. In Step 2 of the Chart Wizard, choose the "Series in Rows" option. In Step 3, change the

Chart title to Mangoes. In Step 4 of the Chart Wizard, choose the "As new sheet" option and enter the name of the chart sheet as "Mangoes".

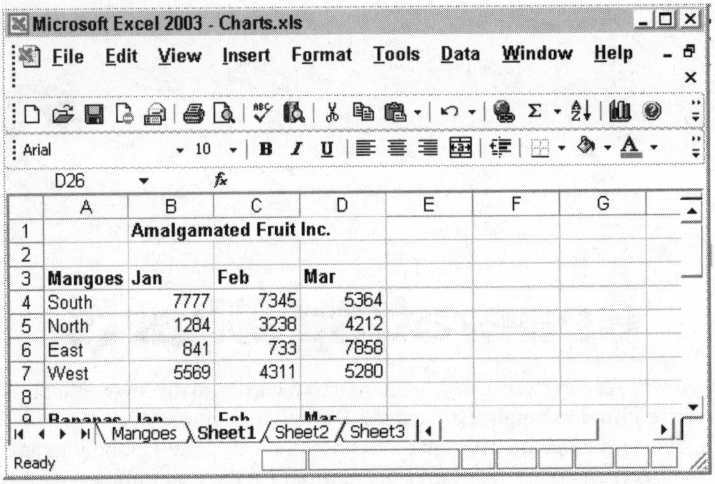

Figure 24-1

The screen in Figure 24-2 shows the chart created.

The Recorded Macro

The recorded macro should look like the following:

```
Sub Macro1()
'
' Macro1 Macro
' Macro recorded 11/23/2003 by Paul Kimmel
'


    Charts.Add
    ActiveChart.ChartType = xlColumnClustered
    ActiveChart.SetSourceData Source:=Sheets("Sheet1").Range("A3:D7"), PlotBy:= _
        xlRows
    ActiveChart.Location Where:=xlLocationAsNewSheet, Name:="Mangoes"
    With ActiveChart
        .HasTitle = True
        .ChartTitle.Characters.Text = "Mangoes"
        .Axes(xlCategory, xlPrimary).HasTitle = False
        .Axes(xlValue, xlPrimary).HasTitle = False
    End With
    ActiveWindow.WindowState = xlMaximized
End Sub
```

The recorded macro uses the Add method of the Charts collection to create a new chart. It defines the active chart's ChartType property, and then uses the SetSourceData method to define the ranges plotted. The macro uses the Location method to define the chart as a chart sheet and assign it a name. It

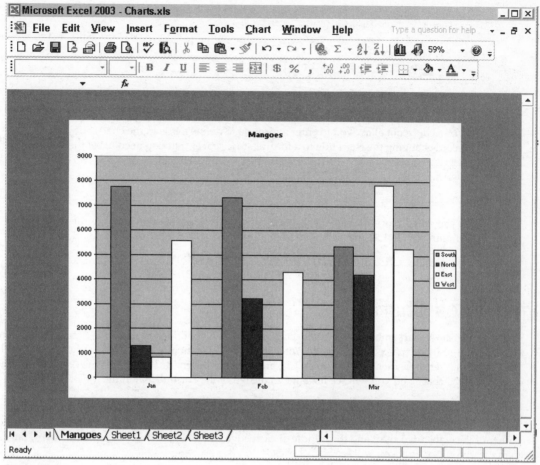

Figure 24-2

sets the `HasTitle` property to `True` so that it can define the `ChartTitle` property. Finally, it sets the `HasTitle` property of the axes back to `False`, a step which is not necessary.

Adding a Chart Sheet Using VBA Code

The recorded code is reasonably good as it stands. However, it is more elegant to create an object variable, so that you have a simple and efficient way of referring to the chart in subsequent code. You can also remove some of the redundant code and add a chart title that is linked to the worksheet. The following code incorporates these changes:

```
Option Explicit

Public Sub AddChartSheet()
  Dim aChart As Chart

  Set aChart = Charts.Add
  With aChart
```

```
        .Name = "Mangoes"
        .ChartType = xlColumnClustered
        .SetSourceData Source:=Sheets("Sheet1").Range("A3:D7"), PlotBy:=xlRows
        .HasTitle = True
        .ChartTitle.Text = "=Sheet1!R3C1"
    End With
End Sub
```

The `Location` method has been removed, as it is not necessary. A chart sheet is produced by default. The Chart Wizard does not allow you to enter a formula to define a title in the chart, but you can separately record changing the chart title to a formula to discover that you need to set the `Text` property of the `ChartTitle` object equal to the formula. In the preceding code, the chart title has been defined as a formula referring to the value in cell R3C1, or A3.

> **When you enter a formula into a chart text element, it must be defined using the row and column (e.g. R3C1) addressing method, not the cell (A1) addressing method.**

Embedded Charts

When you create a chart embedded as a `ChartObject`, it is a good idea to name the `ChartObject` so that it can be easily referenced in later code. You can do this by manually selecting a worksheet cell, so that the chart is not selected, then holding down *Ctrl* and clicking the chart. This selects the `ChartObject`, rather than the chart, and you will see its name to the left of the Formula bar at the top of the screen.

This is how you can tell that you have selected the `ChartObject`: not only does its name appear in the name box to the left of formula bar, but you will also see white boxes (white circles in Excel 2003) at each corner of the embedded chart and the middle of each edge, as shown next. If you select the *chart*, rather than the `ChartObject`, you will see black boxes.

You can select and change the name of the `ChartObject` in the name box and press *Enter* to update it. The embedded chart shown in Figure 24-3 was created using the Chart Wizard. It was then dragged to its new location and had its name changed to `MangoesChart`.

Using the Macro Recorder

If you select cells A3:D7 and turn on the macro recorder before creating the previous chart, including moving the `ChartObject` to the required location and changing its name to `MangoesChart`, you will get code like the following:

```
Sub Macro2()
'
' Macro2 Macro
' Macro recorded 11/23/2003 by Paul Kimmel
'


    Charts.Add
    ActiveChart.ChartType = xlColumnClustered
```

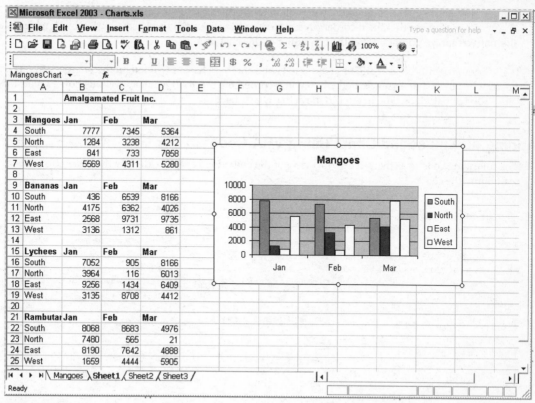

Figure 24-3

```
    ActiveChart.SetSourceData Source:=Sheets("Sheet1").Range("A3:D7"), PlotBy:= _
        xlRows
    ActiveChart.Location Where:=xlLocationAsObject, Name:="Sheet1"
    With ActiveChart
        .HasTitle = True
        .ChartTitle.Characters.Text = "Mangoes"
        .Axes(xlCategory, xlPrimary).HasTitle = False
        .Axes(xlValue, xlPrimary).HasTitle = False
    End With
    ActiveSheet.Shapes("Chart 5").IncrementLeft 81.75
    ActiveSheet.Shapes("Chart 5").IncrementTop -21.75
    ActiveWindow.Visible = False
    Windows("Charts.xls").Activate
    Range("G4").Select
    ActiveSheet.Shapes("Chart 5").Select
    Selection.Name = "MangoesChart"
End Sub
```

The recorded macro is similar to the one that created a chart sheet, down to the definition of the chart title, except that it uses the `Location` method to define the chart as an embedded chart. Up to the `End With`, the recorded code is reusable. However, the code to relocate the `ChartObject` and change its name is not reusable. The code uses the default name applied to the ChartObject to identify the ChartObject. (Note that the recorder prefers to refer to a ChartObject as a Shape object, which is an alternative that we pointed out at the beginning of this chapter.)

If you try to run this code again, or adapt it to create another chart, it will fail on the reference to Chart 30, or whichever shape you created when you recorded the macro. It is not as obvious how to refer to the ChartObject itself as how to refer to the active chart sheet.

Adding an Embedded Chart Using VBA Code

The following code uses the Parent property of the embedded chart to identify the ChartObject containing the chart:

```
Sub AddChart()
  Dim aChart As Chart

  ActiveSheet.ChartObjects.Delete
  Set aChart = Charts.Add
  Set aChart = aChart.Location(Where:=xlLocationAsObject, Name:="Sheet1")
  With aChart
    .ChartType = xlColumnClustered
    .SetSourceData Source:=Sheets("Sheet1").Range("A3:D7"), _
      PlotBy:=xlRows
    .HasTitle = True
    .ChartTitle.Text = "=Sheet1!R3C1"
    With .Parent
        .Top = Range("F3").Top
        .Left = Range("F3").Left
        .Name = "MangoesChart"
    End With
  End With
End Sub
```

AddChart first deletes any existing ChartObjects. It then sets the object variable aChart to refer to the added chart. By default, the new chart is on a chart sheet, so the Location method is used to define the chart as an embedded chart.

> When you use the **Location** method of the **Chart** object, the **Chart** object is recreated and any reference to the original **Chart** object is destroyed. Therefore, it is necessary to assign the return value of the **Location** method to the **aChart** object variable so that it refers to the new **Chart** object.

AddChart defines the chart type, source data, and chart title. Again, the chart title has been assigned a formula referring to cell A3. Using the Parent property of the Chart object to refer to the ChartObject object, AddChart sets the Top and Left properties of the ChartObject to be the same as the Top and Left properties of cell F3. AddChart finally assigns the new name to the ChartObject so that it can easily be referenced in the future.

Editing Data Series

The `SetSourceData` method of the `Chart` object is the quickest way to define a completely new set of data for a chart. You can also manipulate individual series using the `Series` object, which is a member of the chart's `SeriesCollection` object. The following example is designed to show you how to access individual series.

We will take the `MangoesChart` and delete all the series from it, and then replace them with four new series, one at a time. The new chart will contain product information for a region nominated by the user. To make it easier to locate each set of product data, names have been assigned to each product range in the worksheet. For example, A3:D7 has been given the name `Mangoes`, corresponding to the label in A3. The final chart will be similar to Figure 24-4.

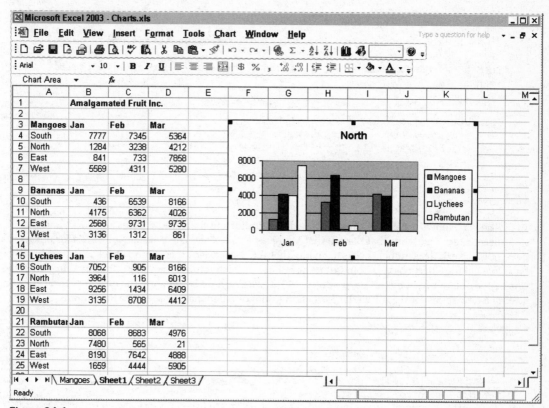

Figure 24-4

The following code converts `MangoesChart` to include the new data (note that the original chart must still be on the spreadsheet for this to work). As `MangoesToRegion` comprises several parts, we'll examine it by section. (The complete for `MangoesToRegion` listing is provided here and the supporting methods are described later.)

```
Public Function PickRegion() As Integer

    Dim Answer As String
```

```
    Do
        Answer = InputBox("Enter Region number (1 to 4)")
        If Answer >= "1" And Answer <= "4" Then
            Exit Do
        Else
            Call MsgBox("Region must be be 1, 2, 3 or 4", vbCritical)
        End If
    Loop

    PickRegion = CInt(Answer)
End Function

Public Sub MangoesToRegion()

    Debug.Assert MangoChartExists()

    ' Sentinel: No point in doing anything if pre-conditions don't exist
    If Not MangoChartExists() Then
        MsgBox "MangoesChart was not found - procedure aborted", vbCritical
        Exit Sub
    End If

    Dim aChart As Chart
    Set aChart = GetMangoChart().Chart
    Debug.Assert (aChart Is Nothing = False)

    Call DeleteSeries(aChart.SeriesCollection)
    Call AddProductsForRegion(PickRegion(), aChart)
End Sub
```

PickRegion shows the user an InputBox with text indicating that valid choices are 1, 2, 3, and 4.
MangoesToRegion asserts that the original Mangoes chart exists. The Debug.Assert is for our use as
developers. Next, the sentinel checks to ensure that the chart exists; this second check is for consumers.
Next, we get the Chart object—from GetMangoChart, which returns the ChartObject—from the
ChartObject returned by GetMangoChart. And, we finish up by deleting the existing chart series and
adding a new series for the selected information (Mangoes, Bananas, Lychees, or Rambutan):

```
Public Sub MangoesToRegion()

    Debug.Assert MangoChartExists()

    ' Sentinel: No point in doing anything if pre-conditions don't exist
    If Not MangoChartExists() Then
        MsgBox "MangoesChart was not found - procedure aborted", vbCritical
        Exit Sub
    End If

    Dim aChart As Chart
    Set aChart = GetMangoChart().Chart
    Debug.Assert (aChart Is Nothing = False)

    Call DeleteSeries(aChart.SeriesCollection)
    Call AddProductsForRegion(PickRegion(), aChart)
End Sub
```

This very concise code is supported by the cast of methods MangoChartExists, GetMangoChart, DeleteSeries, AddProductsForRegion, and PickRegion. Let's review each of those methods in the order introduced:

```
Public Function MangoChartExists() As Boolean
  MangoChartExists = GetMangoChart Is Nothing = False
End Function
```

MangoChartExists call GetMangoChart and tests to ensure that a valid ChartObject is returned. GetMangoChart uses an error handler to attempt to get the chart returning Nothing if an error occurs or the chart is not found:

```
Public Function GetMangoChart() As ChartObject
  On Error GoTo Catch
    Set GetMangoChart = Worksheets("Sheet1").ChartObjects("MangoesChart")
  Exit Function

Catch:
  Set GetMangoChart = Nothing
End Function
```

Next, DeleteSeries accepts a SeriesCollection, which we obtain from the Chart object, and it walks through preexisting series deleting each:

```
Public Sub DeleteSeries(ByVal Series As SeriesCollection)

  Dim I As Integer
  For I = Series.Count To 1 Step -1
    Series(I).Delete
  Next I
End Sub
```

After we delete the existing series, we can create a new series and add all of the products from the selected named group of information and finish up by adding a title and name to the new series:

```
Public Sub AddProductsForRegion(ByVal region As Integer, _
  ByVal Chart As Chart)

  Dim I As Integer
  Dim J As Integer
  Dim rangeY As Range
  Dim rangeX As Range
  Dim products As Variant
  Dim regions As Variant

  products = Array("Mangoes", "Bananas", "Lychees", "Rambutan")
  regions = Array("South", "North", "East", "West")

  For I = LBound(products) To UBound(products)
    Set rangeY = Range(products(I)).Offset(region, 1).Resize(1, 3)
    Set rangeX = Range(products(I)).Offset(0, 1).Resize(1, 3)
```

```
    With Chart.SeriesCollection.NewSeries
        .Name = products(I)
        .Values = rangeY
        .XValues = "=" & rangeX.Address _
            (RowAbsolute:=True, _
            ColumnAbsolute:=True, _
            ReferenceStyle:=xlR1C1, _
            External:=True)
    End With
  Next I

  Chart.ChartTitle.Text = regions(region - 1 + LBound(regions))
  GetMangoChart().Name = "RegionChart"
End Sub
```

That's all there is to it. In a nutshell, we picked an existing chart, deleted the existing series data, and added the new data. We prefer to break up methods as demonstrated in the preceding example because it permits us to legitimately reduce unnecessary comments and eliminate extra local, temporary variables.

If you have been programming for the last 10 years or more then you may be comfortable with a lot of temporary variables and long, monolithic methods. That style of programming isn't wrong, but modern discoveries in software development, including Refactoring—which applies as much to VBA as any other object-oriented language—argue successfully that code is more manageable with shorter methods, fewer temporaries, and well-named methods instead of a lot of temporary variables. We encourage you to read Martin Fowler's *Refactoring: Improving the Design of Existing Code* (Addison-Wesley, 1999) for more information.

Defining Chart Series with Arrays

A chart series can be defined by assigning a VBA array to its `Values` property. This can come in handy if you want to generate a chart that is not linked to the original data. The chart can be distributed in a separate workbook that is independent of the source data.

Figure 24-5 shows a chart of the `Mangoes` data. You can see the definition of the first data series in the Formula bar above the worksheet. The month names and the values on the vertical axis are defined by Excel arrays. The region names have been assigned as text to the series names.

> The size of an array used in the SERIES function is limited to around 250 elements. This limits the number of data points that can be plotted this way.

The 3D chart can be created using the following code:

```
Public Sub MakeArrayChart()
   Dim sourceWorksheet As Worksheet
```

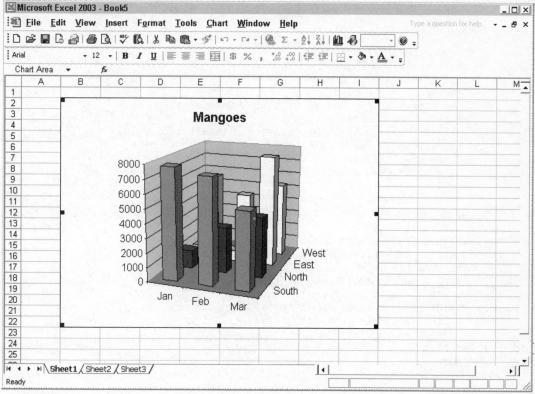

Figure 24-5

```
Dim sourceRange As Range
Dim aWorkbook As Workbook
Dim aWorksheet As Worksheet
Dim aChart As Chart
Dim aNewSeries As Series
Dim I As Integer
Dim SalesArray As Variant
Dim MonthArray As Variant

MonthArray = Array("Jan", "Feb", "Mar")

'Define the data source
Set sourceWorksheet = ThisWorkbook.Worksheets("Sheet1")
Set sourceRange = sourceWorksheet.Range("Mangoes")

'Create a new workbook
Set aWorkbook = Workbooks.Add
Set aWorksheet = aWorkbook.Worksheets(1)

'Add a new chart object and embed it in the worksheet
Set aChart = aWorkbook.Charts.Add
```

```
      Set aChart = aChart.Location(Where:=xlLocationAsObject, Name:="Sheet1")

   With aChart
      'Define the chart type
      .ChartType = xl3DColumn
      For I = 1 To 4
         'Create a new series
         Set aNewSeries = .SeriesCollection.NewSeries
         'Assign the data as arrays
         SalesArray = sourceRange.Offset(I, 1).Resize(1, 3).Value
         aNewSeries.Values = SalesArray
         aNewSeries.XValues = MonthArray
         aNewSeries.Name = sourceRange.Cells(I + 1, 1).Value
      Next I

      .HasLegend = False
      .HasTitle = True
      .ChartTitle.Text = "Mangoes"
      'Position the ChartObject in B2:I22 and name it
      With .Parent
         .Top = aWorksheet.Range("B2").Top
         .Left = aWorksheet.Range("B2").Left
         .Width = aWorksheet.Range("B2:I22").Width
         .Height = aWorksheet.Range("B2:I22").Height
         .Name = "ArrayChart"
      End With
   End With
End Sub
```

(The named range Mangoes was added using the Insert ➪ Name ➪ Define Excel menu
item and specifying the cells A3 to D7 as the Mangoes range.) MakeArrayChart assigns the month
names to MonthArray. This data could have come from the worksheet, if required, like the sales data. A
reference to the worksheet that is the source of the data is assigned to sourceWorksheet. The
Mangoes range is assigned to sourceRange. A new workbook is created for the chart and a reference
to it is assigned to aWorkbook. A reference to the first worksheet in the new workbook is assigned to
aWorksheet. A new chart is added to the Charts collection in aWorkbook and a reference to it assigned
to aChart. The Location method converts the chart to an embedded chart and redefines aChart.

In the With...End With structure, the ChartType property of aChart is changed to a 3D column type.
The For...Next loop creates the four new series. Each time around the loop, a new series is created
with the NewSeries method. The region data from the appropriate row is directly assigned
to the variant SalesArray, and SalesArray is immediately assigned to Values property of the new
series.

MonthArray is assigned to the XValues property of the new series. The text in column A of the
Mangoes range is assigned to the Name property of the new series.

The code then removes the chart legend, which is added by default, and sets the chart title. The final code
operates on the ChartObject, which is the chart's parent, to place the chart exactly over B2:I22, and
name the chart ArrayChart.

The result is a chart in a new workbook that is quite independent of the original workbook and its data. If the chart had been copied and pasted into the new workbook, it would still be linked to the original data.

Converting a Chart to use Arrays

You can easily convert an existing chart to use arrays instead of cell references and make it independent of the original data is was based on. The following code shows how:

```
Public Sub ConvertSeriesValuesToArrays()
  Dim aSeries As Series
  Dim aChart As Chart

  On Error GoTo Catch

  Set aChart = ActiveSheet.ChartObjects(1).Chart
  For Each aSeries In aChart.SeriesCollection
    aSeries.Values = aSeries.Values
    aSeries.XValues = aSeries.XValues
    aSeries.Name = aSeries.Name
  Next aSeries

  Exit Sub
Catch:

  MsgBox "Sorry, the data exceeds the array limits"
End Sub
```

For each series in the chart, the `Values`, `XValues`, and `Name` properties are set equal to themselves. Although these properties can be assigned range references, they always return an array of values when they are interrogated. This behavior can be exploited to convert the cell references to arrays.

Bear in mind that the number of data points that can be contained in an array reference is limited to 250 characters, or thereabouts. The code will fail if the limits are exceeded, so we have set up an error trap to cover this possibility.

Determining the Ranges used in a Chart

The behavior that is beneficial when converting a chart to use arrays is a problem when you need to programmatically determine the ranges that a chart is based on. If the `Values` and `Xvalues` properties returned the strings that you use to define them, the task would be easy.

The only property that contains information on the ranges is the `Formula` property that returns the formula containing the `SERIES` function as a string. The formula would be like the following:

```
=SERIES(Sheet1!$A$4,Sheet1!$B$3:$D$3,Sheet1!$B$4:$D$4,1)
```

The XValues are defined by the second parameter and the Values by the third parameter. You need to locate the commas and extract the text between them as shown in the following code, designed to work with a chart embedded in the active sheet:

```
Public Sub GetRangesFromChart()
  Dim aSeries As Series
  Dim seriesFunction As String
  Dim firstComma As Integer
  Dim secondComma As Integer
  Dim thirdComma As Integer
  Dim rangeValueString As String
  Dim rangeXValueString As String
  Dim rangeValue As Range
  Dim rangeXValue As Range

  On Error GoTo Catch

  'Get the SERIES function from the first series in the chart
  Set aSeries = ActiveSheet.ChartObjects(1).Chart.SeriesCollection(1)
  seriesFunction = aSeries.Formula

  'Locate the commas
  firstComma = InStr(1, seriesFunction, ",")
  secondComma = InStr(firstComma + 1, seriesFunction, ",")
  thirdComma = InStr(secondComma + 1, seriesFunction, ",")
  'Extract the range references as strings
  rangeXValueString = Mid(seriesFunction, firstComma + 1, _
    secondComma - firstComma - 1)

  rangeValueString = Mid(seriesFunction, secondComma + 1, _
    thirdComma - secondComma - 1)

  'Convert the strings to range objects
  Set rangeXValue = Range(rangeXValueString)
  Set rangeValue = Range(rangeValueString)
  'Colour the ranges
  rangeXValue.Interior.ColorIndex = 3
  rangeValue.Interior.ColorIndex = 4
  Exit Sub

Catch:
  MsgBox "Sorry, an error has ocurred" & vbCr & _
         "This chart might contain invalid range references"
End Sub
```

seriesFunction is assigned the formula of the series, which contains the SERIES function as a string. The positions of the first, second, and third commas are found using the InStr function. The Mid function is used to extract the range references as strings and they are converted to Range objects using the Range property.

The conversion of the strings to Range objects works even when the range references are not on the same sheet or in the same workbook as the embedded chart, as long as the source data is in an open workbook.

You could then proceed to manipulate the Range objects. You can change cell values in the ranges, for example, or extend or contract the ranges, once you have programmatic control over them. We have just colored the ranges for illustration purposes.

Chart Labels

In Excel, it is easy to add data labels to a chart, as long as the labels are based on the data series values or X-axis values. These options are available using Chart ⇨ Chart Options.

You can also enter your own text as labels, or you can enter formulas into each label to refer to cells, but this involves a lot of manual work. You would need to add standard labels to the series and then individually select each one and either replace it with your own text, or click in the Formula bar and enter a formula. Alternatively, you can write a macro to do it for you.

Figure 24-6 shows a chart of sales figures for each month, with the name of the top salesperson for each month. The labels have been defined by formulas linked to row 4 of the worksheet, as you can see for Jenny in April. The formula in the Formula bar points to cell E4.

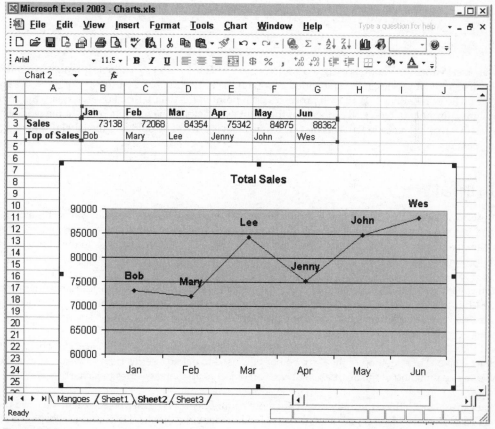

Figure 24-6

Say, you have set up a line chart like the previous one, but without the data labels. You can add the data labels and their formulas using the following code:

```
Public Sub AddDataLabels()
    Dim sales As Series
    Dim points As points
    Dim aPoint As Point
    Dim aRange As Range
    Dim I As Integer

    Set aRange = Range("B4:G4")
    Set sales = ActiveSheet.ChartObjects(1).Chart.SeriesCollection(1)
    sales.HasDataLabels = True
    Set points = sales.points
    For Each aPoint In points
      I = I + 1
      aPoint.DataLabel.Text = "=" & aRange.Cells(I).Address _
          (RowAbsolute:=True, _
          ColumnAbsolute:=True, _
          ReferenceStyle:=xlR1C1, _
          External:=True)
      aPoint.DataLabel.Font.Bold = True
      aPoint.DataLabel.Position = xlLabelPositionAbove
    Next aPoint
End Sub
```

The object variable aRange is assigned a reference to B4:G4. The sales variable is assigned a reference to the first, and only, series in the embedded chart and the HasDataLabels property of the series is set to True. The For Each...Next loop processes each point in the data series. For each point, the code assigns a formula to the Text property of the point's data label. The formula refers to the worksheet cell as an external reference in R1C1 format. The data label is also made bold and the label positioned above the data point.

Summary

It is easy to create a programmatic reference to a chart on a chart sheet. The Chart object is a member of the Charts collection of the workbook. To reference a chart embedded in a worksheet, you need to be aware that the Chart object is contained in a ChartObject object that belongs to the ChartObjects collection of the worksheet.

You can move or resize an embedded chart by changing the Top, Left, Width, and Height properties of the ChartObject. If you already have a reference to the Chart object, you can get a reference to the ChartObject object through the Parent property of the Chart object.

Individual series in a chart are Series objects, and belong to the SeriesCollection object of the chart. The Delete method of the Series object is used to delete a series from a chart. You use the NewSeries method of the SeriesCollection object to add a new series to a chart.

You can assign a VBA array, rather than the more commonly used Range object, to the Values property of a Series object. This creates a chart that is independent of worksheet data and can be distributed without a supporting worksheet.

The Values and XValues properties return data values, not the range references used in a chart. You can determine the ranges referenced by a chart by examining the SERIES function in the Formula property of each series.

The data points in a chart are Point objects and belong to the Points collection of the Series object. Excel does not provide an easy way to link cell values to labels on series data points through the user interface. However, links can be easily established to data point labels using VBA code.

25

Office Files and Folders

Most of the objects discussed in this book come from the Excel Object Model. That is not the only object model available when you are writing Excel VBA code. A number of object models, or type libraries, are automatically associated with each Excel VBA project. You can see them listed in the drop-down menu at the top of the Object Browser or by clicking Tools ⇨ References in the VB Editor window and noting the libraries with check marks. There are libraries for Excel, VBA, Office, OLE Automation and, if you attach a UserForm, there will be a Forms library. You can attach more libraries by checking items in the Tools ⇨ References dialog box. This process is discussed in later chapters such as *Customizing the VBE*.

The Office Object Model is made available to all Microsoft Office applications. It contains objects that are used by all Office applications such as CommandBars, which are discussed in Chapter 26. In this chapter, we will examine two objects contained in the Office Object Model that you use to search for, open and save files and the properties associated with them:

- ❏   FileSearch
  - ❏   FoundFiles
  - ❏   PropertyTests
  - ❏   FileTypes
  - ❏   SearchScopes
  - ❏   ScopeFolders
  - ❏   SearchFolders
- ❏   FileDialog
  - ❏   FileDialogFilters
  - ❏   FileDialogSelectedItems

FileSearch was introduced in Office 97 and was considerably enhanced in Office XP. It allows you to search for files with a wide range of search criteria such as file type, file size, file location, and date of last modification. FileSearch places the names of the files it finds in the FoundFiles collection.

You can use `FileSearch` instead of the VBA `Dir` function for a range of file operations. `FileSearch` is useful for maintenance of files. You can locate files of a certain age and delete them or move them to an archive directory, for example. `FileSearch` is also useful when you need to retrieve data from a number of related files. You can find all the Excel files in a certain directory that start with a client's name, before you consolidate the information in them into a summary file, for example.

`FileDialog` was a new object introduced in Office XP. You use it to display the File Open and File Save As dialog boxes as well as a subdirectory browser. `FileDialog` is a more powerful version of the `GetOpenFileName` and `GetSaveAsFileName` methods of the Excel `Application` object, which have been available in all the previous versions of Excel with VBA, but have not been available to other Office applications. `FileDialog`, being an Office object, is available to all Office XP applications.

FileSearch

The following code searches the `C:\Temp` subdirectory, including any subdirectories beneath it, looking for Excel files:

```
Option Explicit

Public Sub FindClientExcelFiles()
    Dim FileName As Variant
    Dim Message As String
    Dim I As Long
    Dim Count As Long

    With Application.FileSearch

        ' Prepare search criteria
        .NewSearch
        .LookIn = "C:\Temp"
        .SearchSubFolders = True
        .FileType = MsoFileTypeExcelWorkbooks
        .LastModified = MsoLastModified.msoLastModifiedAnyTime
        Count = .Execute

        ' Prepare output text
        Message = Format(Count, "0 ""Files Found""")
        For Each FileName In .FoundFiles
            Message = Message & vbCr & FileName
        Next FileName

        Call MsgBox(Message, vbInformation)

    End With

End Sub
```

In the listing we use the `With End With` construct to obtain a reference to the `Office.FileSearch` object through the `Application.FileSearch` property. One could assign the `Application.FileSearch` property to a local variable, but this generally only adds extra lines of code and little else.

Next, we need to initialize the search criteria. In summary, we provided information like the file location, file masks, and any extra desired parameters. The LookIn property tells FileSearch which subdirectory to search. NewSearch is a method that clears all of the FileSearch properties except LookIn. As these properties persist while you have Excel open, it is a good idea to specifically decide whether you are executing a new search—calling NewSearch if that is the case—each time you use FileSearch. The SearchSubFolders property controls whether we look in subdirectories below the LookIn subdirectory.

FileType determines what file extensions will be included in the search criteria. The constant msoFileTypeExcelWorkbook directs the search to include all the Excel file extensions .xls, .xlt, .xlm, .xlc, and .xla. See the following listing for a table of the other constants available.

msoFileType Constants
MsoFileTypeAllFiles
MsoFileTypeBinders
MsoFileTypeCalendarItem
MsoFileTypeContactItem
MsoFileTypeCustom
MsoFileTypeDatabases
MsoFileTypeDataConnectionFiles
MsoFileTypeDesignerFiles
MsoFileTypeDocumentImagingFiles
MsoFileTypeExcelWorkbooks
MsoFileTypeJournalItem
MsoFileTypeMailItem
MsoFileTypeNoteItem
MsoFileTypeOfficeFiles
MsoFileTypeOutlookItems
MsoFileTypePhotoDrawFiles
MsoFileTypePowerPointPresentations
MsoFileTypeProjectFiles
MsoFileTypePublisherFiles
MsoFileTypeTaskItem
MsoFileTypeTemplates
MsoFileTypeVisioFiles
MsoFileTypeWebPages
MsoFileTypeWordDocuments

The `LastModified` property can use the following constants:

mso Last Modified Constants
MsoLastModifiedAnyTime
MsoLastModifiedLastMonth
MsoLastModifiedLastWeek
MsoLastModifiedThisMonth
MsoLastModifiedThisWeek
MsoLastModifiedToday
MsoLastModifiedYesterday

Instead of the `FileType` property, you can specify the `FileName` property to specify a file mask, as shown below:

```
.FileName = "*.xls"
```

> **FileName** allows you to be more specific than the **FileType** constant. If you use both **FileType** and **FileName**, the **FileName** property overrides the **FileType** property.

You can also search the text contained in the properties of a file or in the body of the file itself by assigning the text to the `TextOrProperty` property of `FileSearch`.

FoundFiles

The `Execute` method of `FileSearch` carries out the search and adds an object representing each file to the `FoundFiles` collection. `Execute` also returns a value that is the number of files found.

You use the `FoundFiles` collection to access the names, including the path, of the files found. The preceding code uses a `For Each...Next` loop to process the list, adding each name to `Message`, separated by a carriage return. The result will look similar to Figure 25-1 (but results will vary based on the actual files on your computer).

Figure 25-1

PropertyTests

When you use the File ⇨ Open dialog box in Office 97 and 2000, you can click the Advanced button to open the Advanced Find dialog box. Here you can specify one or more search criteria for locating files. In VBA, you can use the PropertyTests collection to set up tests that mimic the Advanced Find test criteria.

The Advanced Find dialog box has been superseded by the new File ⇨ Search facilities in Office XP but you can still use the PropertyTests collection in Office XP VBA code.

The following procedure searches for Excel files that are larger than 5,000 bytes (with the new code shown in bold font):

```
Public Sub FindLargeClientExcelFiles()
    Dim FileName As Variant
    Dim Message As String
    Dim I As Long
    Dim Count As Long

    With Application.FileSearch

        .NewSearch
        .LookIn = "C:\WINDOWS"
        .SearchSubFolders = True

        With .PropertyTests
            For I = .Count To 1 Step -1
                .Remove I
            Next I

            .Add Name:="Files of Type", _
                Condition:=msoConditionFileTypeExcelWorkbooks

            .Add Name:="Size", _
                Condition:=msoConditionAtLeast, _
                Value:=5000, _
                Connector:=msoConnectorAnd
        End With

        .LastModified = msoLastModifiedAnyTime
        Count = .Execute

        Message = Format(Count, "0 ""Files Found""")

        For Each FileName In .FoundFiles
            Message = Message & vbCr & FileName
        Next FileName

        Call MsgBox(Message, vbInformation)

    End With

End Sub
```

The `PropertyTests` collection operates independently of any settings in the Advanced Find dialog box. It does not recognize any conditions in that dialog box and it does not change the settings in that dialog box. If you add tests to the `PropertyTests` collection, they persist until you execute `NewSearch`.

The `Add` method of the `PropertyTests` collection adds the new tests, which are specified by assigning a string to the `Name` parameter that is identical to the string that appears in the Property combo box in the Advanced Find dialog box. The first one added is `"Files of Type"`, which gives us yet another way to specify that we want Excel files by providing the appropriate constant for the `Condition` parameter. The available constants are too numerous to tabulate here. IntelliSense ensures that they are listed automatically as you type in your code module and are self-explanatory.

A trap with `PropertyTests` is that there is a default condition defined in the collection when you start an Excel session, and after you execute `NewSearch`, that specifies the `"Files of Type"` parameter to be `msoFileTypeOfficeFiles`. Therefore, it is a good idea to empty the collection before entering new tests so that you are starting from a clear base. The code in the `For...Next` loop removes items in the collection in reverse order. It removes the items with the highest index numbers first so that the index numbers do not change as each item is deleted. The second test specifies that the `"Size"` of the file must be at least 5,000 bytes. The `Connector` parameter, `msoConnectorAnd`, specifies that the second test is joined to the first test with And. The alternative is `msoConnectorOr`. See Appendix C for a complete list of the parameters available.

> If you specify **msoConnectorOr** instead of **msoConnectorAnd** in our example, and you are using Office 97 or 2000, VBA crashes with an error message when you try to execute the code. As usual, the error message is of little help in understanding the problem. The problem is that you are not allowed to combine a "Files of Type" test with any other test using Or. If you try to do it manually in the Advanced Find dialog box you get a clear message telling you this. If you break this rule in Office XP code a runtime error does not occur, but the result is based on **And**. So, beware.

FileTypes

In Office 97 and 2000, you can specify only a single `FileType` property for `FileSearch`. Office XP introduced a `FileTypes` collection that allows you to specify multiple file types. The following Office XP code finds all the Excel and Word files in the directories specified:

```
Public Sub FindClientExcelAndWordFiles()
  Dim FileName As Variant
  Dim Message As String
  Dim I As Long
  Dim Count As Long

  With Application.FileSearch
    .NewSearch

    .FileType = msoFileTypeExcelWorkbooks
    .FileTypes.Add msoFileTypeWordDocuments
    .LookIn = "C:\WINDOWS"
```

```
      .SearchSubFolders = True
      .LastModified = msoLastModifiedAnyTime
     Count = .Execute

     Message = Format(Count, "0 ""Files Found""")

     For Each FileName In .FoundFiles
        Message = Message & vbCr & FileName
     Next FileName

     Call MsgBox(Message, vbInformation)

   End With

End Sub
```

The `FileTypes` collection persists until you execute `NewSearch`, which clears the collection and places the value of `msoFileTypeOfficeFiles` in the collection. However, there is no need to empty the `FileTypes` collection before adding new entries. If you assign an entry to the `FileType` parameter any existing entries in the `FileTypes` collection are destroyed and the new entry becomes the first and only entry in the collection. You can then use the `Add` method of the collection to add more entries. You can use the same file type constants that are listed earlier.

SearchScopes

All of the preceding code assumes that you know the directory organization of the computer you are searching and can specify the subdirectories you want to search. What if you do not know the structure and need to map it for yourself? If you are designing a utility that must run on any computer, you will need to do this.

The `SearchScopes` collection, introduced in Office XP, provides a mechanism for carrying out the directory mapping process. The following code examines each member of the collection. Each member is a `SearchScope` object:

```
Public Sub ListSearchScopeObjects()
   Dim SearchScope As SearchScope
   Dim Message As String

   For Each SearchScope In Application.FileSearch.SearchScopes
      Message = Message & SearchScope.ScopeFolder.Name & vbTab
      Message = Message & " Type=" & SearchScope.Type & vbCr
   Next SearchScope

   Call MsgBox(Message, vbInformation)

End Sub
```

The code will produce something similar to the message box shown in Figure 25-2.

The `SearchScope` objects represent the structures you can examine. The `Type` property identifies the category of each structure. The presence of My Computer and Network Places is no surprise.

Figure 25-2

Help lists the following constants that hold the possible type values:

msoSearchIn Constants
MsoSearchInCustom
MsoSearchInMyComputer
MsoSearchInMyNetworkPlaces
MsoSearchInOutlook

You can't add members to or delete members from the SearchScope collection. The custom type is probably provided for future development.

ScopeFolder

Each SearchScope object has a ScopeFolder property that references a ScopeFolder object. This ScopeFolder object represents the top level of the structure. In the preceding code, the Name property of the ScopeFolder object associated with the top of each structure provides the description of that structure.

The ScopeFolder representing the top of the structure contains a ScopeFolders collection that contains more ScopeFolder objects. The following code displays the Name and Path properties of the ScopeFolders under the top-level ScopeFolder of each structure:

```
Public Sub ListScopeFolderObjects()
  Dim SearchScope As SearchScope
  Dim ScopeFolder As ScopeFolder
  Dim Message As String

  Application.FileSearch.RefreshScopes

  For Each SearchScope In Application.FileSearch.SearchScopes
    Select Case SearchScope.Type

    Case msoSearchInMyComputer
      Message = SearchScope.ScopeFolder.Name & vbCr
      For Each ScopeFolder In SearchScope.ScopeFolder.ScopeFolders
        Message = Message & ScopeFolder.Name & vbTab & vbTab
        Message = Message & "Path=" & ScopeFolder.Path & vbCr
      Next ScopeFolder
```

```
        Case msoSearchInMyNetworkPlaces
          Message = Message & vbCr & SearchScope.ScopeFolder.Name & vbCr
          For Each ScopeFolder In SearchScope.ScopeFolder.ScopeFolders
            Message = Message & ScopeFolder.Name & vbTab
            Message = Message & "Path=" & ScopeFolder.Path & vbCr
          Next ScopeFolder

        Case msoSearchInOutlook
          Message = Message & vbCr & SearchScope.ScopeFolder.Name & vbCr
          For Each ScopeFolder In SearchScope.ScopeFolder.ScopeFolders
            Message = Message & ScopeFolder.Name & vbTab & vbTab
            Message = Message & "Path=" & ScopeFolder.Path & vbCr
          Next ScopeFolder

        Case Else
          Message = Message & vbCr & "Unknown SearchScope object"

      End Select
    Next SearchScope

    Call MsgBox(Message, vbInformation)
  End Sub
```

The code produces a message box like Figure 25-3 (while disconnected from the network).

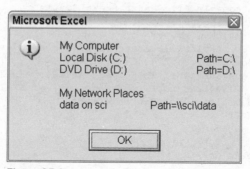

Figure 25-3

The `Select Case` statements provide a convenient way to isolate and examine each of the top-level structures. Each top-level `ScopeFolders` collection contains `ScopeFolder` objects that represent the root directories of the file structures available to it. Each of these `ScopeFolder` objects contains another `ScopeFolders` collection that represents the subdirectories under it. This provides a mechanism for drilling down through the directory trees.

SearchFolders

Another new object in the Office XP object model is the `SearchFolders` collection. You use the `LookIn` property of `FileSearch` to define a single directory path to be searched, by assigning the directory path as a character string to the property. You use the `SearchFolders` collection to define additional directory paths to be searched, by adding `ScopeFolder` objects to the collection.

SearchFolders is not like the FileTypes collection that is recreated when you assign a value to the FileType property. SearchFolders is not affected when you assign a value to the LookIn property or when you execute NewSearch. The LookIn value is additional to the SearchFolders entries.

Because the SearchFolders collection persists during the current Excel session, it is a good idea to empty it before carrying out a new search. The following code searches through all the subdirectories in the root directory of the C drive. When it finds a directory starting with the letters "System32", it adds that directory to the SearchFolders collection:

```
Public Sub SetupSearchFoldersCollection()
  Dim FileSearch As FileSearch
  Dim SearchScope As SearchScope
  Dim ScopeFolder As ScopeFolder
  Dim SubFolder As ScopeFolder
  Dim Message As String
  Dim I As Long

  Set FileSearch = Application.FileSearch

  For I = FileSearch.SearchFolders.Count To 1 Step -1
    FileSearch.SearchFolders.Remove I
  Next I

  For Each SearchScope In FileSearch.SearchScopes
    Select Case SearchScope.Type
      Case msoSearchInMyComputer
        For Each ScopeFolder In SearchScope.ScopeFolder.ScopeFolders
          If (ScopeFolder.Path = "C:\") Then
            For Each SubFolder In ScopeFolder.ScopeFolders
              If UCase(Left(SubFolder.Name, 6)) = "SYSTEM32" Then
                SubFolder.AddToSearchFolders
              End If
            Next SubFolder
          End If
        Next ScopeFolder
    End Select

  Next SearchScope

  PerformSearch

End Sub
```

The code empties the SearchFolders collection and then drills down through the SearchScopes collection and ScopeFolders collection to locate the C drive. It then examines the Name property of each ScopeFolder in the root directory of the C drive to determine if the name begins with "SYSTEM32." It converts the name to upper case so that the comparison is not case-sensitive.

When the code finds a matching directory it uses the AddToSearchFolders method of the ScopeFolder object to add the object to the SearchFolders collection. The code then runs the PerformSearch routine, which is listed in the following, to display the names of the Excel files in the SYSTEM32 directories:

```
Public Sub PerformSearch()
  Dim FileName As Variant
  Dim Message As String
  Dim Count As Long

  With Application.FileSearch
    .NewSearch
    .LookIn = ""
    .SearchSubFolders = True
    .FileName = "*.xls"
    .LastModified = msoLastModifiedAnyTime
    Count = .Execute

    Message = Format(Count, "0 ""Files Found""")

    For Each FileName In .FoundFiles
      Message = Message & vbCr & FileName
    Next FileName
  End With

  MsgBox Message

End Sub
```

PerformSearch sets the LookIn property of FileSearch to a zero-length string to ensure that it does not contain any directory references from previous FileSearch operations.

> Office XP users who have used code to populate the SearchFolders collection should modify the code of the procedures presented earlier in this chapter so that the SearchFolders collection is cleared before the search is executed.

FileDialog

Office XP introduced the FileDialog object that allows you to display the File ⇨ Open and File ⇨ Save As dialog boxes using VBA. Excel users of the previous versions can use the GetOpenFileName and GetSaveAsFileName methods of the Application object to carry out similar tasks and they can continue to do so in 2003 if backward compatibility is required. One advantage of FileDialog is that it has one extra capability that allows you to display a list of directories, rather than files and directories. FileDialog also has the advantage of being available to all Office applications.

We will set up a worksheet to display images that we will allow the user to choose through the File Open dialog box. Figure 25-4 shows how the application looks.

The worksheet contains an Image control created using the Control Toolbox toolbar, with the default name of "Image1". We have set the PictureSizeMode property of the control to zoom so that the picture is automatically fitted in the control. The command button above it uses the default name, and the

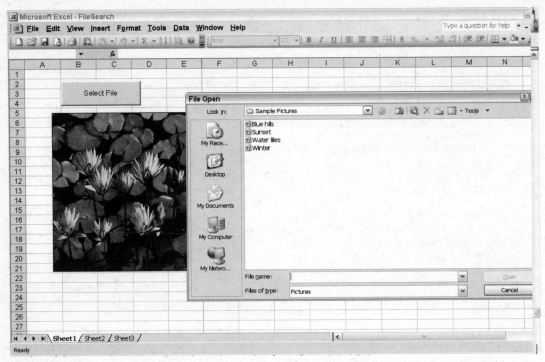

Figure 25-4

caption is modified to "Select File". The class module behind Sheet1 contains the following event procedure:

```
Private Sub CommandButton1_Click()
  Dim Filters As FileDialogFilters
  Dim FileName As String

  On Error GoTo Catch

  With Application.FileDialog(MsoFileDialogType.msoFileDialogOpen)
    Set Filters = .Filters

    With Filters
      .Clear
      .Add "Pictures", "*.jpg"
    End With

    .AllowMultiSelect = False

    If .Show = False Then Exit Sub

    Image1.Picture = LoadPicture(.SelectedItems(1))
  End With
```

```
    Exit Sub

Catch:
  Call MsgBox("Invalid picture file", vbExclamation)
End Sub
```

The `FileDialog` property of the `Application` object returns a reference to the Office `FileDialogs` object. We can use the following `msoFileDialogType` constants to specify the type of dialog box:

MsoFileDialog Constants
MsoFileDialogFilePicker
MsoFileDialogFolderPicker
MsoFileDialogOpen
MsoFileDialogSaveAs

FileDialogFilters

We use the `Filters` property of the `FileDialog` object to return a reference to the `FileDialogFilters` collection for the `FileDialog`. The filters control the types of files that are displayed. By default, there are 24 filters preset that the user can select from the drop-down menu at the bottom of the File Open dialog box. The `Clear` method of the `FileDialogFilters` collection removes the preset filters and we add our own filter that shows only `.jpg` files.

The `Show` method of the `FileDialog` object displays the dialog box. When the user clicks the Open button the `Show` method returns a value of "`True`". If the user clicks the Cancel button, the `Show` method returns "`False`" and we exit from the procedure.

FileDialogSelectedItems

The `Show` method does not actually open the selected file but places the file name and path into a `FileDialogSelectedItems` collection. As we will see later, it is possible to allow multiple file selection. In the present example, the user can only select one file. The name of the file is returned from the first item in the `FileDialogSelectedItems` collection, which is referred to by the `SelectedItems` property of the `FileDialog` object.

We use the `LoadPicture` function to assign the file to the `Picture` property of the image control.

Dialog Types

There is very little difference between the four possible dialog box types apart from the heading at the top of the dialog box. The file picker and folder picker types show Browse in the title bar while the others show File Open and File Save As as appropriate. All the dialog boxes show directories and files except the folder picker dialog box, which shows only directories.

Execute Method

As we have seen, the `Show` method displays the `FileDialog` and the items chosen are placed in the `FileDialogSelectedItems` object without any attempt to open or save any files. You can use the `Execute` method with the File Open and Save As dialog boxes to carry out the required Open or SaveAs operations immediately the user clicks the Open or Save button, as shown in the following code:

```
With Application.FileDialog(xlDialogOpen)
   If .Show Then .Execute
End With
```

MultiSelect

The application shown in Figure 25-5 has been modified to allow the user to select multiple file names by holding down *Shift* or *Control* while clicking file names. The file names are then loaded into the combo box, called *ComboBox1*, at the top of the screen, from which the files can be chosen for viewing.

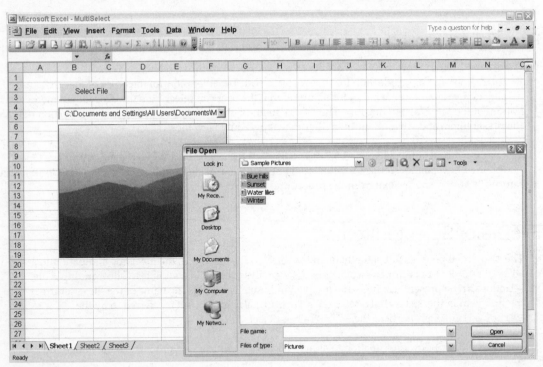

Figure 25-5

The code has been modified as follows:

```
Option Explicit

Private Sub ComboBox1_Change()
   Image1.Picture = LoadPicture(ComboBox1.Text)
End Sub
```

```
Private Sub CommandButton1_Click()
  Dim FileName As String
  Dim Item As Variant

  On Error GoTo Catch

  With Application.FileDialog(msoFileDialogOpen)

    With .Filters
      .Clear
      .Add "Pictures", "*.jpg"
    End With

    .AllowMultiSelect = True

    If .Show = False Then Exit Sub
    ComboBox1.Clear

    For Each Item In .SelectedItems
      Call ComboBox1.AddItem(Item)
    Next Item

    ComboBox1.ListIndex = 0

  End With

  Exit Sub

Catch:
  Call MsgBox(Err.Description, vbExclamation)
End Sub
```

We set the `AllowMultiSelect` property to `True`. The combo box list is cleared of any previous items and we use a `For Each...Next` loop to add the items in the `FileDialogSelectedItems` collection to the combo box list. When we set the combo box `ListIndex` property to zero, it triggers the `Change` event and the event procedure loads the first picture into the image control.

Summary

`FileSearch` and `FileDialog` provide useful facilities to VBA programmers wanting to write file-handling code. Because these objects are part of the Office object model, they have the advantage of being available to all Office VBA applications.

`FileSearch` is available in Excel 97 and all later Windows versions with considerable enhancements since Office XP. You use it to locate files with common characteristics, such as similar file names or similar locations, so that those files can be processed in subsequent code.

`FileDialog` was introduced in Office XP and allows you to display the File Open and File Save As dialog boxes as well as a directory browser. It provides more powerful facilities than the `GetOpenFileName` and `GetSaveAsFileName` functions that are only available in Excel.

Command Bars

The `CommandBars` collection is an object contained in the Office Object Model, documented in Appendix C. It contains all the menus, toolbars, and shortcut popup menus that are already built into Excel and the other Office applications, as well as any of those objects that you create yourself. You access commandbars through the `CommandBars` property of the `Application` object.

Commandbars were first introduced into Office in Office 97. Excel 5 and 95 supported menu bars and toolbars as separate object types. Shortcut menus, or popups, such as those which appear when you right-click a worksheet cell, were a special type of menu bar. In Excel 97 and later versions, the "command bar" is a generic term that includes menu bars, toolbars, and shortcut menus.

Commandbars contain items that are called *controls*. When clicked, some controls execute operations, such as Copy. Until we get down to the nuts and bolts, we will refer to these types of controls as *commands*. There are other controls, such as File, that produce an additional list of controls when clicked. We will refer to these controls as *menus*.

In this chapter, we will show you how to create and manipulate these useful tools.

Toolbars, Menu Bars, and Popups

The screenshot in Figure 26-1 shows the standard Worksheet menu bar at the top of the Excel window.

The Worksheet menu bar contains menus, such as File and Edit. When you click a menu, you see another list containing commands and menus.

- ❑ Cut and Copy are examples of commands in the Edit menu
- ❑ Clear is an example of a menu contained within the Edit menu

Figure 26-2 shows the Standard toolbar.

Toolbars contain controls that can be clicked to execute Excel commands. For example, the button with the scissors icon carries out a Cut. Toolbars can also contain other types of controls such as the

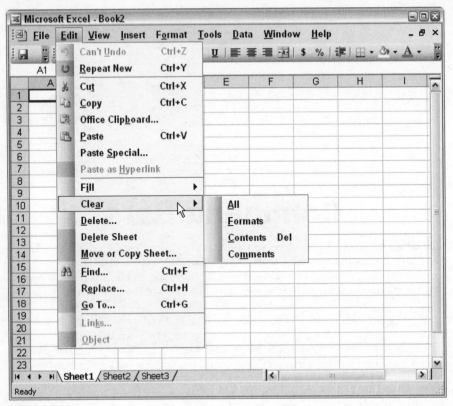

Figure 26-1

Figure 26-2

Zoom combo box (two from the end of the Standard toolbar in the Figure 26-2) that allows you to select, or type in, a zoom factor, displayed as a percentage. Some toolbars contain buttons that display menus, such as the PivotTable button in the PivotTable toolbar.

Figure 26-3 shows the shortcut menu that appears when you right-click a worksheet cell.

This shortcut menu contains commands, such as Paste, and menus, such as Delete . . . , for those operations appropriate to the selected context, in this case, a cell.

Excel 2003 has approximately 124 different built-in command bars containing many thousands of controls. In addition, you can create your own commandbars or tailor existing commandbars to suit your needs. This can be accomplished manually using View ⇨ Toolbars ⇨ Customize . . . , or you can do it programmatically.

Figure 26-3

You may be able to accomplish all the customization you need manually, including attaching commandbars to workbooks, but some tasks can only be carried out using VBA code. For example, you need VBA if you want to:

❑ Automatically remove or hide a command bar when its related workbook is closed or deactivated

❑ Add a custom menu to a built-in menu bar when a workbook is opened and remove it when the workbook is closed

❑ Dynamically change your commandbars in response to user actions

❑ Use some types of controls, such as combo boxes that can only be created and controlled using VBA

To summarize, a command bar can be any one of three types. It can be a menu, toolbar, or shortcut popup menu. When you create a command bar using VBA, you specify which of the three types it will be, using the appropriate parameters of the Add method of the CommandBars collection. You will see examples of this in the following table. You can find out what type an existing command bar is by testing its Type property, which will return a numeric value equal to the value of one of the following intrinsic constants:

Constant	Command Bar Type
MsoBarTypeNormal	Toolbar
MsoBarTypeMenuBar	Menu Bar
MsoBarTypePopup	Shortcut Menu

Controls on commandbars also have a Type property similar to the preceding msoXXX constants. The control that is used most frequently has a Type property of msoControlButton, which represents a command such as the Copy command on the Edit menu of the Worksheet menu bar, or a command button on a toolbar, such as the Cut button on the Standard toolbar. This type of control runs a macro or a built-in Excel action when it is clicked.

The second most common control has a Type property of msoControlPopup. This represents a menu on a menu bar, such as the Edit menu on the Worksheet menu bar, or a menu contained in another menu, such as the Clear submenu on the Edit menu on the Worksheet menu bar. This type of control contains its own Controls collection, to which you can add further controls.

Controls have an Id property. For built-in controls, the Id property determines the internal action carried out by the control. When you set up a custom control, you assign the name of a macro to its OnAction property to make it execute that macro when it is clicked. Custom controls have an Id property of 1.

Many built-in menu items and most built-in toolbar controls have a graphic image associated with them. The image is defined by the FaceId property. The Id and FaceId properties of built-in commands normally have the same numeric value. You can assign the built-in FaceId values to your own controls, if you know what numeric value to use. You can determine these values using VBA, as you will see in the next example.

Excel's Built-In Commandbars

Before launching into creating our own commandbars, it will help to understand how the built-in commandbars are structured and find out just what is already available in Excel 2003. You can use the following code to list the existing commandbars and any that you have added yourself. It lists the name of each command bar in column A and the names of the controls in the commandbar's Controls collection in column B, as shown in Figure 26-4. The code does not attempt to display lower level controls that belong to controls such as the File menu on the Worksheet menu bar, so the procedure has been named ListFirstLevelControls.

The macro also shows the control's Id property value, in all cases, and its image and its FaceId property value when such an image exists. Note that some listed controls might not be visible on your own screen. For example, the Standard toolbar's & Mail Recipient button will not be visible if you do not have a mail system.

> **Make sure you are in an empty worksheet when you run this macro and the following two examples. They contain tests to make sure they will not overwrite any data in the active sheet.**

If you are testing this code, remember that it should be placed in a standard code module, not in a class module. Don't put the code in the ThisWorkbook module or a class module behind a worksheet. You should also include the IsEmptyWorksheet function listed further down:

You will notice in the figure that most, if not all, of the controls have an ampersand in the name. When programming an ampersand defines the shortcut key used to access the command. For example: &File would be displayed as File and an *Alt+F* key combination could be used to access the item.

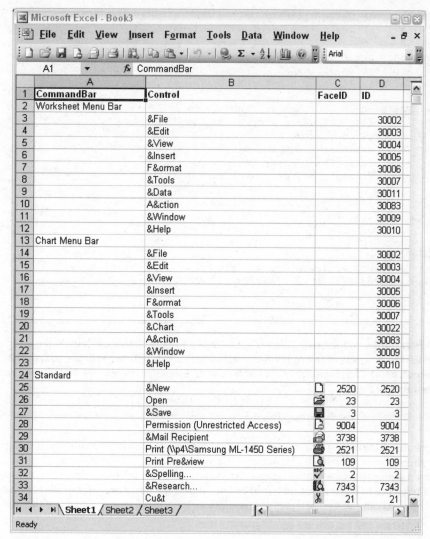

Figure 26-4

Here is the code to list the first level controls:

```
Sub ListFirstLevelControls()
    Dim cbCtl As CommandBarControl
    Dim cbBar As CommandBar
    Dim i As Integer
    If Not IsEmptyWorksheet(ActiveSheet) Then Exit Sub
    On Error Resume Next
    Application.ScreenUpdating = False
    Cells(1, 1).Value = "CommandBar"
    Cells(1, 2).Value = "Control"
    Cells(1, 3).Value = "FaceID"
```

```
        Cells(1, 4).Value = "ID"
        Cells(1, 1).Resize(1,4).Font.Bold = True
        i = 2
        For Each cbBar In CommandBars
            Application.StatusBar = "Processing Bar " & cbBar.Name
            Cells(i, 1).Value = cbBar.Name
            i = i + 1
            For Each cbCtl In cbBar.Controls
                Cells(i, 2).Value = cbCtl.Caption
                cbCtl.CopyFace
                If Err.Number = 0 Then
                    ActiveSheet.Paste Cells(i, 3)
                    Cells(i, 3).Value = cbCtl.FaceID
                End If
                Cells(i, 4).Value = cbCtl.ID
                Err.Clear
                i = i + 1
            Next cbCtl
        Next cbBar
        Range("A:B").EntireColumn.AutoFit
        Application.StatusBar = False
End Sub
```

This example, and the two following, can take a long time to complete. You can watch the progress of the code on the status bar. If you only want to see part of the output, press *Ctrl+Break* after a minute or so to interrupt the macro, click Debug and then Run ⇨ Reset.

ListFirstLevelControls first checks that the active sheet is an empty worksheet using the IsEmptyWorksheet function that is shown next. It then uses On Error Resume Next to avoid runtime errors when it tries to access control images that do not exist. In the outer For Each...Next loop, it assigns a reference to each command bar to cbBar, shows the Name property of the command bar on the status bar so you can track what it is doing, and places the Name in the A column of the current row, defined by i.

The inner For Each...Next loop processes all the controls on cbBar, placing the Caption property of each control in column B. It then attempts to use the CopyFace method of the control to copy the control's image to the clipboard. If this does not create an error, it pastes the image to column C and places the value of the FaceId property in the same cell. It places the ID property of the control in column D. It clears any errors, increments i by one and processes the next control.

The IsEmptyWorksheet function, shown next, checks that the input parameter object Sht is a worksheet. If so, it checks that the count of entries in the used range is 0. If both checks succeed, it returns True. Otherwise, it issues a warning message and the default return value, which is False, is returned:

```
Function IsEmptyWorksheet(Sht As Object) As Boolean
    If TypeName(Sht) = "Worksheet" Then
        If WorksheetFunction.CountA(Sht.UsedRange) = 0 Then
```

```
        IsEmptyWorksheet = True
        Exit Function
      End If
   End If
   MsgBox "Please make sure that an empty worksheet is active"
End Function
```

Controls at All Levels

Figure 26-5 and the accompanying code take the previous procedure to greater levels of detail. All controls are examined to see what controls are contained within them. Where possible, the contained controls are listed. Some controls, such as those containing graphics, can't be listed in greater detail. The information on subcontrols is indented across the worksheet. The code is capable of reporting to as many levels as there are, but Excel does not have controls beyond the third level:

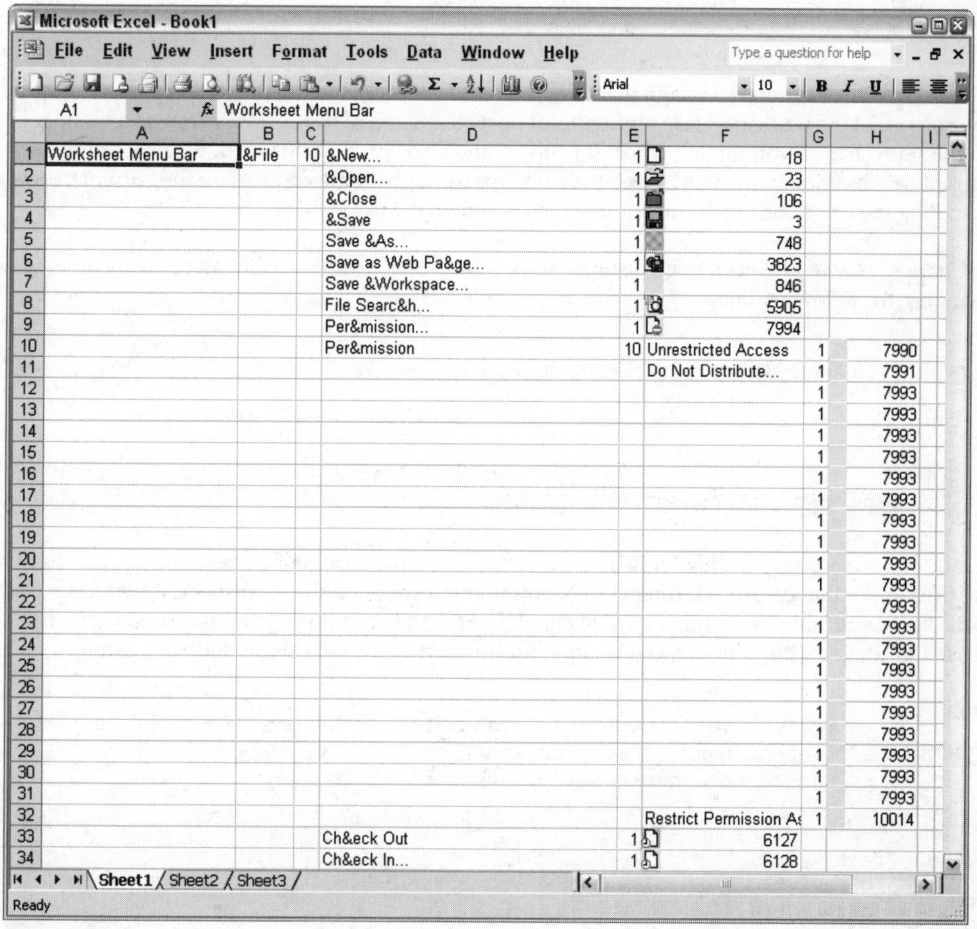

Figure 26-5

Here is the code to list controls at all levels:

```
Sub ListAllControls()
  Dim cbBar As CommandBar
  Dim Rng As Range
  Dim cbCtl As CommandBarControl

  If Not IsEmptyWorksheet(ActiveSheet) Then Exit Sub
  Application.ScreenUpdating = False
  Set Rng = Range("A1")
  For Each cbBar In Application.CommandBars
    Application.StatusBar = "Processing Bar " & cbBar.Name
    Rng.Value = cbBar.Name
    For Each cbCtl In cbBar.Controls
      Set Rng = Rng.Offset(ListControls(cbCtl, Rng))
    Next cbCtl
  Next cbBar
  Range("A:I").EntireColumn.AutoFit
  Application.StatusBar = False
End Sub
```

ListAllControls loops through the CommandBars collection, using Rng to keep track of the current A column cell of the worksheet it is writing to. It posts the name of the current command bar in a message on the status bar, so you can tell where it is up to, and also enters the name of the command bar at the current Rng location in the worksheet. It then loops through all the controls on the current CommandBar, executing the ListControls function, which is shown next.

In Chapter 23, you will need to get listings of the VBE CommandBars. This can be easily accomplished by changing the following line:

```
For Each cBar in Application.CommandBars
```

to:

```
For Each cBar in Application.VBE.CommandBars
```

ListControls is responsible for listing the details of each control it is passed and the details of any controls under that control, starting at the current Rng location in the worksheet. When it has performed its tasks, ListControls returns a value equal to the number of lines that it has used for its list. Offset is used to compute the new Rng cell location for the start of the next commandbar's listing:

```
Function ListControls(cbCtl As CommandBarControl, Rng As Range) As Long
  Dim lOffset As Long 'Tracks current row relative to Rng
  Dim ctlSub As CommandBarControl 'Control contained in cbCtl

  On Error Resume Next
  lOffset = 0
  Rng.Offset(lOffset, 1).Value = cbCtl.Caption
  Rng.Offset(lOffset, 2).Value = cbCtl.Type
  'Attempt to copy control face. If error, don't paste
```

```
      cbCtl.CopyFace
      If Err.Number = 0 Then
        ActiveSheet.Paste Rng.Offset(lOffset, 3)
        Rng.Offset(lOffset, 3).Value = cbCtl.FaceId
      End If
      Err.Clear

      'Check Control Type
      Select Case cbCtl.Type
        Case 1, 2, 4, 6, 7, 13, 18
          'Do nothing for these control types
        Case Else
          'Call function recursively
          'if current control contains other controls
          For Each ctlSub In cbCtl.Controls
            lOffset = lOffset + _
                ListControls(ctlSub, Rng.Offset(lOffset, 2))
          Next ctlSub
          lOffset = lOffset - 1
      End Select
      ListControls = lOffset + 1
   End Function
```

ListControls is a recursive function, and runs itself to process as many levels of controls as it finds. It uses lOffset to keep track of the rows it writes to, relative to the starting cell Rng. It uses very similar code to ListFirstLevelControls, but records the control type as well as the caption, icon, and face ID. Most of the control types are:

- ❑   1 – msoControlButton
- ❑   10 – msoControlPopup

However, you will see other types in the list as well:

- ❑   2 – msoControlEdit
- ❑   4 – msoControlComboBox
- ❑   6 – msoControlSplitDropdown
- ❑   7 – msoControlOCXDropdown
- ❑   13 – msoControlSplitButtonPopup
- ❑   18 – msoControlGrid

The Select Case construct is used to avoid trying to list the subcontrols where this is not possible.

When ListControls finds a control with subcontrols it can list, it calls itself with a Rng starting point that is offset from its current Rng by lOffset lines down and two columns across. ListControls keeps calling itself as often as necessary to climb down into every level of subcontrol and then climbs back to continue with the higher levels. Each time it is called, it returns the number of lines it has written to relative to Rng.

FaceIds

The following code gives you a table of the built-in button faces, shown in Figure 26-6. There are about 3,500 faces in Office 97, about 5,500 faces in Office 2000, about 7,000 faces in Office 2002, and over 10,000 faces in Office 2003. Note that many `FaceId` values represent blank images and that the same images appear repeatedly as the numbers get higher:

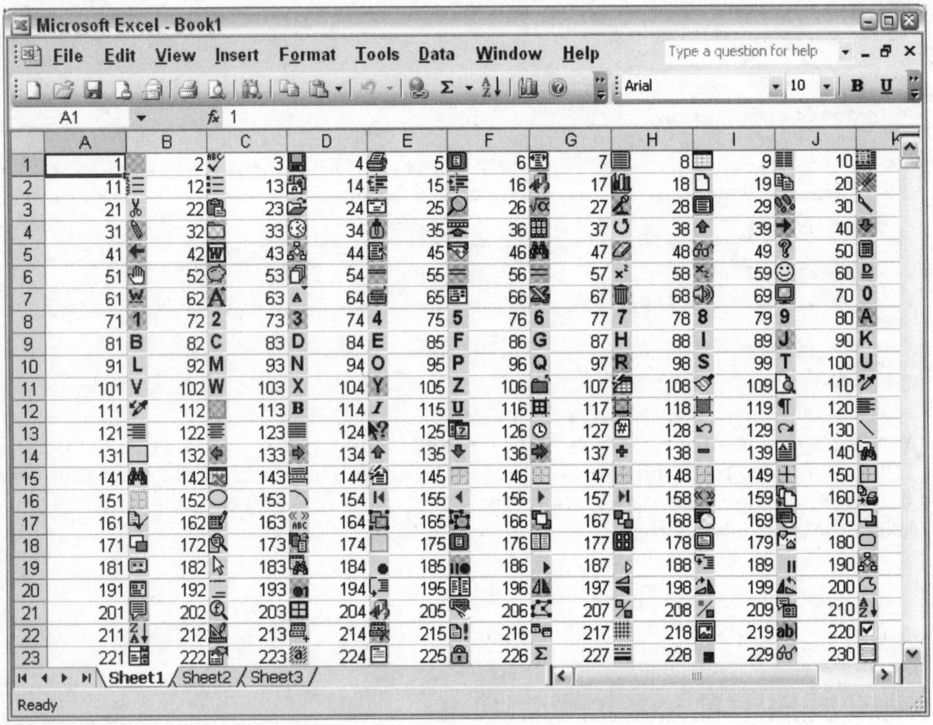

Figure 26-6

Here is the code to list all the `FaceIds`:

```
Sub ListAllFaces()
    Dim i As Integer 'Tracks current FaceId
    Dim j As Integer 'Tracks current column in worksheet
    Dim k As Integer 'Tracks current row in worksheet
    Dim cbCtl As CommandBarControl

    Dim cbBar As CommandBar

    If Not IsEmptyWorksheet(ActiveSheet) Then Exit Sub
    On Error GoTo Recover
    Application.ScreenUpdating = False
    'Create temporary command bar with single control button
    'to hold control button face to be copied to worksheet
    Set cbBar = CommandBars.Add(Position:=msoBarFloating, _
                                MenuBar:=False, _
                                temporary:=True)
```

```
        Set cbCtl = cbBar.Controls.Add(Type:=msoControlButton, _
                               temporary:=True)
    k = 1
    Do
      For j = 1 To 10
        i = i + 1
        Application.StatusBar = "FaceID = " & i

        'Set control button to current FaceId
        cbCtl.FaceId = i
        'Attempt to copy Face image to worksheet
        cbCtl.CopyFace
        ActiveSheet.Paste Cells(k, j + 1)
        Cells(k, j).Value = i
        ' Allow windows messages to process
        DoEvents
      Next j
      k = k + 1
      ' Allow windows messages to process
      DoEvents
    Loop
    Application.StatusBar = "Total Items=" & i

Recover:
  If Err.Number = 1004 Then Resume Next
  Application.StatusBar = False
  cbBar.Delete
End Sub
```

> Note that this code contains two **DoEvents** commands. When these lines are encountered, Windows releases control and allows for standard Windows messages to process. Without these commands it would appear as if Excel had locked up when, in fact, it was just processing the **FaceIDs**. While running this code you should be able to view the status bar of the Excel window which will display a counter of all the totals items processed.

ListAllFaces creates a temporary toolbar, cbBar, using the Add method of the CommandBars collection. The toolbar is declared:

❑   Temporary, which means that it will be deleted when you exit Excel, if it has not already been deleted

❑   Floating, rather than docked at an edge of the screen or a popup

❑   Not to be a menu bar, which means that cbBar will be a toolbar

A temporary control is added to cbBar using the Add method of the Controls collection for the command bar, and assigned to cbCtl.

The Do...Loop continues looping until there are no more valid FaceId values. The Do...Loop increments k, which represents the row numbers in the worksheet. On every row, j is incremented from

1 to 10. j represents the columns of the worksheet. The value of i is increased by one for every iteration of the code in the For...Next loop. i represents the FaceId. The FaceId property of cbCtl is assigned the value of i, and the resulting image is copied to the worksheet.

Some button images are blank and some are missing. The blank images copy without error, but the missing images cause an error number 1004. When an error occurs, the code branches to the error trap at Recover. If the error number is 1004, the code resumes executing at the statement after the one that caused the error, leaving an empty slot for the button image. Eventually, the code gets to the last FaceId in Office. This causes error number –2147467259. At this point, the code clears the status bar, removes the temporary command bar, and exits.

> The information you have gathered with the last three exercises is not documented in any easily obtainable form by Microsoft. It is valuable data when you want to modify the existing command bar structures or alter command bar behavior, and as a guide to the built-in button faces at your disposal. There is an Add-in application, CBList.xla, available with the code that accompanies this book that makes it easy to generate these lists.

Creating New Menus

If you want to provide a user with extra functionality, without removing any of the standard commands, you can add a new menu to the existing Worksheet menu bar. The screen in Figure 26-7 shows a new menu called Custom, inserted between the Window and Help menus:

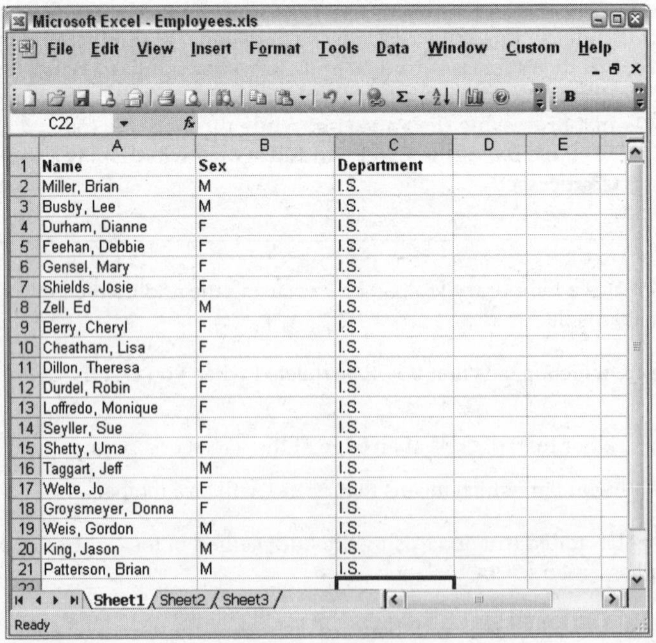

Figure 26-7

The code to create this menu is as follows:

```
Public Sub AddCustomMenu()
    Dim cbWSMenuBar As CommandBar
    Dim muCustom As CommandBarControl
    Dim iHelpIndex As Integer

    Set cbWSMenuBar = Application.CommandBars("Worksheet Menu Bar")
    iHelpIndex = cbWSMenuBar.Controls("Help").Index
    Set muCustom = cbWSMenuBar.Controls.Add(Type:=msoControlPopup, _
                                        Before:=iHelpIndex)
    With muCustom
        .Caption = "&Custom"
        With .Controls.Add(Type:=msoControlButton)
            .Caption = "&Show Data Form"
            .OnAction = "ShowDataForm"
        End With
        With .Controls.Add(Type:=msoControlButton)
            .Caption = "&Print Data List"
            .OnAction = "PrintDataList"
        End With
        With .Controls.Add(Type:=msoControlButton)
            .Caption = "Sort Names &Ascending"
            .BeginGroup = True
            .OnAction = "SortList"
            .Parameter = "Asc"
        End With
        With .Controls.Add(Type:=msoControlButton)
            .Caption = "Sort Names &Descending"
            .OnAction = "SortList"
            .Parameter = "Dsc"
        End With
    End With
End Sub
```

AddCustomMenu creates an object variable cbWSMenuBar referencing the Worksheet menu bar. If you want to add a menu before an existing menu, you need to know the index number of that menu. You can determine the Index property of the control as shown.

AddCustomMenu uses the Add method of the menu bar's Controls collection to add the new menu. The Type property is declared msoControlPopup so that other controls can be attached to the menu. The Before parameter places the new menu just before the Help menu. If you do not specify the position, it will be placed at the end of the menu bar. The Caption property of the new menu is assigned &Custom. The & does not appear in the menu, it causes an underscore to be placed under the character it precedes and indicates that you can activate this menu from the keyboard with *Alt+C*.

The Add method of the new menu's Controls collection is then used to add four commands to the menu. They are all of type msoControlButton so they can each run a macro. Each is given an appropriate Caption property, including shortcut keys indicated with an &. The OnAction property of each command is assigned the name of the macro it is to run. The first of the sort menu items has its BeginGroup property set to True. This places the dividing line above it to mark it as the beginning of a different group. Both sort commands are assigned the same OnAction macro, but also have their Parameter properties assigned text strings that distinguish them.

The Parameter property is a holder for a character string. You can use it for any purpose. Here it is used to hold the strings "Asc", for ascending, and "Dsc", for descending. As you will see next, the SortList procedure will access the strings to determine the sort order required.

The OnAction Macros

The macro assigned to the OnAction property of the Show Data Form menu item is as follows:

```
Private Sub ShowDataForm()
    fmPersonal.Show
End Sub
```

It displays exactly the same data form as in the previous chapter on UserForms. The macro assigned to the Print Data List menu item is as follows:

```
Private Sub PrintDataList()
    Range("Database").PrintPreview
End Sub
```

PrintDataList shows a print preview of the list, from which the user can elect to print the list.

The macro assigned to the Sort menu items is as follows:

```
Private Sub SortList()
    Dim iAscDsc As Integer

    Select Case CommandBars.ActionControl.Parameter
        Case "Asc"
            iAscDsc = xlAscending
        Case "Dsc"
            iAscDsc = xlDescending
    End Select
    Range("Database").Sort Key1:=Range("A2"), Order1:=iAscDsc, Header:=xlYes
End Sub
```

SortList uses the ActionControl property of the CommandBars collection to get a reference to the command bar control that caused SortList to execute. This is similar to Application.Caller, used in user-defined functions to determine the Range object that executed the function.

Knowing the control object that called it, SortList can examine the control's Parameter property to get further information. If the Parameter value is "Asc", SortList assigns an ascending sort. If the Parameter value is "Dsc", it assigns a descending sort. Controls also have a Tag property that can be used, in exactly the same way as the Parameter property, to hold another character string. You can use the `Tag` property as an alternative to the `Parameter` property, or you can use it to hold supplementary data.

Passing Parameter Values

In the previous example, we used the `Parameter` property of the control on the menu to store information to be passed to the `OnAction` macro, and pointed out that you can also use the `Tag` property. If you have more than two items of information to pass, it is more convenient to use a macro procedure that has input parameters.

Say, you wanted to pass three items of data such as a product name and its cost and selling price. The macro might look like the following:

```
Sub ShowProduct(sName As String, dCost As Double, dPrice As Double)
   MsgBox "Product: " & sName & vbCr & _
       "Cost: " & Format(dCost, "$0.00") & vbCr & _
       "Price: " & Format(dPrice, "$0.00")
End Sub
```

To execute this macro from a command bar control, you need to assign something like the following code to the `OnAction` property of the control:

```
'ShowProduct "Apple", 3, 4'
```

The entire expression is enclosed in single quotes. Any string parameter values within the expression are enclosed in double quotes. In order to define this as the `OnAction` property of a control referred to by an object variable, `Ctl`, for example, you need to use the following code:

```
Ctl.OnAction = "'ShowProduct ""Apple"", 3, 4'"
```

The mix of single and double quotes is tricky to get right. The entire string is enclosed in double quotes, while any internal double quotes need to be shown twice.

Deleting a Menu

Built-in and custom controls can be deleted using the control's `Delete` method. The following macro deletes the Custom menu:

```
Public Sub RemoveCustomMenu()
   Dim cbWSMenuBar As CommandBar

   On Error Resume Next
   Set cbWSMenuBar = CommandBars("Worksheet Menu Bar")
   cbWSMenuBar.Controls("Custom").Delete
End Sub
```

`On Error` is used in case the menu has already been deleted.

You can use a built-in commandbar's **Reset** method to make the entire command bar revert to its default layout and commands. This is not a good idea if users have customized their commandbars, or use workbooks or Add-ins that alter the setup, as all their work will be lost.

The following event procedures should be added to the `ThisWorkbook` module to add the Custom menu when the workbook is opened and delete it when the workbook is closed:

```
Private Sub Workbook_BeforeClose(Cancel As Boolean)
    Call RemoveCustomMenu
End Sub

Private Sub Workbook_Open()
    Call AddCustomMenu
End Sub
```

It is important to recognize that command bar changes are permanent. If you do not remove the Custom menu in this example, it will stay in the Excel Worksheet menu bar during the current session and future sessions. Trying to use this menu with another active workbook could cause unexpected results.

Creating a Toolbar

If you are creating a simple toolbar with buttons and drop-downs, you can do it manually. However, there are more complex controls, such as those of type `msoControlEdit`, `msoControlDropdown`, and `msoControlComboBox`, which you can only fully manipulate in VBA code. The toolbar we will create here contains three controls.

The first is of type `msoControlButton` and displays the user form for the data list, as shown in Figure 26-8.

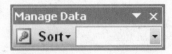

Figure 26-8

The second control, shown in Figure 26-9, is of type `msoControlPopup` and displays two controls of type `msoControlButton`.

The third control, shown in Figure 26-10, is of type `msoControlDropdown` and applies an AutoFilter on Department.

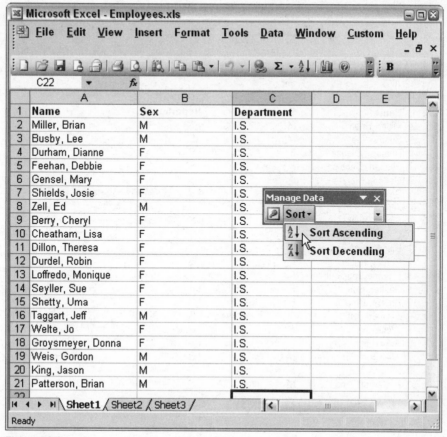

Figure 26-9

The following code creates the toolbar:

```
Public Sub CreateToolbar()
    'Get rid of any existing toolbar called Manage Data
    On Error Resume Next
    CommandBars("Manage Data").Delete
    On Error GoTo 0

    'Create new toolbar
    With CommandBars.Add(Name:="Manage Data")
        With .Controls.Add(Type:=msoControlButton)
            .OnAction = "ShowDataForm"
            .FaceId = 264
            .TooltipText = "Show Data Form"
        End With

        With .Controls.Add(Type:=msoControlPopup)
            .Caption = "Sort"
            .TooltipText = "Sort Ascending or Descending"
```

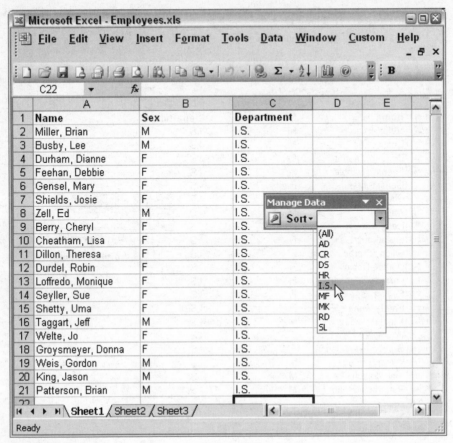

Figure 26-10

```
        With .Controls.Add(Type:=msoControlButton)
          .Caption = "Sort Ascending"
          .FaceId = 210
          .OnAction = "SortList"
          .Parameter = "Asc"
        End With
        With .Controls.Add(Type:=msoControlButton)
          .Caption = "Sort Decending"
          .FaceId = 211
          .OnAction = "SortList"
          .Parameter = "Dsc"
        End With
    End With

    With .Controls.Add(Type:=msoControlDropdown)
        .AddItem "(All)"
        .AddItem "AD"
        .AddItem "CR"
        .AddItem "DS"
```

```
              .AddItem "HR"
              .AddItem "I.S."
              .AddItem "MF"
              .AddItem "MK"
              .AddItem "RD"
              .AddItem "SL"
              .OnAction = "FilterDepartment"
              .TooltipText = "Select Department"
          End With
          .Visible = True
      End With
  End Sub
```

The toolbar itself is very simple to create. `CreateToolbar` uses the `Add` method of the `CommandBars` collection and accepts all the default parameter values apart from the `Name` property. The first control button is created in much the same way as a menu item, using the `Add` method of the `Controls` collection. It is assigned an `OnAction` macro, a `FaceId`, and a ToolTip.

The second control is created as type `msoControlPopup`. It is given the `Caption` of `Sort` and a ToolTip. It is then assigned two controls of its own, of type `msoControlButton`. They are assigned the `SortList` macro and `Parameter` values, as well as `FaceIds` and captions.

Finally, the control of type `msoControlDropdown` is added. Its drop-down list is populated with department codes and its `OnAction` macro is `FilterDepartment`. It is also given a ToolTip. The last action is to set the toolbar's `Visible` property to `True` to display it.

The `FilterDepartment` macro follows:

```
Sub FilterDepartment()
   Dim stDept As String

   With CommandBars.ActionControl
      stDept = .List(.ListIndex)
   End With
   If stDept = "(All)" Then
      Range("Database").Parent.AutoFilterMode = False
   Else
      Range("Database").AutoFilter Field:=5, Criteria1:=stDept
   End If
End Sub
```

A drop-down control has a `List` property that is an array of its list values and a `ListIndex` property that is the index number of the current list value. The `ActionControl` property of the `CommandBars` object, which refers to the currently active control, is a quick way to reference the control and access the `List` and `ListIndex` properties to get the department code required. The code is then used to perform the appropriate AutoFilter operation. If the (All) option is chosen, the `AutoFilterMode` property of the worksheet that is the parent of the `Database Range` object is set to `False`, removing the AutoFilter drop-downs and showing any hidden rows.

It is a good idea to run `CreateToolbar` from the `Workbook_Open` event procedure and to delete the toolbar in the `Workbook_BeforeClose` event procedure. The toolbar will remain permanently in Excel if it is not deleted and will give unexpected results if its buttons are pressed when other workbooks are active. If you do refer to `CommandBars` directly in workbook event procedures, you need to qualify the reference with `Application`:

```
Application.CommandBars("Manage Data").Delete
```

Typically, when the commandbar appears, it will be placed in a location determined by Windows. If you want consistency you could use some standard Win32 API calls to specify the location of the bar when it appears on the screen. To accomplish this, you will need to add a Module to the VBA Project. Within this new module place the following declare statement:

```
Declare Function GetSystemMetrics32 Lib "User32" _
   (ByVal Index As Long) As Long
```

This `Declare` statement defines the `GetSystemMetrics32` call that handles returning the screen size to us in points. Using this information, we can find a center point and display the command bar. Change your command bar code to the following to make use of the Win32 API:

```
Public Sub CreateToolbar()
    'Get rid of any existing toolbar called Manage Data
    On Error Resume Next
    CommandBars("Manage Data").Delete
    On Error GoTo 0

    'Create new toolbar
     With CommandBars.Add(Name:="Manage Data")
        With .Controls.Add(Type:=msoControlButton)
           .OnAction = "ShowDataForm"
           .FaceId = 264
           .TooltipText = "Show Data Form"
        End With

        With .Controls.Add(Type:=msoControlPopup)
           .Caption = "Sort"
           .TooltipText = "Sort Ascending or Descending"
           With .Controls.Add(Type:=msoControlButton)
             .Caption = "Sort Ascending"
             .FaceId = 210
             .OnAction = "SortList"
             .Parameter = "Asc"
           End With
           With .Controls.Add(Type:=msoControlButton)
             .Caption = "Sort Decending"
             .FaceId = 211
             .OnAction = "SortList"
             .Parameter = "Dsc"
           End With
        End With

        With .Controls.Add(Type:=msoControlDropdown)
           .AddItem "(All)"
           .AddItem "AD"
           .AddItem "CR"
           .AddItem "DS"
```

```
                    .AddItem "HR"
                    .AddItem "I.S."
                    .AddItem "MF"
                    .AddItem "MK"
                    .AddItem "RD"
                    .AddItem "SL"
                    .OnAction = "FilterDepartment"
                    .TooltipText = "Select Department"
                End With
                .Visible = True
            End With
```

```
        Dim lWidth As Long
        Dim lHeight As Long
        lWidth = Module1.GetSystemMetrics32(0) ' Width of the screen in points
        lHeight = Module1.GetSystemMetrics32(1) ' Height of the screen in point
        With CommandBars("Manage Data")
            .Position = msoBarFloating
            .Left = lWidth / 2 - .Width / 2
            .Top = lHeight / 2 - .Height / 2
        End With
```

```
        End Sub
```

In this code block, we declare two variables to hold the height and width of the screens. We then return information into these variables using the Win32 API `GetSystemMetrics32`. By passing different parameters to the API we are able to request different information. With this screen size information, we perform the appropriate math and set the properties of the command bar as it is displayed on the screen. API usage in VBA is used in a similar fashion and greatly extends what can be accomplished.

Pop-Up Menus

Excel's built-in shortcut menus are included in the command bar listing created by the macro, `ListFirstLevelControls`, which we saw earlier in this chapter. The modified version of this macro shows only the commandbars of type `msoBarTypePopup`, as displayed in Figure 26-11.

The code to display the pop-ups is shown in the following:

```
Sub ListPopups()
    Dim cbCtl As CommandBarControl
    Dim cbBar As CommandBar
    Dim i As Integer

    If Not IsEmptyWorksheet(ActiveSheet) Then Exit Sub
    On Error Resume Next
    Application.ScreenUpdating = False
    Cells(1, 1).Value = "CommandBar"
    Cells(1, 2).Value = "Control"
    Cells(1, 3).Value = "FaceId"
    Cells(1, 4).Value = "ID"
    Cells(1, 1).Resize(1, 4).Font.Bold = True
    i = 2
```

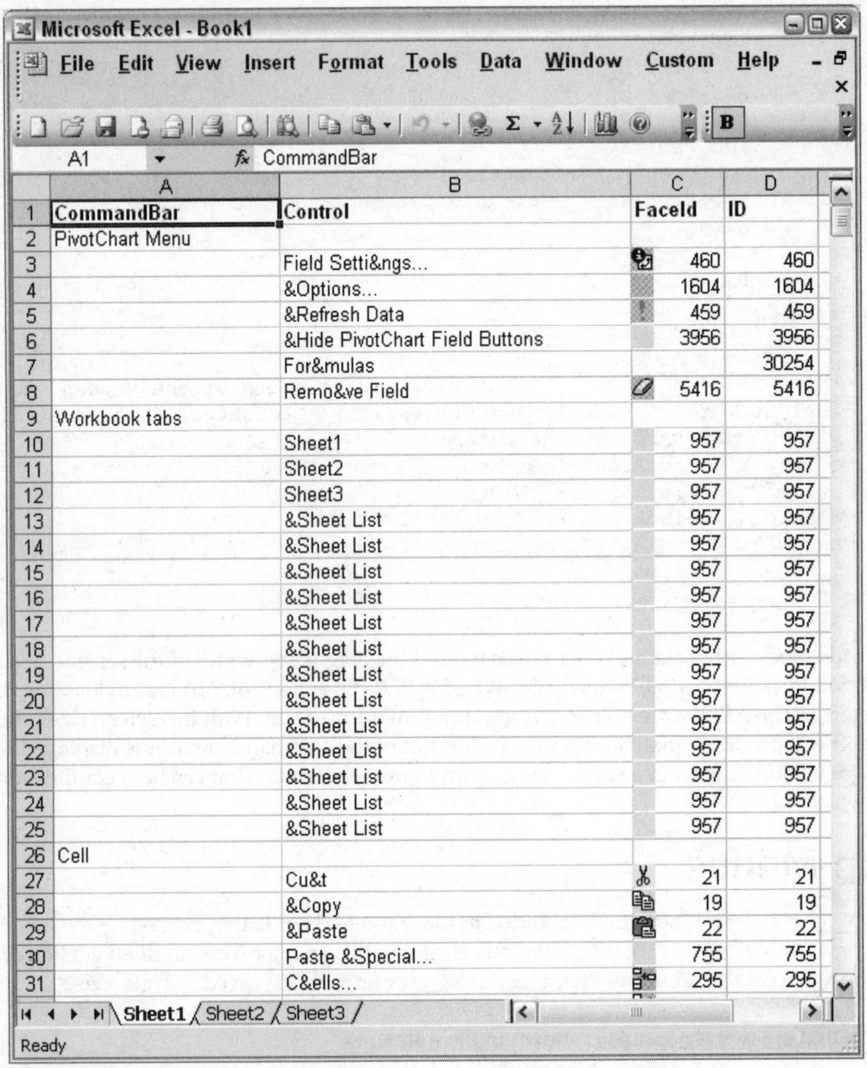

	A	B	C	D
	CommandBar	Control	FaceId	ID
1	**CommandBar**	**Control**	**FaceId**	**ID**
2	PivotChart Menu			
3		Field Setti&ngs...	460	460
4		&Options...	1604	1604
5		&Refresh Data	459	459
6		&Hide PivotChart Field Buttons	3956	3956
7		For&mulas		30254
8		Remo&ve Field	5416	5416
9	Workbook tabs			
10		Sheet1		957	957
11		Sheet2	957	957
12		Sheet3	957	957
13		&Sheet List	957	957
14		&Sheet List	957	957
15		&Sheet List	957	957
16		&Sheet List	957	957
17		&Sheet List	957	957
18		&Sheet List	957	957
19		&Sheet List	957	957
20		&Sheet List	957	957
21		&Sheet List	957	957
22		&Sheet List	957	957
23		&Sheet List	957	957
24		&Sheet List	957	957
25		&Sheet List	957	957
26	Cell			
27		Cu&t	21	21
28		&Copy	19	19
29		&Paste	22	22
30		Paste &Special...	755	755
31		C&ells...	295	295

Figure 26-11

```
For Each cbBar In CommandBars
    Application.StatusBar = "Processing Bar " & cbBar.Name
    If cbBar.Type = msoBarTypePopup Then
        Cells(i, 1).Value = cbBar.Name
        i = i + 1
        For Each cbCtl In cbBar.Controls
            Cells(i, 2).Value = cbCtl.Caption
            cbCtl.CopyFace
            If Err.Number = 0 Then
                ActiveSheet.Paste Cells(i, 3)
                Cells(i, 3).Value = cbCtl.FaceID
            End If
```

```
              Cells(i, 4).Value = cbCtl.ID
              Err.Clear
              i = i + 1
          Next cbCtl
      End If
  Next cbBar
  Range("A:B").EntireColumn.AutoFit
  Application.StatusBar = False
End Sub
```

The listing is identical to `ListFirstLevelControls`, apart from the introduction of a block `If` structure that processes only commandbars of type `msoBarTypePopup`. If you look at the listing produced by `ListPopups`, you will find you can identify the common shortcut menus. For example, there are commandbars named Cell, Row, and Column that correspond to the shortcut menus that popup when you right-click a worksheet cell, row number, or column letter.

You might be confused about the fact that the Cell, Row, and Column commandbars are listed twice. The first set is for a worksheet in Normal view. The second set is for a worksheet in Page Break Preview.

> **Another tricky one is the Workbook Tabs command bar. This is not the shortcut that you get when you click an individual worksheet tab. It is the shortcut for the workbook navigation buttons to the left of the worksheet tabs. The shortcut for the tabs is the Ply command bar.**

Having identified the shortcut menus, you can tailor them to your own needs using VBA code. For example, the screen in Figure 26-12 shows a modified Cell command bar that includes an option to Clear All:

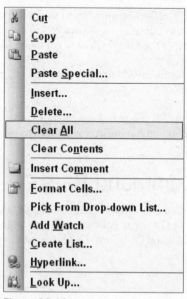

Figure 26-12

The `Clear All` control was added using the following code:

```
Public Sub AddShortCut()
    Dim cbBar As CommandBar
    Dim cbCtl As CommandBarControl
    Dim lIndex As Long

    Set cbBar = CommandBars("Cell")
    lIndex = cbBar.Controls("Clear Contents").Index
    Set cbCtl = cbBar.Controls.Add(Type:=msoControlButton, _
                                   ID:=1964, Before:=lIndex)
    cbCtl.Caption = "Clear &All"
End Sub
```

`AddShortCut` starts by assigning a reference to the `Cell` command bar to `cbBar`.

If you want to refer to the Cell command bar that is shown in Page Break view in Excel 2003, you can use its `Index` property:

```
Set cbBar = CommandBars(31)
```

You need to take care here, if you want code compatible with other versions of Office. In Excel 2000, the `Index` property of the `Cell` command bar in Page Break view is 26 and in Excel 97 it is 24.

`AddShortCut` records the `Index` property of the `Clear Contents` control in `lIndex`, so that it can add the new control before the `Clear Contents` control. `AddShortCut` uses the `Add` method of the `Controls` collection to add the new control to `cbBar`, specifying the `ID` property of the built-in Edit ⇨ Clear ⇨ All menu item on the Worksheet menu bar.

The `Add` method of the `Controls` collection allows you to specify the `Id` property of a built-in command. The listing from `ListAllControls` allows you to determine that the `Id` property, which is the same as the `FaceId` property, of the Edit ⇨ Clear ⇨ All menu item, is 1964.

The built-in `Caption` property for the newly added control is All, so `AddShortCut` changes the `Caption` to be more descriptive.

You can safely leave the modified Cell command bar in your `commandbars` collection. It is not tied to any workbook and does not depend on having access to macros in a specific workbook.

Showing Pop-Up Command Bars

If you want to display a shortcut menu without having to right-click a cell, or chart, you can create code to display the shortcut in a number of ways. For example, you might like to display the shortcut Cell commandbar from the keyboard, using *Ctrl+Shift+C*. You can do this using the following code:

```
Sub SetShortCut()
    Application.OnKey "^+c", "ShowCellShortCut"
End Sub
```

```
Private Sub ShowCellShortCut()
    CommandBars("Cell").ShowPopup x:=0, y:=0
End Sub
```

ShowCellShortCut uses the ShowPopup method to display the Cell shortcut menu at the top-left corner of the screen. The parameters are the x and y screen coordinates for the top left of the menu.

You can also create a popup menu from scratch. The f popup shown in Figure 26-13 appears when you right-click inside the range named Database. Outside the range, the normal Cell popup menu appears.

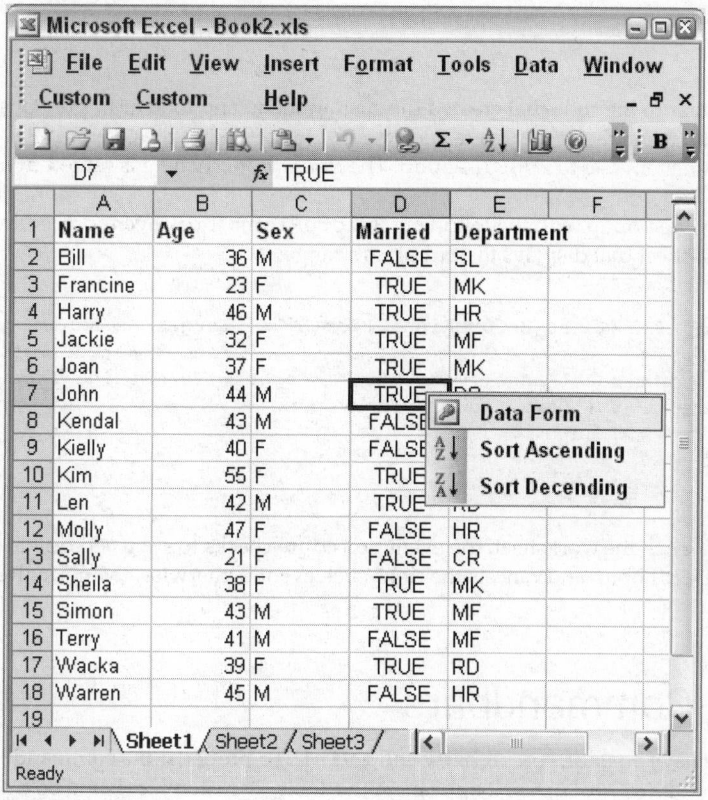

Figure 26-13

The following code created the popup menu:

```
Sub MakePopup()
    With CommandBars.Add(Name:="Data Popup", Position:=msoBarPopup)
        With .Controls.Add(Type:=msoControlButton)
            .OnAction = "ShowDataForm"
            .FaceID = 264
            .Caption = "Data Form"
            .TooltipText = "Show Data Form"
        End With
        With .Controls.Add(Type:=msoControlButton)
```

```
            .Caption = "Sort Ascending"
            .FaceID = 210
            .OnAction = "SortList"
            .Parameter = "Asc"
        End With
        With .Controls.Add(Type:=msoControlButton)
            .Caption = "Sort Decending"
            .FaceID = 211
            .OnAction = "SortList"
            .Parameter = "Dsc"
        End With
    End With
End Sub
```

The code is similar to the code that created the custom menu and toolbar in previous examples. The difference is that, when the popup is created by the Add method of the CommandBars collection, the Position parameter is set to msoBarPopup. The Name property here is set to Data Popup.

You can display the popup with the following BeforeRightClick event procedure in the code module behind the worksheet that displays the Database range:

```
Private Sub Worksheet_BeforeRightClick(ByVal Target As Range, _
                                        Cancel As Boolean)
    If Not Intersect(Range("Database"), Target) Is Nothing Then
        CommandBars("Data Popup").ShowPopup
        Cancel = True
    End If
End Sub
```

When you right-click the worksheet, the event procedure checks to see if Target is within Database. If so, it displays Data Popup and cancels the right-click event. Otherwise, the normal Cell shortcut menu appears.

Disabling Commandbars

Commandbars have an Enabled property and a Visible property. If a commandbar is enabled, and it is not of type msoBarTypePopup, it appears in the Tools ⇨ Customize dialog box. If it is checked in the Tools ⇨ Customize dialog box, it is visible on the screen.

You cannot set the Visible property of a command bar to True unless the Enabled property is also set to True. Setting the Visible property of an enabled command bar of type msoBarTypeNormal to False removes it from the screen. Setting the Worksheet menu bar's Visible property to False does not work. Excel treats it as a special case and insists on showing it when a worksheet is active. The only way to remove the Worksheet menu is to set its Enabled property to False.

The following code removes any visible toolbars and the Worksheet menu bar from the screen:

```
Sub RemoveToolbarsAndWorksheetMenuBar()
    Dim cbBar As CommandBar
```

```
        For Each cbBar In CommandBars
            If cbBar.Enabled And cbBar.Type = msoBarTypeNormal Then
                cbBar.Visible = False
            End If
        Next cbBar
        CommandBars("Worksheet Menu Bar").Enabled = False
        Application.OnKey "%-", ""
    End Sub
```

The screen looks like Figure 26-14.

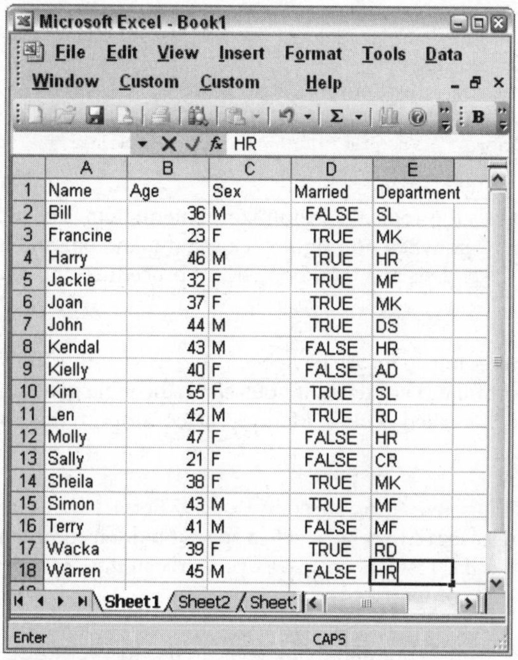

Figure 26-14

The final action carried out by RemoveToolbarsAndWorksheetMenuBar is to disable the *Alt +–* key combination that displays the workbook window's control menu. If you don't do this when you remove the Worksheet menu bar, the user can still access the control menu using *Alt +–*, and then use the cursor movement keys to make a phantom copy of the Worksheet menu bar slowly appear.

You can restore the Worksheet menu bar and the Standard and Formatting toolbars, with the following code, assuming the toolbars have not had their `Enabled` property set to `False`:

```
Sub RestoreToolbarsAndWorksheetMenuBar()
    CommandBars("Worksheet Menu Bar").Enabled = True
```

```
        Application.OnKey "%-"
        CommandBars("Standard").Visible = True
        CommandBars("Formatting").Visible = True
    End Sub
```

Disabling Shortcut Access to Customize

If you want to stop users from making changes to your custom commandbars or built-in commandbars, you can prevent access to the customization dialog box and toolbar with the following code. The code could be placed in the `Personal.xls` workbook so that it is automatically applied at the beginning of an Excel session:

```
Private Sub Workbook_Open()
    'Code to customize commandbars goes here...
    Application.CommandBars("Tools").Controls("Customize...").Enabled = False
    Application.CommandBars("Toolbar List").Enabled = False
End Sub
```

The first line of code disables the Tools ⇨ Customize... menu item. The second line of the code disables the shortcut menu that appears when you right-click a command bar and also disables the View ⇨ Toolbars menu item. As the code is in a workbook event procedure, the reference to `Application` is required.

Note the syntax in the preceding code. We have been able to treat the Tools control on the Worksheet menu bar as if it were a command bar itself. If you search the table generated by `ListAllControls`, you will find a command bar called Built-in Menus. The controls on this command bar can be directly addressed as commandbars.

The Toolbar List command bar was introduced in Excel 97 Service Release 1. You cannot use this command bar in earlier releases of Excel 97—it is a special hidden command bar. Like the Built-in Menus command bar controls, ToolBar List has no `Index` property in the `CommandBars` collection, although it can be addressed by its `Name` property.

If you only want to protect some commandbars, you can use the `Protect` property of the commandbars. The following code applies all protection options to the Standard toolbar. You can omit the constants for any options that are not wanted:

```
Sub ProtectToolbar()
    CommandBars("Standard").Protection = msoBarNoCustomize + _
                                         msoBarNoResize + _
                                         msoBarNoMove + _
                                         msoBarNoChangeVisible + _
                                         msoBarNoChangeDock + _
                                         msoBarNoVerticalDock + _
                                         msoBarNoHorizonaldock
End Sub
```

You can remove the protection with:

```
Sub UnProtectToolbar()
    CommandBars("Standard").Protection = msoBarNoProtection
End Sub
```

Table-Driven Command Bar Creation

Very few professional Excel developers write code to add their menu items and toolbars one-by-one. Most of us use a table-driven approach, whereby we fill out a table with information about the items we want to add, then have a routine which generates all the items based on this table. This makes it much easier to define and modify the design of our commandbars.

Say, we want to create the Custom menu, which we set up earlier in this chapter, using this new method. The first thing we need is a table for the menu information. Insert a new worksheet, change its name to `MenuTable` and fill out the sheet as shown in Figures 26-15 and 26-16. The worksheet named `Data` contains our employee database and DataLists will be used later to define a list of departments.

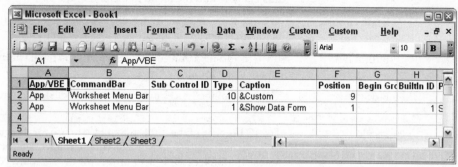

Figure 26-15

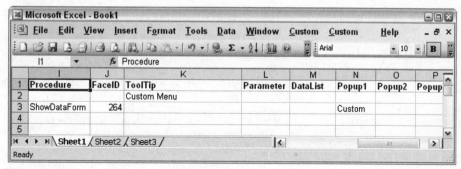

Figure 26-16

The columns of the `MenuTable` are:

Column	Title	Description
A	App / VBE	Either App to add items to Excel's menus or VBE to add them to the VBE. The code to handle VBE entries is provided in Chapter 23
B	CommandBar	The name of the top-level command bar to add our menu to. Get these names from the listings we generated earlier in this chapter

Continues

Column	Title	Description
C	Sub Control ID	The ID number of a built-in pop-up bar to add our menu to. For example, 30002 is the ID of the File popup menu
D	Type	The type of control to add: 1 for a normal button, 10 for a popup and so on. These correspond to the `msoControl...` types listed in the Object Browser
E	Caption	The text to use for the menu item
F	Position	The position in the commandbar to add the menu item. Leave this blank to add the menu to the end of the bar
G	Begin Group	`True` or `False` to specify whether to place a separator line before the item
H	BuiltIn ID	If we're adding a built-in menu item, this is the ID of that menu. Use 1 for all custom menu items
I	Procedure	The name of the procedure to run when a custom menu item is clicked
J	FaceId	The ID number of the built-in tool face to use for the menu. This can also be the name of a picture in the worksheet to use for the button face. 18 is the number for the standard New icon
K	ToolTip	The text of the popup ToolTip to show for the button
L	Parameter	The string to be assigned to the `Parameter` property of the button
M	DataList	Only used with controls that have drop-down lists, such as type `msoControlDropdown` (type 3). It contains the name of a range of cells in the worksheet called DataLists that contains items to be added to the drop-down list
N	Popup1–n	If we add our own popup menus, this is the caption of the custom popup to add further menu items to. We can include as many levels of popup as we like, by simply adding more columns—the code will detect the extra columns

As the MenuTable sheet will be referred to a number of times in code, it is a good idea to give it a meaningful "code name", such as shMenuTable. To do this, locate and select the sheet in the Project Explorer in the VBE, and change its name in the Properties window. It should now be shown as shMenuTable (MenuTable) in the Project Explorer. Using the code name allows you to refer directly to that sheet as an object, so the following two lines are equivalent:

```
Debug.Print ThisWorkbook.Worksheets("MenuTable").Name
Debug.Print shMenuTable.Name
```

The DataLists sheet needs to be renamed as shDataLists in the same way.

The code to create the menu from this table is shown next. The code should be copied into a new module called modSetupBars.

At the top of the module, a number of constants are declared, which correspond to each column of the menu table and you will use these throughout your code. If the menu table structure changes, all you need to do is renumber these constants—you don't need to search through the code:

```
'Constants for the columns in the commandbar creation table
Const miTABLE_APP_VBE           As Integer = 1
Const miTABLE_COMMANDBAR_NAME   As Integer = 2
Const miTABLE_CONTROL_ID        As Integer = 3
Const miTABLE_CONTROL_TYPE      As Integer = 4
Const miTABLE_CONTROL_CAPTION   As Integer = 5
Const miTABLE_CONTROL_POSITION  As Integer = 6
Const miTABLE_CONTROL_GROUP     As Integer = 7
Const miTABLE_CONTROL_BUILTIN   As Integer = 8
Const miTABLE_CONTROL_PROC      As Integer = 9
Const miTABLE_CONTROL_FACEID    As Integer = 10
Const miTABLE_CONTROL_TOOLTIP   As Integer = 11
Const miTABLE_CONTROL_PARAMETER As Integer = 12
Const miTABLE_CONTROL_DATALIST  As Integer = 13
Const miTABLE_POPUP_START       As Integer = 14

'Constant to determine whether commandbars are temporary or permanent
'If you set this to False, users will not loose any additional controls
'that they add to your custom commandbars
Const mbTEMPORARY               As Boolean = False

'The following Application ID is used to identify our menus, making it easy to
'remove them
Const psAppID As String = "TableDrivenCommandBars"
```

The mbTEMPORARY constant allows you to make the menu changes temporary or permanent. psAppID provides an identifying string that will be assigned to the Tag property of our added controls, which makes it easy to find and remove them.

The routine to actually set up the menus is called from our workbook's Auto_Open procedure or Workbook_Open event procedure:

```
' Subroutine: SetUpMenus
' Purpose:    Adds the commandbars defined in the shMenuTable worksheet'

Sub SetUpMenus()
    Dim rgRow As Range
    Dim cbAllBars As CommandBars
    Dim cbBar As CommandBar
    Dim cbBtn As CommandBarControl
    Dim iBuiltInID As Integer, iPopUpCol As Integer, vaData As Variant

    On Error Resume Next 'Just ignore errors in the table definition

    'Remove all of our menus before adding them.
    'This ensures we don't get any duplicated menus
    RemoveMenus

    'Loop through each row of our menu generation table
    For Each rgRow In shMenuTable.Cells(1).CurrentRegion.Rows
```

```
                     'Ignore the header row
                     If rgRow.Row > 1 Then
                         'Read the row into an array of the cells' values
                         vaData = rgRow.Value

                         Set cbBar = Nothing
```

A single routine can be used to add menu items to both the Excel and VBE menus. The only difference is the CommandBars collection that is used – Excel's or the VBE's. This code does not contain all the elements necessary to add VBE menus. We have discussed the additional requirements in Chapter 23:

```
                 'Get the collection of all commandbars, either in the VBE or Excel
                 If vaData(1, miTABLE_APP_VBE) = "VBE" Then
                     Set cbAllBars = Application.VBE.CommandBars
                 Else
                     Set cbAllBars = Application.CommandBars
                 End If

                 'Try to find the commandbar we want
                 Set cbBar = cbAllBars.Item(vaData(1, miTABLE_COMMANDBAR_NAME))

                 'Did we find it - if not, we must be adding one!
                 If cbBar Is Nothing Then
                     Set cbBar = cbAllBars.Add( _
                         Name:=vaData(1, miTABLE_COMMANDBAR_NAME), _
                                                 temporary:=mbTEMPORARY)
                 End If
```

If you want to look for a built-in popup menu to add your control to, you can recursively search for it in the CommandBars collection. For example, if you want to add a menu item to the Edit ⇨ Clear menu, you can enter the ID of the Clear menu (30021) in the Sub Control ID column of the table. Alternatively, you can enter one or more control name entries in the PopUp columns of the table. Entering Edit under PopUp1 and Clear under PopUp2 accomplishes the same result as placing 30021 under Sub Control ID. The first method is convenient when adding controls to the built-in menus. The alternative method is necessary to add items to the menus you create yourself:

```
                 'If set, locate the built-in popup menu bar (by ID) to add our
                 'control to.
                 'e.g. Worksheet Menu Bar > Edit
                 If Not IsEmpty(vaData(1, miTABLE_CONTROL_ID)) Then
                     Set cbBar = cbBar.FindControl(ID:=vaData(1, _
                                 miTABLE_CONTROL_ID), Recursive:=True).CommandBar
                 End If

                 'Loop through the PopUp name columns to navigate down the
                 'menu structure
                 For iPopUpCol = miTABLE_POPUP_START To UBound(vaData, 2)
                     'If set, navigate down the menu structure to the next popup menu
                     If Not IsEmpty(vaData(1, iPopUpCol)) Then
                         Set cbBar = cbBar.Controls(vaData(1, iPopUpCol)).CommandBar
                     End If
                 Next
```

If you are adding an existing Excel control, you can specify its Id property value in the BuiltIn ID column. If you want the control to run your own procedure, you specify the name of the procedure in the Procedure column:

```
'Get the ID number if we're adding a built-in control
iBuiltInID = vaData(1, miTABLE_CONTROL_BUILTIN)

'If it's empty, set it to 1, indicating a custom control
If iBuiltInID = 0 Then iBuiltInID = 1

'Now add our control to the command bar
If IsEmpty(vaData(1, miTABLE_CONTROL_POSITION)) Or _
            vaData(1, miTABLE_CONTROL_POSITION) > _
                                    cbBar.Controls.Count Then
    Set cbBtn = cbBar.Controls.Add(Type:=vaData(1, _
                    miTABLE_CONTROL_TYPE), ID:=iBuiltInID, _
                                temporary:= mbTEMPORARY)
Else
    Set cbBtn = cbBar.Controls.Add(Type:=vaData(1, _
                    miTABLE_CONTROL_TYPE), ID:=iBuiltInID, _
                    temporary:= mbTEMPORARY, _
                    before:=vaData(1, _
                    miTABLE_CONTROL_POSITION))
End If

'Set the rest of button's properties
With cbBtn
    .Caption = vaData(1, miTABLE_CONTROL_CAPTION)
    .BeginGroup = vaData(1, miTABLE_CONTROL_GROUP)
    .TooltipText = vaData(1, miTABLE_CONTROL_TOOLTIP)
```

You can either use one of the standard Office tool faces, by supplying the numeric FaceId, or provide your own picture to use. To use your own picture, just give the name of the Picture object in the FaceId column of the menu table:

```
'The FaceId can be empty for a blank button, the number of
'a standard button face, or the name of a picture object on
'the sheet, which contains the picture to use.
If Not IsEmpty(vaData(1, miTABLE_CONTROL_FACEID)) Then
    If IsNumeric(vaData(1, miTABLE_CONTROL_FACEID)) Then
        'A numeric face ID, so use it
        .FaceId = vaData(1, miTABLE_CONTROL_FACEID)
    Else
        'A textual face ID, so copy the picture to the button
        shMenuTable.Shapes(vaData(1, _
                        miTABLE_CONTROL_FACEID)).CopyPicture
        .PasteFace
    End If
End If
```

It is a good idea to set a property for all your menu items that identifies it as one of yours. If you use the Tag property to do this, you can use the FindControl method of the CommandBars object to locate all of your menu items, without having to remember exactly where you added them. This is done in the RemoveMenus procedure later in the module:

```
'Set the button's tag to identify it as one we created.
'This way, we can still find it if the user moves or renames it
.Tag = psAppID

'Set the control's OnAction property.
'Surround the workbook name with quote marks, in case the
'name includes spaces
If Not IsEmpty(vaData(1, miTABLE_CONTROL_PROC)) Then
    .OnAction = "'" & ThisWorkbook.Name & "'!" & vaData(1, _
                                      miTABLE_CONTROL_PROC)
End If
```

If your procedure expects to find information in the control's Parameter property, you enter that information under the Parameter column of the table:

```
'Assign Parameter property value, if specified
If Not IsEmpty(vaData(1, miTABLE_CONTROL_PARAMETER)) Then
    .Parameter = vaData(1, miTABLE_CONTROL_PARAMETER)
End If
```

For a drop-down control or combo box, you enter a list of values in the DataLists worksheet and assign a name to the list. You enter the name in the DataList column of the table:

```
'Assign data list to ComboBox
If Not IsEmpty(vaData(1, miTABLE_CONTROL_DATALIST)) Then
    For Each Rng In shDatalists.Range(vaData(1, _
                                miTABLE_CONTROL_DATALIST))
        .AddItem Rng.Value
    Next Rng
End If
        End With
    End If
    Next rgRow
End Sub
```

When the application workbook is closed, you need to run some code to remove your menus. Some developers just use CommandBars.Reset, but this removes all other customizations from the commandbars as well as their own. It is much better to locate all the menu items and commandbars that were created for your application and delete them. This takes two routines. The first removes all the menus from a specific CommandBars collection, by searching by its Tag value:

```
Private Sub RemoveMenusFromBars(cbBars As CommandBars)
    Dim cbCtl As CommandBarControl

    'Ignore errors while deleting our menu items
    On Error Resume Next

    'Using the application or VBE CommandBars ...
    With cbBars
```

```
            'Find a CommandBarControl with our tag
            Set cbCtl = .FindControl(Tag:=psAppID)

            'Loop until we don't find one
            Do Until cbCtl Is Nothing
                'Delete the one we found
                cbCtl.Delete

                'Find the next one
                Set cbCtl = .FindControl(Tag:=psAppID)
            Loop
        End With
    End Sub
```

The second removal routine calls the first to remove the menu items from the Excel commandbars and the VBE commandbars and removes any custom bars that might have been created, as long as the user has not added their own controls to them:

```
Sub RemoveMenus()
    Dim cbBar As CommandBar, rgRow As Range, stBarName As String

    'Ignore errors while deleting our menu items and commandbars
    On Error Resume Next

    'Delete our menu items from the Excel and VBE commandbars
    RemoveMenusFromBars Application.CommandBars
    RemoveMenusFromBars Application.VBE.CommandBars

    'Loop through each row of our menu generation table
    For Each rgRow In shMenuTable.Cells(1).CurrentRegion.Rows
        'Ignore the header row
        If rgRow.Row > 1 Then
            stBarName = rgRow.Cells(1, miTABLE_COMMANDBAR_NAME)

            Set cbBar = Nothing
            'Find the command bar, either in the VBE or Excel
            If rgRow.Cells(1, miTABLE_APP_VBE) = "VBE" Then
                Set cbBar = Application.VBE.CommandBars(stBarName)
            Else
                Set cbBar = Application.CommandBars(stBarName)
            End If
            'If we found it, delete it if it is not a built-in bar
            If Not cbBar Is Nothing Then
                If Not cbBar.BuiltIn Then
                    'Only delete blank commandbars - in case user
                    'or other applications added menu items to the
                    'same custom bar
                    If cbBar.Controls.Count = 0 Then cbBar.Delete
                End If
            End If
        End If
    Next
End Sub
```

You should run the `SetUpMenus` procedure from the `Auto_Open` procedure or the `Workbook_Open` event procedure and the `RemoveMenus` procedure from the `Auto_Close` procedure or the `Workbook_BeforeClose` event procedure.

You now have a complete template, which can be used as the basis for any Excel application (or just in a normal workbook where you want to modify the menu structure).

The first table entry, shown previously in Figures 26-15 and 26-16, adds a new popup menu to the Worksheet menu bar called Custom. The second entry adds a menu item called Show Data Form to the Custom menu, as shown in Figure 26-17.

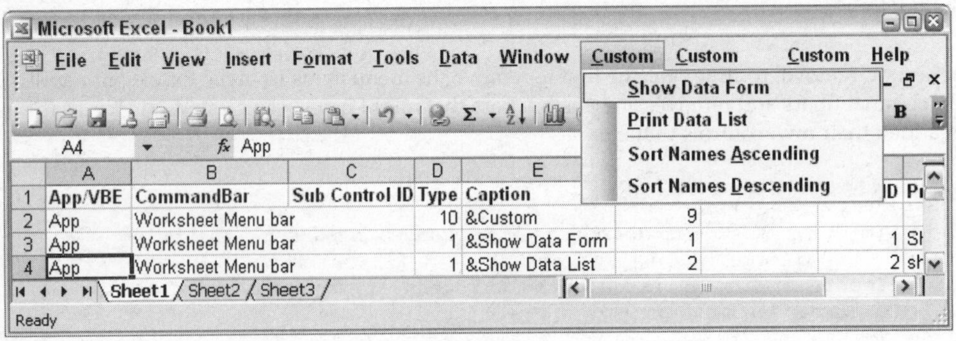

Figure 26-17

You can expand the table to add more items to the custom menu and create new commandbars and controls as shown in Figures 26-18 and 26-19.

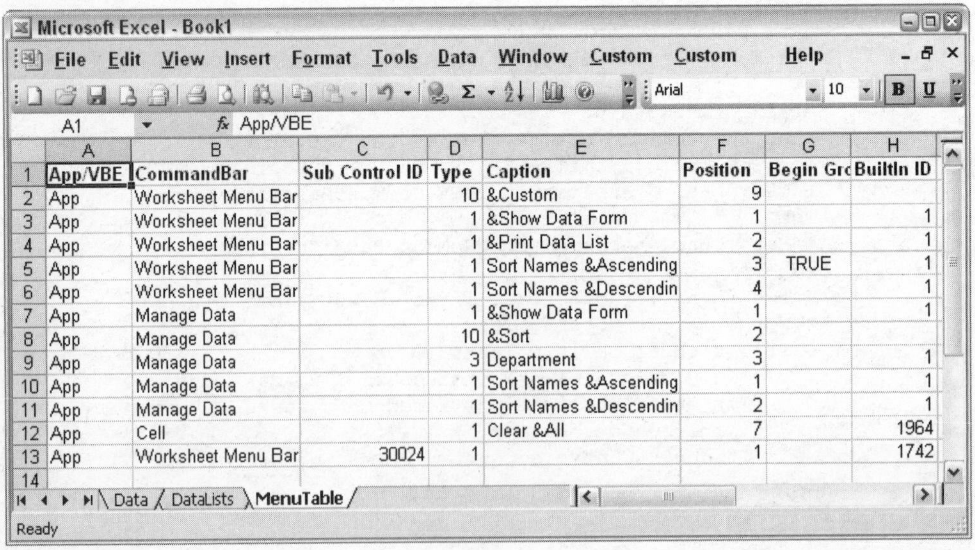

Figure 26-18

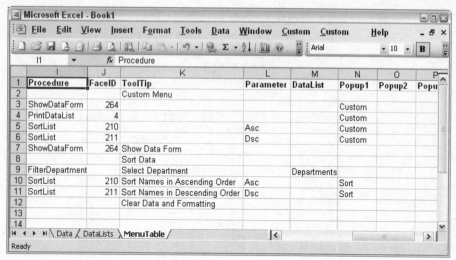

Figure 26-19

The following procedures will automate the running of the code as the workbook is opened and closed:

```
' Subroutine: Auto_Open
' Purpose:    Adds our menus and menuitems to the application
Sub Auto_Open()
    SetUpMenus
    CommandBars("Manage Data").Visible = True
End Sub


' Subroutine: Auto_Close
' Purpose:    Removes our menus and menu items from the application
Sub Auto_Close()
    RemoveMenus
End Sub
```

The data in rows 2 through 6 of the MenuTable table create the Custom menu shown in Figure 26-20, which is identical to the Custom menu we created earlier in this chapter, apart from some added icons.

Rows 7 through 11 create a Manage Data toolbar identical to the one we created earlier. The data required for the drop-down list of departments is in the DataLists worksheet as shown in Figure 26-21. The highlighted range has been given the name Departments.

Row 12 of the table creates a Clear All entry in the popup menu that appears when you right-click a worksheet cell.

Row 13 adds the built-in Merge Across control to the Format ⇨ Row menu, as shown in Figure 26-22.

Although the code we have presented allows you to add items to existing shortcut menus, it is not able to create a new popup shortcut menu. However, you could easily add an extra column that allows you to specify this, as long as you adapt the code accordingly. The technique is flexible enough to accommodate whatever options you need.

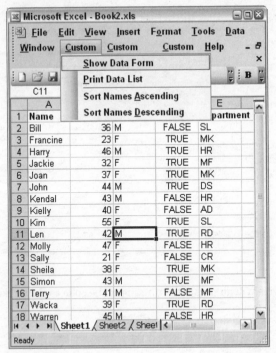

Figure 26-20

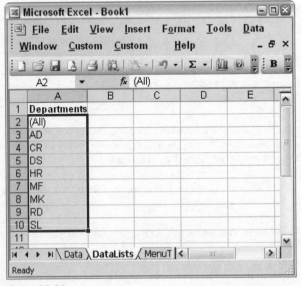

Figure 26-21

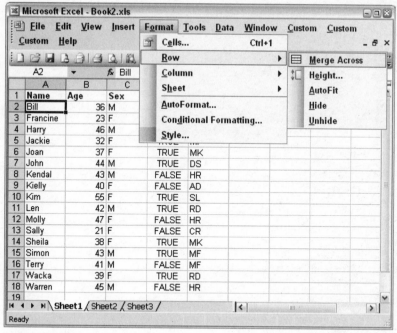

Figure 26-22

Summary

In this chapter, you have seen how the Excel commandbars are structured and learned how to create:

- ❑ Lists of the built-in control images with their Id and FaceId properties
- ❑ An entire list of the FaceIds that are available
- ❑ A complete list of popup menu items

You have also seen how to create your own commandbars and how to add controls to your commandbars. The differences between the three types of commandbars, that is toolbars, menu bars, and popup menus, have been described and methods of creating them programmatically have been presented. In addition, you have been shown how to enable and disable commandbars and controls, as well as how to protect commandbars so that users cannot change them.

Finally, you have seen how you can create a table to define the changes you want to make to a CommandBar structure while your application is open. This approach simplifies the task of customizing menus and makes it very easy to make changes.

27

SmartTags

When something is typed into a worksheet cell, Excel tries to interpret that entry, converting it to something more meaningful than a random set of characters. This is achieved using rules similar to the following:

❑ If the entry contains the characters 0–9, and potentially the local thousand and decimal separators, it's a number that can be used in calculations

❑ If the entry contains the characters 0–9 and the local date separator, it might be date that can be used in calculations (and implies a specific cell format)

❑ If the entry is #N/A, #Value! etc., it's an error value that should propagate through any calculations that refer to it.

❑ If the entry starts with an = sign, it could be a formula to be evaluated or a number

❑ Otherwise, it's a text string—an essentially random set of characters

In each case, Excel is recognizing the entry as a specific data type—a number, date, formula, etc.—and by doing so gives that entry a specific set of behaviors, actions, and properties (those behaviors and actions that are defined for entries of that type). For example, all entries of type "Formula" have the following behaviors:

❑ They need to be checked for "syntax" errors, such as mismatched brackets, etc.

❑ They need to be incorporated into Excel's calculation dependency tree

❑ They need to be evaluated

❑ The cell should show the result of the evaluation, not the text of the formula

Up until Excel 2002, the rules for recognizing entries, and the list of applicable behaviors and properties had been fixed and defined by Excel. The only ways that we were able to extend the recognition was to preformat the cell (to force a specific data type), or by hooking `Worksheet_Change`, `Worksheet_SelectionChange`, and `Worksheet_Calculate` events for specific sheets and checking whatever was typed in, selected, or changed during the recalculation. This was rather cumbersome and it was difficult to detect and respond to every potential way of changing the contents of a cell in a worksheet.

Introduced in Office XP, SmartTags provide a mechanism for us to add our own "data types" (such stock symbols, file names, medical terms, part numbers, etc.), to provide the recognition logic that tells Excel that an entry in a cell is a specific data type, and to provide a list of actions that can be performed on or with that data type.

When an entry is recognized as being of a specific type, the applicable actions are presented to the user as a popup menu when their mouse pointer hovers over the cell, such as the following menu from the standard stock-symbol SmartTag, shown in Figure 27-1, where the characters MSFT are recognized as the stock symbol for Microsoft.

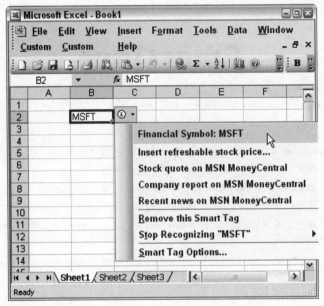

Figure 27-1

To enable SmartTags for a workbook, click Tools ⇨ AutoCorrect Options..., select the SmartTags tab, tick the Label Data with SmartTags checkbox, and tick which of the installed SmartTag recognizers to enable.

There is an official SmartTag Software Development Kit (SDK) available from the Microsoft Web site for Office XP. Though this SDK is useful, at the time of writing, there is no SDK to assist you in building Office 2003 SmartTags. The Office XP SmartTag SDK does, however, include several tools that are compatible with Office 2003 and can help you in tracking down problems or just for general knowledge of SmartTag development. This SDK can be found at http://msdn.microsoft.com/office/.

SmartTag Enhancements

Microsoft Office 2003 has added considerable enhancements to the SmartTags. All enhancements are in the form of a new type library and can coexist with the Office XP type library, so Smart Tags can be created once and work on both Office XP and Office 2003. Before we get into a sample implementation of a SmartTag, let's discuss some of the enhancements that were introduced in Microsoft Office 2003.

Microsoft SmartTags 2.0 Type Library

The Microsoft SmartTags 2.0 Type Library maintains the `ISmartTagAction` and `ISmartTag Recognizer` interfaces for backward compatibility to Office XP. In addition to these legacy interfaces, version 2.0 of this type library exposes the `ISmartTagAction2` and `ISmartTagRecognizer2` interfaces. These new interfaces provide more functionality and allow you to take advantage of new SmartTag features found in Microsoft Office 2003.

To get a better idea of the features introduced in the Microsoft SmartTags 2.0 Type Library, let's take a look at the members in each interface and a description of each one and what is new.

The `ISmartTagRecognizer2` interface contains the following definitions:

❑ *DisplayPropertyPage*—This method is called when the user clicks the Configure button to configure the SmartTag. It accepts an `SmartTagID` (Long) and a `LocaleID` (Long). Since a SmartTag DLL can contain multiple SmartTag objects, the `SmartTagID` parameter can determine which property page is shown.

❑ *PropertyPage*—`ReadOnly` property that informs the host application if your SmartTag control supports property pages. As with the `DisplayPropertyPage` method, this method also contains a `SmartTagID` (Long) and a `LocaleID` (Long) parameter.

❑ *Recognize2*—Very similar to the `Recognize` method, this method contains a few extra parameters that simplify the process of recognizing text. The `Recognize2` method contains a parameter called `TokenList` (`ISmartTagTokenList`) that tokenizes all text into individual words. This frees the programmer from parsing text.

❑ *SmartTagInitialize*—This method is called as soon as the SmartTag in loaded and passes in the name of the host application.

The `ISmartTagAction2` interface contains the follow definitions:

❑ *InvokeVerb2*—This method performs the same function as its predecessor in that it actually carries out an action when a SmartTag action is chosen. `InvokeVerb2` differs from the original `InvokeVerb` method because it also passes a `LocaleID`.

❑ *IsCaptionDynamic*—This method highlights some one of the new features of SmartTags in Office 2003. In Office XP, all SmartTag captions were static, once you defined them, they couldn't be changed. `IsCaptionDynamic` tells the host application if a caption is indeed dynamic. If so, the `SmartTagInitialize` method is called each time the SmartTag menu is displayed. This will give you the opportunity to change the caption at runtime.

❑ *ShowSmartTagIndicator*—This method is of type `Boolean` and determines if the SmartTag indicator is shown.

❑ *SmartTagInitialize*—This is the same as the `SmartTagInitialize` method in the `ISmartTag Recognizer2` interface except this one is fired whenever the Action portion of the SmartTag is loaded.

❑ *VerbCaptionFromID2*—Defines each caption in an action menu for a SmartTag. This method allows for the new cascading menus which will be covered in the sample application.

In a nutshell, the new type library provides more locale information and allows for new features such as cascading menus, dynamic menus and tokenization of host text. Now, we'll build an example SmartTag component that will work with Office XP and Office 2003 and utilize a few of the new features that were introduced.

The FileName SmartTag

Type the following text into a worksheet cell: `C:\mydir\mypic.bmp`.

Following Excel's data entry recognition rules, it's not a number, not a date, not a formula, not an error value, and not anything else that Excel recognizes. It is as meaningful to Excel as a random jumble of characters. To us, though, it's a file, probably a picture—we've recognized that sequence of characters to be a filename and have started to think of it as a `FileName` data type, in the same way that we (and Excel) recognize 123 as an Integer, 123.456 as a Double, 10/5/2001 as a Date, etc. Once we start thinking of those characters as a filename, there are a number of actions that we may like to do with that file:

❑ Check that it exists

❑ Rename it

❑ Open it in its native application

❑ If it's a spreadsheet, open it in the same Excel instance, or a new instance of Excel

By implementing the `FileName` SmartTag that we'll be creating in this chapter, we will:

❑ Extend Excel's recognition routines to recognize cells containing filenames

❑ Provide Excel with a list of actions that can be performed on filenames (and files)

❑ Provide the code to perform those actions

> **Keep in mind that in this particular example, we will be testing the SmartTag with Microsoft Excel but it will also work with Word, Outlook, PowerPoint and Access. In Microsoft Office XP, SmartTags were only compatible with Word, Excel and Outlook. Microsoft Office 2003 now supports Smart Tags in all of the applications listed earlier.**

Anatomy of a SmartTag

Most SmartTags consist of three things:

❑ A unique identifier for the data type (or multiple identifiers for multiple types in the same SmartTag).

❑ A class module that performs the recognition. Excel passes every bit of text entered in a cell to a function in this class that tags the cell with the unique identifier(s) if it passes the recognition tests.

❑ A class module to provide the list of actions applicable to the data type(s) and to perform the selected action when the user clicks the SmartTag action's menu item.

Note that we can extend other SmartTags by providing extra recognition routines that tag the cell with a preexisting identifier (for example, to extend the set of symbols recognized by the standard Stock Symbol SmartTag) and/or providing extra actions that apply to preexisting identifiers (for example, to retrieve stock information from providers other than MSN).

Physically, SmartTags are ActiveX DLLs, usually written in VB or C++. They will typically contain a Recognizer class, an Actions class, and a Globals module to hold constants and enumerations used by both the other classes. The Recognizer and Actions classes each have to implement a specific interface, to provide the hooks through which Excel and the other Microsoft Office applications can call into the class.

We'll start by creating the FileName SmartTag. Open VB6, create a new ActiveX DLL, and call the project FileNameSmartTag. The Recognizer and Actions interfaces are defined in the "Microsoft Smart Tags 2.0 Type Library", which we have to create a reference to using Project ➪ References and selecting that item in the list. These interfaces are for backward compatibility to Microsoft Office XP.

The SmartTag Unique Identifier

When a worksheet cell is tagged, the tag is stored in the workbook in an XML-compliant format. All this means is that the identifier for the SmartTag has to be constructed in a special way—as a Uniform Resource Identifier (URI) followed by a '#' character and the specific SmartTag data type name. The URI string provides a way of identifying the source of the ID and an ID group, which together should provide a globally unique and unambiguous identifier. The full ID string for a specific data type is made up of:

```
urn:schemas-<company>-com:<group>#SmartTagName
```

In this example, we will be recognizing three types of file name:

❑ Files that can be opened in Excel that we'll give the ID of
   "urn:schemas-wrox-com:Excel2003ProgRef#ExcelFile"

❑ Files that can be opened in Word that we'll give the ID of
   "urn:schemas-wrox-com:Excel2003ProgRef#WordFile"

❑ Files that are opened by other applications, that we'll give the ID of
   "urn:schemas-wrox-com:Excel2003ProgRef#NonHostFile"

Add a new module called Globals to the Visual Basic project and add these IDs as constants:

```
'Module to hold global constants and enums used by the SmartTags

'The Uniform Resource Identifiers of the SmartTag data types
Public Const psURIExcel = "urn:schemas-wrox-com:Excel2003ProgRef#ExcelFile"
Public Const psURIWord = "urn:schemas-wrox-com:Excel2003ProgRef#WordFile"
Public Const psURINonHost = _
                    "urn:schemas-wrox-com:Excel2003ProgRef#NonHostFile"
```

Many of the SmartTag procedures that we'll be writing are called multiple times to iterate through a sequence of items—such as Recognizer names or SmartTag actions—passing the sequence number as a parameter. To improve readability, it is a good idea to define Enumerations or Enums in the Globals module to match those sequence numbers. The following Enums will be used later in the chapter, but should be added to the Globals module here:

```
'The sequence numbers for the SmartTag data types
Public Enum peTagSequence
    peTagExcel = 1
    peTagWord = 2
    peTagNonHost = 3
End Enum

'The ID numbers of the actions that we can perform
Public Enum peFileVerbs

    'Four verbs for Excel files
    peXLExists = 11
    peXLRename = 12
    peXLOpen = 13
    peXLOpenNew = 14

    'Four verbs for Word files
    peWordExists = 21
    peWordRename = 22
    peWordOpen = 23
    peWordOpenNew = 24

    'Three verbs for non-host files
    peNHExists = 31
    peNHRename = 32
    peNHOpen = 33
End Enum
```

The SmartTag Recognizer Class

The interaction between Excel (or other Microsoft Office application) and our SmartTag recognition is done through a specific interface—the ISmartTagRecognizer interface—that we have to implement in our class.

To create a class that implements the interface, rename the default Class1 that was created in the VB Project to Recognizer and type in the following code:

```
'Module to recognize File Names
Option Explicit
Implements ISmartTagRecognizer
```

This interface has the following methods and properties, all of which need to be implemented:

Methods and Properties	Description
ProgID	The ID for the Recognizer class, defined as <ProjectName>.<ClassName>
Name	A short name for the SmartTag, shown in the SmartTag list

Methods and Properties	Description
Desc	A long description for the SmartTag
SmartTagCount	The number of SmartTag data types that this class recognizes
SmartTagName	Called once for each data type, to provide the unique ID of the data type
SmartTagDownloadURL	If a tagged file is opened on a machine that does not have the SmartTag DLL installed, this property specifies where the Actions DLL can be downloaded
Recognize	The main routine to perform the recognition and tagging of the text

The first three items are straightforward for most SmartTags:

```
Private Property Get ISmartTagRecognizer_ProgId() As String
   ISmartTagRecognizer_ProgId = "FileNameSmartTag.Recognizer"
End Property

Private Property Get ISmartTagRecognizer_Name( _
                     ByVal LocaleID As Long) As String
   ISmartTagRecognizer_Name = "Filename SmartTag Recognizer"
End Property

Private Property Get ISmartTagRecognizer_Desc( _
                     ByVal LocaleID As Long) As String
   ISmartTagRecognizer_Desc = "SmartTag DLL to recognize filenames"
End Property
```

The SmartTagCount property just returns the number of data types recognized by this class. We're recognizing three data types – Excel files, Word files, and non-host files:

```
Private Property Get ISmartTagRecognizer_SmartTagCount() As Long
   ISmartTagRecognizer_SmartTagCount = 3
End Property
```

The SmartTagName is called multiple times, once for each data type that is being recognized, passing the sequence number of the data type (1, 2, or 3 in our case). It returns the unique ID (URI) for the data type. Many of the SmartTag interface methods use this technique of passing sequence numbers to identify the specific tag or action. To help code readability, we can use enumerated data types to match these sequence numbers; we declared the peTagSequence Enum in the Globals preceding module, to use in the SmartTagName property:

```
Private Property Get ISmartTagRecognizer_SmartTagName( _
                     ByVal SmartTagID As Long) As String

   'Return the required URI name for the SmartTag sequence
   Select Case SmartTagID
```

```
        Case peTagExcel
            ISmartTagRecognizer_SmartTagName = psURIExcel

        Case peTagWord
            ISmartTagRecognizer_SmartTagName = psURIWord

        Case peTagNonHost
            ISmartTagRecognizer_SmartTagName = psURINonHost
    End Select
End Property
```

The `SmartTagDownloadURL` can use similar code to the previous routine, to provide a download location for the Action DLL. In our case, both the Action and Recognizer are located within the same DLL so we won't provide one:

```
Private Property Get ISmartTagRecognizer_SmartTagDownloadURL( _
                    ByVal SmartTagID As Long) As String
    ISmartTagRecognizer_SmartTagDownloadURL = ""
End Property
```

The `Recognizer` class is where all the work is done, and is in many ways the most difficult part of the SmartTag mechanism. The best recognizers should:

❑   Recognize all correct cases

❑   Not give any "false-positives"

❑   Work very quickly

If the recognition is simply a case of recognizing lists of terms (such as part numbers), it's a good idea to get the complete list into an array in one of the startup properties (for example in the `ProgID` property), particularly if that means reading the list from another Web site, or running a database query.

However good the recognition, though, there are likely to be a number of false-positives. For example, TRUE is both a Boolean value in Excel and a valid stock symbol, leading to all cells that contain the Boolean True being tagged as stock symbols. Similarly, a recognizer for car models may recognize the numbers 106, 206, 405, etc. as valid models, even though they may be the result of calculations in Excel's cells.

For our purposes, we will define a string as being recognized as a filename if it passes one of the following tests:

❑   The string has the format of <letter>:\<some text>.<some extension>, without a space after the dot

❑   Alternatively, the string has the format of \\<some text>\<some text>.<some extension>

This could obviously lead to some files not being recognized (for example, if they don't have an extension), and some false-positives. We could improve the algorithm by also checking for invalid characters within any filenames that we find, but the preceding simple rules are a good illustration.

We'll also define a "HostFile" as being one with an `.xls` or `.xla` extension in Excel, or a `.doc` or `.dot` extension in Word (whichever the host is). The following code goes in the `Recognizer` class:

```
Private Sub ISmartTagRecognizer_Recognize(ByVal Text As String, _
            ByVal DataType As SmartTagLib.IF_TYPE, _
            ByVal LocaleID As Long, _
            ByVal RecognizerSite As SmartTagLib.ISmartTagRecognizerSite)

    'Variables used to locate the file name within the text
    Dim iStart As Long, iEnd As Long, iDot As Long, iSlash As Long

    'Variable to hold the file extension
    Dim sExt As String

    'Variable to hold a SmartTag's ProprtyBag
    Dim oPropBag As SmartTagLib.ISmartTagProperties

    iEnd = 1

    'A Word paragraph may contain multiple filenames, so we have to
    'loop through them all
    Do
    iDot = 0

    'Find the characters at the start of a file name
    iStart = InStr(iEnd, Text, ":\")
    If iStart > 0 Then
        iStart = iStart - 1
        iDot = InStr(iStart, Text, ".")
    Else
        iStart = InStr(iEnd, Text, "\\")
        iSlash = InStr(iStart, Text, "\")

        If iSlash > 0 Then
            iDot = InStr(iSlash, Text, ".")
        End If
    End If

    'If we found the start and the end of a file...
    If iStart > 0 And iDot > 0 Then

        '... check that there is something immediately after the dot
        If Trim$(Mid$(Text, iDot + 1, 1)) <> "" Then
            'A valid file!

            'Find the end of the file extension, which may be followed by
            'more text if we're checking a Word paragraph
            For iEnd = iDot + 1 To Len(Text)
                If InStr(1, "\/:*?""<>| ", Mid$(Text, iEnd, 1)) _
                                            <> 0 Then Exit For
            Next

            'Get the extension
            sExt = Mid$(Text, iDot + 1, iEnd - iDot)
```

```
            'Get a property bag for this SmartTag
            Set oPropBag = RecognizerSite.GetNewPropertyBag

            'Add the filename and extension to the property bag,
            'in case we use it later
            oPropBag.Write "FileName", Mid$(Text, iStart, iEnd - iStart)
            oPropBag.Write "Extension", sExt

            'Check if this is a Host or non-host file.
            'Excel's data type is IF_TYPE_CELL while Word's is
            'IF_TYPE_PARA.
            'The CommitSmartTag method is where we actually tag the text.
            If (DataType = IF_TYPE_CELL And _
                    (sExt = "xls" Or sExt = "xla")) Then

                RecognizerSite.CommitSmartTag psURIExcel, _
                                        iStart, iEnd - iStart, oPropBag

            ElseIf (DataType = IF_TYPE_PARA And _
                        (sExt = "doc" Or sExt = "dot")) Then

                RecognizerSite.CommitSmartTag psURIWord, _
                                        iStart, iEnd - iStart, oPropBag
            Else
                RecognizerSite.CommitSmartTag psURINonHost, _
                                        iStart, iEnd - iStart, oPropBag

            End If
        End If
    End If
    Loop Until iDot = 0 Or iEnd >= Len(Text)

End Sub
```

The SmartTag Actions Class

Once an entry has been recognized and tagged by a SmartTag `Recognizer` class, Excel needs to find the items to show for the SmartTag popup menu—the *Actions* that are applicable to the SmartTag data type. When the user selects one of those actions, Excel needs to call the SmartTag DLL to perform the action. All of this is done through the `ISmartTagAction` interface.

To create a class that implements the interface, add a new class module to the project, make sure that its instancing is set to '5 – Multi Use', change its name to `Actions` and type in the following code:

```
'Module for File Names SmartTag Actions

Option Explicit
Implements ISmartTagAction
```

The `ISmartTagAction` interface has the following methods and properties, all of which need to be implemented:

Methods and Properties	Description
ProgID	The ID for the Recognizer class, defined as `<ProjectName>.<ClassName>`
Name	A short name for the SmartTag, shown in the SmartTag list
Desc	A long description for the SmartTag
SmartTagCount	The number of SmartTag data types that this class recognizes
SmartTagName	Called once for each data type, to provide the unique ID of the data type
SmartTagCaption	Called once for each data type, to provide the caption shown on the title of the SmartTag popup menu
VerbCount	Called for each data type, to provide the number of actions appropriate for that type
VerbID	Called for each combination of data type and verb, to provide a unique ID number for that combination
VerbCaptionFromID	Called for each verb ID, to provide the caption to show on the SmartTag popup menu
VerbNameFromID	Called for each verb ID, to provide the programmatic name for the verb (so that the action can be launched using VBA—see later in this chapter for more details)
InvokeVerb	Called when the user clicks one of the SmartTag menus, or the action is called using VBA. This is the main routine to perform the selected action.

The first five properties are the same as the `ISmartTagRecognizer` interface:

```
Private Property Get ISmartTagAction_ProgId() As String
   ISmartTagAction_ProgId = "FileNameSmartTag.Actions"
End Property

Private Property Get ISmartTagAction_Name(ByVal LocaleID As Long) As String
   ISmartTagAction_Name = "Filename SmartTag Actions"
End Property

Private Property Get ISmartTagAction_Desc(ByVal LocaleID As Long) As String
   ISmartTagAction_Desc = "Provides actions to perform on filenames"
End Property

Private Property Get ISmartTagAction_SmartTagCount() As Long
   ISmartTagAction_SmartTagCount = 3
End Property

Private Property Get ISmartTagAction_SmartTagName( _
                ByVal SmartTagID As Long) As String
```

```
      'Return the required URI name for the SmartTag sequence
      Select Case SmartTagID
         Case peTagExcel
            ISmartTagAction_SmartTagName = psURIExcel

         Case peTagWord
            ISmartTagAction_SmartTagName = psURIWord

         Case peTagNonHost
            ISmartTagAction_SmartTagName = psURINonHost
      End Select

   End Property
```

The `SmartTagCaption` property provides the caption shown on the SmartTag popup menu:

```
   Private Property Get ISmartTagAction_SmartTagCaption( _
                ByVal SmartTagID As Long, ByVal LocaleID As Long) As String

      'Return the caption for the SmartTag
      Select Case SmartTagID
         Case peTagExcel
            ISmartTagAction_SmartTagCaption = "Excel files"

         Case peTagWord
            ISmartTagAction_SmartTagCaption = "Word files"

         Case peTagNonHost
            ISmartTagAction_SmartTagCaption = "File names"
      End Select

   End Property
```

The `VerbCount` property provides the number of actions that we define for each SmartTag. In this example, we'll provide the following actions:

❑ Check if the file exists

❑ Rename the file (in which case we'll also update the text in the document)

❑ Open the file in its default editor

❑ If we've recognized an Excel file within Excel, or a Word file within Word, we'll provide an extra action to open the file in a new instance of Excel/Word

To help readability, we defined the `peFileVerbs` enumeration for these actions in the `Globals` module, giving them IDs that correspond to their SmartTag ID and verb sequence.

In the `Actions` class, we use the `VerbCount` property to return the number of actions that we have for each data type:

```
   Private Property Get ISmartTagAction_VerbCount( _
                           ByVal SmartTagName As String) As Long
```

```
        Select Case SmartTagName
          Case psURIExcel
            ISmartTagAction_VerbCount = 4

          Case psURIWord
            ISmartTagAction_VerbCount = 4

          Case psURINonHost
            ISmartTagAction_VerbCount = 3
        End Select

    End Property
```

The VerbID property is used to give a unique ID number to each of our actions. By carefully numbering the actions in our peFileVerbs enumeration, we can calculate the ID from the SmartTag and verb sequence number:

```
    Private Property Get ISmartTagAction_VerbID( _
                      ByVal SmartTagName As String, _
                      ByVal VerbIndex As Long) As Long

        Select Case SmartTagName
          Case psURIExcel
            ISmartTagAction_VerbID = 10 + VerbIndex

          Case psURIWord
            ISmartTagAction_VerbID = 20 + VerbIndex

          Case psURINonHost
            ISmartTagAction_VerbID = 30 + VerbIndex
        End Select

    End Property
```

Now that we've told Excel about all the verbs that we're providing, we're asked to provide a caption for each of them. This caption is the text shown in the SmartTag popup menu:

```
    Private Property Get ISmartTagAction_VerbCaptionFromID( _
                      ByVal VerbID As Long, ByVal ApplicationName As String, _
                      ByVal LocaleID As Long) As String

        Select Case VerbID
          Case peXLExists, peWordExists, peNHExists
            ISmartTagAction_VerbCaptionFromID = "Check if the file exists"

          Case peXLRename, peWordRename, peNHRename
            ISmartTagAction_VerbCaptionFromID = "Rename the file"

          Case peXLOpen, peWordOpen, peNHOpen
            ISmartTagAction_VerbCaptionFromID = "Open the file"
```

```
        Case peXLOpenNew
            ISmartTagAction_VerbCaptionFromID = _
                                "Open the file in a new instance of Excel"

        Case peWordOpenNew
            ISmartTagAction_VerbCaptionFromID = _
                                "Open the file in a new instance of Word"

    End Select

End Property
```

Excel provides a mechanism for us to trigger the SmartTag action from VBA. The `VerbNameFromID` property is used for us to provide a programmatic name for each action. See later in this chapter for more details about using VBA to control and call SmartTags from within Excel:

```
Private Property Get ISmartTagAction_VerbNameFromID( _
                        ByVal VerbID As Long) As String

    Select Case VerbID
        Case peXLExists, peWordExists, peNHExists
            ISmartTagAction_VerbNameFromID = "CheckExists"

        Case peXLRename, peWordRename, peNHRename
            ISmartTagAction_VerbNameFromID = "Rename"

        Case peXLOpen, peWordOpen, peNHOpen
            ISmartTagAction_VerbNameFromID = "Open"

        Case peXLOpenNew, peWordOpenNew
            ISmartTagAction_VerbNameFromID = "OpenNew"

    End Select

End Property
```

The main routine of the `Actions` class is the `InvokeVerb` method, which is where we perform the selected action. Note that one of the parameters passed to the method is the `Target` object. When called from Excel, this is the `Range` object that contains the text, allowing us full access to query or modify any of Excel's objects. In our case, we'll modify the filename text when the `Rename` action is invoked.

We'll use the `ShellExecute` Windows API function to open files in their host application (see Chapter 24 for more about the Windows API). Add is declaration to the top of the `Actions` class:

```
'Use the ShellExecute API call to open a file
Private Declare Function ShellExecute Lib "shell32.dll" _
        Alias "ShellExecuteA" _
        (ByVal hwnd As Long, ByVal lpOperation As String, _
        ByVal lpFile As String, ByVal lpParameters As String, _
        ByVal lpDirectory As String, ByVal nShowCmd As Long) As Long
```

Type in the following code to perform all our actions:

```vb
Private Sub ISmartTagAction_InvokeVerb(ByVal VerbID As Long, _
        ByVal ApplicationName As String, ByVal Target As Object, _
        ByVal Properties As SmartTagLib.ISmartTagProperties, _
        ByVal Text As String, ByVal Xml As String)

    Dim sNewName As String
    Dim oHost As Object
    Dim a As Long

    'All our actions need a check to see if the file exists, so do that first
    If Not FileExists(Text) Then
        MsgBox "The file '" & Text & "' does not exist", _
                vbOKOnly + vbCritical, "FileName Smart Tag"
    Else
        Select Case VerbID
            Case peXLExists, peWordExists, peNHExists

                'If we got this far, the file exists, so say so
                MsgBox "The file '" & Text & "' exists", _
                        vbOKOnly, "FileName Smart Tag"

            Case peXLRename, peWordRename, peNHRename

                'Get the new file name, providing the original as the default
                sNewName = InputBox("Enter the new file name below", _
                                "FileName Smart Tag", Text)

                'If the name was changed (and not cancelled)...
                If sNewName <> "" And sNewName <> Text Then
                    On Error Resume Next

                    '... try to rename the file to be the new name
                    Name Text As sNewName

                    If Err = 0 Then
                        'Successfule change of file name, so change the text
                        'in the source file
                        'Each application (Excel, Word or IE) require a
                        'different syntax:

                        Select Case Left$(LCase$(ApplicationName), 5)
                            Case "excel"
                                Target.Value = sNewName
                            Case "word."
                                Target.Text = sNewName
                            Case Else
                                Target.InnerText = sNewName
                        End Select
                    End If
                End If

            Case peXLOpen
                'Open the Excel file in Excel
                Target.Application.Workbooks.Open Text
```

```
        Case peWordOpen
            'Open the Word file in Word
            Target.Application.documents.Open Text

        Case peNHOpen
            'Use the ShellExecute API call to open the file in its
            'default editor
            On Error Resume Next
            a = ShellExecute(0, vbNullString, Text, vbNullString, _
                        vbNullString, 1)

        Case peXLOpenNew
            'Open the Excel file in a new instance of Excel
            Set oHost = CreateObject("Excel.Application")
            oHost.Workbooks.Open Text
            oHost.Visible = True

        Case peWordOpenNew
            'Open the Word file in a new instance of Word
            Set oHost = CreateObject("Word.Application")
            oHost.documents.Open Text
            oHost.Visible = True


    End Select
End If

End Sub
```

The `InvokeVerb` routine uses a separate function to check if a file exists:

```
Private Function FileExists(sFile As String) As Boolean

    Dim sDir As String

    On Error Resume Next
    sDir = Dir(sFile)
    FileExists = (sDir <> "")

End Function
```

We're done. Save the VB Project and make the DLL file.

Implementing Office 2003 SmartTag Features

Up to this point, we have created fully functional SmartTag component that will work with Microsoft Office XP and Office 2003. Now, we'll add a few more lines of code to each class within our component to enable the Office 2003 SmartTag features. In the Recognizer class, add the following highlighted code thus implementing the `ISmartTagRecognizer2` interface.

```
'Module to recognize File Names
Option Explicit
Implements ISmartTagRecognizer
```

```
Implements ISmartTagRecognizer2

Private Property Get ISmartTagRecognizer_ProgId() As String
    ISmartTagRecognizer_ProgId = "FilenameSmartTag.Recognizer"
End Property
```

As we learned earlier in this chapter, there are four methods required for this interface so let's add the code and briefly discuss what is going on with the code. At the end of the `Recognizer` class, add the following code.

```
' ISmartTagRecognizer2 methods
Public Sub ISmartTagRecognizer2_Recognize2(ByVal Text As String, _
    ByVal DataType As SmartTagLib.IF_TYPE, ByVal LocaleID As Long, ByVal _
    RecognizerSite2 As SmartTagLib.ISmartTagRecognizerSite2, ByVal _
    ApplicationName As String, ByVal TokenList As SmartTagLib.
    ISmartTagTokenList)

    ISmartTagRecognizer_Recognize Text, DataType, LocaleID, RecognizerSite2
End Sub
```

In the `Recognize2` method, we could take advantage of the tokenization but for the sake of clarity, we will simply make a call to the original `Recognize` method so both Office XP and Office 2003 use the same method to determine if a particular block of text should be a SmartTag. Let's add the remaining three to this class before we move on.

```
Public Property Get ISmartTagRecognizer2_PropertyPage(ByVal SmartTagID As _
        Long, ByVal LocaleID As Long) As Boolean

    ISmartTagRecognizer2_PropertyPage = False
End Property

Public Sub ISmartTagRecognizer2_DisplayPropertyPage(ByVal SmartTagID As _
        Long, ByVal LocaleID As Long)
End Sub

Public Sub ISmartTagRecognizer2_SmartTagInitialize(ByVal AppName As String)
End Sub
```

Our `PropertyPage` method will return `False` since we won't be providing a property page for this component. If we would have been providing a property page, the property page would be displayed from the `DisplayPropertyPage` method. All of the required methods for the `ISmartTagRecognizer2` interface have been completed, so let's move on.

Within the `Actions` class, make the following changes so as to implement the `ISmartTagAction2` interface.

```
Option Explicit
Implements ISmartTagAction
Implements ISmartTagAction2
```

```
Private Property Get ISmartTagAction_ProgId() As String
    ISmartTagAction_ProgId = "FilenameSmartTag.Actions"
End Property
```

The `InvokeVerb2` method will have the responsibility of passing off all relevant information to the preceding `InvokeVerb` method. Add the following code to your `Actions` class.

```
Public Sub ISmartTagAction2_InvokeVerb2(ByVal VerbID As Long, ByVal _
        ApplicationName As String, ByVal Target As Object, ByVal Properties As _
        SmartTagLib.ISmartTagProperties, ByVal Text As String, ByVal Xml As _
        String, ByVal LocaleID As Long)

ISmartTagAction_InvokeVerb VerbID, ApplicationName, Target, Properties, _
    Text, Xml

End Sub
```

In this particular example, we will not be showing dynamic captions, and we do want SmartTag underline indicators to be shown which is accomplished from the following code. Add the following code to the bottom of the `Actions` class.

```
Public Property Get ISmartTagAction2_IsCaptionDynamic(ByVal VerbID As Long, _
        ByVal ApplicationName As String, ByVal LocaleID As Long) As Boolean

    ISmartTagAction2_IsCaptionDynamic = False
End Property

Public Property Get ISmartTagAction2_ShowSmartTagIndicator(ByVal VerbID As _
    Long, ByVal ApplicationName As String, ByVal LocaleID As Long) As Boolean

    ISmartTagAction2_ShowSmartTagIndicator = True
End Property

Public Sub ISmartTagAction2_SmartTagInitialize(ByVal ApplicationName
As String)
End Sub
```

We almost have the code completed to enable advanced features within Office 2003. The last item to add is the `VerbCaptionFromID2` method which actually provides the text that is shown in the SmartTag popup menus. Office 2003 supports submenus so we will essentially add the same code as with `VerbCaptionFromID` but with a few minor changes.

```
Public Property Get ISmartTagAction2_VerbCaptionFromID2(ByVal VerbID As
Long, _
        ByVal ApplicationName As String, ByVal LocaleID As Long, ByVal _
        Properties As SmartTagLib.ISmartTagProperties, ByVal recognized_text _
        As String, ByVal Xml As String, ByVal Target As Object) As String

    Select Case VerbID
```

```
        Case peXLExists, peWordExists, peNHExists
            ISmartTagAction2_VerbCaptionFromID2 = "Check if the file exists"

        Case peXLRename, peWordRename, peNHRename
            ISmartTagAction2_VerbCaptionFromID2 = "Rename the file"

        Case peXLOpen, peWordOpen, peNHOpen
            ISmartTagAction2_VerbCaptionFromID2 = "Open///File"

        Case peXLOpenNew
            ISmartTagAction2_VerbCaptionFromID2 = _
                            "Open///In new instance of Excel"

        Case peWordOpenNew
            ISmartTagAction2_VerbCaptionFromID2 = _
                            "Open///Open the file in a new instance of Word"

    End Select
End Property
```

As you can see from this code, it looks almost identical to the `VerbCaptionFromID` method except that three of the menu items now contain a series of forward slashes (///). These forward slashes denote a submenu. In this particular case, our main menu will be Open and the three menu items will be shown as subitems of the Open menu item. You will only see this feature when using Microsoft Office 2003 applications.

Registering SmartTags

Like COM Addins, we have to tell Office that our SmartTag DLL exists by adding entries to the Windows Registry. Unlike COM Addins, Microsoft has not provided us with a tool to make that a simple process. We have to resort to manually scanning the registry and creating our own keys by hand. This can be made slightly easier by using a `.reg` file to create the keys, as shown next.

When Excel starts, it scans the registry for all the keys as shown here:

```
HKEY_CURRENT_USER\Software\Microsoft\Office\Common\Smart Tag\Recognizers
```

If it finds any, they will be either the *ProgID* or the *ClassID* of a SmartTag `Recognizer` class. It uses this ID to create an instance of the class, then, uses the properties defined in the `ISmartTagRecognizer` interface to find out the remaining information about the SmartTag. Excel repeats the process for the `Actions` classes.

The first thing we need to do is to find out the ClassIDs that Visual Basic generated for our SmartTag classes. To do this, click Start ⇨ Run and run a file called `regedit`. In the left-hand list, browse to the registry key `HKEY_CLASSES_ROOT\<ProjectName>.<ClassName>\Clsid` and note the (`Default`) value. That is the ClassID of the class. The easiest way to copy this ID is to double-click the (`Default`) label to edit the value, then use *Ctrl+C* to copy it to the clipboard.

In our `FileName` example, the `Actions` registry key is:

```
HKEY_CLASSES_ROOT\FileNameSmartTag.Actions\Clsid
```

For us, the `Actions` ClassID is:

```
{76C5099E-36E2-4BBE-BA02-6097FAF5CFA2}
```

Repeat this for the `Recognizer` class:

```
HKEY_CLASSES_ROOT\FileNameSmartTag.Recognizer\Clsid
```

Giving the `Recognizer` ClassID:

```
{76C5099E-36E2-4BBE-BA02-6097FAF5CFA2}
```

These ClassIDs are used to register the SmartTag DLL, by including them in a `.reg` file. To do this, start Notepad and copy in the following text, substituting the previous full ClassIDs instead of `ActionClassID` and `RecognizerClassID`:

```
REGEDIT4

[HKEY_CURRENT_USER\Software\Microsoft\Office\Common\Smart Tag]

[HKEY_CURRENT_USER\Software\Microsoft\Office\Common\Smart Tag\Actions]
[HKEY_CURRENT_USER\Software\Microsoft\Office\Common\Smart Tag\Actions
\ActionClassID]

[HKEY_CURRENT_USER\Software\Microsoft\Office\Common\Smart Tag\Recognizers]

[HKEY_CURRENT_USER\Software\Microsoft\Office\Common\Smart
Tag\Recognizers\RecognizerClassID]
```

Remove any blank lines from the top of the file, then save it with a `.reg` extension.

For us, the result is a file called `FileNameSmartTag.reg`, containing the following six lines:

```
REGEDIT4

[HKEY_CURRENT_USER\Software\Microsoft\Office\Common\Smart Tag]

[HKEY_CURRENT_USER\Software\Microsoft\Office\Common\Smart Tag\Actions]

[HKEY_CURRENT_USER\Software\Microsoft\Office\Common\Smart
Tag\Actions\{76C5099E-36E2-4BBE-BA02-6097FAF5CFA2}]

[HKEY_CURRENT_USER\Software\Microsoft\Office\Common\Smart Tag\Recognizers]
```

```
[HKEY_CURRENT_USER\Software\Microsoft\Office\Common\Smart
Tag\Recognizers\{76C5099E-36E2-4BBE-BA02-6097FAF5CFA2}]
```

Double-click the .reg file in Windows Explorer to add those entries to the registry. Excel will now see the FileName SmartTag.

Using the FileName SmartTag

Start Excel 2002, click Tools ➪ AutoCorrect Options..., and click the SmartTags tab. Tick the "Label data with SmartTags" check box to enable SmartTags. There should be an entry in the list for the "Filename SmartTag Recognizer". Tick the box and OK out of the dialog box. Figure 27-2 shows the dialog box you should see, with the boxes checked.

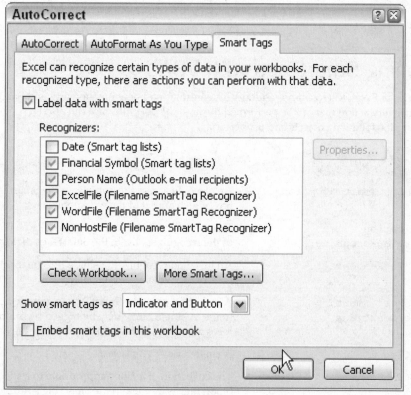

Figure 27-2

Any cells that contain text looking like a filename will then have the SmartTag indicator in the cell (a dark triangle in the bottom-right corner) and our menu of FileName SmartTag actions when the *i* button is clicked (Figure 27-3).

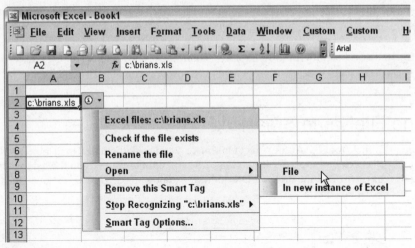

Figure 27-3

Controlling SmartTags with VBA

Historically, in Excel, Microsoft has added VBA control for all new functionality and SmartTags are no exception; every action that can be performed through the user interface can also be performed through code, using the following objects and properties:

Object/Property	Description
Workbook.SmartTagOptions	An object to access the options on the SmartTags dialog box, which are set at the workbook level
Application .SmartTagRecognizers	The collection of all recognizers installed—the contents of the recognizers list in the SmartTags dialog box
SmartTagRecognizer	An installed recognizer (a single recognizer class), controlling whether it is enabled
Worksheet.SmartTags, Range.SmartTags	A collection of all the SmartTags in a worksheet or range. A single range may by tagged by multiple recognizers and so have multiple SmartTags
SmartTag	A single SmartTag object
SmartTag.SmartTagActions	The collection of actions appropriate to a specific SmartTag, as defined in the SmartTag's Actions class
SmartTagAction	A specific action of a specific SmartTag in a specific Range. It has an Execute method to invoke the action
Workbook.RecheckSmartTags	A method to force Excel to rerecognize everything in the workbook

The following examples show how to use some of the more interesting of these objects and properties.

Check if a Recognizer is Active

When working with SmartTags, the first step is often to see if a particular recognizer is installed and active:

```
Function IsRecognizerActive(sProgID As String) As Boolean

    Dim oSTR As SmartTagRecognizer

    'Loop through all the installed recognizers
    For Each oSTR In Application.SmartTagRecognizers

        'Is it the one we're looking for?
        If oSTR.ProgID = sProgID Then

            'If so, return whether it's enabled
            IsRecognizerActive = oSTR.Enabled
            Exit For
        End If
    Next

End Function
```

Remove a Tag from a Range

One of the problems with SmartTags is the issue of false-positives, where a cell is erroneously tagged. An example is the standard Stock Symbol SmartTag that recognizes TRUE as a valid stock symbol, even if that TRUE is a Boolean True. The following code locates all of these false-positives and removes them:

```
Sub RemoveBooleanTrue()

    Dim oSht As Worksheet
    Dim oTag As SmartTag

    'This is the URI of the StockTicker SmartTag
    Const sTicker As String = _
                "urn:schemas-microsoft-com:office:smarttags#stockticker"

    'Loop through all the worksheets in the active workbook
    For Each oSht In ActiveWorkbook.Worksheets

        'Loop through all the tags in the sheet
        For Each oTag In oSht.SmartTags

            'Is it a StockTicker tag with a Boolean value?
            If oTag.Name = sTicker And _
                        TypeName(oTag.Range.Value) = "Boolean" Then

                'Yes, so remove this SmartTag from the cell
                oTag.Delete
            End If
        Next
    Next

End Sub
```

Add a Tag to a Range

If you create a SmartTag Recognizer class to perform the recognition function, it has global scope. This means that the Recognize method will be called for every entry in all workbooks in Excel and all documents in Word. It is possible to distinguish between Word and Excel, but we cannot limit the recognition to specific workbooks, sheets, or ranges.

The SmartTags collection has an Add method, by which we can tag a cell as being a specific SmartTag type. By doing so, we can completely bypass the Recognizer class and perform all of our recognition using VBA; we need only implement an Actions class to provide the popup menu and perform the action.

For example, you may find that the Stock Ticker SmartTag is too pervasive, adding lots of SmartTag indicators to cells that you'd rather not have tagged. Instead, let's assume that you have a PivotTable with a field of stock symbols and you'd like only those items SmartTagged to show the Stock Symbol actions. We first disable the Stock Symbol Recognizer in the SmartTags dialog box, then use the following VBA code to recognize the stock symbols in the PivotTable:

```
Sub AddTickerTagToPivotTableTitles()

    Dim oField As PivotField
    Dim oItem As PivotItem
    Dim oCell As Range

    Const sTicker As String = _
                    "urn:schemas-microsoft-com:office:smarttags#stockticker"

    'Get the 'Symbol' PivotField
    Set oField = ActiveSheet.PivotTables(1).PivotFields("Symbol")

    'Loop through all the PivotItems for that field
    For Each oItem In oField.PivotItems

        'Loop through all the cells in the PivotItems label range
        For Each oCell In oItem.LabelRange

            'If the cell isn't empty ...
            If Not IsEmpty(oCell) Then

                '... tag the cell with the Stock Symbol smart tag
                oCell.SmartTags.Add sTicker
            End If
        Next
    Next

End Sub
```

With this technique, we can combine the interface and power of the SmartTag Actions popup menu with the granularity and control of performing our recognition from within the Excel VBA environment. Once recognized in this way, the cells' tags can be saved within the workbook, by ticking the "Embed SmartTags in this Workbook" check box in the SmartTag Options dialog box.

The Problems with SmartTags

Microsoft has done an excellent job with the new SmartTag technology, but there are a few weaknesses with the current implementation that are worth noting here.

The Recognize Method

By far the biggest problem is the relatively small amount of information that is passed to the `Recognize` method of the `ISmartTagRecognizer` interface:

```
Private Sub ISmartTagRecognizer_Recognize(ByVal Text As String, _
            ByVal DataType As SmartTagLib.IF_TYPE, _
            ByVal LocaleID As Long, _
            ByVal RecognizerSite As SmartTagLib.ISmartTagRecognizerSite)
```

Note that the text is passed to the `Recognize` method `As String`, which gives no indication of the source of that text. For example, the Boolean value `True` and the text value TRUE both come through as the string "TRUE"—the `Recognize` method can not distinguish between them. Though the second version of the SmartTag Type Library does provide more information and tokenize the text for us, it still doesn't provide a source of the text.

A second weakness of the current implementation is that we are not given any informational context. We're just asked if we could recognize a single item of text. If we were able to check the cells around it, we'd be able to make a more accurate judgment. For example, if this was a "Car Model" SmartTag, given the text "206", it would recognize that number as the Peugeot 206. If we could look at the cells around the one we're asked to recognize, we may see that the "206" is just one of a list of numbers, and is not related to models or car.

A third weakness is that we're not given any indication of the "importance", or positional context. For example, we have no way to distinguish between a list header (which we may not want to tag) and an item in the list (which we would want to tag). Similarly, we have to go back to VBA if we want to limit our tagging to specific workbooks (such as only those derived from a specific template), or only cells within PivotTable titles.

All of these problems could be solved by also passing the same `Target` parameter that is passed to the `InvokeVerb` method of the `ISmartTagAction` interface. If we were given the cell that contained the text to be recognized, we could scan the surrounding cells, check the positional context or limit the recognition to specific workbooks.

Coverage

In Office 2003, the only items of text that are being passed to the SmartTag `Recognizer` class are the entire contents of worksheet cells in Excel, or full paragraphs in Word. In most Excel applications, text is presented to the user in many more forms, including:

- ❏ On charts
- ❏ On UserForms

❑   In comment boxes, labels, and other shapes

❑   On VBA `MsgBox` and `InputBox` dialogs

It would be great to see the recognition of text extended to cover those other forms of presentation.

Summary

In Office 2003, Microsoft has made it possible for us to create our own recognition routines for data typed into worksheet cells or Word documents, and provide a list of actions that can be performed on cells recognized by our routines. These actions can be used to operate on the recognized cells, look up relevant information from other sources, or easily integrate our worksheet data with other applications.

SmartTag `Recognizer` and `Actions` classes are fairly easy to create for someone with an understanding of Visual Basic.

SmartTags can be manipulated with a fine degree of precision from within the Excel VBA environment, to the extent of making a `Recognizer` class redundant in some cases.

As always with new functionality, there is room for improvement in the next release.

There are a number of Web sites devoted to SmartTags, including:

❑   `http://www.officesmarttags.com`

❑   `http://www.officezealot.com/smarttags`

❑   `http://msdn.microsoft.com/office`

Excel and the Internet

Historically, a typical Excel-based application was almost entirely contained within Excel itself; the only external interaction would be with the user, from whom we obtained data and to whom we presented our results. If we needed to store data, we'd use separate workbooks and try to mimic a relational database as best we could.

As data access technologies developed from ODBC drivers, through DAO, to the current versions of ADO (documented in Chapter 11), it became more common place to store data in external databases and even retrieve data from (and update data in) other systems across the network. It is now quite common to see Excel used as a front-end querying and analysis tool for large corporate databases, using QueryTables and PivotTables to retrieve the data. The data available to our Excel applications was, however, limited to that available across the company network, and to those databases that we could get permission to access.

Starting with the release of Office 97, Microsoft has slowly extended Excel's reach to include the Internet and associated technologies, either by adding native functionality directly into Excel (such as Web queries), or by ensuring that Excel developers can easily use standard external objects (such as the Internet Transfer Control, the Web browser control, and the MSXML parser), and including those objects within the Office installation.

In Excel 2002, we have sufficient functionality to consider rethinking our approach to developing Excel Applications. We can start to think outside of the pure Excel/ADO environment in terms of obtaining data, publishing results, monitoring our applications, and sharing data with many disparate systems, outside of the corporate network.

This chapter introduces the functionality available to us in Excel 2002 and demonstrates how to use some of it to exploit the Internet within our applications. A complete discussion of all of Excel's Internet-related functionality is beyond the scope of this book.

> Note that throughout this chapter, the term "Internet" is used in its broadest sense, covering both internal and external networks. The chapter assumes a basic understanding of the Internet and how it works. Throughout the examples, we will

> be using a Web server running on a local PC. However, these techniques are equally
> applicable to applications running on a remote server.

So What's all the Hype About?

In a nutshell, it's all about sharing information.

It's about publishing information to unknown consumers, using standard formats and protocols to enable them to access the information you provide in a consistent, reliable, and secure manner.

It's about making that information available globally both inside and outside the organization's networks, while maintaining control over security and access to potentially sensitive information.

It's about retrieving the information that other individuals or organizations provide, from multiple disparate sources, to use as inputs to your application.

It's about sharing information between producers and consumers, suppliers and customers, using standard formats for that exchange.

It's about looking outside of the classic Excel application and adding value to that application by sharing its results with a wider audience than simply the user sitting at the PC.

It's about using Excel as a key component of a larger business process, where that process may span multiple organizations.

Using the Internet for Storing Workbooks

The simplest way of sharing information is to store our workbooks on a Web server. While Excel 97 introduced the ability to download workbooks from Web sites, Excel 2000 and 2002 extended that to allow us to save workbooks as well. They do this by using the FrontPage Server Extensions, which must be running on the server. To open and save a workbook from/to a Web site, we just use the URL instead of the filename:

```
Sub OpenFromWebSiteAndSaveBack()

    Dim oBk As Workbook

    'Open a workbook from a web site
    'The following link should be replaced with a we server for which you
    'have access.
    Set oBk = Workbooks.Open("http://www.MySite.com/book1.xls")

    'Save the workbook to the web site with a new name
    oBk.SaveAs "http://www.MySite.com/Book2.xls"

End Sub
```

If the server requires you to logon, you have the option of letting Excel prompt for the ID and password each time (as in the preceding example), or include the ID and password as part of the URL:

```
Sub OpenFromSecureWebSiteAndSaveBack()

    Dim oBk As Workbook

    'Open a workbook from a web site
    Set oBk = Workbooks.Open("http://UserID:Pwd@www.MySite.com/book1.xls")

    'Save the workbook to the web site with a new name
    oBk.SaveAs "http://UserID:Pwd@www.MySite.com/Book2.xls"

End Sub
```

The URLs can, of course, also be used in Excel's File Open and Save As dialogs.

Using the Internet as a Data Source

The "classic" Excel application has two sources of data—databases on the network, and the user. If an item of data was not available in a database, the user was required to type it in and maintain it. To enable this, the application had to include a number of sheets and dialog boxes to store the information and provide a mechanism for the data entry.

A typical example of this would be maintaining exchange rate information in a financial model; it is usually the user's responsibility to obtain the latest rates and type them into the model. We can add value to the application by automating the retrieval of up-to-date exchange rate information from one of many Web sites.

The following sections demonstrate different techniques for retrieving information from the web, using the USD exchange rates available from http://www.x-rates.com/d/USD/table.html as an example. The Web page looks like Figure 28-1.

Opening Web Pages as Workbooks

The simplest solution is to open the entire Web page as if it were a workbook, then scan the sheet for the required information, such the USD/GBP exchange rate:

```
Sub OpenUSDRatesPage()

    Dim oBk As Workbook
    Dim oRng As Range

    'Open the rates pages as a workbook
    Set oBk = Workbooks.Open("http://www.x-rates.com/d/USD/table.html")


    'Find the British Pounds entry
    Set oRng = oBk.Worksheets(1).Cells.Find("British Pounds")
```

Figure 28-1

```
     'Read off the exchange rate
     MsgBox "The USD/GBP exchange rate is " & oRng.Offset(0, 1).Value

End Sub
```

The problem with using this approach is that we have to load the entire Web page (including graphics, banners, etc.), which may have much more information than we want. The irrelevant data can greatly slow down the speed of data retrieval.

Using Web Queries

Web queries were introduced in Excel 97 and have been enhanced in each subsequent version of Excel. They enable us to retrieve a single table of information from a Web page, with options to automatically refresh the data each time the workbook is opened, or at frequent intervals.

One of the problems with Web queries is that Excel uses the thousands and decimal separators specified in the Windows Regional Settings when attempting to recognize numbers in the page. If the exchange rate Web page was retrieved in many European countries, the period would be treated as a thousand separator, not a decimal separator, resulting in exchange rates that are many times too large. Therefore, Web queries could not be reliably used in versions prior to Excel 2002 in countries that used non-US decimal and thousand separators.

In Excel 2002, Microsoft added three properties to the `Application` object, to temporarily override the settings used when recognizing numbers and you still have access to these properties in Excel 2003:

❑ `Application.DecimalSeparator`—the character to use for the decimal separator

❑ `Application.ThousandsSeparator`—the same for the thousands separator

❑ `Application.UseSystemSeparators`—whether to use the Windows separators, or Excel's

Using these properties, we can set Excel's separators to match those on the Web page, perform the query, then set them back again. If we want to use the Web query's automatic refreshing options, we have to set these separators in the `BeforeRefresh` event, and set them back in the `AfterRefresh` event. This requires advanced VBA techniques, using class modules to trap events, as discussed in Chapter 6.

In our case, we can retrieve just the table of exchange rates, using the following code to create and execute a new Web query. In practice, it's easiest to use the macro recorder to ensure the selections are correct:

```vba
'Retrieve USD exchange rates using a Web Query
Sub GetRatesWithWebQuery()

    Dim oBk As Workbook
    Dim oQT As QueryTable
    'Store the current settings of Excel's number formatting
    Dim sDecimal As String
    Dim sThousand As String
    Dim bUseSystem As Boolean

    'Create a new workbook
    Set oBk = Workbooks.Add

    'Create a query table to download USD rates
    With oBk.Worksheets(1)
        Set oQT = .QueryTables.Add( _
                Connection:="URL; http://www.x-rates.com/d/USD/table.html", _
                Destination:=.Range("A1"))
    End With

    'Set the QueryTable's properties
    With oQT
        .Name = "USD"

        'State that we're selecting a specific table
        .WebSelectionType = xlSpecifiedTables
```

```
            'Import the 5th table on the page
            .WebTables = "5"

            'Ignore the web page's formatting
            .WebFormatting = xlWebFormattingNone

            'Do not try to recognise dates
            .WebDisableDateRecognition = True

            'Don't automatically refresh the query each time the file is opened
            .RefreshOnFileOpen = False

            'Waiting for the query to complete before continuing
            .BackgroundQuery = True

            'Save the query data with the workbook
            .SaveData = True

            'Adjust column widths to autofit new data
            .AdjustColumnWidth = True
        End With

        With Application
            'Remember Excel's current number format settings
            sDecimal = .DecimalSeparator
            sThousand = .ThousandsSeparator
            bUseSystem = .UseSystemSeparators

            'Set Excel's separators to match those of the web site
            .DecimalSeparator = "."
            .ThousandsSeparator = ","
            .UseSystemSeparators = True

            'Ignore any errors raised by the query failing
            On Error Resume Next

            'Perform the query, waiting for it to complete
            oQT.Refresh BackgroundQuery:=False
            'Reset Excel's number format settings
            .DecimalSeparator = sDecimal
            .ThousandsSeparator = sThousand
            .UseSystemSeparators = bUseSystem
        End With

    End Sub
```

The .WebTables = 5 line in the preceding example tells Excel that we want the fifth table on the page. Literally, this is the fifth occurrence of a <TABLE> tag in the source HTML for the page (Figure 28-2).

The sample code parsed the Web page and displayed all relevant information, excluding graphics and non-essential information.

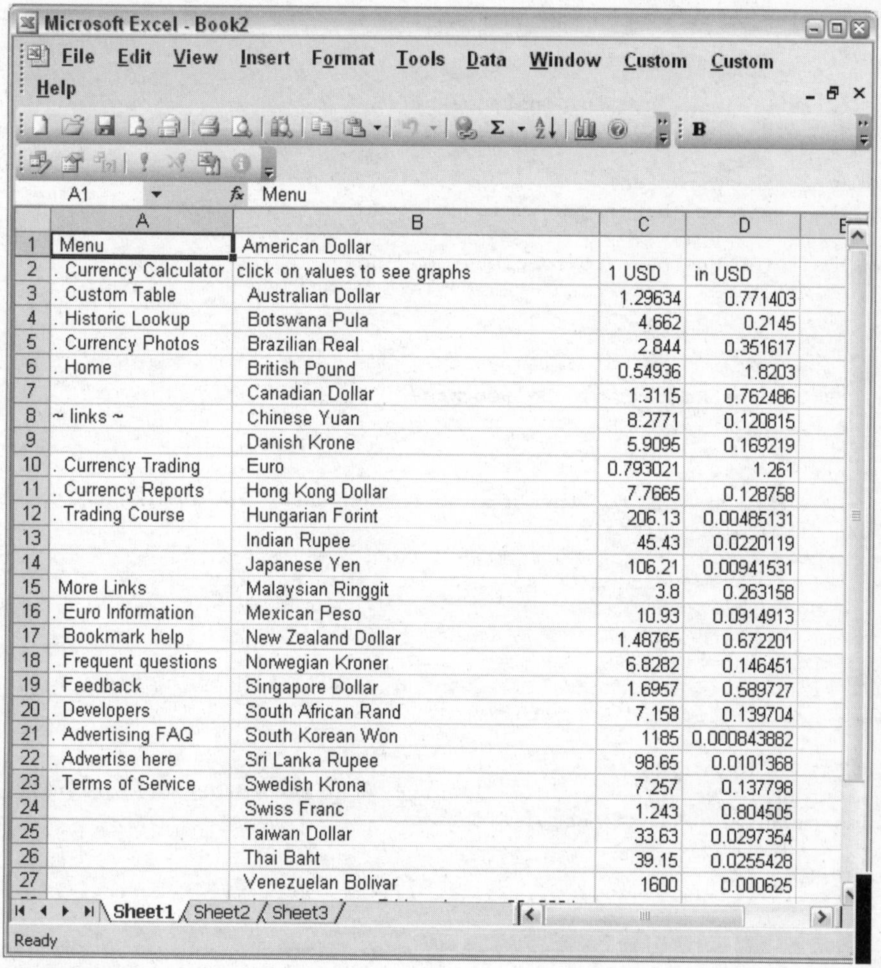

	A	B	C	D
1	Menu	American Dollar		
2	. Currency Calculator	click on values to see graphs	1 USD	in USD
3	. Custom Table	Australian Dollar	1.29634	0.771403
4	. Historic Lookup	Botswana Pula	4.662	0.2145
5	. Currency Photos	Brazilian Real	2.844	0.351617
6	. Home	British Pound	0.54936	1.8203
7		Canadian Dollar	1.3115	0.762486
8	~ links ~	Chinese Yuan	8.2771	0.120815
9		Danish Krone	5.9095	0.169219
10	. Currency Trading	Euro	0.793021	1.261
11	. Currency Reports	Hong Kong Dollar	7.7665	0.128758
12	. Trading Course	Hungarian Forint	206.13	0.00485131
13		Indian Rupee	45.43	0.0220119
14		Japanese Yen	106.21	0.00941531
15	More Links	Malaysian Ringgit	3.8	0.263158
16	. Euro Information	Mexican Peso	10.93	0.0914913
17	. Bookmark help	New Zealand Dollar	1.48765	0.672201
18	. Frequent questions	Norwegian Kroner	6.8282	0.146451
19	. Feedback	Singapore Dollar	1.6957	0.589727
20	. Developers	South African Rand	7.158	0.139704
21	. Advertising FAQ	South Korean Won	1185	0.000843882
22	. Advertise here	Sri Lanka Rupee	98.65	0.0101368
23	. Terms of Service	Swedish Krona	7.257	0.137798
24		Swiss Franc	1.243	0.804505
25		Taiwan Dollar	33.63	0.0297354
26		Thai Baht	39.15	0.0255428
27		Venezuelan Bolivar	1600	0.000625

Figure 28-2

Parsing Web Pages for Specific Information

Web queries are an excellent way of retrieving tables of information from Web pages, but are a little cumbersome if you are only interested in one or two items of information. Another way is to read the page using a hidden instance of Internet Explorer, search within the page for the required information, then return the result. The following code requires a reference to the "Microsoft Internet Controls" object library:

```
Sub GetUSDtoGBPRateUsingIE()

    Dim oIE As SHDocVw.InternetExplorer
    Dim sPage As String
    Dim iGBP As Long, iDec As Long
```

```
       Dim iStart As Long, iEnd As Long
       Dim dRate As Double

       'Create a new (hidden) instance of IE
       Set oIE = New SHDocVw.InternetExplorer

       'Open the web page
       oIE.Navigate "http://www.x-rates.com/d/USD/table.html"

       'Wait for the page to complete loading
       Do Until oIE.readyState = READYSTATE_COMPLETE
           DoEvents
       Loop

       'Retrieve the text of the web page into a variable
       sPage = oIE.Document.body.InnerHTML

       '*********************************************************************
       'The source HTML for the British Pounds entry looks like the following:
       '<tr bgcolor=white>
       '<td>
       '<font face="Verdana" size=-1>  British
       Pound  </font>
       '</td>
       '<td align="right">
       '<font face="Verdana" size=-1> <a href="/d/GBP/USD/graph120.html"
       class="menu">0.54936</a> </font>
       '</td>
       '<td align="right">
       '<font face="Verdana" size=-1> <a href="/d/USD/GBP/graph120.html"
       class="menu">1.8203</a> </font>
       '</td>
       '</tr>
       '*********************************************************************

       'To find the exchange rate, we have to find the entry for British
       'Pounds, then work forwards to find the exchange rate

       'Find the entry for British Pounds in the HTML string.
       iGBP = InStr(1, sPage, " British Pound")

       'Find the next decimal, which will be in the html file
       'extension.
       iDec = InStr(iGBP, sPage, ".")
       'Disregard and continue to look for decimal which will
       'be the decimal in exchange rate
       iDec = InStr(iDec + 1, sPage, ".")

       'Find the start and end of the number
       iStart = InStrRev(sPage, ">", iDec) + 1
       iEnd = InStr(iDec, sPage, "<")

       'Evaluate the number, knowing that it's in US format
       dRate = Val(Mid$(sPage, iStart, iEnd - iStart))
```

```
        'Display the rate
        MsgBox "The USD/GBP exchange rate is " & dRate

End Sub
```

The most appropriate method to use will depend on the precise circumstances, and how much data is required. For single items, it is probably easier to use the last approach. For more than a few items, it will be easier to use a Web query to read the page or table into a workbook, then find the required items on the sheet.

Using the Internet to Publish Results

A Web server can be used as a repository of information, storing your application's results and presenting them to a wider audience than can be achieved with printed reports. By presenting results as Web pages, the reader of those pages can easily use the results as sources of data for their own analysis, and easily pass those results to other interested parties.

Setting Up a Web Server

For all the examples from now on, you will require write access to a Web server. As later examples use Active Server Pages (ASP), we will use Microsoft's IIS 5.1. Open IIS, and right-click the Default Web site node. Select Properties and click the Home Directory tab (Figure 28-3). You will be presented with various configuration options for the default Web site. Make sure that the Read and Write check boxes are selected and click *OK*.

> **IIS 5.1 is the version of IIS included with Windows XP. You can open IIS by going to the Start menu, selecting Run and then typing in inetmgr and then clicking OK. Alternatively, you can go to the Control Panel, double-click Administrative Tools and then open the Internet Information Services control panel.**

Notice the Local Path: box. This is where the root of your Web server is located. By default, it is `C:\inetpub\wwwroot\`. Any Web pages placed in this directory are published at the following URL: `http://localhost/PageName.html`. This is where the first few examples will publish their results. The Timesheet example later in the chapter will require you to set up a Virtual Directory, but we will explain that at the time.

Saving Worksheets as Web Pages

The easiest way to present results as a Web page is to create a template workbook that has all the formatting and links that you'd like to show. When your application produces its results, it is then a

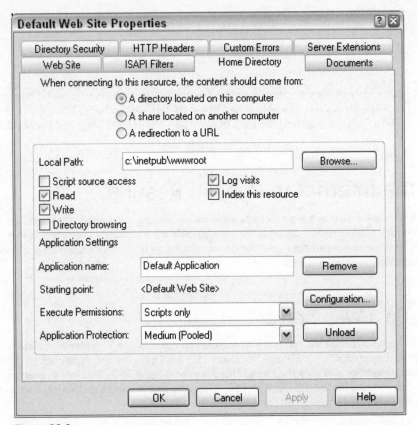

Figure 28-3

simple task to copy the relevant numbers to the template, then save the template direct to the Web server:

```
Sub PublishResultsToWeb()

    Dim oBk As Workbook
    Dim oSht As Worksheet

    'Create a new copy of the Web Template workbook
    Set oBk = Workbooks.Add("c:\mydir\WebTemplate.xls")

    'Get the first sheet in the workbook
    Set oSht = oBk.Worksheets(1)

    'Populate the results
    oSht.Range("Profits").Value = Workbooks("Results.xls") _
            .Worksheets("Financials").Range("Profits").Value

    'Save as a web page, direct to the server
    oSht.SaveAs "http://localhost/ResultsJuly2001.htm", xlHtml
```

```
        'Close the workbook
        oBk.Close False

End Sub
```

Adding Interactivity with the Web Components

The previous example saved a static rendition of the worksheet in HTML format to the Web server. In Excel 2000, Microsoft introduced the Office Web components to create interactive Web pages. When saving a worksheet in interactive form, the following conversions take place:

- ❑ The worksheet, or separate ranges on the sheet, are converted to Spreadsheet Web components.

- ❑ Selected Charts are converted Chart Web components

- ❑ PivotTables are converted to PivotTable Web components

These components are ActiveX controls that are embedded in the HTML page, designed to provide Excel-like levels of interaction, but from within the browser.

It is beyond the scope of this book to document the Web components (which have all been greatly enhanced in Office 2003), but the following code can be used to save a workbook as an interactive Web page, where the workbook contains a range of data to be published (A1:C30), a PivotTable, and an embedded chart:

```
Sub PublishPageInteractive()

    'The PublishObjects collection contains all the parts of the sheet that
    'will be published to web page(s)
    With ActiveWorkbook.PublishObjects

        'Delete any existing publish objects
        .Delete

        'Start with a Pivot Table web component
        .Add(xlSourcePivotTable, "http://localhost/page.htm", "Sheet1", _
             "PivotTable1", xlHtmlList).Publish True

        'Add a worksheet range to the same page
        .Add(xlSourceRange, "http://localhost/page.htm", "Sheet1", _
             "A1:C30", xlHtmlCalc).Publish False

        'Followed by a chart and its source data
        .Add(xlSourceChart, "http://localhost/page.htm", "Sheet1", _
             "Chart 1", xlHtmlChart).Publish False
    End With

End Sub
```

Note that the previous example publishes all the components to the same Web page. By supplying different URLs, multiple pages can be created in this way.

The resulting Web pages are quite simple—being only placeholders for the various Web components (Figure 28-4). It is likely that they would need some post-processing to create presentation-quality pages.

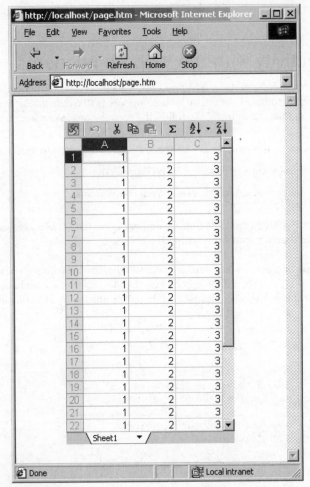

Figure 28-4

Using the Internet as a Communication Channel

Retrieving data from Web pages and publishing results as Web pages is in many ways a passive use of the Internet; the Web server is being used primarily as a storage medium. Web servers are also able to host applications, with which we can interact in a more dynamic manner. The server application acts as a single point of contact for all the client workbooks, to perform the following functions:

❑ A centralized data store

❑ Collation of data from multiple clients

❑ Presentation of that data back to other clients

❑ Workflow management

❑ Calculation engines

As an example, consider a timesheet reporting system, where each member of the staff has an Excel workbook to enter their time on a daily basis. At the end of each month, they connect to the Internet and send their timesheet to an application running on a Web server. That application stores the submitted data in a central database. Some time later, a manager connects to the server and is sent the submitted hours for the staff. The manager checks the numbers and authorizes payment, sending the authorization code back to the server. The payroll department retrieves the authorized timesheet data from the same Web server directly into its accounting system and processes the payments.

In this business process, Excel is used for the frontend client, providing a rich and powerful user interface, yet only fulfils a specific part of the overall process. The server application maintains the data (the completed timesheets) and presents it in whichever format is appropriate for the specific part of the process.

By using the Internet and standard data formats for this two-way communication, we can easily integrate Excel clients with completely separate systems, as in the payroll system in the example, and allow the business process to operate outside of the corporate network.

This section explains how such integration can be achieved with Excel 2003, using a simple error logging application as an example.

Communicating with a Web Server

Within a corporate network, nearly all data transfer takes place using proprietary binary formats, ranging from transferring files to performing remote database queries. Due primarily to security considerations, communication across the Internet has evolved to use textual formats, the simplest being a URL—`http://www.MySite.com/MyPage.htm`.

To be able to communicate with an application running on a Web server, we need to be able to perform some processing on the server and pass information to, and receive information from, that application.

In Excel 2003, the `Workbook` object's `FollowHyperlink` method can be used to communicate with a Web server. There a few problems with using this, including:

❑ Any data returned from the hyperlink is automatically displayed as a new workbook

❑ We have very little control over the communication

A much more flexible alternative is provided by the Microsoft Internet Transfer Control, `msinet.ocx`. This ActiveX control, often referred to as the ITC, is an easy-to-use wrapper for the `wininet.dll` file, which provides low-level Internet-related services for the Windows platform.

Sending Data from the Client to the Server Application

There are two mechanisms that can be used to send information to a Web server. We can either include the information as part of the URL string, or send it as a separate section of the HTTP request.

URL Encoding

Parameters can be included within the URL string by appending them to the end of the URL, with a ? between the URL and the first parameter, and an & between each parameter:

```
http://www.MySite.com/MyPage.asp?param1=value1&param2=value2&param2=value3
```

This has the advantage that the parameters form part of the URL and hence can be stored in the user's Favorites list or typed directly into the browser. It has the disadvantage that there is a limit to the total length of a URL (2083 characters in Internet Explorer), restricting the amount of information than can be passed in this way.

POSTing Data

Whenever a request for a Web page is sent to a Web server, the request contains a large amount of information in various header records. This includes things like the client application type and version, the communication protocol and version, and user IDs and passwords. It also contains a "POST" field which can be used to send information to the server application.

As there is virtually no limit to the amount of data that can be put in a POST field, it is the preferred way of transferring information to the server, and is the method used in the example application shown later in this section.

Sending Data from the Server Application to the Client

Sending information from the application to the client is easy—the data can be presented to the client as a Web page that can be read using the same techniques described earlier in this chapter.

A Web Server Application—Error Logging

There are a number of competing technologies that all provide the ability to perform processing on a Web server, including the .NET Framework, PERL, CGI, JavaServer Pages (JSP), and Active Server Pages (ASP). For the VBA developer, ASP pages written with VBScript will be the most familiar.

In order to use ASP pages, the Web server must be running Microsoft's Internet Information Server on Windows NT, Windows 2000, Windows XP, or Windows 2003 or the Personal Web server on Windows 98 or Windows Me. See the *Setting up a Web Server* section for more details.

In the following example, we will create a Web server application to provide a central error log for any runtime errors that may occur in our Excel applications (or any other application for that matter). The server application has three components:

❏ An Access database to store the error log

❏ An Active Server Page use to write to the error log

❏ An Active Server Page to display a page in the error log

The client, Excel, has a common error-handling routine.

An Access Database to Store the Errors

Start by creating a new database in Access 2002 called `ErrorLog.mdb`, containing a single table called `ErrorData` with the following fields:

Field Name	Data Type	Comment
ErrorID	AutoNumber	Set it to be the Primary Key
ServerTime	Date/Time	
Application	Text	50 characters
ErrSource	Memo	
ErrNumber	Number	Long Integer
ErrDescription	Memo	

In this example, we're only logging the actual error information. In practice, you're likely to store much more information, such as the user name, data file names, workbook and module name, Excel and Windows versions, and Regional settings.

Using FrontPage 2002, create a new Web page and import the database into the Web, using File ➪ Import.... Frontpage will automatically create an "fpdb" folder to store it in and create a database connection for us to use, asking us for the name. Call it ErrorLog.

Virtual Directories

As mentioned in the *Setting up a Web Server* section, we shall be using a Virtual Directory for this example. Open IIS and right-click the Default Web site node. Select New ➪ Virtual Directory. This will start the Virtual Directory Creation Wizard. Click *Next* and fill in the alias as VBA_ProgRef (Figure 28-5).

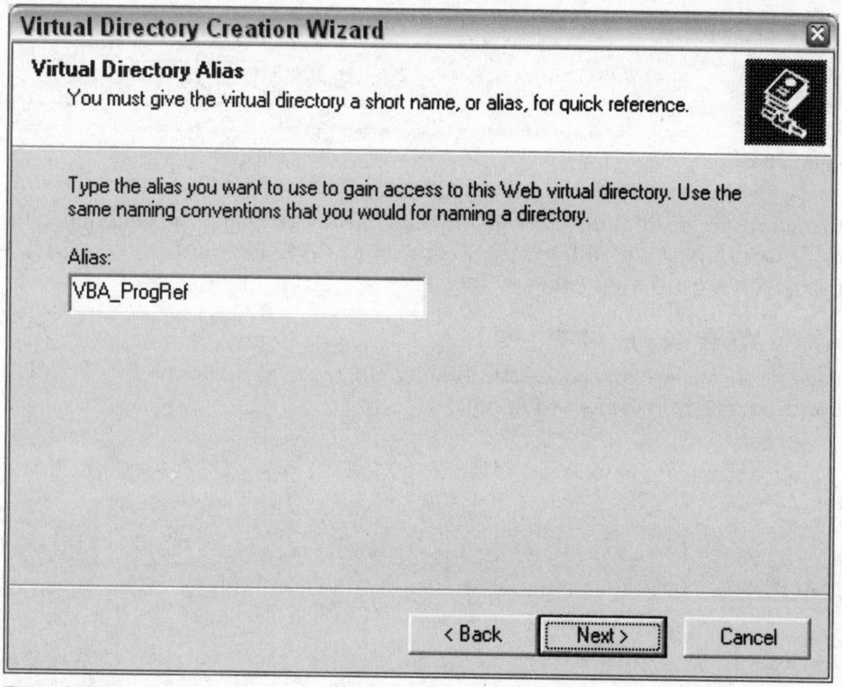

Virtual Directory Creation Wizard

Virtual Directory Alias
You must give the virtual directory a short name, or alias, for quick reference.

Type the alias you want to use to gain access to this Web virtual directory. Use the same naming conventions that you would for naming a directory.

Alias:

VBA_ProgRef

< Back   Next >   Cancel

Figure 28-5

This will map the URL `http://localhost/VBA_ProgRef` to whatever folder on our harddrive we want. This is the next piece of information we need to give to IIS. Enter the directory where FrontPage saved the ASP pages (Figure 28-6).

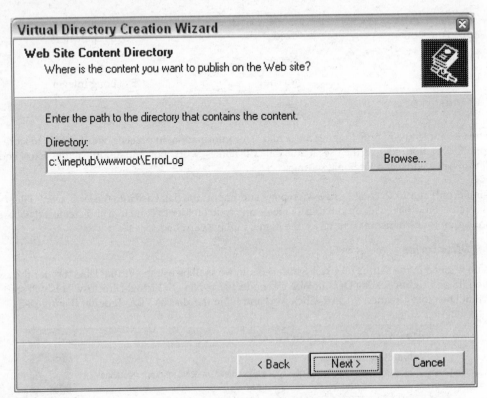

Figure 28-6

Click *Next*, and ensure that this directory gives you write access. That is the final step in the creation of our Virtual Directory. Now the URL `http://localhost/VBA_ProgRef/MyPage.asp` will map to the directory `C:\My Documents\My Webs\myweb\`.

An ASP Page to Write to the Error Log

In FrontPage, create a new blank page, save it as `StoreError.asp`, click on the "HTML" tab to edit the HTML directly and copy in the following code:

```
<%@ LANGUAGE=VBSCRIPT %>
<%

'*********************************************************************************
'*
'* Page name: StoreError.asp
'*
'* Inputs:    The information to store in the error log is supplied within a POST
'*            message (as used by Web forms). A POST file contains information in
```

```
'*              the form:
'*                  Name1=Value1&Name2=Value2&Name3=Value3 etc
'*
'* Outputs:    Returns the record number created to store the error information
'*
'* Purpose:    Receives error information from an application and stores it in
a database on the Server
'*
'***************************************************************************

    Dim objConn, objRS, sTable, lErrID, objField, objID

    'Ignore any errors, such as not being given a specific field in the POST info
    On Error Resume Next

    'Create a reference to the Jet Engine objects, to flush the cache
    Set objJE = Server.CreateObject("JRO.JetEngine")

    'Create a ADO connection
    Set objConn = Server.CreateObject("ADODB.Connection")

    'Use the connection string that FrontPage generated for us
    objConn.Open Application("ErrorLog_ConnectionString")

    'Flush the cache to force a write
    objJE.RefreshCache objConn

    'Create a connection to the error log table
    Set objRS = Server.CreateObject("ADODB.Recordset")
    objRS.ActiveConnection = objConn
    objRS.LockType = 3
    objRS.CursorType = 2
    objRS.Source = "ErrorData"
    objRS.Open

    'Add a new record to the error log table
    objRS.AddNew

    'Fill in all the error information
    For Each objField in objRS.Fields

        Select Case objField.Type
        Case 3    'Long Integer
            If LCase(objField.Name) <> "errorid" Then
                objField.Value = CLng(Request(objField.Name))
            End If
        Case 7, 135    'Date
            If LCase(objField.Name) = "servertime" Then
                objField.Value = Now()
            Else
                objField.Value = CDate(Request(objField.Name))
            End If
        Case 202, 203 'Char, Memo
            objField.Value = Request(objField.Name)
```

```
      End Select
   Next

   'Save the data to the database
   objRS.Update

   'Read off the error ID and return it to the client
objRS.MoveLast
Response.Write objRS.Fields(0).Value

objRS.close
   Set objRS = Nothing

   'Flush the cache to force a write
   objJE.RefreshCache objConn

   objConn.Close
   Set objConn = Nothing

   Set objJE = Nothing
%>
```

The code examines the database file on the server and expects to be given a parameter in the POST string for each field in the table. The Request function retrieves the value of the parameter from the POST string, writing it to the database. The routine ends by using Response.Write to send the error ID back to the client.

An ASP Page to View the Error Log

The ASP script to view a page of the error log is fairly complex, as it generates the HTML required to view the page in the browser and provides a form to assist in navigation between errors. Create a new page called ErrorLog.asp, switch to the HTML view and copy in the following code:

```
<%@ LANGUAGE=VBSCRIPT %>
<%

'***************************************************************************
'*
'* Page name: ErrorLog.asp
'*
'* Inputs:    ErrID - The error number to open in the browser
'*                 Op      - The navigation operation to perform
'*
'* Outputs:   Displays the error information in the browser
'*
'* Purpose:   To enable browsing of the Error Log database
'*
'***************************************************************************

   'Any errors will just bomb through the code, returning zero
   On Error Resume Next

   'Read the parameters passed in the URL
```

```
    sOp = Request.QueryString("Op")
    iErr = Request.QueryString("ErrID")

    'Check the navigation operation
    If sOp = "" Then
        If iErr = "" Then
            sOp = "Last"
        Else
            sOp = "Go"
        End If
    End If

    If iErr = "" Then iErr = 1
    If iErr < 1 Then iErr = 1

    'Create a connection to the error log database
    Set objConn = Server.CreateObject("ADODB.Connection")
    objConn.Open Application("ErrorLog_ConnectionString")

    'Create a connection to the error log table
    Set objRS = Server.CreateObject("ADODB.Recordset")
    objRS.ActiveConnection = objConn
    objRS.CursorType = 3                        'Static cursor.

    objRS.Source = "ErrorData"
    objRS.Open

    'Work out which error to show next
    If objRS.BOF And objRS.EOF Then
        iErr = 0
    Else

        'Find the required error
        objRS.Find "ErrorID = " & iErr

        vBM = objRS.Bookmark

        'Move to the last, next or previous, depending on the required operation
        If objRS.EOF Or sOp = "Last" Then
            objRS.MoveLast

        ElseIf sOp = "Next" Then
            objRS.MoveNext

        ElseIf sOp = "Prev" Then
            objRS.MovePrevious
        End If

        If objRS.EOF Or objRS.BOF Then objRS.Bookmark = vBM

        'Remember which error number we're showing
        iErr = objRS.Fields("ErrorID")
    End If
%>
```

615

```
<%'Write the HTML header information for the web page %>
<HTML>

<head>
<title>Excel 2003 Prog Ref Error Browser</title>
</head>

<%'Start a Web form, so we can allow the user to go to a specific
error ID number %>
<FORM METHOD="GET" ACTION="ErrorLog.asp">

</form>

<table border="0" width="100%">
  <tr>
  <td colspan="2"><p align="center"><b>
    <font face="Arial" size="6">Excel 2003 Prog Ref</font>
    <br>
    <font face="Arial" size="4">Application Error Browser</font></b>
</td>
  </tr>
  <tr>
    <%'Populate the "Error ID" box and Go, Previous and Next links %>
    <td width="20%">Error Number: </td>
    <td width="80%"><INPUT TYPE=TEXT NAME="ErrID" VALUE="<%=iErr%>" SIZE=10>
      <INPUT TYPE=SUBMIT VALUE="Go">
      <a href="ErrorLog.asp?App=<%=sApp%>&ErrID=<%=iErr%>&Op=Prev">Previous</a>
-<a href="ErrorLog.asp?App=<%=sApp%>&ErrID=<%=iErr%>&Op=Next">Next</a> - <a
href="ErrorLog.asp?App=<%=sApp%>&Op=Last">Last</a></td>
  </tr>
<%
    'Loop through all the fields in the table, displaying the name and value to
the page
    For iField = 1 To objRS.Fields.Count - 1
%>
  <tr>
    <td width="20%"><% =objRS.Fields(iField).Name %>: </td>
    <td width="80%">
<%
    If Not objRS.EOF Then
%>
        <%=objRS.Fields(iField).Value %>
<%
    End if
%> </td>
  </tr>
<%
    Next

    'ADO Object clean up.
    objRS.Close
    Set objRS = Nothing
```

```
      objConn.Close
      Set objConn = Nothing

%>
</FORM>
</table>

</body>
</HTML>
```

The Excel Error-Handler Routine

With the database and two ASP pages running on a server, we can now write the Excel error-handler routine to log all our runtime errors to the server database. This routine uses the Microsoft Internet Transfer Control to send the error information to the Web-server application, retrieve the error number, and display it in a simple message box. In practice, you would probably want to send more information to the server, and present a more meaningful error message.

Open a new workbook in Excel 2003, add a reference to the Microsoft Internet Transfer Control (which may require browsing for the msinet.ocx file, usually found in the Windows\System32 directory) and copy in the following code:

```
Option Explicit

'Common error handler
Sub ErrorHandler()

    Dim oInet As Inet
    Dim lContent As Long
    Dim sData As String
    Dim sHeader As String
    Dim sResult As String

    'Create a new instance of the Internet Transfer Control
    Set oInet = New Inet

    'Build the POST string with the error information
    sData = "Application=Excel 2003 Prog Ref" & "&" & _
            "ErrSource=" & Err.Source & "&" & _
            "ErrNumber=" & Err.Number & "&" & _
            "ErrDescription=" & Err.Description

    'Spaces must be replaced with + signs
    sData = Replace(sData, " ", "+")

    'Tell the POST that we're sending an encoded parameter list
    sHeader = "Content-Type: application/x-www-form-urlencoded"

    'Send the error information to the server
    oInet.AccessType = icDirect
    oInet.Execute "http://localhost/VBA_ProgRef/StoreError.asp", "POST", _
                  sData, sHeader
```

```
        'Wait for the server to complete its work
        Do While oInet.StillExecuting
            DoEvents
        Loop

        'Retrieve the returned text (i.e. the error ID)
        lContent = oInet.GetHeader("content-length")
        sResult = oInet.GetChunk(lContent + 100)

        'Display the error ID
        MsgBox "Error logged as number " & sResult

    End Sub

    'Force a division by zero error to test the error handler
    Sub TestIt()

        On Error GoTo errHandler

        'Force division by zero
        Debug.Print 1 / 0

        Exit Sub

    errHandler:

        'Call the common error logging routine
        ErrorHandler

    End Sub
```

Run `TestIt` a few times to test the error handler. If everything was configured correctly, you will get a message showing an incrementing error number. If you open a browser and browse to `http://localhost/VBA_ProgRef/ErrorLog.asp`, you'll see something like Figure 28-7.

The same server-side scripts can be used by many different client applications, and we're not limited to Excel as the client either. By passing the information between the server and the client as a simple list of parameter/value pairs, we have made them very loosely coupled, giving us the flexibility to modify any of the components without requiring changes to any of the others. It is precisely this loose coupling between distributed applications that makes Web-based applications so powerful.

XML

As systems become more and more complex, and require greater and greater amounts of information to be shared between them, it soon becomes too restrictive to pass information between them using the lists of parameter/value pairs that we used earlier. In order to address that restriction, yet maintain the loose coupling of the Web-based architecture, a new format for data exchange was developed, called eXtensible Markup Language, or XML, for short.

XML allows us to structure our data into hierarchical relationships and mark each element as being a specific data type (such as Name, HoursWorked, etc.). The XML for a simple timesheet may look something like the following (where the TS: prefix is used to distinguish our tags from any other).

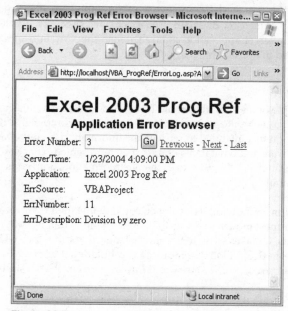

Figure 28-7

```xml
<?xml version="1.0"?>
<!Excel 2003 Prog Ref Timesheet>
<TS:Timesheet xmlns:TS="urn:schemas_wrox_com:ExcelProgRef:Timesheet">
    <TS:Employee>
        <TS:FirstName>Stephen</TS:FirstName>
        <TS:LastName>Bullen</TS:LastName>
        <TS:EmployeeNumber>1234</TS:EmployeeNumber>
    </TS:Employee>
    <TS:ReportingMonth>
        <TS:Year>2001</TS:Year>
        <TS:Month>6</TS:Month>
        <TS:TotalStdHours>157.5</TS:TotalStdHours>
    </TS:ReportingMonth>
    <TS:HoursWorked>
        <TS:Day>1</TS:Day>
        <TS:StdHours>7.5</TS:StdHours>
        <TS:Overtime>2</TS:Overtime>
    </TS:HoursWorked>
    <TS:HoursWorked>
        <TS:Day>4</TS:Day>
        <TS:StdHours>7.5</TS:StdHours>
        <TS:Overtime>1</TS:Overtime>
    </TS:HoursWorked>
    <TS:HoursWorked>
        <TS:Day>5</TS:Day>
        <TS:StdHours>6</TS:StdHours>
        <TS:Overtime/>
    </TS:HoursWorked>
</TS:Timesheet>
```

To send this data to a Web server application, we would use the same POST mechanism that we used above for sending our parameter/value pairs. The `<?xml version="1.0"?>` tag at the top of the data identifies it as XML. The server application could then load the XML into an XML Parser, through which the data can be extracted in a structured manner.

XML Vocabularies

In the preceding example of the XML that could be used to represent a timesheet, all the tag names (`<Timesheet>`, `<Employee>`, `<ReportingMonth>`, etc.) were completely arbitrary, invented for the example. Any application that intended to retrieve the information from the XML text would need to know what those tags were and what items of data they represented. That description of the XML data is known as an "XML Vocabulary". In order to exchange information, both ends of the conversation need to be using the same vocabulary.

While every organization, or individual developer, could define their own vocabulary, there are a number of standards bodies for most industry sectors that are working to define XML vocabularies for their industry's requirements. It makes sense to use these standard vocabularies whenever possible, instead of trying to reinvent the wheel. Start looking for these vocabularies at `http://www.w3.org`, `http://www.BizTalk.org`, `http://www.rosettanet.org`, or your industry's trade bodies.

> **For more information about XML, please refer to Professional XML, Second edition Wrox Press, ISBN 1-861005-05-9.**

The XML-SS Schema

One such XML Vocabulary is the XML-SS schema that Microsoft uses to describe spreadsheet data. Both Excel 2003 and the Office 11 Spreadsheet Web Component can read and write XML using XML-SS. Until recently, the XML-SS schema documentation was available on the Microsoft Web site, but was removed during one of its many reorganizations.

To obtain the XML-SS representation of an Excel `Range`, we use the new optional argument added to the `Range.Value` property:

```
Sub GetRangeXML()

    Dim sRangeXML As String

    sRangeXML = ActiveSheet.Range("A1:C40") _
                .Value(xlRangeValueXMLSpreadsheet)

    'Print to the Immediate window
    Debug.Print sRangeXML

End Sub
```

Consider the following simple timesheet shown in Figure 28-8.

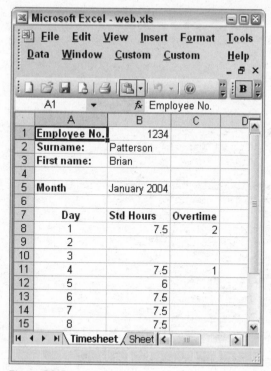

Figure 28-8

This gives the following XML-SS (with some of the days removed):

```
<?xml version="1.0"?>
<?mso-application progid="Excel.Sheet"?>
<Workbook xmlns="urn:schemas-microsoft-com:office:spreadsheet"
 xmlns:o="urn:schemas-microsoft-com:office:office"
 xmlns:x="urn:schemas-microsoft-com:office:excel"
 xmlns:ss="urn:schemas-microsoft-com:office:spreadsheet"
 xmlns:html="http://www.w3.org/TR/REC-html40">
 <DocumentProperties xmlns="urn:schemas-microsoft-com:office:office">
  <Author>Brian Patterson</Author>
  <LastAuthor>Brian Patterson</LastAuthor>
  <Created>2004-01-25T22:20:36Z</Created>
  <LastSaved>2004-01-25T22:23:53Z</LastSaved>
  <Version>11.5606</Version>
 </DocumentProperties>
 <ExcelWorkbook xmlns="urn:schemas-microsoft-com:office:excel">
  <WindowHeight>6810</WindowHeight>
  <WindowWidth>4635</WindowWidth>
  <WindowTopX>120</WindowTopX>
  <WindowTopY>15</WindowTopY>
  <ProtectStructure>False</ProtectStructure>
  <ProtectWindows>False</ProtectWindows>
 </ExcelWorkbook>
```

```xml
 <Styles>
  <Style ss:ID="Default" ss:Name="Normal">
  <Alignment ss:Vertical="Bottom"/>
  <Borders/>
  <Font/>
  <Interior/>
  <NumberFormat/>
  <Protection/>
 </Style>
 <Style ss:ID="s22">
  <Font x:Family="Swiss" ss:Bold="1"/>
 </Style>
 <Style ss:ID="s23">
  <Alignment ss:Horizontal="Center" ss:Vertical="Bottom"/>
  <Font x:Family="Swiss" ss:Bold="1"/>
 </Style>
 <Style ss:ID="s24">
  <Alignment ss:Horizontal="Center" ss:Vertical="Bottom"/>
 </Style>
 <Style ss:ID="s25">
  <NumberFormat ss:Format="@"/>
 </Style>
 </Styles>
 <Worksheet ss:Name="Timesheet">
  <Table ss:ExpandedColumnCount="3" ss:ExpandedRowCount="15" x:FullColumns="1"
   x:FullRows="1">
   <Column ss:AutoFitWidth="0" ss:Width="70.5"/>
   <Column ss:AutoFitWidth="0" ss:Width="61.5"/>
   <Row>
    <Cell ss:StyleID="s22"><Data ss:Type="String">Employee No.</Data></Cell>
    <Cell><Data ss:Type="Number">1234</Data></Cell>
   </Row>
   <Row>
    <Cell ss:StyleID="s22"><Data ss:Type="String">Surname:</Data></Cell>
    <Cell><Data ss:Type="String">Patterson</Data></Cell>
   </Row>
   <Row>
    <Cell ss:StyleID="s22"><Data ss:Type="String">First name:</Data></Cell>
    <Cell><Data ss:Type="String">Brian</Data></Cell>
   </Row>
   <Row ss:Index="5">
    <Cell ss:StyleID="s22"><Data ss:Type="String">Month</Data></Cell>
    <Cell ss:StyleID="s25"><Data ss:Type="String">January 2004</Data></Cell>
   </Row>
   <Row ss:Index="7">
    <Cell ss:StyleID="s23"><Data ss:Type="String">Day</Data></Cell>
    <Cell ss:StyleID="s22"><Data ss:Type="String">Std Hours</Data></Cell>
    <Cell ss:StyleID="s22"><Data ss:Type="String">Overtime</Data></Cell>
   </Row>
   <Row>
    <Cell ss:StyleID="s24"><Data ss:Type="Number">1</Data></Cell>
    <Cell><Data ss:Type="Number">7.5</Data></Cell>
    <Cell><Data ss:Type="Number">2</Data></Cell>
```

```
   </Row>
   <Row>
    <Cell ss:StyleID="s24"><Data ss:Type="Number">2</Data></Cell>
   </Row>
   <Row>
    <Cell ss:StyleID="s24"><Data ss:Type="Number">3</Data></Cell>
   </Row>
   <Row>
    <Cell ss:StyleID="s24"><Data ss:Type="Number">4</Data></Cell>
    <Cell><Data ss:Type="Number">7.5</Data></Cell>
    <Cell><Data ss:Type="Number">1</Data></Cell>
   </Row>
   <Row>
    <Cell ss:StyleID="s24"><Data ss:Type="Number">5</Data></Cell>
    <Cell><Data ss:Type="Number">6</Data></Cell>
   </Row>
   <Row>
    <Cell ss:StyleID="s24"><Data ss:Type="Number">6</Data></Cell>
    <Cell><Data ss:Type="Number">7.5</Data></Cell>
   </Row>
   <Row>
    <Cell ss:StyleID="s24"><Data ss:Type="Number">7</Data></Cell>
    <Cell><Data ss:Type="Number">7.5</Data></Cell>
   </Row>
   <Row>
    <Cell ss:StyleID="s24"><Data ss:Type="Number">8</Data></Cell>
    <Cell><Data ss:Type="Number">7.5</Data></Cell>
   </Row>
  </Table>
  <WorksheetOptions xmlns="urn:schemas-microsoft-com:office:excel">
   <Print>
    <ValidPrinterInfo/>
    <HorizontalResolution>600</HorizontalResolution>
    <VerticalResolution>0</VerticalResolution>
   </Print>
   <Selected/>
   <ProtectObjects>False</ProtectObjects>
   <ProtectScenarios>False</ProtectScenarios>
  </WorksheetOptions>
 </Worksheet>
 <Worksheet ss:Name="Sheet2">
  <WorksheetOptions xmlns="urn:schemas-microsoft-com:office:excel">
   <ProtectObjects>False</ProtectObjects>
   <ProtectScenarios>False</ProtectScenarios>
  </WorksheetOptions>
 </Worksheet>
 <Worksheet ss:Name="Sheet3">
  <WorksheetOptions xmlns="urn:schemas-microsoft-com:office:excel">
   <ProtectObjects>False</ProtectObjects>
   <ProtectScenarios>False</ProtectScenarios>
  </WorksheetOptions>
 </Worksheet>
</Workbook>
```

The XML for a workbook contains the data, formulas, and formatting, but does not include embedded objects, charts, or VBA code.

> **More information about XML support in Excel 2003 is available from the Microsoft Web site at http://msdn.microsoft.com/Office/.**

Using XSLT to Transform XML

Examining the XML-SS data that Excel gives us, we can see that it is expressed in terms of workbooks, worksheets, tables, rows, and cells, while our timesheet XML shown earlier in this section expresses the data in terms of Timesheets, Employees, ReportingMonths, and HoursWorked. Before we can send our timesheet data to our Web server, we need to transform the XML-SS schema into our Timesheet schema. That task is performed by XSLT, which stands for the eXtensible Stylesheet Language: Transformations.

XSLT is a declarative language, in which a stylesheet is applied to the source XML document. The stylesheet is written to select specific items of data out of the source XML in a specific order, such that the result is a new XML document that uses the target schema. In our case:

> **XML-SS + Custom StyleSheet = Timesheet XML**

The following is the XSLT for our transformation:

```
<?xml version="1.0"?>
<xsl:stylesheet version="1.0"
    xmlns:xsl="http://www.w3.org/1999/XSL/Transform"
    xmlns:xl="urn:schemas-microsoft-com:office:spreadsheet"
    xmlns:ss="urn:schemas-microsoft-com:office:spreadsheet"
    exclude-result-prefixes="xl ss">
<xsl:template match="/xl:Workbook/xl:Worksheet/xl:Table">
<TS:Timesheet xmlns:TS="urn:schemas_wrox_com:ExcelProgRef:Timesheet">
  <TS:Employee>
    <TS:FirstName>
      <xsl:value-of
select="xl:Row/xl:Cell[xl:NamedCell[@ss:Name='ForeName']]/xl:Data"/>
    </TS:FirstName>
    <TS:LastName>
      <xsl:value-of
select="xl:Row/xl:Cell[xl:NamedCell[@ss:Name='Surname']]/xl:Data"/>
    </TS:LastName>
    <TS:EmployeeNumber>
      <xsl:value-of
select="xl:Row/xl:Cell[xl:NamedCell[@ss:Name='EmpNo']]/xl:Data"/>
    </TS:EmployeeNumber>
  </TS:Employee>
```

```
    <TS:ReportingMonth>
      <TS:Year>
        <xsl:value-of
select="substring(xl:Row/xl:Cell[xl:NamedCell[@ss:Name='Month']]/xl
:Data,1,4)"/>
      </TS:Year>
      <TS:Month>
        <xsl:value-of
select="substring(xl:Row/xl:Cell[xl:NamedCell[@ss:Name='Month']]/xl
:Data,6,2)"/>
      </TS:Month>
      <TS:TotalStdHours>
        <xsl:value-of
select="xl:Row/xl:Cell[xl:NamedCell[@ss:Name='StdHours']]/xl:Data"/>
      </TS:TotalStdHours>
    </TS:ReportingMonth>
    <xsl:for-each select="xl:Row/xl:Cell[xl:NamedCell[@ss:Name='Days']]">
      <xsl:if
test="string(number(../xl:Cell[xl:NamedCell[@ss:Name='Hours']]/xl
:Data))!= 'NaN'">
        <TS:HoursWorked>
        <TS:Day>
          <xsl:value-of
select="../xl:Cell[xl:NamedCell[@ss:Name='Days']]/xl:Data"/>
          </TS:Day>
          <TS:StdHours>
            <xsl:value-of
select="../xl:Cell[xl:NamedCell[@ss:Name='Hours']]/xl:Data"/>
          </TS:StdHours>
          <xsl:choose>
               <xsl:when
test="string(number(../xl:Cell[xl:NamedCell[@ss:Name='Overtime']]/xl
:Data))!='NaN'"
>
              <TS:Overtime>
                <xsl:value-of
select="../xl:Cell[xl:NamedCell[@ss:Name='Overtime']]/xl:Data"/>
              </TS:Overtime>
            </xsl:when>
            <xsl:otherwise><TS:Overtime/></xsl:otherwise>
          </xsl:choose>
        </TS:HoursWorked>
      </xsl:if>
    </xsl:for-each>
  </TS:Timesheet>
  </xsl:template>
</xsl:stylesheet>
```

The XSLT is almost human-readable. The key to understanding it is to realize the following:

❑   Only tags that start `<xsl>` and `</xsl>` are processing elements, telling the XML parser how to transform the data

❑   All the other tags are copied directly to the output stream

❏   The following expression locates the cell that has been given the range name of ForeName and returns its Data element (i.e. its value), and is equivalent to Range("ForeName").Value in VBA:

```
select="xl:Row/xl:Cell[xl:NamedCell[@ss:Name='ForeName']]/xl:Data"
```

❏   The following expression starts a For...Each loop through all the cells in the named range 'Days', and is equivalent to For Each oCell In Range("Days").Cells in VBA:

```
<xsl:for-each select="xl:Row/xl:Cell[xl:NamedCell[@ss:Name='Days']]">
```

❏   In the XML-SS schema, there is a tree structure of Worksheet > Rows > Cells, so the parent of a cell (../ in XSLT) is the row, so the expression:

```
select="../xl:Cell[xl:NamedCell[@ss:Name='Hours']]/xl:Data"/>
```

is equivalent to the VBA:

```
Application.Intersect(oCell.EntireRow, Range("Hours")).Value
```

❏   The transformation strips out days for which no time was entered. The expression:

```
test="string(number(...))!='NaN'"
```

is the XSLT equivalent of IsNumeric(...) in VBA

We shall be referencing this code by placing it in a cell called "XSLT" in a worksheet called "XSLT", as the screenshot in Figure 28-9 shows.

The VBA code to perform the transformation and send the Timesheet XML to a Web server application is shown next. It uses the MSXML parser to perform the transformation (referenced by the "Microsoft XML, v3.0" object library):

```
'Transfrom the spreadsheet XML-SS format to the TimeSheet XML format
Sub TransformAndPostXML()

    'Define three instances of the MSXML parser

    'One for the source XML - in XML-SS format
    Dim xmlSource As MSXML2.DOMDocument30

    'One for the XSLT transformation
    Dim xmlXSLT As MSXML2.DOMDocument30

    'One for the resultant XML - in Timesheet format
    Dim xmlTimesheet As MSXML2.DOMDocument30

    'Define an instance of the ITC for sending the XML
    Dim oInet As Inet
    Dim sTimesheetXML As String
```

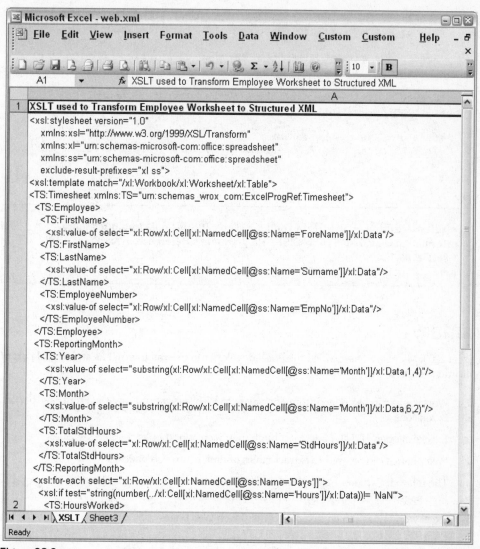

Figure 28-9

```
'Create new instances of the MSXML parsers
Set xmlSource = New MSXML2.DOMDocument30
Set xmlXSLT = New MSXML2.DOMDocument30
Set xmlTimesheet = New MSXML2.DOMDocument30

'Load the source XML from the Timesheet worksheet
xmlSource.loadXML Worksheets("TimeSheet").Range("A1:C40") _
                .Value(xlRangeValueXMLSpreadsheet)

'Load the XSLT from the XSLT worksheet
xmlXSLT.loadXML Worksheets("XSLT").Range("XSLT").Value
```

```
        'Transform the XML-SS using the XSLT, giving the Timesheet XML
        xmlSource.transformNodeToObject xmlXSLT, xmlTimesheet

        'Read the resultant Timesheet XML into a variable
        sTimesheetXML = xmlTimesheet.XML

        'Create a new instance of the Internet Transfer Control
        Set oInet = New Inet

        'Send the XML to the server
        oInet.Execute "http://localhost/MyPage.asp", "POST", sTimesheetXML

End Sub
```

> **A full description of XSLT is beyond the scope of this book, but much more information is available in the XSLT Programmer's Reference, Wrox Press, ISBN 1-861005-06-7.**

Summary

In Excel 2003, Microsoft has enabled the Excel developer to use the Internet as an integral part of an application solution:

❑ Workbooks can be opened from and saved to Web servers running the FrontPage Server Extensions

❑ Excel can open HTML pages as though they were workbooks

❑ Web queries can be used to extract tables of data from Web pages

❑ The Internet Explorer object library can be automated to retrieve individual items of data from a Web page, without the overhead of using a workbook

❑ Excel workbooks can be saved as content-rich Web pages

❑ Interactive Web pages can easily be produced, providing Excel-like interaction within the Web browser.

❑ The Microsoft Internet Transfer Control can be used to exchange data between Excel applications and Web servers, either using a simple parameter list or more structured XML.

❑ Excel 2003 supports the XML-SS schema for describing spreadsheets, and the MSXML parser can use XSLT to transform XML-SS to other XML schemas, prior to sending the data to the Web server.

Together, these tools enable us to develop new types of business solution, where Excel is one key part of a larger business process, which may span multiple organizations and geographical locations.

29

XML and Excel

Sometimes it is difficult to tell which technologies one should care about and which one can ignore. Do you remember DDE? Have you ever heard of SGML? In truth, some technologies (DDE but not SGML completely) can be safely ignored because they are waystation technologies that are stepping stones to something better. Then, sometimes a technology arrives and really can't be ignored. XML is such a time.

A refined question is can Excel VBA programmers afford to ignore XML? And an equally refined answer is probably not for long. XML is quickly becoming the definitive language of the Internet much as English has become the language of technology. In this chapter we will explore XML, beginning with a brief discussion of what it is, and we will show you a few of the things you can do with XML vis-à-vis Excel.

What Is XML?

XML, or eXtensible Markup Language, is a derivative of SGML, or Standard Generalized Markup Language. XML is a markup language like HTML that contains data and things that describe the data. What is important about XML is that XML is self-describing in nature and that XML is just text. Because XML is self-describing it can be used to describe just about anything, and because XML is text it can easily be transported across networks very easily, including the biggest network, the Internet. The Internet will handle other things besides text, but TCP/IP networks really like text.

Because XML is text, it is very easy to manage and transmit. Because XML contains data and elements that describe the data, it is a very convenient package for conveying information. Don't get me wrong, binary files (graphics, video, music) are great, but XML is for the foreseeable future the language of the Internet.

At first sight, an XML file can be shocking. However, if you are even vaguely familiar with HTML then XML won't take so long to get used to. The next listing is a complete XML file:

```
<?xml version="1.0" standalone="yes"?>
<snapshot>
  <Recording>
```

```
        <Id>0</Id>
        <Count>0</Count>
        <When>2004-02-01T09:27:42.7096378-05:00</When>
        <InstanceId>0</InstanceId>
        <DealerHand>QD,JS</DealerHand>
        <PlayerHand>QC,10D</PlayerHand>
        <HandNumber>0</HandNumber>
        <CurrentBet>25</CurrentBet>
        <Money>500</Money>
        <PlayState>Push</PlayState>
        <Hints>Stand</Hints>
    </Recording>
  </snapshot>
```

Unfortunately, we can't provide a complete XML tutorial here, but Wrox has some very good books on XML if you are interested in becoming an expert at reading and writing it. One of those things we can defer that we talked about though is becoming an expert at reading and writing XML, because most XML tools will do that for us. The XML text has simple format in which the data is conveyed.

In the listing, the first document indicates that the text is an XML document. The first line may vary some, but, in general, XML documents contain a first line very similar to the one shown. The words in <>, like <snapshot> are tags. These tags are the descriptors that tell us what the data is. To some extent one can think of these tag descriptors in much the same way we think of object-oriented technology. Outer descriptors like <snapshot> make up what might be called a namespace (think named area). Nested, inner descriptors like <Recording> might be part of a namespace or a class. In the example, we can think of <Recording> as being analogous to a user-defined data type or class. Thus, in the <snapshot> namespace or named area we have a type named <Recording>. Finally, the innermost elements are members. Collectively, a snapshot.Recording has members Id, Count, When, InstanceId, DealerHand, PlayerHand, HandNumber, CurrentBet, Money, PlayState, and Hints.

Perhaps a better outer element might be <BlackJackhand> or something, but be that as it may, even this relatively simple XML file conveys quite a bit of meaning about the data we are looking at. The names of things are expressly indicated, as well as the values of things. The data types can be inferred from the data itself. (XML does support explicitly indicating data types and more, too.)

What Is XSD?

XSD, or XML Schema Definition, is the technology that supports describing an XML document without the data. Similar to database technologies—and in some sense XML is sort of a universal database mechanism—there are tables and schemas. A table contains data and a schema contains data that is contained in the associated data table. Symmetrically, an XSD file contains a schema that describes the kinds, types, and organization of data in a related XML file.

If we were to infer or extract just the schema for XML files containing recordings of BlackJack hands, then that schema might appear as shown in the next listing:

```
<?xml version="1.0" ?>
<xs:schema id="snapshot" targetNamespace="http://tempuri.org/game.xsd"
```

```
 xmlns:mstns="http://tempuri.org/game.xsd"
   xmlns="http://tempuri.org/game.xsd" xmlns:xs="http://www.w3.org/2001/XMLSchema"
 xmlns:msdata="urn:schemas-microsoft-com:xml-msdata"
   attributeFormDefault="qualified" elementFormDefault="qualified">
   <xs:element name="snapshot" msdata:IsDataSet="true"
 msdata:EnforceConstraints="False">
     <xs:complexType>
       <xs:choice maxOccurs="unbounded">
         <xs:element name="Recording">
           <xs:complexType>
             <xs:sequence>
               <xs:element name="Id" type="xs:integer" minOccurs="0" />
               <xs:element name="Count" type="xs:integer" minOccurs="0" />
               <xs:element name="When" type="xs:dateTime" minOccurs="0" />
               <xs:element name="InstanceId" type="xs:integer" minOccurs="0" />
               <xs:element name="DealerHand" type="xs:string" minOccurs="0" />
               <xs:element name="PlayerHand" type="xs:string" minOccurs="0" />
               <xs:element name="HandNumber" type="xs:string" minOccurs="0" />
               <xs:element name="CurrentBet" type="xs:double" minOccurs="0" />
               <xs:element name="Money" type="xs:double" minOccurs="0" />
               <xs:element name="PlayState" type="xs:string" minOccurs="0" />
               <xs:element name="Hints" type="xs:string" minOccurs="0" />
             </xs:sequence>
           </xs:complexType>
         </xs:element>
       </xs:choice>
     </xs:complexType>
   </xs:element>
 </xs:schema>
```

Arguably, the schema looks worse than the XML data itself; however, remember that the benefit here is that the text we are looking at completely describes what data associated with this schema will look like and it is really just plain text. Again, as plain text it is very easy to move XSD files across networks, making it a very good common denominator.

What Is XMLSS?

Excel doesn't use XSD directly. Instead, Excel converts schemas into XMLSS, or XML Spreadsheet Schemas. In part, what Excel does is convert types expressed in XML schemas to types that are convenient for Excel to work with and displays the XMLSS in the XML Source Task Pane. In effect, the schema, as far as Excel is concerned, is expressed or viewed by Excel in the way that it shows the Spreadsheet Schema in the XML Source Task Pane (see Figure 29-1).

If you look at the XML Source Task Pane (accessible from Data ⇨ XML ⇨ XML Source), then you will see that XML Spreadsheet Schema simply shows the descriptors without the data. The difference is that an XML file may have 0 to many instances of elements defined by the schema. For example, there would only be one <snapshot> </snapshot> tag pair, but there can be as many repetitions of <Recording> </Recording> pairs as desired. It is a reasonably good metaphor to think of a schema file as a class definition and the XML file as containing captured instances of that class.

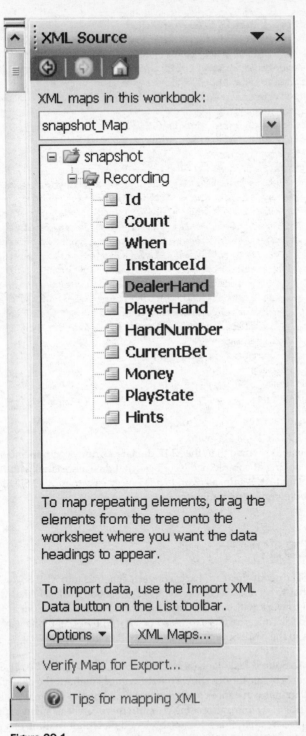

Figure 29-1

Importing XML Data

The real benefit of XML and XSD is that it represents a common denominator that—in part because it is an open standard, not owned by anybody—for the most part everyone seems to agree is a good, common means of interchanging data. The result is that any application that can read and write XML can communicate with any other application that can also read and write XML. This is true regardless of the language, the platform, the operating system, tools, or the means in which the data is transported.

Having a common data interchange language for all the tools is a good thing. Just remember a few years ago it was difficult, if not impossible, to convey data between Word, Excel, and other applications, especially custom applications. Sure, comma-delimited files worked okay, and Automation supported wiring code directly to Excel, but comma delimited files didn't convey anything about their information, that is, they had no standardized schema, and Automation required a special knowledge of Excel itself. By standardizing the data and schema, any program can export or import XML and any other program can share that data without requiring special knowledge about the consumer of the data. That is, an application doesn't have to talk to Excel VBA through Automation to share its data with Excel. To demonstrate the versatility of XML we will use a simple game that we created recently.

BlackJack: Data Versatility

BlackJack is a game that takes "a minute to learn and a lifetime to master." BlackJack seems to offer a pretty good return as gambling goes, but being a competitive sort we are always looking to improve. To that end we wrote a BlackJack game (shown in Figure 29-2) with .NET, including some pretty good hints

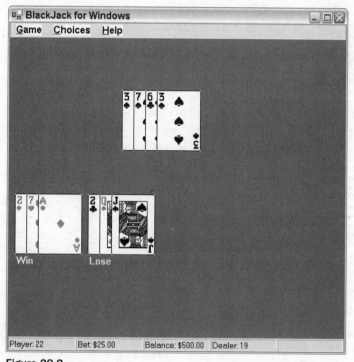

Figure 29-2

based on probability and a game recorder that streams the dealer and player hand, bet, and outcome to an XML file. However, writing an engine to analyze the game and perhaps graph the outcome is a bit more effort than we want to expend on a game, but we do want the ability to examine the data.

This is where Excel comes in. Whether you are writing a game and analyzing game play to take a few hundred extra bucks from a Vegas casino or writing a mission critical application for analyzing Mars dust, Excel is a powerful analytical tool. If you use XML as the means of persisting the data, then you can easily import that XML data into Excel.

While it is possible to implement the BlackJack game in Excel with VBA and using the `cards.dll` that ships with Windows, that's really not what this chapter is about. (You can find the BlackJack source code on `http://www.softcocnepts.com/BlackJack/`.)

Figure 29-3 shows an imported round of BlackJack where the starting amount of money was increased from $500 to $2,520. This is a pretty successful round of BlackJack, so we'd like to review the data and get a handle on what went right. From the figure we can see that the schema was inferred from the XML file (shown in the XML Source Task Pane), and the rows and columns were converted to lists, including Auto Filter column headers and insert rows (not shown).

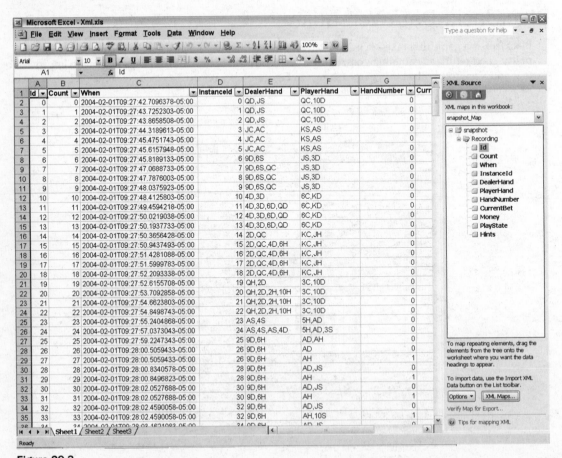

Figure 29-3

Importing an XML File

Our implementation of OpenXML calls the `Application.Workbooks` collection's version of OpenXML. OpenXML takes three arguments: an XML source file, an XSLT (XML Style Sheet Transformation file), and a `LoadOption`. The XML file contains the XML data. The XSLT file contains an XSL Transform document (which we will come back to in a moment), and an `XlXmlLoadOption` that describes how to treat the XML data. The code in the listing simulates the behavior we get by selecting the Data ⇨ XML ⇨ Import menu item:

```
Public Sub OpenXML()
   Dim aWorkbook As Workbook
   Set aWorkbook = Application.Workbooks.OpenXML( _
      Filename:="game.xml", LoadOption:= XlXmlLoadOption.XlXmlLoadImportToList)
End Sub
```

In the example, we declare a Workbook object and invoke the `Application.Workbooks.OpenXML` method. This method returns a new Workbook containing the imported XML and the inferred Excel XML Spreadsheet Schema.

What Is XSL and XSLT?

XSL is the acronym that refers to the eXtensible Style Language. The XSL separates the presentation of the data—the stylesheet—from the actual data—the XML file. For example, by passing the `XlXMLLoadOption.XlXMLLoadImportToList` option we cause the XML data to be formatted as a collection of lists.

Now that you have an idea of what an XSL file is, what is an XSLT file? As we said, XXSL is a stylesheet for XML. It describes how XML data will be displayed. An XSLT (XSL Transform) file describes how XML data is formatted and displayed. To master XMLS and XSL, try Wrox's very fine book *"XSLT: Programmer's Reference"*, 2nd edition, by Michael Kay.

There are two things you need to know here: the first is that we can use XML in Excel without mastering XML, XSL, and XSLT, but these are all very powerful technologies. The second thing is that Mr. Kay's book is 900 pages long and is just one of many. Which, unfortunately, means the subject is too complicated to describe in detail here. That said we have revised the `OpenXML` method to include an XSL `Transform` file, so that you can see the difference between a basic import of XML data and an example of how XSLT can format and transmogrify the data. The first listing is a slightly revised first few lines of the `game.xml` file that indicates the XSLT file to use for formatting. The second listing is the new `game.xsl` transform file, and the third listing is the new `OpenXML` procedure that accommodates the new XSLT file:

```
<?xml version='1.0' ?>
<?xml-stylesheet type='text/xsl' href='game.xsl' ?>
<snapshot>
  <Recording>
    <Id>0</Id>
    <Count>0</Count>
    <When>2004-02-01T09:27:42.7096378-05:00</When>
    <InstanceId>0</InstanceId>
    <DealerHand>QD,JS</DealerHand>
    <PlayerHand>QC,10D</PlayerHand>
' ... intentionally ellided
```

The second line in bold font indicates the new information. This tells the game.xml file to use game.xsl for formatting. Remember here that we are separating data from formatting. We can quickly substitute a different XSL file and get a different subset of data and completely different presentation:

```
<xsl:stylesheet xmlns:xsl="http://www.w3.org/1999/XSL/Transform"
version="1.0">
  <xsl:template match="/">
    <HTML>
     <body>
       <table>
         <COLGROUP WIDTH="100" ALIGN="CENTER"></COLGROUP>
             <COLGROUP WIDTH="100" ALIGN="CENTER"></COLGROUP>
         <COLGROUP WIDTH="100" ALIGN="CENTER"></COLGROUP>
             <COLGROUP WIDTH="100" ALIGN="CENTER"></COLGROUP>
         <COLGROUP WIDTH="100" ALIGN="CENTER"></COLGROUP>
             <COLGROUP WIDTH="100" ALIGN="CENTER"></COLGROUP>
         <COLGROUP WIDTH="100" ALIGN="CENTER"></COLGROUP>
             <TD><B>Dealer Hand</B></TD>
             <TD><B>Player Hand</B></TD>
             <TD><B>Hand #</B></TD>
             <TD><B>Bet</B></TD>
             <TD><B>Player Funds</B></TD>
             <TD><B>Result</B></TD>
             <xsl:for-each select="snapshot/Recording">
         <tr>
             <td><xsl:value-of select="DealerHand"/></td>
             <td><xsl:value-of select="PlayerHand"/></td>
           <td><xsl:value-of select="HandNumber"/></td>
             <td><xsl:value-of select="CurrentBet"/></td>
             <td><xsl:value-of select="Money"/></td>
             <td><xsl:value-of select="PlayState"/></td>
         </tr>
         </xsl:for-each>
       </table>
     </body>
    </HTML>
    </xsl:template>
</xsl:stylesheet>
```

The game.xsl file contains the formatting information. A common practice is to use HTML to describe the appearance of the information. As shown in the preceding listing, we are formatting the data as an HTML file with bold case column headers and in an HTML table. The result is that the data will look like a Web page. The bold case for each XSLT statement is defined to only select specific columns in the game.xml file. We can also write advanced XSLT that can perform arithmetic operations on the data, in effect, adding new information derived from the static game.xml data.

Finally, we have the revised subroutine, OpenXML. In the next listing, you will see that the X1XmlLoadOption was left out and a dynamic array—Array(1 —is used. This argument indicates which stylesheet to use from the .XML file. For example, if we had a second, statement
<?xml-stylesheet type='text/xsl' href='game2.xsl' ?> and passed Array(2) then the latter, game2.xsl, stylesheet would be used to format our data. Here is the revised OpenXML subroutine:

```
Public Sub OpenXML()
  Dim path As String
  path = ThisWorkbook.path + "\game.xml"
  Dim aWorkbook As Workbook
  Set aWorkbook = Application.Workbooks.OpenXML(path, Array(1))
End Sub
```

While we can't cram 900 pages of XML, XSL, and XSLT information within this text, what we can learn from the text is that XML, in addition to being an easy means of transporting data over networks and between applications, supports a separate formatting and transformation file that permits one copy of the data and many variations on the presentation of that data. Figure 29-4 shows what our dynamic page looks like in Excel.

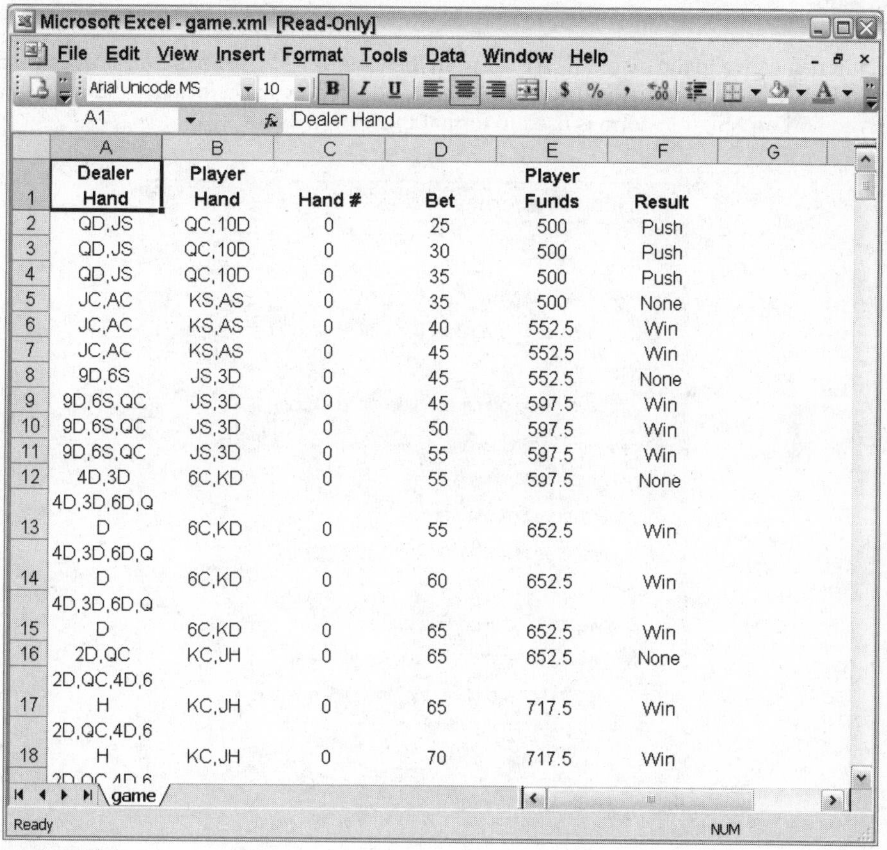

Figure 29-4

The Excel window titled "Microsoft Excel - game.xml [Read-Only]" displays the following worksheet data:

	A Dealer Hand	B Player Hand	C Hand #	D Bet	E Player Funds	F Result	G
2	QD,JS	QC,10D	0	25	500	Push	
3	QD,JS	QC,10D	0	30	500	Push	
4	QD,JS	QC,10D	0	35	500	Push	
5	JC,AC	KS,AS	0	35	500	None	
6	JC,AC	KS,AS	0	40	552.5	Win	
7	JC,AC	KS,AS	0	45	552.5	Win	
8	9D,6S	JS,3D	0	45	552.5	None	
9	9D,6S,QC	JS,3D	0	45	597.5	Win	
10	9D,6S,QC	JS,3D	0	50	597.5	Win	
11	9D,6S,QC	JS,3D	0	55	597.5	Win	
12	4D,3D	6C,KD	0	55	597.5	None	
13	4D,3D,6D,Q D	6C,KD	0	55	652.5	Win	
14	4D,3D,6D,Q D	6C,KD	0	60	652.5	Win	
15	4D,3D,6D,Q D	6C,KD	0	65	652.5	Win	
16	2D,QC	KC,JH	0	65	652.5	None	
17	2D,QC,4D,6 H	KC,JH	0	65	717.5	Win	
18	2D,QC,4D,6 H	KC,JH	0	70	717.5	Win	
	2D,QC,4D,6						

Exporting a Worksheet to an XML File

Suppose, we make changes to a version of our data, for example, removing sensitive values, and want to export that data to a new XML file for the consumption of our customers. We can use the Workbook. SaveAsXMLData method to export the new data file.

637

The next listing offers some code that exports the game.xml file using the XMLSS map created by Excel, saving the new file as newgame.xml:

```
Public Sub ExportXML()
  Dim map As XmlMap
  Set map = ThisWorkbook.XmlMaps("snapshot_Map")
  Dim newPath As String
  newPath = ThisWorkbook.path + "\newgame.xml"
  If (map.IsExportable) Then
    Call ThisWorkbook.SaveAsXMLData(newPath, map)
  Else
    MsgBox "Can't use " & map.Name & " to export data"
  End If
End Sub
```

The default name give to the map can be read from the Data ⇨ XML ⇨ XML Map Properties dialog box (shown in Figure 29-5). This dialog box can be used to adjust how Excel formats and transforms the data similarly to how an XSL transform is used to format the XML data.

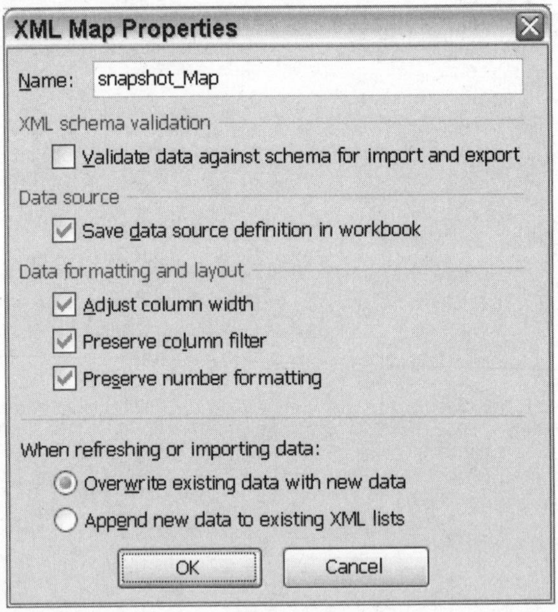

Figure 29-5

Summary

XML, XSL, and XSLT represent a powerful shift in the way data can now be represented in a non-proprietary way. Many modern applications and developer tools are defined to read and write XML. This means that applications in the future will require less and less effort to intracommunicate because they will all work on a common standard understood by all others.

For Excel VBA programmers, we now have a way of reading XML data produced by any other application without writing a lot of custom and proprietary code to do so. One benefit seen in Chapter 21 is SharePoint services. SharePoint services uses XML to transport data, making it easy to publish shared lists on the Internet.

With the added technology for formatting and transforming data—XSL and XSLT—data is now separated from the formatting and layout of the data permitting one instance of XML data to be presented in many different ways.

Excel 2003 Object Model

Most of the objects in the Excel Object Model have objects with associated collections. The collection object is usually the plural form of the associated object. For example, the Worksheets collection holds a collection of Worksheet objects. For simplicity, each object and associated collection will be grouped together under the same heading.

Common Properties with Collections and Associated Objects

In most cases the purpose of the collection object is only to hold a collection of the same objects. The common properties and methods of the collection objects are listed in the following section. Only unique properties, methods, or events will be mentioned in each object section.

Common Collection Properties

Name	Returns	Description
Application	Application	Read-only. Returns a reference to the owning Application of the current object. Excel, in this case
Count	Long	Read-only. Returns the number of objects in the collection
Creator	Long	Read-only. Returns a Long number that describes whether the object was created in Excel or not
Parent	Object	The Parent object is the owning object of the collection object. For example, Workbooks.Parent returns a reference to the Application object

Common Collection Methods

Name	Returns	Parameters	Description
Item	Single	Index as Variant	Returns the object from the collection with the Index value specified by the Index parameter. The Index value may also specify a unique string key describing one of the objects in the collection

Common Object Properties

Objects also have some common properties. To avoid redundancy the common properties and methods of all objects are listed next. They will be mentioned in each object description as existing but are only defined here.

Name	Returns	Description
Application	Application	Read-only. Returns a reference to the owning Application of the current object—Excel, in this case
Creator	Long	Read-only. Returns a Long number that describes whether the object was created in Excel or not
Parent	Object	Read-only. The owning object of the current object. For example, Characters. Parent may return a reference to a Range object, since a Range object is one of the possible owners of a Characters object

Excel Objects and Their Properties, Methods and Events

The objects are listed in alphabetical order. Each object has a general description of the object and possible parent objects. This is followed by a table format of each of the object's properties, methods, and events. The last section of each object describes some code examples of the object's use.

Addin Object and the Addins Collection

The Addins collection holds all of the Addin objects available to Excel. Each Addin object represents an Addin shown in Excel's Addins dialog box under the Tools ⇨ Add-Ins... menu. The Addin must be installed (AddIn.Installed = True) to be able to use it in the current session. Examples of available Addin objects in Excel include the Analysis Toolpack, the MS Query Addin, and the Conditional Sum Wizard.

The Add method of the Addins collection can be used to add a new Addin to the collection. The Add method requires a FileName to be specified (usually with a XLL or XLA file extension). The Count property of the Addins collection returns the number of Addins that are available for use by the current Excel session.

Addin Common Properties

The Application, Creator, and Parent properties are defined at the beginning of this Appendix.

Addin Properties

Name	Returns	Description
CLSID	String	Read-only. Returns a unique identifier for the Addin
FullName	String	Read-only. Returns the full path and filename of the associated Addin
Installed	Boolean	Set/Get whether the Addin can be used in the current session
Name	String	Read-only. Returns the file name of the Addin
Path	String	Read-only. Returns the full file path of the associated Addin
Title	String	Read-only. This hidden property returns the string shown in the Addin Manager dialog box

Example: AddIn Object and the AddIns Collection

This example ensures that the Analysis Toolpack is installed:

```
Sub UseAnalysisToolpack()
    Dim oAddin As AddIn
    'Make sure the Analysis Toolpack is installed
    For Each oAddin In AddIns
        If oAddin.Name = "ANALYS32.XLL" Then
            oAddin.Installed = True
        End If
    Next
End Sub
```

Note that instead of looping through the Addins collection, you could follow the online Help and use:

```
AddIns("Analysis Toolpak").Installed = True
```

Unfortunately, this approach may not work with a non-English User-Interface language, if the Addin's title has been localised.

Adjustments Object

The `Adjustments` object holds a collection of numbers used to move the adjustment "handles" of the parent `Shape` object. Each `Shape` object can have up to eight different adjustments. Each specific adjustment handle can have one or two adjustments associated with it depending on if it can be moved both horizontally and vertically (two) or in just one dimension. Adjustment values are between 0 and 1 and hence are percentage adjustments—the absolute magnitude of a 100% change is defined by the shape being adjusted.

Adjustments Common Properties

The `Application`, `Creator`, and `Parent` properties are defined at the beginning of this Appendix.

Adjustments Properties

Name	Returns	Description
Count	Long	Read-only. Returns the number of adjustments values associated with the parent `Shape` object
Item	Single	Parameters: `Index As Long`. Set/Get the adjustment value or values indicated by the `Index` parameter

Example: Adjustments Object

This example draws a block arrow on the sheet, then modifies the dimensions of the arrow head:

```
Sub AddArrow()
    Dim oShp As Shape

    'Add an arrow head to the sheet
    Set oShp = ActiveSheet.Shapes.AddShape( _
                msoShapeRightArrow, 10, 10, 100, 50)

    'Set the 'head' of the arrow to start 30% of the way across
    'and the 'shaft' to start 40% of the way down.
    oShp.Adjustments(1) = 0.3      'Left/right
    oShp.Adjustments(2) = 0.4      'Up/down
End Sub
```

AllowEditRange Object and the AllowEditRanges Collection

The `AllowEditRange` object represents a range of cells on a worksheet that can still be edited when protected. Each `AllowEditRange` object can have permissions set for any number of users on your network and can have a separate password.

Be aware of the `Locked` property of the `Range` object when using this feature. When you unlock cells, then protect the worksheet, you are allowing any user access to those cells, regardless of the `AllowEditRange` objects. When each `AllowEditRange` object's cells are locked, any user can still edit them unless you assign a password or add users and deny them permission without using a password.

The `AllowEditRanges` collection represents all `AllowEditRange` objects that can be edited on a protected worksheet. See the `AllowEditRange` object for more details.

AllowEditRanges Collection Properties

Name	Returns	Description
Count	Long	Read-only. Returns the number of `AllowEditRange` objects that are contained in the area
Item	AllowEdit Range	Parameter: `Index As Variant`. Returns a single `AllowEditRange` object in the `AllowEditRanges` collection

AllowEditRanges Collection Methods

Name	Returns	Parameters	Description
Add	AllowEdit Range	Title As String, Range As Range, [Password]	Adds an `AllowEditRange` object to the `AllowEditRanges` collection

AllowEditRange Properties

Name	Returns	Description
Range	Range	Returns a subset of the ranges that can be edited on a protected worksheet
Title	String	Returns or sets the title of the Web page when the document is saved as a Web page
Users	UserAccess List	Returns the list of users who are allowed access to the protected range on a worksheet

AllowEditRange Methods

Name	Returns	Parameters	Description
ChangePassword		Password As String	Sets the password for a range that can be edited on a protected worksheet
Delete			Deletes the object
Unprotect		[Password]	Removes any protection from a sheet or workbook

Example: AllowEditRange Object

The following routine loops through a list of range names in a worksheet and adds an `AllowEditRange` item for each one whose name begins with `"pc"`. It also denies access to the `pcNetSales` range to all but one user, who can only edit the range with a password.

```
Sub CreateAllowRanges()

    Dim lPos As Long
    Dim nm As Name
    Dim oAllowRange As AllowEditRange
    Dim sName As String

    With wksAllowEditRange
        'Loop through the worksheet level
        ' range names
        For Each nm In .Names
            'Store the name
            sName = nm.Name

            'Locate the position of the "!"
            lPos = InStr(1, sName, "!", vbTextCompare)

            'If there was an "!"...
            If lPos > 0 Then
                'Is there a "pc" just after the exclamation point
                'If so, it's a range we want to create an AllowEditRange
                ' object for
                If Mid(sName, lPos + 1, 2) = "pc" Then
                    'Make sure the cells are locked
                    'Unlocking them will allow any user
                    ' access to them.
                    nm.RefersToRange.Locked = True

                    'Pull out the worksheet reference (including the "!")
                    ' from the range name
                    sName = Right(sName, Len(sName) - lPos)

                    'Create the AllowEditRange
                    'Remove the old one if it exists
                    On Error Resume Next
                        Set oAllowRange = Nothing
                        Set oAllowRange = .Protection.AllowEditRanges(sName)
                    On Error GoTo 0
                    If Not oAllowRange Is Nothing Then oAllowRange.Delete
                    Set oAllowRange = .Protection.AllowEditRanges.Add(sName, _
                                                        nm.RefersToRange)
                    'If it's the sales range name...
                    If sName = "pcNetSales" Then
                        'Add a password, then
                        'Add a user and deny them from editing the range
                        ' without the password
                        oAllowRange.ChangePassword "pcnsw"
```

```
                              oAllowRange.Users.Add "RCR\AgamaOffice", False
                    End If
                End If
            End If
        Next nm
    End With

End Sub
```

Application Object

The `Application` object is the root object of the Excel Object Model. All the other objects in the Excel Object Model can only be accessed through the `Application` object. Many objects, however, are globally available. For example, the `ActiveSheet` property of the `Application` object is also available globally. That means that the active WorkSheet can be accessed by at least two ways: `Application.ActiveSheet` and `ActiveSheet`.

The `Application` object holds most of the application level attributes that can be set through the Tools ⇨ Options menu in Excel. For example, the `DefaultFilePath` is equivalent to the Default File Location text box in the General tab of the Options dialog box.

Many of the `Application` object's properties and methods are equivalent to things that can be set with the Options dialog box.

The `Application` object is also used when automating Excel from another application, such as Word. The `CreateObject` function, `GetObject` function or the `New` keyword can be used to create a new instance of an Excel `Application` object from another application. Please refer to Chapter 15 for examples of automation from another application.

The `Application` object can also expose events. However, `Application` events are not automatically available for use. The following three steps must be completed before `Application` events can be used:

Create a new class module, say, called `cAppObject`, and declare a `Public` object variable in a class, say, called `AppExcel`, to respond to events. For example:

```
Public WithEvents AppExcel As Excel.Application
```

Now the `Application` object events will be available in the class for the `AppExcel` object variable. Write the appropriate event handling code in the class. For example, if you wanted a message to appear whenever a worksheet is activated then you could write the following:

```
Private Sub AppExcel_SheetActivate(ByVal Sh As Object)
    'display worksheet name
    MsgBox "The " & Sh.Name & " sheet has just been activated."
End Sub
```

Finally, in a procedure in a standard module instantiate the class created above with a current `Application` object:

```
Private App As New cAppObject 'class with the above code snippets
Sub AttachEvents()
    Set App.AppExcel = Application
End Sub
```

The `EnableEvents` property of the `Application` object must also be set to `True` for events to trigger at the appropriate time.

Application Common Properties

The `Application`, `Creator`, and `Parent` properties are defined at the beginning of this Appendix.

Application Properties

Name	Returns	Description
ActiveCell	Range	Read-only. Returns the cell in the active sheet where the cursor is located
ActiveChart	Chart	Read-only. Returns the currently selected chart in the active workbook. If no chart is currently selected, nothing is returned
ActivePrinter	String	Set/Get the name of the printer currently being used
ActiveSheet	Object	Read-only. Returns the currently active sheet in the active workbook
ActiveWindow	Window	Read-only. Returns the currently selected Excel window, if any
ActiveWorkbook	Workbook	Read-only. Returns the workbook that is currently active, if any
AddIns	AddIns	Read-only. Returns the collection of Addins currently available for use in Excel
AlertBefore Overwriting	Boolean	Set/Get whether a message pops up any time an attempt to overwrite non-blank cells by a drag-and-drop operation is made
AltStartupPath	String	Set/Get the alternative startup file location folder for Excel
AnswerWizard	Answer Wizard	Read-only. Returns an object allowing manipulation of the Answer Wizard
ArbitraryXML Support Available	Boolean	Returns a Boolean value indicating if the XML feature is available in Excel
AskToUpdate Links	Boolean	Set/Get whether the user is prompted to update links whenever a workbook with links is opened

Name	Returns	Description
Assistant	Assistant	Read-only. Returns an object allowing manipulation of the Office Assistant
AutoCorrect	AutoCorrect	Read-only. Returns an object allowing modification of Excel's AutoCorrect features
AutoFormatAs You TypeReplace Hyperlinks	Boolean	Set/Get whether Excel automatically formats/creates hyperlinks as you type
Automation Security	Mso Automation Security	Set/Get the level of macro security used when Excel opens a file programmatically. This setting is independent of the macro security setting found in Security dialog box in the Tools ⇨ Macro command, though the msoAutomationSecurityByUI constant instructs the property to use the setting found there
AutoPercent Entry	Boolean	Set/Get whether Excel automatically adds a % sign when typing a number into a cell that has a Percentage format applied
AutoRecover	AutoRecover	Set/Get AutoRecover options such as Path and Time interval
Build	Long	Read-only. Returns the exact build number of Excel
Calculate BeforeSave	Boolean	Set/Get whether workbooks are calculated before they are saved to disk. This assumes that formula calculation is not set to automatic (Calculation property)
Calculation	Xl Calculation	Set/Get when calculations are made automatically, manually, or semi-automatically
Calculation InterruptKey	Xl Calculation Interrupt Key	Set/Get the key that can interrupt Excel when performing calculations
Calculation State	Xl Calculation State	Read-only. Indicates whether Excel calculations are in progress, pending, or done
Calculation Version	Long	Read-only. Returns the Excel version and calculation engine version used when the file was last saved
Caller	Variant	Read-only. Parameters: [Index]. Returns information describing what invoked the current Visual Basic code (for example, cell function, document event)
CanPlaySounds	Boolean	Read-only. Returns whether sound notes are heard in Excel. Property unused from Excel 2000 onwards

Continues

Name	Returns	Description
CanRecord Sounds	Boolean	Read-only. Returns whether sound notes can be recorded in Excel. Property unused from Excel 2000 onwards
Caption	String	Set/Get the caption that appears in the main Excel window
CellDragAnd Drop	Boolean	Set/Get whether dragging and dropping cells is possible
Cells	Range	Read-only. Returns all the cells in the active sheet
Charts	Sheets	Read-only. Returns all the charts in the active workbook
Clipboard Formats	Variant	Read-only. Parameters: [Index]. Returns an array of format values (XlClipboardFormat) that are currently in the clipboard
Columns	Range	Read-only. Returns all the columns in the currently active sheet
COMAddIns	COMAddIns	Read-only. Returns the collection of installed COM Addins
CommandBars	CommandBars	Read-only. Returns the collection of commandbars available to Excel
Command Underlines	XlCommand Underlines	Set/Get how commands are underlined in Excel. Used only on Macintosh systems
Constrain Numeric	Boolean	Set/Get whether only numbers and punctuation marks are recognized by handwriting recognition. Used only by Windows for Pen Computing
Control Characters	Boolean	Set/Get whether control characters are displayed for right-to-left languages. (Language support must be installed)
CopyObjects WithCells	Boolean	Set/Get whether objects (such as embedded objects) can be cut, copied, and sorted along with cell data
Cursor	XlMouse Pointer	Set/Get which mouse pointer is seen in Microsoft Excel
Cursor Movement	Long	Set/Get what type of cursor is used: visual or logical
CustomList Count	Long	Read-only. Returns the number of custom and built-in lists used in Excel (for example, Monday, Tuesday, Wednesday...)
CutCopyMode	XlCutCopy Mode	Set/Get whether a cut or copy operation is currently happening
DataEntry Mode	Long	Set/Get whether locked cells can be edited (xlOff for editing allowed, xlOn for editing of unlocked cells only, xlStrict for editing of unlocked cells only that can not be canceled by pressing Escape)
DDEAppReturn Code	Long	Read-only. Returns the result (confirmation/error) of the last DDE message sent by Excel

Name	Returns	Description
DefaultFile Path	String	Set/Get the default folder used when opening files
DefaultSave Format	XlFile Format	Set/Get the default file format used when saving files
DefaultSheet Direction	Long	Set/Get which direction new sheets will appear in Excel
DefaultWeb Options	DefaultWeb Options	Read-only. Returns an object allowing manipulation of the items associated with the Web Options dialog box
Decimal Separator	String	Set/Get the character used for the decimal separator. This is a global setting and will affect all workbooks when opened. Use Application UseSystemSeparators = True to globally reset custom separators
Dialogs	Dialogs	Read-only. Returns a collection of all the built-in dialog boxes
DisplayAlerts	Boolean	Set/Get whether the user is prompted by typical Excel messages (for example, "Save Changes to Workbook?") or no prompts appear and the default answer is always chosen
Display Clipboard Window	Boolean	Set/Get whether the Clipboard window is displayed. Used in Microsoft Office Macintosh Edition
Display Comment Indicator	XlComment DisplayMode	Set/Get how Excel displays cell comments and indicators
Display Document Action TaskPane	Boolean	Set to True to display the Document Actions task pane
DisplayExcel4 Menus	Boolean	Set/Get whether Excel display Excel 4.0 menus
Display Formula Bar	Boolean	Set/Get whether the formula bar is displayed
DisplayFull Screen	Boolean	Set/Get whether the Excel is in full screen mode
Display Function ToolTips	Boolean	Set/Get whether ToolTips for arguments appear in the cell when typing a function
DisplayInsert Options	Boolean	Set/Get whether the Insert Options drop-down button appears next to a range after inserting cells, rows, or columns

Continues

Name	Returns	Description
DisplayNote Indicator	Boolean	Set/Get whether comments inserted into cells have a little note indicator at the top right corner of the cell
DisplayPaste Options	Boolean	Set/Get whether the Paste Options drop-down button appears next to a range after a paste operation. This is an Office XP setting and therefore affects all other Office applications that use this feature
DisplayRecent Files	Boolean	Set/Get whether the most recently opened files are displayed under the File menu
DisplayScroll Bars	Boolean	Set/Get whether scroll bars are displayed for all open workbooks in the current session
Display StatusBar	Boolean	Set/Get whether the status bar is displayed
EditDirectly InCell	Boolean	Set/Get whether existing cell text can be modified directly in the cell. Note that cell text can still be overwritten directly
Enable Animations	Boolean	Set/Get whether adding and deleting cells, rows, and columns are animated
EnableAuto Complete	Boolean	Set/Get whether the AutoComplete feature is enabled
EnableCancel Key	XlEnable CancelKey	Set/Get how an Excel macro reacts when the user tries to interrupt the macro (for example, *Ctrl-Break*). This can be used to disable any user interruption, send any interruption to the error handler, or to just stop the code (default). *Use with care*
EnableEvents	Boolean	Set/Get whether events are triggered for any object in the Excel Object Model that supports events
EnableSound	Boolean	Set/Get whether sounds are enabled for Excel
ErrorChecking Options	Error Checking Options	Set/Get error checking properties such as BackgroundChecking, IndicatorColorIndex, and InconsistentFormula. These options mirror rules found on the Error Checking tab of the Tools ⇨ Options command
Excel4Intl MacroSheets	Sheets	Read-only. Returns the collection of sheets containing Excel 4 International macros
Excel4Macro Sheets	Sheets	Read-only. Returns the collection of sheets containing Excel 4 macros
ExtendList	Boolean	Set/Get whether formatting and formulas are automatically added when adding new rows or columns to the existing lists of rows or columns

Name	Returns	Description
FeatureInstall	MsoFeature Install	Set/Get how Excel reacts when an Excel feature is accessed that is not installed (through the interface or programmatically)
FileConverters	Variant	Read-only. Parameters: [Index1], [Index2]. Returns an array of all the file converters available in Excel
FileDialog	FileDialog	Parameters: [fileDialogType]. Returns an object that represents an instance of one of several types of file dialog boxes
FileFind	IFind	Returns an object that can be used to search for files. Used in Microsoft Office Macintosh Edition
FileSearch	FileSearch	Read-only. Returns an object that can be used to search for files
FindFormat	FindFormat	Set/Get search criteria for the types of cell formats to look for when using the Find and Replace methods
FixedDecimal	Boolean	Set/Get whether any numbers entered in the future will have the decimal points specified by FixedDecimalPlaces
FixedDecimal Places	Long	Set/Get the decimals places used for any future numbers
GenerateGet PivotData	Boolean	Set/Get whether Excel can get PivotTable report data
Height	Double	Set/Get the height of Excel's main application window. The value cannot be set if the main window is maximized or minimized
Hinstance	Long	Read-only. Returns the instance handle of the instance that is calling Excel. Used mainly by other custom applications like those written in Visual Basic
Hwnd	Long	Read-only. Returns the top-level window handle of the Excel window. Used mainly by other custom applications like those written in Visual Basic
IgnoreRemote Requests	Boolean	Set/Get whether remote requests through DDE are ignored
Interactive	Boolean	Set/Get whether Excel accepts keyboard and mouse input
International	Variant	Read-only. Parameters: [Index]. Returns international settings for Excel. Use the XlApplicationInternational constants as one of the values of Index

Continues

Name	Returns	Description
Iteration	Boolean	Set/Get whether Excel will iterate through and calculate all the cells in a circular reference trying to resolve the circular reference. Use with MaxIterations and MaxChange
Language Settings	Language Settings	Read-only. Returns an object describing the language settings in Excel
Left	Double	Set/Get the left edge of Excel's main application window. The value cannot be set if the main window is maximized or minimized
LibraryPath	String	Read-only. Returns the directory where Addins are stored
MailSession	Variant	Read-only. Returns the hexadecimal mail session number or Null if mail session is active
MailSystem	XlMail System	Read-only. Returns what type of mail system is being used by the computer (for example, xlMapi, xlPowerTalk)
MapPaperSize	Boolean	Set/Get whether documents formatted for another country's/region's standard paper size (for example, A4) are automatically adjusted so that they're printed correctly on your country's/region's standard paper size (for example, Letter)
Math Coprocessor Available	Boolean	Read-only. Returns whether a math coprocessor is available
MaxChange	Double	Set/Get the minimum change between iterations of a circular reference before iterations stop
MaxIterations	Long	Set/Get the maximum number of iterations allowed for circular references before iterations stop
MemoryFree	Long	Read-only. Returns how much free memory (in bytes) Excel can use
MemoryTotal	Long	Read-only. Returns how much total memory (in bytes) is available to Excel (including memory in use)
MemoryUsed	Long	Read-only. Returns how much memory (in bytes) Excel is using
MouseAvailable	Boolean	Read-only. Returns whether the mouse is available
MoveAfter Return	Boolean	Set/Get whether the current cell changes when the user hits Enter
MoveAfter Return Direction	XlDirection	Set/Get which direction the cursor will move when the user hits *Enter* changing the current cell
Name	String	Read-only. Returns "Microsoft Excel"

Name	Returns	Description
Names	Names	Read-only. Returns the collection of defined names in an active workbook
Network Templates Path	String	Read-only. Returns the location on the network where the Excel templates are kept, if any
NewWorkbook	Start Working	Read-only. Returns a `StartWorking` object
ODBCErrors	ODBCErrors	Read-only. Returns the collection of errors returned by the most recent query or `PivotTable` report that had an ODBC connection
ODBCTimeout	Long	Set/Get how long, in seconds, an ODBC connection will be kept before timing out
OLEDBErrors	OLEDBErrors	Read-only. Returns the collection of errors returned by the most recent query or `PivotTable` report that had an OLEDB connection
OnWindow	String	Set/Get the procedure that is executed every time a window is activated by the end user
Operating System	String	Read-only. Returns the name and version of the operating system
Organization Name	String	Read-only. Returns the organization name as seen in the About Microsoft Excel dialog box
Path	String	Read-only. Returns the path where Excel is installed
PathSeparator	String	Read-only. Returns a backslash ("\") on a PC or a colon ":" on a Macintosh
PivotTable Selection	Boolean	Set/Get whether PivotTables use structured selection. For example, when selecting a `Row` field title the associated data is selected with it
Previous Selections	Variant	Read-only. Parameters: `[Index]`. Returns an array of the last four ranges or named areas selected by using Name dialog box or `Goto` feature
ProductCode	String	Read-only. Returns the Guid for Excel
PromptFor SummaryInfo	Boolean	Set/Get whether the user is prompted to enter summary information when trying to save a file
Range	Range	Read-only. Parameters: `Cell1, [Cell2]`. Returns a `Range` object containing all the cells specified by the parameters
Ready	Boolean	Read-only. Determines whether the Excel application is ready

Continues

Name	Returns	Description
RecentFiles	RecentFiles	Read-only. Returns the collection of recently opened files
RecordRelative	Boolean	Read-only. Returns whether recorded macros use relative cell references (True) or absolute cell references (False)
ReferenceStyle	XlReference Style	Set/Get how cells are referenced: Letter-Number (for example, A1, A3) or RowNumber-ColumnNumber (for example, R1C1, R3C1)
Registered Functions	Variant	Read-only. Parameters: [Index1], [Index2]. Returns the array of functions and function details relating to external DLLs or code resources. Using Addins will add external DLLs to your workbook
ReplaceFormat	Replace Format	Set/Get replacement criteria for the types of cell formats to replace when using the Replace method
RollZoom	Boolean	Set/Get whether scrolling with a scroll mouse will zoom instead of scroll
Rows	Range	Read-only. Returns all the rows in the active sheet
RTD	RTD	Read-only. Returns a reference to a real-time date (RTD) object connected to a RTD Server
ScreenUpdating	Boolean	Set/Get whether Excel updates its display while a procedure is running. This property can be used to speed up procedure code by turning off screen updates (setting the property to False) during processing. Use with the ScreenRefresh method to manually refresh the screen
Selection	Object	Read-only. Returns whatever object is currently selected (for example, sheet, chart)
Sheets	Sheets	Read-only. Returns the collection of sheets in the active workbook
SheetsInNew Workbook	Long	Set/Get how many blank sheets are put in a newly created workbook
ShowChartTip Names	Boolean	Set/Get whether charts show the tip names over data points
ShowChartTip Values	Boolean	Set/Get whether charts show the tip values over data points
ShowStartup Dialog	Boolean	Set/Get whether the New Workbook task pane appears when loading the Excel application
ShowToolTips	Boolean	Set/Get whether ToolTips are shown in Excel
ShowWindowsIn Taskbar	Boolean	Set/Get whether each workbook is visible on the taskbar (True) or only one Excel item is visible in the taskbar (False)

Name	Returns	Description
SmartTag Recognizers	SmartTag Recognizers	Read-only. Returns a collection of SmartTag recognition engines (recognizers) currently being used in the application
Speech	Speech	Read-only. Allows access to the properties and methods used to programmatically control the Office speech tools
Spelling Options	Spelling Options	Read-only. Allows access to the spelling options of the application
StandardFont	String	Set/Get what font is used as the standard Excel font
Standard FontSize	Double	Set/Get what font size is used as the standard Excel font size (in points)
StartupPath	String	Read-only. Returns the folder used as the Excel startup folder
StatusBar	Variant	Set/Get the status bar text. Returns `False` if Excel has control of the status bar. Set to `False` to give control of the status bar to Excel
TemplatesPath	String	Read-only. Returns the path to the Excel templates
ThisCell	Range	Set/Get the cell in which a user-defined function is being called
ThisWorkbook	Workbook	Read-only. Returns the workbook that contains the currently running VBA code
Thousands Separator	String	Set/Get the character used for the thousands separator. This is a global setting and will affect all workbooks when opened. Use `Application UseSystemSeparators = True` to globally reset custom separators
Top	Double	Set/Get the top of Excel's main application window. The value cannot be set if the main window is maximized or minimized
Transition MenuKey	String	Set/Get what key is used to bring up Excel's menu. The forward slash key ("/") is the default
Transition MenuKeyAction	Long	Set/Get what happens when the Transition Menu key is pressed. Either Excel menus appear (`xlExcelMenu`) or the Lotus Help dialog box (`xlLotusHelp`) appears
Transition NavigKeys	Boolean	Set/Get whether the Transition Navigation keys are active. These provide different key combinations for moving and selecting within a worksheet
UsableHeight	Double	Read-only. Returns the vertical space available in Excel's main window, in points, that is available to a sheet's Window. The value will be 1 if there is no space available

Continues

Name	Returns	Description
UsableWidth	Double	Read-only. Returns the horizontal space available in Excel's main window, in points, that is available to a sheet's Window. This property's value will be invalid if no space is available. Check the value of the UsableHeight property to check to see if there is any space available (>1)
UsedObjects	UsedObjects	Read-only. Represents objects allocated in a workbook
UserControl	Boolean	Read-only. True if the current Excel session was started by a user, and False if the Excel session was started programmatically
UserLibrary Path	String	Read-only. Returns the location of Excel's COM Addins
UserName	String	Set/Get the user name in Excel. Note that this is the name shown in the General tab of the Options dialog box and *not* the current user's network ID or the name shown in the Excel splash screen
UseSystem Separators	Boolean	Set/Get whether the system operators in Excel are enabled. When set to False, you can use Application .DecimalSeparator and Application .ThousandsSeparator to override the system separators, which are located in the Regional Settings/Options applet in the Windows Control Panel
Value	String	Read-only. Returns "Microsoft Excel"
VBE	VBE	Read-only. Returns an object allowing manipulation of the Visual Basic Editor
Version	String	Read-only. Returns the version of Excel
Visible	Boolean	Set/Get whether Excel is visible to the user
Watches	Watches	Read-only. Returns a Watches object that represents all of the ranges that are tracked when a worksheet is calculated
Width	Double	Set/Get the width of Excel's main application window. The value cannot be set if the main window is maximized or minimized
Windows	Windows	Read-only. Returns all the Windows open in the current Excel session
WindowsForPens	Boolean	Read-only. Returns whether Excel is running in a Windows for Pen Computing environment
WindowState	XlWindow State	Set/Get whether the window is maximized, minimized, or in a normal state
Workbooks	Workbooks	Read-only. Returns all the open workbooks (not including Addins) in the current Excel session

Name	Returns	Description
Worksheet Function	Worksheet Function	Read-only. Returns an object holding all the Excel's worksheet functions that can be used in VBA
Worksheets	Sheets	Read-only. Returns all the worksheets in the active workbook

Application Methods

Name	Returns	Parameters	Description
Activate MicrosoftApp		Index As XlMS Application	Activates an application specified by XlMSApplication. Opens the application if it is not open. Acts in a similar manner as the GetObject function in VBA
AddChartAuto Format		Chart, Name As String, [Description]	Adds the formatting and legends of the Chart specified by the parameter to the custom chart types
AddCustomList		ListArray, [ByRow]	Adds the array of strings specified by ListArray to Excel's custom lists. The ListArray may also be a cell range
Calculate			Calculates all the formulas in all open workbooks that have changed since the last calculation. Only applicable if using manual calculation
CalculateFull			Calculates all the formulas in all open workbooks. Forces recalculation of every formula in every workbook, regardless of whether or not it has changed since the last calculation
CalculateFull Rebuild			Completely calculates all open workbooks, including all formulas with dependencies
CalculateFull Rebuild			Forces a full calculation of the data and rebuilds the dependencies for all open workbooks. Note that dependencies are the formulas that depend on other cells
CentimetersTo Points	Double	Centimeters As Double	Converts the Centimeters parameter to points where 1 cm = 28.35 points

Continues

659

Name	Returns	Parameters	Description
CheckAbort	—	[KeepAbort]	Stops any recalculations in an Excel application
CheckSpelling	Boolean	Word As String, [Custom Dictionary], [Ignore Uppercase]	Checks the spelling of the Word parameter and returns True if the spelling is correct or False if there are errors
Convert Formula	Variant	Formula, FromReference Style As XlReference Style, [ToReference Style], [ToAbsolute], [RelativeTo]	Converts the Formula parameter between R1C1 references and A1 references and returns the converted formula. Also can change the Formula parameter between relative references and absolute references using the ToReferenceStyle parameter and the XlReferenceStyle constants
DDEExecute		Channel As Long, String As String	Sends a Command to an application using DDE through the given Channel number. The properties starting with DDE are associated with the older technology, Dynamic Data Exchange, which was used to share data between applications
DDEInitiate	Long	App As String, Topic As String	Returns a channel number to use for DDE given an application name and the DDE topic
DDEPoke		Channel As Long, Item, Data	Sends Data to an item in an application using DDE through the given Channel number
DDERequest	Variant	Channel As Long, Item As String	Returns information given a specific DDE channel and a requested item
DDETerminate		Channel As Long	Closes the specified DDE channel
DeleteChart AutoFormat		Name As String	Deletes the custom chart type specified by the Name parameter
DeleteCustom List		ListNum As Long	Deletes the custom list specified by the list number. The first four lists are built-in to Excel and cannot be removed
DoubleClick			Triggered by a double-click to the active cell in the active sheet

Name	Returns	Parameters	Description
Evaluate	Variant	Name	Evaluates the Name string expression as if it were entered into a worksheet cell
ExecuteExcel4 Macro	Variant	String As String	Executes the Excel 4 macro specified by the String parameter and returns the results
FindFile	Boolean		Shows the Open dialog box allowing the user to choose a file to open. True is returned if the file opens successfully
GetCustomList Contents	Variant	ListNum As Long	Returns the custom list specified by the ListNum parameter as an array of strings
GetCustom ListNum	Long	ListArray	Returns the list number for the custom list that matches the given array of strings. A zero is returned if nothing matches
GetOpen Filename	Variant	FileFilter], [FilterIndex], [Title], [ButtonText], [MultiSelect]	The Open dialog box is displayed with the optional file filters, titles, and button texts specified by the parameters. The filename and path are returned from this method call. Optionally, can return an array of filenames if the MultiSelect parameter is True. Does not actually open the file
GetPhonetic	String	[Text]	Returns the phonetic text of the Japanese characters in the Text parameter. If no Text parameter is specified then an alternate phonetic text of the previous Text parameter is returned
GetSaveAs Filename	Variant	[Initial Filename], [FileFilter], [FilterIndex], [Title], [ButtonText]	The Save As dialog box is displayed with the optional default file name, file filters, titles, and button texts specified by the parameters. The filename and path are returned from this method call. Does not actually save the file
Goto		[Reference], [Scroll]	Selects the object specified by the Reference parameter and activates the sheet containing that object. The Reference parameter can be a cell, range, or the name of a VBA procedure. The Scroll parameter, if set to True, will scroll the selected object to the top left corner of the Excel window

Continues

Name	Returns	Parameters	Description
Help		[HelpFile], [HelpContext ID]	Displays the Help topic specified by the HelpContextID parameter in the Help file HelpFile
InchesTo Points	Double	Inches As Double	Converts the Inches parameter to points and returns the new value. (1 inch = 72 points)
InputBox	Variant	Prompt As String, [Title], [Default], [Left], [Top], [HelpFile], [HelpContext ID], [Type]	Displays a simple input box very similar to a standard VBA one. However, the [Type] parameter can be used to set the return type to a formula (0), number (1), text (2), Boolean (4), cell reference (8), an error value (16), or an array of values (64)
Intersect	Range	Arg1 As Range, Arg2 As Range, [Arg3], ... [Arg30]	Returns the intersection or overlap of the ranges specified by the parameters as a Range object
MacroOptions		[Macro], [Description], [HasMenu], [MenuText], [HasShortcut Key], [ShortcutKey], [Category], [StatusBar], [HelpContext ID], [HelpFile]	Allows modification of macro attributes such as the name, description, shortcut key, category and associated Help file. Equivalent to the Macro Options dialog box
MailLogoff			Logs off the current MAPI mail session (for example, Exchange, Outlook)
MailLogon		[Name], [Password], [DownloadNew Mail]	Logs on to the default MAPI mail client (for example, Exchange, Outlook). Credentials such as name and password can be specified
NextLetter	Workbook		Used in Macintosh systems with PowerTalk mail extensions to open the oldest unread workbook from the In Tray. Generates an error in Windows
OnKey		Key As String, [Procedure]	Executes the procedure specified by the Procedure parameter whenever the keystroke or key combination described in the Key parameter is pressed

Name	Returns	Parameters	Description
OnRepeat		Text As String, Procedure As String	Specifies the text to appear by the Edit ⇨ Repeat menu item and the procedure to run when the user chooses Edit ⇨ Repeat
OnTime		EarliestTime, Procedure As String, [LatestTime], [Schedule]	Chooses a procedure to run at the time specified by the EarliestTime parameter. Uses the LatestTime parameter to specify a time range
OnUndo		Text As String, Procedure As String	Specifies the text to appear by the Edit ⇨ Undo menu item and the procedure to run when the user chooses Edit ⇨ Undo
Quit			Shuts down Microsoft Excel
RecordMacro		[BasicCode], [XlmCode]	If the user is currently recording a macro, running this statement will put the code specified in the BasicCode parameter into the currently recording macro
RegisterXLL	Boolean	Filename As String	Loads the code resource specified by the Filename parameter and registers all the functions and procedures in that code resource
Repeat			Repeats the last user action made. Must be the first line of a procedure
Run	Variant	[Macro], [Arg1], [Arg2], ... [Arg30]	Runs the macro or procedure specified by the Macro parameter. Can also run Excel 4.0 macros with this method
SaveWorkspace		[Filename]	Saves the current workspace to the Filename parameter
SendKeys		Keys, [Wait]	Sends the keystrokes in the Keys parameter to Microsoft Excel user interface
SetDefault Chart		[FormatName], [Gallery]	Set the default chart type added when programmatically adding a chart. The FormatName parameter can be a built-in chart type or a custom chart type name
Undo			Undoes the last action done with the user interface

Continues

Name	Returns	Parameters	Description
Union	Range	Arg1 As Range, Arg2 As Range, [Arg3], ... [Arg30]	Returns the union of the ranges specified by the parameters
Volatile		[Volatile]	Sets the function that currently contains this statement to be either volatile (Volatile parameter to True) or not. A volatile function will be recalculated whenever the sheet containing it is calculated, even if its input values have not changed
Wait	Boolean	Time	Pauses the macro and Excel until the time in the Time parameter is reached

Application Events

Name	Parameters	Description
NewWorkbook	Wb As Workbook	Triggered when a new workbook is created. The new workbook is passed into the event
SheetActivate	Sh As Object	Triggered when a sheet is activated (brought up to front of the other sheets). The activated sheet is passed into the event
SheetBefore DoubleClick	Sh As Object, Target As Range, Cancel As Boolean	Triggered when a sheet is about to be double-clicked. The sheet and the potential double-click spot are passed into the event. The double-click action can be canceled by setting the Cancel parameter to True
SheetBefore RightClick	Sh As Object, Target As Range, Cancel As Boolean	Triggered when a sheet is about to be right-clicked. The sheet and the potential right-click spot are passed into the event. The right-click action can be canceled by setting the Cancel parameter to True
Sheet Calculate	Sh As Object	Triggered when a sheet is recalculated passing in the recalculated sheet
SheetChange	Sh As Object, Target As Range	Triggered when a range on a sheet is changed, for example, by clearing the range, entering data, deleting rows or columns, pasting data etc. *Not* triggered when inserting rows/columns
Sheet Deactivate	Sh As Object	Triggered when a sheet loses focus. Passes in the sheet

Name	Parameters	Description
SheetFollow Hyperlink	Sh As Object, Target As Hyperlink	Triggered when the user clicks a hyperlink on a sheet. Passes in the sheet and the clicked hyperlink
SheetPivot TableUpdate	ByVal Sh As Object, Target As PivotTable	Triggered by an update of the PivotTable report. Passes in the sheet and the PivotTable report
Sheet Selection Change	Sh As Object, Target As Range	Triggered when the user selects a new cell in a worksheet. Passes in the new range and the sheet where the change occurred
Window Activate	Wb As Workbook, Wn As Window	Triggered when a workbook window is activated (brought up to the front of other workbook windows). The workbook and the window are passed in
Window Deactivate	Wb As Workbook, Wn As Window	Triggered when a workbook window loses focus. The related workbook and the window are passed in
WindowResize	Wb As Workbook, Wn As Window	Triggered when a workbook window is resized. The resized workbook and window are passed into the event. Not triggered when Excel is resized
Workbook Activate	Wb As Workbook	Triggered when a workbook is activated (brought up to the front of other workbook windows). The workbook is passed in
WorkbookAddin Install	Wb As Workbook	Triggered when an Addin is added to Excel that is also a workbook. The Addin workbook is passed into the event
WorkbookAddin Uninstall	Wb As Workbook	Triggered when an Addin is removed to Excel that is also a workbook. The Addin workbook is passed into the event
Workbook BeforeClose	Wb As Workbook, Cancel As Boolean	Triggered just before a workbook is closed. The workbook is passed into the event. The closure can be canceled by setting the Cancel parameter to True
Workbook BeforePrint	Wb As Workbook, Cancel As Boolean	Triggered just before a workbook is printed. The workbook is passed into the event. The printing can be canceled by setting the Cancel parameter to True
Workbook BeforeSave	Wb As Workbook, SaveAsUI As Boolean, Cancel As Boolean	Triggered just before a workbook is saved. The workbook is passed into the event. The saving can be canceled by setting the Cancel parameter to True. If the SaveAsUI is set to True then the Save As dialog box appears

Continues

Name	Parameters	Description
Workbook Deactivate	Wb As Workbook	Triggered when a workbook loses focus. The related workbook and the window are passed in
WorkbookNew Sheet	Wb As Workbook, Sh As Object	Triggered when a new sheet is added to a workbook. The workbook and new sheet are passed into the event
WorkbookOpen	Wb As Workbook	Triggered when a workbook is opened. The newly opened workbook is passed into the event
WorkbookPivot TableClose Connection	ByVal Wb As Workbook, Target As PivotTable	Triggered when a PivotTable report connection is closed. The selected workbook and PivotTable report are passed in to this event
WorkbookPivot TableOpen Connection	ByVal Wb As Workbook, Target As PivotTable	Triggered when a PivotTable report connection is opened. The selected workbook and PivotTable report are passed in to this event

Example: Application Object

This example demonstrates how to use `Application.GetOpenFilename` to get the name of a file to open. The key to using this function is to assign its return value to a `Variant` data type:

```
Sub UsingGetOpenFilename()
    Dim sFilter As String
    Dim vaFile As Variant
    'Build a filter list. If you omit the space before the first comma,
    'Excel will not display the pattern, (*.New)
    sFilter = "New Files (*.New) ,*.new," & _
              "Old Files (*.Old) ,*.old," & _
              "All Files (*.*) ,*.*"
    'Display the File Open dialog, putting the result in a Variant
    vaFile = Application.GetOpenFilename(FileFilter:=sFilter, FilterIndex:=1, _
                             Title:="Open a New or Old File",
MultiSelect:=False)
    'Did the user cancel?
    If vaFile <> False Then
        MsgBox "You want to open " & vaFile
    End If
End Sub
'The Application object is used to store and retrieve custom sort orders:
Sub UsingACustomSortOrder()
    Dim vaSortList As Variant
    Dim iListNum As Integer
    Dim bAdded As Boolean
    'Sort the products in this order
    vaSortList = Array("Oranges", "Mangoes", "Apples", "Pears")
    'Get the number of this custom sort, if it exists.
    iListNum = Application.GetCustomListNum(vaSortList)
    'If it doesn't exist, we get zero, NOT an error
    If iListNum = 0 Then
```

```
        'Create a custom list for this sort order
        Application.AddCustomList vaSortList

        'And retrieve its number (the last one!)
        iListNum = Application.CustomListCount

        'Remember that we added it - delete it after use
        bAdded = True
    End If
    'Sort the range using this custom list. Note that we have to
    'add 1 to the list number, as 'ordercustom:=1' means to use the
    'standard sort order (which is not a custom list)
    ActiveCell.CurrentRegion.Sort key1:=ActiveCell, _
                            ordercustom:=iListNum + 1, header:=xlYes
    'If we added the list, remove it.
    If bAdded Then Application.DeleteCustomList iListNum
End Sub
```

Chapter 3 in the first section of this book contains more examples of using the Application object.

Areas Collection

The Areas collection holds a collection of Range objects. Each Range object represents a block of cells (for example, A1:A10) or a single cell. The Areas collection can hold many ranges from different parts of a workbook. The parent of the Areas collection is the Range object.

Areas Common Properties

The Application, Creator, and Parent properties are defined at the beginning of this Appendix.

Areas Properties

Name	Returns	Description
Count	Long	Read-only. Returns the number of Range objects that are contained in the area
Item	Range	Parameter: Index As Long. Returns a single Range object in the Areas collection. The Index parameter corresponds to the order of the ranges selected

Example: Areas Collection

When using a Range containing a number of different areas, we cannot use code like rgRange.Cells(20).Value if the twentieth cell is not inside the first area in the range. This is because Excel only looks at the first area, implicitly doing rgRange.Areas(1).Cells(20).Value, as this example shows—with a function to provide a workaround:

```
Sub TestMultiAreaCells()
    Dim oRNg As Range
    'Define a multi-area range
```

```
        Set oRNg = Range("D2:F5,H2:I5")
        'The 12th cell should be F5.
        MsgBox "Rng.Cells(12) is " & oRNg.Cells(12).Address & _
                vbCrLf & "Rng.Areas(1).Cells(12) is " & _
                        oRNg.Areas(1).Cells(12).Address & _
                vbCrLf & "MultiAreaCells(Rng, 12) is " & _
                        MultiAreaCells(Rng, 12).Address

        'The 13th cell of the multi-area range should be H2,
        'that is the first cell in the second area.
        MsgBox "Rng.Cells(13) is " & oRNg.Cells(13).Address & _
                vbCrLf & "Rng.Areas(1).Cells(13) is " & _
                        oRNg.Areas(1).Cells(13).Address & _
                vbCrLf & "MultiAreaCells(Rng, 13) is " & _
                        MultiAreaCells(Rng, 13).Address
End Sub
Function MultiAreaCells(oRange As Range, iCellNum As Long) As Range
    Dim iTotCells As Long, oArea As Range
    'Loop through all the areas in the range,
    'starting again from the first if we run out
    Do
        For Each oArea In oRange.Areas
            'Is the cell we want in this area?
            If iTotCells + oArea.Cells.Count >= iCellNum Then

                'Yes - return it and exit the function
                Set MultiAreaCells = oArea.Cells(iCellNum - iTotCells)
                Exit Function
            Else
                'No - count up the cells we've checked and carry on
                iTotCells = iTotCells + oArea.Cells.Count
            End If
        Next
    Loop
End Function
```

AutoCorrect Object

The AutoCorrect object represents all of the functionality of the Excel's AutoCorrect features.

AutoCorrect Common Properties

The Application, Creator, and Parent properties are defined at the beginning of this Appendix.

AutoCorrect Properties

Name	Returns	Description
AutoExpand ListRange	Boolean	Set to True to enable automatic expansion in lists
Capitalize NamesOfDays	Boolean	Set/Get whether the first letter of days of the weeks are capitalized

Name	Returns	Description
CorrectCaps Lock	Boolean	Set/Get whether typing mistakes made with leaving the Caps Lock on are automatically corrected
Correct SentenceCap	Boolean	Set/Get whether the first letter of a sentence is capitalized if accidentally left in small case
DisplayAuto Correct Options	Boolean	Displays / Hides the AutoCorrect Options button. The default value is True. This is an Office-wide setting. Changing it in Excel will also affect all the other Office applications
ReplaceText	Boolean	Set/Get whether Excel will automatically replace certain words with words from the AutoCorrect list
TwoInitial Capitals	Boolean	Set/Get whether Excel will automatically change the second letter of a word to lowercase if the first letter is uppercase

AutoCorrect Methods

Name	Returns	Parameters	Description
Add Replacement	Variant	What As String, Replacement As String	Adds a word (the What parameter) that will be automatically replaced with another word (the Replacement parameter) to the ReplacementList list array
Delete Replacement	Variant	What As String	Deletes a word from the ReplacementList list so that it does not get replaced with another word automatically
Replacement List	Variant	[Index]	Returns a multidimensional array of strings. The first column of the array holds the word that will be changed and the second column holds the replaced text. The Index parameter can be used to return an array containing a single word and its replacement

Example: AutoCorrect Object

This example uses the AutoCorrect object to find the replacement to use for a given word:

```
Sub TestAutoCorrect()
    MsgBox "'(c)' is replaced by " & UseAutoCorrect("(c)")
End Sub
```

```
Function UseAutoCorrect(ByVal sWord As String) As String
    Dim i As Integer
    Dim vaRepList As Variant
    Dim sReturn As String
    'Default to returning the word we were given
    sReturn = sWord
    'Get the replacement list into an array
    vaRepList = Application.AutoCorrect.ReplacementList
    'Go through the replacement list
    For i = LBound(vaRepList) To UBound(vaRepList)
        'Do we have a match?
        If vaRepList(i, 1) = sWord Then
            'Return the replacement text
            sReturn = vaRepList(i, 2)
            'Jump out of the loop
            Exit For
        End If
    Next
    'Return the word, or its replacement if it has one
    UseAutoCorrect = sReturn
End Function
```

AutoFilter Object

The `AutoFilter` object provides the functionality equivalent to the `AutoFilter` feature in Excel. This object can programmatically filter a range of text for specific types of rows, hiding the rows that do not meet the filter criteria. Examples of filters include top 10 rows in the column, rows matching specific values, and non-blank cells in the row. Using the Data ➪ Filter ➪ AutoFilter submenu in Excel can access this feature. The parent of the `AutoFilter` object is the `Worksheet` object (implying that a worksheet can have only one `AutoFilter`).

The `AutoFilter` object is used with the `AutoFilter` method of the `Range` object and the `AutoFilterType` property of the `Worksheet` object.

AutoFilter Common Properties

The `Application`, `Creator`, and `Parent` properties are defined at the beginning of this Appendix.

AutoFilter Properties

Name	Returns	Description
Filters	Filters	Read-only. Returns the collection of filters associated with the range that was autofiltered (for example, non-blank rows)
Range	Range	Read-only. Returns the group of cells that have an `AutoFilter` applied to it

Example: AutoFilter Object

This example demonstrates how to use the `AutoFilter`, `Filters` and `Filter` objects, by displaying the complete set of auto-filters currently in use:

```vba
Sub ShowAutoFilterCriteria()
    Dim oAF As AutoFilter, oFlt As Filter
    Dim sField As String
    Dim sCrit1 As String, sCrit2 As String
    Dim sMsg As String, i As Integer
    'Check if the sheet is filtered at all
    If ActiveSheet.AutoFilterMode = False Then
        MsgBox "The sheet does not have an AutoFilter"
        Exit Sub
    End If
    'Get the sheet's AutoFilter object
    Set oAF = ActiveSheet.AutoFilter
    'Loop through the Filters of the AutoFilter
    For i = 1 To oAF.Filters.Count
        'Get the field name from the first row
        'of the AutoFilter range
        sField = oAF.Range.Cells(1, i).Value
        'Get the Filter object
        Set oFlt = oAF.Filters(i)
        'If it is on...
        If oFlt.On Then
            'Get the standard filter criteria
            sMsg = sMsg & vbCrLf & sField & oFlt.Criteria1
            'If it's a special filter, show it
            Select Case oFlt.Operator
                Case xlAnd
                    sMsg = sMsg & " And " & sField & oFlt.Criteria2
                Case xlOr
                    sMsg = sMsg & " Or " & sField & oFlt.Criteria2
                Case xlBottom10Items
                    sMsg = sMsg & " (bottom 10 items)"
                Case xlBottom10Percent
                    sMsg = sMsg & " (bottom 10%)"
                Case xlTop10Items
                    sMsg = sMsg & " (top 10 items)"
                Case xlTop10Percent
                    sMsg = sMsg & " (top 10%)"
            End Select
        End If
    Next
    If sMsg = "" Then
        'No filters are applied, so say so
        sMsg = "The range " & oAF.Range.Address & " is not filtered."
    Else
        'Filters are applied, so show them
        sMsg = "The range " & oAF.Range.Address & " is filtered by:" & sMsg
    End If
    'Display the message
    MsgBox sMsg
End Sub
```

AutoRecover Object

This object allows access to the AutoRecover settings for the Excel application. These settings can be found on the Save tab of the Tools ➪ Options command and apply to all workbooks. Note that each workbook can choose whether or not to have AutoRecover applied to it—also located on the Save tab.

AutoRecover Common Properties

The Application, Creator, and Parent properties are defined at the beginning of this Appendix.

AutoRecover Properties

Name	Returns	Description
Enabled	Boolean	True if the AutoRecover object is enabled
Path	String	Set/Get the complete path to where the AutoRecover temporary files are saved
Time	Long	Set/Get the time interval for the AutoRecover object. Permissible values are integers from 1 to 120 minutes (default 10)

Example: AutoRecover Object

The following subroutine and function sets AutoRecover properties, then ensures that the workbook the code is in uses them:

```
Sub SetAutoRecoverOptions()
    'Set the AutoRecover options for the application
    ChangeAutoRecoverSettings True, "C:\Documents and Settings\AgamaOffice\My
Documents\Backup Files\AutoRecover\Excel", 2

    'Make sure this workbook uses them
    ThisWorkbook.EnableAutoRecover = True
End Sub
Function ChangeAutoRecoverSettings(Optional ByVal vEnable As Variant,
Optional ByVal vPath As Variant, Optional ByVal vTime As Variant)
    With Application.AutoRecover
        'Only set the property if a value was passed
        If Not IsMissing(vEnable) Then
            'Enable AutoRecover
            .Enabled = vEnable
        End If

        'Only set the property if a value was passed
        If Not IsMissing(vPath) Then
            'Change the path to a central backup files area
            .Path = vPath
        End If
```

```
                'Only set the property if a value was passed
            If Not IsMissing(vTime) Then
                'Save every AutoRecover file every 2 minutes
                .Time = vTime
            End If
        End With
    End Function
```

Axis Object and the Axes Collection

The Axes collection represents all of the Axes in an Excel chart. Each Axis object is equivalent to an axis in an Excel chart (for example, X axis, Y axis, etc.). The parent of the Axes collection is the Chart object.

Besides the typical properties and methods associated with a collection object, the Axes collection also has a Count property that returns the number of Axis objects in the collection. Also, unlike most other collections, the Item method of the Axes collection has two parameters: Type and AxisGroup. Use one of the xlAxisType constants for the Type parameter (xlValue, xlCategory, or xlSeriesAxis). The optional second parameter, AxisGroup, can take one of the xlAxisGroup constants (xlPrimary or xlSecondary).

Axis Common Properties

The Application, Creator, and Parent properties are defined at the beginning of this Appendix.

Axis Properties

Name	Returns	Description
AxisBetween Categories	Boolean	Set/Get whether the value axis crosses the category axis between categories (as in Column charts) or aligned with the category label (as in Line charts)
AxisGroup	XlAxis Group	Read-only. Returns whether the current axis is of the primary group (xlPrimary) or the secondary group (xlSecondary)
AxisTitle	AxisTitle	Read-only. Returns an object manipulating the axis title properties
BaseUnit	XlTime Unit	Set/Get what type of base units to have for a category axis. Use with BaseUnitIsAuto property. Fails on a value axis
BaseUnitIsAuto	Boolean	Set/Get whether the Excel automatically chooses the base units for a category axis. Fails on a value axis
Border	Border	Read-only. Returns the border's properties around the selected axis
CategoryNames	Variant	Set/Get the category names for the axis as a string array

Continues

Name	Returns	Description
CategoryType	XlCategory Type	Set/Get what type of axis to make the category axis. Fails on a value axis
Crosses	XlAxis Crosses	Set/Get where one axis crosses with the other axis: at the minimum value, maximum value, Excel automatic, or some custom value
CrossesAt	Double	Set/Get what value the other axis crosses the current one. Use when the Crosses property is xlAxisCrossesCustom
DisplayUnit	XlDisplay Unit	Set/Get what sort of unit to display for the axis (for example xlThousands)
DisplayUnit Custom	Double	Set/Get the value to display units if the DisplayUnit property is set to xlCustom
DisplayUnit Label	DisplayUnit Label	Read-only. Returns an object that manipulates a unit label for an axis
HasDisplay UnitLabel	Boolean	Set/Get whether a display unit label created using the DisplayUnit or DisplayUnitCustom property is visible on the axis
HasMajor Gridlines	Boolean	Set/Get whether major gridlines are displayed on the axis
HasMinor Gridlines	Boolean	Set/Get whether minor gridlines are displayed on the axis
HasTitle	Boolean	Set/Get whether the axis has a title
Height	Double	Read-only. Returns the height of the axis
Left	Double	Read-only. Returns the position of the axis from the left edge of the chart
Major Gridlines	Gridlines	Read-only. Returns an object to manipulate the major gridlines formatting associated
MajorTickMark	XlTickMark	Set/Get how the major ticks should look like (for example, inside the axis, outside the axis)
MajorUnit	Double	Set/Get what the value is between major blocks of a unit
MajorUnitIs Auto	Boolean	Set/Get whether the value of MajorUnit is set automatically
MajorUnit Scale	XlTimeUnit	Set/Get what type to set for the major units
MaximumScale	Double	Set/Get what the maximum value is for the axis
MaximumScale IsAuto	Boolean	Set/Get whether the maximum value for the axis is determined automatically

Name	Returns	Description
MinimumScale	Double	Set/Get what the minimum value is for the axis
MinimumScale IsAuto	Boolean	Set/Get whether the minimum value for the axis is determined automatically
Minor Gridlines	Gridlines	Read-only. Returns an object to manipulate major gridline formatting associated
MinorTickMark	XlTickMark	Set/Get what the minor ticks should look like (for example, inside the axis, outside the axis)
MinorUnit	Double	Set/Get what the value is between minor blocks of a unit
MinorUnitIs Auto	Boolean	Set/Get whether the value of MinorUnit is set automatically
MinorUnitScale	XlTimeUnit	Set/Get what scale to set for the minor units
ReversePlot Order	Boolean	Set/Get whether the unit values on the axis should be reversed
ScaleType	XlScale Type	Set/Get the type of scale to use for the units: Linear or Logarithmic
TickLabel Position	XlTickLabel Position	Set/Get the position that the tick marks will appear in relation to the axis (for example, low, high)
TickLabels	TickLabels	Read-only. Returns an object to manipulate properties of the tick labels of an axis
TickLabel Spacing	Long	Set/Get how often to display the tick labels
TickMark Spacing	Long	Set/Get how often to display tick marks on an axis. Fails on a value axis
Top	Double	Read-only. Returns the top of the axis in relation to the top edge of the chart
Type	XlAxisType	Set/Get the type of axis (xlCategory, xlSeriesAxis, or xlValue)
Width	Double	Read-only. Returns the width of the axis

Axis Methods

Name	Returns	Parameters	Description
Delete	Variant		Deletes the axis from the axes collection
Select	Variant		Selects the axis on the chart

Example: Axis Object and the Axes Collection

This example sets the labels for the X-axis (independently of the data that's plotted) and applies some formatting:

```
Sub FormatXAxis()
    Dim oCht As Chart, oAxis As Axis
    'Get the first embedded chart on the sheet
    Set oCht = ActiveSheet.ChartObjects(1).Chart
    'Get it's X axis
    Set oAxis = oCht.Axes(xlCategory)
    'Format the X axis
    With oAxis
        .CategoryNames = Array("Item 1", "Item 2", "Item 3")
        .TickLabels.Orientation = 45
        .AxisBetweenCategories = True
        .ReversePlotOrder = False
        .MinorTickMark = xlTickMarkNone
    .MajorTickMark = xlTickMarkCross
    End With
End Sub
```

AxisTitle Object

The `AxisTitle` object contains the formatting and words associated with a chart axis title. The parent of the `AxisTitle` object is the `Axis` object. The `AxisTitle` object is used in coordination with the `HasTitle` property of the parent `Axis` object. The `HasTitle` property must be `True` for a child `AxisTitle` object to exist.

AxisTitle Common Properties

The `Application`, `Creator`, and `Parent` properties are defined at the beginning of this Appendix.

AxisTitle Properties

Name	Returns	Description
AutoScaleFont	Variant	Set/Get whether the font size will change automatically if the parent chart changes sizes
Border	Border	Read-only. Returns the border's properties around the selected axis title
Caption	String	Set/Get the axis title's text
Characters	Characters	Read-only. Parameters: [Start], [Length]. Returns an object containing all the characters in the axis title. Allows manipulation on a character-by-character basis
Fill	ChartFillFormat	Read-only. Returns an object containing fill formatting options for the chart axis title

Name	Returns	Description
Font	Font	Read-only. Returns an object containing Font options for the chart axis title
Horizontal Alignment	Variant	Set/Get how you want the axis title horizontally aligned. Use the xlAlign constants
Interior	Interior	Read-only. Returns an object containing options to format the area in the chart title text area (for example, interior color)
Left	Double	Set/Get the distance from the left edge of the axis title text area to the chart's left edge
Name	String	Read-only. Returns the name of the axis title object
Orientation	Variant	Set/Get the angle of the text for the axis title. The value can be in degrees (from –90 to 90) or one of the XlOrientation constants
ReadingOrder	Long	Set/Get how the text is read (from left to right or right to left). Only applicable in appropriate languages
Shadow	Boolean	Set/Get whether the axis title has a shadow effect
Text	String	Set/Get the axis title's text
Top	Double	Set/Get the distance from the top edge of the axis title text area to the chart's top edge
Vertical Alignment	Variant	Set/Get how you want the axis title horizontally aligned. Use the xlVAlign constants

AxisTitle Methods

Name	Returns	Parameters	Description
Delete	Variant		Deletes the axis title from the axis
Select	Variant		Selects the axis title on the chart

Example: AxisTitle Object

This example ensures the X-axis has a title and sets the X-axis title's caption and formatting:

```
Sub FormatXAxisTitle()
    Dim oCht As Chart, oAT As AxisTitle
    'Get the first embedded chart on the sheet
    Set oCht = ActiveSheet.ChartObjects(1).Chart
    'Give the X axis a title
    oCht.Axes(xlCategory).HasTitle = True
    'Get the title
    Set oAT = oCht.Axes(xlCategory).AxisTitle
```

```
    'Format the title
    With oAT
        .AutoScaleFont = False
        .Caption = "X Axis Title"
        .Font.Bold = True
    End With
End Sub
```

Border Object and the Borders Collection

The Borders collection contains the properties associated with four borders around the parent object. Parent objects of the Borders collection are the Range and the Style object. A Borders collection always has four borders. Use the xlBordersIndex constants with the Item property of the Borders collection to access one of the Border objects in the collection.

Each Border object corresponds to a side or some sides of a border around a parent object. Some objects only allow access to all four sides of a border as a whole (for example, left side of border can not be accessed independently). The following objects are parents of the Border object (not the Borders collection): Axis, AxisTitle, ChartArea, ChartObject, ChartTitle, DataLabel, DataTable, DisplayUnitLabel, Downbars, DropLines, ErrorBars, Floor, GridLines, HiLoLines, LeaderLines, Legend, LegendKey, OleObject, PlotArea, Point, Series, SeriesLines, TrendLine, UpBars, and Walls. The following collections are also possible parents of the Border object: DataLabels, ChartObjects, and OleObjects.

The Borders collection has a few properties besides the typical collection attributes. They are listed in the following table.

Borders Collection Properties

Name	Returns	Description
Color	Variant	Set/Get the color for all four of the borders in the collection. Use the RGB function to set the color
ColorIndex	Variant	Set/Get the color for all four of the borders in the collection. Use the index number of a color in the current color palette to set the Color value
Count	Long	Read-only. Returns the number of Border objects in the collection. Always returns four
LineStyle	Variant	Set/Get the style of line to use for the borders (for example, xlDash). Use the xlLineStyle constants to set the value
Value	Variant	Set/Get the style of line to use for the borders (for example, xlDash). Use the xlLineStyle constants to set the value. Same as LineStyle
Weight	Variant	Set/Get how thick to make the borders in the collection (for example, xlThin, xlThick). Use the xlBorderWeight constants

Border Common Properties

The `Application`, `Creator`, and `Parent` properties are defined at the beginning of this Appendix.

Border Properties

Name	Returns	Description
Color	Variant	Set/Get the color for a border. Use the RGB function to set the color
ColorIndex	Variant	Set/Get the color for a border. Use the index number of a color in the current color palette to set the color value
LineStyle	Variant	Set/Get the style of line to use for a border (for example, xlDash). Use the xlLineStyle constants to set the value
Weight	Variant	Set/Get how thick to make the border (for example, xlThin, xlThick). Use the xlBorderWeight constants

Example: Border Object and the Borders Collection

Applies a 3D effect to a range:

```
Sub TestFormat3D()
    'Format the selected range as 3D sunken
    Format3D Selection
End Sub
Sub Format3D(oRange As Range, Optional bSunken As Boolean = True)
    'Using the range...
    With oRange
        'Surround it with a white border
        .BorderAround Weight:=xlMedium, Color:=RGB(255, 255, 255)

        If bSunken Then
            'Sunken, so make the left and top dark-grey
            .Borders(xlEdgeLeft).Color = RGB(96, 96, 96)
            .Borders(xlEdgeTop).Color = RGB(96, 96, 96)
        Else
            'Raised, so make the right and bottom dark-grey
            .Borders(xlEdgeRight).Color = RGB(96, 96, 96)
            .Borders(xlEdgeBottom).Color = RGB(96, 96, 96)
        End If
    End With
End Sub
```

CalculatedFields Collection

See the *PivotField Object*, *PivotFields Collection*, and the *CalculatedFields Collection* section.

CalculatedItems Collection

See the *PivotItem Object, PivotItems Collection,* and the *CalculatedItems Collection* section.

CalculatedMember Object and the CalculatedMembers Collection

The `CalculatedMembers` collection is a collection of all the `CalculatedMember` objects on the specified `PivotTable`. Each `CalculatedMember` object represents a calculated field, or calculated item.

CalculatedMembers Common Properties

The `Application`, `Creator`, and `Parent` properties are defined at the beginning of this Appendix.

CalculatedMembers Collection Properties

Name	Returns	Description
Count	Long	Returns the number of objects in the collection
Item	Calculated Member	Parameter: Index As Variant. Returns a single CalculatedMember object in the CalculatedMembers collection

CalculatedMembers Collection Methods

Name	Returns	Parameters	Description
Add	Calculated Member	Name As String, Formula As String, [SolveOrder], [Type]	Adds a CalculatedField or CalculatedItem to a PivotTable

CalculatedMember Common Properties

The `Application`, `Creator`, and `Parent` properties are defined at the beginning of this Appendix.

CalculatedMember Properties

Name	Returns	Description
Formula	String	Returns the CalculatedMember's formula in multidimensional expressions (MDX) syntax
IsValid	Boolean	Indicates whether the specified CalculatedMember object has been successfully instantiated with the OLAP provider during the current session. Will return True even if the PivotTable is not connected to its data source

Name	Returns	Description
Name	String	Set/Get the name of the object
SolveOrder	Long	Gets the value of the CalculatedMember's MDX (multidimensional expression) argument (default is zero)
SourceName	String	Gets the object's name as it appears in the original source data for the specified PivotTable report
Type	Xl Calculated MemberType	Gets the CalculatedMember object's type

CalculatedMember Methods

Name	Returns	Parameters	Description
Delete			Deletes the selected object

Example: CalculatedMembers Collection and CalculatedMember Object

The following routine returns information about each CalculatedMember from the data source used by the PivotTable on the wksPivotTable worksheet. It returns messages if either the data source is not an OLAP type or if there are no CalculatedMembers:

```
Sub ReturnCalculatedMembers()
    Dim lIcon As Long, lCount As Long
    Dim ptTable As PivotTable
    Dim oCalcMember As CalculatedMember
    Dim oCalcMembers As CalculatedMembers
    Dim sInfo As String
    'Set the reference to the PivotTable
    Set ptTable = wksPivotTable.PivotTables("WroxSales1")
    On Error Resume Next
        Set oCalcMembers = ptTable.CalculatedMembers
    On Error GoTo 0

    'Did we return a reference to Calculated Members?
    If Not oCalcMembers Is Nothing Then
        'If there's at least one Calculated Member...
        If oCalcMembers.Count > 0 Then
            'Initialize the Count
            ' and message variables
            lCount = 1
            lIcon = vbInformation

            'Loop through each Calculated Member
            ' And store its name and formula
            For Each oCalcMember In oCalcMembers
                With oCalcMember
```

```
                          sInfo = sInfo & lCount & ") " & .Name & ": " & .Formula
                          lCount = lCount + 1
                      End With
                  Next oCalcMember

          Else
              'It's a valid OLAP data source, but no
              ' Calculated Members are there
              lIcon = vbExclamation
              sInfo = "No Calculated Members found."
          End If
      Else
          'oCalcMembers returned nothing. Not an OLAP data source
          lIcon = vbCritical
          sInfo = "Could not retrieve Calculated Members. Data Source may not be
  OLAP type."
      End If

      MsgBox sInfo, lIcon, "Calculated Members"

  End Sub
```

CalloutFormat Object

The CalloutFormat object corresponds to the line callouts on shapes. The parent of the CalloutFormat object is the Shape object.

CalloutFormat Common Properties

The Application, Creator, and Parent properties are defined at the beginning of this Appendix.

CalloutFormat Properties

Name	Returns	Description
Accent	MsoTriState	Set/Get whether a vertical accent bar is used to separate the callout box from the line
Angle	MsoCallout AngleType	Set/Get the angle of the callout line in relation to the callout box
AutoAttach	MsoTriState	Set/Get whether a callout line automatically changes where it is attached to the callout box depending on the where the line is pointing (left or right of the callout box)
AutoLength	MsoTriState	Read-only. Return whether the callout line changes size automatically if the multisegment callout box is moved
Border	MsoTriState	Set/Get whether the callout box has a border around it
Drop	Single	Read-only. Returns the distance from the callout box to the spot where the callout line is pointing

Name	Returns	Description
DropType	MsoCallout DropType	Read-only. Returns the spot on the callout box that attaches to the callout line
Gap	Single	Set/Get the distance between the callout line end and the callout box
Length	Single	Read-only. Returns the length of the first part of a callout line. AutoLength must be False
Type	MsoCallout Type	Set/Get the type of line callout used

CalloutFormat Methods

Name	Returns	Parameters	Description
Automatic Length			Sets the AutoLength property to True
CustomDrop		Drop As Single	Uses the Drop parameter to set the distance from the callout box to the spot where the callout line is pointing
CustomLength		Length As Single	Sets the length of the first part of a callout line to the Length parameter and sets AutoLength to False
PresetDrop		DropType As MsoCallout DropType	Sets the spot on the callout box that attaches to the callout line using the DropType parameter

Example: CalloutFormat Object

This example applies the same formatting to all the callouts in a worksheet:

```
Sub FormatAllCallouts()
    Dim oShp As Shape
    Dim oCF As CalloutFormat
    'Loop through all the shapes in the sheet
    For Each oShp In ActiveSheet.Shapes
        'Is this a callout?
        If oShp.Type = msoCallout Then
            'Yes - set its text box to autosize
            oShp.TextFrame.AutoSize = True

            'Get the CalloutFormat object
            Set oCF = oShp.Callout

            'Format the callout
            With oCF
                .Gap = 0
                .Border = msoFalse
```

```
                    .Accent = msoTrue
                    .Angle = msoCalloutAngle30
                    .PresetDrop msoCalloutDropCenter
                End With
            End If
        Next
    End Sub
```

CellFormat Object

Represents both the FindFormat and ReplaceFormat property settings of the Application object, which are then used by the Find and Replace methods (respectively) of the Range object.

Set the FindFormat property settings before using the Find method to search for cell formats within a range. Set the ReplaceFormat property settings if you want the Replace method to replace formatting in cells. Any values specified in the What or Replacement arguments of either the Find or Replace methods will involve an And condition. For example, if you are searching for the word "wrox" and have set the FindFormat property to search for Bold, only those cells containing both will be found.

When searching for formats, make sure the SearchFormat argument of the Find method is set to True. When replacing formats, make sure the ReplaceFormat argument of the Replace method is set to True.

When you want to search for formats only, make sure the What argument of the Find method contains nothing. When you only want to replace formats, make sure the Replace argument of the Replace method contains nothing.

When replacing one format with another, make sure you explicitly specify formats you no longer want. For example, if you are searching for cells containing both bold and red and want to replace both formats with just blue, you'll need to make sure you set the bold property of the ReplaceFormat property to False. If you don't, you'll end up with blue and bold text.

When you need to search or replace using different format settings (or none at all), be sure to use the Clear method of either the CellFormat object—if you've declared a variable as such, or by directly accessing the Clear methods of the FindFormat and ReplaceFormat properties. Setting the SearchFormat and ReplaceFormat arguments to False for the Find and Replace methods will *not* prevent the FindFormat and/or ReplaceFormat settings from being used.

CellFormat Common Properties

The Application, Creator, and Parent properties are defined at the beginning of this Appendix.

CellFormat Properties

Name	Returns	Description
AddIndent	Variant	Gets whether the text in a cell is automatically indented when the text alignment is set to equal distribution either horizontally or vertically
Borders	Borders	Set/Get the search criteria based on the cell's border format

Name	Returns	Description
Font	Font	Set/Get the search criteria based on the cell's font format
Formula Hidden	Variant	Gets whether the formula will be hidden when the worksheet is protected. Returns Null if the specified range contains some cells with hidden formulas and some cells without
Horizontal Alignment	Variant	Set/Get the horizontal alignment for the specified object
IndentLevel	Variant	Set/Get the indent level for the cell or range
Interior	Interior	Set/Get the search criteria based on the cell's interior format
Locked	Variant	Set/Get whether cells in the range can be modified if the sheet is protected. Returns Null if only some of the cells in the range are locked
MergeCells	Variant	Returns True if the range or style contains merged cells
NumberFormat	Variant	Set/Get the number format associated with the cells in the range. Null if all the cells don't have the same format
NumberFormat Local	Variant	Set/Get the number format associated with the cells in the range in the language of the end user. Null if all the cells don't have the same format
Orientation	Variant	Set/Get the text orientation for the cell text. A value from −90 to 90 degrees can be specified, or use an XlOrientation constant
ShrinkToFit	Variant	Set/Get whether the cell text will automatically shrink to fit the column width. Returns Null if the rows in the range have different ShrinkToFit properties
Vertical Alignment	Variant	Set/Get how the cells in the range are vertically aligned. Use the XLVAlign constants
WrapText	Variant	Set/Get whether cell text wraps in the cell. Returns Null if the cells in the range contain different text wrap properties

CellFormat Methods

Name	Returns	Parameters	Description
Clear			Removes the criteria set in the FindFormat and ReplaceFormat properties

Example: CellFormat Object

The following routine searches through the used range in a worksheet replacing any cells containing both a Tahoma font and a light blue background with Arial light green background:

```
Sub ReplaceFormats()

    Dim oCellFindFormat As CellFormat
    Dim oCellReplaceFormat As CellFormat
    Dim rngReplace As Boolean, sMessage As String

    'Define variables for Find and Replace formats
    Set oCellFindFormat = Application.FindFormat
    Set oCellReplaceFormat = Application.ReplaceFormat

    'Set the Search criteria for the Find Formats
    With oCellFindFormat
        .Clear
        .Font.Name = "Tahoma"
        .Interior.ColorIndex = 34
    End With

    'Set the Replace criteria for the Replace Formats
    With oCellReplaceFormat
        .Clear
        .Font.Name = "Arial"
        .Interior.ColorIndex = 35
    End With

    'Perform the replace
    wksAllowEditRange.UsedRange.Replace What:="", Replacement:="", _
                                SearchFormat:=True, _
                                ReplaceFormat:=True

    'Reset the Find and Replace formats
    oCellFindFormat.Clear
    oCellReplaceFormat.Clear

End Sub
```

Characters Object

The `Characters` object allows access to individual characters in a string of text. Characters can have some of the visual properties modified with this object. Possible parents of the `Characters` object are the `AxisTitle`, `ChartTitle`, `DataLabel`, and the `Range` object. Each of the parent objects can use the `Characters([Start], [Length])` property to access a part of their respective texts. The `Start` parameter can specify which character to start at and the `Length` parameter can specify how many to take from the `Start` position.

Characters Common Properties

The `Application`, `Creator`, and `Parent` properties are defined at the beginning of this Appendix.

Characters Properties

Name	Returns	Description
Caption	String	Set/Get the full string contained in the Characters object
Count	Long	Read-only. Returns the number of characters in the object
Font	Font	Read-only. Returns an object allowing manipulation of the character's font
Phonetic Characters	String	Set/Get the phonetic characters contained in the Characters object
Text	String	Set/Get the full string contained in the Characters object

Characters Methods

Name	Returns	Parameters	Description
Delete	Variant		Deletes the characters in the collection
Insert	Variant	String As String	Replaces the characters in the collection with the specified string

Example: Characters Object

This example formats all the capital letters in the active cell in red with 16 point bold text:

```
Sub FormatCellCapitals()
    Dim sText As String
    Dim oChars As Characters
    Dim i As Integer
    'Get the text of the active cell
    sText = ActiveCell.Text
    'Loop through the text
    For i = 1 To Len(sText)
        'Is this character a capital letter?
        If Asc(Mid(sText, i, 1)) > 64 And Asc(Mid(sText, i, 1)) < 91 Then

            'Yes, so get the Characters object
            Set oChars = ActiveCell.Characters(i, 1)

            'Format the Characters object in Red, 16pt Bold.
            With oChars
                .Font.Color = RGB(255, 0, 0)
                .Font.Size = 16
                .Font.Bold = True
            End With
        End If
    Next
End Sub
```

Chart Object and the Charts Collection

The Charts collection holds the collection of chart sheets in a workbook. The Workbook object is always the parent of the Charts collection. The Charts collection only holds the chart sheets. Individual charts can also be embedded in worksheets and dialog sheets. The Chart objects in the Charts collection can be accessed using the Item property. Either the name of the chart can be specified as a parameter to the Item's parameter or an index number describing the position of the chart in the workbook (from left to right).

The Chart object allows access to all of the attributes of a specific chart in Excel. This includes chart formatting, chart types, and other charting properties. The Chart object also exposes events that can be used programmatically.

The Charts collection has a few properties and methods besides the typical collection attributes. These are listed in the following table.

Charts Collection Properties and Methods

Name	Returns	Description
Count	Long	Read-only. Returns the number of charts in the collection
HPageBreaks	HPageBreaks	Read-only. Returns a collection holding all the horizontal page breaks associated with the Charts collection
VPageBreaks	VPageBreaks	Read-only. Returns a collection holding all the vertical page breaks associated with the Charts collection
Visible	Variant	Set/Get whether the charts in the collection are visible. Also can set this to xlVeryHidden to not allow a user to make the charts in the collection visible
Add	Chart	Method. Parameters: [Before], [After], [Count] Adds a chart to the collection. You can specify where the chart goes by choosing which sheet object will be before the new chart object (Before parameter) or after the new chart (After parameter). The Count parameter decides how many charts are created
Copy		Method. Parameters: [Before], [After]. Adds a new copy of the currently active chart to the position specified at the Before or After parameters
Delete		Method. Deletes all the charts in the collection
Move		Method. Parameters: [Before], [After]. Moves the current chart to the position specified by the parameters

Name	Returns	Description
PrintOut		Method. Parameters: [From], [To], [Copies], [Preview], [ActivePrinter], [PrintToFile], [Collate], [PrToFileName].
		Prints out the charts in the collection. The printer, number of copies, collation, and whether a print preview is desired can be specified with the parameters. Also, the sheets can be printed to a file using the PrintToFile and PrToFileName parameters. The From and To parameters can be used to specify the range of printed pages
PrintPreview		Method. Parameters: [EnableChanges]. Displays the current chart in the collection in a print preview mode. Set the EnableChanges parameter to False to disable the Margins and Setup buttons, hence not allowing the viewer to modify the chart's page setup
Select		Method. Parameters: [Replace]. Selects the current chart in the collection

Chart Common Properties

The Application, Creator, and Parent properties are defined at the beginning of this Appendix.

Chart Properties

Name	Returns	Description
Area3DGroup	ChartGroup	Read-only. Returns a ChartGroup object containing the area chart group for a 3D chart
AutoScaling	Boolean	Set/Get whether Excel will stretch a 3D chart to match its 2D chart equivalent. RightAngleAxes must be true
Bar3DGroup	ChartGroup	Read-only. Returns a ChartGroup object containing the bar chart group for a 3D chart
BarShape	XlBarShape	Set/Get the basic shape used in 3D bar or column charts (for example, box, cylinder, pyramid, etc.)
ChartArea	ChartArea	Read-only. Returns the part of a chart containing axes, titles, legends, and formatting properties
ChartTitle	ChartTitle	Read-only. Returns an object manipulating the chart title's properties. Use with the HasTitle property
ChartType	XlChart Type	Set/Get what the type of chart is. This property determines what other chart properties are valid. For example, if the ChartType is set to xl3DBarClustered then the Bar3DGroup property can be used to access the chart group properties

Continues

Name	Returns	Description
CodeName	String	Read-only. Returns the programmatic name of the chart set at design-time in the VBA editor
Column3DGroup	ChartGroup	Read-only. Returns a ChartGroup object containing the column chart group for a 3D chart
Corners	Corners	Read-only. Returns an object holding all the corners of a 3D chart
DataTable	DataTable	Read-only. Returns an object to manipulate a chart's data table
DepthPercent	Long	Set/Get the percentage that a 3D chart depth (y-axis) is in relation to its width (x-axis)
Display BlanksAs	XlDisplay BlanksAs	Set/Get how blank cells are treated when plotting data in a chart. (for example, xlNotPlotted, xlZero, or xlInterpolated)
Elevation	Long	Set/Get what angle of elevation, in degrees, the viewer sees a 3D chart. Valid degrees vary depending on the type of 3D chart
Floor	Floor	Read-only. Returns an object with the formatting properties of the floor (base) of a 3D chart
GapDepth	Long	Set/Get the percentage depth of a data series in relation to the marker width
HasAxis	Variant	Parameters: [Index1], [Index2]. Set/Get whether axes exist for the chart. The parameters can be used to specify the axis type (using the xlAxisType constants with the first parameter) and the axis group (using the xlAxisGroup constants with the second parameter)
HasDataTable	Boolean	Set/Get whether a data table is associated (and therefore displayed). Use with the DataTable property
HasLegend	Boolean	Set/Get whether the chart has a legend. Use with the Legend property
HasPivot Fields	Boolean	Set/Get whether PivotChart controls are displayed for the PivotChart. Can only set to True if using a PivotChart report
HasTitle	Boolean	Set/Get whether the chart has a title. Use with the ChartTitle property
Height Percent	Long	Set/Get the percentage that a 3D chart height (z-axis) is in relation to its width (x-axis)
Hyperlinks	Hyperlinks	Read-only. Returns the collection of hyperlinks associated with the chart
Index	Long	Read-only. Returns the spot in the parent collection where the current chart is located

Name	Returns	Description
Legend	Legend	Read-only. Returns the formatting properties for a Legend. Use with the HasLegend property
Line3DGroup	ChartGroup	Read-only. Returns a ChartGroup object containing the line chart group for a 3D chart
MailEnvelope	MsoEnvelope	Set/Get the e-mail header for a document
Name	String	Set/Get the name of the chart
Next	Object	Read-only. Returns the next sheet in the workbook (from left to right) as an object
PageSetup	PageSetup	Read-only. Returns an object to manipulate the page setup properties for the chart
Perspective	Long	Sets the perspective, in degrees, that a 3D chart will be viewed as if the RightAngleAxes property is set to False
Pie3DGroup	ChartGroup	Read-only. Returns a ChartGroup object containing the pie chart group for a 3D chart
PivotLayout	Pivot Layout	Read-only. Returns an object to manipulate the location of fields for a PivotChart report
PlotArea	PlotArea	Read-only. Returns an object to manipulate formatting, gridlines, data markers and other visual items for the area where the chart is actually plotted. Inside the chart area
PlotBy	XlRowCol	Set/Get whether columns in the original data are used as individual data series (xlColumns) or if the rows in the original data are used as data series (xlRows)
PlotVisible Only	Boolean	Set/Get whether only visible cells are plotted or if invisible cells are plotted too (False)
Previous		Read-only. Returns the previous sheet in the workbook (from right to left) as an object
Protect Contents	Boolean	Read-only. Returns whether the chart and everything in it is protected from changes
ProtectData	Boolean	Set/Get whether the source data can be redirected for a chart
Protect Drawing Objects	Boolean	Read-only. Returns whether the shapes in the chart can be modified (ProtectDrawingObjects = False)
Protect Formatting	Boolean	Set/Get whether formatting can be changed for a chart

Continues

Name	Returns	Description
Protect GoalSeek	Boolean	Set/Get whether the user can modify the points on a chart with a mouse action
Protection Mode	Boolean	Read-only. Returns whether protection has been applied to the user interface. Even if a chart has user interface protection on, any VBA code associated with the chart can still be accessed
Protect Selection	Boolean	Set/Get whether parts of a chart can be selected and if shapes can be put into a chart
RightAngle Axes	Variant	Set/Get whether axes are fixed at right angles for 3D charts even if the perspective of the chart changes
Rotation	Variant	Set/Get what angle of rotation around the z-axis, in degrees, the viewer sees on a 3D chart. Valid degrees vary depending on the type of 3D chart
Scripts	Scripts	Read-only. Returns the collection of VBScript code associated with a chart (typically to later use on Web pages)
Shapes	Shapes	Read-only. Returns all the shapes contained by the chart
ShowWindow	Boolean	Set/Get whether an embedded chart is shown in a separate window and not as an embedded object in the worksheet
SizeWith Window	Boolean	Set/Get whether chart sheets automatically change sizes to match the window size
SurfaceGroup	ChartGroup	Read-only. Returns a ChartGroup object containing the surface chart group for a 3D chart
Tab	Tab	Read-only. Returns a Tab object for a chart or a worksheet
Visible	XlSheet Visibility	Set/Get whether the chart is visible or not. The Visible property can also be set to xlVeryHidden to make the chart inaccessible to the end user
Walls	Walls	Read-only. Returns an object to manipulate the formatting of the walls on a 3D chart
WallsAnd Gridlines2D	Boolean	Set/Get whether gridlines and walls are drawn in a 2D manner on a 3D bar charts, 3D stacked area charts, and 3D clustered column charts

Chart Methods

Name	Returns	Parameters	Description
Activate			Activates the chart making it the `ActiveChart`
ApplyCustom Type		ChartType As XlChartType, [TypeName]	Changes the chart type to the one specified in the `ChartType` parameter. If the `ChartType` is `xlUserDefined` then the second parameter can specify the custom chart type name
ApplyData Labels		[Type As Xl DataLabels Type], [Legend Key], [Auto Text], [Has LeaderLines], [ShowSeries Name], [Show CategoryName], [ShowValue], [Show Percentage], [ShowBubble Size], [Separator]	Sets the point labels for a chart. The `Type` parameter specifies whether no label, a value, a percentage of the whole, or a category label is shown. The legend key can appear by the point by setting the `LegendKey` parameter to `True`
AreaGroups	Object	[Index]	Returns either a single area chart group (`ChartGroup`) or a collection of area chart groups (`ChartGroups`) for a 2D chart
Axes	Object	Type, AxisGroup As XlAxisGroup	Returns the `Axis` object or the `Axes` collection for the associated chart. The type of axis and the axis group can be specified with the parameters
BarGroups	Object	[Index]	Returns either a single bar chart group (`ChartGroup`) or a collection of bar chart groups (`ChartGroups`) for a 2D chart
ChartGroups	Object	[Index]	Returns either a single chart group (`ChartGroup`) or a collection of chart groups (`ChartGroups`) for a chart
ChartObjects	Object	[Index]	Returns either a single embedded chart (`ChartObject`) or a collection of embedded charts (`ChartObjecs`) in a chart

Continues

Name	Returns	Parameters	Description
ChartWizard		[Source], [Gallery], [Format], [PlotBy], [Category Labels], [Series Labels], [HasLegend], [Title], [Category Title], [ValueTitle], [ExtraTitle]	A single method to modify the key properties associated with a chart. Specify the properties that you want to change. The Source specifies the data source. Gallery specifies the chart type. Format can specify one of the 10 built-in chart auto-formats. The rest of the parameters set up how the source will be read, the source of category labels, the source of the series labels, whether a legend appears, and the titles of the chart and the axis. If Source is not specified this method can only be used if the sheet containing the chart is active
CheckSpelling		[Custom Dictionary], [Ignore Uppercase], [Always Suggest], [SpellLang]	Checks the spelling of the text in the chart. A custom dictionary can be specified (CustomDictionary), all *uppercase* words can be ignored (IgnoreUppercase), and Excel can be set to display a list of suggestions (AlwaysSuggest)
ColumnGroups	Object	[Index]	Returns either a single column chart group (ChartGroup) or a collection of column chart groups (ChartGroups) for a 2D chart
Copy		[Before], [After]	Adds a new copy of the chart to the position specified at the Before or After parameters
CopyPicture		[Appearance As XlPicture Appearance], [Format As Xl-CopyPicture Format], [Size As XlPicture Appearance]	Copies the chart into the clipboard as a picture. The Appearance parameter can be used to specify whether the picture is copied as it looks on the screen or when printed. The Format parameter can specify the type of picture that will be put into the clipboard. The Size parameter is used when dealing with chart sheets to describe the size of the picture

Name	Returns	Parameters	Description
Create Publisher		Edition, Appearance As XlPicture Appearance, Size As XlPictureA ppearance, [Contains PICT], [Contains BIFF], [Contains RTF], [Contains VALU]	Used on the Macintosh to create an image of the chart in a standard format. Equivalent to CopyPicture on the PC
Delete			Deletes the chart
Deselect			Unselects the chart object
Doughnut Groups	Object	[Index]	Returns either a single doughnut chart group (ChartGroup) or a collection of doughnut chart groups (ChartGroups) for a 2D chart
Evaluate	Variant	Name	Evaluates the Name string expression as if it were entered into a worksheet cell
Export	Boolean	Filename As String, [FilterName], [Interactive]	Saves the chart as a picture (jpg or gif format) at the name specified by Filename
GetChart Element		x As Long, y As Long, ElementID As Long, Arg1 As Long, Arg2 As Long	Returns what is located at the coordinates x and y of the chart. Only the first two parameters are sent. Variables must be put in the last three parameters. After the method is run, the last three parameters can be checked for return values. The ElementID parameter will return one of the XlChartItem parameters. The Arg1 and Arg2 parameters may or may not hold data depending on the type of element
LineGroups	Object	[Index]	Returns either a single line chart group (ChartGroup) or a collection of line chart groups (ChartGroups) for a 2D chart

Continues

Name	Returns	Parameters	Description
Location	Chart	Where As XlChart Location, [Name]	Moves the chart to the location specified by the Where and Name parameters. The Where can specify if the chart is moving to become a chart sheet or an embedded object
Move		[Before], [After]	Moves the chart to the position specified by the parameters
OLEObjects	Object	[Index]	Returns either a single OLE Object (OLEObject) or a collection of OLE objects (OLEObjects) for a chart
Paste		[Type]	Pastes the data or pictures from the clipboard into the chart. The Type parameter can be used to specify if only formats, formulas or everything is pasted
PieGroups	Object	[Index]	Returns either a single pie chart group (ChartGroup) or a collection of pie chart groups (ChartGroups) for a 2D chart
PrintOut		[From], [To], [Copies], [Preview], [Active Printer], [PrintToFile], [Collate], [PrToFile Name]	Prints out the chart. The printer, number of copies, collation, and whether a print preview is desired can be specified with the parameters. Also, the sheets can be printed to a file by using the PrintToFile and PrToFileName parameters. The From and To parameters can be used to specify the range of printed pages
PrintPreview		[Enable Changes]	Displays the current chart in the collection in a print preview mode. Set the EnableChanges parameter to False to disable the Margins and Setup buttons, hence not allowing the viewer to modify the page setup

Name	Returns	Parameters	Description
Protect		[Password], [Drawing Objects], [Contents], [Scenarios], [User Interface Only]	Protects the chart from changes. A case-sensitive Password can be specified. Also, whether shapes are protected (DrawingObjects), the entire contents are protected (Contents), and whether only the user interface is protected (UserInterfaceOnly)
RadarGroups	Object	[Index]	Returns either a single radar chart group (ChartGroup) or a collection of radar chart groups (ChartGroups) for a 2D chart
Refresh			Refreshes the chart with the data source
SaveAs		Filename As String, [FileFormat], [Password], [WriteRes Password], [ReadOnly Recommended], [Create Backup], [AddToMru], [Text Codepage], [TextVisual Layout], [Local]	Saves the current chart into a new workbook with the file name specified by the Filename parameter. A file format, password, write-only password, creation of backup files, and other properties of the saved file can be specified with the parameters
Select		[Replace]	Selects the chart
Series Collection	Object	[Index]	Returns either a single series (Series) or a collection of series (SeriesCollection) for a chart
SetBackground Picture		FileName As String	Sets the chart's background to the picture specified by the FileName parameter
SetSourceData		Source As Range, [PlotBy]	Sets the source of the chart's data to the range specified by the Source parameter. The PlotBy parameter uses the XlRowCol constants to choose whether rows or columns of data will be plotted

Continues

Name	Returns	Parameters	Description
Unprotect		[Password]	Deletes the protection set up for a chart. If the chart was protected with a password, the password must be specified now
XYGroups	Object	[Index]	Returns either a single scatter chart group (ChartGroup) or a collection of scatter chart groups (ChartGroups) for a 2D chart

Chart Events

Name	Parameters	Description
Activate		Triggered when a chart is made to have focus
BeforeDouble Click	ElementID As XlChartItem, Arg1 As Long, Arg2 As Long, Cancel As Boolean	Triggered just before a user double-clicks a chart. The element that was double-clicked in the chart is passed in to event procedure as ElementID. The Arg1 and Arg2 parameters may or may not hold values depending on the ElementID. The double-click action can be canceled by setting the Cancel parameter to True
BeforeRight Click	Cancel As Boolean	Triggered just before a user right-clicks a chart. The right-click action can be canceled by setting the Cancel parameter to True
Calculate		Triggered after new or changed data is plotted on the chart
Deactivate		Triggered when the chart loses focus
DragOver		Triggered when a cell range is dragged on top of a chart. Typically used to change the mouse pointer or give a status message
DragPlot		Triggered when a cell range is dropped onto a chart. Typically used to modify chart attributes
MouseDown	Button As XlMouse Button, Shift As Long, x As Long, y As Long	Triggered when the mouse button is pressed down on a chart. Which mouse button is pressed is passed in with the Button parameter. The Shift parameter holds information regarding the state of the Shift, Ctrl, and Alt keys. The x and y parameters hold the x and y coordinates of the mouse pointer

Name	Parameters	Description
MouseMove	Button As XlMouse Button, Shift As Long, x As Long, y As Long	Triggered when the mouse is moved on a chart. Which mouse button is pressed is passed in with the Button parameter. The Shift parameter holds information regarding the state of the Shift, Ctrl, and Alt keys. The x and y parameters hold the x and y coordinates of the mouse pointer
MouseUp	Button As XlMouse Button, Shift As Long, x As Long, y As Long	Triggered when the mouse button is released on a chart. Which mouse button is pressed is passed in with the Button parameter. The Shift parameter holds information regarding the state of the Shift, Ctrl, and Alt keys. The x and y parameters hold the x and y coordinates of the mouse pointer
Resize		Triggered when the chart is resized
Select	ElementID As XlChartItem, Arg1 As Long, Arg2 As Long	Triggered when one of the elements in a chart is selected. The element that was selected in the chart is passed in to event procedure as ElementID. The Arg1 and Arg2 parameters may or may not hold values depending on the ElementID
SeriesChange	SeriesIndex As Long, PointIndex As Long	Triggered when the value of a point on a chart is changed. SeriesIndex returns the location of the series in the chart series collection. PointIndex returns the point location in the series

Example: Chart Object and the Charts Collection

This example creates a 3D chart from the table containing the active cell, formats it and saves a picture of it as a .jpg image:

```
Sub CreateAndExportChart()
    Dim oCht As Chart
    'Create a new (blank) chart
    Set oCht = Charts.Add
    'Format the chart
    With oCht
        .ChartType = xl3DColumnStacked
        'Set the data source and plot by columns
        .SetSourceData Source:=Selection.CurrentRegion, PlotBy:=xlColumns

        'Create a new sheet for the chart
        .Location Where:=xlLocationAsNewSheet
        'Size and shape matches the window it's in
        .SizeWithWindow = True
        'Turn of stretching of chart
        .AutoScaling = False
        'Set up a title
        .HasTitle = True
```

```
        .ChartTitle.Caption = "Main Chart"
        'No titles for the axes
        .Axes(xlCategory).HasTitle = False
        .Axes(xlSeries).HasTitle = False
        .Axes(xlValue).HasTitle = False
        'Set the 3D view of the chart
        .RightAngleAxes = False
        .Elevation = 50    'degrees
        .Perspective = 30 'degrees
        .Rotation = 20      'degrees
        .HeightPercent = 100
        'No data labels should appear
        .ApplyDataLabels Type:=xlDataLabelsShowNone
        'Save a picture of the chart as a jpg image
        .Export "c:\" & .Name & ".jpg", "jpg", False
    End With
End Sub
```

ChartArea Object

The `ChartArea` object contains the formatting options associated with a chart area. For 2D charts `ChartArea` includes the axes, axes titles and chart titles. For 3D charts, `ChartArea` includes the chart title and its legend. The part of the chart where data is plotted (plot area) is not part of the `ChartArea` object. Please see the `PlotArea` object for formatting related to the plot area. The parent of the `ChartArea` is always the `Chart` object.

ChartArea Common Properties

The `Application`, `Creator`, and `Parent` properties are defined at the beginning of this Appendix.

ChartArea Properties

Name	Returns	Description
AutoScaleFont	Variant	Set/Get whether the font size changes in the `ChartArea` whenever the `Chart` changes sizes
Border	Border	Read-only. Returns the border's attributes around the selected chart area
Fill	ChartFillFormat	Read-only. Returns an object to manipulate the fill attributes of the chart area
Font	Font	Read-only. Returns access to `Font` properties such as `Type` and `Size`
Height	Double	Set/Get the height of the chart area in points
Interior	Interior	Read-only. Returns an object containing options to format the inside area of the chart area (for example, interior color)

Name	Returns	Description
Left	Double	Set/Get the left edge of the chart area in relation to the chart in points
Name	String	Read-only. Returns the name of the chart area
Shadow	Boolean	Set/Get whether a shadow effect appears around the chart area
Top	Double	Set/Get the top edge of the chart area in relation to the chart in points
Width	Double	Set/Get the width of the chart area in points

ChartArea Methods

Name	Returns	Parameters	Description
Clear	Variant		Clears the chart area
ClearContents	Variant		Clears the data from the chart area without affecting formatting
ClearFormats	Variant		Clears the formatting from the chart area without affecting the data
Copy	Variant		Copies the chart area into the clipboard
Select	Variant		Activates and selects the chart area

Example: ChartArea Object

Apply formatting to the chart area:

```
Sub FormatChartArea()
    Dim oCA As ChartArea
    Set oCA = Charts(1).ChartArea
    With oCA
        .Border.LineStyle = xlContinuous
        .Fill.PresetTextured msoTextureCanvas
        .Fill.Visible = msoTrue
    End With
End Sub
```

ChartColorFormat Object

The ChartColorFormat object describes a color of the parent ChartFillFormat. For example, the ChartFillFormat object contains a BackColor property that returns a ChartColorFormat object to set the color.

ChartColorFormat Common Properties

The `Application`, `Creator`, and `Parent` properties are defined at the beginning of this Appendix.

ChartColorFormat Properties

Name	Returns	Description
RGB	Long	Read-only. Returns the red-green-blue value associated with color
SchemeColor	Long	Set/Get the color of `ChartColorFormat` using an index value corresponding to the current color scheme
Type	Long	Read-only. Returns whether the color is an RGB, mixed, or scheme type

Example: ChartColorFormat Object

This example sets a chart's fill pattern to built-in colour number 6, then displays the RGB values for the color.

```
Sub SetChartColorFormat()
    Dim oCCF As ChartColorFormat
    With Charts(3).PlotArea.Fill
        'Make sure we're using a Fill pattern
        .Visible = True

        'Get the ChartColorFormat for the ForeColor
        Set oCCF = .ForeColor
        'Set it to built-in colour #6
        oCCF.SchemeColor = 6

        'Read off colour 6's RGB values
        MsgBox "ForeColor #6 RGB is:" & vbCrLf & _
        "Red = " & ((oCCF.RGB And &HFF0000) / &H10000) & vbCrLf & _
        "Green = " & ((oCCF.RGB And &HFF00) / &H100) & vbCrLf & _
        "Blue = " & ((oCCF.RGB And &HFF))
    End With
End Sub
```

ChartFillFormat Object

The `ChartFillFormat` object represents the fill formatting associated with its parent object. This object allows manipulation of foreground colors, background colors and patterns associated with the parent object.

ChartFillFormat Common Properties

The `Application`, `Creator`, and `Parent` properties are defined at the beginning of this Appendix.

ChartFillFormat Properties

Name	Returns	Description
BackColor	ChartColor Format	Read-only. Returns the background color through the `ChartColorFormat` object
ForeColor	ChartColor Format	Read-only. Returns the foreground color through the `ChartColorFormat` object
GradientColor Type	Mso Gradient ColorType	Read-only. Returns what type of gradient fill color concept is used
GradientDegree	Single	Read-only. Returns how dark or light the gradient fill is
GradientStyle	Mso Gradient Style	Read-only. Returns the orientation of the gradient that is used
Gradient Variant	Long	Read-only. Returns the variant used for the gradient from the center
Pattern	MsoPattern Type	Read-only. Returns the pattern used for the fill, if any
PresetGradient Type	MsoPreset Gradient Type	Read-only. Returns the type of gradient that is used
PresetTexture	MsoPreset Texture	Read-only. Returns the non-custom texture of the fill
TextureName	String	Read-only. Returns the custom texture name of the fill
TextureType	MsoTexture Type	Read-only. Returns whether the texture is custom, preset, or mixed
Type	MsoFillType	Set/Get how transparent the fill is. From 0 (opaque) to 1 (clear)
Visible	MsoTriState	Read-only. Returns if the fill is a texture, gradient, solid, background, picture or mixed

ChartFillFormat Methods

Name	Returns	Parameters	Description
OneColor Gradient		Style As MsoGradient Style, Variant As Long, Degree As Single	Sets the style, variant and degree for a one-color gradient fill

Continues

Name	Returns	Parameters	Description
Patterned		Pattern As MsoPattern Type	Set the pattern for a fill
Preset Gradient		Style As MsoGradient Style, Variant As Long, Preset GradientType As MsoPreset GradientType	Choose the style, variant, and preset gradient type for a gradient fill
Preset Textured		PresetTexture As MsoPreset Texture	Set the preset texture for a fill
Solid			Set the fill to a solid color
TwoColor Gradient		Style As MsoGradient Style, Variant As Long	Set the style for a two-color gradient fill
UserPicture		[PictureFile], [Picture Format], [Picture StackUnit], [Picture Placement]	Set the fill to the picture in the PictureFile format
UserTextured		TextureFile As String	Set the custom texture for a fill with the TextureFile format

Example: ChartFillFormat Object

```
Sub FormatPlotArea()
    Dim oCFF As ChartFillFormat
    'Get the ChartFillFormat for the plot area
    Set oCFF = ActiveSheet.ChartObjects(1).Chart.PlotArea.Fill
    'Format the fill area
    With oCFF
        .TwoColorGradient Style:=msoGradientDiagonalUp, Variant:=1
        .Visible = True
        .ForeColor.SchemeColor = 6
        .BackColor.SchemeColor = 7
    End With
End Sub
```

ChartGroup Object and the ChartGroups Collection

The `ChartGroups` collection holds all the plotting information associated with the parent chart. A chart can have more than one `ChartGroup` associated with it. For example, a single chart can contain both a line and a bar chart associated with it. The `ChartGroups` property of the `Chart` object can be used to access the `ChartGroups` collection. Also, the `PieGroups` and `LineGroups` properties of the `Chart` object will also return only chart groups of pie chart types and line chart types, respectively.

Besides the typical properties associated with a collection, the `ChartGroups` collection also has a `Count` property that returns the number of `ChartGroup` objects in the collection. The parent of the `ChartGroups` collection or the `ChartGroup` object is the `Chart` object.

The `ChartGroup` object includes all of the plotted points associated with a particular chart type. A `ChartGroup` can hold many series of points (each column or row of the original data). Each series can contain many points (each cell of the original data). A `Chart` can contain more than one `ChartGroup` associated with it. The `Bar3DGroup`, `Column3DGroup`, `Line3DGroup`, `Pie3DGroup`, and the `SurfaceGroup` properties of the `Chart` object can be used to access a particular chart group of the corresponding chart type. The `AreaGroups`, `BarGroups`, `ColumnGroups`, `DoughnutGroups`, `LineGroups`, `PieGroups`, `RadarGroups`, and `XYGroups` methods of the `Chart` object can be used to return either a `ChartGroup` object or a `ChartGroups` collection.

ChartGroup Common Properties

The `Application`, `Creator`, and `Parent` properties are defined at the beginning of this Appendix.

ChartGroup Properties

Name	Returns	Description
AxisGroup	XlAxis Group	Set/Get whether the chart group is primary or secondary
BubbleScale	Long	Set/Get the percentage increase in the size of bubbles from the default size. Valid values from 0 to 300 percent. Valid only for bubble chart group
DoughnutHole Size	Long	Set/Get how large the hole in a doughnut chart group is. The value is a percentage of the size of the chart. Valid values from 10 to 90 percent. Valid only on doughnut chart groups
DownBars	DownBars	Read-only. Returns an object to manipulate the formatting options of down bars on a line chart group. Valid only on line chart groups. Use with the `HasUpDownBars` property
DropLines	DropLines	Read-only. Returns an object to manipulate the formatting options of drop lines on a line or area chart group. Valid only on line or area chart groups. Use with the `HasDropLines` property

Continues

Name	Returns	Description
FirstSlice Angle	Long	Set/Get what angle to use for the first slice of a pie or doughnut chart groups (the first data point plotted on the chart)
GapWidth	Long	Set/Get how big to make the gap between the columns of different data series. Also, when dealing with Bar of Pie charts or Pie of Pie charts, the GapWidth describes the distance from the main chart to the secondary chart (when the ChartType is xlPieOfPie or xlBarOfPie for the parent chart)
Has3Dshading	Boolean	Set/Get whether 3D shading is applied to the chart group visuals
HasDropLines	Boolean	Set/Get whether the chart group has drop lines. Use with the DownLines property
HasHiLoLines	Boolean	Set/Get whether the chart group has high-low lines. Use with the HiLoLines property
HasRadarAxis Labels	Boolean	Set/Get whether axis labels are put on a radar chart. Valid only for radar chart groups
HasSeries Lines	Boolean	Set/Get whether the chart group has series lines. Use with the SeriesLines property
HasUpDownBars	Boolean	Set/Get whether the chart group has up and down bars. Use with the DownBars and UpBars property
HiLoLines	HiLoLines	Read-only. Returns an object to manipulate the formatting of high-low lines in a line chart. Valid only for line charts
Index	Long	Read-only. Returns the spot in the parent collection that the current ChartGroup object is located
Overlap	Long	Set/Get whether bars and columns in a series will overlap each other or have a gap between them. A value from −100 to 100 can be specified where −100 will put a gap between each bar / column equal to the bar / column width and 100 will stack the bars / columns on top of each other. Valid only for 2D bar and column chart groups
RadarAxis Labels	TickLabels	Read-only. Returns an object to manipulate the formatting and labels associated with radar axis labels. Valid only for radar chart groups
SecondPlot Size	Long	Set/Get the percentage of size of the secondary part of a Pie of Pie or Bar of Pie chart group as a percentage of the main Pie

Name	Returns	Description
SeriesLines	SeriesLines	Read-only. Returns an object to manipulate the formatting associated with the series lines in a chart group. A series line connects same series of data appearing in a stacked column chart groups, stacked bar chart groups, Pie of Pie chart groups, or Bar of Pie chart groups. Use with the HasSeriesLines property
ShowNegative Bubbles	Boolean	Set/Get whether bubbles with negative data values are shown. Valid only on bubble chart groups
Size Represents	XlSizeRepresents	Set/Get whether the value of the data points are represented by the size or the area of bubbles on a bubble chart group. Valid only on bubble chart groups
SplitType	XlChartSplitType	Set/Get how the two charts in Pie of Pie chart group and Bar of Pie chart group are split up. For example, the chart can be split by percentage of value (xlSplitByPercentValue) or be split by value (xlSplitByValue)
SplitValue	Variant	Set/Get the value that will be combined in the main pie chart but split up in the secondary chart in a Pie of Pie or Bar of Pie chart group
UpBars	UpBars	Returns an object to manipulate the formatting options of up bars on a line chart group. Valid only on line chart groups. Use with the HasUpDownBars property
VaryBy Categories	Boolean	Set/Get whether different colors are assigned to different categories in a single series of a chart group. The chart can only contain a single data series for this to work

ChartGroup Methods

Name	Returns	Parameters	Description
Series Collection	Object	[Index]	Returns either a single series (Series) or a collection of series (SeriesCollection) for a chart

Example: ChartGroup Object and the ChartGroups Collection

This sets the gap width of all column groups in the chart to 10% and set each column to have a different color:

```
Sub FormatColumns()
    Dim oCht As Chart
    Dim oCG As ChartGroup
    For Each oCG In Charts(1).ColumnGroups
        oCG.GapWidth = 10
        oCG.VaryByCategories = True
    Next
End Sub
```

ChartObject Object and the ChartObjects Collection

The ChartObjects collection holds all of the embedded Chart objects in a worksheet, chart sheet, or dialog sheet. This collection does not include the actual chart sheets themselves. Chart sheets can be accessed through the Charts collection. Each Chart in the ChartObjects collection is accessed through the ChartObject object. The ChartObject acts as a wrapper for the embedded chart itself. The Chart property of the ChartObject is used to access the actual chart. The ChartObject object also contains properties to modify the formatting of the embedded chart (for example, Height, Width).

The ChartObjects collection contains many properties besides the typical collection attributes. These properties are listed next.

ChartObjects Collection Properties and Methods

Name	Returns	Description
Border	Border	Read-only. Returns the border's properties around the collection of chart objects
Count	Long	Read-only. Returns the number of ChartObject objects in the collection
Enabled	Boolean	Set/Get whether any macros associated with each ChartObject object in the collection can be triggered by the user
Height	Double	Set/Get the height of the ChartObject in the collection if there is only one object in the collection
Interior	Interior	Read-only. Returns an object containing options to format the inside area of all the Chart objects in the collection (for example, interior color)
Left	Double	Set/Get the distance from the left edge of the ChartObject to the left edge of the parent sheet. This property only works if there is only one ChartObject in the collection
Locked	Boolean	Set/Get whether the ChartObject is locked when the parent sheet is protected. This property only works if there is only one ChartObject in the collection

Name	Returns	Description
Placement	Variant	Set/Get how the ChartObject object is anchored to the sheet (for example, free floating, move with cells). Use the XlPlacement constants to set this property. This property only works if there is only one ChartObject in the collection
PrintObject	Boolean	Set/Get whether the embedded chart on the sheet will be printed when the sheet is printed. This property only works if there is only one ChartObject in the collection
Rounded Corners	Boolean	Set/Get whether the corners of the embedded chart are rounded (True) or right angles (False). This property only works if there is only one ChartObject in the collection
Shadow	Boolean	Set/Get whether a shadow appears around the embedded chart. This property only works if there is only one ChartObject in the collection
ShapeRange	ShapeRange	Read-only. Returns the ChartObjects in the collection as Shape objects
Top	Double	Set/Get the distance from top edge of the ChartObject to the top of the parent sheet. This property only works if there is only one ChartObject object in the collection
Visible	Boolean	Set/Get whether all the ChartObject objects in the collection are visible
Width	Double	Set/Get the width of the ChartObject in the collection if there is only one ChartObject object in the collection
Add	ChartObject	Method. Parameters: Left As Double, Top As Double, Width As Double, Height As Double. Adds a ChartObject to the collection of ChartObjects. The position of the new ChartObject can be specified by using the Left, Top, Width, and Height parameters
BringToFront	Variant	Method. Brings all the ChartObject objects in the collection to the front of all the other objects
Copy	Variant	Method. Copies all the ChartObject objects in the collection into the clipboard
CopyPicture	Variant	Method. Parameters: Appearance As XlPictureAppearance, Format As XlCopyPictureFormat. Copies the Chart objects in the collection into the clipboard as a picture. The Appearance parameter can be used to specify whether the picture is copied as it looks on the screen or when printed. The Format parameter can specify the type of picture that will be put into the clipboard

Continues

Name	Returns	Description
Cut	Variant	Method. Cuts all the ChartObject objects in the collection into the clipboard
Delete	Variant	Method. Deletes all the ChartObject objects in the collection into the clipboard
Duplicate		Method. Duplicates all the ChartObject objects in the collection into the parent sheet. (for example, if you had two ChartObject objects in the parent sheet and used this method then you would have four ChartObject objects)
Select	Variant	Method. Parameters: [Replace]. Selects all the ChartObject objects in the collection
SendToBack	Variant	Method. Brings the ChartObject objects in the collection to the back of other objects

ChartObject Common Properties

The Application, Creator, and Parent properties are defined at the beginning of this Appendix.

ChartObject Properties

Name	Returns	Description
Border	Border	Read-only. Returns the border's properties around the embedded chart
BottomRight Cell	Range	Read-only. Returns the single cell range located under the lower-right corner of the ChartObject
Chart	Chart	Read-only. Returns the actual chart associated with the ChartObject
Enabled	Boolean	Set/Get whether a macro associated with the ChartObject is capable of being triggered
Height	Double	Set/Get the height of embedded chart
Index	Long	Read-only. Returns the position of the ChartObject among the parent collection
Interior	Interior	Read-only. Returns an object containing options to format the inside area of the chart object (for example, interior color)
Left	Double	Set/Get the distance from the left edge of the ChartObject to the left edge of the parent sheet

Name	Returns	Description
Locked	Boolean	Set/Get whether the ChartObject is locked when the parent sheet is protected
Name	String	Set/Get the name of the ChartObject
Placement	Variant	Set/Get how the ChartObject object is anchored to the sheet (for example, free floating, move with cells). Use the XlPlacement constants to set this property
PrintObject	Boolean	Set/Get whether the embedded chart on the sheet will be printed when the sheet is printed
ProtectChart Object	Boolean	Set/Get whether the embedded chart can change sizes, be moved, or deleted from the parent sheet
Rounded Corners	Boolean	Set/Get whether the corners of the embedded chart are rounded (True) or right angles (False)
Shadow	Boolean	Set/Get whether a shadow appears around the embedded chart
ShapeRange	ShapeRange	Read-only. Returns the ChartObject as a Shape object
Top	Double	Set/Get the distance from top edge of the ChartObject to the top of the parent sheet
TopLeftCell	Range	Read-only. Returns the single cell range located above the top-left corner of the ChartObject
Visible	Boolean	Set/Get whether the ChartObject object is visible
Width	Double	Set/Get the width of embedded chart
ZOrder	Long	Read-only. Returns the position of the embedded chart among all the other objects on the sheet. The ZOrder also matches the location of the ChartObject in the parent collection

ChartObject Methods

Name	Returns	Parameters	Description
Activate	Variant		Makes the embedded chart the active chart
BringToFront	Variant		Brings the embedded chart to the front of all the other objects on the sheet. Changes the ZOrder
Copy	Variant		Copies the embedded chart into the clipboard

Continues

Name	Returns	Parameters	Description
CopyPicture	Variant	Appearance As XlPicture Appearance, Format As XlCopyPicture Format	Copies the Chart object into the clipboard as a picture. The Appearance parameter can be used to specify whether the picture is copied as it looks on the screen or when printed. The Format parameter can specify the type of picture that will be put into the clipboard. The Size parameter is used when dealing with chart sheets to describe the size of the picture
Cut	Variant		Cuts the embedded chart into the clipboard
Delete	Variant		Deletes the embedded chart from the sheet
Duplicate			Duplicates the embedded chart and places the duplicate in the same parent sheet
Select	Variant	[Replace]	Sets focus to the embedded chart
SendToBack	Variant		Sends the embedded object to the back of the other objects on the sheet

Example: ChartObject Object and the ChartObjects Collection

This example creates .jpg images from all the embedded charts in the active worksheet:

```
Sub ExportChartObjects()
    Dim oCO As ChartObject
    For Each oCO In ActiveSheet.ChartObjects
        'Export the chart as a jpg image, giving it the
        'name of the embedded object
        oCO.Chart.Export "c:\" & oCO.Name & ".jpg", "jpg"
    Next
End Sub
```

ChartTitle Object

The ChartTitle object contains all of the text and formatting associated with a chart's title. The parent of the ChartTitle object is the Chart object. This object is usually used along with the HasTitle property of the parent Chart object.

ChartTitle Common Properties

The Application, Creator, and Parent properties are defined at the beginning of this Appendix.

ChartTitle Properties

Name	Returns	Description
AutoScaleFont	Variant	Set/Get whether the font size will change automatically if the parent chart changes sizes
Border	Border	Read-only. Returns the border's properties around the selected chart title
Caption	String	Set/Get the chart title's text
Characters	Characters	Read-only. Parameters: [Start], [Length]. Returns an object containing all the characters in the chart title. Allows manipulation on a character-by-character basis
Fill	ChartFill Format	Read-only. Returns an object containing fill formatting options for the chart title
Font	Font	Read-only. Returns an object containing Font options for the chart title
Horizontal Alignment	Variant	Set/Get how the chart title is horizontally aligned. Use the xlAlign constants
Interior	Interior	Read-only. Returns an object containing options to format the area in the chart title text area (for example, interior color)
Left	Double	Set/Get the distance from the left edge of the chart title text area to the chart's left edge
Name	String	Read-only. Returns the name of the chart title object
Orientation	Variant	Set/Get the angle of the text for the chart title. The value can either be in degrees (from −90 to 90) or one of the XlOrientation constants
ReadingOrder	Long	Set/Get how the text is read (from left to right or right to left). Only applicable in appropriate languages
Shadow	Boolean	Set/Get whether the chart title has a shadow effect
Text	String	Set/Get the chart title's text
Top	Double	Set/Get the distance from the top edge of the chart title text area to the chart's top edge
Vertical Alignment	Variant	Set/Get how you want the chart title horizontally aligned. Use the xlVAlign constants

ChartTitle Methods

Name	Returns	Parameters	Description
Delete	Variant		Deletes the chart title from the chart
Select	Variant		Selects the chart title on the chart

Example: ChartTitle Object

This example adds a chart title to a chart and formats it:

```
Sub AddAndFormatChartTitle()
    Dim oCT As ChartTitle
    'Make sure the chart has a title
    Charts(1).HasTitle = True
    'Get the ChartTitle object
    Set oCT = Charts(1).ChartTitle
    'Format the chart title
    With oCT
        .Caption = "Hello World"
        .Font.Name = "Times New Roman"
        .Font.Size = 16
        .Characters(1, 1).Font.Color = RGB(255, 0, 0)
        .Characters(7, 1).Font.Color = RGB(255, 0, 0)
        .Border.LineStyle = xlContinuous
        .Border.Weight = xlThin
        .Shadow = True
    End With
End Sub
```

ColorFormat Object

The ColorFormat object describes a single color used by the parent object. Possible parents of the ColorFormat object are the FillFormat, LineFormat, ShadowFormat, and ThreeDFormat objects.

ColorFormat Common Properties

The Application, Creator, and Parent properties are defined at the beginning of this Appendix.

ColorFormat Properties

Name	Returns	Description
RGB	Long	Read-only. Returns the red-green-blue value associated with color
SchemeColor	Integer	Set/Get the color of the ColorFormat using an index value corresponding to the current color scheme

Name	Returns	Description
TintAndShade	Single	Set/Get a value that lightens or darkens the color of a specified shape. The values can be from −1 (darkest) to 1 (lightest). Zero is neutral
Type	MsoColor Type	Read-only. Returns whether the color is an RGB, mixed, or scheme type

Example: ColorFormat Object

Set the ForeColor of a shape's fill effect:

```
Sub FormatShapeColour()
   Dim oShp As Shape
   Dim oCF As ColorFormat
   Set oShp = ActiveSheet.Shapes(1)
   Set oCF = oShp.Fill.ForeColor
   oCF.SchemeColor = 53
End Sub
```

Comment Object and the Comments Collection

The Comments collection holds all of the cell comments in the parent Range object. Each Comment object represents a single cell comment.

Comment Common Properties

The Application, Creator, and Parent properties are defined at the beginning of this Appendix.

Comment Properties

Name	Returns	Description
Author	String	Read-only. Returns the name of the person who created the comment.
Shape	Shape	Read-only. Returns the comment box as a Shape object allowing manipulation of the comment box.
Visible	Boolean	Set/Get whether the comment is visible all the time (True) or only when the user hovers over the cell containing the comment.

Comment Methods

Name	Returns	Parameters	Description
Delete			Deletes the comment from the cell
Next	Comment		Returns the next cell comment in the parent collection

Continues

Name	Returns	Parameters	Description
Previous	Comment		Returns the previous cell comment in the parent collection
Text	String	[Text], [Start], [Overwrite]	Sets the text associated with the comment. The Text parameter is used to set the comment text. Use the Start parameter to specify the starting point for Text in the existing comment. Set the Overwrite parameter to True to overwrite existing text

Example: Comment Object and the Comments Collection

This example removes the user name added by Excel at the start of the comment and formats the comment to make it more readable:

```
Sub FormatComments()
    Dim oComment As Comment, i As Integer
    'Loop through all the comments in the sheet
    For Each oComment In ActiveSheet.Comments
        'Using the text of the comment...
        With oComment.Shape.TextFrame.Characters

            'Find and remove the user name inserted by Excel
            i = InStr(1, .Text, ":" & vbLf)
            If i > 0 Then
                .Text = Mid(.Text, i + 2)
            End If

            'Increase the font size
            With .Font
                .Name = "Arial"
                .Size = 10
                .Bold = False
            End With
        End With

        'Make the text frame auto-fit
        oComment.Shape.TextFrame.AutoSize = True
    Next
End Sub
```

ConnectorFormat Object

The ConnectorFormat object represents the connector line used between shapes. This connector line connects two shapes together. If either of the shapes are moved, the connector automatically readjusts so the shapes still look visually connected. The parent of a ConnectorFormat object is the Shape object.

ConnectorFormat Common Properties

The Application, Creator, and Parent properties are defined at the beginning of this Appendix.

ConnectorFormat Properties

Name	Returns	Description
Begin Connected	MsoTri State	Read-only. Returns whether the beginning of the connector has a shape attached. Use with `BeginConnectedShape`
Begin Connected Shape	Shape	Read-only. Returns the shape that is connected to the beginning of the connector. Use with `BeginConnected`
Begin Connection Site	Long	Read-only. Returns which connection site (connection spot) on the shape that the beginning of the connector is connected to. Use with `BeginConnected`
EndConnected	MsoTri State	Read-only. Returns whether the end of the connector has a shape attached. Use with `BeginConnectedShape`
EndConnected Shape	Shape	Read-only. Returns the shape that is connected to the end of the connector. Use with `EndConnected`
EndConnection Site	Long	Read-only. Returns which connection site (connection spot) on the shape that the end of the connector is connected to. Use with `EndConnected`
Type	Mso Connector Type	Set/Get what type of connector is being used (for example, `msoConnectorStraight`, `msoConnectorCurve`)

ConnectorFormat Methods

Name	Returns	Parameters	Description
BeginConnect		Connected Shape As Shape, Connection Site As Lon	Sets the beginning of the connector to the shape specified by the `ConnectedShape` parameter at the connection site specified by the `ConnectionSite` parameter
Begin Disconnect			Disconnects the shape that was at the beginning of the connection. This method does not move the connection line
EndConnect		Connected Shape As Shape, Connection Site As Lon	Sets the end of the connector to the shape specified by the `ConnectedShape` parameter at the connection site specified by the `ConnectionSite` parameter
End Disconnect			Disconnects the shape that was at the end of the connection. This method does not move the connection line

Example: ConnectorFormat Object

This example formats all fully-connected connectors as curved lines:

```
Sub FormatConnectors()
    Dim oShp As Shape
    Dim oCF As ConnectorFormat
    'Loop through all the Shapes in the sheet
    For Each oShp In ActiveSheet.Shapes
        'Is it a Connector?
        If oShp.Connector Then

            'Yes, so get the ConnectorFormat object
            Set oCF = oShp.ConnectorFormat

            'If the connector is connected at both ends,
            'make it a curved line.
            With oCF
                If .BeginConnected And .EndConnected Then
                    .Type = msoConnectorCurve
                End If
            End With
        End If
    Next
End Sub
```

ControlFormat Object

The ControlFormat object contains properties and methods used to manipulate Excel controls such as textboxes and listboxes. This object's parent is always the Shape object.

ControlFormat Common Properties

The Application, Creator, and Parent properties are defined at the beginning of this Appendix.

ControlFormat Properties

Name	Returns	Description
DropDown Lines	Long	Set/Get how many lines are displayed in the drop-down part of a combo box. Valid only if the control is a combo box
Enabled	Boolean	Set/Get whether the control is enabled
LargeChange	Long	Set/Get the value that is added or subtracted every time the user clicks inside the scroll bar area for a scroll box. Valid only if the control is a scroll box
LinkedCell	String	Set/Get the range where the results of the control are placed
ListCount	Long	Read-only. Returns the number of items in the list box of combo box. Valid only for list box and combo box controls
ListFill Range	String	Set/Get the range that contains the items for a list box or combo box. Valid only for list box and combo box controls

Name	Returns	Description
ListIndex	Long	Set/Get the item that is currently selected in the list box or combo box. Valid only for list box and combo box controls
LockedText	Boolean	Set/Get whether the control text can be changed if the workbook is locked
Max	Long	Set/Get the maximum value allowed for a scroll bar or spinner. Valid only on a control that is a scroll bar or spinner
Min	Long	Set/Get the minimum value allowed for a scroll bar or spinner. Valid only on a control that is a scroll bar or spinner
MultiSelect	Long	Set/Get how a list box reacts to user selection. The property can be set to xlNone (only one item can be selected), xlSimple (each item the user clicks one is added to the selection), or xlExtended (the user has to hold down the *Ctrl* key to select multiple items). Valid only on list boxes
PrintObject	Boolean	Set/Get whether the control will be printed when the sheet is printed
SmallChange	Long	Set/Get the value that is added or subtracted every time the user clicks on the arrow button associated with the scroll bar. Valid only if the control is a scroll box
Value	Long	Set/Get the value of the control

ControlFormat Methods

Name	Returns	Parameters	Description
AddItem		TextAs String, [Index]	Adds the value of the Text parameter into a list box or combo box. Valid only for list box and combo box controls
List	Variant	[Index]	Set/Get the string list array associated with a combo box or list box. Can also Set/Get individual items in the list box or combo box if the Index parameter is specified. Valid only for list box and combo box controls
RemoveAll Items			Removes all the items from a list box or combo box. Valid only for list box and combo box controls
RemoveItem		Index As Long, [Count]	Removes the item specified by the Index parameter from a list box or combo box. Valid only for list box and combo box controls

Example: ControlFormat Object

This example resets all the list boxes, drop-downs, scrollbars, spinners, and check boxes on the sheet:

```
Sub ResetFormControls()
    Dim oShp As Shape
    Dim oCF As ControlFormat
    'Loop through all the shapes in the sheet
    For Each oShp In ActiveSheet.Shapes
        'Is this a Forms control?
        If oShp.Type = msoFormControl Then

            'Yes, so get the ControlFormat object
            Set oCF = oShp.ControlFormat

            'Reset the control as appropriate
            Select Case oShp.FormControlType
                Case xlListBox, xlDropDown
                    oCF.RemoveAllItems

                Case xlSpinner, xlScrollBar
                    oCF.Value = oCF.Min

                Case xlCheckBox
                    oCF.Value = xlOff

            End Select
        End If
    Next
End Sub
```

Corners Object

The Corners object represents the corners of a 3D chart. The parent of the Corners object is the Chart object. The parent chart must be a 3D chart. Individual corners cannot be accessed.

Corners Common Properties

The Application, Creator, and Parent properties are defined at the beginning of this Appendix.

Corners Properties

Name	Returns	Description
Name	String	Read-only. Returns the name of the Corners object—usually "Corners"

Corners Methods

Name	Returns	Parameters	Description
Select	Variant		Sets the corners on the chart

Example: Corners Object

No example—its only method is to select it, which is not particularly useful.

CubeField Object and the CubeFields Collection

The CubeFields collection holds all of the PivotTable report fields based on an OLAP cube. Each CubeField object represents a measure or hierarchy field from the OLAP cube. The parent of the CubeFields collection is the PivotTable object.

The CubeFields collection contains a Count property besides the typical collection attributes. The Count property returns the number of objects in the collection.

CubeFields Collection Methods

Name	Returns	Parameters	Description
AddSet	CubeField	Name As String, Caption As String	Adds a new CubeField object to the CubeFields collection

CubeField Common Properties

The Application, Creator, and Parent properties are defined at the beginning of this Appendix.

CubeField Properties

Name	Returns	Description
Caption	String	Read-only. Returns the text label to use for the cube field
CubeField Type	XlCube FieldType	Read-only. Returns whether the cube field is a hierarchy field (xlHierarchy) or a measure field (xlMeasure)
DragToColumn	Boolean	Set/Get whether the field can be dragged to a column position. False for measure fields
DragToData	Boolean	Set/Get whether the field can be dragged to the data position
DragToHide	Boolean	Set/Get whether the field can be dragged off the PivotTable report and therefore hidden
DragToPage	Boolean	Set/Get whether the field can be dragged to the page position. False for measure fields
DragToRow	Boolean	Set/Get whether the field can be dragged to a row position. False for measure fields
Enable Multiple PageItems	Boolean	Set/Get whether multiple items in the page field area for OLAP PivotTables can be selected

Continues

Name	Returns	Description
HasMember Properties	Boolean	Read-only. Returns True when there are member properties specified to be displayed for the cube field
HiddenLevels	Long	Set/Get the top levels of the hierarchy cube field that are hidden. Set the value to 0 before setting it a value greater than 0 (displays all the levels then hide some)
LayoutForm	XlLayout FormType	Set/Get the way the specified PivotTable items appear
Layout Subtotal Location	XlSubtotal Location Type	Set/Get the position of the PivotTable field subtotals in relation to the specified field
Name	String	Read-only. Returns the name of the field
Orientation	XlPivot Field Orientation	Set/Get where the field is located in the PivotTable report
PivotFields	PivotFields	Read-only. Returns the PivotFields collection
Position	Long	Set/Get the position number of the hierarchy field among all the fields in the same orientation
ShowInField List	Boolean	Set/Get whether a CubeField object will be shown in the field list
Treeview Control	Treeview Control	Read-only. Returns an object allowing manipulation of the cube on an OLAP PivotTable report
Value	String	Read-only. Returns the name of the field

CubeField Methods

Name	Returns	Parameters	Description
AddMember PropertyField		Property As String, [Property Order]	Adds a member property field to the display for the cube field. Note that the property field specified will not be viewable if the PivotTable view has no fields
Delete			Deletes the object

CustomProperty Object and the CustomProperties Collection

This object allows you to store information within a worksheet or SmartTag. This information can then be used as metadata for XML, or can be accessed by any routine that needs information specific to the worksheet or SmartTag.

More important to a developer is the ability of this new object to store specifics regarding a worksheet or group of worksheets so that any routine can call up the `CustomProperty`, analyze the information contained within, then make decisions on how to handle that worksheet. In the past, many developers used worksheet level range names to store information about a worksheet. Worksheet level range names only reside in that worksheet, enabling each worksheet to have the same range name, but store different values.

For example, each worksheet in a workbook containing a dozen budget worksheets and three report worksheets could contain the same range name called `IsBudget`. All of the budget sheets would store the value of `True` in the range name while the report sheets would store `False`. Routines that need to loop through the worksheets applying different formats or calculations to budget sheets can call on the value of the range name to determine if it's a budget sheet before running code on it.

This new `CustomProperty` object makes storing such information (or any information for that matter) simpler than creating worksheet level range names, or storing such information in a hidden worksheet or in the Registry.

The `CustomProperties` collection represents `CustomProperty` objects for either worksheets or SmartTags. `CustomProperties` can store information within either a worksheet or SmartTag. They are similar to the `DocumentProperties` object in the Office XP model, except they are stored with a worksheet or SmartTag instead of the whole document.

CustomProperties Common Properties

The `Application`, `Creator`, and `Parent` properties are defined at the beginning of this Appendix.

CustomProperties Collection Properties

Name	Returns	Description
Count	Long	Read-only. Returns the number of objects in the collection
Item	Custom Property	Read-only. `Index As Variant`. Returns a single object from a collection

CustomProperties Collection Methods

Name	Returns	Parameters	Description
Add	Custom Property	Name As String, Value As Variant	Adds custom property information

CustomProperty Common Properties

The `Application`, `Creator`, and `Parent` properties are defined at the beginning of this Appendix.

CustomProperty Properties

Name	Returns	Description
Name	String	Set/Get the name of the object
Value	Variant	Set/Get the style of line to use for the borders (for example, xlDash). Use the xlLineStyle constants to set the value. Same as LineStyle

CustomProperty Methods

Name	Returns	Parameters	Description
Delete			Deletes the object

Example: CustomProperty Object

This routine loops through the worksheets in a workbook and creates a CustomProperty called IsBudget. The value of IsBudget depends on whether or not the worksheet contains the phrase "Budget Analysis". It then lists the results:

```
Sub CreateCustomProperties()
    Dim bBudget As Boolean
    Dim lRow As Long
    Dim oCustomProp As CustomProperty
    Dim rng As Range, wks As Worksheet

    'Turn off the screen and clear the search formats
    With Application
        .FindFormat.Clear
        .ScreenUpdating = False
    End With

    'Clear the worksheet that will contain the
    ' Custom Property list
    wksCustomProperties.UsedRange.Offset(1, 0).ClearContents

    'Initialize the row counter
    lRow = 2     'Row 1 contains the Column Headings

    'Loop through the worksheet in this workbook
    For Each wks In ThisWorkbook.Worksheets

        'Supress errors resulting in no cells found and
        ' no Custom Property
        On Error Resume Next
            bBudget = False
```

```
            bBudget = _
                    (Len(wks.UsedRange.Find(What:="Budget
Analysis").Address) > 0)

            'Unfortunately, we cannot refer to a Custom Property by
            ' its name, only its numeric index
            Set oCustomProp = wks.CustomProperties(1)
        On Error GoTo 0

        'If the Custom Property exists, delete it and
        ' add it again
        If Not oCustomProp Is Nothing Then oCustomProp.Delete

        'Note the value of bBudget is encased in double quotes.
        'If we don't, True will be stored as -1 and False 0 (their
        'numeric values).
        Set oCustomProp = wks.CustomProperties.Add(Name:=
"IsBudget", Value:="" _
                                                & bBudget & "")

        'List the Custom Property settings on the worksheet
        With wksCustomProperties
            'Parent.Name returns the name of the object
            ' holding the Custom Property - the worksheet name in this case
            .Cells(lRow, 1).Value = oCustomProp.Parent.Name
            .Cells(lRow, 2).Value = oCustomProp.Name
            .Cells(lRow, 3).Value = oCustomProp.Value
        End With

        'Move down one row
        lRow = lRow + 1

    Next wks

End Sub
```

CustomView Object and the CustomViews Collection

The CustomViews collection holds the list of custom views associated with a workbook. Each CustomView object holds the attributes associated with a workbook custom view. A custom view holds settings such as window size, window position, column widths, hidden columns, and print settings of a workbook. The parent object of the CustomViews collection is the Workbook object.

The CustomViews collection has two other properties besides the typical collection attributes. The Count property returns the number of CustomView objects in the collection. The Add method adds a custom view to the CustomViews collection. The Add method accepts a name for the view with the ViewName parameter. Optionally, the Add method accepts whether print settings are included (PrintSettings) and whether hidden rows and columns are included (RowColSettings).

CustomView Common Properties

The Application, Creator, and Parent properties are defined at the beginning of this Appendix.

CustomView Properties

Name	Returns	Description
Name	String	Read-only. Returns the name of the custom view
PrintSettings	Boolean	Read-only. Returns whether print settings are included in the custom view
RowCol Settings	Boolean	Read-only. Returns whether hidden rows and columns are included in the custom view

CustomView Methods

Name	Returns	Parameters	Description
Delete			Deletes the custom view
Show			Shows the custom view and the settings associated with it

Example: CustomView Object and the CustomViews Collection

Display all the custom views in the workbook as a screen-show, pausing for two seconds between each one:

```
Sub ShowCustomView()
    Dim oCV As CustomView
    'Cycle through all the custom views in the sheet
    'that contain row/column information
    For Each oCV In ActiveWorkbook.CustomViews
        If oCV.RowColSettings Then
            oCV.Show
        End If

        'Pause for 2 seconds between each view
        Application.Wait Now + TimeValue("00:00:02")
    Next
End Sub
```

DataLabel Object and the DataLabels Collection

The DataLabels collection holds all the labels for individual points or trendlines in a data series. Each series has only one DataLabels collection. The parent of the DataLabels collection is the Series object. Each DataLabel object represents a single data label for a trendline or a point. The DataLabels collection is used with the HasDataLabels property of the parent Series object.

The DataLabels collection has a few properties and methods besides the typical collection attributes. They are listed in the following table.

DataLabels Collection Properties and Methods

Name	Returns	Description
AutoScaleFont	Variant	Set/Get whether the font size will change automatically if the parent chart changes sizes
AutoText	Boolean	Set/Get whether Excel will generate the data label text automatically
Border	Border	Read-only. Returns the border's properties around the data label collection
Count	Long	Read-only. Returns the number of data labels in the collection
Fill	ChartFill Format	Read-only. Returns an object containing fill formatting options for the data labels in the collection
Font	Font	Read-only. Returns an object containing Font options for the data labels in the collection
Horizontal Alignment	Variant	Set/Get how the data labels are horizontally aligned. Use the xlAlign constants
Interior	Interior	Read-only. Returns an object containing options to format the inside area of the data labels in the collection (for example, interior color)
Name	String	Read-only. Returns the name of the collection
NumberFormat	String	Set/Get the numeric formatting to use if the data labels are numeric values or dates
NumberFormat Linked	Boolean	Set/Get whether the same numerical format used for the cells containing the chart data is used by the data labels
NumberFormat Local	Variant	Set/Get the name of the numeric format being used by the data labels in the language being used by the user
Orientation	Variant	Set/Get the angle of the text for the data labels. The value can be in degrees (from –90 to 90) or one of the XlOrientation constants
Position	XlDataLabel Position	Set/Get where the data labels are going to be located in relation to points or trendlines
ReadingOrder	Long	Set/Get how the text is read (from left to right or right to left). Only applicable in appropriate languages
Separator	Variant	Set/Get the separator used for the data labels on a chart
Shadow	Boolean	Set/Get whether the data labels have a shadow effect
ShowBubble Size	Boolean	Set/Get whether to show the bubble size for the data labels on a chart

Continues

Name	Returns	Description
ShowCategory Name	Boolean	Set/Get whether to display the category name for the data labels on a chart
ShowLegendKey	Boolean	Set/Get whether the key being used in the legend, usually a specific color, will show along with the data label
Show Percentage	Boolean	Set/Get whether to display the percentage value for the data labels on a chart
ShowSeries Name	Boolean	Set/Get whether to show the series name
ShowValue	Boolean	Set/Get whether to display the specified chart's data label values
Type	Variant	Set/Get what sort of data label to show for the collection (for example, labels, percent, values)
Vertical Alignment	Variant	Set/Get how you want the data labels horizontally aligned. Use the xlVAlign constants
Delete	Variant	Method. Deletes the data labels
Select	Variant	Method. Selects the data labels on the chart

DataLabel Common Properties

The Application, Creator, and Parent properties are defined at the beginning of this Appendix.

DataLabel Properties

Name	Returns	Description
AutoScaleFont	Variant	Set/Get whether the font size will change automatically if the parent chart changes sizes
AutoText	Boolean	Set/Get whether Excel will generate the data label text automatically
Border	Border	Read-only. Returns the border's properties around the data label
Caption	String	Set/Get the data label text
Characters	Characters	Read-only. Parameters: [Start], [Length]. Returns an object that represents a range of characters within the text
Fill	ChartFill Format	Read-only. Returns an object containing fill formatting options for the data label
Font	Font	Read-only. Returns an object containing Font options for the data label

Name	Returns	Description
Horizontal Alignment	Variant	Set/Get how the data labels are horizontally aligned. Use the xlAlign constants
Interior	Interior	Read-only. Returns an object containing options to format the inside area of the data label (for example, interior color)
Left	Double	Set/Get the distance from the left edge of the data label to the parent chart's left edge
Name	String	Read-only. Returns the name of the data label
NumberFormat	String	Set/Get the numeric formatting to use if the data label is a numeric value or a date
NumberFormat Linked	Boolean	Set/Get whether the same numerical format used for the cells containing the chart data is used by the data label
NumberFormat Local	Variant	Set/Get the name of the numeric format being used by the data label in the language being used by the user
Orientation	Variant	Set/Get the angle of the text for the data label. The value can be in degrees (from –90 to 90) or one of the XlOrientation constants
Position	XlDataLabel Position	Set/Get where the data label is going to be located in relation to points or trendlines
ReadingOrder	Long	Set/Get how the text is read (from left to right or right to left). Only applicable in appropriate languages
Separator	Variant	Set/Get the separator used for the data labels on a chart
Shadow	Boolean	Set/Get whether the data label has a shadow effect
ShowBubble Size	Boolean	Set/Get whether to show the bubble size for the data labels on a chart
ShowCategory Name	Boolean	Set/Get whether to display the category name for the data labels on a chart
ShowLegendKey	Boolean	Set/Get whether the key being used in the legend, usually a specific color, will show along with the data label
Show Percentage	Boolean	Set/Get whether to display the percentage value for the data labels on a chart
ShowSeries Name	Boolean	Set/Get whether to show the series name
ShowValue	Boolean	Set/Get whether to display the specified chart's data label values
Text	String	Set/Get the data label text

Continues

Name	Returns	Description
Top	Double	Set/Get the distance from the top edge of the data label to the parent chart's top edge
Type	Variant	Set/Get what sort of data label to show (for example, labels, percent, values)
Vertical Alignment	Variant	Set/Get how you want the data label horizontally aligned. Use the xlVAlign constants

DataLabel Methods

Name	Returns	Parameters	Description
Delete	Variant		Deletes the data label
Select	Variant		Selects the data label on the chart

Example: DataLabel Object and the DataLabels Collection

This example adds data labels to all the points on the chart, using the column to the left of the X values range:

```
Sub AddDataLabels()
    Dim oSer As Series
    Dim vaSplits As Variant
    Dim oXRng As Range
    Dim oLblRng As Range
    Dim oLbl As DataLabel
    'Loop through all the series in the chart
    For Each oSer In Charts(1).SeriesCollection
        'Get the series formula and split it into its
        'constituent parts (Name, X range, Y range, order)
        vaSplits = Split(oSer.Formula, ",")

        'Get the X range
        Set oXRng = Range(vaSplits(LBound(vaSplits) + 1))

        'Get the column to the left of the X range
        Set oLblRng = oXRng.Offset(0, -1)

        'Show data labels for the series
        oSer.ApplyDataLabels

        'Loop through the points
        For i = 1 To oSer.Points.Count

            'Get the DataLabel object
            Set oLbl = oSer.Points(i).DataLabel
```

```
            'Set its text and alignment
        With oLbl
            .Caption = oLblRng.Cells(i)
            .Position = xlLabelPositionAbove
        End With
    Next
    Next
End Sub
```

DataTable Object

A DataTable object contains the formatting options associated with a chart's data table. The parent of the DataTable object is the Chart object.

DataTable Common Properties

The Application, Creator, and Parent properties are defined at the beginning of this Appendix.

DataTable Properties

Name	Returns	Description
AutoScaleFont	Variant	Set/Get whether the font size will change automatically if the parent chart changes sizes.
Border	Border	Read-only. Returns the border's properties around the data table
Font	Font	Read-only. Returns an object containing Font options for the data table
HasBorder Horizontal	Boolean	Set/Get whether the data table has horizontal cell borders
HasBorder Outline	Boolean	Set/Get whether the data table has a border around the outside
HasBorder Vertical	Boolean	Set/Get whether the data table has vertical cell borders
ShowLegendKey	Boolean	Set/Get whether the legend key is shown along with the data table contents

DataTable Methods

Name	Returns	Parameters	Description
Delete			Deletes the data table
Select			Selects the data table on the chart

Example: DataTable Object

Adds a data table to a chart and formats it to only have vertical lines between the values:

```
Sub FormatDataTable()
    Dim oDT As DataTable
    'Display the data table
    Charts(1).HasDataTable = True
    'Get the DataTable object
    Set oDT = Charts(1).DataTable
    'Format the data table to only have vertical lines
    With oDT
        .HasBorderOutline = False
        .HasBorderHorizontal = False
        .HasBorderVertical = True
    End With
End Sub
```

DefaultWebOptions Object

Allows programmatic changes to items associated with the default settings of the Web Options dialog box. These options include what Excel does when opening an HTML page and when saving a sheet as an HTML page.

DefaultWebOptions Common Properties

The `Application`, `Creator`, and `Parent` properties are defined at the beginning of this Appendix.

DefaultWebOptions Properties

Name	Returns	Description
AllowPNG	Boolean	Set/Get whether Portable Network Graphics Format PNG is allowed as an output format. PNG is a file format for the lossless, portable, well-compressed storage of images
AlwaysSaveIn DefaultEncoding	Boolean	Set/Get whether Web pages are always saved in the default encoding
CheckIfOfficeIs HTMLEditor	Boolean	Set/Get whether Office is the default Web editor for Office created pages
Download Components	Boolean	Set/Get whether Office components are downloaded to the end user's machine when viewing Excel files in a Web browser
Encoding	MsoEncoding	Set/Get the type of encoding to save a document as
FolderSuffix	String	Read-only. Returns what the suffix name is for the support directory created when saving an Excel document as a Web page. Language dependent

Name	Returns	Description
Fonts	WebPage Fonts	Read-only. Returns a collection of possible Web type fonts
LoadPictures	Boolean	Set/Get whether images are loaded when opening up an Excel file
LocationOf Components	String	Set/Get the URL or path that contains the Office Web components needed to view documents in a Web browser
Organize InFolder	Boolean	Set/Get whether supporting files are organized in a folder
PixelsPer Inch	Long	Set/Get how dense graphics and table cells should be when viewed on a Web page
RelyOnCSS	Boolean	Set/Get whether Cascading Style Sheets (CSS) is used for font formatting
RelyOnVML	Boolean	Set/Get whether image files are not created when saving a document with drawn objects. Vector Markup Language is used to create the images on the fly. VML is an XML-based format for high-quality vector graphics on the Web
SaveHidden Data	Boolean	Set/Get whether all hidden data is saved in the Web page along with the regular data
SaveNewWeb PagesAsWeb Archives	Boolean	Set/Get whether a new Web page can be saved as a Web archive
ScreenSize	MsoScreen Size	Set/Get the target monitor's screen size
Target Browser	MsoTarget Browser	Set/Get the browser version
UpdateLinks OnSave	Boolean	Set/Get whether links are updated every time the document is saved
UseLongFile Names	Boolean	Set/Get whether long file names are used whenever possible

Example: DefaultWebOptions Object

This example shows how to open a Web page, without loading the pictures:

```
Sub OpenHTMLWithoutPictures()
    Dim bLoadImages As Boolean
    Dim oDWO As DefaultWebOptions
    'Get the Default Web options
    Set oDWO = Application.DefaultWebOptions
```

```
        'Remember whether to load pictures
        bLoadImages = oDWO.LoadPictures
        'Tell Excel not to load pictures, for faster opening
        oDWO.LoadPictures = False
        'Open a web page, without pictures
        Workbooks.Open "http://www.wrox.com"
        'Restore the setting
        oDWO.LoadPictures = bLoadImages
    End Sub
```

Diagram Object

A `Diagram` represents a preset collection of shapes surrounded by an invisible border. It's a cross between adding shapes using the Drawing toolbar and an enhanced version of the Org Chart program used in previous versions of Microsoft Office. Within each `Diagram` are `Nodes`. Each Node represents an individual shape in the `Diagram`.

There are several different types of preset `Diagrams` you can choose from: `Cycle`, `Target`, `Radial`, `Venn`, `Pyramid`, and `OrgChart`.

It's important to note that the `Diagram` object belongs to the `Shape(s)` object, which, in turn, belongs to the `Worksheet` object. Consequently, to add a `Diagram` object to a worksheet, you go through the `Shapes` collection using the `AddDiagram` method:

```
ActiveSheet.Shapes.AddDiagram(msoDiagramOrgChart, 2, 2, 400, 300)
```

If you set the preceding code to an object variable, it returns a `Shape` object. To add shapes to the `Diagram`, use the `DiagramNode` object within the `Shape` object:

```
ActiveSheet.Shapes(1).DiagramNode.Children.AddNode
```

To reference the properties and methods of the `Diagram` object itself (listed next), you access the `Diagram` object through the `Shape` object, like so:

```
ActiveSheet.Shapes(1).Diagram.Nodes(1).TextShape.Fill.BackColor.
SchemeColor = 17
```

Diagram Common Properties

The `Application`, `Creator`, and `Parent` properties are defined at the beginning of this Appendix.

Diagram Properties

Name	Returns	Description
AutoFormat	MsoTriState	Get/Set the automatic formatting state for a diagram
AutoLayout	MsoTriState	Get/Set the constant which determines the automatic positioning of the nodes and connectors in a diagram
Nodes	Diagram Nodes	Read-only. Returns a DiagramNodes object that contains a flat list of all the nodes in the specified diagram

Name	Returns	Description
Reverse	MsoTriState	Set/Get whether to reverse the order of the nodes
Type	MsoDiagram Type	Read-only. Returns the diagram type

Diagram Methods

Name	Returns	Parameters	Description
Convert		Type As Mso DiagramType	Converts the current diagram to a different diagram

Example: Diagram Object

The following routine creates a diagram and adds and formats several shapes (called nodes) to the diagram. The shape color and font name come from a table on a worksheet, allowing you to easily experiment with different looks.

As of this writing, any attempt to programmatically add text to nodes in a Diagram results in an error:

```
Sub CreateDiagram()

    Const sRANGE_LEVELS As String = "Levels"

    Dim lCount As Long
    Dim oDiagramShape As Shape
    Dim oDiagramNode As DiagramNode
    Dim oDiagramNodeChild As DiagramNode

    'Clear the current shapes (except the Command Button)
    On Error Resume Next
        For Each oDiagramShape In wksDiagrams.Shapes
            If oDiagramShape.HasDiagram Then oDiagramShape.Delete
        Next oDiagramShape
    On Error GoTo 0

    'Turn off the screen
    Application.ScreenUpdating = False

    'Create the Diagram
    Set oDiagramShape = wksDiagrams.Shapes.AddDiagram(msoDiagramOrgChart, 2, 2,
300, 250)

    'Remove the transparent background
    oDiagramShape.Fill.Visible = msoTrue

    'Create the top level node
    Set oDiagramNode = oDiagramShape.DiagramNode.Children.AddNode

    With oDiagramNode
```

```
                    'Format the top level node
            With .Shape
                .AutoShapeType = msoShapeBevel
                .TextFrame.Characters.Font.Name = _
                    wksDiagrams.Range(sRANGE_LEVELS).Cells(1, 2).Text
                .Fill.ForeColor.SchemeColor = _
                    wksDiagrams.Range(sRANGE_LEVELS).Cells(1, 3).Value
            End With

            'Create a child node under the top level node
            Set oDiagramNodeChild = .Children.AddNode

            'Format the child node
            With oDiagramNodeChild
                .Shape.TextFrame.Characters.Font.Name = _
                    wksDiagrams.Range(sRANGE_LEVELS).Cells(2, 2).Text
                .Shape.Fill.ForeColor.SchemeColor = _
                    wksDiagrams.Range(sRANGE_LEVELS).Cells(2, 3).Value
            End With

            'Place two child nodes under the top level's child
            For lCount = 1 To 2
                With oDiagramNodeChild.Children.AddNode
                    .Shape.TextFrame.Characters.Font.Name = _
                        wksDiagrams.Range(sRANGE_LEVELS).Cells(3, 2).Text
                    .Shape.Fill.ForeColor.SchemeColor = _
                        wksDiagrams.Range(sRANGE_LEVELS).Cells(3, 3).Value
                End With
            Next lCount

            'Create another child under the top level node
            Set oDiagramNodeChild = .Children.AddNode

            With oDiagramNodeChild
                .Shape.TextFrame.Characters.Font.Name = _
                    wksDiagrams.Range(sRANGE_LEVELS).Cells(2, 2).Text
                .Shape.Fill.ForeColor.SchemeColor = _
                    wksDiagrams.Range(sRANGE_LEVELS).Cells(2, 3).Value
            End With

            'Place two child nodes under this child
            '(which is under top level)
            For lCount = 1 To 2
                With oDiagramNodeChild.Children.AddNode
                    .Shape.TextFrame.Characters.Font.Name = _
                        wksDiagrams.Range(sRANGE_LEVELS).Cells(3, 2).Text
                    .Shape.Fill.ForeColor.SchemeColor = _
                        wksDiagrams.Range(sRANGE_LEVELS).Cells(3, 3).Value
                End With
            Next lCount

    End With

    End Sub
```

DiagramNode Object and the DiagramNodes Collection

The `DiagramNode` object represents one shape inside a `Diagram`. Shapes underneath a specific node are called children. Use the `AddNode` method of the `Children` property of this object to add nodes to the current node.

The `DiagramNodes` collection consists of all of the `Nodes` in a `Diagram` object. Each `Node` is a shape within the `Diagram`.

DiagramNodes Common Properties

The `Application`, `Creator`, and `Parent` properties are defined at the beginning of this Appendix.

DiagramNodes Collection Properties

Name	Returns	Description
Count	Long	Read-only. Returns the number of objects in the collection

DiagramNodes Collection Methods

Name	Returns	Parameters	Description
Item	Diagram Node	Index As Variant	Returns a single object from a collection
SelectAll			Selects all the shapes in the collection

DiagramNode Common Properties

The `Application`, `Creator`, and `Parent` properties are defined at the beginning of this Appendix.

DiagramNode Properties

Name	Returns	Description
Children	Diagram NodeChildren	Read-only. Returns the collection of child nodes of a particular node
Diagram	IMso Diagram	Read-only. Returns a representation of a diagram
Layout	MsoOrg Chart LayoutType	Set/Get the formatting style of the child nodes of an organization chart
Root	Diagram Node	Read-only. Returns the root of the root diagram node

Continues

Name	Returns	Description
Shape	Shape	Read-only. Returns the shape attached to the specified comment, diagram node, or hyperlink
TextShape	Shape	Read-only. Returns the shape of the text box associated with a diagram node

DiagramNode Methods

Name	Returns	Parameters	Description
AddNode	Diagram Node	[pos As MsoRelative NodePosition], [nodeType As MsoDiagram NodeType]	Creates a diagram node and returns a DiagramNode object that represents the new node
CloneNode	Diagram Node	copyChildren As Boolean, [pTarget Node As DiagramNode], [pos As MsoRelative NodePosition]	Clones a diagram node and returns a DiagramNode object representing the cloned node
Delete			Deletes the object
MoveNode		pTargetNode As DiagramNode, pos As MsoRelative NodePosition	Moves a diagram node and any of its child nodes, within a diagram
NextNode	Diagram Node		Selects the next diagram node in a series of nodes and returns a DiagramNode object representing the newly-selected node
PrevNode	Diagram Node		Returns the previous diagram node in a collection of diagram nodes
ReplaceNode		pTargetNode As DiagramNode	Replaces a target diagram node with the source diagram node
SwapNode		pTargetNode As DiagramNode, [swapChildren As Boolean]	Swaps the source diagram node with a target diagram node
Transfer Children		pReceiving Node As DiagramNode	The child nodes of a source diagram node are transferred to a receiving diagram node

DiagramNodeChildren Object

The DiagramNodeChildren object represents a Child shape one level below a DiagramNode object. Each DiagramNodeChildren object is a DiagramNode object itself. If a DiagramNodeChildren object contains Children below it (in the hiercharchy), then each of those would be considered DiagramNodeChildren objects.

DiagramNodeChildren Common Properties

The Application, Creator, and Parent properties are defined at the beginning of this Appendix.

DiagramNodeChildren Properties

Name	Returns	Description
Count	Long	Read-only. Returns the number of objects in the collection
FirstChild	Diagram Node	Read-only. Returns the first child node of a parent node
LastChild	Diagram Node	Read-only. Returns the last child node of a parent node

DiagramNodeChildren Methods

Name	Returns	Parameters	Description
AddNode	Diagram Node	[Index], [nodeType As MsoDiagram NodeType]	Makes a new DiagramNode
SelectAll			Selects all the shapes in the collection

Dialog Object and the Dialogs Collection

The Dialogs collection represents the list of dialog boxes that are built-in to Excel. The XlBuiltinDialog constants are used to access an individual Dialog object in the Dialogs collection. A Dialog object represents a single built-in Excel dialog box. Each Dialog object will have additional custom properties depending on what type of Dialog object it is. Besides the typical collection attributes, the Dialogs collection also has a Count property that returns the number of Dialog objects in the collection.

Dialog Common Properties

The Application, Creator, and Parent properties are defined at the beginning of this Appendix.

Dialog Methods

Name	Returns	Parameters	Description
Show	Boolean	[Arg1], [Arg2], ...[Arg30]	Displays and executes the dialog box settings. True is returned if the user chose *OK* and False is returned if the user chose *Cancel*. The arguments to pass depend on the dialog box

Example: Dialog Object and the Dialogs Collection

```
Sub ShowPrinterSelection()
    'Show printer selection dialog
    Application.Dialogs(xlDialogPrinterSetup).Show
End Sub
```

DisplayUnitLabel Object

The DisplayUnitLabel object contains all of the text and formatting associated with the label used for units on axes. For example, if the values on an axis are in the millions it would be messy to display such large values on the axis. Using a unit label such as "Millions" would allow much smaller numbers to be used. The parent of the DisplayUnitLabel object is the Axis object. This object is usually used along with the HasDisplayUnit property of the parent Axis object.

DisplayUnitLabel Common Properties

The Application, Creator, and Parent properties are defined at the beginning of this Appendix.

DisplayUnitLabel Properties

Name	Returns	Description
AutoScaleFont	Variant	Set/Get whether the font size will change automatically if the parent chart changes sizes
Border	Border	Read-only. Returns the border's properties around the unit label
Caption	String	Set/Get the unit label's text
Characters	Characters	Read-only. Parameters: [Start], [Length]. Returns an object containing all the characters in the unit label. Allows manipulation on a character-by-character basis
Fill	ChartFill Format	Read-only. Returns an object containing fill formatting options for the unit label
Font	Font	Read-only. Returns an object containing Font options for the unit label

Name	Returns	Description
Horizontal Alignment	Variant	Set/Get how you want the unit label horizontally aligned. Use the xlAlign constants
Interior	Interior	Read-only. Returns an object containing options to format the area in the unit label text area (for example, interior color)
Left	Double	Set/Get the distance from the left edge of the unit label text area to the chart's left edge
Name	String	Read-only. Returns the name of the DisplayUnitLabel object
Orientation	Variant	Set/Get the angle of the text for the unit label. The value can be in degrees (from −90 to 90) or one of the XlOrientation constants
ReadingOrder	Long	Set/Get how the text is read (from left to right or right to left). Only applicable in appropriate languages
Shadow	Boolean	Set/Get whether the unit label has a shadow effect
Text	String	Set/Get the unit label's text
Top	Double	Set/Get the distance from the top edge of the unit label text area to the chart's top edge
Vertical Alignment	Variant	Set/Get how you want the unit label horizontally aligned. Use the xlVAlign constants

DisplayUnitLabel Methods

Name	Returns	Parameters	Description
Delete	Variant		Deletes the unit label from the axis
Select	Variant		Selects the unit label on the chart

Example: DisplayUnitLabel Object

```
Sub AddUnitLabel()
    Dim oDUL As DisplayUnitLabel
    'Format the Y axis to have a unit label
    With Charts(1).Axes(xlValue)
        .DisplayUnit = xlThousands
        .HasDisplayUnitLabel = True
        'Get the unit label
        Set oDUL = .DisplayUnitLabel
    End With
    'Format the unit label
```

```
      With oDUL
         .Caption = "Thousands"
         .Font.Name = "Arial"
         .VerticalAlignment = xlCenter
      End With
   End Sub
```

DownBars Object

The DownBars object contains formatting options for down bars on a chart. The parent of the DownBars object is the ChartGroup object. To see if this object exists, use the HasUpDownBars property of the ChartGroup object.

DownBars Common Properties

The Application, Creator, and Parent properties are defined at the beginning of this Appendix.

DownBars Properties

Name	Returns	Description
Border	Border	Read-only. Returns the border's properties around the down bars
Fill	ChartFill Format	Read-only. Returns an object containing fill formatting options for the down bars
Interior	Interior	Read-only. Returns an object containing options to format the inside area of the down bars (for example, interior color)
Name	String	Read-only. Returns the name of the down bars

DownBars Methods

Name	Returns	Parameters	Description
Delete	Variant		Deletes the down bars
Select	Variant		Selects the down bars in the chart

DropLines Object

The DropLines object contains formatting options for drop lines in a chart. The parent of the DropLines object is the ChartGroup object. To see if this object exists, use the HasDropLines property of the ChartGroup object.

DropLines Common Properties

The Application, Creator, and Parent properties are defined at the beginning of this Appendix.

DropLines Properties

Name	Returns	Description
Border	Border	Read-only. Returns the border's properties around the drop lines
Name	String	Read-only. Returns the name of the drop lines

DropLines Methods

Name	Returns	Parameters	Description
Delete	Variant		Deletes the drop lines
Select	Variant		Selects the drop lines in the chart

Example: DropLines Object

```
Sub AddAndFormatDropLines()
    Dim oDLine As DropLines
    'Show the drop lines
    Charts(1).ChartGroups(1).HasDropLines = True
    'Get the DropLines object
    Set oDLine = Charts(1).ChartGroups(1).DropLines
    'Format the drop lines
    With oDLine
        .Border.Weight = xlMedium
        .Border.LineStyle = xlDash
        .Border.ColorIndex = 3
    End With
End Sub
```

Error Object and the Errors Collection

The Error object contains one error in the Errors collection representing one error in a cell containing possible errors.

The Errors collection represents all the errors contained within a cell. Each cell can contain multiple errors.

These errors are analogous to the new Error Checking feature in Excel 2003. The different types of errors that Excel can check can be found on the Error Checking Tab of the Tools ⇨ Options command. In the Excel application, cells containing errors appear with a small triangle in their upper left corner. The default color of the triangle on most systems is green, but can be changed using the Error Indicator Color option on the Error Checking Tab of the Options command.

When a user selects a range containing an error, a drop-down icon containing an exclamation point inside a yellow diamond appears. The user can then click the icon and choose how to handle the errors in the range. If action was taken, like ignoring the error or clicking one of the recommended choices, the green indicator disappears for all cells containing that error. Any cells still containing the green triangle indicate other error types are still present in those cells.

As of this writing, the `Errors Collection` object and `Error` object do not have the ability to handle multiple errors in a multicell range as described earlier. The Help file and object model indicate that the Parent object of the `Errors Collection` is a `Range` object. However, any attempt to reference the `Errors` in a multicell range results in an error. Since each cell can contain multiple errors, for all intent and purposes, the `Error Collection` object stores all the errors contained within one cell, not a range of cells. This requires that you loop through a range of cells if you need to programmatically handle errors in a multicell range.

Note that neither the `Error` nor `Errors` objects contains a count or Boolean property that would allow us to test whether an error even exists in a cell. For this reason, additional code would be needed to loop through each error type for every desired cell checking for the `Error` object's `Value` property, which returns `True` if that type of error occurs in the cell.

Use the `Item` property of the `Errors Collection` object to loop through the error types to determine which errors might have occurred.

Errors Common Properties

The `Application`, `Creator`, and `Parent` properties are defined at the beginning of this Appendix.

Errors Collection Properties

Name	Returns	Description
Item	Error	Returns an `Error` object that is contained in the `Errors` collection

Error Common Properties

The `Application`, `Creator`, and `Parent` properties are defined at the beginning of this Appendix.

Error Properties

Name	Returns	Description
Ignore	Boolean	Get/Set whether error checking is enabled for a range
Value	Boolean	Read-only. Returns whether all the validation criteria are met

ErrorBars Object

The `ErrorBars` object contains formatting options for error bars in a chart. The parent of the `Errors` object is the `SeriesCollection` object.

ErrorBars Common Properties

The Application, Creator, and Parent properties are defined at the beginning of this Appendix.

ErrorBars Properties

Name	Returns	Description
Border	Border	Read-only. Returns the border's properties around the error bars
EndStyle	XlEndStyle Cap	Set/Get the style used for the ending of the error bars
Name	String	Read-only. Returns the name of the error bars

ErrorBars Methods

Name	Returns	Parameters	Description
ClearFormats	Variant		Clears the formatting set on the error bar
Delete	Variant		Deletes the error bars
Select	Variant		Selects the error bars in the chart

Example: ErrorBars Object

```
Sub AddAndFormatErrorBars()
    Dim oSer As Series
    Dim oErrBars As ErrorBars
    'Add error bars to the first series (at +/- 10% of the value)
    Set oSer = Charts(1).SeriesCollection(1)
    oSer.ErrorBar xlY, xlErrorBarIncludeBoth, xlErrorBarTypePercent, 10
    'Get the ErrorBars object
    Set oErrBars = oSer.ErrorBars
    'Format the error bars
    With oErrBars
        .Border.Weight = xlThick
        .Border.LineStyle = xlContinuous
        .Border.ColorIndex = 7
        .EndStyle = xlCap
    End With
End Sub
```

ErrorCheckingOptions Collection Object

Represents all of the Error Checking possibilities found on the Error Checking Tab of the Tools ➪ Options command. Using the BackgroundChecking property of this object hides all of the error indicators (small triangle in the upper right corner of cells).

Use the other properties in this object to specify which type of error checking you want Excel to perform.

The `ErrorCheckingOptions` object can be referenced through the `Application` object and therefore affect all open workbooks.

ErrorCheckingOptions Common Properties

The `Application`, `Creator`, and `Parent` properties are defined at the beginning of this Appendix.

ErrorCheckingOptions Collection Properties

Name	Returns	Description
Background Checking	Boolean	Set/Get whether background error checking is set, that is whether the autocorrect button will apear in cells that contain errors
EmptyCell References	Boolean	Set/Get whether error checking is on for cells containing formulas that refer to empty cells
EvaluateToError	Boolean	Set/Get whether error checking is on for cells that evaluate to an error value
Inconsistent Formula	Boolean	Set/Get whether error checking is on for cells containing an inconsistent formula in a region
IndicatorColor Index	XlColor Index	Set/Get the color of the indicator for error checking options
ListDataVali dation	Boolean	The property will return `True` if data validation is enabled for a list.
NumberAsText	Boolean	Set/Get whether error checking is on for numbers written as text
OmittedCells	Boolean	Set/Get whether error checking is on for cells that contain formulas referring to a range that omits adjacent cells that could be included
TextDate	Boolean	Set/Get whether error checking is on for cells that contain a text date with a two-digit year
UnlockedForm ulaCells	Boolean	Set/Get whether error checking is on for cells that are unlocked and contain a formula

Example: ErrorCheckingOptions Object

The following routine uses a table on a worksheet to set the Error Checking Options:

```
Sub SetErrorCheckingOptions()

    Dim rngSettings As Range
    Dim vSetting As Variant
```

```
        'Locate the start of the Settings table
        Set rngSettings = wksErrors.Range("ErrorSettings")

        'Go through each ErrorChecking Property and
        ' set it according to the values placed in teh table
        With Application.ErrorCheckingOptions

            vSetting = rngSettings.Cells(1, 2).Value
            If Len(vSetting) And (vSetting = True Or vSetting = False) Then
                .BackgroundChecking = vSetting
            End If

            vSetting = rngSettings.Cells(2, 2).Value
            If Len(vSetting) And (vSetting = True Or vSetting = False) Then
                .EvaluateToError = vSetting
            End If

            vSetting = rngSettings.Cells(3, 2).Value
            If Len(vSetting) And (vSetting = True Or vSetting = False) Then
                .TextDate = vSetting
            End If

            vSetting = rngSettings.Cells(4, 2).Value
            If Len(vSetting) And (vSetting = True Or vSetting = False) Then
                .NumberAsText = vSetting
            End If

            vSetting = rngSettings.Cells(5, 2).Value
            If Len(vSetting) And (vSetting = True Or vSetting = False) Then
                .InconsistentFormula = vSetting
            End If

            vSetting = rngSettings.Cells(6, 2).Value
            If Len(vSetting) And (vSetting = True Or vSetting = False) Then
                .OmittedCells = vSetting
            End If

            vSetting = rngSettings.Cells(7, 2).Value
            If Len(vSetting) And (vSetting = True Or vSetting = False) Then
                .UnlockedFormulaCells = vSetting
            End If

            vSetting = rngSettings.Cells(8, 2).Value
            If Len(vSetting) And (vSetting = True Or vSetting = False) Then
                .EmptyCellReferences = vSetting
            End If

            vSetting = rngSettings.Cells(9, 2).Value
            If LCase(vSetting) = "xlcolorindexautomatic" Then
                .IndicatorColorIndex = xlColorIndexAutomatic
            ElseIf Len(vSetting) And (vSetting > 1 And vSetting < 100) Then
                .IndicatorColorIndex = vSetting
            End If

        End With
```

```
      'Indicators sometimes don't appear
      ' after the routine finishes unless you
      ' update the screen
      Application.ScreenUpdating = True

End Sub
```

FillFormat Object

The `FillFormat` object represents the fill effects available for shapes. For example, a `FillFormat` object defines solid, textured, and patterned fill of the parent shape. A `FillFormat` object can only be accessed through the parent `Shape` object.

FillFormat Common Properties

The `Application`, `Creator`, and `Parent` properties are defined at the beginning of this Appendix.

FillFormat Properties

Name	Returns	Description
BackColor	ColorFormat	Read-only. Returns the background color through the `ColorFormat` object
ForeColor	ColorFormat	Read-only. Returns the foreground color through the `ColorFormat` object
GradientColor Type	MsoGradient ColorType	Read-only. Returns what type of gradient fill color concept is used
GradientDegree	Single	Read-only. Returns how dark or light the gradient fill is
GradientStyle	MsoGradient Style	Read-only. Returns the orientation of the gradient that is used
GradientVariant	Integer	Read-only. Returns the variant used for the gradient from the center
Pattern	MsoPattern Type	Read-only. Returns the pattern used for the fill, if any
PresetGradient Type	MsoPreset Gradient Type	Read-only. Returns the type of gradient that is used
PresetTexture	MsoPreset Texture	Read-only. Returns the non-custom texture of the fill
TextureName	String	Read-only. Returns the custom texture name of the fill
TextureType	MsoTexture Type	Read-only. Returns whether the texture is custom, preset, or mixed
Transparency	Single	Set/Get how transparent the fill is. From 0 (opaque) to 1 (clear)

Name	Returns	Description
Type	MsoFillType	Read-only. Returns if the fill is a texture, gradient, solid, background, picture or mixed
Visible	MsoTriState	Set/Get whether the fill options are visible in the parent shape

FillFormat Methods

Name	Returns	Parameters	Description
OneColor Gradient		Style As MsoGradient Style, Variant As Integer, Degree As Single	Set the style, variant and degree for a one-color gradient fill
Patterned		Pattern As MsoPattern Type	Set the pattern for a fill
Preset Gradient		Style As MsoGradient Style, Variant As Integer, Preset GradientType As MsoPreset GradientType	Choose the style, variant, and preset gradient type for a gradient fill
Preset Textured		Preset Texture As MsoPreset Texture	Set the preset texture for a fill
Solid			Set the fill to a solid color
TwoColor Gradient		Style As MsoGradient Style, Variant As Integer	Set the style for a two-color gradient fill
UserPicture		PictureFile As String	Set the fill to the picture in the PictureFile format
UserTextured		TextureFile As String	Set the custom texture for a fill with the TextureFile format

Example: FillFormat Object

```
Sub FormatShape()
   Dim oFF As FillFormat
```

```
    'Get the Fill format of the first shape
    Set oFF = ActiveSheet.Shapes(1).Fill
    'Format the shape
    With oFF
        .TwoColorGradient msoGradientFromCorner, 1
        .ForeColor.SchemeColor = 3
        .BackColor.SchemeColor = 5
    End With
End Sub
```

Filter Object and the Filters Collection

The Filters collection holds all of the filters associated with the specific parent AutoFilter. Each Filter object defines a single filter for a single column in an autofiltered range. The parent of the Filters collection is the AutoFilter object.

The Filters collection has one other property besides the typical collection attributes. The Count property returns the number of Filter objects in the collection.

Filter Common Properties

The Application, Creator, and Parent properties are defined at the beginning of this Appendix.

Filter Properties

Name	Returns	Description
Criteria1	Variant	Read-only. Returns the first criteria defined for the filter (for example, ">=5")
Criteria2	Variant	Read-only. Returns the second criteria for the filter, if defined
On	Boolean	Read-only. Returns whether the filter is in use
Operator	XlAuto Filter Operator	Read-only. Returns what sort of operator has been defined for the filter (for example, xlTop10Items)

Example: Filter Object and the Filters Collection

See the AutoFormat object for an example of using the Filter object and the Filters collection.

Floor Object

The Floor object contains formatting options for the floor area of a 3D chart. The parent of the Floor object is the Chart object.

Floor Common Properties

The Application, Creator, and Parent properties are defined at the beginning of this Appendix.

Floor Properties

Name	Returns	Description
Border	Border	Read-only. Returns the border's properties around the floor of the 3D chart
Fill	ChartFill Format	Read-only. Returns an object containing fill formatting options for the floor of a 3D chart
Interior	Interior	Read-only. Returns an object containing options to format the inside area of the chart floor (for example, interior color)
Name	String	Read-only. Returns the name of the Floor object
PictureType	Variant	Set/Get how an associated picture is displayed on the floor of the 3D chart (for example, stretched, tiled). Use the XlPictureType constants

Floor Methods

Name	Returns	Parameters	Description
ClearFormats	Variant		Clears the formatting made on the Floor object
Paste			Pastes the picture in the clipboard into the Floor object
Select	Variant		Selects the floor on the parent chart

Example: Floor Object

```
Sub FormatFloor()
    Dim oFlr As Floor
    'Get the chart's Floor
    Set oFlr = Charts(1).Floor
    'Format the floor in white marble
    With oFlr
        .Fill.PresetTextured msoTextureWhiteMarble
        .Fill.Visible = True
    End With
End Sub
```

Font Object

The Font object contains all of the formatting attributes related to fonts of the parent including font type, size and color. Possible parents of the Font object are the AxisTitle, Characters, ChartArea, ChartTitle, DataLabel, Legend, LegendEntry, Range, Style, and TickLabels objects. Also, the DataLabels collection is another possible parent of the Font object.

Font Common Properties

The Application, Creator, and Parent properties are defined at the beginning of this Appendix.

Font Properties

Name	Returns	Description
Background	Variant	Set/Get the type of background used behind the font text (xlBackgroundAutomatic, xlBackgroundOpaque, and xlBackgroundTransparent). Use the XlBackground constants. Valid only for text on charts
Bold	Variant	Set/Get whether the font is bold
Color	Variant	Set/Get the color of the font. Use the RGB function to create the color value
ColorIndex	Variant	Set/Get the color of the font. Use the XlColorIndex constants or an index value in the current color palette
FontStyle	Variant	Set/Get what style to apply to the font (for example, "Bold")
Italic	Variant	Set/Get whether the font is italic
Name	Variant	Set/Get the name of the font
OutlineFont	Variant	Set/Get whether the font is an outline font. Not used in Windows
Shadow	Variant	Set/Get whether the font is a shadow font. Not used in Windows
Size	Variant	Set/Get the font size of the font
Strikethrough	Variant	Set/Get whether the font has a strikethrough effect
Subscript	Variant	Set/Get whether the font characters look like a subscript
Superscript	Variant	Set/Get whether the font characters look like a superscript
Underline	Variant	Set/Get whether the font is underlined

Example: Font Object

```
Sub FormatCellFont()
    Dim oFont As Font
    'Get the font of the currently selected range
    Set oFont = Selection.Font
    'Format the font
    With oFont
        .Name = "Times New Roman"
        .Size = 16          'Points
        .ColorIndex = 5     'Blue
        .Bold = True
        .Underline = xlSingle
    End With
End Sub
```

FormatCondition Object and the FormatConditions Collection

The `FormatConditions` collection contains the conditional formatting associated with the particular range of cells. The `Parent` of the `FormatConditions` collection is the `Range` object. Up to three `FormatCondition` objects can be contained in the `FormatConditions` collection. Each `FormatCondition` object represents some formatting that will be applied if the condition is met.

The `FormatConditions` collection has one property and two methods besides the typical collection attributes. The `Count` property returns how many `FormatCondition` objects are in the collection. The `Add` method can be used to add a formatting condition to the collection. The `Type` parameter must be specified (`XlFormatConditionType` constants) and the condition may be specified with the `Operator`, `Formula1`, and `Formula2` parameters.

Name	Returns	Description
Count	Long	Read-only. Returns the number of objects in the collection
Add	Format Condition	Method. Parameters: `Type As XlFormatConditionType`, `[Operator], [Formula1], [Formula2]`
Delete		Method

FormatCondition Common Properties

The `Application`, `Creator`, and `Parent` properties are defined at the beginning of this Appendix.

FormatCondition Properties

Name	Returns	Description
Borders	Borders	Read-only. Returns a collection holding all the individual border attributes for the formatting condition
Font	Font	Read-only. Returns an object containing `Font` options for the formatting condition
Formula1	String	Read-only. Returns the value that the cells must contain or an expression or formula evaluating to `True/False`. If the formula or expression evaluates to `True` then the formatting is applied
Formula2	String	Read-only. Returns the value that the cells must contain or an expression evaluating to `True/False`. Valid only if the `Operator` property is `xlBetween` or `xlNotBetween`
Interior	Interior	Read-only. Returns an object containing options to format the inside area for the formatting condition (for example, interior color)
Operator	Long	Read-only. Returns the operator to apply to the `Formula1` and `Formula2` property. Use the `XlFormatConditionOperator` constants

Continues

Name	Returns	Description
Type	Long	Read-only. Returns whether the `FormatCondition` is applying formatting based on cell values or a formula. Use the `XlFormatConditionType` constants

FormatCondition Methods

Name	Returns	Parameters	Description
Delete			Deletes the formatting condition
Modify		Type As XlFormat Condition Type, [Operator], [Formula1], [Formula2]	Modifies the formatting condition. Since all the properties are read-only, this is the only way to modify the format condition

Example: FormatCondition Object and the FormatConditions Collection

```
Sub AddConditionalFormat()
   Dim oFC As FormatCondition
   'Remove any existing conditions
   For Each oFC In Selection.FormatConditions
       Selection.FormatConditions(1).Delete
   Next
   'Add first condition
   Set oFC = Selection.FormatConditions.Add(Type:=xlCellValue,
Operator:=xlLess, _
                                                Formula1:="10")

   With oFC
       .Font.ColorIndex = 2            'white
       .Font.Bold = True
       .Interior.Pattern = xlSolid
       .Interior.Color = RGB(255, 0, 0)   'red
   End With
   'Add second condition
   Set oFC = Selection.FormatConditions.Add(Type:=xlCellValue,
Operator:=xlBetween, _
                                    Formula1:="10", Formula2:="40")

   With oFC
       .Font.Color = RGB(0, 255, 0)
       .Font.Bold = False
       .Interior.Pattern = xlNone
   End With
   'Add third condition
   Set oFC = Selection.FormatConditions.Add(Type:=xlCellValue,
Operator:=xlGreater, _
                                                Formula1:="40")
```

```
        With oFC
            .Font.Color = RGB(0, 0, 255)
            .Font.Bold = True
            .Interior.Pattern = xlNone
        End With
End Sub
```

FreeformBuilder Object

The FreeformBuilder object is used by the parent Shape object to create new "free hand" shapes. The BuildFreeform method of the Shape object is used to return a FreeformBuilder object.

FreeformBuilder Common Properties

The Application, Creator, and Parent properties are defined at the beginning of this Appendix.

FreeformBuilder Methods

Name	Returns	Parameters	Description
AddNodes		SegmentType As MsoSegment Type, EditingType As MsoEditing Type, X1 As Single, Y1 As Single, [X2], [Y2], [X3], [Y3]	This method adds a point in the current shape being drawn. A line is drawn from the current node being added to the last node added. SegmentType describes the type of line to add between the nodes. X1, Y1, X2, Y2, X3, Y3 is used to define the position of the current node being added. The coordinates are taken from the upper left corner of the document
ConvertTo Shape	Shape		Converts the nodes added above into a Shape object

Example: FreeformBuilder Object

```
Sub MakeArch()
    Dim oFFB As FreeformBuilder
    'Create a new freeform builder
    Set oFFB = ActiveSheet.Shapes.BuildFreeform(msoEditingCorner, 100, 300)
    'Add the lines to the builder
    With oFFB
        .AddNodes msoSegmentLine, msoEditingAuto, 100, 200
        .AddNodes msoSegmentCurve, msoEditingCorner, 150, 150, 0, 0, 200, 200
        .AddNodes msoSegmentLine, msoEditingAuto, 200, 300
        .AddNodes msoSegmentLine, msoEditingAuto, 100, 300

        'Convert it to a shape
        .ConvertToShape
    End With
End Sub
```

Graphic Object

Represents a picture that can be placed in any one of the six locations of the Header and Footer in the Page Setup of a sheet. It's analogous to using both the Insert Picture and Format Picture buttons in the Header or Footer dialogs inside the Page Setup command.

It's important to note that none of the Property settings of this object will result in anything appearing in the Header or Footer unless you insert "&G" (via VBA code) in any of the six different areas of the Header or Footer.

Graphic Common Properties

The `Application`, `Creator`, and `Parent` properties are defined at the beginning of this Appendix.

Graphic Properties

Name	Returns	Description
Brightness	Single	Set/Get the brightness of the specified picture. This property's value must be from 0.0 (dimmest) to 1.0 (brightest)
ColorType	MsoPicture ColorType	Set/Get the color transformation applied to the specified picture or OLE object
Contrast	Single	Set/Get the contrast of the specified picture. This property's value must be from 0.0 (least) to 1.0 (greatest)
CropBottom	Single	Set/Get the number of points that are cropped off the bottom of the specified picture or OLE object
CropLeft	Single	Set/Get the number of points that are cropped off the left-hand side of the specified picture or OLE object
CropRight	Single	Set/Get the number of points that are cropped off the right-hand side of the specified picture or OLE object
CropTop	Single	Set/Get the number of points that are cropped off the top of the specified picture or OLE object
Filename	String	Set/Get the URL or path to where the specified object was saved
Height	Single	Set/Get the height of the object
LockAspectRatio	MsoTriState	Set/Get whether the specified shape retains its original proportions when you resize it
Width	Single	Set/Get the width of the object

Example: Graphic Object

The following routine prompts the user for a graphic file. If chosen, it places the graphic in the header of the active sheet as a Watermark and sizes it to fit the page:

```
Sub AddWatermark()
    Dim oSheet As Object
    Dim sFile As String

    On Error Resume Next
        Set oSheet = ActiveSheet
    On Error GoTo 0

    'Make sure there is an active sheet
    If Not oSheet Is Nothing Then

        'Set the properties of the File Open dialog
        With Application.FileDialog(msoFileDialogFilePicker)

            'Change the default dialog title
            .Title = "Insert Graphic In Center Header"

            'Allow only one file
            .AllowMultiSelect = False

            'Clear the filters and create your own
            'Switch to the custom filter before showing the dialog
            .Filters.Add "All Pictures", "*.gif; *.jpg; *.jpeg; *.bmp; *.wmf; _
                                  *.gif; *.emf; *.dib; *.jfif; *.jpe", 1

            'Show thumbnails to display small representations
            ' of the images
            .InitialView = msoFileDialogViewThumbnail

            'Show the dialog
            '-1 means they didn't cancel
            If .Show = -1 Then
                'Store the chosen file
                sFile = .SelectedItems(1)

                'Set up the graphic in the Header
                With oSheet.PageSetup
                    With .CenterHeaderPicture
                        .Filename = sFile
                        .ColorType = msoPictureWatermark
                        .LockAspectRatio = True

                        'Make it fill the page
                        'c Assumes a letter size portrait)
                        .Width = Application.InchesToPoints(17)
                    End With

                    'Make the graphic appear
                    'Without this, nothing happens
                    .CenterHeader = "&G"
                End With
```

```
                End If

                'Remove the filter when done
                .Filters.Clear

            End With

        End If

    End Sub
```

Gridlines Object

The `Gridlines` object contains formatting properties associated with the major and minor gridlines on a chart's axes. The gridlines are an extension of the tick marks seen in the background of a chart allowing the end user to more easily see what a chart object's value is. The parent of the `Gridlines` object is the `Axis` object. To make sure the object is valid and to create the `Gridlines` object use the `HasMajorGridlines` and `HasMinorGridlines` properties of the `Axis` object first.

Gridlines Common Properties

The `Application`, `Creator`, and `Parent` properties are defined at the beginning of this Appendix.

Gridlines Properties

Name	Returns	Description
Border	Border	Read-only. Returns the border's properties around the gridlines
Name	String	Read-only. Returns the name of the `Gridlines` object

Gridlines Methods

Name	Returns	Parameters	Description
Delete	Variant		Deletes the `Gridline` object
Select	Variant		Selects the gridlines on the chart

Example: Gridlines Object

```
Sub FormatGridlines()
    Dim oGL As Gridlines
    'Make sure the Y axis has gridlines
    With Charts(1).Axes(xlValue)
        .HasMajorGridlines = True

        'Get the Gridlines object for the major gridlines
        Set oGL = .MajorGridlines
    End With
```

```
        'Format the gridlines
        With oGL
            .Border.ColorIndex = 5
            .Border.LineStyle = xlDash
            .Border.Weight = xlThin
        End With
End Sub
```

GroupShapes Collection

The `GroupShapes` collection holds all of the shapes that make up a grouped shape. The `GroupShapes` collection holds a collection of `Shape` objects. The parent of the `GroupShapes` object is the `Shape` object.

The `GroupShapes` collection only has two properties besides the typical collection attributes. The `Count` property returns the number of `Shape` objects in the `GroupShapes` collection, and the `Range` property returns a subset of the shapes in the `Shapes` collection.

HiLoLines Object

The `HiLoLines` object contains formatting attributes for a chart's high-low lines. The parent of the `HiLoLines` object is the `ChartGroup` object. High-low lines connect the largest and smallest points on a 2D line chart group.

HiLoLines Common Properties

The `Application`, `Creator`, and `Parent` properties are defined at the beginning of this Appendix.

HiLoLines Properties

Name	Returns	Description
Border	Border	Read-only. Returns the border's properties around the high-low lines
Name	String	Read-only. Returns the name of the `HiLoLines` object

HiLoLines Methods

Name	Returns	Parameters	Description
Delete	Variant		Deletes the high-low lines
Select	Variant		Selects the high-low lines on the chart

Example: HiLoLines Object

```
Sub AddAndFormatHiLoLines()
    Dim oHLL As HiLoLines
    'Add high-low lines to the first group
```

```
        Charts(1).ChartGroups(1).HasHiLoLines = True
        'Get the HiLoLines object
        Set oHLL = Charts(1).ChartGroups(1).HiLoLines
        'Format the lines
        With oHLL
            .Border.Weight = xlMedium
            .Border.LineStyle = xlContinuous
            .Border.ColorIndex = 3
        End With
    End Sub
```

HPageBreak Object and the HPageBreaks Collection

The HPageBreaks collection contains all of the horizontal page breaks in the printable area of the parent object. Each HPageBreak object represents a single horizontal page break for the printable area of the parent object. Possible parents of the HPageBreaks collection are the WorkSheet and the Chart objects.

The HPageBreaks collection contains one property and one method besides the typical collection attributes. The Count property returns the number of HPageBreak objects in the collection. The Add method is used to add a HPageBreak object to the collection (and horizontal page break to the sheet). The Add method has a Before parameter to specify the range above where the horizontal page break will be added.

HPageBreak Common Properties

The Application, Creator, and Parent properties are defined at the beginning of this Appendix.

HPageBreak Properties

Name	Returns	Description
Extent	XlPageBreak Extent	Read-only. Returns whether the horizontal page break is full screen or only for the print area
Location	Range	Set/Get the cell that the horizontal page break is located. The top edge of the cell is the location of the page break
Type	XlPageBreak	Set/Get whether the page break is automatic or manually set

HPageBreak Methods

Name	Returns	Parameters	Description
Delete			Deletes the page break
DragOff		Direction As XlDirection, RegionIndex As Long	Drags the page break out of the printable area. The Direction parameter specifies the direction the page break is dragged. The RegionIndex parameter specifies which print region the page break is being dragged out of

Example: HPageBreak Object and the HPageBreaks Collection

```
Sub AddHPageBreaks()
    Dim oCell As Range
    'Loop through all the cells in the first column of the sheet
    For Each oCell In ActiveSheet.UsedRange.Columns(1).Cells
        'If the font size is 16, add a page break above the cell
        If oCell.Font.Size = 16 Then
            ActiveSheet.HPageBreaks.Add oCell
        End If
    Next
End Sub
```

Hyperlink Object and the Hyperlinks Collection

The `Hyperlinks` collection represents the list of hyperlinks in a worksheet or range. Each `Hyperlink` object represents a single hyperlink in a worksheet or range. The `Hyperlinks` collection has an `Add` and `Delete` method besides the typical collection of properties and methods. The `Add` method takes the text or graphic that is to be converted into a hyperlink (`Anchor`) and the URL address or filename (`Address`) and creates a `Hyperlink` object. The `Delete` method deletes the `Hyperlinks` in the collection. The `Hyperlinks` collection also has a `Count` property that returns the number of `Hyperlink` objects in the collection.

Hyperlink Common Properties

The `Application`, `Creator`, and `Parent` properties are defined at the beginning of this Appendix.

Hyperlink Properties

Name	Returns	Description
Address	String	Set/Get the file name or URL address of the hyperlink
EmailSubject	String	Set/Get the e-mail subject line if the address is an e-mail address
Name	String	Read-only. Returns whether the `ExtraInfo` property needs to be filled
Range	Range	Read-only. Returns the name of the hyperlink
ScreenTip	String	Read-only. Returns the spot in the document where the hyperlink is
Shape	Shape	Set/Get the text that appears when the mouse hovers over the hyperlink
SubAddress	String	Read-only. Returns the shape associated with the hyperlink, if any
TextToDisplay	String	Set/Get the spot in the target location that the hyperlink points to
Type	Long	Set/Get the target location of the HTML frame of the Address

Hyperlink Methods

Name	Returns	Parameters	Description
AddTo Favorites			Adds the `Address` property to the `Favorites` folder
CreateNew Document		Filename As String, EditNow As Boolean, Overwrite As Boolean	Creates a new document with the `FileName` name from the results of the hyperlink's address. Set the `EditNow` property to `True` to open up the document in the appropriate editor. Set `Overwrite` to `True` to overwrite any existing document with the same name
Delete			Deletes the `Hyperlink` object
Follow		[NewWindow], [AddHistory], [ExtraInfo], [Method], [HeaderInfo]	Opens up the target document specified by the `Address` property. Setting `NewWindow` to `True` opens up a new window with the target document. Set `AddHistory` to `True` to display the item in history folder. Use the `Method` parameter to choose if the `ExtraInfo` property is sent as a `Get` or a `Post`

Example: Hyperlink Object and the Hyperlinks Collection

This example creates a hyperlink-based "Table of Contents" worksheet:

```
Sub CreateHyperlinkTOC()
    Dim oBk As Workbook
    Dim oShtTOC As Worksheet, oSht As Worksheet
    Dim iRow As Integer
    Set oBk = ActiveWorkbook
    'Add a new sheet to the workbook
    Set oShtTOC = oBk.Worksheets.Add
    With oShtTOC
        'Add the title to the sheet
        .Range("A1").Value = "Table of Contents"

        'Add Mail and web hyperlinks
        .Hyperlinks.Add .Range("A3"), "mailto:Me@MyISP.com", _
                    TextToDisplay:="Email your comments"
        .Hyperlinks.Add .Range("A4"), "http://www.wrox.com", _
                    TextToDisplay:="Visit Wrox Press"
    End With
    'Loop through the sheets in the workbook
    'adding location hyperlinks
    iRow = 6
    For Each oSht In oBk.Worksheets
```

```
            If oSht.Name <> oShtTOC.Name Then
                oShtTOC.Hyperlinks.Add oShtTOC.Cells(iRow, 1), "", _
                        SubAddress:="'" & oSht.Name & "'!A1", _
                        TextToDisplay:=oSht.Name
                iRow = iRow + 1
            End If
        Next
End Sub
```

Interior Object

The `Interior` object contains the formatting options associated with the inside area of the parent object. Possible parents of the `Interior` object are the `AxisTitle`, `ChartArea`, `ChartObject`, `ChartTitle`, `DataLabel`, `DownBars`, `Floor`, `FormatCondition`, `Legend`, `LegendKey`, `OLEObject`, `PlotArea`, `Point`, `Range`, `Series`, `Style`, `Upbars`, and `Walls` objects. The `ChartObjects`, `DataLabels`, and `OLEObjects` collections also are possible parents of the `Interior` object.

Interior Common Properties

The `Application`, `Creator`, and `Parent` properties are defined at the beginning of this Appendix.

Interior Properties

Name	Returns	Description
Color	Variant	Set/Get the color of the interior. Use the RGB function to create the color value
ColorIndex	Variant	Set/Get the color of the interior. Use the XlColorIndex constants or an index value in the current color palette
InvertIf Negative	Variant	Set/Get whether the color in the interior of the parent object is inverted if the values are negative
Pattern	Variant	Set/Get the pattern to use for the interior of the parent object. Use one of the XlPattern constants
PatternColor	Variant	Set/Get the color of the interior pattern. Use the RGB function to create the color value
PatternColor Index	Variant	Set/Get the color of the interior pattern. Use the XlColorIndex constants or an index value in the current color palette

Example: Interior Object

```
Sub FormatRange()
    Dim oInt As Interior
    'Get the interior of the current selection
    Set oInt = Selection.Interior
```

```
      'Format the interior in solid yellow
      '(colour depends on the workbook palette)
      With oInt
         .Pattern = xlSolid
         .ColorIndex = 6
      End With
End Sub
```

IRtdServer Object

This object allows the ability to connect to a Real-Time Data Server (RTD). This type of server allows Excel to receive timed interval data updates without the need for extra coding. In prior versions of Excel, when regular updates were needed, you could use the OnTime method to set up regular data update intervals. RTDs send updates automatically based on an interval set within the server or by using the HeartbeatInterval method of the IRTDUpdateEvent object.

This object is similar in nature to using the RTD worksheet function, which displays data at regular intervals in a worksheet cell.

Note that to use this object you must instantiate it using the Implements keyword.

IRtdServer Methods

Name	Returns	Parameters	Description
ConnectData		TopicID, Strings, GetNewValues	Called when a file is opened that contains real-time data (RTD) functions or when a new formula which contains a RTD function is entered
Disconnect Data		TopicID	Used to notify the RTD server that a topic is no longer in use
Heartbeat	Long		Checks to see if the RTD server is still active. Negative numbers or zero are a failure, while positive numbers indicate success
RefreshData		ByRef TopicCount As Long	This method is called to get new data, but only after being notified by the RTD server that there is new data
ServerStart	Long	Callback Object	Called immediately after a RTD server is instantiated. Negative numbers or zero are a failure, while positive numbers indicate success
Server Terminate			Used to terminate the connection to the server

IRTDUpdateEvent Object

Represents Real-Time update events. This object is used to set the interval between updates for an `IrtdServer` object using the `HeartbeatInterval` property. This object is returned when you use the `ServerStart` method of the `IrtdServer` object to connect to a Real-Time Data server.

IRTDUpdateEvent Properties

Name	Returns	Description
Heartbeat Interval	Long	Set/Get the interval between updates for RTD

IRTDUpdateEvent Methods

Name	Returns	Parameters	Description
Disconnect			Instructs the RTD server to disconnect from the specified object
UpdateNotify			Excel is informed by the RTD server that new data has been received

LeaderLines Object

The `LeaderLines` object contains the formatting attributes associated with leader lines on charts connecting data labels to the actual points. The parent of the `LeaderLines` object is the `Series` object. Use the `HasLeaderLines` property of the `Series` object to create a `LeaderLines` object and make sure one exists.

LeaderLines Common Properties

The `Application`, `Creator`, and `Parent` properties are defined at the beginning of this Appendix.

LeaderLines Properties

Name	Returns	Description
Border	Border	Read-only. Returns the border's properties around the leader lines

LeaderLines Methods

Name	Returns	Parameters	Description
Delete			Deletes the LeaderLines object
Select			Selects the leader lines on the chart

Example: LeaderLines Object

```
Sub AddAndFormatLeaderLines()
    Dim oLL As LeaderLines
    'Using the first series of the PIE chart
    With Charts(1).SeriesCollection(1)
        'Add labels with leader lines (if required)
        .ApplyDataLabels HasLeaderLines:=True

        'Position the labels
        .DataLabels.Position = xlLabelPositionBestFit

        'Get the LeaderLines Object. If all labels are
        'in their default position, this will give an error
        Set oLL = .LeaderLines
    End With
    'Format the leader lines
    With oLL
        .Border.LineStyle = xlContinuous
        .Border.ColorIndex = 5
    End With
End Sub
```

Legend Object

The Legend object contains the formatting options and legend entries for a particular chart. The parent of the Legend object is the Chart object. Use the HasLegend property of the Chart object to create a Legend object and to make sure one exists.

Legend Common Properties

The Application, Creator, and Parent properties are defined at the beginning of this Appendix.

Legend Properties

Name	Returns	Description
AutoScaleFont	Variant	Set/Get whether the font size will change automatically if the parent chart changes sizes
Border	Border	Read-only. Returns the border's properties around the legend
Fill	ChartFill Format	Read-only. Returns an object containing fill formatting options for the legend of a chart
Font	Font	Read-only. Returns an object containing Font options for the legend text
Height	Double	Set/Get the height of the legend box
Interior	Interior	Read-only. Returns an object containing options to format the inside area of a legend (for example, interior color)
Left	Double	Set/Get the distance from the left edge of the legend box to the left edge of the chart containing the legend

Name	Returns	Description
Name	String	Read-only. Returns the name of the Legend object
Position	XlLegend Position	Set/Get the position of the legend on the chart (for example, xlLegendPositionCorner, xlLegendPositionLeft)
Shadow	Boolean	Set/Get whether the legend has a shadow effect
Top	Double	Set/Get the distance from the top edge of the legend box to the top edge of the chart containing the legend
Width	Double	Set/Get the width of the legend box

Legend Methods

Name	Returns	Parameters	Description
Clear	Variant		Clears the legend
Delete	Variant		Deletes the legend
LegendEntries	Object	[Index]	Returns either one LegendEntry object or a LegendEntries collection depending if an Index parameter is specified. Contains all the legend text and markers
Select	Variant		Selects the legend on the chart

Example: Legend Object

```
Sub PlaceLegend()
    Dim oLgnd As Legend
    'Make sure the chart has a legend
    Charts(1).HasLegend = True
    'Get the Legend
    Set oLgnd = Charts(1).Legend
    'Position and format the legend
    With oLgnd
        .Position = xlLegendPositionRight
        .Border.LineStyle = xlNone
        .AutoScaleFont = False
    End With
End Sub
```

LegendEntry Object and the LegendEntries Collection

The LegendEntries collection contains the collection of entries in a legend. Each LegendEntry object represents a single entry in a legend. This consists of the legend entry text and the legend entry marker. The legend entry text is always the associated series name or trendline name. The parent of the LegendEntries collection is the Legend object.

The LegendEntries collection contains one property besides the typical collection attributes. The Count property returns the number of LegendEntry objects in the collection.

LegendEntry Common Properties

The Application, Creator, and Parent properties are defined at the beginning of this Appendix.

LegendEntry Properties

Name	Returns	Description
AutoScaleFont	Variant	Set/Get whether the font size will change automatically if the parent chart changes sizes
Font	Font	Read-only. Returns an object containing Font options for the legend entry text
Height	Double	Read-only. Returns the height of the legend entry
Index	Long	Read-only. Returns the position of the LegendEntry in the LegendEntries collection
Left	Double	Read-only. Returns the distance from the left edge of the legend entry box to the left edge of the chart
LegendKey	LegendKey	Read-only. Returns an object containing formatting associated with the legend entry marker
Top	Double	Read-only. Returns the distance from the top edge of the legend entry box to the top edge of the chart
Width	Double	Read-only. Returns the width of the legend entry

LegendEntry Methods

Name	Returns	Parameters	Description
Delete	Variant		Deletes the LegendEntry object
Select	Variant		Selects the legend entry on the chart

Example: LegendEntry Object and the LegendEntries Collection

```
Sub FormatLegendEntries()
    Dim oLE As LegendEntry
    'Make sure the chart has a legend
    Charts(1).HasLegend = True
    'Loop through all the legend entries
    For Each oLE In Charts(1).Legend.LegendEntries
        'Format each entry with a different font style
        With oLE
            .Font.Size = 10 + .Index * 4
```

```
            .Font.Bold = (.Index Mod 2) = 0
            .Font.ColorIndex = .Index
        End With
    Next
End Sub
```

LegendKey Object

The LegendKey object contains properties and methods to manipulate the formatting associated with a legend key entry marker. A legend key is a visual representation, such as a color, that identifies a specific series or trendline.

LegendKey Common Properties

The Application, Creator, and Parent properties are defined at the beginning of this Appendix.

LegendKey Properties

Name	Returns	Description
Border	Border	Read-only. Returns the border's properties around the legend key
Fill	ChartFill Format	Read-only. Returns an object containing fill formatting options for the legend key of a series or trendline in a chart
Height	Double	Read-only. Returns the height of the legend entry key
Interior	Interior	Read-only. Returns an object containing options to format the inside area of the legend key (for example, interior color)
InvertIf Negative	Boolean	Set/Get whether the color in the legend key is inverted if the values are negative
Left	Double	Read-only. Returns the distance from the left edge of the legend key entry box to the left edge of the chart
Marker Background Color	Long	Set/Get the color of the legend key background. Use the RGB function to create the color value
Marker Background ColorIndex	XlColor Index	Set/Get the color of the legend key background. Use the XlColorIndex constants or an index value in the current color palette
Marker Foreground Color	Long	Set/Get the color of the legend key foreground. Use the RGB function to create the color value
Marker Foreground ColorIndex	XlColor Index	Set/Get the color of the legend key foreground. Use the XlColorIndex constants or an index value in the current color palette

Continues

Name	Returns	Description
MarkerSize	Long	Set/Get the size of the legend key marker
MarkerStyle	XlMarker Style	Set/Get the type of marker to use as the legend key (for example, square, diamond, triangle, picture, etc.)
PictureType	Long	Set/Get how an associated picture is displayed on the legend (for example, stretched, tiled). Use the XlPictureType constants
PictureUnit	Long	Set/Get how many units a picture represents if the PictureType property is set to xlScale
Shadow	Boolean	Set/Get whether a shadow effect appears around the legend entry key
Smooth	Boolean	Set/Get whether the legend key has smooth curving enabled
Top	Double	Read-only. Returns the distance from the top edge of the legend entry key box to the top edge of the chart
Width	Double	Read-only. Returns the width of the legend entry key box.

LegendKey Methods

Name	Returns	Parameters	Description
ClearFormats	Variant		Clears the formatting made on the LegendKey object
Delete	Variant		Deletes the LegendKey object
Select	Variant		Selects the legend key on the parent chart

Example: LegendKey Object

```
Sub FormatLegendKeys()
    Dim oLE As LegendEntry
    Dim oLK As LegendKey
    'Make sure the chart has a legend
    Charts(1).HasLegend = True
    'Loop through all the legend entries
    For Each oLE In Charts(1).Legend.LegendEntries
        'Get the legend key for the entry
        Set oLK = oLE.LegendKey

        'Format each legend key with a different colour and size
        With oLK
            .MarkerForegroundColor = oLE.Index
            .MarkerSize = oLE.Index * 2 + 1
        End With
    Next
End Sub
```

LineFormat Object

The LineFormat object represents the formatting associated with the line of the parent Shape object. The Line property of the Shape object is used to access the LineFormat object. The LineFormat object is commonly used to change line properties such as arrowhead styles and directions.

LineFormat Common Properties

The Application, Creator, and Parent properties are defined at the beginning of this Appendix.

LineFormat Properties

Name	Returns	Description
BackColor	Color Format	Read-only. Returns an object allowing manipulation of the background color of the line
Begin Arrowhead Length	Mso Arrowhead Length	Set/Get the arrowhead length on the start of the line
Begin Arrowhead Style	Mso Arrowhead Style	Set/Get how the arrowhead looks on the start of the line
Begin Arrowhead Width	Mso Arrowhead Width	Set/Get the arrowhead width on the start of the line
DashStyle	MsoLine Dash Style	Set/Get the style of the line
EndArrowhead Length	Mso Arrowhead Length	Set/Get the arrowhead length on the end of the line
EndArrowhead Style	Mso Arrowhead Style	Set/Get how the arrowhead looks on the end of the line
EndArrowhead Width	Mso Arrowhead Width	Set/Get the arrowhead width on the end of the line
ForeColor	Color Format	Read-only. Returns an object allowing manipulation of the background color of the line
Pattern	MsoPattern Type	Set/Get the pattern used on the line
Style	MsoLine Style	Set/Get the line style
Transparency	Single	Set/Get how transparent (1) or opaque (0) the line is
Visible	MsoTri State	Set/Get whether the line is visible
Weight	Single	Set/Get how thick the line is

Example: LineFormat Object

```
Sub AddAndFormatLine()
    Dim oShp As Shape
    Dim oLF As LineFormat
    'Add a line shape
    Set oShp = ActiveSheet.Shapes.AddLine(100, 100, 200, 250)
    'Get the line format object
    Set oLF = oShp.Line
    'Set the line format
    With oLF
        .BeginArrowheadStyle = msoArrowheadOval
        .EndArrowheadStyle = msoArrowheadTriangle
        .EndArrowheadLength = msoArrowheadLong
        .EndArrowheadWidth = msoArrowheadWide
        .Style = msoLineSingle
    End With
End Sub
```

LinkFormat Object

The LinkFormat object represents the linking attributes associated with an OLE object or picture. The LinkFormat object is associated with a Shape object. Only Shape objects that are valid OLE objects can access the LinkFormat object.

LinkFormat Common Properties

The Application, Creator, and Parent properties are defined at the beginning of this Appendix.

LinkFormat Properties

Name	Returns	Description
AutoUpdate	Boolean	Set/Get whether the parent Shape object is updated whenever the source file changes or when the parent object is opened
Locked	Boolean	Set/Get whether the parent Shape object does not update itself against the source file

LinkFormat Methods

Name	Returns	Parameters	Description
Update			Updates the parent Shape object with the source file data

Example: LinkFormat Object

```
Sub UpdateShapeLinks()
    Dim oShp As Shape
```

```
      Dim oLnkForm As LinkFormat
      'Loop through all the shapes in the sheet
      For Each oShp In ActiveSheet.Shapes
          'Is it a linked shape?
          If oShp.Type = msoLinkedOLEObject Or oShp.Type = msoLinkedPicture Then

              'Yes, so get the link format
              Set oLnkForm = oShp.LinkFormat

              'and update the link
              oLnkForm.Update
          End If
      Next
  End Sub
```

ListColumn Object

The ListColumn object represents a column in a List. The ListColumns Collection contains all columns within in list, represented by many ListColumn objects.

ListColumn Common Properties

The Application, Creator, and Parent properties are defined at the beginning of this Appendix.

ListColumn Properties

Name	Returns	Description
Index	Integer	Index number of ListColumn object in the List
ListDataFormat	ListDataFormat Object	Returns a ListDataFormat for the ListColumn object
Name	String	Name of this object
Range		Returns a range representing the range for which the current ListColumn applies to the current list
SharePointFormula	String	Returns a string which is the formula for a calculated field
TotalsCalulation		Determines the type of calculation in the totals row
XPath		Returns an XPath object for the element mapped to the specific Range

ListColumn Methods

Name	Returns	Parameters	Description
Delete			Deletes a column of data in the list

ListDataFormat Object

The ListDataFormat holds all of the data type properties for a `ListColumn` object.

ListDataFormat Common Properties

The Application, Creator, and Parent properties are defined at the beginning of this Appendix.

ListDataFormat Properties

Name	Returns	Description
AllowFillIn	Boolean	Determines if the user can provide values or if they are restricted to use information from a list
Choices	String Array	Contains a string array of choices
DecimalPlaces	Long	Determines the number of decimal places to show
DefaultValue	Variant	Default value to use for this item
IsPercent	Boolean	Determines if this item should be displayed as a percentage
LCID	Long	Determines the currency symbol that is used
MaxCharacters	Long	The maximum number of characters that can be entered
MaxNumber	Variant	The largest number used
MinNumber	Variant	The minimum number that can be used
ReadOnly	Boolean	Determines if the item should be read-only and therefore disallow changes
Required	Boolean	Determines if the item is required
Type	XlListDataType	Used when a item is links to a SharePoint site

ListObject Object

The `ListObject` represents a list object within a workbook.

ListObject Properties

Name	Returns	Description
Application	Object	Returns an Application object which represents the Excel application
Count	Integer	Return the number of items within the collection
Creator	Long	Returns a Long value that represents the application that created the object. This value can then be converted to a hexadecimal value and then to ASCII

Name	Returns	Description
Item	Object	Returns a single object from a collection of objects
Parent	Object	Returns a reference to the parent of the object

ListObject Methods

Name	Returns	Parameters	Description
Delete			Deletes an item from the collection
Publish	String	[Target – String Array] [LinkSource – Boolean]	Publishes the object to a Windows Sharepoint Server. The Target string array must contain the following elements: 0 – URL of SharePoint Server 1 – ListName 2 – Description of list
Refresh			Refreshes the current data from a Windows SharePoint Server
Resize		Range	Allows a ListObject to be resized of a certain range
Unlink			Removes the current link to a Windows SharePoint Server
Unlist			Removes the list functionality from a ListObject thus turning all data into a regular range of data
Update Change			Updates all information on a Windows SharePoint Server by synchronizing all changes

ListRow Object

The ListRow, as the name implies, represents a Row within a List object.

ListRow Properties

Name	Returns	Description
Application	Object	Returns an Application object which represents the Excel application
Creator	Long	Returns a Long value that represents the application that created the object. This value can then be converted to a hexadecimal value and then to ASCII

Continues

Name	Returns	Description
Index	Long	Returns an index number for an item within a collection
InvalidData	Boolean	Returns a Boolean value for a row in a list that determines if the row has or has not passed validation
Parent	Object	Returns a reference to the parent of the object
Range	Range	Returns a range to which the current object applies

ListRow Methods

Name	Returns	Parameters	Description
Delete			Deletes an item from the collection

Mailer Object

The Mailer object is used on the Macintosh to mail Excel files using the PowerTalk Mailer.

Mailer Common Properties

The Application, Creator, and Parent properties are defined at the beginning of this Appendix.

Mailer Properties

Name	Returns	Description
BCCRecipients	Variant	Set/Get the list of blind copies
CCRecipients	Variant	Set/Get the list of carbon copies
Enclosures	Variant	Set/Get the list of enclosures
Received	Boolean	Read-only. Returns whether the mail message was received
SendDateTime	Date	Read-only. Returns the date and time the message was sent
Sender	String	Read-only. Returns the name of the mail message sender
Subject	String	Set/Get the subject line of the mail message
ToRecipients	Variant	Set/Get the array of recipient names
WhichAddress	Variant	Set/Get the address that the mail message originates from

Name Object and the Names Collection

The Names collection holds the list of named ranges in a workbook. Each Name object describes a range of cells in a workbook that can be accessed by the name. Some Name objects are built-in (for example,

Print_Area) and others are user defined. The parent of the Names collection can be the WorkBook, Application, and Worksheet object. The Name object can also be accessed through the Range object.

The Names collection has an Add method besides the typical collection attributes. The Add method adds a Name object to the collection. The parameters of the Add method correspond to the properties of the Name object.

Name Common Properties

The Application, Creator, and Parent properties are defined at the beginning of this Appendix.

Name Properties

Name	Returns	Description
Category	String	Set/Get the category of the Name in the language used to create the macro. Valid only if the Name is a custom function or command
CategoryLocal	String	Set/Get the category of the Name in the language of the end user. Valid only if the Name is a custom function or command
Index	Long	Read-only. Returns the spot that Name is located in the Names collection
MacroType	XlXLMMacroType	Set/Get if the Name refers to command, function, or just a range
Name	String	Set/Get the name of the Name object in the language of the macro
NameLocal	String	Set/Get the name of the Name object in the language of the end user
RefersTo	Variant	Set/Get the range text that the Name refers to in the language of the macro and in A1 notation style
RefersToLocal	Variant	Set/Get the range text that the Name refers to in the language of the user and in A1 notation style
RefersToR1C1	Variant	Set/Get the range text that the Name refers to in the language of the macro and in R1C1 notation style
RefersToR1C1 Local	Variant	Set/Get the range text that the Name refers to in the language of the user and in R1C1 notation style
RefersToRange	Range	Read-only. Returns the range that the Name refers to
ShortcutKey	String	Set/Get the shortcut key to trigger a Microsoft Excel 4.0 macro associated with a Name
Value	String	Set/Get the range text that the Name refers to in the language of the macro and in A1 notation style
Visible	Boolean	Set/Get whether the name of the Name object appears in the Names dialog box in Excel

Name Methods

Name	Returns	Parameters	Description
Delete			Deletes the Name object from the collection

Example: Name Object and the Names Collection

```
Sub DeleteInvalidNames()
    Dim oName As Name
    'Loop through all the names in the active workbook
    For Each oName In ActiveWorkbook.Names
        'Is it an invalid name?
        If InStr(1, oName.RefersTo, "#REF") > 0 Then

            'Yes, so log it
            Debug.Print "Deleted name " & oName.Name & " - " & oName.RefersToLocal

            'and delete it from the collection
            oName.Delete
        End If
    Next
End Sub
```

ODBCError Object and the ODBCErrors Collection

The ODBCErrors collection contains a list of errors that occurred by the most recent query using an ODBC connection. Each ODBCError object contains information describing an error that occurred on the most recent query using an ODBC connection. If the most recent query against an ODBC source did not generate any errors then the collection is empty.

The ODBCErrors collection has a Count property besides the typical collection attributes. The Count property returns the number of ODBCError objects in the collection.

ODBCError Common Properties

The Application, Creator, and Parent properties are defined at the beginning of this Appendix.

ODBCError Properties

Name	Returns	Description
ErrorString	String	Read-only. Returns the error string generated from the ODBC connection
SqlState	String	Read-only. Returns the SQL state error generated from the ODBC connection

Example: ODBCError Object and the ODBCErrors Collection

```
Sub CheckODBCErrors()
    Dim oErr As ODBCError
    Dim sMsg As String
    'Continue after errors
    On Error Resume Next
    'Don't show logon prompts etc
    Application.DisplayAlerts = False
    'Update an ODBC query table
    ActiveSheet.QueryTables(1).Refresh
    'Any errors?
    If Application.ODBCErrors.Count = 0 Then
        'No, so all OK
        MsgBox "Updated OK"
    Else
        'Yes, so list them all
        sMsg = "The following error(s) occured during the update"
        For Each oErr In Application.ODBCErrors
            sMsg = sMsg & vbCrLf & oErr.ErrorString & " (" & oErr.SqlState & ")"
        Next
        MsgBox sMsg
    End If
End Sub
```

OLEDBError Object and the OLEDBErrors Collection

The OLEDBErrors collection contains a list of errors that occurred by the most recent query using an OLE DB provider. Each OLEDBError object contains information describing an error that occurred on the most recent query using an OLE DB provider. If the most recent query against an OLE DB provider did not generate any errors then the collection is empty.

The OLEDBErrors collection has a Count property besides the typical collection attributes. The Count property returns the number of OLEDBError objects in the collection.

OLEDBError Common Properties

The Application, Creator, and Parent properties are defined at the beginning of this Appendix.

OLEDBError Properties

Name	Returns	Description
ErrorString	String	Read-only. Returns the error string generated from the OLE DB provider
Native	Long	Read-only. Returns a provider-specific error number describing the error
Number	Long	Read-only. Returns the error number describing the error

Continues

Name	Returns	Description
SqlState	String	Read-only. Returns the SQL state error generated from the OLE DB provider
Stage	Long	Read-only. Returns the stage of an error generated from the OLE DB provider

Example: OLEDBError Object and the OLEDBErrors Collection

```
Sub CheckOLEDbErrors()
    Dim oErr As OLEDBError
    Dim sMsg As String
    'Continue after errors
    On Error Resume Next
    'Don't show logon prompts etc
    Application.DisplayAlerts = False
    'Update an OLE DB pivot table
    ActiveSheet.PivotTables(1).Refresh
    'Any errors?
    If Application.OLEDBErrors.Count = 0 Then
        'No, so all OK
        MsgBox "Updated OK"
    Else
        'Yes, so list them all
        sMsg = "The following error(s) occured during the update"
        For Each oErr In Application.OLEDBErrors
            sMsg = sMsg & vbCrLf & oErr.ErrorString & " (" & oErr.SqlState & ")"
        Next
        MsgBox sMsg
    End If
End Sub
```

OLEFormat Object

The OLEFormat object represents all attributes associated with an OLE object or ActiveX object for linking. Linking characteristics are taken care of by the LinkFormat object. The Shape object is the parent of the OLEFormat object. The parent Shape object must be a linked or embedded object to be able to use this object.

OLEFormat Common Properties

The Application, Creator, and Parent properties are defined at the beginning of this Appendix.

OLEFormat Properties

Name	Returns	Description
Object	Object	Read-only. Returns a reference to the parent OLE object
ProgId	String	Read-only. Returns the ProgId of the parent OLE object

OLEFormat Methods

Name	Returns	Parameters	Description
Activate			Activates and opens the parent OLE object
Verb		[Verb]	Performs an action on the parent OLE object that triggers a reaction in the OLE object (for example, xlOpen)

Example: OLEFormat Object

```
Sub PrintEmbeddedWordDocuments1()
    Dim oShp As Shape
    Dim oOF As OLEFormat
    'Loop through all the shapes in the sheet
    For Each oShp In ActiveSheet.Shapes
        'Is it an embedded object
        If oShp.Type = msoEmbeddedOLEObject Then
            'Get the embedded object's format
            Set oOF = oShp.OLEFormat

            'Is it a Word document?
            If oOF.ProgId Like "Word.Document*" Then

                'Yes, so print the Word document.
                'The first .Object gives us the generic
                'OLEObject contained in the Shape.
                'The second .Object gives us the Word object
                'contained within the OLEObject
                oOF.Object.Object.PrintOut
            End If
        End If
    Next
End Sub
```

OLEObject Object and the OLEObjects Collection

The OLEObjects collection holds all the ActiveX controls, linked OLE objects and embedded OLE objects on a worksheet or chart. An OLE object represents an ActiveX control, a linked OLE object, or an embedded OLE object on a worksheet or chart.

The OLEObjects collection has many properties and methods besides the typical collection attributes. These are listed in the following table.

OLEObjects Collection Properties and Methods

Name	Returns	Description
AutoLoad	Boolean	Set/Get whether the OLE object is automatically loaded when the workbook is opened. Not valid for ActiveX controls. Usually set to False. This property only works if there is one OLEObject in the collection

Continues

Name	Returns	Description
Border	Border	Read-only. Returns the border's properties around the OLE object. This property only works if there is one OLEObject in the collection
Count	Long	Read-only. Returns the number of OLEObject objects in the collection
Enabled	Boolean	Set/Get whether the OLEObject is enabled. This property only works if there is one OLEObject in the collection
Height	Double	Set/Get the height of OLEObject frame. This property only works if there is one OLEObject in the collection
Interior	Interior	Read-only. Returns an object containing options to format the inside area of the OLE object (for example, interior color). This property only works if there is one OLEObject in the collection
Left	Double	Set/Get the distance from the left edge of the OLEObject frame to the left edge of the sheet. This property only works if there is one OLEObject in the collection
Locked	Boolean	Set/Get whether editing will be possible when the parent sheet is protected. This property only works if there is one OLEObject in the collection
Placement	Variant	Set/Get how the OLEObject object is anchored to the sheet (for example, free floating, move with cells). Use the XlPlacement constants to set this property. This property only works if there is one OLEObject in the collection
PrintObject	Boolean	Set/Get whether the OLEObject on the sheet will be printed when the sheet is printed. This property only works if there is one OLEObject in the collection
Shadow	Boolean	Set/Get whether a shadow appears around the OLE object. This property only works if there is one OLEObject in the collection
ShapeRange	ShapeRange	Read-only. Returns the OLE object as a Shape object. This property only works if there is one OLEObject in the collection
SourceName	String	Set/Get the link source name of the OLE object. This property only works if there is one OLEObject in the collection
Top	Double	Set/Get the distance from top edge of the OLE object to the top of the parent sheet. This property only works if there is one OLEObject in the collection
Visible	Boolean	Set/Get whether all the OLEObjects in the collection are visible

Name	Returns	Description
Width	Double	Set/Get the width of the OLE object frame. This property only works if there is one OLEObject in the collection
ZOrder	Long	Read-only. Returns the position of the OLE object among all the other objects on the sheet. This property only works if there is one OLEObject in the collection
Add	OLEObject	Method. Parameters: [ClassType], [Filename], [Link], [DisplayAsIcon], [IconFileName], [IconIndex], [IconLabel], [Left], [Top], [Width], [Height]. Adds an OLE object to the collection of OLEObjects. The position of the new OLE object can be specified by using the Left, Top, Width, and Height parameters. The type of OLEObject (ClassType) or its location (FileName) can be specified as well. The other parameters have equivalent OLEObject properties
BringToFront	Variant	Method. Brings all the OLE objects in the collection to the front of all the other objects
Copy	Variant	Method. Copies all the OLE objects in the collection into the clipboard
CopyPicture	Variant	Method. Parameters: Appearance As XlPictureAppearance, Format As XlCopyPictureFormat. Copies the OLE objects in the collection into the clipboard as a picture. The Appearance parameter can be used to specify whether the picture is copied as it looks on the screen or when printed. The Format parameter can specify the type of picture that will be put into the clipboard
Cut	Variant	Method. Cuts all the OLE objects in the collection into the clipboard
Delete	Variant	Method. Deletes all the OLEObject objects in the collection into the clipboard
Duplicate		Method. Duplicates all the OLEObject objects in the collection into the parent sheet
Select	Variant	Method. Parameters: [Replace]. Selects all the OLEObject objects in the collection
SendToBack	Variant	Method. Brings the OLEObject objects in the collection to the back of other objects

OLEObject Common Properties

The Application, Creator, and Parent properties are defined at the beginning of this Appendix.

OLEObject Properties

Name	Returns	Description
AltHTML	String	Set/Get what HTML to use when the document is saved as a Web page instead of embedding the OLE control
AutoLoad	Boolean	Set/Get whether the OLE object is automatically loaded when the workbook is opened. Not valid for ActiveX controls. Usually set to False
AutoUpdate	Boolean	Set/Get whether the OLE object is automatically updated when the source changes. Valid only for linked objects (OLEType=xlOLELink)
Border	Border	Read-only. Returns the border's properties around the OLE object
BottomRight Cell	Range	Read-only. Returns the single cell range located under the lower-right corner of the OLE object
Enabled	Boolean	Set/Get whether the OLEObject is enabled
Height	Double	Set/Get the height of OLEObject frame
Index	Long	Read-only. Returns the spot in the collection where the current OLEObject is located
Interior	Interior	Read-only. Returns an object containing options to format the inside area of the OLE object (for example, interior color)
Left	Double	Set/Get the distance from the left edge of the OLEObject frame to the left edge of the sheet
LinkedCell	String	Set/Get the range that receives the value from the results of the OLE object
ListFill Range	String	Set/Get the range that holds the values used by an ActiveX list box
Locked	Boolean	Set/Get whether editing will be possible when the parent sheet is protected
Name	String	Set/Get the name of the OLE object
Object		Read-only. Returns access to some of the properties and methods of the underlying object in the OLE object
OLEType	Variant	Read-only. Returns the type OLE object: xlOLELink or xlOLEEmbed. Use the XlOLEType constants
Placement	Variant	Set/Get how the OLEObject object is anchored to the sheet (for example, free floating, move with cells). Use the XlPlacement constants to set this property
PrintObject	Boolean	Set/Get whether the OLEObject on the sheet will be printed when the sheet is printed

Name	Returns	Description
ProgId	String	Read-only. Returns the programmatic identifier associated with the OLE object (for example, "Excel.Application")
Shadow	Boolean	Set/Get whether a shadow appears around the OLE object
ShapeRange	ShapeRange	Read-only. Returns the OLE object as a Shape object
SourceName	String	Set/Get the link source name of the OLE object
Top	Double	Set/Get the distance from top edge of the OLE object to the top of the parent sheet
TopLeftCell	Range	Read-only. Returns the single cell range located above the top-left corner of the OLE object
Visible	Boolean	Set/Get whether the OLEObject is visible
Width	Double	Set/Get the width of the OLE object frame
ZOrder	Long	Read-only. The position of the OLE object among all the other objects on the sheet

OLEObject Methods

Name	Returns	Parameters	Description
Activate	Variant		Sets the focus and activates the OLE object
BringToFront	Variant		Brings the OLE object to the front of all the other objects
Copy	Variant		Copies the OLE object into the clipboard
CopyPicture	Variant	Appearance As XlPictureAppearance, Format As XlCopyPictureFormat	Copies the OLE object into the clipboard as a picture. The Appearance parameter can be used to specify whether the picture is copied as it looks on the screen or when printed. The Format parameter can specify the type of picture that will be put into the clipboard
Cut	Variant		Cuts the OLE object into the clipboard
Delete	Variant		Deletes the OLEObject object into the clipboard
Duplicate			Duplicates the OLEObject object into the parent sheet
Select	Variant	[Replace]	Selects the OLEObject object
SendToBack	Variant		Brings the OLEObject object to the back of other objects

Continues

Name	Returns	Parameters	Description
Update	Variant		Updates the OLE object link, if applicable
Verb	Variant	Verb As XlOLEVerb	Performs an action on the parent OLE object that triggers a reaction in the OLE object (for example, xlOpen)

OLEObject Events

Name	Parameters	Description
GotFocus		Triggered when the OLE object gets focus
LostFocus		Triggered when the OLE object loses focus

Example: OLEObject Object and the OLEObjects Collection

```
Sub PrintEmbeddedWordDocuments2()
    Dim oOLE As OLEObject
    'Loop through all the shapes in the sheet
    For Each oOLE In ActiveSheet.OLEObjects
        'Is it a Word document?
        If oOLE.ProgId Like "Word.Document*" Then
            'Yes, so print the Word document.
            oOLE.Object.PrintOut
        End If
    Next
End Sub
```

Outline Object

The Outline object represents the outline feature in Excel. The parent of the Outline object is the WorkSheet object.

Outline Common Properties

The Application, Creator, and Parent properties are defined at the beginning of this Appendix.

Outline Properties

Name	Returns	Description
Automatic Styles	Boolean	Set/Get whether the outline has styles automatically assigned by Excel
Summary Column	XlSummary Column	Set/Get whether the summary columns are to the left (xlLeft) or the right (xlRight) of the detail columns
SummaryRow	XlSummary Row	Set/Get whether the summary rows are above (xlAbove) or below (xlBelow) the detail rows

Outline Methods

Name	Returns	Parameters	Description
ShowLevels	Variant	[RowLevels], [Column Levels]	Show the detail of rows and columns at a higher level as specified by the RowLevels and ColumnLevels parameters, respectively. The rest of the detail for the other levels is hidden

Example: Outline Object

```
Sub ShowOutlines()
   Dim oOutl As Outline
   'Group some rows
   ActiveSheet.Range("4:5").Group
   'Get the Outline object
   Set oOutl = ActiveSheet.Outline
   'Format the outline display
   With oOutl
      .ShowLevels 1
      .SummaryRow = xlSummaryAbove
   End With
End Sub
```

PageSetup Object

The PageSetup object contains the functionality of the Page Setup dialog box. Possible parents of the PageSetup object are the Chart and Worksheet object.

PageSetup Common Properties

The Application, Creator, and Parent properties are defined at the beginning of this Appendix.

PageSetup Properties

Name	Returns	Description
BlackAndWhite	Boolean	Set/Get whether worksheet items will be printed in black and white only. Not valid when parents are Chart objects
BottomMargin	Double	Set/Get the bottom margin of the page in points
CenterFooter	String	Set/Get the text for the center part of the footer
CenterFooter Picture	Graphic	Read-only. Returns the picture for the center section of the footer

Continues

Name	Returns	Description
CenterHeader	String	Set/Get the text for the center part of the header
CenterHeader Picture	Graphic	Read-only. Returns the picture for the center section of the footer
Center Horizontally	Boolean	Set/Get whether the worksheet or chart will be horizontally centered on the page
Center Vertically	Boolean	Set/Get whether the worksheet or chart will be vertically centered on the page
ChartSize	XlObjectSize	Set/Get how the chart is scaled to fit one page (xlFullPage or xlFitToPage) or the same way it appears on the screen (xlScreenSize). Not valid when parents are Worksheet objects
Draft	Boolean	Set/Get whether graphics will be printed. True means graphics will not be printed
FirstPage Number	Long	Set/Get which number will be used as the first page number. Use xlAutomatic to have Excel choose this (default)
FitToPages Tall	Variant	Set/Get how many pages tall the sheet will be scaled to. Setting this property to False will mean the FitToPagesWide property will be used
FitToPages Wide	Variant	Set/Get how many pages wide the sheet will be scaled to. Setting this property to False will mean the FitToPagesTall property will be used
FooterMargin	Double	Set/Get the distance from the page bottom to the footer of the page in points
HeaderMargin	Double	Set/Get the distance from the page top to the header of the page in points
LeftFooter	String	Set/Get the text for the left part of the footer
LeftFooter Picture	Graphic	Read-only. Returns the picture for the left section of the footer
LeftHeader	String	Set/Get the text for the center part of the header
LeftHeader Picture	Graphic	Read-only. Returns the picture for the left section of the header
LeftMargin	Double	Set/Get the left margin of the page in points
Order	XlOrder	Set/Get the manner that Excel numbers pages for large worksheets (for example, xlDownTheOver, xlOverThenDown). Not valid for parents that are Chart objects

Name	Returns	Description
Orientation	XlPage Orientation	Set/Get the page orientation: xlLandscape or xlPortrait
PaperSize	XlPaper Size	Set/Get the paper size (for example, xlPaperLetter, xlPaperLegal, etc.)
PrintArea	String	Set/Get the range on a worksheet that will be printed. If this property is set to False then the entire sheet is printed. Not valid for parents that are Chart objects
PrintComments	XlPrint Location	Set/Get how comments are printed or if they are at all (for example, xlPrintInPlace, xlPrintNoComments)
PrintErrors	XlPrint Errors	Set/Get the type of print error displayed. This allows the suppression of error values when printing a worksheet
Print Gridlines	Boolean	Set/Get whether cell gridlines are printed for a worksheet. Not valid for parents that are Chart objects
PrintHeadings	Boolean	Set/Get whether row and column headings are printed
PrintNotes	Boolean	Set/Get whether notes attached to the cells are printed at the end as endnotes. Not valid if parents are Chart objects
PrintTitle Columns	String	Set/Get which columns to repeat on the left side of every printed page
PrintTitleRows	String	Set/Get which rows to repeat on the top of every page
RightFooter	String	Set/Get the text for the right part of the footer
RightFooter Picture	Graphic	Read-only. Returns the picture for the right section of the footer
RightHeader	String	Set/Get the text for the center part of the header
RightHeader Picture	Graphic	Read-only. Returns the picture for the right section of the header
RightMargin	Double	Set/Get the right margin of the page in points
TopMargin	Double	Set/Get the top margin of the page in points
Zoom	Variant	Set/Get the percentage scaling that will occur for the worksheet. Not valid for parents that are Chart objects. (10 to 400 percent)

PageSetup Methods

Name	Returns	Parameters	Description
PrintQuality	Variant	[Index]	Set/Get the print quality. The Index parameter can be used to specify horizontal (1) or vertical (2) print quality

Example: PageSetup Object

```
Sub SetUpPage()
    Dim oPS As PageSetup
    'Get the sheet's PageSetup object
    Set oPS = ActiveSheet.PageSetup
    'Set up the page
    With oPS
        'Set the paper size to the local default
        .PaperSize = fnLocalPaperSize
        .Orientation = xlPortrait
        'etc.
    End With
End Sub
Function fnLocalPaperSize() As XlPaperSize
    'Remember the paper size when we've read it
    Static iPaperSize As XlPaperSize
    'Is it set?
    If iPaperSize = 0 Then
        'No, so create a new workbook and read off the paper size
        With Workbooks.Add
            iPaperSize = .Worksheets(1).PageSetup.PaperSize
            .Close False
        End With
    End If
    'Return the paper size
    fnLocalPaperSize = iPaperSize
End Function
```

Pane Object and the Panes Collection

The Panes collection allows manipulation of the different panes of a window. A Pane object is equivalent to the single pane of a window. The parent object of the Panes collection is the Window object.

Besides the typical collection properties and methods, the Panes collection has a Count property. The Count property returns the number of Pane objects in the collection.

Pane Common Properties

The Application, Creator, and Parent properties are defined at the beginning of this Appendix.

Pane Properties

Name	Returns	Description
Index	Long	Read-only. Returns the spot in the collection where Pane object is located
ScrollColumn	Long	Set/Get which column number is the leftmost column in the pane window
ScrollRow	Long	Set/Get which row number is the top row in the pane window
VisibleRange	Range	Read-only. Returns the cell range that is visible in the pane

Pane Methods

Name	Returns	Parameters	Description
Activate	Boolean		Activates the pane
LargeScroll	Variant	[Down], [Up], [ToRight], [ToLeft]	Causes the document to scroll in a certain direction a screen-full at a time, as specified by the parameters
ScrollInto View		Left As Long, Top As Long, Width As Long, Height As Long, [Start]	Scrolls the spot specified by the Left, Top, Width, and Height parameters to either the upper-left corner of the pane (Start = True) or the lower-right corner of the pane (Start = False). The Left, Top, Width, and Height parameters are specified in points
SmallScroll	Variant	[Down], [Up], [ToRight], [ToLeft]	Causes the document to scroll in a certain direction a document line at a time, as specified by the parameters

Example: Pane Object and the Panes Collection

```
Sub ScrollActivePane()
    Dim oPane As Pane
    Dim oRNg As Range
    'The range to show in the pane
    Set oRNg = Range("G3:J10")
    'Get the active pane
    Set oPane = Application.ActiveWindow.ActivePane
    'Scroll the pane to show the range in the top-left corner
    oPane.ScrollColumn = oRNg.Column
    oPane.ScrollRow = oRNg.Row
End Sub
```

Parameter Object and the Parameters Collection

The `Parameters` collection holds the list of parameters associated with a query table. If no parameters exist then the collection has no `Parameter` objects inside of it. Each `Parameter` object represents a single parameter for a query table. The parent of the `Parameters` collection is the `QueryTable` object.

The `Parameters` collection has a few extra properties and methods besides the typical collection attributes. They are listed in the following table.

Parameters Collection Properties and Methods

Name	Returns	Description
Count	Long	Read-only. Returns the number of `Parameter` objects in the collection
Add	Parameter	Method. Parameters: `Name As String, [iDataType]`. Adds a parameter to the collection creating a new query parameter for the parent query table. The type of parameter can be specified by `iDataType`. Use the `XlParamaterDataType` constants for `iDataType`
Delete		Method. Deletes the parameters in the collection

Parameter Common Properties

The `Application`, `Creator`, and `Parent` properties are defined at the beginning of this Appendix.

Parameter Properties

Name	Returns	Description
DataType	XlParameter DataType	Set/Get the data type of the parameter
Name	String	Set/Get the name of the parameter
Prompt String	String	Read-only. Returns the prompt that is displayed to the user when prompted for a parameter value
RefreshOn Change	Boolean	Set/Get whether the query table results are refreshed when the parameter value changes
Source Range	Range	Read-only. Returns the range of text that contains the parameter value
Type	XlParameter Type	Read-only. Returns the type of parameter (for example, `xlConstant, xlPrompt, or xlRange`). `XlConstant` means that the `Value` parameter has the value of the parameter. `XlPrompt` means that the user is prompted for the value. `XlRange` means that the value defines the cell range that contains the value
Value	Variant	Read-only. Returns the parameter value

Parameter Methods

Name	Returns	Parameters	Description
SetParam		Type As XlParameter Type, Value	Set/Get the type of the parameter and the value of the parameter

Example: Parameter Object and the Parameters Collection

```
Sub UpdateQuery()
    Dim oParam As Parameter
    'Using the Query Table...
    With ActiveSheet.QueryTables(1)
        'Get the first parameter
        Set oParam = .Parameters(1)

        'Set its value
        oParam.SetParam xlConstant, "Company"

        'Refresh the query
        .Refresh
    End With
End Sub
```

Phonetic Object and the Phonetics Collection

The Phonetics collection holds all of the phonetic text in a range. The Phonetic object represents a single phonetic text string. The parent of the Phonetics object is the Range object.

The Phonetics collection has a few properties and methods besides the typical collection attributes. They are listed in the following table.

Phonetics Collection Properties and Methods

Name	Returns	Description
Alignment	Long	Set/Get the alignment for the phonetic text. Use the XlPhoneticAlignment constants
Character Type	Long	Set/Get the type of phonetic text to use. Use the XLPhoneticCharacterType constants
Count	Long	Read-only. Returns the number of Phonetic objects in the collection
Font	Font	Read-only. Returns an object containing Font options for the text in the Phonetics collection

Continues

Name	Returns	Description
Length	Long	Read-only. Returns the number of phonetic text characters starting from the Start parameter
Start	Long	Read-only. Returns what the position is that represents the first character of the phonetic text strings. Valid only if there is only one Phonetic object in the collection
Text	String	Set/Get the phonetic text. Valid only if there is only one Phonetic object in the collection
Visible	Boolean	Set/Get whether the phonetic text is visible to the end user. Valid only if there is only one Phonetic object in the collection
Add		Method. Parameters: Start As Long, Length As Long, Text As String. Adds a Phonetic object to the collection at the cell specified by the parent Range object
Delete		Method. Deletes all the Phonetic objects in the collection

Phonetic Common Properties

The Application, Creator, and Parent properties are defined at the beginning of this Appendix.

Phonetic Properties

Name	Returns	Description
Alignment	Long	Set/Get the alignment for the phonetic text. Use the XlPhoneticAlignment constants
CharacterType	Long	Set/Get the type of phonetic text to use. Use the XLPhoneticCharacterType constants
Font	Font	Read-only. Returns an object containing Font options for the phonetic text
Text	String	Set/Get the phonetic text
Visible	Boolean	Set/Get whether the phonetic text is visible to the end user

PictureFormat Object

The PictureFormat object allows manipulation of the picture properties of the parent Shape object.

PictureFormat Common Properties

The Application, Creator, and Parent properties are defined at the beginning of this Appendix.

PictureFormat Properties

Name	Returns	Description
Brightness	Single	Set/Get the brightness of the parent shape (0 to 1 where 1 is the brightest)
ColorType	MsoPicture ColorType	Set/Get the type of color setting of the parent shape
Contrast	Single	Set/Get the contrast of the parent shape (0 to 1 where 1 is the greatest contrast)
CropBottom	Single	Set/Get how much is cropped off the bottom
CropLeft	Single	Set/Get how much is cropped off the left
CropRight	Single	Set/Get how much is cropped off the right
CropTop	Single	Set/Get how much is cropped off the top
Transparency Color	Long	Set/Get the color used for transparency
Transparent Background	MsoTriState	Set/Get whether transparent colors appear transparent

PictureFormat Methods

Name	Returns	Parameters	Description
Increment Brightness		Increment As Single	Increases the brightness by the Increment value
Increment Contrast		Increment As Single	Increases the contrast by the Increment value

Example: PictureFormat Object

```
Sub SetPictureFormat()
    Dim oShp As Shape
    Dim oPF As PictureFormat
    For Each oShp In ActiveSheet.Shapes
        If oShp.Type = msoPicture Then

            'Get the PictureFormat
            Set oPF = oShp.PictureFormat

            'Format the picture
            With oPF
                .TransparentBackground = msoTrue
                .TransparencyColor = RGB(255, 0, 0)
```

```
            .ColorType = msoPictureWatermark
        End With
    End If
  Next
End Sub
```

PivotCache Object and the PivotCaches Collection

The PivotCaches collection holds the collection of memory "caches" holding the data associated with a PivotTable report. Each PivotCache object represents a single memory cache for a PivotTable report. The parent of the PivotCaches collection is the Workbook object. Also a possible parent of the PivotCache object is the PivotTable object.

The PivotCaches has a Count property and Add method besides the typical collection attributes. The Count property returns the number of items in the collection. The Add method takes a SourceType constant (from the XlPivotTableSourceType constants) and SourceData to add a PivotCache to the collection.

PivotCache Common Properties

The Application, Creator, and Parent properties are defined at the beginning of this Appendix.

PivotCache Properties

Name	Returns	Description
ADOConnection	Object	Read-only. Returns an ADO connection object if the PivotCache is connected to an OLE DB data source
Background Query	Boolean	Set/Get if the processing of queries in a PivotTable report is done asynchronously. False for OLAP data sources
CommandText	Variant	Set/Get the SQL command used to retrieve data
CommandType	XlCmdType	Set/Get the type of ComandText (for example, xlCmdSQL, xlCmdTable)
Connection	Variant	Set/Get the OLE DB connection string, the ODBC string, Web data source, path to a text file, or path to a database
EnableRefresh	Boolean	Set/Get whether the PivotTable cache data can be refreshed. Always False for OLAP data sources
Index	Long	Read-only. Returns the spot in the collection for the specific cache
IsConnected	Boolean	Read-only. Returns whether the PivotCache is still connected to a data source
Local Connection	String	Set/Get the connection string to an offline cube file. Blank for non-OLAP data sources. Use with UseLocalConnection

Name	Returns	Description
Maintain Connection	Boolean	Set/Get whether the connection to the data source does not close until the workbook is closed. Valid only against an OLE DB source
MemoryUsed	Long	Read-only. Returns the amount of bytes used by the `PivotTable` cache
MissingItems Limit	XlPivot Table Missing Items	Set/Get the maximum number of unique items that are retained per `PivotTable` field, even when they have no supporting data in the cache records
OLAP	Boolean	Read-only. Returns whether the `PivotCache` is connected to an OLAP server
OptimizeCache	Boolean	Set/Get whether the `PivotTable` cache is optimized when it is built. Always `False` for OLE DB data sources
QueryType	xlQuery Type	Read-only. Returns the type of connection associated with the query table. (For example, `xlOLEDBQuery`, `xlDAOQuery`, `xlTextImport`)
RecordCount	Long	Read-only. Returns the number of records in the `PivotTable` cache
Recordset		Set/Get the recordset used as the data source for the `PivotTable` cache
RefreshDate	Date	Read-only. Returns the date the cache was last refreshed
RefreshName	String	Read-only. Returns the name of the person who last refreshed the cache
RefreshOnFile Open	Boolean	Set/Get whether the `PivotTable` cache is refreshed when the workbook is opened
RefreshPeriod	Long	Set/Get how long (minutes) between automatic refreshes from the data source. Set to 0 to disable
RobustConnect	XlRobust Connect	Set/Get the method by which the `PivotCache` connects to its data source
SavePassword	Boolean	Set/Get whether an ODBC connection password is saved with the query table
Source Connection File	String	Set/Get the name of the file that was used to create the `PivotTable`
SourceData	Variant	Set/Get the data source for the `PivotTable` report
SourceData File	String	Read-only. Returns the name of the source data file for the `PivotCache`

Continues

Name	Returns	Description
SourceType	XlPivot TableSource Type	Read-only. Returns a value that identifies the type of item being published
UseLocal Connection	Boolean	Set/Get if the `LocalConnection` property is used to set the data source. `False` means the `Connection` property is used. Allows you to store some data sources offline

PivotCache Methods

Name	Returns	Parameters	Description
CreatePivot Table	PivotTable	Table Destination As Variant, [TableName], [ReadData], [Default Version]	Creates a `PivotTable` report that is based on the current `PivotCache` object. The `TableDestination` parameter specifies where the new `PivotTable` report will be located. A `TableName` can also be specified. Set `ReadData` to `True` to fill the cache with all the records from the external database. Set `ReadData` to `True` to only retrieve some of the data. `DefaultVersion` is the default version of the `PivotTable` report
Make Connection			Makes a connection for the specified `PivotCache`
Refresh			Refreshes the data in the `PivotTable` cache with the latest copy of the external data. Set the `BackgroundQuery` parameter to `True` to get the data to refresh asynchronously
ResetTimer			Resets the time for the automatic refresh set by `RefreshPeriod` property
SaveAsODC		ODCFileName As String, [Description], [Keywords]	Saves the `PivotCache` source as an Office Data Connection (ODC) file. `ODCFileName` is the location where the file is to be saved. `Description` is the description that will be saved in the file. `Keywords` is a list of space-separated keywords that can be used to search for this file

Example: PivotCache Object and the PivotCaches Collection

```
Sub RefreshPivotCache()
    Dim oPC As PivotCache
    Set oPC = ActiveWorkbook.PivotCaches(1)
    With oPC
        'Refresh in the foreground
        .BackgroundQuery = False

        'Only refresh if the data is over 1 hour old
        If .RefreshDate < Now - TimeValue("01:00:00") Then
            .Refresh
        End If
    End With
End Sub
```

PivotCell Object

Represents a cell somewhere inside a `PivotTable`. Use access the `PivotCell` object through the range object. Once obtained, you can use the various properties of the `PivotCell` object to retrieve data from a `PivotTable`. For example, you can use the `PivotCellType`, `ColumnItems`, and `RowItems` properties to locate a particular sales person's total sales for a specific region.

This object mirrors the functionality of the `GETPIVOTDATA` worksheet function and the `GetPivotData` method of the `PivotTable` object. The difference is the `PivotCell` object can render information about where the cell is in the report. The `GETPIVOTDATA` worksheet function and the `GetPivotData` method do just the opposite. They yield the value associated with row and column heading you provide.

PivotCell Common Properties

The `Application`, `Creator`, and `Parent` properties are defined at the beginning of this Appendix.

PivotCell Properties

Name	Returns	Description
ColumnItems	PivotItemList	Read-only. Returns the items which represent the selected range on the column axis
Custom Subtotal Function	Xl Consolidation Function	Read-only. Returns the custom subtotal function field setting of the `PivotCell`
DataField	PivotField	Read-only. Returns the selected data field
PivotCellType	XlPivotCell Type	Read-only. Returns the `PivotTable` entity that the selected cell corresponds to
PivotField	PivotField	Read-only. Returns the `PivotTable` field containing the upper-left corner of the specified range

Continues

799

Name	Returns	Description
PivotItem	PivotItem	Read-only. Returns the PivotTable item containing the upper-left corner of the specified range
PivotTable	PivotTable	Read-only. Returns the PivotTable report containing the upper-left corner of the specified range, or the PivotTable report associated with the PivotChart report
Range	Range	Read-only. Returns the range to which the specified PivotCell applies
RowItems	PivotItemList	Read-only. Returns the items which represent the selected range on the row axis

PivotField Object, PivotFields Collection and the CalculatedFields Collection

The PivotFields collection holds the collection of fields associated with the parent PivotTable report. The CalculatedFields collection holds the collection of calculated fields associated with the parent PivotTable report. Each PivotField object represents single field in a PivotTable report. The parent of the PivotFields and CalculatedFields collection is the PivotTable object.

The PivotFields and CalculatedFields collections have one extra property besides the typical collection attributes. The Count property returns the number of fields in the parent collection. The CalculatedFields collection also has an Add method that adds a new calculated field to the collection given a Name and a Formula.

PivotField Common Properties

The Application, Creator, and Parent properties are defined at the beginning of this Appendix.

PivotField Properties

Name	Returns	Description
AutoShowCount	Long	Read-only. Returns the number of top or bottom items that are automatically displayed in the PivotTable field
AutoShowField	String	Read-only. Returns the name of the data field used to figure out what top or bottom items to show automatically for a PivotTable field
AutoShowRange	Long	Read-only. Returns either xlTop if the top items are shown automatically or xlBottom if the bottom items are shown

Name	Returns	Description
AutoShowType	Long	Read-only. Returns either xlAutomatic if AutoShow is True or xlManual if AutoShow is disabled
AutoSortField	String	Read-only. Returns the data field name that will be used to sort the PivotTable field automatically
AutoSortOrder	Long	Read-only. Returns one of the XLSortOrder constants specifying the automatic sort order type used for the field
BaseField	Variant	Set/Get the base field used for a calculation. Data fields only
BaseItem	Variant	Set/Get the base item in the base field used for a calculation. Data fields only
Calculation	XlPivotField Calculation	Set/Get the type of calculation to do on the data field
Caption	String	Set/Get the text label to use for the field
ChildField	PivotField	Read-only. Returns the child field of the current field, if any
ChildItems	Variant	Read-only. Parameters: [Index]. Returns an object or collection containing a single PivotTable item (PivotItem) or group of PivotTable items (PivotItems) associated with the field
CubeField	CubeField	Read-only. Returns the cube field that the current PivotTable field comes from.
CurrentPage	Variant	Set/Get the current page showing for the page field. Page fields only
Current PageList	Variant	Set or Get an array of strings corresponding to the list of items included in a multiple-item page field of a PivotTable report
CurrentPageName	String	Set/Get the displayed page of the PivotTable report
DataRange	Range	Read-only. Returns a range containing the data or items in the field
DataType	XlPivotField DataType	Read-only. Returns the data type of the PivotTable field
DatabaseSort	Boolean	Set/Get whether manual repositioning of items in a PivotField is allowed. Returns True, if the field has no manually positioned items

Continues

Name	Returns	Description
DragToColumn	Boolean	Set/Get whether the field can be dragged to a column position
DragToData	Boolean	Set/Get whether the field can be dragged to the data position
DragToHide	Boolean	Set/Get whether the field can be dragged off the PivotTable report and therefore hidden
DragToPage	Boolean	Set/Get whether the field can be dragged to the page position
DragToRow	Boolean	Set/Get whether the field can be dragged to a row position
DrilledDown	Boolean	Set/Get whether the PivotTable field can be drilled down
EnableItem Selection	Boolean	Set/Get whether the ability to use the field dropdown in the user interface is enabled
Formula	String	Set/Get the formula associated with the field, if any
Function	Xl Consolidation Function	Set/Get the type of function used to summarize the PivotTable field
GroupLevel	Variant	Read-only. Returns how the field is placed within a group of fields
HiddenItems	Variant	Read-only. Parameters: [Index]. Returns an object or collection containing a single hidden PivotTable item (PivotItem) or group of hidden PivotTable items (PivotItems) associated with the field
HiddenItems List	Variant	Set/Get an array of strings that are hidden items for the PivotField
IsCalculated	Boolean	Read-only. Returns whether the PivotTable field is calculated
IsMember Property	Boolean	Read-only. Returns whether the PivotField contains member properties
LabelRange	Range	Read-only. Returns the cell range containing the field's label
LayoutBlank Line	Boolean	Set/Get whether a blank row is added just after the current row field
LayoutForm	XlLayoutForm Type	Set/Get how the items will appear in the field

Name	Returns	Description
LayoutPage Break	Boolean	Set/Get whether a page break is inserted after each field
LayoutSubtotal Location	XlSubtotal LocationType	Set/Get the location for the field subtotals as compared to the current field
MemoryUsed	Long	Read-only. Returns the number of bytes of computer memory being used for the field
Name	String	Set/Get the name of the field
NumberFormat	String	Set/Get the format used for numbers in the field
Orientation	XlPivotField Orientation	Set/Get where the field is located in the PivotTable report
ParentField	PivotField	Read-only. Returns the parent field of the current field, if any
ParentItems	Variant	Read-only. Parameters: [Index]. Returns an object or collection containing a single parent PivotTable item (PivotItem) or group of parent PivotTable items (PivotItems) associated with the field
Position	Variant	Set/Get the position number of the field among all the fields in the same orientation
PropertyOrder	Long	Set/Get the display position of the member property within the cube field to which it belongs (setting will rearrange the order). Valid only for PivotField objects that are member property fields
PropertyParent Field	PivotField	Read-only. Returns the field to which the properties in this field are linked
ServerBased	Boolean	Set/Get whether only items that match the page field selection are retrieved from the external data source
ShowAllItems	Boolean	Set/Get whether all items in the field are displayed
SourceName	String	Read-only. Returns the name of the source data for the field
Standard Formula	String	Set/Get the formulas with standard US formatting
SubtotalName	String	Set/Get the label used for the subtotal column or row for this field

Continues

Name	Returns	Description
Subtotals	Variant	Parameters: [Index]. Set/Get the subtotals displayed for the field
TotalLevels	Variant	Read-only. Returns the total number of fields in the current field group
Value	String	Set/Get the name of the field
VisibleItems	Variant	Read-only. Parameters: [Index]. Returns an object or collection containing a single visible PivotTable item (PivotItem) or group of visible PivotTable items (PivotItems) associated with the field

PivotField Methods

Name	Returns	Parameters	Description
AddPageItem		Item As String, [ClearList]	Adds an additional item to a multiple item page field. Item is the source name of a PivotItem object, corresponding to the specific OLAP member unique name. ClearList indicates whether to delete all existing items before adding the new item
AutoShow		Type As Long, Range As Long, Count As Long, Field As String	Set the number of top or bottom items to display for a row, page, or column field. Type describes whether the items are shown as xlAutomatic or xlManual. Range is the location to start showing items. Count is the number of items to show for the field. Field is the base data field name
AutoSort		Order As Long, Field As String	Sets the field to automatically sort based on the Order specified (using XlSortOrder constants) and the base data Field
Calculated Items	Calculated Items		Returns the group of calculated PivotTable items associated with the field
Delete			Deletes the PivotField object

Name	Returns	Parameters	Description
PivotItems	Variant	[Index]	Returns an object or collection containing a single PivotTable item (PivotItem) or group of PivotTable items (PivotItems) associated with the field

Example: PivotField Object, PivotFields Collection and the CalculatedFields

```
Sub AddField()
    Dim oPT As PivotTable
    Dim oPF As PivotField
    Set oPT = ActiveSheet.PivotTables(1)
    'Set the UseStandardFormula argument to true
    'This will format the field names in the formula for
    ' Standard U.S.English instead of using Local Settings
    'Note that running/debugging this workbook in versions of Excel
    ' prior to Excel 2003 will result in a "Wrong number of arguments" error.
    Set oPF = oPT.CalculatedFields.Add("Total", "=Price * Volume", True)
    oPF.Orientation = xlDataField
End Sub
```

PivotFormula Object and the PivotFormulas Collection

The PivotFormulas collection holds the formulas associated with the PivotTable. Each PivotFormula object represents a formula being used in a PivotTable report. The parent of the PivotFormulas collection is the PivotTable object.

The PivotFormulas collection has a Count property and an Add method besides the typical collection attributes. The Count property returns the number of items in the collection. The Add method takes a Formula string and adds a PivotFormula to the collection.

PivotFormula Common Properties

The Application, Creator, and Parent properties are defined at the beginning of this Appendix.

PivotFormula Properties

Name	Returns	Description
Formula	String	Set/Get the formula associated with the table. Use the A1-style reference notation
Index	Long	Read-only. Returns the order that the formulas in the parent collection will be processed
Standard Formula	String	Set/Get the formulas with standard US formatting
Value	String	Set/Get the formula associated with the table

PivotFormula Methods

Name	Returns	Parameters	Description
Delete			Deletes the formula from the parent collection

PivotItem Object, PivotItems Collection, and the CalculatedItems Collection

The `PivotItems` collection holds the collection of individual data entries in a field. The `CalculatedItems` collection holds the collection of individual calculated entries in a field. Each `PivotItem` object represents a single entry in a data field. The parent of the `PivotItems` and `CalculatedItems` collections is the `PivotField` object.

The `PivotItems` and `CalculatedItems` have one extra property besides the typical collection attributes. The `Count` property returns the number of objects in the collection. Also, the `Add` method of the `PivotItems` collection adds another item to the collection (only a `Name` is required). The `Add` method of the `CalculatedItems` collection adds another item to the collection but requires a `Name` and a `Formula` to be specified.

PivotItem Common Properties

The `Application`, `Creator`, and `Parent` properties are defined at the beginning of this Appendix.

PivotItem Properties

Name	Returns	Description
Caption	String	Set/Get the label text associated with the item
ChildItems	Variant	Read-only. Parameters: [Index]. Returns an object or collection containing a single `PivotTable` item (`PivotItem`) or group of `PivotTable` items (`PivotItems`) associated with the item
DataRange	Range	Read-only. Returns a range containing the data or items in the item
DrilledDown	Boolean	Set/Get whether the `PivotTable` item can be drilled down
Formula	String	Set/Get the formula associated with item, if any
IsCalculated	Boolean	Read-only. Returns whether the item that was calculated is a data item
LabelRange	Range	Read-only. Returns the cell range containing the field's item

Name	Returns	Description
Name	String	Set/Get the name of the item
ParentItem	PivotItem	Read-only. Returns the parent item of the current item, if any
ParentShowDetail	Boolean	Read-only. Returns whether the current item is being shown because the one of the item's parents is set to show detail
Position	Long	Set/Get the position number of the item among all the items in the same orientation
RecordCount	Long	Read-only. Returns the number of records in the PivotTable cache that contain the item
ShowDetail	Boolean	Set/Get whether the detail items are being displayed
SourceName	Variant	Read-only. Returns the name of the source data for the item
SourceName Standard	String	Read-only. Returns the PivotItem's source name in standard US format settings
StandardFormula	String	Set/Get the formulas with standard US formatting
Value	String	Set/Get the name of the specified item
Visible	Boolean	Set/Get whether the item is visible

PivotItem Methods

Name	Returns	Parameters	Description
Delete			Deletes the item from the collection

Example: PivotItem Object, PivotItems Collection, and the CalculatedItems Collection

```
Sub ShowPivotItemData()
   Dim oPT As PivotTable
   Dim oPI As PivotItem
   'Get the pivot table
   Set oPT = ActiveSheet.PivotTables(1)
   'Get the pivot item
   Set oPI = oPT.PivotFields("Product").PivotItems("Oranges")
   'Show all the source data rows for that pivot item
   oPI.ShowDetail = True
End Sub
```

PivotItemList Object

Represents a list of `PivotItems` associated with a particular cell in a `PivotTable`. You access the list through the `PivotCell` object. `PivotItemLists` are accessed either through the `ColumnItems` or `RowItems` properties of the `PivotCell` object. How many row and column items in the `PivotItemList` depends on the structure of the `PivotTable`.

For example, cell D5 is in a `PivotTable` called `WroxSales1`. In the row area to the left of cell D5 is the row heading OR (Oregon). To the left of OR is another row label called Region1. Based on this information the following will yield 2:

```
MsgBox wksPivotTable.Range("D5").PivotCell.RowItems.Count
```

The following will yield Region1, the farthest label to the left of cell D5:

```
MsgBox wksPivotTable.Range("D5").PivotCell.RowItems(1)
```

Finally, the following will yield OR, the second farthest label to the left of cell D5:

```
MsgBox wksPivotTable.Range("D5").PivotCell.RowItems(2)
```

We have yet to find a use for both the `PivotItemList` and `PivotCell` objects. Normally, we are looking for the opposite. We want to retrieve information based on row or column items (headings) we provide, something the `GetPivotData` method and the `GETPIVOTDATA` worksheet function can obtain.

PivotItemList Common Properties

The `Application`, `Creator`, and `Parent` properties are defined at the beginning of this appendix.

PivotItemList Properties

Name	Returns	Description
Count	Long	Returns the number of objects in the collection

PivotItemList Methods

Name	Returns	Parameters	Description
Item	PivotItem	Index As Variant	Returns a single `PivotItem` from the `PivotItemList`

PivotLayout Object

The `PivotLayout` object describes how the fields of a `PivotChart` are placed in the parent chart. Either the `Chart` object or the `ChartGroup` object is the parent of the `PivotChart` object.

PivotLayout Common Properties

The `Application`, `Creator`, and `Parent` properties are defined at the beginning of this Appendix.

PivotLayout Properties

Name	Returns	Description
ColumnFields		Read-only. Parameters: [Index]. Returns an object or collection containing the PivotTable field (PivotField) or PivotTable fields (PivotFields) associated with the columns of the PivotChart
CubeFields	CubeFields	Read-only. Returns the collection of cube fields associated with the PivotChart
DataFields		Read-only. Parameters: [Index]. Returns an object or collection containing the PivotTable field (PivotField) or PivotTable fields (PivotFields) associated with the data fields of the PivotChart
HiddenFields		Read-only. Parameters: [Index]. Returns an object or collection containing the PivotTable field (PivotField) or PivotTable fields (PivotFields) associated with the hidden fields of the PivotChart
InnerDetail	String	Set/Get the name of the field that will show the detail when the ShowDetail property is True
PageFields		Read-only. Parameters: [Index]. Returns an object or collection containing the PivotTable field (PivotField) or PivotTable fields (PivotFields) associated with the page fields of the PivotChart
PivotCache	PivotCache	Read-only. Returns the PivotChart's data cache
PivotFields		Read-only. Parameters: [Index]. Returns an object or collection containing the PivotTable field (PivotField) or PivotTable fields (PivotFields) associated with the fields of the PivotChart
PivotTable	PivotTable	Read-only. Returns the PivotTable associated with the PivotChart
RowFields		Read-only. Parameters: [Index]. Returns an object or collection containing the PivotTable field (PivotField) or PivotTable fields (PivotFields) associated with the rows of the PivotChart
Visible Fields		Read-only. Parameters: [Index]. Returns an object or collection containing the PivotTable field (PivotField) or PivotTable fields (PivotFields) associated with the visible fields of the PivotChart

PivotLayout Methods

Name	Returns	Parameters	Description
AddFields		[RowFields], [Column Fields], [PageFields], [AppendField]	Adds row, column, and page fields to a PivotChart report RowFields, ColumnFields, and PageFields can hold a single string field name or an array of string field names. Set AppendField to True to add the fields to the chart. Set AppendField to False to replace the fields in the chart

Example: PivotLayout Object

```
Sub SetPivotLayout()
    Dim oPL As PivotLayout
    'Get the pivot layout
    Set oPL = Charts(1).PivotLayout
    'Show sales of Oranges by region
    With oPL
        .AddFields RowFields:="Region", PageFields:="Product"
        .PageFields("Product").CurrentPage = "Oranges"
    End With
End Sub
```

PivotTable Object and the PivotTables Collection

The PivotTables collection contains the collection of PivotTables in the parent worksheet. Each PivotTable object in the collection allows manipulation and creation of Excel PivotTables. The parent of the PivotTables collection is the Worksheet object.

The PivotTables collection has a Count property and an Add method besides the typical collection attributes. The Count property returns the number of PivotTable objects in the collection. The Add method takes a new PivotTable cache (containing the data) and the destination single cell range determining the upper-left corner of the PivotTable report to create a new PivotTable report. The name of the new PivotTable report can also be specified in the Add method.

PivotTable Common Properties

The Application, Creator, and Parent properties are defined at the beginning of this Appendix.

PivotTable Properties

Name	Returns	Description
CacheIndex	Long	Set/Get the index number pointing to the PivotTable cache of the current PivotTable
Calculated Members	Calculated Members	Read-only. Returns all the calculated fields and calculated items for the PivotTable

Name	Returns	Description
ColumnFields	Object	Read-only. Parameters: [Index]. Returns an object or collection containing the PivotTable field (PivotField) or PivotTable fields (PivotFields) associated with the columns of the PivotTable
ColumnGrand	Boolean	Set/Get whether grand totals are shown for columns in the PivotTable
ColumnRange	Range	Read-only. Returns the range of cells containing the column area in the PivotTable report
CubeFields	CubeFields	Read-only. Returns the collection of cube fields associated with the PivotTable report
DataBody Range	Range	Read-only. Returns the range of cells containing the data area of the PivotTable report
DataFields	Object	Read-only. Parameters: [Index]. Returns an object or collection containing the PivotTable field (PivotField) or PivotTable fields (PivotFields) associated with the data fields of the PivotTable
DataLabel Range	Range	Read-only. Returns the range of cells that contain the labels for the data fields in the PivotTable report
DataPivot Field	PivotField	Read-only. Returns all the data fields in a PivotTable
DisplayEmpty Column	Boolean	Read-only. Returns whether the non-empty MDX keyword is included in the query to the OLAP provider for the value axis
DisplayEmptyRow	Boolean	Read-only. Returns whether the non-empty MDX keyword is included in the query to the OLAP provider for the category axis
DisplayError String	Boolean	Set/Get whether the string in the ErrorString property is displayed in cells that contain errors
Display Immediate Items	Boolean	Set/Get whether items in the row and column areas are visible when the data area of the PivotTable is empty
DisplayNull String	Boolean	Set/Get whether the string in the NullString property is displayed in cells that contain null values
EnableData ValueEditing	Boolean	Set/Get whether to show an alert when the user overwrites values in the data area of the PivotTable

Continues

Name	Returns	Description
Enable Drilldown	Boolean	Set/Get whether drilldown in the PivotTable report is enabled
EnableField Dialog	Boolean	Set/Get whether the PivotTable Field dialog box is displayed when the user double-clicks a PivotTable field
EnableField List	Boolean	Set/Get whether to disable the ability to display the field well for the PivotTable. If the list was already visible, it disappears
EnableWizard	Boolean	Set/Get whether the PivotTable Wizard is available
ErrorString	String	Set/Get the string that is displayed in cells that contain errors. Use with the DisplayErrorString property
GrandTotal Name	String	Set/Get the string label that will be displayed on the grand total column or row heading of a PivotTable report. Default is "Grand Total"
HasAuto Format	Boolean	Set/Get whether the PivotTable report is automatically reformatted when the data is refreshed or the fields are moved around
HiddenFields	Object	Read-only. Parameters: [Index]. Returns an object or collection containing the PivotTable field (PivotField) or PivotTable fields (PivotFields) associated with the hidden fields of the PivotTable
InnerDetail	String	Set/Get the name of the field that will show the detail when the ShowDetail property is True
MDX	String	Read-only. Returns the MDX (Multidimensional Expression) that would be sent to the provider to populate the current PivotTable view
ManualUpdate	Boolean	Set/Get whether the PivotTable report is only recalculated manually
MergeLabels	Boolean	Set/Get whether the outer-row item, column item, subtotal, and grand total labels of a PivotTable report have merged cells
Name	String	Set/Get the name of the PivotTable report
NullString	String	Set/Get the string that is displayed in cells that contain null strings. Use with the DisplayNullString property
PageField Order	Long	Set/Get how new page fields are added to a PivotTable report's layout. Use the XLOrder constants

Name	Returns	Description
PageFields	Object	Read-only. Parameters: [Index]. Returns an object or collection containing the PivotTable field (PivotField) or PivotTable fields (PivotFields) associated with the page fields of the PivotTable
PageField Style	String	Set/Get the style used for a page field area in a PivotTable
PageField WrapCount	Long	Set/Get how many page fields are in each column or row of the PivotTable report
PageRange	Range	Read-only. Returns the range containing the page area in the PivotTable report
PageRange Cells	Range	Read-only. Returns the range containing the page fields and item drop-down lists in the PivotTable report
Pivot Formulas	Pivot Formulas	Read-only. Returns the collection of formulas used in the PivotTable report
Pivot Selection	String	Set/Get the data and label selection in the PivotTable using the standard PivotTable report selection format. For example, to select the data and label for the Country equal to "Canada" then the string would be "Country[Canada]"
Pivot Selection Standard	String	Set/Get the PivotTable selection in standard PivotTable report format using US settings
Preserve Formatting	Boolean	Set/Get whether formatting of the PivotTable report is preserved when the report is changed, sorted, pivoted, refreshed or recalculated
PrintTitles	Boolean	Set/Get whether the print title set on the PivotTable report is printed whenever the parent worksheet is printed
RefreshDate	Date	Read-only. Returns the date that the PivotTable report data was refreshed last
RefreshName	String	Read-only. Returns the name of the user who last refreshed the PivotTable report data
RepeatItems OnEachPrinted Page	Boolean	Set/Get whether row, column, and item labels appear on the first row of each page when the PivotTable report is printed
RowFields		Read-only. Parameters: [Index]. Returns an object or collection containing the PivotTable field (PivotField) or PivotTable fields (PivotFields) associated with the rows of the PivotTable

Continues

813

Name	Returns	Description
RowGrand	Boolean	Set/Get whether grand totals are shown for rows in the PivotTable
RowRange	Range	Read-only. Returns the range of cells containing the row area in the PivotTable report
SaveData	Boolean	Set/Get whether the PivotTable report data is saved with the workbook
Selection Mode	XlPT Selection Mode	Set/Get how the PivotTable report selection mode is set (for example, xlLabelOnly)
ShowCell Background FromOLAP	Boolean	Set/Get whether the MDX that Excel asks for includes the BackColor property for each cell in the data area that corresponds to a cell in the OLAP data set
ShowPage MultipleItem Label	Boolean	Set/Get whether "(Multiple Items)" will appear in the PivotTable cell whenever items are hidden and an aggregate of non-hidden items is shown in the PivotTable view
SmallGrid	Boolean	Set/Get whether a two-by-two grid is used for a newly created PivotTable report (True) or a blank stencil outline (False)
SourceData	Variant	Set/Get the source of the PivotTable report data. Can be a cell reference, an array, multiple ranges, and another PivotTable report. Not valid to use with OLE DB data sources
Subtotal HiddenPage Items	Boolean	Set/Get whether hidden page fields are included in row and column subtotals, block totals, and grand totals
TableRange1	Range	Read-only. Returns the range containing the whole PivotTable report, not including page fields
TableRange2	Range	Read-only. Returns the range containing the whole PivotTable report, with page fields
TableStyle	String	Set/Get the PivotTable report body style
Tag	String	Set/Get a string to be saved with the PivotTable report (for example, a description of the PivotTable report)
VacatedStyle	String	Set/Get the style to use for vacated cells when a PivotTable report is refreshed
Value	String	Set/Get the name of the PivotTable report

Name	Returns	Description
Version	XlPivot Table VersionList	Read-only. Returns the version number of Excel
View Calculated Members	Boolean	Set/Get whether calculated members for OLAP PivotTables can be viewed
Visible Fields		Read-only. Parameters: [Index]. Returns an object or collection containing the PivotTable field (PivotField) or PivotTable fields (PivotFields) associated with the visible fields of the PivotTable
VisualTotals	Boolean	Set/Get whether PivotTables should retotal after an item has been hidden from view

PivotTable Methods

Name	Returns	Parameters	Description
AddDataField	PivotField	Field As Object, [Caption], [Function]	Adds a data field to a PivotTable report. Field is the unique field on the server, Caption is the label used to identify this data field, and Function is the function performed in the added data field
AddFields	Variant	[RowFields], [Column Fields], [PageFields], [AddToTable]	Adds row, column, and page fields to a PivotTable report. The RowFields, ColumnFields, and PageFields can hold a single string field name or an array of string field names. Set AddToTable to True to add the fields to the report. Set AddToTable to False to replace the fields in the report
Calculated Fields	Calculated Fields		Returns the collection of calculated fields in the PivotTable Report

Continues

Name	Returns	Parameters	Description
CreateCube File	String	File As String, [Measures], [Levels], [Members], [Properties]	Creates a cube file from a PivotTable report connected to an OLAP data source. File is the name of the cube file to be created, Measures is an array of unique names of measures that are to be part of the slice, and Levels an array of strings, where each array item is a unique level name. Members is an array of string arrays, where the elements correspond, in order, to the hierarchies represented in the Levels array. Properties should be set to False if you don't want member properties being included in the slice
Format		Format As xlPivotFormat Type	Set the PivotTable report format to the predefined style specified in the Format parameter
GetData	Double	Name As String	Get the value of a specific cell in the PivotTable report. The Name parameter must be in the standard PivotTable report selection format
GetPivotData	Range	[DataField], [Field1], [Item1], [Field2], [Item2], [Field3], [Item3], [Field4], [Item4], [Field5], [Item5], [Field6], [Item6], [Field7], [Item7], [Field8], [Item8], [Field9], [Item9], [Field10], [Item10], [Field11], [Item11], [Field12], [Item12], [Field13], [Item13], [Field14], [Item14]	Returns information about a data item in a PivotTable report. FieldN is the name of a column or row field in the PivotTable report, and ItemN is the name of an item in FieldN
ListFormulas			Creates a separate worksheet with the list of all the calculated PivotTable items and fields

Name	Returns	Parameters	Description
PivotCache	PivotCache		Returns a data cache associated with the current PivotTable
PivotFields	Object	[Index]	Returns an object or collection containing the PivotTable field (PivotField) or PivotTable fields (PivotFields) associated with the fields of the PivotTable
PivotSelect		Name As String, [Mode As XlPTSelectionMode], [UseStandard Name]	Selects the part of the PivotTable specified by Name parameter in the standard PivotTable report selection format. Mode decides which part of the PivotTable to select (for example, xlBlanks). Set UseStandardName to True for recorded macros that will play back in other locales
PivotTableWizard		[SourceType], [SourceData], [Table Destination], [TableName], [RowGrand], [ColumnGrand], [SaveData], [HasAuto Format], [AutoPage], [Reserved], [Background Query], [Optimize Cache], [PageField Order], [PageField WrapCount], [ReadData], [Connection]	Creates a PivotTable report. The SourceType uses the XLPivotTableSourceType constants to specify the type of SourceData being used for the PivotTable. The TableDestination holds the range in the parent worksheet that the report will be placed. TableName holds the name of the new report. Set RowGrand or ColumnGrand to True to show grand totals for rows and columns, respectively. Set HasAutoFormat to True for Excel to format the report automatically when it is refreshed or changed. Use the AutoPage parameter to set if a page field is created for consolidation automatically. Set BackgroundQuery to True for Excel to query the data source asynchronously.

Continues

Name	Returns	Parameters	Description
			Set `OptimizeCache` to `True` for Excel to optimize the cache when it is built. Use the `PageFieldOrder` with the `XLOrder` constants to set how new page fields are added to the report. Use the `PageFieldWrapCount` to set the number of page fields in each column or row. Set `ReadData` to `True` to copy the data from the external database into a cache. Finally, use the `Connection` parameter to specify an ODBC connection string for the `PivotTable`'s cache
`RefreshTable`	Boolean		Refreshes the `PivotTable` report from the source data and returns `True`, if successful
`ShowPages`	Variant	`[PageField]`	Creates a new `PivotTable` report for each item in the page field (`PageField`) in a new worksheet
`Update`			Updates the `PivotTable` report

Example: PivotTable Object and the PivotTables Collection

```
Sub PreviewPivotTable()
    Dim oPT As PivotTable
    'Get the pivot layout
    Set oPT = ActiveSheet.PivotTables(1)
    'Add column and row titles, then printpreview the table
    With oPT
        .ColumnGrand = False
        .RowGrand = True
        .TableRange2.PrintPreview
    End With
End Sub
```

PlotArea Object

The `PlotArea` object contains the formatting options associated with the plot area of the parent chart. For 2D charts the `PlotArea` includes trendlines, data markers, gridlines, data labels, and the axis labels—but not titles. For 3D charts the `PlotArea` includes the walls, floor, axes, axis titles, tick-marks, and all of the items mentioned for the 2D charts. The area surrounding the plot area is the chart area. Please see the `ChartArea` object for formatting related to the chart area. The parent of the `PlotArea` is always the `Chart` object.

PlotArea Common Properties

The Application, Creator, and Parent properties are defined at the beginning of this Appendix.

PlotArea Properties

Name	Returns	Description
Border	Border	Read-only. Returns the border's properties around the plot area
Fill	ChartFill Format	Read-only. Returns an object containing fill formatting options for a chart's plot area
Height	Double	Set/Get the height of the chart plot area
InsideHeight	Double	Read-only. Returns the height inside the plot area that does not include the axis labels
InsideLeft	Double	Read-only. Returns the distance from the left edge of the plot area, not including axis labels, to the chart's left edge
InsideTop	Double	Read-only. Returns the distance from the left edge of the plot area, not including axis labels, to the chart's left edge
InsideWidth	Double	Read-only. Returns the width inside the plot area that does not include the axis labels
Interior	Interior	Read-only. Returns an object containing options to format the inside area of the plot area (for example, interior color)
Left	Double	Set/Get the distance from the left edge of the plot area to the chart's left edge
Name	String	Read-only. Returns the name of the plot area
Top	Double	Set/Get the distance from the top edge of the plot area to the chart's top edge
Width	Double	Set/Get the width of the chart plot area

PlotArea Methods

Name	Returns	Parameters	Description
ClearFormats	Variant		Clears any formatting made to the plot area
Select	Variant		Selects the plot area on the chart

Example: PlotArea Object

This example uses the `PlotArea` object to make all the charts in the workbook have the same size and position plot area, regardless of the formatting of the axes (for example, different fonts and number scales):

```
Sub MakeChartAreasSameSizeAsFirst()
    Dim oCht As Chart, oPA As PlotArea
    Dim dWidth As Double, dHeight As Double
    Dim dTop As Double, dLeft As Double
    'Get the dimensions of the inside of the
    'plot area of the first chart
    With Charts(1).PlotArea
        dWidth = .InsideWidth
        dHeight = .InsideHeight
        dLeft = .InsideLeft
        dTop = .InsideTop
    End With
    'Loop through the charts in the workbook
    For Each oCht In Charts
        'Get the PlotArea
        Set oPA = oCht.PlotArea

        'Size and move the plot area
        With oPA
            If .InsideWidth > dWidth Then
                'Too big, make it smaller
                .Width = .Width - (.InsideWidth - dWidth)
            Else
                'Too small, move it left and make bigger
                .Left = .Left - (dWidth - .InsideWidth)
                .Width = .Width + (dWidth - .InsideWidth)
            End If

            If .InsideHeight > dHeight Then
                'Too big, make it smaller
                .Height = .Height - (.InsideHeight - dHeight)
            Else
                'Too small, move it left and make bigger
                .Top = .Top - (dHeight - .InsideHeight)
                .Height = .Height + (dHeight - .InsideHeight)
            End If
            'Set the position of the inside of the plot area
            .Left = .Left + (dLeft - .InsideLeft)
            .Top = .Top + (dTop - .InsideTop)
        End With
    Next
End Sub
```

Point Object and the Points Collection

The `Points` collection holds all of the data points of a particular series of a chart. In fact, a chart (`Chart` object) can have many chart groups (`ChartGroups` / `ChartGroup`) that can contain many series (`SeriesCollection` / `Series`), which, in turn, can contain many points (`Points` / `Point`). A `Point` object describes the particular point of a series on a chart. The parent of the `Points` collection is the `Series` object.

The `Points` collection contains a `Count` property besides the typical collection attributes. The `Count` property returns the number of `Point` objects in the collection.

Point Common Properties

The `Application`, `Creator`, and `Parent` properties are defined at the beginning of this Appendix.

Point Properties

Name	Returns	Description
ApplyPictTo End	Boolean	Set/Get whether pictures are added to the end of the point
ApplyPictTo Front	Boolean	Set/Get whether pictures are added to the front of the point
ApplyPictTo Sides	Boolean	Set/Get whether pictures are added to the sides of the point
Border	Border	Read-only. Returns the border's properties around the point
DataLabel	DataLabel	Read-only. Returns an object allowing you to manipulate the data label attributes (for example, formatting, text). Use with `HasDataLabel`
Explosion	Long	Set/Get how far out a slice (point) of a pie or doughnut chart will explode out. 0 for no explosion
Fill	ChartFill Format	Read-only. Returns an object containing fill formatting options for a point
HasDataLabel	Boolean	Set/Get whether the point has a data label. Use with `DataLabel`
Interior	Interior	Read-only. Returns an object containing options to format the inside area of the point (for example, interior color)
InvertIfNegative	Boolean	Set/Get whether the point's color will be inverted if the point value is negative
Marker Background Color	Long	Set/Get the color of the point marker background Use the `RGB` function to create the color value
Marker Background ColorIndex	XlColor Index	Set/Get the color of the point marker background. Use the `XlColorIndex` constants or an index value in the current color palette

Continues

Name	Returns	Description
Marker Foreground Color	Long	Set/Get the color of the point marker foreground. Use the RGB function to create the color value
Marker Foreground ColorIndex	XlColor Index	Set/Get the color of the point marker foreground. Use the XlColorIndex constants or an index value in the current color palette
MarkerSize	Long	Set/Get the size of the point key marker
MarkerStyle	XlMarker Style	Set/Get the type of marker to use as the point key (for example, square, diamond, triangle, picture, etc.)
PictureType	XlChart PictureType	Set/Get how an associated picture is displayed on the point (for example, stretched, tiled). Use the XlPictureType constants
PictureUnit	Long	Set/Get how many units a picture represents if the PictureType property is set to xlScale
Secondary Plot	Boolean	Set/Get if the point is on the secondary part of a Pie of Pie chart of a Bar of Pie chart
Shadow	Boolean	Set/Get whether the point has a shadow effect

Point Methods

Name	Returns	Parameters	Description
ApplyData Labels	Variant	[Type As XlDataLabels Type], [LegendKey], [AutoText], [HasLeader Lines], [ShowSeries Name], [ShowCategory Name], [ShowValue], [Show Percentage], [ShowBubble Size], [Separator]	Applies the data label properties specified by the parameters to the point. The Type parameter specifies whether no label, a value, a percentage of the whole, or a category label is shown. The legend key can appear by the point by setting the LegendKey parameter to True. Set AutoText to True if the object automatically generates appropriate text based on content. HasLeaderLines should be set to True if the series has leader lines. All the other parameters are simply the property of the data label that they describe
ClearFormats	Variant		Clears the formatting made to a point

Name	Returns	Parameters	Description
Copy	Variant		Cuts the point and places it in the clipboard
Delete	Variant		Deletes the point
Paste	Variant		Pastes the picture in the clipboard into the current point so it becomes the marker
Select	Variant		Selects the point on the chart

Example: Point Object and the Points Collection

```
Sub ExplodePie()
    Dim oPt As Point
    'Get the first data point in the pie chart
    Set oPt = Charts(1).SeriesCollection(1).Points(1)
    'Add a label to the first point only and
    'set it away from the pie
    With oPt
        .ApplyDataLabels xlDataLabelsShowLabelAndPercent
        .Explosion = 20
    End With
End Sub
```

Protection Object

Represents the group of the much-needed sheet protection options new to Excel 2003. When you protect a sheet, you now have the option to only allow unlocked cells selected, allow cell, column, and row formatting, allow insertion and deletion of rows and columns, allow sorting, and more.

Setting Protection options is done via the `Protect` method of the `Worksheet` object. Use the `Protection` property of the `Worksheet` object to check the current protection settings:

```
MsgBox ActiveSheet.Protection.AllowFormattingCells
```

Protection Properties

Name	Returns	Description
AllowDeleting Columns	Boolean	Read-only. Returns whether the deletion of columns is allowed on a protected worksheet
AllowDeleting Rows	Boolean	Read-only. Returns whether the deletion of rows is allowed on a protected worksheet
AllowEdit Ranges	AllowEdit Ranges	Read-only. Returns an `AllowEditRanges` object

Continues

Name	Returns	Description
Allow Filtering	Boolean	Read-only. Returns whether the user is allowed to make use of an AutoFilter that was created before the sheet was protected
Allow Formatting Cells	Boolean	Read-only. Returns whether the formatting of cells is allowed on a protected worksheet
AllowFormatting Columns	Boolean	Read-only. Returns whether the formatting of columns is allowed on a protected worksheet
AllowFormatting Rows	Boolean	Read-only. Returns whether the formatting of rows is allowed on a protected worksheet
AllowInserting Columns	Boolean	Read-only. Returns whether the inserting of columns is allowed on a protected worksheet
AllowInserting Hyperlinks	Boolean	Read-only. Returns whether the inserting of hyperlinks is allowed on a protected worksheet
AllowInserting Rows	Boolean	Read-only. Returns whether the inserting of rows is allowed on a protected worksheet
AllowSorting	Boolean	Read-only. Returns whether the sorting option is allowed on a protected worksheet
AllowUsing PivotTables	Boolean	Read-only. Returns whether the manipulation of PivotTables is allowed on a protected worksheet

Example: Protection Object

The following routine sets Protection options based on the user name found on the General tab of the Tools ➪ Options command and that user's settings on a table on the worksheet. If the user isn't found, a message appears and the default settings are used:

```
Sub ProtectionSettings()
    Dim rngUsers As Range, rngUser As Range
    Dim sCurrentUser As String

    'Grab the current username
    sCurrentUser = Application.UserName

    'Define the list of users in the table
    With wksAllowEditRange
        Set rngUsers = .Range(.Range("Users"), .Range("Users").End(xlToRight))
    End With

    'Locate the current user on the table
    Application.FindFormat.Clear
    Set rngUser = rngUsers.Find(What:=sCurrentUser, SearchOrder:=xlByRows,
MatchCase:=False, SearchFormat:=False)

    'If current user is found on the table...
```

```
        If Not rngUser Is Nothing Then
            'Set the Protection properties based
            ' on a table
            wksAllowEditRange.Protect Password:="wrox1", _
            DrawingObjects:=True, _
            Contents:=True, _
            AllowFormattingCells:=rngUser.Offset(1, 0).Value, _
            AllowFormattingColumns:=rngUser.Offset(2, 0).Value, _
            AllowFormattingRows:=rngUser.Offset(3, 0).Value, _
            AllowSorting:=rngUser.Offset(4, 0).Value, _
            UserInterfaceOnly:=True

            'Select Unlocked cells, Locked and Unlocked cells, or neither
            ' is NOT part of the Protection object
            If rngUser.Offset(5, 0).Value = True Then
                wksAllowEditRange.EnableSelection = xlUnlockedCells
            Else
                wksAllowEditRange.EnableSelection = xlNoRestrictions
            End If
        Else
            'Current user is not on the table
            MsgBox "User not found on User Table. Default Options will be used.", _
    vbExclamation, "Protection Settings"
            wksAllowEditRange.Protect , True, True, False, False, False, _
                                 False, False, False, False, False, _
                                 False, False, False, False, False

            wksAllowEditRange.EnableSelection = xlNoRestrictions

        End If

End Sub
```

PublishObject Object and the PublishObjects Collection

The PublishObjects collection holds all of the things in a workbook that have been saved to a Web page. Each PublishObject object contains items from a workbook that have been saved to a Web page and may need some occasional refreshing of values on the Web page side. The parent of the PublishObjects collection is the Workbook object.

The PublishObjects collection has a few properties and methods besides the typical collection attributes. The unique attributes are listed in the following table.

PublishObjects Properties and Methods

Name	Returns	Description
AutoRepublish	Boolean	Set/Get whether an item in the PublishObjects collection should be republished when a workbook is saved
Count	Long	Read-only. Returns the number of PublishObject objects in the collection

Continues

Name	Returns	Description
Add	Publish Object	Method. Parameters: SourceType As XlSourceType, Filename As String, [Sheet], [Source], [HtmlType], [DivID], [Title]. Adds a PublishObject to the collection
Delete		Method. Deletes the PublishObject objects from the collection
Publish		Method. Publishes all the items associated with the PublishObject objects to a Web page

PublishObject Common Properties

The Application, Creator, and Parent properties are defined at the beginning of this Appendix.

PublishObject Properties

Name	Returns	Description
DivID	String	Read-only. Returns the id used for the <DIV> tag on a Web page
Filename	String	Set/Get the URL or path that the object will be saved to as a Web page
HtmlType	XlHtmlType	Set/Get what type of Web page to save (for example, xlHtmlStatic, xlHtmlChart). Pages saved as other than xlHtmlStatic need special ActiveX components
Sheet	String	Read-only. Returns the Excel sheet that will be saved as a Web page
Source	String	Read-only. Returns the specific item, like range name, chart name, or report name from the base type specified by the SourceType property
SourceType	XlSource Type	Read-only. Returns the type of source being published (for example, xlSourceChart, xlSourcePrintArea, etc.)
Title	String	Set/Get the Web page title for the published Web page

PublishObject Methods

Name	Returns	Parameters	Description
Delete			Deletes the PublishObject object
Publish		[Create]	Publishes the source items specified by the PublishObject as a Web file. Set the Create parameter to True to overwrite existing files. False will append to the existing Web page with the same name, if any

Example: PublishObject Object and the PublishObjects Collection

```
Sub UpdatePublishedCharts()
    Dim oPO As PublishObject
    For Each oPO In ActiveWorkbook.PublishObjects
        If oPO.SourceType = xlSourceChart Then
            oPO.Publish
        End If
    Next
End Sub
```

QueryTable Object and the QueryTables Collection

The QueryTables collection holds the collection of data tables created from an external data source. Each QueryTable object represents a single table in a worksheet filled with data from an external data source. The external data source can be an ODBC source, an OLE DB source, a text file, a Data Finder, a Web-based query, or a DAO/ADO recordset. The parent of the QueryTables collection is the Worksheet object.

The QueryTables collection has a few properties and methods not typical of a collection. These atypical attributes are listed next.

QueryTables Properties and Methods

Name	Returns	Description
Count	Long	Read-only. Returns the number of items in the collection
Add	QueryTable	Method. Parameters: Connection, Destination As Range, [Sql]. Adds a QueryTable to the collection. The Connection parameter can specify the ODBC or OLE DB connection string, another QueryTable object, a DAO or ADO recordset object, a Web-based query, a Data Finder string, or a text file name. The Destination parameter specifies the upper-left corner that the query table results will be placed. The SQL parameter can specify the SQL for the connection, if applicable

QueryTable Common Properties

The Application, Creator, and Parent properties are defined at the beginning of this Appendix.

QueryTable Properties

Name	Returns	Description
AdjustColumn Width	Boolean	Set/Get whether the column widths automatically adjust to best fit the data every time the query table is refreshed

Continues

Name	Returns	Description
Background Query	Boolean	Set/Get if the query table processing is done asynchronously
CommandText	Variant	Set/Get the SQL command used to retrieve data
CommandType	XlCmdType	Set/Get the type of ComandText (for example, xlCmdSQL, xlCmdTable)
Connection	Variant	Set/Get the OLE DB connection string, the ODBC string, Web data source, path to a text file, or path to a database
Destination	Range	Read-only. Returns the upper-left corner cell that the query table results will be placed
EditWebPage	Variant	Set/Get the Webpage URL for a Web query
Enable Editing	Boolean	Set/Get whether the query table data can be edited or only refreshed (False)
Enable Refresh	Boolean	Set/Get whether the query table data can be refreshed
FetchedRow Overflow	Boolean	Read-only. Returns whether the last query table refresh retrieved more rows than available on the worksheet
FieldNames	Boolean	Set/Get whether the field names from the data source become column headings in the query table
FillAdjacent Formulas	Boolean	Set/Get whether formulas located to the right of the query table will update automatically when the query table data is refreshed
ListObject	Range	Returns a Range object
Maintain Connection	Boolean	Set/Get whether the connection to the data source does not close until the workbook is closed. Valid only against an OLE DB source
Name	String	Set/Get the name of the query table
Parameters	Parameters	Read-only. Returns the parameters associated with the query table
PostText	String	Set/Get the post message sent to the Web server to return data from a Web query
Preserve Column Info	Boolean	Set/Get whether column location, sorting and filtering does not disappear when the data query is refreshed
Preserve Formatting	Boolean	Set/Get whether common formatting associated with the first five rows of data are applied to new rows in the query table

Name	Returns	Description
QueryType	xlQuery Type	Read-only. Returns the type of connection associated with the query table. (For example, xlOLEDBQuery, xlDAOQuery, xlTextImport)
Recordset		Read-only. Returns a recordset associated with the data source query
Refreshing	Boolean	Read-only. Returns whether an asynchronous query is currently in progress
RefreshOn FileOpen	Boolean	Set/Get whether the query table is refreshed when the workbook is opened
Refresh Period	Long	Set/Get how long (minutes) between automatic refreshes from the data source. Set to 0 to disable
RefreshStyle	XlCell Insertion Mode	Set/Get how worksheet rows react when data rows are retrieved from the data source. Worksheet cells can be overwritten (xlOverwriteCells), cell rows can be partial inserted / deleted as necessary (xlInsertDeleteCells), or only cell rows that need to be added are added (xlInsertEntireRows)
ResultRange	Range	Read-only. Returns the cell range containing the results of the query table
Robust Connect	XlRobust Connect	Set/Get how the PivotCache connects to its data source
RowNumbers	Boolean	Set/Get whether a worksheet column is added to the left of the query table containing row numbers
SaveData	Boolean	Set/Get whether query table data is saved with the workbook
SavePassword	Boolean	Set/Get whether an ODBC connection password is saved with the query table
SourceConnection File	String	Set/Get the name of the file that was used to create the PivotTable
SourceData File	String	Read-only. Returns the name of the source data file for the PivotCache
TextFile Column DataTypes	Variant	Set/Get the array of column constants representing the data types for each column. Use the XlColumnDataType constants. Used only when QueryType is xlTextImport
TextFile Comma Delimiter	Boolean	Set/Get whether a comma is the delimiter for text file imports into a query table. Used only when QueryType is xlTextImport and for a delimited text file

Continues

829

Name	Returns	Description
TextFile Consecutive Delimiter	Boolean	Set/Get whether consecutive delimiters (for example, ",,,") are treated as a single delimeter. Used only when QueryType is xlTextImport
TextFile Decimal Separator	String	Set/Get the type of delimeter to use to define a decimal point. Used only when QueryType is xlTextImport
TextFile Fixed ColumnWidths	Variant	Set/Get the array of widths that correspond to the columns. Used only when QueryType is xlTextImport and for a fixed width text file
TextFile Other Delimiter	String	Set/Get the character that will be used to delimit columns from a text file. Used only when QueryType is xlTextImport and for a delimited text file
TextFile ParseType	XlText ParsingType	Set/Get the type of text file that is being imported: xlDelimited or xlFixedWidth. Used only when QueryType is xlTextImport
TextFilePlatform	XlPlatform	Set/Get which code pages to use when importing a text file (for example, xlMSDOS, xlWindows). Used only when QueryType is xlTextImport
TextFile PromptOn Refresh	Boolean	Set/Get whether the user is prompted for the text file to use to import into a query table every time the data is refreshed. Used only when QueryType is xlTextImport. The prompt does not appear on the initial refresh of data
TextFile Semicolon Delimiter	Boolean	Set/Get whether the semicolon is the text file delimiter for importing text files. Used only when QueryType is xlTextImport and the file is a delimited text file
TextFile Space Delimiter	Boolean	Set/Get whether the space character is the text file delimiter for importing text files. Used only when QueryType is xlTextImport and the file is a delimited text file
TextFile StartRow	Long	Set/Get which row number to start importing from a text file. Used only when QueryType is xlTextImport
TextFileTab Delimiter	Boolean	Set/Get whether the tab character is the text file delimiter for importing text files. Used only when QueryType is xlTextImport and the file is a delimited text file
TextFileText Qualifier	XlText Qualifier	Set/Get which character will be used to define string data when importing data from a text file. Used only when QueryType is xlTextImport

Name	Returns	Description
TextFile Thousands Separator	String	Set/Get which character is used as the thousands separator in numbers when importing from a text file (for example, ",")
TextFile TrailingMinus Numbers	Boolean	Set/Get whether to treat numbers imported as text that begin with a "-" symbol as negative numbers
TextFile VisualLayout	Long	Returns 1 or 2 depending on the visual layout of the file. A value of 1 represents left-to-right while 2 represents right-to-left
Web Consecutive DelimitersAsOne	Boolean	Set/Get whether consecutive delimiters are treated as a single delimeter when importing data from a Web page. Used only when QueryType is xlWebQuery
WebDisable Date Recognition	Boolean	Set/Get whether data that looks like dates are parsed as text when importing Web page data. Used only when QueryType is xlWebQuery
WebDisable Redirections	Boolean	Set/Get whether Web query redirections are disabled for the QueryTable object
WebFormatting	xlWeb Formatting	Set/Get whether to keep any of the formatting when importing a Web page (for example, xlAll, xlNone). Used only when QueryType is xlWebQuery
WebPre Formatted TextToColumns	Boolean	Set/Get whether HTML data with the <PRE> tag is parsed into columns when importing Web pages. Used only when QueryType is xlWebQuery
WebSelection Type	xlWeb Selection Type	Set/Get what data from a Web page is imported. Either all tables (xlAllTables), the entire page (xlEntirePage), or specified tables (xlSpecifiedTables). Used only when QueryType is xlWebQuery
WebSingleBlock TextImport	Boolean	Set/Get whether all the Web page data with the <PRE> tags are imported all at once. Used only when QueryType is xlWebQuery
WebTables	String	Set/Get a comma-delimited list of all the table names that will be imported from a Web page. Used only when QueryType is xlWebQuery and WebSelectionType is xlSpecifiedTables

QueryTable Methods

Name	Returns	Parameters	Description
CancelRefresh			Cancels an asynchronously running query table refresh
Delete			Deletes the query table
Refresh	Boolean	[Background Query]	Refreshes the data in the query table with the latest copy of the external data. Sets the BackgroundQuery parameter to True to get the data to refresh asynchronously
ResetTimer			Resets the time for the automatic refresh set by RefreshPeriod property
SaveAsODC		ODCFileName As String, [Description], [Keywords]	Saves the PivotCache source as an Office Data Connection file. ODCFileName is the location of the source file. Description is the description that will be saved in the file. Keywords is a list of space-separated keywords that can be used to search for this file

Example: QueryTable Object and the QueryTables Collection

```
Sub UpdateAllWebQueries()
    Dim oQT As QueryTable
    For Each oQT In ActiveSheet.QueryTables
        If oQT.QueryType = xlWebQuery Then
            oQT.BackgroundQuery = False
            oQT.Refresh
        End If
    Next
End Sub
```

Range Object

The Range object is one of the more versatile objects in Excel. A range can be a single cell, a column, a row, a contiguous block of cells, or a non-contiguous range of cells. The main parent of a Range object is the Worksheet object. However, most of the objects in the Excel Object Model use the Range object. The Range property of the Worksheet object can be used to choose a certain range of cells using the Cell1 and Cell2 parameters.

Range Common Properties

The Application, Creator, and Parent properties are defined at the beginning of this Appendix.

Range Properties

Name	Returns	Description
AddIndent	Variant	Set/Get whether text in a cell is automatically indented if the text alignment in a cell is set to equally distribute
Address	String	Read-only. Parameters: RowAbsolute, ColumnAbsolute, ReferenceStyle As XlReferenceStyle, [External], [RelativeTo]. Returns the address of the current range as a string in the macro's language. The type of address (reference, absolute, A1 reference style, R1C1 reference style) is specified by the parameters
AddressLocal	String	Read-only. Parameters: RowAbsolute, ColumnAbsolute, ReferenceStyle As XlReferenceStyle, [External], [RelativeTo]. Returns the address of the current range as a string in the user's language. The type of address (reference, absolute, A1 reference style, R1C1 reference style) is specified by the parameters
AllowEdit	Boolean	Read-only. Returns True if the range can be edited on a protected worksheet
Areas	Areas	Read-only. Returns an object containing the different non-contiguous ranges in the current range
Borders	Borders	Read-only. Returns all the individual borders around the range. Each border side can be accessed individually in the collection
Cells	Range	Read-only. Returns the cells in the current range. The Cells property will return the same range as the current range
Characters	Characters	Read-only. Parameters: [Start], [Length]. Returns all the characters in the current range, if applicable
Column	Long	Read-only. Returns the column number of the first column in the range
Columns	Range	Read-only. Returns a range of the columns in the current range
ColumnWidth	Variant	Set/Get the column width of all the columns in the range. Returns Null if the columns in the range have different widths
Comment	Comment	Read-only. Returns an object representing the range comment, if any

Continues

Name	Returns	Description
Count	Long	Read-only. Returns the number of cells in the current range
CurrentArray	Range	Read-only. Returns a Range object that represents the array associated with the particular cell range, if the cell is part of an array
CurrentRegion	Range	Read-only. Returns the current region that contains the Range object. A region is defined as an area that is surrounded by blank cells
Dependents	Range	Read-only. Returns the dependents of a cell on the same sheet as the range
Direct Dependents	Range	Read-only. Returns the direct dependents of a cell on the same sheet as the range
Direct Precedents	Range	Read-only. Returns the direct precedents of a cell on the same sheet as the range
End	Range	Read-only. Parameters: Direction As XlDirection. Returns the cell at end of the region containing the Range object. Which end of the region is specified by the Direction parameter
EntireColumn	Range	Read-only. Returns the full worksheet column(s) occupied by the current range
EntireRow	Range	Read-only. Returns the full worksheet row(s) occupied by the current range
Errors	Errors	Read-only. Returns the Errors collection associated with the Range object
Font	Font	Read-only. Returns an object containing Font options for the text in the range
Format Conditions	Format Conditions	Read-only. Returns an object holding conditional formatting options for the current range
Formula	Variant	Set/Get the formula in the cells of the range
FormulaArray	Variant	Set/Get the array formula of the cells in the range
Formula Hidden	Variant	Set/Get whether the formula will be hidden if the workbook/worksheet is protected
FormulaLabel	XlFormula Label	Set/Get the type of formula label to use for the specified range
FormulaLocal	Variant	Set/Get the formula of the range in the language of the user using the A1 style references
FormulaR1C1	Variant	Set/Get the formula of the range in the language of the macro using the R1C1 style references

Name	Returns	Description
FormulaR1C1 Local	Variant	Set/Get the formula of the range in the language of the user using the R1C1 style references
HasArray	Variant	Read-only. Returns whether a single cell range is part of an array formula
HasFormula	Variant	Read-only. Returns whether all the cells in the range contain formulas (True). If only some of the cells contain formulas then Null is returned
Height	Variant	Read-only. Returns the height of the range
Hidden	Variant	Set/Get whether the cells in the range are hidden. Only works if the range contains whole columns or rows
Horizontal Alignment	Variant	Set/Get how the cells in the range are horizontally aligned. Use the XLHAlign constants
Hyperlinks	Hyperlinks	Read-only. Returns the collection of hyperlinks in the range
ID	String	Set/Get the ID used for the range if the worksheet is saved as a Web page
IndentLevel	Variant	Set/Get the indent level for the range
Interior	Interior	Read-only. Returns an object containing options to format the inside area of the range if applicable (for example, interior color)
Left	Variant	Read-only. Returns the distance from the left edge of the left-most column in the range to the left edge of ColumnA
ListHeader Rows	Long	Read-only. Returns the number of header rows in the range
ListOject	Range	Returns a Range object
LocationIn Table	XlLocation InTable	Read-only. Returns the location of the upper-left corner of the range
Locked	Variant	Set/Get whether cells in the range can be modified if the sheet is protected. Returns Null if only some of the cells in the range are locked
MergeArea	Range	Read-only. Returns a range containing the merged range of the current cell range
MergeCells	Variant	Set/Get whether the current range contains merged cells
Name	Variant	Set/Get the Name object that contains the name for the range

Continues

Name	Returns	Description
Next	Range	Read-only. Returns the next range in the sheet
NumberFormat	Variant	Set/Get the number format associated with the cells in the range. Null if all the cells don't have the same format
NumberFormat Local	Variant	Set/Get the number format associated with the cells in the range in the language of the end user. Null if all the cells don't have the same format
Offset	Range	Read-only. Parameters: [RowOffset], [ColumnOffset]. Returns the cell as a Range object that is the offset from the current cell as specified by the parameters. A positive RowOffset offsets the row downward. A negative RowOffset offsets the row upward. A positive ColumnOffset offsets the column to the right and a negative ColumnOffset offsets the column to the left
Orientation	Variant	Set/Get the text orientation for the cell text. A value from −90 to 90 degrees can be specified, or use an XlOrientation constant
OutlineLevel	Variant	Set/Get the outline level for the row or column range
PageBreak	Long	Set/Get how page breaks are set in the range. Use the XLPageBreak constants
Phonetic	Phonetic	Read-only. Returns the Phonetic object associated with the cell range
Phonetics	Phonetics	Read-only. Returns the Phonetic objects in the range
PivotCell	PivotCell	Read-only. Returns a PivotCell object that represents a cell in a PivotTable report
PivotField	PivotField	Read-only. Returns the PivotTable field associated with the upper-left corner of the current range
PivotItem	PivotItem	Read-only. Returns the PivotTable item associated with the upper-left corner of the current range
PivotTable	PivotTable	Read-only. Returns the PivotTable report associated with the upper-left corner of the current range
Precedents	Range	Read-only. Returns the range of precedents of the current cell range on the same sheet as the range
Prefix Character	Variant	Read-only. Returns the character used to define the type of data in the cell range. For example, "'" for a text label

Name	Returns	Description
Previous	Range	Read-only. Returns the previous range in the sheet
QueryTable	QueryTable	Read-only. Returns the query table associated with the upper-left corner of the current range
Range	Range	Read-only. Parameters: Cell1, [Cell2]. Returns a Range object as defined by the Cell1 and optionally Cell2 parameters. The cell references used in the parameters are relative to the range. For example, Range.Range ("A1") would return the first column in the parent range but not necessarily the first column in the worksheet
ReadingOrder	Long	Set/Get whether the text is from right-to-left (x1RTL), left-to-right (x1LTR), or context-sensitive (x1Context)
Resize	Range	Read-only. Parameters: [RowSize], [ColumnSize]. Returns a new resized range as specified by the RowSize and ColumnSize parameters
Row	Long	Read-only. Returns the row number of the first row in the range
RowHeight	Variant	Set/Get the height of the rows in the range. Returns Null if the rows in the range have different row heights
Rows	Range	Read-only. Returns a Range object containing the rows of the current range
ShowDetail	Variant	Set/Get if all the outline levels in the range are expanded. Applicable only if a summary column or row is the range
ShrinkToFit	Variant	Set/Get whether the cell text will automatically shrink to fit the column width. Returns Null if the rows in the range have different ShrinkToFit properties
SmartTags	SmartTags	Read-only. Returns a SmartTags object representing the identifier for the specified cell
SoundNote	SoundNote	Property is kept for backwards compatibility only
Style	Variant	Read-only. Returns the Style object associated with the range
Summary	Variant	Read-only. Returns whether the range is an outline summary row or column

Continues

Name	Returns	Description
Text	Variant	Read-only. Returns the text associated with a range cell
Top	Variant	Read-only. Returns the distance from the top edge of the topmost row in the range to the top edge of RowA
UseStandard Height	Variant	Set/Get whether the row height is the standard height of the sheet. Returns Null if the rows in the range contain different heights
UseStandard Width	Variant	Set/Get whether the column width is the standard width of the sheet. Returns Null if the columns in the range contain different widths
Validation	Validation	Read-only. Returns the data validation for the current range
Value	Variant	Parameters: [RangeValueDataType]. Set/Get the value of a cell or an array of cells depending on the contents of the Range object
Value2	Variant	Set/Get the value of a cell or an array of cells depending on the contents of the Range object. No Currency or Date types are returned by Value2
Vertical Alignment	Variant	Set/Get how the cells in the range are vertically aligned. Use the XLVAlign constants
Width	Variant	Read-only. Returns the height of the range
Worksheet	Worksheet	Read-only. Returns the worksheet that has the Range object
WrapText	Variant	Set/Get whether cell text wraps in the cell. Returns Null if the cells in the range contain different text wrap properties
XPath	Object	Represents the XPath element of the object at the current range

Range Methods

Name	Returns	Parameters	Description
Activate	Variant		Selects the range cells
AddComment	Comment	[Text]	Adds the text specified by the parameter to the cell specified in the range. Must be a single cell range

Name	Returns	Parameters	Description
Advanced Filter	Variant	Action As XlFilter Action, [Criteria Range], [CopyToRange], [Unique]	Copies or filters the data in the current range. The Action parameter specifies whether a copy or filter is to take place. CriteriaRange optionally specifies the range containing the criteria. CopyToRange specifies the range that the filtered data will be copied to (if Action is xlFilterCopy)
ApplyNames	Variant	Names, Ignore Relative Absolute, UseRowColumn Names, OmitColumn, OmitRow, Order As XlApplyNames Order, [AppendLast]	Applies defined names to the formulas in a range. For example, if a cell contained =$A$1*100 and $A$1 was given the name "TopLeft", you could apply the "TopLeft" name to the range, resulting in the formula changing to =TopLeft*100. Note that there is no UnApplyNames method
ApplyOutline Styles	Variant		Applies the outline styles to the range
AutoComplete	String	String As String	Returns and tries to AutoComplete the word specified in the String parameter. Returns the complete word, if found. Returns an empty string if no word or more than one word is found
AutoFill	Variant	Destination As Range, Type As XlAutoFill Type	Uses the current range as the source to figure out how to AutoFill the range specified by the Destination parameter. The Type parameter can also be used to specify the type of fill to use (for example, xlFillCopy, xlFillDays)

Continues

Name	Returns	Parameters	Description
AutoFilter	Variant	Field, Criteria1, Operator As XlAutoFilter Operator, [Criteria2], [Visible Drop Down]	Creates an auto-filter on the data in the range. See the AutoFilter object for details on the parameters
AutoFit	Variant		Changes the column widths in the range to best fit the data in the cells. The range must contain full rows or columns
AutoFormat	Variant	Format As XlRangeAuto Format, [Number], [Font], [Alignment], [Border], [Pattern], [Width]	Formats the range using the format specified by the Format parameter. The other parameters are Boolean indicators to specify: if numbers are formatted appropriately (Number), fonts applied (Font), alignments applied (Alignment), border formats applied (Border), pattern formats applied (Pattern), and if row/column widths are applied from the autoformat
AutoOutline	Variant		Creates an outline for the range
BorderAround	Variant	LineStyle, Weight As XlBorder Weight, ColorIndex As XlColorIndex, [Color]	Creates a border around the range with the associated line style (LineStyle), thickness (Weight), and color (ColorIndex)
Calculate	Variant		Calculates all the formulas in the range

Name	Returns	Parameters	Description
CheckSpelling	Variant	[Custom Dictionary], [Ignore Uppercase], [Always Suggest], [SpellLang]	Checks the spelling of the text in the range. A custom dictionary can be specified (CustomDictionary), all UPPERCASE words can be ignored (IgnoreUppercase), and Excel can be set to display a list of suggestions (AlwaysSuggest)
Clear	Variant		Clears the text in the cells of the range
ClearComments			Clears all the comments in the range cells
ClearContents	Variant		Clears the formulas and values in a range
ClearFormats	Variant		Clears the formatting in a range
ClearNotes	Variant		Clears comments from the cells in the range
ClearOutline	Variant		Clears the outline used in the current range
Column Differences	Range	Comparison	Returns the range of cells that are different to the cell specified by the Comparison parameter
Consolidate	Variant	[Sources], [Function], [TopRow], [Left Column], [Create Links]	Consolidates the source array of range reference strings in the Sources parameter and returns the results to the current range. The Function parameter can be used to set the consolidation function. Use the XLConsolidation Function constants
Copy	Variant	[Destination]	Copies the current range to the range specified by the parameter or to the clipboard if no destination is specified

Continues

Name	Returns	Parameters	Description
CopyFrom Recordset	Long	Data As Recordset, [MaxRows], [MaxColumns]	Copies the records from the ADO or DAO recordset specified by the Data parameter into the current range. The recordset can't contain OLE objects
CopyPicture	Variant	Appearance As XlPicture Appearance, Format As XlCopyPicture Format	Copies the range into the clipboard as a picture. The Appearance parameter can be used to specify whether the picture is copied as it looks on the screen or when printed. The Format parameter can specify the type of picture that will be put into the clipboard
CreateNames	Variant	[Top], [Left], [Bottom], [Right]	Creates a named range for the items in the current range. Set Top to True to make the first row hold the names for the ranges below. Set Bottom to True to use the bottom row as the names. Set Left or Right to True to make the left or right column contain the Names, respectively
Create Publisher	Variant	Edition, Appearance As XlPicture Appearance, [Contains PICT], [Contains BIFF], [ContainsRTF], [Contains VALU]	Creates a publisher based on the range. Available only on the Macintosh with System 7 or later
Cut	Variant	[Destination]	Cuts the current range to the range specified by the parameter, or to the clipboard if no destination is specified

Name	Returns	Parameters	Description
DataSeries	Variant	Rowcol, Type As XlDataSeries Type, Date As XlDataSeries Date, [Step], [Stop], [Trend]	Creates a data series at the current range location
Delete	Variant	[Shift]	Deletes the cells in the current range and optionally shifts the cells in the direction specified by the Shift parameter. Use the XlDeleteShift Direction constants for the Shift parameter
DialogBox	Variant		Displays a dialog box defined by an Excel 4.0 macro sheet
Dirty			Selects a range to be recalculated when the next recalculation occurs
Edition Options	Variant	Type As XlEdition Type, Option As XlEdition Options Option, Name, Reference, Appearance As XlPicture Appearance, ChartSize As XlPicture Appearance, [Format]	Used on the Macintosh. EditionOptions set how the range should act when being used as the source (publisher) or target (subscriber) of the link. Editions are basically the same as Windows' DDE links
FillDown	Variant		Copies the contents and formatting from the top row into the rest of the rows in the range
FillLeft	Variant		Copies the contents and formatting from the rightmost column into the rest of the columns in the range

Continues

843

Name	Returns	Parameters	Description
FillRight	Variant		Copies the contents and formatting from the leftmost column into the rest of the columns in the range
FillUp	Variant		Copies the contents and formatting from the bottom row into the rest of the rows in the range
Find	Range	What As Variant, [After], [LookIn], [LookAt], [SearchOrder], [Search Direction As XlSearch Direction], [MatchCase], [MatchByte], [Search Format]	Looks through the current range for the text of data type specified by the What parameter. Use a single cell range in the After parameter to choose the starting position of the search. Use the LookIn parameter to decide where the search is going to take place
FindNext	Range	[After]	Finds the next instance of the search criteria defined with the Find method
FindPrevious	Range	[After]	Finds the previous instance of the search criteria defined with the Find method
Function Wizard	Variant		Displays the Function Wizard for the upper-left cell of the current range
GoalSeek	Boolean	Goal, ChangingCell As Range	Returns True if the value specified by the Goal parameter is returned when changing the ChangingCell cell range
Group	Variant	[Start], [End], [By], [Periods]	Either demotes the outline in the range or groups the discontinuous ranges in the current Range object

Name	Returns	Parameters	Description
Insert	Variant	[Shift], [CopyOrigin]	Inserts the equivalent rows or columns in the range into the range's worksheet
InsertIndent		InsertAmount As Long	Indents the range by the amount specified by the InsertAmount parameter
Justify	Variant		Evenly distributes the text in the cells from the current range
ListNames	Variant		Pastes the names of all the named ranges in the current range starting at the top-left cell in the range
Merge		[Across]	Merges the cells in the range. Set the Across parameter to True to merge each row as a separate cell
Navigate Arrow	Variant	[Toward Precedent], [ArrowNumber], [LinkNumber]	Moves through the tracer arrows in a workbook from the current range, returning the range of cells that make up the tracer arrow destination. Tracer arrows must be turned on. Use the ShowDependents and ShowPrecendents methods
NoteText	String	[Text], [Start], [Length]	Set/Get the cell notes associated with the cell in the current range
Parse	Variant	[ParseLine], [Destination]	Parses the string specified by the ParseLine parameter and returns it to the current range parsed out by column. Optionally, can specify the destination range with the Destination parameter. The ParseLine string should be in the "[ColumnA] [ColumnB]" format

Continues

Name	Returns	Parameters	Description
PasteSpecial	Variant	Paste As XlPasteType, Operation As XlPaste Special Operation, [SkipBlanks], [Transpose]	Pastes the range from the clipboard into the current range. Use the Paste parameter to choose what to paste (for example, formulas, values). Use the Operation parameter to specifiy what to do with the paste. Set SkipBlanks to True to not have blank cells in the clipboard's range pasted. Set Transpose to True to transpose columns with rows
PrintOut	Variant	[From], [To], [Copies], [Preview], [Active Printer], [PrintToFile], [Collate], [PrToFile Name]	Prints out the charts in the collection. The printer, number of copies, collation, and whether a print preview is desired can be specified with the parameters. Also, the sheets can be printed to a file with using the PrintToFile and PrToFileName parameters. The From and To parameters can be used to specify the range of printed pages
PrintPreview	Variant	[Enable Changes]	Displays the current range in a print preview. Set the EnableChanges parameter to False to disable the Margins and Setup buttons, hence not allowing the viewer to modify the page setup
Remove Subtotal	Variant		Removes subtotals from the list in the current range
Replace	Boolean	What As Variant, Replacement As Variant, [LookAt], [SearchOrder], [MatchCase], [MatchByte], [Search Format], [Replace Format]	Finds the text specified by the What parameter in the range. Replaces the found text with the Replacement parameter. Use the SearchOrder parameters with the XLSearchOrder constants to choose whether the search occurs by rows or by columns

Name	Returns	Parameters	Description
Row Differences	Range	Comparison.	Returns the range of cells that are different to the cell specified by the Comparison parameter
Run	Variant	[Arg1], [Arg2], ... [Arg30]	Runs the Excel 4.0 macro specified by the current range. The potential arguments to the macro can be specified with the Argx parameters
Select	Variant		Selects the cells in the range
SetPhonetic			Creates a Phonetic object for each cell in the range
Show	Variant		Scrolls the Excel window to display the current range. This only works if the range is a single cell
ShowDependents	Variant	[Remove]	Displays the dependents for the current single cell range using tracer arrows
ShowErrors	Variant		Displays the source of the errors for the current range using tracer arrows
ShowPrecedents	Variant	[Remove]	Displays the precedents for the current single cell range using tracer arrows
Sort	Variant	[Key1], [Order1 As XlSortOrder], [Key2], [Type], [Order2 As XlSortOrder], [Key3], [Order3 As XlSortOrder], [Header As XlYesNoGuess], [OrderCustom], [MatchCase],	Sorts the cells in the range. If the range contains only one cell then the active region is searched. Use the Key1, Key2, and Key3 parameters to set which columns will be the sort columns. Use the Order1, Order2, and Order3 parameters to set the sort order. Use the Header parameter to set whether the first row contains headers. Set the

Continues

Name	Returns	Parameters	Description
		[Orientation As XlSort Orientation], [SortMethod As XlSortMethod], [DataOption1 As XlSortData Option], [DataOption2 As XlSortData Option], [DataOption3 As XlSortData Option]	MatchCase parameter to True to sort data and to treat uppercase and lowercase characters differently. Use the Orientation parameter to choose whether rows are sorted or columns are sorted. Finally, the SortMethod parameter is used to set the sort method for other languages (for example, xlStroke or xlPinYin). Use the SortSpecial method for sorting in East Asian languages
SortSpecial	Variant	[SortMethod As XlSortMethod], [Key1], [Order1 As XlSortOrder] [Type], [Key2], [Order2 As XlSortOrder], [Key3], [Order3 As XlSortOrder] [Header As XlYesNoGuess], [OrderCustom], [MatchCase], [Orientation As XlSort Orientation], [DataOption1 As XlSortData Option], [DataOption2 As XlSortData Option], [DataOption3 As XlSortData Option]	Sorts the data in the range using East Asian sorting methods. The parameters are the same as the Sort method
Speak		[Speak Direction], [Speak Formulas]	Causes the cells of the range to be spoken in row order or column order

Name	Returns	Parameters	Description
SpecialCells	Range	Type As XlCellType, [Value]	Returns the cells in the current range that contain some special attribute as defined by the Type parameter. For example, if Type is xlCellTypeBlanks then a Range object containing all of the empty cells are returned
SubscribeTo	Variant	Edition As String, Format As XlSubscribeTo Format	Only valid on the Macintosh. Defines the source of a link that the current range will contain
Subtotal	Variant	GroupBy As Long, Function As Xl Consolidation Function, TotalList, Replace, PageBreaks, SummaryBelow Data As XlSummaryRow	Creates a subtotal for the range. If the range is a single cell then a subtotal is created for the current region. The GroupBy parameter specifies the field to group (for subtotaling). The Function parameter describes how the fields will be grouped. The TotalList parameter uses an array of field offsets that describe the fields that will be subtotaled. Set the Replace parameter to True to replace existing subtotals. Set the PageBreaks to True for page breaks to be added after each group. Use the SummaryBelowData parameter to choose where the summary row will be added
Table	Variant	[RowInput], [Column Input]	Creates a new data table at the current range

Continues

Name	Returns	Parameters	Description
TextToColumns	Variant	[Destination], [DataType As XlTextParsing Type], [Text Qualifier As XlText Qualifier], [Consecutive Delimiter], [Tab], [Semicolon], [Comma], [Space], [Other], [OtherChar], [FieldInfo], [Decimal Separator], [Thousands Separator], [Trailing MinusNumbers]	Parses text in cells into several columns. The Destination specifies the range that the parsed text will go into. The DataType parameter can be used to choose whether the text is delimited or fixed width. The TextQualifier parameter can specify which character denotes string data when parsing. Set the Consecutive Delimiter to True for Excel to treat consecutive delimiters as one. Set the Tab, Semicolon, Comma, or Space parameter to True to use the associated character as the delimiter. Set the Other parameter to True and specify an OtherChar to use another character as the delimiter. FieldInfo takes a two-dimensional array containing more parsing information. The DecimalSeparator and ThousandsSeparator can specify how numbers are treated when parsing
Ungroup	Variant		Either promotes the outline in the range or ungroups the range in a PivotTable report
UnMerge			Splits up a merged cell into single cells

Example: Range Object

See Chapter 5 for examples of working with the Range object.

RecentFile Object and the RecentFiles Collection

The `RecentFiles` collection holds the list of recently modified files. Equivalent to the files listed under the File menu in Excel. Each `RecentFile` object represents one of the recently modified files.

`RecentFiles` has a few attributes besides the typical collection ones. The `Maximum` property can be used to set or return the maximum number of files that Excel will "remember" modifying. The value can range from 0 to 9. The `Count` property returns the number of `RecentFile` objects in the collection. The `Add` method is used to add a file (with the `Name` parameter) to the collection.

RecentFile Common Properties

The `Application`, `Creator`, and `Parent` properties are defined at the beginning of this Appendix.

RecentFile Properties

Name	Returns	Description
Index	Long	Read-only. Returns the spot in the collection that the current object is located
Name	String	Read-only. Returns the name of the recently modified file
Path	String	Read-only. Returns the file path of the recently modified file

RecentFile Methods

Name	Returns	Parameters	Description
Delete			Deletes the object from the collection
Open	Workbook		Opens up the recent file and returns the opened workbook

Example: RecentFile Object and the RecentFiles Collection

```
Sub CheckRecentFiles()
    Dim oRF As RecentFile
    'Remove any recent files that refer to the floppy drive
    For Each oRF In Application.RecentFiles
        If Left(oRF.Path, 2) = "A:" Then
            oRF.Delete
        End If
    Next
End Sub
```

RoutingSlip Object

The `RoutingSlip` object represents the properties and methods of the routing slip of an Excel document. The parent object of the `RoutingSlip` object is the `Workbook` object. The `HasRoutingSlip` property of the `Workbook` object has to set to `True` before the `RoutingSlip` object can be manipulated.

RoutingSlip Common Properties

The `Application`, `Creator`, and `Parent` properties are defined at the beginning of this Appendix.

RoutingSlip Properties

Name	Returns	Description
Delivery	XlRouting Slip Delivery	Set/Get how the delivery process will proceed
Message	Variant	Set/Get the body text of the routing slip message
Recipients	Variant	Parameters: [Index]. Returns the list of recipient names to send the parent workbook to
ReturnWhen Done	Boolean	Set/Get whether the message is returned to the original sender
Status	XlRouting SlipStatus	Read-only. Returns the current status of the routing slip
Subject	Variant	Set/Get the subject text for the routing slip message
TrackStatus	Boolean	Set/Get whether the message is sent to the original sender each time the message is forwarded

RoutingSlip Methods

Name	Returns	Parameters	Description
Reset	Variant		Reset the routing slip

RTD Object

Represents a Real-Time Data object, like one referenced using the `IrtdServer` object. As of this writing, there was very little documentation.

RTD Properties

Name	Returns	Description
Throttle Interval	Long	Set/Get the time interval between updates

RTD Methods

Name	Returns	Parameters	Description
RefreshData	RTD		Requests an update of RTD from the RTD server
Restart Servers	RTD		Reconnects to servers for RTD

Scenario Object and the Scenarios Collection

The `Scenarios` collection contains the list of all the scenarios associated with a worksheet. Each `Scenario` object represents a single scenario in a worksheet. A scenario holds the list of saved cell values that can later be substituted into the worksheet. The parent of the `Scenarios` collection is the `Worksheet` object.

The `Scenarios` collection has a few extra properties and methods besides the typical collection attributes. These are listed in the following table.

Scenarios Properties and Methods

Name	Returns	Description
Count	Long	Read-only. Returns the number of `Scenario` objects in the collection
Add	Scenario	Method. Parameters: `Name As String`, `ChangingCells`, `[Values]`, `[Comment]`, `[Locked]`, `[Hidden]`. Adds a scenario to the collection. The `Name` parameter specifies the name of the scenario. See the `Scenario` object for a description of the parameters
CreateSummary	Variant	Method. Parameters: `ReportType As XlSummaryReportType`, `[ResultCells]`. Creates a worksheet containing a summary of all the scenarios of the parent worksheet. The `ReportType` parameter can specify the report type. The `ResultCells` parameter can be a range of cells containing the formulas related to the changing cells
Merge	Variant	Method. Parameters: `Source`. Merges the scenarios in the `Source` parameter into the current worksheet

Scenario Common Properties

The `Application`, `Creator`, and `Parent` properties are defined at the beginning of this Appendix.

Scenario Properties

Name	Returns	Description
ChangingCells	Range	Read-only. Returns the range of cells in the worksheet that will have values plugged in for the specific scenario
Comment	String	Set/Get the scenario comment
Hidden	Boolean	Set/Get whether the scenario is hidden
Index	Long	Read-only. Returns the spot in the collection that the current Scenario object is located
Locked	Boolean	Set/Get whether the scenario cannot be modified when the worksheet is protected
Name	String	Set/Get the name of the scenario
Values	Variant	Read-only. Parameters: [Index]. Returns an array of the values to plug in to the changing cells for this particular scenario

Scenario Methods

Name	Returns	Parameters	Description
Change Scenario	Variant	Changing Cells, [Values]	Changes which set of cells in the worksheet are able to change for the scenario. Optionally, can choose new values for the scenario
Delete	Variant		Deletes the Scenario object from the collection
Show	Variant		Shows the scenario results by putting the scenario values into the worksheet

Example: Scenario Object and the Scenarios Collection

```
Sub GetBestScenario()
    Dim oScen As Scenario
    Dim oBestScen As Scenario
    Dim dBestSoFar As Double
    'Loop through the scenarios in the sheet
```

```
For Each oScen In ActiveSheet.Scenarios
    'Show the secnario
    oScen.Show

    'Is it better?
    If Range("Result").Value > dBestSoFar Then
        dBestSoFar = Range("Result").Value

        'Yes - remember it
        Set oBestScen = oScen
    End If
Next
'Show the best scenario
oBestScen.Show
MsgBox "The best scenario is " & oBestScen.Name
End Sub
```

Series Object and the SeriesCollection Collection

The SeriesCollection collection holds the collection of series associated with a chart group. Each Series object contains a collection of points associated with a chart group in a chart. For example, a simple line chart contains a series (Series) of points brought in from the originating data. Since some charts can have many series plotted on the same chart, the SeriesCollection is used to hold that information. The parent of the SeriesCollection is the ChartGroup.

The SeriesCollection has a few attributes that are not typical of a collection. These are listed in the following table.

SeriesCollection Properties and Methods

Name	Returns	Description
Add	Series	Method. Parameters: Source, Rowcol As XlRowCol, [SeriesLabels], [CategoryLabels], [Replace]. Adds a Series to the collection. The Source parameter specifies either a range or an array of data points describing the new series (and all the points in it). The Rowcol parameter sets whether the row or the column of the Source contains a series of points. Set SeriesLabels or CategoryLabels to True to make the first row or column of the Source contain the labels for the series and category, respectively
Count	Long	Read-only. Returns the number of Series objects in the collection

Continues

Name	Returns	Description
Extend	Variant	Method. Parameters: Source, [Rowcol], [CategoryLabels]. Adds the points specified by the range or array of data points in the Source parameter to the SeriesCollection. See the Add method for details on the other parameters
Paste	Variant	Method. Parameters: Rowcol As XlRowCol, [SeriesLabels], [CategoryLabels], [Replace], [NewSeries]. Pastes the data from the Clipboard into the SeriesCollection as a new Series. See the Add method for details on the other parameters
NewSeries	Series	Method. Creates a new series and returns the newly created series

Series Common Properties

The Application, Creator, and Parent properties are defined at the beginning of this Appendix.

Series Properties

Name	Returns	Description
ApplyPictToEnd	Boolean	Set/Get whether pictures are added to the end of the points in the series
ApplyPictTo Front	Boolean	Set/Get whether pictures are added to the front of the points in the series
ApplyPictTo Sides	Boolean	Set/Get whether pictures are added to the sides of the points in the series
AxisGroup	XlAxis Group	Set/Get the type of axis type being used by the series (primary or secondary)
BarShape	XlBarShape	Set/Get the type of shape to use in a 3D bar or column chart (for example, xlBox)
Border	Border	Read-only. Returns the collection of borders (sides) around the series. Each border's attributes can be accessed individually
BubbleSizes	Variant	Set/Get the cell references (A1 reference style) that contain data relating to how big the bubble should be for bubble charts
ChartType	XlChartType	Set/Get the type of chart to use for the series
ErrorBars	ErrorBars	Read-only. Returns the error bars in a series. Use with HasErrorBars

Name	Returns	Description
Explosion	Long	Set/Get how far out the slices (points) of a pie or doughnut chart will explode out. 0 for no explosion
Fill	ChartFill Format	Read-only. Returns an object containing fill formatting options for the series of points on a chart
Formula	String	Set/Get the type of formula label to use for the series
FormulaLocal	String	Set/Get the formula of the series in the language of the user using the A1 style references
FormulaR1C1	String	Set/Get the formula of the series in the language of the macro using the R1C1 style references
FormulaR1C1 Local	String	Set/Get the formula of the series in the language of the user using the R1C1 style references
Has3DEffect	Boolean	Set/Get if bubble charts have a 3D appearance
HasDataLabels	Boolean	Set/Get if the series contains data labels
HasErrorBars	Boolean	Set/Get if the series contains error bars. Use with the ErrorBars property
HasLeader Lines	Boolean	Set/Get if the series contains leader lines. Use with the LeaderLines property
Interior	Interior	Read-only. Returns an object containing options to format the inside area of the series (for example, interior color)
InvertIf Negative	Boolean	Set/Get whether the color of the series' points should be the inverse if the value is negative
LeaderLines	Leader Lines	Read-only. Returns the leader lines associated with the series
Marker Background Color	Long	Set/Get the color of the series points marker background. Use the RGB function to create the color value
Marker Background ColorIndex	XlColor Index	Set/Get the color of the series points marker background. Use the XlColorIndex constants or an index value in the current color palette
Marker Foreground Color	Long	Set/Get the color of the series points marker foreground. Use the RGB function to create the color value
Marker Foreground ColorIndex	XlColor Index	Set/Get the color of the series points marker foreground. Use the XlColorIndex constants or an index value in the current color palette
MarkerSize	Long	Set/Get the size of the point key marker
MarkerStyle	XlMarker Style	Set/Get the type of marker to use as the point key (for example, square, diamond, triangle, picture, etc.)

Continues

857

Name	Returns	Description
Name	String	Set/Get the name of the series
PictureType	XlChart Picture Type	Set/Get how an associated picture is displayed on the series (for example, stretched, tiled). Use the XlPictureType constants
PictureUnit	Long	Set/Get how many units a picture represents if the PictureType property is set to xlScale
PlotOrder	Long	Set/Get the plotting order for this particular series in the SeriesCollection
Shadow	Boolean	Set/Get whether the points in the series will have a shadow effect
Smooth	Boolean	Set/Get whether scatter or line charts will have curves smoothed
Type	Long	Set/Get the type of series
Values	Variant	Set/Get the range containing the series values or an array of fixed values containing the series values
XValues	Variant	Set/Get the array of x values coming from a range or an array of fixed values

Series Methods

Name	Returns	Parameters	Description
ApplyCustom Type		ChartType As XlChartType	Changes the chart type to the one specified in the ChartType parameter
ApplyData Labels	Variant	[Type As XlDataLabels Type], [LegendKey], [AutoText], [HasLeader Lines], [ShowSeries Name], [ShowCategory Name], [ShowValue], [Show Percentage], [ShowBubble Size], [Separator]	Applies the data label properties specified by the parameters to the series. The Type parameter specifies whether no label, a value, a percentage of the whole, or a category label is shown. The legend key can appear by the point by setting the LegendKey parameter to True. Set the HasLeaderLines to True to add leader lines to the series

Name	Returns	Parameters	Description
ClearFormats	Variant		Clears the formatting made on the series
Copy	Variant		Copies the series into the clipboard
DataLabels	Object	[Index]	Returns the collection of data labels in a series. If the Index parameter is specified then only a single data label is returned
Delete	Variant		Deletes the series from the series collection
ErrorBar	Variant	[Direction As XlErrorBar Direction], [Include As XlErrorBar Include], [Type As XlErrorBar Type], [Amount], [MinusValues]	Adds error bars to the series. The Direction parameter chooses whether the bar appears on the x or y axis. The Include parameter specifies which error parts to include. The Type parameter decides the type of error bar to use. The Amount parameter is used to choose an error amount. The MinusValues parameter takes the negative error amount to use when the Type parameter is xlErrorBarTypeCustom
Paste	Variant		Uses the picture in the Clipboard as the marker on the points in the series
Points		[Index]	Returns either the collection of points associated with the series or a single point if the Index parameter is specified
Select	Variant		Selects the series' points on the chart
Trendlines		[Index]	Returns either the collection of trendlines associated with the series or a single trendline if the Index parameter is specified

Example: Series Object and the SeriesCollection Collection

See the `DataLabel` object for an example of using the `Series` object.

SeriesLines Object

The `SeriesLines` object accesses the series lines connecting data values from each series. This object only applies to 2D stacked bar or column chart groups. The parent of the `SeriesLines` object is the `ChartGroup` object.

SeriesLines Common Properties

The `Application`, `Creator`, and `Parent` properties are defined at the beginning of this Appendix.

SeriesLines Properties

Name	Returns	Description
Border	Border	Read-only. Returns the border's properties around the series lines
Name	String	Read-only. Returns the name of the `SeriesLines` object

SeriesLines Methods

Name	Returns	Parameters	Description
Delete	Variant		Deletes the `SeriesLines` object
Select	Variant		Selects the series lines in the chart

Example: SeriesLines Object

```
Sub FormatSeriesLines()
    Dim oCG As ChartGroup
    Dim oSL As SeriesLines
    'Loop through the column groups on the chart
    For Each oCG In Charts(1).ColumnGroups
        'Make sure we have some series lines
        oCG.HasSeriesLines = True
        'Get the series lines
        Set oSL = oCG.SeriesLines
        'Format the lines
        With oSL
            .Border.Weight = xlThin
            .Border.ColorIndex = 5
        End With
    Next
End Sub
```

ShadowFormat Object

The `ShadowFormat` object allows manipulation of the shadow formatting properties of a parent `Shape` object. Use the `Shadow` property of the `Shape` object to access the `ShadowFormat` object.

ShadowFormat Common Properties

The `Application`, `Creator`, and `Parent` properties are defined at the beginning of this Appendix.

ShadowFormat Properties

Name	Returns	Description
ForeColor	ColorFormat	Read-only. Allows manipulation of the shadow forecolor
Obscured	MsoTriState	Set/Get whether the shape obscures the shadow or not
OffsetX	Single	Set/Get the horizontal shadow offset
OffsetY	Single	Set/Get the vertical shadow offset
Transparency	Single	Set/Get the transparency of the shadow (0 to 1 where 1 is clear)
Type	MsoShadowType	Set/Get the shadow type
Visible	MsoTriState	Set/Get whether the shadow is visible

ShadowFormat Methods

Name	Returns	Parameters	Description
Increment OffsetX		Increment As Single	Changes the horizontal shadow offset
Increment OffsetY		Increment As Single	Changes the vertical shadow offset

Example: ShadowFormat Object

```
Sub AddShadow()
    Dim oSF As ShadowFormat
    Set oSF = ActiveSheet.Shapes.Range(1).Shadow
    With oSF
        .Type = msoShadow6
        .OffsetX = 5
        .OffsetY = 5
        .ForeColor.SchemeColor = 2
        .Visible = True
    End With
End Sub
```

Shape Object and the Shapes Collection

The Shapes collection holds the list of shapes for a sheet. The Shape object represents a single shape such as an AutoShape, a free-form shape, an OLE object (like an image), an ActiveX control or a picture. Possible parent objects of the Shapes collection are the Worksheet and Chart object.

The Shapes collection has a few methods and properties besides the typical collection attributes. They are listed in the following table.

Shapes Collection Properties and Methods

Name	Returns	Description
Count	Long	Read-only. Returns the number of shapes in the collection
Range	ShapeRange	Read-only. Parameters: Index. Returns a ShapeRange object containing only some of the shapes in the Shapes collection
AddCallout	Shape	Method. Parameters: Type As MsoCalloutType, Left As Single, Top As Single, Width As Single, Height As Single. Adds a callout line shape to the collection
AddConnector	Shape	Method. Parameters: Type As MsoConnectorType, BeginX As Single, BeginY As Single, EndX As Single, EndY As Single. Adds a connector shape to the collection
AddCurve	Shape	Method. Parameters: SafeArrayOfPoints. Adds a Bezier curve to the collection
AddDiagram	Shape	Method. Parameters: Type As MsoDiagramType, Left As Single, Top As Single, Width As Single, Height As Single. Adds a new AutoShape to the worksheet
AddFormControl	Shape	Method. Parameters: Type As XlFormControl, Left As Long, Top As Long, Width As Long, Height As Long. Adds an Excel control to the collection
AddLabel	Shape	Method. Parameters: Orientation As MsoTextOrientation, Left As Single, Top As Single, Width As Single, Height As Single. Adds a label to the collection
AddLine	Shape	Method. Parameters: BeginX As Single, BeginY As Single, EndX As Single, EndY As Single. Adds a line shape to the collection
AddOLEObject	Shape	Method. Parameters: [ClassType], [Filename], [Link], [DisplayAsIcon], [IconFileName], [IconIndex], [IconLabel], [Left], [Top], [Width], [Height]. Adds an OLE control to the collection

Name	Returns	Description
AddPicture	Shape	Method. Parameters: `Filename As String, LinkToFile As MsoTriState, SaveWithDocument As MsoTriState, Left As Single, Top As Single, Width As Single, Height As Single`. Adds a picture object to the collection
AddPolyline	Shape	Method. Parameters: `SafeArrayOfPoints`. Adds an open polyline or a closed polygon to the collection
AddShape	Shape	Method. Parameters: `Type As MsoAutoShapeType, Left As Single, Top As Single, Width As Single, Height As Single`. Adds a shape using the `Type` parameter to the collection
AddTextbox	Shape	Method. Parameters: `Orientation As MsoTextOrientation, Left As Single, Top As Single, Width As Single, Height As Single`. Adds a textbox to the collection
AddText Effect	Shape	Method. Parameters: `PresetTextEffect As MsoPresetTextEffect, Text As String, FontName As String, FontSize As Single, FontBold As MsoTriState, FontItalic As MsoTriState, Left As Single, Top As Single`. Adds a `WordArt` object to the collection
Build Freeform	Freeform Builder	Method. Parameters: `EditingType As MsoEditingType, X1 As Single, Y1 As Single`. Accesses an object that allows creation of a new shape based on `ShapeNode` objects
SelectAll		Method. Selects all the shapes in the collection

Shape Common Properties

The `Application`, `Creator`, and `Parent` properties are defined at the beginning of this Appendix.

Shape Properties

Name	Returns	Description
Adjustments	Adjustments	Read-only. An object accessing the adjustments for a shape
Alternative Text	String	Set/Get the alternate text to appear if the image is not loaded. Used with a Web page
AutoShape Type	MsoAuto ShapeType	Set/Get the type of `AutoShape` used

Continues

Name	Returns	Description
BlackWhite Mode	MsoBlack WhiteMode	Property used for compatibility to other drawing packages only. Does not do anything
BottomRight Cell	Range	Read-only. Returns the single cell range that describes the cell under the lower-right corner of the shape
Callout	Callout Format	Read-only. An object accessing the callout properties of the shape
Child	MsoTriState	Read-only. Returns whether the specified shape is a child shape, or if all shapes in a shape range are child shapes of the same parent
Connection SiteCount	Long	Read-only. Returns the number of potential connection points (sites) on the shape for a connector
Connector	MsoTriState	Read-only. Returns whether the shape is a connector
Connector Format	Connector Format	Read-only. Returns an object containing formatting options for a connector shape. Shape must be a connector shape
Control Format	Control Format	Read-only. Returns an object containing formatting options for an Excel control. Shape must be an Excel control
Diagram	Diagram	Read-only. Returns a Diagram object
DiagramNode	DiagramNode	Read-only. Returns a node in the diagram
Fill	FillFormat	Read-only. Returns an object containing fill formatting options for the Shape object
FormControl Type	XlForm Control	Read-only. Returns the type of Excel control the current shape is (for example, xlCheck Box). Shape must be an Excel control
GroupItems	GroupShapes	Read-only. Returns the shapes that make up the current shape
HasDiagram	MsoTriState	Read-only. Returns whether a shape or shape range contains a diagram
HasDiagram Node	MsoTriState	Read-only. Returns whether a diagram node exists in a given shape or shape range
Height	Single	Set/Get the height of the shape
Horizontal Flip	MsoTriState	Read-only. Returns whether the shape has been flipped

Name	Returns	Description
Hyperlink	Hyperlink	Read-only. Returns the hyperlink of the shape, if any
ID	Long	Read-only. Returns the type for the specified object
Left	Single	Set/Get the horizontal position of the shape
Line	LineFormat	Read-only. An object accessing the line formatting of the shape
LinkFormat	LinkFormat	Read-only. An object accessing the OLE linking properties
LockAspect Ratio	MsoTriState	Set/Get whether the dimensional proportions of the shape is kept when the shape is resized
Locked	Boolean	Set/Get whether the shape can be modified if the sheet is locked (True = cannot modify)
Name	String	Set/Get the name of the Shape object
Nodes	ShapeNodes	Read-only. An object accessing the nodes of the free-form shape
OLEFormat	OLEFormat	Read-only. An object accessing OLE object properties, if applicable
OnAction	String	Set/Get the macro to run when the shape is clicked
ParentGroup	Shape	Read-only. Returns the common parent shape of a child shape or a range of child shapes
Picture Format	Picture Format	Read-only. An object accessing the picture format options
Placement	XlPlacement	Set/Get how the object will react with the cells around the shape
Rotation	Single	Set/Get the degrees rotation of the shape
Script	Script	Read-only. Returns the VBScript associated with the shape
Shadow	Shadow Format	Read-only. An object accessing the shadow properties
TextEffect	TextEffect Format	Read-only. An object accessing the text effect properties
TextFrame	TextFrame	Read-only. An object accessing the text frame properties
ThreeD	ThreeD Format	Read-only. An object accessing the 3D effect formatting properties

Continues

Name	Returns	Description
Top	Single	Set/Get the vertical position of the shape
TopLeftCell	Range	Read-only. Returns the single cell range that describes the cell over the upper-left corner of the shape
Type	MsoShape Type	Read-only. Returns the type of shape
VerticalFlip	MsoTriState	Read-only. Returns whether the shape has been vertically flipped
Vertices	Variant	Read-only. Returns a series of coordinate pairs describing the Freeform's vertices
Visible	MsoTriState	Set/Get whether the shape is visible
Width	Single	Read-only. Returns the type of shape
ZOrder Position	Long	Read-only. Returns where the shape is in the zorder of the collection (for example, front, back)

Shape Methods

Name	Returns	Parameters	Description
Apply			Activates the shape
Copy			Copies the shape to the clipboard
CopyPicture		[Appearance As XLPicture Appearance], [Format As XlCopyPicture Format]	Copies the range into the clipboard as a picture. The Appearance parameter can be used to specify whether the picture is copied as it looks on the screen or when printed. The Format parameter can specify the type of picture that will be put into the clipboard
Cut			Cuts the shape and places it in the clipboard
Delete			Deletes the shape
Duplicate	Shape		Duplicates the shape returning the new shape
Flip		FlipCmd As MsoFlipCmd	Flips the shape using the FlipCmd parameter

Name	Returns	Parameters	Description
Increment Left		Increment As Single	Moves the shape horizontally
Increment Rotation		Increment As Single	Rotates the shape using the Increment parameter as degrees
IncrementTop		Increment As Single	Moves the shape vertically
PickUp			Copies the format of the current shape so another shape can then apply the formats
Reroute Connections			Optimizes the route of the current connector shape connected between two shapes. Also, this method may be used to optimize all the routes of connectors connected to the current shape
ScaleHeight		Factor As Single, RelativeTo OriginalSize As MsoTriState, [Scale]	Scales the height of the shape by the Factor parameter
ScaleWidth		Factor As Single, RelativeTo OriginalSize As MsoTriState, [Scale]	Scales the width of the shape by the Factor parameter
Select		[Replace]	Selects the shape in the document
SetShapes Default Properties			Sets the formatting of the current shape as a default shape in Word
Ungroup	ShapeRange		Breaks apart the shapes that make up the Shape object
ZOrder		ZOrderCmd As MsoZ OrderCmd	Changes the order of the shape object in the collection

Example: Shape Object and the Shapes Collection

The Shape object is a generic container object for other object types. Examples of using the Shapes collection and Shape object are included under the specific objects.

ShapeNode Object and the ShapeNodes Collection

The ShapeNodes collection has the list of nodes and curved segments that make up a free-form shape. The ShapeNode object specifies a single node or curved segment that makes up a free-form shape. The Nodes property of the Shape object is used to access the ShapeNodes collection.

The ShapeNodes collection has a few methods besides the typical collection attributes listed in the following table.

ShapeNodes Collection Properties and Methods

Name	Returns	Description
Count	Integer	Read-only. Returns the number of ShapeNode objects in the collection
Delete		Method. Parameters: Index As Integer. Deletes the node specified by the Index
Insert		Method. Parameters: Index As Integer, SegmentType As MsoSegmentType, EditingType As MsoEditingType, X1 As Single, Y1 As Single, X2 As Single, Y2 As Single, X3 As Single, Y3 As Single. Inserts a node or curved segment in the Nodes collection
SetEditing Type		Method. Parameters: Index As Integer, EditingType As MsoEditingType. Sets the editing type for a node
SetPosition		Method. Parameters: Index As Integer, X1 As Single, Y1 As Single. Moves the specified node
SetSegment Type		Method. Parameters: Index As Integer, SegmentType As MsoSegmentType. Changes the segment type following the node

ShapeNode Common Properties

The Application, Creator, and Parent properties are defined at the beginning of this Appendix.

ShapeNode Properties

Name	Returns	Description
EditingType	MsoEditing Type	Read-only. Returns the editing type for the node
Points	Variant	Read-only. Returns the positional coordinate pair
SegmentType	MsoSegment Type	Read-only. Returns the type of segment following the node

Example: ShapeNode Object and the ShapeNodes Collection

```
Sub ToggleArch()
    Dim oShp As Shape
    Dim oSN As ShapeNodes
    Set oShp = ActiveSheet.Shapes(1)
    'Is the Shape a freeform?
    If oShp.Type = msoFreeform Then

        'Yes, so get its nodes
        Set oSN = oShp.Nodes
        'Toggle segment 3 between a line and a curve
        If oSN.Item(3).SegmentType = msoSegmentCurve Then
            oSN.SetSegmentType 3, msoSegmentLine
        Else
            oSN.SetSegmentType 3, msoSegmentCurve
        End If
    End If
End Sub
```

ShapeRange Collection

The ShapeRange collection holds a collection of Shape objects for a certain range or selection in a document. Possible parent items are the Range and the Selection object. The ShapeRange collection has many properties and methods besides the typical collection attributes. These items are listed next.

However, some operations will cause an error if performed on a ShapeRange collection with multiple shapes.

ShapeRange Properties

Name	Returns	Description
Adjustments	Adjustments	Read-only. An object accessing the adjustments for a shape
Alternative Text	String	Set/Get the alternative text to appear if the image is not loaded. Used with a Web page

Continues

Name	Returns	Description
AutoShape Type	MsoAuto ShapeType	Set/Get the type of AutoShape used
BlackWhite Mode	MsoBlack WhiteMode	Property used for compatibility to other drawing packages only. Does not do anything
Callout	Callout Format	Read-only. An object accessing the callout properties of the shape
Child	MsoTriState	Read-only. Returns whether the specified shape is a child shape, or if all shapes in a shape range are child shapes of the same parent
Connection SiteCount	Long	Read-only. Returns the number of potential connection points (sites) on the shape for a connector
Connector	MsoTriState	Read-only. Returns whether the shape is a connector
Connector Format	Connector Format	Read-only. Returns an object containing formatting options for a connector shape. Shape must be a connector shape
Count	Long	Read-only. Returns the number of shapes in the collection
Diagram	Diagram	Read-only. Returns a Diagram object
DiagramNode	DiagramNode	Read-only. Returns a node in the diagram
Fill	FillFormat	Read-only. An object accessing the fill properties of the shape
GroupItems	GroupShapes	Read-only. Returns the shapes that make up the current shape
HasDiagram	MsoTriState	Read-only. Returns whether a shape or shape range contains a diagram
HasDiagram Node	MsoTriState	Read-only. Returns whether a diagram node exists in a given shape or shape range
Height	Single	Set/Get the height of the shape
Horizontal Flip	MsoTriState	Read-only. Returns whether the shape has been flipped
ID	Long	Read-only. Returns the type for the specified object
Left	Single	Set/Get the horizontal position of the shape
Line	LineFormat	Read-only. An object accessing the line formatting of the shape
LockAspect Ratio	MsoTriState	Set/Get whether the dimensional proportions of the shape are kept when the shape is resized
Name	String	Set/Get the name of the shape

Name	Returns	Description
Nodes	ShapeNodes	Read-only. Returns the nodes associated with the shape
ParentGroup	Shape	Read-only. Returns the common parent shape of a child shape or a range of child shapes
Picture Format	Picture Format	Read-only. An object accessing the picture format options
Rotation	Single	Set/Get the degrees rotation of the shape
Shadow	Shadow Format	Read-only. An object accessing the shadow properties
TextEffect	TextEffect Format	Read-only. An object accessing the text effect properties
TextFrame	TextFrame	Read-only. An object accessing the text frame properties
ThreeD	ThreeD Format	Read-only. An object accessing the 3D effect formatting properties
Top	Single	Set/Get the vertical position of the shape
Type	MsoShape Type	Read-only. Returns the type of shape
VerticalFlip	MsoTriState	Read-only. Returns whether the shape has been vertically flipped
Vertices	Variant	Read-only. Returns a series of coordinate pairs describing the Freeform's vertices
Visible	MsoTriState	Set/Get whether the shape is visible
Width	Single	Set/Get the width of the shape
ZOrderPosition	Long	Read-only. Changes the order of the object in the collection

ShapeRange Methods

Name	Returns	Parameters	Description
Align		AlignCmd As MsoAlignCmd, RelativeTo As MsoTriState	Aligns the shapes in the collection to the alignment properties set by the parameters
Apply			Applies the formatting that was set by the PickUp method

Continues

Name	Returns	Parameters	Description
Delete			Deletes the shape
Distribute		DistributeCmd As MsoDistribute Cmd, RelativeTo As MsoTriState	Distributes the shapes in the collection evenly either horizontally or vertically
Duplicate	ShapeRange		Duplicates the shape and returns a new ShapeRange
Flip		FlipCmd As MsoFlipCmd	Flips the shape using the FlipCmd parameter
Group	Shape		Groups the shapes in the collection
IncrementLeft		Increment As Single	Moves the shape horizontally
Increment Rotation		Increment As Single	Rotates the shape using the Increment parameter as degrees
IncrementTop		Increment As Single	Moves the shape vertically
PickUp			Copies the format of the current shape so another shape can then apply the formats
Regroup	Shape		Regroups any previously grouped shapes
Reroute Connections			Optimizes the route of the current connector shape connected between two shapes. Also, this method may be used to optimize all the routes of connectors connected to the current shape
ScaleHeight		Factor As Single, RelativeTo OriginalSize As MsoTriState, [Scale]	Scales the height of the shape by the Factor parameter
ScaleWidth		Factor As Single, RelativeTo OriginalSize As MsoTriState, [Scale]	Scales the width of the shape by the Factor parameter
Select		[Replace]	Selects the shape in the document

Name	Returns	Parameters	Description
SetShapes Default Properties			Sets the formatting of the current shape as a default shape in Word
Ungroup	ShapeRange		Breaks apart the shapes that make up the Shape object
ZOrder		ZOrderCmd As MsoZOrderCmd	Changes the order of the shape object in the collection

Example: ShapeRange Collection

```
Sub AlignShapeRanges()
    Dim oSR As ShapeRange
    'Get the first two shapes on the sheet
    Set oSR = ActiveSheet.Shapes.Range(Array(1, 2))
    'Align the left-hand edges of the shapes
    oSR.Align msoAlignLefts, msoFalse
End Sub
```

Sheets Collection

The Sheets collection contains all of the sheets in the parent workbook. Sheets in a workbook consist of chart sheets and worksheets. Therefore, the Sheets collection holds both the Chart objects and Worksheet objects associated with the parent workbook. The parent of the Sheets collection is the Workbook object.

Sheets Common Properties

The Application, Creator, and Parent properties are defined at the beginning of this Appendix.

Sheets Properties

Name	Returns	Description
Count	Long	Read-only. Returns the number of sheets in the collection (and therefore workbook)
HPageBreaks	HPageBreaks	Read-only. Returns a collection holding all the horizontal page breaks associated with the Sheets collection
VPageBreaks	VpageBreaks	Read-only. Returns a collection holding all the vertical page breaks associated with the worksheets of the Sheets collection
Visible	Variant	Set/Get whether the sheets in the collection are visible. Also, can set this to xlVeryHidden to not allow a user to make the sheets in the collection visible

Sheets Methods

Name	Returns	Parameters	Description
Add		[Before], [After], [Count], [Type]	Adds a sheet to the collection. You can specify where the sheet goes by choosing which sheet object will be before the new sheet object (Before parameter) or after the new sheet (After parameter). The Count parameter decides how many sheets are created. The Type parameter can be used to specify the type of sheet using the XLSheetType constants
Copy		[Before], [After]	Adds a new copy of the currently active sheet to the position specified at the Before or After parameters
Delete			Deletes all the sheets in the collection. Remember a workbook must contain at least one sheet
FillAcross Sheets		RangeAs Range, Type As XlFillWith	Copies the values in the Range parameter to all the other sheets at the same location. The Type parameter can be used to specify whether cell contents, formulas or everything is copied
Move		[Before], [After]	Moves the current sheet to the position specified by the parameters. See the Add method
PrintOut		[From], [To], [Copies], [Preview], [Active Printer], [Print ToFile], [Collate], [PrToFile Name]	Prints out the sheets in the collection. The printer, number of copies, collation, and whether a print preview is desired can be specified with the parameters. Also, the sheets can be printed to a file using the PrintToFile and PrToFileName parameters. The From and To parameters can be used to specify the range of printed pages
PrintPreview		[Enable Changes]	Displays the current sheet in the collection in a print preview mode. Set the EnableChanges parameter to False to disable the Margins and Setup buttons, hence not allowing the viewer to modify the page setup
Select		[Replace]	Selects the current sheet in the collection

SmartTag Object and the SmartTags Collection Object

The `SmartTag` object represents an identifier that is assigned to a cell. Excel comes with many SmartTags, such as the Stock Ticker or Date recognizer, built in. However, you may also write your own SmartTags in Visual Basic. SmartTags are covered in detail in Chapter 18, but note that a degree of familiarity with XML is required to work with SmartTags.

The `SmartTags` collection represents all the SmartTags assigned to cells in an application.

SmartTag Common Properties

The `Application`, `Creator`, and `Parent` properties are defined at the beginning of this Appendix.

SmartTag Properties

Name	Returns	Description
DownloadURL	String	Read-only. Returns a URL to save along with the corresponding SmartTag
Name	String	Read-only. Returns name of the SmartTag
Properties	Custom Properties	Read-only. Returns the properties for the SmartTag
Range	Range	Read-only. Returns the range to which the specified SmartTag applies
SmartTag Actions	SmartTag Actions	Read-only. Returns the type of action for the selected SmartTag
XML	String	Read-only. Returns a sample of the XML that would be passed to the action handler

SmartTag Methods

Name	Returns	Parameters	Description
Delete			Deletes the object

Example: SmartTag Object

Note: This example is repeated in Chapter 18, in the *Remove a Tag from a Range* section.

One of the problems with SmartTags is the issue of false-positives, where a cell is erroneously tagged. An example is the standard Stock Symbol SmartTag that recognizes TRUE as a valid stock symbol, even if that TRUE is a Boolean `True`. The following code locates all of these false-positives and removes them:

```
Sub RemoveBooleanTrue()
    Dim oSht As Worksheet
    Dim oTag As SmartTag
```

```
        'This is the URI of the StockTicker SmartTag
        Const sTicker As String = _
                    "urn:schemas-microsoft-com:office:smarttags#stockticker"
        'Loop through all the worksheets in the active workbook
        For Each oSht In ActiveWorkbook.Worksheets
            'Loop through all the tags in the sheet
            For Each oTag In oSht.SmartTags
                'Is it a StockTicker tag with a Boolean value?
                If oTag.Name = sTicker And _
                            TypeName(oTag.Range.Value) = "Boolean" Then
                    'Yes, so remove this SmartTag from the cell
                    oTag.Delete
                End If
            Next
        Next
    End Sub
```

SmartTagAction Object and the SmartTagActions Collection Object

The SmartTagAction object represents an action that can be performed by a SmartTag. This may involve displaying the latest price for a stock symbol, or setting up an appointment on a certain date.

The SmartTagActions collection represents all of the SmartTagAction objects in the application.

SmartTagAction Common Properties

The Application, Creator, and Parent properties are defined at the beginning of this Appendix.

SmartTagAction Properties

Name	Returns	Description
ActiveXControl	Object	Reference to an ActiveX control that is currently in the Document Actions task pane
CheckboxState	Boolean	Returns True if the check box is checked, otherwise False is returned
ExpandHelp	Boolean	Returns True if the smart document help control is currently expanded. If not, False is returned
ListSelection	Long	Returns a index number for an item within a List control
Name	String	Read-only. Returns name of the SmartTag
PresentInPane	Boolean	Returns a Boolean value indicating if a smart document control is currently being shown in the Document Actions task pane

Name	Returns	Description
RadioGroup Selection	Long	Returns an index number to the currently selected radio button within a RadioGroup control
TextboxText	String	Returns the text within a TextBox control

SmartTagAction Methods

Name	Returns	Parameters	Description
Execute			Activates the SmartTag action

SmartTagOptions Collection Object

The SmartTagOptions collection represents all the options of a SmartTag. For instance, it holds whether SmartTags should be embedded in the worksheet, or if they should be displayed at all.

SmartTagOptions Collection Properties

Name	Returns	Description
DisplaySmart Tags	XlSmartTag DisplayMode	Set/Get the display features for SmartTags
EmbedSmartTags	Boolean	Set/Get whether to embed SmartTags on the specified workbook

SmartTagReconizer Object and the SmartTagRecognizers Collection Object

The SmartTagReconizer object represents the recognizer engines that label the data in the worksheet. These can be user-defined, and as such any kind of information can be identified by SmartTags. See Chapter 18 for more details.

The SmartTagRecognizers collection represents all of the SmartTagRecognizer objects in the application.

SmartTagRecognizers Collection Properties

Name	Returns	Description
Recognize	Boolean	Set/Get whether data can be labeled with a SmartTag

SmartTagRecognizer Common Properties

The `Application`, `Creator`, and `Parent` properties are defined at the beginning of this Appendix.

SmartTagRecognizer Properties

Name	Returns	Description
Enabled	Boolean	Set/Get whether the object is recognized
FullName	String	Read-only. Returns the name of the object, including its path on disk, as a string
ProgId	String	Read-only. Returns the programmatic identifiers for the object

SoundNote Object

The `SoundNote` object is not used in the current version of Excel. It is kept here for compatibility purposes only. The list of its methods is shown next.

SoundNote Methods

Name	Returns	Parameters
Delete	Variant	
Import	Variant	Filename As String
Play	Variant	
Record	Variant	

Speech Object

Represents the Speech recognition applet that comes with Office XP. This new Speech feature allows text to be read back on demand, or when you enter data on a document. For Excel, you have the option of having each cell's contents read back as they are entered on the worksheet. Use the `SpeakCellOnEnter` property of this object to enable this feature.

`Speech` is accessible through the `Application` object.

Speech Properties

Name	Returns	Description
Direction	XlSpeak Direction	Set/Get the order in which the cells will be spoken
SpeakCellOn Enter	Boolean	Set/Get whether to turn on Excel's mode where the active cell will be spoken when the *Enter* key is pressed, or when the active cell is finished being edited

Speech Methods

Name	Returns	Parameters	Description
Speak		Text As String, [SpeakAsync], [SpeakXML], [Purge]	The Text is spoken by Excel. If Purge is True the current speech will be terminated and any buffered text to be purged before Text is spoken

Example: Speech Object

The following routine reads off the expense totals for all items that are greater than a limit set in another cell on the sheet:

```
Sub ReadHighExpenses()

    Dim lTotal As Long
    Dim lLimit As Long
    Dim rng As Range

    'Grab the limitation amount
    lLimit = wksAllowEditRange.Range("Limit")

    'Loop through the expense totals
    For Each rng In wksAllowEditRange.Range("Expenses")
        'Store the current expense total
        lTotal = rng.Offset(0, 5).Value

        'If the current total is greater than
        ' the limit, read it off
        If lTotal > lLimit Then
            Application.Speech.Speak rng.Text
            Application.Speech.Speak lTotal
        End If
    Next rng

End Sub
```

SpellingOptions Collection Object

Represents the spelling options in Excel. These options can be found on the Spelling tab of the Tools ⇨ Options command and are accessed through the Application object. Hence this object is accessible through the Application object.

SpellingOptions Collection Properties

Name	Returns	Description
ArabicModes	XlArabic Modes	Set/Get the mode for the Arabic spelling checker
DictLang	Long	Set/Get the dictionary language used by Excel for checking spelling

Continues

Name	Returns	Description
GermanPost Reform	Boolean	Set/Get whether to check the spelling of words using the German post-reform rules
HebrewModes	XlHebrew Modes	Set/Get the mode for the Hebrew spelling checker
IgnoreCaps	Boolean	Set/Get whether to check for uppercase words, or lowercase words during spelling checks
IgnoreFile Names	Boolean	Set/Get whether to check for Internet and file addresses during spelling checks
IgnoreMixed Digits	Boolean	Set/Get whether to check for mixed digits during spelling checks
KoreanCombine Aux	Boolean	Set/Get whether to combine Korean auxiliary verbs and adjectives when using the spelling checker
KoreanProcess Compound	Boolean	Set/Get whether to process Korean compound nouns when using the spelling checker
KoreanUseAuto ChangeList	Boolean	Set/Get whether to use the auto-change list for Korean words when using the spelling checker
SuggestMain Only	Boolean	Set/Get whether to suggest words from only the main dictionary, for using the spelling checker
UserDict	String	Set/Get whether to create a custom dictionary to which new words can be added, when performing spelling checks

Example: SpellingOptions Collection Object

The following routine sets some spelling options and creates a new custom dictionary where added words during a spellcheck can be found:

```
Sub SetSpellingOptions()

    'This one is as simple as it gets
    With Application.SpellingOptions
        .IgnoreCaps = True
        .IgnoreFileNames = True
        .IgnoreMixedDigits = True
        .SuggestMainOnly = False

        'This property creates a custom dictionary
        ' called Wrox.dic, which can be found and directly edited
        ' in C:\WINDOWS\Application Data\Microsoft\Proof.
        'Added words during a spellcheck will now appear
        ' in this custom dictionary.
    End With
```

Style Object and the Styles Collection

The `Styles` collection holds the list of user-defined and built-in formatting styles, such as `Currency` and `Normal`, in a workbook or range. Each `Style` object represents formatting attributes associated with the parent object. There are some Excel built-in `Style` objects, such as `Currency`. Also, new styles can be created. Possible parents of the `Styles` collection are the `Range` and `Workbook` objects.

Styles can be accessed by the end user using the Style dialog box from the Format ⇨ Style menu.

The `Styles` collection has three extra attributes besides the typical collection ones. The `Count` property returns the number of `Style` objects in the collection. The `Add` method uses the `Name` parameter to add a new style to the collection. The `BasedOn` parameter of the `Add` method can be used to specify a range that the new style will be based on. The `Merge` method merges the styles in the workbook specified by the `Workbook` parameter into the current parent workbook.

Style Common Properties

The `Application`, `Creator`, and `Parent` properties are defined at the beginning of this Appendix.

Style Properties

Name	Returns	Description
AddIndent	Boolean	Set/Get whether text associated with the style is automatically indented if the text alignment in a cell is set to equally distribute
Borders	Borders	Read-only. Returns the collection of borders associated with the style. Each border side can be accessed individually
BuiltIn	Boolean	Read-only. Returns whether the style is built-in
Font	Font	Read-only. Returns an object containing `Font` options for the associated style
FormulaHidden	Boolean	Set/Get whether formulas associated with the style will be hidden if the workbook/worksheet is protected
Horizontal Alignment	XlHAlign	Set/Get how the cells associated with the style are horizontally aligned. Use the `XlHAlign` constants
IncludeAlignment	Boolean	Set/Get whether the styles include properties associated with alignment (that is, `AddIndent`, `HorizontalAlignment`, `Vertical Alignment`, `WrapText`, and `Orientation`)
IncludeBorder	Boolean	Set/Get whether border attributes are included with the style (that is, `Color`, `ColorIndex`, `LineStyle`, and `Weight`)

Continues

Name	Returns	Description
IncludeFont	Boolean	Set/Get whether font attributes are included in the style (that is, Background, Bold, Color, ColorIndex, FontStyle, Italic, Name, OutlineFont, Shadow, Size, Strikethrough, Subscript, Superscript, and Underline)
IncludeNumber	Boolean	Set/Get whether the NumberFormat property is included in the style
Include Pattern	Boolean	Set/Get whether interior pattern related properties are included in the style (that is, Color, ColorIndex, InvertIfNegative, Pattern, PatternColor, and PatternColorIndex)
Include Protection	Boolean	Set/Get whether the locking related properties are included with the style (that is, FormulaHidden and Locked)
IndentLevel	Long	Set/Get the indent level for the style
Interior	Interior	Read-only. Returns an object containing options to format the inside area of the style (for example, interior color)
Locked	Boolean	Set/Get whether the style properties can be changed if the workbook is locked
MergeCells	Variant	Set/Get whether the current style contains merged cells
Name	String	Read-only. Returns the name of the style
NameLocal	String	Read-only. Returns the name of the style in the language of the user's computer
NumberFormat	String	Set/Get the number format associated with the style
NumberFormat Local	String	Set/Get the number format associated with the style in the language of the end user
Orientation	Xl Orientation	Set/Get the text orientation for the cell text associated with the style. A value from –90 to 90 degrees can be specified or an XlOrientation constant
ReadingOrder	Long	Set/Get whether the text associated with the style is from right-to-left (xlRTL), left-to-right (xlLTR), or context sensitive (xlContext)
ShrinkToFit	Boolean	Set/Get whether the cell text associated with the style will automatically shrink to fit the column width

Name	Returns	Description
Value	String	Read-only. Returns the name of the style
Vertical Alignment	XlVAlign	Set/Get how the cells associated with the style are vertically aligned. Use the XlVAlign constants
WrapText	Boolean	Set/Get whether cell text wraps in cells associated with the style

Style Methods

Name	Returns	Parameters	Description
Delete	Variant		Deletes the style from the collection

Example: Style Object and the Styles Collection

```
Sub UpdateStyles()
    Dim oStyle As Style
    Set oStyle = ActiveWorkbook.Styles("Editing")
    'Update the Editing style to be unlocked with a default background
    With oStyle
        .IncludePatterns = True
        .IncludeProtection = True
        .Locked = False
        .Interior.Pattern = xlNone
    End With
End Sub
```

Tab Object

Represents the Sheet tab at the bottom of an Excel chart sheet or worksheet. Excel 2003 now allows you to customize the sheet's tab color by using either the Color or ColorIndex properties of this object.

Note that when setting ColorIndex property of this object to xlColorIndexAutomatic (which appears on the AutoComplete list for the property), an error will occur.

Tab Common Properties

The Application, Creator, and Parent properties are defined at the beginning of this Appendix.

Tab Properties

Name	Returns	Description
Color	Variant	Set/Get the primary color of the Tab object. Use the RGB function to create a color value
ColorIndex	XlColor Index	Set/Get the color of the interior

Example: Tab Object

The following routine changes the tab color for all budget worksheet in a workbook based on a setting in a custom property for each worksheet:

```
Sub ColorBudgetTabs()
    Dim bBudget As Boolean
    Dim oCustomProp As CustomProperty
    Dim oCustomProps As CustomProperties
    Dim wks As Worksheet

    'Loop through each worksheet in this workbook
    For Each wks In ThisWorkbook.Worksheets
        'Loop through all of the custom properties
        ' for the current worksheet until the
        ' "IsBudget" proeprty name is found
        For Each oCustomProp In wks.CustomProperties
            If oCustomProp.Name = "IsBudget" Then
                'Grab its value and exit the loop
                bBudget = CBool(oCustomProp.Value)
                Exit For
            End If
        Next oCustomProp

        'Use the value in the custom property to determine
        ' whether the tab should be colored.
        If bBudget Then wks.Tab.ColorIndex = 20 'Light blue

    Next wks

End Sub
```

TextEffectFormat Object

The TextEffectFormat object contains all the properties and methods associated with WordArt objects. The parent object of the TextEffectFormat is always the Shape object.

TextEffectFormat Common Properties

The Application, Creator, and Parent properties are defined at the beginning of this Appendix.

TextEffectFormat Properties

Name	Returns	Description
Alignment	MsoText Effect Alignment	Set/Get the alignment of the WordArt
FontBold	MsoTriState	Set/Get whether the WordArt is bold
FontItalic	MsoTriState	Set/Get whether the WordArt is italic
FontName	String	Set/Get the font used in the WordArt

Name	Returns	Description
FontSize	Single	Set/Get the font size in the WordArt
KernedPairs	MsoTriState	Set/Get whether the characters are kerned in the WordArt
Normalized Height	MsoTriState	Set/Get whether both the uppercase and lowercase characters are the same height
PresetShape	MsoPreset TextEffect Shape	Set/Get the shape of the WordArt
PresetText Effect	MsoPreset TextEffect	Set/Get the effect associated with the WordArt
RotatedChars	MsoTriState	Set/Get whether the WordArt has been rotated by 90 degrees
Text	String	Set/Get the text in the WordArt
Tracking	Single	Set/Get the spacing ratio between characters

TextEffectFormat Methods

Name	Returns	Parameters	Description
Toggle VerticalText			Toggles the text from vertical to horizontal and back

Example: TextEffectFormat Object

```
Sub FormatTextArt()
   Dim oTEF As TextEffectFormat
   Dim oShp As Shape
   Set oShp = ActiveSheet.Shapes(1)
   If oShp.Type = msoTextEffect Then
      Set oTEF = oShp.TextEffect

      With oTEF
         .FontName = "Times New Roman"
         .FontBold = True
         .PresetTextEffect = msoTextEffect14
         .Text = "Hello World!"
      End With
   End If
End Sub
```

TextFrame Object

The TextFrame object contains the properties and methods that can manipulate text-frame shapes. Possible parent objects of the TextFrame object are the Shape and ShapeRange objects.

TextFrame Common Properties

The Application, Creator, and Parent properties are defined at the beginning of this Appendix.

TextFrame Properties

Name	Returns	Description
AutoMargins	Boolean	Set/Get whether Excel will calculate the margins of the text frame automatically. Set this property to False to use the MarginLeft, MarginRight, MarginTop, and MarginBottom properties
AutoSize	Boolean	Set/Get whether the size of the text frame changes to match the text inside
Horizontal Alignment	XlHAlign	Set/Get how the text frame is horizontally aligned. Use the XLHAlign constants
MarginBottom	Single	Set/Get the bottom spacing in a text frame
MarginLeft	Single	Set/Get the left spacing in a text frame
MarginRight	Single	Set/Get the right spacing in a text frame
MarginTop	Single	Set/Get the top spacing in a text frame
Orientation	MsoText Orientation	Set/Get the orientation of the text in the text frame
ReadingOrder	Long	Set/Get whether the text in the frame is read from right-to-left (xlRTL), left-to-right (xlLTR), or context sensitive (xlContext)
Vertical Alignment	XlVAlign	Set/Get how the text frame is vertically aligned. Use the XlVAlign constants

TextFrame Methods

Name	Returns	Parameters	Description
Characters	Characters	[Start], [Length]	Returns an object containing all the characters in the text frame. Allows manipulation on a character-by-character basis and to retrieve only a subset of text in the frame

Example: TextFrame Object

```
Sub SetShapeAutoSized()
    Dim oTF As TextFrame
    Dim oShp As Shape
```

```
      Set oShp = ActiveSheet.Shapes(1)
      Set oTF = oShp.TextFrame
      oTF.AutoSize = True
   End Sub
```

ThreeDFormat Object

The ThreeDFormat object contains all of the three-dimensional formatting properties of the parent Shape object. The ThreeD property of the Shape object is used to access the ThreeDFormat object.

ThreeDFormat Common Properties

The Application, Creator, and Parent properties are defined at the beginning of this Appendix.

ThreeDFormat Properties

Name	Returns	Description
Depth	Single	Set/Get the "depth" of a 3D shape
ExtrusionColor	ColorFormat	Read-only. An object manipulating the color of the extrusion
ExtrusionColor Type	MsoExtrusion ColorType	Set/Get how the color for the extrusion is set
Perspective	MsoTriState	Set/Get whether the shape's extrusion has perspective
Preset Extrusion Direction	MsoPreset Extrusion Direction	Read-only. Returns the direction of the extrusion
Preset Lighting Direction	MsoPreset Lighting Direction	Set/Get the directional source of the light source
Preset Lighting Softness	MsoPreset Lighting Softness	Set/Get the softness of the light source
Preset Material	MsoPreset Material	Set/Get the surface material of the extrusion
PresetThreeD Format	MsoPreset ThreeD Format	Read-only. Returns the preset extrusion format
RotationX	Single	Set/Get how many degrees the extrusion is rotated
RotationY	Single	Set/Get how many degrees the extrusion is rotated
Visible	MsoTriState	Set/Get whether the 3D shape is visible

ThreeDFormat Methods

Name	Returns	Parameters	Description
Increment RotationX		Increment As Single	Changes the RotationX property
Increment RotationY		Increment As Single	Changes the RotationY property
ResetRotation			Resets the RotationX and RotationY to 0
SetExtrusion Direction		Preset Extrusion Direction As MsoPreset Extrusion Direction	Changes the extrusion direction
SetThreeD Format		PresetThreeD Format As MsoPreset ThreeDFormat	Sets the preset extrusion format

Example: ThreeDFormat Object

```
Sub SetShape3D()
    Dim o3DF As ThreeDFormat
    Dim oShp As Shape
    Set oShp = ActiveSheet.Shapes(1)
    Set o3DF = oShp.ThreeD
    With o3DF
        .Depth = 10
        .SetExtrusionDirection msoExtrusionBottomRight
    End With
End Sub
```

TickLabels Object

The TickLabels object contains the formatting options associated with the tick-mark labels for tick marks on a chart axis. The parent of the TickLabels object is the Axis object.

TickLabels Common Properties

The Application, Creator, and Parent properties are defined at the beginning of this Appendix.

TickLabels Properties

Name	Returns	Description
Alignment	Long	Set/Get the alignment of the tick labels. Use the XlHAlign constants
AutoScaleFont	Variant	Set/Get whether the font size will change automatically if the parent chart changes sizes
Depth	Long	Read-only. Returns how many levels of category tick labels are on the axis
Font	Font	Read-only. Returns an object containing Font options for the tick label text
Name	String	Read-only. Returns the name of the TickLabels object
NumberFormat	String	Set/Get the numeric formatting to use if the tick labels are numeric values or dates
NumberFormat Linked	Boolean	Set/Get whether the same numerical format used for the cells containing the chart data is used by the tick labels
NumberFormat Local	Variant	Set/Get the name of the numeric format being used by the tick labels in the language being used by the user
Offset	Long	Set/Get the percentage distance between levels of labels as compared to the axis label's font size
Orientation	XlTickLabel Orientation	Set/Get the angle of the text for the tick labels. The value can be in degrees (from –90 to 90) or one of the XlTickLabelOrientation constants
ReadingOrder	Long	Set/Get how the text is read (from left to right or right to left). Only applicable in appropriate languages

TickLabels Methods

Name	Returns	Parameters	Description
Delete	Variant		Deletes the tick labels from the axis labels
Select	Variant		Selects the tick labels on the chart

Example: TickLabels Object

```
Sub FormatTickLabels()
   Dim oTL As TickLabels
   Set oTL = Charts(1).Axes(xlValue).TickLabels
   With oTL
      .NumberFormat = "#,##0"
      .Font.Size = 12
   End With
End Sub
```

TreeviewControl Object

The `TreeviewControl` object allows manipulation of the hierarchical member-selection of a cube field. This object is usually used by macro recordings and not when building VBA code. The parent of the `TreeviewControl` object is the `CubeField` object.

TreeviewControl Common Properties

The `Application`, `Creator`, and `Parent` properties are defined at the beginning of this Appendix.

TreeviewControl Properties

Name	Returns	Description
Drilled	Variant	Set/Get a string array describing the drilled status of the members of the parent cube field
Hidden	Variant	Set/Get the hidden status of the members in a cube field

Trendline Object and the Trendlines Collection

The `Trendlines` collection holds the collection of trendlines in a chart. Each `TrendLine` object describes a trendline on a chart of a particular series. `Trendlines` are used to graphically show trends in the data and help predict future values. The parent of the `Trendlines` collection is the `Series` object.

The `Trendlines` collection has one property and one method besides the typical collection attributes. The `Count` property returns the number of `TrendLine` objects in the collection. The `Add` method adds a trendline to the current chart. The `Add` method has a `Type`, `Order`, `Period`, `Forward`, `Backward`, `Intercept`, `DisplayEquation`, `DispayRSquared`, and `Name` parameter. See the *Trendline Properties* section for more information.

Trendline Common Properties

The `Application`, `Creator`, and `Parent` properties are defined at the beginning of this Appendix.

Trendline Properties

Name	Returns	Description
Backward	Long	Set/Get how many periods the trendline extends back
Border	Border	Read-only. Returns the border's properties around the trendline
DataLabel	DataLabel	Read-only. Returns an object to manipulate the trendline's data label
Display Equation	Boolean	Set/Get whether the equation used for the trendline is displayed on the chart
Display RSquared	Boolean	Set/Get whether the R-squared value for the trendline is displayed on the chart
Forward	Long	Set/Get how many periods the trendline extends forward
Index	Long	Read-only. Returns the spot in the collection that the current object is
Intercept	Double	Set/Get at which point the trendline crosses the value (y) axis
InterceptIs Auto	Boolean	Set/Get whether the point the trendline crosses the value axis is automatically calculated with regression
Name	String	Set/Get the name of the Trendline object
NameIsAuto	Boolean	Set/Get whether Excel automatically chooses the trendline name
Order	Long	Set/Get the order of a polynomial trendline. The Type property must be xlPolynomial
Period	Long	Set/Get what the period is for the moving-average trendline
Type	XlTrendline Type	Set/Get the type of the trendline (for example, xlExponential, xlLinear, etc.)

Trendline Methods

Name	Returns	Parameters	Description
ClearFormats	Variant		Clears any formatting made on the trendlines
Delete	Variant		Deletes the trendlines
Select	Variant		Selects the trendlines on the chart

Example: Trendline Object and the Trendlines Collection

```
Sub AddTrendLine()
   Dim oSer As Series
   Dim oTL As Trendline
   Set oSer = Charts(1).SeriesCollection(1)
   Set oTL = oSer.Trendlines.Add(xlLinear)
   With oTL
      .DisplayEquation = True
      .DisplayRSquared = True
   End With
End Sub
```

UpBars Object

The UpBars object contains formatting options for up bars on a chart. The parent of the UpBars object is the ChartGroup object. To see if this object exists, use the HasUpDownBars property of the ChartGroup object.

UpBars Common Properties

The Application, Creator, and Parent properties are defined at the beginning of this Appendix.

UpBars Properties

Name	Returns	Description
Border	Border	Read-only. Returns the border's properties around the up bars
Fill	ChartFill Format	Read-only. Returns an object containing fill formatting options for the up bars of a chart
Interior	Interior	Read-only. Returns an object containing options to format the inside area of the up bars (for example, interior color)
Name	String	Read-only. Returns the name of the up bars

UpBars Methods

Name	Returns	Parameters	Description
Delete	Variant		Deletes the up bars
Select	Variant		Selects the up bars in the chart

Example: UpBars Object

```
Sub AddAndFormatUpBars()
    Dim oUpBars As UpBars
    'Add Up/Down bars to the chart
    Charts(1).ChartGroups(1).HasUpDownBars = True
    'Get the collection of UpBars
    Set oUpBars = Charts(1).ChartGroups(1).UpBars
    'Format the up bars
    With oUpBars
        .Interior.ColorIndex = 3
        .Interior.Pattern = xlSolid
    End With
End Sub
```

UsedObjects Collection Object

Represents the total amount of objects currently being used in all open workbooks. Used objects can be worksheets, chart sheets, the workbook itself, and any ActiveX controls placed on worksheets. This object can be referenced through the `Application` object.

Note that in addition to the common collection properties defined earlier, `UsedObjects` has the `Item` and `Count` properties.

Example: UsedObjects Collection Object

The following routine lists all of the parent objects of the `UsedObjects` collection:

```
Sub CountUsedObjects()
    Dim lCount As Long
    Dim oUsedObjs As UsedObjects
    'Turn off the screen
    Application.ScreenUpdating = False

    'Store the used object collection
    Set oUsedObjs = Application.UsedObjects

    'Clear the old list
    wksUsedObjects.UsedRange.Offset(1, 0).Resize(, 1).ClearContents
    'Loop through and list the parents of all of the objects
    'Cannot seem to grab the name/caption/... of the object itself
    For lCount = 1 To oUsedObjs.Count
        wksUsedObjects.Range("ListStart").Cells(lCount, 1) =
oUsedObjs.Item(lCount).Parent.Name
    Next lCount
End Sub
```

UserAccess Collection Object

Represents one user within a possible group of users who have permission to access a range specified by the `AllowEditRange` object. You can refer to a user by using the `Item` property of the

`UserAccessList` object. Once referenced, you use the properties of this object to change the user's settings.

UserAccess Collection Properties

Name	Returns	Description
AllowEdit	Boolean	Set/Get whether the user is allowed access to the specified range on a protected worksheet
Name	String	Read-only. Returns the name of the `UserAccess` object

UserAccess Collection Methods

Name	Returns	Parameters	Description
Delete			Deletes the object

UserAccessList Collection Object

Represents a list of users who have access to a protected range on a worksheet. This object can be accessed via the `AllowEditRange` object after it's been created. Use the `Add` method of this object to add a user to the list, which contains an argument that determines whether or not they need a password to access the range.

Note that the password is set using the `ChangePassword` method of the `AllowEditRange` object. This means that all of the users for an `AllowEditRange` use the same password. Note that this collection only has `Count` and `Item` properties.

UserAccessList Methods

Name	Returns	Parameters	Description
Add	UserAccess	Name As String, AllowEdit As Boolean	Adds a user access list to the collection. Name is the name of the list, and if `AllowEdit` is `True` users on the access list are allowed to edit the editable ranges on a protected worksheet
DeleteAll			Removes all users associated with access to a protected range on a worksheet

Example: UserAccessList Object

The following routine loops through all of the `AllowEditRange` objects on a specified worksheet and removes all of the users except for the range `pcNetSales`:

```
Sub DeleteAllUsers()

    Dim oAllowRange As AllowEditRange

    'Loop through all of the AllowEditRange objects on the
    ' specified worksheet
    For Each oAllowRange In wksAllowEditRange.Protection.AllowEditRanges
        'Remove all names from all AllowEditRanges
        ' except for the range whose AllowEditRange Title
        ' is pcNetSales
        If oAllowRange.Title <> "pcNetSales" Then
            oAllowRange.Users.DeleteAll
        End If
    Next oAllowRange

End Sub
```

Validation Object

The `Validation` object contains properties and methods to represent validation for a range in a worksheet. The `Range` object is the parent of the `Validation` object.

Validation Common Properties

The `Application`, `Creator`, and `Parent` properties are defined at the beginning of this Appendix.

Validation Properties

Name	Returns	Description
AlertStyle	Long	Read-only. Returns how the user will be alerted if the range includes invalid data. Uses the XlDVAlertStyle constants
ErrorMessage	String	Set/Get the error message to show for data validation
ErrorTitle	String	Set/Get what the title is for the error data validation dialog box
Formula1	String	Read-only. Returns the value, cell reference, or formula used for data validation
Formula2	String	Read-only. Returns the second part of the value, cell reference, or formula used for data validation. The Operator property must be xlBetween or xlNotBetween

Continues

Name	Returns	Description
IgnoreBlank	Boolean	Set/Get whether a blank cell is always considered valid
IMEMode	Long	Set/Get how the Japanese input rules are described. Use the XlIMEMode constants
InCell Dropdown	Boolean	Set/Get whether a drop-down list of valid values is displayed in the parent range. Used when the Type property is xlValidateList
InputMessage	String	Set/Get the validation input message to prompt the user for valid data
InputTitle	String	Set/Get what the title is for the input data validation dialog box
Operator	Long	Read-only. Returns the operator describing how Formula1 and Formula2 are used for validation. Uses the XlFormatConditionOperator constants
ShowError	Boolean	Set/Get whether the error message will be displayed when invalid data is entered in the parent range
ShowInput	Boolean	Set/Get whether the input message will be displayed when the user chooses one of the cells in the parent range
Type	Long	Read-only. Returns the data validation type for the range. The XlDVType constants can be used (for example, xlValidateDecimal, xlValidateTime)
Value	Boolean	Read-only. Returns if the validation is fulfilled for the range

Validation Methods

Name	Returns	Parameters	Description
Add		Type As XlDVType, [Alert Style], [Operator], [Formula1], [Formula2]	Adds data validation to the parent range. The validation type (Type parameter) must be specified. The type of validation alert (AlertStyle) can be specified with the XlDVAlertStyle constants. The Operator parameter uses the XlFormatCondition Operator to pick the type of operator to use. The Formula1 and Formula2 parameters pick the data validation formula
Delete			Deletes the Validation method for the range

Name	Returns	Parameters	Description
Modify		[Type], [AlertStyle], [Operator], [Formula1], [Formula2]	Modifies the properties associated with the Validation. See the properties of the Validation object for a description of the parameters

Example: Validation Object

```
Sub AddValidation()
   Dim oValid As Validation
   Set oValid = Selection.Validation
   With oValid
      .Delete
      .Add Type:=xlValidateWholeNumber, AlertStyle:=xlValidAlertStop, _
         Operator:=xlBetween, Formula1:="10", Formula2:="20"
      .ShowInput = False
      .ShowError = True
      .ErrorTitle = "Error"
      .ErrorMessage = "Number must be between 10 and 20"
   End With
End Sub
```

VPageBreak Object and the VPageBreaks Collection

The VPageBreaks collection contains all of the vertical page breaks in the printable area of the parent object. Each VPageBreak object represents a single vertical page break for the printable area of the parent object. Possible parents of the VPageBreaks collection are the WorkSheet and the Chart objects.

The VPageBreaks collection contains one property and one method besides the typical collection attributes. The Count property returns the number of VPageBreak objects in the collection. The Add method is used to add a VPageBreak object to the collection (and vertical page break to the sheet). The Add method has a Before parameter to specify the range to the right of where the vertical page break will be added.

VPageBreak Common Properties

The Application, Creator, and Parent properties are defined at the beginning of this Appendix.

VPageBreak Properties

Name	Returns	Description
Extent	XlPageBreak Extent	Read-only. Returns whether the vertical page break is full screen or only for the print area
Location	Range	Set/Get the cell where the vertical page break is located. The left edge of the cell is the location of the page break
Type	XlPageBreak	Set/Get whether the page break is automatic or manually set

VPageBreak Methods

Name	Returns	Parameters	Description
Delete			Deletes the page break
DragOff		Direction As XlDirection, RegionIndex As Long	Drags the page break out of the printable area. The Direction parameter specifies the direction the page break is dragged. The RegionIndex parameter specifies which print region the page break is being dragged out of

Example: VPageBreak Object and the VPageBreaks Collection

```
Sub AddVPageBreaks()
    Dim oCell As Range
    'Loop through all the cells in the first column of the sheet
    For Each oCell In ActiveSheet.UsedRange.Rows(1).Cells
        'If the font size is 16, add a page break to the left of the cell
        If oCell.Font.Size = 16 Then
            ActiveSheet.VPageBreaks.Add oCell
        End If
    Next
End Sub
```

Walls Object

The Walls object contains formatting options for all the walls of a 3D chart. The walls of a 3D chart cannot be accessed individually. The parent of the Walls object is the Chart object.

Walls Common Properties

The Application, Creator, and Parent properties are defined at the beginning of this Appendix.

Walls Properties

Name	Returns	Description
Border	Border	Read-only. Returns the border's properties around the walls of the 3D chart
Fill	ChartFill Format	Read-only. Returns an object containing fill formatting options for the walls of a 3D chart
Interior	Interior	Read-only. Returns an object containing options to format the inside area of the walls (for example, interior color)
Name	String	Read-only. Returns the name of the Walls object

Name	Returns	Description
PictureType	Variant	Set/Get how an associated picture is displayed on the walls of the 3D chart (for example, stretched, tiled). Use the XlPictureType constants
PictureUnit	Variant	Set/Get how many units a picture represents if the PictureType property is set to xlScale

Walls Methods

Name	Returns	Parameters	Description
ClearFormats	Variant		Clears the formatting made on the Walls object
Paste			Deletes the Walls object
Select	Variant		Selects the walls on the parent chart

Example: Walls Object

```
Sub FormatWalls()
    Dim oWall As Walls
    Set oWall = Charts(1).Walls
    With oWall
        .Fill.PresetTextured msoTextureCork
        .Fill.Visible = True
    End With
End Sub
```

Watch Object and the Watches Collection Object

The Watch object represents one Watch in the Watch window (View ➪ Toolbars ➪ Watch Window). Each Watch can be a cell or cell range you need to keep track of as other data on the worksheet changes. A Watch object is an auditing tool similar to the watches you can create in the VBE. Watches do just that, they keep track of a cell or cell range, allowing you to study changes to those cells when other data on the worksheet changes.

The Watches collection contains all the Watch objects that have been set in the application.

Watches Collection Methods

Name	Returns	Parameters	Description
Add	Watch	Source As Variant	Adds a range which is tracked when the worksheet is recalculated
Delete			Deletes the object

Watch Common Properties

The `Application`, `Creator`, and `Parent` properties are defined at the beginning of this Appendix.

Watch Properties

Name	Returns	Description
Source	Variant	Read-only. Returns the unique name that identifies items that have a `SourceType` property value of `xlSourceRange`, `xlSourceChart`, `xlSourcePrintArea`, `xlSourceAutoFilter`, `xlSourcePivotTable`, or `xlSourceQuery`

Watch Methods

Name	Returns	Parameters	Description
Delete			Deletes the object

Example: Watch Object

The following routine prompts the user for a range, then loops through each cell in the range and adds it to the Watch Window. It then displays the Watch Window:

```
Sub AddWatches()
    Dim oWatch As Watch
    Dim rng As Range
    Dim rngWatches As Range

    'Prompt the user for a range
    'Supress the error if they cancel
    On Error Resume Next
        Set rngWatches = Application.InputBox(_
            "Please select a cell or cell range to watch", "Add Watch", , , , , , 8)
    On Error GoTo 0

    'If they selected a range
    If Not rngWatches Is Nothing Then
        'Loop through each cell and
        ' add it to the watch list
        For Each rng In rngWatches
            Application.Watches.Add rng
        Next rng
    End If
    'View the watch window based on their answer
    Application.CommandBars("Watch Window").Visible = (Not rngWatches
 Is Nothing)

End Sub
```

WebOptions Object

The WebOptions object contains attributes associated with opening or saving Web pages. The parent of the WebOptions object is the Workbook object. The properties set in the WebOptions object override the settings of the DefaultWebOptions object.

WebOptions Common Properties

The Application, Creator, and Parent properties are defined at the beginning of this Appendix.

WebOptions Properties

Name	Returns	Description
AllowPNG	Boolean	Set/Get whether Portable Network Graphics Format (PNG) is allowed as an output format. PNG is a file format for the lossless, portable, well-compressed storage of images
Download Components	Boolean	Set/Get whether Office components are downloaded to the end user's machine when viewing Excel files in a Web browser
Encoding	MsoEncoding	Set/Get the type of code page or character set to save with a document
FolderSuffix	String	Read-only. Returns what the suffix name is for the support directory created when saving an Excel document as a Web page. Language dependent
LocationOf Components	String	Set/Get the URL or path that contains the Office Web components needed to view documents in a Web browser
OrganizeIn Folder	Boolean	Set/Get whether supporting files are organized in a separate folder from the document
PixelsPer Inch	Long	Set/Get how dense graphics and table cells should be when viewed on a Web page
RelyOnCSS	Boolean	Set/Get whether Cascading Style Sheets (CSS) is used for font formatting
RelyOnVML	Boolean	Set/Get whether image files are not created when saving a document with drawn objects. Vector Markup Language is used to create the images on the fly. VML is an XML-based format for high-quality vector graphics on the Web
ScreenSize	MsoScreen Size	Set/Get the target monitor's screen size

Continues

Name	Returns	Description
Target Browser	MsoTarget Browser	Set/Get the browser version
UseLongFile Names	Boolean	Set/Get whether links are updated every time the document is saved

WebOptions Methods

Name	Returns	Parameters	Description
UseDefault FolderSuffix			Tells Excel to use its default naming scheme for creating supporting folders

Example: WebOptions Object

```
Sub SetWebOptions()
   Dim oWO As WebOptions
   Set oWO = ActiveWorkbook.WebOptions
   With oWO
      .ScreenSize = msoScreenSize800x600
      .RelyOnCSS = True
      .UseDefaultFolderSuffix
   End With
End Sub
```

Window Object and the Windows Collection

The Windows collection holds the list of windows used in Excel or in a workbook. Each Window object represents a single Excel window containing scrollbars and gridlines for the window. The parents of the Windows collection can be the Application object and the Workbook object.

The Windows collection has a Count property and an Arrange method besides the typical collection attributes. The Count property returns the number of Window objects in the collection. The Arrange method arranges the windows in the collection in the manner specified by the ArrangeStyle parameter. Use the XlArrangeStyle constants to set the ArrangeStyle parameter. Set the ActiveWorkbook parameter to True to arrange only the windows associated with the open workbook. Set the SyncHorizontal parameter or the SyncVertical parameter to True so the windows will scroll horizontally or vertically together, respectively.

Window Common Properties

The Application, Creator, and Parent properties are defined at the beginning of this Appendix.

Window Properties

Name	Returns	Description
ActiveCell	Range	Read-only. Returns the cell in the window where the cursor is
ActiveChart	Chart	Read-only. Returns the currently selected chart in the window. If no chart is currently selected, nothing is returned
ActivePane	Pane	Read-only. Returns the active pane in the window
ActiveSheet		Read-only. Returns the active sheet in the window
Caption	Variant	Set/Get the caption that appears in the window
Display Formulas	Boolean	Set/Get whether formulas are displayed in the window. Not valid in a Chart sheet
Display Gridlines	Boolean	Set/Get whether worksheet gridlines are displayed
Display Headings	Boolean	Set/Get whether row and column headings are displayed. Not valid in a Chart sheet
Display Horizontal ScrollBar	Boolean	Set/Get whether the horizontal scrollbar is displayed in the window
Display Outline	Boolean	Set/Get whether outline symbols are displayed
Display RightToLeft	Boolean	Set/Get whether the window contents are displayed from right to left. Valid only with languages that support right-to-left text
Display Vertical ScrollBar	Boolean	Set/Get whether the vertical scrollbar is displayed in the window
Display WorkbookTabs	Boolean	Set/Get whether workbook tabs are displayed
DisplayZeros	Boolean	Set/Get whether zero values are displayed. Not valid with Chart sheets
EnableResize	Boolean	Set/Get whether a user can resize the window
FreezePanes	Boolean	Set/Get whether split panes are frozen. Not valid with Chart sheets
GridlineColor	Long	Set/Get the color of the gridlines. Use the RGB function to create the color value

Continues

Name	Returns	Description
GridlineColor Index	XlColor Index	Set/Get the color of the gridlines. Use the XlColorIndex constants or an index value in the current color palette
Height	Double	Set/Get the height of the window
Index	Long	Read-only. Returns the spot in the collection where the current object is located
Left	Double	Set/Get the distance from the left edge of the client area to the window's left edge
OnWindow	String	Set/Get the name of the procedure to run whenever a window is activated
Panes	Panes	Read-only. Returns the panes that are contained in the window
RangeSelection	Range	Read-only. Returns the selected range of cells or object in the window
ScrollColumn	Long	Set/Get the column number of the left-most column in the window
ScrollRow	Long	Set/Get the row number of the top-most row in the window
SelectedSheets	Sheets	Read-only. Returns all the selected sheets in the window
Selection	Object	Read-only. Returns the selected object in the window
Split	Boolean	Set/Get whether the window is split into panes
SplitColumn	Long	Set/Get at which column number the window split is going to be located
Split Horizontal	Double	Set/Get where the horizontal split of window will be located, in points
SplitRow	Long	Set/Get at which row number the window split is going to be located
SplitVertical	Double	Set/Get where the vertical split of window will be located, in points
SyncScrolling SideBySide	Boolean	When documents are compared, setting this to True will allow both documents to be scrolled at the same time
TabRatio	Double	Set/Get how big a workbook's tab is as a ratio of a workbook's tab area width to the window's horizontal scrollbar width

Name	Returns	Description
Top	Double	Set/Get the distance from the top edge of the client area to the window's top edge
Type	XlWindow Type	Read-only. Returns the window type
UsableHeight	Double	Read-only. Returns the maximum height that the window can be
UsableWidth	Double	Read-only. Returns the maximum width that the window can be
View	XlWindow View	Set/Get the view in the window (for example, xlNormalView, xlPageBreakPreview)
Visible	Boolean	Set/Get whether the window is visible
VisibleRange	Range	Read-only. Returns the range of cells that are visible in the current window
Width	Double	Set/Get the width of the window
WindowNumber	Long	Read-only. Returns the number associated with a window. Typically used when the same workbook is opened twice (for example, MyBook.xls:1 and MyBook.xls:2)
WindowState	XlWindow State	Set/Get the state of window: minimized, maximized, or normal
Zoom	Variant	Set/Get the percentage window zoom

Window Methods

Name	Returns	Parameters	Description
Activate	Variant		Sets focus to the window
ActivateNext	Variant		Activates the next window in the z-order
Activate Previous	Variant		Activates the previous window in the z-order
BreakSideBySide	Boolean		Disables side-by-side mode. The return value indicates if the operation was successful

Continues

Name	Returns	Parameters	Description
Close	Boolean	[SaveChanges], [Filename], [Route Workbook]	Closes the window. Set SaveChanges to True to automatically save changes in the window's workbook. If SaveChanges is False then all changes are lost. The Filename parameter can be used to specify the filename to save to. RouteWorkbook is used to automatically route the workbook onto the next recipient, if applicable
CompareSideBy SideWith	Boolean		Opens two windows in side-by-side mode
LargeScroll	Variant	[Down], [Up], [ToRight], [ToLeft]	Causes the document to scroll a certain direction a screen-full at a time, as specified by the parameters
NewWindow	Window		Creates and returns a new window
PointsTo Screen PixelsX	Long	Points As Long	Converts the horizontal document coordinate Points parameter to screen coordinate pixels
PointsTo Screen PixelsY	Long	Points As Long	Converts the vertical document coordinate Points parameter to screen coordinate pixels
PrintOut	Variant	[From], [To], [Copies], [Preview], [Active Printer], [PrintToFile], [Collate], [PrToFile Name]	Prints out the document in the window. The printer, number of copies, collation, and whether a print preview is desired can be specified with the parameters. Also, the sheets can be printed to a file using the PrintToFile and PrToFileName parameters. The From and To parameters can be used to specify the range of printed pages
PrintPreview	Variant	[Enable Changes]	Displays the current workbook in the window in a print preview mode. Set the EnableChanges parameter to False to disable the Margins and Setup buttons, hence not allowing the viewer to modify the page setup
RangeFrom Point	Object	x As Long, y As Long	Returns the shape or range located at the x and y coordinates. Returns nothing if there is no object at the x, y coordinates

Name	Returns	Parameters	Description
ResetPositions SideBySide			Resets the positions of two windows that are currently in side-by-side mode
ScrollInto View		Left As Long, Top As Long, Width As Long, Height As Long, [Start]	Scrolls the spot specified by the Left, Top, Width, and Height parameters to either the upper-left corner of the window (Start = True) or the lower-right corner of the window (Start = False). The Left, Top, Width, and Height parameters are specified in points
Scroll Workbook Tabs	Variant	[Sheets], [Position]	Scrolls through the number of sheets specified by the Sheets parameter or goes to the sheet specified by the position parameter (xlFirst or xlLast)
SmallScroll	Variant	[Down], [Up], [ToRight], [ToLeft]	Causes the document to scroll a certain direction one document line at a time, as specified by the parameters

Example: Window Object and the Windows Collection

```
Sub MinimiseAllWindows()
    Dim oWin As Window
    For Each oWin In Windows
        oWin.WindowState = xlMinimized
    Next
End Sub
```

Workbook Object and the Workbooks Collection

The Workbooks collection contains the list of open workbooks. A Workbook object represents a single workbook. The parent of the Workbook is the Application object.

Workbooks Properties

Name	Returns	Description
Count	Long	Read-only. Returns the number of Workbook objects in the collection
DisplayInk Comments	Boolean	Setting this to True will display ink comments

Continues

Name	Returns	Description
Document LibraryVersions		Returns a collection that represents all versions of shared workbooks that have versioning enabled
InactiveList BorderVisible	Boolean	Determines if the border of a list control is visible when the list control isn't active
Permission		Returns a Permission object that represents all permission settings
SharedWorkspace		A link to the document workspace in which a document is located
SmartDocument		Returns all settings for a smart document
Sync		The Sync property provides access to all methods and properties for documents that are part of a document workspace
XmlMaps		Represents all schema maps that have been added to the document workbook
XmlNamespaces		Represents all XML namespaces that have been added to the document workbook

Workbooks Methods

Name	Returns	Parameters	Description
Add	Workbook	[Template]	Adds a new workbook to the collection. Using a template name in the Template parameter can specify a template. Also, the XlWBATemplate constants can be used to open up a type of workbook
CanCheckOut	Boolean	Filename As String	Returns whether Excel can check out a specified workbook from a server
CheckOut		Filename As String	Returns a specified workbook from a server for editing

Name	Returns	Parameters	Description
Close			Closes the workbook
Discard Conflict		Filename As String	This keyword is reserved for future use
Offline Conflict	Boolean	Filename As String	This keyword is reserved for future use
Open	Workbook	Filename As String, [UpdateLinks], [ReadOnly], [Format], [Password], [WriteRes Password], [IgnoreRead Only Recommended], [Origin], [Delimiter], [Editable], [Notify], [Converter], [AddToMru], [Local], [CorruptLoad], [OpenConflict Document]	Opens a workbook specified by the Filename parameter and adds it to the collection. Use the UpdateLinks parameter to choose how links in the file are updated. Set ReadOnly to True to open up the workbook in read-only mode. If the file requires a password, use the Password or WriteResPassword parameters. Set AddToMru to True to add the opening workbook to the recently used files list. If the file to open is a delimited text file then there are some parameters that can be used. Use the Format parameter to choose the text delimiter character if opening a text file. Use the Origin parameter to choose the code page style of the incoming delimited text file. Use the Delimiter parameter to specify a delimiter if 6 (custom) was chosen for the Format parameter
OpenDatabase	Workbook	Filename As String, [CommandText], [CommandType], [Background Query], [ImportData As]	Returns a Workbook representing a database specified by the Filename parameter. The CommandText and CommandType parameters set the text and the type of the query

Continues

Name	Returns	Parameters	Description
OpenText		Filename As String, [Origin], [StartRow], [DataType], [Text Qualifier As XlText Qualifier], [Consecutive Delimiter], [Tab], [Semicolon], [Comma], [Space], [Other], [OtherChar], [FieldInfo], [TextVisual Layout], [Decimal Separator], [Thousands Separator], [Trailing MinusNumbers], [Local]	Opens the text file in Filename and parses it into a sheet on a new workbook. Origin is used to choose the code page style of the file (XlPlatform constant). StartRow decides the first row to parse. DataType decides if the file is xlDelimited or xlFixedWidth. Set ConsecutiveDelimiter to True to treat consecutive delimiters as one. Set Tab, Semicolon, Comma, Space, or Other to True to pick the delimiter character. Use the DecimalSeparator and ThousandsSeparator to pick the numeric characters to use
OpenXML	Workbook	Filename As String, [Stylesheets]	Returns an XML file in Microsoft Excel. Use the Stylesheets parameter to specify which XSLT stylesheet processing instructions to apply

Workbook Common Properties

The Application, Creator, and Parent properties are defined at the beginning of this Appendix.

Workbook Properties

Name	Returns	Description
AcceptLabelsIn Formulas	Boolean	Set/Get whether labels can be used in worksheet formulas
ActiveChart	Chart	Read-only. Returns the active chart in the workbook

Name	Returns	Description
ActiveSheet		Read-only. Returns the active sheet (chart or workbook) in the workbook
AutoUpdate Frequency	Long	Set/Get how often a shared workbook is updated automatically, in minutes
AutoUpdate SaveChanges	Boolean	Set/Get whether changes made to a shared workbook are visible to other users whenever the workbook is automatically updated
Builtin Document Properties	Document Properties	Read-only. Returns a collection holding all the built-in properties of the workbook. Things like title, subject, author, and number of words of the workbook can be accessed from this object
Calculation Version	Long	Read-only. Returns the version number of Excel that was last used to recalculate the Excel spreadsheet
ChangeHistory Duration	Long	Set/Get how far back, in days, a shared workbook's change history is visible
Charts	Sheets	Read-only. Returns the charts in the workbook
CodeName	String	Read-only. Returns the name of the workbook that was set at design time in the VBE
Colors	Variant	Parameters: [Index]. Set/Get the color palette colors for the workbook. There are 56 possible colors in the palette
CommandBars	CommandBars	Read-only. Returns an object to manipulate the commandbars in Excel
Conflict Resolution	XlSave Conflict Resolution	Set/Get how shared workbook conflicts are resolved when they are being updated (for example, xlLocalSessionChanges means that the local user's changes are always accepted)
Container		Read-only. Returns the object that contains the workbook, if applicable
CreateBackup	Boolean	Read-only. Returns whether a backup file is created whenever the workbook is saved
Custom Document Properties	Document Properties	Read-only. Returns a collection holding all the user-defined properties of the workbook
CustomViews	CustomViews	Read-only. Returns the collection of custom views in a workbook

Continues

Name	Returns	Description
Date1904	Boolean	Set/Get whether the 1904 date system is used in the workbook
Display Drawing Objects	xlDisplay Drawing Objects	Set/Get if shapes are displayed, placeholders are displayed or shapes are hidden
EnableAuto Recover	Boolean	Set/Get whether the option to save changed files, of all formats, on a timed interval, is switched on
Envelope Visible	Boolean	Set/Get whether the envelope toolbar and e-mail composition header are visible
Excel4Intl MacroSheets	Sheets	Read-only. Returns the collection of Excel 4.0 international macro sheets in the workbook
Excel4Macro Sheets	Sheets	Read-only. Returns the collection of Excel 4.0 macro sheets in the workbook
FileFormat	XlFile Format	Read-only. Returns the file format of the workbook
FullName	String	Read-only. Returns the path and file name of the workbook
FullNameURL Encoded	String	Read-only. Returns the name of the object, including its path on disk, as a string
HasPassword	Boolean	Read-only. Returns whether the workbook has a protection password
HasRouting Slip	Boolean	Set/Get whether the workbook has a routing slip. Use with the RoutingSlip object
Highlight Changes OnScreen	Boolean	Set/Get whether changes in a shared workbook are visibley highlighted
HTMLProject	HTMLProject	Read-only. Returns an object to access the project explorer of the script editor
IsAddin	Boolean	Set/Get whether the current workbook is running as an Addin
IsInplace	Boolean	Read-only. Returns whether the workbook is being edited as an object (True) or in Microsoft Excel (False)
KeepChange History	Boolean	Set/Get whether changes are tracked in a shared workbook
ListChangesOn NewSheet	Boolean	Set/Get whether a separate worksheet is used to display changes of a shared workbook
Mailer	Mailer	Read-only

Name	Returns	Description
MultiUser Editing	Boolean	Read-only. Returns whether a workbook is being shared
Name	String	Read-only. Returns the file name of the workbook
Names	Names	Read-only. Returns the collection of named ranges in the workbook
Password	String	Set/Get the password that must be supplied to open the specified workbook
Password Encryption Algorithm	String	Read-only. Returns the algorithm used by Excel to encrypt passwords for the specified workbook
Password EncryptionFile Properties	Boolean	Read-only. Returns whether Excel encrypts file properties for the specified password-protected workbook
Password EncryptionKey Length	Long	Read-only. Returns the key length of the algorithm that Excel uses when encrypting passwords for the specified workbook
Password Encryption Provider	String	Read-only. Returns the name of the algorithm encryption provider that Excel uses when encrypting passwords for the specified workbook
Path	String	Read-only. Returns the file path of the workbook
PersonalViewList Settings	Boolean	Set/Get whether a user's view of the workbook includes filters and sort settings for lists
PersonalView PrintSettings	Boolean	Set/Get whether a user's view of the workbook includes print settings
PrecisionAs Displayed	Boolean	Set/Get whether the precision of numbers in the workbook are as displayed in the cells. Used for calculations
Protect Structure	Boolean	Read-only. Returns whether the sheet order cannot be changed in the workbook
Protect Windows	Boolean	Read-only. Returns whether the workbook windows are protected
Publish Objects	Publish Objects	Read-only. Returns access to an object used to publish objects in the workbook as Web pages
ReadOnly	Boolean	Read-only. Returns whether the workbook is in read-only mode
ReadOnly Recommended	Boolean	Read-only. Returns whether the user is prompted with a message recommending that you open the workbook as read-only

Continues

Name	Returns	Description
Remove Personal Information	Boolean	Set/Get whether personal information can be removed from the specified workbook
Revision Number	Long	Read-only. Returns how many times a shared workbook has been saved while open
Routed	Boolean	Read-only. Returns whether a workbook has been routed to the next recipient
RoutingSlip	RoutingSlip	Read-only. Returns access to a RoutingSlip object that can be used to add a routing slip for the workbook. Use with the HasRoutingSlip property
Saved	Boolean	Set/Get whether a workbook does not have changes that need saving
SaveLink Values	Boolean	Set/Get whether values linked from external sources are saved with the workbook
Sheets	Sheets	Read-only. Returns the collection of sheets in a workbook (Chart or Worksheet)
ShowConflict History	Boolean	Set/Get whether the sheet containing conflicts related to shared workbooks are displayed
ShowPivot Table FieldList	Boolean	Set/Get whether the PivotTable field list can be shown
SmartTag Options	SmartTag Options	Read-only. Returns the options that can be performed with a SmartTag
Styles	Styles	Read-only. Returns the collection of styles associated with the workbook
Template Remove ExtData	Boolean	Set/Get whether all the external data references are removed after a workbook is saved as a template
UpdateLinks	XlUpdate Links	Set/Get the workbook's setting for updating embedded OLE links
UpdateRemote References	Boolean	Set/Get whether remote references are updated for the workbook
UserStatus	Variant	Read-only. Returns the name of the current user
VBASigned	Boolean	Read-only. Returns whether the VBA Project for the workbook has been digitally signed
VBProject	VBProject	Read-only. Returns access to the VBE and associated project

Name	Returns	Description
WebOptions	WebOptions	Read-only. Returns an object allowing manipulation of Web related properties of the workbook
Windows	Windows	Read-only. Returns the collection of windows that make up the workbook
Worksheets	Sheets	Read-only. Returns the collection of worksheets that make up the workbook
WritePassword	String	Set/Get the write password of a workbook
WriteReserved	Boolean	Read-only. Returns whether the workbook can be modified
Write ReservedBy	String	Read-only. Returns the name of the person with write permission to the workbook

Workbook Methods

Name	Returns	Parameters	Description
Accept AllChanges		[When], [Who], [Where]	Accepts all the changes made by other people in a shared workbook
Activate			Activates the workbook
AddTo Favorites			Adds the workbook shortcut to the Favorites folder
BreakLink		Name As String, Type As XlLinkType	Converts formulas linked to other Excel sources or OLE sources to values
CanCheckIn	Boolean		Set/Get whether Excel can check in a specified workbook to a server
ChangeFile Access		Mode As Xl FileAccess, [Write Password], [Notify]	Changes access permissions of the workbook to the one specified by the Mode parameter. If necessary, the WritePassword can be specified. Set Notify to True to have the user notified if the file cannot be accessed
ChangeLink		Name As String, NewName As String, Type As XlLinkType	Changes the link from the workbook specified by the Name parameter to the NewName workbook. Type chooses the type of link (for example, OLE, Excel)

Continues

Name	Returns	Parameters	Description
CheckIn		[SaveChanges], [Comments], [MakePublic]	Performs a check-in or undo-check-out of the working copy on the server
Close		[SaveChanges], [Filename], [Route Workbook]	Closes the workbook. Set SaveChanges to True to automatically save changes in the workbook. If SaveChanges is False then all changes are lost. The Filename parameter can be used to specify the filename to save to. RouteWorkbook is used to automatically route the workbook onto the next recipient, if applicable
DeleteNumber Format		NumberFormat As String	Deletes the number format in the NumberFormat parameter from the workbook
EndReview			Ends the review of a file that has been sent for review
Exclusive Access	Boolean		Gives the current user exclusive access to a shared workbook
Follow Hyperlink		Address As String, [SubAddress], [NewWindow], [AddHistory], [ExtraInfo], [Method], [HeaderInfo]	Opens up the appropriate application with the URL specified by the Address parameter. Set NewWindow to True to open up a new window for the hyperlink. Use the ExtraInfo and Method parameters to send more information to the hyperlink (say, for an ASP page). The Method parameter uses the MsoExtraInfoMethod constants
Highlight Changes Options		[When], [Who], [Where]	Set/Get when changes are viewed in a shared workbook (When), whose workbook changes can be viewed (Who), and the range that the changes should be put in (Where). Use the XlHighlighChangesTime constants with the When parameter

Name	Returns	Parameters	Description
LinkInfo	Variant	Name As String, LinkInfo As XlLinkInfo, [Type], [EditionRef]	Returns the link details mentioned in the LinkInfo parameter for the link specified by the Name parameter. Use the Type parameter with the XlLinkInfoType constants to pick the type of link that will be returned
LinkSources	Variant	[Type]	Returns the array of linked documents, editions, DDE and OLE servers in a workbook. Use the Type parameter with the XlLinkInfoType constants to pick the type of link that will be returned
Merge Workbook		Filename	Merges the changes from the Filename workbook into the current workbook
NewWindow	Window		Opens up a new window with the current workbook
OpenLinks		Name As String, [ReadOnly], [Type]	Opens the Name link and supporting documents. Set ReadOnly to True to open the documents as read-only. Use the Type parameter with the XlLinkInfoType constants to pick the type of link that will be returned
PivotCaches	PivotCaches		Returns the collection of PivotTable caches in the workbook
Post		[DestName]	Posts the workbook into a Microsoft Exchange public folder
PrintOut		[From], [To], [Copies], [Preview], [Active Printer], [PrintToFile], [Collate], [PrToFile Name]	Prints out the workbook. The printer, number of copies, collation, and whether a print preview is desired can be specified with the parameters. Also, the sheets can be printed to a file using the PrintToFile and PrToFileName parameters. The From and To parameters can be used to specify the range of printed pages

Continues

Name	Returns	Parameters	Description
PrintPreview		[Enable Changes]	Displays the current workbook in a print preview mode. Set the EnableChanges parameter to False to disable the Margins and Setup buttons, hence not allowing the viewer to modify the page setup
Protect		[Password], [Structure], [Windows]	Protects the workbook from user changes. A protect Password can be specified. Set the Structure parameter to True to protect the relative position of the sheets. Set the Windows to True to protect the workbook windows
Protect Sharing		[Filename], [Password], [WriteRes Password], [ReadOnly Recommended], [Create Backup], [Sharing Password]	Protects and saves the workbook for sharing. The file is saved to the Filename parameter with the optional passwords in Password, WriteResPassword, and SharingPassword parameters. Set ReadOnlyRecommended to True to display a message to the user every time the workbook is opened. Set CreateBackup to True to create a backup of the saved file
PurgeChange HistoryNow		Days As Long, [Sharing Password]	Deletes the entries in the change log for the shared workbook. The Days parameter specifies how many days back to delete the entries. A SharingPassword may be required
RecheckSmart Tags			Does a foreground SmartTag check. Any data that was not annotated before will now be annotated
RefreshAll			Refreshes any external data source's data into the workbook
RejectAll Changes		[When], [Who], [Where]	Rejects all the changes in a shared workbook
ReloadAs		Encoding As MsoEncoding	Reopens the workbook using the Web page related Encoding parameter

Name	Returns	Parameters	Description
RemoveUser		Index As Long	Disconnects the user (specified by the user index in the Index parameter) from a shared workbook
ReplyAll			Replies to all recipients of the sent workbook. Valid only in the Macintosh Edition of Excel
ReplyWith Changes		[ShowMessage]	E-mails a notification to the author of a workbook telling them that a reviewer has completed review of the workbook
ResetColors			Resets the colors in the color palette to the default colors
Route			Routes the workbook using the routing slip
RunAuto Macros		Which As XlRunAuto Macro	Runs the auto macro specified by the Which parameter
Save			Saves the workbook
SaveAs		Filename, FileFormat, Password, WriteRes Password, ReadOnly Recommended, CreateBackup, AccessMode As XlSaveAs AccessMode, [Conflict Resolution], [AddToMru], [Text Codepage], [TextVisual Layout], [Local]	Saves the workbook as FileName. The type of file to be saved can be specified with the FileFormat parameter. The file can be saved with the optional passwords in the Password and WriteResPassword parameters. Set ReadOnlyRecommended to True to display a message to the user every time the workbook is opened. Set CreateBackup to True to create a backup of the saved file. Use the AccessMode to choose how the workbook is accessed (for example, xlShared, xlExclusive). Use the ConflictResolution parameter to decide how shared workbooks resolve change conflicts. Set the AddToMru parameter to True to add the workbook to the recently opened files list

Continues

Name	Returns	Parameters	Description
SaveCopyAs		[Filename]	Saves a copy of the workbook as the FileName
SendForReview		[Recipients], [Subject], [ShowMessage], [Include Attachment]	Sends a workbook in an e-mail message for review to the specified recipients
SendMail		Recipients, [Subject], [Return Receipt]	Sends the workbook through the default mail system. The recipient or recipients and subject can be specified with the parameters. Set ReturnReceipt to True to request a return receipt
SendMailer		FileFormat, Priority As XlPriority	
SetLinkOnData		Name As String, [Procedure]	Runs the procedure in the Procedure parameter whenever the DDE or OLE link in the Name parameter is updated
SetPassword Encryption Options		[Password Encryption Provider], [Password Encryption Algorithm], [Password EncryptionKey Length], [Password Encryption File Properties]	Sets the options for encrypting workbooks using passwords
Unprotect		[Password]	Unprotects the workbook with the password, if necessary
Unprotect Sharing		[Sharing Password]	Unprotects the workbook from sharing and saves the workbook
UpdateFrom File			Reloads the current workbook from the file if the file is newer then the workbook

Name	Returns	Parameters	Description
UpdateLink		[Name], [Type]	Updates the link specified by the Name parameter. Use the Type parameter with the XlLinkInfoType constants to pick the type of link that will be returned
WebPagePreview			Previews the workbook as a Web page

Workbook Events

Name	Parameters	Description
Activate		Triggered when the workbook is activated
AddinInstall		Triggered when the workbook is opened as an Addin
Addin Uninstall		Triggered when the workbook opened as an Addin is uninstalled
BeforeClose	Cancel As Boolean	Triggered just before the workbook closes. Set the Cancel parameter to True to cancel the closing
BeforePrint	Cancel As Boolean	Triggered just before the workbook is printed. Set the Cancel parameter to True to cancel the printing
BeforeSave	SaveAsUI As Boolean, Cancel As Boolean	Triggered just before the workbook is saved. Set the Cancel parameter to True to cancel the saving. Set the SaveAsUI to True for the user to be prompted with the Save As dialog box
Deactivate		Triggered when the workbook loses focus
NewSheet	Sh As Object	Triggered when a new sheet is created in the workbook. The Sh parameter passes in the new sheet
Open		Triggered when the workbook is opened

Continues

Name	Parameters	Description
PivotTable Close Connection	ByVal Target As PivotTable	Triggered when a PivotTable report closes the connection to its data source. Target is the selected PivotTable
PivotTable Open Connection	ByVal Target As PivotTable	Triggered when a PivotTable report opens the connection to its data source. Target is the selected PivotTable
SheetActivate	Sh As Object	Triggered when a sheet is activated in the workbook. The Sh parameter passes in the activated sheet
SheetBefore DoubleClick	Sh As Object, Target As Range, Cancel As Boolean	Triggered when a sheet is about to be double-clicked. The sheet and the potential double-click spot are passed into the event. The double-click action can be canceled by setting the Cancel parameter to True
SheetBefore RightClick	Sh As Object, Target As Range, Cancel As Boolean	Triggered when a sheet is about to be right-clicked. The sheet and the potential right-click spot are passed into the event. The right-click action can be canceled by setting the Cancel parameter to True
Sheet Calculate	Sh As Object	Triggered when a sheet is recalculated passing in the recalculated sheet
SheetChange	Sh As Object, Target As Range	Triggered when the contents of a cell are changed in any worksheet in the workbook, for example, triggered by entering new data, clearing the cell, deleting a row/column. *Not* triggered when inserting rows/columns
Sheet Deactivate	Sh As Object	Triggered when a sheet loses focus. Passes in the sheet
SheetFollow Hyperlink	Sh As Object, Target As Hyperlink	Triggered when the user clicks on a hyperlink on a sheet. Passes in the sheet and the clicked hyperlink
SheetPivot TableUpdate	ByVal Sh As Object, Target As PivotTable	Triggered when the sheet of the PivotTable report has been updated
Sheet Selection Change	Sh As Object, Target As Range	Triggered when the user selects a different cell on the sheet. Passes in the new range and the sheet where the change occurred

Name	Parameters	Description
Window Activate	Wn As Window	Triggered when a workbook window is activated (brought up to the front of other workbook windows). The workbook and the window are passed in
Window Deactivate	Wn As Window	Triggered when a workbook window loses focus. The related workbook and the window are passed in
WindowResize	Wn As Window	Triggered when a workbook window is resized. The resized workbook and window are passed into the event

Example: Workbook Object and the Workbooks Collection

Please refer to Chapter 4 for `Workbook` object examples.

Worksheet Object and the Worksheets Collection

The `Worksheets` collection holds the collection of worksheets in a workbook. The `Workbook` object is always the parent of the `Worksheets` collection. The `Worksheets` collection only holds the worksheets. The `Worksheet` objects in the `Worksheets` collection can be accessed using the `Item` property. Either the name of the worksheet can be specified as a parameter to the `Item`'s parameter or an index number describing the position of the worksheet in the workbook (from left to right).

The `Worksheet` object allows access to all of the attributes of a specific worksheet in Excel. This includes worksheet formatting and other worksheet properties. The `Worksheet` object also exposes events that can be used programmatically.

The `Worksheets` collection has a few properties and methods besides the typical collection attributes. These are listed in the following table.

Worksheets Collection Properties and Methods

Name	Returns	Description
Count	Long	Read-only. Returns the number of worksheets in the collection
HPageBreaks	HPage Breaks	Read-only. Returns a collection holding all the horizontal page breaks associated with the `Worksheets` collection

Continues

Name	Returns	Description
VpageBreaks	VPage Breaks	Read-only. Returns a collection holding all the vertical page breaks associated with the `Worksheets` collection
Visible	Variant	Set/Get whether the worksheets in the collection are visible. Also can set this to `xlVeryHidden` to not allow a user to make the worksheets in the collection visible
Add		Method. Parameters: `[Before]`, `[After]`, `[Count]`, `[Type]`. Adds a worksheet to the collection. You can specify where the worksheet goes by choosing which sheet object will be before the new worksheet object (`Before` parameter) or after the new worksheet (`After` parameter). The `Count` parameter decides how many worksheets are created
Copy		Method. Parameters: `[Before]`, `[After]`. Adds a new copy of the currently active worksheet to the position specified at the `Before` or `After` parameters
Delete		Method. Deletes all the worksheets in the collection
FillAcross Sheets		Method. Parameters: `Range As Range`, `Type As XlFillWith`. Copies the range specified by the `Range` parameter across all the other worksheets in the collection. Use the `Type` parameter to pick what part of the range is copied (for example, `xlFillWithContents`, `xlFillWithFormulas`)
Move		Method. Parameters: `[Before]`, `[After]`. Moves the current worksheet to the position specified by the parameters
PrintPreview		Method. Parameters: `[EnableChanges]`. Displays the current worksheet in the collection in a print preview mode. Set the `EnableChanges` parameter to `False` to disable the Margins and Setup buttons, hence not allowing the viewer to modify the page setup

Name	Returns	Description
PrintOut		Method. Parameters: `[From]`, `[To]`, `Copies]`, `[Preview]`, `[ActivePrinter]`, `[PrintToFile]`, `[Collate]`, `[PrToFileName]`. Prints out the worksheets in the collection. The printer, number of copies, collation, and whether a print preview is desired can be specified with the parameters. Also, the sheets can be printed to a file using the `PrintToFile` and `PrToFileName` parameters. The `From` and `To` parameters can be used to specify the range of printed pages
Select		Method. Parameters: `[Replace]`. Selects the current worksheet in the collection

Worksheet Common Properties

The `Application`, `Creator`, and `Parent` properties are defined at the beginning of this Appendix.

Worksheet Properties

Name	Returns	Description
AutoFilter	AutoFilter	Read-only. Returns an `AutoFilter` object if filtering is turned on
AutoFilter Mode	Boolean	Set/Get whether `AutoFilter` drop-down arrows are currently displayed on the worksheet
Cells	Range	Read-only. Returns the cells in the current worksheet
Circular Reference	Range	Read-only. Returns the cell range that contains the first circular reference on the worksheet
CodeName	String	Read-only. Returns the name of the worksheet set at design time in the VBE
Columns	Range	Read-only. Returns a range of the columns in the current worksheet
Comments	Comments	Read-only. Returns the collection of comments in the worksheet
Consolidation Function	Xl Consolidation Function	Read-only. Returns the type of consolidation being used in the worksheet (for example, `xlSum`, `xlMax`, `xlAverage`)

Continues

Name	Returns	Description
Consolidation Options	Variant	Read-only. Returns a one-dimensional array containing three elements of Booleans. The first element describes whether the labels in the top row are used; the second element describes whether the labels in the left-most column are used; and the third element describes whether links are created to the source data
Consolidation Sources	Variant	Read-only. Returns the array of strings that describe the source sheets for the current worksheet's consolidation
Custom Properties	Custom Properties	Read-only. Returns the identifier information associated with a worksheet
DisplayPage Breaks	Boolean	Set/Get whether page breaks are displayed
DisplayRight ToLeft	Boolean	Set/Get whether the worksheet contents are displayed from right to left. Valid only with languages that support right-to-left text
EnableAuto Filter	Boolean	Set/Get whether the AutoFilter arrows are enabled when a worksheet is user interface-only protected
Enable Calculation	Boolean	Set/Get whether Excel will automatically recalculate the worksheet as necessary
EnableOut lining	Boolean	Set/Get whether outlining symbols are enabled when a worksheet is user interface-only protected
EnablePivot Table	Boolean	Set/Get whether PivotTable controls and related actions are enabled when a worksheet is user interface-only protected
Enable Selection	XlEnable Selection	Set/Get what objects can be selected when a worksheet is protected (for example, xlNoSelection, xlNoRestrictions)
FilterMode	Boolean	Read-only. Returns whether a worksheet is in a filter mode
HPageBreaks	HPageBreaks	Read-only. Returns a collection holding all the horizontal page breaks associated with the Worksheet
Hyperlinks	Hyperlinks	Read-only. Returns the collection of hyperlinks in the worksheet
Index	Long	Read-only. Returns the spot in the parent collection where the current worksheet is located
ListObjects	Range	Returns a Range object

Name	Returns	Description
MailEnvelope	MsoEnvelope	Set/Get the e-mail header for a document
Name	String	Set/Get the name of the worksheet
Names	Names	Read-only. Returns the collection of ranges with names in the worksheet
Next		Read-only. Returns the next sheet in the workbook (from left to right) as an object
Outline	Outline	Read-only. Returns an object to manipulate an outline in the worksheet
PageSetup	PageSetup	Read-only. Returns an object to manipulate the page setup properties for the worksheet
Previous		Read-only. Returns the previous sheet in the workbook (from right to left) as an object
Protect Contents	Boolean	Read-only. Returns whether the worksheet and everything in it is protected from changes
Protect Drawing Objects	Boolean	Read-only. Returns whether the shapes in the worksheet can be modified (ProtectDrawingObjects = False)
Protection	Protection	Read-only. Returns the protection options of the worksheet
Protection Mode	Boolean	Read-only. Returns whether protection has been applied to the user interface. Even if a worksheet has user interface protection on, any VBA code associated with the worksheet can still be accessed
Protect Scenarios	Boolean	Read-only. Returns whether the worksheet scenarios are protected
QueryTables	QueryTables	Read-only. Returns the collection of query tables associated with the worksheet
Range	Range	Read-only. Parameters: Cell1, [Cell2]. Returns a Range object as defined by the Cell1 and optionally Cell2 parameters
Rows	Range	Read-only. Returns a Range object containing the rows of the current worksheet
Scripts	Scripts	Read-only. Returns the collection of VBScript code associated with a worksheet (typically to later use on Web pages)
ScrollArea	String	Sets the A1-style reference string describing the range in the worksheet that can be scrolled. Cells not in the range cannot be selected

Continues

Name	Returns	Description
Shapes	Shapes	Read-only. Returns all the shapes contained by the worksheet
SmartTags	SmartTags	Read-only. Returns the identifier for the specified cell
Standard Height	Double	Read-only. Returns the default height of the rows in the worksheet, in points
Standard Width	Double	Read-only. Returns the default width of the columns in the worksheet, in points
Tab	Tab	Read-only. Returns the Tab object for the selected chart or worksheet
TransitionExp Eval	Boolean	Set/Get whether evaluates expressions using Lotus 1-2-3 rules in the worksheet
TransitionForm Entry	Boolean	Set/Get whether formula entries can be entered using Lotus 1-2-3 rules
Type	XlSheetType	Read-only. Returns the worksheet type (for example, xlWorksheet, xlExcel4MacroSheet, xlExcel4IntlMacroSheet)
UsedRange	Range	Read-only. Returns the range in the worksheet that is being used
Visible	XlSheet Visibility	Set/Get whether the worksheet is visible. Also can set this to xlVeryHidden to not allow a user to make the worksheet visible
VPageBreaks	VPageBreaks	Read-only. Returns a collection holding all the vertical page breaks associated with the worksheet

Worksheet Methods

Name	Returns	Parameters	Description
Activate			Activates the worksheet
Calculate			Calculates all the formulas in the worksheet
ChartObjects		[Index]	Returns either a chart object (ChartObject) or a collection of chart objects (ChartObjects) in a worksheet

Name	Returns	Parameters	Description
CheckSpelling		[Custom Dictionary], [Ignore Uppercase], [Always Suggest], [SpellLang]	Checks the spelling of the text in the worksheet. A custom dictionary can be specified (CustomDictionary), all uppercase words can be ignored (IgnoreUppercase), and Excel can be set to display a list of suggestions (AlwaysSuggest)
CircleInvalid			Circles the invalid entries in the worksheet
ClearArrows			Clears out all the tracer arrows in the worksheet
ClearCircles			Clears all the circles around invalid entries in a worksheet
Copy		[Before], [After]	Adds a new copy of the worksheet to the position specified at the Before or After parameters
Delete			Deletes the worksheet
Evaluate	Variant	Name	Evaluates the Name string expression as if it were entered into a worksheet cell
Move		[Before], [After]	Moves the worksheet to the position specified by the parameters
OLEObjects		[Index]	Returns either a single OLE object (OLEObject) or a collection of OLE objects (OLEObjects) for a worksheet
Paste		[Destination], [Link]	Pastes the contents of the clipboard into the worksheet. A specific destination range can be specified with the Destination parameter. Set Link to True to establish a link to the source of the pasted data. Either the Destination or the Link parameter can be used

Continues

929

Name	Returns	Parameters	Description
PasteSpecial		[Format], [Link], [DisplayAs Icon], [IconFile Name], [IconIndex], [IconLabel], [NoHTML Formatting]	Pastes the clipboard contents into the current worksheet. The format of the clipboard data can be specified with the string Format parameter. Set Link to True to establish a link to the source of the pasted data. Set DisplayAsIcon to True to display the pasted data as an icon and the IconFileName, IconIndex, and IconLabel to specify the icon and label. A destination range must be already selected in the worksheet
PivotTables		[Index]	Returns either a single PivotTable report (PivotTable) or a collection of PivotTable reports (PivotTables) for a worksheet
PivotTable Wizard	Pivot Table	[SourceType], [SourceData], [Table Destination], [TableName], [RowGrand], [ColumnGrand], [SaveData], [HasAuto Format], [AutoPage], [Reserved], [Background Query], [Optimize Cache], [PageField Order], [PageField WrapCount], [ReadData], [Connection]	Creates a PivotTable report. The SourceType uses the XLPivotTableSourceType constants to specify the type of SourceData being used for the PivotTable. Table Destination holds the range in the parent worksheet that report will be placed. TableName holds the name of the new report. Set RowGrand or ColumnGrand to True to show grand totals for rows and columns, respectively. Set HasAutoFormat to True for Excel to format the report automatically when it is refreshed or changed. Use the AutoPage parameter to set if a page field is created automatically for consolidation.

Name	Returns	Parameters	Description
			Set `BackgroundQuery` to `True` for Excel to query the data source asynchronously. Set `OptimizeCache` to `True` for Excel to optimize the cache when it is built. Use the `PageFieldOrder` with the `xlOrder` constants to set how new page fields are added to the report. Use the `PageFieldWrapCount` to set the number of page fields in each column or row. Set `ReadData` to `True` to copy the data from the external database into a cache. Finally, use the `Connection` parameter to specify an ODBC connection string for the `PivotTable`'s cache
PrintOut		[From], [To], [Copies], [Preview], [Active Printer], [PrintToFile], [Collate], [PrToFile Name]	Prints out the worksheet. The printer, number of copies, collation, and whether a print preview is desired can be specified with the parameters. Also, the sheets can be printed to a file using the `PrintToFile` and `PrToFileName` parameters. The `From` and `To` parameters can be used to specify the range of printed pages
PrintPreview		[Enable Changes]	Displays the worksheet in a print preview mode. Set the `EnableChanges` parameter to `False` to disable the Margins and Setup buttons, hence not allowing the viewer to modify the page setup
Protect		[Password], [Drawing Objects], [Contents], [Scenarios], [User Interface Only], [Allow Formatting Cells], [Allow Formatting	Protects the worksheet from changes. A case-sensitive `Password` can be specified. Also, whether shapes are protected (`DrawingObjects`), the entire contents are protected (`Contents`), and whether only the user interface is protected (`UserInterfaceOnly`)

Continues

931

Name	Returns	Parameters	Description
		Columns], [Allow Formatting Rows], [Allow Inserting Columns], [Allow Inserting Rows], [Allow Inserting Hyperlinks], [Allow Deleting Columns], [Allow DeletingRows], [Allow Sorting], [Allow Filtering], [AllowUsing PivotTables]	
ResetAllPage Breaks			Resets all the page breaks in the worksheet
SaveAs		Filename As String, [FileFormat], [Password], [WriteRes Password], [ReadOnly Recommended], [Create Backup], [AddToMru], [Text Codepage], [TextVisual Layout] , [Local]	Saves the worksheet as FileName. The type of file to be saved can be specified with the FileFormat parameter. The file can be saved with the optional passwords in the Password and WriteResPassword parameters. Set ReadOnly Recommended to True to display a message to the user every time the worksheet is opened. Set CreateBackup to True to create a backup of the saved file. Set the AddToMru parameter to True to add the worksheet to the recently-opened files list
Scenarios		[Index]	Returns either a single scenario (Scenario) or a collection of scenarios (Scenarios) for a worksheet

Name	Returns	Parameters	Description
Select		[Replace]	Selects the worksheet
SetBackground Picture		Filename As String	Sets the worksheet's background to the picture specified by the FileName parameter
ShowAllData			Displays all of the data that is currently filtered
ShowDataForm			Displays the data form that is part of the worksheet
Unprotect		[Password]	Deletes the protection set up for a worksheet. If the worksheet was protected with a password, the password must be specified now
XmlDataQuery	Range	[XPath] [Selection Namespaces] [Map]	Represents cells mapped to a particular XPath
XmlMapQuery	Range	[XPath] [Selection Namespaces] [Map]	Represents cells mapped to a particular XPath

Worksheet Events

Name	Parameters	Description
Activate		Triggered when a worksheet is made to have focus
BeforeDouble Click	Target As Range, Cancel As Boolean	Triggered just before a user double-clicks a worksheet. The cell closest to the point double-clicked in the worksheet is passed in to the event procedure as Target. The double-click action can be canceled by setting the Cancel parameter to True
BeforeRight Click	Cancel As Boolean	Triggered just before a user right-clicks a worksheet. The cell closest to the point right-clicked in the worksheet is passed in to the event procedure as Target. The right-click action can be canceled by setting the Cancel parameter to True
Calculate		Triggered after the worksheet is recalculated

Continues

Name	Parameters	Description
Change	Target As Range	Triggered when the worksheet cell values are changed. The changed range is passed into the event procedure as `Target`
Deactivate		Triggered when the worksheet loses focus
Follow Hyperlink	Target As Hyperlink	Triggered when a hyperlink is clicked on the worksheet. The hyperlink that was clicked is passed into the event procedure as `Target`
PivotTable Update	ByVal Target As Pivot Table	Triggered when a `PivotTable` report is updated on a worksheet
Selection Change	Target As Range	Triggered when the selection changes in a worksheet. The new selected range is passed into the event procedure as `Target`

Example: Worksheet Object and the Worksheets Collection

Please refer to Chapter 4 for `Worksheet` object examples.

WorksheetFunction Object

The `WorksheetFunction` object contains all of the Excel worksheet function. The `WorksheetFunction` object allows access to Excel worksheet function in Visual Basic code. The parent of the `WorksheetFunction` object is the `Application` object.

WorksheetFunction Common Properties

The `Application`, `Creator`, and `Parent` properties are defined at the beginning of this Appendix.

WorksheetFunction Methods

Name	Returns	Parameters	Description
Acos	Double	Arg1 As Double	Returns the arccosine of the `Arg1` number. Arg1 must be between –1 to 1
Acosh	Double	Arg1 As Double	Returns the inverse hyperbolic cosine of the `Arg1` number. Arg1 must be >= 1
And	Boolean	Arg1, [Arg2], ... [Arg30]	Returns `True` if all the arguments (from Arg1 up to Arg30) evaluate to `True`

Name	Returns	Parameters	Description
Asc	String	Arg1 As String	Returns the half-width character equivalent of the full width characters in the Arg1 string. Not the same as the VBA Asc function which returns the ASCII code of the first character in the string
Asin	Double	Arg1 As Double	Returns the arcsine of the Arg1 number. Arg1 must be between −1 and 1
Asinh	Double	Arg1 As Double	Returns the inverse hyperbolic sine of the Arg1 number
Atan2	Double	Arg1 As Double, Arg2 As Double	Returns the arctangent of the x and y coordinates specified in the Arg1 and Arg2 parameters, respectively
Atanh	Double	Arg1 As Double	Returns the inverse hyperbolic tangent of the Arg1 number. Arg1 must be between −1 and 1
AveDev	Double	Arg1, [Arg2], ... [Arg30]	Returns the average of the absolute deviation from the mean of the Arg1 to Arg30 number parameters
Average	Double	Arg1, [Arg2], ... [Arg30]	Returns the average of the numbers in Arg1 to Arg30
BahtText	String	Arg1 As Double	Returns a number in Thai text with a "Baht." suffix. Arg1 is the number to be converted
BetaDist	Double	Arg1 As Double, Arg2 As Double, Arg3 As Double, [Arg4], [Arg5]	Returns the cumulative beta probability. Arg1 is the number to evaluate. Arg2 is the Alpha part of the distribution. Arg3 is the Beta part of the distribution. Arg4 and Arg5 can be the lower and upper bounds of the interval in Arg1

Continues

Name	Returns	Parameters	Description
BetaInv	Double	Arg1 As Double, Arg2 As Double, Arg3 As Double, [Arg4], [Arg5]	Returns the inverse of the cumulative beta probability density. Arg1 is the probability of the distribution. Arg2 is the Alpha part of the distribution. Arg3 is the Beta part of the distribution. Arg4 and Arg5 can be the lower and upper bounds of the evaluated number
BinomDist	Double	Arg1 As Double, Arg2 As Double, Arg3 As Double, Arg4 As Boolean	Returns the individual term binomial distribution probability. Arg1 is the number of successes in the trials. Arg2 holds the total number of trials. Arg3 is the probability of success on a single trial. Arg4 sets whether the method returns the cumulative distribution function (True) or the probability mass function (False)
Ceiling	Double	Arg1 As Double, Arg2 As Double	Returns the nearest number to Arg1 that is a multiple of Arg2, rounded positively
ChiDist	Double	Arg1 As Double, Arg2 As Double	Returns the one-tail probability of the chi-squared distribution. Arg1 is the number to evaluate. Arg2 is the number of degrees of freedom
ChiInv	Double	Arg1 As Double, Arg2 As Double	Returns the inverse of the one-tail probability of the chi-squared distribution. Arg1 is the probability. Arg2 is the number of degrees of freedom
ChiTest	Double	Arg1, Arg2	Returns the chi-squared distribution test for independence. Arg1 holds the range of data that will be tested against the expected values. Arg2 holds the range of expected data
Choose	Variant	Arg1, Arg2, [Arg3], ... [Arg30]	Returns one of the parameter values (Arg2 to Arg30) given the index value in Arg1. For example, if Arg1 is 2 then the value in Arg3 is returned
Clean	String	Arg1 As String	Returns the string in Arg1 without any nonprintable characters

Name	Returns	Parameters	Description
Combin	Double	Arg1 As Double, Arg2 As Double	Returns the total possible number of combinations of a group of Arg2 items in a total number of Arg1 items
Confidence	Double	Arg1 As Double, Arg2 As Double, Arg3 As Double	Returns a range on either side of a sample mean for a population mean. Arg1 is the Alpha value used to determine the confidence level. Arg2 is the standard deviation for the data range. Arg3 is the sample size
Correl	Double	Arg1, Arg2	Returns the correlation coefficient of the arrays in Arg1 and Arg2. The parameters can also be cell ranges
Cosh	Double	Arg1 As Double	Returns the hyperbolic cosine of the Arg1 number
Count	Double	Arg1, [Arg2], ... [Arg30]	Returns the number of numeric values in the arguments. Arg1 to Arg30 can be values or range references
CountA	Double	Arg1, [Arg2], ... [Arg30]	Returns the number of non-empty values in the arguments. Arg1 to Arg30 can be values or range references
CountBlank	Double	Arg1 As Range	Returns the number of empty values in the range in Arg1
CountIf	Double	Arg1 As Range, Arg2	Counts the number of cells in the Arg1 range that meet the criteria in Arg2
Covar	Double	Arg1, Arg2	Returns the covariance of the arrays or ranges in Arg1 and Arg2
CritBinom	Double	Arg1 As Double, Arg2 As Double, Arg3 As Double	Returns the smallest value where the cumulative binomial distribution is greater than or equal to the criterion value. Arg1 is the number of Bernoulli trials. Arg2 is the probability of success for each trial. Arg3 is the criterion value

Continues

Name	Returns	Parameters	Description
DAverage	Double	Arg1 As Range, Arg2, Arg3	Returns the average of the column specified by Arg2 in the range of cells in Arg1. Arg3 contains the criteria used to choose rows of records to be averaged
Days360	Double	Arg1, Arg2, [Arg3]	Returns the difference of days between the Arg1 and Arg2 dates (Arg1 – Arg2). If the Arg3 method is set to True then the European method of calculation is used. If Arg3 is set to False or omitted then the US method of calculation is used
Db	Double	Arg1 As Double, Arg2 As Double, Arg3 As Double, Arg4 As Double, [Arg5]	Returns depreciation for a specified period using the fixed-declining balance method. Arg1 is the initial cost to depreciate. Arg2 is the final salvage cost (cost at end of depreciation). Arg3 is the number of periods to depreciate. Arg4 is the specific period from Arg3 to depreciation. Arg5 can be the number of months in the first year that depreciation will start
Dbcs	String	Arg1 As String	Returns the Double-Byte-Character-Set string of the given ASCII string. Opposite of the Asc function
DCount	Double	Arg1 As Range, Arg2, Arg3	Returns the number of cells that match the criteria in Arg3. Arg1 specifies the range of rows and columns to count and Arg2 is used to choose the field name or number to count
DCountA	Double	Arg1 As Range, Arg2, Arg3	Returns the number of non-blank cells that match the criteria in Arg3. Arg1 specifies the range of rows and columns to count and Arg2 is used to choose the field name or number to count

Name	Returns	Parameters	Description
Ddb	Double	Arg1 As Double, Arg2 As Double, Arg3 As Double, Arg4 As Double, [Arg5]	Returns depreciation for a specified period using the double-declining balance method. Arg1 is the initial cost to depreciate. Arg2 is final salvage cost (cost at end of depreciation). Arg3 is the number of periods to depreciate. Arg4 is the specific period from Arg3 to depreciation. Arg5 can be the rate at which the balance declines
Degrees	Double	Arg1 As Double	Converts the radians in Arg1 into degrees and returns the degrees
DevSq	Double	Arg1, [Arg2], ... [Arg30]	Returns the sum of the squares of deviations of the Arg1 to Arg30 from their mean
DGet	Variant	Arg1 As Range, Arg2, Arg3	Returns the cell value that matches the criteria in Arg3. Arg1 specifies the range of rows and columns to count and Arg2 is used to choose the field name or number to count. Criteria must match a single cell
DMax	Double	Arg1 As Range, Arg2 , Arg3	Returns the largest value that matches the criteria in Arg3. Arg1 specifies the range of rows and columns to count and Arg2 is used to choose the field name or number to count
DMin	Double	Arg1 As Range, Arg2, Arg3	Returns the smallest value that matches the criteria in Arg3. Arg1 specifies the range of rows and columns to count and Arg2 is used to choose the field name or number to count
Dollar	String	Arg1 As Double, [Arg2]	Returns a currency-type string of the number in Arg1 with the decimal points specified in Arg2

Continues

Name	Returns	Parameters	Description
DProduct	Double	Arg1 As Range, Arg2, Arg3	Returns the multiplication product of the values that match the criteria in Arg3. Arg1 specifies the range of rows and columns to count and Arg2 is used to choose the field name or number to count
DStDev	Double	Arg1 As Range, Arg2, Arg3	Returns the estimated standard deviation of the values that match the criteria in Arg3. Arg1 specifies the range of rows and columns to count and Arg2 is used to choose the field name or number to count
DStDevP	Double	Arg1 As Range, Arg2, Arg3	Returns the standard deviation of the values that match the criteria in Arg3 assuming the entire population is given. Arg1 specifies the range of rows and columns to count and Arg2 is used to choose the field name or number to count
DSum	Double	Arg1 As Range, Arg2, Arg3	Returns the sum of the values that match the criteria in Arg3. Arg1 specifies the range of rows and columns to count and Arg2 is used to choose the field name or number to count
DVar	Double	Arg1 As Range, Arg2, Arg3	Returns the variance of the values that match the criteria in Arg3. Arg1 specifies the range of rows and columns to count and Arg2 is used to choose the field name or number to count
DVarP	Double	Arg1 As Range, Arg2, Arg3	Returns the variance of the values that match the criteria in Arg3 assuming that the entire population is given. Arg1 specifies the range of rows and columns to count and Arg2 is used to choose the field name or number to count
Even	Double	Arg1 As Double	Converts the Arg1 number into the nearest even whole number, rounded up, and returns it

Name	Returns	Parameters	Description
ExponDist	Double	Arg1 As Double, Arg2 As Double, Arg3 As Boolean	Returns the exponential distribution of a value. Arg1 is the value of the function. Arg2 is the Lambda parameter value. Set Arg3 to True for the method to return the cumulative distribution. Set Arg3 to False to return the probability density
Fact	Double	Arg1 As Double	Returns the factorial of Arg1
FDist	Double	Arg1 As Double, Arg2 As Double, Arg3 As Double	Returns the F probability distribution of a value. Arg1 is the value to evaluate the function. Arg2 is the numerator degrees of freedom and Arg3 is the denominator degrees of freedom
Find	Double	Arg1 As String, Arg2 As String, [Arg3]	Finds the text in Arg1 from the text in Arg2 and returns the starting position of the found text. Arg3 can specify the starting position to search in Arg2
FindB	Double	Arg1 As String, Arg2 As String, [Arg3]	Finds the text in Arg1 from the text in Arg2 and returns the starting position of the found text. Arg3 can specify the starting byte position to search in Arg2
FInv	Double	Arg1 As Double, Arg2 As Double, Arg3 As Double	Returns the inverse of the F probability distribution. Arg1 is the probability that is associated with the F cumulative distribution. Arg2 is the numerator degrees of freedom and Arg3 is the denominator degrees of freedom
Fisher	Double	Arg1 As Double	Returns the Fisher transformation at the Arg1 value
FisherInv	Double	Arg1 As Double	Returns the inverse of the Fisher transformation given the value of Arg1
Fixed	String	Arg1 As Double, [Arg2], [Arg3]	Rounds the number Arg1 to the decimal points Arg2 and returns the value as a string. Set Arg3 to True to put commas in the returned text. Set Arg3 to False to not put commas in the returned text

Continues

Name	Returns	Parameters	Description
Floor	Double	Arg1 As Double, Arg2 As Double	Returns the nearest number to Arg1 that is a multiple of Arg2, rounded down towards 0
Forecast	Double	Arg1 As Double, Arg2, Arg3	Returns a predicted y value for a given x value (Arg1) by using the existing value pairs. Arg2 is an array or range corresponding to the y's known values. Arg3 is an array or range corresponding to the x's known values
Frequency	Variant	Arg1, Arg2	Returns an array of numbers describing the frequency of values in the array Arg1 that are in the intervals specified by the Arg2 array. Arg1 and Arg2 can also be references to a range
FTest	Double	Arg1, Arg2	Returns the result of an F-test of the arrays in Arg1 and Arg2. Arg1 and Arg2 can also be references to a range
Fv	Double	Arg1 As Double, Arg2 As Double, Arg3 As Double, [Arg4], [Arg5]	Returns the future value of an investment for a time period. Arg1 is the interest rate per period. Arg2 is the total number of payment periods. Arg3 is the payment per period. Arg4 is the initial value. Arg5 determines if payments are due at the end of the period (0) or the beginning of the period (1)
GammaDist	Double	Arg1 As Double, Arg2 As Double, Arg3 As Double, Arg4 As Boolean	Returns the gamma distribution. Arg1 is the value to evaluate. Arg2 is the alpha parameter to the distribution. Arg3 is the beta parameter to the distribution. Set Arg4 to True for the method to return the cumulative distribution. Set Arg4 to False to return the probability density
GammaInv	Double	Arg1 As Double, Arg2 As Double, Arg3 As Double	Returns the inverse of the gamma cumulative distribution. Arg1 is the gamma distribution probability. Arg2 is the alpha parameter to the distribution. Arg3 is the beta parameter to the distribution
GammaLn	Double	Arg1 As Double	Returns the natural logarithm of the gamma function with the Arg1 number

Name	Returns	Parameters	Description
GeoMean	Double	Arg1, [Arg2], ... [Arg30]	Returns the geometric mean of the numbers in Arg1 to Arg30. Arg1 to Arg30 can also be a reference to a range
Growth	Variant	Arg1, [Arg2], [Arg3], [Arg4]	Returns the predicted exponential growth of y values (Arg1) for a series of new x values (Arg3). Arg2 can be used to set the series of existing x values. Arg4 can be set to False to make the 'b' part of the equation equal to one
HarMean	Double	Arg1, [Arg2], ... [Arg30]	Returns the harmonic mean of the numbers in Arg1 to Arg30. Arg1 to Arg30 can also be a reference to a range
HLookup	Variant	Arg1, Arg2, Arg3, [Arg4]	Looks up the value specified by Arg1 in the table array (or range reference); Arg2 first row. Arg3 specifies the row number in the table array that contains the matching value. Set Arg4 to True to find approximate data or set Arg4 to False to only lookup exact values
HypGeom Dist	Double	Arg1 As Double, Arg2 As Double, Arg3 As Double, Arg4 As Double	Returns the hypergeometric distribution probability. Arg1 is the number of successes in the trials. Arg2 holds the total number of trials. Arg3 is the number of successes in the trial. Arg4 is the size of the population
Index	Variant	Arg1, Arg2 As Double, [Arg3], [Arg4]	May return the cell or array of cells from Arg1 that has a row number of Arg2 and a column number of Arg3. May also return the cell or range of cells that have a row number of Arg2 and a column number of Arg3. If Arg1 contains many areas then Arg4 can be used to specify the area

Continues

Name	Returns	Parameters	Description
Intercept	Double	Arg1, Arg2	Returns the point where the x-axis and y-axis coordinates intersect. Arg1 represents the array of known y values and Arg2 represents the array of known x values
Ipmt	Double	Arg1 As Double, Arg2 As Double, Arg3 As Double, Arg4 As Double, [Arg5], [Arg6]	Returns the interest amount paid for an investment for a time period. Arg1 is the interest rate per period. Arg2 is the period that you want to find the amount of interest for. Arg3 is the total number of payment periods. Arg4 is the initial value. Arg5 is the future value that is wanted to be attained. Arg6 determines if payments are due at the end of the period (0) or the beginning of the period (1)
Irr	Double	Arg1, [Arg2]	Returns the rate of return for an array of values in Arg1. Arg2 can be used to specify a guess of the Irr result
IsErr	Boolean	Arg1	Returns whether the cell Arg1 contains an error value (except #N/A)
IsError	Boolean	Arg1	Returns whether the cell Arg1 contains any error value
IsLogical	Boolean	Arg1	Returns whether the cell or value Arg1 contains a logical value
IsNA	Boolean	Arg1	Returns whether the cell Arg1 contains the #N/A value
IsNonText	Boolean	Arg1	Returns whether the cell Arg1 does not contain text
IsNumber	Boolean	Arg1	Returns whether the cell Arg1 contains a numeric value
Ispmt	Double	Arg1 As Double, Arg2 As Double, Arg3 As Double, Arg4 As Double	Returns the interest amount paid for an investment at a particular period. Used for compatibility purposes. Arg1 is the interest rate per period. Arg2 is the period that you want to find the amount of interest for. Arg3 is the total number of payment periods. Arg4 is the initial value

Name	Returns	Parameters	Description
IsText	Boolean	Arg1	Returns whether the cell Arg1 contains a text value
Kurt	Double	Arg1, Arg2], ... [Arg30]	Returns the kurtosis of the values in Arg1 to Arg30. Also, Arg1 can be a reference to a cell range
Large	Double	Arg1, Arg2 As Double	Returns the Arg2 largest value in the array or cell reference specified by Arg1 (for example, second largest, third largest)
LinEst	Variant	Arg1, [Arg], [Arg3], [Arg4]	Returns an array describing a straight line that best fits the data of known y values (Arg1) and known x values (Arg2). Set Arg3 to False to make the 'b' part of the calculations equal to 0. Set Arg4 to True to return additional statistics
Ln	Double	Arg1 As Double	Returns the natural logarithm of the Arg1 number
Log	Double	Arg1 As Double, [Arg2]	Returns the logarithm of the Arg1 number to the base specified in Arg2. Arg2 is 10 by default
Log10	Double	Arg1 As Double	Returns the base-10 logarithm of the Arg1 number
LogEst	Variant	Arg1, [Arg2], [Arg3], [Arg4]	Returns an array describing the curved line that best fits the data of known y values (Arg1) and known x values (Arg2). Set Arg3 to False to make the 'b' part of the calculations equal to 0. Set Arg4 to True to return additional statistics
LogInv	Double	Arg1 As Double, Arg2 As Double, Arg3 As Double	Returns the inverse of the lognormal cumulative distribution of a value. Arg1 is the probability that will have to be inversed. Arg2 is the mean of ln(value). Arg3 is the standard deviation of ln(value)

Continues

Name	Returns	Parameters	Description
LogNormDist	Double	Arg1 As Double, Arg2 As Double, Arg3 As Double	Returns the cumulative lognormal distribution of Arg1. Arg2 is the mean of ln(Arg1) and Arg3 is the standard deviation of ln(Arg1)
Lookup	Variant	Arg1, Arg2, [Arg3]	The value Arg1 is searched for in the single row or column in Arg2. A value from the matching spot in another array, Arg3, is returned
Match	Double	Arg1, Arg2, [Arg3]	Returns the relative position of an item in an array, Arg2, which matches a specific value, Arg1. Use Arg3 to set the type of match
Max	Double	Arg1, [Arg2], ... [Arg30]	Returns the largest value in the numbers Arg1 to Arg30. Arg1 can also be a cell range
MDeterm	Double	Arg1	Returns the matrix determinant of the matrix array specified by Arg1. Arg1 can also be a cell range. Cell elements cannot contain text or be empty. There must be an equal amount of rows to columns
Median	Double	Arg1, [Arg2], ... [Arg30]	Returns the median value in the numbers Arg1 to Arg30. Arg1 can also be a cell range
Min	Double	Arg1, [Arg2], ... [Arg30]	Returns the smallest value in the numbers Arg1 to Arg30. Arg1 can also be a cell range
MInverse	Variant	Arg1	Returns the inverse matrix for the matrix array in Arg1. Arg1 can also be a cell range. Cell elements cannot contain text or be empty. There must be an equal amount of rows to columns

Name	Returns	Parameters	Description
MIrr	Double	Arg1, Arg2 As Double, Arg3 As Double	Returns the modified rate or return for a series of values in Arg1. Arg2 is the interest rate paid. Arg3 is the interest rate received as the cash flow values are reinvested
MMult	Variant	Arg1, Arg2	Returns the matrix product of the two matrix arrays Arg1 and Arg2. The number of columns in Arg1 must be the same as the number of rows in Arg2. Arg1 and Arg2 can also be a cell range. Cell elements cannot contain text or be empty
Mode	Double	Arg1, [Arg2], ... [Arg30]	Returns the most frequently occurring number in Arg1 to Arg30. Arg1 can also be a cell range
NegBinom Dist	Double	Arg1 As Double, Arg2 As Double, Arg3 As Double	Returns the negative binomial distribution of the arguments. Arg1 is the number of failures in the trials. Arg2 holds the threshold number of successes. Arg3 is the probability of success on a single trial
NormDist	Double	Arg1 As Double, Arg2 As Double, Arg3 As Double, Arg4 As Boolean	Returns the normal cumulative distribution for the value to distribute (Arg1), the mean (Arg2), and the standard deviation (Arg3). Set Arg4 to True to return the cumulative distribution and False to return the probability mass
NormInv	Double	Arg1 As Double, Arg2 As Double, Arg3 As Double	Returns the inverse of the normal cumulative distribution given a probability (Arg1), the mean (Arg2), and the standard deviation (Arg3)
NormSDist	Double	Arg1 As Double	Returns the standard normal cumulative distribution for the value to distribute (Arg1)

Continues

Name	Returns	Parameters	Description
NormSInv	Double	Arg1 As Double	Returns the inverse of the standard normal cumulative distribution for a given probability (Arg1)
NPer	Double	Arg1 As Double, Arg2 As Double, Arg3 As Double, [Arg4], [Arg5]	Returns the number of periods for an investment. Arg1 is the interest rate per period. Arg2 is the payment amount made each period. Arg3 is the initial value. Arg4 is the future value that is wanted to be attained. Arg5 determines if payments are due at the end of the period (0) or the beginning of the period (1)
Npv	Double	Arg1 As Double, Arg2, [Arg3], ... [Arg30]	Returns the net present value of an investment using a discount rate (Arg1) and many future payments and income (Arg2 to Arg30)
Odd	Double	Arg1 As Double	Converts the Arg1 number into the nearest odd whole number, rounded up, and returns it
Or	Boolean	Arg1, [Arg2], ... [Arg30]	Returns True if any of the expressions in Arg1 to Arg30 returns True
Pearson	Double	Arg1, Arg2	Returns the Pearson product moment correlation coefficient containing an array of values. Arg1 is the array of independent values and Arg2 is the array of dependent values. Arg1 and Arg2 can also be cell references
Percentile	Double	Arg1, Arg2 As Double	Returns the Arg2 percentile of values in the Arg1 range of cells or array
Percent Rank	Double	Arg1, Arg2 As Double, [Arg3]	Returns how the value Arg2 ranks in the Arg1 range of cells or array. Arg3 can specify the number of significant digits for the returned percentage

Name	Returns	Parameters	Description
Permut	Double	Arg1 As Double, Arg2 As Double	Returns the total possible number of permutations of a group of Arg2 items in a total number of Arg1 items
Phonetic	String	Arg1 As Range	Returns the phonetic characters from the Arg1 text string
Pi	Double		Returns pi (3.14) to 15 decimal places
Pmt	Double	Arg1 As Double, Arg2 As Double, Arg3 As Double, [Arg4], [Arg5]	Returns the payment for a loan. Arg1 is the interest rate per period. Arg2 is the number of payments for the loan. Arg3 is the initial value. Arg4 is the future value that is wanted to be attained. Arg5 determines if payments are due at the end of the period (0) or the beginning of the period (1)
Poisson	Double	Arg1 As Double, Arg2 As Double, Arg3 As Boolean	Returns the Poisson distribution given the number of events (Arg1) and the expected numeric value (Arg2). Set Arg3 to True to return the cumulative probability and False to return the probability mass
Power	Double	Arg1 As Double, Arg2 As Double	Returns the base number Arg1 raised to the power of Arg2
Ppmt	Double	Arg1 As Double, Arg2 As Double, Arg3 As Double, Arg4 As Double, [Arg5], [Arg6]	Returns the payment on the principal of an investment for a given period of time. Arg1 is the interest rate per period. Arg2 specifies the period to look at. Arg3 is the total number of payments. Arg4 is the initial value. Arg5 is the future value that is wanted to be attained. Arg6 determines if payments are due at the end of the period (0) or the beginning of the period (1)
Prob	Double	Arg1, Arg2, Arg3 As Double, [Arg4]	Returns the probability that the values in the Arg1 array and associated Arg2 array are within the lower limit (Arg3) and upper limit (Arg4)

Continues

Name	Returns	Parameters	Description
Product	Double	Arg1, [Arg2], ... [Arg30]	Returns the multiplication product of all the values in Arg1 to Arg30
Proper	String	Arg1 As String	Capitalizes the start of every word in Arg1 and makes everything else lowercase
Pv	Double	Arg1 As Double, Arg2 As Double, Arg3 As Double, [Arg4], [Arg5]	Returns the present value of an investment. Arg1 is the interest rate per period. Arg2 is the number of payments for the loan. Arg3 is the payment amount made per period. Arg4 is the future value that is wanted to be attained. Arg5 determines if payments are due at the end of the period (0) or the beginning of the period (1)
Quartile	Double	Arg1, Arg2 As Double	Returns the quartile specified by Arg2 of the array in Arg1. Arg2 can be 0 (Minimum value), 1 (first quartile), 2 (second quartile), 3 (third quartile), or 4 (maximum value)
Radians	Double	Arg1 As Double	Converts the Arg1 number from degrees to radians and returns the new value
Rank	Double	Arg1 As Double, Arg2 As Range, [Arg3]	Returns the rank of Arg1 in the range Arg2. Arg3 can be used to set how to rank Arg1
Rate	Double	Arg1 As Double, Arg2 As Double, Arg3 As Double, [Arg4], [Arg5], [Arg6]	Returns the interest rate per period for a value. Arg1 is the total number of payments. Arg2 is the payment amount per period. Arg3 is the initial value. Arg4 is the future value that is wanted to be attained. Arg5 determines if payments are due at the end of the period (0) or the beginning of the period (1)

Name	Returns	Parameters	Description
Replace	String	Arg1 As String, Arg2 As Double, Arg3 As Double, Arg4 As String	Replaces part of the text in `Arg1` with the text in `Arg4`. The starting character of the replacement is at the number `Arg2` and `Arg3` specifies the number of replaced characters in `Arg1`
ReplaceB	String	Arg1 As String, Arg2 As Double, Arg3 As Double, Arg4 As String	Replaces part of the text in `Arg1` with the text in `Arg4`. The starting character of the replacement is at the number `Arg2` and `Arg3` specifies the number of replaced bytes in `Arg1`
Rept	String	Arg1 As String, Arg2 As Double	Repeats the string in `Arg1` by `Arg2` number of times and returns that new string
Roman	String	Arg1 As Double, [Arg2]	Returns the number in `Arg1` to a Roman numeral equivalent. `Arg2` can specify the style of Roman numerals. 0 or `True` is the classic style. 4 or `False` is the simplified style. The other options are 2, 3, and 4 that set the style to varying degrees of simplification
Round	Double	Arg1 As Double, Arg2 As Double	Returns the `Arg1` number rounded to the number of digits specified in `Arg2`
RoundDown	Double	Arg1 As Double, Arg2 As Double	Returns the `Arg1` number rounded to the number of digits specified in `Arg2`. The number is rounded down towards 0
RoundUp	Double	Arg1 As Double, Arg2 As Double	Returns the `Arg1` number rounded to the number of digits specified in `Arg2`. The number is rounded up towards 0

Continues

Name	Returns	Parameters	Description
RSq	Double	Arg1, Arg2	Returns the square of the Pearson product moment correlation coefficient containing an array of values. Arg1 is the array of y values and Arg2 is the array of x values. Arg1 and Arg2 can also be cell references
RTD	Variant	progID As Variant, server As Variant, topic1 As Variant, [topic2], [topic3], [topic4], [topic5], [topic6], [topic7], [topic8], [topic9], [topic10], [topic11], [topic12], [topic13], [topic14], [topic15], [topic16], [topic17], [topic18], [topic19], [topic20], [topic21], [topic22], [topic23], [topic24], [topic25], [topic26], [topic27], [topic28]	Connects to a source to receive RTD. progID is the real-time server programmatic identifier, server is the server name, and topic1 is the topic to look up
Search	Double	Arg1 As String, Arg2 As String, [Arg3]	Finds the text in Arg1 from the text in Arg2 and returns the starting position of the found text. Arg3 can specify the starting position to search in Arg2

Name	Returns	Parameters	Description
SearchB	Double	Arg1 As String, Arg2 As String, [Arg3]	Finds the text in Arg1 from the text in Arg2 and returns the starting position of the found text. Arg3 can specify the starting byte position to search in Arg2
Sinh	Double	Arg1 As Double	Returns the hyperbolic sine of the Arg1 number
Skew	Double	Arg1, [Arg2], ... [Arg30]	Returns how skewed the numbers in Arg1 to Arg30 are. The arguments can also be a range reference
Sln	Double	Arg1 As Double, Arg2 As Double, Arg3 As Double	Returns the simple straight-line depreciation of an asset costing Arg1 with a salvage value of Arg3 over Arg2 number of periods
Slope	Double	Arg1, Arg2	Returns the slope of the linear regression line through the data points of the x values (Arg1) and y values (Arg2)
Small	Double	Arg1, Arg2 As Double	Returns the Arg2 smallest value in the array or cell reference specified by Arg1 (for example, second smallest, third smallest)
Standardize	Double	Arg1 As Double, Arg2 As Double, Arg3 As Double	Returns the normalized value from a distribution given a value (Arg1), a mean (Arg2), and a standard deviation (Arg3)
StDev	Double	Arg1, [Arg2], ... [Arg30]	Returns the estimated standard deviation of the values in Arg1 to Arg30. The arguments can also be a range reference
StDevP	Double	Arg1, [Arg2], ... [Arg30]	Returns the standard deviation of the values in Arg1 to Arg30 based on all the values. The arguments can also be a range reference

Continues

Name	Returns	Parameters	Description
StEyx	Double	Arg1, Arg2	Returns the standard error of the predicted y values for each of the x values in the regression given some know y values (Arg1) and x values (Arg2)
Substitute	String	Arg1 As String, Arg2 As String, Arg3 As String, [Arg4]	Substitutes all occurrences of the Arg2 text with the Arg3 text in the original Arg1 text string. Arg4 can be used to specify which occurrence to replace
Subtotal	Double	Arg1 As Double, Arg2 As Range, [Arg3], ... [Arg30]	Returns subtotals for the ranges or references specified in the Arg2 to Arg30 parameters. Arg1 is a number describing what type of function to use for calculating the subtotal. Valid function numbers are from 1 to 10 representing Average, Count, CountA, Max, Min, Product, StcDev, StDevP, Sum, Var, and VarP in numerical order
Sum	Double	Arg1, [Arg2], ... [Arg30]	Returns the sum of all the numbers in Arg1 to Arg30
SumIf	Double	Arg1 As Range, Arg2, [Arg3]	Returns the sum of the cells in the range Arg1 with the criteria matching Arg2. A different range to sum can be specified with Arg3. The columns or rows in Arg1 and Arg3 have to be the same
SumProduct	Double	Arg1, [Arg2], ... [Arg30]	Multiplies each corresponding element in the arrays Arg1 to Arg30 and returns the sum of the products. The arrays in Arg1 to Arg30 must have the same dimension
SumSq	Double	Arg1, [Arg2], ... [Arg30]	Returns the sum of the square roots of the number in Arg1 to Arg30

Name	Returns	Parameters	Description
SumX2MY2	Double	Arg1, Arg2	Subtracts the squares of the corresponding elements in the arrays `Arg1` and `Argc2` and returns the sum of all the new elements
SumX2PY2	Double	Arg1, Arg2	Adds the squares of the corresponding elements in the arrays `Arg1` and `Arg2` and returns the sum of all the new elements
SumXMY2	Double	Arg1, Arg2	Subtracts the corresponding elements in the arrays `Arg1` and `Arg2`, squares the difference and returns the sum of all the new elements
Syd	Double	Arg1 As Double, Arg2 As Double, Arg3 As Double, Arg4 As Double	Returns the sum-of-years digits depreciation of an asset over a specified period. `Arg1` is the initial cost. `Arg2` is the salvage cost. `Arg3` is the number of periods to depreciate the asset over. `Arg4` is the specified period to return
Tanh	Double	Arg1 As Double	Returns the hyperbolic tangent of the `Arg1` number
Tdist	Double	Arg1 As Double, Arg2 As Double, Arg3 As Double	Returns the probability for the student t-distribution for a value, `Arg1`, is a calculated value of 't'. `Arg2` indicates the number of degrees of freedom. Set `Arg3` to 1 to return a one-tailed distribution. Set `Arg3` to 2 to return a two-tailed distribution
Text	String	Arg1, Arg2 As String	Converts the value in `Arg1` into text using the formatting in `Arg2`
Tinv	Double	Arg1 As Double, Arg2 As Double	Returns the t-value of the Student's t-distribution given the probability (`Arg1`) and the degrees of freedom (`Arg2`)
Transpose	Variant	Arg1	Transposes the range specified by `Arg1` from column to row or vice versa and returns the new range

Continues

Name	Returns	Parameters	Description
Trend	Variant	Arg1, [Arg2], [Arg3], [Arg4]	Returns the values associated with a linear trend given some y values (Arg1), some x values (Arg2), and some new x values (Arg3). Set Arg4 to False to make 'b' equal to 0 in the equation
Trim	String	Arg1 As String	Returns the string in Arg1 without leading and trailing spaces
TrimMean	Double	Arg1, Arg2 As Double	Returns the mean of the interior of the data array in Arg1. Use Arg2 to specify the fractional part of the data array to exclude
Ttest	Double	Arg1, Arg2, Arg3 As Double, Arg4 As Double	Returns the probability associated with a student's t-Test given the two sets of data in Arg1 and Arg12. Set Arg3 to 1 to return a one-tailed distribution. Set Arg3 to 2 to return a two-tailed distribution. Set Arg4 to 1, 2, or 3 to set the type of t-Test to paired, two-sample equal variance, or two-sample unequal variance, respectively
USDollar	String	Arg1 As Double, Arg2 As Double	Returns a currency-type string of the number in Arg1 with the decimal points specified in Arg2
Var	Double	Arg1, [Arg2] ... [Arg30]	Returns the estimated variance based on the numbers in Arg1 to Arg30. The arguments can also be range references
VarP	Double	Arg1, [Arg2] ... [Arg30]	Returns the variance based on the numbers in Arg1 to Arg30 as an entire population. The arguments can also be range references
Vdb	Double	Arg1 As Double, Arg2 As Double, Arg3 As Double, Arg4 As Double, Arg5 As Double, [Arg6], [Arg7]	Returns the double-declining balance method depreciation (unless otherwise specified) of an asset for specified periods. Arg1 is the initial cost. Arg2 is the salvage cost. Arg3 is the number of periods to depreciate the asset over. Arg4 is the starting period to calculate depreciation. Arg5 is the ending period to calculate depreciation. Arg6 is the rate at which the balance declines. Set Arg7 to True to keep the calculation using the double-declining balance method. Set Arg7 to False to have Excel switch to straight-line depreciation, when necessary

Name	Returns	Parameters	Description
Vlookup	Variant	Arg1, Arg2, Arg3, [Arg4]	Looks up the value specified by Arg1 in the table array (or range reference) Arg2 first column Arg3 specifies the column number in the table array that contains the matching value. Set the Arg4 to True to find approximate data or set Arg4 to False to only lookup exact values
Weekday	Double	Arg1, [Arg2]	Returns the numerical day of the week for the date in Arg1. Arg2 specifies which day is the start of the week
Weibull	Double	Arg1 As Double, Arg2 As Double, Arg3 As Double, Arg4 As Boolean	Returns the Weibull distribution using the value (Arg1). Arg2 is the alpha parameter to the distribution. Arg3 is the beta parameter to the distribution. Set Arg4 to True to return the cumulative probability and False to return the probability mass
Ztest	Double	Arg1, Arg2 As Double, [Arg3]	Returns the two-tailed P-value of a z-test. Arg1 is the array or range of data to test against Arg2. Arg2 is the value to test. Arg3 is the population standard deviation

Example: WorksheetFunction Object

```
Sub GetBiggest()
    Dim oWSF As WorksheetFunction
    Dim vaArray As Variant
    Set oWSF = Application.WorksheetFunction
    vaArray = Array(10, 20, 13, 15, 56, 12, 8, 45)
    MsgBox "Biggest is " & oWSF.Max(vaArray)
End Sub
```

XmlDataBinding Object

Represents the connection to a data soure for an XML Map.

Name	Returns	Description
Application	Object	Returns a reference to the Microsoft Excel application
Creator	Long	Returns a long integer which denotes the application that created this object
Parent	Object	Reference to the parent object
SourceUrl	String	Returns a string representing the XML data file

XmlDataBinding Methods

Name	Returns	Parameters	Description
ClearSettings	Boolean		Clears all settings for the current object
LoadSettings	Boolean		Loads a set of settings in
Refresh			Refreshes all data

XmlMap Object

The XMLMap object represents an XML Map that has been added to a workbook.

XmlMap Properties

Name	Returns	Description
AdjustColumn Width	Boolean	Set this to True to automatically adjust column widths when data is refreshed
AppendOnImport	Boolean	Set this to True and imported data will be appended to current data. Otherwise imported data will overwritten
Application	Long	Reference to the Excel Application
Creator	Long	Value representing the creator of the object
DataBinding	XmlDataBinding	
IsExportable	Boolean	Determines if the current data is exportable
Name	String	Name of this object
Parent	Object	Reference to the parent of this object
PreserveColumn Filter	Boolean	Determines if column filters are persisted
PreserveNumber Formatting	Boolean	Determines if number formatting is persisted
RootElement Name	String	Returns a string representing the root element name in the XML tree
RootElement Namespace	XmlNamespace	Returns a XmlNamespace object that represents the namespace of the current root element
SaveDataSource Definition	Boolean	Determines if the data source information is saved

Name	Returns	Description
Schemas	XmlSchemas	Returns a collection of XmlSchema objects that have been applied to the current workbook
ShowImport Export Validation Errors	Boolean	Set this to True and during import and export operations—any validation errors will be displayed

XmlMap Methods

Name	Returns	Parameters	Description
Delete			Deletes the current XmlMap object
Export			Exports the current XmlMap object
ExportXml			Exports the current XmlMap object as XML which can be persisted to a file
Import			Imports an XmlMap object
ImportXml			Imports an XmlMap object from XML

VBE Object Model

Officially known as "*Microsoft Visual Basic for Applications Extensibility 5.3*", the VBE object library provides access to the code and forms within an application and to the various objects that compose the *Visual Basic Integrated Development Environment (VBIDE)*. By default, this object library is *not* included in the list of referenced libraries for new projects. In order to use the objects referred to in this chapter, a reference to the Microsoft Visual Basic for Applications Extensibility 5.3 library must be created using the Tools ⇨ References menu in the VBE. If you had done development with Office XP, the VBE should be familiar to you since the version included with Office 2003 remains the same.

Many of the objects in the VBE object model have the same names as objects in the Excel object model. To distinguish the libraries and to ensure that you have the object from the VBE library you need to include the VBIDE library name in any Dim statements you may use:

```
Dim oWinVB As VBIDE.Window      'Always gives a VBE Window
Dim oWinXL As Excel.Window      'Always gives an Excel Window
Dim oWin As Window              'Gives an Excel Window
```

All of the applications in Office 2003 share the same development environment—the VBE. The code and forms that belong to each Excel workbook, Word document, Access database, PowerPoint presentation (i.e. the "host document"), or Access Database are grouped into Visual Basic projects (the VBProject object). There is one project for each host document. FrontPage and Outlook have a single Project each, which "belongs" to the application.

Links Between the Excel and VBE Object Models

There are a number of properties of Excel objects that provide links to the VBE object model. Similarly, there are a number of properties in the VBE object model that provide a link back into Excel. Many of the code examples in this Appendix and in Chapter 14 use these links:

Excel to VBE Excel Property	Resulting VBE Item
Application.VBE	VBE object
Workbook.VBProject	VBProject object
Workbook.CodeName	The name of the workbook-level VBComponent in the workbook's VBProject, usually "ThisWorkbook" in English versions of Excel 2002
Worksheet.CodeName Chart.CodeName	The name of the sheet-level VBComponent in the workbook's VBProject, usually "Sheet1", "Chart1" etc. in English versions of Excel 2002

VBE to Excel VBE Property	Resulting Excel Item
VBProject.FileName	The full name of the workbook, if the VBProject is an Excel workbook project and the workbook has been saved
VBComponent.Properties("Name")	The file name of the workbook, if the VBComponent is the workbook-level item (for example, "ThisWorkbook"), or the name of the sheet for sheet-level VBComponents
VBComponent.Properties("<Other Properties>")	The properties associated with the Excel object to which the VBComponent applies (if any)

Common Properties and Methods

Most of the objects in the VBE object library have the following common properties. To avoid redundancy, these properties will be listed for each object, but will not be explained. Generally speaking, when objects share common properties it means that all derive from the same base class. If you are familiar with Object Oriented Development, base classes and inheritance should be common knowledge. If you'd like to know more about Object Oriented Development, the Microsoft Development Network (http://msdn.microsoft.com) is an excellent reference.

Name	Returns	Description
Collection		Read-only. Returns the collection to which an object belongs. For example, a Reference object belongs to the References collection. The Collection property is used for objects that belong to collections. To clarify, Collections are a grouping of similar objects

Name	Returns	Description
Parent		Read-only. Return the object to which an object belongs. For example, a References collection belongs to a VBProject object. The Parent property is used for objects that do not belong to collections
VBE	VBE	Read-only. Returns the Visual Basic Editor object, which is analogous to the Application object in the Excel Object Model

> Collections can be thought of as a grouping of similar objects. For example, if you wanted to store phone book information you could create a class object that holds all information for a particular contact. A collection could then be used to group all Contact information together. Using a collection you could use the VB commands for each to iterate through each contact record in your collection.

Most of the objects in the VBE Object Model are contained in associated collections. The collection object is usually the plural form of the associated object. For example, the Windows collection holds a collection of Window objects. For simplicity, each object and associated collection will be grouped together under the same heading. The common properties and methods of the collection objects are the same as in the Excel Object Model, and are listed in Appendix A. Only unique properties, methods or events will be mentioned for each object.

AddIn Object and AddIns Collection

Not to be confused with Excel's Addin object, VBE Addins are DLLs that conform to Microsoft's Component Object Model architecture and are more commonly known as "COM Addins". These Addins are typically created using C++, Visual Basic, or the any of the languages based on the .NET Framework. If you have any installed, they can be found under the VBE's Add-Ins menu and can be loaded and unloaded using the Add-Ins ⇨ Add-In Manager ... menu item.

Some examples of VBE Addins would be code generation tools, the API Viewer that generates Declare statements for methods within the Win32 API and so on. There are literally thousands of Addins for the VBE and a list of many can be found on the Microsoft Web site.

AddIn Common Properties

The Collection and VBE properties are defined at the beginning of this section.

AddIn Properties

Name	Returns	Description
Connect	Boolean	Whether the COM Addin is currently connected (that is, active). Can be set to `True` to load and run the Addin. Similar to the `Installed` property of an Excel Addin
Description	String	The text that appears in the "Description" box of the VBE Addinn Manager
Guid	String	Read-only. Returns the globally unique identifier for the Addin. The `Guid` is created by Excel/VB when the Addin is compiled. Guid are based on several factors and it is almost impossible to have two separate machines generate the same Guid
Object		In the Addin's `OnConnection` method, it can expose an object to the VBE (typically the root class of its object model, if it has one). You can then use the Addin's `Object` property to access this object and through it, the rest of the Addin's object model. Few Addins currently expose an `Object`
ProgId	String	Read-only. Returns the program ID for the Addin, which comprises the name of the Addin project and the name of the connection class (usually a connection designer). For example, if you have an Addin project called `MyAddin` and an Addin `Designer` class called dsrMyConnection, the `ProgId` will be `"MyAddin.dsrMyConnection"`

AddIns Collection Methods

Name	Returns	Description
Item	Addin	Read-only. Parameters: `Item As Variant`. Returns an Addin associated with the item. The parameter can be either a number or the `ProgId` of the Addin (for example, `MyAddin.dsrMyConnection`)
Update		Method. Updates the list of available COM Addins from the Registry. This should only need to be used if you are compiling an Addin through code (for example, using `VBProject.MakeCompiledFile`)

AddIn Examples

The following example iterates through all the Addins registered for use in the VBE and prints information about those that are active.

```
Sub ListRunningAddins()
    'Define as a VBE Addin, not an Excel one
    Dim oAddin As VBIDE.Addin

    'Loop through the VBE's addins
    For Each oAddin In Application.VBE.AddIns

        'Is it active (i.e. connected)?
        If oAddin.Connect Then

            'Yes, so show it's ID and description
            Debug.Print oAddin.ProgId, oAddin.Description
        End If
    Next
End Sub
```

Note that VBE Addins do not have a property to provide their name, as shown in the list in the Addin Manager dialog box.

CodeModule Object

The CodeModule object contains all of the code for a single VBComponent (i.e., Module, UserForm, Class Module, or Excel sheet). There is only ever one CodeModule for a component—its methods and properties enable you to locate, identify, modify, and add lines of code to a project's components. There can be more than one procedure of the same name in a module, if they are Property procedures:

```
Dim msSelection As String
Property Get TheSelection() As String
    TheSelection = msSelection
End Property

Property Let TheSelection(NewString As String)
    MsSelection = NewString
End Property
```

Hence, to uniquely identify a procedure, you need to supply both its name ("TheSelection" in this example) and the type of procedure you're looking for (vbext_pk_Get for Property Get, vbext_pk_Let for Property Let, vbext_pk_Set for Property Set, or vbext_pk_proc for Subs and Functions). The ProcOfLine function provides this information for a given line number – the name of the procedure is the return value of the function and the type of procedure is returned in the variable you supply to its ProcKind argument. It is one of the few properties in the whole of Office 2002 that returns values by modifying the arguments passed to it.

CodeModule Common Properties

The Parent and VBE properties are defined at the beginning of this section (its Parent being the VBComponent).

CodeModule Properties

Name	Returns	Description
CodePane	CodePane	Read-only. Returns the active CodePane for the module. If there is no visible CodePane, one is created and displayed. Note that a CodeModule can have up to two code panes, but there is no CodePanes collection for them!

CountOf Declaration Lines	Long	Read-only. Returns the number of lines at the top of the module used for Dim, Type, and Option statements. If there are any such items at the top of the module, any comments following them are considered to be part of the following procedure, not the declarations. The following has two declaration lines:
		
		`Option Explicit`
		
		`Dim msSelection As String`
		
		`'My Comment`
		
		`Sub ProcedureStart()`
		
		If no such statements exist, comments appearing at the top of the module are counted as declaration lines, if they are followed by a blank line. The following has one declaration line:
		
		`'My Comment`
		
		`Sub ProcedureStart()`
		
		If the comment is immediately followed by the procedure, it is included in the procedure's lines, so the following has no declaration line:
		
		`'My Comment`
		
		`Sub ProcedureStart()`

CountOf Lines	Long	Read-only. Returns the total number of lines of code in the module, with line continuations counted as separate lines
Lines	String	Read-only. Parameters: StartLine As Long, Count As Long. Returns a block of code, starting from Startline and continuing for Count lines

Name	Returns	Description
Name	String	(Hidden) Read-only. Returns the name of the associated `VBComponent`
ProcBody Line	Long	Read-only. Parameters: `ProcName As String`, `ProcKind As vbext_ProcKind`. Returns the line number of the start of the procedure, not including any preceding comments—that is it gives the line number of the `Sub`, `Function`, or `Property` statement
ProcCount Lines	Long	Read-only. Parameters: `ProcName As String`, `ProcKind As vbext_ProcKind`. Returns the number of lines used by the procedure, including preceding comments, up to the `End Sub`, `End Function`, or `End Property` statement
ProcOfLine	String	Read-only. Parameters: `Line As Long [in]`, `ProcKind As Long [out]`. Returns the name of the procedure that a line is located within. The `ProcKind` argument is also modified to return the type of procedure (`Sub/Function`, `Property Let`, `Get` or `Set`). This is usually the first property to be called; the name and type returned from this are then used in calls to the other methods
ProcStart Line	Long	Read-only. Parameters: `ProcName As String`, `ProcKind As vbext_ProcKind`. Returns the line number of the start of the procedure, including comments. Hence, `ProcBodyLine - ProcStartLine` gives you the number of preceding comment lines

CodeModule Methods

Name	Returns	Parameters	Description
AddFromFile		`FileName As String`	Reads code from a text file and adds it to the end of the code module. It does not check if the names of procedures read from a file already existing in the module
AddFrom String		`String As String`	Adds code from a string to the end of the code module

Continues

Name	Returns	Parameters	Description
CreateEventProc	Long	EventName As String, ObjectName As String	Creates an empty event procedure in a module, filling in the event parameters for you. Cannot be used on standard modules, as they do not support events. The ObjectName must be a valid object for the class module, and the EventName must be a valid event for that object
DeleteLines		StartLine As Long, Count As Long	Deletes lines from a code module, starting at StartLine, for Count lines
Find	Boolean	Target As String, StartLine As Long, StartColumn As Long, EndLine As Long, EndColumn As Long, WholeWord As Boolean, MatchCase As Boolean, PatternSearch As Boolean	Locates a string within a code module, or section of a code module. It provides the same functionality as the VBE's Find dialog box
InsertLines		Line As Long, String As String	Adds code from a string into the middle of a code module, inserting the code before the Line given
ReplaceLine		Line As Long, String As String	Adds code from a string into the middle of a code module, replacing the Line given

CodeModule Examples

There are a number of CodeModule examples in the chapter on "*Programming the VBE*". The following example identifies the procedure for a given line and displays its type, name, and line count:

```
Sub WhichProc()
    Dim lLine As Long, iProcKind As Long, lLineCount As Long
    Dim sProc As String, sMsg As String
    Dim oActiveCM As VBIDE.CodeModule
```

```
        lLine = CLng(InputBox("Which line?"))

        'Cancelled?
        If lLine = 0 Then Exit Sub

        'Get the currently active code module
        Set oActiveCM = Application.VBE.ActiveCodePane.CodeModule

        'Get the name and type of the procedure at
        'that line - iProcKind is filled in
        sProc = oActiveCM.ProcOfLine(lLine, iProcKind)

        If sProc = "" Then
            'We didn't get a name, so you must be in the Declarations section
            sMsg = "You are in the Declarations section"
            lLineCount = oActiveCM.CountOfDeclarationLines
        Else
            sMsg = "You are in "

            'Display the type of the procedure...
            Select Case iProcKind
                Case vbext_pk_Proc
                    sMsg = sMsg & "Sub or Function procedure"
                Case vbext_pk_Get
                    sMsg = sMsg & "Property Get procedure"
                Case vbext_pk_Let
                    sMsg = sMsg & "Property Let procedure"
                Case vbext_pk_Set
                    sMsg = sMsg & "Property Set procedure"
            End Select

            '... its name ...
            sMsg = sMsg & " '" & sProc & "'"

            '... and how many lines it has.
            lLineCount = oActiveCM.ProcCountLines(sProc, iProcKind)
        End If

    'Display the message
    MsgBox sMsg & vbCrLf & "which has " & lLineCount & " lines."
End Sub
```

CodePane Object and CodePanes Collection

A CodePane is a view of a CodeModule, providing you with access to the interaction layer between the developer and the code being edited. Most VBE Addins use this layer to identify which line in which CodePane is currently being edited, and then modify the code at the line, using CodeModule's methods and properties. Note that there can be more than one CodePane for a CodeModule (for example, by splitting a code window into two panes with the horizontal splitter bar).

CodePane Common Properties

The Collection and VBE properties are defined at the beginning of this section.

CodePane Properties

Name	Returns	Description
CodeModule	CodeModule	Read-only. Returns the CodeModule that contains the code being viewed in the CodePane
CodePaneView	vbext_Code Paneview	Read-only. Returns whether the CodePane is set to show one procedure at a time, or a full-module view with separator lines between procedures
CountOf VisibleLines	Long	Read-only. Returns the number of lines visible in the CodePane. This and the TopLine property can be used to center a line in the CodePane window (see the following example)
TopLine	Long	The CodeModule line number of the first line visible in the CodePane window
Window	Window	Read-only. Returns the Window object containing the CodePane(s)

CodePane Methods

Name	Parameters	Description

GetSelection	StartLine As Long, StartColumn As Long EndLine As Long, EndColumn As Long	Used to retrieve the currently selected text. All of the arguments are passed ByRef and are modified within the procedure to return the selection. All arguments are required, but it is only required to pass arguments for those items you want to retrieve. For example, to get only the start line, you can use:
		
		`Dim lStart As Long`
		
		`Application.VBE.ActiveCodePane.Get`
		`Selection - lStart, 0, 0, 0`

SetSelection	StartLine As Long, StartColumn As Long, EndLine As Long, EndColumn As Long	Used to set the position of the currently selected text. A program would typically read the selection using GetSelection, modify the code, then set the selection back again using SetSelection. See the "PrintProcedure" routine in the Chapter 23 for an example of this
Show		Opens and displays the CodePane, making it active

CodePanes Collection Properties

The `CodePanes` collection contains all of the open `CodePane` objects in the VBE.

Name	Returns	Description
Current	CodePane	Read-only. Returns the currently active `CodePane`, and is the same as `Application.VBE.ActiveCodePane`

CodePane Examples

There are a number of `CodePane` examples in Chapter 23 of this book. The following example identifies the current selection and centers it in the `CodePane` window:

```
Sub CenterSelectionInWindow()
    Dim oCP As VBIDE.CodePane
    Dim lStartLine As Long, lEndLine As Long
    Dim lVisibleLines As Long, lNewTop As Long

    'Get the active CodePane
    Set oCP = Application.VBE.ActiveCodePane

    'Using the CodePane object...
    With oCP
        'Get the start and end lines of the selection
        .GetSelection lStartLine, 0, lEndLine, 0

        'How many lines fit in the window?
        lVisibleLines = .CountOfVisibleLines

        'So what should the new top line be?
        lNewTop = (lStartLine + lEndLine - lVisibleLines)\2

        'Set the window to display code from that line
        .TopLine = lNewTop
    End With
End Sub
```

CommandBarEvents Object

Within the VBE, the `OnAction` property of a command bar button has no effect – the routine named in this property is *not* run when the button is clicked. Instead, the VBE object model provides you with the `CommandBarEvents` object, which hooks into whichever command bar button you tell it to, either your own custom buttons or built-in items, and raises events for the button's actions. In Office 2002, it only raises the `Click` event, and hence provides exactly the same functionality as Excel's `OnAction`. The main difference is that the `Click` event has some arguments to enable you to modify its behavior. The `CommandBarEvents` object also provides an extensible interface, allowing Microsoft to provide a richer event model in future versions of the VBE (such as `BeforePopUp`, `BeforeRightClick`, and standard mouse events).

CommandBarEvents Events

Name	Parameters	Description
Click	CommandBarControl As Object, handled As Boolean, CancelDefault As Boolean	Triggered when a hooked command bar button is clicked. The CommandBarControl is passed to the event. A single control can be hooked by many CommandBarEvents objects. The events are fired in reverse order of setting up (most recently set up fires first). An event handler can set the handled flag to True to tell subsequent handlers that the event has already been processed. The CommandBarEvents object can also be used to hook into built-in menu items. If you want to handle the event through code, you can set the CancelDefault flag to True to stop the menu's normal action

CommandBarEvents Examples

In a class module called CBarEvents, add the following code:

```
Public WithEvents oCBEvents As VBIDE.CommandBarEvents

'Hook into the Click event for the menu item
Private Sub oCBEvents_Click(ByVal CommandBarControl As Object, _
        handled As Boolean, CancelDefault As Boolean)

    Debug.Print "Clicked " & CommandBarControl.Caption
End Sub
```

In a normal module, add the following code:

```
'Declare a collection to hold all the instances of our events class
Dim ocolMenus As New Collection

Sub AddMenus()

    'Declare some CommandBar items
    Dim oBar As CommandBar
    Dim oBtn1 As CommandBarButton, oBtn2 As CommandBarButton

    'And an object to hold instances of your events class
    Dim oCBE As CBarEvents
```

```
       'Get the VBE's menu bar
       Set oBar = Application.VBE.CommandBars("Menu Bar")

       'Add a menu item to it
       Set oBtn1 = oBar.Controls.Add(Type:=msoControlButton, temporary:=True)
       oBtn1.Caption = "Menu1"
       oBtn1.Style = msoButtonCaption

       'Create a new instance of your CommandBarEvent handler
       Set oCBE = New CBarEvents

       'Link your CommandBarEvent handler to the menu item you just created
       Set oCBE.oCBEvents = Application.VBE.Events.CommandBarEvents(oBtn1)

       'And add the instance of your event handler to the collection
       ocolMenus.Add oCBE

       'Repeat for a second menu
       Set oBtn2 = oBar.Controls.Add(Type:=msoControlButton, temporary:=True)
       oBtn2.Caption = "Menu2"
       oBtn2.Style = msoButtonCaption

       Set oCBE = New CBarEvents
       Set oCBE.oCBEvents = Application.VBE.Events.CommandBarEvents(oBtn2)
       ocolMenus.Add oCBE
    End Sub
```

When you run the AddMenus routine, two menus are added to the VBE standard menu bar, which both use your CommandBarEvents handling class to hook into their Click event. When you click each of the menu items, the Immediate window displays the menu's caption.

Events Object

The Events object is a high-level container for the VBE's event model. In Office 2002, it contains event objects associated with clicking a command bar button and adding/removing references. The VBE extensibility model is based on the Visual Basic extensibility model, which contains a much richer set of events.

Events Properties

Name	Returns	Description
CommandBar Events	CommandBar Events	Read-only. Parameters: CommandBarControl. Performs the linking required to hook a CommandBarEvents object to a specific command bar button
References Events	References Events	Read-only. Parameters: VBProject. Performs the linking required to hook a ReferencesEvents object to a specific project

Events Examples

Examples of the Events object are included in the CommandBarEvents and ReferencesEvents sections.

LinkedWindows Collection

The LinkedWindows collection contains all the docked windows in the VBE workspace. COM Addins written in VB5/6 (but not in the Developer edition of Office 2002) can add their own windows to this collection. Within the Office environment, you are limited to docking or undocking the built-in windows. Note that if you undock, then dock a built-in window, it does *not* go back to its original position.

LinkedWindows Collection Methods

Name	Returns	Description
Add		Method. Parameters: Window As Window. Docks the specified window
Remove		Method. Parameters: Window As Window. Undocks the specified window

Property Object and Properties Collection

All of the VBComponents in a project have a Properties collection. The properties contained in the collection correspond to the items shown in the Properties Window of the VBE. For the VBComponents that correspond to the Excel objects, the Properties collection of the VBComponents also includes many of the properties of the Excel object.

Property Common Properties

The Collection, Parent, and VBE properties are defined at the beginning of this section.

Property Properties

Name	Returns	Description
IndexedValue	Variant	Parameters: Index1, [Index2], [Index3], [Index4]. The Property's Value can be an array of up to four indices. The IndexedValue can be used to read a single item in the returned array
Name	String	Read-only. Returns the name of the property, and is also used to refer to a specific property

Name	Returns	Description
NumIndices	Integer	Read-only. If the `Property`'s value is an array, this returns the number of indices (dimensions) in the array. If not an array, it returns zero
Object	Object	The `Object` property is used to obtain a reference to the object returned by the `Property`, if any
Value	Variant	The `Property`'s value

It is easy to get confused with the `Name` property:

Item	Refers to
`Worksheet.CodeName`	The code name of the `VBComponent` (Read-only)
`VBComponent.Name`	The code name of the `VBComponent` (Read/write)
`VBComponent` `.Properties("CodeName")`	The code name of the `VBComponent` (Read-only)
`VBComponent` `.Properties("_CodeName")`	The code name of the `VBComponent` (Read/write)[1]
`VBComponent` `.Properties("Name")`	The name of the worksheet (Read/write)
`VBComponent` `.Properties("Name").Name`	`"Name"`

Property Examples

This simple example identifies the workbook containing a given `VBComponent`:

```
Sub IdentifyWorkbook()
    Dim oBk As Workbook

    'Get the workbook containing a given VBComponent
    Set oBk =
Application.VBE.ActiveVBProject.VBComponents("Sheet1").Properties("Parent")
.Object

    MsgBox oBk.Name
End Sub
```

[1] This was the only reliable way to change a worksheet's *CodeName* in Excel 97.

Reference Object and References Collection

A Reference is a link from your VBProject to an external file, which may be an object library (for example, linking to the Word object library), a control (for example, Windows Common Controls), an ActiveX DLL, or another VBProject. By creating a reference to the external object, you can implement early binding—meaning that the referenced objects run in the same memory area, all the links are evaluated at compile time, and Excel provides ToolTip programming help when working with the referenced objects.

When you run your application on another machine, it may not have all the objects that your application requires. The Reference object and References collection provide access to these references, allowing you to check that they are all present and working before you try to use them.

Reference Common Properties

The Collection and VBE properties are defined at the beginning of this section.

Reference Properties

Name	Returns	Description
BuiltIn	Boolean	Read-only. Returns if the reference is built-in or added by the developer. The "Visual Basic for Applications" and "Microsoft Excel 10.0 Object Library"_references are built-in and cannot be removed
Description	String	Read-only. Returns the description of the reference, which is the text shown in the Object Browser
FullPath	String	Read-only. Returns the path to the workbook, DLL, OCX, TLB or OLB file that is the source of the reference
Guid	String	Read-only. Returns the globally unique identifier for the reference
IsBroken	Boolean	Read-only. Returns True if the reference is broken (is not available on the machine)
Major	Long	Read-only. Returns the major version number of the referenced file
Minor	Long	Read-only. Returns the minor version number of the referenced file
Name	String	Read-only. Returns a short name for the reference (for example, "VBA" or "Excel")
Type	vbext_RefKind	Read-only. Returns the reference type, vbext_rk_TypeLib for DLLs etc, or vbext_rk_Project for other VBProjects

References Collection Methods

Name	Returns	Description
AddFromFile	Reference	Method. Parameters: `FileName As String`. Adds a reference between the `VBProject` and a specific file. This should only be used to create references between workbooks
AddFromGuid	Reference	Method. Parameters: `Guid As String`, `Major As Long`, `Minor As Long`. Adds a reference between the `VBProject` and a specific DLL, Typelib, etc. A library's file name, location and version may change over time, but its `Guid` is guaranteed to be constant. Hence, when adding a reference to a DLL, Typelib, etc, the `Guid` should be used. If you require a specific version of the DLL, you can request the major and minor version numbers
Remove		Method. Parameters: `Reference As Reference`. Removes a reference from the `VBProject`

References Collection Events

The `References` collection provides two events, which you can use to detect when items are added to or removed from the collection. You could use this, for example, to create a "Top 10 References" dialog box, by using the `Application`'s events to detect when a workbook is opened or created and hooking into the workbook's `VBProject`'s `References` collection events to detect when a particular `Reference` is added to a project. You could maintain a list of these and display them in a dialog box, similar to the existing Tools ➪ References dialog box in the VBE (but without all the clutter).

Name	Parameters	Description
ItemAdded	Reference As VBIDE.Reference	Triggered when a `Reference` is added to the `VBProject` being watched
ItemRemoved	Reference As VBIDE.Reference	Triggered when a `Reference` is removed from the `VBProject` being watched

Reference Examples

This example checks for broken references and alerts the user.

```
Function HasMissingRefs() As Boolean
    Dim oRef As VBIDE.Reference


    'Loop through all the references for the project
    For Each oRef In ThisWorkbook.VBProject.References
```

```
            'Is it missing?
            If oRef.IsBroken Then

                'Yes - show different messages for workbook and DLL references
                If oRef.Type = vbext_rk_Project Then
                    MsgBox "Could not find the workbook " & oRef.FullPath & _
                            ", which is required by this application."
                Else
                    MsgBox "This application requires the object library '" & _
                            oRef.Description & "', which has not been installed."
                End If

                'Return that there are some missing references
                HasMissingRefs = True
            End If
        Next
End Function
```

The following example shows the core code to watch when the user adds or removes references
to any project (so that you could, for example, create a "Top 10" references picker). There are four steps to
take:

❑   When started, hook into the References events of the VBProjects in all open workbooks.

❑   Hook into the Application's events to detect workbooks being created or opened.

❑   When a workbook is created or opened, hook its VBProject's References events.

❑   When a References event is triggered, do something (here, you just print it out)

In a class module, CRefEvents (for the fourth step):

```
'The WithEvents object to hook the References events
Public WithEvents oRefEvt As VBIDE.References

'We'll also store the workbook you're tracking
Public oWorkbook As Workbook

'We added a reference to a workbook
Private Sub oRefEvt_ItemAdded(ByVal Reference As VBIDE.Reference)
    Debug.Print "Added Reference '" & _
                Reference.Description & _
                "' to " & oWorkbook.Name
End Sub

'We removed a reference from a workbook
Private Sub oRefEvt_ItemRemoved(ByVal Reference As VBIDE.Reference)
    Debug.Print "Removed Reference '" & _
                Reference.Description & _
                "' from " & oWorkbook.Name
End Sub
```

In a class module, CAppEvents (for the third step):

```
'WithEvents object to hook the Application's events
Public WithEvents oApp As Application

'Hook the References events for new workbooks
Private Sub oApp_NewWorkbook(ByVal Wb As Workbook)

    'A new References event handler instance
    Dim oRefEvents As New CRefEvents

    'Tell it which workbook you're hooking
    Set oRefEvents.oWorkbook = Wb

    'And give it the References object to hook into
    Set oRefEvents.oRefEvt = Wb.VBProject.References

    'Add the event handler to your collection of such handlers
    oRefHooks.Add oRefEvents
End Sub

'Hook the References events for opened workbooks
Private Sub oApp_WorkbookOpen(ByVal Wb As Workbook)
    Dim oRefEvents As New CRefEvents

    Set oRefEvents.oWorkbook = Wb
    Set oRefEvents.oRefEvt = Wb.VBProject.References
    oRefHooks.Add oRefEvents
End Sub
```

In a normal module (for the first and second steps):

```
'One instance of Application events hook
Public oAppHooks As New CAppEvents

'Lots of instances of References events hooks
Public oRefHooks As New Collection

Sub SetUpReferenceHooking()
    Dim oRefEvents As CRefEvents
    Dim oBk As Workbook

    Set oRefHooks = Nothing

    'Step 1: Loop through the existing projects,
    'hooking their references events
    For Each oBk In Workbooks
        If Not oBk Is ThisWorkbook Then
            Set oRefEvents = New CRefEvents
            Set oRefEvents.oWorkbook = oBk
            Set oRefEvents.oRefEvt = oBk.VBProject.References
            oRefHooks.Add oRefEvents
        End If
    Next

    'Step 2: Hook the Application events to watch for new projects to hook
    Set oAppHooks.oApp = Application
End Sub
```

ReferencesEvents Object

In a similar manner to the way in which the `CommandBarEvents` object provides the `Click` event for a command bar, the `ReferencesEvents` object provides two events related to a `VBProject`'s `References` collection. The `ReferencesEvents` object appears to be redundant—all of the events it handles are also included in a `VBProject`'s `References` object. The only difference (apart from the definition) is that the `ReferencesEvents` object works with a `VBProject` object instead of the `VBProject`'s `References` collection. Note that a `VBProject` is compiled when a `Reference` is added or removed, resulting in the loss of any variables and instances of classes. Hence a `VBProject` cannot monitor its own `References` events.

ReferencesEvents Events

Name	Parameters	Description
ItemAdded	Reference As VBIDE.Reference	Triggered when a Reference is added to the VBProject being watched
ItemRemoved	Reference As VBIDE.Reference	Triggered when a Reference is removed from the VBProject being watched

ReferencesEvents Examples

The examples for the `ReferencesEvents` object are the same as the `References Collection Events`. The only difference is the way the events are handled (shown in bold in the code):

In the `CRefEvents` class:

```
'The WithEvents object to hook the References events
Public WithEvents oRefEvt As VBIDE.References Events
```

In the `CAppEvents` class:

```
'Hook the References events for opened workbooks
Private Sub oApp_WorkbookOpen(ByVal Wb As Workbook)
    Dim oRefEvents As New CRefEvents

    Set oRefEvents.oWorkbook = Wb
    Set oRefEvents.oRefEvt = _
        Application.VBE.Events.ReferencesEvents(Wb.VBProject)
    oRefHooks.Add oRefEvents
End Sub
```

In the normal module:

```
Set oRefEvents.oWorkbook = oBk
Set oRefEvents.oRefEvt = _
    Application.VBE.Events.ReferencesEvents(oBk.VBProject)
```

VBComponent Object and VBComponents Collection

The VBComponents collection contains all the modules, class modules (including code behind worksheets), and UserForms in a VBProject; they are all different types of VBComponent. Every VBComponent has a CodeModule to store its code and some VBComponents (such as a UserForm) have a graphical development interface, called its Designer. Through the Designer, you can modify the graphical elements of the VBComponent, such as adding controls to a UserForm.

VBComponent Common Properties

The Collection and VBE properties are defined at the beginning of this section.

VBComponent Properties

Name	Returns	Description
CodeModule	CodeModule	Read-only. Returns the CodeModule for the component, used to store its VBA code.
Designer		Read-only. Returns the Designer object for the component, which provides access to the design-time graphical elements of the component
DesignerID	String	Read-only. Returns an identifier for the Designer, so you know what sort of designer it is. For example, a UserForm's designer ID is Forms.Form, while that of the Addin Connection designer in Office 2002 Developer is MSAddnDr.AddInDesigner
Designer Window	Window	Read-only. Returns a Window object, representing the Window displaying the Designer. (Shown as a method in the Object Browser, as it opens the Window if not already open)
HasOpen Designer	Boolean	Read-only. Identifies if the component's Designer is open
Name	String	The name of the VBComponent
Properties	Properties	Read-only. Returns the component's Properties collection, providing access to the items shown in the Property window and to many of the associated Excel object's properties if the VBComponent represents the code behind an Excel object. See the Property Object for more information
Saved	Boolean	Read-only. Returns whether the contents of the VBComponent has changed since the last save. It is analogous to an Excel workbook's Saved property, but applies to each component individually

Continues

Name	Returns	Description
Type	vbext_ Component Type	Read-only. Returns the type of the component: vbext_ct_StdModule — Normal module vbext_ct_ClassModule — Class module vbext_ct_MSForm — UserForm vbext_ct_Document — Excel object vbext_ct_ActiveXDesigner — All other types

VBComponent Methods

Name	Parameters	Description
Activate		Displays the VBComponent's main window (code module or designer) and sets the focus to it
Export	FileName As String	Saves the component as a file, separate from the workbook

VBComponents Collection Methods

Name	Returns	Description
Add	VBComponent	Parameters: ComponentType. Add a new, built-in, VBComponent to the project. The ComponentType can be one of vbext_ct_StdModule, vbext_ct_ClassModule, and vbext_ct_MSForm
AddCustom	VBComponent	Parameters: ProgId. Add a new, custom, VBComponent to the project. The result is always of type vbext_ct_ActiveXDesigner. It seems that custom VB components can only be added to ActiveX DLL projects and not to Excel workbook projects
Import	VBComponent	Parameters: FileName. Add a new VBComponent to the project from a file (usually a previously-exported VBComponent)
Remove		Parameters: VBComponent. Removes a VBComponent from a project

VBComponent Examples

Many of the examples in this section and in Chapter 23 use the `VBComponent` object and its properties and methods. The following below exports a UserForm from the workbook containing the code, imports it into a new workbook and renames it. It then adds a standard module, fills in some code to show the form, then calls the routine to show the form in the new workbook:

```
Sub CopyAndShowUserForm()
    Dim oNewBk As Workbook, oVBC As VBIDE.VBComponent

    'Create a new workbook
    Set oNewBk = Workbooks.Add

    'Export a UserForm from this workbook to disk
    ThisWorkbook.VBProject.VBComponents("UserForm1").Export "c:\temp.frm"

    'Import the UserForm into the new workbook
    Set oVBC = oNewBk.VBProject.VBComponents.Import("c:\temp.frm")

    'Rename the UserForm
    oVBC.Name = "MyForm"

    'Add a standard module to the new workbook
    Set oVBC = oNewBk.VBProject.VBComponents.Add(vbext_ct_StdModule)

    'Add some code to the standard module, to show the form
    oVBC.CodeModule.AddFromString _
            "Sub ShowMyForm()" & vbCrLf & _
            "    MyForm.Show" & vbCrLf & _
            "End Sub" & vbCrLf

    'Close the code pane the Excel opened when you added code to the module
    oVBC.CodeModule.CodePane.Window.Close

    'Delete the exported file
    Kill "c:\temp.frm"

    'Run the new routine to show the imported UserForm
    Application.Run oNewBk.Name & "!ShowMyForm"
End Sub
```

VBE Object

The VBE object is the top-level object in the VBIDE object library and hence is analogous to the `Application` object in the Excel library. Its main jobs are to act as a container for the VBIDE's commandbars, Addins, windows etc. and to provide information about the objects currently being modified by the user. Unfortunately, it does not expose any of the VBIDE's options settings (code settings, edit formats, error handling etc.), nor does it provide any editing events (such as selecting a different project, adding or deleting lines of code, etc.).

VBE Properties

Name	Returns	Description
ActiveCode Pane	CodePane	Returns or sets the CodePane currently being edited by the user. Typically used to identify which object is being worked on, or to force the user to work with a specific code pane
Active VBProject	VBProject	Returns or sets the VBProject selected in the Project Explorer window. If the Project Explorer is showing a VBComponent selected, this property returns the VBProject containing the component
Active Window	Window	Read-only. Returns the active Window, which may be a code pane, designer or one of the VBIDE windows (that is, Project Explorer, Immediate window etc.)
Addins	Addins	Read-only. Returns a collection of all the COM Addins registered for use in the VBIDE. See the AddIn object for more information
CodePanes	CodePanes	Read-only. Returns a collection of all the open CodePanes in the VBIDE. See the CodePane object for more information
CommandBars	CommandBars	Read-only. Returns a collection of all the commandbars in the VBIDE
Events	Events	Read-only. Returns an object containing all the events in the VBIDE. See the Events object for more information
MainWindow	Window	Read-only. Returns a Window object representing the main window of the VBIDE
Selected VBComponent	VBComponent	Read-only. Returns the VBComponent object that is shown as selected in the Project Explorer window. Note that this usually, but not always, corresponds to the ActiveCodePane
VBProjects	VBProjects	Read-only. Returns a collection of all the VBProjects in the VBIDE, both Excel workbooks and ActiveX DLLs
Version	String	Read-only. Returns the version number of the Extensibility library (shows 6.0 for Office 2002)
Windows	Windows	Read-only. Returns a collection of all the open windows in the VBIDE. See the Windows object for more information

VBE Examples

Most of the examples in this section and in Chapter 23 include the VBE's properties. The following line displays the VBE:

```
Application.VBE.MainWindow.Visible = True
```

VBProject Object and VBProjects Collection

A `VBProject` represents all of the code for a workbook, including code behind sheets, modules, class modules, and User Forms. In the Developer edition of Office 2002, a `VBProject` can also be a stand-alone project, compiled as an ActiveX DLL.

VBProject Common Properties

The `Collection` and `VBE` properties are defined at the beginning of this section.

VBProject Properties

Name	Returns	Description
BuildFile Name	String	For ActiveX DLLs only, get/set the name of the DLL file to compile the project into
Description	String	For ActiveX DLLs only, the description of the DLL, as it will appear in the Tools ⇨ References list
FileName	String	Read-only. For workbook projects, returns the full name of the workbook. For ActiveX DLL projects, returns the name of the source code version of the project *.vba. If the file has not been saved, a runtime error occurs if you try to read this property
HelpContext ID	Long	Identifies the default Help-file context ID for the project
HelpFile	String	Get/Set the Help file for a project. Each of the User Forms and controls within the project can be assigned a context ID to show a page from this Help file

Continues

Name	Returns	Description
Mode	vbext_VBAMode	Read-only. Returns the VBProject's operation mode (Design, Run or Break). Note that VBProjects can have different execution modes (for example, an ActiveX COM Addin project can be running while you are in Design mode on a different project)
Name	String	The name of the project
Protection	vbext_ Project Protection	Read-only. Returns whether the project is locked for viewing. Locked projects only expose their VBProject object. Any attempt to navigate below the VBProject level results in an error. Note that if a VBProject is set to Protected, but is unprotected by the user during a session, its Protection property shows as vbext_pp_none for the remainder of that session
References	References	Read-only. Returns the collection of References for the VBProject. See the References object for more information
Saved	Boolean	Read-only. Returns whether the VBProject has been changed since the last save. For Excel projects, this should agree with the workbook's Saved property
Type	vbext_ ProjectType	Read-only. Returns the type of project – host project (an Excel workbook, Word document, Access database etc.) or an ActiveX DLL project
VBComponents	VBComponents	Read-only. Returns the collection of VBComponents in the project. See the VBComponent object for more information

VBProject Methods

Name	Returns	Parameters	Description
MakeCompiledFile			For ActiveX DLL projects only. Compiles the project and makes the DLL file
SaveAs		FileName As String	For ActiveX DLL projects only. Saves the project file

VBProjects Collection Methods

Name	Returns	Description
Add	VBProject	Method. Parameters: `Type`. Adds a new project to the VBE. Can only successfully add stand-alone (ActiveX DLL) projects using this method
Remove		Method. Parameters: `lpc As VBProject`. Removes a `VBProject` from the VBE. Can only be used for ActiveX DLL projects

VBProject Examples

Most of the examples in this section use the `VBProject` object and its properties. This example lists the names of all the `VBComponents` in all the unlocked projects in the VBE:

```
Sub PrintComponents()
    Dim oVBP As VBIDE.VBProject
    Dim oVBC As VBIDE.VBComponent

    'Loop through all the projects in the VBE
    For Each oVBP In Application.VBE.VBProjects

        'If the project is not protected...
        If oVBP.Protection = vbext_pp_none Then

            '... loop through its components
            For Each oVBC In oVBP.VBComponents
                Debug.Print oVBP.Name & "." & oVBC.Name
            Next
        End If
    Next
End Sub
```

Window Object and Windows Collection

The `Window` object represents a single window in the VBE, including the VBE's main window, the built-in Project Explorer, Immediate, Debug, and Watch Windows etc., as well as all open `CodePanes` and Designer Windows.

Window Common Properties

The `Collection` and `VBE` properties are defined at the beginning of this section.

Window Properties

Name	Returns	Description
Caption	String	Read-only. Returns the caption of the Window, as shown in its title bar
Height	Long	The height of the Window, in twips (1 twip = 1/20 points). Does not affect docked windows
HWnd	Long	Read-only. Returns a handle to the Window, for use in Windows API calls
Left	Long	The left edge of the Window on the screen, in twips (1 twip = 1/20 points). Does not affect docked windows
Linked WindowFrame	Window	Read-only. Multiple windows can be linked together in the VBE (for example, while docking them). This property returns another Window that represents the frame surrounding the docked windows. Returns Nothing if the window is not linked
Linked Windows	Linked Windows	Read-only. Returns a collection of windows linked to the Window (for example, when docked)
Top	Long	The top of the Window on the screen, in twips (1 twip = 1/20 points). Does not affect docked windows
Type	vbext_ WindowType	Read-only. Returns the window type, such as CodePane, Immediate window, Main window, etc.
Visible	Boolean	Get/Set whether or not the window is visible
Width	Long	The width of the Window, in twips (1 twip = 1/20 points). Does not affect docked windows
WindowState	vbext_ WindowState	The Window state – minimized, maximized, or normal

Window Methods

Name	Returns	Description
Close		Closes the window
SetFocus		Opens and activates the window, displays it, and gives it the focus

Windows Collection Methods

Name	Returns	Description
CreateTool Window	Window	Parameters: AddInInst, ProgId, Caption, GuidPosition, DocObj. This method is only used when creating COM Addins using VB5/6, to create a dockable window in the VBE

Window Examples

This example closes all code and designer windows in the VBE:

```
Sub CloseAllCodeWindows()
    Dim oWin As VBIDE.Window

    'Loop through all the open windows in the VBE
    For Each oWin In Application.VBE.Windows

        'Close the window, depending on its type
        Select Case oWin.Type
            Case vbext_wt_Browser, vbext_wt_CodeWindow, vbext_wt_Designer

                'Close the Object Browser, code windows and designer windows
                Debug.Print "Closed '" & oWin.Caption & "' window."
                oWin.Close

            Case Else
                'Don't close any other windows
                Debug.Print "Kept '" & oWin.Caption & "' window open."
        End Select
    Next
End Sub
```

Office 2003 Object Model

Common Properties with Collections and Associated Objects

Most of the objects in the Office Object Model have objects with associated collections. The collection object is usually the plural form of the associated object. For example, the CommandBars collection holds a collection of CommandBar objects. For simplicity, each object and associated collection will be grouped together under the same heading.

In most cases, the purpose of the collection object is only to hold a collection of the same objects. The common properties of the collection objects are listed in the following section. Only unique properties, methods, or events will be mentioned in each object section.

Common Collection Properties

Name	Returns	Description
Application	Application	Read Only. Returns a reference to the Application owning the current object
Count	Long	Read Only. Returns the number of objects in the collection
Creator	Long	Read Only. Returns a Long number that describes which application the object was created in. MacIntosh only
Parent	Object	Read Only. The Parent object is the container object of the collection object. For example, Workbooks .Parent returns a reference to the Application object

Common Object Properties

Objects also have some common properties. To avoid redundancy, the common properties of all objects are listed next. They will be mentioned in each object description as existing but are only defined here.

Name	Returns	Description
Application	Application	Read Only. Returns a reference to the Application owning the current object
Creator	Long	Read Only. Returns a Long number that describes which application the object was created in. MacIntosh only
Parent	Object	Read Only. The container object of the current object. For example, in Excel Shapes(1).Parent may return a reference to a Worksheet object, since a Worksheet object is one of the possible containers of a Shapes object

Office Objects and Their Properties and Events

The objects are listed in alphabetical order. Each object has a general description of the object and possible parent objects. This is followed by a table format of each of the object's properties and methods. The last section of each object describes some code examples of the object's use.

AnswerWizard Object

The AnswerWizard object is part of the AnswerWizardFiles collection. It's used to control which files are used when using the Answer Wizard dialog box.

AnswerWizard Common Properties

The Application, Creator, and Parent properties are defined at the beginning of this Appendix.

AnswerWizard Properties

Name	Returns	Description
Files	AnswerWizardFiles	Read Only. Returns the list of files available to the current AnswerWizard

AnswerWizard Methods

Name	Returns	Parameters	Description
ClearFileList			Clears the list of files for the current AnswerWizard, including the default list of files for the Microsoft Office host application
ResetFileList			Resets the list of files for the current AnswerWizard to the default list of files for the Microsoft Office host application

AnswerWizardFiles Collection Object

A collection of references to Answer Wizard files: the `AnswerWizardFiles` collection contains all of the Answer Wizard files (with the file name extension `.AW`) available to the active Microsoft Office application.

AnswerWizardFiles Collection Common Properties

The `Application`, `Count`, `Creator`, and `Parent` properties are defined at the beginning of this Appendix.

AnswerWizardFiles Properties

Name	Returns	Parameters	Description
Item	String	Index as Long	Read Only. Returns a file name string from an `AnswerWizardFiles` collection

AnswerWizardFiles Collection Methods

Name	Returns	Parameters	Description
Add		FileName as String	Creates a new reference (a String value) to an Answer Wizard file and adds it to the `AnswerWizardFiles` collection
Delete		FileName as String	Deletes the specified Answer Wizard file from the `AnswerWizardFiles` collection

Assistant Object

The `Assistant` object controls how the Office Assistant appears and what it displays. For example, you can use the `Assistant` object to display your own custom messages as an alternative to the `MsgBox` function. Many of the `Assistant`'s properties relate to the choices found in the `Assistant`'s Options dialog box.

Assistant Common Properties

The `Application`, `Creator`, and `Parent` properties are defined at the beginning of this Appendix.

Assistant Properties

Name	Returns	Description
Animation	Mso AnimationType	Set/Get which animation to run for the Office Assistant
Assist WithAlerts	Boolean	Set/Get whether the Office Assistant balloon displays application alerts when the Office Assistant is visible. When set to `False`, the alerts will appear in the Application's default dialog boxes

Continues

Name	Returns	Description
Assist WithHelp	Boolean	Set/Get whether the Office Assistant appears when the user presses the *F1* key to display Help. If `False`, the Microsoft Help Window displays
Assist WithWizards	Boolean	Set/Get whether the Office Assistant appears and provides online Help when wizards appear
BallonError	MsoBalloon ErrorType	Read Only. Returns a value that indicates the last recorded balloon error
FeatureTips	Boolean	Set/Get whether the Office Assistant provides information about using application features more effectively
FileName	String	Set/Get the filename and location of the current Office Assistant
GuessHelp	Boolean	Set/Get whether the Office Assistant balloon presents a list of Help topics based on keywords the user selects before clicking the Assistant window or pressing *F1*. If the Assistant is disabled (see the `On` property overleaf), the Help topics appear in the standard Help window
High Priority Tips	Boolean	Set/Get whether the Office Assistant displays highpriority tips
Item	String	Read Only. Returns the text associated with the object
Keyboard Shortcut Tips	Boolean	Set/Get whether the Office Assistant displays Help about keyboard shortcuts
Left	Long	Set/Get the horizontal position of the Office Assistant window (in points) from the left edge of the screen
MouseTips	Boolean	Set/Get whether the Office Assistant provides suggestions for using the mouse effectively
MoveWhenIn TheWay	Boolean	Set/Get whether the Office Assistant window automatically moves when it's in the way of the user's work area
Name	String	Read Only. Returns the name of the current Office Assistant. If the Assistant is disabled either via the Assistant's Options dialog box or via the `Assistant` `.On` property, `Name` returns `Nothing`
NewBalloon	Balloon	Read Only. Returns a reference to a new `Balloon` object. Though you can have multiple `Balloon` objects, only one can be displayed at a time
On	Boolean	Set/Get whether the Office Assistant is enabled

Name	Returns	Description
Reduced	Boolean	Set/Get whether the Office Assistant window appears in its smaller size. This does not appear to have any effect on Office XP applications
SearchWhen Programming	Boolean	Set/Get whether the Office Assistant displays application and programming Help while the user is working in Visual Basic
Sounds	Boolean	Set/Get whether the Office Assistant produces the sounds that correspond to animations
TipOfDay	Boolean	Set/Get whether the Office Assistant displays a special tip each time the Office application is opened
Top	Long	Set/Get the distance (in points) from the top of the Office Assistant to the top edge of the screen
Visible	Boolean	Set/Get whether the Office Assistant is visible. This property has no effect if Assistant.On is set to False

Assistant Methods

Name	Returns	Parameters	Description
Activate Wizard		WizardID as Long, Act as MsoWizard ActType, [Animation]	Resumes or suspends Office Assistant Help during a custom wizard. Use this method only with the StartWizard method
DoAlert	Long	BstrAlertTitle as String, bstrAlertText as String, alb as MsoAlertButton Type, alc as MsoAlertIcon Type, ald as MsoAlertDefault Type, alq as MsoAlert CancelType, varfSysAlert as Boolean	Displays an alert either through the Office Assistant or as a normal message box. Returns a Long that indicates which button the user pressed. When the Office Assistant is enabled, it displays the message (using a balloon). If the Assistant is disabled, the message appears and works like a regular message box. This method is very similar to the Balloon property, which only displays a message when the Office Assistant is enabled
EndWizard		WizardID as Long, varfSuccess, Animation	Releases the variable returned by the StartWizard method. Use this method only with the StartWizard method

Continues

Name	Returns	Parameters	Description
Help			Displays the Office Assistant and the builtin "What would you like to do?" Assistant balloon for standard Office online Help
Move		XLeft as Integer, yTop as Integer	Moves the Office Assistant to the specified location. Assistant must be enabled and visible for this to work, though no error occurs if either are `False`
ResetTips			Resets the application tips that appear in the Office Assistant balloon
StartWizard	Long	On as Boolean, Callback as String, PrivateX as Long, [Animation], [CustomTeaser], [Top], [Left], [Bottom], [Right]	Starts the Office Assistant and returns a `Long` value that identifies the session. You should use this method only to run the Office Assistant in a custom wizard The number returned by `StartWizard` method is used by the `ActivateWizard` and `EndWizard` methods

Example: Assistant Object

The following routine uses some of the properties of the `Assistant` object to display the Assistant, ask a question, and then react to the user's response:

```
'Public user defined type used to hold current Assistant's properties
Public Type AssistInfo
    bOn As Boolean
    bVisible As Boolean
    sFileName As String
End Type

Sub Opening()

    Dim lReturnValue As Long
    Dim oBalloon As Balloon
    Dim udAssistCurr As AssistInfo

    'Store current Assistant settings
    With udAssistCurr
        .bOn = Assistant.On
        .bVisible = Assistant.Visible
        .sFileName = Assistant.Filename
    End With

    'Customize the Assistant and display a custom balloon
```

```
        With Assistant
            .On = True
            .Visible = True
            .Filename = "C:\Program Files\Microsoft Office\Office10\dot.acs"
            .Animation = msoAnimationCheckingSomething

            'Create a new balloon
            Set oBalloon = .NewBalloon

            'Customize the new balloon
            With oBalloon
                .Heading = "Wrox Press Welcomes You"
                .Text = "Do you want to load the Wrox Press custom workbook?"
                .Button = msoButtonSetYesNo
                lReturnValue = .Show
            End With

            If lReturnValue = msoBalloonButtonYes Then 'They clicked Yes
                'Open the workbook and display a custom animation
                Workbooks.Open "C:\My Documents\Wrox\Wrox Examples.xls"
                .Animation = msoAnimationGetTechy
                .Animation = msoAnimationAppear
            Else
                'Reset the Assistant properties
                If udAssistCurr.bOn Then .Animation = msoAnimationGoodbye
                If Len(udAssistCurr.sFileName) Then _
                    .Filename = udAssistCurr.sFileName
                .Visible = udAssistCurr.bVisible
                .On = udAssistCurr.bOn
            End If
        End With

End Sub
```

Balloon Object

The `Balloon` object is used to reference and create messages using the Office Assistant. In most cases, it's used to create a custom balloon containing text, labels, check boxes, and/or command buttons by setting an object variable equal to the `NewBalloon` property. See `Assistant` object for an example.

Balloon Common Properties

The `Application`, `Creator`, and `Parent` properties are defined at the beginning of this Appendix.

Balloon Properties

Name	Returns	Description
Animation	Mso Animation Type	Set/Get an animation action for the Office Assistant. When this property is applied to the `Balloon` object, the Assistant is animated only while the balloon is displayed

Continues

Name	Returns	Description
Balloon Type	MsoBalloon Type	Set/Get the type of balloon the Office Assistant uses. When you create a Balloon object, this property is initially set to msoBalloonTypeButtons
Button	MsoButton SetType	Set/Get the type and number of buttons displayed at the bottom of the Office Assistant balloon. When you create a Balloon object, this property is initially set to msoButtonSetOK
Callback	String	Set/Get the name of the procedure to run from a modeless balloon. If you use the Callback property with a modeless balloon, you must write the procedure to receive three arguments: the Balloon object that called the procedure; a long integer that represents the msoBalloonButtonType value of the button the user clicked; and a long integer that uniquely identifies the balloon that called the procedure, as denoted in the balloon's Private property
Heading	String	Set/Get the heading text that appears in the Office Assistant balloon
Icon	MsoIcon Type	Set/Get the type of icon that appears in the upper-left portion of the Office Assistant balloon
Labels	Balloon Labels	Read Only. Returns a BalloonLabels collection that represents the button labels, number labels, and bullet labels contained in the specified Office Assistant balloon
Mode	MsoMode Type	Set/Get the modal behavior of the Office Assistant balloon. When you create a Balloon object, this property is initially set to msoModeModal, which means the balloon must be dismissed before the user can continue working with the application
Name	String	Read Only. Returns the name of the Balloon object
Private	Long	Set/Get an integer that identifies the Office Assistant Balloon object that initiated the callback procedure. Used to identify the modeless Balloon object when running a callback procedure, which must include this property's value as one of its arguments
Text		Set/Get the text displayed next to a checkbox or label in the Office Assistant balloon. Applies to the BalloonLabel and BalloonCheckBox objects

Balloon Methods

Name	Returns	Parameters	Description
Close	Balloon		Closes the active modeless balloon. You should use this method only in `callback` procedures
SetAvoid Rectangle	Assistant	Left as long, Top as Long, Right as Long, Bottom as Long	Prevents the Office Assistant balloon from being displayed in a specified area of the screen
Show	MsoBalloon ButtonType		Displays the specified `Balloon` object

BalloonCheckBox Collection

This collection comprises all of the check boxes that appear in a `Balloon` object. It's used to iterate through all of the `BalloonCheckBox` objects to determine which ones were checked when the `Balloon` object was closed.

BalloonCheckBox Collection Common Properties

The `Application`, `Count`, `Creator`, and `Parent` properties are defined at the beginning of this Appendix.

BalloonCheckBox Collection Properties

Name	Returns	Description
Item	Balloon CheckBox	Read Only. Returns a specific item in the collection with the `Index` value specified by the `Index` parameter
Name	String	Read Only. Returns the name of the `BalloonCheckBox` object

BalloonCheckBox Object

Represents one of the check boxes in a collection of check boxes that appear in a `Balloon` object.

BalloonCheckBox Common Properties

The `Application`, `Creator`, and `Parent` properties are defined at the beginning of this Appendix.

BalloonCheckBox Properties

Name	Returns	Description
Checked	Boolean	Set/Get whether the specified check box in the Office Assistant balloon was checked
Item	String	Read Only. Returns a text associated with the BalloonCheckBox object
Name	String	Read Only. Returns the name of the BalloonCheckBox object
Text	String	Set/Get the text displayed next to a check box in an Office Assistant balloon

BalloonLabels Collection

This collection comprises all of the labels that appear in a Balloon object. It's used to iterate through all of the BalloonLabels objects to determine which ones were checked when the Balloon object was closed.

BalloonLabels Collection Common Properties

The Application, Count, Creator, and Parent properties are defined at the beginning of this Appendix.

BalloonLabels Collection Properties

Name	Returns	Description
Item	Balloon CheckBox	Read Only. Returns a specific item in the collection with the Index value specified by the Index parameter
Name	String	Read Only. Returns the name of the BalloonLabels object

BalloonLabels Object

Represents one of the check boxes in a collection of check boxes that appear in a Balloon object.

BalloonLabels Common Properties

The Application, Creator, and Parent properties are defined at the beginning of this Appendix.

BalloonLabels Properties

Name	Returns	Description
Checked	Boolean	Set/Get whether the specified check box in the Office Assistant balloon was checked
Item	String	Read Only. Returns a text associated with the BalloonLabel object

Name	Returns	Description
Name	String	Read Only. Returns the name of the `BalloonLabels` object
Text	String	Set/Get the text displayed next to a label in an Office Assistant balloon

Example: BalloonCheckBox Collection Object

The following routine uses both the `BalloonCheckBox` Collection and `BalloonCheckBox` to display a list of city choices in a custom `Balloon` object, then reports the results using the `DoAlert` method of the `Assistant` object:

```
Sub CustomBalloon()

    Dim lItem As Long
    Dim lReturnValue As Long
    Dim oBalloon As Balloon
    Dim oCheckBox As BalloonCheckbox
    Dim sMessage As String
    Dim vCities As Variant

    'Create an array of cities you want displayed in the balloon
    vCities = Array("New York", "London", "Paris")

    'Display a custom balloon
    With Assistant
        .On = True
        .Visible = True

        'Create a new balloon
        Set oBalloon = .NewBalloon

        'Customize the new balloon
        With oBalloon
            'Add heading text with both blue color and underlined
            .Heading = "{cf 252}{ul 1}Wrox Press{ul 0}{cf 0}"
            'Add a picture to the balloon,
            ' then two lines below add green instructional text
            .Text = _
"{WMF ""C:\Program Files\Microsoft Office\Clipart\Office\TRAVEL.WMF""}" & _
                vbCrLf & vbCrLf & _
                "{cf 2}Please check the cities you want to visit.{cf 0}"

            'Create a series of checkboxes with each checkbox's text
            ' equal to one of the cities in the array
            For lItem = 1 To 3
                'Arrays start at 0 by default
                .CheckBoxes(lItem).Text = vCities(lItem - 1)
            Next lItem

            'Show the balloon
            .Show
```

```
                    ' Loop through the BalloonCheckBox collection and
                    ' determine which ones were checked
                    For Each oCheckBox In .CheckBoxes
                        If oCheckBox.Checked Then _
                            sMessage = sMessage & oCheckBox.Text & vbCrLf
                    Next oCheckBox

            End With

            'Report the results using the .DoAlert method
            If Len(sMessage) Then
                'They chose at least one of the cities
                sMessage = "Cities chosen:" & vbCrLf & vbCrLf & sMessage
            Else
                'Report that they chose none
                sMessage = "Guess you're a hermit!"
            End If

            .DoAlert "{cf 2}Wrox{cf 0}", "{cf 1}" & sMessage & "{cf 0}", _
                    msoAlertButtonOK, msoAlertIconInfo, _
                    msoAlertDefaultFirst, msoAlertCancelDefault, False

        End With

    End Sub
```

COMAddins Collection Object

The COMAddins collection is a list of all COMAddins objects for a Microsoft Office host application, in this case, Excel. COMAddins are custom solutions for use with several Office applications like Excel, Access, Word, and Outlook developed in any language (VB, C++, or J++) that supports COM (Component Object Model) components.

COMAddins Collection Common Properties

The Application, Count, Creator, and Parent properties are defined at the beginning of this Appendix.

COMAddins Collection Methods

Name	Returns	Parameters	Description
Item	COMAddIn	Index as Variant	Returns a member of the specified COMAddins collection
Update			Updates the contents of the COMAddins collection from the list of Addins stored in the Windows registry

COMAddinObject

Represents a single COM Addin in the Microsoft Office host application and is also a member of COMAddins collection. COMAddins are custom solutions for use with several Office applications like Excel, Access, Word, and Outlook developed in any language (VB, C++, or J++) that supports COM (Component Object Model) components.

COMAddin Common Properties

The Application, Creator, and Parent properties are defined at the beginning of this Appendix.

COMAddinProperties

Name	Returns	Description
Connect	Boolean	Set/Get the state of the connection for the specified COMAddIn object
Description	String	Set/Get a descriptive String value for the specified COMAddIn object
Guid	String	Read Only. Returns the globally unique class identifier (Guid) for the specified COMAddIn object
Object	Object	Set/Get the object that is the basis for the specified COMAddIn object. Used primarily to communicate with other COMAddins
ProgId	String	Read Only. Returns the programmatic identifier (ProgID) for the specified COMAddIn object

Example: COMAddin Object

The following routine loops through the list of COMAddins and displays its relevant information in a table on Sheet1 of the workbook containing the code:

```
Sub COMAddinInfo()

    Dim lRow As Long
    Dim oCom As COMAddIn

    ' Set up the headings on Sheet1 of this workbook
    With Sheet1.Range("A1:D1")
        .Value = Array("Guid", "ProgId", "Creator", "Description")
        .Font.Bold = True
        .HorizontalAlignment = xlCenter
    End With

    ' Loop through the COMAddins collection and place
    ' its information in cells below the headings
    If Application.COMAddIns.Count Then
        For Each oCom In Application.COMAddIns
```

```
            With Sheet1.Range("A2")
                .Offset(lRow, 0).Value = oCom.GUID
                .Offset(lRow, 1).Value = oCom.progID
                .Offset(lRow, 2).Value = oCom.Creator
                .Offset(lRow, 3).Value = oCom.Description
                lRow = lRow + 1
            End With
        Next oCom
    End If

    ' Autofit the table
    Sheet1.Range("A1:D1").EntireColumn.AutoFit

End Sub
```

CommandBars Collection Object

The Commandbars collection contains a list of all Commandbars (known as Toolbars to most users) in the container application. See Commandbars object for more information. It contains properties related to the settings found in the Options tab of the Customize command.

CommandBars Collection Common Properties

The Application, Count, Creator, and Parent properties are defined at the beginning of this Appendix.

CommandBars Collection Properties

Name	Returns	Description
Action Control	CommandBar Control	Read Only. Returns the CommandBarControl object whose OnAction property is set to the running procedure. If the running procedure was not initiated by a command bar control, this property returns Nothing
Active MenuBar	CommandBar	Read Only. Returns a CommandBar object that represents the active menu bar in the container application. This almost always returns the application's Worksheet menu bar
AdaptiveMenus	Boolean	Set/Get whether adaptive (abbreviated) menus are enabled
DisableAskA QuestionDrop down	Boolean	Set/Get whether the Answer Wizard drop-down menu is enabled, which appears on the right side of the container application's Worksheet menu bar. When set to True, the drop-down disappears from the menu bar
Disable Customize	Boolean	Set/Get whether toolbar customization is disabled. When True, the Customize command becomes disabled on the Tools menu and disappears from the Toolbar's shortcut (right-click) menu

Name	Returns	Description
DisplayFonts	Boolean	Set/Get whether the font names in the Font box are displayed in their actual fonts. Recommend setting this to False on older computer systems with fewer resources
DisplayKeys InTooltips	Boolean	Set/Get whether shortcut keys are displayed in the ToolTips for each command bar control. This property has no effect on Excel's commandbars
DisplayTool tips	Boolean	Set/Get whether ScreenTips are displayed whenever the user positions the pointer over command bar controls
Item	CommandBar	Read Only. Returns a CommandBar object from the CommandBars collection with the Index value specified by the Index parameter. Index can also be a string representing the name of the CommandBar
LargeButtons	Boolean	Set/Get whether the toolbar buttons displayed are larger than normal size
MenuAnimation Style	MsoMenu Animation	Set/Get the animation type of all CommandBarPopup controls (menus) in the CommandBars collection

CommandBars Collection Methods

Name	Returns	Parameters	Description
Add	CommandBar	[Name], [Position], [MenuBar], [Temporary]	Creates a new command bar and adds it to the collection of commandbars
FindControl	CommandBar Control	[Type], [Id], [Tag], [Visible]	Returns a single CommandBarControl object that fits a specified criterion based on the parameters
FindControls	CommandBar Controls	[Type], [Id], [Tag], [Visible]	Returns a series of CommandBarControl objects in a collection that fits the specified criteria based on the parameters
ReleaseFocus			Releases the user interface focus from all commandbars

CommandBars Collection Events

Name	Parameters	Description
OnUpdate		The OnUpdate event is recognized by the CommandBar object and all command bar controls. Due to the large number of OnUpdate events that can occur during normal usage, Excel developers should exercise caution when using this event

Example: CommandBars Collection Object

The following routine sets some options for all CommandBars, then displays a count of CommandBars for the current container application as well as which menu bar is active:

```
Sub CountCommandBars()

    'Customize some settings for all CommandBars
    With CommandBars
        ' Enable the recently used menus feature
        .AdaptiveMenus = True

        ' Remove the Help box that appears on the right side of the Menu
        ' Note: This does not affect the VBE's Help box
        .DisableAskAQuestionDropdown = True

        ' Don't allow any customization of any CommandBar
        .DisableCustomize = True

        ' Don't display the look of the Fonts in the Font Dropdown button
        ' Saves resources and speeds up computer
        .DisplayFonts = False

        ' Have the menus randomly animate when clicked
        .MenuAnimationStyle = msoMenuAnimationRandom

        ' Display tooltip text when hovering over CommandBar controls
        .DisplayTooltips = True

        ' Display shortcut keys in the ToolTips (Has no effect in Excel)
        .DisplayKeysInTooltips = True

        ' Have CommandBar buttons appear large for easier readability
        .LargeButtons = True

        ' Tell the user how many CommandBars there are and which menu is
active.
        MsgBox "There are " & .Count & " CommandBars in " _
            & .Parent.Name & "." & vbCrLf _
            & "The active menu is the " _
```

```
              & .ActiveMenuBar.Name & "." _
              , vbInformation, "Wrox"

      End With

End Sub
```

CommandBar Object

This object holds the properties and methods for a specific `Commandbar` in the `CommandBars` collection. The properties and methods are similar to the `Commandbars` collection but only apply to the individual `Commandbar` referenced. Use `Commandbars (Index)` to return a reference to a specific `CommandBar`, like:

```
Dim oBar As CommandBar
Set oBar = CommandBars("Wrox")
```

CommandBar Common Properties

The `Application`, `Creator`, and `Parent` properties are defined at the beginning of this Appendix.

CommandBar Properties

Name	Returns	Description
Adaptive Menu	Boolean	Read Only. Returns a `CommandBar` object that represents the active menu bar in the container application
BuiltIn	Boolean	Read Only. Returns `True` if the specified command bar or command bar control is a built-in command bar or control of the container application. Returns `False` if it's a custom command bar or control, or if it's a built-in control whose `OnAction` property has been set
Context	String	Set/Get a string that determines where a command bar will be saved. The string is defined and interpreted by the application
Controls	CommandBar Controls	Read Only. Returns a `CommandBarControl` object that represents all the controls on a command bar
Enabled	Boolean	Set/Get whether the `CommandBar` is enabled. Setting this property to `True` causes the name of the command bar to appear in the list of available commandbars
Height	Long	Set/Get the height of the `CommandBar`
ID	Long	Read Only. Returns the `ID` for a built-in command bar
Index	Long	Read Only. Returns the index number for a `CommandBar` in the `CommandBars` collection
Left	Long	Set/Get the distance (in pixels) of the left edge of the command bar relative to the screen

Continues

Name	Returns	Description
Name	String	Set/Get the name of the CommandBar
NameLocal	String	Set/Get the name of a built-in command bar as it's displayed in the language version of the container application, or the name of a custom command bar
Position	MsoBarPosition	Set/Get the position of the command bar
Protection	MsoBar Protection	Set/Get the way a command bar is protected from user customization
RowIndex	Long	Set/Get the docking order of a command bar in relation to other commandbars in the same docking area. Can be an integer greater than zero, or either of the following MsoBarRow constants: msoBarRowFirst or msoBarRowLast
Top	Long	Set/Get the distance (in points) from the top of the command bar to the top edge of the screen
Type	MsoBar Type	Read Only. Returns the type of command bar
Visible	Boolean	Set/Get whether the command bar is visible. The Enabled property for a command bar must be set to True before the visible property is set to True
Width	Long	Set/Get the width (in pixels) of the specified command bar

CommandBar Methods

Name	Returns	Parameters	Description
Delete			Deletes the specified CommandBar from the CommandBars collection
Find Control	CommandBar Control	[Type], [Id], [Tag], [Visible], [Recursive]	Returns a CommandBar that fits the specified criteria
Reset			Resets a built-in CommandBar to its default configuration
ShowPopup		[x], [y]	Displays the CommandBar as a shortcut menu at specified coordinates or at the current pointer coordinates

Example: CommandBar Object

The following routine customizes a custom toolbar (CommandBar) called "Wrox":

```
Sub CustomizeWroxBar()

    Dim oBar As CommandBar
    Dim oMenu As CommandBarPopup

    ' Determine if the CommandBar exists.
    On Error Resume Next
    Set oBar = Application.CommandBars("Wrox")

    On Error GoTo Error

    ' If CommandBar exists, go ahead and customize it
    If Not oBar Is Nothing Then
        With oBar
            ' Add a separator before the 2nd control on the bar
            .Controls(2).BeginGroup = True

            ' Move it to the right
            .Position = msoBarRight

            ' Don't allow it to be customized by the user
            .Protection = msoBarNoCustomize

            ' Make it visible
            .Visible = True

            ' Obtain a reference to the first control on the Wrox bar,
            ' which is a menu holding additional controls
            Set oMenu = CommandBars("Wrox").Controls(1)
            With oMenu
                ' Change the menu text
                .Caption = "Member Info"

                ' Change the text for the popup tooltip
                .TooltipText = "Insert Member Info"

                ' Add a separator before the 3rd control on the menu
                .Controls(3).BeginGroup = True
            End With

        End With
    Else
        ' A CommandBar named "Wrox" doesn't exist.
        ' Error out and display the custom error message
        Err.Raise Number:=glERROR_CUSTOM, _
                Description:="Wrox commandbar not found."
    End If

    Exit Sub
```

```
Error:
    ' Display the error
    MsgBox Err.Number & vbLf & Err.Description

End Sub
```

CommandBarButton Object

A `CommandBarButton` is any button or menu item on any `CommandBar`. You access a specific `CommandBarButton` by referencing the `Commandbar` it's located in and by using `Controls(Index)`. Index can either be the `CommandBarButton`'s number position on the menu or toolbar or its Caption.

For example, we can refer to the first control on a `Commandbar` called "Wrox" using:

```
CommandBars("Wrox").Controls(1)
```

or:

```
CommandBars("Wrox").Controls("Member Info")
```

CommandBarButton Common Properties

The `Application`, `Creator`, and `Parent` properties are defined at the beginning of this Appendix.

CommandBarButton Properties

Name	Returns	Description
BeginGroup	Boolean	Set/Get whether the specified `CommandBarButton` appears at the beginning of a group of controls on the command bar
BuiltIn	Boolean	Read Only. Returns `True` if the specified command bar or command bar control is a built-in command bar or control of the container application. Returns `False` if it's a custom command bar or control, or if it's a built-in control whose `OnAction` property has been set
BuiltInFace	Boolean	Set/Get whether the face of the `CommandBarButton` control is its original built-in face. This property can only be set to `True`, which will reset the face to the built-in face
Caption	String	Set/Get the caption text of the `CommandBarButton`
Description Text	String	Set/Get the description for a `CommandBarButton`. The description is not displayed to the user, but it can be useful for documenting the behavior of the control for other developers
Enabled	Boolean	Set/Get whether the `CommandBarButton` object is enabled

Name	Returns	Description
FaceId	Long	Set/Get the Id number for the face of the CommandBarButton
Height	Long	Set/Get the height of the CommandBarButton
HelpContextId	Long	Set/Get the Help context Id number for the Help topic attached to the CommandBarButton
HelpFile	String	Set/Get the file name for the Help topic for the CommandBarButton
HyperlinkType	MsoCommand BarButton Hyperlink Type	Set/Get the type of hyperlink associated with the specified CommandBarButton
Id	Long	Read Only. Returns the ID for a built-in CommandBarButton
Index	Long	Read Only. Returns the index number for a CommandBarButton in the CommandBars collection
IsPriority Dropped	Boolean	Read Only. Returns whether the CommandBarButton is currently dropped from the menu or toolbar based on usage statistics and layout space. (Note that this is not the same as the control's visibility, as set by the Visible property.) A CommandBarButton with Visible set to True, will not be immediately visible on a Personalized menu or toolbar if IsPriorityDropped is True
Left	Long	Read Only. Returns the horizontal position of the CommandBarButton (in pixels) relative to the left edge of the screen. Returns the distance from the left side of the docking area
Mask	IpictureDisp	Returns an IPictureDisp object representing the mask image of a CommandBarButton object. The mask image determines what parts of the button image are transparent
OLEUsage	MsoControl OLEUsage	Set/Get the OLE client and OLE server roles in which a CommandBarButton will be used when two Microsoft Office applications are merged
OnAction	String	Set/Get the name of a Visual Basic procedure that will run when the user clicks or changes the value of a CommandBarButton
Parameter	String	Set/Get a string that an application can use to execute a command
Picture	IPictureDisp	Set/Get an IPictureDisp object representing the image of the CommandBarButton

Continues

Name	Returns	Description
Priority	Long	Set/Get the priority of a CommandBarButton
ShortcutText	String	Set/Get the shortcut key text displayed next to the CommandBarButton control when the button appears on a menu, submenu, or shortcut menu
State	MsoButton State	Set/Get the appearance of the CommandBarButton
Style	MsoButton Style	Set/Get the way a CommandBarButton is displayed
Tag	String	Set/Get information about the CommandBarButton, for example, data to be used as an argument in procedures
TooltipText	String	Set/Get the text displayed in the CommandBarButton's ScreenTip
Visible	Boolean	Set/Get whether the CommandBarButton is visible
Width	Long	Set/Get the width (in pixels) of the specified CommandBarButton

CommandBarButton Methods

Name	Returns	Parameters	Description
Copy	CommandBar Control	[Bar], [Before]	Copies a CommandBarButton to an existing command bar
CopyFace			Copies the face of a CommandBarButton to the Clipboard
Delete		[Temporary]	Deletes the specified CommandBarButton from its collection. Set Temporary to True to delete the control for the current session only—the application will display the control again in the next session
Execute			Runs the procedure or built-in command assigned to the specified CommandBarButton. For custom controls, use the OnAction property to specify the procedure to be run
Move	CommandBar Conrol	[Bar], [Before]	Moves the specified CommandBarButton to an existing command bar
PasteFace			Pastes the contents of the Clipboard onto a CommandBarButton

Name	Returns	Parameters	Description
Reset			Resets a built-in `CommandBarButton` to its default configuration, or resets a built-in `CommandBarButton` to its original function and face
SetFocus			Moves the keyboard focus to the specified `CommandBarButton`. If the control is disabled or isn't visible, this method will fail

CommandBarButton Events

Name	Parameters	Description
Click	ByVal Ctrl As CommandBarButton, ByVal CancelDefault As Boolean	Triggered when a user clicks a `CommandBarButton`. `Ctrl` denotes the control that initiated the event. `CancelDefault` is `False` if the default behavior associated with the `CommandBarButton` control occurs, unless cancelled by another process or Addin

Example: CommandBarButton Object

The following first routine creates a `CommandBarButton` on the custom `Wrox` `CommandBar`, assigns it a ToolTip text and a button image, then assigns it the `SelectNumericValues` routine:

```
Sub AddCommandBarButton()

    Const sSELECT_NUMERIC As String = "SelectNumericValues"

    Dim ctlButton As CommandBarButton

    ' Add the CommandBarButton
    Set ctlButton = CommandBars("Wrox").Controls.Add(msoControlButton)

    With ctlButton

        ' Assign it the same button image as the
        ' Select Visible Cells button in Excel
        .FaceId = 441

        ' Add ToolTip text
        .TooltipText = "Select Numeric Values"

        ' Store a custom name in its Tag property which can be
        ' used by the FindControl method to locate the control without
        ' knowing its position
        .Tag = sSELECT_NUMERIC
```

```
            ' Assign the CommandBarButton control the routine
            .OnAction = sSELECT_NUMERIC
    End With

End Sub

Sub SelectNumericValues()

    Dim rng As Range

    ' Suppress any errors (like no worksheet/workbook active)
    On Error Resume Next

    ' Make sure the current selection is a Range
    If TypeOf Selection Is Range Then

        If Selection.Cells.Count = 1 Then
            ' If they're only selecting one cell,
            ' grab all of the numeric constants for the worksheet
            ActiveSheet.UsedRange.SpecialCells( _
                xlCellTypeConstants, xlNumbers).Select
        Else
            ' Grab the selection's numeric constants
            Selection.SpecialCells(xlCellTypeConstants, xlNumbers).Select
        End If
    End If

End Sub
```

CommandBarComboBox Object

This object represents a drop-down list, custom edit box, or ComboBox (combination of the first two) control on any CommandBar. These types of controls only appear on the command bar—when it's either floating or docked at either the top or bottom of the Application window.

CommandBarComboBox Common Properties

The Application, Creator, and Parent properties are defined at the beginning of this Appendix.

CommandBarComboBox Properties

Name	Returns	Description
BeginGroup	Boolean	Set/Get whether the specified CommandBarComboBox appears at the beginning of a group of controls on the command bar
BuiltIn	Boolean	Read OnlyRead only. Returns True if the specified command bar or command bar control is a built-in command bar or control of the container application. Returns False if it's a custom command bar or control, or if it's a built-in control whose OnAction property has been set

Name	Returns	Description
Caption	String	Set/Get the caption text of the CommandBarComboBox
Description Text	String	Set/Get the description for a CommandBarComboBox The description is not displayed to the user, but it can be useful for documenting the behavior of the control for other developers
DropDown Lines	Long	Set/Get the number of lines in a CommandBarComboBox. The ComboBox control must be a custom control. Note that an error occurs if you attempt to set this property for a ComboBox control that's an edit box or a built-in ComboBox control
DropDown Width	Long	Set/Get the width (in pixels) of the list for the specified CommandBarComboBox. Note that an error occurs if you attempt to set this property for a built-in control
Enabled	Boolean	Set/Get whether the CommandBarComboBox object is enabled
Height	Long	Set/Get the height of the CommandBarComboBox
HelpContext Id	Long	Set/Get the Help context Id number for the Help topic attached to the CommandBarComboBox
HelpFile	String	Set/Get the file name for the Help topic for the CommandBar ComboBox
Id	Long	Read OnlyRead only. Returns the ID for a built-in CommandBarComboBox
Index	Long	Read OnlyRead Only. Returns a Long representing the index number for the CommandBarComboBox object in the CommandBars collection
IsPriority Dropped	Boolean	Read OnlyRead Only. Returns whether the CommandBarComboBox is currently dropped from the menu or toolbar based on usage statistics and layout space. (Note that this is not the same as the control's visibility, as set by the Visible property.) A CommandBarComboBox with Visible set to True, will not be immediately visible on a Personalized menu or toolbar if IsPriorityDropped is True
Left	Long	Read OnlyRead Only. Returns the horizontal position of the CommandBarComboBox (in pixels) relative to the left edge of the screen. Returns the distance from the left side of the docking area

Continues

Name	Returns	Description
List	String	Set/Get a specified item in the CommandBarComboBox. Read OnlyRead Only for built-in CommandBarComboBox controls. Required parameter: Index as Long
ListCount	Long	Read OnlyRead Only. Returns the number of list items in a CommandBarComboBox
ListHeader Count	Long	Set/Get the number of list items in a CommandBar ComboBox that appears above the separator line. Read OnlyRead Only for built-in ComboBox controls
ListIndex	Long	Set/Get the index number of the selected item in the list portion of the CommandBarComboBox. If nothing is selected in the list, this property returns zero
OLEUsage	Mso Control OLEUsage	Set/Get the OLE client and OLE server roles in which a CommandBarComboBox will be used when two Microsoft Office applications are merged
OnAction	String	Set/Get the name of a Visual Basic procedure that will run when the user clicks or changes the value of a CommandBarComboBox
Parameter	String	Set/Get a string that an application can use to execute a command
Priority	Long	Set/Get the priority of a CommandBarComboBox
Style	MsoCombo Style	Set/Get the way a CommandBarComboBox control is displayed. Can be either of the following MsoComboStyle constants: msoComboLabel or msoComboNormal
Tag	String	Set/Get information about the CommandBarComboBox, for example, data to be used as an argument in procedures
Text	String	Set/Get the text in the display or edit portion of the CommandBarComboBox control
TooltipText	String	Set/Get the text displayed in the CommandBarComboBox's ScreenTip
Top	Long	Read OnlyRead Only. Returns the distance (in pixels) from the top edge of the CommandBarComboBox to the top edge of the screen
Type	MsoControl Type	Read OnlyRead Only. Returns the type of CommandBarComboBox
Visible	Boolean	Set/Get whether the CommandBarComboBox is visible
Width	Long	Set/Get the width (in pixels) of the specified CommandBarComboBox

CommandBarComboBox Methods

Name	Returns	Parameters	Description
AddItem		Text as String, [Index as Variant]	Adds a list item to the specified CommandBarComboBox. The combo box control must be a custom control and must be a drop-down list box or a combo box. This method will fail if it's applied to an edit box or a built-in combobox control
Clear			Removes all list items from a CommandBarComboBox (drop-down list box or combo box) and clears the text box (edit box or combo box). This method will fail if it's applied to a built-in command bar control
Copy	Object	[Bar], [Before]	Copies a CommandBarComboBox to an existing command bar
Delete		[Temporary]	Deletes the specified CommandBarComboBox from its collection. Set Temporary to True to delete the control for the current session only—the application will display the control again in the next session
Execute			Runs the procedure or built-in command assigned to the specified CommandBarComboBox. For custom controls, use the OnAction property to specify the procedure to be run
Move	CommandBar Control	[Bar], [Before]	Moves the specified CommandBarComboBox to an existing command bar
RemoveItem		Index As Long	Removes a specified item from a CommandBarComboBox
Reset			Resets a built-in CommandBarComboBox to its default configuration, or resets a built-in CommandBarComboBox to its original function and face
SetFocus			Moves the keyboard focus to the specified CommandBarComboBox. If the control is disabled or isn't visible, this method will fail

CommandBarComboBox Events

Name	Parameters	Description
Change	ByVal Ctrl As CommandBarComboBox	Triggered when the end user changes the selection in a CommandBarComboBox

Example: CommandBarComboBox Object

The following routine adds a CommandBarComboBox control to a custom Commandbar named Wrox. It populates the control's list using an e-mail address list on a worksheet in the workbook containing the code. We assign a MailTo routine to the combo box, which then sends the activeworkbook to the person chosen in the combo box:

```
Sub AddComboBox()

    Const sTAG_RUN As String = "MailTo"

    Dim ctlCombo As CommandBarComboBox
    Dim lItem As Long
    Dim vaItems As Variant
    Dim szttt As String

    ' Grab the list of items from a list on a worksheet in this workbook
    vaItems = wksListData.Range("Items")

    ' Add the CommandBarComboBox
    Set ctlCombo = CommandBars("Wrox").Controls.Add(msoControlComboBox)

    With ctlCombo
        ' Add the list of items from the worksheet to
        ' the CommandBarComboBox
        For lItem = LBound(vaItems) To UBound(vaItems)
            .AddItem vaItems(lItem, 1), lItem
        Next lItem

        ' Add ToolTip text
        .TooltipText = "Send Workbook To"

        ' Store a custom name in its Tag property which can be used by the
        ' FindControl method to locate control without knowing its position
        .Tag = sTAG_RUN

        ' Assign the CommandBarComboBox control the routine
        .OnAction = sTAG_RUN
    End With

End Sub

Sub MailTo()

    Dim ctlCombo As CommandBarComboBox
    Dim lChoice As Long
```

```
    ' Suppress errors in case there is no active workbook
    On Error Resume Next

    ' Access the control
    Set ctlCombo = CommandBars.ActionControl

    ' Which one on the list did they choose?
    lChoice = ctlCombo.ListIndex

    If lChoice Then
        ' They chose someone Send the active workbook using the name chosen
        ' from the combo box
        ActiveWorkbook.SendMail _
            Recipients:=ctlCombo.List(lChoice), _
            Subject:=ActiveWorkbook.Name, ReturnReceipt:=True
    End If

End Sub
```

CommandBarControls Collection Object

This collection holds all of the controls on a CommandBar. This collection's name can only be seen when declaring it as a variable type. You can access all the controls for a Commandbar directly using:

```
CommandBars(Index).Controls
```

Where Index can either be an number representing its position on the list of Commandbars or a String representing the Name of the CommandBar.

CommandBarControls Collection Common Properties

The Application, Count, Creator, and Parent properties are defined at the beginning of this Appendix.

CommandBarControls Collection Properties

Name	Returns	Parameters	Description
Item	Object	Index as Variant	Returns a CommandBarControl object from the CommandBarControls collection

CommandBarControls Collection Methods

Name	Returns	Parameters	Description
Add	CommandBar Control	[Type], [Id], [Parameter], [Before], [Temporary]	Creates a new CommandBarControl object and adds it to the collection of controls on the specified command bar

Example: CommandBarControls Collection Object

The following routine lists all of the controls on a custom CommandBar named Wrox with some of its property information on a worksheet:

```
Sub ListAllControls()

    Dim ctl As CommandBarControl
    Dim ctlAll As CommandBarControls
    Dim lRow As Long

    ' Store all of the controls for the Wrox CommandBar
    Set ctlAll = CommandBars("Wrox").Controls

    ' Initialize the Row Counter
    lRow = 2

    ' On a worksheet in this workbook...
    With wksControls
        ' Clear the old list
        .UsedRange.ClearContents

        ' Place the headings on the worksheet
        .Cells(1, 1).Value = "CAPTION"
        .Cells(1, 2).Value = "BUILTIN"
        .Cells(1, 3).Value = "ID"
        .Cells(1, 4).Value = "TAG"
        .Cells(1, 5).Value = "TOOLTIP"
        .Cells(1, 6).Value = "TYPE"

        ' Loop through all of the controls placing information about each
        ' control in columns on the worksheet
        For Each ctl In ctlAll
            .Cells(lRow, 1).Value = ctl.Caption
            .Cells(lRow, 2).Value = ctl.BuiltIn
            .Cells(lRow, 3).Value = ctl.ID
            .Cells(lRow, 4).Value = ctl.Tag
            .Cells(lRow, 5).Value = ctl.TooltipText
            .Cells(lRow, 6).Value = ctl.Type
            lRow = lRow + 1 'Increment the row counter
        Next

        ' AutoFit the columns
        .UsedRange.EntireColumn.AutoFit

    End With

End Sub
```

CommandBarControl Object

Represents a generic control on a CommandBar. A control usually consists of a CommandBarButton, CommandBarComboBox, or a CommandBarPopup. When using one of these controls, you can work with them directly using their own object reference. Doing so will yield all of the properties and methods specific to that control.

Use the `Control` object when you are unsure which type of `Commandbar` object you are working with or when using controls other than the three mentioned earlier. Most of the methods and properties for the `CommandBarControl` Object can also be accessed via the `CommandBarButton`, `CommandBarComboBox`, and `CommandBarPopup` controls.

CommandBarControl Common Properties

The `Application`, `Creator`, and `Parent` properties are defined at the beginning of this Appendix.

CommandBarControl Properties

Name	Returns	Description
BeginGroup	Boolean	Set/Get whether the specified `CommandBarControl` appears at the beginning of a group of controls on the command bar
BuiltIn	Boolean	Read Only. Returns `True` if the specified command bar or command bar control is a built-in command bar or control of the container application. Returns `False` if it's a custom command bar or control, or if it's a built-in control whose `OnAction` property has been set
Caption	String	Set/Get the caption text of the `CommandBarControl`
Description Text	String	Set/Get the description for a `CommandBarControl`. The description is not displayed to the user, but it can be useful for documenting the behavior of the control for other developers
Enabled	Boolean	Set/Get whether the `CommandBarControl` object is enabled
Height	Long	Set/Get the height of the `CommandBarControl`
Help ContextId	Long	Set/Get the Help context `Id` number for the Help topic attached to the `CommandBarControl`
HelpFile	String	Set/Get the file name for the Help topic for the `CommandBarControl`
Id	Long	Read Only. Returns the `Id` for a built-in `CommandBarControl`
Index	Long	Read Only. Returns a `Long` representing the index number for the `CommandBarControl` object in the `CommandBarControls` collection
IsPriority Dropped	Boolean	Read Only. Returns whether the CommandBar Control is currently dropped from the menu or toolbar based on usage statistics and layout space. (Note that this is not the same as the control's visibility, as set by the `Visible` property.) A `CommandBarControl` with `Visible` set to `True`, will not be immediately visible on a Personalized menu or toolbar if `IsPriorityDropped` is `True`

Continues

Name	Returns	Description
Left	Long	Read Only. Returns the horizontal position of the CommandBarControl (in pixels) relative to the left edge of the screen. Returns the distance from the left side of the docking area
OLEUsage	MsoControl OLEUsage	Set/Get the OLE client and OLE server roles in which a CommandBarControl will be used when two Microsoft Office applications are merged
OnAction	String	Set/Get the name of a Visual Basic procedure that will run when the user clicks or changes the value of a CommandBarControl
Parameter	String	Set/Get a string that an application can use to execute a command
Priority	Long	Set/Get the priority of a CommandBarControl
Tag	String	Set/Get information about the CommandBarControl, for example, data to be used as an argument in procedures
Tooltip Text	String	Set/Get the text displayed in the CommandBarControl's ScreenTip
Top	Long	Read Only. Returns the distance (in pixels) from the top edge of the CommandBarControl to the top edge of the screen
Type	MsoControl Type	Read Only. Returns the type of CommandBarControl
Visible	Boolean	Set/Get whether the CommandBarControl is visible
Width	Long	Set/Get the width (in pixels) of the specified CommandBarControl

CommandBarControl Methods

Name	Returns	Parameters	Description
Copy	CommandBar Control	[Bar],[Before]	Copies a CommandBarControl to an existing command bar
Delete		[Temporary]	Deletes the specified CommandBarControl from its collection. Set Temporary to True to delete the control for the current session only – the application will display the control again in the next session

Name	Returns	Parameters	Description
Execute			Runs the procedure or built-in command assigned to the specified CommandBarControl. For custom controls, use the OnAction property to specify the procedure to be run
Move	CommandBar Control	[Bar], [Before]	Moves the specified CommandBarControl to an existing command bar
Reset			Resets a built-in CommandBarControl to its default configuration, or resets a built-in CommandBarControl to its original function and face
SetFocus			Moves the keyboard focus to the specified CommandBarControl. If the control is disabled or isn't visible, this method will fail

Example: CommandBarControl Object

The following routine searches for a CommandBarControl using its Tag property, then depending on the type of control found, accesses a unique property or method for that control. The State and Commandbar properties as well as the Clear method used next will not appear on the Properties/ Methods list of a generic CommandBarControl object, but still work assuming the control is the correct type:

```
Sub FindCommandBarControl()

    Dim ctl As CommandBarControl

    ' Find a control on the Wrox CommandBar based on its Tag property
    ' Recursive:=True means search through the controls in any
    ' submenus(CommandBarPopup)
    Set ctl = CommandBars("Wrox").FindControl(Tag:="MailTo", _
                                              Recursive:=True)

    If Not ctl Is Nothing Then 'We found the control
        ' Access a property or method unique to that control
        Select Case ctl.Type
            Case msoControlButton
                ' Make the button appear pressed
                ctl.State = msoButtonDown
            Case msoControlComboBox
                ' Clear the items in the combo box
                ctl.Clear
            Case msoControlButtonPopup
```

```
                    ' Access the 2nd control on this menu/submenu
                    ' using its unique CommandBar property
                    ctl.CommandBar.Controls(2).Enabled = False
            Case Else
                MsgBox ctl.Type
        End Select
    End If

End Sub
```

CommandBarPopup Object

This object represents a menu or submenu on a CommandBar, which can contain other Commandbar controls within them. For example, the File and Edit menus on the menu bar are both considered CommandBarPopup controls. The SendTo submenu on the File menu and the Fill submenu on the Edit menu are also CommandBarPopup controls.

Because CommandBarPopup controls can have other controls added to them, they are in effect a separate CommandBar. For example, assuming the first control on a custom Commandbar named Wrox is a CommandBarPopup control, the following code can be used to reference and treat the control as if it were just another CommandBar:

```
Dim oBar as CommandBar
Set oBar = CommandBars("Wrox").Controls(1).CommandBar
```

To reference the same control as a CommandBarPopup:

```
Dim ctl As CommandBarPopup
Set ctl = CommandBars("Wrox").Controls(1)
```

CommandBarPopup Common Properties

The Application, Creator, and Parent properties are defined at the beginning of this Appendix.

CommandBarPopup Properties

Name	Returns	Description
BeginGroup	Boolean	Set/Get whether the specified CommandBarPopup appears at the beginning of a group of controls on the command bar
BuiltIn	Boolean	Read Only. Returns True if the specified command bar or command bar control is a built-in command bar or control of the container application. Returns False if it's a custom command bar or control, or if it's a built-in control whose OnAction property has been set
Caption	String	Set/Get the caption text of the CommandBarPopup
CommandBar	CommandBar	Read Only. Returns a CommandBar object that represents the menu displayed by the specified popup control

Name	Returns	Description
Controls	CommandBar Controls	Read Only. Returns a CommandBarControls object that represents all the controls on a command bar popup control
Description Text	String	Set/Get the description for a CommandBarPopup. The description is not displayed to the user, but it can be useful for documenting the behavior of the control for other developers
Enabled	Boolean	Set/Get whether the CommandBarPopup object is enabled
Height	Long	Set/Get the height of the CommandBarPopup
HelpContext Id	Long	Set/Get the Help context Id number for the Help topic attached to the CommandBarPopup
HelpFile	String	Set/Get the file name for the Help topic for the CommandBarPopup
Id	Long	Read Only. Returns the Id for a built-in CommandBarPopup
Index	Long	Read Only. Returns a Long representing the index number for the CommandBarPopup object in the CommandBars collection
IsPriority Dropped	Boolean	Read Only. Returns whether the CommandBarPopup is currently dropped from the menu or toolbar based on usage statistics and layout space. (Note that this is not the same as the control's visibility, as set by the Visible property.) A CommandBarPopup with Visible set to True, will not be immediately visible on a Personalized menu or toolbar if IsPriorityDropped is True
Left	Long	Read Only. Returns the horizontal position of the Command BarPopup (in pixels) relative to the left edge of the screen. Returns the distance from the left side of the docking area
OLEMenu Group	MsoOLEMenu Group	Set/Get the menu group that the specified CommandBarPopup belongs to when the menu groups of the OLE server are merged with the menu groups of an OLE client. Read Only for built-in controls
OLEUsage	MsoControlOLE Usage	Set/Get the OLE client and OLE server roles in which a CommandBarPopup will be used when two Microsoft Office applications are merged
OnAction	String	Set/Get the name of a Visual Basic procedure that will run when the user clicks or changes the value of a CommandBarPopup
Parameter	String	Set/Get a string that an application can use to execute a command

Continues

Name	Returns	Description
Priority	Long	Set/Get the priority of a CommandBarPopup
Tag	String	Set/Get information about the CommandBarPopup, for example, data to be used as an argument in procedures
TooltipText	String	Set/Get the text displayed in the CommandBarPopup's ScreenTip
Top	Long	Read Only. Returns the distance (in pixels) from the top edge of the CommandBarPopup to the top edge of the screen
Type	MsoControl Type	Read Only. Returns the type of CommandBarPopup
Visible	Boolean	Set/Get whether the CommandBarPopup is visible
Width	Long	Set/Get the width (in pixels) of the specified CommandBarPopup

CommandBarPopup Methods

Name	Returns	Parameters	Description
Copy	CommandBar Control	[Bar], [Before]	Copies a CommandBarPopup to an existing command bar
Delete		[Temporary]	Deletes the specified CommandBarPopup from its collection. Set Temporary to True to delete the control for the current session only—the application will display the control again in the next session
Execute			Runs the procedure or built-in command assigned to the specified CommandBarPopup. For custom controls, use the OnAction property to specify the procedure to be run
Move	CommandBar Control	[Bar], [Before]	Moves the specified CommandBar Popup to an existing command bar
Reset			Resets a built-in CommandBarPopup to its default configuration, or resets a built-in CommandBarPopup to its original function and face
SetFocus			Moves the keyboard focus to the specified CommandBarPopup. If the control is disabled or isn't visible, this method will fail

Example: CommandBarPopup Object

The following routine adds a custom Popup menu with three CommandBarButtons to an existing Popup menu on the custom Wrox CommandBar. The information used to add the three CommandBarButtons is drawn from a table located on a worksheet inside the workbook containing the code:

```
Sub AddCommandBarPopup()

    Dim ctlButton As CommandBarButton
    Dim ctlPopup As CommandBarPopup
    Dim ctlMenuPopup As CommandBarPopup
    Dim rngControls As Range, rngControl As Range

    ' Find the Special popup (menu) on the Wrox CommandBar
    Set ctlMenuPopup = CommandBars("Wrox").FindControl( _
                        Type:=msoControlPopup, _
                        Tag:="PopupSpecial", _
                        Recursive:=True)

    ' Continue if found
    If Not ctlMenuPopup Is Nothing Then
        ' Add a popup control to the Special popup control found,
        ' placing it in the first position
        Set ctlPopup = ctlMenuPopup.Controls.Add( _
                        Type:=msoControlPopup, _
                        Before:=ctlMenuPopup.Controls(1).Index)

        ' Set the range to the table containing the
        ' information for the controls I want added
        With wksPopup
            Set rngControls = .Range(.Range("A2"), .Range("A2").End(xlDown))
        End With

        ' Set the caption to the new popup with the letter E underlined (&E)
        ctlPopup.Caption = "&Edit"

        ' Loop through the table adding the controls to the new popup
        For Each rngControl In rngControls
            ' If it's a built-in control,
            ' use the ID parameter of the Add method
            If Len(rngControl.Offset(0, 3).Value) Then
                Set ctlButton = ctlPopup.Controls.Add( _
                                Type:=rngControl.Offset(0, 1).Value, _
                                ID:=rngControl.Offset(0, 3).Value)
            Else
                Set ctlButton = ctlPopup.Controls.Add( _
                                Type:=rngControl.Offset(0, 1).Value)
            End If

            ' Set the properties for the new control
            With ctlButton
                ' Add a separator if there's something in
                ' the BeginGroup column of the table
                .BeginGroup = (Len(rngControl.Offset(0, 2).Value) > 0)
```

```
                        ' Set the control's picture face if there's something
                        ' in the FaceID column of the table. If it's a built-in
                        ' control, there should be nothing in this column.
                        If Len(rngControl.Offset(0, 4).Value) Then _
                            .FaceId = rngControl.Offset(0, 4).Value

                        ' If it's a custom control, assign it a macro
                        If Len(rngControl.Offset(0, 5).Value) Then _
                            .OnAction = rngControl.Offset(0, 5).Text

                        ' Set a Tag value for future searches of the control
                        If Len(rngControl.Offset(0, 6).Value) Then _
                            .Tag = rngControl.Offset(0, 6).Text

                        ' If there's ToolTip text, use it to set the
                        ' control's Caption and ToolTip
                        If Len(rngControl.Offset(0, 7).Value) Then
                            .Caption = rngControl.Offset(0, 7).Text
                            .TooltipText = rngControl.Offset(0, 7).Text
                        End If
                    End With
                Next rngControl

        Else
            'Special Popup not found, report it
            MsgBox "Could not locate Member Info control", vbCritical, "Wrox"
        End If

    End Sub
```

Below is the table used to generate the three CommandBarButtons in the routine above.

Sub Menu	Type	Begin Group	ID	Face ID	On Action	Tag	ToolTip Text
&Select Numeric Values	1			441	Select Numeric Values	Select Numeric Values	Select Numeric Values
Paste Special &Values	1	TRUE	370				
Paste Special &Formulas	1		5836				

DocumentLibraryVersion Object

The DocumentLibraryVersion object represents a single saved version of a shared document which has versioning enabled and which is stored in a document library on the server. Each DocumentLibraryVersion object is a member of the active document's DocumentLibraryVersions collection.

DocumentLibraryVersion Properties

Name	Returns	Description
Comments	String	Returns any optional comments associated with the specified version of the shared document
Index	Long	Returns a **Long** representing the index number for an object in the collection. Read Only
Modified	Date/Time	
ModifiedBy	String	Returns the name of the user who last saved the specified version of the shared document to the server. Read Only **String**

DocumentLibraryVersion Methods

Name	Returns	Parameters	Description
Delete			Removes a document library version from the DocumentLibrary Versions collection
Open			Opens the specified version of the shared document from the DocumentLibraryVersions collection in Read Only mode
Restore			Restores a previous saved version of a shared document from the DocumentLibraryVersions collection

DocumentLibraryVersions Collection Object

Represents a collection of DocumentLibraryVersion objects.

DocumentProperties Collection Object

Represents all of the Document Properties listed in the host application's Summary and Custom tabs of the Properties command (File menu) for a document. The document would be the Workbook object in Excel and the Document object in Word.

The DocumentProperties collection consists of two distinct types: Built-in properties and Custom properties. Built-in properties are native to the host application and are found on the Summary tab of the Properties command. Custom properties are those created by the user for a particular document and are found on the Custom tab of the Properties command.

It's important to note that when accessing DocumentProperties for a document, you must use either the BuiltinDocumentProperties property for properties native to the host application, or the CustomDocumentProperties property for properties created by the user. Strangely enough, BuiltinDocumentProperties and CustomDocumentProperties are not found in the Office object model but are part of the host application's model. In other words, you will not find these two properties within the DocumentProperties or DocumentProperty objects of the Microsoft Office XP model.

To access the built-in author document property, you use:

```
MsgBox ActiveWorkbook.BuiltinDocumentProperties("Author").Value
```

or:

```
MsgBox ActiveWorkbook.BuiltinDocumentProperties(3).Value
```

You need to know that the Index value for Author is 3. See the following DocumentProperties Collection example for more details.

To access a custom property in a document, use:

```
MsgBox ActiveWorkbook.CustomDocumentProperties("BillingNumber").Value
```

or:

```
MsgBox ActiveWorkbook.CustomDocumentProperties(1).Value
```

The assumption here is that BillingNumber is the first custom property.

The Custom Tab of the Properties command in Excel contains numerous suggestions for custom properties, but only those suggested custom properties that are assigned a value will be part of the CustomDocumentProperties list.

Several built-in properties are specific to certain host applications. For example, the Number of Paragraphs property is native to Microsoft Word and any attempt to reference it from another application will result in a runtime error.

DocumentProperties Collection Common Properties

The Application, Count, Creator, and Parent properties are defined at the beginning of this Appendix.

DocumentProperties Collection Properties

Name	Returns	Parameters	Description
Item	Document Property	Index as Variant	Index can also be a string representing the DocumentProperty's name

DocumentProperties Collection Methods

Name	Returns	Parameters	Description
Add	Document Property	Name As String, LinkToContent As Boolean, [Type], [Value], [LinkSource]	Creates a new custom document property. You can only add a new document property to the custom DocumentProperties collection

Example: DocumentProperties Collection Object

The following routine creates a list of all document properties. It includes the property's Name, whether it's a built-in or custom property, its Type, Index and Value. The Index was obtained using a counter variable. The Index specifies its position in the list and can be used to access the property without knowing its name. For example, the previous code used the number 3 to access the Author built-in property:

```
Sub ListDocumentProperties()

    Dim oProperty As DocumentProperty
    Dim lIndex As Long, lRow As Long

    ' Disable the screen
    Application.ScreenUpdating = False

    ' Start the counters
    lIndex = 1
    lRow = 2

    ' Access a worksheet within this workbook. Note that a worksheet can be
    ' accessed directly using its Property Name (in the Properties box of
    ' the VBE) so long as the code is in the same workbook as the worksheet
    With wksBuiltInProperties

        ' Clear the worksheet except for the titles in the first row
        .UsedRange.Offset(1, 0).ClearContents

        ' Supress errors when a value from a
        ' property cannot be accessed from Excel
        On Error Resume Next

        ' Loop through the Built in properties
        For Each oProperty In .Parent.BuiltinDocumentProperties
            .Cells(lRow, 1) = oProperty.Name
            .Cells(lRow, 2) = "Built in"
            .Cells(lRow, 3) = oProperty.Type
            .Cells(lRow, 4) = lIndex
            .Cells(lRow, 5) = oProperty.Value
```

```
            lIndex = lIndex + 1
            lRow = lRow + 1
    Next oProperty

    ' Reset the Index counter and loop through the custom properties
    lIndex = 1
    For Each oProperty In .Parent.CustomDocumentProperties
        .Cells(lRow, 1) = oProperty.Name
        .Cells(lRow, 2) = "Custom"
        .Cells(lRow, 3) = oProperty.Type
        .Cells(lRow, 4) = lIndex
        .Cells(lRow, 5) = oProperty.Value
        lIndex = lIndex + 1
        lRow = lRow + 1
    Next oProperty

    ' Select the 1st cell in the worksheet
    .Cells(1, 1).Select

    End With

End Sub
```

DocumentProperty Object

Represents a single property in the DocumentProperties collection. The property can either be a built-in or custom property. Use BuiltinDocumentProperties or CustomDocumentProperties to reference a single DocumentProperty.

DocumentProperty Common Properties

The Application, Creator, and Parent properties are defined at the beginning of this Appendix.

DocumentProperty Properties

Name	Returns	Description
LinkSource	String	Set/Get the source of a linked custom document property
LinkTo Content	Boolean	Returns whether the custom document property is linked to the content of the container document
Name	String	Set/Get the name of the Document property
Type	MsoDoc Properties	Set/Get the document property type. Read Only for built-in document properties; Read/Write for custom document properties
Value	Variant	Set/Get the value of a document property. If the container application doesn't define a value for one of the built-in document properties, reading the Value property for that document property causes an error

DocumentProperty Methods

Name	Returns	Parameters	Description
Delete	Result		Removes a custom document property

Example: DocumentProperty Object

The following routine adds a custom document property called `BillingNumber` and sets the `Value` property based on a user prompt:

```
Sub AddDocumentProperty()

    Dim oProperty As DocumentProperty
    Dim vAnswer As Variant
    Dim wkb As Workbook

    ' Check for an active workbook
    On Error Resume Next
        Set wkb = ActiveWorkbook
    On Error GoTo 0

    ' If a workbook is active...
    If Not wkb Is Nothing Then

        ' Prompt the user to select a cell or type a number
        ' If user selects a range, only the first cell will be used
        vAnswer = Application.InputBox("Billing Number?", _
                                "Billing Number", , , , , , 1)

        ' If they didn't cancel...
        If vAnswer <> "False" Then

            ' Check to see if the custom property already exists
            On Error Resume Next
                Set oProperty = _
                    ActiveWorkbook.CustomDocumentProperties("BillingNumber")
            On Error GoTo 0

            ' If it doesn't exist, create it
            If oProperty Is Nothing Then
                Set oProperty = ActiveWorkbook.CustomDocumentProperties.Add _
                            (Name:="BillingNumber", _
                            LinkToContent:=False, _
                            Type:=msoPropertyTypeNumber, Value:=1)
            End If

            ' Set the value based on the InputBox return value
            oProperty.Value = vAnswer

        End If
```

```
      Else
          ' No Book is active. Tell them.
          MsgBox "No Workbook active.", vbCritical, "Add Property"
      End If

End Sub
```

FileDialog Object

This object is now a more structured and more flexible alternative to both the `GetSaveAsFilename` and `GetOpenFilename` methods. It includes the ability to customize the action button (for example, the Save button in Save As dialog), choose from a list of different dialog types (above and beyond the Open & Save As), adds more flexibility when using custom file types/filters (for example, "*.bil"), and allows you to set a default view that the user will see when the dialog appears (for example, Detail or Large Icon views).

Note that some of the properties and methods for this object depend on the `MsoFileDialogType` chosen in the `FileDialogType` property. For example, the following will encounter an error when attempting to use the `Add` method of the `Filters` property with the `msoFileDialogSaveAs` dialog type:

```
Application.FileDialog(msoFileDialogSaveAs).Filters.Add _
    "Billing Files", "*.bil", 1
```

FileDialog Common Properties

The `Application`, `Creator`, and `Parent` properties are defined at the beginning of this Appendix.

FileDialog Properties

Name	Returns	Description
AllowMulti Select	Boolean	Set/Get whether the user is allowed to select multiple files from a file dialog box
Button Name	String	Set/Get the text that is displayed on the action button of a file dialog box. By default, this property is set to the standard text for the type of file dialog box
Dialog Type	MsoFile DialogType	Read Only. Returns an `MsoFileDialogType` constant representing the type of file dialog box that the `FileDialog` object is set to display
Filter Index	Long	Set/Get the default file filter of a file dialog box. The default filter determines which types of files are displayed when the file dialog box is first opened
Filters	FileDialog Filters	Returns a `FileDialogFilters` collection
Initial FileName	String	Set/Get the path and/or file name that is initially displayed in a file dialog box

Name	Returns	Description
Initial View	MsoFile DialogView	Set/Get an `MsoFileDialogView` constant representing the initial presentation of files and folders in a file dialog box
Item	String	Read Only. Returns the text associated with the `FileDialog` object
Selected Items	FileDialog SelectedItems	Returns a `FileDialogSelectedItems` collection. This collection contains a list of the paths of the files that a user selected from a file dialog box displayed using the `Show` method of the `FileDialog` object
Title	String	Set/Get the title of a file dialog box displayed using the `FileDialog` object

FileDialog Methods

Name	Returns	Parameters	Description
Execute			For `FileDialog` objects of type `msoFileDialogOpen` or `msoFileDialogSaveAs`, carries out a user's action right after the `Show` method is invoked
Show	Long		Displays a file dialog box. Returns a `Long` indicating whether the user pressed the action button (−1) or the cancel button (0). When the `Show` method is called, no more code will execute until the user dismisses the file dialog box. With Open and SaveAs dialog boxes, use the `Execute` method right after the `Show` method to carry out the user's action

Example: FileDialog Object

The following routine prompts the user to save the active workbook using the `FileDialog` object. Once the user exits the Save As dialog, the routine converts the billing workbook filled with formulas and range names to values with only no range names:

```
Sub ConvertBillingStatement()

    ' Use this constant to insure that the company's keyword used for
    ' Billing remains consistent throughout this procedure
    Const sNAME_BILLING As String = "Billing"

    Dim nm As Excel.Name
```

```
Dim sPath As String
Dim wks As Excel.Worksheet
Dim wkb As Excel.Workbook

' Check whether this is a billing workbook
' by checking for the existence of a hidden name
On Error Resume Next
    Set wkb = ActiveWorkbook
On Error GoTo 0

' If a workbook is active...
If Not wkb Is Nothing Then
    On Error Resume Next
        Set nm = wkb.Names(sNAME_BILLING)

    ' If this is a billing file...
    If Not nm Is Nothing Then

        ' Store the current path
        sPath = CurDir

        ' Set the properties of the File Save As dialog
        With Application.FileDialog(msoFileDialogSaveAs)

            ' Change the default dialog title
            .Title = "Save " & sNAME_BILLING & " Number"

            ' Change the name of the Save button in the Dialog
            .ButtonName = "Save " & sNAME_BILLING

            ' Switch to the Billing folder
            .InitialFileName = "C:\" & sNAME_BILLING & "\"

            ' Display the Details view in the dialog
            .InitialView = msoFileDialogViewDetails

            ' Show the dialog -1 means they didn't cancel
            If .Show = -1 Then
                ' Convert all formulas to values
                For Each wks In wkb.Worksheets
                    wks.UsedRange.Copy
                    wks.UsedRange.PasteSpecial xlPasteValues
                Next wks

                ' Remove all range names except the one that
                ' identifies it as a Billing workbook
                For Each nm In wkb.Names
                    If nm.Name <> sNAME_BILLING Then nm.Delete
                Next nm

                ' Save the file
                .Execute

            End If
```

```
                        ' Return the current path to its original state
                        ChDir sPath

                End With
        Else
                ' The Billing range name is not there,
                ' so this cannot be a Billing file
                MsgBox wkb.Name & " is not a " & sNAME_BILLING & " workbook", _
                        vbInformation, "Convert " & sNAME_BILLING & " Statement"
        End If
    End If

End Sub
```

FileDialogFilters Collection Object

Represents all the filters shown in the new `FileDialog` object, including custom filters created using the `Add` method of the `Filters` property for the `FileDialog` object.

Note that filters created using the `Add` method of the `Filters` property do not appear in the standard Open and Save As dialogs.

FileDialogFilters Collection Common Properties

The `Application`, `Count`, `Creator`, and `Parent` properties are defined at the beginning of this Appendix.

FileDialogFilters Collection Methods

Name	Returns	Parameters	Description
Add	File Dialog Filter	Description As String, Extensions As String, [Position]	Adds a new file filter to the list of filters in the Files of type drop-down list box in the File dialog box. Returns a `FileDialogFilter` object that represents the newly added file filter
Clear			Removes all the file filters in the `FileDialogFilters` collection
Delete		[filter]	Removes a specified file filter from the `FileDialogFilters` collection
Item	FileDialog Filter	[Index As Long]	Returns the specified `FileDialogFilter` object from a `FileDialogFilters` collection

Example: *FileDialogFilters Collection Object*

The following routine uses the `FileDialog` object to display an Open dialog. The routine uses the `Add` method of the `Filters` property to add a custom Billing file type to the Files of Type drop-down in the Open dialog. Note that the custom filter is persistent, which is why this routine removes the filter once the dialog box is dismissed:

```
Sub UsingFileDialogOpen()

    Const lFILTER_POSITION As Long = 1

    Dim lCount As Long
    Dim sChosen As String

    ' Set the properties of the File Open dialog
    With Application.FileDialog(msoFileDialogOpen)
        ' Change the default dialog title
        .Title = "Open Billing Files"

        ' Allow the user to select multiple files
        .AllowMultiSelect = True

        ' Set the filter description and filter position
        .Filters.Add "Billing Files", "*.bil", lFILTER_POSITION

        ' Switch to the custom filter before showing the dialog
        .FilterIndex = lFILTER_POSITION

        ' Show the dialog -1 means they didn't cancel
        If .Show = -1 Then
            ' Initialize the message string
            sChosen = "The following files were chosen:" & vbCrLf

            ' Dump filename (and path) of each file chosen in the
            ' message string
            For lCount = 1 To .SelectedItems.Count
                sChosen = sChosen & vbCrLf & .SelectedItems(lCount)
            Next lCount

            ' Display the list of each file chosen
            MsgBox sChosen, vbInformation

        End If

        ' Remove the filter when done
        .Filters.Delete lFILTER_POSITION

    End With
End Sub
```

FileDialogFilter Object

Represents a single filter in the `FileDialogFilter` collection. To reference an individual filter, use:

```
Application.FileDialog(msoFileDialogOpen).Filters(lIndex)
```

FileDialogFilter Common Properties

The `Application`, `Creator`, and `Parent` properties are defined at the beginning of this Appendix.

FileDialogFilter Properties

Name	Returns	Description
Description	String	Read Only. Returns the description displayed in the file dialog box of each `Filter` object as a `String` value
Extensions	String	Read Only. Returns a String value containing the extensions that determine which files are displayed in a file dialog box for each `Filter` object

Example: FileDialogFilter Object

The following routine removes all custom billing file types from the list of filters in the `msoFileDialogSaveAs` type `FileDialog`:

```
Sub RemoveCustomBillingFilters()

    Dim lIndex As Long

    With Application.FileDialog(msoFileDialogOpen)
        ' Loop through the filter list backwards. When looping from top to
        ' bottom, deleted filters cause the filter below it (on the list)
        ' to move up one, causing the loop to skip over all filters
        ' below the deleted ones.
        For lIndex = .Filters.Count To 1 Step -1
            ' If the extension has a "bi" in it, it's our
            ' custom filter. Remove it.
            If .Filters(lIndex).Extensions Like "*.bi*" Then
                .Filters.Delete lIndex
            End If
        Next lIndex
    End With

End Sub
```

FileDialogSelectedItems Collection Object

This collection returns all of the chosen items in a `FileDialog`. It consists of more than one item when the `FileDialog`'s `AllowMultiSelect` property is set to `True`, unless the `msoFileDialogSaveAs` `FileDialog` is used (where only one item is always returned). The `FileDialogSelectedItems` collection is a collection of strings.

FileDialogSelectedItems Collection Common Properties

The `Application`, `Count`, `Creator`, and `Parent` properties are defined at the beginning of this Appendix.

FileDialogSelectedItems Collection Methods

Name	Returns	Parameters	Description
Item	String	Index as long	Returns the path of one of the files that the user selected from a file dialog box that was displayed using the Show method of the FileDialog object

Example: FileDialogSelectedItems Collection Object

The following routine is an altered version of the previous ConvertBillingStatement procedure. This version uses the SelectedItems collection to return the path and filename from the msoFileDialogSaveAs FileDialog. It then checks the return value to insure that the phrase "Wrox Billing" appears and redisplays the FileDialog if it does not:

```
Sub ConvertBillingStatement2()

    ' Use this constant to insure that the company's keyword used for
    ' Billing remains consistent throughout this procedure
    Const sNAME_BILLING As String = "Billing"

    Dim bBillName As Boolean
    Dim nm As Excel.Name
    Dim sPath As String
    Dim wks As Excel.Worksheet
    Dim wkb As Excel.Workbook

    ' Check whether this is a billing workbook
    ' by checking for the existence of a hidden name
    On Error Resume Next
        Set wkb = ActiveWorkbook
    On Error GoTo 0

    ' If a workbook is active...
    If Not wkb Is Nothing Then
        On Error Resume Next
            Set nm = wkb.Names(sNAME_BILLING)

        ' If this is a billing file...
        If Not nm Is Nothing Then

            ' Store the current path
            sPath = CurDir

            ' Set the properties of the File Save As dialog
            With Application.FileDialog(msoFileDialogSaveAs)

                ' Change the default dialog title
                .Title = "Save " & sNAME_BILLING & " Number"

                ' Change the name of the Save button in the Dialog
                .ButtonName = "Save " & sNAME_BILLING
```

```
                    ' Switch to the Billing folder
                    .InitialFileName = "C:\" & sNAME_BILLING & "\"
                    .AllowMultiSelect = True

                    ' Display the Details view in the dialog
                    .InitialView = msoFileDialogViewDetails

                    ' Loop until the path or filename has the phrase
                    ' Wrox Billing in it (or they cancel)
                    Do
                        ' Assume the path or filename does have the phrase "Wrox
                        ' Billing" in it by setting the BillName check to True
                        bBillName = True

                        ' Show the dialog -1 means they didn't cancel
                        If .Show = -1 Then

                            ' Set the boolean check by searching for the
                            ' phrase Wrox Billing in the path or filename
                            bBillName = (InStr(1, .SelectedItems(1), _
                                        "Wrox " & sNAME_BILLING, vbTextCompare) > 0)

                            ' If the phrase is there...
                            If bBillName Then
                                ' Convert all formulas to values
                                For Each wks In wkb.Worksheets
                                    wks.UsedRange.Copy
                                    wks.UsedRange.PasteSpecial xlPasteValues
                                Next wks

                                ' Remove all range names except the one that
                                ' identifies it as a Billing workbook
                                For Each nm In wkb.Names
                                    If nm.Name <> sNAME_BILLING Then nm.Delete
                                Next nm

                                ' Save the file
                                .Execute

                            Else
                                ' Warn them that they need the phrase "Wrox Billing"
                                ' in the path or filename
                                MsgBox "The filename must contain the phrase " & _
                                        "'Wrox Billing'", vbExclamation, _
                                        "Convert Workbook"
                            End If
                        End If
                    Loop Until bBillName

                    ' Return the current path to its original state
                    ChDir sPath

                End With
        Else
```

```
                ' Billing range name is not there, so this is not a Billing file.
            MsgBox wkb.Name & " is not a " & sNAME_BILLING & " workbook", _
                    vbInformation, "Convert " & sNAME_BILLING & " Statement"
        End If
    End If

End Sub
```

FileSearch Object

The `FileSearch` object programmatically mimics the search feature in the host applications Open dialog (Tools ➪ Search command). This feature allows you to search for any file type in any group of folders, based on almost any criteria. Note that search settings are persistent and should be reset using the `NewSearch` method each time the `FileSearch` object is used. Note also that the `NewSearch` method does not reset the `LookIn` property.

FileSearch Common Properties

The `Application`, `Creator`, and `Parent` properties are defined at the beginning of this Appendix.

FileSearch Properties

Name	Returns	Description
FileName	String	Set/Get the name of the file to look for during a file search. The name of the file may include the * (asterisk) or ? (question mark) wildcards
FileType	MsoFileType	Set/Get the type of file to look for during a file search
FileTypes	FileTypes	Returns a `FileTypes` collection
FoundFiles	FoundFiles	Read Only. Returns a `FoundFiles` object that contains the names of all the files found during a search
Last Modified	MsoLast Modified	Set/Get a constant that represents the amount of time since the specified file was last modified and saved
LookIn	String	Set/Get the folder to be searched during the specified file search
MatchAll WordForms	Boolean	Set/Get whether the file search is expanded to include all forms of the specified word contained in the body of the file, or in the file's properties
MatchText Exactly	Boolean	Set/Get whether the specified file search will find only files whose body text or file properties contain the exact word or phrase that you've specified
Property Tests	Proper Tests	Read Only. Returns the `PropertyTests` collection that represents all the search criteria for a file search

Name	Returns	Description
Search Folders	Search Folders	Returns a SearchFolders collection
Search Scopes	Search Scopes	Returns a SearchScopes collection
SearchSub Folders	Boolean	Set/Get whether the search includes all the subfolders in the folder specified by the LookIn property
TextOr Property	String	Set/Get the word or phrase to be searched for, in either the body of a file or the file's properties, during the file search. The word or phrase can include the * (asterisk) or ? (question mark) wildcard character

FileSearch Methods

Name	Returns	Parameters	Description
Execute	Long	[SortBy], [SortOrder], [Always Accurate]	Begins the search for the specified file(s). Returns zero if no files are found, or a positive number if one or more files are found
NewSearch			Resets all the search criteria settings to their default settings
Refresh Scopes			Refreshes the list of currently available ScopeFolder objects

Example: FileSearch Object

The following routine searches for any files containing the word "billing" in a billing folder that were modified in the last seven days and displays the results in a message box:

```
Sub SearchForRecentBilling()

    Dim lCount As Long
    Dim sFiles As String

    With Application.FileSearch

        ' Clear the previous search settings
        .NewSearch

        ' Search for any xls file with the word Billing
        .Filename = "*Billing*.xls"

        ' Search for Billing files this week
```

```
        .LastModified = msoLastModifiedThisWeek

        ' Look in the billing folder including subfolders
        .LookIn = "C:\Billing"
        .SearchSubFolders = True

        ' Perform the search and return the results
        If .Execute > 0 Then
            sFiles = "Files Found:" & vbCrLf
            For lCount = 1 To .FoundFiles.Count
                sFiles = sFiles & vbCrLf & .FoundFiles(lCount)
            Next lCount
            MsgBox sFiles, vbInformation, "Billing Files"
        End If

    End With

End Sub
```

FileTypes Collection Object

Represents a set of file types you want to search for when using the FileSearch object. The file types in this collection persist from one search to another, so when searching for new or different file types, it's important to remove all of the file types from the FileTypes collection by using either the Remove method of this collection object or by setting a new file type using the FileType property.

FileTypes Collection Common Properties

The Application, Count, and Creator properties are defined at the beginning of this Appendix.

FileTypes Collection Properties

Name	Returns	Parameters	Description
Item	MsoFile Type	Index as Long	Read Only. Returns a value that indicates which file type will be searched for by the Execute method of the FileSearch object

FileTypes Collection Methods

Name	Returns	Parameters	Description
Add		FileType As MsoFileType	Adds a new file type to a file search
Remove		Index As Long	Removes the specified file type from the FileTypes collection

Example: FileTypes Collection Object

The following function resets the `FileSearch` object by calling the `NewSearch` method, resetting the `LookIn` property to a default path of `C:\` and by removing each `FileType` from the `FileTypes` collection using a backward loop:

```
Sub NewSearch()

    ' Reset the FileSearch Object
    ResetFileSearch

    With Application.FileSearch
        ' Place code here for your new search
    End With

End Sub

Function ResetFileSearch()

    Dim lCount As Long
    Dim oFileTypes As FileTypes
    Dim oPropertyTests As PropertyTests

    With Application.FileSearch

        ' Clear the previous search settings
        .NewSearch

        ' Reset the Lookin property by setting it to a default
        ' The NewSearch method does not reset this property
        .LookIn = "C:\"

        ' Remove all FileType items from the FileTypes Collection
        Set oFileTypes = .FileTypes

        ' When removing FileTypes, PropertyTests, and SearchFolders the
        ' index of the Type below the one you remove changes (decreases by
        ' one), so you need to step backwards in the collection to prevent
        ' the Subscript Out of Range error
        For lCount = oFileTypes.Count To 1 Step -1
            oFileTypes.Remove lCount
        Next lCount

        ' Remove the Property Tests
        Set oPropertyTests = .PropertyTests
        For lCount = oPropertyTests.Count To 1 Step -1
            oPropertyTests.Remove lCount
        Next lCount

        ' Reset the SearchFolders collection
        For lCount = .SearchFolders.Count To 1 Step -1
            .SearchFolders.Remove lCount
```

```
        Next lCount

    End With

End Function
```

FoundFiles Object

The `FoundFiles` object contains the list of files returned from a file search.

FoundFiles Common Properties

The `Application`, `Creator`, and `Parent` properties are defined at the beginning of this Appendix.

FileTypes Collection Properties

Name	Returns	Parameters	Description
Item	String	Index as Long	Read Only. Returns the file name from the list of file names represented by the `FoundFiles` object

HTMLProject Object

Represents the HTML code used to display the Office document as an HTML document. You can use Microsoft's Script Editor to access the HTML version of the Office document.

Learning how to manipulate objects and settings using Microsoft's Script Editor and programming using HTML is beyond the scope of this book. However, a brief description is warranted before you using the Office model's HTML objects.

The Script Editor is similar the Visual Basic Editor (VBE). It contains a Project Explorer, a Properties window, a Toolbox for adding controls, and a Code window for creating HTML code, similar to the VBE. Changing settings and manipulating the document via the Script Editor changes the office document itself, similar to using the VBE to change settings and using VBA code to manipulate the document. In Excel, the data is displayed in a worksheet format, with WYSIWYG (What You See Is What You Get) formatting displayed. The Script Editor gives you access to all of the formatting, settings, data, and HTML code in one window. You don't see the formatting, but can see the HTML code that comprises the formatting.

You use the Script Editor to customize the HTML version of the Office Document similar to using the VBE to customize—a Workbook in the VBE—by adding/editing HTML code, changing object settings, adding events, etc. Editing the settings and HTML code in the Script Editor will in most cases change the Office document itself.

An HTML Project holds objects similar to that of a VBProject for a Workbook. For example, each VBProject for a Workbook contains `Sheet` objects for each Sheet in the Workbook. The HTML Project for the same Workbook also contains an object for each Sheet in the Workbook. The Script Editor allows you to edit the properties of the HTML objects using a Properties window, just like the Properties window in the VBE, though most of the properties between Editors don't match. For example, in the Script Editor, you can double-click one of the Sheet objects and in the Properties window change the Background setting so that it points to an image on the harddrive. When you save the project from within the Script Editor, you can see the new background appear when viewing that sheet in the Excel window. There is no such Property for the Sheet object in the VBE, but in Excel this feature can be accessed using the Format ➪ Sheet ➪ Background command or by using VBA code to programmatically change the background.

The HTML objects in this Office model allow access to and manipulation of the HTML objects of an Office document, similar to the VBE object model allowing access to the VBProject and its objects.

HTMLProject Common Properties

The Application, Creator, and Parent properties are defined at the beginning of this Appendix.

HTMLProject Properties

Name	Returns	Description
HTMLProject Items	HTMLProject Items	Read Only. Returns the HTMLProjectItems collection that is included in the specified HTML project
State	MsoHTML ProjectState	Read Only. Returns the current state of an HTMLProject object

HTMLProject Methods

Name	Returns	Parameters	Description
Open		[OpenKind As MsoHTML Project Open]	Opens the specified HTML project in the Microsoft Script Editor in one of the views specified by the optional MsoHTMLProjectOpen constants. If no constant is specified, the project item is opened in the default view
Refresh Document		Refresh As Boolean = True	Refreshes the specified HTML project in the Microsoft Office host application. True if all changes are to be saved; False if all changes are to be ignored
Refresh Project		Refresh As Boolean = True	Using this method is equivalent to clicking the Refresh button on the Refresh toolbar in the Microsoft Script Editor. When refreshing the document by setting RefreshDocument to True, all changes to the HTML source made in the Office host application are saved to the HTML project in the Microsoft Script Editor. If RefreshDocument is set to False, all changes to the HTML source are ignored

Example: HTMLProject Object

The following routine sets a reference to the `ActiveWorkbook`'s `HTMLProject` and then uses that reference to provide a count of items, the locked state of the project. It then displays the project in the Script Editor:

```
Sub HTMLProjectInfo()

    Dim oHTMLProject As HTMLProject

    ' Store a reference to the HTML project
    Set oHTMLProject = ActiveWorkbook.HTMLProject
    With oHTMLProject
        ' Display the number of items in the project and
        ' whether the document or project is locked or not
        MsgBox "Project Items: " & .HTMLProjectItems.Count & vbCrLf & _
               "Locked State: " & .State, vbInformation, _
               "HTML Project Details"

        ' Display the Project in the Script Editor
        .Open (msoHTMLProjectOpenSourceView)
    End With

End Sub
```

HTMLProjectItems Collection Object

Represents all of the objects (items) contained in an `HTMLProject`. All projects contain a `StyleSheet` object, which contains styles used by the entire project (similar to the Styles feature in Excel and Word). All projects contain an object representing the document (workbook).

For example, a workbook called "Wrox Examples.xls" will contain an `HTMLProjectItem` called `WroxExamples.xls` in the `HTMLProjectItems` Collection for that workbook's `HTMLProject`. This item in the project stores information about the application it runs in, the objects inside the project (for example, sheets in workbook), as well as Document Properties (both built-in and custom) like those discussed in the `DocumentProperties` collection section of this index. In addition, each Sheet in Excel is also an object in the `HTMLProjectItems` collection.

HTMLProjectItems Collection Common Properties

The `Application`, `Count`, `Creator`, and `Parent` properties are defined at the beginning of this Appendix.

HTMLProjectItems Collection Methods

Name	Returns	Parameters	Description
Item	HTMLProject Item	Index as Variant	Returns the `HTMLProjectItem` object that represents a particular project in the Microsoft Script Editor

HTMLProjectItem Object

Represents one item in the `HTMLProjectItems` collection.

HTMLProjectItem Common Properties

The `Application`, `Creator`, and `Parent` properties are defined at the beginning of this Appendix.

HTMLProjectItem Properties

Name	Returns	Description
IsOpen	Boolean	Read Only. Returns whether the specified HTML project item is open in the Microsoft Script Editor
Name	String	Read Only. Returns the name of the `HTMLProjectItem` object
Text	String	Set/Get the HTML text in the HTML editor

HTMLProjectItem Methods

Name	Returns	Parameters	Description
LoadFrom File		FileName As String	Updates the text in the Microsoft Script Editor with text from the specified file (on disk)
Open		[OpenKind As MsoHTMLProject Open]	Opens the specified HTML project item in the Microsoft Script Editor in one of the views specified by the optional `MsoHTMLProjectOpen` constants. If no constant is specified, the project item is opened in the default view
SaveCopyAs		FileName As String	Saves the specified HTML project item using a new file name

Example: HTMLProjectItem Object

The following routine stores the HTML code for the `Workbook` item in the `HTMLProjectItems` Collection in a text file and then displays the code in the Script Editor:

```
Sub OpenAndExportWorkbookItem()

    Dim oHTMLItem As HTMLProjectItem

    ' Store a reference to the Workbook object of this project
    ' Note: Use 1 when running this code in a multi-language environment
    ' 1 is always the Workbook (Document) object in the HTMLProject
```

```
    Set oHTMLItem = _
            ThisWorkbook.HTMLProject.HTMLProjectItems("WroxExamples.xls")

    With oHTMLItem
        ' Store the HTML code for the Workbook Item
        .SaveCopyAs "C:\Billing\WorkbookSettings.txt"

        ' Display it in the Scrip Editor
        .Open
    End With

End Sub
```

LanguageSettings Object

Returns information about the language settings currently being used in the host application. These are Read Only and can affect how data is viewed and edited in certain host applications.

LanguageSettings Common Properties

The `Application`, `Creator`, and `Parent` properties are defined at the beginning of this Appendix.

LanguageSettings Properties

Name	Returns	Description
LanuguageID	Long	Read Only. Returns the locale identifier (LCID) for the install language, the user interface language, or the Help language
Language Preferred ForEditing	Boolean	Read Only. Returns True if the value for the msoLanguageID constant has been identified in the Windows registry as a preferred language for editing

Example: LanguageSettings Object

The following routine displays a message if additional language modes are not available. In Access and Excel, additional language modes can affect how the program is viewed and edited:

```
Sub ChangeLanguageID()

    Dim oLanguage As LanguageSettings

    ' Grab the reference to the Language Settings
    Set oLanguage = Application.LanguageSettings

    ' Test for any additional language support and report
    ' the result if none are available
    If oLanguage.LanguageID(msoLanguageIDExeMode) = 0 Then
        MsgBox "Support for multiple language viewing and editing is " & _
                "not currently available. Please install additional " & _
                "languages to enable. See search for LanguageID in your " & _
```

```
                      "application's VBA help for more details", _
                      vbInformation, "Language ID"
        End If

    End Sub
```

MsoEnvelope Object

This new Office object allows you to send data from a host application using an Outlook mail item without having to reference and connect to the Outlook Object model. Using the Index property of this object allows access to a host of Outlook features not available through the SendMail feature, such as Voting Options, CC, and BCC fields, Body Formatting choices (HTML, Rich text, Plain text) and much more.

Note that the MsoEnvelope object sends the document as inline (formatted) text. It does not attach the document to an e-mail, though you can add attachments using the Attachments property of the MailItem object, which you can access via this object's Index property. For Excel, this object can only be accessed through a Worksheet or a Chart object, which means it only sends those objects (and not the entire workbook). Similar to the SendMail feature in Excel, except that this exposes a CommandBar object associated with this feature and allows for setting of Introduction text.

The properties you set are saved with the document/workbook and are therefore persistent.

MsoEnvelope Common Properties

The Parent property is defined at the beginning of this Appendix.

MsoEnvelope Properties

Name	Returns	Description
Command Bars	Command Bars	Returns a CommandBars collection
Introduction	String	Set/Get the introductory text that is included with a document that is sent using the MsoEnvelope object. The introductory text is included at the top of the document in the e-mail
Item	Object	Returns a MailItem object that can be used to send the document as an e-mail

MsoEnvelope Events

Name	Parameters	Description
EnvelopeHide		Triggered when the user interface that corresponds to the MsoEnvelope object is hidden
EnvelopeShow		Triggered when the user interface that corresponds to the MsoEnvelope object is displayed

Example: MsoEnvelope Object

The following routine creates an Outlook MailItem for a worksheet (using its Name property from the Properties window in the VBE) and sets the subject, introduction text and recipient, adds the entire workbook as an attachment, and sends it:

```
Sub SendSheet()
    SendMsoMail "Robert Rosenberg"
End Sub

Function SendMsoMail(ByVal strRecipient As String)

    Dim oMailEnv As MsoEnvelope
    Dim oMailItem As MailItem

    ' Grab a reference to the MsoEnvelope
    Set oMailEnv = wksIncome.MailEnvelope

    ' Set up the Envelope
    With oMailEnv

        ' Add intro text, which appears just above the data
        ' in the Outlook Mail Item
        .Introduction = "Here are the figures you asked for." & _
            "Attached is the entire workbook for your convenience."

        ' Grab a reference to the MailItem which allows us access to
        ' Oulook MailItem properties and methods
        Set oMailItem = .Item

        ' Set up the MailItem
        With oMailItem

            ' Attach this workbook
            .Attachments.Add ThisWorkbook.FullName

            ' Make sure the email format is HTML
            .BodyFormat = olFormatHTML

            ' Add the recipient name and resolve it using
            ' Outlook's Check Name feature)
            .Recipients.Add strRecipient
            .Recipients.ResolveAll

            ' Add the Subject
            .Subject = "Here is the document."

            ' Send it off. The Display method does not work
            .Send

        End With

    End With

End Function
```

NewFile Object

Represents a new document listing in the Task Pane of the host application. In Excel, this object allows you to add workbooks to any of the five sections in the Task Pane: Open a Workbook, New, New from existing workbook, New from template, or the bottom section (which has no name). When clicking added workbooks in the New, New from existing workbook, or New from template sections, Excel, by default, creates a copy of the file unless you override it using the `Action` parameter of the `Add` method.

NewFile Common Properties

The `Application` and `Creator` properties are defined at the beginning of this Appendix.

NewFile Methods

Name	Returns	Parameters	Description
Add	Boolean	FileName As String, [Section], [DisplayName], [Action]	Adds a new item to the New Item task pane
Remove	Boolean	FileName As String, [Section], [DisplayName], [Action]	Removes a new item to the New Item task pane

Example: NewFile Object

The following routine adds a new file to the New From Existing Workbook section of the Task Pane. It will display on the Task Pane as New Billing Workbook, but when clicked will open a copy of the `NewFile.xls` workbook in the Billing folder on the harddrive:

```
Sub AddNewWorkbookToTaskPane()

    Dim oNewFile As NewFile

    ' Grab a reference to the NewFile object
    Set oNewFile = Application.NewWorkbook

    ' Add the file to the task pane. It places it in the New From Existing
    ' Workbook section of the Task Pane
    oNewFile.Add Filename:="C:\Billing\NewFile.xls", _
                Section:=msoNewfromExistingFile, _
                DisplayName:="New Billing Workbook", _
                Action:=msoCreateNewFile

    ' The new listing on the Task Pane will not show up
    ' until you hide and display the Task pane
    Application.CommandBars("Task Pane").Visible = False
    Application.CommandBars("Task Pane").Visible = True

End Sub
```

ODSOColumns Collection Object

Represents a set of data fields (columns) in a Mail Merge Data Source.

> Cannot be implemented at this time. Requires that the *OfficeDataSourceObject* be referenced via the *Application* object of the host application. No *OfficeData SourceObject* exists in any of the *Application* objects in Microsoft Office XP.

ODSOColumn Object

Represents a single field in a MailMerge Data Source.

> Cannot be implemented at this time. Requires that the *OfficeDataSourceObject* be referenced via the *Application* object of the host application. No *OfficeData SourceObject* exists in any of the *Application* objects in Microsoft Office XP.

ODSOFilters Collection Object

Represents a set of filters applied to a Mail Merge Data Source. Filters are essentially queries that restrict which records are returned when a Mail Merge is performed.

> Cannot be implemented at this time. Requires that the *OfficeDataSourceObject* be referenced via the *Application* object of the host application. No *OfficeData SourceObject* exists in any of the *Application* objects in Microsoft Office XP.

ODSOFilter Object

Represents a single Filter in the ODSO (Office Data Source Object) Filters collection.

> Cannot be implemented at this time. Requires that the *OfficeDataSourceObject* be referenced via the *Application* object of the host application. No *OfficeData SourceObject* exists in any of the *Application* objects in Microsoft Office XP.

OfficeDataSourceObject Object

Represents a data source when performing a Mail Merge operation. Allows you to return a set of records that meet specific criteria.

Cannot be implemented at this time. Requires that the *OfficeDataSourceObject* be referenced via the *Application* object of the host application. No *OfficeData SourceObject* exists in any of the *Application* objects in Microsoft Office XP.

Permission Object

Use the *Permission* object to restrict permissions to the active document and to return or set specific permissions settings.

Permission Properties

Name	Returns	Description
Application	Object	Returns an **Application** object that represents the container application this object
Count	Long	Returns or sets a Long value representing the number of items in the collection
Creator	Long	Returns a Long value that indicates which application created the object
Document Author	String	Returns or sets the name in email form of the author of the active document.
Enabled	Boolean	Returns or sets a Boolean value that indicates whether permissions are enabled on the active document
Enable Trusted Browser	Boolean	Determines if a user can view document with restricted permission in a Web browser if client application is not installed
Item	User Permission	Returns a **UserPermission** object that is a member of the **Permission** collection. The **UserPermission** object associates a set of permissions on the active document with a single user and an optional expiration date
Parent	Object	Returns a reference to the parent object for this particular object
Permission FromPolicy	Boolean	Returns a Boolean value indicating if a permission has been applied to the active document
Policy Description	String	Returns a description of the permission policy that is applied the currently active document
PolicyName	String	Returns the name indicating the permission policy that is currently applied to the active document
Request PermissionURL	String	When users need additional permission for the current document, this property can contain aWeb address or email address for the person to contact

Name	Returns	Description
StoreLicenses	Boolean	Returns a Boolean value that indicates whether the user's license to view the active document should be cached to allow offline viewing when the user cannot connect to a rights management server

Permission Methods

Name	Returns	Parameters	Description
Add	User Permission	[UserID], [Permission], [Expiration Date]	Creates a new set of permissions on the active document for the specified user
ApplyPolicy		[Filename]	Applies the specified permission policy to the active document
RemoveAll			Removes all UserPermission objects from the Permission collection of the active document

PropertyTests Collection Object

This collection object represents the list of search criteria when using the FileSearch object. They are analogous to viewing the list of criteria on the Advanced tab of the Search dialog box (accessed via the Tools ➪ Search command inside the File ➪ Open dialog box. This object collection is used when you need to set multiple criteria during a File Search.

Use the Add method of this collection object to add advanced criteria to your file search.

PropertyTests Collection Common Properties

The Application, Count, and Creator properties are defined at the beginning of this Appendix.

PropertyTests Collection Properties

Name	Returns	Parameters	Description
Item	Property Test	Index as Long	Returns a PropertyTest object from the PropertyTests collection

PropertyTests Collection Methods

Name	Returns	Parameters	Description
Add		Name As String, Condition As MsoCondition, [Value], [SecondValue], [Connector]	Adds a PropertyTest object to the PropertyTests collection
Remove		Index As Long	Removes a PropertyTest object from the PropertyTests collection.

Example: PropertyTests Collection Object

The following routines prompt a user for a billing number, then search for all Excel workbooks in a billing folder on the harddrive whose custom document property called BillingNumber is greater than or equal to their answer:

```
Sub SearchBillingNumber()

    Dim lCount As Long, lNumber As Long
    Dim oFiles As FoundFiles
    Dim sFiles As String

    ' Ask them which number they want for the lower bound of the
    ' Billing Number search
    lNumber = Application.InputBox( _
                "What billing number (starting with 1) do you" & _
                "want the search to start with?", _
                "Search for Billing Numbers", , , , , 1)

    ' If they gave a number greater than 1...
    If lNumber > 0 Then
        ' Assume no files were found
        sFiles = "No Files found"

        ' Use the ReturnBillingNumbers function to return a list of billing
        ' files with Billing Numbers greater than lNumber
        Set oFiles = ReturnBillingNumbers(lNumber)

        ' Report the results
        If Not oFiles Is Nothing Then
            sFiles = "Files Found:" & vbCrLf
            For lCount = 1 To oFiles.Count
                sFiles = sFiles & vbCrLf & oFiles(lCount)
            Next lCount
        End If

        ' Display the search results
        MsgBox sFiles, vbInformation, "Billing Files"

    End If
End Sub
```

```
Function ReturnBillingNumbers(1Number As Long) As FoundFiles

    With Application.FileSearch

        ' Reset the previous search including the FileTypes, Lookin values,
        ' and property tests
        ' See the FileTypes Collection example for this routine.
        ResetFileSearch

        ' Add 1st condition: Excel Workbooks only. Use the And value of
        ' Connector parameter to insure that both conditions are met
        .PropertyTests.Add _
            Name:="Files of Type", _
            Condition:=msoConditionFileTypeExcelWorkbooks, _
            Connector:=msoConnectorAnd

        ' Add 2nd Condition:
        'CustomDocumentProperty called BillingNumber is greater than 1Number
        .PropertyTests.Add _
            Name:="BillingNumber", _
            Condition:=msoConditionMoreThan, _
            Value:=1Number

        ' Search the Billing folder
        .LookIn = "C:\Billing"

        ' Perform the search and return the results
        If .Execute > 0 Then
            Set ReturnBillingNumbers = .FoundFiles
        End If

    End With

End Function
```

PropertyTest Object

Represents a single criteria in the `PropertyTests` collection.

PropertyTest Common Properties

The `Application`, `Creator`, and `Parent` properties are defined at the beginning of this Appendix.

PropertyTest Properties

Name	Returns	Description
Condition	MsoCondition	Read Only. Returns the condition of the specified search criteria
Connector	MsoConnector	Read Only. Returns the connector between two similar property test values. The default value is `msoConnectorAnd`

Name	Returns	Description
Name	String	Read Only. Returns the name of the PropertyTest object
SecondValue	Variant	Read Only. Returns an optional second value property test (as in a range) for the file search
Value	Variant	Read Only. Returns the value of a property test for a file search

Example: PropertyTest Object

The following routine removes the PropertyTest that is searching for Excel workbooks:

```
Sub RemoveExcelPropertyTest()

    Dim lItem As Long
    Dim oProperty As PropertyTest

    ' Initialize the property test counter
    lItem = 1

    With Application.FileSearch
        ' Loop through the PropertTests collection
        For Each oProperty In .PropertyTests
            ' Remove the property test that's searching for Excel workbooks
            If oProperty.Condition = msoConditionFileTypeExcelWorkbooks Then
                .PropertyTests.Remove lItem
                Exit For
            Else
                lItem = lItem + 1
            End If
        Next oProperty
    End With

End Sub
```

ScopeFolders Collection Object

This collection contains a list of subfolders in a ScopeFolder object. It's used by the FileSearch object's SearchFolders collection to determine which folders and subfolders are used in a search. Each item in a ScopeFolders collection is a ScopeFolder, a folder that can be (but is not necessarily) used in a search. Each ScopeFolder that contains subfolders has in effect its own ScopeFolders collection, similar to folders having subfolders having more subfolders and so on.

ScopeFolders Collection Common Properties

The Application, Count, and Creator properties are defined at the beginning of this Appendix.

ScopeFolders Collection Properties

Name	Returns	Parameters	Description
Item	ScopeFolder	Index as Long	Returns a ScopeFolder object that represents a subfolder of the parent object

ScopeFolder Object

Represents a single folder in a ScopeFolders collection. Each ScopeFolder can contain a ScopeFolders collection, which represents a ScopeFolder's subfolders. Both ScopeFolder and the ScopeFolders collection can be analyzed to determine whether they will be used in a search by the FileSearch object. Any ScopeFolder you want used in a search is added to the SearchFolders collection using the ScopeFolder's AddToSearchFolders method.

ScopeFolder Common Properties

The Application and Creator properties are defined at the beginning of this Appendix.

ScopeFolder Properties

Name	Returns	Description
Name	String	Read Only. Returns the name of the ScopeFolder object
Path	String	Read Only. Returns the full path of a ScopeFolder object
Scope Folders	Scope Folder	Returns a ScopeFolders collection. The items in this collection correspond to the subfolders of the parent ScopeFolder object

ScopeFolder Methods

Name	Returns	Parameters	Description
AddTo SearchFolders			Adds a ScopeFolder object the SearchFolders collection

Example: ScopeFolder Object

The following routines dump a list of Excel workbooks from all of the folders in the harddrive that contain the word billing:

```
Sub FindBillingFiles()

    Dim lCount As Long
    Dim oSearchFolders As SearchFolders
    Dim sFiles As String

    With Application.FileSearch

        ' Reset the Search. See FileTypes collection for this routine
        ResetFileSearch

        ' Search for Excel workbooks
        .FileType = msoFileTypeExcelWorkbooks
```

```
        ' Search all folders containing the word "Billing" in the hard drive
        Set oSearchFolders = BillingFolders("RCOR HD (C:)", "Billing")
        If Not oSearchFolders Is Nothing Then
             .LookIn = oSearchFolders(1)
        End If

        ' Assume no files will be found
        sFiles = "No Files found"

        ' If we found any files, list them
        If .Execute > 0 Then
             sFiles = "Files Found:" & vbCrLf
             For lCount = 1 To .FoundFiles.Count
                 sFiles = sFiles & vbCrLf & .FoundFiles(lCount)
             Next lCount
        End If

    End With

    ' Report the results
    MsgBox sFiles, vbInformation, "Billing Files"

End Sub
```

This function is called by the main `FindBillingFiles` routine and creates the set of Search Folders for the `FileSearch` object.

```
Function oSetSearchFolders(sDrive As String, _
                        sKeyName As String) As SearchFolders

    Dim lCount As Long
    Dim oSearchScope As Searchscope
    Dim oScopeFolder As ScopeFolder

    With Application.FileSearch

        ' Search only the local machine (not Network neighborhood)
        For Each oSearchScope In .SearchScopes
            ' Only look in the local hard drive
            If oSearchScope.Type = msoSearchInMyComputer Then
                'Loop through each ScopeFolder in the ScopeFolders
                ' collection within the SearchScope object.
                For Each oScopeFolder In _
                        oSearchScope.ScopeFolder.ScopeFolders
                    If oScopeFolder.Name = sDrive Then
                        ' This function adds any folders containing
                        ' the word Billing to the SearchFolders collection.
                        AddFolders oScopeFolder.ScopeFolders, sKeyName
                    End If
                Next oScopeFolder
            End If
        Next oSearchScope
```

```
            ' If any billing folders were found pass the search folders back to
            ' the calling routine
            If .SearchFolders.Count > 0 Then
                Set oSetSearchFolders = .SearchFolders
            End If

        End With

    End Function
```

This routine is called by the `oSetSearchFolders` function and adds a `ScopeFolder` to the `SearchFolders` collection:

```
    Sub AddFolders(ByVal oScopeFolders As ScopeFolders, ByRef sFolder As String)

        ' Declare a variable as a ScopeFolder object
        Dim oScopeFolder As ScopeFolder

        ' Loop through each ScopeFolder object in the ScopeFolders collection.
        For Each oScopeFolder In oScopeFolders
            ' Don't bother looking in the WINNT or Windows folders
            If LCase(oScopeFolder.Name) <> "winnt" And _
                    LCase(oScopeFolder.Name) <> "windows" Then
                ' Test to see if the folder name of the ScopeFolder
                ' matches the value of sFolder. Use LCase to ensure
                ' that case does not affect the match.
                If InStr(1, LCase(oScopeFolder.Name), _
                        LCase(sFolder), vbTextCompare) > 0 Then

                    ' Add the ScopeFolder to the SearchFolders collection.
                    oScopeFolder.AddToSearchFolders

                End If

                ' Allow this process to continue handling events
                DoEvents

                ' If the current ScopeFolder has ScopeFolders (subfolders)...
                ' Supress errors resulting from certain folders not being
                ' perceived as folders
                On Error Resume Next
                If oScopeFolder.ScopeFolders.Count > 0 Then
                    ' Call this routine again (recursively) to handle the
                    ' subfolders
                    AddFolders oScopeFolder.ScopeFolders, sFolder
                End If

                On Error GoTo 0

            End If

        Next oScopeFolder

    End Sub
```

Scripts Collection Object

Represents all of the scripts in a document, like an Excel worksheet, a PowerPoint slide, or a Word document. Scripts are blocks of code written in ASP, Java, Visual Basic, or any other language able to run in an HTML environment. Scripts are run when the document they are contained within is displayed as an HTML document.

Understanding how to create HTML scripts is beyond the scope of this book.

Scripts Collection Common Properties

The `Application`, `Count`, `Creator`, and `Parent` properties are defined at the beginning of this Appendix.

Scripts Collection Methods

Name	Returns	Parameters	Description
Add	Script	[Anchor], [Location], [Language], [Id], [Extended], [ScriptText]	Adds a `Script` object to the `Scripts` collection of `Worksheet` or `Chart` object
Delete			Removes all scripts from the specified worksheet
Item	Script	Index As Variant	Returns the specified member of the `Scripts` collection

Example: Scripts Collection Object

The following routine adds a simple script to the body (cell A1) of a worksheet called Income Report. When the page is displayed in either a browser or in Excel's Web Page Preview, a simple message box is displayed warning the user that the figures are based on last year's data:

```
Sub AddScriptToReport()

    Const sSCRIPT_NAME As String = "DataWarning"

    Dim oScript As Script

    On Error Resume Next
        ThisWorkbook.Worksheets("Income Report").Scripts(sSCRIPT_NAME).Delete
    On Error GoTo 0

    ThisWorkbook.Worksheets("Income Report").Scripts.Add _
        Anchor:=ThisWorkbook.Worksheets("Income Report").Range("A1"), _
        Location:=msoScriptLocationInBody, _
        ID:=sSCRIPT_NAME, _
        ScriptText:="MsgBox ""Income Report based on last year's data"""

End Sub
```

Script Object

A `Script` object represents one block of HTML code within the `Scripts` collection. You can reference a `Script` object using the `Item` method of the `Scripts` collection object, as follows:

```
ThisWorkbook.Worksheets("Income Report").Scripts(1)
```

or:

```
ThisWorkbook.Worksheets("Income Report").Scripts.Item(1)
```

You can also reference a `Script` object by specifying its `ID`:

```
ThisWorkbook.Worksheets("Income Report").Scripts("DataWarning")
```

Script Common Properties

The `Application`, `Creator`, and `Parent` properties are defined at the beginning of this Appendix.

Script Properties

Name	Returns	Description
Extended	String	Set/Get attributes added to the `<SCRIPT>` tag, with the exception of the `LANGUAGE` and `ID` attributes
Id	String	Set/Get the `ID` of a `Script` object. The ID returned is the ID attribute of the `<SCRIPT>` tag in HTML, or an empty string if there is no `ID` attribute specified
Language	MsoScript Language	Set/Get the scripting language of the active script
Location	MsoScript Location	Read Only. Returns the location of the script anchor in the specified HTML document
ScriptText	String	Set/Get the text contained in a block of script
Shape	Object	Read Only. Returns a `Shape` object

Script Methods

Name	Returns	Parameters	Description
Delete			Deletes the specified Script from the `Scripts` collection.

Example: Script Object

The following routine removes all of the scripts from every sheet (chart or worksheet) in the active workbook:

```
Sub RemoveScripts()

    Dim oScript As Script
    Dim sh As Object

    ' Suppress errors (ex: no active workbook)
    On Error Resume Next

    ' Remove all of the scripts objects in this workbook
    For Each sh In ActiveWorkbook.Sheets
        For Each oScript In sh.Scripts
            oScript.Delete
        Next oScript
    Next sh

End Sub
```

SearchFolders Collection Object

Represents all of the folders used in a File Search (by the FileSearch object). SearchFolders consist of ScopeFolder objects (with the corresponding ScopeFolders collection), which are simply folders. Use the Add method of the SearchFolders object to add ScopeFolder objects to its collection.

SearchFolders Collection Common Properties

The Application, Count, and Creator properties are defined at the beginning of this Appendix.

SearchFolders Collection Properties

Name	Returns	Parameters	Description
Item	Scope Folder	Index as Long	Returns a ScopeFolder object that represents a subfolder of the parent object

SearchFolders Collection Methods

Name	Returns	Parameters	Description
Add		ScopeFolder as ScopeFolder	Adds a search folder to a file search
Remove		Index As Long	Removes a search folder from a file search

Example: SearchFolders Collection Object

The following routine searches for all Excel workbooks in folders containing the word "billing" on the F drive (on the network) and displays the results on a worksheet:

```
Sub ReportBillingFilesFromNetWorkDrive()

    Dim lCount As Long, lRow As Long
```

```vbnet
Dim oSearchScope As SearchScope
Dim oScopeFolder As ScopeFolder
Dim oScopeSubFolder As ScopeFolder

With Application.FileSearch

    ' Reset FileSearch object. See FileTypes collection for this routine
    ResetFileSearch

    ' Loop through the SearchScopes collection
    ' looking for the My Computer area (scope)
    For Each oSearchScope In .SearchScopes
        If oSearchScope.Type = msoSearchInMyComputer Then
            Set oScopeFolder = oSearchScope.ScopeFolder
            Exit For
        End If
    Next oSearchScope

    ' Now loop through the My computer area (scope)
    ' until we find the mapped "F Billing" drive on the network
    For Each oScopeSubFolder In oScopeFolder.ScopeFolders
        If oScopeSubFolder.Name = "Billing (F:)" Then
            Set oScopeFolder = oScopeSubFolder
            Exit For
        End If
    Next oScopeSubFolder

    ' Now loop through each top-level folder in the F drive adding any
    ' folder that contains the name Billing to the SearchFolders
    ' collection
    Set oScopeSubFolder = Nothing
    For Each oScopeSubFolder In oScopeFolder.ScopeFolders
        If InStr(1, oScopeSubFolder.Name, _
                "billing", vbTextCompare) > 0 Then
            .SearchFolders.Add oScopeSubFolder
        End If
    Next oScopeSubFolder

    ' Look for Excel workbooks
    .FileType = msoFileTypeExcelWorkbooks

    ' Don't search subfolders. Setting this to True will override the
    ' SearchFolders collection and will search the entire contents of
    ' the F drive
    .SearchSubFolders = False

    If .Execute > 0 Then 'Files were found
        ' Dump the files found on the wksBillingFiles worksheet
        wksBillingFiles.UsedRange.Offset(1, 0).ClearContents

        ' The first row contains the column heading
        lRow = 2
        For lCount = 1 To .FoundFiles.Count
            wksBillingFiles.Cells(lRow, 1).Value = .FoundFiles(lCount)
```

```
                    lRow = lRow + 1
                Next lCount
            Else
                MsgBox "No Files found", vbInformation, "Billing Files"
            End If

        End With

    End Sub
```

SearchScopes Collection Object

Represents the list of top-level searchable areas when performing a File Search using the `FileSearch` object. Top level areas include My Computer, My Network Places, Outlook (folders), and Custom, if available.

SearchScopes Collection Common Properties

The `Application`, `Count`, and `Creator` properties are defined at the beginning of this Appendix.

SearchScopes Collection Properties

Name	Returns	Parameters	Description
Item	SearchScope	Index as Long	Returns a `SearchScope` object that corresponds to an area in which to perform a file search, such as local drives or Microsoft Outlook folders

Example: SearchScopes Collection Object

The following routine lists all of the `SearchScopes` on the current computer.

```
Sub FindSearchScopes()

    Dim lRow As Long
    Dim oSearchScope As SearchScope

    With Application.FileSearch

        ' Clear the old results
        wksSearchScopes.Range("Info").ClearContents

        ' Set the starting row
        lRow = wksSearchScopes.Range("Info").Cells(1, 1).Row

        ' Loop through the SearchScopes collection
        ' looking for the My Computer area (scope)
        For Each oSearchScope In .SearchScopes
            ' Dump the info found on the wksSearchScopes worksheet
```

```
        wksSearchScopes.Cells(1Row, 1).Value = _
            oSearchScope.ScopeFolder.Name
        wksSearchScopes.Cells(1Row, 2).Value = oSearchScope.Type
        1Row = 1Row + 1
    Next oSearchScope

    ' Sort the list by Scope Type
    With wksSearchScopes
        .Range("Info").Sort Key1:=.Cells(1, 2), Order1:=xlAscending
    End With

    End With

End Sub
```

SearchScope Object

An individual top-level area in the SearchScopes Collection object that can be searched when using the FileSearch object.

SearchScope Common Properties

The Application and Creator properties are defined at the beginning of this Appendix.

SearchScope Properties

Name	Returns	Description
ScopeFolder	ScopeFolder	Returns a ScopeFolder object
Type	MsoSearchIn	Read Only. Returns a value that corresponds to the type of SearchScope object. The type indicates the area in which the Execute method of the FileSearch object will search for files

SharedWorkspace Object

The SharedWorkspace property returns a SharedWorkspace object which allows the developer to add the active document to a Microsoft Windows SharePoint Services document workspace on the server and to manage other objects in the shared workspace.

SharedWorkspace Properties

Name	Returns	Description
Application	Object	Returns an **Application** object that represents the container application this object
Connected	Boolean	Indicates if the current document is save in and connected to a workspace. Read-only

Name	Returns	Description
Creator	Long	Returns a Long value that indicates which application created the object
Files	SharedWorkspace Files	Returns a collection of SharedWorkspaceFiles. Read-only
Folders	SharedWorkspace Folders	Returns a collection of SharedWorkspaceFolders. Read-only
LastRefreshed	Date/Time	Returns a date and time indicating the last time the Refresh was most recently called. Read-only
Links	SharedWorkspace Links	Returns a collection of SharedWorkspaceLinks. Read-only
Members	SharedWorkspace Members	Returns a collection of SharedWorkspaceMembers. Read-only
Name	String	Returns or sets the name of the object. Read/Write
Parent	Object	Returns a reference to the parent object for this particular object
SourceURL	String	Designates the location of a shared document. Read-only
Tasks	SharedWorkspace Tasks	Returns a collection of SharedDocumentTasks. Read-only
URL	String	Returns the URL of the shared workspace. Read-only

SharedWorkspace Methods

Name	Returns	Parameters	Description
CreateNew		[URL], [Name]	Creates a new SharedWorkspace object
Delete			Deletes a SharedWorkspace object from the collection
Disconnect			Disconnects from the shared workspace
Refresh			Refreshes the current copy of a document from the shared workspace
RemoveDocument			Removes the current document from the shared workspace

SharedWorkspaceFile Object

The SharedWorkSpaceFile object represents a file that has been saved in a shared document workspace. This shared document workspace would typically be a Sharepoint server.

SharedWorkspaceFile Properties

Name	Returns	Description
Application	Object	Returns an **Application** object that represents the container application this object
CreatedBy	String	Read-only
CreatedDate	Variant	Read Only Read Only
Creator	Long	Returns a Long value that indicates which application created the object
ModifiedBy	String	Read Only Read Only
ModifiedDate	Variant	Read Only Read Only
Parent	Object	Returns a reference to the parent object for this particular object
URL	String	Read Only Read Only

SharedWorkspaceFile Methods

Name	Returns	Parameters	Description
Delete			Deletes a SharedWorkspaceFile object

SharedWorkspaceFolder Object

Represents a folder in a shared document workspace.

SharedWorksapceFolder Properties

Name	Returns	Description
Application	Object	Returns an **Application** object that represents the container application this object
Creator	Long	Returns a Long value that indicates which application created the object
FolderName	String	Read-only
Parent	Object	Returns a reference to the parent object for this particular object

SharedWorkspaceFolder Methods

Name	Returns	Parameters	Description
Delete			Deletes the current object

SharedWorkspaceLink Object

Represents a URL link saved in a shared document workspace.

SharedWorkspaceLink Properties

Name	Returns	Description
Application	Object	Returns an **Application** object that represents the container application this object
CreatedBy	String	Read Only Read Only
CreatedDate	Variant	Read Only Read Only
Creator	Long	Returns a Long value that indicates which application created the object
Description	String	Read/Write
ModifiedBy	String	Read Only Read Only
ModifiedDate	Variant	Read Only Read Only
Notes	String	Read/Write
Parent	Object	Returns a reference to the parent object for this particular object
URL	String	Read Only Read Only

SharedWorkspaceLink Methods

Name	Returns	Parameters	Description
Delete			Deletes the current object
Save			Saves the current object

SharedWorkspaceMember Object

The SharedWorkspaceMember object represents a user who has rights in a shared document workspace.

SharedWorkspaceMember Properties

Name	Returns	Description
Application	Object	Returns an **Application** object that represents the container application this object
Creator	Long	Returns a Long value that indicates which application created the object
DomainName	String	Read Only Read Only
Email	String	Read Only Read Only
Name	String	Read Only Read Only
Parent	Object	Returns a reference to the parent object for this particular object

SharedWorkspaceMember Methods

Name	Returns	Parameters	Description
Delete			Deletes the current object

SharedWorkspaceMembers Collection Object

Contains a collection of SharedWorkspaceMember objects.

SharedWorkspaceTask Object

Represents a task saved in a shared document workspace.

SharedWorkspaceTask Properties

Name	Returns	Description
Application	Object	Returns an **Application** object that represents the container application this object
AssignedTo	String	Read/Write
CreatedBy	String	Read Only Read Only
CreatedDate	Variant	Read Only Read Only
Creator	Long	Returns a Long value that indicates which application created the object
Description	String	Read/Write

Name	Returns	Description
DueDate	Variant	Read/Write
ModifiedBy	String	Read Only Read Only
ModifiedDate	Variant	Read Only Read Only
Parent	Object	Returns a reference to the parent object for this particular object
Priority	msoShared Workspace TaskPriority	Read/Write
Status	msoShared Workspace TaskStatus	Read/Write
Title	String	Read/Write

SharedWorkspaceTask Methods

Name	Returns	Parameters	Description
Delete			Deletes the current object
Save			Saves the current object

SharedWorkspaceTasks Collection Object

Contains a collection of SharedWorkspaceTask objects.

Signature Object

This object represents a digital signature attached to a document. Digital Signatures are electronic versions of handwritten signatures. They enable other users of your document to uniquely identify and validate the source of the document.

When a document containing a digital signature contains macros, users who open the document have the option of trusting the author, or source of the signature. When macro security for an Office application is set to high, only macros from trusted sources are enabled. This protects those other users from opening documents that could contain macro viruses by allowing them to choose which sources they wish to trust.

Digital Signatures also add a level protection for the author of the document by insuring that the contents of the document remained unchanged. When you digitally sign a document, an encrypted key is added to the signature. When other users change the document, a message appears informing them that they do not have the key to unlock the signature. This causes the document to lose its signature.

This object is currently not accessible in Microsoft Excel, though it is available through the Document object in Microsoft Word and the Presentation object in Microsoft PowerPoint.

Signature Common Properties

The `Application`, `Creator`, and `Parent` properties are defined at the beginning of this Appendix.

Signature Properties

Name	Returns	Description
Attach Certificate	Boolean	Set/Get whether the digital certificate that corresponds to the specified `Signature` object is attached to the document
ExpireDate	Variant	Read Only. Returns the date on which the digital signature that corresponds to the `Signature` object will expire
Is Certificate Expired	Boolean	Read Only. Returns whether the digital certificate that corresponds to the `Signature` object has expired
Is Certificate Revoked	Boolean	Read Only. Returns whether the digital certificate that corresponds to the `Signature` object has been revoked by the issuer of the certificate
Issuer	String	Read Only. Returns the name of the issuer of the digital certificate that corresponds to the `Signature` object
IsValid	Boolean	Read Only. Returns whether the digital certificate that corresponds to the `Signature` object is a valid certificate. A certificate may be invalid for several reasons ranging from its having expired to changes in the document that contains it
SignDate	Variant	Read Only. Returns the date and time that the digital certificate corresponding to the `Signature` object was attached to the document
Signer	String	Read Only. Returns the name of the person who attached the digital certificate that corresponds to the `Signature` object to the document

Signature Methods

Name	Returns	Parameters	Description
Delete			Deletes the specified signature from the `SignatureSet` collection

SignatureSet Collection Object

Represents all of the `Signature` objects in a document.

SignatureSet Collection Common Properties

The `Application`, `Count`, `Creator`, and `Parent` properties are defined at the beginning of this Appendix.

SignatureSet Collection Properties

Name	Returns	Parameters	Description
Item	Signature	iSig as Long	Returns a `Signature` object that corresponds to one of the digital signatures with which the document is currently signed

SignatureSet Collection Methods

Name	Returns	Parameters	Description
Add	Signature		Returns a `Signature` object that represents a new e-mail signature
Commit			Commits all changes of the specified `SignatureSet` collection to disk. Until this method is executed, none of the changes to the collection are saved

Example: SignatureSet Collection Object

The following routine adds a digital signature to the active PowerPoint presentation, then displays the information contained within the signature chosen. Note that the `Add` method of the `Signatures` property prompts the user with a dialog box containing a list of digital signatures:

```
Sub AddSig()

    Dim lIcon As Long
    Dim ppt As Presentation
    Dim oSignature As Signature
    Dim sInfo As String

    ' Check for an active presentation
    On Error Resume Next
        Set ppt = ActivePresentation
    On Error GoTo 0
```

```
        'If there's a presentation active...
        If Not ppt Is Nothing Then

            ' Set the icon that will appear in the message box to information
            lIcon = vbInformation

            ' Add the signature to the presentation. This will prompt the user
            ' to select a signature and return all of the property settings to
            ' the oSignature object
            Set oSignature = ppt.Signatures.Add

            ' Commit the changes to disk. This will display a "Signed" message
            ' next to the presentation name
            ppt.Signatures.Commit

            ' Initialize the message string
            sInfo = "Signature Information:" & vbCrLf & vbCrLf

            ' Add the signature info to the message
            With oSignature
                sInfo = sInfo & "Issuer: " & .Issuer & vbCrLf
                sInfo = sInfo & "Signer: " & .Signer & vbCrLf
                sInfo = sInfo & "Sign Date: " & .SignDate & vbCrLf
                sInfo = sInfo & "Expire Date: " & .ExpireDate
            End With
        Else
            ' No presentation active, so set the message box icon to exclamation
            ' and the message to inform the user
            lIcon = vbExclamation
            sInfo = "No presentation is currently active"
        End If

        ' Display the message
        MsgBox sInfo, lIcon, "Add Signature"

End Sub
```

SmartDocument

This is used to manage the XML expansion pack attached to the currently active document.

SmartDocument Properties

Name	Returns	Description
Application	Object	Returns an **Application** object that represents the container application this object
Creator	Long	Returns a Long value that indicates which application created the object
SolutionID	String	Read/Write
SolutionURL	String	Read/Write

SmartDocument Methods

Name	Returns	Parameters	Description
PickSolution		[ConsiderAllSchemas]	
RefreshPane			

Sync Object

Use the Sync object to manage the synchronization of the local and server copies of a shared document stored in a Windows SharePoint Services document workspace. The Status property returns important information about the current state of synchronization. Use the GetUpdate method to refresh the sync status. Use the LastSyncTime, ErrorType, and WorkspaceLastChangedBy properties to return additional information.

Sync Properties

Name	Returns	Description
Application	Object	Returns an **Application** object that represents the container application this object
Creator	Long	Returns a Long value that indicates which application created the object
ErrorType	MsoSyncErrorType	Read Only Read Only
LastSyncTime	Variant	Read Only Read Only
Parent	Object	Returns a reference to the parent object for this particular object
Status	MsoSyncStatusType	Read Only Read Only
WorkspaceLastChangedBy	String	Read Only Read Only

Sync Methods

Name	Returns	Parameters	Description
GetUpdate			
OpenVersion		[SyncVersionType]	
PutUpdate			
ResolveConflict		[SyncConflictResolution]	
Unsuspend			

UserPermission

Represents a set of permissions on a document for a single user.

UserPermission Properties

Name	Returns	Description
EdxpirationDate	Variant	Read/Write
Permission	Long	Read/Write
UserId	String	Read Only Read Only

UserPermission Methods

Name	Returns	Parameters	Description
Remove			Removes the current UserPermission object from the collection of Permissions.

WebPageFonts Collection Object

Represents a set of WebPageFont objects that allow you to set both the proportional and fixed font style and size used when documents are saved as Web pages. See the WebPageFont object for more details.

The collection can be referenced using the Fonts property of the DefaultWebOptions property in the host's Application object, like so:

```
Set oWebPageFonts = Application.DefaultWebOptions.Fonts
```

Note that as of this writing, the count property of the WebPageFonts Collection object always returns zero, even though there are 12 WebPageFont objects (Character Sets) in the collection.

WebPageFonts Collection Common Properties

The Application, Count, and Creator properties are defined at the beginning of this Appendix.

WebPageFonts Collection Properties

Name	Returns	Parameters	Description
Item	WebPage Font	Index as MsoCharacter Set	Returns a WebPageFont object from the WebPageFonts collection for a particular value of MsoCharacterSet

WebPageFont Object

This object represents which fixed and proportional font and size are used when the host application's documents are saved as Web pages. Microsoft Excel and Microsoft Word also use these settings when you open a Web page within the application, but the settings only take effect when the Web page being opened cannot display its own font settings or when no font information is contained within the HTML code.

Be aware that the `FixedWidthFont` and `ProportionalFont` properties will accept any valid String and `FixedWidthFontSize` and `ProportionalFontSize` will accept any valid Single value. For example, the following will not encounter an error, even though they aren't valid font and size settings.

```
Application.DefaultWebOptions.Fonts(msoCharacterSetEnglishWesternEuropean
OtherLatinScript).ProportionalFont = "XXXXXXXX"

Application.DefaultWebOptions.Fonts(msoCharacterSetEnglishWesternEuropean
OtherLatinScript).ProportionalFontSize = 1200
```

An error will occur when the application attempts to use these settings.

WebPageFont Common Properties

The `Application` and `Creator` properties are defined at the beginning of this Appendix.

WebPageFont Properties

Name	Returns	Description
FixedWidth Font	String	Set/Get the fixed-width font setting in the host application
FixedWidth FontSize	Single	Set/Get the fixed-width font size setting (in points) in the host application
ProportionalFont	String	Set/Get the proportional font setting in the host application
Proportional FontSize	Single	Set/Get the proportional font size setting (in points) in the host application

Example: WebPageFont Object

The following routine loops through the `WebPageFonts` collection, and for each `WebPageFont` (character set), establishes the proportional and fixed font name and size based on data entered in a `FontInfo` range located on the `wksWebPageFonts` worksheet in the workbook containing this code:

```
Sub SetWebPageFonts()

    Const sRANGE_FONT_INFO As String = "FontInfo"

    Dim lCalc As Long
    Dim lCount As Long, lRow As Long
    Dim oWebFont As WebPageFont
```

```
        ' Turn off the screen and Calculation
    With Application
        ' Store the calculation mode
        lCalc = .Calculation
        ' Turn calculation off
        .Calculation = xlCalculationManual
        ' Turn off the screen
        .ScreenUpdating = False
    End With

    ' Set the row counter based on the input range's first cell
    lRow = wksWebPageFonts.Range("InputRange").Cells(1, 1).Row

    ' Clear the old info
    wksWebPageFonts.Range("InputRange").ClearContents

    ' There are twelve Font character sets. Need to use a hard-coded upper
    ' range (12) because Application.DefaultWebOptions.Fonts.Count
    ' always returns zero
    For lCount = 1 To 12
        ' Grab a reference to a single WebPageFont (or character set)
        Set oWebFont = Application.DefaultWebOptions.Fonts(lCount)

        With oWebFont
            ' Use the settings on the wksWebPageFonts worksheet to
            ' set the WebPageFont font settings
            .ProportionalFont = _
                wksWebPageFonts.Range(sRANGE_FONT_INFO).Cells(1, 1).Value
            .ProportionalFontSize = _
                wksWebPageFonts.Range(sRANGE_FONT_INFO).Cells(1, 2).Value
            .FixedWidthFont = _
                wksWebPageFonts.Range(sRANGE_FONT_INFO).Cells(1, 3).Value
            .FixedWidthFontSize = _
                wksWebPageFonts.Range(sRANGE_FONT_INFO).Cells(1, 4).Value

            ' Display the new WebPageFont settings in a table
            ' on the wksWebPageFonts worksheet
            wksWebPageFonts.Cells(lRow, 2) = lCount
            wksWebPageFonts.Cells(lRow, 3) = .ProportionalFont
            wksWebPageFonts.Cells(lRow, 4) = .ProportionalFontSize
            wksWebPageFonts.Cells(lRow, 5) = .FixedWidthFont
            wksWebPageFonts.Cells(lRow, 6) = .FixedWidthFontSize

            ' Move one row down for the next Character set
            lRow = lRow + 1
        End With
    Next lCount

    ' Reset the calculation mode
    Application.Calculation = lCalc

End Sub
```

Index

D

P

S